The Roug

Mexico

written and researched by

John Fisher, Daniel Jacobs, Stephen Keeling and Zora O'Neill

www.roughguides.com

Contents

◀◀ Paseo de la Reforma, Mexico City ◀ Puerto Escondido, Baja California

Introduction to Mexico

Mexico enjoys a cultural blend which is wholly unique. It has experienced an oil-based economic miracle which has created vast modern cities and one of the fastest growing industrial powers on earth. Yet, in places, it can still feel like a forgotten Spanish colony, while more than five hundred years after the Conquest, the influence of indigenous American culture is all-pervasive. You can see different aspects of Mexico's diversity within a space as small as a few city blocks: traditional markets, barely changed since the Conquest, thrive in the shadow of massive colonial churches and steel-and-glass skyscrapers, while teenagers skateboard to a soundtrack of *rock en español* past Maya women laying out their handmade wares on colourful blankets.

Occasionally the mix is an uneasy one, but for the most part it works remarkably well. The people of Mexico reflect this variety, too: there are communities of full-blooded **indígenas**, and there are a few – very few – Mexicans of pure **Spanish** descent. The great majority of the population, though, is **mestizo**, combining in themselves both traditions with, to a greater or lesser extent, a veneer of urban sophistication. Add in a multitude of distinct regional identities and you have a thrilling, constantly surprising place to travel.

Despite the inevitable influence of the US, looming to the north, and close links with the rest of the Spanish-speaking world (an avid audience for

▲ Kayaking near Filo Bobos

Mexican soap operas), the country remains resolutely individual. The music that fills the plazas in the evenings, the buildings that circle around them, even the smells emanating from a row of taco carts: they all leave you without any doubt about where you are. The strength of **Mexican identity** perhaps hits most clearly if you travel overland across the border with the US, as the ubiquitous Popsicle vendors suddenly appear from nowhere, and the pace of life slows perceptibly.

Many first-time visitors are surprised to find that Mexico is far from being a "developing" nation. If you're the type of traveller who gauges the level of "adventure" in terms of squalor endured, then you may be disappointed: the country has a robust economy, a remarkably thorough and efficient internal transport system and a vibrant contemporary arts and music scene. Adventure comes instead through happening upon a **village fiesta**, complete with a muddy bullfight and rowdy dancing, or hopping on a rural bus, packed with

Fact file

- Bordering the US, Guatemala and Belize, Mexico is technically part of **North America**. The country covers an **area** of virtually two million square kilometres – about a quarter the size of the continental US and eight times the size of the UK – and has a **population** of more than 110 million. Well over 20 million live in the capital and its immediate vicinity in the Valley of México.
- Mexico is a country of tremendous geographical variety. The north is largely arid **semi-desert**, the south **tropical** and forested. The **volcanic mountains** of the centre rise to 5700m.
- The **economy** is among the most successful in the region, based on free-trade agreements with most countries in the Americas. Chief **exports** are oil and related products, silver (it's the world's largest source) and other metals and minerals, as well as manufactured goods produced using Mexican labour in the border zone.
- Mexico is a **federal republic**, with a presidential system loosely based on that of the US. A single party, the PRI, governed from the establishment of the modern constitution in 1917 until the conservative opposition party PAN won the presidential election in 2000; they have remained in power since.

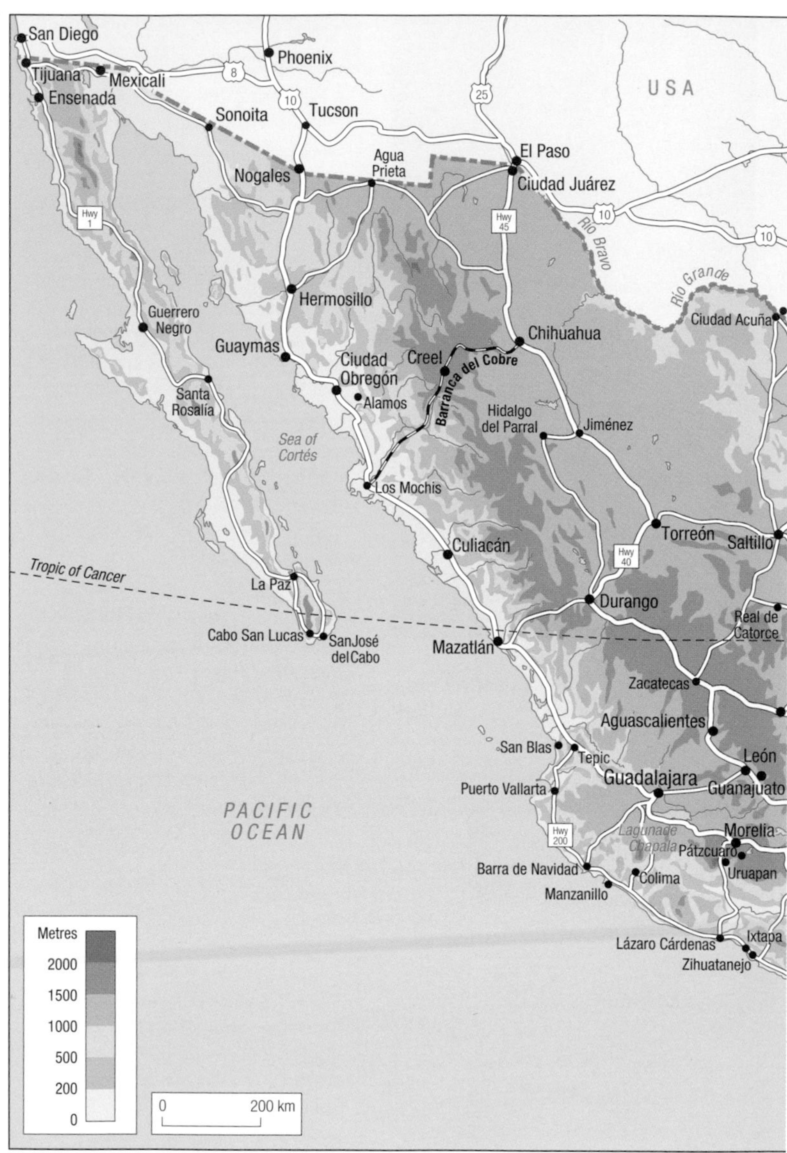

farmers all carrying machetes half their height and curious about how you've wound up going their way.

This is not to say that Mexico is always an easy place to travel around. The power may go off, the water may not be drinkable. Occasionally it can seem that there's incessant, inescapable noise and dirt. And although the **mañana**

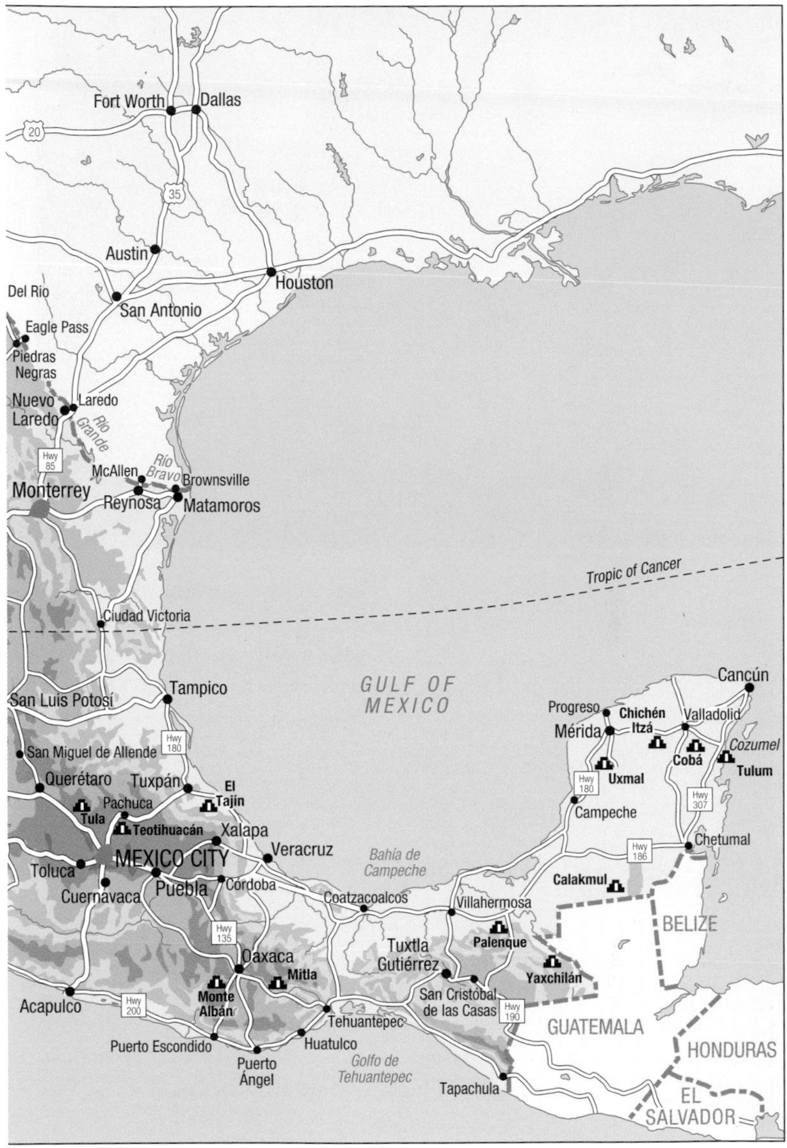

mentality is largely an outsiders' myth, Mexico is still a country where timetables are not always to be entirely trusted, where anything that can break down will break down (when it's most needed) and where any attempt to do things in a hurry is liable to be frustrated. You simply have to accept the local temperament: work may be necessary to live but it's not life's central focus,

◄ Rodeo at sunset, Puerto Vallarta

minor annoyances really are minor and there's always something else to do in the meantime. More deeply disturbing are the extremes of ostentatious wealth and grim poverty, most poignant in the big cities, where unemployment is high and living conditions beyond crowded. But for the most part, you'll find this is a friendly, fabulously varied and enormously enjoyable place in which to travel.

Where to go

Physically, Mexico resembles a vast horn, curving away south and east from the US border, with its final tip bent right back round to the north. It is an extremely mountainous country: two great ranges, the Sierra Madre Occidental in the west and the Sierra Madre Oriental in the east, run parallel to the coasts, enclosing a high, semi-desert plateau. About halfway down they are crossed by the volcanic highland area in which stand Mexico City and the major centres of population. Beyond, the mountains run together as a single range through the southern states of Oaxaca and Chiapas. Only the eastern tip – the Yucatán Peninsula – is consistently low-lying and flat.

For most visitors central and southeastern Mexico are the main attractions. Many find the arid and sparsely populated north – a region heavily influenced by the neighbouring US and dominated by industrial cities such as **Monterrey** – relatively dull. The major exceptions are the shores and wilderness of **Baja**

¿Habla usted Náhuatl?

Spanish may be the language of officialdom in Mexico, but it's not the **official language**. Rather it's just one of 63 languages legally recognized in the country. These other languages range from Náhuatl, spoken by more than 1.6 million people descended from the ancient Aztecs, to Kiliwa, kept alive by about fifty people in Baja California. All told, more than ten million people speak an indigenous language – a number second only to Peru. And this isn't even taking into account the numerous languages spoken by immigrant groups, many of whom have been in Mexico for a century or more: Old Order Mennonites converse in Plautdietsch (Low German), Lebanese families speak Arabic and the village of Chipilo, settled by Italians in 1882, has preserved an obscure Venetian dialect. You'll have to visit remote villages to hear Rarámuri, Chuj or Paipai, but in Chiapas and the Yucatán Peninsula, radio and TV programs are broadcast in various Maya strains.

California, a destination in its own right, and the **Copper Canyon**, with its spectacular rail journey. And the border cities can provide a bit of (sometimes sleazy) excitement.

It's in the highlands north of the capital that the first really worthwhile stops come, with the bulk of the historic colonial towns and an enticing spring-like climate year-round. Coming through the **Bajío**, the heart of the country, you'll pass the silver-mining towns of **Zacatecas** and **Guanajuato**, the historic centres of **San Miguel de Allende** and **Querétaro**, and many smaller places with a legacy of superb colonial architecture. **Mexico City,** though a

▲ The cathedral, Mérida

nightmare of urban sprawl, is totally fascinating, and in every way – artistic, political, cultural – the capital of the nation. Around the city lie the chief relics of the pre-Hispanic cultures of central Mexico: the massive pyramids of **Teotihuacán**; the main Toltec site at **Tula**; and **Tenochtitlán**, heart of both the Aztec empire and the modern capital. **Guadalajara**, to the west, is a

Mercados Mexicanos

The colour and bustle of Mexico's **markets** is hard to beat. Even if you've no intention of buying, half an hour is always well spent meandering through narrow aisles surrounded by heaps of perfectly ripe fruit and stacks of *nopal* cactus leaves (though stay away from the meat sections if you're at all squeamish). In small villages, like those around Oaxaca (see p.638), inhabitants still recognize one day of the week as the traditional market day, coming from miles around to sell their wares and stock up for the week ahead. The main square comes to life in the early morning, and returns to its dozy ways only when all the day's transactions have been completed, usually in mid-afternoon. Larger villages may have two or three official market days, but the rest of the week is often so busy it seems that every day is market day. In the cities, each *barrio* has its own vibrant market: among the best are Guadalajara's **Libertad** (see p.328), Mexico City's enormous **La Merced** (p.451) and Oaxaca's **mercados Abastos** (p.626) and **20 de Noviembre** (p.626). You'll soon find that each village or city's market has its own special character: while they primarily sell food, most will have a section devoted to local handicrafts, and in cities you'll often find specialist artesanía markets dedicated to goods such as hammocks, tin ornaments, glassware and clothing. For further details on markets and hints on bargaining, see Basics, p.58.

▲ Museo Nacional de Anthropología, Mexico City

city on a more human scale, capital of the state of **Jalisco** and in easy reach of **Michoacán**: between them, these states share some of the most gently scenic country in Mexico, where the thickly forested hills are studded with lakes and ancient villages. This area also has a reputation for producing some of the finest crafts, glassware and ceramics above all, in a country renowned for them.

South of the capital, the states of Oaxaca and Chiapas, home to some of the largest populations of pure indigenous groups, are mountainous and beautiful, too, but in a far wilder way. The city of **Oaxaca**, especially, is one of the country's most enticing destinations. It has an extraordinary mix of colonial and indigenous life, superb markets and fascinating archeological sites. **Chiapas** is still associated with the Zapatista uprising of the mid-1990s, though visitors are little affected these days, and the strength of indigenous traditions in and around the market town of **San Cristóbal de las Casas**, together with a number of lesser-known yet romantically tumbledown ancient Maya cities, continue to make it a big travellers' centre. It's typically the stop before the picturesque ruins of **Palenque**. East into the **Yucatán** there is also traditional indigenous life, side-by-side with a tourist industry based around the truly magnificent Maya cities – **Chichén Itzá** and **Uxmal** above all – and the burgeoning Caribbean resorts that stretch down the coast from **Cancún**. The capital of Yucatán state, **Mérida**, is a particular gem, both cosmopolitan and old-fashioned.

On the Pacific coast, where the surf is wilder and the scenery more rugged than in the Caribbean, **Acapulco** is just the best known of the beach

◀ Chac-mool figure, Cancún

destinations. Along the ocean to the north, hundreds of miles of relatively empty sand are broken up only by resort cities like **Mazatlán** and **Puerto Vallarta**; the south is even less developed, and the state of Oaxaca has some equally enticing shores. Few tourists venture over to the Gulf coast, despite the attractions of **Veracruz** and its mysterious ruins. The scene here is largely dominated by oil, the weather too humid most of the time and the beaches sometimes a disappointment. For music and general bonhomie, however, the city's central plaza is one of the country's finest destinations.

When to go

To a great extent, the physical terrain in Mexico determines the **climate** – certainly far more than the expected indicator of latitude. You can drive down the coast all day without conditions changing noticeably, but turn inland to the mountains, and the contrast is immediate: in temperature, scenery, vegetation, even the mood and character of the people around you. Generalizations, therefore, are difficult.

Summer, from June to October, is in theory the **rainy season**, but just how wet it is varies wildly from place to place. In the heart of the country you can expect a heavy but short-lived downpour virtually every afternoon; in the north hardly any rain falls, ever. Chiapas is the wettest state, with many minor roads washed out in the autumn, and in the south and low-lying coastal areas summer is stickily humid too. Along the beaches, September through mid-October is **hurricane season** – you'll usually get wet weather, choppy seas and mosquitoes, if not a full-on tropical storm. Late **winter** is the traditional tourist season, and in the big resorts like Acapulco and Cancún, December through April are the busiest months. Mountain areas, though, can get very cold then; in fact, nights in the mountains can be extremely cold at any time of year.

In effect, visitors come all year round – sticking on the whole to the highlands in summer and the coasts in winter. November is probably the ideal time to visit, with the rains over, the land still fresh and the peak season not yet begun. Overall, though, the climate is so benign that any time of year will do, so long as you're prepared for some rain in the summer, some cold in winter and the sudden changes which go with the altitude at any time.

Average temperatures and rainfall

	Jan	Mar	May	Jul	Sep	Nov
Acapulco						
Max/Min (°C)	31/22	31/22	32/25	33/25	32/25	32/24
Max/Min (°F)	88/72	88/72	90/77	91/77	90/77	90/75
Rainfall (mm)	13	5	0	203	279	15
Guadalajara						
Max/Min (°C)	23/7	28/9	31/14	26/15	26/15	25/10
Max/Min (°F)	73/45	82/48	88/57	79/59	79/59	77/50
Rainfall (mm)	13	8	25	178	178	13
Mérida						
Max/Min (°C)	28/18	32/20	34/21	33/23	32/23	29/19
Max/Min (°F)	82/64	90/68	93/70	91/73	90/73	84/66
Rainfall (mm)	25	13	76	127	178	25
Mexico City						
Max/Min (°C)	22/6	27/10	27/13	24/13	23/13	23/9
Max/Min (°F)	72/43	81/50	81/55	75/55	73/55	73/48
Rainfall (mm)	13	13	76	152	127	13
Monterrey						
Max/Min (°C)	20/9	26/13	31/20	34/22	34/22	23/12
Max/Min (°F)	68/48	79/55	88/68	93/72	93/72	73/54
Rainfall (mm)	25	25	51	76	102	25
Oaxaca						
Max/Min (°C)	28/8	32/12	32/15	28/15	27/15	28/10
Max/Min (°F)	82/46	90/54	90/59	82/59	81/59	82/50
Rainfall (mm)	51	25	127	203	279	51
Tijuana						
Max/Min (°C)	20/6	21/8	23/12	27/16	27/16	23/10
Max/Min (°F)	68/43	70/46	73/54	81/61	81/61	73/50
Rainfall (mm)	51	25	5	0	13	25

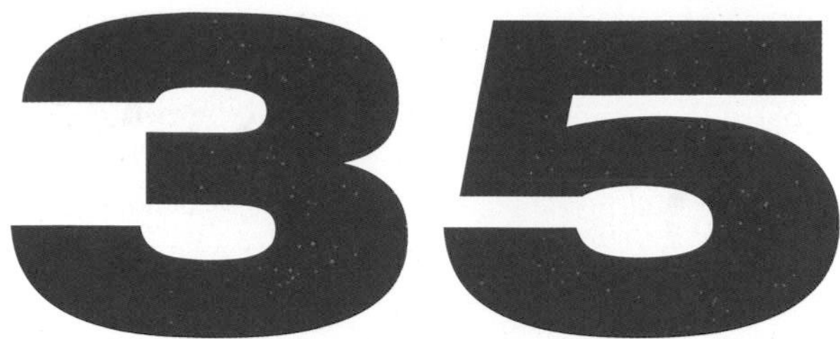

35 things not to miss

It's not possible to see everything Mexico has to offer in one trip – and we don't suggest you try. What follows, in no particular order, is a selective taste of the country's highlights: ancient ruins, vibrant cities and spectacular landscapes. They're arranged in five colour-coded categories to help you find the very best things to see, do and experience. All highlights have a page reference to take you straight into the guide, where you can find out more.

01 **Cenotes, Valladolid** Page **799** • Take a refreshing dip in these crystal-clear sinkholes, one of which has the roots of a huge *alamo* tree stretching down into it.

02 Tulum Page **832** • Poised dramatically overlooking the Caribbean, this important Maya spiritual and cultural centre is one of the most picturesque of all the ancient sites.

03 Voladores de Papantla Page **598** • An ancient religious ritual, this spectacle is now performed as much for tourists as it is for locals, but it's still breathtaking.

04 The Bonampak murals Page **723** • Hidden deep in the forest until 1946, the ancient temples at Bonampak are home to renowned paintings depicting vivid scenes of Maya life, including human sacrifice.

05 The Rivera murals Page **399** • Diego Rivera's work is inextricably linked with Mexico's national identity, which is a particularly powerful theme in his classic murals at the Palacio Nacional in Mexico City.

06 Coffee Page **591** • Some of the country's best produce is grown in Veracruz state, and the coffee is no exception.

07 Palenque Page **717** • This Maya site is remarkable not only for its distinct architectural style but also for its setting – surrounded by jungle-covered hills, right at the edge of the great Yucatán plain.

08 Nightlife in Playa del Carmen Page **822** • At Christmas and Spring Break the wild parties take over: the rest of the year you can dance on the sand or in super-hip small clubs alongside stylish Mexico City weekenders and European expats in this Caribbean boomtown.

09 The Copper Canyon Page **155** • Whether you take the awe-inspiring train ride here from the west coast or hike along the canyon floor, a visit to this vast chasm is the definite highlight of any trip to northern Mexico.

10 Lago de Pátzcuaro Page **360** • Most famous for its Day of the Dead celebrations, the enchanting lake is a worthy destination year-round.

11 Guanajuato Page **268** • This gorgeous colonial town, sandwiched into a narrow ravine, is home to one of the country's finest Baroque churches, a thriving student scene and a relaxed café and bar culture.

12 El Tajín Page **597** • Once the most important city on the Gulf coast, by the time of the Conquest it had been forgotten, and was only rediscovered by accident in 1785. Even now it remains one of the most mysterious archeological sites in Mexico.

13 Tula Page **472** • The ancient city of Tula, where the giant Atlantes stand atop the main pyramid, succeeded Teotihuacán as the Valley of México's great power.

14 Football Page **452** • Fan or not, you can't afford to miss out on the buzz generated by matches at Mexico City's Estadio Azteca, site of the 1970 and 1986 World Cups.

15 The Zócalo, Mexico City Page **395** • The eternal heart of the city, the capital's main plaza is surrounded by its oldest streets, its cathedral, the Palacio Nacional and the ruins of Aztec Tenochtitlán.

16 Charreada Page **452** • If bullfights aren't for you, head to a *charreada* (rodeo) instead; the ultimate charro (cowboy) event, traditional *charreadas* make a brilliant spectator sport.

17 Museo Nacional de Antropología Page **419** • Mexico's best and most important museum, with an enormous collection of artefacts from all the major pre-Hispanic cultures.

18 Diving Page **824** • Mexico has numerous fantastic diving opportunities: the coral reefs off Isla Cozumel provide some of the best.

19 Silver jewellery from Taxco Page **503** • The town of Taxco, an interesting place in itself, offers the most exquisite silver products in the country.

20 Xochimilco Page **438** • Take in the carnival atmosphere and dazzling colours while being punted around the canals and serenaded by mariachi bands, then wander the streets of Xochimilco town to visit the flower and fruit market.

21 Las Pozas, Xilitla Page **310** • Built by English arts patron Edward James, this crumbling architectural experiment is a weird juxtaposition of modern concrete and timeless jungle.

22 The zócalo in Veracruz Page **580** • One of the most enjoyable places in the republic to chill out. In the evening, the tables under the *portales* of the plaza fill up, and the drinking and marimba music begin.

23 Acapulco's cliff divers Page **562** • Watch the *clavadistas* plunge into the sea from precipitous cliffs – a spotlit tourist display, but one requiring undeniable skill.

24 Mariachi Page **449** • Probably the best known of all Mexican music styles, you'll find mariachi played the length and breadth of the country. In the evening, hundreds of bands compete for attention in a blur of silver-spangled finery in Mexico City's Plaza Garibaldi.

25 Calakmul Page **763** • Deep in the heart of the jungle and only partially restored, this is the largest-known archeological zone in Mesoamerica, with a stunning seven thousand buildings in its central area alone.

26 Turquoise waters and white-sand beaches Page **109** • The Pacific coast around Bahía Concepción is classic picture-postcard material and a must for all beach lovers.

27 Museo Frida Kahlo Page **431** • Politics, art and national identity combine at the home of Frida Kahlo and her husband Diego Rivera, two of Mexico's most iconic artists.

28 Hammocks Page **771** • String a hammock from one tree to another and relax as locals do. Mérida, in the Yucatán, is one of the best places in the country to pick one up.

29 Sian Ka'an Biosphere Reserve Page **839** • A huge, stunning coastal nature reserve with eco-systems ranging from tropical forest through fresh- and salt-water marshes to barrier reef. Wildlife of every sort lives here, but it's especially good for bird watching.

30 Whale watching Page **100** • From December to April, thousands of grey whales come to mate in the lagoons of Guerrero Negro, San Ignacio and Bahía Magdalena, where they can be observed at close quarters.

31 Real de Catorce Page **236** • This picturesque ghost-town once thrived on the wealth of its silver mines, as the magnificent churches attest. Each year Huichol pilgrims visit the nearby desert in search of peyote.

32 Oaxaca markets Page **638** • Any market in Mexico is a feast for the senses, but Oaxaca's are especially vibrant, with heaps of everything from fresh produce to some of the country's best-made and most imaginative textiles.

33 Fiestas Page **54** • Local fiestas, often featuring traditional dances whose roots go back to the pre-colonial era, can be a colourful highlight of a trip. Every town and village, no matter how small, will celebrate with costumes, fireworks and marching bands at least once a year.

34 Monarch Butterfly Sanctuary Page **372** • Witness the amazing sight of millions of monarch butterflies settling on the landscape, turning it a vibrant orange, every year between November and April.

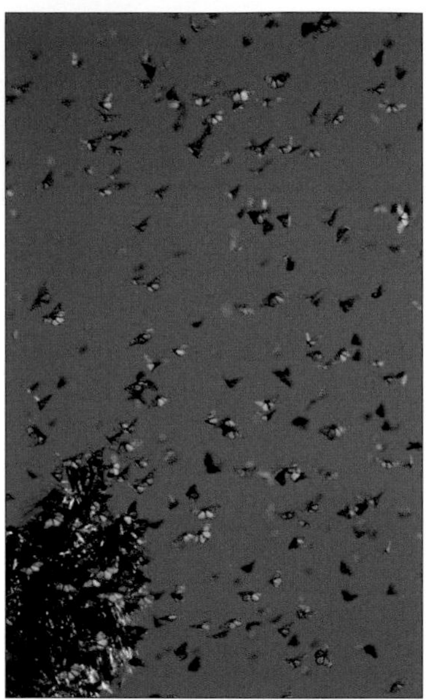

35 Chichén Itzá Page **790** • The most famous of the Maya sites. It's well worth staying nearby so you can see the sprawling ruins and complex carvings over a couple of days.

Basics

Basics

Getting there

The quickest and easiest way to get to Mexico is to fly. Going overland from the US won't save you much money, if any, but becomes more convenient the nearer you live to the border.

To some extent, airfares to Mexico depend on the **season**. Though ticket prices to Mexico City and other non-resort destinations show little, if any, fluctuation, some fares, especially to resort areas, do vary, and are highest around Easter, from early June to mid-September and at Christmas and New Year. Prices drop during the "shoulder" seasons – mid-September to early November and mid-April to early June – and you'll get the best deals during the low season (November to April, excluding Christmas and New Year). Note also that flying at weekends may add to round-trip fares. The round-trip prices quoted here assume midweek travel.

Barring special offers, the best **airfares** carry certain restrictions, such as advance booking and fixed departure dates. You can often cut costs by going through a **discount flight agent**. Some agents specialize in **charter flights**, which may be cheaper than any available scheduled flight, but again with fixed departure dates, and typically a maximum two- or three-week stay. Agents may also offer special student or youth fares. Don't automatically assume that tickets purchased through a travel specialist will be cheapest, however – once you get a quote, check directly with the airlines and you may turn up a better deal.

From the US and Canada

From most places in North America, flying is the most convenient way to reach Mexico. If you're willing to have your journey take a little longer, it is also possible to reach Mexico overland, via train, bus or car, or by water – several cruise lines stop along the country's Pacific coast.

By air

There are **flights** to Mexico from just about every major **US** city, with the cheapest and most frequent leaving from "gateway" cities in the south and west, especially Dallas, Houston, Los Angeles and Miami.

If you live close to the border, it's usually cheaper to cross into Mexico and take an **internal flight** (which you can arrange through your local travel agent). If it's a resort that you want, you'll probably find that one of the airlines offers an attractive deal including a few nights' lodging.

Aeroméxico and Mexicana fly direct to dozens of destinations in Mexico, and can make connections to many others; the bigger US airlines have connections to Mexico City and the more popular resorts. For the lowest-priced round trip to Mexico City in high season, expect to pay (including tax) around US$250 out of Dallas, US$270 from Miami, US$280 from Houston, US$285 from New York or US$310 from LA. For a flight to Cancún, you'll be looking at around US$245 from Dallas, US$255 from Miami, US$295 from Houston, US$270 from New York or US$345 from LA. There are direct flights to many parts of Mexico from numerous other US airports, but adding a feeder flight from any US or Canadian city to one of the main gateways should be straightforward.

There are fewer direct scheduled flights from **Canada** to Mexico, although Air Canada, Aeroméxico and Mexicana fly to Mexico City from Toronto, and Mexicana flies there from Montréal and Vancouver too, and Air Canada flies from Toronto, Montréal and Vancouver to Cancún and Toronto to Cozumel, along with plentiful winter charter flights. Your options expand greatly if you fly via the US. Typical lowest high-season round-trip fares to Mexico City are around Can$360 from Toronto, Can$345 Montréal or Can$425 from Vancouver. To Cancún, expect to pay around Can$370 from Toronto or Montréal and Can$415 from Vancouver.

By train

US passenger **train** services reach the border at El Paso, on the LA–Dallas line. El Paso is served by Amtrak's *Texas Eagle* (three times weekly from Chicago, St Louis, Little Rock and Dallas) and *Sunset Limited* (three times weekly from New Orleans, Houston, Tucson and LA). The journey takes seventeen hours from LA (US$99), twenty from Houston (US$91), 29 from Dallas (US$87) and 51 from Chicago (US$117).

Arrivals on these services give you plenty of time to get across the frontier, have something to eat in Ciudad Juárez and get a bus on to Mexico City.

Check current timetables with Amtrak (Ⓣ1-800/USA-RAIL, Ⓦwww.amtrak.com).

By bus

North American **bus** travel is pretty grim compared to the relative comfort of Amtrak, but you have a wider range of US border posts to choose from. Count on at least 52 hours' journey time from New York to El Paso (US$83 if purchased two weeks in advance), or twelve hours from San Francisco to Tijuana (US$58 if purchased two weeks in advance) – and at least a further day's travel from either point to Mexico City.

Greyhound (Ⓣ1-800/231-2222 or 1-214/849-8100, Ⓦwww.greyhound.com) runs regularly to all the major border crossings. Some of their buses will also take you over the frontier to a Mexican bus station, which saves a lot of hassle. Greyhound agents abroad should be able to reserve your through tickets with their Mexican counterparts, which is even more convenient but involves pre-planning. Additionally, many Mexican bus companies cross the border into the US, so that you can pick up a bus to Mexico as far north as Houston or LA.

More countercultural, and arguably better value, are overland tours from San Francisco with Green Tortoise Adventure Travel (Ⓣ1-800/TORTOISE or 1-415/956-7500, Ⓦwww.greentortoise.com). Converted school buses provide reasonably comfortable transport and sleeping space for up to 35 people; the clientele comes from all over the world, and communal cookouts are the rule.

By car

Taking your own **car** into Mexico will obviously give you a great deal more freedom, but it's an option fraught with complications. Aside from border formalities, you'll also have to contend with the state of the roads, the style of driving and the quality of the fuel.

Licences and permits

Driving licences from the US, Canada, the UK, Ireland, Australia, New Zealand and most European countries are valid in Mexico, but it's a good idea to arm yourself with an **International Driving Licence** – available from motoring organizations such as the AAA in the US, the CAA in Canada, or the AA in Britain. If you fall foul of a Mexican traffic cop for any reason, show that first; if they abscond with it you at least still have your own licence.

As a rule, you can drive in Baja California, western Sonora and the Zona Libre (the border area extending roughly 25km into Mexico) without any special formalities. To drive elsewhere in Mexico, however, you must obtain a temporary **importation permit** (US$27 for an ordinary car, US$45 for a camper) at the border, or online at Ⓦwww.banjercito.com.mx/site/siteBanjer/iitv/iitv/english.html. To make sure you don't sell the car in Mexico or a neighbouring country, you'll also be required either to post a cash bond, the amount of which will depend on the make and age of your vehicle, though it will be at least US$400 for a car less than eight years old, or to give an imprint of a major credit card (Visa, MasterCard, Diners Club or American Express).

This is done using the credit or debit card of the owner of the vehicle (who must be in it) at Banjército, the Mexican army bank, which has offices at border posts specifically for the purpose. You'll need to show registration and title documents for the car, plus your driver's licence and passport, and you'll probably be asked to supply two photocopies of these as well as your tourist card. The permits are good for 180 days, during which time you can drive your car out of Mexico and return, but there are penalties in force if you exceed the limit, including forfeiture of your vehicle. More detailed information on importing a vehicle to Mexico can be found at ⓦwww.mexonline.com/drivemex.htm.

Insurance

US and Canadian **auto insurance** policies don't cover Mexico, so you will need to take out a Mexican policy, available from numerous agencies on either side of every border post. Rates depend on the value of the vehicle and what kind of coverage you want, but figure on US$11 or so a day for basic liability (fourteen days' basic liability coverage for a US$10,000 vehicle is around US$110, with full coverage for around US$150). To arrange a policy before leaving the US, call Instant Mexico Insurance Services (ⓣ1-800/345-4701, ⓦwww.mexonline.com/instant1.htm); International Gateway (ⓣ1-619/271-0572, ⓦwww.igib.com); Oscar Padilla Mexican Insurance (ⓣ1-800/466-7227, ⓦwww.mexicaninsurance.com); or Sanborn's Insurance (ⓣ1-800/222-0158, ⓦwww.sanbornsinsurance.com). The last is the acknowledged leader in the field.

To get discounts on insurance, it might be worthwhile joining a travel club, such as Discover Baja Travel Club (ⓣ1-800/727-2252, ⓦwww.discoverbaja.com) or Sanborn's Sombrero Club (ⓣ1-800/222-0158, ⓦwww.sanbornsinsurance.com). These clubs typically also offer discounts on accommodation and free travel advice. Annual dues are US$25–39.

The American and Canadian Automobile Associations produce road maps and route planners for travel to Mexico, and members may qualify for discounted insurance at affiliated border agencies, but their emergency/breakdown services do not cover you once you are inside Mexico.

Border crossings

There are some forty **frontier posts** along the US–Mexico border. Many of them are only open during the day, and are more or less inaccessible without your own transport. For a full list, see ⓦapps.cbp.gov/bwt or www.mexico.us/bordercrossings".htm. The main ones, open 24 hours a day, seven days a week, are, from west to east:

San Diego, California–**Tijuana**, Baja California.
Calexico, California–**Mexicali**, Baja California.
Nogales, Arizona–**Nogales**, Sonora.
Douglas, Arizona–**Agua Prieta**, Sonora.
El Paso, Texas–**Ciudad Juárez**, Chihuahua.
Laredo, Texas–**Nuevo Laredo**, Tamaulipas.
Brownsville, Texas–**Matamoros**, Tamaulipas.

By boat

If you want to **sail** to Mexico in your own boat, similar conditions apply to those in effect for motor vehicles (see opposite) – for

Border practicalities

Crossing the border, especially on foot, it's easy to go straight past the immigration and customs checks. There's a free zone south of the frontier, and you can cross at will and stay for up to three days. Make sure you get your **tourist card** stamped and your bags checked, though, or when you try to continue south you'll be stopped after some 20km and sent back to complete the formalities. See "Entry requirements", on p.59, for more information.

Troubled areas

The area bordering the US, and particularly **Ciudad Juárez**, but also Tijuana, is the biggest hotspot in Mexico's **drugs war** (see p.187). Extra caution should be exercised when crossing this area, especially by car.

further details, see Ⓦwww.tijuana.com/boatcrossing.

Alternatively, you could take a **cruise**. Several lines offer cruises on the Pacific coast, most popularly between LA and Acapulco, stopping at Los Cabos, Mazatlán, Puerto Vallarta and Zihuatanejo. Others ply the Caribbean side out of Miami, taking in Cozumel, Playa del Carmen and other Mexican destinations. Prices start at US$400 per person for a week-long cruise, plus airfare to the starting point, and go (way) up from there. Agencies specializing in cruises include those listed below.

Cruiseboat contacts

Carnival Cruise Lines US & Canada Ⓣ1-888/227-6482, Ⓦwww.carnival.com.
Cruise West Ⓣ1-888/851-8133, Ⓦwww.cruisewest.com.
Cruise World Ⓣ1-800/228-1153, Ⓦwww.cruiseworldtours.com.
Norwegian Cruise Line US & Canada Ⓣ1-866/234-7350, UK Ⓣ0845/658 8010; Ⓦwww.ncl.com.
Royal Caribbean Cruises US & Canada Ⓣ1-866/562-7625, UK Ⓣ0845/165 8414, Australia Ⓣ02/4331 5400; Ⓦwww.royalcaribbean.com.

From the UK and Ireland

The only direct scheduled flights from the British Isles to Mexico are from London to Mexico City, with BA out of Heathrow, or Mexicana out of Gatwick. Flying from anywhere else in Britain or Ireland, or to any other destination in Mexico, means you will have to change planes somewhere.

From London, though a direct flight is easiest, it may well be cheaper to take an indirect flight with a European or American carrier (Lufthansa frequently offers the lowest rates). From other British and Irish airports, you can either fly to London and pick up BA's direct flight there, or use a European or American airline, changing planes at their hub cities. Of American carriers, Continental offers the widest choice of Mexican destinations, with twice as many as the next contender, American Airlines. Another possibility is to fly via the US and either continue overland or buy an onward flight once in the country. LA and Houston are logical points from which to set off overland, and along with Miami, have reasonably priced onward flights to several Mexican destinations. **Prices** for scheduled return flights from London to Mexico City (including tax) start at around £470.

Charter flights to Mexico are fairly common, flying from Gatwick, Birmingham, Glasgow or Manchester to Cancún, or occasionally Acapulco or Puerto Vallarta. Charter fares, sometimes under £450 in the low season, can also be very good value any time outside school holidays, though they can go as high as £800 in August, and your stay will probably be limited to one or two weeks. The best way to find out about charters is to call or log on to Sky Deals (Ⓣ0800/757 757, Ⓦwww.skydeals.com), who sell tickets for all the main operators, or My Travel (Ⓣ0871/895 0055, Ⓦwww.mytravel.co.uk), the main charter operator to Mexico.

If flying via the US, it's worth checking if your transatlantic carrier has an **airpass** deal for non-US residents – most major US airlines do – by which you purchase coupons at a flat rate for a certain number of flights in North America (with a usual minimum of three). Depending on the airline, the pass will usually also include one or more destinations in Mexico and Canada.

From Australia, New Zealand and South Africa

The **high season** for flights to Mexico from the southern hemisphere is mid-June to mid-July and mid-December to mid-January, though prices do not vary vastly between seasons. There are no direct flights to Mexico from Australia, New Zealand or South Africa, so you will have to change planes somewhere en route.

From **Australia**, most options involve changing planes in Los Angeles. Your widest choice of flights is from Sydney, where you can fly with Delta via LA, or LAN via Santiago de Chile. United flies via LA from both Sydney and Melbourne, and Qantas flies from almost all Australian airports to LA, where you can continue to Mexico with Mexicana, American or United. You can also take an Air New Zealand/Mexicana combination, with an extra change of planes at Auckland. Prices start at around Aus$1200 (including tax) for the round trip.

Six steps to a better kind of travel

At Rough Guides we are passionately committed to travel. We feel strongly that only through travelling do we truly come to understand the world we live in and the people we share it with – plus tourism has brought a great deal of **benefit** to developing economies around the world over the last few decades. But the extraordinary growth in tourism has also damaged some places irreparably, and of course **climate change** is exacerbated by most forms of transport, especially flying. This means that now more than ever it's important to **travel thoughtfully** and **responsibly**, with respect for the cultures you're visiting – not only to derive the most benefit from your trip but also to preserve the best bits of the planet for everyone to enjoy. At Rough Guides we feel there are six main areas in which you can make a difference:

- Consider what you're contributing to the **local economy**, and how much the services you use do the same, whether it's through employing local workers and guides or sourcing locally grown produce and local services.
- Consider the **environment** on holiday as well as at home. The biodiversity of local flora and fauna can be adversely affected by tourism. Try to patronize businesses that take account of this.
- Travel with a purpose, not just to tick off experiences. Consider **spending longer** in a place, and getting to know it and its people.
- Give thought to how often you **fly**. Try to avoid short hops by air and more harmful night flights.
- Consider **alternatives to flying**, travelling instead by bus, train, boat and even by bike or on foot where possible.
- Make your trips **"climate neutral"** via a reputable carbon-offset scheme. All Rough Guide flights are offset, and every year we donate money to a variety of charities devoted to combating the effects of climate change.

From **New Zealand**, your choice is very similar: either LAN Chile from Auckland via Santiago, or else Auckland to LA with Air New Zealand, or with Qantas via Sydney, continuing with Mexicana or United. From other New Zealand airports, you will probably need to change planes additionally at Auckland or Sydney. Prices start from around NZ$2400 return (including tax).

From **South Africa**, your most direct route is with Delta or United from Johannesburg via the US, though European airlines such as Air France, Iberia, Lufthansa and British Airways will fly you via their respective hubs in Europe. From other South African airports, you'll usually have to fly via Johannesburg. Fares start at around R14,000.

Packages and tours

Hundreds of companies – particularly in the US – offer good-value **package trips** to Mexican resorts, as do the tour arms of most major North American airlines. Packages are generally only available for the more commercialized destinations, such as Cabo San Lucas, Mazatlán, Puerto Vallarta, Acapulco, Ixtapa and Cancún, and travel agents usually only give you one or two weeks. In addition, literally hundreds of specialist companies offer **tours** of Mexico based around hiking, biking, diving, bird watching and the like. Remember that bookings made through a travel agent cost no more than going through the tour operator – indeed, many tour companies sell only through agents. See p.32 for information on tour operators.

Airlines, agents and operators

Airlines

Aeromar Ⓦwww.aeromar.com.mx.
Aeroméxico Ⓦwww.aeromexico.com.
Air Canada Ⓦwww.aircanada.com.
Air France Ⓦwww.airfrance.com.
Air New Zealand Ⓦwww.airnz.co.nz.
Alaska Airlines Ⓦwww.alaskaair.com.

American Airlines Ⓦwww.aa.com.
British Airways Ⓦwww.ba.com.
Continental Airlines Ⓦwww.continental.com.
Delta Ⓦwww.delta.com.
Iberia Ⓦwww.iberia.com.
JetBlue Ⓦwww.jetblue.com.
KLM Ⓦwww.klm.com.
LAN Ⓦwww.lan.com.
Lufthansa Ⓦwww.lufthansa.com.
Mexicana Ⓦwww.mexicana.com.
Northwest Ⓦwww.nwa.com.
Qantas Ⓦwww.qantas.com.
South African Airways Ⓦwww.flysaa.com.
Sun Country Airlines Ⓦwww.suncountry.com.
United Airlines Ⓦwww.united.com.
US Airways Ⓦwww.usair.com.

Agents

North South Travel UK ⓣ01245/608 291, Ⓦwww.northsouthtravel.co.uk. Friendly, competitive travel agency, offering discounted fares worldwide. Profits are used to support projects in the developing world, especially the promotion of sustainable tourism.

Trailfinders UK ⓣ0845/058 5858, Ⓦwww.trailfinders.com; Ireland ⓣ01/677 7888, Ⓦwww.trailfinders.ie; Australia ⓣ1300/780 212, Ⓦwww.trailfinders.com.au. One of the best-informed and most efficient agents for independent travellers.

Travel CUTS Canada ⓣ1-866/246-9762, US ⓣ1-800/592-2887; Ⓦwww.travelcuts.com. Canadian youth and student travel firm.

STA Travel US ⓣ1-800/781-4040, Ⓦwww.statravel.com; UK ⓣ020/7361 6162, Ⓦwww.statravel.co.uk; Australia ⓣ13/4782, Ⓦwww.statravel.com.au; NZ ⓣ0800/474 400, Ⓦwww.statravel.co.nz; South Africa ⓣ0861/781 781, Ⓦwww.statravel.co.za. Specialists in independent travel (especially student and under-26); also student IDs and travel insurance.

USIT Ireland ⓣ01/602 1906, Northern Ireland ⓣ028/9032 7111; Ⓦwww.usit.ie. Ireland's main student and youth travel specialists.

Tour operators

Baja Expeditions US & Canada ⓣ1-800/843-6967, Ⓦwww.bajaex.com. Sea kayaking, whale watching, snorkelling and scuba diving, among other tours in Baja California.

Cathy Matos Mexican Tours UK ⓣ020/8492 0000, Ⓦwww.cathymatosmexico.co.uk. Wide variety of tailor-made tours, including colonial cities, beaches, sightseeing and archeology, whale watching and destination weddings.

G.A.P. Adventures US & Canada ⓣ1-800/708-7761, UK ⓣ0870/999 0144, Australia ⓣ1300/796 618, New Zealand ⓣ0800 333 307; Ⓦwww.gapadventures.com. Guided adventure trips, some involving camping, mostly centred on the Yucatán.

Global Exchange US ⓣ1-415/255-7296, Ⓦwww.globalexchange.org. Organization campaigning on international issues and offering "Reality Tours" to increase American travellers' awareness of real life in Mexico (especially Oaxaca and Chiapas) and other countries.

South America Destinations Australia ⓣ03/9725 4655, Ⓦwww.south-america.com.au. Latin America specialists offering a range of Mexico tours, including a colonial cities tour, a Copper Canyon rail trip and a week in the Yucatán.

South America Travel Centre Australia ⓣ03/9642 5353, Ⓦwww.satc.com.au. Tours on offer include a ten-day Maya ruins tour (also visiting Monte Albán and Oaxaca), an eight-day colonial cities tour and a six-day Copper Canyon trip.

Trips Worldwide UK ⓣ0800/840 0850, Ⓦwww.tripsworldwide.co.uk. Friendly, experienced company with an inspired range of tailor-made itineraries to Mexico.

Wilderness Travel US ⓣ1-800/368-2794, Ⓦwww.wildernesstravel.com. Cultural and wildlife trips including a twelve-day "World of the Maya" tour, or eight days' sea kayaking in Baja California.

Wild Oceans UK ⓣ0117/965 8333, Ⓦwww.wildwings.co.uk. Naturalist-led tours to observe whales (including blue whale research project), sea lions and other wildlife in the Sea of Cortés.

Getting around

Distances in Mexico can be huge, and if you're intending to travel on public transport, you should be prepared for some very long journeys. Getting from Tijuana to Mexico City, for example, can take nearly two days nonstop by bus. Although public transport at ground level is frequent and reasonably efficient everywhere, taking an internal flight at least once may be worthwhile for the time it saves.

By bus

Within Mexico, **buses** (long-distance buses are called *camiones*, rather than *autobuses*, in Mexican Spanish) are by far the most common and efficient form of public transport. There are an unbelievable number of them, run by a multitude of companies and connecting even the smallest of villages. Intercity services generally rely on very comfortable and dependable vehicles; remote villages are more commonly connected by what look like (and often are) recycled school buses from north of the border.

The legendary craziness of Mexican bus drivers is largely a thing of the past, and many bus companies have installed warning lights and buzzers to indicate when the driver is exceeding the speed limit (though these are often ignored by the driver). In recent years the government has been trying to improve the safety record through regular mechanical checks and also with random alcohol and drug tests on the drivers.

Classes

There are basically two **classes** of bus, first (*primera*) and second (*segunda*), though on major long-distance routes there's often little to differentiate them. First-class vehicles have reserved seats, videos and air-conditioning, though an increasing number of second-class lines have the same comforts. The main differences will be in the number of stops – second-class buses call at more places, and consequently take longer to get where they're going – and the fare, which is about ten percent higher on first-class services, and sometimes a lot more. You may be able to get a discount with a student card, though it's unlikely. Most people choose first class for any appreciably long distance, and second for short trips or for destinations not served by a first-class bus, but you should not be put off second class if it seems more convenient.

On important routes there are also **deluxe**, or **pullman**, buses, with names like Primera Plus or Turistar Plus and fares around thirty percent higher than those of first-class buses. They have few, if any, stops, waitress service and free snacks and drinks over longer distances, comfortable airline-style seating and air-conditioning that works – be sure to keep a sweater handy, as they can get very cold. They may also be emptier, which could mean more space to stretch out and sleep. Almost all pullman services have computerized reservations and may accept credit cards; these facilities are increasingly common with the larger regular bus lines too.

Stations

Most towns of any size have a modern **bus station**, known as the **Central Camionera** or **Central de Autobuses**. Don't let the word "central" fool you, as they are usually located a long way from the town centre. Where there is no unified terminus you may find separate first- and second-class terminals, or individual ones for each company, sometimes little more than bus stops at the side of the road. There is some form of baggage deposit (left luggage) office in every bus station – usually known as a **guardería**, **consigna** or simply **equipaje**, and costing about M$40–100 per item per day. Before leaving anything, make sure that the place will be open when you come to collect your bags. If there's no formal facility, staff at the bus companies' baggage dispatching offices can often be persuaded to look after your things for a short while.

Tickets

Always check your route and arrival time, and whenever possible buy **tickets** from the bus station in advance to get the best (or any) seats; count on paying about M$75–120 for every 100km covered. There are very rarely problems getting a place on a bus from its point of origin or from really big towns. In smaller, mid-route places, however, you may have to wait for the bus to arrive (or at least to leave the previous stop) before discovering if there are any seats – the increased prevalence of computerized ticketing is easing the problem. Often there are too few seats, and without fluent and loud Spanish you may lose out in the fight for the ticket clerk's attention. Alternatively, there's almost always a bus described as *local*, which means it originates from where you are (as opposed to a *de paso* bus, which started somewhere else), and tickets for these can be bought well in advance.

Weekends, holiday season, school holidays and fiestas also overload services to certain destinations: again the only real answer is to buy tickets in advance. However, you could also try the cheaper second-class lines, where they'll pack you in standing, or take whatever's going to the next town along the way and try for a *local* from there. A word with the driver and a small tip can sometimes work wonders.

Timetables

Terms to look out for on the timetable, besides *local* and *de paso*, include *vía corta* (by the short route) and *directo* or *expreso* (direct/nonstop – in theory at least). *Salida* is departure, *llegada* arrival. A decent road map will be extremely helpful in working out which buses are going to pass through your destination.

By air

There are more than fifty airports in Mexico with regular passenger **flights** run by local airlines, plus several smaller airports with feeder services. The two big companies, both formerly state-owned and with international as well as domestic flights, are Aeroméxico and Mexicana, which between

Distance chart (in km)

	Acapulco	Aguascalientes	Cancún	Chihuahua	Ciudad Juárez	Durango	Guadalajara	Matamoros	Mérida
Acapulco	–	889	1951	1732	2109	1281	859	1361	1647
Aguascalientes	889	–	2144	979	1356	417	250	819	1840
Cancún	1951	2144	–	3086	3463	2524	2174	2331	304
Chihuahua	1732	979	3086	–	377	632	1188	1097	2782
Ciudad Juárez	2109	1356	3463	377	–	1009	1565	1474	3159
Durango	1281	417	2524	632	1009	–	556	880	2220
Guadalajara	859	250	2174	1188	1565	556	–	995	1870
Matamoros	1361	819	2331	1097	1474	880	995	–	2027
Mérida	1647	1840	304	2782	3159	2220	1870	2027	–
Mexico City	390	514	1630	1456	1833	894	544	971	1326
Monterrey	1341	582	2349	790	1167	573	771	307	2046
Nogales	2572	1748	3855	769	635	1508	1698	2050	3551
Oaxaca	653	984	1702	1938	2315	1376	1026	1368	1398
San Luis Potosí	800	168	2043	1043	1420	481	344	651	1739
Tampico	863	575	1833	1307	1684	888	751	498	1529
Tijuana	3151	2504	4597	1532	1294	2087	2777	2629	4293
Tuxtla Gutiérrez	967	1389	1155	2331	2708	1769	1419	1764	851
Veracruz	711	898	1332	1808	2185	1279	929	999	1028
Villahermosa	1090	1283	861	2225	2602	1663	1313	1470	557

them connect most places to Mexico City, usually several times a day. Their monopoly is being challenged by a handful of smaller airlines such as Aeromar and Interjet, which also cover most major destinations, as well as Mexicana's no-frills carrier Click. The competition between the companies keeps prices steady and relatively low. Information about the independent operators is available online and through travel agents.

Internal **airfares** reflect the popularity of the route: the more popular the trip, the lower the price. Thus the flight from Tijuana to Mexico City costs much the same as the much shorter, but less popular flight from Tijuana to Chihuahua, but even the more expensive routes can be worthwhile for the time they save. While the smaller airlines might be cheaper, the price of a ticket on a particular flight doesn't normally vary from agent to agent. There are few discounts, and it's usually twice as much for a round-trip as a one-way ticket.

Mexicana and Aeroméxico offer a multi-flight airpass, available only outside Mexico.

Domestic airlines

Aerolitoral Mexico ⓣ01-800/800-2376, ⓦwww.aerolitoral.com.mx.
Aeromar Mexico ⓣ01-800/237-6627 or 55/5133-1111, ⓦwww.aeromar.com.mx.
Aeroméxico Mexico ⓣ01-800/021-4010 or 55/5133-4010, US ⓣ1-800/237-6639, UK c/o ⓣ020/7367 0900, Australia c/o ⓣ02/8666 4666, NZ c/o ⓣ09/623 4298, South Africa c/o ⓣ011/781-2111; ⓦwww.aeromexico.com.
Aeroservicio Guerrero Mexico ⓣ01-800/823-3153 or 615/157-0137, ⓦwww.aereoserviciosguerrero.com.mx.
Aerovega Mexico ⓣ951/516-4982, ⓦwww.oaxaca-mio.com/aerovega.
Click Mexico ⓣ01-800/112-5425 or 55/2282-6262, ⓦwww.clickmx.com (outside Mexico, contact Mexicana).
Interjet Mexico ⓣ01-800/ 011-2345 or 55/1102-5555, US ⓣ1-866/285-9525; ⓦwww.interjet.com.mx.
Mexicana Mexico ⓣ01-800/801-2030 or 55/2881-0000, US ⓣ1-800/531-7921; ⓦwww.mexicana.com.mx.
VivaAerobus Mexico ⓣ81/8215 0150, US ⓣ1-889/9-FLY-VIVA; ⓦwww.vivaaerobus.com.

Mexico City	Monterrey	Nogales	Oaxaca	San Luis Potosí	Tampico	Tijuana	Tuxtla Gutiérrez	Veracruz	Villa-hermosa
390	1341	2572	653	800	863	3151	967	711	1090
514	582	1748	984	168	575	2504	1389	898	1283
1630	2349	3855	1702	2043	1833	4597	1155	1332	861
1456	790	769	1938	1043	1307	1532	2331	1808	2225
1833	1167	635	2315	1420	1684	1294	2708	2185	2602
894	573	1508	1376	481	888	2087	1769	1279	1663
544	771	1698	1026	344	751	2777	1419	929	1313
971	307	2050	1368	651	498	2629	1764	999	1470
1326	2046	3551	1398	1739	1529	4293	851	1028	557
–	954	2242	482	413	473	2821	875	385	769
954	–	1743	1387	541	517	2322	1783	1018	1489
2242	1743	–	2707	1812	2076	817	3100	2577	2994
482	1387	2707	–	895	870	3303	547	369	841
413	541	1812	895	–	407	2568	1288	798	1182
473	517	2076	870	407	–	2839	1266	501	972
2821	2322	817	3303	2568	2839	–	1070	305	776
875	1783	3100	547	1288	1266	1070	–	765	294
385	1018	2577	369	798	501	305	765	–	471
769	1489	2994	841	1182	972	776	294	471	–

Volaris Mexico ⓣ01-800/122-8000 or 55/1102-8000, US ⓣ1-866/988-3527; ⓦwww.volaris.com.mx.

By rail

Since Mexico's railways were privatized in 1995, all passenger services have been withdrawn bar one suburban service out of Mexico City and two lines run especially for tourists: the **Copper Canyon railway** in Chihuahua, an amazing scenic journey and one of the country's top tourist attractions (see p.157), and the **Tequila Express** from Guadalajara to Amatitán (see p.340).

By boat

Ferries connect Baja California with a trio of ports on the Pacific mainland: Santa Rosalía to Guaymas, and La Paz to Mazatlán and Topolobampo (for Los Mochis). For detailed information on schedules see ⓦwww.mexconnect.com/mex_/mexicoferryw.html. There are also smaller boats to islands off the Caribbean and Gulf coasts: from Chiquilá to Holbox, from Cancún to Isla Mujeres and from Playa del Carmen to Cozumel. Though not as cheap as they once were, all these services are still pretty reasonable: see the relevant chapters for current fares.

By car

Getting your **car** into Mexico (see "Getting there", p.28) is just the beginning of your problems. Although most people who venture in by car both enjoy their trip and get out again with no more than minor incidents, driving in Mexico does require a good deal of care and concentration, and almost inevitably involves at least one brush with bureaucracy or the law. Hitchhiking is possible, but due to safety concerns, the scarcity of lifts and the vast distances involved, it's not recommended.

Car rental

Renting a car in Mexico – especially if done with a short, specific itinerary in mind – avoids many problems and is often an extremely good way of seeing quickly a small area that would take days to explore using public transport. There are any number of competing agencies in all the tourist resorts and major cities; the local operations usually charge less than the well-known names. Always check **rates** carefully to make sure they include insurance, tax and the mileage you need. Daily rates with unlimited mileage start around US$20/£12; weekly rates usually cost around the same as six days. In some resorts **mopeds** and **motorbikes** are also available for short distances, but most of the large, international companies don't deal with them because of the high frequency of accidents.

Licences and insurance

Drivers from Australia, Canada, most European countries, Ireland, New Zealand, the UK and the US (but not South Africa) will find that their **licences** are valid in Mexico, though an international licence (available from the motoring organizations listed on p.28) can be useful, especially if your domestic one has no photo on it. You are required to have all your documents with you when driving. **Insurance** is not compulsory, but you'd be foolhardy not to get some sort of policy (see p.29 for more on motor insurance).

Petrol

The government oil company, PEMEX, has a monopoly and sells two types of **petrol**: Magna Sin (regular unleaded), and Premium (high-octane unleaded). Both of these cost slightly more than regular unleaded north of the border, at about US$2.50 per US gallon.

Roads and traffic

Mexican **roads and traffic** are your chief worries. Traffic circulates on the right, and the normal speed limit is 40kph (25mph) in built-up areas, 70kph (43mph) in open country and 110kph (68mph) on the freeway. Some of the new highways are excellent, and the toll (*cuota*) superhighways are better still, though extremely expensive to drive on (check prices online at ⓦwww.sct.gob.mx/autotransporte/index.htm). Away from the major population centres, however, roads are often narrow, winding

Banditry: a warning

You should be aware when driving in Mexico, especially in a foreign vehicle, of the danger of **bandits**. Robberies and even more serious assaults on motorists do occur, above all in the northwest and especially in the state of Sinaloa, though for private motorists and buses the problem is nothing like as bad as it once was. Robbers may try to make you stop by indicating that there is something wrong with your vehicle; they've also been known to pose as policemen, hitchhikers and motorists in distress, so think twice about offering a lift or a helping hand. On the other hand, there are plenty of legitimate police checkpoints along the main roads, where you must stop, and increased security (to combat the drug cartels) has very much reduced hold-ups of buses. Robbers nowadays mainly target cargo trucks rather than private cars, but it is nonetheless best to avoid driving at night on the worst-affected roads, notably: **Hwy-15** (Los Mochis–Mazatlán) and express **Hwy-1** in Sinaloa; **Hwy-5** (Mexico City–Acapulco) in Guerrero; **Hwy-200** along the Pacific coast of Jalisco, Michoacán, Guerrero and Oaxaca; **Hwy-75** (Oaxaca–Tuxtepec) and **Hwy 175** (Oaxaca–Pochutla) in Oaxaca; **Hwy-150** (Mexico City–Veracruz); **Hwy-57** (Mexico City–San Luis Potosí–Matahuela); and near the border, in particular on **Hwy-2** (Mexicali–Agua Prieta) and **Hwy-40** (Matamoros–Monterrey). It's always safer to use a toll (*cuota*) highway than a free one. The US State Department nonetheless advises its citizens to avoid travelling at night anywhere in the country.

and potholed, with livestock wandering across at unexpected moments. Get out of the way of Mexican bus and truck drivers – if you signal left to them on a stretch of open road, it means it's clear to overtake. Every town and village limits the speed of through traffic with a series of *topes* (concrete or metal speed bumps) across the road. Look out for the warning signs and take them seriously; the bumps are often huge. It's wise to avoid driving at night, not only for road safety reasons, but also because of the threat of hold-ups (see box above). Any good road map should provide details of the more common symbols used on Mexican **road signs**, and SECTUR has a pamphlet on driving in Mexico in which they're also featured. One convention of note: the first driver to flash their lights at a junction, or where only one vehicle can pass, has the right of way – you're not being invited to go first.

Most large towns have extensive **one-way systems**. Traffic direction is often poorly marked (look for small arrows affixed to lampposts), though this is less of a problem than it sounds: simply note the direction in which the parked cars, if not the moving cars, are facing.

Parking

Parking in cities is another hassle – the restrictions are complicated and foreigners are easy pickings for traffic police, who usually remove one or both plates in lieu of a ticket (retrieving them can be an expensive and time-consuming business). Since **theft** is also a real threat, you'll usually have to pay extra for a hotel with secure parking. You may well also have to fork out over on-the-spot "fines" for traffic offences (real or concocted). In Mexico City, residents' cars are banned from driving on one day of every week, determined by their licence number: the ban also applies to foreign cars, but rented vehicles are exempt.

Breakdowns and accidents

Unless your car is a basic-model VW, Ford or Dodge (all of which are manufactured in Mexico), **spare parts** are expensive and hard to come by – bring a basic spares kit. Tyres in particular suffer on burning-hot Mexican roads, so you should carry at least one good spare. Roadside *vulcanizadoras* and *llanteros* can do temporary repairs; new tyres are expensive, but remoulds aren't a good idea on hot roads at high speed. If you have a breakdown on any highway between 8am and 8pm, there is a free mechanic service known as the **Ángeles Verdes** (Green Angels). As well as patrolling major routes looking for beleaguered motorists, they can be reached by phone on ⓣ078 or on local state hotlines, or by email at ⓔangelesverdes@sectur.gob.mx, and they speak English.

Should you have a minor **accident**, try to come to some arrangement with the other party – involving the police will only make matters worse, and Mexican drivers will be just as anxious to avoid doing so. If you witness an accident, you may want to consider the gravity of the situation before getting involved. Witnesses can be locked up along with those directly implicated to prevent them from leaving before the case comes up – so consider if your involvement is necessary to serve justice. In a serious incident, contact your consulate and your Mexican insurance company as soon as possible.

Cycling

Mexico is not big on **cycling**, and with its vast size and the heavy and inconsiderate traffic in big cities, not to mention the danger of banditry, few tourists travel the country by bicycle. Nonetheless, there's now a free bike hire scheme in Mexico City (see p.390), and Guadalajara's main youth hostel, the *Hostel Guadalajara Centro* (see p.322), rents out bikes for free. The Yucatán peninsula, being quite flat, also lends itself to cycling, and bicycles can be rented in Campeche, Isla Mujeres, Playa del Carmen, Isla Cozumel and Tulum (see p.757, p.812, p.819, p.824 & p.837). So does the area around Oaxaca, where you can also rent bikes (see p.618). Bicycle tour firms in Mexico include Bicicletas Pedro Martinez (ⓦwww.bicicletaspedromartinez.com), !El Tours (ⓦwww.bikemexico.com) and Backroads (ⓦwww.backroads.com).

Local transport

Public transport within Mexican towns and cities is always plentiful and inexpensive, though crowded and not particularly user-friendly. Mexico City has an extensive, excellent **Metro** system (M$2 per journey), and there are smaller metros in Guadalajara (M$5 per journey) and Monterrey (M$4.50 per journey), but elsewhere you'll be reliant on buses (usually around M$5 per journey), which pour out clouds of choking diesel fumes; often there's a flat-fare system, but this varies from place to place. Wherever possible we've indicated which bus to take and where to catch it, but often only a local will fully understand the intricacies of the system and you may well have to ask: the main destinations of the bus are usually marked on the windscreen, which helps.

In bigger places *combis* or **colectivos** offer a faster and perhaps less crowded alternative for only a little more money. These are minibuses, vans or large sport utility vehicles that run along fixed routes to set destinations; they'll pick you up and drop you off wherever you like along the way, and you simply pay the driver for the distance travelled. In Mexico City, *combis* are known as **peseros**.

Regular **taxis** can also be good value, but be aware of rip-offs – unless you're confident

Addresses

In Mexico **addresses** are frequently written with just the street name and number (thus: Madero 125), which can lead to confusion as many streets are known only as numbers (C 17). Calle (C) means "street"; Avenida (Av), Bulevar (Blv), Calzada and Paseo are other common terms – most are named after historical figures or dates. An address such as Hidalgo 39 8° 120, means Hidalgo no. 39, 8th floor, room 120 (a ground-floor address would be denoted PB for *planta baja*). Many towns have all their streets laid out in a **numbered grid** fanning out from a central point – often with odd-numbered streets running east–west, even ones north–south. In such places a suffix – Ote (for *Oriente*, East), Pte (for *Poniente*, West), Nte (for *Norte*, North) or Sur (South) – may be added to the street number to tell you which side of the two central dividing streets it is.

that the meter is working, fix a price before you get in. In the big cities, there are often tables of fixed prices posted at prominent spots. At almost every airport and at some of the biggest bus stations you'll find a booth selling vouchers for taxis into town at a fixed price depending on the part of town you want to go to – sometimes there's a choice of paying more for a private car or less to share. This will invariably cost less than just hailing a cab outside the terminal, and will certainly offer extra security. In every case you should know the name of a hotel to head for, or they'll take you to the one that pays the biggest commission. Never accept a ride in any kind of unofficial or unmarked taxi.

Accommodation

Finding a room is rarely difficult – in areas that are not overly touristy the cheap places to stay are usually concentrated around the main plaza (the zócalo), with others near the market, train station or bus station (or where the bus station used to be, before it moved to the outskirts of town). In bigger cities, there's usually a relatively small area in which you'll find the bulk of the less expensive possibilities. The more modern and expensive places often lie on the outskirts of towns, accessible only by car or taxi. The only times you're likely to have big problems finding somewhere to stay are in coastal resorts over the peak Christmas season, at Easter, on Mexican holidays and almost anywhere during a local fiesta, when it's well worth trying to reserve ahead.

Hotels

Mexican hotels may describe themselves as anything from *paradores*, *posadas* and *casas de huéspedes* to plain *hoteles*, all terms that are used more or less interchangeably. A *parador* is totally unrelated to its upmarket Spanish namesake, for example, and although in theory a *casa de huéspedes* means a small cheap place like a guesthouse, you won't find this necessarily to be the case.

All rooms should have an official **price** displayed, though this is not always a guide to quality – a filthy fleapit and a beautifully run converted mansion may charge exactly the same, even if they're right next door to each other. The only recourse for guaranteeing quality is seeing your room first. You should never pay more than the official rate (though just occasionally the sign may not have kept up with inflation) and in the low season you can often pay less. The charging system varies: sometimes it's per person, but usually the price quoted will be for the room regardless of how many people occupy it, so sharing can mean big savings. A room with one double bed (*cama matrimonial*) is almost always cheaper than a room with two singles (*doble* or *con dos camas*), and most hotels have large "family" rooms with several beds, which are tremendous value for groups. In the big resorts, there are lots of apartments that sleep six or more and include cooking facilities, for yet more savings. A little gentle haggling rarely goes amiss, and many places will have some rooms that cost less, so just ask ("*Tiene un cuarto mas barato*?").

Air-conditioning (*aire acondicionado*) is a feature that inflates prices – it is frequently optional. Unless it's unbearably hot and humid, a room with a simple ceiling fan (*ventilador*) is generally better; except in the most expensive places, the air-conditioning units are almost always noisy and inefficient, whereas a fan can be left running silently all night and the draught helps to keep insects away. It might seem too obvious to mention, but be careful of the **ceiling fans**, which are often quite low. In winter, especially at altitude

Accommodation price codes

All the accommodation listed in this book has been categorized into one of nine **price codes**, as set out below. The codes normally refer to the price of the cheapest room for two people in high season.

❶ M$149 and under	❹ M$400–599	❼ M$1200–1599
❷ M$150–249	❺ M$600–899	❽ M$1600–1999
❸ M$250–399	❻ M$900–1199	❾ M$2000 and over

or in the desert, it will of course be **heating** rather than cooling that you want – if there isn't any, make sure there's enough bedding and ask for extra blankets if necessary.

When looking at a room, you should always check its **insect proofing**. Cockroaches and ants are common, and there's not much you can do about them, but decent netting will keep mosquitoes and worse out and allow you to sleep.

Campsites, hammocks and cabañas

Camping is easy enough if you are hiking in the backcountry, or happy simply to crash on a beach, but **robberies** are common, especially in places with a lot of tourists. There are very few organized campsites, and those that do exist are first and foremost trailer parks, not particularly pleasant to pitch tents in. Of course, if you have a van or **RV** you can use these or park just about anywhere else – there are a good number of facilities in the well-travelled areas, especially down the Pacific coast and Baja.

If you're planning to do a lot of camping, an **international camping card** is a good investment, serving as useful ID and getting you discounts at member sites. It is available from home motoring organizations.

In a lot of less official campsites, you will be able to rent a hammock and a place to sling it for the same price as pitching a tent (around US$5/£3), maybe less, and certainly less if you're packing your own hammock (Mexico is a good place to buy these, especially in and around Mérida in the Yucatán).

Beach huts, or **cabañas**, are found at the more rustic, backpacker-oriented beach resorts, and sometimes inland. Usually just a wooden or palm-frond shack with a hammock slung up inside (or a place to sling your own), they are frequently without electricity, though as a resort gets more popular, they tend to transform into sturdier beach bungalows with modern conveniences and higher prices. At backwaters and beaches too untouristed for even cabañas, you should still be able to sling a hammock somewhere (probably the local bar or restaurant, where the palapa serves as shelter and shade).

Hostels

There are fifteen official **youth hostels** in Mexico, charging around M$100 per person for basic, single-sex dorm facilities. A **YH card** is not usually necessary, but you usually pay slightly more without one. Rules are strict in some places (no booze, 11pm curfew, up and out by 9am) but others are open 24 hours and provide kitchen facilities, laundry, travel advice, internet and other services. At holiday periods they may be taken over by Mexican groups. There's a list of official youth hostels (with contact details, prices, location maps and online booking), on the HIM website (Ⓦwww.hostellingmexico.com), but most hostels are not YHA-affiliated, and generally have mixed dorms, liberal alcohol policies and no curfews.

Crime and personal safety

Despite soaring crime rates and dismal-sounding statistics, you are unlikely to run into trouble in Mexico if you stick to well-travelled paths. Even in Mexico City, which has an appalling reputation, the threat is not that much greater than in many large North American and European cities. Obviously there are areas in cities where you wander alone, or at night, at your peril; but the best precaution is common sense. The narco war (see opposite), and the still rumbling conflict in Chiapas do not generally affect tourists.

Avoiding theft

Petty theft and **pickpockets** are your biggest worry in Mexico, so don't wave money around, try not to look too obviously affluent, don't leave cash or cameras in hotel rooms and deposit your valuables in your hotel's safe if it has one (make a note of what you've deposited and ask the hotelier to sign it if you're worried). Crowds, especially on public city transport, are obvious hot spots: thieves tend to work in groups and target tourists. Distracting your attention, especially by pretending to look for something (always be suspicious of anyone who appears to be searching for something near you), or having one or two people pin you down while another goes through your pockets, are common ploys. Razoring of bags and pockets is another gambit, as is the more brutish grabbing of handbags, or anything left unattended even for a split second. **Mugging** is less common than pickpocketing, but you should steer clear of obvious danger spots, such as deserted pedestrian underpasses in big cities – indeed, avoid all deserted areas in big cities. When using ATM machines, use those in shopping malls or enclosed premises, and only in daylight when there are plenty of people around. **Robbery and sexual assault** on tourists by cab drivers are not unknown, and it is not a good idea to hail a cab in the street in Mexico City (see p.380). Instead, phone for a radio cab or, failing that, take the next best option and get a cab from an official *sitio*. At night the beaches in tourist areas are also potentially dangerous.

When travelling, keep an eye on your bags (which are safe enough in the luggage compartments underneath most buses). Hold-ups of buses happen from time to time, and you may well be frisked on boarding to check for arms, since the bandits are most often passengers on the bus.

Drivers are likely to encounter problems if they leave anything in their car. The **vehicle** itself is less likely to be stolen than broken into for the valuables inside. To avoid the worst, always park legally (and preferably off the street) and never leave anything visible inside the car.

Police

Mexican **police** are not well paid, and **graft** is an accepted part of the job, though often difficult for foreign visitors to accept. If a policeman accuses you of some violation (this is almost bound to happen to drivers at some stage), explain that you're a tourist, not used to the ways of the country – you may get off scot-free, but more likely the subject of a "**fine**" will come up. Such on-the-spot fines are open to negotiation, but only if you're confident you've done nothing seriously wrong and have a reasonable command of Spanish. Otherwise pay up and get out.

These small bribes, known as *mordidas* (bites), may also be extracted by border officials or bureaucrats (in which case, you could get out of paying by asking for a receipt, but it won't make life easier). In general, it is always wise to back off from any sort of confrontation with the police and to be extremely polite to them at all times.

Far more common than the *mordida* is the **propina**, or tip, a payment made entirely on your initiative. There's no need to do this, but it's remarkable how often a few pesos complete paperwork that would otherwise take weeks, open firmly locked doors or even find a seat on a previously full bus. All such transactions are quite open, and it's up to you to literally put your money on the table.

Should a crime be committed against you – in particular if you're robbed – your relationship with the police will obviously be different, although even in this eventuality it's worth considering whether the lengthy hassles you'll go through make it worth reporting. Some insurance companies will insist on a police report if you're to get any refund – in which case you may practically have to dictate it to the officer and can expect little action – but others will be understanding of the situation. Travellers' cheque issuers, for example, may accept that your cheques have been stolen and the theft was not reported to the police, though they are within their rights to demand that you do report it. The department you need in order to *presentar una denuncia* (report the theft officially) is the Procuradoría General de Justicia.

The Mexican **legal system** is based on the Napoleonic code, which assumes your guilt until you can prove otherwise. Should you be jailed, your one phone call should be to your **consulate** – if nothing else, they'll arrange an English-speaking lawyer. You can be held for up to 72 hours on suspicion before charges have to be brought. Mexican jails are grim, although lots of money and friends on the outside can ameliorate matters slightly.

Drugs

Drug offences are the most common cause of serious trouble between tourists and the authorities. Under heavy pressure from the US to clamp down on the trade, local authorities are particularly happy to throw the book at foreign offenders.

A good deal of **marijuana** (known as *mota*) – grown primarily in Guerrero ("Acapulco Gold"), Oaxaca and Michoacán (redder in colour, and generally considered the best), and to a lesser extent in other states – continues to be cultivated in Mexico, despite US-backed government attempts to stamp it out (at one time, imports of Mexican marijuana were so high that the DEA had crops sprayed with paraquat). A new law has decriminalized small quantities of cannabis (up to 5g), cocaine (up to 0.5g) and heroin (up to 0.05g), but for quantities reckoned to be for distribution you can wave goodbye to daylight for a long time, and don't expect much help or sympathy from your consulate.

Other naturally occurring drugs – Mexico has more species of psychoactive plants than anywhere else in the world – still form an important part of many indigenous rituals. **Hallucinogenic mushrooms** can be found in many parts of the country, especially in the states of Oaxaca, Chiapas and México, while the **peyote cactus** from the northern deserts is used primarily by the Huichol, but also by other indigenous peoples. The authorities turn a blind eye to traditional use, but use by non-indigenous Mexicans and tourists is as strongly prohibited as that of any other illegal drug, and heavily penalized. Expect searches and hotel raids by police if staying in areas known for peyote.

Americans have been travelling to the border region, especially Tijuana, to buy **prescription medicines**, but can be arrested and imprisoned if they are controlled drugs such as Valium, Vicodin and codeine, unless bought with a legitimate Mexican (*not* American) prescription. Taking them back to the US may also be illegal.

The drugs war

Mexico is a major staging post on the cocaine-smuggling route from Colombia to the US, and use of cocaine is widespread and growing, with **crack** a blight in parts of the capital and some northern cities. Powerful, well-connected cocaine- and methamphetamine-smuggling cartels, known as "**narcos**" have long fought over territory, with each gang having its own pet politicians and police in the states it controls. The situation changed radically in 2007 when President Felipe Calderón declared war on the *narcos*, who have since turned their guns on the police and army as well as each other, and innocent civilians often get caught in the crossfire. Thousands of people a year are now being killed in incidents related to the **drugs war**, with the biggest hotspots in areas bordering the US, and in major drug-producing states such as Sinaloa, but nowhere is safe. Tourists are not usually affected, but June 2009 saw tourist hotels hurriedly evacuated as a two-hour gun battle engulfed a section of Acapulco. Ironically, the increased presence of police and army patrols has led to better security in some ways (less highway banditry for example), but particularly in hotspots such as Ciudad Juárez, Tijuana, Nuevo Laredo, Monterrey, Matamoros, Nogales and Reynosa, it is best to avoid areas you don't know and anywhere associated with the drugs trade, though shootings have occurred in those cities at ordinary restaurants and busy road junctions.

Health

Most travellers visit Mexico without catching anything more serious than a dose of Montezuma's Revenge. You will still want the security of health insurance (see p.61), but the important thing is to keep your resistance high and to be aware of the health risks linked to poor hygiene, untreated water, mosquito bites, undressed open cuts and unprotected sex.

Lack of sanitation in Mexico is much exaggerated, but a degree of caution is wise. Avoid food that looks like it has been on display for a while or not freshly cooked, and always peel fruit before eating it. Avoid raw shellfish, and don't eat anywhere that is obviously dirty (easily spotted, since most Mexican restaurants are scrupulously clean). Salads are healthy, but think twice before eating them if you have a sensitive stomach. In general, keep an eye out for cleanliness of street stalls – beware of food that has been left out to breed germs rather than food that has been freshly cooked. For advice on water, see the box opposite.

There are no required vaccinations for Mexico, but it's worth visiting your doctor at least four weeks before you leave to check that you are up to date with **tetanus**, **typhoid** and **hepatitis A** shots, as well as a **rabies** shot and **anti-malarial** pills if you're going to be in areas where they are recommended.

For comprehensive coverage of the sort of health problems encountered by travellers, consult the *Rough Guide to Travel Health* by Dr Nick Jones.

Diarrhoea

Diarrhoea (Montezuma's Revenge, or simply *turista* as it's also known in Mexico) is the medical problem you're most likely to encounter, and no one, however cautious, seems to avoid it altogether. If you go down with a mild dose unaccompanied by other symptoms, it may simply be due to your body being unfamiliar with the local bacteria, but if your diarrhoea is accompanied by cramps and vomiting, it could be **food poisoning** of some sort. Either way, it will probably pass of its own accord in 24 to 48 hours without treatment. In the meantime, it's essential to replace the fluid and salts you're losing, so drink lots of water. If you have severe diarrhoea, and whenever young children have it, add **oral rehydration salts** – *suero oral* (brand names: Dioralyte, Electrosol, Rehidrat). If you can't get these, dissolve half a teaspoon of salt and three of sugar in a litre of water. Avoid greasy food, heavy spices, caffeine and most fruit and dairy products; some say bananas, papayas, guavas and prickly pears (*tunas*) help, while plain yogurt or a broth made from yeast extract (such as Marmite or Vegemite, if you happen to have some with you) can be easily absorbed by your body when you have diarrhoea. Drugs like Lomotil or Imodium plug you up – and thus undermine the body's efforts to rid itself of infection – but they can be a temporary stop-gap if you

What about the water?

In a hot climate and at high altitudes, it's essential to increase **water** intake to prevent dehydration. Most travellers, and most Mexicans if they can, stay off the tap water. A lot of the time it is in fact drinkable, and in practice may be impossible to avoid completely: ice made with it, unasked for, may appear in drinks, utensils are washed in it, and so on.

Most restaurants and *licuaderías* use **purified water** (*agua purificada*), but always check; most hotels have a supply and will often provide bottles of water in your room. Bottled water (generally purified with ozone or ultraviolet) is widely available, but stick with known brands, and always check that the seal on the bottle is intact since refilling empties with tap water for resale is common (carbonated water is generally a safer bet in that respect).

There are various methods of **treating water** while you are travelling, whether your source is from a tap or a river or stream. Boiling it for a minimum of five minutes is the time-honoured method, but it is not always practical, will not remove unpleasant tastes and is a lot less effective at higher altitudes – including much of central Mexico – where you have to boil it for much longer.

Chemical sterilization, using either chlorine or iodine tablets or a tincture of iodine liquid, is more convenient, but leaves a nasty aftertaste (which can to some extent be masked with lime juice). Chlorine kills bacteria but, unlike iodine, is not effective against amoebic dysentery and giardiasis. Pregnant women or people with thyroid problems should consult their doctor before using iodine sterilizing tablets or iodine-based purifiers. Too many iodine tablets can cause gastrointestinal discomfort. Inexpensive iodine removal filters are available and are recommended if treated water is being used continuously for more than a month or is being given to babies.

Purification, involving both filtration and sterilization, gives the most complete treatment. Portable water purifiers range in size from units weighing as little as 60g, which can be slipped into a pocket, up to 800g for carrying in a backpack.

have to travel. If symptoms persist for more than three days, or if you have a fever or blood in your stool, seek medical advice (see "Getting medical help", p.47).

Malaria and dengue fever

Malaria, caused by a parasite that lives in the saliva of female *Anopheles* mosquitoes, is endemic in some parts of Mexico. Areas above 1000m (such as the capital) are malaria-free, as are Cancún, Cozumel, Isla Mujeres and all the beach resorts of the Baja and the Pacific coasts. Daytime visits to archeological sites are risk-free, too, but low-lying inland areas can be risky, especially at night. The main risk areas are Chiapas, Tabasco, the Yucatán Peninsula, Oaxaca, Guerrero, Michoacán, northern Jalisco, Nayarit, Sinaloa and parts of Sonora, Chihuahua and Durango. Chloroquine (brand names: Nivaquin, Resochin, Avloclor, Aralen) is the recommended malaria prophylactic for travellers to Mexico; you need to start taking the pills one week before you arrive and continue for one month after you depart. Chloroquine is unsuitable for sufferers from various complaints such as epilepsy and psoriasis but daily proguanil (brand name Paludrine) can be used in its place. Consult a physician before beginning any course of medication; see ⓦwwwn.cdc.gov/travel/destinations/Mexico.aspx for more information on malaria in Mexico.

If you go down with malaria, you'll probably know. The fever, shivering and headaches are like severe flu and come in waves, usually beginning in the early evening. Malaria is not infectious, but can be dangerous and sometimes even fatal if not treated quickly. If no doctor is available, take 600mg of quinine sulphate three times daily for seven days, followed on the eighth day (or sooner if the quinine isn't working) by three Fansidar (available from local pharmacies).

The most important thing, obviously, is to avoid **mosquito** bites altogether. Though active from dusk till dawn, female *Anopheles* mosquitoes prefer to bite in the evening. Wear long sleeves, skirts or trousers, avoid dark colours, which attract mosquitoes, and put **repellent** on all exposed skin, especially feet and ankles, which are their favourite targets. Plenty of good brands are sold locally, though health departments recommend carrying high-DEET brands available from travel clinics at home. An alternative is to burn coils of **pyrethrum** incense such as Raidolitos (these are readily available and burn all night if whole, but break easily). Sleep under a **net** if you can – one that hangs from a single point is best if you're going to buy one (you can usually find a way to tie a string across your room to hang it from). Special mosquito nets for hammocks are available in Mexico.

Another illness spread by mosquito bites is **dengue fever**, whose symptoms are similar to those of malaria, plus a headache and aching bones. Dengue-carrying mosquitoes are particularly prevalent during the rainy season and fly during the day, so wear insect repellent in the daytime if mosquitoes are around. The only treatment is complete rest, with drugs to assuage the fever – and take note that a second infection can be fatal.

Other bites and stings

Other biting insects can also be a nuisance. These include bed bugs, sometimes found in cheap hotels – look for squashed ones around the bed. Sandflies, often present on beaches, are quite small, but their bites, usually on feet and ankles, itch like hell and last for days. Head or body lice can be picked up from people or bedding, and are best treated with medicated soap or shampoo.

Scorpions are mostly nocturnal and hide during the day under rocks and in crevices, so poking around in such places when in the countryside is generally ill-advised. If sleeping in a place where they might enter (such as a beach cabaña), shake your shoes out before putting them on in the morning, and try not to wander round barefoot. Some scorpion stings are dangerous and medical treatment should always be sought – cold-pack the sting in the meantime. Snakes are unlikely to bite unless accidentally disturbed – walk heavily and they will usually slither away. A fifth or so of Mexico's snake species are venomous, the most dangerous being rattlesnakes (cascabel, found in the north), coral snakes (coralillo, found particularly in Guerrero, Oaxaca, Veracruz and Chiapas), and the nauyacas (found mainly in the south and the Yucatán). If you do get bitten or stung, remember what the snake or scorpion looked like (kill it if you can do so without receiving more bites), try not to move the affected part (tourniquets are not recommended due to dangerous risk of gangrene – if you do use one, it is vital to relieve it for at least ninety seconds every fifteen minutes), and seek medical help: antivenins are available in most hospitals. Black widow spiders also exist in Mexico; tarantulas are more fearsome-looking, but a lot less dangerous.

Altitude and heat problems

Two other common causes of health problems in Mexico are altitude and the sun. The solution in both cases is to take it easy. Especially if you arrive in Mexico City (2240m), you may find any activity strenuous, and the thin air is made worse by the high concentration of pollutants. Allow yourself time to acclimatize. If going to higher altitudes (climbing Popocatépetl, for example), you may develop symptoms of **Acute Mountain Sickness (AMS)**, such as breathlessness, headaches, dizziness, nausea and appetite loss. More extreme cases may include vomiting, disorientation, loss of balance and coughing up of pink frothy phlegm. A slow descent almost always brings immediate recovery.

Tolerance to the sun, too, takes a while to build up: use a strong **sunscreen** and, if you're walking during the day, wear a hat or keep to the shade. Be sure to avoid dehydration by drinking enough (water or fruit juice rather than beer or coffee and aim to drink at least three litres a day), and don't exert yourself for long periods in the hot sun. Be aware that overheating can cause **heatstroke**, which is potentially fatal. Signs are a very high body temperature without a feeling of fever, accompanied by headaches, disorientation and even irrational behaviour. Lowering body temperature (a tepid shower, for example) is the first step in treatment.

Less serious is **prickly heat**, an itchy rash that is in fact an infection of the sweat ducts caused by excessive perspiration that doesn't dry off. A cool shower, zinc oxide powder and loose cotton clothes should help.

Hepatitis

Hepatitis A is transmitted through contaminated food and water, or through saliva, and thrives in conditions of poor hygiene. It can lay a victim low for several months with exhaustion, fever and diarrhoea, and can even cause liver damage. The Havrix vaccine has been shown to be extremely effective; with a booster after six months, protection lasts for ten years.

Hepatitis symptoms include a yellowing of the whites of the eyes, general malaise, orange urine (though dehydration can also cause this) and light-coloured stools. If you think you have it and are unable immediately to see a doctor, it is important to get lots of rest, avoid alcohol and do your best not to spread the disease. If medical insurance coverage is an issue, you can go to a pathology lab (most towns have them) to get blood tests before paying a greater amount to see a doctor.

More serious is **hepatitis B**, which is passed through blood or sexual contact, in the same way as HIV but more easily. A hepatitis B jab is recommended if you will be in contact with those with weaker immunity systems, for example, working around medical patients or with children. Ideally three doses are given over six months but if time is short, there are other options that take one to two months, with a booster given after a year.

Other diseases

Typhoid and cholera are spread in the same way as hepatitis A. **Typhoid** produces a persistent high fever with malaise, headaches and abdominal pains, followed by diarrhoea. Vaccination can be by injection or orally, though the oral alternative is less effective, more expensive and only lasts a year, as opposed to three for a shot in the arm. **Cholera** appears in epidemics rather than isolated cases – if it's about, you will probably hear about it. Cholera is characterized by sudden attacks of watery diarrhoea with severe cramps and debilitation. The vaccination is no longer given, as it is ineffective.

Immunizations against **mumps**, **measles**, **TB** and **rubella** are a good idea for anyone who wasn't vaccinated as a child and hasn't had the diseases, and it's worth making sure you are covered for **tetanus**. You don't need a shot for **yellow fever** unless you're coming from a country where it's endemic (in which case you need to carry your vaccination certificate).

Rabies exists in Mexico and the rabies vaccine is advised for anyone who will be more than 24 hours away from medical help, for example if going trekking in remote areas. The best advice is simply to give dogs a wide berth, and not to play with animals at all, no matter how cuddly they may look. A bite, a scratch or even a lick from an infected animal could spread the disease – rabies can be fatal, so if you are bitten, assume the worst and get medical help as quickly as possible. While waiting, wash any such wound immediately but gently with soap or detergent and apply alcohol or iodine if possible. If you decide to get the vaccination, you'll need three shots spread over a four-week period prior to travel.

Getting medical help

For minor medical problems, head for a **farmacia** – look for a green cross and the *Farmacia* sign. Pharmacists are knowledgeable and helpful, and many speak some English. One word of warning however: in many Mexican pharmacies you can still buy drugs such as Entero-Vioform and Mexaform, which can cause optic nerve damage and have been banned elsewhere; it is not a good idea, therefore, to use local brands unless you know what they are. Note that the purchase of prescription drugs without a Mexican prescription is illegal; a US prescription will not suffice.

For more serious complaints you can get a list of English-speaking **doctors** from your government's nearest consulate. Big hotels and tourist offices may also be able to recommend medical services. Every Mexican border town has hundreds of doctors experienced in treating gringos (dentists, too), since they charge less than their colleagues across the border. Every reasonably sized town should also have a state- or Red Cross-run **health centre** (*centro de salud*), where treatment is free. Treatment at health centres should be adequate for minor problems, but for anything involving an overnight stay, go to a private hospital (for which your travel insurance should cover you).

Medical resources for travellers

US and Canada

Canadian Society for International Health ⓣ613/241-5785, ⓦwww.csih.org. Extensive list of travel health centres.
CDC ⓣ1-800/232 4636, ⓦwww.cdc.gov/travel. Official US government travel health site.
International Society for Travel Medicine ⓣ1-770/736-7060, ⓦwww.istm.org. Has a full list of travel health clinics.

Australia, New Zealand and South Africa

Travellers' Medical and Vaccination Centre ⓣ1300/658 844, ⓦwww.tmvc.com.au. Lists travel clinics in Australia, New Zealand and South Africa.

UK and Ireland

Hospital for Tropical Diseases Travel Clinic ⓣ0845/155 5000, 020/7388 9600 (Travel Clinic), ⓦwww.thehtd.org.
MASTA (Medical Advisory Service for Travellers Abroad) ⓣ0870/606 2782, ⓦwww.masta.org for the nearest clinic.
Travel Medicine Clinic ⓣ028/9031 5220.
Tropical Medical Bureau ⓣ1850/487 674, ⓦwww.tmb.ie. Ireland.

Food and drink

Whatever your preconceptions about Mexican food, if you've never eaten in Mexico, they will almost certainly be wrong. Food here bears very little resemblance to the concoctions served in "Mexican" restaurants or fast-food joints in other parts of the world – you certainly won't find *chile con carne* outside the tourist spots. Nor, as a rule, is it especially spicy; indeed, a more common complaint from visitors is that after a while it all seems rather bland. Drinking options range from coffee or juices to beer and, of course, tequila.

Where to eat

Basic meals are served at **restaurantes**, but you can get breakfast, snacks and often full meals at cafés too; there are **takeaway** and **fast-food** places serving sandwiches, tortas (filled rolls) and tacos (tortillas folded over with a filling), as well as more international-style food; there are establishments called **jugerías** (look for signs saying "Jugos y Licuados") serving nothing but wonderful juices (*jugos*), *licuados* (fruit blended with water or milk) and fruit salads; and there are **street stalls** dishing out everything from tacos to orange juice to ready-made vegetable salads sprinkled with chile-salt and lime. Just about every **market** in the country has a cooked-food section, too, and these are invariably the cheapest places to eat, if not always the most enticing surroundings. Big cities and resorts have international restaurants – **pizza** and **Chinese** food are ubiquitous. **Argentinian** restaurants are the places to go for well-cooked, quality steaks.

On buses (especially second-class ones), people clamber on at stops with home-made foods, local specialities, cold drinks or coffee. You'll find wonderful things this way that you won't come across in restaurants, but they should be treated with caution, and with an eye to hygiene.

Salsa

A good guide to the quality of a restaurant is their **salsa**. A restaurant with a superior salsa on the table will probably serve up some decent food, whereas a place that takes no pride in its salsa often treats its food in the same manner. To a certain extent you can tell from the presentation: a place that has grubby, rarely changed salsa dishes probably just refills them from a supermarket-bought can, and will not take the same pride in its food as a *casero* (home-cooking) restaurant that proudly puts its own salsa on the table in a nice bowl.

Frequently you will be served a variety of salsa and other sauces, including bottles of commercial hot sauce (Tapatío, Tabasco, Yucateco), but there should always be at least one home-made salsa among them. Increasingly this is **raw**, California-style salsa: tomato, onion, chile and cilantro (coriander leaves) finely chopped together. More common, though, are the traditional **cooked** salsas: either green or red, and relatively mild (though start eating with caution, just in case). The recipes are – of course – closely guarded secrets, but the basic ingredients are tomato (the verdant Mexican tomatillo in green versions), onion and one or more of the hundreds of varieties of chile.

What to eat

The basic Mexican diet is essentially one of **corn** (*maíz* as a crop, *elote* when eaten), supplemented by **beans** and **chiles**. These three things appear in an almost infinite variety of guises.

Mexican cooks use at least a hundred different types of **chiles**, fresh or dried, in colours ranging from pale green to almost black, and all sorts of different sizes (large, mild ones are often stuffed with meat or cheese and rice to make **chiles rellenos**). Each has a distinct flavour and by no means all are hot (which is why we don't use the English term "chilli" for them), although the most common, **chiles jalapeños**, small and either green or red, certainly are. Chile is also the basic ingredient of more complex cooked sauces, notably **mole**, which is Mexico's version of a curry, traditionally served with turkey or chicken, but also sometimes with enchiladas (rolled, filled tortillas). There are several types of *mole*, the two most common being the rather bland *mole verde*, and the far richer and more exciting **mole poblano**, a speciality of Puebla. Half of the fifty or so ingredients in this extraordinary mixture are different types of chile, but the most notable ingredient is chocolate. Another speciality to look out for is **chiles en nogada**, a bizarre combination of stuffed green peppers in a white sauce made of walnuts and cream cheese or sour cream, topped with red pomegranate: the colours of the national flag.

Beans (*frijoles*), an invariable accompaniment to egg dishes – and pretty much everything else too – are usually of the pinto or kidney variety and are almost always served **refritos**, ie boiled up, mashed and "refried" (though actually it is the first time they're fried). They're even better if you can get them whole in some kind of country-style soup or stew, often with pork or bacon, as in **frijoles charros**.

You'll find **corn** in soups and stews such as **pozole** (with meat), or roasted on the cob at street stalls. It's also ground into flour for **tortillas**, flat maize pancakes of which you will get a stack to accompany your meal in any cheap restaurant, though posher places provide bread rolls (*bolillos*) instead. Tortillas made of wheat flour (*de harina*) are rare except in the north.

Tortillas form the basis of most **antojitos** (appetizers or light courses). Simplest of these are **tacos**, tortillas filled with almost anything, from beef and chicken to green vegetables, and then fried (they're usually still soft, not at all like the baked taco shells you may have had at home). With cheese, either alone or in addition to other fillings, they are called **quesadillas**. **Enchiladas** are rolled, filled tortillas covered in salsa and baked; **enchiladas suizas** are filled with chicken and have sour cream over them. **Tostadas** are flat tortillas toasted crisp and piled with ingredients – usually meat, salad vegetables and cheese (smaller bite-size versions are known as *sopes*). Tortillas torn up and cooked together with meat and (usually hot) sauce are called **chilaquiles**; this is a traditional way of using up leftovers. Especially in the north, you'll also come across **burritos** (large wheat-flour tortillas, stuffed with anything, but usually beef and potatoes or beans) and **gorditas** (delicious fat corn tortillas, sliced open, stuffed and baked or fried). Also short and fat are **tlacoyos**, tortillas made with a stuffing of mashed beans, often using blue-corn flour, which gives them a rather bizarre colour.

Corn flour, too, is the basis of **tamales** – found predominantly in central and southern Mexico – which are a sort of cornmeal pudding, stuffed, flavoured and steamed in corn or banana leaves. They can be either savoury, with additions like shrimp or corn kernels, or sweet when made with something like coconut.

Except in the north, **meat** is not especially good – beef in particular is usually thin and tough; pork, goat and occasionally lamb are better. If the menu doesn't specify what kind of meat it is, it's usually pork – even steak (*bistec*) can be pork unless it specifies *bistec de res*. For thick American-style steaks, look for a sign saying "Carnes Hereford" or for a "New York Cut" description (only in expensive places or in the north or at fancier resorts). **Seafood** is almost always fresh and delicious, especially the spicy shrimp or octopus cocktails which you find in most coastal areas (**coctél/campechana de camarón** or **pulpo**), but beware of eating uncooked shellfish, even *ceviche* (though the lime juice it is marinaded in does kill off most of the nasties). **Eggs** in country areas are genuinely free-range and flavoursome. They feature on every menu as the most basic of meals, and at some time you must try the classic Mexican combinations of **huevos rancheros** (fried eggs on a tortilla with red salsa) or **huevos a la mexicana** (scrambled with onion, tomato and chile).

Vegetarian food

Vegetarians can eat well in Mexico, although it does take caution to avoid meat altogether. Many Mexican dishes are naturally meat-free and there are always fabulous fruits and vegetables available. Most restaurants serve vegetable soups and rice, and items like quesadillas, *chiles rellenos* and even tacos and enchiladas often come with non-meat fillings. Another possibility is **queso fundido**, simply (and literally) melted cheese, served with tortillas and salsa. Eggs, too, are served anywhere at any time, and many *jugerías* serve huge mixed **salads** to which grains and nuts can be added.

However, vegetarianism, though growing, is not particularly common, and a simple cheese and chile dish may have some meat added to "improve" it. Worse, most of the fat used for frying is animal fat (usually lard), so that even something as unadorned as refried beans may not be strictly vegetarian (especially as a bone or some stock may have been added to the water the beans were originally boiled in). Even "vegetarian" restaurants, which can be found in all the big cities, often include chicken on the menu. You may well have better luck in pizza places and Chinese or other ethnic restaurants.

Meals

Traditionally, Mexicans eat a light breakfast very early, a snack of tacos or eggs in mid-morning, lunch (the main meal of the day) around 2pm or later – in theory followed by a siesta, but decreasingly so, it seems – and a late, light supper. Eating a large meal at lunch time can be a great way to save money – almost every restaurant serves a cut-price **comida corrida** (set meal, varied daily).

Breakfast (*desayuno*) in Mexico can consist simply of coffee (see opposite) and *pan dulce* – sweet rolls and pastries that usually come in a basket; you pay for as many as you eat. More substantial breakfasts consist of eggs in any number of forms (many set breakfasts include *huevos al gusto*: eggs any way you like them), and at fruit-juice places you can have a simple *licuado* (see opposite) fortified with raw egg (*blanquillo*). Freshly squeezed orange juice (*jugo de naranja*) is always available from street stalls in the early morning.

Snacks mostly consist of some variation on the taco/enchilada theme (stalls selling them are called *taquerías*), but tortas – rolls heavily filled with meat or cheese or both, garnished with avocado and chile and toasted on request – are also wonderful, and you'll see takeout torta stands everywhere. Failing that, you can of course always make your own snacks with bread or tortillas, along with fillings such as avocado or cheese, from shops or markets.

At **lunch time** (around 1–5pm) many restaurants serve a *comida corrida* (cut-price set menu, known in more upmarket places the the *menu del día* or *menu turístico*), usually consisting of three or four courses for US$5/£3 or less – sometimes even half that price. A typical *comida* will consist of "wet" soup, probably vegetable, followed by "dry" soup – most commonly *sopa de arroz* (rice seasoned with tomato or chile), or perhaps a plate of vegetables, pasta, beans or guacamole (avocado mashed with onion, and maybe tomato, lime juice and chile). Then comes the main course, followed by pudding, usually fruit, *flan* or *pudin* (crème caramel-like concoctions), or rice pudding. Other Mexican deserts worth looking out for include meringue made with pulque, and *capirotada* (bread pudding, especially popular during Lent).

Some restaurants also offer set meals in the evening, but this is rare, and on the whole going out to **eat at night** is much more expensive.

Drinks

The basic drinks to accompany food are water or beer. If you're drinking **water**, stick to bottled stuff (*agua mineral* or *agua de Tehuacán*) – it comes either plain (*sin gas*) or carbonated (*con gas*).

Jugos, licuados and refrescos

Soft drinks (*refrescos*) – including Coke, Pepsi, Squirt (fun to pronounce in Spanish), and Mexican brands like apple-flavoured Sidral (which are usually extremely sweet) – are on sale everywhere. Far more tempting are the real **fruit juices** and *licuados* sold at shops and stalls displaying the "Jugos y Licuados" sign and known as *jugerías* or *licuaderías*. Juices (**jugos**) can be squeezed from anything that will go through the extractor. Orange (**naranja**) and carrot (**zanahoria**) are the staples, but you should also experiment with some of the more obscure tropical fruits such as soursop or mamey. *Licuados* are made of fruit mixed with water (**licuado de agua** or simply **agua de**...) or milk (**licuado de leche**) in a blender, usually with sugar added, and are always fantastic. **Limonada** (fresh lemonade) is also sold in many of these places, as are **aguas frescas** – flavoured cold drinks, of which the most common are **horchata** (rice milk flavoured with cinnamon) and **agua de arroz** (like an iced rice-pudding drink – delicious), **agua de jamaica** (hibiscus) or **de tamarindo** (tamarind). These are also often served in restaurants or sold in the streets from great glass jars. Make sure that any water and ice used is purified – street stalls are especially suspect in this regard. Juices and *licuados* are also sold at many ice-cream parlours – *neverías* or *paleterías*. The ice cream, more like Italian *gelato* than the heavy-cream US varieties, can also be fabulous and comes in a huge range of flavours.

Coffee and tea

A great deal of **coffee** is produced in Mexico, and in the growing areas, especially the state of Veracruz, as well as in the traditional coffeehouses in the capital, you will be served superb coffee. In its basic form, **café solo** or **negro**, it is strong, black, often sweet (ask for it *sin azúcar* for no sugar), and comes in small cups. For weaker black coffee ask for **café americano**, though this may mean instant (if you do want instant, ask for "Nescafé"). White is **café cortado** or **con un pocito de leche**; **café con leche** can be delicious, made with all milk and no water (ask if it's "hecho de leche"). **Espresso** and **cappuccino** are often available too, or you may be offered **café de olla** – stewed in the pot for hours with cinnamon and sugar, it's thick, sweet and tasty. Outside traditional coffee areas, however, the coffee is often terrible, with only instant available.

Tea (té) is often available too, and you may well be offered a cup at the end of a comida. Usually it's some kind of herb tea like **manzanillo** (camomile) or **yerbabuena** (mint). If you get the chance to try traditional **hot chocolate** ("the drink of the Aztecs"), then do so – it's an extraordinary, spicy, semi-bitter concoction, quite unlike the milky bedtime drink of your childhood.

Alcohol

Mexican beer (*cerveza*) is mostly light lager (*cerveza clara*) – usually light in flavour as well as colour. Sol, Tecate and Dos Equis are typical brands; if you want something more flavoursome try Modelo, Bohémia or Corona, or a dark (*oscura*) beer, of which the best are Negra Modelo, Indio and Tres Equis. Pacífico, originally from the west coast, is gaining popularity among the national brands. Try a *michelada*, a beer cocktail made by adding ice, lime and Worcestershire and Tabasco sauces to dark beer and rimming the glass with salt. The milder *chelada* is a light beer mixed with plenty of lime and salt, and both are refreshing on a sunny day.

You'll normally be drinking in **bars**, but if you don't feel comfortable – this applies to women, in particular (see below for more on this topic) – you can also buy alcohol from most shops, supermarkets and, cheapest of all, *agencias*, which are normally agents for just one brand. For bottles you pay a deposit: to get it back, keep your receipt and return your bottles to the same store. Bigger, 940ml bottles are known as *caguamas* (turtles), or in the case of Pacífico, *ballenas* (whales).

Wine (*vino – tinto* is red, *blanco* is white) is not seen a great deal, although Mexico does produce a fair number of perfectly good vintages. You're safest sticking to brand names like Hidalgo or Domecq, although it may also be worth experimenting with some of the new labels, especially those from Baja California, such as Lacetto, which are attempting to emulate the success of their neighbours across the border and in many cases have borrowed American techniques and wine-makers.

Tequila, distilled from the cactus-like agave plant and produced mainly in the state of Jalisco, is the most famous Mexican spirit, usually taken with lime and salt, or a chile and tomato chaser called sangrita, but *añejo* or *reposado* tequila (aged in the vat), should be sipped straight, and not wasted in cocktails such as margarita (tequila, lime juice and triple sec – considered a ladies' drink). Mexican law allows up to 49 percent cane or corn to be added to the agave from which tequila is made, so unless the label says "100% de agave", it won't be. The proprietary brands, José Cuervo and Sauza, make bog-standard white tequilas as well as smoother, aged versions (Cuervo Tradicional and Sauza Hornitos), but connoisseurs prefer posher makes such as Herradura or Don Julio. "Gold" tequila contains extraneous colourants and is worth avoiding. For more on tequila see the box on p.341.

Mescal (often spelled mezcal) is basically the same thing as tequila, but is made from a slightly different variety of plant, the maguey, and is younger and less refined. In fact, tequila was originally just a variety of mescal. The spurious belief that the worm in the mescal bottle is hallucinogenic is based on confusion between the drink and the peyote cactus, which is also called mescal, but by the time you've got down as far as the worm, you'll be too far gone to notice anyway.

Pulque, a mildly alcoholic milky beer made from the same cactus, is the traditional drink of the poor and sold in special bars called *pulquerías*. The best comes from the state of Mexico City, and is thick and viscous – it's a little like palm wine, and definitely an acquired taste. Unfermented *pulque*, called *aguamiel*, is sweet and non-alcoholic.

Drinking other spirits, you should always ask for **nacional**, as anything imported is fabulously expensive. **Rum** (*ron*), **gin** (*ginebra*) and **vodka** are made in Mexico, as are some very palatable **brandies** (brandy or coñac – try San Marcos or Presidente). Most of the **cocktails** for which Mexico is known – margaritas, piñas coladas and so on – are available only in tourist areas or hotel bars, and are generally pretty strong.

For drinking any of these, the least heavy atmosphere is in **hotel bars**, tourist areas or anything that describes itself as a "ladies' bar". **Cantinas** are for serious drinking, traditionally macho places that were closed to women (they typically had a sign above the door prohibiting entry to "women, members of the armed forces and anyone in uniform"). Especially in big cities they are now more liberal, but in small, conservative places they remain exclusively male preserves with an atmosphere of drunken bonhomie and an undercurrent of readiness for a fight, where women may not be welcome and are sometimes still even banned.

The media

The Mexican media can be very sensationalist, and news is mostly local, and often heavily slanted towards the government, but for those who know Spanish there is an independent press, and some interesting programmes on TV.

Newspapers

Few domestic **newspapers** carry much foreign news, and the majority of international coverage does not extend beyond Latin America. Most papers are lurid scandal sheets, brimming with violent crime depicted in full colour. Each state has its own press, however, and they do vary: while most are little more than government mouthpieces, others are surprisingly independent.

If you read Spanish, the best national paper is *Reforma*, with a good reputation for independence and political objectivity. Also worth a read is the left-wing *La Jornada*, which is quite daringly critical of government policy, especially in Chiapas (its journalists regularly face death threats as a result). The press has gradually been asserting its independence since the mid-1990s, tackling such subjects as human rights, corruption and drug trafficking, though journalists still face danger if they speak out, not only from shady government groups but also from drug traffickers. Reporting on links between the two is particularly dangerous. Over 45 journalists have been killed in Mexico since 2000, including nine in the state of Tamaulipas alone; press freedom campaign group Reporters Without Borders rates Mexico the most dangerous country for journalists on the American continent, and the second most dangerous in the world after Iraq.

Television

You can usually pick up a dozen channels in Mexico without cable or satellite. Four are run by the main **TV** company, Televisa, and another two by TV Azteca. Canal 22 tends to show cultural programmes, though they are often rather dry. Canal Once is the most original and independent channel, and frequently has something quite interesting on, especially late in the evening. **Cable** and **satellite** are now widespread, and even quite downmarket hotels offer numerous channels, many of them American.

On Mexican TV you can watch any number of US shows dubbed into Spanish, but far and away the most popular programmes are the *telenovelas* – soap operas that dominate the screens from 6pm to 10pm and pull in millions of viewers. Each episode takes melodrama to new heights, with nonstop action and emotions hammed up to the maximum for riveted fans. Plot lines make national news, and *telenovela* stars are major celebrities, despite their ludicrously over-the-top acting styles.

Radio

Radio stations in the capital and Guadalajara (among others) have programmes in English for a couple of hours each day, and in many places US broadcasts can also be picked up. Reactor (105.7MHz FM, and on line at Ⓦ www.reactor.imer.com.mx), plays a mix of music including modern Mexican sounds, and in México state, Radio Chapingo (1610kHz AM) plays the traditional music of Indigenous ethic groups as well as modern Mexican music of various genres. If you have a short-wave radio, you can get the BBC World Service (check Ⓦ www.bbc.co.uk/worldservice for times and frequencies), the Voice of America (Ⓦ www.voa.gov) and at certain times, Radio Canada (Ⓦ www.rcinet.ca).

Festivals

Stumbling, perhaps accidentally, onto some Mexican village fiesta may prove to be the highlight of your travels. Everywhere, from the remotest Indian village to the most sophisticated city suburb, devotes at least one day annually to partying. Usually it's in honour of the local saint's day, but many fiestas have pre-Christian origins and any excuse – from harvest celebrations to the coming of the rains – will do.

Details of the most important local fiestas can be found at the end of each chapter. In addition to these, there are plenty of lesser local festivals, as well as certain major festivals celebrated throughout the country. Traditional dances and music form an essential part of almost every fiesta, and most include a procession behind some revered holy image or a more celebratory secular parade with fireworks. No two fiestas will be quite the same.

Carnaval, the week before Lent, is celebrated throughout the Roman Catholic world, and is at its most exuberant in Latin America. It is the last week of taking one's pleasures before the forty-day abstinence of Lent, which lasts until Easter. Like Easter, its date is not fixed, but it generally falls in February or early March. Carnaval is celebrated with costumes, parades, eating and dancing, most spectacularly in Veracruz and Mazatlán, and works its way up to a climax on the last day, Mardi Gras (Shrove Tuesday).

The country's biggest holiday, however, is **Semana Santa** – Holy Week – beginning on Palm Sunday and continuing until the following Sunday, Easter Day. Still a deeply religious festival in Mexico, it celebrates the resurrection of Christ, and has also become an occasion to venerate the Virgin Mary, with processions bearing her image now a hallmark of the celebrations. Expect transport to be totally disrupted during this week as virtually the whole country is on the move; you will definitely need to plan ahead if travelling then. Many places close for the whole of Holy Week, and certainly from Thursday to Sunday.

Secular Independence Day (Sept 16) is in some ways more solemn than the religious festivals. While Easter and Carnaval are popular, this one is more official, marking the historic day in 1810 when Manuel Hidalgo y Costilla issued the *Grito* (Cry of Independence) from his parish church in Dolores, now Dolores Hidalgo, Guanajuato, which is still the centre of commemoration. You'll also find the day marked in the capital with mass recitation of the *Grito* in the Zócalo, followed by fireworks, music and dancing.

The **Day of the Dead** is All Saints' or All Souls' Day and its eve (Nov 1–2), when offerings are made to ancestors' souls, frequently with picnics and all-night vigils at their graves. People build shrines in their homes to honour their departed relatives, but it's the cemeteries to head for if you want to see the really spectacular stuff. Sweetmeats and papier-mâché statues of dressed-up skeletons give the whole proceedings a rather gothic air.

Christmas is a major holiday, and another time when people are on the move and transport is booked solid for weeks ahead. Gringo influence is heavy nowadays, with Santa Claus and Christmas trees, but the Mexican festival remains distinct in many ways, with a much stronger religious element (virtually every home has a Nativity crib). **New Year** is still largely an occasion to spend with family, the actual hour being celebrated with the eating of grapes. Presents are traditionally given on Twelfth Night or **Epiphany** (Reyes; Jan 6), which is when the Magi of the Bible arrived bearing gifts – though things are shifting into line with Yankee custom, and more and more people are exchanging gifts on December 25. One of the more bizarre Christmas events takes place in Oaxaca, where there is a public display of Nativity cribs and other sculptures made of radishes.

Sports and outdoor activities

You'll find facilities for golf, tennis, sailing, surfing, scuba diving and deep-sea fishing – even horseback riding and hunting – provided at all the big resorts.

Sport fishing is enormously popular in Baja California and the big Pacific coast resorts, while freshwater bass fishing is growing in popularity too, especially behind the large dams in the north of the country. **Diving** and **snorkelling** are big on the Caribbean coast, with world-famous dive sites at Cozumel and on the reefs further south. The Pacific coast has become something of a centre for **surfing**, with few facilities as yet (though you can rent surfboards in major tourist centres such as Acapulco and Mazatlán) but plenty of Californian surfers who follow the weather south over the winter. The most popular places are in Baja California and on the Oaxaca coast, but the biggest waves are to be found around Lázaro Cárdenas in Michoacán. A more minority-interest activity for which Mexico has become a major centre is **caving**. With a third of the country built on limestone, there are caverns in most states that can be explored by experienced potholers or spelunkers.

The Ministry of Tourism publishes a leaflet on participatory sports in Mexico, and can also advise on licences and seasons.

Spectator sports

Mexico's chief spectator sport is soccer (*fútbol*; see box, p.477). Mexican teams have not been notably successful on the international stage, but going to a game can still be a thrilling experience. The capital and Guadalajara are the best places to see a match and the biggest game in the domestic league, "El Clásico", between Chivas from Guadalajara and América from Mexico City, fills the city's 150,000-seater Aztec stadium to capacity. **Baseball** (*béisbol*) is also popular, as is **American football** (especially on TV). **Jai alai** (also known as **frontón**, or **pelota vasca**) is Basque handball, common in big cities and played at a very high speed with a small hard ball and curved scoop attached to the hand; it's a big gambling game.

Mexican rodeos (*charreadas*), mainly seen in the north of the country, are as spectacular for their style and costume as they are for the events, while **bullfights** remain an obsession: every city has a bullring – Mexico City's Plaza México is the world's largest – and the country's *toreros* are said to be the world's most reckless, much in demand in Spain. Another popular blood sport, usually at village level, is **cockfighting**, still legal in Mexico and mainly attended for the opportunity to bet on the outcome.

Masked **wrestling** (*lucha libre*) is very popular in Mexico, too, with the participants, Batman-like, out of the game for good should their mask be removed and their secret identity revealed. Nor does the resemblance to comic-book superheroes end in the ring: certain masked wrestlers have become popular social campaigners out of the ring, always ready to turn up just in the nick of time to rescue the beleagured poor from eviction by various landlords or persecution by corrupt politicians. For more on wrestling, see p.453.

Culture and etiquette

Mexicans are generally very courteous, and in some ways quite formal. It is common, for example, to address people as señor or señora, while being too brusque can give quite a bad impression.

Most Mexicans are also quite religious, and about three-quarters are **Roman Catholic**; you will often see little altars by the roadside, and many people cross themselves whenever they pass a church. It is wise to avoid open disrespect for religion unless you are sure of your company. While male travellers will find the country very easy-going, women may encounter a few difficulties arising from traditional Latin machismo.

Homosexuality

There are no federal laws governing **homosexuality** in Mexico, and hence it's **legal**. There are, however, laws enforcing "public morality", which although they are supposed only to apply to prostitution, are often used against gays. 1997 saw the election of Mexico's first "out" congresswoman, the left-wing PRD's Patria Jiménez, and in 2003 the federal parliament passed a law against discrimination on various grounds including sexual preference. In 2005, however, a gay man from Tampico successfully claimed political asylum in the US after demonstrating the extent of persecution he faced in his hometown.

Nonetheless, there are a large number of **gay groups** and **publications** in Mexico – we've supplied two contact addresses below. The **lesbian** scene is not as visible or as large as the gay scene for men, but it's there and growing. There are gay bars and clubs in the major resorts and US border towns, and in large cities such as the capital, and also Monterrey, Guadalajara, Veracruz and Oaxaca; elsewhere, private parties are where it all happens, and you'll need a contact to find them.

As far as popular **attitudes** are concerned, religion and machismo are the order of the day, and prejudice is rife, but attitudes are changing. Soft-core porn magazines for gay men are sold openly on street stalls and, while you should be careful to avoid upsetting macho sensibilities, you should have few problems if you are discreet. In Juchitán, Oaxaca, on the other hand, gay male transvestites, known as *muxes*, are accepted as a kind of third sex, and the town even has a transvestite basketball team.

You can check the latest gay rights situation in Mexico on the International Gay and Lesbian Human Rights Commission website at ⓦwww.iglhrc.org, and information on the male gay scene in Mexico (gay bars, meeting places and cruising spots) can be found in the annual *Spartacus Gay Guide*, available in specialist bookshops at home. As for **contacts** within Mexico: lesbians can get in touch with Grupo Patlatonalli, Apartado Postal 1-623, Guadalajara, 44100 Jalisco (ⓣ33/3632-0507, ⓔpatlas@mail.udg.mx); while for gay men, CIDHOM (Centro de Información y Documentación de las Homosexualidades en México), Cerrada Cuauhnochtli 11, Col. Pueblo Quieto, Tlalpan, México DF 14040 (ⓣ55/5666-5436, ⓔcidhom@prodigy.net.mx), can offer information.

Sexual harassment and discrimination

Machismo is engrained in the Mexican mentality and, although it's softened to some extent by the gentler mores of indigenous culture, most women will find that a degree of harassment is inevitable.

On the whole, most hassles will be limited to **comments** (*piropos*, supposedly compliments) in the street, but situations that might be quite routine at home can seem threatening without a clear understanding of the nuances of Mexican Spanish. Avoid eye contact – wearing sunglasses helps. Any provocation is best ignored – Mexican women are rarely slow with a stream of retaliatory abuse, but it's a dangerous strategy unless you're very sure of your ground, and coming from a foreigner, it may be taken as racism.

Public transport can be one of the worst places for harassment, especially groping in crowded situations. On the Mexico City Metro, there are separate women's carriages and passages during rush hours. Otherwise, if you get a seat, you can hide behind a newspaper.

Problems are aggravated in the big tourist spots, where legendarily "easy" tourists attract droves of would-be gigolos. Away from resorts and big cities, though, and especially in indigenous areas, there is rarely any problem – you may as an outsider be treated as an object of curiosity, and usually, such curiosity can also extend to friendliness and hospitality. On the whole, the further from the US border you get, the easier things will become.

The restrictions imposed on drinking are without a doubt irksome: women can now drink in most cantinas, but some still maintain a ban, and even in so-called "ladies' bars", "unescorted" women may be looked at with suspicion or even refused service.

Tipping

At expensive restaurants in tourist resorts, waiters and waitresses are used to American tipping levels (15–20 percent), but elsewhere levels are more like those in Europe (10–15 percent). In mid-range and upmarket hotels, you will be expected to tip chambermaids (a few dollars, depending on the standard of the hotel and the length of your stay) and porters (ten pesos or a dollar is fine). It is not usual to tip taxi drivers, but small tips are expected by gas-station and car-park attendants and the bagboys at supermarkets (all of these will be happy with a few pesos of small change).

Shopping

The craft tradition of Mexico, much of it descended directly from arts practised long before the Spanish arrived, is still extremely strong. Regional and highly localized specialities survive, with villages throughout the republic jealously guarding their reputations – especially in the states of Michoacán, Oaxaca, Chiapas and the Yucatán. There's a considerable amount of Guatemalan textiles and embroidery about, too.

Crafts

To buy crafts, there is no need to visit the place of origin – **craft shops** in Mexico City and all the big resorts gather the best and most popular items from around the country. On the other hand, it's a great deal more enjoyable to see where the articles come from, and certainly the only way to get any real bargains. The good stuff is rarely cheap wherever you buy it, however, and there is an enormous amount of dross produced specifically for tourists.

FONART shops, in major centres throughout Mexico, are run by a government agency (Ⓦwww.fonart.gob.mx) devoted to the promotion and preservation of crafts; their wares are always excellent, if expensive, and the shops should be visited to get an idea of what is available. Where no such store exists, you can get a similar idea by looking at the best of the tourist shops.

Among the most popular items are: **silver**, the best of which is wrought in Taxco, although rarely mined there; **pottery**, made almost everywhere, with different techniques, designs and patterns in each region; **woollen goods**, especially blankets, which are again made everywhere, and *sarapes* from Oaxaca – always check the fibres and go for more expensive natural dyes; **leather**, especially tyre-tread-soled *huaraches* (sandals), sold cheaply wherever you go; **glass** from Jalisco; **lacquerware**, particularly from Uruapán; and **hammocks**, the best of which are sold in Mérida.

It is illegal to buy or sell antiquities, and even more criminal to try taking them out of the country (moreover, many items sold as valuable antiquities are little more than worthless fakes) – best to just look.

Markets

For bargain hunters, the **mercado** (market) is the place to head. There's one in every Mexican town, which on the traditional market day, will be at its busiest with villagers from the surrounding area bringing their produce for sale or barter. Mercados are mainly dedicated to food and everyday necessities, but most have a section devoted to crafts, and in larger towns you may find a separate crafts bazaar.

Unless you're completely hopeless at bargaining, prices will always be lower in the market than in shops, but shops do have a couple of advantages. First, they exercise a degree of quality control, whereas any old junk can be sold in the market; and second, many established shops will be able to ship purchases home for you, which saves an enormous amount of frustrating bureaucracy.

Bargaining and haggling are very much a matter of personal style, highly dependent on your command of Spanish, aggressiveness and, to some extent, experience. The old tricks (never show the least sign of interest – let alone enthusiasm, and walking away, will always cut the price dramatically) do still hold true; but make sure you know what you want, its approximate value and how much you are prepared to pay. Never start to haggle for something you definitely don't intend to buy – it'll end in bad feelings on both sides. In shops there's little chance of significantly altering the official price unless you're buying in bulk, and even in markets most food and simple household goods have a set price (though it may be doubled at the sight of an approaching gringo).

Travel essentials

Costs

The developed tourist resorts and big cities are invariably more expensive than more remote towns, and certain other areas also have noticeably higher prices – among them the industrialized north. Prices can also be affected by **season** and many hotels raise their prices during busy times of the year. Summer, Christmas and Easter are the peak times for Mexican tourists and areas like Acapulco and Cancún, which attract large numbers of overseas visitors, put their prices up during the high season. Special events are also likely to be marked by price hikes.

Nonetheless, wherever you go you can probably get by on US$300/£200 a week (you could reduce that if you hardly travel around, stay only on campsites or in hostels, live on basic food and don't buy any souvenirs, though this requires a lot of discipline); you'd be living well on US$600/£400.

As always, if you're **travelling alone** you'll end up spending more – sharing rooms and food saves a substantial amount. In the larger resorts, you can get apartments for up to six people for even greater savings. If you have an **International Student** or **Youth Card**, you might find the occasional reduction on a museum admission price, but don't go out of your way to obtain one, since most concessions are, at least in theory, only for Mexican students. Cards available include the ISIC card for full-time students and the Go-25 youth card for under-26s, both of which carry health and emergency insurance benefits for Americans, and are available from youth travel firms such as STA Travel. Even a college photo ID card might work in some places.

Most restaurant bills come with **fifteen percent IVA** (Impuesto de Valor Añadido, or Valued Added Sales Tax) added; this may not always be included in prices quoted on the menu. **Service** is hardly ever added to bills, and the amount you tip is entirely up to you – in cheap places, it's just the loose change, while expensive venues tend to expect a full fifteen percent. See p.57 for more on tipping.

Entry requirements

Citizens of the US, Canada, the UK, Ireland, Australia, New Zealand and some Western European countries do not need **visas** to enter Mexico as tourists for less than 180 days. Other Europeans can stay for ninety days. Non-US citizens travelling via the US, however, may need a US visa (p.60). Visitors entering by land and passing beyond the Zona Libre (see p.186) are subject to a M$210 **entry fee** (*derecho de no inmigrante*), which will be included in your ticket if arriving by air.

Visas, obtainable only through a consulate (in person or by mail), are required by nationals of South Africa and most poor countries, as well as by anyone entering Mexico to work, to study or for stays longer than six months. Business visitors usually need a Business Authorization Card available from consulates, but nationals of countries exempt from a tourist visa can enter on business for up to 30 days on a tourist card (see below). Anyone under the age of 18 needs written consent from their parents if not accompanied by both of them (if accompanied by one, they need written consent from the other). For more detailed information on who needs a visa, visit the website of the Insituto Nacional de Migración at Ⓦwww.inm.gob.mx/EN.

Tourist cards

All visitors, regardless of nationality, need a valid **passport** and a **tourist card** (or FMT – *folleto de migración turística*). Tourist cards are free, and if you're flying direct, you should get one on the plane, or from the airline before leaving. A good travel agent should be able to arrange one for you, too. Otherwise, they're issued by Mexican consulates, in person or by post. Every major US city and most border towns have a Mexican consulate. Finally, failing all these options, you should be able to get tourist cards at airports or border crossings on arrival. However, if they've run out, you'll have to twiddle your thumbs until the next batch comes in, and if your passport is not issued by a rich Western country, you may encounter difficulty in persuading border officials to give you a card at all; it's therefore preferable to get one in advance. Entering from Belize or Guatemala, it's not at all uncommon for border posts to run out of tourist cards, or for officials to (illegally) demand a fee for issuing them.

Most people officially need a **passport** to pick up their tourist card, but for US and Canadian citizens entering by land, all that's required is proof of citizenship (an original birth certificate or notarized copy, for instance, or naturalization papers), along with some form of photo ID (such as a driver's licence). Passports are still best, however.

A tourist card is valid for a **single entry** only, so if you intend to enter and leave Mexico more than once you should pick up two or three. On the card, you are asked how long you intend to stay. Always apply for longer than you need, since getting an extension is a frustrating and time-consuming business. You don't always get the time you've asked for and at land borders with Belize and Guatemala, you'll probably only get thirty days (though they may give you more if you ask); entering via Chiapas, you may only get fifteen days (extensions unlikely), especially if you look like a Zapatista sympathizer. Immigration officers sometimes ask to see bank statements or other proof of sufficient funds for your stay, especially if you look poor (or are from a poor country).

A tourist card isn't strictly necessary for anyone who only intends to visit the northern border towns and stay less than three days (though you still need a passport or photo ID). In fact, the twenty-kilometre strip adjoining the US border is a duty-free area into which you can come and go more or less as you please; heading further south beyond this zone, however, there are checkpoints on every road, and you'll be sent back if you haven't brought the necessary documents and been through customs and immigration.

Don't lose the tourist card stub that is given back to you after immigration inspection. You are legally required to carry it at all times, and if you have to show your papers, it's more important than your passport. It also has to be handed in on leaving the country – without it, you may encounter hassle and delay.

Should you lose your tourist card, or need to have it renewed, head for the nearest **immigration department office** (Departamento de Migración); there are branches in the biggest cities. In the case of renewal, it's far simpler to cross the border for a day and get a new card on re-entry than to apply for an extension; if you do apply to the immigration department, it's wise to do so a couple of weeks in advance, though you may be told to come back nearer the actual expiration date. Whatever else you may be told, branches of SECTUR (the tourist office) cannot renew expired tourist cards or replace lost ones – they will only direct you to the nearest immigration office.

US visas

Non-US citizens travelling through the US on the way to or from Mexico, or stopping over there, may need a **US visa**. If there's even a possibility you might stop in the US, unless you are Canadian or from a country on the US visa waiver programme (this includes Britain, Ireland, Australia, New Zealand, Singapore, the Netherlands, Denmark, Sweden, Norway and Germany, but not South Africa), obtaining a visa in advance is a sensible precaution. Application will normally involve making an appointment for an interview at a US embassy or consulate, which should be arranged as far in advance as possible; visit the website of the US embassy in your country of residence for further details. Citizens of countries on the visa waiver programme will need to have a machine-readable passport and to apply on line for authorization to travel via the Electronic System for Travel Authorization at ⓦwww.cbp.gov/xp/cgov/travel/id_visa/esta (this does not apply to arriving in the US by land); also, if your passport was issued after October 26, 2006, it must have an integrated information chip (further details can be found online at ⓦtravel.state.gov/visa/temp/without/without_1990.html). On entry you will be given an I-94 or I-94W form. Be sure to return it when you leave the US: if it isn't returned within the visa expiry time, computer records automatically log you as an illegal alien. You can keep the same form while travelling through Mexico so long as it will still be valid to hand in when you finally leave the US – otherwise, hand it in when you leave the US for Mexico and get a new one ($6) when you re-enter the US. If for any reason you do not manage to hand in your form when you leave the US, you can mail it (with a letter of explanation and evidence of your departure from the US) to: DHS-CBP SBU, 1084 South Laurel Road, London, KY 40744, USA.

Many US airports do not have transit lounges, so even if you are on a through flight you may have to go through US immigration and customs. This can easily take two hours, so bear the delay in mind if you have an onward flight to catch.

Mexican consulates and embassies abroad

The following all issue visas and tourist cards. To find the address of an embassy or consulate not listed here, see under "Representaciones" at ⓦwww.sre.gob.mx.

Australia

14 Perth Ave, Yarralumla, Canberra, ACT 2600 ⓣ02/6273 3963, ⓦwww.mexico.org.au.

Belize

Corner of Wilson St and Newtown Barracks, Belize City ⓣ223 0193, ⓦwww.sre.gob.mx/belice.

Canada

45 O'Connor St, Suite 1500, Ottawa, ON K1P 1A4 ⓣ1-613/233-8988, ⓦwww.sre.gob.mx/canada; 2055 Peel, Suite 1000, Montréal, PQ H3A 1V4 ⓣ1-514/288-2502, ⓦportal.sre.gob.mx/montreal; 199 Bay St, Suite 4440, Commerce Court W, Toronto, ON M5L 1E9 ⓣ1-416/368-2875, ⓦwww.consulmex.com; 1177 W Hastings St, Suite 411, Vancouver, BC V6E 2K3 ⓣ1-604/684-3547, ⓦwww.consulmexvan.com.

Cuba

1206 Ave 7ma (at the corner of 12 & 14), Reparto Miramar, Municipio Playa, Havana ⓣ07/207 9889, ⓦportal.sre.gob.mx/cuba.

Guatemala

7–57 2a Avenida, Zona 10, Apartado Postal 1455, Guatemala City ⓣ2420 3400, ⓦwww.sre.gob.mx/guatemala; 21 Av 8–64, Zona 3, Quetzaltenango

Ⓣ7767 5542 to 4, Ⓦwww.sre.gob.mx/quetzaltenango.

Ireland

19 Raglan Rd, Ballsbridge, Dublin 4 Ⓣ01/667 3105, Ⓦwww.sre.gob.mx/irlanda.

New Zealand

185–187 Featherston St, Level 2 (AMP Chambers), Wellington Ⓣ04/472 0555, Ⓦwww.sre.gob.mx/nuevazelandia.

South Africa

Parkdev Building, Brooklyn Bridge, 570 Fehrsen St, Brooklyn, Pretoria 0181 Ⓣ012/460 1004, Ⓦportal.sre.gob.mx/sudafrica.

UK

16 St George St, London W1S 1FD Ⓣ020/7499-8586, Ⓦwww.sre.gob.mx/reinounido.

US

2827 16th St NW, Washington, DC 20009–4260 Ⓣ1-202/736-1000, Ⓦportal.sre.gob.mx/washington; and in nearly 50 other US towns and cities, among them those in the border states listed below:

Arizona 1201 F Ave, Douglas, AZ 85607 Ⓣ1-520/364-3107, Ⓦportal.sre.gob.mx/douglas; 571 N Grand Ave, Nogales, AZ 85621 Ⓣ1-602/287-2521, Ⓦportal.sre.gob.mx/nogales.

California 408 Heber Ave, Calexico, CA 92231 Ⓣ1-760/357-3863, Ⓦwww.sre.gob.mx/calexico; 1549 India St, San Diego, CA 92101 Ⓣ1-619/231-8414, Ⓦportal.sre.gob.mx/sandiego.

Texas 301 Mexico Blvd, Suite F-2, Brownsville, TX 78520 Ⓣ1-956/542-4431, Ⓦwww.sre.gob.mx/brownsville; 2398 Spur 239, Del Rio, TX 78840 Ⓣ1-830/775-2352 or 1-866/701-7777, Ⓦportal.sre.gob.mx/delrio; 2252 E Garrison St, Eagle Pass, TX 78852 Ⓣ1-830/773-9255 or 6, Ⓦportal.sre.gob.mx/eaglepass; 910 E San Antonio Ave, El Paso, TX 79901 Ⓣ1-915/533-3644, Ⓦwww.sre.gob.mx/elpaso; 1612 Farragut St, Laredo, TX 78040 Ⓣ1-956/723-6369, Ⓦwww.sre.gob.mx/laredo; 600 S Broadway St, McAllen, TX 78501 Ⓣ1-956/686-0243, Ⓦwww.sre.gob.mx/mcallen; 127 Navarro St, San Antonio, TX 78205 Ⓣ210/227-9145 or 6, Ⓦportal.sre.gob.mx/sanantonio.

Customs

Duty-free allowances into Mexico are three litres of liquor (including wine), plus four hundred cigarettes or 25 cigars or 200g of tobacco, plus twelve rolls of camera film or camcorder tape. The monetary limit for duty-free goods is US$300 ($50 if arriving by land). If you are carrying more than US$10,000 with you, you must declare it. For full details, see Ⓦwww.aduanas.gob.mx/aduana_mexico (click on "English"). It is illegal to take antiquities out of the country, and penalties are serious.

Electricity

Theoretically 110 volts AC, with simple two-flat-pin rectangular plugs – most North American appliances can be used as they are. Travellers from the UK, Ireland, Australasia, South Africa and Europe should bring along a converter and a plug adapter. Cuts in service and fluctuations in current do occur, and in cheap hotels an appliance that draws a lot of current may blow a fuse when turned on.

Insurance

There are no reciprocal health arrangements between Mexico and any other country, so travel **insurance** is essential. Credit cards (particularly American Express) often have certain levels of medical or other insurance included, and travel insurance may also be included if you use a major credit card to pay for your trip. Some package tours, too, may include insurance.

Before paying for a new policy, it's worth checking whether you are already covered: some all-risks home insurance policies may cover your possessions when overseas, and many private medical schemes include cover when abroad. In Canada, provincial health plans usually provide partial cover for medical mishaps overseas, while holders of official student/teacher/youth cards in Canada and the US are entitled to meagre accident coverage and hospital inpatient benefits. Students will often find that their student health coverage extends during the vacations and for one term beyond the date of last enrolment.

After exhausting the possibilities above, you might want to contact a specialist travel insurance company, or consider the travel insurance deal offered by Rough Guides (see box, p.62). A typical travel insurance policy usually provides cover for the loss of baggage, tickets and – up to a certain limit – cash or cheques, as well as cancellation or curtailment of your journey. Most of them exclude so-called **dangerous sports** unless an extra premium is paid: in Mexico this can mean scuba diving, whitewater rafting, windsurfing and trekking, though probably not kayaking or jeep safaris. Many policies can be chopped and changed to exclude coverage you don't need – for example, sickness and accident benefits can often be excluded or included at will. If you do take medical coverage, ascertain whether benefits will be paid as treatment proceeds or only after your return home, and whether there is a 24-hour medical emergency number. When securing **baggage cover**, make sure that the per-article limit – typically under US$1000/£500 – will cover your most valuable possession. If you need to make a claim, you should keep receipts for medicines and medical treatment, and in the event you have anything stolen, you must make an official statement to the police and obtain a copy of the declaration (*copia de la declaración*) for your insurance company.

Internet

Internet cafés are easy to find in all the larger cities and resort destinations, and the level of service is usually excellent. A fair few offer cheap VOIP phone calls too. In smaller towns and villages, such facilities are still rare. Depending on where you are, internet access can cost anything from M$5 to M$25 an hour. Major tourist resorts can be the most expensive places, and in these areas it's best to look for cheaper internet cafés around the town centre and avoid those in the luxury hotel zones. Internet facilities in large cities are usually open from early morning until late at night, but in smaller towns they have shorter opening hours and may not open on Sundays. Most home **email** accounts can be accessed from computers in Mexican cybercafés.

Laundry

Lavanderías (**laundromats**) are ubiquitous in Mexico, as the majority of households don't own a washing machine. Most *lavanderías* charge by the kilo, and for a few dollars you'll get your clothes back clean, pressed and perfectly folded, in less than 24 hours. Many hotels also offer laundry services that, although convenient, tend to charge by the item, adding up to a considerably greater cost.

Living and working in Mexico

There's virtually no chance of finding temporary **work** in Mexico unless you have some very specialized skill and have arranged the position beforehand. Work **permits** are almost impossible to obtain. The few foreigners who manage to find work do so mostly in language schools. It may be possible, though not legal, to earn money as a private English tutor by advertising in a local newspaper or at a university.

The best way to extend your time in Mexico is on a **study programme** or **volunteer project**. A US organization called AmeriSpan selects language schools throughout Latin America, including Mexico, to match the needs and requirements of students, and provides advice and support. For further information, call (from the US or Canada) ⓣ1-800/879-6640 or 215/751-1100, or see ⓦwww.amerispan.com.

Rough Guides travel insurance

Rough Guides has teamed up with WorldNomads.com to offer great **travel insurance** deals. Policies are available to residents of over 150 countries, with cover for a wide range of **adventure sports**, 24-hour emergency assistance, high levels of medical and evacuation cover and a stream of **travel safety information**. Roughguides.com users can take advantage of their policies online 24/7, from anywhere in the world – even if you're already travelling. And since plans often change when you're on the road, you can extend your policy and even claim online. Roughguides.com users who buy travel insurance with WorldNomads.com can also leave a positive footprint and donate to a community development project. For more information go to ⓦ**www.roughguides.com/shop**.

Volunteers need to apply for a voluntary work visa (FM3), for which you will need to present a letter of invitation from the organization for whom you are volunteering.

Study and work programmes

AFS Intercultural Programs US ⓣ1-800/AFS-INFO, Canada ⓣ1-800/361-7248, UK ⓣ0113/242 6136, Australia ⓣ1300/131 736, New Zealand ⓣ0800/600 300, South Africa ⓣ011/447 2673, international enquiries ⓣ+1-212/352-9810; ⓦwww.afs.org. Intercultural exchange organization with programmes in over fifty countries, including Mexico.

Council on International Educational Exchange (CIEE) US ⓣ1-800/40-STUDY or 1-207/553-4000, UK ⓣ020/8939 9057, Ireland ⓣ0818/200 020, Australia ⓣ02/9997 0700, South Africa ⓣ021/424 3866; ⓦwww.ciee.org. Leading NGO offering study programmes around the world including Mexico.

Earthwatch Institute US ⓣ1-800/776-0188, UK ⓣ01865/318 838, Australia ⓣ03/9682 6828; ⓦwww.earthwatch.org. Matches volunteers with scientists working on particular projects; recent programmes in Mexico have included tracking turtles in Baja California and searching for fossils in Guanajuato. It's not cheap: volunteers must raise a minimum contribution of US$1500–4000 (average about US$2500) for each one- to two-week stint as a contribution to the cost of research.

Studyabroad.com US ⓣ01-484/766-2920, ⓦwww.studyabroad.com. Language programmes, semester-long and year-long courses and internships in Guadalajara, Cuernavaca, Puebla and Mexico City.

World Learning US ⓣ1-888/272-7881 or 802/258-3212, ⓦwww.worldlearning.org. Its School for International Training (ⓦwww.sit.edu) runs accredited college semesters in Oaxaca, comprising language and cultural studies, homestay and other academic work.

Mail

Mexican **postal services** (*correos*) are reasonably efficient. Airmail to the capital should arrive within a few days, but it may take a couple of weeks to get anywhere at all remote. **Post offices** (generally open Mon–Fri 8am–4pm, Sat 8am–1pm) usually offer a **poste restante/general delivery** service: letters should be addressed to Lista de Correos at the Correo Central (main post office) of any town; all mail that arrives for the Lista is put on a list updated daily and displayed in the post office, but is held for only two weeks. You may get around that by sending it to "Poste Restante" instead of "Lista de Correos" and having letter-writers put "Favor de retener hasta la llegada" (please hold until arrival) on the envelope; letters addressed thus will not appear on the Lista. Letters are often filed incorrectly, so you should have staff check under all your initials, preferably use only two names on the envelope (in Hispanic countries, the second of people's three names, or the third if they've four names, is the paternal surname and the most important, so if three names are used, your mail will probably be filed under the middle one) and capitalize and underline your surname. To collect, you will need your passport or some other official ID with a photograph. There is no fee.

For personal mail, Mexican **addresses** begin with the street and house number. The number goes after the street name (Juárez 123 rather than 123 Juárez), and is followed if appropriate by the floor or apartment number (*planta baja* means ground floor). After that comes the *cólonia* (the immediate neighbourhood), then the town, then finally the zip code and the state (on one line in that order – in the case of Mexico City, "México DF" is the equivalent of the state).

Sending letters and cards home is also easy enough, if slow. Anything sent **abroad** by air should have an airmail (*por avión*) stamp on it or it is liable to go by surface mail. Letters should take around a week to North America, two to Europe or Australasia, but can take much longer (postcards in particular are likely to be slow). Anything at all important should be taken to the post office and preferably registered rather than dropped in a mailbox, although the dedicated airmail boxes in resorts and big cities are supposed to be more reliable than ordinary ones. Postcards or letters up to 20g cost M$9.50 to the US or Belize, M$10.50 to Canada or the Caribbean, M$13 to the British Isles, Europe or South America, M$14.50 to Australasia, Asia, Africa or the Pacific.

Sending **packages** out of the country is drowned in bureaucracy. Regulations about the thickness of brown paper wrapping and the amount of string used vary from state to state, but any package must be checked by customs and have its paperwork stamped by at least three other departments. Take your package (unsealed) to any post office and they'll set you on your way. Many stores will send your purchases home for you, which is much easier. Within the country, you can send a package by bus if there is someone to collect it at the other end.

Maps

Rough Guides, in conjunction with the World Mapping Project, produce a **Mexico map** on a scale of 1:2,250,000, with roads, contours and physical features all clearly shown, and printed on rip-proof, waterproof plastic. Obviously we recommend it. However, other reliable alternatives include those published by Globetrotter (1:3,500,000), Geocenter (1:2,500,000), Hallwag (1:2,500,000) and Freytag & Berndt (1:2,500,000).

In Mexico itself, the best maps are those published by Guía Roji, who also publish a Mexican road atlas and a Mexico City street guide. Guía Roji maps are widely available – try branches of Sanborn's or large Pemex stations – and can also be ordered on line at ⓦtienda.guiaroji.com.mx.

More detailed, large-scale maps – for hiking or climbing – are harder to come by. The most detailed, easily available area maps are produced by International Travel Map Productions, whose 1:1,000,000 Travellers' Reference Map series includes the peninsulas of Baja California and the Yucatán. INEGI, the Mexican government map-makers, also produce very good topographic maps on various scales. They have an office in every state capital (addresses on their website at ⓦwww.inegi.org.mx – click on "Centros de información" under "Servicios a usuarios") and an outlet at Mexico City's airport. Unfortunately, stocks can run rather low, so don't count on being able to buy the ones that you want.

Money

The Mexican **peso**, usually written $, is made up of 100 centavos (¢, like a US cent). Bills come in denominations of $20, $50, $100, $200, $500 and $1000, with coins of 10¢, 20¢, 50¢, $1, $2, $5 and $10. The use of the dollar symbol for the peso is occasionally confusing; the initials MN (*moneda nacional* or national coin) are occasionally used to indicate that it's Mexican, not American money that is being referred to. Prices in this book are generally quoted in Mexican pesos (M$). Note, however, that these will be affected by factors such as inflation and exchange rates. Check the Universal Currency Converter (ⓦwww.xe.com) for up-to-date rates. At the time of writing, one US dollar (US$) was worth approximately M$13, one pound sterling (£) approximately M$20 and one euro M$18. Some tour operators and large hotels quote prices in US dollars, and accept payment in that currency.

Carrying your money

The easiest way to access your money in Mexico is in the form of **plastic**, though it's a good idea to also have some back-up (cash and/or travellers' cheques). Using a Visa, MasterCard, Plus or Cirrus card, you can draw cash from **ATMs** in most towns and tourist resorts. By using these you get trade exchange rates, which are somewhat better than those charged by banks for changing cash, though your card issuer may well add a foreign transaction fee, and these can be as much as five percent, so check with your issuer before leaving home. Local ATM providers may also charge a transaction fee, typically US$0.75. If you use a credit card rather than a debit card, note all cash advances and ATM withdrawals obtained are treated as loans, with interest accruing daily from the date of withdrawal. It is possible to get a **prepaid card**, like a form of travellers' cheques in plastic, which you charge up with funds at home and then use to withdraw money from ATMs – Mastercard, Visa and American Express all issue them.

It's wise to make sure your card is in good condition and, before you leave home, to check that the card and your personal identification number (**PIN**) will work overseas. Technical hitches at ATMs occasionally occur – though rare, it has been known for machines not to dispense cash but to debit your account anyway. Take extra care when withdrawing money from ATMs, especially at night; it's best done during the day, in a busy area and preferably with a friend beside you.

As far as other forms of money are concerned (the latter having the advantage that you can get them refunded if lost or stolen), the easiest kind of **foreign currency** to change in Mexico, obtaining the best rates, is **cash** US dollars. US dollar **travellers' cheques** come second. Euros and Canadian dollars are next best, with other international currencies such as pounds sterling (English notes, not Scottish or Northern Irish), Japanese yen and Swiss francs a poor fourth – and you'll find it hard to change travellers' cheques in those currencies. Quetzales and Belize dollars are best got rid of before entering Mexico (otherwise, your best bet for changing them is with tourists heading the other way). It is a good idea to change other currencies into US dollars at home before coming to Mexico, since the difference in the exchange rate more than outweighs the amount you lose in changing your money twice. In some touristy places, such as Acapulco and Tijuana, US dollar bills are almost as easy to spend as pesos.

Banks and exchange

Banks are generally open Monday to Friday from 9.30am to 5pm, often with shorter hours for **exchange**. Commission on currency exchange varies but the exchange rate is fixed daily by the government. Generally, only larger branches of the big banks, plus some in tourist resorts, will change currencies other than dollars – and even then at worse rates than you would get for the dollar equivalent. A very few ATMs in big city centres and resorts can issue US dollars as well as pesos.

Casas de cambio (exchange offices) have varying exchange rates and commission charges, and tend to have shorter queues, less bureaucratic procedures and longer opening hours. The exchange rates are generally better than at banks, but always worth checking, especially for travellers' cheques. Some casas de cambio will change only US dollars, but others take euros, Canadian dollars, sterling and other currencies. Again, it's worth shopping around, especially if you intend to change a large sum.

If you're desperate, hotels, shops and restaurants that are used to tourists may change dollars or accept them as payment, but rates will be very low.

Opening hours

It's almost impossible to generalize about **opening hours** in Mexico; even when times are posted at museums, tourist offices and shops, they're not always adhered to.

The **siesta** is still around, and many places will close for a couple of hours in the early afternoon, usually from 1pm to 3pm. Where it's hot – especially on the Gulf coast and in the Yucatán – everything may close for up to four hours in the middle of the day, and then reopen until 8pm or 9pm. In central Mexico, the industrial north and highland areas, hours are more like the standard nine-to-five, and shops do not close for lunch.

Shops tend to keep fairly long hours, say from 9am to 8pm. Post offices are open Monday to Friday from 8am to 4pm and Saturday from 8am to 1pm, and the central post office in a large town will usually be open until 6pm weekdays. Banks are generally open Monday to Friday from 9.30am to 5pm.

Museums and galleries tend to open from about 9am or 10am to 5pm or 6pm. Many have reduced entry fees – or are free – on Sunday, and most are closed on Monday. Some museums close for lunch, but archeological sites are open all day.

Public holidays

The main **public holidays**, when virtually everything will be closed, are listed below. Many places also close on January 6 (Twelfth Night/Reyes).

Jan 1 New Year's Day
Feb 5 Anniversary of the Constitution
March 21 Birthday of Benito Juárez
Late March/early April Maundy Thursday and Good Friday
May 1 Labour Day
May 5 Battle of Puebla
Sept 16 Independence Day
Oct 12 Día de la Raza/Columbus Day
Nov 1–2 Day of the Dead
Nov 20 Anniversary of the Revolution
Dec 12 Virgin of Guadalupe
Dec 25 Christmas Day

Phones

Local **phone** calls in Mexico are cheap, and some hotels will let you call locally for free. Coin-operated **public phones** exist but internal long-distance calls are best made with a **phonecard** (sold at newsstands and usable in public phones on almost every street corner). Slightly more expensive, but often less for international calls, are *casetas de teléfono*, phone offices, mainly found at bus stations and airports. Calling abroad with a phonecard or from a *caseta* is expensive. Some internet offices offer **VOIP international calls**, which are much cheaper (typically M$2 a minute to the US or Canada, M$3 to the rest of the world), but the line will not be as good.

It is also possible to **call collect** (*por cobrar*). In theory, you should be able to make an international collect call from any public phone, by dialling the international operator (ⓣ090). If you have a calling card from your home phone company, you can also use the person-to-person direct-dial numbers listed in the box below.

Calling Mexico from abroad, dial the international access code (ⓣ011 from the US or Canada, ⓣ00 from Britain, Ireland or New Zealand, ⓣ0011 from Australia, ⓣ09 from South Africa), followed by the **country code** for Mexico, which is 52. Mexican **numbers** consist of an area code (usually three digits, though Mexico City's, for example, is just ⓣ55), followed by a number, usually seven digits (though Mexico City's, for example, are eight digits). If dialling from abroad, you dial the area code immediately after the 52 for Mexico. If dialling long-distance within Mexico, or from a mobile, you need to dial ⓣ01, then the area code and the number. If dialling from a landline with the same area code, you omit it. The area code for toll-free numbers is ⓣ800, always preceded by the ⓣ01.

To use a **mobile phone** in Mexico is expensive if you simply take your own phone and use it under a roaming agreement. If you are there for any length of time, either buy a prepaid cellphone (around M$500, including a varying amount of call credit). You can buy a Mexican SIM-card (around M$100) to get a Mexican number for your own handset, but this involves registering your identity (so you'll need a passport) and that doesn't always work for a foreigner, so make sure your mobile works before you leave the store. Your phone charger will not work in Mexico if it is designed for a 220–240v electricity supply. Calls from mobiles are pricey and with a SIM-card from abroad you pay to receive as well as make international calls. Mexican cellphone numbers have ten digits of which the first two or three are the area code (55 for Mexico City, for example). To call a cellphone from a landline, first dial ⓣ044 if it has the same area code, ⓣ045 if not, or the international access code plus 52-1 if calling from abroad, and then the ten-digit number.

Useful and emergency numbers

National operator ⓣ020
Police ⓣ060
International operator ⓣ090
Fire ⓣ068
Directory enquiries ⓣ040
Ambulance ⓣ065
Tourist information ⓣ078
Green Angels Emergency (general) ⓣ080 (tourist highway breakdown) ⓣ078

Dialling codes

Mexico long-distance ⓣ01 + area code + number
US & Canada ⓣ001 + area code + number
UK ⓣ00 44 + area code (minus initial zero) + number
Ireland ⓣ00 353 + area code (minus initial zero) + number
Australia ⓣ00 61 + area code (minus initial zero) + number
New Zealand ⓣ00 64 + area code (minus initial zero) + number
South Africa ⓣ00 27 + area code (minus initial zero) + number

Photography

Film is manufactured in Mexico and, if you buy it from a chain store like Woolworth's or Sanborn's rather than at a tourist store, costs no more than at home (if you buy it elsewhere, be sure to check the date on the box, and be suspicious if you can't see it). Up to twelve rolls of film can be brought into Mexico, and spare batteries are also a wise precaution. Purchasing any sort of camera hardware, though, will be prohibitively expensive. Slide film is hard to come by, too.

Senior travellers

Mexico is not a country that offers any special difficulties – or any special advantages – to **older travellers**, but the same considerations apply here as to anywhere else in the world. If choosing a package tour, consider one run by firms such as Elderhostel (Ⓦwww.elderhostel.org) or Saga (Ⓦwww.saga.co.uk), which specialize in holidays for the over-50s.

Do remember that Mexico's high altitude, desert heat and tropical humidity can tire you out a lot faster than you might otherwise expect. As far as comfort is concerned, first-class buses are generally pretty pleasant, with plenty of legroom. Second-class buses can be rather more boneshaking, and you won't want to take them for too long a journey.

Senior citizens are often entitled to **discounts** at tourist sights, and on occasion for accommodation and transport, something which it's always worth asking about.

Time

Four **time zones** exist in Mexico. Most of the country is on GMT–6 in winter, GMT–5 in summer (first Sunday in April till last Sunday in October), the same as US Central Time. Baja California Sur, Sinaloa, Nayarit and Chihuahua are on GMT–7 in winter, GMT–6 in summer (the same as US Mountain Time). Baja California is on GMT–8 in winter, GMT–7 in summer, the same as the US West Coast (Pacific Time); and finally, Sonora is on GMT–7 all year round, and does not observe daylight saving time.

Toilets

Public toilets in Mexico can be quite filthy, and often there's no paper, although there may be someone selling it outside for a couple of pesos. It's therefore wise to carry toilet paper with you. Toilets are usually known as *baños* (literally bathrooms) or as *excusados* or *sanitarios*. The most common signs are "Damas" (Ladies) and "Caballeros" (Gentlemen), though you may find the more confusing "Señoras" (Women) and "Señores" (Men) or even symbols of the moon (women) and sun (men).

Tourist information

The first place to head for **information**, and for free maps of the country and many towns, is the Mexican Government Ministry of Tourism (**Secretaría de Turismo**, abbreviated to **SECTUR**; Ⓦwww.sectur.gob.mx, but information at Ⓦwww.visitmexico.com), which has offices throughout Mexico and abroad. Stock up with as many relevant brochures and plans as they'll let you have, since offices in Mexico are frequently closed or have run out.

Once you're in Mexico, you'll find tourist offices (sometimes called *turismos*) run by SECTUR, in addition to some run by state and municipal authorities; quite often there'll be two or three rival ones in the same town. Some are extremely friendly and helpful, with free information and leaflets by the cart-load; others are barely capable of answering the simplest enquiry. We have listed these in the relevant city and regional sections throughout the guide. You can also call SECTUR toll-free round the clock in Mexico at Ⓣ078 or 01-800/903-9200, from the US or Canada on Ⓣ1-800/446-3942, or from the UK Ⓣ00-800/1111-2266.

Mexican tourist offices overseas

Canada

1 Place Ville Marie, Suite 2409, Montréal, PQ H3B 2C3 Ⓣ01-450/871-1103, Ⓔmontreal@visitmexico.com; 2 Bloor St W, Suite 1502, Toronto, ON M4W 3E2 Ⓣ01-416/925-2753, Ⓔtoronto@visitmexico.com; 999 W Hastings St, Suite 1110, Vancouver, BC V6C 2W2 Ⓣ01-604/669-2845, Ⓔvancouver@visitmexico.com.

UK

Wakefield House, 41 Trinity Square, London EC3N 4DT Ⓣ020/7488 9392, Ⓔgayala@visitmexico.com.

US

225 N Michigan Ave, 18th floor, Suite 1850, Chicago, IL 60601 ⓣ01-312/228-0517, ⓔchicago@visitmexico.com; 4507 San Jacinto, Suite 308, Houston, TX 77004 ⓣ01-713/772-2581, ⓔhouston@visitmexico.com; 1880 Century Park East, Suite 511, Los Angeles, CA 90067 ⓣ01-310/282-9112, ⓔlosangeles@visitmexico.com; 400 Madison Ave, Suite 11C, New York, NY 10017 ⓣ01-212/308-2110, ⓔnewyork@visitmexico.com; 5975 Sunset Drive, Suite 305, South Miami, FL 33143 ⓣ01-786/621-2909, ⓔmiami@visitmexico.com.

Government websites

Australian Department of Foreign Affairs ⓦwww.dfat.gov.au, www.smartraveller.gov.au.
British Foreign & Commonwealth Office ⓦwww.fco.gov.uk.
Canadian Department of Foreign Affairs ⓦwww.international.gc.ca.
Irish Department of Foreign Affairs ⓦwww.foreignaffairs.gov.ie.
New Zealand Ministry of Foreign Affairs ⓦwww.mft.govt.nz.
US State Department ⓦwww.travel.state.gov.
South African Department of Foreign Affairs ⓦwww.dfa.gov.za.

Travellers with disabilities

Mexico is not well equipped for people with disabilities, but it is improving. Especially at the top end of the market, it shouldn't be too difficult to find accommodation and tour operators who can cater for your particular needs.

If you stick to **beach resorts** – Cancún and Acapulco in particular – and upmarket tourist hotels, you should be able to find places that are wheelchair-friendly and used to disabled guests. US chains are very good for this, with Choice, Days Inn, Holiday Inn, Leading Hotels of the World, Marriott, Radisson, Ramada, Sheraton and Westin claiming to have the necessary facilities for at least some disabilities in some of their hotels. Check in advance with tour companies, hotels and airlines that they can accommodate you specifically.

Unless you have your own **transport**, the best way to travel in Mexico may be by air; buses rarely cater for disabled people and not for wheelchairs. Travelling on a lower budget, or getting off the beaten track, you'll find few facilities. Ramps are rare, streets and pavements not in a very good state and people no more likely to volunteer help than at home. Depending on your disability, you may want to find an able-bodied helper to accompany you.

Travelling with children

A minor under the age of 18 can enter the country with either their own passport or on the passport of a parent with whom they are travelling, but if they are not accompanied by both parents, they will need written consent from whichever parent is not with them (or from both if they are on their own).

Travelling with younger kids is not uncommon – most Mexicans dote on children and they often help to break the ice with strangers. The main problem, especially with small children, is their extra vulnerability. They need protecting from the sun, unsafe drinking water, heat and unfamiliar food. Chile peppers in particular may be a problem for kids who are not used to them. Diarrhoea can also be dangerous for younger children: rehydration salts (see p.44) are vital. Ensure that your child is aware of the dangers of rabies and other animal-borne illnesses; keep children away from all animals and consider a rabies shot.

For touring, hiking or walking, child-carrier backpacks are ideal: they can weigh less than 2kg and start at around US$90/£60 new, though you should be able to find cheaper used ones online. If the child is small enough, a fold-up buggy is also well worth packing – especially if they will sleep in it while you have a meal or a drink.

Guide

Guide

Baja California

CHAPTER 1 Highlights

* **The Transpeninsular Highway** One of the world's great road-trips, Highway 1 runs the length of Baja California for 1711km, a witheringly beautiful drive of starry nights, vast deserts and empty beaches. See p.74

* **Fish tacos** The seafood in this part of Mexico is always exceptional, but the real star is the humble fish taco, found all over Baja but best experienced in Ensenada See p.89

* **Valle de Guadalupe** Tour the vineyards of this rapidly maturing wine area, from giants like Vinos L.A. Cetto to boutique producers like Casa De Piedra. See p.92

* **Cave art** The wild, rugged mountains of Baja California protect some of the most spell-binding prehistoric cave art in the world, best explored with a local guide. See p.100

* **Whale-watching at Laguna San Ignacio** Each winter migrating grey whales journey from the Arctic Circle to nurse their calves in the warm waters of this pristine inlet. See p.103

* **Bahía Concepcíon** Camp underneath a star-filled sky, lounge on gorgeous beaches and kayak alongside dolphins in serene aquamarine waters. See p.109

* **La Paz** All of the Baja's best qualities: great restaurants, cheap rooms, vibrant street life and outdoor adventure opportunities. See p.113

▲ Fish taco stand, Ensenada

Baja California

Graced with tantalizing desert landscapes, lush oases and rich marine life, **Baja California** is one of the most compelling and popular destinations in Mexico. Its human history is no less enticing, with a legacy of remote cave paintings, crumbling Spanish missions, top-notch beach resorts and fabulous seafood. Yet even today, Baja maintains a palpable air of isolation from the rest of Mexico. Much of this remoteness can be attributed to geographical factors: the peninsula lies over 1300 kilometres west of Mexico City, and the sheer distances involved in traversing its length – it's over 1700 kilometres long – are not conducive to quick exploration.

Baja was virtually ignored by the Spanish until 1697, when Jesuit missionaries under **Juan María de Salvatierra** began the painstaking process of establishing isolated churches across the peninsula. By 1840, the indigenous population was virtually extinct thanks to disease, and Baja remained a desolate place well into the twentieth century. Popularized by American adventurers in the 1940s (author John Steinbeck among them), Baja underwent sluggish development until the completion of the **Transpeninsular Highway** (Hwy-1) in 1973, the first paved road connecting the north and south. Since then development in its two states – and Baja California Sur – has largely been restricted to the areas that lie within easy reach of southern California and to Los Cabos, but you need to explore the interior to experience the peninsula at its most captivating.

Between December and April, visitors flock to the peninsula's west coast, near Guerrero Negro, to witness hordes of **whales** congregating to calve. Further south, you'll find turquoise waters and white-sand beaches; most coastal towns in Baja California Sur offer fantastic opportunities for diving, fishing and kayaking, but **Loreto**, **La Paz** and the remote settlements on the **East Cape** are the standouts among them. Right at the end of the peninsula, a booming resort industry in **Los Cabos** attracts crowds that fly in for week-long stays at self-contained hotels.

If you're entering Mexico from California with the intention of heading to the rest of the country, there's a straightforward choice of **routes**: down from Tijuana through the Baja peninsula on Hwy-1 and onwards by ferry from La Paz or Santa Rosalía; or sticking to the mainland via Hwy-2 and Hwy-15. If travelling by car, Baja's Hwy-1 is generally safer and less busy, and the narrow strip of land that it traverses ranks as one of Mexico's most beautiful drives.

The Transpeninsular Highway (Hwy-1)

The **Transpeninsular Highway** stands as one of North America's last great road trips. Part of the thrill comes from the long spaces separating major towns, the narrow segments of highway that snake along precarious cliffsides and the animals and washouts that can block the road. But the biggest draw is the near-constant beauty of the desert, mountain, sea and ocean vistas and their illumination by brilliant blue skies and starry nights. The times below include necessary stops for petrol and army inspections; all cars and buses are searched at military checkpoints stationed between Tijuana and Ensenada (2); north of El Rosario; north of Guerrero Negro; north of San Ignacio; and north of La Paz.

Tijuana to Mexicali	1hr 50min	(198km)
Mexicali to San Felipe	2hr 15min	(195km)
San Felipe to Ensenada	3hr 10min	(245km)
Tijuana to Ensenada	55min	(109km)
Ensenada to San Quintín	3hr	(190km)
San Quintín to El Rosario	55min	(56km)
El Rosario to Cataviña	1hr 50min	(123km)
Cataviña to Parador Punta Prieta	1hr	(103km)
Parador Punta Prieta to Bahía de los Angeles	45min	(69km)
Parador Punta Prieta to Guerrero Negro	1hr 50min	(135km)
Guerrero Negro to San Ignacio	1hr 30min	(146km)
San Ignacio to Santa Rosalía	45min	(72km)
Santa Rosalía to Mulegé	40min	(62km)
Mulegé to Loreto	1hr 45min	(138km)
Loreto to Ciudad Insurgentes	1hr 20min	(141km)
Ciudad Insurgentes to La Paz	2hr 20min	(209km)
La Paz to Todos Santos	45min	(77km)
Todos Santos to Cabo San Lucas	55min	(77km)
Cabo San Lucas to San José del Cabo	25min	(32km)

Tijuana

Known for years as the definitive booze-soaked border town, **TIJUANA** is a city of contradictions, a window into the soul of modern Mexico. American day-trippers have been coming here in significant numbers since the 1950s, but visits crashed 90 percent between 2005 and 2009, and the main commercial drag, **Avenida Revolución**, or **La Revo**, is a shadow of its former raucous self. Escalating drug-related violence (see p.187) of the kind portrayed in *Traffic* (2000) and *La Linea* (2008) – largely shot in Tijuana – led to US government travel warnings in 2008 that devastated the cross-border tourist trade.

Tijuana's real problem, though, is one of perception. Founded in 1889, the city has grown to have a population of almost two million, and despite its often shabby appearance, the region's duty-free status and its legion of **maquiladores** (assembly plants) have helped make Tijuana one of the richest cities in Mexico. The reality is that beautification schemes and police crackdowns have left central Tijuana safer and smarter than ever before, and lurid stories of drug violence and kidnappings are highly exaggerated and rarely affect tourist areas (at least during the day). The tackiness, pushy vendors and painted donkeys are still there, but downtown is flooded with police and has become largely free of the violence. The city is fast developing a dynamic **arts** scene, and enterprising newcomers have breathed life into

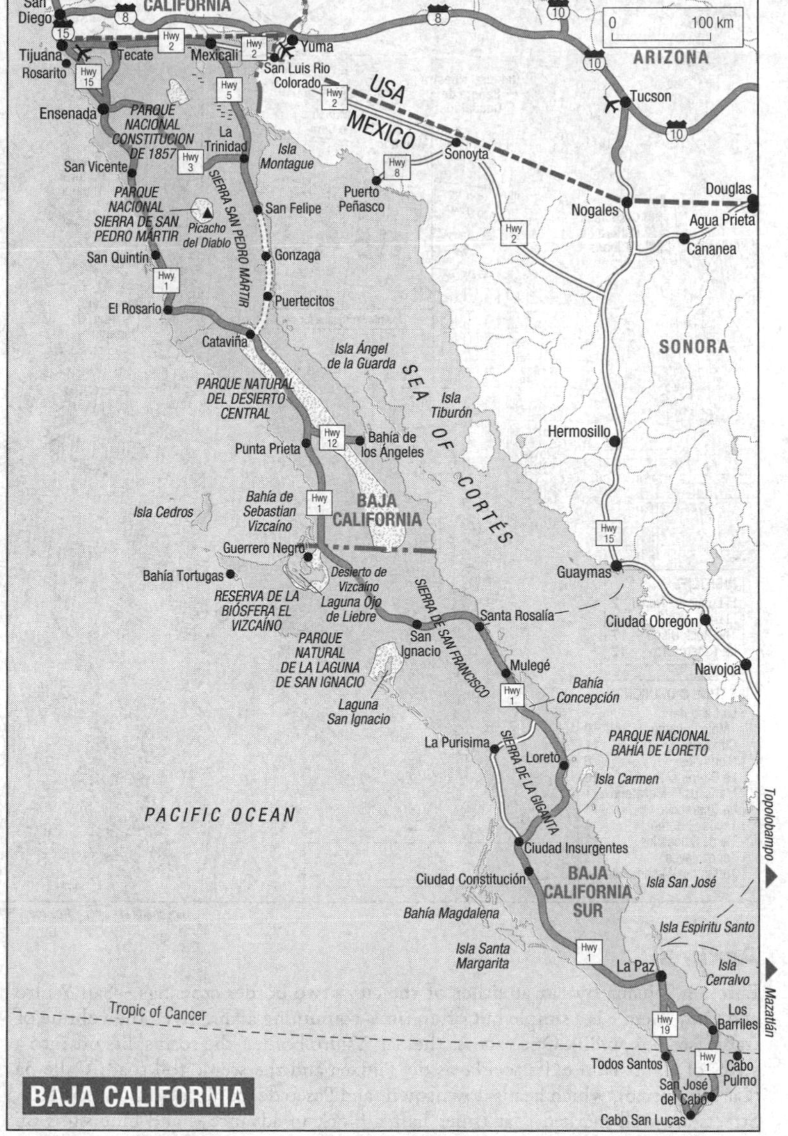

the city's restaurant industry, using cultural institutions like Centro Cultural Tijuana (CECUT) as a breeding ground for home-grown artistic and cultural movements. In the **Zona Río**, beyond the areas where most tourists venture, you'll find sophisticated restaurants, clubs and modern concrete and glass buildings, offering the best glimpse of Tijuana's other life – one that has more in common with San Diego than the adult-themed carnival atmosphere of La Revo. And the **food** is fabulous – Tijuana excels at tasty tacos and can claim some of the best burritos in Mexico.

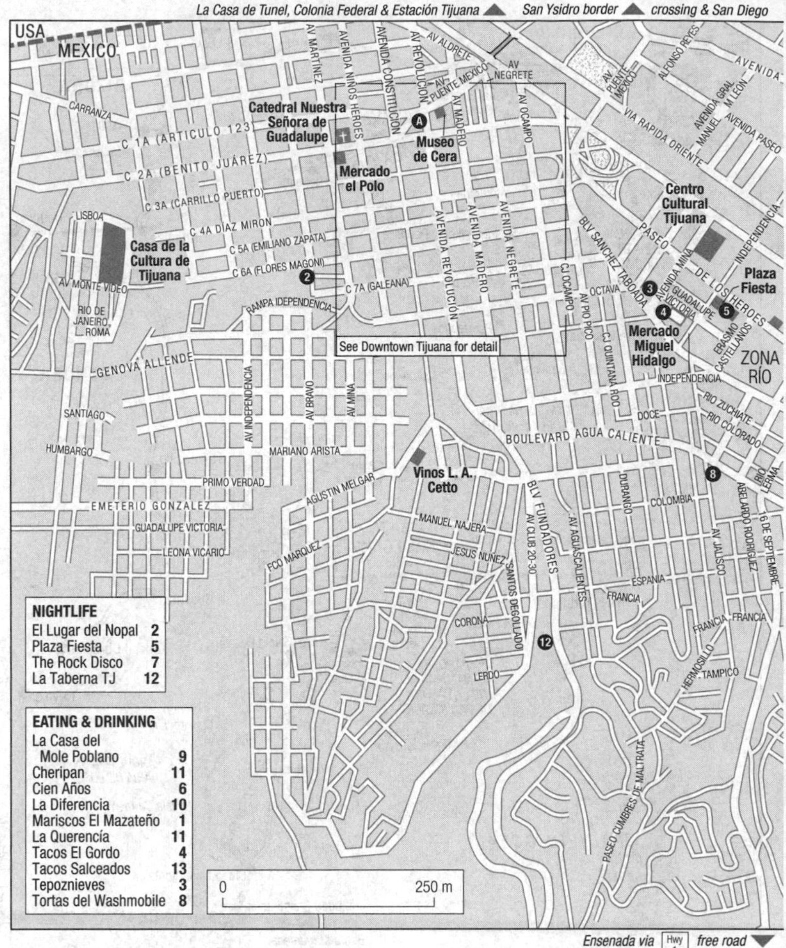

Arrival

Entering Tijuana **by car** at either of the city's two border crossings – San Ysidro and Otay Mesa – is a simple but often time-consuming affair, given the volume of traffic (see box, p.80). Once across the San Ysidro border, the road splits off into a series of right-hand exits to Playas de Tijuana and the scenic toll road; Calle 3a (Carillo Puerto), which heads downtown; and Paseo de los Héroes into Zona Río. Streets are well marked – at times half a block in advance – and blue signs on lampposts identify the distance to prominent locations. Around 8km east of San Ysidro, Otay Mesa is typically used by drivers of passenger cars and RVs who don't mind driving a little further to avoid San Ysidro's long queues.

The **San Diego Trolley** (US$2.50) connects downtown San Diego to the border, or you can leave your car at Border Station Parking, 4570 Camino de la Plaza (US ⓣ619/428-1422; US$8) in San Ysidro. From here Mexicoach operates a convenient **shuttle service** from the parking lot and trolley station on the US side of the border to the centrally located Terminal Turístico at Revolución and Calle 6 (daily

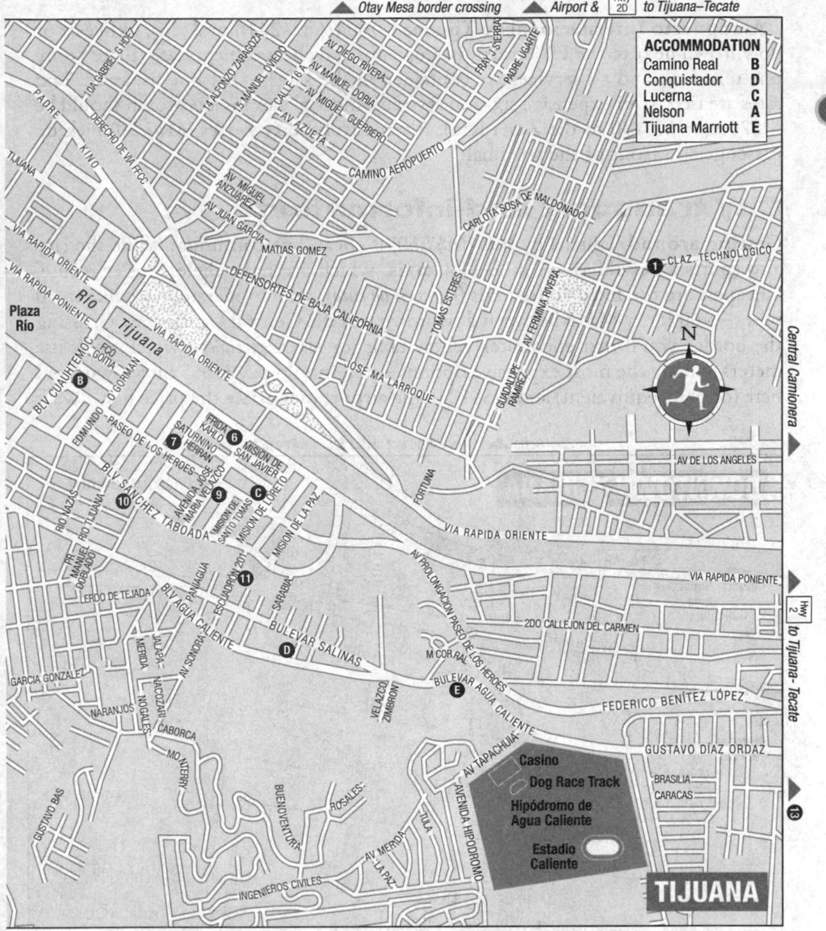

8am–9pm; every 30min; US$4; ⓣ664/685-1470; ⓦwww.mexicoach.com), and on to Rosarito (daily 9am–7pm; every 2hr; US$13). You can also walk across the border, using the pedestrian route through the Viva Tijuana shopping mall, over the footbridge, and along Calle Comercio to Avenida Revolución in downtown. Alternatively, once across the border, you can catch a bus (M$7.50) headed downtown (look for those marked "Centro" or "Revolución") or to the Central Camionera (blue-and-white buses marked "Cam Cen" or "Cam Central") from the public bus and taxi terminal right by the entrance to Viva Tijuana. If you're planning to head straight out of the city by plane or bus (see p.80), it makes more sense to take the regular Greyhound service (1hr 10min; US$15; US ⓣ619/515-1100) from the San Diego terminal at 120 West Broadway direct to Tijuana's airport or the long-distance bus station, **Central Camionera** (ⓣ664/621-2982), at Lázaro Cárdenas 15751, north of the river and 6km east of the city centre (near the airport). Arriving at the latter, the local bus marked "Centro" takes thirty minutes to get to the centre of Tijuana via Calle 2a; taxis charge around M$100.

Aeropuerto Internacional de Tijuana (☎664/683-2418 or 2118), 6km east of downtown next to the US border, is simple for travellers to negotiate: there's only one terminal, and all services are contained in the kiosks that line its walls. Taxi rates are tied to an expensive six-zone system; most places in downtown should be M$200 (or M$180 to the Zona Río). Alternatively, **city buses** (M$7.50) pick up passengers in front of the terminal.

City transport and information

Getting around Tijuana by **bus** (M$7.50) is cheap but confusing, while the city also sports a bewildering number of **taxis**, which are nevertheless easier to use. Cheapest are the fixed-route taxis (*los taxis de ruta*), which operate more like small buses – you'll pay M$13 between downtown and the Central Camionera. Crossing the border you'll first encounter yellow taxis (or *taxis especiales*), which don't use meters and are the most expensive options – you should pay US$5 into town from here (or peso-equivalent) and US$10 to the airport (negotiate the price first). Walk

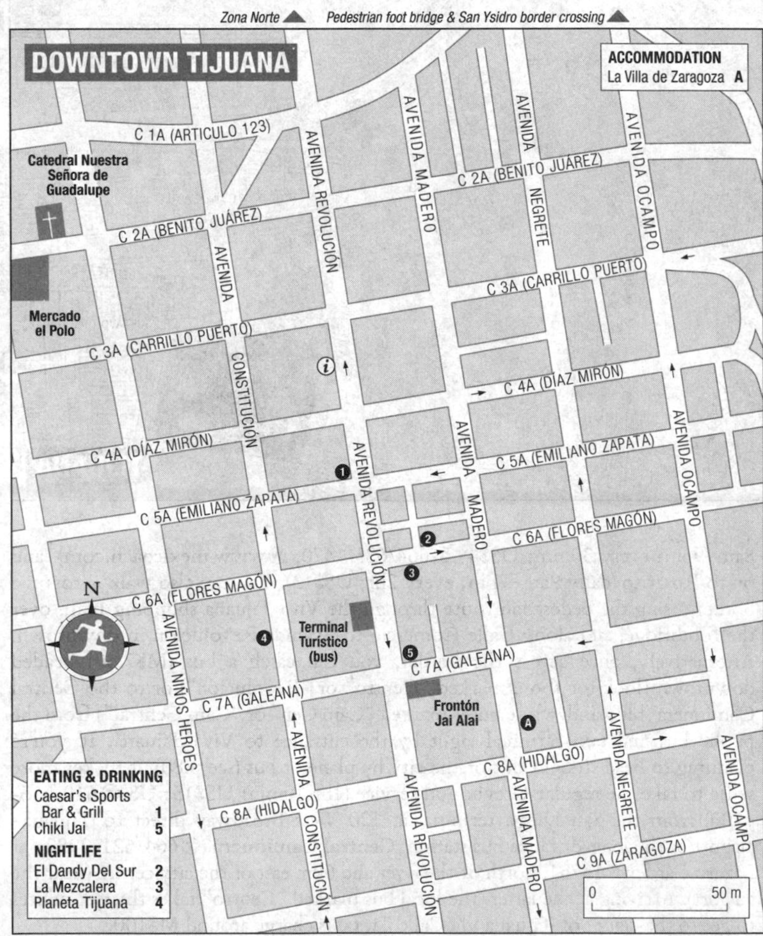

a little further and you'll see the stand for white *taxis libres*, which do use meters (starting at M$6) and are about half the price.

The most convenient **tourist office** is right at the border, at the pedestrian entry point (Mon–Sat 9am–6pm, Sun 9am–1pm; ⓣ664/607-3097). The **main tourist office** is in the centre of downtown on Revolución between calles 3a and 4a (daily 9am–6pm; ⓣ664/685-2210). For general information call ⓣ1-888/775-2417.

Accommodation

Since a sizeable proportion of Tijuana's visitors leave before nightfall, the city offers fewer types of **accommodation** than one would expect. None of the budget places along Calle 1a heading west from Revolución or north of Calle 1a (Zona Norte) is recommended – particularly not for lone women. The hotels listed below are generally safe, but note that petty theft can be a problem anywhere in Tijuana – never leave valuables in your room.

Camino Real Paseo de los Héroes 10305 ⓣ664/633-4000, ⓦwww.caminoreal.com/tijuana. The *Real*'s exterior walls are electric with colour, and the rooms – with satellite TVs and marble bathrooms – have more character than most chains, though some are starting to show their age. Live music and cocktails pull locals into the lobby bar, but there's also a tequila-centric cantina and a tapas bar. ⑤

Conquistador Agua Caliente 10750 ⓣ664/681-7955, ⓦwww.hotelconquistador-tij.com. The *Conquistador*'s two-storey white stucco building, red roof tiles, heavy wood furniture and tapestries may evoke a colonial era Tijuana never really had, but they give it character otherwise absent from the neighbourhood. Rooms open onto the parking area or the pool. ⑤

Lucerna Paseo de los Héroes 10902 ⓣ664/633-3900, ⓦwww.hoteleslucerna.com/tijuana. The six-storey main building and three annexes surround an outdoor pool with a mini waterfall. The best rooms, along with two restaurants and a bar, face this courtyard area. Every room has satellite TV, a balcony, coffee-maker, a/c and purified water. ⑥

Nelson Revolución 721 at C 1a ⓣ664/685-4302. Smack dab at the top of La Revo, this stucco palace can't be beat for location, but the street noise can be relentless at times. *Nelson* is one of La Revo's oldest hotels, so although the rooms have cable TV, they're otherwise quite dated and worn. ④

Tijuana Marriott Agua Caliente 11553 ⓣ664/6226600, ⓦwww.marriott.com. The former *Emporio* has been revamped as an upmarket Marriott with all the extras – wi-fi, business centre, gym and pool – though the rooms are fairly standard business hotel affairs. Free parking for guests and reasonable on-line rates make this a good deal. ⑥

La Villa de Zaragoza Madero 1120 (between C7 and C8) ⓣ664/685-1832, ⓦwww.hotellavilla.biz. This conveniently located US-style motel/hotel complex sits just to the east of the Jai Alai Frontón Palace, and is usually blissfully quiet despite its proximity to La Revo. Rooms, some with kitchenettes, are ageing a bit, and the staff can seem a bit stiff at times. A security guard watches over the parking lot (24hr) and they offer free wi-fi. ④

The City

If you're only in town to spend a few hours gawking at the city's historic tackiness, you need not wander far from the uninterrupted stream of bars, dance clubs, malls and markets on **Avenida Revolución** between calles 1a and 8a. When the lure of cheap souvenirs begin to pall, you'll do yourself a favour by heading east to the **Zona Río**; the district's backbone, Paseo de los Héroes, is Tijuana's grandest boulevard and contains the city's finest institutions.

The prestigious **Centro Cultural Tijuana**, or CECUT, Paseo de los Héroes at Avenida Independencia (ⓣ664/687-9635, ⓦwww.cecut.gob.mx) is home to a major performance space, recital halls, a lobby for temporary visual art exhibits (Tues–Sun 10am–8pm; free) and an **IMAX** movie theatre (Mon–Fri 4–9pm, Sat & Sun 11am–7pm; M$45) – the brown globe it is housed in gives the complex its nickname "La Bola". There's also a tranquil garden dotted with replicas of Meso-american sculpture (daily 10am–6pm), a decent bookshop (Mon–Sat 9am–9pm,

Crossing the border at Tijuana

If you have the right documentation, passing through either Tijuana **border post** is normally a breeze, though, depending on the day and hour, you may have to wait in a very long queue before returning to the States; non-US citizens should allow more time if you require new I-94 or I-94W (visa-waiver) forms (see p.29 for more on border formalities). Because of its proximity to the Tijuana airport and nearby factories, trucks tend to use the **Otay Mesa** crossing. While heading into the US at Otay Mesa seldom takes more than an hour, it's a 25-minute drive from downtown Tijuana and about as long from Otay on I-805 to reach central San Diego. Both San Ysidro and Otay Mesa crossings are open 24 hours.

Moving further into Mexico

If you're taking your **car** off the **Baja Peninsula** (which is part of the visa- and duty-free zone) you'll need to get a **temporary importation vehicle permit** at the branch of Banjercito at the border, though you can also do this on-line up to 180 days in advance (for details see "Getting there", p.28). The permit is U$29.70 at the border (plus US$16.50 processing fee) and US$49.50 at Ⓦwww.banjercito.com.mx by credit card only; otherwise cash deposits range US$200–400.

From the border, taxis to Tijuana airport should cost M$150–200 (depending on the type of cab). Tijuana is a hub for Aeroméxico, which operates around 70 daily flights to/from 15 Mexican cities (it also flies to Tokyo and Shanghai). The airport also serves as hub for low-cost Volaris, and has flights by Interjet, VivaAerobus and Mexicana. Note many of these airlines run buses to the airport direct from San Diego.

Mexicoach (see p.84) runs **buses** between Tijuana and Rosarito (US$7 or peso-equivalent) every two hours. Tijuana's long-distance bus station, **Central Camionera** (see p.77) has regular services to Guadalajara (36hr) and Mexico City (42hr), and most major cities in between. You can also catch buses here for destinations in Baja California, though it pays to remember that La Paz is a 24hr ride away. Buses to Ensenada take around 90min.

Sun 10am–8pm) and the absorbing **Museo de las Californias** (Tues–Sun 10am–6.30pm; M$25), with exhibits highlighting the history of the region from pre-Columbian times. The newest attraction, **El Cubo** (Tues–Sun 10am–7pm; M$45) is an imaginative building designed by local architect Eugenio Velásquez, which houses innovative contemporary artwork.

Mercado Miguel Hidalgo, Independencia at Guadalupe Victoria (daily 7am–7pm), is the city's largest outdoor market and the last real remnant of the zone's pre-spruced-up period. You can buy produce, seafood, desserts, piñatas, toys and clothing at the colourful stalls that line its perimeter. Some of the stalls double as restaurants, but if you can't find anything to your liking, there are a number of bakeries and fish taco joints along the nearby streets Guadalupe Victoria and Mina. The Mercado is within walking distance of the adjacent **Plaza del Zapato** (for cheap name-brand trainers) and the city's largest mall, the **Plaza Río**, Paseo de los Héroes 9698 (Ⓣ664/684-0402).

Just under 1km southeast of here, at the end of Bulevar Agua Caliente, lies the vast **Hipódromo de Agua Caliente** at Agua Caliente 12027 (races daily at 6.30pm or 7.45pm; Mon & Tues 1pm; Sat & Sun 2pm; grandstand seating free; Ⓣ664/633-7300). Initially erected in 1929 for horse racing (Seabiscuit won the Caliente Handicap here in 1938) and, in the smaller in-field track, dog racing, it now only features **greyhound** (*galgos*) **racing** and off-track betting; horse races were eliminated in 1992 after a labour dispute. Billionaire track owner and ex-mayor Jorge Hank Rhon has redeveloped the whole site as a lavish entertainment centre, complete with the largest casino in Mexico, bars and restaurants; in 2009 he finished building the Estadio Caliente inside for **Club Tijuana** (tickets M$70–100; Ⓦwww.xoloitzcuintlesdecaliente.com), the city's Primera División soccer team (which he also owns).

Colonia Federal

For a taster of Tijuana's vibrant art scene, head for the Colonia Federal, a small neighbourhood frequented by artists, sandwiched between the US border and Tijuana River north of downtown. La Casa de Túnel at Chapo Márquez 133 (Ⓣ664/682-9570, Ⓦwww.cofac101.org/index.html) was once the site of an illegal tunnel across the frontier (those responsible were arrested in 2004), and today operates as an illuminating gallery for mainly local artists. Nearby, at Jose Maria Larroque 271 (3°), the Estación Tijuana (Ⓦestaciontijuana.blogspot.com) is also worth a look – check the website for the latest exhibitions.

Eating and drinking

The best by-product of Tijuana's population boom is its flourishing **restaurant scene**. For the tastiest meals, avoid **La Revo** almost entirely. **Zona Río** has the most enticing selection of restaurants, with several sandwiched between Paseo de los Héroes and Sánchez Taboada. The city also has plenty of addictive street food, while beer fans should check out the *Cerveza Tijuana* brewpub, where you can also eat (see p.83).

If you're not planning to visit any of Mexico's wine-growing regions, stop in at Vinos L.A. Cetto (Mon–Sat 10am–5pm; Ⓣ664/685-3031, Ⓦwww.cettowines.com), 3km southwest of La Revo at Cañón Johnson Av 2108. One of the largest producers in the Valle de Guadaloupe (see p.92), their Tijuana outpost offers tastings (*traditionales* M$20, *reserva* M$50) and the chance to tour the packaging area and underground cellars.

La Revo and around

Caesar's Sports Bar & Grill Revolución 1071 Ⓣ664/638-4562. Legend has it that Caesar Cardini first whipped up his eponymous salad in Tijuana in 1924, and this shrine to his memory still prepares the dish tableside with raw egg and garlic, Parmesan cheese, anchovies and hearts of Romaine lettuce (around M$70) in an elaborate ceremony.

Chiki Jai Revolución 1388, at Calle 7 Ⓣ664/685-4955. Enticing Spanish *taberna*, draped with bullfighting memorabilia, fading photos of Tijuana and paintings of Don Quixote.Come here for decent tapas, sangria and *vino tinto*. Open since 1947, and the likes of Errol Flynn, Rita Hayworth and Ava Gardner once ate here. Daily for lunch and dinner.

Tortas del Washmobile Agua Caliente, at Jalisco (15 blocks south of La Revo). This famous stall was established over forty years ago next to a gas station with a car wash (now defunct), and serves only one thing: a mouth-watering mesquite grilled beef sandwich marinated in a secret sauce. Served on *pambaso* rolls; ask for *con todo* and you'll also get heaps of guacamole and a topping of red onions, tomatoes and salsa (less than M$30). Open daily 8am–4pm, or until they run out of bread.

Zona Río

La Casa del Mole Poblano Paseo de los Héroes 10511 Ⓣ664/634-6920. Dark chocolate and hot chiles flavour the Oaxacan sauce this restaurant uses to coat chicken legs and breasts (M$75) and other meat dishes. The lighting and decor are a pleasant surprise for a bargain spot, with waterfalls, plants and, on weekends, roving musicians.

Cheripan Escuadrón 201, no. 3151 Ⓣ664/622-9730, Ⓦwww.cheripan.com. Argentine grill lauded for its succulent steaks (M$175), chops and extensive wine list, as well as the city's best fries, coated in parsley and garlic (M$35). Try the *martini de tamarindo*.

Cien Años José María Velazco 1407 Ⓣ664/634-3039, Ⓦwww.cien.info. This tourist favourite has drawn notice for its use and adaptation of Aztec recipes – as the name suggests, every recipe served is supposed to be more than a hundred years old. Gourmands swear by the cactus salad and stingray tacos; tamer items such as honey-roasted duck or chicken *mole* are available for the less intrepid. Dishes average M$100–250.

La Diferencia Sánchez Taboada 10611-A ⓣ664/634-7078, ⓦwww.ladiferencia.com.mx. Along with *Cien Años*, *Diferencia* has a more daring menu than most places in Tijuana, with satisfying takes on pre-Columbian meals. Unfamiliar dishes like beef-tongue strips with chiles, the Aztec delicacy crepes Cuitlacoche (an edible corn fungus) and prickly-pear salad are made more appealing within a romantic setting complete with a courtyard and fountain. Entrées M$140–280.

Mariscos El Mazateño Calzada Tecnologico 473-E, Tomas Aquino (20min drive from La Revo). Take a taxi to this iconic taquería for their spicy Sinaloan-style *Taco Mazatena* (*camarón enchilado* or shrimp taco), and filling smoked marlin tacos (M$18–20). Some seating inside, but most locals eat standing up or crouched on the sidewalk outside.

La Querencia Escuadrón 201, no. 3110 ⓣ664/972-9935, ⓦwww.laquerenciatj.com. Established in 2006 by celebrity chef Miguel Guerrero, this fancy restaurant with lacquered steel dining tables and open kitchens is one of the creators of contemporary Baja Med cuisine, a blend of traditional Mexican ingredients with Mediterranean flavours. Try the betabel (beet) carpaccio (M$50), oyster (ostión) tacos (M$20–25) or more substantial fish of the day. Open from 1pm Mon–Sat, closed Sun.

Tacos El Gordo Sánchez Taboada (at Javier Mina next to Mercado Hidalgo). There are many *El Gordo* taco shops in Tijuana (and now southern California), but this place is one of the best. Feast on a tempting range of zesty tacos, including *suadero* (fried breastbone meat), *carne asada* and tacos *al pastor*, all complimented by a fabulous range of salsas. Most tacos are less than M$25. Open daily 10am–5am.

Tacos Salceados Ermita Nte 30-A. Known locally as *La Ermita*, after the street, this knocks out the best beef tacos in the city with at least fifteen spicy salsas to choose from. Chef Javier Campos Guttiérez is also known for his gourmet creations such as shrimp and strawberry tacos, or nopal tacos (prickly-pear cactus).Seating is available here, but it's so popular there's almost always a wait for tables.

Tepoznieves Sánchez Taboada 4002 ⓣ664/634-6532. Enjoy a scoop of Beso de Ángel ice cream ("angel's kiss"), a sumptuous blend of mamey, pine nut, strawberry and cherry, or choose from an equally innovative list of all-natural flavours such as Primavera (cheese, mango, nuts and flowers).

Nightlife

Traditionally, the rowdiest action in Tijuana is along **La Revo**, where numerous bars pump out rock music and hip-hop for primarily US visitors. After the slump in 2009, it remains to be seen whether the strip's glory days are now over. In any case, most locals and visitors in the know shun La Revo in favour of the clubs and bars clustered around the shopping areas of **Zona Río**, where the beats are louder, the clubs larger and the scene doesn't slow down until morning. If you're lucky, you may get to see a performance by **Javier Batiz**, one of Tijuana's rock legends, or electronica merchants **Nortec Collective**, who scored big hits across Latin America with their 2005 album *Tijuana Sessions Vol. 3*. Check ⓦwww.myspace.com/nortec or www.milrecords.com for more information. Discover smaller shows by picking up the free Spanish-language weekly *Bitácora*, available beginning Wednesdays at most cafés and bars around town as well as online at ⓦwww.bitacoracultural.com. Get tickets for bigger events through **Ticketmovil** (ⓣ664/681-7084, ⓦwww.ticketmovil.com.mx). You should avoid Tijuana's red-light district, known as "La Coahuila" or **Zona Norte** (beyond the northern end of La Revo) – this area is dodgy even during the day and is littered with brothels and strip clubs.

El Dandy Del Sur Calle 6a no. 2030 ⓣ664/688-0052. Open since 1957 but immortalized by local techno group the Nortec Collective in 2005, this jukebox bar on the corner of 6th and La Revo is popular with artists and plenty of locals escaping the tourist drag. The walls are decorated with mirrors and pictures of movie stars; tends to attract serious drinkers long into the early hours.

El Lugar del Nopal Callejón 5 de Mayo 1328 ⓣ664/685-1264, ⓦwww.lugardelnopal.com. This café-cum-performance space is a gathering place for Tijuana's creative class, who turn up for exhibits, screenings and live music. Closed Sun & Mon.

La Mezcalera Calle 6 no. 8267 (between Revolución and Madero). Friendly bar and restaurant featuring, unsurprisingly, mescal, the traditional and extremely potent Mexican spirit made from the agave plant. They usually have at least six different brands of the stuff and nine different types of crema de mescal (a blend of mescal and agave syrup). Daily 5pm–2am.

Planeta Tijuana Constitución 1033 ⓣ664/688-3272, ⓦwww.naza.com.mx. Formerly *Multikulti*, this gutted, 1950s open-air cinema now hosts small concerts, underground arts festivals and DJ events such as the regular *Club Lobby* nights. Cover usually ranges M$70–100.

Plaza Fiesta Paseo de los Héroes 1001. Can't decide where to go? Locals often head here without a specific place in mind, preferring to wander between the bars and clubs until they find a scene that appeals to them. Standouts include *La Cantina* (ⓣ664/634-3065), reggae and ska specialists *Berlin Bar* (ⓣ664/700-2184, ⓦwww.berlintijuana.com) and Swiss-themed *Sótano Suizo* (ⓣ664/684-8834, ⓦwww.sotanosuizo.com.mx). Most spots are quiet before 11pm.

The Rock Disco Diego Rivera 1482 ⓣ664/634-3784. The exterior and fake boulders say *Flintstones* but the inside is all lasers and techno beats. Cover starts around M$100; for an extra M$50 they'll park your car. Open Thurs–Sat 9pm–3am.

La Taberna TJ at the Consorcio Cervecero de Baja California, Fundadores 2951 ⓣ664/638-8662, ⓦwww.tjbeer.com. Home of *Cerveza Tijuana*, the city's acclaimed microbrewery houses a congenial pub, a few minutes south of La Revo by taxi. Decked out with dark wood panelling and hardwood floors, the pub usually offers five or six hand-crafted Czech-style lagers and a menu of decent bar food. You can look into the brewery floor through a window, but tours must be arranged in advance. Live music Wed–Sat night, closed Sun.

Listings

Airlines Aeroméxico, Plaza Río, Paseo de los Héroes ⓣ664/638-8444 or 684-9268, ⓦwww.aeromexico.com; InterJet, Aeropuerto Internacional de Tijuana ⓣ01800/01-12345, ⓦwww.interjet.com.mx; Mexicana, Diego Rivera 1511 ⓣ664/634-6545 or 6566, ⓦwww.mexicana.com.mx; Viva Aerobus, Aeropuerto Internacional de Tijuana ⓣ81/8215-0150, ⓦwww.vivaaerobus.com; Volaris ⓣ01800/122-8000, ⓦwww.volaris.com.mx.

American Express There's an office in Viajes Carrousel travel agency (Mon–Fri 9am–8pm, Sat 9am–2pm; ⓣ664/684-0556) way out at Sánchez Taboada 10116 and Clemente Orozco, but their rates are poor.

Banks and exchange US dollars are accepted almost everywhere in Tijuana, but you do get a slightly better return on pesos. If you're visiting no further south than Ensenada there's really no reason to change your currency – you'll lose in the exchange rate whatever savings you'd get buying in shops. If you do change it's no problem, with casas de cambio on virtually every corner. Most offer good rates – almost identical to those north of the border – though few of them accept travellers' cheques, and if they do, they charge a heavy commission. For cheques you're better off with a bank, most of which are on Constitución, a block over from Revolución. ATMs along both of these blocks dispense both dollars and pesos.

Books Sanborn's department store, at Revolución 1102 and Calle 8a (ⓣ664/688-1433), has books and magazines, some from across the border. The Gandhi bookshop at Paseo Héroes 9111 and General M. Márquez in Zona Río also has a good selection.

Consulates Canada, Germán Gedovius 10411 ⓣ664/684-0461; Germany, Cantera 400-305, Playas de Tijuana ⓣ664/680-2512; UK, Salinas 1500 ⓣ664/686-5320; US, Tapachula 96 ⓣ664/622-7400, ⓦwww.tijuana.usconsulate.gov.

Hospital Centro Medico Excel, Paseo de los Héroes 2507 ⓣ664/634-7001.

Internet access The most convenient internet cafés can be found along Revolución; try Word Net at Calle 2a no. 8174 (ⓣ664/685-6514) which has English-speaking staff and free bread when you buy coffee (M$20/hr).

Left luggage Bags can be left at the Central Camionera (daily 6am–10.30pm), or in lockers over the border in the Greyhound station (24hr).

Police If you become a victim of crime, a rip-off or simply want to make a complaint, pick up any phone and dial ⓣ078.

Post office Negrete and C 11a (Mon–Fri 8am–4pm, Sat & Sun 9.30am–1pm), though to send international mail you're better off crossing the border.

Rosarito

If you want to escape the hectic pace and noise of Tijuana, head for the coastal city of **ROSARITO** about 45 minutes' bus ride south on the old road to Ensenada. **Beaches** in Tijuana are invariably crowded and dirty, so Rosarito's longer and sandier beach is a good alternative and provides a more restful atmosphere during the week (and a lively party scene on weekends). Rosarito was also hit hard by US travel warnings in 2009, though tourists (and the city's 14,000 expats) rarely experience any trouble. The main exception is during March and April, when US spring-breakers make the town difficult to bear for anyone who wishes to remain sober.

Information and getting around

The **state tourist office**, Hwy-1 km 28, is a good twenty-minute walk from the centre (Mon–Fri 8am–8pm, Sat & Sun 8am–1pm; ⓣ661/612-5222), but the **Rosarito Convention and Visitors' Bureau** also runs three tourist information booths during US holidays and special events, the most convenient of which can be found outside Oceana Towers at Juárez 907 (ⓣ1-800/962-2252, ⓦwww.rosarito.org), just across from *Señor Frog's*. Getting around Rosarito is easy enough on foot, as most of the action centres on a six-kilometre stretch of Bulevar Benito Juárez, which runs north–south a few blocks inland from the beach. Taxis are plentiful at night, and should take you back to your hotel for a few pesos. As in Tijuana, US dollars are accepted virtually everywhere.

Accommodation

Accommodation prices are highest during spring break (March and April) and the week after Christmas, but drop considerably the rest of the year. Throughout the year it's advisable to reserve at least a week in advance if you plan on staying Friday or Saturday night. The classic place to stay is the *Rosarito Beach Hotel*, Benito Juárez 31 (ⓣ661/612-0144, US ⓣ1-800/343-8582, ⓦwww.rosaritohtl.com; ❼), which was established in 1926 and gave the city its name; it's now a mini-village with a spa, restaurants, bars, two pools, time-share apartments, a racquetball court, craft shops, liquor stores, a history museum and an internet café. Many of the rooms have ocean views but are otherwise without charm; request an older room with garden view – they've managed to retain some character. The hotel's charismatic owner, Hugo Torres, became mayor of the city for the second time in 2007. Elsewhere, the stellar beachfront location and terrace bar overlooking the ocean at *Los Pelicanos*, Cedros 115 (ⓣ661/612-0445, ⓦwww.lospelicanosrosarito.net; ❻), make up for rather lacklustre, standard three-star rooms, while the *La Paloma Beach & Tennis Club* (US ⓣ1-562/491-5203, ⓦwww.bajak28.com; ❼), just south of the

Getting to Rosarito

To get to Rosarito from Tijuana, drive south along either the toll (*cuota*; M$26) or free (*libre*) road for 25km, or take a Mexicoach bus from the Terminal Turístico on La Revo (see p.76). Taxis from the border charge M$200–250, but a *taxi libre* from downtown Tijuana should be M$150–180. You can also take one of the cheaper *taxi de ruta* vans that leave from Madero between calles 3 and 4 (around M$20 per person); to get back, try flagging down a *taxi de ruta* on Juárez, Rosarito's main street. If you're **continuing south** to Ensenada and beyond, you can pick up long-distance buses (at least hourly) at the autopista tollbooth 1km south of the tourist office, past the *Rosarito Beach Hotel*.

city at Hwy-1 km 28.5, rents a selection of modern one- to three-bedroom condo apartments close to the seafront, with three pools, jacuzzis and a gym on site.

Baja Studios

Until 1995 Rosarito was part of the city of Tijuana, but it became a municipality when local politicians like Hugo Torres realized that it was capable of generating its own tourism dollars. Conventional sights are lacking in the city itself, but movie aficionados come to see the **Baja Studios**, 4km south of town at km 32.5 on the free highway to Ensenada. This bit of Hollywood-in-Mexico, originally created by Fox for the filming of *Titanic*, was sold to a group of private investors in 2007. Since then its massive production facilities and seventeen-million-gallon oceanfront tank (also used to shoot films such as *Pearl Harbor* and *Master and Commander*) have seen little action, and have instead become a major tourist attraction. The **Xploration** theme park (Wed–Fri 9am–4.30pm, Sat & Sun 10am–5.30pm; US$12, kids US$9 or peso-equivalents; ⓣ661/612-4294, US ⓣ866/369-2252, ⓦwww.xploration.com.mx) offers a range of exhibits and experiences based around the studios, from an interactive journey through the process of movie-making to the kitschy X-Men exhibit. The *Titanic* model, created at 95 percent scale, has been disassembled, but much of the set is viewable at the park's Titanic Museum.

Eating and drinking

You'll find plenty of **restaurants**, cafés and bars in the blocks behind the seafront and the *Rosarito Beach Hotel*, but there are some extra special treats worth seeking out; Rosarito is another Baja town known for its **tacos**, but you should also head down to Puerto Nuevo for the **lobster** (see box, p.86).

The Castle Carretera Libre Rosarito–Ensenada km 36.6 ⓣ661/613-2022, ⓦwww.thecastleatrosarito.com. For an upmarket but kitsch experience, reserve a table at this romantic beachside restaurant in a mock Romanesque summer house built by Al Capone in the 1920s. Expect haute Mexican dishes such as chicken *poblano* and flounder in white wine; budget around M$400 per head.

La Flor de Michoacan Benito Juárez 291 ⓣ661/612-1858. Founded in 1950 on the north side of town, this popular family restaurant pulls in tourists and locals alike for its piles of crispy *carnitas* (fried pork) served with rice, beans, guacamole, and fresh tortillas. You'll spend around M$150 a person; throw in a pitcher or two of strawberry margaritas.

Ruben's Fish and Shrimp Stand Benito Juárez 28 (no phone). Fabulous taco stall just across from the *Rosarito Beach Hotel*, specializing in bulging fish and shrimp tacos (less than M$20), as well as deep-fried crab, *ceviches*, and fried local fish. Whole fish dinners, priced by the kilo, cost less than M$100 and include rice, beans and salad. Summer daily 6am–7pm; winter Thurs–Mon 8am–5pm.

Tacos Tijuana Junior Popotla 3103, Carretera Libre Rosarito–Ensenada km 30 ⓣ661/100-2598. Another local favourite, this diner-like place stands on the main road south of downtown. Try their *Plato Fiesta* which comes with local fish, shrimp, calamari, octopus and tacos (enough for two people). Their trademark tacos are pretty good too; the *taco gobernador* is crammed with shrimp marinated in chiles and lemons.

Tacos El Yaqui Las Palmas 51 ⓣ661-612-1352. This small taco stand knocks out some of the best (and biggest) *carne asada* tacos on the coast. Tacos with all the toppings are around M$23; you can add cheese for a couple more pesos. You'll find it one block off Juárez at the south end of town (across from Festival Plaza's parking lot). Usually open Mon–Fri 7.30am–4pm, and till 9pm Sat & Sun.

Nightlife

Rosarito's most popular **bars** and **clubs** are contained within what's known as the Barbachano Zone, the area between Juárez and Coronado downtown. Party-goers flock to *Papas and Beer*, at Coronado and Eucalipto 400 (ⓣ664/612-0444,

Lobster town

Once not much more than a dusty roadside settlement between Rosarito and Ensenada at Hwy-1 km 44, **Puerto Nuevo** is nowadays known the length of the peninsula for its near-fanatical devotion to the local speciality that bears its name: Puerto Nuevo-style grilled Pacific **lobster**. Found off the coast and throughout the rest of the Pacific Rim, these lobsters don't grow as large as their Atlantic counterparts (actually, they're giant langoustines more closely related to shrimps) and they don't have claws, but they're just as delicious.

Choosing where to sample the revered dish is made easy enough by the town's one-way street plan, which juts to the west from Hwy-1. Though every one of the more than thirty restaurants serves lobsters the same basic way – grilled and split in half with beans, rice and warm flour tortillas – *Puerto Nuevo #2* (Ⓣ661/614-1454), directly to your south on the second block, and *Ortega's Patio* at the southwest corner of the grid (Ⓣ661/614-0345) are consistently good bets – the latter also gets you ocean views, low lighting and a wood-beam ceiling. Expect to pay M$150–300 depending on the size of the lobster. Most restaurants open 10am to 8pm on weekdays, with some open until 11pm Fri & Sat. Cash only.

Ⓦwww.papasandbeer.com), and nearby *Iggy's*, Coronado 11327 (Ⓣ661/612-0537), where beach volleyball and knocking back as much Corona as possible are the order of the day. One of the more recent additions to the scene is *Coco Beach Club* (Ⓦwww.cocobeachrosarito.com) behind *Papas and Beer*, a cavernous mega-club with three dancefloors and a decent line-up of DJs and live acts, though as with all these places, Spring Break drives the biggest parties. You can also grab a beer and soak up the action in one of numerous open-air cantinas on the beach, where there's usually plenty of live music.

Ensenada and around

Perched on the edge of the Bahía de Todos Santos, 100km south of Tijuana, the affable port town of **ENSENADA** is traditionally packed at weekends with groups of partying southern Californians and crowds of cruise-ship passengers. This all changed in 2009, when, like many other Mexican resorts, it was disproportionately affected by the double whammy of swine flu and US travel warnings. Nevertheless, it remains far calmer, cheaper and smaller than Tijuana and makes a fun jumping-off spot for ecotourism destinations further south.

The first Spaniard to stay for any length of time – at least long enough to notice the indigenous Kumai who fished regularly in the bay – was **Franciscan Junípero Serra**, who rode through in 1769 on his way from Loreto to San Diego. By around 1870 Ensenada had developed into a supply point for missionaries working along the northern Mexican frontier. When gold reserves were discovered that year in nearby Real de Castillo, miners rushed in, but at the beginning of the twentieth century the mines closed and the population dwindled, leaving the town to revert to little more than a small fishing village. A renaissance came in the late 1930s with the rise of agriculture in the Mexicali Valley, and the port became a point of export for the produce. When the paved highway down from Tijuana opened some forty years later, American tourist dollars began to pour in. Today the city is a major port and fish-processing centre.

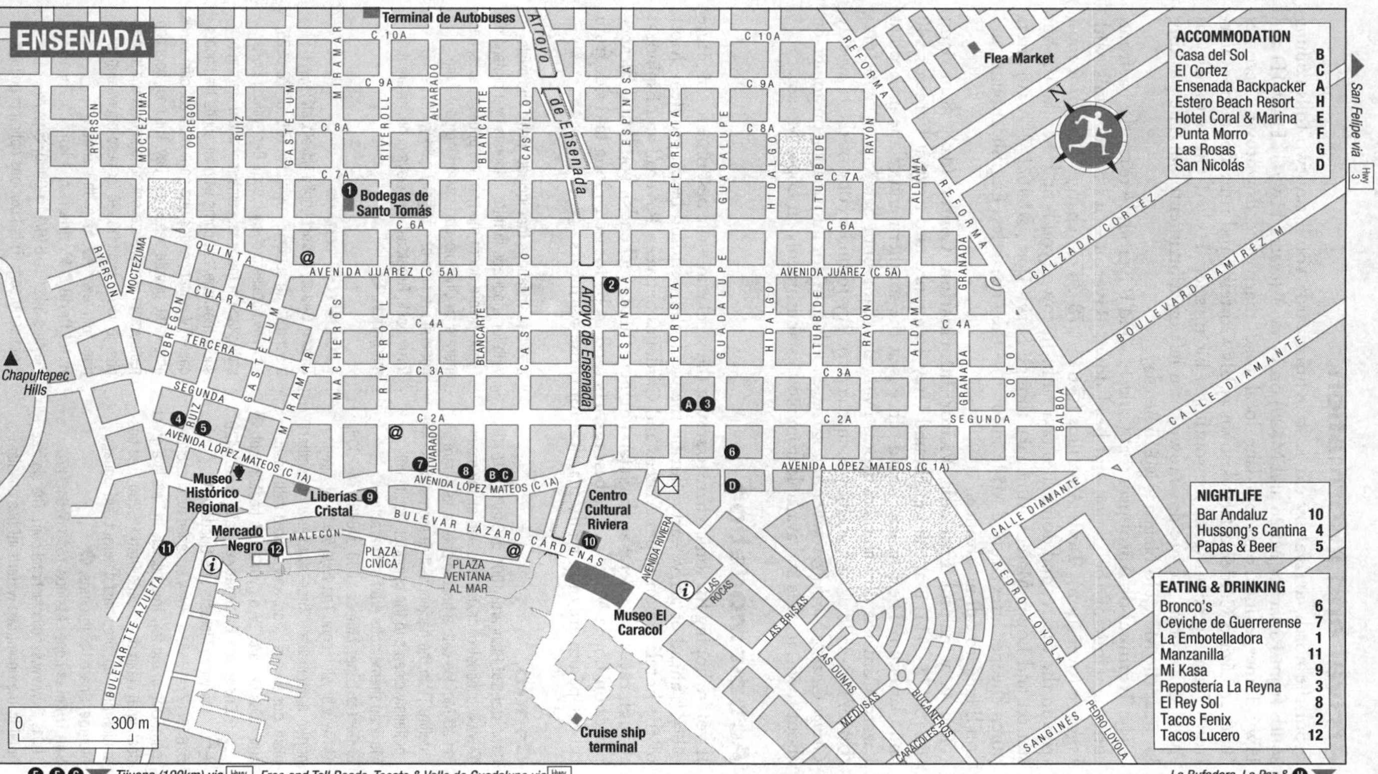

ENSEADA
ACCOMMODATION
Casa del Sol B
El Cortez C
Ensenada Backpacker A
Estero Beach Resort H
Hotel Coral & Marina E
Punta Morro F
Las Rosas G
San Nicolás D
NIGHTLIFE
Bar Andaluz 10
Hussong's Cantina 4
Papas & Beer 5
EATING & DRINKING
Bronco's 6
Ceviche de Guerrerense 7
La Embotelladora 1
Manzanilla 11
Mi Kasa 9
Repostería La Reyna 3
El Rey Sol 8
Tacos Fenix 2
Tacos Lucero 12
Terminal de Autobuses
Flea Market
Bodegas de Santo Tomás
Museo Histórico Regional
Liberías Cristal
Mercado Negro
Centro Cultural Riviera
Museo El Caracol
Cruise ship terminal
Chapultepec Hills
PLAZA CIVÍCA
PLAZA VENTANA AL MAR
Arroyo de Ensenada
AVENIDA JUÁREZ (C 5A)
AVENIDA LÓPEZ MATEOS (C 1A)
BULEVAR LÁZARO CÁRDENAS
BULEVAR TTE AZUETA
MALECÓN
CALZADA CORTEZ
BOULEVARD RAMÍREZ M
CALLE DIAMANTE
PEDRO LOYOLA
REFORMA
SEGUNDA
AVENIDA RIVIERA
0 300 m
San Felipe via Hwy 3
E, F, G, Tijuana (100km) via Hwy 1 Free and Toll Roads, Tecate & Valle de Guadalupe via Hwy 3
La Bufadora, La Paz & H

Arrival and information

From the north, **arrival by car** is straightforward. You'll pay two tolls coming south from Rosarito (M$26 and M$29) on Hwy-1 (*cuota*). Hwy-1, Hwy-1D and Hwy-3 merge into one four-lane local road that, once downtown, becomes Bulevar Lázaro Cárdenas (also known as Blv Costero) and runs along the waterfront. Entering town from the south is a bit messier. Hwy-1 enters the city as Avenida Reforma; to get downtown, turn left on Libramiento Sur.The **parking** lot near the Mercado Negro is M$15 per day.

The **Terminal de Autobuses** is at Calle 11a and Riveroll; to reach the bayfront, turn right out of the station and head down Riveroll – it's a long walk with luggage (over 1km). **Taxis** Amarillos (Ⓣ646/178-3475) charges M$60 for most trips in the centre, and dominates taxi ranks in town (you'll find them at the bus station and López Mateos/Miramar), though Servi Taxi (Ⓣ646/172-7310) offers much cheaper rates (around M$45 in town) – they speak less English, though, and you'll have to call in advance.

The very helpful **Ensenada Visitor Information Center** (daily 8am–8pm; Ⓣ646/178-2411) is at the southbound Hwy-1 entrance into town at Cárdenas 540 and Gastélum. The **tourism board** office is at the southern end of the malecón at Lazaro Cárdenas 609 and Los Rocas (Mon–Fri 8am–6pm Sat & Sun 9am–1pm; Ⓣ646/178-8578, Ⓦwww.enjoyensenada.com). Try to find a copy of the bi-weekly *Gringo Gazette North* (Ⓦwww.gringogazettenorth.com) for information on goings-on about town; it's free and available from most establishments on López Mateos.

Accommodation

If you're hoping for somewhere to **stay** at the weekend – the best time for nightlife – book ahead or arrive early; during the week there should be no problem. Most of the hotels are on López Mateos and Cárdenas between Riveroll and Espinoza; though **rates** in general are high (and higher still at weekends), you'll find cheaper places on López Mateos. The best **resorts** tend to be located a long taxi ride from the strip, and are only really practical for those with cars.

Centro

Casa del Sol Blancarte 1001 Ⓣ646/178-1570, Ⓦwww.casadelsolmexico.net. Two-storey motor inn off Mateos with a heated pool at its centre and satellite TV in the hacienda-style rooms; these are spotlessly clean and the colourful, traditional Mexican theme adds a bit of character. ❺

El Cortez López Mateos 1089 Ⓣ646/178-2306, Ⓦwww.bajainn.com. The *Baja Inn* hotels are the northern peninsula's three-star stalwarts: rather plain, but always clean, and packed with basic amenities like a/c, TV, a gym and a heated pool. ❺

Ensenada Backpacker Calle 2, no. 1429 (between Floresta and Guadalupe) Ⓣ646/177-1758, Ⓦwww.ensenadabackpacker.com. One of the few true hostels in Baja is a great deal, with clean dorm beds from M$250, free bus station pick-up, breakfast, internet and luggage storage. Shared bathrooms. ❸

San Nicolás López Mateos 1536 Ⓣ646/176-1901, Ⓦwww.sannicolashotel.com. The closest hotel to the downtown waterfront has popular package vacations that include meals and deals with local aquatic outfitters. Murals by a protégé of Diego Rivera adorn many of the public spaces, and there's an Olympic-size swimming pool – the general effect is of a slightly quirky, 1970s throwback. Breakfast is always good, as are the margaritas. ❺

Outside town

Estero Beach Resort Lupita Novelo, off Hwy-1 around 13km south of downtown Ⓣ646/176-6225, Ⓦwww.hotelesterobeach.com. Best-value resort-style place in the area; some rooms are starting to show their age, but come with terracotta tiled floors, cable TV, private patios and gardens. Most offer views across the private beach and bay. The pool, bars and restaurants are all excellent, though taxis will try and charge you at least US$20 (or peso-equivalent) for rides into town. ❺, ❼ (with sea view).

Hotel Coral & Marina Hwy-1 km 103, Zona Playitas 3421 Ⓣ646/175-0000, Ⓦwww.hotelcoral.com. This luxurious option is popular with American yachties for the excellent on-site marina facilities, and is a great choice for families or for those looking for a smart resort; standard rooms come with breezy ocean views and all the amenities, but it will cost you at least M$100 to take a taxi into town. ❼

Punta Morro Hwy-1 km 106 ⓣ800/526-6676, ⓦwww.punta-morro.com. The ocean-view studios and suites here have fireplaces, which may explain why guests don't mind the 30min walk to downtown. Rooms also have satellite TV, a/c and sitting areas. There's an on-site restaurant for the nights you want to skip the downtown commute. ❽

Las Rosas Hwy-1 km 105 ⓣ646/174-4310, ⓦwww.lasrosas.com. This white- and pink-stucco resort has balconies and ocean views from every room. The location is fabulous, but be prepared for some traffic noise from the highway. The hotel caters to the same clientele as *Punto Morro*, but manages to differentiate itself with a small, on-site spa and enticing infinity pool. 5–10min drive to town. ❼

The Town

The focal point for Ensenada's municipal and tourist activities is the **waterfront** – almost all of the city's attractions are squeezed into the streets near the malecón. The six-block long promenade is where the city's residents come to see and be seen, gathering for sunset strolls and special events; the centrepiece is the Plaza Ventana al Mar, with its monumental Mexican flag visible all over town. Starting at 8am at the northernwestern end of the malecón, the Mercado de Mariscos (aka **Mercado Negro**), contains numerous merchants selling the day's catches. The diversity of what's on display – from squirming eel to giant abalone – is staggering and it's a good place to try the town's lauded **fish tacos**, which were supposedly invented in Ensenada and have been served at the market since it opened in 1958.

North of the malecón, Ensenada's downtown is shaped roughly as a narrow rectangle that runs northwest to southeast, corresponding to the parallel **Bulevar Lázaro Cárdenas** and lively **Avenida López Mateos** (or Calle 1a, "La Primera"). On the latter you'll find scores of souvenir shops and outfits offering sport-fishing trips, as well as the bulk of the bars, hotels and restaurants – the majority of visitors come here to eat, drink and shop. In recent years, Ensenada has worked hard to widen its tourist appeal with a string of cultural attractions, most notably the Riviera del Pacifico, a former casino and hotel completed in lavish Spanish Revival style in 1930 and now the **Centro Cívico Social y Cultural Riviera de Ensenada** (ⓣ646/176-4233) on Cárdenas and Riviera. You can wander through the tranquil gardens, grab a drink at the *Bar Andaluz* (see p.91), or visit the absorbing **Museo de Historia** inside (daily 10am–5pm; M$10; ⓣ646/177-0594). Exhibition rooms here focus on prehistoric and native cultures of Baja California, the eighteenth-century Spanish missions and the ultimate decimation of the native population through disease all via old photos, objects and labelling in Spanish and English – note the sobering fact that as recently as the 1870s, 95 percent of northern Baja's population was *indio* (around 15 percent today). On the other side of Cárdenas, the **Museo El Caracol** is the latest city attraction, a fancy science museum showcasing the geology and environments of Baja slated to open in 2010 – check ⓦwww.caracol.org.mx for the latest news. For a more general look at the peoples and cultures of Baja and Mesoamerica, head over to the **Museo Histórico Regional**, at Gastélum off Mateos (Tues–Sun 9am–5pm; free; ⓣ646/178-3692), built in 1886 as a military headquarters and serving as the Ensenada jail until 1986.

Finally, the Bodegas de Santo Tomás **winery**, one of the peninsula's largest, offers regular tastings at Miramar 666 between calles 6a and 7a (daily 10am–5pm; M$100 for five wines; ⓣ646/178-3333, ⓦwww.santo-tomas.com). You can also visit the main **vineyard** and winery, south of Ensenada in the Santo Tomás valley, for a more comprehensive tour of the estate and cellars (same times and price). It's the only major producer not located in the Valle de Guadalupe (see p.92) – you'll find it off Hwy-1 at km 49.

Beaches and La Bufadora

Although it enjoys an enviable position on the Pacific, Ensenada lacks good **beaches**, and to find a decent stretch of sand you'll have to head about half an hour south. As in other parts of Baja it can be difficult to get to many of the best beaches without your own transport; however, you can catch a local bus from Cárdenas (every 30min; M$9.50) to **San Miguel**, 11km north of downtown. Devotees claim San Miguel has the **best waves** in northern Baja and it's been a hotspot for years; huge swells barrel down a rocky headland here, so it's definitely not for beginners. It also gets very crowded, so arrive early. Taxis charge around M$120. The best **beaches** for swimming and sunbathing are at **Estero**, some 10km to the south and 2km off the main road.

The most popular attraction in the area, though, is **La Bufadora**. Often described as a geyser, "the snorter" is actually a blowhole, where the combined action of wind, waves and an incoming tide periodically forces a huge jet of sea water up through a vent in the roof of an undersea cavern, in ideal conditions reaching 25–30m. Even though it's more than 20km off the main road (40km from town), and encircled by souvenir stands that rather spoil the atmosphere, it's worth a visit. To get there, flag down a local bus on Cárdenas and Macheros labelled "Maneadero" and tell the driver you want to visit La Bufadora. Where he drops you you'll be able to catch another local bus to the blowhole. The whole trip should take around one hour and cost around M$12. Taxis are open to negotiation, but tend to ask for M$400 round-trip, including an hour at the site.

Activities

From December to March, the California grey whale migration from the Arctic to the peninsula's Pacific coast can be seen on daily **whale-watching tours** from Ensenada, although what you'll see is nothing compared to Baja California Sur. There are several tour companies in the harbour that offer half-day excursions for about M$300 per person.

Baja Pro Scuba Divers at Cardenas 1094, between Castillo and Blancarte (Ⓣ646/1757527, Ⓦwww.bajapro-scubadivers.com) offers **diving**, **snorkelling** and **kayaking** in the waters off Ensenada, as well as the chance to dive with **whale sharks** (Aug–Oct) off Bahía de Los Angeles.

Ensenada itself hosts numerous events aimed squarely at the large US encampment in town, from sporting contests to food and wine festivals. The **Newport to Ensenada Yacht Race** (Ⓦwww.nosa.org) in April, is one of the largest international regattas in the world, with yachts leaving Newport, California, on a Friday afternoon and finishing in Ensenada a day later, when the partying commences and the town gets packed. April (and September) is also when the **Rosarito–Ensenada Bike Ride** (Ⓦwww.rosaritoensenada.org) draws thousands of cyclists here for the scenic eighty-kilometre "fun ride" from Playa de Rosarito to Ensenada, while off-road racing is the theme du jour during the Baja 500 (June) and the Baja 1000 (Nov). The town celebrates **Independence Day** (Sept 16) with a week of festivities.

Eating and drinking

La Primera (López Mateos) has the largest share of straightforward **restaurant** options, but steer away from the cavernous spaces promising every kind of continental indulgence. Be sure to trawl the Mercado Negro for **fish tacos** (see p.89), and for fresh bread and **pastries** try *Repostería La Reyna*, Calle 2 no. 1449. When it comes to **nightlife** Ensenada offers many of the same opportunities for clubbing and drinking as Tijuana but within a smaller area and without the edge (although you should still exercise caution) – many of the restaurants below also double as bars and clubs.

Restaurants

Bronco's López Mateos 1525 ⓣ646/176-4900, ⓦwww.broncossteakhouse.net. The five blocks that separate *Bronco's* from the heart of the tourist district will save you a good M$100 on a filet mignon (M$204). With spurs everywhere, the Wild West theme is over the top, but the spirit is genuine, and live bands on weekends add to the authenticity. Breakfast served.

Ceviche de Guerrerense López Mateos and Alvarado. You'll see tiny mobile seafood stalls all over Ensenada, but you should definitely try this one: fresh fish, shrimp, clam, sea urchin, mussel and crab *ceviche*, as well sea cucumber for the more adventurous, has been served here since the 1960s. Wed–Mon 10am–4pm.

La Embotelladora Vieja Miramar 666 ⓣ646/174-0807. *Vieja*'s association with Santo Tomás Winery gives it an edge on rare and small-batch Baja wines – served by the glass and bottle – that are well paired with the progressive Mexican-Mediterranean menu. Dinner only.

Manzanilla Teniente Azueta 139 ⓣ646/175-7073, ⓦwww.rmanzanilla.com. This outpost of celebrity chef Benito Molina moved near the port entrance in 2008, but retains its spacious, antique bar decorated with local art. More importantly, the food, from posh Spanish bar snacks like fresh sardines on toast to dinners featuring specials such as *pescado en caldo* and seafood risotto, has maintained its freshness and exceptional quality. Wed–Sat noon–midnight.

Mi Kasa Riveroll 87 ⓣ646/178-8211. This cafeteria opens to a busy breakfast crowd and finishes with family dinners. In three meals you can get a broad sampling of Mexican home cooking, from *huevos con nopales* (eggs with cactus) in the morning, to chicken in *mole* at lunch and deep-fried tacos or *menudo* (stewed tripe and peppers) at dinner, all for less than M$100.

El Rey Sol López Mateos 1000 ⓣ646/178-1733, ⓦwww.elreysol.com. This venerable French-style seafood restaurant opened in 1947 and despite the hype remains an essential Ensenada experierence. Stick with classics such as French onion soup, Caesar salad and clams "El Rey Sol". Entrées M$150–300.

Tacos Lucero Mercado Negro. The market is littered with stalls selling fish tacos, but this is one of the more dependable vendors, a small stand tucked away near the southern entrance. The fish is fresh and succulent, but the tubs of help-yourself salsas on each table really make this a stand-out option (fish tacos M$10, shrimp tacos M$15).

Tacos Fenix Espinosa at Juárez. This three-person stand operates from a sidewalk next to the Ferretería Fenix tyre shop, from which it derives its name. The superb fish tacos are made to order with home-made batter and angelito shark (angel shark), and in your hands before they have time to cool (M$11). Daily 7am–9pm. Not to be confused with the almost as good *Tacos Mi Ranchito "Fenix"* at the corner of Espinosa and Calle 6.

Nightlife

Bar Andaluz Centro Cultural Riviera, Cárdenas at Riviera. This elegant Spanish Revival bar is one of the most appealing watering holes in Baja, with tiled floors, vivid murals, a wooden bar and sunny courtyard. Glasses of wine from M$33, coffee M$11. Closed Sun.

Hussong's Cantina Ruiz 113 ⓣ646/178-3210. Established in 1892 and a tourist destination with its own line in T-shirts, *Hussong's* is still an honest bar packed with locals and gringos alike. The floors are covered in sawdust, the bands are *norteña* and the drink of choice is a margarita – legend has it the tequila cocktail was invented here in 1941, though there are numerous other claimants in Mexico.

Papas & Beer López Mateos and Ruiz ⓣ646/174-0145, ⓦwww.papasandbeer.com. It's hard to ignore the ubiquitous Baja party chain, but at least it delivers; plenty of wild boozing, live music and themed party nights, especially during Spring Break.

Listings

Banks Most are on Ruiz, a few blocks north of López Mateos.

Books Librerías de Cristal, López Mateos 690, at Macheros (Mon–Sat 10am–8pm, Sun 10am–6pm), has a great selection of books and magazines.

Buses The terminal at C 11a and Riveroll handles all long-distance buses for Baja towns including San Felipe, Guerrero Negro, La Paz and Loreto. Buses to Tijuana (M$130) leave every 30min. Buses to Guadalajara and Mexico City are less frequent, and you have to change in Mexicali for most other destinations.

Internet access Try Eksezoo, at C 4a no. 409-B and Miramar (Mon–Sat 9am–10pm; M$5/30min); La Web on Cardenas between Castillo and Blancarte (Mon–Sat 8am–9pm, Sun 9am–8pm; M$12/hr); or Compunet, next to Hertz (Mon–Sat

9am–7pm; M$15/hr). Free wireless hotspots are all over town – try the malecón.
Post office Riviera and Mateos (Mon–Fri 8am–7pm, Sat 9am–1pm).

Spanish courses Baja California Language College, Riveroll 1287 (Ⓣ646/174-1741, Ⓦwww.bajacal.com).

Around Ensenada: Valle de Guadalupe

The vineyards of the **Valle de Guadalupe** are so heavily drenched in hype that on first visit anyone but the most optimistic – or wine-soaked – visitor will be disappointed. The region is clearly on the right track, though, as illustrated by growing international acclaim and the pioneering work of French-trained winemaker Hugo d'Acosta since the 1990s.

The villages of **San Antonio de las Minas** in the southwest and **Francisco Zarco** and **El Porvenir** in the northeast are the centres of the valley's production. Wine has been produced here since the Spanish introduced it in the sixteenth century, though modern production began with **Molokan Russian** immigrants who settled in Baja in 1904. Only a handful of current residents claim Russian ancestry, but you can get grips with their legacy at the **Museo Comunitario Ruso Del Valle De Guadalupe** (Tues–Sun 9am–5pm; free; Ⓣ646/155-2030) in Francisco Zarco, which preserves a small collection of Russian bits and pieces in a restored Russian home dating from 1905. Ask here about the **Panteón Ruso,** the old cemetery nearby, where you'll find fifteen ageing Russian tombstones.

In August, some of the vineyards host the ten-day **Fiestas de la Vendimia** (Ⓦwww.fiestasdelavendimia.com) where tastings and wine-themed competitions are held in the valley and in Ensenada; for information about tickets ask at the latter's tourist office or check the website.

The vineyards

Though you can show up at the major wineries without a reservation, it is best to call ahead everywhere before visiting, especially if you're coming in the warmer months (July–Sept).

▲ The road to Valle de Guadalupe

Bibayoff Bodegas from Hwy-3, exit west at the sign to El Tigre, follow the dirt road 4km and turn north; proceed 5.6km to Rancho Bibayoff ⓣ646/176-1008, ⓔbibayoff@prodigy.net.mx. The Russians were responsible for resurrecting the wine industry here, but this is the only Russian-run vineyard still open to the public. Bibayoff sells many of his grapes to other producers but keeps enough around to produce five estate wines, including a Nebbiolo and Colombard. Tours and wine tasting by appointment, usually on Sat & Sun only (free).

Casa de Piedra Hwy-3 km 93.5 ⓣ646/178-2173, ⓦwww.vinoscasadepiedra.com. Boutique producer owned by Hugo d'Acosta, producing the highly respected Vino de Piedra. Tastings by appointment only, but worth setting up (free).

Chateau Camou from Hwy-3, follow main road into Francisco Zarco, turn north after 3km ⓣ646/177-2221, ⓦwww.chateau-camou.com.mx. Two hundred acres of vineyards surround the mission-style building housing a modern winery and small tasting room. From here Camou turns out 30,000 cases of Bordeaux, Zinfandel and a dessert blend of Chardonnay, Chenin Blanc and Sauvignon Blanc. Reservations required; some tours include lunch (M$140). Basic tours from M$70. Daily 9am–4.30pm.

Domecq Hwy-3 km 73.5, Francisco Zarco ⓣ646/155-2249 ext 110, ⓦwww.vinosdomecq.com.mx. In 1972 Domecq was the first commercial winery to open in the valley, though it was purchased by Pernod Ricard in 2005. Like L.A. Cetto – with whom Domecq's wines make up eighty percent of the region's total output – its setup will be familiar to visitors used to California- and Australia-style vineyard tours. The tasting area also includes a store with merchandise. Tasting fees are M$50 per person (for three red and two white wines), but the winery tour is free. Mon–Fri 10am–4pm, Sat 10am–1.30pm.

L.A. Cetto Hwy-3 km 73.5, Francisco Zarco ⓣ646/155-2179, ⓦwww.cettowines.com. Although the Cetto family has been bottling wine in Baja California since 1928, they didn't set up their current operation in the valley until 1974; they're now the largest producer of table wines in Mexico, noted for their outstanding Nebbiolo, Petite Sirah, Cabernet Sauvignon and Zinfandel. For first-timers, Cetto offers a great introduction to the process through its free wine tours and tastings; it's also one of the few wineries to have food and a dining area. Daily 11am–5pm.

Monte Xanic from Hwy-3, follow main road into Francisco Zarco, turn north after 2.7km ⓣ646/174-6769, ⓦwww.montexanic.com.mx. Thirty thousand cases of wine from estate-grown grapes roll out of Xanic every year, some with price tags north of M$1500. Its speciality is Bordeaux, but it also bottles Chenin Blanc and Syrah, the latter used for cheaper wines. Wine tasting and tours of the spectacular new premises should start in 2010 – call in advance to get the latest.

Practicalities

To reach the valley from Ensenada, leave the city along Cárdenas and follow Hwy-1 (north) through El Sauzal and exit on Hwy-3 (La Ruta del Vino) towards Tecate, just prior to the beginning of the Hwy-1D toll road north of San Miguel.

Mexican wine tasting

Once derided for its watery grapes and poor vintage, Mexican wines have gathered a loyal following since the late 1990s, when producers such as Hugo d'Acosta started to focus on small-production, high-quality boutique wines such as Casa de Piedra in the Valle de Guadalupe. These are five of the best:

Vino de Piedra, Casa de Piedra Tones of black fruit lace this blend of Tempranillo and Cabernet Sauvignon.

Viñas de Camou, Chateau Camou Bordeaux-style blend of Cabernet Sauvignon, Cabernet Franc and Merlot.

Cabernet Sauvignon/Merlot, Monte Xanic Smooth, dark red wine with a peppery aroma.

Special Reserve Chardonnay, Chateau Camou One of the best white wines in the valley.

Gabriel, Adobe Guadalupe Another exquisite red wine blend (55 percent Merlot) produced by Hugo d'Acosta.

The vineyards and stores begin in about 10km, near San Antonio de las Minas. With a few exceptions, the valley's vineyards are located on dirt roads that branch off a 25km stretch of the main highway. Detailed signs direct visitors how to navigate the unmarked dirt roads that link the vineyards.

If you don't have a car your only option is to join an **organized tour** from San Diego, Ensenada or Tijuana though you'll have to reserve in advance; Eco Baja Tours runs day trips from Ensenada for US$45 (or peso-equivalent) on most Saturdays (Ⓦwww.ecobajatours.com), while Prime Baja Tours does a slightly bigger and more frequent tour for US$99 (Ⓣ646/178-2232, Ⓦwww.primebajatours.com).

If you want **to stay**, try the romantic six-room *Adobe Guadalupe* (Ⓣ646/155-2094, US Ⓣ949/863-9776, Ⓦwww.adobeguadalupe.com; ⑧), which also produces wine (see box, p.93). To get here, follow the main road into Francisco Zarco from Hwy-3 and turn north after 5.7km at the second stop sign in El Porvenir. Perched on a hilltop at Hwy-3 km 89, *La Villa del Valle* (Ⓣ646/156-8007, Ⓦwww.lavilladelvalle.com; ⑧) is another gorgeous hotel managed by US expats. Note also that *Banyan Tree* hotel chain is expected to open a luxury **resort** inside the Monte Xanic winery in 2011.

Of the few **dining** options in the valley, the best one – as well as one of the best on the entire peninsula – is *A Laja*, Hwy-3 km 83, Francisco Zarco (Ⓣ646/155-2556, Ⓦwww.lajamexico.com; Wed lunch only, Thurs–Sat dinner; reservations essential). Former *Daniel* and *Four Seasons* New York chef Jair Téllez, along with partner Laura Reinert, opened this prix-fixe destination (M$550 per person) restaurant in 2001, and it continues to draw eager diners with its changing, seasonally influenced menu – expect dishes like sea trout (*curvina*) with roasted peppers and courgettes, and oven-roasted pig with butternut squash and beets.

Mexicali and San Felipe

If the peninsula of Baja California is desolate, the northern part of the state is infinitely, yet spectacularly, more so. The drive from Tijuana to **MEXICALI** is worthwhile for the views alone, as the mountains suddenly drop away to reveal a huge salt lake and hundreds of miles of desert below. Mexicali is unbearably hot in summer, and winter nights can drop below freezing, but despite its natural disadvantages it's a large, wealthy city, the capital of the state of Baja California and an important road and rail junction along the US border. While there may be an exotic ring to the name (a hybrid of Mexico and California; its step-sibling, **CALEXICO**, is just across the border), there's nothing exotic about the city and it's not a place where you'd choose to spend time; you might pass through to cross the US border, or to take the two hour thirty-minute bus ride down to the more appealing resort of San Felipe.

Practicalities

There is a **tourist information booth** (daily 8am–7pm) opposite the vehicle entrance at the border, but it's not always open in the late summer, especially in the afternoon. The more helpful Comité de Turismo y Convenciones de Mexicali (Mon–Fri 9am–5pm; Ⓣ686/551-9800, Ⓦwww.cotuco.com.mx) is off López Mateos at Camelias in the Centro Cívico, the city's municipal headquarters, 3km south of the border. You can also visit the **city tourist office** at Obregón 1257 (Ⓣ686/552-4401, Ⓦwww.mexicaliturismo.com), which is usually open the same

Getting to and from Mexicali

The primary Mexicali border crossing (known as Calexico West) is open 24 hours and tends to get very congested, especially during morning and evening rush hours, though the wait is much longer coming into the US (up to 2hr). A second crossing known as Calexico East (daily 6am–midnight) connects with Mexicali's main industrial park, east of downtown (this is where buses now cross the border), but this is almost as busy. Coming from the US, if you're just taking the bus as far as Calexico, it's easy to walk to Calexico West and straight into downtown Mexicali: US Hwy-111 crosses the border here, becoming Bulevar Adolfo López Mateos.

Moving further into Mexico

Most buses into Mexico use the **Central de Autobuses** (Ⓣ686/557-2410), 4km from the border at Anahuac and Calzada Independencia. To get to the border take any "Centro" bus (M$7.50); to get back, take a "Calle 6" bus from the local bus stand off Mateos. Well over fifty buses a day head **south** (at least twenty to Mexico City), and there's at least one local service an hour to **Tijuana**.

Buses from California and Arizona use the Greyhound station in Calexico, 123 First St (US Ⓣ760/357-1895) just across the street from the border and much closer to the new Mar de Cortez Group bus station in Mexicali (Terminal Turística; Ⓣ686/582-0134), at Av Mexico 343, on the corner of López Mateos; Peninsula Ejecutivo, ABC and Águila buses serve this more convenient location (best for buses to San Felipe). Taxis around town usually charge M$50, but agree the price first.

The Aeropuerto Internacional de Mexicali, Mesa de Andrade km 23.5 (Ⓣ686/552-2148, Ⓦwww.aeropuertosgap.com.mx), is 20km east of the city off the Mexicali–Los Algodones highway. **Flights** with Aeromexico, Mexicana and Volaris serve Cancún, Culiacán, Guadalajara, Hermosillo, Mexico City, Monterrey and Toluca. Budget, Dollar, Hertz and Alamo have car rental desks on the east side of the building. Buy tickets from a booth in the terminal for shared taxis that leave every fifteen minutes; fares into downtown Mexicali are around M$300.

hours. There are several **banks** and casas de cambio very close to the border – Bancomer, on Madero, is closest, and Banamex a couple of blocks up Madero near the **post office**.

If you have to spend the night in Mexicali, the best choice is *Crowne Plaza*, López Mateos at Av de los Héroes, (Ⓣ686/557-3600, Ⓦwww.crowneplaza.com; ❼), which has modern rooms with satellite TV and internet. The *Del Norte* at Madero 205 (Ⓣ686/552-8101, US Ⓣ1-888/227-8504, Ⓦwww.hoteldelnorte.com.mx; ❹) is the one border hotel worth staying at, located just south of the west crossing; you can walk to all the nearby restaurants and the rooms are old but clean.

Mexicali has more Chinese restaurants than any other in Mexico, most located in **Chinatown**, known locally as Chinesca, in the blocks immediately south of the Calexico West border crossing; *Restaurant El Dragón* Juárez 1830 at the Centro Cívico (Ⓣ686/566-2020) is the grandest, with a mock imperial pagoda outside and a tricked-out dining hall. *Cenaduría Selecta*, Arista 1510 at Calle G (Ⓣ686/552-4047), tucked away in a quieter area a short taxi ride from downtown, is a popular Mexican diner that has been serving classics since 1945; the tacos, burritos and *mole poblano* all standout (mains from M$100). For something cheaper, try *Hot Dogs Oscarin*, Juárez at Normal, a popular stall that comes alive after 9pm with the smell of sizzling franks. The double-length outdoor grill serves up loaded hot dogs wrapped in bacon from M$25 (something of a Mexicali tradition) to walk-up or dine-in customers.

San Felipe

With so few places in northern Baja boasting a decent beach, the prospect of **SAN FELIPE**, a Sea of Cortés resort and growing retirement community, 200km south of Mexicali, might seem attractive. In truth, its appeal is limited: the entire bay is strung with RV parks, and the dunes between here and the encircling folded ridges of the San Pedro Martír mountains reverberate to the screaming engines of dune buggies and balloon-tyred ATVs. If you're planning to continue south down Baja, then do just that. But San Felipe does have good swimming – at least at high tide – and if you are confined to the north, it's an enjoyable place to relax for a day or so.

Established in 1916, San Felipe first came to the attention of sport fishermen who, in the early 1950s, started to exploit the vast schools of tortuava, a species now fished onto the endangered list. Since the 1980s, the fishing village has grown to accommodate the November-to-April influx of around 250,000 American and Canadian holiday-makers and college students on Spring Break. Apart from lying on the beach, you can rent **dirt bikes** and ATVs from a couple of places along the malecón (try San Felipe Off Road ⓣ646/577-3022, ⓦwww.sanfelipeoffroad.com; M$500/hr), or indulge in a little **sport fishing**; contact Tony Reyes Sports Fishing (US ⓣ1-714/538-8010; ⓦwww.tonyreyes.com).

The mostly gravel road through the cactus desert south of here to Hwy-1 is gradually improving, and though rough in parts can be negotiated by low-clearance vehicles and motorbikes (assuming you take it slow), making an interesting alternative route to southern Baja. The main road goes as far as **Puertecitos**, 85km south (1hr; no public transport) – you'll find a basic restaurant here (Sat & Sun only) and by 2010, a gas station. Beyond here, gas is available at Gonzaga Bay (another 2hr), one of the most alluring stretches of coast in Baja; stay and eat at *Alfonsina's* (ⓣ664/648-1951, ⓔalfonsinas@hotmail.com; M$800).

Practicalities

Most visitors **drive** to San Felipe along Hwy-5 from Mexicali and the US border (around 2hr); fill up in Mexicali because there are no gas stations on the way. **Buses** from Mexicali (5 daily; 2hr 30min), Tijuana (4 daily; 5–6hr) and Ensenada (2 daily; 3hr 30min) arrive at the bus station 1km inland on Mar Caribe South, near the PEMEX gas station: turn left out of the bus station and right down Manzanillo to get to Avenida Mar de Cortés, which runs parallel to the sea. At the junction, the **tourist office** (Mon–Fri 8am–7pm, Sat 9am–3pm, Sun 10am–1pm; ⓣ646/577-1155, ⓦwww.visitsanfelipebc.com) gives out a map of the town but little else. Better is the Instituto de Informatica de San Felipe (aka The Net), next to the *El Cortez* hotel on Mar de Cortés (ⓣ686/577-1600, ⓦwww.sanfelipe.com.mx), which offers advice, free internet, maps and books. Also along Cortés there's a Bancomer and Banamex, both with ATMs (though US$s are accepted everywhere). The **post office** is on Mar Blanco just off Chetumal, five blocks inland.

Hotels in San Felipe are not particularly cheap, though there are a couple of decent mid-range choices: the three-storey *La Hacienda de la Langosta Roja*, Chetumal 125 (ⓣ686/577-1608, US ⓣ1-800/967-0005, ⓦwww.sanfelipelodging.com; ❻), is the cleanest downtown hotel and has rooms overlooking the sea. On the beach, *El Cortez* (ⓣ686/577-1055; ❺), has plenty of atmosphere, the patio is a great place to eat and the old-world ★ *Barefoot Bar* on the sand is perfect for drinks. If you have a car and want to be near a quieter strip of beach, head to the ★ *Casa La Vida* (ⓣ686/577-2807, ⓦwww.casalavida.com; ❻), 3km south of downtown in Playas de San Felipe; managed by friendly US expats, the three spacious suites come with US cable TV, wi-fi and kitchens.

Not surprisingly, **seafood** is the staple diet here, with San Felipe best known for its **fish tacos** and shellfish cocktails; you'll find the best stands at an area known as

Plaza Maristacos at the south end of the malecón, near the *Costa Azul Hotel*. On the northern end of the malecón, *Rice and Beans* (Mon–Fri 7am–11pm) has a veranda and serves good-value fresh fish, all sorts of omelettes and fabulous margaritas. For a posh sit-down meal, try the Italian-style seafood restaurant at *La Hacienda de la Langosta Roja* (see opposite).

South to La Paz

South of Ensenada, the topography around Hwy-1 shifts from suburban sprawl to farmland and then into curvy, hilly passes that eventually drop into the Santo Tomás valley. From here it's around 1375km to La Paz, a journey which can take twenty hours direct or preferably several days, taking in the entrancing landscapes and small towns along the way – you'll see far fewer tourists on this stretch of the **Transpeninsular Highway** (see box, p.74).

Parque Nacional Sierra San Pedro Martír

Sixty-five kilometres past Santo Tomás, just beyond Colonet, a road at km 141 heads inland towards the **Parque Nacional Sierra San Pedro Martír** (mid May–Nov daily 7am–7pm; M$40 per vehicle), a tranquil alpine reserve that resembles the high sierras of California. The side road winds 100km up into the mountains (the park entrance is at km 84; the road is unsurfaced but in good condition beyond here), which includes the peninsula's highest peak, **Picacho del Diablo** (3095m) – where it snows in winter. As you climb, the land becomes increasingly green and wooded, and at the end of the road (2830m) the **Observatorio Astronómico Nacional** (Sat 11am–1pm by reservation; ⓣ646/174-4580, ⓦwww.astrossp.unam.mx) takes advantage of the piercingly clear air – there are mesmerizing views in every direction. Numerous poorly defined trails wind through the park, but again, there's no public transport (or food and gas stations) and you need to be fully equipped for wilderness camping if you want to linger. Contact **Ecotur** in Ensenada (Costero 1094 ⓣ646/178-3704, ⓔecoturbc@ens.com.mx) for organized hiking tours of the park (from M$2000).

San Quintín

Baja's pismo clam capital, **SAN QUINTÍN** is the first town of any size south of Ensenada, and even here, though there are a couple of big hotels, most of the buildings look temporary. Apart from a pit-stop to sample the **clams**, there's no reason to overnight here unless you are one of the many weekend fishermen destined for the **Bahía San Quintín**, which is undeniably attractive, with five cinder-cone volcanoes as a backdrop to a series of small sandy beaches, and endless fishing (fishing licences can be obtained from local tackle shops or from ⓦwww.conapescasandiego.org; around M$350/week) and superb clam digging that draw campers and RV tourists. The closest beaches are some 20km from town, 5km from the highway, and there's no public transport to reach them.

Buses from Ensenada stop at **Lázaro Cárdenas**, 5km south of town, but without your own car there's little point in getting off here. If you want a **place to stay**, try *The Old Mill* (ⓣ616/165-3376 or US ⓣ1-800/479-7962, ⓔoldmill@telnor.net; ❸); exit west from Hwy-1 directly across from the transformer station on the south side of Lázaro Cárdenas (there will be a sign for *Don Eddie's* motel at the turn-off) and follow directions to *Don Eddie's* until you see the marked turn-off to *The Old Mill*.

Most of the thirty million clams harvested here end up north of the border, but you can sample the smoked, over-sized molluscs at numerous roadside vendors in town or at *Palapa de Mariscos el Paraíso* (ⓣ616/165-2906) along the main highway at the north end of San Quintín. The best **restaurant** for seafood in general is at the *Old Mill* – giant plates of clams cost around M$100.

El Rosario

Some 60km beyond San Quintín, the highway passes through **EL ROSARIO**, the original site of a Dominican mission founded in 1774. Nowadays, however, the old mission site is little more than a BMX track for local kids, and definitely not worth getting off the bus for; modern **El Rosario de Arriba** is essentially another pit-stop, comprising a couple of petrol stations, a few restaurants and small **motels**. If you're **driving**, it's absolutely necessary to fill up your tank here: there's no dependable pump until just north of the state border with Baja California Sur. The *Baja Cactus Motel*, Hwy-1 km 55 San Quintín–Punta Prieta (ⓣ616/165-8850, ⓦwww.bajacactus.com; ④) is one of the best bargains in Mexico, with plush rooms, satellite TV and wi-fi access at less than M$500. It's conveniently positioned between the PEMEX station and *Mama Espinosa's* restaurant and cabañas (ⓣ616/165-8770; ④). *Espinosa's* is one of the oldest **restaurants** on the peninsula, opened in 1930 – Mama Espinosa herself, though over 100 years old, usually entertains the bus-loads of tourists that stop here. Their famous **lobster burritos** (M$150) are rather over-priced, but everything else – beef and pork tacos and big burritos – qualifies as the best food between here and Bahía de los Angeles.

Beyond El Rosario, the road turns sharply inland and runs down the centre of the peninsula for some 350km to Guerrero Negro, cutting through the protected **Parque Natural del Desierto Central de Baja California**. This is where you head into Baja California proper – barren and god-forsaken. For the most part the scenery is dry, brown desert, with the peninsula's low mountain spine to the left and nothing else but sand, a bizarre landscape of cactus – particularly yucca, *cirios*, unique to this area, and *cardones*, which can grow over 16m tall – and rock, with plenty of strange giant formations.

Bahía de los Ángeles

The turn-off for **BAHÍA DE LOS ÁNGELES** (also known as L.A. Bay), a growing community on the Sea of Cortés, is about 224km further on from El Rosario, followed by a 69km trip east along well-maintained Hwy-6. Still a small place with an underdeveloped, frontier feeling, the town sits on the eponymous bay, which teems with sea life and is hemmed in by contorted mountains. There's little here other than a few hotels, cafés and fishing boats; the one exception is the small bilingual **Museo de Naturaleza y Cultura**, two blocks west of the main drag (winter daily 9am–noon & 2–4pm; summer daily 9am–noon & 3–5pm; free). Its location is marked by a narrow-gauge locomotive, a relic of the gold and copper mines that first attracted Europeans to the area. Mining history and that of the local *ranchero* life is well covered, along with details of sea life in the bay.

Isla Ángel de la Guarda, the largest island in the Sea of Cortés, dominates the bay and is the real focus of the settlement's leisure activities; it's the best place on the sea's northern coast for diving and kayaking trips. Though you'll plenty of **fishing** outfits, there aren't any other speciality operators in town, and any activity you'd like to indulge in is typically arranged through the campground or motel you're staying at – *Daggett's* (see opposite) rents kayaks for around M$70/day. Note that the islands offshore are part of the **Área de Protección de Flora y Fauna Islas del**

Golfo de California, and visiting or camping on them requires a permit (M$40/day). You can obtain one from the reserve office (Mon–Fri 8am–2pm & 4–6pm, Sat 9am–1pm; ⓣ200/124-9106) in town, near the *Hotel Villa Vitta*, which also can advise on boat operators and fishing guides (who typically charge M$1500/day).

Practicalities

Because of the difficulty in getting supplies to the bay, lodging and food are more expensive than you'd expect, and there are no banks or ATMs here, so make sure you have enough cash. *Los Vientos Spa & Resort* (ⓣ646/178-2614, ⓦwww.losvientosspaandresort.com; ❻), which opened in 2005, is the first deluxe **hotel** option in town, but as yet has not drastically altered the languid vibe. Two of the better cheaper **places to stay** are just off crumbling asphalt roads on the north side of town. *Larry and Raquel's Motel on the Beach*, on La Gringa 3km north of the Hwy-6 junction (ⓣ619/423-3454, ⓔbahiatours@yahoo.com; ❺), has nine rooms in two storeys just 50m from the sea. The rooms are spare and clean, without phones or TVs, though the restaurant does have satellite TV, an internet connection and some of the best fish tacos between Ensenada and San José del Cabo. The most comfortable, modern accommodation is supplied by *Costa del Sol* (ⓣ200/124-9110, ⓔcostadelsolhotel@hotmail.com; ❺), while *Camp Daggett's* (ⓣ200/124-9101, ⓦwww.campdaggetts.com; camping M$50/person, cabins ❹), between *Larry's* and the town, is primarily an RV community, but they've reserved the beachfront for palapa-shaded plots (with barbecues) for campers and have cabins with one to three beds, air-conditioning and showers.

The best **place to eat** or grab a cold drink is *Guillermo's* (ⓣ619/124-9104); the burgers are good (M$55) but the beachside location and views of the offshore islands are spectacular. Otherwise try the cheap **taco stands** on the main road – *Taquería Carreta* is a local favourite for fish and shrimp tacos. The town now has two **PEMEX** stations, both open daily.

Guerrero Negro

Continuing on the main highway, there's little between El Rosario and the 28th parallel, where an enormous metal monument and a hotel mark the border between the states of Baja California and **Baja California Sur**; you'll have to set your watch forward an hour when you cross. **GUERRERO NEGRO**, just across the border, offers little in the way of respite from the heat and aridity that has gone before (winters, however, can find the town quite chilly). Flat and dust-blown, it was only established in the 1950s as a supply centre for Exportadora de Sal, the world's largest salt manufacturer, and is surrounded by vast saltpans and stark storage warehouses. At most times of year you'll want to do little more than grab a drink and carry straight on, especially if you don't have a car – it's a dispiriting place to navigate on foot. In January and February (and, peripherally, Dec & March–April), however, Guerrero Negro is home to one of Mexico's most extraordinary natural phenomena, the congregation of scores of **grey whales** just off the coast.

The whales, which spend most of their lives in the icy Bering Sea around Alaska, can be watched (at remarkably close quarters) from an area within the **Reserva de la Biosfera Complejo Lagunar Ojo de Liebre**, which encompasses the **Laguna Ojo de Liebre**. During the season there are organized **whale-watching trips**, and an observation tower that guarantees at least a distant sighting. Although talk turns every year to restricting numbers or banning boats altogether, there are currently more tours and **boat trips** than ever. If you can take one, then do so – it's an exceptional experience, and many visitors actually get to touch the whales, which sometimes come right up to bobbing vessels after

Ecotourism in Baja California Sur

With so many natural sights, **ecotourism** has become big business in **Baja California Sur**, which stretches from Guerrero Negro nearly 1000km south to Cabo San Lucas. The plankton-rich waters that surround the peninsula support an amazingly diverse aquatic culture and a host of watersports possibilities, while inland, the five mountain ranges that constitute the backbone of the peninsula contain the petroglyphs of some of the region's first inhabitants.

Whale watching

One of the most magical sights in this part of the world is the annual grey whale migration: from December to April, thousands of **grey whales** travel some 10,000km to mate and breed in the warm-water lagoons of Baja California. There are three main "sanctuaries" where you can see them. Most whales congregate in **Ojo de Liebre** (see p.99), just off Guerrero Negro, where **tours** are plentiful and cost around M$700 for transport to the lagoon, four hours of boat travel and lunch. Many people, though, prefer the lagoon near **San Ignacio** (see p.103), 150km south; where the town itself is a further attraction, as are the local birds, caves and mission church. The least-visited of the three sanctuaries is the more isolated **Bahía Magdalena**, 140km south of Loreto and 216km north of La Paz, located near the far less interesting town of Ciudad Constitución. Most southern towns offer whale-watching tours as well, but keep in mind that these charge exorbitant prices for transport to the west coast, where they are likely to take you to one of the sanctuaries. If you can't make a boat trip, you can sometimes spy whales from the shore: **Todos Santos** (see p.120) and the western side of **Cabo San Lucas** (see p.122) are particularly good for this.

Cave-painting tours

Baja California is home to some of the most bewitching and thought-provoking cave art in the world – the **Sierra de San Francisco**, between Bahía de los Angeles and Loreto, was declared a World Heritage Site by Unesco in 1993 because of five hundred particularly vivid rock-art sites contained within it. Not much is known about the provenance of these designs; largely ignored until the 1960s, when an amateur archeologist named Harry Crosby started exploring them, it's really been within the last fifty years that the paintings have been subjected to examination. A 2003 study backed by the National Geographic Society concluded that the designs in the Sierra de San Francisco region were about 7500 years old – pre-dating any other known Mexican society. In general, the cave paintings are extremely hard to visit, reachable only by

the engines are switched off. Whale-watching trips are run from *Mario's* (Ⓣ615/157-1940, Ⓦwww.mariostours.com), costing around M$700 per person for a three-hour trip (8am and 11am), including a complimentary drink or two. Malarrimo Eco-Tours (Ⓣ615/157-0100, Ⓦwww.malarrimo.com) also runs whale tours (M$700), as well as eight-hour tours to the Sierra de San Francisco to see cave paintings (Oct–Dec; M$900) from the hotel of the same name (see opposite).

To watch the whales from the shore, you'll need your own vehicle (preferably 4WD): head south from town until you see the park sign, from where a poor sand track leads 24km down to the lagoon. Midway there's a **checkpoint** where you must register your vehicle and its occupants, and at the park entrance a fee of around M$50 (or US$4) is charged. To see the whales you'll need to get up early or stay late, as they move out to the deeper water in the middle of the day.

Practicalities

If you want to stay in Guerrero Negro, you can choose from numerous **hotels and motels** strung out along the main drag, Zapata, which runs for 5km between tracks or mule paths and almost impossible to find without a guide (which is also a legal requirement for most visits). Many of the famed paintings are 45km north of **San Ignacio** (see p.103), so most people choose that town as their base for the excursion. Tours are also a good option from **Guerrero Negro** in the north, and **Mulegé** in the south (see p.106); operators are listed with the relevant entries. **Tours** generally last anywhere from five hours to several days; a five-hour tour will cost M$400–900 per person, depending on the length of your hike and the transport required for the tour. Having your own transport will usually cut these costs in half.

Watersports

The waters around Baja are so picturesque and rich in marine life that nearly everyone will be drawn to try their hand at sea kayaking, diving or fishing. For **kayaking**, the first real spot for even a novice to put in would be **Mulegé** (see p.106). The standard open-top kayaks go for about M$500 per day; wet suit and fins are another M$60 or so. **Loreto** (see p.110) and **La Paz** (see p.113) are also phenomenal options for sea kayaking. Trips to Isla del Carmen off Loreto and to Isla Espíritu Santo off La Paz pose more extended challenges and attract their share of experienced kayakers – see the relevant entries for details.

The most popular **diving** areas in the south are off the coast of **Mulegé** and **Bahía Concepción**, **Loreto**, **La Paz** and **Los Cabos**. In the waters off San José del Cabo, the giant reef known as **Cabo Pulmo** offers the chance to dive amidst schools of hammerheads, whale sharks, tunas and sea lions; many claim it to be the peninsula's best diving spot. From August to November you'll find the ideal combination of water clarity and warmth. Diving is not cheap, though, and having your own gear will cut costs in half. The average two-tank all-inclusive outing will cost you M$800–1000, and the prices generally increase the closer to Los Cabos you choose to dive.

Fishing in Baja can be spectacular, especially so in the south. The favourite holes have always been near **La Paz** and around **Cabo San Lucas**, the small fishing village of **La Playita**, just east of **San José del Cabo**, and the rest of the **East Cape**, where the nearby Gordo Banks seamount produces more marlin, tuna, wahoo, sailfish and dorado than anywhere else in Mexico. **Fishing charters** offer one of two services: either less formal fishing from a *panga* that can carry up to three anglers, or the larger marina-based fleets with boats that can accommodate up to six. *Pangas* charge anywhere from M$1500 to M$2000 for six hours, the larger boats upwards of M$5000, including food, drinks and gratuity.

Hwy-1 and the salt-mining company town known as Communidad ESSA. The best is *Los Caracoles*, Zapata at Calz de la República, (ⓣ615/157-1088, ⓦwww.hotelloscaracoles.com.mx; ❹), on the right as you enter town (before the bus station), with spotless rooms, satellite TV and friendly staff, as well as three computers in reception with free internet access, free coffee and excellent whale-watching trips. *Malarrimo*, a block further along Zapata at Pipila (ⓣ615/857-0250, ⓦwww.malarrimo.com; ❹), is another solid option, with clean rooms with TV, and RV spaces (M$300) – you can also **camp** here for M$150. Further into town, the *Baja Mision Hotel & Hostel* (ⓣ615/157-1110; ❸) is a funkier budget option further along Zapata, with simple singles and doubles with bath, and the friendly *Black Warrior* café on site.

There are plenty of **restaurants** along the main street, though most close between lunch and dinner. *Malarrimo* has a bar and excellent seafood (lunch specials from M$70); *Mario's* (ⓣ615/157-0788), on Hwy-1 just before Zapata, is a solid option for breakfast and the basics; and you can also try *Don Gus* (ⓣ615/157-1762), an agreeable place just off Zapata, close to the bus station, where you can eat huge M$270 shrimp platters while gazing at one of the region's salt flats. The best taco stand is *Tacos El Muelle* (fish tacos M$15) on Zapata. Fresh produce can also be purchased from Mercado Tianguis supermarket, also on Zapata.

The **Terminal de Autobuses** is on Rubio, just off Zapata at the eastern end of town near Hwy-1. **Buses** from Guerrero Negro are often full upon arrival; try to buy your ticket at least a day in advance. The six services (one local) which head north to Tijuana (12hr; M$723), with two going on to Mexicali, leave at night and morning; the eight southbound services – two local, running all the way to La Paz (12hr; M$826) – depart either early in the morning or in the late afternoon and evening. The **taxis** at the stand in front of the Mercado Tianguis supermarket on Zapata adjust their rates depending on how long you'll have to wait for a bus – a ride to San Ignacio is about M$1000 per car. **Internet** cafés go out of business frequently here; try Internet.com (Mon–Sat 9am–8pm; M$10/hr) on Zapata, beyond the Tianguis supermarket on the left. You'll find a branch of **Bancomer** (with ATM) on Zapata, 3km from Hwy-1 just before the company town. The tiny **airport** is 2km north of town (taxis should be around M$130), with Aeroservicio Guerrero (Ⓣ615/157-0137, Ⓦwww.aereoserviciosguerrero.com.mx) flying Cessna aircraft to Ensenada (Mon, Wed & Fri), Hermosillo (Thurs) and Guayamas (Tues, Thurs & Sat).

San Ignacio

Leaving Guerrero Negro, the highway heads 142km inland for the hottest, driest stage of the journey, across the Desierto Vizcaíno. In the midst of this landscape, **SAN IGNACIO**'s appeal is immediate even from a distance. Gone are the dust and concrete that define the peninsula, replaced by green palms and a cool breeze; it's an oasis any desert traveller would hope for, and another excellent base for **whale-watching** and **cave-painting tours**.

The settlement was founded by the Jesuits in 1728, but the area had long been populated by the indigenous **Cochimí**, attracted by the tiny stream, the only fresh water for hundreds of miles. Underneath the surfaced road between the highway and town is the small dam that the settlers built to form the lagoon that still sustains the town's agricultural economy, mostly based on the Mediterranean staples of dates, figs, grapes, olives, limes and oranges. Early missionaries were responsible, too, for the attractive palm trees that give the town its character.

In town, the central Plaza Ecoturismo, shaded by six huge Indian laurel trees, plays hosts to concerts, festivals and children's soccer games, and is dominated by **Misión San Ignacio de Kadakaamán** (usually open during services only) a gorgeous church constructed of lava-block walls – carved out of the output from Volcan las Tres Virgenes to the east – over one metre thick. Completed in 1786, it's probably the best example of colonial architecture in the whole of Baja California. The left wing of the mission now houses the exquisite **Museo de Pinturas Rupestres de San Ignacio** (May–Oct Mon–Sat 8am–5pm; Nov–April daily 8am–5pm; free), which contains photos and cave art exhibits, with a focus on the nearby Sierra de San Francisco (Spanish-only captions).

Practicalities

The centre of San Ignacio lies almost 3km off the main highway, where all the **buses** stop. Upon arrival you may be lucky enough to pick up a taxi (M$50); otherwise it's a thirty-minute walk down the road through the palms. The bus stop is actually in San Lino, a little settlement anchored by the campground and restaurant *Ricardo's Rice & Beans*, just west of the intersection along a road parallel to the highway (Ⓣ615/154-0283; ❹). There are old but clean rooms here, with hot showers, and plenty of space to **camp** outside (M$50 per car and all passengers, M$110 if you want to use the showers). Camping at *Ignacio Springs Bed and Breakfast* on the northern side of Río San Ignacio (Ⓣ615/154-0333, Ⓦwww.ignaciosprings.com; ❺ includes breakfast and kayaks) is a rather glamorous and comfortable affair. The well-appointed yurts have queen-size beds, tile floors, air-conditioning and patios; some even have their own bath. Guests have use of kayaks and easy access to the only espresso in town. If you can get in, the most enticing place to

Tours and trips from San Ignacio

Whale watching

Although whales are most in evidence in January and February, **whale-watching** tours to the nearby Laguna San Ignacio (2hr drive) are offered from December to April – prices are usually slightly cheaper December to January and April.

Tour operators

Ecoturismo Kuyima Ⓣ615/154-0070, Ⓦwww.kuyima.com. Located opposite the church (daily 8am–8pm Dec–April; 9am–1pm May–Nov), this the best tour operator in town. Charges about US$495 all-inclusive for its four-day, three-night package (or peso-equivalent), and just M$560 for whale-watching tours only (no transport); it's an extra US$130 (or peso-equivalent) per van for day-trippers – if you have your own car you can cut your expenses considerably, though until the dirt road to Laguna San Ignacio from San Ignacio is upgraded, this can be tough on a small vehicle. Kuyima also offers accommodation at the lagoon, with tents and clean palapas with solar power, plus they serve food. It's possible to visit and return in one day, but it's better to stay the night (US$165 all-inclusive per night) as the whales are best seen in the early morning when they venture into the shallow waters. You camp with your own equipment for just M$150 (or rent tents for M$560).

Antonio's Ecotours Ⓣ615/154-0089, Ⓦwww.wildcoastecotourism.com. Located on the road between the river and plaza, directly opposite the *Desert Inn*. Charges M$560 for tours, M$630 for one night in a cabaña, and M$120 for camping. Transport is an additional M$420 per person, but day packages (for a minimum four people), which include transport and lunch, start at M$1200.

Cave art

Cave-art tours from San Ignacio focus on the area of Sierra de San Francisco about 45km north of San Ignacio, where nearly five hundred sites exist across 11,000 square kilometres; tour operators usually pass through the little town of San Francisco de la Sierra and head for the easily accessible Cueva del Ratón, or remoter caves such as the Cueva Pintada and Cueva de las Flechas in Canón San Pablo, which require a minimum of two days. Tours are expensive (up to M$6000 for three days), so if you want to save some cash you can arrange a mule trip yourself at San Francisco.

Tours

Independent tours are possible, but you must always be accompanied by a guide and are required to get **INAH permission**, gained in San Ignacio from the INAH office next to the church (Mon–Sat 8am–3pm; Ⓣ615/154-0215 or 0222); the park entry fee is M$34, and guide fee M$70. You'll then need your own transport to get there: at km 118, 45km north of San Ignacio, you'll find a road heading east to San Francisco de la Sierra, and the first site is just over 2km further on. Once you've sorted out a guide and a mule, you'll be able to camp in the area – an excellent way to see a variety of paintings. Note that **flash photography** is not allowed in the caves (bringing a camera costs M$35). Ecoturismo Kuyima (see above) offers hassle-free **guided day trips** from M$700.

stay in San Ignacio itself is the *Casa Lereé* guesthouse, on Madero behind the plaza (Ⓣ615/154-0158, Ⓦwww.murrietawebdesign.com/test/leree/index.html; no credit cards; ❺ private bath, ❸ shared bath). The three rooms are clean and brightly painted, and look out onto a garden courtyard.

For **food**, *La Mision Kadakaamán* on the central plaza (opposite the church) has some outside plastic tables and a menu of all the usual Mexican favourites from M$80, while *Rene's*, just past the plaza on La Correa, serves *desayuna* to gringos' liking (scrambled eggs and French toast) along with *chilaquiles* and *huevos rancheros*. Some of the best food is cooked up in the tacos stalls on the plaza; try the juicy *carne asada* at *Taquería Lupita* or the frozen *raspado de tamarindo* and hot dogs at *El Capu*. Don't miss the addictive *pan de datil* (date pie) and date empanadas sold by Luz Romero from her kitchen on the edge of the plaza (M$20).

There are **no banks** in town, few places accept credit cards and people are reluctant to take travellers' cheques – it's best to come with a supply of cash. There is **internet** access, though, on the north side of the plaza at the Whale Watching Tours office (daily 9am–10pm; M$20/hr). The Tienda Mesa general store, on the main road just off the plaza, sells hats, drinks, maps, machetes, camping gear and anything else you'd need before heading down to the lagoon or into the Sierra de San Francisco.

Santa Rosalía

South of San Ignacio, the highway emerges on the east coast at **SANTA ROSALÍA**, the largest town in central Baja (with a population of around 14,000), and one of the most intriguing places to explore on the peninsula. Established by French miners in the 1880s, it has something of a transient air, and many of its buildings look strikingly un-Mexican. The streets are narrow and crowded, with the workers' houses in the valley, which feature low, angled roofs and hibiscus-flanked porches, resembling French Caribbean dwellings, and grander colonial residences for the managers lining the hill to the north.

Wedged in the narrow river valley of the Arroyo de Santa Rosalía, today the town serves as the terminal for ferries to Guaymas, but it was once a busy port used to ship copper from the nearby French-run mines of the Compagnie du Boléo (see box opposite). The French left in 1954 and the mines were finally closed thirty years later, though much of the equipment still lies around town, including parts of a rusting narrow-gauge railway. Canadian-listed Baja Mining is currently developing a copper-cobalt-zinc-manganese project at the old Boleo workings, and if it opens as expected in 2011, will dramatically transform the town – the company has promised to work with local authorities to develop housing, infrastructure and utilities, as well as hire locals for the expected 650 to 700 mine workforce.

Arrival and information

Hwy-1 enters Santa Rosalía in both directions from along the coast, passing the harbour and the eastern border of the triangle-shaped **Parque Morelos**. Four avenidas – the main commercial drag Obregón, along with Constitución, Carranza and Montoya – run inland from here, crossing the numbered calles that intersect at right angles. The **ferry terminal** lies two minutes' walk south of Parque Morelos. The terminal also serves as the town's transport hub: **taxis** (Ⓣ615/152-0266) wait here and **buses** use the parking lot to drop off and take on passengers, making it one of the few centrally located stations on the entire peninsula. If you can't wait for a bus, you should be able to negotiate a taxi to San Ignacio for around M$570, and Mulegé for M$500. Both **banks** are on Obregón, and have ATMs: Bancomer (at Calle 5; Mon–Fri 8.30am–4pm) and Banamex (opposite; Mon–Fri 9am–4pm). The **post office** is on Constitución at Calle 2, and there's a

phone outside the *Hotel del Real*. There are a few places with **internet** access: try *Café Internet*, on Obregón and Calle Playa, just off Parque Morelos (Mon–Sat 10am–9pm; M$20/hr).

Accommodation

Accommodation options in Santa Rosalía are fairly limited so try to book ahead. Taxis charge around M$40 to shuttle between the bus and ferry terminal and the hotels.

Blanco y Negro Sarabia at Calle 3 ⓣ615/152-0080. A long-time backpackers' favourite whose cheapest rooms share a bath. To get there, walk down Obregón or Constitución and turn left at Calle 3. ❷

Las Casitas Hwy-1 km 195 Santa Rosalía–Loreto ⓣ615/152-3023, ⓦwww.santarosaliacasitas.com. A long walk uphill from downtown, but the excellent views of the sea from its hillside perch make it worthwhile. The large, ceramic-tiled rooms have modern amenities (free wi-fi) and large windows overlooking the water. ❹

Hotel Francés Jean M.Cousteau 15 ⓣ615/152-2052. A charming colonial-style building on the hill to the north of town, beyond the museum. Built in 1920, it's worth the extra for its relative luxury. ❺

Hotel del Real Montoya Calle Playa on Parque Morelos ⓣ615/152-0068. Rooms come with satellite TV and a/c, and there's a plantation-style porch for morning coffee. ❸

The Town

Spend some time wandering the streets of Santa Rosalía, as the town has retained much of its original wood-frame housing and the odd piece of mining equipment. The premier sight is the **Iglesia de Santa Bárbara** at Obregón and Pedro Altamirano, three blocks from Parque Morelos, a prefabricated iron church said to have been designed by Gustave Eiffel and exhibited in Paris before it was shipped here in 1895. The rather austere interior is softened somewhat by vivid stained-glass windows reflecting its Art Nouveau style, though some experts now believe Eiffel was not the designer – just don't say that to the locals. Follow Progreso up the hill from here and you'll see more leftovers from the mining period, culminating with the **Museo El Boleo** (Mon–Fri 8am–2pm & 5–7pm; M$20) at the top, housed in the old mining offices. The museum

Santa Rosalía's copper mines

While walking in the hills around Santa Rosalía in 1868, legend has it that one José Villavicencio chanced upon a **boleo**, a blue-green globule of rock that proved to be just a taster of a mineral vein containing more than twenty percent copper. By 1880, the wealth of the small-scale mining concessions came to the notice of the **Rothschilds**, who provided financing for the French Compagnie du Boléo (or "El Boleo") to buy the rights and found a massive extraction and smelting operation in 1885. Six hundred kilometres of tunnels were dug, a foundry was shipped out from Europe, and a new wharf built to transport the smelted ore north to Washington State for refining. Ships returned with lumber for the construction of a new town, laid out with houses built to a standard commensurate with their occupier's status within the company. Water was piped from the Santa Agueda oasis 15km away, and labour was brought in: Yaqui from Sonora as well as two thousand Chinese and Japanese who supposedly found that Baja was too arid to grow rice and soon headed off to the Mexican mainland. By 1954, falling profits from the nearly spent mines forced the French to sell the pits and smelter to the Mexican government who, though the mines were eventually left idle, continued to smelt ore from the mainland until the 1990s. Since 2004, Canadian-owned Baja Mining Corp has been working hard to reopen the mine – despite local cynicism, it expects to start production in 2011.

Moving on by ferry from Santa Rosalía

The **ferry** from Santa Rosalía to Guaymas (see p.145), across the Sea of Cortés in the state of Sonora, departs on Tuesdays and Wednesdays at 9am, and Fridays and Sundays at 8pm, arriving 7hr later. Always call in advance, though, as schedules often change. One-way tickets are M$605 (returns are M$1090), but you'll often get a discount on Sundays. A cabin is an additional M$825, while cars cost M$2730 (one-way). The ticket office (Ⓣ800/672-9053, Ⓦwww.ferrysantarosalia.com) inside the terminal is open daily 10am–7pm. You can also take an Aeroservicio Guerrero (Ⓣ615/155-1453, Ⓦwww.aereoserviciosguerrero.com.mx) **flight** to Guaymas for M$850 (tickets include transport to the airport); buy tickets at the office in the ferry terminal (daily 8am–1pm & 3–6pm).

outlines the history of the mine and the town through old photos and mining curios. The area around the museum is known as the **Mesa Francés**, and contains the grandest examples of the town's French architectural legacy.

Eating

Sadly, no French **restaurants** remain as a reminder of the town's beginnings. The *Panadería El Boleo* (closed Sun) Obregón 30 between calles 3 and 4, dates back to 1901 but is definitely past its prime – the cakes are fresh enough in the morning (M$5) but the bread is nothing like the real thing. Restaurants in general aren't up to much either, though you can eat well enough at *Terco's Pollito* (Ⓣ615/152-0075), Obregón on Parque Morelos, which serves succulent barbecue chicken and well-prepared Mexican dishes. *El Muelle* at Calle Plaza and Constitución (Ⓣ615/152-0931) is an old wooden building with an outdoor patio serving decent *carne asada* and arrachera steaks. Several inexpensive stalls are scattered along Obregón: *Super Tacos*, on Obregón just off Parque Morelos serves tasty beef tacos for M$13, while *Tacos El Arabe*, on the south side of Parque Morelos, is noted for its similarly priced fish tacos.

Mulegé

Some 60km to the south of Santa Rosalía lies **MULEGÉ**, a rural town on the site of one of the original Jesuit missions. Like San Ignacio, it's a real oasis: tucked into a lush valley, the town sits on the north bank of the palm-fringed Río Santa Rosalía and has clung onto its small town atmosphere, despite a growing US expat community. The calm was shattered somewhat in September 2009, when Hurricane Jimena caused extensive damage, the worst storm to hit Mulegé for fifty years.

Outside of hurricane season the town makes a good base for the superb **beaches** strung out along the Bahía Concepción (p.109). Yet again you'll miss out on the best of them without your own transport, but here hitching is at least a realistic possibility – many visitors commute to the beaches daily, particularly during the high season (mid-Oct to April).

Arrival and information

Mulegé's streets branch eastward from Hwy-1 and surround both sides of the estuary, though the old centre and Plaza Corona lies on the north bank – base yourself here if you don't have a car. There are two **PEMEX** stations in and around town: one in the center on Avenida Martínez at Zaragoza, and another 2.5km south of town along Hwy-1. The **bus terminal** is at the junction of Hwy-1 and Martínez, a good ten-minute walk southwest of Plaza Corona; to get to the plaza, follow Martínez (under the *faux* city gate), then take a right fork, and finally a second right onto Zaragoza. **Taxis** will charge around M$35. **Moving on,** six buses head south to La Paz (three go on to Los Cabos) from 8am, but only five go north and only three to Tijuana; the first leaves at 2.55pm. If you can't wait, taxis will charge M$450–500 to Santa Rosalía.

The best place for **information** is *Las Casitas* (see below), though they don't speak much English. Mulegé has a Bancomer (Mon–Fri 8.30am–4pm) with an **ATM** on Zaragoza between Martínez and Moctezuma. The small **post office** is at Zaragoza and Madero, and outside it you'll find long-distance **phones**. If you need a **laundry**, Lavamática Claudia (Mon–Sat 8am–7pm), at Zaragoza and Moctezuma, charges M$20 per load (plus M$9 for drying). There are several **internet** cafés in town: *Carlos Place* opposite *Los Equipales* on Moctezuma (Mon–Sat 9am–1pm & 4–8pm; M$30/hr), or the cheaper *Cuesta* next door to *Hotel Hacienda* on Madero (Mon–Sat 9am–10pm; M$20/hr).

Accommodation

If you want to **stay** in Mulegé, you have a choice of either cheap and very basic *casas de huéspedes* or comfortable mid-range hotels, but all of them are pretty good value. Since the flooding of the Río Mulegé in 2006, **camping** in town has been difficult, though you can try the *Villa María Isabel RV Park* (☎615/153-0246) inside the *Hotel Serenidad* complex (see below); RV spaces with full hookups are M$200, and tent sites around M$100.

Casa de Huéspedes Manuelita Moctezuma s/n (left fork as you head into town from the highway) ☎615/153-0175. Slightly more comfortable than the nearby *Nachita*, but otherwise similar with basic rooms and (usually) hot showers. ❸

Casa de Huéspedes Nachita Moctezuma (next to *Los Equipales*) ☎615/153-0140. A family-run place with the most laid-back staff you'll find in Baja – it's a bit more spartan than nearby *Manuelita*, but a little cheaper. ❷

Las Casitas Madero 50 ☎615/153-0019, ⓦwww.historicolascasitas.com.mx. The former home of Mexican poet José Gorosave has been a hotel since 1962, and is the best place to stay in the centre (5min from the plaza). The gift shop and restaurant give way to an orchard-like yard and dribbling fountains at the back, while the charming rooms come with TVs, ceiling fans and bathroom. ❹

Hotel Cuesta Real Hwy-1 km 132 ☎615/153-0321, ⓦcuestarealhotel.tripod.com. Friendly place near the river, with twelve rooms featuring spotless tiled floors, cable TV and wi-fi. Has on-site restaurant, gift shop, laundry facilities, and a swimming pool. RV full hookup M$180. ❹

Hotel Hacienda Madero 3 (just off the plaza), ☎615/153-0021. One of the classic Baja hotels; the front section dates back to the 1770s and it's been a hotel since the 1950s. Rooms are fading a bit, but its small pool, pleasant courtyard and on-site parking make this an attractive option. ❸

Serenidad Hwy-1 km 139 ☎615/153-0530, ⓦwww.serenidad.com. Just south of town on the east side of the Transpeninsular, the most luxurious hotel in Mulegé is another stalwart from the 1960s, though it's also starting to show its age. Look out for the summer three-night-stay specials, and the legendary Saturday night pig roast, a tradition since 1970 (M$200). Closed Sept. ❻

The Town

There's not a great deal to see in Mulegé, though once the ambitious restoration of the **Museo de Mulegé** is complete, the former prison should prove an absorbing attraction – work on the local history museum should be finished by 2011. Built in 1907, it was known as "prison without doors", as it allowed its inmates to work in town in the mornings and afternoons – and some were even married there. Perched on a hillside (walk up Zaragoza and follow the signs), it offers decent views across Mulegé.

For a slightly longer hike (20–30min) but a much better panorama, visit the **Misión de Santa Rosalía de Mulegé**. Founded by the Jesuits in 1705, the current building was completed sixty years later and sits atop a hill 3km on the other side of town – like most of the Baja missions, it was abandoned in 1828 after the indigenous population died out. The church only opens for the occasional Mass, but it's still well worth the hike up for the spectacular view from above the palms. Follow Zaragoza south underneath the highway bridge and take the dirt road on the right that climbs to the mission.

Eating and drinking

Mulegé doesn't offer a huge amount of **eating and drinking** options, but what there is is quite good. The majority of the North American long-stayers and many Mexicans gravitate towards the decent, reasonably priced restaurant and bar at *Las Casitas* (see p.107), which also does Friday night "Fiesta" buffets with live music.

Asadero Danny's Madero and Rubio (no phone). Cute family-owned diner at the end of Madero overlooking the road, noted for its home-style cooking and scrumptious tacos – shrimp and fish.

Eduardo's Martínez near Zaragoza, opposite the PEMEX station (☎615/153-0258). You can try freshly baked pizzas here most nights, but the real highlight is on Sunday, when the kitchens prepare some of the best Chinese food south of Mexicali. Dinner only.

Los Equipales Moctezuma (near Zaragoza) ☎615/153-0330. The best Mexican restaurant in town, offering large steaks and seafood portions on an open second-floor terrace – a steak complete with soup, salad and potatoes costs M$130–220. Great bar for drinks also.

Scott's El Candil Zaragoza 8 (near the plaza) ☎615/104-2547. Less formal and cheaper gringo rendezvous spot that does excellent breakfasts of fruit, eggs, ham, bacon, toast and potatoes for M$40, set in stone building with wood beams and thatch roof.

Taquitos Mulegé Plaza Corona. The best fish and shrimp tacos in town are usually available at this stall from 9am to 1pm, or until the seafood runs out; tacos are around M$12.

Activities and trips around Mulegé

Other than as a springboard for the beaches to the south, the main reason to stop at Mulegé is to go **diving** or take one of the **cave-painting tours** out to the Sierra de Guadalupe. This range boasts the densest collection of rock art in Baja (at least 700 paintings), as well as some of the most accessible at La Trinidad, requiring as little as five hours for the round trip. Getting a group together to cut costs shouldn't prove a problem in high season, but you still need to shop around as the tours differ considerably. Expect to pay M$400 per person or half that with your own transport. Overnight excursions are possible too, including a night at a 260-year-old ranch and two different cave locations. Head to *Las Casitas* (see p.107), which also acts as an informal tourist office for information on other local attractions and tours. They can connect you with Mulegé Tours, run by Salvador Castro Drew (☎615/161-4985, Ⓔmulegetours@hotmail.com) – Salvador grew up in the area and is one of the most knowledgable local guides. The hotel can also arrange kayak rentals (M$200/3hr, M$300/6hr) and horseriding (☎615/153-0019).

For **snorkelling and diving trips,** head to Cortez Explorers (daily 4–7pm; ☎615/153-0500, Ⓦwww.cortez-explorers.com) at Moctezuma 75-A; boat dives start at M$1000 per person (shore dives M$700). An open-water PADI course is M$5400 (4–5 days), while snorkelling trips start at M$600 (including equipment). If you're qualified, you can also rent snorkel gear from them (M$300/24hr) and go about it yourself: **Punta Prieta** – north of the lighthouse, a short walk from town – is still fairly unknown, even though it's really the only place you can dive or snorkel that can be reached by the shore (other spots must be accessed by boat). Follow Madero as it hugs the river, and before you reach the lighthouse you'll meet a dirt road; take a left and it will take you past an old hotel and a school before you reach Punta Prieta.

Bahía Concepción

There is good diving and fishing immediately around Mulegé, but the best beaches are between 10km and 50km south of town along the shore of **Bahía Concepción**, for once easily accessible from Hwy-1 – the drive down to Loreto along this stretch of road is truly spectacular. The bay ranges from 3km to 6.5km wide, is 48km long and is enclosed on three sides and dotted with islands. The blue-green waters, tranquil bays and white-sand beaches are gorgeous and relatively undeveloped – though you will at times find teams of RVs lining the waters – and it's a good place to break your journey for a day or so before travelling south. As far as **kayaking** goes, there are few places better than Bahía Concepción.

The best stretches of sand include **Playa Punta Arena**, at Hwy-1 km 118, 2km along a dirt road, where there should be some basic palapa shelters to rent (around M$80). In 2008 arsonists torched most of the units on the beach, allegedly to make way for a private buyer – ask in Mulegé for the latest situation. **Playa Santispac**, some 5km further on, is right on the highway – despite the early stages of development and occasional crowds of RVs, it still has plenty of room to **camp** (M$60) and enough life to make staying here longer-term a realistic option (toilets, showers, basic groceries), though there are free open palapas to hang out under during the day if you just want to swim. Stop at *Ana's* for cheap fish tacos and potent Bloody Marys; you can also rent **kayaks** (M$250–350/day) and snorkelling gear (M$100/day). **Posada Concepción**, just south of Santispac, shows the beginnings of Cabo-style development and has permanent residents; full RV hookups are around M$100. If you follow the road to the right from Posada Concepción you'll pass a bend and 1km thereafter arrive at the rather secluded **Playa Escondida**. Few trailers can make it over the hump, so the campground is more hospitable to tent campers (M$60). It is rustic (cold showers and outhouses) and there are no services. Escondida Kayak Rental (Dec–April daily 7am–7pm) has kayaks to hire for M$300/day and snorkelling gear for M$150/day.

Further south there are few facilities for anything other than camping: **Playa El Coyote** and **Playa El Requesón**, another couple of popular, bone-white beaches, are the last and the best opportunities for this (M$60 for each). Note that there's no fresh water (pit toilets and palapas only) available at either, but locals drop by in the early morning and afternoon selling everything from water to fresh shrimps. One exception to the camping rule is *Hotel San Buenaventura* at km 94.5 (Ⓣ615/155-6126, Ⓦwww.hotelsanbuenaventura.com; ❼), a small resort in

▲ Kayaking, Bahía Concepción

between Coyote and Requesón with a campground (M$250) and restaurant. The motel-type rooms have air-conditioning and ceiling fans. The beach here is clean but gravelly.

Loreto

Another popular escape for fishing and diving enthusiasts, **LORETO** is enjoying something of a renaissance. Some 138km down the coast from Mulegé, this was the site of the earliest permanent settlement in the Californias, founded in 1697 by Juan María Salvatierra as the first Jesuit mission to the region. Loreto served as the administrative capital of the entire California territory until a devastating hurricane struck in 1829 and La Paz took on the role. Eight kilometres south of town, the new "town" of **Nopoló** has evolved into the largely expat community of **Loreto Bay**, the largest residential development by a foreign builder in Mexico. Construction was placed on hold in 2009, in part due to the US recession, but once a new buyer is found it should provide a massive economic boost to the entire region (and support for the town through the Loreto Bay Foundation). Critics, however, claim that the project threatens to overwhelm the already limited water supply and Loreto's delicate natural assets: Mexico's largest marine park, **Parque Nacional Bahía de Loreto**, lies just offshore, while the weathered landscapes of the **Sierra de la Giganta** provide a stunning backdrop.

Arrival, information and getting around

Loreto's **airport** (☎613/135-0454) is 5km south of town off Hwy-1. Aereo Calafia and Aereoservicios Guerrero offer domestic flights, while Alaska Airlines and its subsidiary Horizon Air operate flights from Los Angeles. Hertz, Avis and National have **car rental** counters at the entrance, while Budget, Europcar and these firms also have offices downtown. **Taxi** shuttles downtown cost around M$200; there's no regular bus service to or from the airport.

Loreto's **bus terminal** is at Salvatierra and Paseo Pedro de Ugarte (☎613/135-0767), just in front of the baseball field. It's a hot twenty-minute walk east along Salvatierra to the Plaza Cívica, and a further ten minutes in the same direction to the beach – taxis usually meet buses and charge M$40–45 anywhere in town. The taxi stand at Hildalgo near Madero serves both Sitio Loreto (☎613/135-0424) and Sitio Juárez (☎613/135-0915). **Moving on**, only 4–5 buses a day depart north or south; northbound services all leave in the afternoon (first departure 12.30pm). Taxis will ask for M$1300 to drive to Mulegé (90min), but you can usually negotiate a much lower price.

The English-speaking **tourist office** (Mon–Fri 8am–8pm; ☎613/135-0411) is located in the Palacio de Gobierno at Madero and Salvatierra, on the west side of the pedestrian Plaza Cívica. Bancomer, just across the street, has the **only ATM** between Santa Rosalía and Ciudad Insurgentes; the staff will change travellers' cheques Monday to Friday from 8.30am to 3.30pm. The **post office** is on Deportiva 13, just off Salvatierra on the way into town, not far from the bus terminal. More spots in town are adding wi-fi **internet** access; just walk the streets with your laptop until you've picked up a signal. Established locations include *Caseta Soledad Internet Café* on Salvatierra a short walk before the pedestrianized section (Mon–Sat 8am–9pm & Sun 9am–1pm; M$20/hr), and *Ricardo's Sport Fishing* at Madero and Juárez (Mon–Sat 9am–10pm & Sun 9am–2pm; M$20/hr).

Accommodation

Loreto has a wide range of **accommodation**, from cute B&Bs to four-star resort hotels, some exceptionally good value, though the handful of truly budget options seem very scruffy in comparison.

Baja Outpost López Mateos (malecón) between Hidalgo and Jordán ⓣ613/125-1134, ⓦwww.bajaoutpost.com. No-frills accommodation that fills up because of the all-inclusive packages of whale watching, kayaking and diving – it's a bit shabby and can be noisy but the activities are excellent value. Packages start at around U$223 for three nights. ❺

Coco Cabañas Davis s/n, at Constituyentes ⓣ613/135-1729, ⓦwww.cococabanasloreto.com. All eight cabañas surround a patio with a lovely sunken pool and barbecue area. The rooms have kitchens and private baths (no TVs), but the real draw here are the welcoming owners Stephen and Barrett, who can set up virtually any activity and are experts on the local area. ❺

Iguana Inn Juárez s/n, at Davis ⓣ613/135-1627, ⓦwww.iguanainn.com. Another friendly, bargain inn near the centre of town. The owners live in the front house, guests stay in the four spotless cabañas situated around a gurgling fountain and courtyard in the back. The relatively modern rooms, with tile floors, a/c, TV and ceiling fans, have kitchenettes and private baths. ❹

El Junípero Hidalgo s/n ⓣ613/135-0122. *Junípero*'s location just off the plaza and the relatively cheap prices are its best assets; rooms are rather plain and sparse, but each has a/c and a private bath. ❹

La Mision Rosendo Robles, at the malecón ⓣ613/134-0350, ⓦwww.lamisionloreto.com. This newly renovated behemoth has retained some of its former charm (it originally opened in the 1960s), and is certainly the most luxurious option on the malecón. The colonial-style rooms feature marble floors and baths, hardwood furnishings, flat-screen TVs and patios or balconies overlooking the ocean. ❻

Posada de las Flores Salvatierra, at Madero and Plaza Cívica ⓣ613/135-1162, ⓦwww.posadadelasflores.com. Alluring boutique hotel in the centre of town, set in an old building with courtyard smothered in blossoms – the theme is eighteenth-century Mexico, with rooms decked out with antiques and a wonderful rooftop pool and bar area. Rates are very reasonable. ❻

The Town

Neat and tidy, Loreto has a strong sense of history, though there's little left of its glory days. The town is shaped roughly like a triangle pointing west from the malecón; all points of interest are near the wide end closest to the shore. Salvatierra turns into a tree-lined pedestrian mall at Independencia and the few buildings of note are along this six-block-long promenade to the sea, including the mission church, the **Misión de Nuestra Señora de Loreto Conchó**. Still standing, though heavily restored after centuries of earthquake damage, its basic structure – solid, squat and simple – is little changed since 1752. The inscription over the door, which translates as "The head and mother church of the missions of upper and lower California", attests to its former importance, as does the richly adorned Baroque *retablo* originally transported here from Mexico City.

Next door to the mission, in a former storage house and courtyard complex, stands the thoroughly engaging **Museo de las Misiones** (Tues–Sun 9am–6pm; ⓣ613/135-0441; M$37). The museum chronicles the early conversion and colonization of Baja California in five rooms that are accessed via a covered path. Much of Loreto's centre is otherwise given over to craft shops and galleries, many selling silver. *El Caballo Blanco* (daily 8.30am–7pm; ⓣ613/116-5374), at Hidalgo and Madero, is an excellent little bookshop with lots of material on Baja.

Misión San Francisco Xavier de Viggé-Biaundó

If you have a car (preferably a 4WD), make time for the detour to the **Misión San Francisco Javier de Viggé-Biaundó**, 36km southwest of Loreto in the heart of the mountains. Established in 1699, it became the base of Father Juan de Ugarte two years later, one of the leading Jesuit pioneers in Baja. The current church, completed in 1758, is one of the most isolated and evocative on the peninsula. Mass is heard here once a month, but the church is usually open – you'll find fine gilded *retablos* and a gracious statue of San Javier. The mission is signposted at km 118 on Hwy-1, south of Loreto. The gravel road snakes between vast desert mountains, dry arroyos and massive faces of cracked rock.

Parque Nacional Bahía de Loreto

Loreto's greatest asset is the giant body of protected waters along its eastern shore – you'll get an entrancing view of the islands from the breezy malecón. The **Parque Nacional Bahía de Loreto** was established in 1996 to protect over 2000 square kilometres of the Sea of Cortés from overfishing, and it's become another superb place for **diving** and **kayaking**. If you just want a closer look at the islands, try the Parque Marino Lareto Fisherman's Co-Op Eco Union Tours (daily 6am–8pm; ⓣ613/135-1664, ⓔecounionadventures@hotmail.com), who give 90 percent of their earnings to the captains that actually take out the boats (21 local fishermen). Tours of **Isla Coronados** take 5hr and cost M$1000 for a boat that can take four – you'll be able to snorkel and see the sea lion colony here. Tours of **Isla Carmen** take 7hr and cost M$1100 for the near side and M$2000 for the far side; tours of **Isla Danzante** take 6hr and cost M$1300 – you'll see a lot more marine life here, such as sea lions, whale sharks, dolphins, manta rays and whales. The daily park fee is around M$23 (usually set at US$2-equivalent). They have a booth at the marina, at the top end of the malecón, and also on Hidalgo next to *El Junípero*.

The Dolphin Dive Center (ⓣ613/135-1914, ⓦwww.dolphindivebaja.com), Juárez between Mateos and Davis, runs two-tank **dive trips** to Isla Coronados (M$990), Isla Carmen (M$1090) and Isla Danzante (M$1200) that include tanks, all gear, snacks, guide, boat and park fees – they do **snorkelling** off Coronados for M$650 and PADI open-water certification for M$4000 (4 days). *Baja Outpost* does diving, snorkelling and kayaking trips, as well as package deals that include its B&B-style rooms (see p.111).

Eating and drinking

Finding simple Mexican **food** is no problem at taco stands along Hidalgo or Juárez, while the best views can be found along the malecón. The best supermarket is El Pescador, on the corner of Salvatierra and Independencia, while Mercado Juárez is just around the corner from the bus station (on Juárez). For a romantic drink, try the roof-top *Antigua Casa del Negro Mesa* bar at the *Posada de las Flores* (see p.111).

Café Olé Madero, just off Plaza Cívica. Popular place under a shady palapa that does good-value breakfasts (M$45) and *antojitos* like burritos (M$60) and fresh fish (M$75) – beers are M$20. Closes at 1pm on Sun.

El Cañaveral Salvatierra, opposite the museum. Refreshing *jugos* and *liquidados* served in a whimsical garden laden with pink blossoms, fresh fruit, orange trees, coconuts and caged parrots. Drinks from M$25.

Las Cascada Salvatierra at Zapata ⓣ613/135-0550. Though this English-speaking place is mainly frequented by tourists, it's not a bad introduction to the town, with attentive service, a great location on the tree-lined main drag and decent food: filling fish tacos (M$60), chiles stuffed with seafood (M$100) and happy hour 3–5pm daily. Closed Wed.

Mc Lulu's Tacos Hidalgo, near the junction with Salvatierra. Another exceptional tacos stand, basically a tin hut with a couple of stools, knocking out tasty fish and *carne asada* for M$15, and shrimp tacos for M$20.

Mediterraneo Malecón at Hidalgo ⓣ613/135-2577, ⓦwww.mediterraneo-loreto.com. Fine Italian food, posh service and fabulous second-floor views across the sea and the islands; they also serve Mexican classics, paella, steaks and decent wines by the glass (burritos and sandwiches range from M$95–185, dinner mains from M$200). The backyard Tex-Mex barbecue (Thurs–Mon 3–10pm) is worth a second trip.

Mexico Lindo y Que Rico Hidalgo, near Colegio ⓣ613/135-1175. Solid choice for lunch or dinner, with a big English menu offering everything from local fish to Mexican classics, all served in an enticing courtyard away from the main road – the original well and wrought-iron gates add to the sense of antiquity. Entrées M$50–120.

El Rey de Taco Juárez, near Misioneros. This takeout place (there are a few seats inside) has garnered a loyal following for its fresh fish tacos and tacos *carne asada* (M$15), though opening hours can be erratic.

La Paz

Everyone ends up in **LA PAZ** eventually, if only to get the ferry out, and it seems that most of the population of Baja California Sur is gravitating to the state capital, too. The outskirts are an ugly sprawl, their development outpacing the spread of paved roads and facilities, but the old town centre near the languid malecón, modernized as it is, has managed to preserve something of its sleepy provincial atmosphere. During the last week in February, La Paz livens up with its boisterous **carnival**, a plethora of colourful parades and cultural events that transform the town, while **eating** here is a real pleasure at any time.

Some history

The bay of La Paz was explored by **Cortés** himself in 1535, but the town wasn't permanently settled until the end of the eighteenth century. It then grew rapidly, however, thanks to the riches of the surrounding sea; for a time it was a major **pearl-fishing** centre. American troops occupied the town in 1847 during the Mexican–American War, and six years later it was again invaded, this time by the US freebooter **William Walker** in one of his many attempts to carve himself out a Central American kingdom; by this time it was already capital of the territory of California. He changed his mind and left by ship for the Ensenada area in the spring, but not without taking the former and current governors as hostages, as well as the town's archives.

John Steinbeck visited La Paz in 1940, a trip he recorded in *The Log from the Sea of Cortez* (he also based his seminal 1947 novel *The Pearl* in the city), but by this time the pearl trade had almost completely dried up, most likely due to a disease among the oysters. Since the 1960s La Paz has prospered again; in part due to the ferry service to the mainland, and also because of fly-in US fishermen attempting to emulate John Wayne and Bing Crosby, who dropped their own hooks in the sea from here. Though visitors continue to come, like most of Baja the economic downturn hit the city hard in 2009, best symbolized by the bitter labour dispute that shuttered *Hotel Los Arcos*, and the growing number of closed stores downtown.

Arrival and information

Car and **bus** traffic from northbound Hwy-1 comes into the city via Calzada Forjadores (which ends up as 5 de Febrero), the epicentre of new development and shopping malls in the city, but of little interest to most travellers; southbound Hwy-1 enters along Abasolo, which turns into the waterfront Obregón and adjacent malecón– this is the most appealing area to visit. Most buses arrive at the modern **Terminal Turística** on the malecón at Calle Independencia. The station serves ABC, Águila and Ejecutivo lines, can help arrange tours, and has internet terminals (M$15/hr). Most buses will also pull in at the Central Camionera (main bus station) at Jalisco and Héroes de la Independencia first, but don't get off here – it's around 25 blocks from the best bit of the malecón. ATP buses arrive at a separate terminal at Degollado and Prieto.

Ferry passengers arriving at Pichilingue (see box, p.119) can take taxis into La Paz for about M$200. The **Aeropuerto Internacional General Manuel Márquez de León**, Hwy-1 km 10 Ciudad Insurgentes–La Paz (☎612/122-2959), is 12km southwest of the city. Hertz, Avis and Dollar **rental car** companies have desks in the airport's only terminal. You can also rent cars downtown at one of the international chain agencies clustered along the malecón – if you plan to see all the beaches renting a car is a good idea. Transporte Terrestre (☎612/125-1156) has a monopoly on all transport from the airport (though other firms can take you back); taxis charge around M$300 to hotels on the malecón, while shared minibus

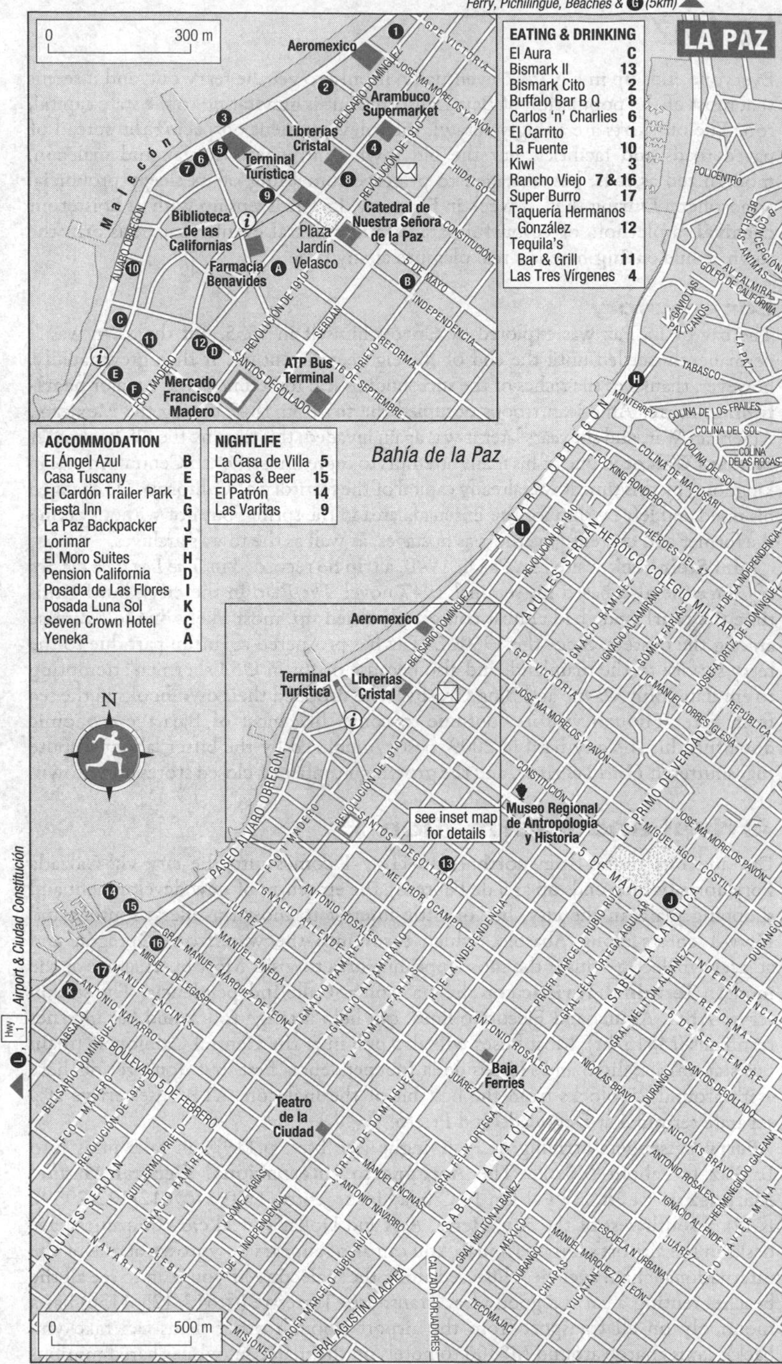
LA PAZ
Ferry, Pichilingue, Beaches & G (5km)
EATING & DRINKING
El Aura C
Bismark II 13
Bismark Cito 2
Buffalo Bar B Q 8
Carlos 'n' Charlies 6
El Carrito 1
La Fuente 10
Kiwi 3
Rancho Viejo 7 & 16
Super Burro 17
Taquería Hermanos González 12
Tequila's Bar & Grill 11
Las Tres Vírgenes 4
ACCOMMODATION
El Ángel Azul B
Casa Tuscany E
El Cardón Trailer Park L
Fiesta Inn G
La Paz Backpacker J
Lorimar F
El Moro Suites H
Pension California D
Posada de Las Flores I
Posada Luna Sol K
Seven Crown Hotel C
Yeneka A
NIGHTLIFE
La Casa de Villa 5
Papas & Beer 15
El Patrón 14
Las Varitas 9
Bahía de la Paz
Aeromexico
Arambuco Supermarket
Librerías Cristal
Terminal Turística
Biblioteca de las Californias
Plaza Jardín Velasco
Catedral de Nuestra Señora de la Paz
Farmacia Benavides
ATP Bus Terminal
Mercado Francisco Madero
Malecón
Museo Regional de Antropología y Historia
see inset map for details
Baja Ferries
Teatro de la Ciudad
L, Hwy 1, Airport & Ciudad Constitución
Central Camionera (bus terminal 1km)
Hwy 1, Los Cabos & Todos Santos
0 300 m
0 500 m

rides start around M$200 per person. As always, confirm the price before entering the taxi or shuttle. Unless you have a big group, you'll have to pay at least M$200 for the return trip by taxi.

The most useful **tourist office** (daily Mon–Fri 9am–7pm, Sat 9am–1pm; ⓣ612/125-6844, ⓦwww.visitlapaz.net) is housed in the attractively restored 1910 Palacio Municipal (old city hall) at 16 de Septiembre and Dominguez and is being developed as a cultural centre. Though the tourist police post on the waterfront at Obregón and Mutualismo also stocks brochures and is usually open longer hours, the staff speak less English.

Getting a **taxi** in town is never difficult, especially if you use one of the many stands along the waterfront or on Plaza Jardín Velasco; there are stands on the malecón in front of *Hotel Perla* and *Seven Crown Hotel* and on both sides of the cathedral on the plaza. They don't use meters, but you shouldn't pay more than M$70 for most trips in the city.

Accommodation

Most of the inexpensive **hotels**, are within a few blocks of the main plaza and malecón; some of the older fancier places are downtown too, but the newer ones, such as the *Crown Plaza Resort*, tend to be out along the coast. It's best to stay near the malecón if you are travelling by bus – those with cars have a few more options.

Note that the popular *Hotel Los Arcos* closed in November 2008 due to a labour dispute – check ⓦwww.losarcos.com for the latest news (the same thing happened in 2006, but this looks like a more serious incident).

El Ángel Azul Independencia 518 at Prieto ⓣ612/125-5130, ⓦwww.elangelazul.com. A tastefully restored 150-year-old courthouse with sparsely furnished rooms around a garden courtyard. The nine rooms and two suites have a/c and free wi-fi access, while the front of the inn has an art gallery and a small café for breakfast, lunch and evening cocktails. ❻

El Cardón Trailer Park Hwy-1 km 4 ⓣ612/124-0078, ⓔelcardon@latinmail.com. The closest campsite to town has plenty of pitches, all with full hookups for around M$200; the site comes with laundry, pool, hot showers and an internet café. ❷

Casa Tuscany Nicolás Bravo 110, between Mutualismo and Madero ⓣ612/128 8103, ⓦwww.tuscanybaja.com. The distinctive decorations that adorn the four bedrooms in this B&B come from Guatemala and Italy and all rooms have access to the rooftop terrace. There's also a shared library of books and videos. ❻

Fiesta Inn Carretera Pichilingue km 7.5 at the Marina Costa Baja ⓣ612/123-6000, ⓦwww.fiestainn.com. Worth considering if you have wheels (30min from the malecón), this newish chain hotel is currently one of the best in town, but not that expensive; the amenities are excellent (pool, gym, wi-fi) and most rooms have seaviews, though they tend to be fairly standard three-star fare. ❻

La Paz Backpacker 5 de Mayo 1386, between Isabel La Católica and Félix Ortega ⓣ612/123-5619, ⓦwww.lapazbackpacker.com. This popular hostel offers clean a/c six- or eight-bed dorms (from M$75) and camping a short walk from the malecón; you also get free pick-up from the bus station. ❶

Lorimar Nicolás Bravo 110 ⓣ612/125-3822. This small hotel two blocks from the malecón is La Paz's best budget option, especially when you factor in the helpful desk staff. Each immaculate room has a private bath, but no TV. ❹, or ❸ in the old wing.

El Moro Suites Carretera Pichilingue km 2 ⓣ612/122-4084, ⓦwww.clubelmoro.com. This two-storey hotel is set around a large central courtyard with a pool, hot tub and bar. Rooms range from inexpensive doubles with satellite TV and private bath to multi-room suites with kitchenettes and patios. Breakfast is included in some packages, and there's free wi-fi around the pool. ❺

Pension California Degollado 209 ⓣ612/122-2896, ⓔpensioncalifornia@prodigy.net.mx. The aged but wonderful *Pension California* is in an old building with a courtyard. The spare rooms all have bath and fan, and public areas include a communal kitchen, laundry and free high-speed internet access. ❸

Posada de Las Flores Obregón 440 ⓣ612/125-5871, ⓦwww.posadadelasflores.com. Well-designed rooms with Mexican-Colonial chic decor, plush bath products and a mini-bar; you'll pay more here for the boutique hotel experience than it's worth, but the location on the malecón and the view from the attached second-storey restaurant are superb. ⑦

Posada Luna Sol Topete 564, between 5 de Febrero and Navarro ⓣ612/123-0559, ⓦposadalunasol.com. The location, along a residential block west of the marina, is a bit removed from the action, but the rooms – with artisan-tiled private baths, flat-screen TVs and a/c – break from the cookie-cutter hotel norm and the knowledgeable staff are excellent local resources. There's also secure, on-site parking. ⑤

Seven Crown Hotel Obregón 1710 ⓣ612/123-0559, ⓦwww.sevencrownlapaz.com. Top location right on the malecón, with fairly simple but stylish rooms done out in minimalist furnishings and tiled floors (and satellite TV). The fourth floor restaurant and rooftop bar have fabulous views of the bay. Parking on site. ⑥

Yeneka Madero 1520 ⓣ612/125-4688, ⓔynkmacias@prodigy.net.mx. The funkiest hotel on the peninsula is liberally sprinkled with folk art and eccentric furniture in the comfortable, clean rooms, some of which come with a/c and TV – the owners are gradually renovating them. You also get internet, laundry, complimentary coffee and a free shot of tequila in the evening. ④

The town and around

The **malecón** in La Paz is one of the most attractive in Mexico; a tranquil promenade overlooking small strips of sand with ravishing views of the mountains across the bay, it becomes the centre of life at night, especially at weekends. There's not a great deal to see in the city itself but if you're just hanging around waiting for a ferry, you can happily fill a day window-shopping in the centre – dozens of stores selling everything from clothes, cosmetics and varied bric-a-brac. The **Plaza Jardín Velasco**, three blocks inland from the malecón on 5 de Mayo, stands as the city's rather faded main square, presided over by the modest **Catedral de Nuestra Señora de la Paz**; the striking twin-towered structure is open most days for a quick peek, though there's little to see inside. It was completed in 1865 near the site of the old mission, but the towers were added in the 1920s.

The small **Museo Regional de Antropología y Historia**, nearby at 5 de Mayo and Altamirano (daily 9am–6pm; ⓣ612/122-0162; M$31), is also worth a passing look: the permanent exhibits begin with geology and prehistory, take in the colonial Spanish period (with a scale model of the La Paz Mission), a section on William Walker and the Mexican-American War, and end with the pearl and coal industries circa 1920s (no English captions).

Beaches ring the bay all around La Paz, but the easiest to get to are undoubtedly those to the north, served by the local bus that runs along Obregón to the ferry terminal at Pichilingue. Decent ones are **Playa del Tesoro**, shortly before Pichilingue, and **Playa Pichilingue**, just beyond the ferry station. Both have simple facilities, including a restaurant. The best, however, is **Playa de Balandra**, actually several beaches around a saltwater lagoon with eight shallow bays, most of which are no more than waist deep: five buses leave the bus station from 10am daily and traverse the beach route, taking you to Pichilingue for M$20 and Balandra for M$23; the last bus back is at 5pm.

There are plenty of opportunities for fishing, diving and **boat trips** in the bay; go to the malecón opposite the *Seven Crown Hotel* to find people offering the latter from around M$700 – the **Parque Nacional Archipiélago de Espíritu Santo** is a popular destination, comprising the main Isla Espíritu Santo and nearby **Los Islotes**, a small group of islands that hosts a colony of **sea lions**; see Listings on p.118 for details on specific operators.

Eating and drinking

While sights are thin on the ground, **eating** is a real pleasure in La Paz – the seafood, especially, is excellent. The cheapest stalls lie inside the **Mercado Municipal Francisco Madero** – look for the "Area de Comedores" facing Revolución (at Degollado) for tacos (around M$40). Just inside the market you'll find *Jugos Mary* where fresh juices are M$14. Most of the best places to eat and drink line the malecón or the streets immediately behind it. Locals also swear by the **hot dog cart** usually perched outside *Carlos 'n' Charlies*.

El Aura *Seven Crown Hotel*, Obregón 1710 at Degollado ⓣ612/128-7787. This minimalist hotel has a stylish roof bar and restaurant, open to non-guests, with fabulous views of the bay and several small terraces for those seeking private sunset inebriation. Entrées M$190–300.

Bismark II Altamirano and Degollado ⓣ612/122-4854. Excellent seafood – order the fresh catch grilled (M$105–150) – without having to pay inflated waterfront prices. Also runs an open-air restaurant and *taquería* called *Bismark Cito* towards the northern end of Obregón and Hildalgo, with some of the best tacos in town (M$15 fish, M$65 lobster). Open for breakfast.

Buffalo Bar B Q Madero 1240 ⓣ612/128-8755 Local favourite for its juicy steaks (from M$275) and burgers (M$110); they even serve a luscious Kobe beef burger for M$200. The ribs are also worth a try. Mon–Fri open at 6pm, Sat & Sun opens 2–4pm.

Carlos 'n' Charlies Obregón and 16 de Septiembre ⓣ612/122-9290. As everyone walks by during early evening and late night, it's more about the social scene here – and the drinks, too – than the food, a pan-Mexican hodgepodge of a menu. Two levels of outdoor space along Obregón give it the edge over other malecón pub-crawl stops. Serves decent fish from M$130, and steaks from M$175.

El Carrito Obregón at Morelos ⓣ612/125-5720. Unpretentious and popular with locals who come for the *ceviche* and other great seafood, all reasonably priced. Basically a tacos stand set in a small garden facing the malecón, with plastic tables and chairs, and huge plates of stuffed potatoes for M$45. Open from lunch till late.

La Fuente Obregón (malecón), in between Arreola and Lerdo de Tejeda. Always busy thanks to the sumptuous home-made ice cream on offer, from simple but tasty vanilla to delicious chocolate chip concoctions for M$21 (bowl) and M$24 (cone). Look out for the painted white tree with polka dots at the entrance.

Kiwi Obregón at 5 de Mayo ⓣ612/123-3282. Great local and regional cuisine for decent prices, with tables set right above the sand on the beach. Try the scrumptious stuffed fish fillet, a house speciality. Does decent breakfasts at M$50–80.

Rancho Viejo Márquez de León at Dominguez. One of the most famous tacos joints in La Paz, renowned for its arrachera (steak) tacos and roast potatoes stuffed with cheese, mushroom and marinated *al pastor*. Open 24hr and particularly busy at 2am on the weekends. Also serves beer, unusually for a *taquería*, and has a convenient branch on the malecón (Obregón 460-D), next to *Carlos 'n' Charlies* where fish tacos plates are M$50, marlin M$70, and good breakfasts M$50, all with a nice view of the bay.

Super Burro Absalo at Encinas (opposite the PEMEX gas station). Another fabulous *taquería*, well worth the walk south along the malecón for its smoky *carne asada* tacos (M$14) and giant burritos. The meat is flame-grilled and served with luscious salsas, guacamole and a generous plate of fresh salad. Also known for their *charros frijoles* soup (bean soup with salsa).

Taquería Hermanos González Lerdo de Tejada, at Madero. Delicious fried fish tacos (M$12) and tacos *carne asada* (M$13) are the essential eats at this popular stand (also known as "Super Tacos de Baja California"), accompanied by dollops of the help-yourself salsa and salads; shrimp tacos go for M$15. Usually closed by 5.30pm.

Tequila's Bar and Grill Ocampo 310 ⓣ612/121-5217. Equally enjoyed by tourists and locals, *Tequila's* is one of the few places you can play pool while the kitchen cooks up what you've caught in the bay (price according to size of fish). There's a full seafood-centric menu for those who haven't been fishing, too. Still the locals' bar of choice, and lively most nights.

Las Tres Vírgenes Madero 1130 ⓣ612/165-6265. Great choice for a splurge, with a romantic courtyard and posh menu of "Baja High Cuisine" featuring fine meats, seafood, poultry and exceptional dishes such as blue crab enchiladas; expect big portions.

Nightlife

The malecón gets particularly lively at the weekends, when locals and tourists mingle to trawl for snacks and drinks, plenty of live music and boozing to the early hours.

La Casa de Villa Obregón and 16 de Septiembre ⓣ612/128-5742. The evening begins at happy hour at this multilevel dance club and pool hall with a split personality; sink the stripes indoors or head up to the roof deck for dancing amongst a mix of locals and visitors.

Papas & Beer Obregón at Márquez de León (in the Vista Coral complex) ⓣ612/128-5145, ⓦwww.lapaz.papasandbeer.com. This Spring Break stalwart serves up the usual blend of dance music, plenty of booze and themed party nights, though you'll see far more locals at this outpost of the chain – go on Sun for Banda Sinaloense night, or for cheap M$13 vodka shots on Wed (8–11pm).
El Patrón Obregón at Márquez de León (in the Vista Coral complex) ⓣ612/165-5312, ⓦwww.ladivinauva.com. Refined bar and restaurant overlooking the bay, with daily live mariachi music 3–5pm and 8–11pm (except Wed); the food is good, but this is the place for a sunset cocktail.
Las Varitas Independencia 111 ⓣ612/125-2025. The city's premier live music club tends to be crowded even when there isn't a show. A second-storey covered balcony overlooks the street below and provides a temporary escape if the music starts going downhill. Cover M$40; opens Thurs–Sat 9pm–3am, and occasionally earlier in the week.

Listings

Airlines and flights Aeroméxico has an office at Obregón near Hidalgo (Mon–Fri 9am–7pm Sat 9am–3pm; ⓣ612/122-0091); for comprehensive flight details, contact the Viajes Perla travel agency, on the malecón, inside the *Seven Crown Hotel* (Mon–Fri 9am–7.15pm, Sat 9am–3.45pm; ⓣ612/122-8601) – they also represent American Express.
Banks Most banks and ATMs are on 16 de Septiembre near the waterfront.
Books Librerías de Cristal, Constitución 195 (at Madero), sells many English-language newspapers and books, as does Librerías Educal (daily 10am–8pm) on 16 de Septiembre, inside the old city hall. You can also try the bookshop inside the Museo Regional (see p.116).
Buses Five regular daily services head north as far as Tijuana, 22 hours away (first at 7am) two to Mexicali (7am & 8pm) and a handful of other services that terminate at points along the way. Buses leave roughly hourly (5am–8.15pm; 3hr) for Cabo San Lucas and San José del Cabo; some are routed via Todos Santos (Corta), others take the eastern route direct to San José (Larga). The western route is quicker to San Lucas, and more scenic as it follows the coast for quite a way below Todos Santos. ATP also runs buses to the same destinations every 2hr. Peninsular Ejecutivo is the most expensive but generally faster – other buses stop along the way to pick people up.
Car rental Most car rental agents have offices at the airport or on the malecón, including: Alamo ⓣ612/122-6262; Avis ⓣ612/122-2651; Budget ⓣ612/123-1919; Dollar ⓣ612/122-6060; Europcar 122-3107; Hertz ⓣ612/122-0919; National ⓣ612/125-6585; and Thrifty ⓣ612/125-9696.
Internet access As usual, internet joints go in and out of business with alarming regularity here. Café Callejón, just in from the water on the pedestrian-only El Callejón (next to La Perla), has a terminal which sometimes works (daily 8.30am–10pm; M$15/hr); otherwise your best bet is the bus station (M$15/hr). Wi-fi is offered at most cafés for those with laptops.
Laundry La Paz Lava, Mutualismo 260 ⓣ612/122-3112 (daily 8am–8pm; M$16/small load), is just behind *Seven Crown Hotel* and the malecón.
Pharmacy Farmacia Benavides (daily 8am–10pm), at 16 de Septiembre between Dominguez and Madero.
Post office On Revolución at Constitución (Mon–Fri 8am–5pm, Sat 8am–1pm).
Spanish courses Se Habla La Paz, Madero 540 ⓣ612/122-7763, ⓦwww.sehablalapaz.com. Students appreciate the balance between conversation and grammar, the relaxed surroundings and friendly teachers and staff.
Tours and activities Baja Diving and Service at the Club Cantamar Resort at Pichilingue Bay (ⓣ612/122-1826, ⓦwww.clubcantamar.com), offers good diving (M$1150) and snorkelling tours (M$500), and courses (from M$1250) – they'll pick you up from town (they have an office on the malecón, at Obregón 1665-2, Plaza Cerralvo). For decent kayak rental (M$350/day) and kayak expeditions to nearby volcanic islands, or to the sea lion colony at Los Islotes, try Baja Outdoor Activities (BOA), Madero and Campeche y Tamaulipas (ⓣ612/125-5636, ⓦwww.kayactivities.com), a 30min walk from downtown La Paz on the road to Pichilingue next to the *Hotel El Moro*. Otherwise, operators include: Funbaja (ⓣ612/106-7148, ⓦwww.funbaja.com), km 2.5 on the road to Pichilingue, which runs all kinds of aquatic outings; the Cortez Club (ⓣ612/121-6120, ⓦwww.cortezclub.com), at *La Concha Beach Resort* at km 5 on the road to Pichilingue, which runs beginner's through to divemaster courses for PADI dive certification; Baja Challenge Tours at Obregón 460 between Ocampo and Degollado (ⓣ612/128-6089, ⓦwww.bajachallengetours.com) which does mountain biking tours; and the Carey Dive Center (ⓣ612/128-4048, ⓦwww.buceocarey.com) at Obregón and Ocampo.

Moving on by ferry from La Paz

If you're planning to take the **Baja Ferries** (Ⓦwww.bajaferries.com) services from Terminal Pichilingue across the Sea of Cortés to Mazatlán or Topolobampo (the port for Los Mochis), you should buy tickets as far ahead of time as possible. You should also scour the internet for updates to routes and schedules, as they change often and routes can close unexpectedly for months at a time. If you have a vehicle, it's worth checking out the alternative service to Mazatlán provided by TMC (Ⓦwww.ferrytmc.com), which specializes in trucks and freight but also takes cars from M$2950.

The routes

Ferries currently depart from La Paz at 2am Tuesday to Sunday and arrive in **Mazatlán** 12 hours later. *Turista*-class seats start at M$1190; for a four-person *cabina* it's an additional M$760, while suites start at an additional M$900. Ferries currently make the journey to **Topolobampo** Tuesday to Sunday at 8am (arriving 6hr later at 2pm). *Salón*-class seats are M$1065; *cabinas* and suites cost the same as on the Mazatlán route.

Getting tickets

Baja Ferries has a **ticket office** downtown at Ignacio Allende 1025 at Marcelo Rubio (daily 8am–5pm; Ⓣ612/125-7443 or 1-800/337-7437). Tickets can be paid for with major credit cards. Bicycles go free. Tickets for the TMC ferry must be purchased in cash or with Visa and MasterCard at its counter at Terminal Pichilingue (Ⓣ01-800/744-5050, 612/123-9226).

Before buying tickets, car drivers to should ensure they have a **permit** (US$29.70) to drive on the mainland. This should have been obtained when crossing the border into Mexico (see p.29), but if not, take your vehicle and all relevant papers to the branch of Banjercito at the ferry terminal (daily 9am–2pm) a couple of days before you sail. If for some reason you've managed to get this far without having your tourist card stamped, you should also attend to that before sailing – there's an immigration office at Obregón 2140 (Mon–Fri 8am–8pm), between Juárez and Allende.

To get to Terminal Pichilingue catch a bus from the Central Camionera (5 times daily 10am–5pm; M$20), or take a **taxi** from town (M$200), and aim to arrive at the ferry three hours in advance of the departure time. According to signs at the terminal, it is illegal to take your own **food** on board, but since the catering is so poor, everyone does and nobody seems to mind. Try one of the *loncheros* by the docks for quesadillas, burritos and drinks to take along.

Los Cabos and the eastern cape

South of La Paz, Baja California finally runs out of land where the Pacific Ocean and the Sea of Cortés come together in spectacular fashion. After running parallel for over 1300 kilometres, the ocean and sea meet at the sister towns of **Cabo San Lucas** and **San José del Cabo**, known collectively as **Los Cabos** – easily the most exclusive parcel of land in Baja California. Undeniably beautiful and home to the lion's share of the peninsula's lavish resorts, golf courses and oft-photographed beaches, the area carries a hefty price tag. It is also one of the fastest-developing regions in Mexico, supporting a sizeable US expat population and hordes of timeshare owners.

But Los Cabos is just a tiny part of the cape. Many of its most remarkable areas still require a great deal of time and preparation to access, and many travellers rent cars to drive the **loop** created by three roads north of Cabo San Lucas: the fast Hwy-19 running straight up the Pacific coast through increasingly upmarket **Todos Santos**; the older Transpeninsular Highway route trailing north from San José del Cabo to La Paz; and the third, most exhausting route along the **eastern Cape**.

Todos Santos

The farming town of **TODOS SANTOS**, located just north of the Tropic of Cancer, marks the halfway point between Cabo San Lucas and La Paz. It's also relatively unusual in the cape region, with great beaches in easy reach, relatively affordable hotels and a bus service, though it's a lot more convenient if you have a car.

Founded in 1723 as a Jesuit mission, the fortunes of Todos Santos have risen and fallen ever since: it was destroyed by an eighteenth-century indigenous uprising, then gained (and subsequently lost) status as a major place for sugar-cane growing. In the 1970s, with the creation of the Transpeninsular Highway, throngs of surfers came in search of giant waves, followed in the 1980s by an artistic crowd, many of whom settled here. There's also some great **whale watching** from the shore: sit on any of the beaches in the winter months and you are bound to see several of the creatures.

Today, the pleasant, leisurely paced town is home to a thriving community of local and North American artists, despite undergoing rapid change: it became part of the government's Pueblo Mágico programme in 2006 (Ⓦ www.todossantos.cc), so tourism and infrastructure development has been ramped up and a spate of condo and hotel projects are in the works, many controversially located on the beaches.

Arrival and information

The highway runs through the middle of Todos Santos at Calle Colegio Militar. Here, and on parallel Juárez, are the **bank**, shops, **post office** and telephones. El Tecolote (Ⓣ 612/145-0295) on Hidalgo at Juárez has a great selection of new and used **books**, and sells local maps. The tiny **bus station** is at the corner of Colegio Militar and Zaragoza. Buses leave every hour for Cabo San Lucas (1hr) and La Paz (2hr).

Accommodation

Hotel California Juárez btw Morelos and Márquez de León Ⓣ 612/145-0525, Ⓦ www.hotelcaliforniabaja.com. An evening's stay at this gem might make it worth parting with some of those pesos you've been setting aside for a rainy day. Rooms are multicultural *mestizos* of Mexican and Moorish decor. There's a pool and restaurant, as well as ocean views from the top floor, though claims that this is the inspiration behind the Eagles famous 1970s hit have long been dismissed by Don Henley and co. ⑨

Hotel María Bonita Hotel Colegio Militar at Hidalgo Ⓣ 612/145-0850, Ⓔ mariabonitahotel@prodigy.net.mx. Best of the budget hotels in town, with twelve simple but clean rooms with small bathrooms above cosy *Café Brown*. The road can be a bit noisy, but you do get free internet. ④

Hotelito on a dirt track north of town (take Calle Topete off Juárez) Ⓣ 612/145-0099, Ⓦ www.thehotelito.com. Fabulous boutique hotel, with a hip contemporary Mexican style, bold colours and four individual cottages set around a central courtyard. Each comes with a terrace and seating area (with hammock), and you can opt for in-room massages. ⑦

Motel Guluarte Juárez at Morelos Ⓣ 612/825-0006. Still one of the cheapest places in town. Fifteen older rooms with fridge and fan (some have a/c and TV), and a block of newer units that are much smarter. Also has a small pool and car park, and sits next to a nice little market. ④

Pescadero Surf Camp Hwy-19 km 64 (at Pescadero, between Playa Los Cerritos and Playa San Pedrito) Ⓣ 612/134-0480, Ⓦ www.pescaderosurf.com. Perfectly located to make the most of the beaches and the surf, this collection of cosy palapas, each with electricity, water and bathroom, also has a pool with swim-up bar and can organize surf lessons (M$500) and rentals (M$200/day). ④, camping M$130.

Posada La Poza Cerro La Poza (take Olachea off Hwy-19/Degollado, south of the centre) Ⓣ 612/145-0400, Ⓦ www.lapoza.com. This tranquil boutique is justly lauded for its high quality and extra touches: binoculars and bird guide in each room, sweat lodge, saltwater swimming pool, free kayaks, bikes, fishing gear and internet. All suites have ocean or lagoon views, CD players and smart furnishings – no TVs or phones though. ⑨

Todos Santos Inn Legaspi 33, between Topete and Obregón Ⓣ 612/145-0040, Ⓦ www.todossantosinn.com. This US-expat-run inn is surrounded by many of the town's art galleries. The late nineteenth-century structure houses eight elegantly decorated rooms, a lush garden patio and an enticing pool. ⑨

A taste of Mexico

If you're a fan of 'Mexican' restaurants, prepare for a few surprises – you won't find many dishes you're familiar with here. Instead, there's a fabulous array of tasty treats that varies significantly from region to region. Even the basics – tortillas, chiles, beans – which can be uninspiring on their own, appear in different and delicious guises. A plain tortilla can be transformed into a marvellous taco with a dab of salsa, some shredded *nopales* (cactus leaves) or a smear of *huitlacoche* (a kind of corn fungus).

Chiles at a market in Chetumal ▲

Eating out in Playa del Carmen ▼

Salsa ▼

Tortillas

Tortillas are Mexico's staple food. These unleavened flatbreads accompany most meals – half a dozen will come in a basket wrapped in a cloth or in a special, though less elegant, plastic container. Most Mexicans eat **corn** tortillas. These are prepared from a *masa* (paste) of ground maize, salt and water which is pressed or patted flat by hand, then heated on a *comal*, a flat steel sheet. Corn tortillas are at their best – soft on the inside but with a slightly crisp exterior – when served fresh off the *comal*. In the northern states, however, tortillas are typically made with **wheat** flour and rolled rather than pressed.

Chiles

Chiles have been cultivated in Mexico for over 5000 years, and there are now some 300 varieties used. Different types are associated with different regions: they come in all shapes, sizes and colours and vary dramatically in potency. The hottest is the **habanero**, 25 times hotter than the more common **jalapeño**, which is traditionally grown around the city of Xalapa. Far less intimidating is the **poblano**, a large, mild chile used in dishes such as *chiles rellenos* and *chiles en nogada*.

Salsa

Most first-time visitors don't realize how tame most Mexican fare actually is. The heat usually comes from one of several chile-based **salsas** supplied as condiments on the table. If you want your food to stay mild, go easy on the salsa. Even if you prefer things a bit spicy, it's worth tasting a little salsa before you go slopping it all over the place – they can be devilishly *picante*. For more on salsa composition, see the box on p.49.

Chocolate

The Olmecs of the Gulf coast began mixing cacao beans into a bitter **chocolate** drink around 3000 years ago. By the time Cortés and the conquistadors reached New Spain in the early sixteenth century, the use of cacao had spread to the Aztecs, who consumed *chocoatl* cold and mixed with spices – this "drink of the gods" was said to be a favourite of Aztec emperor Moctezuma. Chocolate remains a popular drink in Mexico today (now with lots of added sugar), but its most distinctive use is in **mole poblano**, a thick sauce of chocolate and chiles that accompanies otherwise savoury dishes – particularly chicken. Though found all over the country, *mole* remains a speciality of Puebla in central Mexico, where the dish originated in the colonial era.

▲ Chocolate for Day of the Dead celebrations

▼ Tequila

Tequila tasting

Tequila, a distilled extract of the agave plant, is part of Mexico's national identity: though its manufacture is confined to the state of Jalisco and its immediate environs, it has become one of the country's most important, and most famous, exports. Tequila's well-entrenched reputation as a potent spirit to enliven parties has earned it a bad name over the years, but that's beginning to change. While you can still buy a bottle of firewater for under M$100, connoisseurs are increasingly paying big bucks for sophisticated tipples, and thoughtful sipping is making inroads into the shot-glass tradition. Tequila is traditionally served with salt and lemon; there are no strict rules about the order in which to take these, but most people finish with the lemon.

For more on tequila styles and manufacture, see p.341.

▼ Chicken with *mole poblano*

Guacamole ▲

Condiments at the *Rio Nlzuc* bar, Cancún ▲

A taco stand ▼

Oranges at a market, Chetumal ▼

Regional cuisine

It's easy to think of Mexican food as one cuisine. In reality, while there are common themes, each region has its own excellent specialities. Here are a few regional highlights.

▸▸ **Baja California** In Baja, the sea is all around, so it makes sense that *mariscos* (seafood) and *pescado* (fish) dominate menus – the fish taco is an eternal favourite. Northern Baja is home to Mexico's wine industry, and drinking wine with your meal is far more common here than elsewhere in the country.

▸▸ **The north** Dining in the north, where the land is too dry to grow produce, tends to revolve around grilled meat: the *asado* (barbecue) is king. *Cabrito asado* (roast kid) is the classic dish, often served in gargantuan portions and accompanied only by tortillas and salsa. These basic ingredients combine into burritos and fajitas, dishes that have travelled north of the border to become what most of the world thinks of as "Mexican food".

▸▸ **Central Mexico** With fertile valleys and highlands that receive enough rain to sustain agriculture, central Mexico has the widest range of local ingredients. This is the land of the avocado (and therefore guacamole) and the birthplace of tequila. Mexico's second city, Guadalajara, excels with its *birria*, a soupy stew, while coastal towns dish up tasty *camarones* (shrimps). Further south, Oaxaca claims the country's finest tamales, stuffed corn-meal dough cooked in banana leaves.

▸▸ **The Yucatán** Influenced by the flavours of the Caribbean, an abundance of tropical fruits and the all-powerful burn of the *habanero* chile, Yucatecan cuisine is a world apart from that of central Mexico. The most celebrated dish is *cochinita pibil*, pork marinated in a *recado* made from garlic, chiles, black pepper, cumin, cinnamon, oregano and vinegar, then wrapped in plantain leaves and grilled.

The town and beaches

Todos is crammed with **art galleries and studios**, and if you feel like trying your own hand at being creative, you can join any of the local **workshops** that teach everything from writing to watercolours, pottery and even improvisational theatre. Check the local monthly publication *El Calendario* (Ⓦwww.elcalendariodetodos santos.com) for details. The town has little else to see, though the otherwise unexceptional **Iglesia de Nuestra Señora del Pilar** contains a venerated image of the Virgin of the Pillar, a manifestation of Mary associated with Zaragoza, Spain, and celebrated with vigour every October 12. Though the mission was founded in 1723, the church was rebuilt in the nineteenth century. You can also check out the **Centro Cultural Profesor Nestor Agúndez Martínez** (Mon–Fri 8am–5pm, Sat & Sun 10am–3pm; free) on Juárez at Obregón, which displays a modest but absorbing collection of historical artefacts from the area, as well as local art and handicrafts.

As for **beaches**, **Punta Lobos** is the first of several strung out between here and Cabo San Lucas, a bumpy ten-minute ride west along any unmarked dirt road; 2km south of Todos on Hwy-19, look for the signs to Punta Lobos, a further 2.5km west. From here, the rest of the beaches line the coast for 10km south, most of them prime **surfing** country. The two most popular surf breaks are San Pedrito (also known as **Las Palmas**) and Los Cerritos, a popular beach break 12km further south (50m beyond km 64). Note that due to riptides, steeply shelving beaches and rogue waves, only **San Pedrito** and **Los Cerritos** are safe for **swimming**.

Tours and activities

Todos Santos Eco Adventures (Ⓣ612/14-50189, Ⓦwww.tosea.net) arranges a vast range of activities, from horseriding (M$1000), birdwatching (M$300) and nature walks through the Sierra de la Laguna Biosphere Reserve (Nov–June; M$550), to historical tours of the town (M$150), surf lessons (M$600/hr) and multi-day adventures. Mario's Surf School (Ⓣ612/142-6156, Ⓦwww.mariosurfschool.com) rents surf boards for M$200/day and offers lessons for M$600/hr. You'll find it at Los Cerritos beach. Todos Caballos (Ⓣ612/154-5588, Ⓦwww.todoscaballos.com) offers a variety of horseriding expeditions and lessons.

Eating and drinking

Cheap places to eat are mainly on Colegio Militar and Juárez, though Todos also has a surprisingly high number of upscale places to spend those pesos.

Los Adobes Hidalgo, between Juárez and Colegio Militar Ⓣ612/145-0203, Ⓦwww.losadobes detodossantos.com. Expect pricey but high-quality *alta cocina* such as hearty *sopa de marisco* (M$165), *mole poblano* (M$150) and organic *chiles rellenos* (M$135), served in a serene desert garden dining room.

Barajas Tacos Degollado (Hwy-19) at Cuauhtémoc. The most popular tacos stand in town serves all the classics for M$12–20: *carnitas* (fried pork), *carne asada*, fish and shrimp tacos, with heaps of home-made salsa – it closes late, usually at midnight. Closed Tues.

Café Santa Fe Centenario 4, on the plaza Ⓣ612/145-0340. One of the cape's best restaurants, *Santa Fe*'s Northern Italian menu showcases locally grown ingredients and a stellar wine list that combines vintages from the Valle de Guadalupe and abroad. Dinner costs about M$700 a person, with wine, and tables are set inside an old hacienda or outside on the courtyard patio. Closed Tues.

Caffé Todos Santos Centenario 33, at Topete Ⓣ612/145-0340, Ⓦwww.caffetodossantos.com. Decorated by local artists, this expat-run café does fine breakfasts (M$40–100), coffees, teas, muffins and bagels. Lunch and dinner (M$60–130) are a few steps above deli fare. Closes at 2pm Mon.

La Copa Wine Bar Legaspi 33, at *Todos Santos Inn* Ⓣ612/145-0040. Good by-the-glass selections as well as the town's most satisfying margaritas. Intimate and cosy, it's one of the few romantic hideaways in Todos.

La Coronela *Hotel California* (see opposite). Good, slightly highbrow Mexican cuisine – such as seared tuna – with a country slant, and tapas on a separate menu. The bar is a great place to grab a drink.

Miguel's Degollado and Rangel. Rustic Mexican restaurant under a palapa, popular with surfers and locals for its fish tacos and superb battered *chiles rellenos* smothered in salsa. The menu also features burritos, cheeseburgers (M$60–100) and ice-cold margaritas.

Shut-up Frank's Degollado s/n, between Rangel and Cuauhtémoc ⓣ612/145-0707, ⓦwww.shutupfranks.com. The town's only sports bar and a popular hangout for US expats, with great burgers and some traditional Mexican food. Happy hour Mon–Fri 3–7pm.

Tacos Chilakos Juárez and Hidalgo. Cheap, easy and open-air, *Chilakos* is regarded as one of the best places for tacos on the peninsula; sublime *carne asada* tacos, and *papas rellenas* in the evenings (from about M$15). Closed Sun.

Cabo San Lucas

The bay of **Cabo San Lucas**, at the southernmost tip of Baja, 73km from Todos, was once a base for pirate vessels waiting to pounce on Spanish treasure ships. Until the 1980s it was little more than a village occasionally visited by adventurous sports fishermen. Today it's more like an enclave of the US than part of Mexico, with almost all aspects of civilization geared to tourism – millions of North Americans vacation here, many flying down from LA for the weekend or disgorging from a constant stream of cruise ships, and it's a well-established Spring Break party town. Transactions are conducted in US currency, multi-million-dollar second homes occupy the best vantage points and everywhere is kept pristine. If you can handle the crowds and aggressive touts, spending a day or two here can still be fun, and the jagged cape which gave the town its name is still entrancing – if you're looking to fish or dive, the allure will probably last a bit longer.

Arrival and information

From Todos Santos, Hwy-19 ends northwest of Cabo San Lucas at Avenida Reforma before entering into a confusing warren of city streets – it's easier to take the less direct bypass road Bulevar Constituyentes (on some signs it is marked Calle Hidalgo) around Cabo's eastern edge and then double back into town via a right on Hwy-1. **Buses** into Cabo arrive at the station at Hidalgo and Reforma (ⓣ624/143-5020), a long walk from downtown; taxis charge around M$70. Surprisingly, Cabo has **no official tourist office**, just dozens of places dishing out maps and drink coupons, and usually throwing in some time-share patter while they're at it. For information about **arrival by air**, see San José del Cabo, p.129.

Accommodation

Most of the resorts occupy the prime real estate immediately around the marina, while downtown has a healthy selection of budget **accommodation**. The resorts to the east of the marina empty out onto the active Playa El Médano; those to the west have the beautiful but unswimmable Playa Solmar at their doors. Note that total **hotel taxes** should be 13 percent (10 percent sales tax plus 3 percent room tax) – anything extra is being added as a **service charge** by the hotel (typically another 10 percent).

Bungalows Hotel Libertad, near Herrera ⓣ624/143-5035, ⓦwww.cabobungalows.com. Perennial favourite and one of the best deals in Cabo; even the smallest rooms are cosy suites, the location is perfect (just far enough from the madness), the breakfasts are incredible, the staff are super-helpful and you get free wi-fi. ❼

Casa Rafael Médano and Camino Pescador ⓣ624/143-0739, ⓦwww.mexonline.com/rafael1.htm. Funky budget option (at least for Cabo), close to all the action and the beach, with clean rooms, a small restaurant and cigar room. ❺

Grand Solmar Land's End Solmar 1, at Playa Solmar ⓣ624/146-7700, US ⓣ1-800/344-3349, ⓦwww.solmar.com. The venerable *Solmar* has been given a comprehensive facelift and should emerge as a flashy new resort in 2011 – check the website for progress (the hotel will be open throughout). The oceanfront location will still be stunning, with two heated swimming pools,

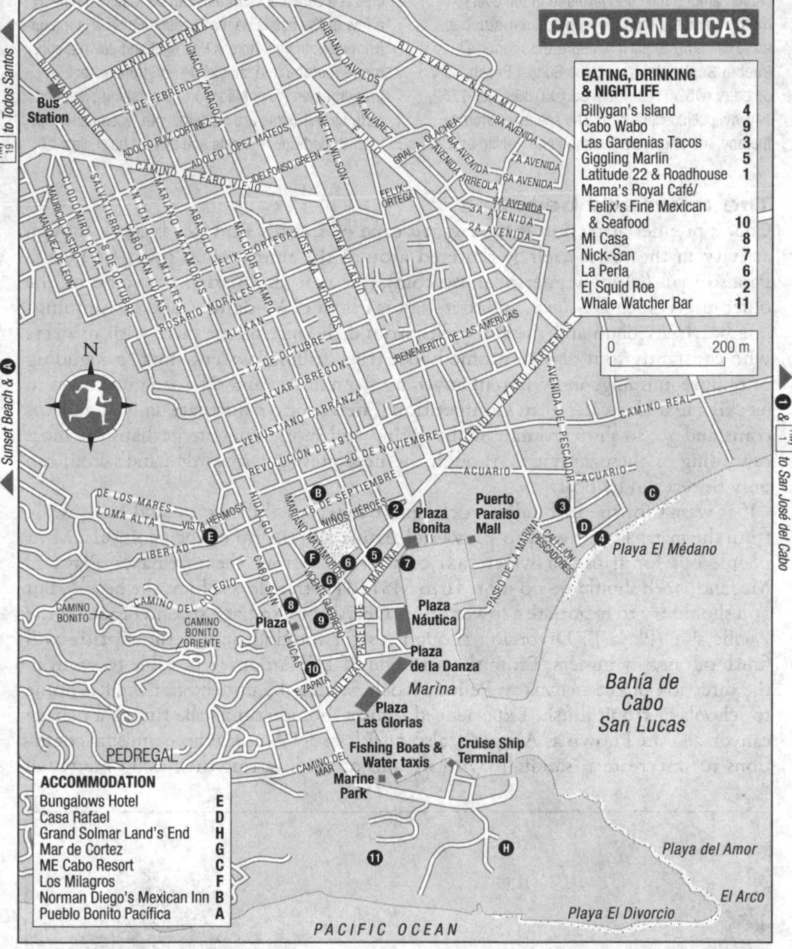

swim-up bars and the best sport-fishing fleet in Los Cabos. The new rooms should be fabulous, all with spell-binding ocean views. 9

Mar de Cortez Lázaro Cárdenas, between Guerrero and Matamoros ⓣ624/143-0032, ⓦwww.mardecortez.com. Colonial-style decor in a lovely planted setting with a mix of older and modern, larger rooms around a pool; some have terraces and all have a/c. Also has a good restaurant, free wi-fi and free parking. Closed Sept. 4

ME Cabo Resort Playa Médano s/n, off Paseo del Pescador ⓣ624/145-7800, US ⓣ1-888/95-MELIA, ⓦwww.me-cabo.com. More South Beach, Miami, than Mexico, this style-heavy resort has two pools and an outdoor bar and club scene that will disturb light sleepers. Many rooms have views of the water and balconies; inside they're fitted with LCD TVs, DVD players, iPod docks and wi-fi. 9

Los Milagros Matamoros 116 ⓣ624/143-4566, ⓦwww.losmilagros.com.mx. Tasteful, studio-like rooms with high-speed internet connections, a small pool and a sun deck make this a real find, just a few blocks from the action. Reservations recommended. 5

Norman Diego's Mexican Inn 16 de Septiembre and Abasolo ⓣ624/143-4987, ⓦwww.themexicaninn.com. The dirt road just outside the door gives a false impression of the comfort at this small B&B. Coffee and *postres* are served around the courtyard's fountain every morning and Mexican tile work, queen-size beds, a/c, TVs and DVD players adorn the rooms. ⑥

Pueblo Bonito Pacífica Cabo Sunset Beach, off Via de Lerry ⓣ624/142-9696, US ⓣ1-866/585-1752, ⓦwww.pueblobonito.com. The scents of aromatherapy, trickling water features and Pacific breezes create a sense of calm that can be matched only by a few of the hotels on the Corridor. *Pacífica* is a haul from downtown – across Pedregal and down a curvy road – but the free shuttles to and from sister properties on Playa Médano make getting back and forth easy. Rooms are modern, with wood panelling, high-thread-count sheets and private balconies. ⑨

The town and beaches

Cabo's premier attraction is the rugged cape of **Land's End** (see below), though activity in the town itself is centered around the **marina** and open-air Puerto Paraíso mall (ⓦwww.puertoparaiso.com). West of the marina are some of the older resorts such as *Solmar*, and to its east is **Playa El Médano**, Cabo's swimming-safe beach. Médano and the sidewalks around the marina are busy with hawkers who constantly tout glass-bottomed boat trips, fishing, water-skiing, paragliding or bungee jumping, and will rent anything from horses and off-road quad bikes to jet skis and underwater gear. Competition is fierce, prices fluctuate daily and places come and go, so shop around. Scuba diving and snorkelling are perhaps the most rewarding of these activities, though the best sites (out towards Land's End) can only be reached by boat.

If it wasn't for the forbidding rocks and dangerous cliffs, you could easily walk from the marina southwest to **Playa del Amor** and the tip of the peninsula. Most people opt for trips via water taxi or tour boat from the marina or Playa El Médano: both should be no more than M$150 (with at least 2hr at the beach), but you should try to negotiate a lower price. Del Amor also has a second beach on the Pacific side (Playa El Divorcio), though it's for looking only – the **riptide** will finish off any swimmers. From the safe side of Del Amor it's possible to swim in the direction of the marina to Pelican Rock, where the underwater shelf is home to schools of tropical fish. Experienced **divers** shouldn't miss the rim of a marine canyon at a site known as Anegada, also off Playa del Amor, where unusual conditions at 30m create a "sandfall" with streams of sand starting their 2000-metre fall

▲ Land's End, Cabo San Lucas

to the canyon bottom. El Arco, the huge rock arch at *Finisterra* or **Land's End** itself, not far from Del Amor – where the Sea of Cortés meets the Pacific – is an extraordinary place, with a clear division between the shallow turquoise seawater on the east and the profound blue of the ocean out to the west; a colony of sea lions lives on the surrounding rocks. You'll need to take a boat trip to get close.

Eating, drinking and nightlife

For reasonably inexpensive **food**, head for Morelos and the streets away from the waterfront. The more touristy places – some of them the most expensive in Baja – cluster around the marina and along Hidalgo. At night, such places compete for partying patrons by offering **happy hours** (often 6–8pm) and novel cocktails. There's little difference between them; stroll along and take your pick.

Billygan's Island Playa Médano s/n, at Paseo del Pescador ⓣ624/143-4830, ⓦwww.billygans.com. One of the three beach bar-restaurants that caters to partygoers all day (8am–11pm). Breakfast, lunch and dinner (M$90–220) are served right on the sand, and tropical drinks are poured and consumed nonstop.

Cabo Wabo Vicente Guerrero at Lázaro Cárdenas ⓣ624/143-1188, ⓦwww.cabowabocantina.com. Rocker Sammy Hagar (of *Van Halen* fame) owns this boisterous club, which makes a popular tequila of the same name (also used on his Tequila Shrimp). Loud, but still a good place to hear live music – and if you're going here around a holiday, perhaps you can catch Sammy himself on stage.

Las Gardenias Tacos Playa Médano. Serves the best tacos in Los Cabos, on the main road back from the beach. One side knocks out sublime fish, chicharrón (both M$18) and shrimp tacos (around M$20) while the other features a menu of standard Mexican classics like stuffed chiles. If you take a taxi, make sure you don't end up at the condo of the same name.

Giggling Marlin Marina s/n, at Matamoros ⓣ624/143-1182, ⓦwww.gigglingmarlin.com. A Cabo institution, drawing an older set than other places on the strip. Mostly a place to drink and dance to Latin standards: chances of getting out without hearing *La Bamba* are slim.

Latitude 22+ Roadhouse Hwy-1 km 4.5 (next to Costco) ⓣ624/143-1516, ⓦwww.lat22nobaddays.com. Classic old Baja bar and diner, despite the incongruous location, draped with fishing memorabilia and offering a menu of slow-roasted prime rib, Philly cheese steak, burgers and pastas. Entrées range M$75–160. Closed Tues.

Mama's Royal Cafe/Felix's Fine Mexican & Seafood Hidalgo at Zapata ⓣ624/143-4290, ⓦwww.felixcabosanlucas.com. Breakfast, lunch and brunch are served under the *Mama's* moniker, with dinner and drinks going by *Felix*; either way, this restaurant is cheaper (about M$150/person) and better than most of what Cabo has to offer. Both menus are large, with two-dozen *huevos* choices in the morning and a dozen shrimp variations in the evening. The centrepiece is the 37-strong salsa bar that sounds much hokier than it tastes.

Mi Casa Cabo San Lucas at Lázaro Cárdenas ⓣ624/143-1933. This old Cabo joint has new Cabo prices in its otherwise low-key open-air restaurant decorated with handmade lanterns. The pan-Mexican menu – Yucatán-style baked fish, chicken in *mole*, Puerto Nuevo-style lobster – runs close to M$200 per entrée. Lunchtime provides some decent deals.

Nick-San Marina s/n, Plaza de la Danza ⓣ624/143-4484, ⓦwww.nicksan.com. Plenty of restaurants in Baja will sell you raw fish without knowing what they're doing with it – *Nik-San* is the exception. In addition to the extensive selection of locally caught sushi and sashimi – try the tuna – the Indonesian-inspired lobster soup is especially tasty. Dinner for two around M$1000.

La Perla Lázaro Cárdenas, between Matamoros and Abasolo. Very inexpensive and surprisingly untouristy place right in the tourist zone; tortas, tacos and burgers for less than M$70.

El Squid Roe Lázaro Cárdenas s/n, at Zaragoza ⓣ624/143-0655, ⓦwww.elsquidroe.com. If you just want to go nuts, this Cabo classic should be your first stop; a wild party atmosphere where table dancing is allowed, if not encouraged. There's a full dinner menu of Tex-Mex dishes alongside cocktails such as the yard-long margarita. Open late.

Whale Watcher Bar Marina s/n, at Hotel *Finisterra* ⓣ624/143-3333. They serve food here, but everyone comes for the stunning views of the Pacific Ocean. The bar is on the hotel's top floor – the highest point in Cabo – and lines up tables along its outdoor balcony and flush against sliding glass doors.

Listings

Airlines For airport enquiries, call ⓣ624/142-0341. Airlines include: Aeroméxico ⓣ624/142-0397; Alaska ⓣ624/149-5800; Continental ⓣ624/142-3890; Mexicana ⓣ624/143-5352; and United ⓣ624/142-2880.

Banks and exchange There's an ATM, and the best exchange rates, at Bancomer (cheques cashed 8.30am–noon) on Lázaro Cárdenas at Hidalgo; after hours, several casas de cambio (one by *Giggling Marlin*; see above) offer decent rates until 11pm.

Car rental Avis ⓣ624/143-4606 or 146-0201; Budget ⓣ624/143-4190 or 1522; Hertz ⓣ624/146-5088 or 142-0375; National ⓣ624/143-1414; and Thrifty ⓣ624/146-5030 or 143-1666.

Consulates Canada ⓣ624/142-4333; US ⓣ624/143-3566.

Emergencies Police ⓣ624/143-3997 or 142-0361; hospital ⓣ624/143-1594.

Internet access and phones *Corner Café* at Matamoros and Lázaro Cárdenas (daily 7am–midnight) is fairly dependable, though not cheap (M$10/15min); there are also several small internet places near the old bus station at Zaragoza and 16 de Septiembre, as well as a number of good but expensive internet providers along the strip. You can pick up free wi-fi all over town.

Post office On Lázaro Cárdenas, east of the marina (Mon–Fri 9am–5pm).

Taxis Expensive; taxis will try to charge US$ rates if they can, which are always higher. Trips to San José will be at least M$350; the airport will set you back M$640 (or US$60), though a full mini-van, should you be able to arrange one, tends to charge M$170 (US$17) per person.

Tours and activities Land's End Divers (ⓣ624/143-2200, ⓦwww.mexonline.com/landsend.htm), at A-5 in the marina, has good rates for diving (from M$450). Snorkelling (M$450), diving and kayaking combos are offered by Cabo Expeditions (ⓣ624/143-2700, ⓦcaboexpeditions.com.mx), behind *Hotel Tesoro* on the marina. Pisces Fleet (ⓣ624/143-1288, ⓦwww.piscessportfishing.com), in the marina, runs marlin-fishing trips (from M$4450/person).

The Corridor

The distinction between Cabo San Lucas and San José del Cabo blurs further each year as new resorts are erected along the **CORRIDOR** separating the two towns. Even with the construction, though, the Corridor is not packed with glass, steel and stucco eyesores but is a series of rolling and rocky hills, wide beaches, manicured golf courses and rather tame resorts hidden behind bougainvillea-covered gates. For non-guests, the picture-perfect **beaches** are the real attractions here, accessible by car or, with more time, local bus (see box, p.128).

Practicalities

Taxis wait outside most hotels and charge around M$300 to get to Cabo San Lucas or the airport, and M$200 to San José. You can also flag down local **buses** along Hwy-1 (M$15–23). The Corridor offers no real budget **accommodation**; the only way to get a bed under M$2500 here is to book a package trip ahead of time with an airline or consolidator. Midway between Cabo San Lucas and San José del Cabo is *Las Ventanas al Paraíso*, Hwy-1 km 19.5 (ⓣ624/144-2800, US ⓣ888/767-3966, ⓦwww.lasventanas.com; ⑨). Suites here – some with roof decks and private jacuzzis – skip the Mexican craft style for John Pawson-like aesthetics. You're likely to run into a celebrity at either the *ceviche* bar or swim-up cantina. The ★ *One & Only Palmilla*, Hwy-1 km 27.5 (ⓣ624/146-7000, US ⓣ1-800/637-2226, ⓦwww.oneandonlyresorts.com; ⑨), is one of the continent's best resorts, with unparalleled service and rooms that, even at their most basic, are first class, as well as two pools, a beach and a spa. The cheapest option on the Corridor (but still relatively pricey) is the *Suites Terrazas de Positano*, Hwy-1 km 4 (ⓣ624/143-9383, ⓔplazapositano@yahoo.com; ⑧), on the second floor of a shopping plaza. All eight suites look out onto the sea and have kitchenettes, TV and air-conditioning, and the owners gladly prepare custom Italian dinners.

The region's best **restaurants** are in the resorts along the Corridor. But, like the resorts, price tags are exorbitant. If you're going to splash out at one Corridor

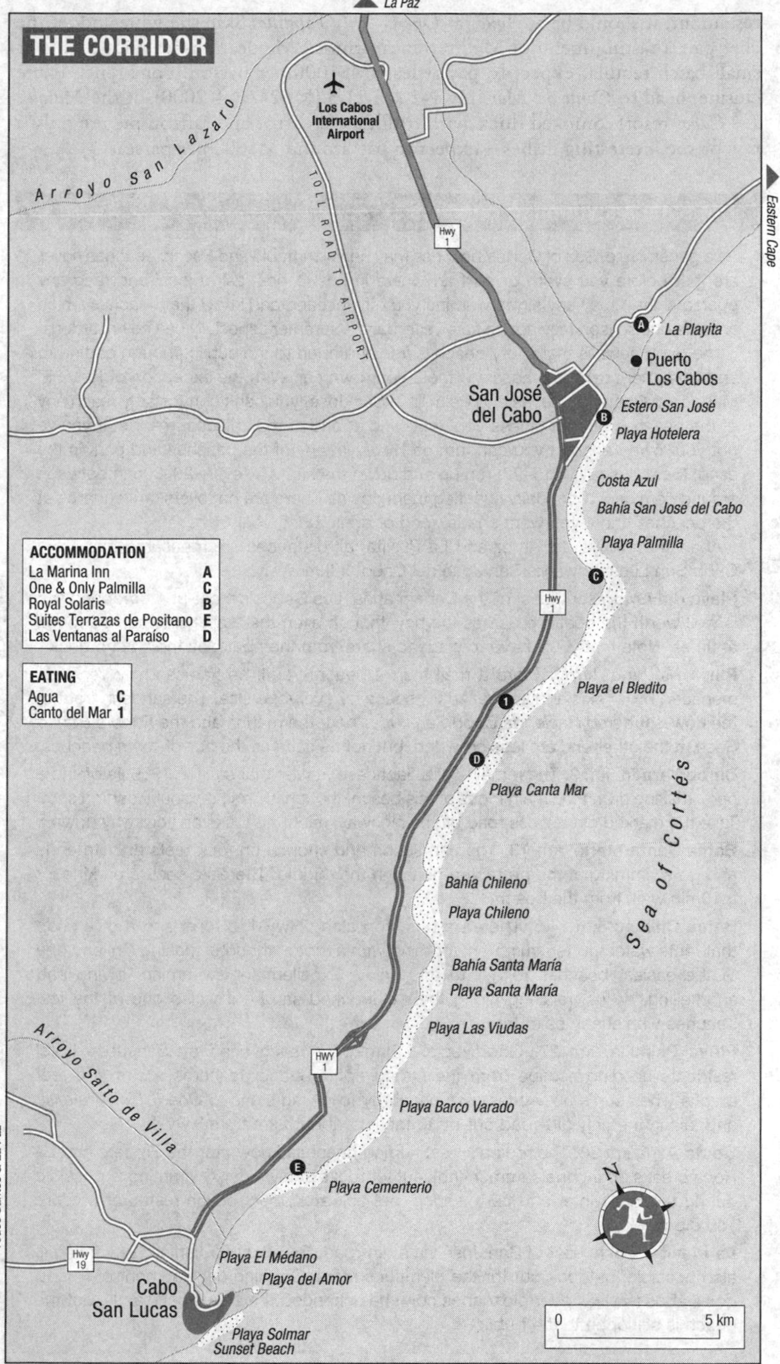
THE CORRIDOR
La Paz
Los Cabos International Airport
Arroyo San Lazaro
TOLL ROAD TO AIRPORT
Hwy 1
Eastern Cape
La Playita
Puerto Los Cabos
San José del Cabo
Estero San José
Playa Hotelera
Costa Azul
Bahía San José del Cabo
Playa Palmilla
ACCOMMODATION
La Marina Inn A
One & Only Palmilla C
Royal Solaris B
Suites Terrazas de Positano E
Las Ventanas al Paraíso D
EATING
Agua C
Canto del Mar 1
Playa el Bledito
Playa Canta Mar
Sea of Cortés
Bahía Chileno
Playa Chileno
Bahía Santa María
Playa Santa María
Playa Las Viudas
Arroyo Salto de Villa
Playa Barco Varado
Playa Cementerio
Todos Santos & La Paz
Hwy 19
Playa El Médano
Playa del Amor
Cabo San Lucas
Playa Solmar
Sunset Beach
0 5 km
N

restaurant, it should be at *Agua*, at *One & Only Palmilla*. Skip the wine and let the chef pair a tasting menu of Mediterranean-tinged Mexican dishes with flights of small-batch tequila; expect to pay at least M$1000 per person. For French haute cuisine, head to *Canto del Mar*, Hwy-1 km 21.5 (Ⓣ624/144-2000), at the *Marquis Los Cabos* resort. Smoked duck with truffles and carrot and saffron pie are only a few of the interesting dishes – expect to pay around M$600 per person.

The cape's swimming beaches

As a general rule, Sea of Cortés beaches may be swimmable and Pacific beaches never are, but before you **swim** or **surf** anywhere in Los Cabos, ask a local and read any posted signs. Obey any **signs** warning you off wet sand and know that beaches which are safe one season may not be safe year-round – summer especially can be hazardous.

The good news is that every beach is free and open to the public, though getting to and from them can be a hassle without your own car. With the exception of Playa El Médano in Cabo San Lucas and Palmilla in San José, you can't comfortably reach any of the beaches on foot unless you're staying at one of the adjacent resorts. If you've got your own transport you can turn off Hwy-1 at any of the beaches and park in the sand; **local buses** (M$15–23) run up and down the highway every 20–30min between around 5am and 10pm daily (just flag them down). There are no toilets or lifeguards at the beaches and if you want shade, food or drink, bring your own.

Apart from Playa del Amor and La Playita, all distances are measured east from Cabo San Lucas towards San José del Cabo, 33km away.

Playa del Amor, southeast of the Cabo marina. Los Cabos's most-photographed site is well worth the boat trip across the bay, though even the "safe" side can be rough at times. Note that you'll have to wade to shore from the boats, as there is no dock.

Playa Médano, km 1. More a mall than a beach; you'll be harassed by vendors, menaced by jet skis and squeezed for space by everyone else. The sands in front of the now-shuttered *Hacienda Cabo San Lucas* near the marina and the *Pueblo Bonito Rosé* at the other end are less crowded, but not as calm as the out-of-town beaches.

Barco Varado, km 9. The remains of a Japanese trawler that sank in 1966 lie offshore here, making diving the main focus of this beach, though it's also a popular surfing spot. Take the marked dirt access road off the highway; mind the rocks on your way down.

Bahía Santa María, km 13. You can scuba and snorkel on rock reefs at both ends and go swimming at the protected beach in the middle. There's a secure parking lot a 10min walk from the beach.

Bahía Chileno, km 14.5. There's a bus stop along Hwy-1, a toilet and a dive shop that rents watersports equipment (nothing with a motor, though), making Chileno one of the easiest beaches to get to and enjoy. Excellent for swimming, diving and snorkelling, or just relaxing along the well-packed sand – it's also one of the few beaches with shady palm trees.

Playa Palmilla, km 27. Good, safe 1.5km-long beach used by San José hotel residents needing escape from the strong riptide closer to home. Point and reef breaks when surf's up. Access the beach by following signs to *One & Only Palmilla* and taking the only dirt-road cut-off to the left, about 2km from Hwy-1.

Costa Azul, km 28. The region's best surfing beach is known for the Zippers and La Roca breaks during the summer (look out for rocks at low tide). Swimming is possible during the late winter and early spring, but ask at *Zippers* beach restaurant before you dip in.

La Playita, 2.5km east of San José via a dirt road. Excellent for fishing; swimming is also possible, but look out for the plentiful surfers. Ongoing development of Puerto Los Cabos (Ⓦwww.puertoloscabos.com) has changed the area significantly, but the beach is still open to the public.

San José del Cabo

SAN JOSÉ DEL CABO, 33km east of Cabo San Lucas, is the older and altogether more sedate of the two towns and a far more attractive place to spend time. Founded as a mission in 1730 by Jesuits, it was abandoned after the Pericú revolt in 1734. A mix of ex-pirates, lapsed missionaries and drop-out miners began to repopulate the town in the early nineteenth century and turned the area into an agricultural centre and small port. Although frequently referred to as colonial, modern San José, like Cabo, is a product of late nineteenth-century construction and planning. No traces remain of its first settlement, and none of the buildings dates further back than the late 1880s.

Arrival and information

Aeropuerto Internacional de Los Cabos, Hwy-1 km 42 La Paz–Cabo San Lucas (Ⓣ624/146-5097), serves several Mexican, US and Canadian cities. It lies 19km north of downtown San José del Cabo and a further 32km from Cabo San Lucas. Arrival at Los Cabos can be a rather confusing and stressful experience, thanks to the mobs of timeshare salesmen that greet you in the terminal, and the cartel-controlled transport system. If you're not renting a car (see below), try and arrange a ride in advance: taxi unions prevent hotels from running their own shuttles to the airport, though approved companies can do so on their behalf – you'll pay around M$350 round-trip to Cabo San Lucas. Alternatively, contact Los Cabos Airport Shuttle (Ⓣ624/142-3238, Ⓦwww.loscabosairportshuttle.com) or Trans Baja (USⓉ1-877/BAJA-123, Ⓦwww.transbaja.com) directly, which charge around M$100–120 to San José, M$140–150 to the Corridor and M$170–190 to Cabo San Lucas for shared van rides. If you arrive without a ride don't worry – ignore the timeshare booths when you arrive (which offer rides plus sales pitch), and make for one of the many **shuttles** waiting outside the terminal, for about the same rates as Trans Baja. Public **buses** (M$7) run down Hwy-1 into San José, but this involves a ten-minute hike from the terminal to catch one, and a much longer walk from the bus station into the town centre. Airport **taxis** are a real rip-off: they'll ask for around M$600 to San José, M$900 to Cabo and M$750 for Corridor resorts (it's much cheaper coming back). Whatever you opt for, try to pay in pesos (US$ rates are always higher) and always negotiate the price beforehand.

Renting a car is the sensible option if you want to make the most of the area. **Car rental** agencies have kiosks in the arrivals section of each terminal; rates start at around M$600/day, insurance included. The fastest way from the airport to any other location is along the nineteen-kilometre toll road (M$26) that connects with Hwy-1 at Paseo de Los Cabos, right where San José begins to give way to the Corridor. This four-lane highway zips through grazing pastures, taking about a third of the time the free Hwy-1 takes to cover the same distance.

The **Terminal de Autobuses** in San José is on González Conseco just off Hwy-1, a long, hot walk from the central Plaza Mijares. Taxis will take you anywhere in town for around M$50 (M$100–150 for the Corridor). To save money, you can try and flag down a *colectivo* outside the terminal (M$5), which will usually end up at the depot on Coronado and Hidalgo, a bit closer to the plaza. **Peninsular Ejecutivo** drops you off much closer to the centre, at Juárez and Paseo Mijares. The **tourist office**, Mauricio Castro at Plaza San José (Mon–Fri 8am–3pm; Ⓣ624/146-9628, Ⓦloscabostourismoffice.com), is quite far out on Hwy-1, and only offers basic information.

Accommodation

It's difficult to tell where the Corridor ends and San José begins, except by your wallet – there is some more affordable lodging to be found in San José.

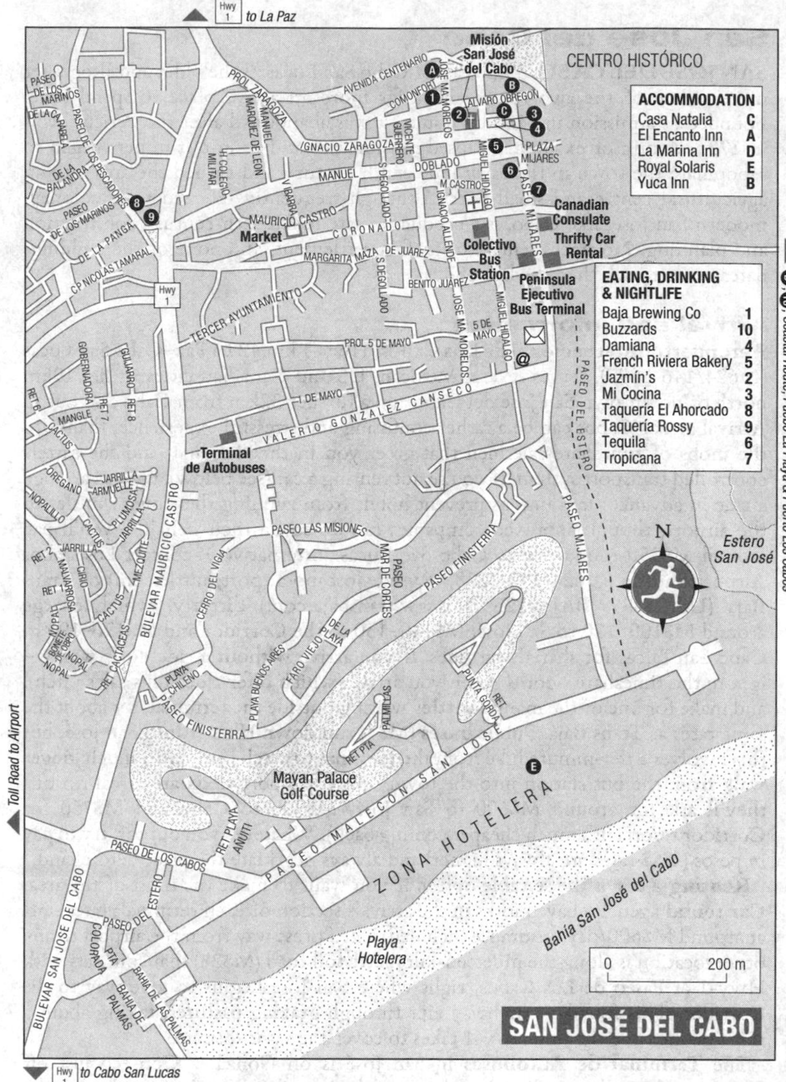

Casa Natalia Mijares 4 ⓣ624/142-5100, ⓦwww.casanatalia.com. Upmarket boutique hotel right on the plaza, with luxurious rooms festooned with bold, contemporary local artwork and sporting tiny, flower-draped terraces. Breakfast is delivered to your terrace, and there's a shuttle service to the beach. ❾

El Encanto Inn Morelos 133 ⓣ624/142-0388, ⓦwww.elencantoinn.com. Comfortable option, just north of the plaza in the art gallery district and set inside two separate buildings, both with courtyards overflowing with blossoms and plants. Hacienda-style rooms have charm, though some are ageing a little; the pool is a great place to relax. ❼

La Marina Inn Paseo de Pescadores, Puerto Los Cabos (Pueblo la Playa) ⓣ624/142-4166, ⓦwww.lamarinahotel.com. The former *Playita Resort* is now part of the new Puerto Los Cabos marina, but remains a pleasant waterside alternative and a great base for fishermen; the hotel can arrange fishing trips for you and the restaurant will cook your catch. Free wi-fi. ❻

Royal Solaris Zona Hotelera ⓣ624/145-6800, ⓦwww.clubsolaris.com. Numerous pools, activities and some in-house childcare facilities make this a good spot for families – as does the all-inclusive deal. All rooms have balconies and at least partial views of the Sea of Cortés, which makes up for the dated decor. ❾

Yuca Inn Obregón at Plaza Mijares ⓣ624/142-0462, ⓦwww.yucainn.com.mx. Backpacker-friendly hostel, just off the plaza with a laid-back second-floor café. The small pool, hammocks and common kitchen areas with lockable pantry cabinets are nice extras, and the English-speaking owner is a mine of information. Rooms are basic but adequate. ❹

The town and around

Though increasingly hemmed in by sterile shopping centres and resorts, sleepy old **Plaza Mijares** and **Paseo Mijares** (which now leads to the modern **Zona Hotelera** about 1km seaward) are still more or less intact, though there's little to see beyond the numerous high-end shops, art galleries and restaurants that line the streets and shady courtyards, aimed squarely at well-heeled tourists. The church, **La Misión de San José del Cabo Añuití**, was built in 1932 on roughly the site of the original 1730 Jesuit foundation, and though it isn't much to look at from the outside, the interior offers a tranquil and cool respite from the afternoon heat. On the other side of the plaza, the **Jardín de los Cabeños Ilustres** proudly displays statues of the region's most famous sons, including Antonio Mijares (local hero of the Mexican-American War), though non-Mexicans will have a hard time recognizing any of them.

Most visitors tend to come here for the aquatic flora and fauna outside the town, for which most of the hotels can help arrange tours, guides and equipment, but you'd be wise to shop around – see Listings p.132 for suggestions. Some 2km east of the plaza (and clearly signposted), the condos and giant marina of the **Puerto Los Cabos** (ⓦwww.puertoloscabos.com) development haven't quite swallowed up **Pueblo La Playa** (**La Playita**), a hundred-year-old fishing village that offers numerous options for sport fishing; try Gordo Banks Pangas (ⓣ624/142-1147, ⓦwww.gordobanks.com). The waters at the seamount of Gordo Banks just offshore house the highest concentrations of gamefish in the waters of Los Cabos.

Eating, drinking and nightlife

There's a huge variety of upmarket **restaurants** downtown along Mijares, but it's more difficult to find places with local prices – look around Zaragoza and Obregón. **Nightlife** is far tamer here than in San Lucas, but there are a few decent bars in the centre of town.

Baja Brewing Co Morelos, near Obregón ⓣ624/146-9995, ⓦwww.bajabrewingcompany.com. Baja Sur's only microbrewery serves its fresh beers in an open, wood-covered bar. Excellent happy hour (daily 4–8pm) offers beers for just M$25 and there's live music Thurs–Sat.

Buzzards East Cape Rd, 20min drive from San José ⓣ951/302-1735, ⓦwww.buzzardsbar.com. If you're spending a day surfing on the eastern cape (beyond La Playita), this is one of the few places you can get a beer, margarita and a bite to eat. It closes by 9pm, but what surfer stays up that late?

Damiana Mijares 8 ⓣ624/142-0499. The candlelit, bougainvillea-covered courtyard helps take the sting out of pricey takes on Mexican basics like fish tacos (M$150) and *enchiladas suizas* (M$120). Lunch and dinner.

French Riviera Bakery Manuel Doblado at Miguel Hidalgo ⓣ624/142-3350, ⓦwww.frenchrivieraloscabos.com. Its popularity has spawned fancier Corridor and Cabo outposts, but people keep coming to this original location just off the square for coffee, French pastries, cakes and both savoury and sweet crepes (M$60) – try the Hawaiian (pineapple and coconut) for M$95. Breakfasts from M$145.

Jazmín's Morelos, between Zaragoza and Obregón ⓣ624/142-1760, ⓦwww.jazminrestaurant.com. The best-value traditional Mexican food in town (fresh fish from M$165), in a pretty dining room decorated with brightly coloured *papel picado* (paper art) and Pancho Villa memorabilia. Also has excellent breakfasts – perhaps the best *chilaquiles* on the cape (from M$44).

Mi Cocina Mijares 4, inside *Casa Natalia* ☎624/142-5100. The torch-lit atmosphere is captivating, and Chef Loïc Tenoux's French-influenced Mexican dishes are inspired. Charred *poblano* chiles stuffed with lamb share the menu with crayfish over couscous and a grilled Romaine Caesar salad. Entrées range M$220–360; expect to pay M$1200 for a meal for two. Dinner only.

Taquería El Ahorcado Pescadores and Marinos ☎624/172-2093. AKA "Tacos the Hangman", this popular local stall serves juicy roasted meat, Pibil pork, quesadillas and for the adventurous, beef tongue and even brain tacos for M$15.Walk to the end of Doblado, cross Hwy-1 and take the first right (on Pescadores). Dinner only; closed Mon.

Taquería Rossy Hwy-1 at Manuel Doblado ☎624/142-6755. This storefront on the west side of Hwy-1 just before downtown San José is the lunch spot of choice for budget travellers after fish tacos – worth the 20min walk from the plaza. Battered pieces of fillets, marlin, dorado and *carne asada* tacos go for less than M$15 each.

Tequila Manuel Doblado 1011, between Mijares and Hidalgo ☎624/142-1155, Ⓦwww.tequilarestaurant.com. The top choice in town for Mexican *alta cocina*, with a gorgeous courtyard, garden dining area and attentive waiting staff. Seafood entrées range M$280–400. Cigar fans should check-out the walk-in humidor.

Tropicana Mijares 38 ☎624/142-1580. A colonial-style restaurant with an attractive tiled, palapa-covered sitting area on the main drag that's a popular choice for meals or afternoon drinks. Serves excellent seafood and usual Tex-Mex fare (M$120 up to M$600 for lobster), often with dancers providing entertainment.

Listings

Airlines For airport enquiries, call ☎624/142-0341. For airlines see p.31.

Banks and exchange You'll find both ATMs and the town's best rates at Bancomer, on Zaragoza and Morelos (Mon–Fri 8.30am–4pm, Sat 10am–4pm), and Banamex, Mijares and Coronado (Mon–Fri 9am–4pm, Sat 10am–2pm).

Books Librerías de Cristal, Mijares 41 (Mon–Sat 10am–7.50pm, Sun 10am–6pm).

Buses Águila ☎624/142-1100 runs buses to Cabo San Lucas (30min; M$37) and on to La Paz, via Corta (3hr–3hr 30min; M$120) hourly from the terminal near Hwy-1 from 5.15am to 9.15pm. It also has buses via Los Barriles (1hr 30min) for M$65 and on to La Paz (via Larga), every 2hr. You can also board direct buses to Tijuana and all points in between from here, for around M$900 (6.15am, 9.15am, 12.15pm & 2pm; 24hr). Slightly more convenient, but less frequent and more expensive, Peninsular Ejecutivo runs to Cabo San Lucas (M$43) and La Paz (M$200) from Juárez and Mijares, five times daily from 6.30am to 7.30pm. Local buses run up and down the Corridor between San José and Cabo for M$23 – flag them down on Hwy-1.

Car rental Avis ☎624/142-1180 or 146-0201; Hertz ☎624/142-0375; National ☎624/142-2424; Quick ☎624/142-4600, Ⓦwww.quickrentacar.com; Thrifty ☎624/142-1671. See Ⓦwww.cabaja.com for one-way rentals to the US border.

Emergencies Police ☎624/143-3997 or 142-0361; hospital ☎624/143-1594.

Internet access Ciber Spacio, on González Canseco, just off Mijares, has cheap rates (daily 10am–9pm; M$20/hr), but otherwise ask around – as elsewhere in Mexico, places open and close depressingly fast. Free wi-fi is increasingly available for those with lap-tops.

Post office On Mijares, on the way to the hotel zone from the beach (Mon–Fri 9am–6pm).

Taxis You'll pay M$350 to get to Cabo San Lucas (or US$35), about M$200 to the Corridor beaches and at least M$200 (or US$20) to get to the airport. Each company has its own stand; there's one on the plaza, while most of the others line Mijares, but they all tend to charge the same rates. Your hotel should be able to negotiate slightly cheaper rates.

Tours and activities Motosol (☎624/143-9310, Ⓦwww.atvsmotosol.com) arranges horseriding (M$245/hr), scooter rentals (M$150/day), ATV rentals (M$250/day) and tours to the beach and mountains for M$245; head to the corner of Mijares and Cansesco. Bajawild, at Hwy-1 km 28, Plaza Costa Azul 5, arranges snorkelling and kayaking tours (M$850/half-day), surfing lessons (M$900/half-day) and a range of other activities (☎624/148-2222, Ⓦwww.bajawild.com).

Los Barriles

The **eastern cape** is mostly known for its stunningly beautiful and largely undeveloped 120km of coastline between Bahía de los Muertos and San José's estuary. Within these few hundred kilometres there are only a handful of towns of note, along the water and inland.

The largest and most accessible resort is **LOS BARRILES**, a major **fishing** and **windsurfing** centre 66km north of Los Cabos airport on Hwy-1 that takes advantage of the near-constant strong breeze in the bay. The wind, best in winter, is brilliant for experienced windsurfers (less so for beginners) and makes this a regular venue for international competitions.

Vela Windsurf (Nov–March; Ⓦwww.velawindsurf.com) is the best place to rent equipment or take lessons (M$700/hr), operating out of the comfortable *Playa del Sol* (Ⓣ624/141-0050; ❼) **hotel** on the beach. Nearby *Hotel Palmas de Cortés* (Ⓣ624/141-0050, US Ⓣ1-877/777-8862; ❽) is the landmark **resort** here, well established and able to arrange activities and outings for you. You can also get package deals that include all meals. Both properties are managed by Van Wormer Resorts (US Ⓣ818/224-4744, Ⓦwww.vanwormerresorts.com). You'll find simple, clean and cheaper lodgings at the congenial *Hotel Los Barriles,* 20 de Noviembre, north of Calle Los Barriles (Ⓣ624/141-0024, Ⓦwww.losbarrileshotel.com; ❺). RVs should make for *East Cape RV Resort* (Ⓣ624/141-0231, Ⓦwww.eastcaperv.com; ❷), near the beach, while **campers** can pitch a tent at *Martin Verdugo's Beach Resort* on 20 de Noviembre (Ⓣ612/141-0054, Ⓦwww.verdugosbeachresort.com) for around M$150.

The growing number of condos in the area means that **eating** options continue to grow in Los Barriles, but *Tío Pablo's*, 20 de Noviembre (Ⓣ612/142-1214), a US-expat-run restaurant with a mammoth menu of delicious burgers, fish and salads, remains a dependable choice.

Taxis will charge at least M$800 from Los Cabos airport to Los Barriles; try to arrange transport with your hotel if you can. The "Via Larga" buses between San José and La Paz drop you at the intersection of the highway (2hr), from where there's a half-kilometre walk into town. If you're driving on to La Paz or Todos from here as part of the Los Cabos "loop", be sure to make a lunch stop at **San Bartolo** where *El Oasis* is renowned for its local sweets or *dulces* made of guava and mango, as well as delicious empanadas and quesadillas.

Major fiestas

February

Carnaval (week before Lent; variable Feb–March). Celebrated with particular gusto in La Paz (see p.113) and Ensenada (see p.86).

March

Fiesta de San José (March 19). Saint's day celebrations in San José del Cabo (see p.129) with horse races, cockfights and fireworks.

September

Independence Day (Sept 16). Celebrated everywhere. Tijuana (see p.74) has horse and motor races, mariachi, dancing, gambling and fireworks, as does Ensenada (see p.86).

Travel details

Buses

Services on the main highways south from Tijuana are excellent, with constant fast traffic and regular express services, if you want them, from the border all the way to Mexico City. Baja California has fewer services. The following frequencies and times are for first-class services. Second-class buses usually cover the same routes, running ten to twenty percent slower.

Cabo San Lucas to: La Paz via San José del Cabo (6 daily; 3–4hr); La Paz via Todos Santos (8 daily; 2hr 30min); San José del Cabo (roughly hourly; 30min); Todos Santos (8 daily; 1hr).

Ensenada to: Guerrero Negro (7 daily; 9hr); La Paz (4 daily; 20hr); Loreto (4 daily; 15hr); Mexicali (4 daily; 4hr); San Felipe (2 daily; 3hr 30min); Tijuana (hourly; 1hr 30min).

Guerrero Negro to: Ensenada (7 daily; 9hr); La Paz (3 daily; 12hr); San Ignacio (7 daily; 2hr); Santa Rosalía (7 daily; 3hr); Tijuana (7 daily; 12hr).

La Paz to: Cabo San Lucas via Todos Santos (8 daily; 2hr 30min); Ensenada (5 daily; 20hr); Guerrero Negro (6 daily; 12hr); Loreto (7 daily; 5hr); Mexicali (2 daily; 28hr); Mulegé (6 daily; 7hr); San Ignacio (6 daily; 9hr); San José del Cabo via eastern route (6 daily; 3–4hr); Santa Rosalía (5 daily; 8hr); Tijuana (5 daily; 22hr); Todos Santos (8 daily; 1hr).

Mexicali to: Chihuahua (1 daily; 19hr); Ensenada (4 daily; 4hr); Guadalajara (1 daily; 30hr); Guaymas (every 30min; 11hr); Hermosillo (every 30min; 9–10hr); Los Mochis (every 30min; 17hr); Mazatlán (every 30min; 18hr); Mexico City (1 daily; 48hr); Monterrey (1 daily; 29hr); San Felipe (4 daily; 3hr); Tijuana (every 30min; 3hr).

Santa Rosalía to: Guerrero Negro (7 daily; 3hr); La Paz (5 daily; 8hr); Loreto (8 daily; 3hr); Mulegé (8 daily; 1hr); San Ignacio (7 daily; 1hr); Tijuana (4 daily; 14hr).

Tijuana to: Ensenada (hourly; 1hr 30min); Guadalajara (every 30min; 36hr); Guaymas (every 30min; 14hr); Guerrero Negro (7 daily; 12hr); Hermosillo (every 30min; 12–13hr); La Paz (1 daily; 24hr); Los Mochis (every 30min; 19hr); Loreto (4 daily; 17hr); Los Angeles (12 daily; 4hr); Mazatlán (every 30min; 26hr); Mexicali (every 30min; 3hr); Mexico City (hourly; 42hr); Mulegé (4 daily; 15hr); Navojoa (every 30min; 17hr); El Rosario (4 daily; 6hr); San Ignacio (4 daily; 13hr); Santa Rosalía (4 daily; 14hr); Tepic (every 30min; 30hr).

Flights

Almost every town of any size has an airport, with flights, not necessarily direct, to Mexico City. Busiest are Tijuana, with half a dozen flights a day to the capital by a variety of routings and a couple direct to Guadalajara; Los Cabos, and La Paz, with flights to Mexico City and many towns along the mainland coast. Mexicana and Aeroméxico operate flights to major Mexican cities, while low-cost carrier Volaris uses Tijuana as a major hub.

La Paz to: Guadalajara (1 daily); Los Angeles via Loreto (1 daily); Los Angeles direct (2 daily); Mexico City (1 daily); Phoenix (1 daily); San Diego (1 daily); Tijuana (2 daily); Tucson (1 daily).

Los Cabos to: Houston (2 daily); Los Angeles (many daily); Minneapolis (1 daily); Salt Lake City (1 daily); San Diego (many daily); San Francisco (2 daily); Tijuana (2 daily).

Ferries

Purchase tickets as far in advance as possible, thereby avoiding long queues during the busy summer months. All services are subject to change, so always check the schedule in advance.

La Paz to: Mazatlán (2am Tues–Sun; 12hr); Topolobampo (Tues–Sun 8am; 6hr).

Santa Rosalía to: Guaymas (9am Tues & Wed, 8pm Fri & Sun; 7hr).

2

The northwest and Copper Canyon

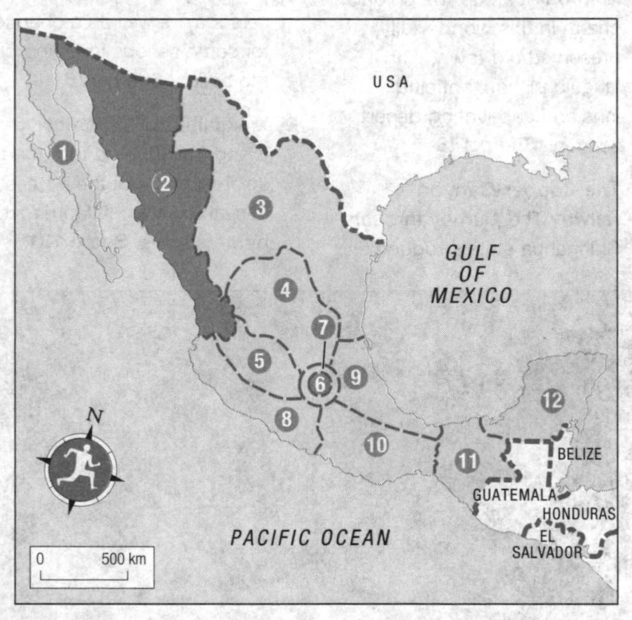

CHAPTER 2

Highlights

✱ **Reserva de la Biosfera El Pinacate** Explore this barren, moon-like reserve, a fifty-kilometre-wide volcanic field of mesmerizing craters, home to all manner of wildlife. See p.140

✱ **Bahía de Kino** This likeable, low-key resort offers 15km of pristine, empty beaches and some of the most dazzling sunsets in the country. See p.144

✱ **Álamos** Soak up the colonial charm in this wonderfully preserved old town, with languid plazas, enticing inns and captivating desert scenery. See p.148

✱ **The Copper Canyon railway** The journey through Chihuahua state's rugged canyons offers one of the world's most awe-inspiring train experiences. See p.157

✱ **Creel and the Sierra Tarahumara** For real adventure and a window into Mexico's past, hike or bike to the waterfalls and Rarámuri villages around Creel. See p.161

✱ **San Blas** Tranquil backwater offering phenomenal bird watching, surfing and seafood, as well as a chance for some serious lounging on the beach. See p.176

✱ **Mexcaltitán** This intriguing island town claims to be the spiritual home of the Aztecs, a miniature Tenochtitlán ringed by waterways. See p.181

▲ The Copper Canyon railway

2

The northwest and Copper Canyon

Divided from Baja California by the Sea of Cortés, Mexico's **northwest** mainland is something of a bizarre – and initially uninviting – introduction to the country. At once fertile, wealthy and heavily Americanized, in parts it is also strikingly impoverished, drab and barren. The climate's not exactly welcoming, either – summer temperatures can hit 50°C (122°F), while winter nights in the desert drop to freezing levels. Indeed, it's the extraordinary desert scenery that first grabs your attention, and as you continue south through the states of Sonora and Sinaloa, the desert becomes rockier, which, along with the huge cacti, makes for some archetypal Mexican landscapes.

Travellers who choose to enter Mexico here tend to stick rigidly to the highway all the way to Tepic. On the whole, the best advice is to push through the northern part, perhaps stopping at the shrimping port and burgeoning resort of **Puerto Peñasco**, or at the quieter beaches in **Bahía de Kino** and **San Carlos**. You should definitely visit **Álamos**, once a silver-mining city and now a charming retreat for expats and artists, or **El Fuerte**, a colonial town rich in history. Continuing down the highway you'll pass through **Los Mochis**, gateway to the region's principal natural attraction, the **Sierra Tarahumara**. Wonderfully wild, pristine and remote, the sierra conceals six dizzying chasms known collectively as the Barranca del Cobre (or **Copper Canyon**). Mexico's last surviving passenger train, nicknamed "El Chepe", steers a phenomenal course around its rim – one of the world's ultimate train rides.

South of Los Mochis you cross the Tropic of Cancer, and here you begin to come across resorts that can be regarded as destinations in their own right, including **Mazatlán** with its wealth of beaches, bars and fine seafood restaurants, and **San Blas**, a small, friendly town surrounded by steamy jungles and peaceful strips of sand.

Sonora

From Mexicali, Hwy-2 trails the US border eastwards towards **Sonora**, the second largest state in Mexico; you'll have to put your watch forward an hour when you cross the state line, unless Baja California is on Daylight Saving Time (April–Oct), in which case there's no change. The Colorado River marks the boundary, and

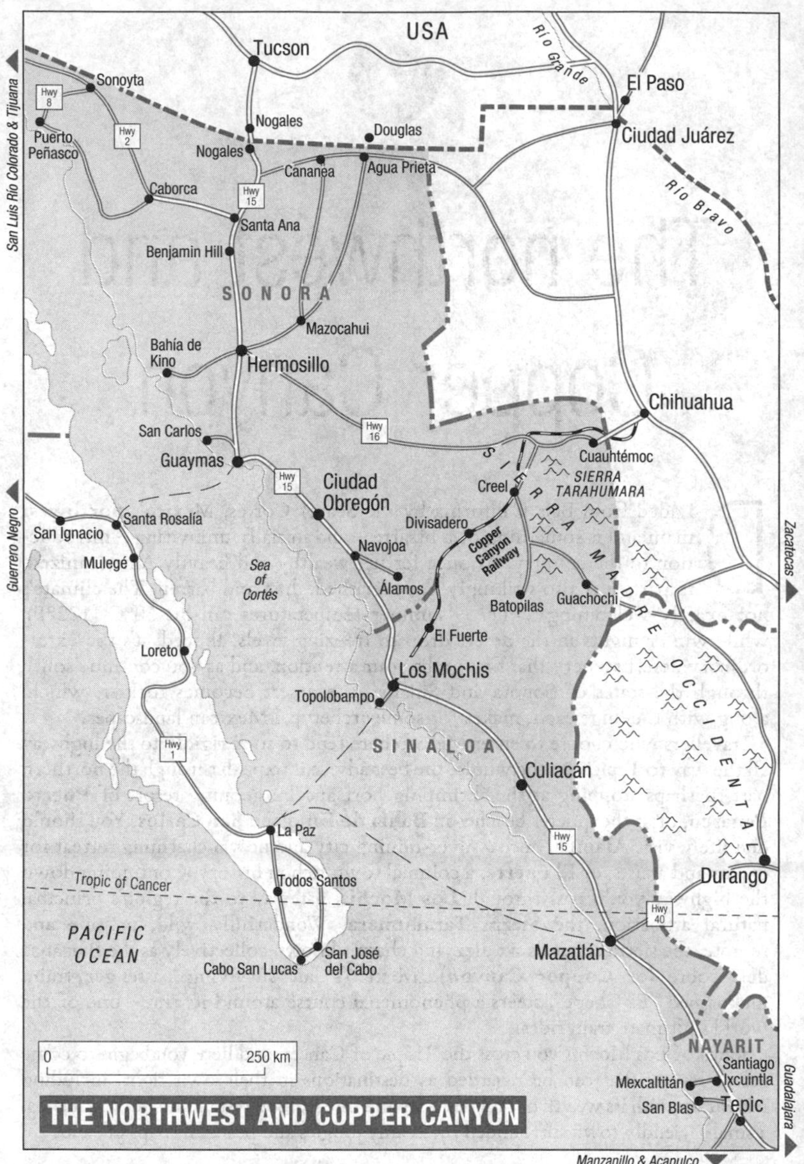

beyond here lies the parched **Gran Desierto de Altar**, an area so desolate that it was used by American astronauts to simulate lunar conditions.

There's little to stop for on the road. You'll pass through **San Luis Río Colorado**, something of an oasis on the Colorado River, and **Sonoyta**, a minor border crossing into Arizona. Both are pretty dull, though they have plenty of facilities for travellers passing through. Beyond Sonoyta the road splits: Hwy-8 heads south towards the Sea of Cortés and the resort town of **Puerto Peñasco**, while Hwy-2 cuts inland before turning south and hitting the first foothills of the Sierra Madre Occidental and Hwy-15, which then hugs the coast all the way to Tepic and Guadalajara. Coming from Arizona and Nogales on Hwy-15, there's little to see; however, you do pass through the small town of **Magdalena**. Here there's a mausoleum containing the remains of **Padre Kino**, "Conquistador of the Desert", a Spanish Jesuit priest who came to Mexico in 1687 and is credited with having founded 25 missions and converting at least seven local indigenous tribes to Catholicism. From here the highway cuts straight south, passing through several small towns on the way to **Hermosillo**, the state capital.

Puerto Peñasco

Not long ago, **PUERTO PEÑASCO** was little more than an inoffensive shrimping port, a mere handful of rudimentary houses. It was so unknown, in fact, that Al Capone used it as a secret base for his liquor-smuggling racket during Prohibition. In the past few years, though, the town has exploded into a major resort for Arizona's beach-starved masses, and it is now filled with high-rise condominiums. Events in 2009 (see p.869) and the US recession hit Puerto Peñasco hard, but once things settle down the development is sure to continue: a new highway along the coast (reducing driving times from California) opened in 2008, and the Mar de Cortés International Airport should be open by 2011. If you like resorts, golf or just fancy a couple of days on the beach before heading south, "Rocky Point" (as the expat community calls it) can be fun. Note that temperatures regularly top 40°C (104°F) in the summer.

Arrival and information

Puerto Peñasco is just 100km south of the US border and around four hours' drive from Phoenix, Arizona – most visitors drive here on Hwy-8. The main **bus stations** are located on Benito Juárez (the main road into town) in the centre, around 1km from the seafront; ABC and Transportes Norte de Sonora are at Constitución and Juárez, while Albatros (for buses within Sonora) is further up at Benito Juárez 292. One of the omnipresent white **taxis** (locals pay around M$20 for a ride anywhere in town; fix the price first) should get you to wherever you need to be.

The **Rocky Point Tourism & Visitor Assistance Bureau** (Mon–Sat 9am–5pm; phone 24hr ⓣ638/388-8207, ⓦwww.tourismrockypoint.com), at Suite 204, California Building, at Juárez and Calle 12, has maps and plenty of information; it also offers free 24 hour assistance in the event of an emergency (via bilingual volunteers), free internet and free international calls. The **Puerto Peñasco Convention and Visitors' Bureau** (Mon–Fri 9am–2pm & 4pm–7pm, Sat 9am–3pm; ⓣ638/388-0444, ⓦwww.cometorockypoint.com), on the corner of Juárez and Calle 11 (next to the PEMEX station), also has an ample assortment of flyers and glossy brochures. *Join us Here in Rocky Point* (ⓦwww.joinusrockypoint.com) and *The Rocky Point Times* (ⓦwww.rptimes.com) are two English-language publications that have helpful information on the town.

Accommodation

There isn't much cheap (or good-value) accommodation in Puerto Peñasco, with most options starting at around M$400. Many of the town's more reasonable hotels can be found around Calle 13, between Juárez and the colossal *Hotel Peñasco del Sol* on the water. Prices can double or triple at the weekends and high season, and even quadruple at spring break, Christmas and Semana Santa. Many **RV parks** front the beach along Matamoros, south of the port. **Condo rentals** are worth considering: try Sea Side Reservations (ⓣ1-888/262-4508, ⓦwww.seasidemexico.com) or Oceano Luxury Vacation Rentals (ⓣ1-888/328-8491, ⓦwww.gooceano.com).

La Casa del Puerto Primero de Junio 13 block from the church in the old port ⓣ638/383-6209. Tasteful studios and one-bedroom suites with jacuzzi, sun deck, palapas and bar. A good deal for groups, the rooms here have luxurious touches, and prices drop slightly out of season. They also rent out kayaks and boogie boards at reasonable rates. ❺

Laos Mar Balboa 90 ⓣ638/383-4700. Best mid-range option, with pool and jacuzzi on Sandy Beach – the spotless rooms come with desert or sea views, and a basic breakfast is included. ❹

Motel Alexander Zapata 89, at Calle 13 ⓣ638/383-3749. This budget motel offers neat rooms with en-suite bathrooms, a/c and cable TV. A stone's throw from the action on C 13. ❹

Posada La Roca Primero de Junio 2, in the old port ⓣ638/383-3199. This is the oldest building in town, frequented by Al Capone during Prohibition. A great budget option with cool, if plain quarters, and a cosy living room. Capone stayed in no.10. ❹

Sonoran Spa Resort Camino a la Choya km 3 ⓣ1-877/629-3750, ⓦwww.sonoran-spa-resort.com. There's no shortage of luxury lodgings in Puerto Peñasco, and this is one of the best, right on Sandy Beach with three pools and all the extras; rooms are one- to three-bedroom suites with kitchens and sea views. ❼

The town and around

Though the **Old Port** used to be the centre of town, tourist dollars are pushing development along the coast in both directions, and now the action is divided between the malecón on the waterfront, and Calle 13 to the north of the harbour. From the malecón and the Old Port, the main Bulevar Juárez runs nearly parallel to the water before heading off towards Sonoyta, while the town's main attraction, **Sandy Beach,** stretches off to the northwest, an eight-kilometre strip backed by condos and resort hotels ending at **La Choya** (or Cholla Bay in English).

There are plenty of opportunities for **fishing**, **diving** and **sailing** here. Ocean-bound activities are best arranged in the Old Port; the Sun and Fun Dive Shop (ⓣ602/476-8066 or 1-888/381-7720, ⓦwww.sunandfundivers.com), at Juárez between Calle 13 and Fremont, rents fishing, scuba-diving and snorkelling gear, as well as skim and boogie boards. **San Jorge Island** is the most popular offshore destination, frequented by hordes of sea lions. If they're feeling up to it, and haven't been laid low by the daytime heat, you can swim with them. Otherwise, there are usually numerous dolphins frolicking around.

If you don't have the inclination to get in the water, you can visit the **Centro Intercultural de Estudios de Desiertos y Océanos** (CEDO; Mon–Sat 9am–5pm, Sun 10am–2pm; free; ⓦwww.cedointercultural.org), in Las Conchas residential zone 4km east of the harbour, the foremost authority on local wildlife, and currently researching the harmful effects of development on regional ecology. Inside you can check out the Gran Desierto de Altar Botanical Gardens, a 20-metre fin whale skeleton and the Earthship Visitors' Center (which houses various ecological exhibits), or even attend natural history lectures (Tues 2pm & Sat 4pm; free). CEDO also runs expert-led tours of the Botanical Gardens (M$100), the local tidepools (M$100; 2hr), the Punta Roja oyster farms (M$300), the Estero Morúa coastal wetlands (M$150; 3–4hr), the Estero Morúa for bird watching (M$300; 6–7hr), Estero Morúa kayaking (M$400; 6hr), the Gran Desierto dunes (M$500; 5hr), San Jorge Island (M$700–900; 6–7hr) and the Pinacate Biosphere Reserve (M$350–400; 6hr).

The region's most impressive natural attraction, the **Reserva de la Biosfera El Pinacate y Gran Desierto de Altar** (ranger station daily 9am–5pm; M$40; ⓣ638/384-9007), lies 52km north of Puerto Peñasco on Hwy-8. NASA used this otherworldly expanse of volcanic cinder cones and craters to train its astronauts for lunar landings. One of Pinacate's largest and most awe-inspiring craters, "El Elegante", is 1.6km wide and 250m deep and can be seen from space. Camping is allowed by arrangement with the **ranger station** at the edge of the park; permits are given on a first-come, first-served basis but there are no facilities. No public transport runs to Pinacate, so you'll have to drive or join a tour.

Eating and drinking

Basic eating options line Calle 13, where liquor flows copiously and young gringo folk gather. More sophisticated dining can be had in the Old Port, where restaurants proliferate along and around the malecón, or within the resorts along Sandy Beach.

Aqui Es Con Flavio's Malecón and Primero de Junio in the Old Port ⓣ638/383-5252. Unpretentious place right on the boardwalk, where most people come for the margaritas, frolicking pelicans and the views rather than the food. The seafood is not bad, though – groups should opt for the seafood combo.

Blue Marlin Malecón, Old Port ⓣ638/388-0056. Fabulous family-owned seafood restaurant popular with locals, actually specializing in marlin (local, when they can get it fresh); try the smoked marlin, one of the town's best dishes, or the Neptune platter for two, loaded with a variety of seafood (around M$350). Noon–10pm, closed Wed.

La Casa del Capitán Av del Agua 1, Cerro de la Ballena (follow Juárez to Antonio's liquor store; from there you'll see the entrance to the path leading to the top of "Whale Hill", a 15min walk), ⓣ638/383-5698. One of the most popular restaurants in town to view the sunset (when it's always packed with tourists), with gorgeous views across the sea, great for romantic dinners. There's a full international and Mexican menu.

Coffee's Haus Benito Juárez 216-B ⓣ638/388-1065, ⓦwww.coffeeshaus.com. This friendly European-style café serves rich coffee, wonderful breakfasts and addictive pastries such as apple-strudel with vanilla sauce and cherry coconut cake. Tues–Sat 7.30am–4pm, Sun 7.30am–2pm.

The Friendly Dolphin Alcantar 44 in the Old Port ⓣ638/383-2608, ⓦwww.friendlydolphin.com. Local favourite with a full seafood menu and reasonable prices. Adorned with antique pictures of Mexico. Food is also served on an outdoor patio upstairs. Occasionally one of the owners will play guitar and sing to the tables. Mains average M$150–200. Daily 10am–11pm.

JJ's Cantina 58 Seaside Av, La Choya (Cholla Bay) ⓣ638/383-2785, ⓦwww.jjscantina.com. A beach-bar and seafood joint that does great fish, tacos and burgers (all for less than M$100), about 20min drive from the malecón. If you don't mind the expat crowd – monthly events include chile cook-offs and "Bathtub Races" – an excellent place to watch the sun set over the bay. Cash only.

Lapa Lapa Kino and Zaragoza ⓣ638/388-0599. Tasty food in a stunning setting, with heart-melting views of the sunset and the ocean. Try the exceptional coconut shrimp or pecan-crusted fish (mains M$120–200). Wed–Mon 10am–10pm.

Pollo Lucas Juárez at Sonora (near the bus stations) ⓣ638/388-8172. No-frills *asadero*, under a huge palapa billowing smoke from the enormous grill – the main event here is *pollo asado al carbon*, sumptuous roast chicken served with salsas, beans and tortillas (M$45). No booze, but you can bring your own.

Sushi Sun C 13 and Elias Callas ⓣ638/383-2772. Locals swear by the sushi at this mid-range place (sets from M$150). Specialities include tempura and Matsuri rolls, both made with local *camarones*. They also deliver. Closed Mon.

Listings

Banks There are several strung along Juárez, with ATMs; US$s are accepted everywhere.

Buses Services out of Puerto Peñasco are becoming more frequent, with daily buses to Hermosillo, Mexicali, Tijuana and Nogales. Several outfits also run minibuses to Arizona: Head Out to Rocky Point (ⓣ1-866/443-2368, ⓦwww.headouttorockypoint.com) runs buses from Phoenix (4hr) for US$190 return; Mercedes Shuttle Rocky Point Mexico (ⓣ602/956-5696, ⓦmercedesshuttle.com) offers a similar service and price, while Rocky Point Rides (ⓦwww.rockypointrides.com) runs from Tucson for the same rates.

Internet access Your best bet is the free internet at the Rocky Point Tourism & Visitor Assistance Bureau (see p.139).

Post office 1285 Chiapas Av, off Fremont (Mon–Fri 8am–3pm; ⓣ638/383-2350).

Nogales

Like most of the other border towns, **NOGALES** is a fast-growing melange of cheap stores, *maquiladoras* (factories), street hustlers and rough bars. Though the tourist areas are safe enough during the day, the day-trip crowd largely

disappeared in 2009. Things are likely to improve, but there's little point in hanging around in any case – move on as quickly as possible.

Practicalities

The main **bus station**, which is close to several smaller terminals, sits on the highway about 5km south of the border; inside you'll find a guardería (M$5/hr). **Taxis** to the border are around M$80. Local buses (M$6) also do the journey: for trips back to the bus station look for buses marked "Central Camionera" from López Mateos between Campillo and Ochoa. Southbound departures from the bus station are frequent, going as far south as Guadalajara (26hr) and Mexico City (34hr) via Hermosillo (3hr).

On the other side of the border (in Nogales, Arizona), the **Greyhound** station is right by the customs office at 35 N Terrace Av (☎520/287-5628); buses (operated by Autobuses Crucero) leave four times daily for Tucson (1hr) and Phoenix (3hr 40min).

Crossing the border (24hr) into Mexico is straightforward; remember to have your tourist card stamped by *migración* if you're heading further south (see p.29). Immediately inside the border, the small **tourist office** (Wed–Mon 9am–1pm & 2–6pm; ☎631/312-0666) has a limited amount of local information and maps. From here López Mateos and Av Sonora (Hwy-15) lead south towards the main bus stations, while the two main commercial streets are a couple of blocks west: Obregón and Juárez. There are several **banks**, most with ATMs (some giving US dollars), and casas de cambio along López Mateos and Obregón, but if you want to make a phone call or send mail you're better off doing so back in the US. You can use the **internet** at Café Yajar, on Plaza Niños Heroes close to the church (daily 9.30am–8pm; M$20/hr) or at the main bus station ($20/hr).

Hermosillo is only three hours away, but if you do get stuck in Nogales, there are a couple of decent **places to stay**. Possibilities include the *Hotel San Carlos*, Juárez 22 (☎631/312-1557; ❹), with air-conditioning and free internet access for guests, and the *Hotel Fray Marcos de Niza*, Campillo 91 (☎631/312-1651; ❺), a slightly pricier option with fantastic decor.

There are plenty of cafés and **restaurants** in town; the best place to eat is the elegant *La Roca*, Elias 91, which serves fine Sonoran cuisine in a colonial building, half built into the rock face just across the Mexican side of the border – a good meal here should be less than M$500. You can also try the cheaper *La Posada*, Pierson 116, (just off Obregón), which has been serving hearty Mexican food since 1963 – dishes average M$60 (cash only).

Hermosillo

The thriving state capital of Sonora, **HERMOSILLO** is a smart, affluent but rather odd-looking place, home to one of the largest Ford manufacturing plants outside the US. It's surrounded by strange rock formations and presided over, right in the centre, by the **Cerro de la Campana**, a tall outcrop crowned by radio masts and surreally illuminated at night to resemble a giant, spiral snail-shell. The city has a turbulent history, and some of the earliest **presidents** of revolutionary Mexico were *Sonorenses*: Adolfo de la Huerta, born here in 1881, Álvaro Obregón, who was born in the southern part of the state, and Plutarco Elías Calles and Abelardo Rodríguez (both born in nearby Guaymas). Though their many monuments and the streets named after them reflect pride in this glorious past, Hermosillo will now be remembered for a heart-breaking tragedy: in 2009 a fire destroyed a government-run day-care centre in the city, killing at least 47 young children. While there's little to see in the way of traditional sights, Hermosillo's laurel-lined avenues, overflowing meat markets, shops full of cowboy paraphernalia and tasty snack food make for an engaging stopover on the route south. Note that **summers** here are fierce, with temperatures often exceeding 47 °C (117 °F).

Arrival and information

Although the city itself sprawls, **downtown** Hermosillo is relatively compact. Hwy-15 from Nogales (270km to the north) comes into town as Bulevar Eusebio Kino, known as Bulevar Rosales as it runs north–south through the centre of town. Crossing it, Bulevar Luis Encinas passes the **Central Camionera** (Ⓣ662/212-5952), 3km east of the centre, then leaves town to the west, past the airport towards Bahía de Kino (see p.144). Virtually everything you might want to see lies to the south near Plaza Zaragoza or Serdán, the main commercial street downtown.

To get downtown from the rather isolated Central Camionera, take a "Ruta 1" microbus, or a "Multirutas" town bus (all M$6) across the main road. To get back, catch a bus marked "Central Camionera" from Juárez (on east side of Jardín Juárez). **Taxis** are a fixed M$70. The busy international **airport**, an important Aeroméxico hub (with flights to Los Angeles, Phoenix and Las Vegas), is 10km out at Carretera Bahía de Kino km 9.5. You can pick up fixed-fare taxis here; it's M$170 for anywhere within the city or M$430 to Nogales. *Colectivos* are just M$60 into the centre.

The inconveniently located **tourist office** (Mon–Fri 8am–3pm & 5–7pm; Ⓣ662/217-0060 or 1-800/716-2555, Ⓦwww.sonoraturismo.gob.mx) is in the Edificio Sonora Norte (north wing) at the Centro de Gobierno, Comonfort and Paseo del Canal (500m south of Plaza Zaragoza); they generally prove helpful, though they have little printed information and seem to come across few visitors.

Accommodation

Nearly all the cheaper **hotels** in Hermosillo are strikingly poor value, but some very pleasant mid-range places cater to business people and the wealthy *rancheros* who come here for the markets. The most expensive hotels, such as the *Fiesta Americana*, and a number of motels, are almost all in the **Zona Hotelera**, a long way from the centre on Kino (Hwy-15).

Colonial Hotel Vado del Río 9 Ⓣ662/259-0000 or 1-800/849-9007, Ⓦwww.hotelescolonial.com. Plush, modern motel on the southern edge of downtown, worth the extra walk if you're not driving; includes breakfast, satellite TV, internet, laundry, gym and even a small pool on site. ❺

Hotel Niza Plutarco Elías Calles 66, just off Serdán near the market Ⓣ662/217-2028. Solid budget option, with comfy en-suite rooms equipped with a/c and TV; good location with views of Cerro de la Compana, but lacking in atmosphere. Cash only. ❸

Hotel Suites Kino Pino Suárez 151, just off Rosales near Plaza Zaragoza Ⓣ662/213-3131, Ⓦwww.hotelsuiteskino.com. Colonial-style hotel set in a nineteenth-century building with standard, motel-style rooms and all the facilities, including cable TV, free internet, coffee, parking and a pool. ❺

Hotel Washington Noriega 68 near Guerrero Ⓣ662/213-1183. Best budget option in town: ageing but good-value rooms, excellent hot showers, a very helpful staff and free coffee in the lobby. ❷

The town and around

The spacious **Plaza Zaragoza** is the venerable, shaded heart of the city and a good place to begin any wanderings around the centre. The plaza is framed by the stately **Palacio de Gobierno** (Mon–Fri 8am–8pm, Sat 8am–3pm; free), completed in 1906 and boasting a series of florid murals highlighting the history of Sonora (painted in the 1980s), and the striking **Catedral de Nuestra Señora de la Asunción**, a grand edifice completed in 1908 but added to throughout the twentieth century.

On the east side of the Cerro de la Campana you'll find the **Museo Regional de Sonora**, Jesús García Final (Wed–Sat 10am–5pm, Sun 9am–4pm; M$37, free Sun; Ⓣ662/217-2580), which houses exhibits charting the historical development of Sonora from the conception of the Earth to the construction of *maquiladora* plants. Alternatively, check out the **Centro Ecológico de Sonora**, a 220 acres ecological preserve that is home to exotic fauna including lions, tigers and panthers. It's about 5km south on Bulevar Rosales (daily 8am–5pm; M$30;

Ⓦ www.centroecologico.gob.mx); take the "Luis Orcí" bus from Jardín Juárez. If you visit between October and December, catch the local baseball team in action: **Los Naranjeros de Hermosillo** is one of the best teams in Mexico. They play at the **Estadio De Beisbol Héctor Espino** on Luís Encinas and Solidaridad (Ⓦ www.naranjeros.com.mx).

Eating and drinking

Downtown Hermosillo is surprisingly short of decent **places to eat**: Serdán and the surrounding streets are lined with plenty of juice bars, places selling tortas and, oddly enough, Chinese restaurants. Locals in search of fancier food tend to get in their cars and head for the restaurants situated on the main boulevards (such as Morelos) and the Zona Hotelera, now flooded with all the major US chains. Nevertheless, you shouldn't leave the city without trying some of the local specialties: **hot dogs** are fabulously over-the-top here, wrapped in bacon and piled with all sorts of toppings – some of the best stalls are around the entrance to the Universidad de Sonora, at Luís Encinas and Rosales. Also try some of the **carne asada** – this is beef country after all – and the **coyotas**, sweet cookies made from flour, brown sugar, molasses and milk (best sampled on the stalls along Obregón). The student population also drives the local nightlife, with plenty of **bars** and clubs near the university.

Gordo's Olivares, between Colosio and Encinas. This stall is a local institution thanks to the best hot dogs in town – huge, juicy, masterpieces of bacon-wrapped dogs and ground beef in a giant bun, slathered in an array of zesty condiments. Open from around 7pm.

Mariachisimo Periférico Pte 325, Col Palmar del Sol ☎662/218-3555. The newer sister restaurant of *Xochimilco* (see below), serving the same high-quality *carne asada* but with the added bonus of later opening hours and live mariachi bands (Mon–Sat 3.30pm, 10pm & midnight). Mon–Sat noon–2am, Sun noon–7pm.

El Pescadito Colosio and Olivares, in front of Costco; also Naranjo and Veracruz. Just north of the centre, but worth the taxi ride for excellent fresh fish and shrimp tacos – they have five outlets in the city, but these two are the closest to downtown. They tend to open daily 7am–2pm.

Tacos Jaas Gómez Farías, at Mariscal not far from the Zona Hotelera. The place to gorge on prime *tacos de carne asada* (M$20), from around 7pm daily. They have several locations, but this is the best, though it's a no-frills open-air place with plastic tables and chairs. "Light" versions, wrapped in lettuce leaves are also available.

La Tequilera Pino Suárez 72 ☎662/217-5337. Popular club and pub playing traditional music as well as all the latest international hits. Men usually pay a cover of M$25 weekends (women free), but pitchers of beer are just M$200 (cash only). Open Thurs–Sat from 9pm.

Xochimilco Obregón 51 ☎662/250-4089. A Hermosillo *carne asada* favourite since 1949, serving great sit-down meals and "special plates" of charcoal-broiled beef, ribs, beans and giant tortillas. Daily 11am–9pm.

Listings

Banks and exchange There are numerous casas de cambio and banks on Serdán, and a handy Bancomer with ATM at Matamoros and Sonora, on Jardín Juarez a block from the *Monte Carlo* hotel.

Buses Most intercity buses passing through Hermosillo are *de paso*, and it can be very hard to get on. However, TBC (depot left of the Central Camionera) runs a local service to Guaymas, Navojoa and, four times daily, to Álamos.

Consulate US (☎662/289-3500), Monterrey 141, between Galeana and Rosales.

Post office At the corner of Serdán and Rosales.

Bahía de Kino

Boasting more than 15km of pristine Sea of Cortés coastline, 110km west of Hermosillo, **BAHÍA DE KINO** is a popular weekend escape for locals and increasingly a winter resort for Americans. For good reason; the seafront is padded with miles of inviting sands, the placid waters are perfect for swimming and kayaking, the offshore islets and strange rock formations make the sunsets particularly memorable and the resort remains relatively low-key and laid-back – for now. There are two settlements around the bay: the old fishing village of **Kino Viejo**, a dusty collection of corrugated-iron huts, passed over by the fruits of development, and the younger **Kino Nuevo** – an eight-kilometre strip of one-storey seafront houses, trailer parks and a couple of hotels and restaurants.

This whole area used to be inhabited by the **Seri** people, and there are still a few communities living round about: their former home on the offshore **Isla del Tiburón** (Shark Island), was made into a wildlife refuge in the 1960s but is still administered by the tribal government. You may come across Seri hawking traditional (and not so traditional) ironwood carvings along the beach in Kino Nuevo, though their main settlement is Punta Chueca, 35km north – you can buy genuine crafts here, but you'll need your own wheels to reach the settlement. The tiny **Museo de los Seris** (Tues–Fri 8am–3pm; M$6), on the plaza in the middle of Kino Nuevo, gives a little more information on Seri history.

Practicalities

Buses ($55) leave Hermosillo from the small Costa Expresso bus station on Sonora, a block and a half east of the *Monte Carlo* near Jardín Juárez, between Jesús García and Gonzalez. There are about nine a day – hourly from 5.30am to 1.30pm, then every two or three hours up to 6.30pm – with more at busy weekends; they take around two hours and end up in Kino Nuevo near the helpful **tourist office** (Thurs–Tues 9am–5pm).

There are several hotels in town, though none cater to anyone on a budget. At the southern fringes of town, on the edge of Kino Viejo, you'll find *Posada del Mar Hotel* (Ⓣ662/242-0155; ④), which has a pool and basic rooms with exposed brick walls. Further north, *La Playa RV & Hotel* (Ⓣ662/242-0273, Ⓦwww.laplayarvhotel.com; ⑦), at Mar de Cortés 101, is a gorgeous Mediterranean-style resort right on the beach, its rooms equipped with tiled-floor, marble-clad bathrooms, satellite TV, fridge and microwave. Sicilian-run *Hotel Saro* (Ⓣ662/242-0007; ④) has big, apartment-style rooms across from the beach with tiled floors, air-conditioning, kitchens and basic TVs. *Kino Bay RV Trailer Park* lies at the far northern edge of town (Ⓣ662/242-0216, Ⓦwww.kinobayrvpark.net) and offers 200 full hook-up sites from M$215/day. Opposite it you'll find *Jorge's Restaurant*, one of a handful of places that dish up local **seafood**. Head south from *Jorge's* and you'll arrive at *El Pargo Rojo,* another popular and reputable restaurant. *La Palapa del Pescador*, also offering quality fish dishes, lies at the other end of town, south of *Hotel Saro*.

Guaymas

The next major stop on Hwy-15 is **GUAYMAS**, around 120km south of Hermosillo – an important port that claims some proud history but has little to offer visitors. Guaymas port is rough, shabby and vaguely depressing, though the old fishing harbour downtown is being transformed by the new *malecón turistico*, a fancy marina project, and the beginnings of regular cruise-ship visits. Once complete, the marina should brighten the seafront considerably (or destroy what little charm Guaymas had left, depending on your point of view), but there are otherwise few concessions to tourism. There's the **Plaza de los Tres Presidentes** where you can look out over scores of boats at anchor, and the nearby **Plaza 13 de Julio** with its church and some old Porfiriano bank buildings. But the best thing about Guaymas is its **sunset**, one of the finest in Mexico – try to be here to see the sun sink behind the mountain ridges that surround the town. The best beach near Guaymas, and the one the locals use, is at **Miramar**, an upmarket suburb on Bacochibampo Bay, a few kilometres north of the town. The resort town of **San Carlos** is also just a short bus ride away.

Practicalities

The **airport** is off García López (Hwy-15) 7km north of town; taxis charge a highly inflated flat rate of M$300 into the centre of Guaymas or San Carlos, though you can take local buses to both (M$7 and M$9 respectively). To reach the airport from Guaymas, catch a "San José" bus along Serdán. Budget and Hertz also have counters at the airport. For arrivals by **bus**, most companies have terminals on Calle 14 near Calle 12, a couple of blocks south of Serdán and within walking distance of the waterfront. Tufesa and TAP have terminals 1km west at García López 927 and 915 respectively (near Calle Jaiba). **Ferries** from Santa Rosalía (see opposite) arrive at the docks 2km east of the centre, easily reached on local buses (M$5) along Serdán. **Taxis** tend to charge between M$30 and M$50 for trips within town, and M$150 between Guaymas and San Carlos, but always fix the price in advance.

Accommodation in Guaymas is relatively poor, and unless you're looking for somewhere to crash for one night, it's advisable to head for the beaches. If you have to stay, aim for the well-equipped *Armida Hotel*, Carretera Internacional Salida al Norte S/N (Ⓣ622/225-2800, Ⓦhotelarmida.com.mx; ④), close to the TAP and Tufesa terminals, or the cheaper *Hotel del Sol* at Calz García López 995 (Ⓣ622/224-9411, Ⓔsuitesdelsol@hotmail.com; ③). The **Mercado Municipal**, a block off Serdán on Calle 20, sells fresh food good for picnics, but Guaymas has plenty of fun, inexpensive **places to eat** (most are cash only). *Los Barcos* on the malecón between Calles 21 and 22 (Ⓣ622/222-7650) is the best place to sample the local seafood (including over fifteen plump shrimp dishes) for M$100–125 (closes 1pm on Sun), while *Coctelería El Doug Out* on García López between calles 11 and 12 (Ⓣ622/222-2626) is a no-frills food court offering excellent crab and various *ceviche*, *pulpo cocido* and other shellfish, all for well under M$100. *Lonchería Doney Serdán*, on the corner of Calle 25 (Ⓣ622/222-4270) is a justly popular local *comedor* at the far end of Serdán, lauded for its giant *papas locas* (huge baked potatoes stuffed with meat, cheese and cream) and *tacos carne asada* (open from 4pm).

Listings

Banks Mostly on Serdán, including Bancomer at C 18, and Banamex at C 20. Both have 24hr ATMs.

Internet access Available at Mundo Internet, just off Serdán on C 20 (Mon–Fri 9am–9pm, Sat 9am–7pm, Sun 10am–7pm; M$10/hr).

Post office Av 10 just off C 20 (C Miguel Alemán), which runs south from Serdán and round the side of the bay.

Taxis Ⓣ622/224-0466 or 622/222-7859.

Tourist information A tiny booth is at Serdán and C 25, right across from the waterfront – it's nominally open 9am–6pm, but actual hours tend to be erratic.

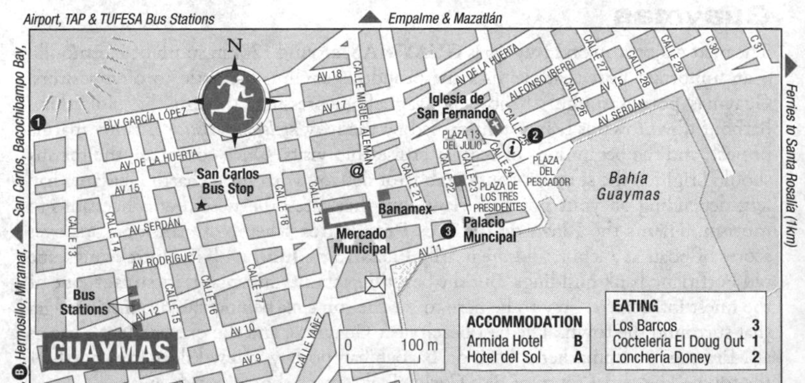

Moving on from Guaymas

The **ferry** from Guaymas to Santa Rosalía (see p.104), across the Sea of Cortés in Baja California, departs on Mondays, Tuesdays, Thursdays and Saturdays at 8pm; the crossing takes seven hours. Always call in advance, though, as schedules often change. One-way tickets are M$605 (returns are M$1090), but you'll often get a discount on Sundays. A cabin is an additional M$825, while cars cost M$2730 (one way). The ticket office inside the terminal is open Mon–Sat 8am–3pm (ⓣ622/222-0204, ⓦwww.ferrysantarosalia.com). You can also take an Aero Servicio Guerrero (ⓣ622/221-2800, ⓦwww.aereoserviciosguerrero.com.mx) **flight** to Santa Rosalía for M$850 (tickets usually include transport to the airport). To get to the ferry dock, take any local bus headed east on Serdán. For long-distance **buses**, make for the TAP terminal at García López 915; you'll find plenty of services to Guadalajara (20hr), Hermosillo (2hr), Los Mochis (5hr), Mexico City (26hr) and Tijuana (15hr).

San Carlos

Around 16km north of Guaymas, the town of **SAN CARLOS** is in the infant stages of becoming a larger resort geared towards a mainly retired clientele. The chief attraction here is the scenery: the resort is dominated by the barren, jagged peaks of Cerro Tatakawi, and the scorched desert landscape makes a stunning backdrop to a series of inviting bays and calm, cobalt-blue waters. Though access to the shore is difficult, and most beaches you can reach are stony, there's a modern marina, a golf course and scores of villas and developments linked by a long avenue of transplanted palms. The main activities here are **diving** and **fishing**.

Practicalities

Visit Gary's Dive Shop at Manlio Beltrones km 10 (ⓣ622/226-0049, ⓦwww.garysdivemexico.com), which runs various dive trips starting at around M$540 for a basic two-tank drive, fishing from around M$650 and **cruises** around Seal Island (a sea lion colony) for M$810. They also have a fast broadband **internet** connection upstairs (Mon–Sat 8am–6pm; M$30/hr). The best source of **information** here is the Conventions and Visitors Bureau at Manlio Beltrones km 9.2 (Mon–Fri 9am–1pm & 2–5pm, Sat 9am–2pm; ⓣ622/226-0202, ⓦwww.go2sancarlos.com).

If you want to **stay**, there's no shortage of smart resorts along the shore, though the *Best Western Hacienda Tetakawi* (ⓣ622/226-0220, ⓦwww.bwtetakawi.com; ❺) with pool, restaurant and all the trimmings, is great value, as is the *Fiesta San Carlos* (ⓣ622/226-1314; ❺) at Manlio Beltrones km 8 (though there are no TVs or telephones here). For something a little cheaper, aim for the *Totonaka RV Park* (ⓣ622/226-0481, ⓦwww.totonakarv.com; ❺), on the right-hand side as you enter San Carlos; it also offers free internet usage from its office and basic apartments, as well as RV and tent sites.

There are some decent **eating** options: *Rosa's Cantina* (ⓣ622/226-1000) on the main strip at Manlio Beltrones km 9.5 serves fine tortas and other Mexican dishes, and *Tacos JJ* over the road does sublime *tacos carne asada*. If you're in the mood for seafood, try *Charly's Rock* across from the *Totonaka RV Park*; the restaurant serves enormous lobsters and is also a good spot to have a margarita and watch the sun go down. *Blackie's* (ⓣ622/226-1525; closed Mon) at Beltrones km 10 is an expat favourite and a good choice for dinner, with juicy steaks, seafood and the odd local dish – count on paying around M$180 for the signature rib-eye.

Buses (M$9) for Miramar and San Carlos leave Guaymas every thirty minutes or so from Calle 19 by the post office, but it's easier to catch them as they head up Serdán (try the corner of Calle 18). It can take up to an hour to reach San Carlos.

Álamos

Another "*Pueblo Magico*", some 250km south of Guaymas, the enchanting colonial town of **ÁLAMOS** hasn't escaped the notice of scores of North Americans – predominantly artists and retirees – who have chosen to settle here over the last forty years or so, often renovating the otherwise doomed-to-decay Spanish architecture. A ride out to this patch of green makes a very pleasant respite from the monotony of the coastal road, and it's a great place to do nothing for a while: a tour of the town takes no longer than a couple of hours, and there's little else to do but soak up the languid atmosphere. Everything changes in January each year, when thousands of people descend upon Álamos for the week-long **Ortiz Tirado music festival**, in honour of the late Dr Alfonso Ortiz Tirado, sometimes referred to as the "Mexican Pavarotti". Accommodation is usually booked solid at this time, so reservations are a must. In the cooler winter months, Álamos is also a good base for exploring the fairly distinct ecosystem hereabouts; the meeting of Sonoran and Sinaloan deserts, at the foot of the Sierra Madre Occidental, has created a home for a broad range of flora and fauna. In particular, this is a **bird watching** mecca, boasting several hundred different species.

Some history

Coronado was the first European to pass through this area in 1540, spending most of his time trying to subjugate the Yoreme and Yaqui, unaware that below his feet lay some of the richest **silver ore** in Mexico. When the ore was discovered in the late 1600s, Álamos became Mexico's northernmost silver-mining town; officially founded in 1684, within a century it was a substantial city with its own mint, and the most prosperous town north of Guadalajara. Following Mexican independence, control of the area fell into the hands of the Almada family who, despite having initially productive mines, spent most of the nineteenth century protecting their property from political wranglings and petty feuds, and watching over the region's decline. The mint closed in 1896, and even the brief existence of a railway only served to help depopulate a dying town – the ravages of the Revolution

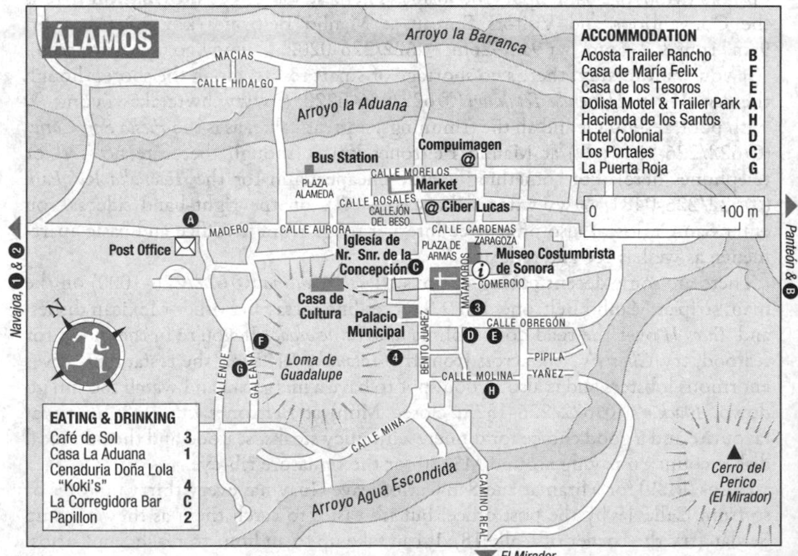

finished off what business was left. Álamos languished until the 1940s, when an American, **William Levant Alcorn**, bought numerous houses here and set about selling the property to his countryfolk. A bank was built in 1958 and an airstrip opened, and a paved road from Navojoa was finished two years later. Today the population hovers around the 10,000 mark.

Arrival and information

Hourly **buses** run to Álamos (6.30am–6.30pm; 1hr; M$26; ⓣ647/428-0096) from **NAVOJOA**, arriving at the bus station on Morelos at Plaza Alameda. Most long-distance buses heading north or south along the Hwy-15 corridor stop at Navojoa, pulling in at either the TBC and Transportes de Pacífico stations, around the junction of Guerrero and Calle No Reelección, or at the TAP/Elite bus station three blocks away. Local buses to Álamos leave from the TBC station.

In Álamos there is a **Bancomer**, with an ATM, across the Alameda on Rosales. Follow Rosales east, then Juárez south to reach the Plaza de Armas and the enthusiastic **tourist office** at Victoria 5 (daily 8am–7pm; ⓣ647/428-0450, ⓦwww.alamosmexico.com). The **post office** is on the approach into town, opposite the *Dolisa Motel and Trailer Park*. There are a few places with **internet** access; try Compuimagen, Morelos 37 (8am–9.30pm; M$8/hr), or Ciber Lucas, just off the plaza on the Callejón del Beso (8am–10pm; M$10/hr). **Moving on from Álamos**, there are frequent TBC buses back to Navojoa, from where you can pick up a variety of buses on the busy north–south coastal route; Los Mochis is just two hours south (M$100).

Accommodation

Low-cost accommodation in Álamos is hard to come by, but there are some enticing, moderately priced hacienda-style places with orchid-draped courtyards. You'll pay ten to twenty percent less outside the high season (Nov–April). The town also boasts two **trailer parks**, both offering some rooms: *Dolisa Motel and Trailer Park* (ⓣ647/428-0131, ⓔdolisa@prodigy.net.mx; ❹), Madero 72, a convenient though often crowded site at the entrance to town (open all year); and *Acosta Trailer Rancho*, about 1km east of town (Oct–April; ⓣ647/428-0246, ⓔranchoacosta@hotmail.com; ❹), a secluded park with camping spots and a pool. To get there, follow Morelos east across the usually dry Arroyo La Aduana, then turn left at the cemetery.

Casa de María Felix Galeana 41 ⓣ647/428-0929, ⓦwww.casademariafelix.com. This charming hotel occupies the birthplace of legendary Mexican actress María Felix (1914–2002), and features a small museum in her honour; most of the six suites, dressed in vivid pinks, greens and indigo, come with kitchens, fireplaces, internet and jacuzzi. ❺

Casa de los Tesoros Obregón 10, at Gutierrez ⓣ647/428-0400, ⓦwww.tesoros-hotel.com. This eighteenth-century former convent now has a pool and tastefully decorated rooms, a/c for summer, fireplace for winter; there's also live music in the restaurant every night. ❺

Hacienda de los Santos Molina 8 ⓣ647/428-0222, ⓦhaciendadelossantos.com. The best hotel in town, with gorgeous colonial architecture (carved out of three Spanish mansions and an eighteenth-century sugar mill), enhanced with modern amenities and antique furnishings in every room, tranquil gardens and a pool – the restaurant is also excellent. ❾

Hotel Colonial Obregón 4 ⓣ647/428-1371, ⓦwww.alamoshotelcolonial.com. This elegant American-owned hotel was built in 1875, one block from the plaza, and offers ten sumptuous rooms, all decorated with antiques and furniture from around the world. There's a restaurant and a pool. ❽

Los Portales Juárez, on the Plaza de Armas ⓣ647/428-0211. Splendid old hacienda dating from 1720, formerly owned by the Almada family (owners of the silver mines) and the first place to be restored by the Alcorns in 1948, with pleasant rooms around a broad stone courtyard, but no a/c or pool. ❺

La Puerta Roja Galeana 46 ⓣ647/428-0142, ⓦwww.lapuertarojainn.com. This fabulous B&B is a casual, flower-strewn affair run by Teri and Pat Shannon, with five cosy and highly distinctive rooms – check out the Pink Room. The aromas of the wonderful home-cooked breakfasts are a great wake-up call. ❻

The town and around

The town's focal point is the arcaded **Plaza de Armas** and elegant **Iglesia de Nuestra Señora de Concepción**, dating from 1786 – check out the graceful altar inside, with a silver and gold communion rail made in Oaxaca. The antique wrought-iron kiosk in the centre of the plaza is also worth a quick look, with surprisingly elaborate murals decorating its ceiling, created in Mazatlán. Opposite the kiosk on the east side of the plaza, the mildly diverting **Museo Costumbrista de Sonora** (Wed–Sun 10am–5pm; M$10) illustrates the town's zenith through a mock-up of La Quintera mine, coins from the old mint and grainy photos of moustachioed workers (all in Spanish). There's also a whole shrine-like section dedicated to acclaimed singer **Dr Alfonso Ortiz Tirado,** who was born in Álamos in 1893 – his sombrero is preserved along with photos.

From the plaza, the **Callejón del Beso** (Kissing Alley) isn't as narrow as the famous street in Guanajuato, but leads to the busy market (mostly fruit and meat). The **Palacio Municipal**, down Juárez from the plaza in the other direction, is an odd but striking red-brick affair from 1899, and you can also stroll up to the **Casa de Cultura** (Mon–Fri 8am–3pm; free), Loma Guadalupe, which houses a mix of art exhibitions and holds events in the old eighteenth-century stone jail, **El Cárcel**, with stellar views of the town. Take the side street at the Palacio Municipal, turn right at the end and climb the steps up the hill. You can also hike up to **El Mirador** south of the centre for the best vantage point in town (get directions from the tourist office), from where you can see all of Álamos and enthralling vistas of the surrounding Sierra Madre.

One of the most appealing aspects of Álamos is its magnificent old Andalucian-style **mansions**, brooding and shuttered from the outside, but enclosing beautiful flower-filled patios. If poking your head through gaping doorways and visiting the restaurants or bars of houses converted into swanky hotels doesn't satisfy your curiosity, you can take an hour-long **house tour** (Nov–April Sat 10am; US$10 or peso equivalent), which leaves from the museum on the plaza and visits three of the finest, predominantly American-owned, homes. You could also hire one of the informative, English-speaking **guides** who work at the tourist office (see p.149);

▲ Iglesia de Nuestra Señora de Concepción, Álamos

Hurtado Solis (aka "Joe") will show you around the town and inside a couple of the houses (M$100; 2hr), any day of the week.

Eating and drinking

Most of the top **restaurants** in Álamos are at the town's fancier hotels: particularly good are the ones at the *Casa de los Tesoros* and *Hacienda de los Santos*. Cheaper fare can be found outside the market and around the main plaza, where *raspados* sellers ply their wares, and locals line up for roaming taco stand *Fortino's* when it lands in front of the tourist office at weekends (from around 6–7pm).

Café de Sol Obregón 3 ⓣ647/428 0466. Take a break from Mexican fare at this bright café around a courtyard, serving healthy breakfasts (M$50–66) and lunches, as well as hamburgers (M$55), tostadas (M$45) and frappucinos (M$25). Main dishes M$65–80. Tues–Sun 7.30am–6pm.

Casa La Aduana La Aduana ⓣ647/404-3473, ⓦwww.casaladuana.com. If you have transport, it's worth making reservations at this isolated restaurant and inn, 3km on a dirt road off the main Álamos highway. Housed in a romantic adobe building dating from the 1630s, the restaurant does a superb fixed-price menu (M$170–280) of "new Sonoran cuisine" highlighting local produce: dishes like chicken in apple, *chipotle* and cream, and *shrimps al ajillo*. Wed–Sun 1–7.30pm.

Cenaduria Doña Lola "Koki's" Volantín, behind the Palacio Municipal. Popular local diner, serving excellent home-cooked Mexican classics for under M$45. Open for dinner only 6pm–midnight.

La Corregidora Bar Juárez 6, Plaza de Armas (at *Hotel Los Portales*). Atmospheric old bar and the best spot to people-watch on the plaza. Has pool table, big-screen TV and karaoke. Tues–Sun 4pm–2am.

Papillon Madero 74 ⓣ647/428-1387. Located on the main road into town (near the hospital), this is a fine dining alternative to the hotels, especially good for steaks and ribs, but also decent Mexican fare and drinks.

Into Sinaloa

Beyond Navojoa, Hwy-15 maintains its southbound course, soon crossing the state line into **Sinaloa**. The next place of any size is **Los Mochis**, an uninteresting destination in itself, but as the western terminus of the Copper Canyon railway, an important transport hub. There are plenty of places to stay in Los Mochis should you need to spend a night, but many train passengers prefer to head inland to **El Fuerte**, a tranquil colonial backwater some two hours east. Back on Hwy-15, the prosperous city of **Culiacán** lies about 200km south of Los Mochis. Though it's the state capital, you'll find little to do here and it's been known as "narco city" for its role in the illegal drug trade since the 1950s – most travellers choose to press on to the resort of Mazatlán. Note that Sinaloa is one hour ahead of Sonora in the summer (April–Oct), as the latter does not observe daylight savings.

Los Mochis

The modern agricultural centre of **LOS MOCHIS** is a relatively new creation by Mexican standards, its origins going back to the establishment of a utopian colony on Topolobampo Bay in 1881, led by American socialist Albert Kimsey Owen. The colony was abandoned in the early 1900s, and Los Mochis really owes its existence to the Sinaloa Sugar Company, a US-owned monolith that was established by Benjamin Johnston in the 1890s (the founder and his wife are commemorated with reverential portraits in the lobby of *Hotel Santa Anita*). The town grew up around the extensive company works, and today it's a broad-streeted, prosperous, but rather dull place with few attractions, notable only as a major crossing point for road, rail and ferry, and above all the western terminus of the incomparable **Copper Canyon railway** (see p.157). If you're planning to take the ferry or train you'll have

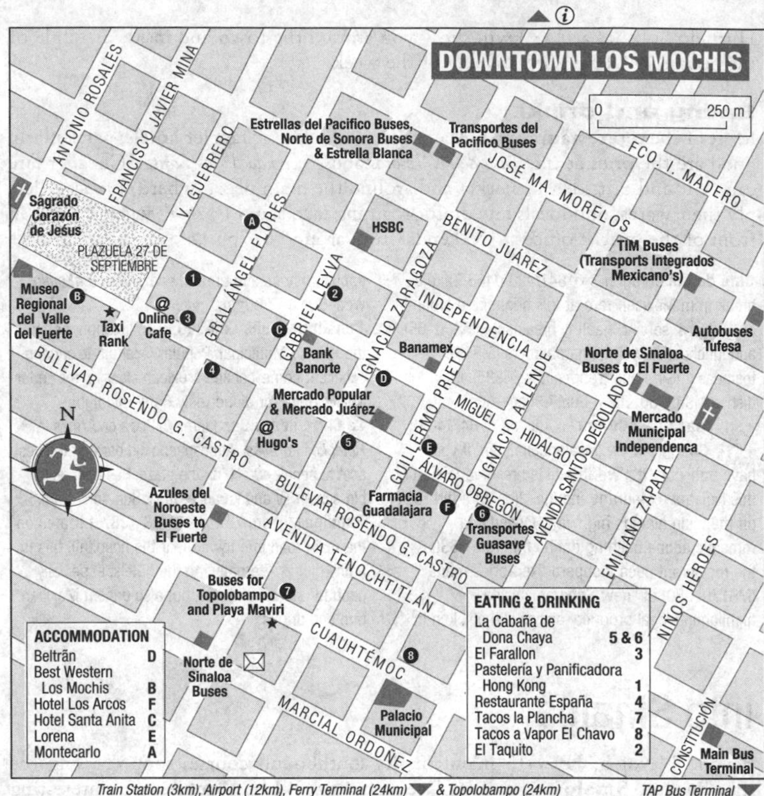

little choice but to stay at least one night here – don't expect much excitement. The sweltering grid of streets that makes up Los Mochis has no real focus, but what there is of a **town centre** is on Hidalgo and Obregón, between Allende and Leyva.

Arrival and information

The main first-class **bus station**, serving Elite, Futura and Transportes Chihuahuenses, is at Castro and Constitución, south of the centre, while TAP has its own plush terminal just south of here. Estrella del Pacifico, Norte de Sonora and Transportes del Pacifico have terminals on Morelos between Zaragoza and Leyva, while first-class Tufesa is at Zapata between Juárez and Morelos. Second-class Norte de Sinaloa is at Zaragoza and Ordonez. All of these stations are within walking distance of most downtown hotels and restaurants. **Taxis** will charge M$50 from most bus stations for trips around the centre.

The **Federal del Valle del Fuerte International Airport** is southwest of town off the Topolobampo highway at km 12.5. Taxis should be around M$175, but fix the price first. The La Paz **ferry**, meanwhile, arrives at **TOPOLOBAMPO** itself, 24km south. Local buses ply back and forth, terminating at Cuauhtémoc in Los Mochis, between Zaragoza and Prieta (M$15), or you can take a taxi (no more than M$200). The **train station** is 3km southeast of the centre; although there are frequent buses (M$5) during the day, you can't rely on them to meet the late-evening arrival of trains from Chihuahua. While you should be charged around M$70 for a **taxi** ride from the station into town, you might have a struggle to get this price.

Despite the number of visitors who come through Los Mochis on the way to the Copper Canyon, there are few concessions to tourism, and the **tourist office** (Mon–Fri 9am–4pm; ⓣ668/812-1336, ⓦwww.vivesinaloa.com) is inconveniently located at Edificio San Isidro, Zaragoza 444, a long walk north of Obregón.

Accommodation

Given that the only reason most people come here is to overnight before taking the train, your **hotel** options in Los Mochis are fairly limited, and the best hotels regularly fill up – book ahead.

Beltrán Hidalgo and Zaragoza ⓣ668/812-0688, ⓦwww.losmochishotel.com. Clean, comfortable rooms, all with a/c and en-suite bathrooms. Tidy, professional and efficient, if uninspiring. ❸

Best Western Los Mochis Obregón 691 ⓣ668/816-3000, ⓦwww.bestwestern.com. The town's best hotel is regularly packed out with tour groups, offering smart but standard chain fare right on the main plaza, 1km from the main bus station. The restaurant does a decent buffet for M$75 on Mon. ❻

Hotel Los Arcos Allende 534 Sur ⓣ668/817-1424. This is the cheapest option in town, although it's not the friendliest or most comfortable place – last resort only. ❶

Hotel Santa Anita Leyva and Hidalgo ⓣ668/818-7046, ⓦwww.mexicoscoppercanyon.com. This is the second luxury option in town, owned by the same people who operate many of the fancier lodges along the Copper Canyon rail line. Rooms are comfy, with cable TV, free wi-fi and a mountainous breakfast buffet (extra). There's also a rather expensive restaurant, a bar and a travel agency. They often fill up with tour groups in the high season. ❻

Lorena Obregón, at the corner of Prieto ⓣ668/812-0239, ⓦwww.hotellorena.com.mx. The fifty mid-sized rooms at this hotel have a/c and TV, and if you ask nicely they will fix you a lunch for the train ride. There's also a good, cheap restaurant upstairs. ❹

Montecarlo Flores at Independencia ⓣ668/812-1818, ⓔsinaloanorte@infosel.net.mx. The plain, clean rooms here are set around a colonial-style courtyard. Make sure you get one of the larger rooms – their rooms vary in size, but not in price. ❷

Eating

Eating in Los Mochis is not particularly exciting, but there are plenty of cheap and cheerful taco stalls and basic restaurants in the centre, and a couple of smarter places. The **Mercado Municipal Independencia** on Independencia between Zapata and Degollado has a handful of cheap *loncherías* in the northwest corner, serving *comidas* for under M$40. Most restaurants close relatively early, but you'll find plenty of US fast-food chains (many open 24hr) on the outskirts, if you get desperate (head down Obregón beyond Plazuela 27 de Septiembre).

La Cabaña de Dona Chaya corner of Obregón and Allende. This basic diner, established in the 1960s, specializes in tacos *carne asada* or tacos *moreno* (dried beef), with quesadilla versions of both (M$23–30); you get a lot of succulent meat for the price, but the salsas are not as fresh as on the street stalls. There's a second branch on Zaragoza and Obregón (this is more famous for roast chicken, M$150 for two).

El Farallon corner of Obregón and Flores ⓣ668/812-1273, ⓦrestaurantelfarallon.com. Founded in 1961, this is still the best restaurant in Los Mochis with an intriguing and delicious seafood menu (fish fillet cooked in numerous ways), and *Sinaloenses* classics. Mains from around M$120.

Pastelería y Panificadora Hong Kong Hidalgo 569 ⓣ668/812-2737. Not a Chinese restaurant but a local bakery chain selling delicious pastries, cakes and bread. The name is just a gimmick.

Restaurante España Obregón 525 ⓣ668/812-2335. This reliable Mexican-Spanish restaurant has international pretensions and prices to match, though the M$75 breakfast buffet is good value, and it knocks out decent paella (mains average M$100).

Tacos la Plancha Cuauhtémoc between Zaragoza and Prieto. This bargain stall cooks up huge plates of five *tacos al pastor* for M$16, with salsa, guacamole and all the works. Open later than most stalls, with a few plastic tables and chairs under the nearby trees.

Tacos a Vapor El Chavo Cuauhtémoc and Allende ⓣ668/815-68 16, ⓦwww.tacoselchavo.com. This venerable stall has a chequered history that goes back to the early 1960s (charted on its own website, no less). It is the best place to grab

Moving on from Los Mochis

By bus

The most comfortable **buses** depart from the main first-class station on Castro and Constitución (☎668/812-5749) and the TAP terminal behind it, but there are also several second-class terminals scattered around town (see p.152). First-class buses cost around M$340 to **Mazatlán** (6hr), M$885 to **Mexico City** (19hr), M$635 to **Guadalajara** (12hr), M$95 to **Navojoa** (2hr), M$200 to **Guaymas** (5hr), M$280 to **Hermosillo** (7hr), and M$810 to **Tijuana** (21hr). For **Álamos**, take a first-class bus to Navajoa and change there. Buses to **El Fuerte** (2hr) are supplied by two competing services, both costing M$60 and departing roughly every hour (usually with a/c but no toilets): Azules del Noreste runs from the terminal on Leyva at Tenochtitlán, while Norte de Sinaloa leaves from the small station inside the Mercado Independencia, at Independencia and Degollado.

By train

The only way to get to Chihuahua from Los Mochis is by train, cutting through the awe-inspiring Copper Canyon (see opposite). Both trains are relatively expensive compared to bus travel, but take second-class if you want to save money – it's not as rough as travel agents make out. The Primera (or Estrella, Vista or plain no. 73) leaves for Chihuahua daily at 6am (scheduled to arrive at Creel 4.10pm, Chihuahua 9.30pm) and the second-class Económica (or Mixto or no. 75) leaves at 7am on Tuesday, Friday and Sunday (scheduled to arrive at Creel 6pm, Chihuahua 11.40pm), though they are usually subject to delays en route, especially on the second-class service. Fares on the Primera are currently M$1083 to Creel and M$1981 to Chihuahua; on the second class train it costs M$542 to Creel and M$991 to Chihuahua. The **ticket office** at the station opens at 5am for same-day sales for both trains; tickets for the *Primera* can also be bought the previous day at Viajes Flamingo (☎668/812-1613, Ⓦwww.mexicoscoppercanyon.com), in the *Hotel Santa Anita* in town (see p.153), or direct from Ferrocarril Chihuahua Pacifico (☎614/439-7212, Ⓦwww.chepe.com.mx).

If you want to take a city bus to the station (M$5), ask your hotel for the closest stop; you should allow at least an hour to get there in time. If you're aiming to catch the 6am train, try to gather a group of people and arrange in advance for a driver to pick you up – taking the bus at this time is a little risky time-wise. Normally, though, taxis are easy enough to find, especially around the bus stations and *Hotel Santa Anita* – the latter also lays on a minibus to the station for guests (5.15am; M$50). Taxis are around M$70.

By air

The **airport** (☎668/818-68-70) at Los Mochis is surprisingly well-connected; Aeroméxico currently offers the only international flight, to San Francisco, but also flies to Guadalajara, Hermosillo, Mazatlán, Mexico City and Tijuana. InterJet flies to Mexico City, while Viva Aerobus goes to Guadalajara. Aéreo Servicio Guerrero and Aéreo Calafia offer useful connections across to Baja California, and Mexicana also flies to the capital. Taxis to the airport should be around M$175.

By ferry

Current Baja Ferries (Ⓦwww.bajaferries.com) departures for the six-hour **crossing to La Paz** from Topolobampo are daily at 5pm; you can buy tickets as you board, but as ever it's safest to purchase tickets and **check the timetable** in advance. Tickets cost M$1065 for a reclining seat, an additional M$760 for a cabin and over M$2000 for a small car; they can be bought at their office at Plaza Encuentro, Centenario and Rosales (daily 9am–5pm; ☎668/818-6893), or at their offices at Topolobampo port (daily 9am–11pm; ☎668/862-1003). Buses (M$15) for the forty-minute journey to Topolobampo operate every fifteen minutes from Cuauhtémoc and Prieto (Mon–Sat), and Cuahtémoc and Allende (Sun).

cheap and tasty *tacos a vapor*, smothered in rich sauce – closes by early afternoon. Tacos just M$4–7.
El Taquito Leyva at Barrera, near the *Hotel Santa Anita* ⓣ 668/812-8119. No-frills canteen with formica tables and cheap Mexican food (*comida* from M$50); though on the bland side, it's clean, safe and open 24hr.

Listings

Banks and exchange There's a Banamex with an ATM (Mon–Fri until 2pm) at the corner of Prieto and Hidalgo.
Internet access Try Hugo's Internet, just past Obregón on Leyva (Mon–Fri 9am–7.30pm, Sat 9am–6.30pm; M$12/hr), or Online Café Internet (Mon–Sat 9am–8pm) at Obregón near *Hotel Corintios* at Obregón 580 (at Guerrero).
Post office Ordoñez 226 between Zaragoza and Prieto (Mon–Fri 9am–2pm & 4–6pm, Sat 9am–1pm).

The Copper Canyon

The 653-kilometre, fourteen-hour **train trip** that starts on the sweaty Pacific coast at Los Mochis, fights its way up to cross the Continental Divide amidst the peaks of the Sierra Madre Occidental, then drifts down across the high plains of Chihuahua, is one of the world's most extraordinary rail journeys. Mesmerizing views come thick and fast as the line hangs over the vast canyons of the **Río Urique** and its tributaries, with jagged peaks smothered in dense forest, and narrow, precipitous gorges falling away on both sides. Somewhat confusingly, this region of over eleven major canyons is collectively dubbed the Barrancas del Cobre (or Copper Canyon System) – the actual **Barranca del Cobre** usually refers to the northern valley of the Río Urique. The main gorges boast depths of more than 2000m, and if you include the whole area the Grand Canyon is a midget by comparison.

Scenically, however, there's no comparison with the great canyons of the southwestern US, and if you've visited them you may find the canyons here a little disappointing. Part of the difficulty is in getting a true sense of their size and beauty: though the train cuts across some spectacular valleys, you only get a glimpse of the actual **Barranca del Cobre** once, at **Divisadero**. The line only brushes the northern edge of the Parque Nacional Barranca del Cobre, which is hard to access: there are no well-marked hiking tracks and official campsites, and serious hikers need to devote the best part of a week to their endeavours. Creel makes a sensible base from which to organize further exploration.

Even when the bare mountain peaks here are snow-covered, the climate on the canyon floors is semitropical – a fact that the indigenous **Rarámuri** (also known, incorrectly, as the Tarahumara), depend on, migrating in winter to the warmth of the deep canyons. The Rarámuri, who were driven here after the Spanish Conquest and whose population now totals some 60,000, live in isolated communities along the rail line and in the surrounding Sierra Tarahumara, eking out an existence from the sparse patches of cultivatable land. Although their isolation is increasingly encroached upon by commercial forestry interests, ranchers and growing numbers of travellers, they remain an independent people, close to their traditions. Despite centuries of missionary work, their religious life embraces only token aspects of Catholicism and otherwise remains true to its animist roots, their chief deities being the gods of the sun, moon and rain. Above all, the tribe is renowned for running: a common feature of local festivals are the **foot races** between villages that last at least one day and sometimes several on end, with the runners kicking a wooden ball ahead of them as they go (Norogachi is one of the best places to see this, see p.166).

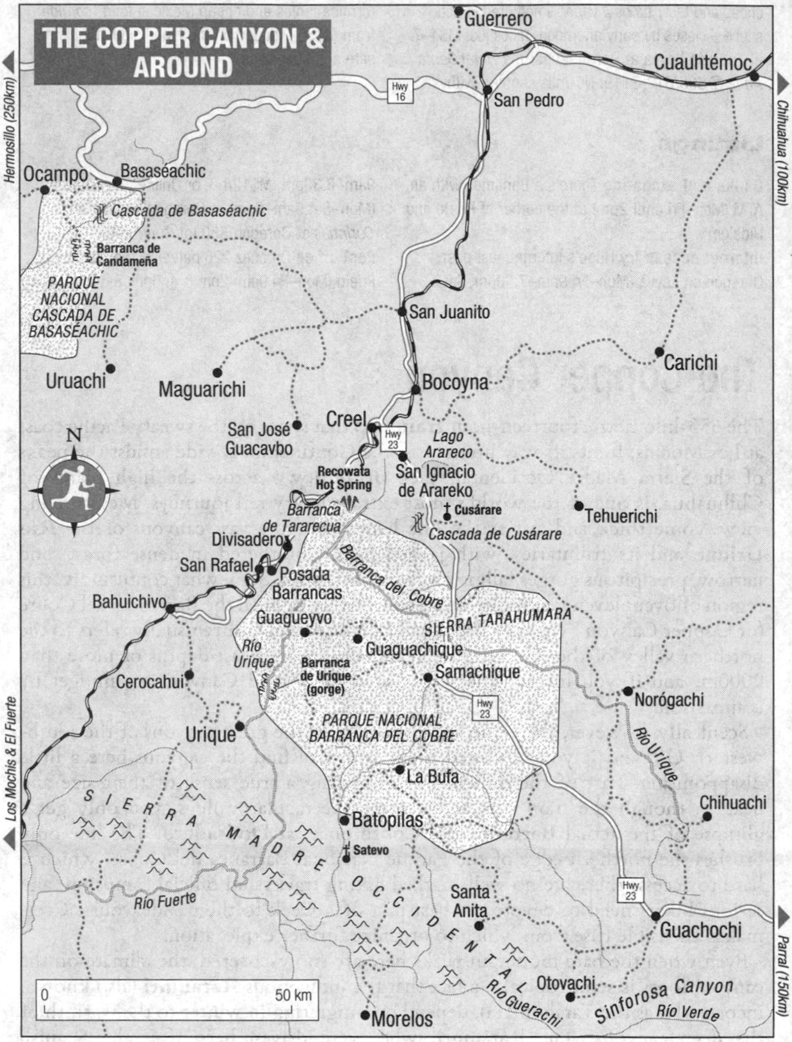

THE COPPER CANYON & AROUND

The train route

If you're travelling *clase económica*, the train timetable (see box, p.158) more or less dictates that you tackle the journey eastbound from the coast to the mountains; otherwise, you may well find yourself travelling along the most dramatic stretch of the line in the dark. Travelling first class it doesn't make a lot of difference. From Los Mochis (see p.151) or El Fuerte (p.158), the start of the journey is an inauspicious grind across the humid coastal plain, with passengers in the first-class, air-conditioned train settling back in their reclining seats while the economy train passengers just sweat. The first-class cosseting becomes less of a benefit as the line breaks into the mountains and you start climbing into ever-cooler air (at least in winter – summer days are still burning hot up here). It was this section of the route that defeated the original builders, and, from the passenger's point of view, the bit you've been waiting for. For six hours, the train zigzags dizzily upwards, clinging to the canyon wall, rocketing across bridges, plunging into tunnels, only to find itself constantly just a few metres above the track it covered twenty minutes earlier. Eventually, you arrive at **Divisadero**, where there's a halt of about fifteen minutes to marvel at the view of the Copper Canyon itself. At first it seems a perverse choice for a stop, with nothing around but the mountaintops and crowds of Rarámuri hawking their crafts and delicious gorditas. But walk a little way down the path and you're suddenly standing on the edge of space, on the lip of a vast chasm. Below you are the depths of the **Barranca del Cobre** and, adjoining it, the **Barranca de Urique** and the **Barranca de Tararecua**. There are a couple of absurdly expensive places to stay here and a few bare-bones cheaper ones as well, but for most people it's all too rapidly back on the train, which clanks on for an hour to **Creel**, just past the halfway stage and, at 2330m, close to the highest point of the line (note, though, after Divisadero the scenery is far less scintillating). This is the place to stop if you want seriously to explore the **Sierra Tarahumara** and the canyons.

From Creel, the train takes a further six hours to reach Chihuahua – though beautiful, it's not a truly spectacular run. In fact, if the train timetable doesn't suit, there's no reason why you shouldn't take the **bus** from Creel to Chihuahua: it's cheaper than even the second-class train fare, is quicker and covers much the same ground.

Rail practicalities

The Copper Canyon line is operated by the Ferrocarril de Chihuahua al Pacífico (CHP), from which the train derives its affectionate nickname, "El Chepe". There are two daily services running in each direction: the first-class **Primera** (also known as *Estrella*), which is primarily a tourist service, and the second-class **Económica** (also known as *Mixto*), half the price but considerably slower and less comfortable. The *Primera* service has air-conditioning and reserved, reclining seats, while the *Económica* tends to run late – on the other hand, the views are the same from either train, and if you'd rather squeeze up with the locals, you'll save a lot of cash and practise more Spanish on the second-class service.

Tickets for the *Económica* can only be bought from the station on the morning of departure, but *Primera* tickets can be pre-booked one week in advance either at the station (Los Mochis: Mon–Fri 5–7am & 9am–5.30pm, Sat 5–7am & 10am–12.30pm, Sun 5–7am & 8–10am; Chihuahua: Mon–Fri 5–7am & 10am–5.30pm, Sat 5–7am & 9am–12.30pm, Sun 5–7am), from travel agents (see *Hotel Santa Anita* in Los Mochis), or from Ferrocarril Mexicano direct (Ⓣ614/439-7212, Ⓦwww.chepe.com.mx). Reserve early to be sure of a first-class seat, especially from May to September and during Semana Santa. **Prices** for the whole journey from Los Mochis to Chihuahua have risen dramatically in the past few years – to nearly M$854 on the *Económica* and about M$1708 on the *Primera* (M$934 to Creel). It's advisable to break up the journey, not only to get the most out of it, but also because the trip, even travelling first class, can become very tedious either side of the dramatic central section. Section costs are based on a per-kilometre rate, so you'll pay hardly any more no matter how often you break the journey.

You'll save money by taking along your own **food and drink**; though technically you are not allowed to eat in first-class cars, snacks are generally tolerated. It's not essential in any case; meals, snacks and drinks are available on the train (though not cheaply), and throughout the journey people stand on the platforms selling tacos, *chiles rellenos*, fresh fruit, hot coffee and whatever local produce comes to hand.

The CHP timetable

Currently the *Primera* and *Económica* travel daily in both directions, but always check to see if the service is running. The official **times** below are not entirely reliable, and trains (particularly the *Económica*) frequently run some hours late. The *Primera* train is rarely, if ever, on time to connect with the La Paz ferry in Los Mochis.

	Primera (no.73)		*Económica* (no.75)	
Los Mochis	6am	9.30pm	7am	11.30pm
El Fuerte	8.50am	6.45pm	9.42am	8.40pm
Bahuichivo	12.55pm	2.45pm	2.40pm	4.25pm
Divisadero	2.40pm	1pm	4.15pm	2.28pm
Creel	4.10pm	11.25am	5.53pm	12.55pm
Cuauhtémoc	7.10pm	8.25am	9.11pm	9.39am
Chihuahua	9.30pm	6am	11.40pm	7am

El Fuerte

Founded in the sixteenth century, **EL FUERTE** is a tranquil, verdant town full of handsome colonial architecture and lush mango trees. In the 1800s it became rich from mining, and was made a city in 1906; the Revolution devastated the place and it's been a backwater ever since. In 2009 the town became the latest addition to Mexico's burgeoning *Pueblos Mágicos* programme, and a frenzy of publicly funded restoration and regeneration has engulfed the centre. Located 75km east of Los Mochis on the rail line (2hr 50min by train), El Fuerte makes a pleasant alternative start (or end) to the Copper Canyon train ride, and is a far more appealing place to stay than Los Mochis.

Aside from being "the gateway to the canyons", the town is an attractive destination in itself, rich in historical and natural diversions. El Fuerte grew up around a Spanish **fort** (from which it takes its name) completed in 1615 to suppress the local rebellious tribes. Though the original has been lost, a reasonably authentic replica was completed in 2001 on its possible location, supplying commanding views of the streets and surrounding countryside. It houses the **El Fuerte Mirador Museum** (Tues–Sun 9am–5pm; M$5), where you'll find an array of historical artefacts and old photos of the town, with mostly English labelling.

Over 150 species of **birds** are supported by El Fuerte's green surroundings, best seen by boat at dawn when their activity is most intense. The region is also home to several indigenous **Yoreme** (Mayo) villages, where it is possible to witness traditional dances or purchase pottery and other crafts. Ancient Indian **petroglyphs** depicting geometric and anthropomorphic shapes are scattered throughout the area, most notably at the Cerro de la Máscara. Most hotels offer tours to any or all of these attractions; ask at the popular *Posada del Hidalgo* or *Hotel Río Vista* (see opposite), or enquire at *3 Amigos Too*.

Arrival and information

The town centre is small and easy to navigate, being focused on the main plaza, with the Río Fuerte and old fort to the south. The **train station** is a few kilometres out of town, and you'll need to arrange transport if you hope to catch the morning train to Chihuahua or Creel – the pricier hotels should do this for you, but otherwise you should scout around for a taxi near the plaza or market (around M$100). Note that there are no buses to either Creel or Chihuahua from here. **Buses** from Los Mochis (see p.151) arrive and depart frequently at Juárez (until 7pm), next to the town market, where you'll find **banks** with ATMs and the main plaza a couple of blocks away.

The **post office** (Mon–Fri 8am–4pm) is inside the Palacio Municipal on 5 de Mayo. The best place for information and maps is **3 Amigos Too** (Mon–Fri 8am–5pm; ⓣ698/893-5028, ⓦwww.amigos3.com), along the river three blocks from the plaza at Reforma 100 – follow the signs (the "Amigo Trail") from the plaza. They also rent kayaks (M$350/day), run guided kayak trips (from M$400), rent bikes (M$160/day) and run tours down the El Fuerte River with a petroglyphs hike (from M$300). You can check the **internet** at *Urias Ciber Café*, Juárez 103 (Mon–Sat 8am–8pm, Sun 9am–3pm; M$10/hr).

Accommodation

Hotel La Choza 5 de Mayo 101 ⓣ698/893-12-74, ⓦwww.hotellachoza.com. Charming, mid-range option, with 32 a/c rooms simply decorated with tiled floors and colourful bedspreads – you get TV, a gorgeous little pool and decent restaurant on site. ❺

Hotel El Fuerte Monteclaros 37 ⓣ698/893-0226, ⓦwww.hotelelfuerte.com.mx. A beautiful 300-year-old hacienda once owned by the wealthy Ibarra family, with exquisite rooms and a jacuzzi fed by illuminated waterfalls. Loads of colour, elegance and style make this the best luxury hotel in town. ❺

Hotel Río Vista Cerro de las Pilas ⓣ698/893-0413, ⓦwww.hotelriovista.com.mx. Housed in the old fort stables, this pleasant hotel has excellent views over the Río Fuerte and is popular with bird watchers. There's the *Mirador* restaurant, a cooling-off pool and lots of rustic antiques. ❹

Posada del Hidalgo Hidalgo 101 ⓣ698/893-0242, ⓦwww.hotelposadadelhidalgo.com. First-class service is provided by a small army of staff in this grand old hotel, the former 1890 home of the Almada family. There are spa facilities, a restaurant, pool and plenty of quiet, leafy patios. ❼

Posada Don Porfirio Juárez 104 ⓣ698/893-0044, ⓦwww.posadadonporfirio.com.mx. Best budget option in town (with one M$300 room), a tranquil hotel with clean, bright a/c rooms and a shady courtyard slung with hammocks. Ask the owners for a copy of *Legends of the City*, a small booklet that tells the history of El Fuerte. ❹

Torres del Fuerte Robles 102 ⓣ698/893-1974, ⓦwww.hotelestorres.com. Gorgeous old hotel that drips with colonial charm: lavish period rooms come with marble floors, stone sinks, rugs and Mudéjar -influenced antiques, but with modern amenities – the patio bar and gardens are a great place to relax. ❼

Eating and drinking

Eating options are as yet fairly uninspiring in El Fuerte – the whole scene is set to change with the new *mágico* status of the town, hopefully for the better. Cheap *comedores*, **restaurants** and taco stands can be found on Juárez, close to the market. If you want to sample the town's culinary specialities, which include *lobina* (black bass) and *cauque* (crayfish), there are several decent upmarket restaurants, mostly in the pricier hotels.

Asadero Mi Casita Robles and Zaragoza (no phone). Locals flock here for the fabulous *papa asada*, roast potatoes with barbecued beef, cheese and salsas. Mexican dishes for less than M$50. Wed–Mon 6pm–1am.

Mesón del General Juárez 202 ⓣ698/893-0260. Relatively economical option serving a range of seafood (including *lobina*) and steak dishes in a charming old courtyard and mansion, enhanced by plants and murals. Mains average around M$80.

Restaurant Diligencias *Hotel La Choza* (see above) ⓣ698/893-12-74. For a posh meal and the best bar in town head to *La Choza* on 5 de Mayo, where delectable local delicacies (including the ubiquitous *lobina* and crayfish) are served in a bright, friendly dining room. Expect to pay around M$400 to M$500 for dinner for two.

El Supremo Constitución and Rosales. For unpretentious, reasonably priced home-cooked fare, head to this local diner – it looks a bit dark and dingy from the outside, but the food is good (M$40–100).

Cerocahui and Urique

Four hours beyond El Fuerte, the first place worth considering as a base in the mountains is the minuscule town of **CEROCAHUI**, accessed from the station at **Bahuichivo** (7hr and M$662 from Los Mochis, and 10km by road from Cerocahui). Very much in the formative stages of tourist development, Cerocahui gives access to the **Urique** canyon system and a range of attractions including overlooks, waterfalls and disused mines. The four-hour drive from Cerocahui to the bottom of the canyon is stunning, and the town of **URIQUE** at its conclusion marks the start (or end) of the popular two-day trek to Batopilas (see p.165). At Urique, rather lovely and economical accommodation can be had at the Munos-family run *San Isidro Lodge* (ⓣ635/456-5257, ⓦwww.coppercanyonamigos.com; ❻), who have ties to the local Rarámuri, while more pricey and luxurious quarters can be found in Cerocahui at the *Hotel Misión* (ⓣ635/456-0294, ⓦwww.hotelmision.com; ❼). Both hotels provide tours and will collect you from Bahuichivo station.

Divisadero

Around 50km east of Cerocahui lies **DIVISADERO**, where the train pauses for fifteen minutes for the mind-blowing "one-hundred-mile" view of the canyons – this is the closest you'll get to that Grand Canyon-like panorama, at least on the rail line. The platform is smothered in snack stalls, most of them selling variations of gorditas – absolutely scrumptious and crammed with a variety of home-made fillings, chilis, beans and cheeses. The most popular stalls are *Gorditas Doña Esther* and *Antojitos Lucy* (both charge M$20 per gordita). A slightly bizarre, carnival atmosphere pervades when the train arrives, with Rarámuri children begging for change, mariachi singers serenading snack eaters and trinket stalls lining the steps down to the *mirador* – munch your gorditas at the latter to soak up the mesmerizing views (finish them before you reboard).

Practicalities

Several **buses** a day run to Creel from Divisadero (1hr; M$50), the last one passing through at about 4pm; it's always worth checking the schedule for changes, though, so you don't get stuck.

If you decide to break your journey here, you'll find some stunning but rather over-priced accommodation near the station, and more options 5km southwest near the **Posada Barrancas** station, which serves the sleepy village of Areponápuchi. The *Cabañas Díaz* at Posada Barrancas (ⓣ635/578-3008; ❸ shared bath; ❹ bath) is a congenial family-run inn with economical, cosy rooms equipped with fireplaces, and amazing home-cooked meals (from M$70) served in the Díaz family kitchen – they keep several friendly dogs, can arrange all manner of guided trips (on foot or horseback), and will drop you off in Divisadero for free. The *Hotel Mansión Tarahumara* also in Posada Barrancas (ⓣ614/415-4721, ⓦwww.lasierratarahumara.com.mx; ❼) is a rather surreal and pricey hotel resembling a fairy-tale castle (it's known as *El Castillo*); the Alpine-style cabins are clean and bright, but only the new rooms have the stunning canyon views. Steps away from Divisadero station, and perched right on the edge of the canyon, the *Hotel Divisadero Barrancas* (ⓣ614/415-1199, ⓦwww.hoteldivisadero.com; ❾) is a tour-group favourite featuring spacious rooms with wood-beam ceilings, most with spectacular views of the gorges – only some have balconies, though, so always ask when you make a reservation. Rates at least include three meals and a couple of walking tours.

Creel and the Sierra Tarahumara

Once nothing more than a rough-and-ready backwater, **CREEL** has rapidly transformed into full-blown mountain resort. Indeed, Creel is yet another "*pueblo mágico*" and has seen tourism all but replace logging as its main industry; on most days (but especially Sundays) you'll be greeted by a weird juxtaposition of laid-back Western backpackers, smartly dressed locals, rich Mexican tourists in their 4WDs and ragged Rarámuri trinket sellers and their children, trying to make a buck or two. In July and August the town is invaded by Mexican tour groups – the best hotels often get completely booked up at this time. This is not to say that the town has become completely commercial; beneath the facade of development, Creel is still a rural mountain town at heart, and an ideal base from which to explore the area.

There isn't much to do in Creel itself, other than enjoy the refreshing, pine-scented mountain air, though the **Museo de la Casa de las Artesanías** across the rail tracks from the plaza (Mon–Sat 9am–7pm, Sun 9am–1pm; M$10) is certainly worth a visit. It contains displays on Rarámuri culture that give intriguing insights into their archaic philosophy, most notably with a series of black and white photos revealing their vivid ceremonial and religious life. If you're in the market for handicrafts, the Jesuit mission shop **Artesanías Misión**, right on the plaza (Mon–Sat 9am–1pm & 3–6pm, Sun 9.30am–1pm), has a host of wares including blankets, baskets, dolls, drums and violins; their products lack the vibrancy of other Mexican crafts, but make up for it with rustic charm.

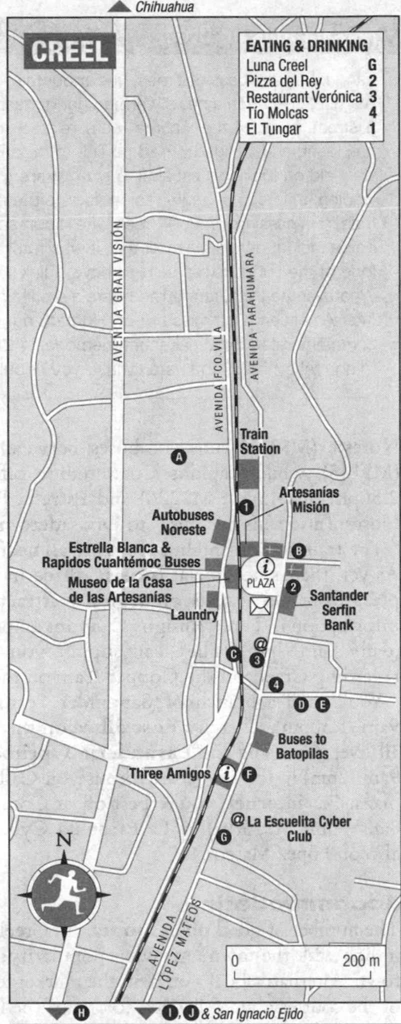

ACCOMMODATION			
Casa Margarita's	B	Nuevo Barrancas del Cobre	A
Complejo Eco-Turístico Arareko	J	Parador de la Montaña Hotel	F
Hotel Margarita's Plaza Mexicana	D	La Posada de Creel	C
Hotel Los Valles	E	Sierra Bonita	H
The Lodge at Creel	G	Villa Mexicana Creel Mountain Lodge	I

Arrival and information

The train is obviously the way to **arrive** but, wonderful though it is, the vagaries of the timetable may induce you to catch one of the frequent daily buses that run between Creel and Chihuahua (4hr 30min). Three companies offer services:

Masacradas en Creel

Languid at the best of times, the mountain calm of Creel was brutally shattered in August 2008 when a heavily armed gang massacred thirteen locals as they chatted on a street. Most of the victims were related to Eliseo Loya Ochoa, Creel's sectional president, and (allegedly) had no link to organized crime. One was just a baby. Blame was laid on Mexico's escalating **drug wars** (p.187). None of the culprits was caught, leading hundreds of angry residents to protest and, for a few hours at least, block the train from passing through Creel. One report suggested the killings were linked to illegal horse racing; others claimed that it was retribution for a hit a couple of weeks before (one of the thirteen was said to have a link to the group that carried out that killing). Whatever the truth, family members are still fighting for justice (taking their case to the Inter-American Commission of Human rights in 2009) and the *masacrados* are commemorated by a makeshift memorial in Chihuahua (see p.195). Things were back to normal by 2009, and as a tourist, you should have nothing to worry about.

Noreste (M$215) runs six buses between 6.45am and 5pm via Cuauhtémoc (M$145), while Rapidos Cuauhtémoc offers four services (6.30am, 12.40pm, 2.50pm & 4.45pm; M$226) and Estrella Blanca just two (8.45am & 11.15am). Noreste also runs five buses to Divisadero from 10.30am to 6.50pm (M$50).

The train station and bus stops are all near the main plaza in the centre of town. As yet, there's no official **tourist office** in Creel, though the small kiosk on the plaza dispenses leaflets on regional attractions. The best place to go for local information is Three Amigos Canyons Expeditions (see p.162), López Mateos 46 (daily 9am–7pm). They can supply you with maps, information and advice regarding Creel and the Copper Canyon more generally.

You'll find a branch of Santander Serfín **bank** on López Mateos (Mon–Fri 9am–1.30pm). There's a **post office** on the main plaza, long-distance **telephones** all over town and the **Lavandería Optima** (Mon–Fri 9am–2pm & 3–6pm, Sat 9am–2pm) in the two-storey house on Calle Villa, across the rail tracks from the plaza. For **internet**, you're best off at Compucenter, López Mateos 33 (Mon–Sat 8am–9pm; M$15/hr) or La Escuelita Cyber Club (daily 8am–10pm; M$15/hr), also on López Mateos.

Accommodation

The number of good **places to stay** in Creel grows every year, and prices are rising in line with the town's growing popularity; the cheaper places are on the edge of town. Alternatively, if you're in the market for something luxurious, take advantage of the courtesy buses that run to one of the **lodges** out in the nearby countryside.

Casa Margarita's López Mateos and Parroquia 11 ⓣ635/456-0045, ⓦcasamargaritas.tripod.com. A Creel institution and the place for backpackers to meet, *Margarita's* services run the gamut from tour guides to laundry. Breakfast and supper is included. Dorms (M$70) and rooms with bathroom. ❸

Complejo Eco-Turístico Arareko Carr Creel–Guachochi km 7 ⓣ635/456-0126, ⓦwww.sanignacioarareko.tripod.com. If you fancy staying in more natural surroundings, this Rarámuri-run accommodation agency has an office on López Mateos and rents out the basic *Cabañas Batosarachi* (M$150) and the more comfortable *Cabañas de Segorachi* (M$250) around Lake Arareco, part of the San Ignacio de Arareko *ejido* (7km south of Creel on the Batopilas road).

Hotel Margarita's Plaza Mexicana Elfido Batista off López Mateos ⓣ635/456-0245, ⓦwww.hotelesmargaritas.com. The fancier sibling of *Casa Margarita's* has spacious heated rooms set around a courtyard, each decorated with murals. Popular bar on site; again the price includes breakfast and dinner. Discounts are possible in the low season, depending on demand. ❹

Hotel Los Valles Elfido Batista s/n, next to *Margarita's Plaza Mexicana* ⓣ635/456-0092, ⓦwww.hotellosvalles.com.mx. This newish motel off the main drag has eight small, clean rooms with satellite TV for decent prices; one of the better bargains in town. ❸

The Lodge at Creel López Mateos 61 ☎635/456-0071, US ☎1-877/844-0409, ⓦwww.thelodgeatcreel.com. Easily the best place to stay in town, run by Best Western and offering cabin-style rooms with spa, sauna, jacuzzi, and full restaurant and bar (there's also *Luna Creel* on site, see below). The wood-trimmed, rustic huts are ample and full of amenities, including coffee-makers, purified water and telephones. ❽

Nuevo Barrancas del Cobre Francisco Villa 121, right across from the train station; look for the "Nuevo" sign ☎635/456-0042. Handsome log-cabin-style rooms that sleep up to four, complete with carpets, heaters and woody aromas. The rooms inside the main building are cheaper, more basic and less appealing. Rooms ❸, cabins ❺

Parador de la Montaña Hotel López Mateos 44 ☎635/456-0023, ⓦwww.hotelparadorcreel.com. This once posh hotel has seen better days, but though the motel-style cabañas could do with a refit, you still get lots of space, showers and cable TV in reasonably comfy surroundings. The restaurant and bar are OK, but the whole place is packed in the summer with Mexican families. ❺

La Posada de Creel Vías del Ferrocarril ☎635/456-0805, ⓦwww.laposadadecreel.com. Excellent backpacker-friendly hotel behind the station, with cheap singles (shared bath) and simple but clean en-suite singles and doubles; breakfast included. ❷ shared bath, ❹ en suite

Sierra Bonita Gran Visión, about 1km out of town ☎614/410-4015, ⓦwww.sierrabonita.com.mx. Perched on a hill overlooking Creel, this four-star hotel is one of the most luxurious in town. Its best rooms have a fireplace and jacuzzi – perfect for unwinding after a hard, long day of hiking. ❻

Villa Mexicana Creel Mountain Lodge López Mateos, on the edge of town ☎614/456-0665, ⓦwww.vmcoppercanyon.com. Creel's only RV park and campground offers full hook-up and a host of facilities including a communal kitchen. Its other accommodation ranges from cheap log cabins to luxury rooms. Hook-ups ❷, cabins ❺, rooms ❻

Eating and drinking

Restaurants in Creel are all fairly similar, with the majority strung along López Mateos and serving economical home-cooked fare. The **cantinas** in Creel tend to be the preserve of locals, though if you behave discreetly you'll probably be free to frequent them (women too), and there are a couple of decent places for a drink listed below – otherwise the big hotels all have passable though not particularly exciting bars serving all the usual drinks.

Luna Creel *The Lodge at Creel*, López Mateos 61 ☎614/456-0071. The most congenial place to hang out at night in Creel; live music from 7pm (*trova*, rock, oldies and jazz) and a decent selection of drinks. It serves Columbian coffee, Mexican hot chocolate and pastries during the day; the affable hosts (English-speaking) also run a craft shop. Open 9am–2pm & 4–11pm or later – usually closed Mon.

Pizza del Rey López Mateos, on the plaza ☎635/456-0538. This small place serves reasonable enough pizzas (M$140–180 for a large one), but also popular ice creams in summer. Takeout or eat in the pleasant second-floor lodge-like dining area.

Restaurant Verónica López Mateos 33 ☎635/456-0631. Solid bet for all the usual Mexican classics; try their speciality, the "Norteño" – fried beef and vegetables topped with melted cheese. Daily 7.30am–10.30pm.

Tío Molcas López Mateos 35 ☎635/456-0033. Serves Mexican food but is most popular as a bar catering primarily to travellers. Open 7am–11pm.

El Tungar next to the train station. This burrito specialist dubs itself *hospital para crodas* or "hangover hospital"; true to the description, it also serves reviving *birria* and spicy *menudo* (regarded as a classic Mexican hangover cures). Mon–Sat 8am–5pm, Sun 8am–1pm.

Around Creel

For anyone who wants to explore the Sierra Tarahumara independently, the *ejido* (a collectively owned community) of **San Ignacio de Arareko**, a Rarámuri land-owning cooperative on the edge of Creel, contains many of the attractions normally covered by tours. Get there by following López Mateos towards the highway, taking a left onto the dirt road and continuing past the cemetery and uphill into the pine forest. A few kilometres from the *ejido* entrance (M$15), you'll encounter the eighteenth-century **Misión de San Ignacio** and a series of

Exploring the Sierra Tarahumara

If you have the time and are reasonably fit, independent exploration of the **Sierra Tarahumara** around Creel is both feasible and recommended. Whether you plan to see the sights of the sierra on your own or as part of a group, be sure to visit **Three Amigos Canyon Expeditions**, López Mateos 46 (ⓣ635/456-0179, ⓦwww.amigos3.com), the most professional and best-equipped outfit in town. They can advise on your trip, organize a well-priced tour or rent you vehicles; a five-person-capacity pick-up truck, with a cooler, maps and information costs M$1300 a day, a well-maintained mountain bike M$150–200 a day (M$90–130/half-day) and a two-person moped is M$550 a day or M$100/hr. Customers also get free internet use at the shop.

If you're not up to strenuous activity, or have only limited time in Creel, an **organized tour** is the best way to see the canyons (though these normally require at least four to six people to run). Try the booth on the main plaza, Three Amigos or the more popular hotels like *Casa Margarita's*. Rates should be about the same, but it's worth shopping around. Roughly speaking, a four-hour spin through the San Ignacio *ejido* should cost around M$120; a two- to three-hour trip to Cusárare M$170; a full-day trip to La Bufa and all the other nearby attractions M$350 and a day-long trip to Basaséachic around M$350 (seven-person minimum). Find out if food is included with your tour and if there are additional costs like museum entrance or toll fees before you set out. If you don't speak Spanish, check that your guide speaks English before parting with any money.

Hardcore adventure enthusiasts should contact Chito Arturo at Umárike Expediciones (ⓣ635/456-0632, ⓦwww.umarike.com.mx). A reputable guide with over ten years of experience, he can organize extensive backcountry hikes, **rock-climbing** lessons and biking and **canyoning** trips. A truly memorable way of exploring the canyons is on **horseback**, and if you want to be assured of animals that are cared for, speak to Norberto at El Adventurero on López Mateos (ⓣ635/456-0557, ⓦwww.ridemexico.com). Decent, professional tours start at M$140 for a two-hour ride through the San Ignacio *ejido* (two-person minimum).

otherworldly rock formations, including the **Valley of the Mushrooms**, which contains surreal structures closely resembling giant toadstools, and the **Valley of the Frogs**, with its squat amphibian-like boulders. The **Valley of the Monks** lies 5km away (M$10 toll), and has tall upright stones revered by the Rarámuri as symbols of fertility. Serene **Lago de Arareco**, 7km from Creel on the main highway to Batopilas, is a beautiful spot for fishing (largemouth bass) and camping – you can stay in a cabin on the lake (see p.162).

The **Recowata hot springs** are 22km from Creel and within biking or riding distance; follow the road to Divisadero for 7km and look for the turning on the left. Here you can bathe in three pools of steamy, clean, sulphurous water. Note that the hour-long descent to (and return from) the pools can be very strenuous, and shouldn't be undertaken by the faint of heart (or when it's wet).

The **Cascada de Cusárare** (M$15; tickets include entry to the Cusárare mission and museum), 30m high and most impressive during the rainy season, lies some 22km from Creel on the Batopilas road, and a 40min walk from the highway. The village of Cusárare is 3km further along the road and contains the seventeenth-century Jesuit **Misión de Cusárare** (Tues–Sun 9am–6pm; M$15, includes museum and waterfall) adorned with Rarámuri wall paintings completed in the 1970s; the mission's original art, including a set of twelve rare oil paintings by Miguel Correa (painted around 1713), were painstakingly restored in the 1990s and are now housed in the **Museo de Loyola** next door (same hours). You can reach the falls and village by bike, or on the daily Batopilas bus (see opposite), though you'll have a long hike back to Creel if you don't stay overnight, which you can do by camping or checking into the pricey *Sierra Lodge* (Ⓣ435/259-3999, Ⓦwww.coppercanyonlodges.com, reservations through Three Amigos; ⑧). Hitching is a possibility, though you should exercise the usual precautions.

Furthest from Creel and actually outside the canyonlands is the jaw-dropping 312m **Cascada de Basaséachic**, protected in the Parque Nacional Cascada de Basaséachic. The second-highest waterfall in Mexico (though the highest, Piedra Volada, only flows during the rainy season), it makes a long, but spectacularly rewarding day's excursion – about four hours' drive to the north (163km via San Pedro), and two hours on foot.

Batopilas

If you want to get a true idea of the sierra's size, a trip to isolated **BATOPILAS** is all but compulsory. Located 123km south of Creel, the town is accessible only via a nerve-wrenching five-hour drive on primitive dirt roads. The route rises and falls through four of the sierra's six canyons before commencing a final, convoluted descent to the floor of Batopilas canyon. Founded in 1632, the town emerged as a prosperous silver-mining centre, with production peaking in the nineteenth century under the auspices of the Batopilas Mining Company. By the early twentieth century, the surrounding mineral reserves were exhausted and the population had plummeted. For many years Batopilas was forgotten by the outside world – the town only received road connections in the 1970s and electricity in 1988. Today it's a peaceful, subtropical place with a population of about eight hundred. Resplendent with bougainvillea, palm and citrus trees and strung along a single two-kilometre road by the Río Batopilas, it's a world away from the fresh pine forests of Creel. There are several worthwhile **hikes** here, leading to everything from Rarámuri villages to abandoned mines and waterfalls. The best of these go to the "Lost Cathedral", the huge **Misión de San Miguel de Satevó**, 8km away in a desolate landscape of cacti and dust. A longer, two-day trek leads to the town of **Urique**, and can be easily organized with an operator in Creel (see opposite).

Practicalities

Buses and vans leave Creel six times a week from El Towi artesanía shop on López Mateos (buses: Tues, Thurs & Sat 7.30am; vans: Mon, Wed & Fri 9.30am; both M$200; 5hr). Return buses leave from outside the church in Batopilas at 5am, but always check for changes in the schedule. There is no official tourist office in Batopilas – Three Amigos in Creel (see opposite) can supply you with a map and other useful information. **Telephones** and a **post office** can be found on the main plaza. Most importantly, there is no bank here, so bring enough pesos for your stay.

The Mennonites

Towards the eastern end of the Copper Canyon rail line, the city of Cuauhtémoc contains Mexico's largest **Mennonite community** (around 50,000). You'll come across Mennonites throughout Chihuahua and Durango – the men in bib-and-tucker overalls and straw stetsons, as often as not trying to sell the tasty cheese that is their main produce, and the women, mostly silent, wrapped in long, nineteenth-century dresses with a headscarf. The Christian sect, founded in the sixteenth century by a Dutchman, Menno Simons, believe only in the Bible and their personal conscience: their refusal to do military service or take national oaths of loyalty has led to a long history of persecution. The Mennonites arrived in Mexico in the 1920s from Manitoba, Canada, but among themselves they still speak a form of German, although so divergent as to be virtually unintelligible to a modern German-speaker.

Casa Monse (Ⓣ649/456-9027; ❶), on the plaza itself, has clean, cheap rooms in a courtyard overflowing with plants. Next door you'll find *Juanita's* (Ⓣ649/456-9043; ❹), which has large, comfy rooms, and many quiet enclaves in which to relax. The best mid-range option is *Real de Minas* (Ⓣ649/456-9045; ❺) at Donato Guerra 1 (one block south of the plaza), which has bright, beautifully decorated rooms around a central courtyard. The exquisite blue-domed *Riverside Lodge* (Ⓣ01-800-776-3942, Ⓦwww.coppercanyonlodges; ❽), two blocks north of the plaza next to the church, is the most luxurious place in town but is only open September to April. **Dining** in Batopilas is fairly simple. *Restaurant Carolina* at the small Plaza de la Constitución (south of the main plaza), does decent and affordable home-cooked Mexican staples, as does *Casa Doña Mica* opposite. *El Puente Colgante*, just off the main plaza, is the place for a cold beer, and also serves wine, steaks and fresh trout.

Guachochi

Like Creel, rustic **GUACHOCHI**, about 170km to the south, made headlines in 2008 for drug-related killings, but don't be put off; this is a normally unexciting (and safe) ranching town providing access to the sierra's most remote and awe-inspiring locale, the **Cañon de la Sinforosa** (a further 18km south). Some of the hikes in Sinforosa are fairly hardcore – the canyon is 1830m deep and a trek along its length, for example, can take up to three weeks – while easier walks lead to stunning vantage points overlooking the valleys; in either case, hire a local guide in Guachochi or contact Cristina's Canyon Tours (Ⓣ668/818-8421, Ⓦwww.cristinascanyontours.com). There are also various hot springs and waterfalls in the region; the most spectacular is the **Cascada Rosalinda** with an eighty-metre drop. Rarámuri culture is thriving in this region, with **Norogachi**, 60km from Guachochi, one of the last remaining Rarámuri ceremonial centres, especially renowned for the vivid celebrations that occur during Semana Santa.

Just one Estrella Blanca bus to **Hidalgo de Parral**, via Guachochi, leaves Creel daily (1.45pm). Once in Guachochi, there are direct buses to Chihuahua from the Estrella Blanca bus station, located in a pink building around a kilometre from the plaza, near where you'll find the Transportes Ballezanos station, which also runs several daily services to Parral.

There are plenty of **accommodation** options in Guachochi. Around half a kilometre from the plaza, you'll find *Hotel Melina*, Dominguez 14 (Ⓣ649/543-0255; ❹), with clean, comfortable rooms and an adjoining restaurant. *Doña Lucha*, Agustin Melgar 306 (Ⓣ649/543-0182; ❷), is a solid budget option, while the more upmarket *Las Cumbres* (Ⓣ649/543-0200; ❹) is located on the highway (Av de las Garzas), with good access to the canyon. For **food**, be sure to try the town's speciality – fresh **trucha** (trout). *Los Adobes* on 20 de Noviembre is an excellent, if slightly expensive place for this. If you need to **change money** or withdraw cash, there's a branch of Scotiabank on Francisco Villa.

Cuauhtémoc

As the Copper Canyon Railway winds its way east, the pine trees, canyons and mountains of the Sierra Tarahumara gradually give way to ranching country, centred on the town of **CUAUHTÉMOC**, 70km from Creel and 130km from Chihuahua. This is also one of the chief centres for **Mennonites** (see box, p.165). There's not much to the town itself, but if the curious Mennonite connection interests you, make a trip to the Museo y Centro Cultural Menonita at Hwy-5 km 10 (Mon–Sat 9am–6pm; M$25; Ⓣ625/586-1895), which displays traditional artefacts (mostly farm tools) and sells Mennonite crafts, jams and the famous cheese. You'll need to take a taxi (around M$200 return) from the Estrella Blanca bus station at Calle 9 and

Allende. To see Mennonite cheese being made, visit *La Quesería América* (Mon–Sat 8am–6pm; ⓣ625/587 7249) at Campo 2-B, north of the town.

Mazatlán

The burgeoning resort of **MAZATLÁN** seems far less dominated by tourism than Acapulco or Puerto Vallarta, its direct rivals, though hotels stretch further every year along the coast road to the north, flanking a series of excellent sandy beaches. Mazatlán peaked in the 1980s, and today much of the downtown seafront looks decidedly tired, despite the steady flow of visitors. There are few activities or sights here – you certainly wouldn't come for the architecture – but it is a pleasant enough place and the shabby *centro histórico* has preserved much of its traditional, congenial atmosphere, despite ongoing attempts to spruce it up.

Remember to book accommodation well ahead if you are planning to be here around **Semana Santa**, when Mexicans descend on the city for massive celebrations, or July and August, when families pack the hotels and beaches. You should also plan around the massive **carnival** held here in February, one of the world's largest.

Unusually for Mexico, little is known about the establishment of Mazatlán – in part because it started life as a base for smugglers and pirates. By the early 1800s it was a more respectable mining port, but in the 1920s the beaches started attracting rich *norteamericanos* and its future was assured. Most tourists stay in the **Zona Dorada**, the "Golden Zone", and penetrate the **centro histórico** only on brief forays, though the latter has far more character.

Arrival and city transport

The **bus station** lies on the main west coast route linking Tijuana and Mexicali in the north with Guadalajara and Mexico City in the south. The station has all

Mazatlán narco tours

Mazatlán may be a languid tropical town where the biggest dangers to tourists are sunburn and hangovers, but it does have a darker side; like many parts of the country, this relates to the drug trade (see p.187). While most Mexicans are thoroughly opposed to the drug cartels, there remains a fascination with some of the more colourful characters and in many places enterprising locals have created **"narco tours"**. It sounds dangerous but isn't – most of the sites included are not currently connected to the cartels and the biggest draw is the enthusiasm and commentary of the guides (note that most drivers speak very little English). Mazatlán has been one of the Tijuana and Sinaloa cartels' favourite vacation spots for years, and resourceful (or unethical, depending on how you see it) cab drivers have started offering tours of drug-related hot spots; highlights include the seafront *Frankie Oh* disco, once owned by Tijuana cartel boss Francisco Arellano Félix (now closed); the house once owned by Félix; and the spot where his brother Ramón was infamously murdered in 2002. More uncomfortably perhaps, you may be shown what locals believe is one of the hideaways of Mexico's most wanted drug trafficker and the current head of the Sinaloa cartel, Joaquín Guzmán Loera (aka *El Chapo*) – even if he does own the place he's highly unlikely to be there.

It's usually just Mexican tourists that take these tours and needless to say, you won't find information on them at the tourist office, which is totally opposed to the practice – just ask any cab or *pulmonía* driver on the street (they usually charge M$150–200/hr).

facilities, including guardería (M$3/hr) and long-distance phones, and there are constant arrivals and departures to and from all points north and south. From the bus station, head up the hill to the main road and get on just about any bus heading to the right – they'll get you, by a variety of routes, to the **Mercado Pino Suárez** in the *centro histórico*, effectively the terminus for local buses. For the Zona Dorada, walk downhill a few blocks from the bus station and catch a "Sábalo" bus heading to the right along the coast road. Smaller city **buses** (daily 5.30am–10.30pm; every 15min) are M$5.50, while the larger air-conditioned buses are M$8. **Taxis** charge around M$50 to the old town, and M$70 to the Zona Dorada.

Arriving by **ferry** you'll be at the docks, south of the centre: there are buses here, but getting an entire ferry-load of people and their baggage onto two or three of them always creates problems. Taxis (M$35 to the old town) are in demand, too, so try to be among the first off the boat. If you do get stranded, don't despair: the one-kilometre walk to the *centro histórico* isn't too bad. Mazatlán's **General Rafael Buelna International Airport** (Ⓦ www.airport.mazatlan.com.mx) is some 20km south of town, served by the usual system of fixed-price vans (around M$73–160 per person or M$800 per van) and taxis (about M$290 to the old town and most of Zona Dorada). Taxis charge M$250 for the return journey from the *centro histórico* (rank on Serdán north of Flores). You'll find Budget, Hertz and Europcar **car rental** desks at the airport.

Downtown, you can walk just about everywhere, but the rest of the resorts are stretched out 15km along the coast road northwards. These are all linked by a single bus route and patrolled by scores of taxis, little open *pulmonías* (they look like overgrown golf carts but are usually modified VW Beetles) and larger pick-up trucks (*aurigas*); prices depend on your negotiation skills (and the season) but locals pay just M$30–50 between Zona Dorada and the old town (foreigners are asked for at least M$70). *Pulmonías* and *aurigas* are not necessarily cheaper, but the latter can fit in a lot more people (eight adults).

Information

Mazatlán's **tourist office** (Mon–Fri 9am–5pm, July & Aug also Sat & Sun; Ⓣ 669/981-8883, Ⓦ www.sinaloa-travel.com) is on the corner of Olas Altas and Flores, right on the malecón in the *centro histórico*. The staff speak English and have plenty of information on local and state-wide diversions, including Mazatlan's lively **carnival** which involves a massive firework display known as the Combate Naval. You'll also find a mobile information booth in the Plaza República (daily 10.30am–5.30pm). In the Zona Dorada, commercial information booths pop up on almost every corner – most sell tours and condos, but some give friendly, free advice. If you have any trouble – theft, accident and so forth – seek help from the tourist **police** (Ⓣ 669/914-8444). There are a couple of free English-language publications worth checking out if you're here for more than just a day: look for bi-monthly *Pacific Pearl* (Ⓦ www.pacificpearl.com) and *Mazatlán Interactivo* (Ⓦ www.mazatlaninteractivo.com), both of which contain useful information about events and attractions.

Accommodation

Almost all Mazatlán's cheaper **hotels** are in the *centro histórico*, within a short walk of the market. There's also a small group around the bus station which are convenient for transport and beaches, but not in the most appealing part of town. Many have two classes of rooms, with and without air-conditioning. The fancier hotels are all in the Zona Dorada and in **Nuevo Mazatlán** much further north, but you'll also find some exceptional boutiques and B&Bs in the *centro histórico*.

If you're in a group, it's worth considering an **apartment rental**, as these can be great value: check the Sinaloa Sun Properties website (ⓦwww.mazinfo.com/sinaloasun) for ideas. **Trailer parks** tend not to last very long, occupying vacant lots and then moving north to keep ahead of development. One of the more permanent sites is the *Mar Rosa Trailer Park*, right on the beach in the Zona Dorada at Camarón Sábalo 702 (ⓣ669/983-6187; RV sites M$300–400).

Centro histórico

Best Western Hotel Posada Freeman Express Olas Altas 79 ⓣ669/985-6060. This 1940s monolith has been given a Best Western makeover with modern, smart rooms with wi-fi, cable TV, a/c and free, fairly substantial buffet breakfasts – the rooftop pool is tiny but a great place to hang out with a beer. ❼

Casa Lucila Hotel Boutique Olas Atlas 16 ⓣ669/982-1100, ⓦwww.casalucila.com. Fabulous place to stay, and not as expensive as you might think; you get wonderful ocean views, a top-floor infinity pool and eight elegant rooms enhanced with flat-screen TVs, marble-clad bathrooms and jacuzzis. ❻

Hotel del Río Juárez and Quijano ⓣ669/982-4430. This popular budget option is always very clean and tidy, and rooms even have cable TV. A good deal for groups of four. ❸

Hotel Lerma Bolivar 622 between Serdán and Juárez ⓣ669/981-2436. Still the best deal in town. Sizeable, clean rooms (with fan) around a very spacious courtyard with parking, and very hospitable staff. The café across the

street has good, cheap breakfasts and comida corrida. ❶

Mazatlán Ocean Front Inn Paseo Claussen 127 ⓣ669/982-6876, ⓦwww.mazatlanoceanfrontinn.com. Inviting B&B right on the oceanfront, a couple of blocks north of Zaragoza, with six comfortable rooms, three with sea views, a small pool, full breakfast and super-helpful owners. The free bikes, laundry and free calls to the US are thoughtful extras. ❻

Old Mazatlán Inn Pedregoso 18 ⓣ669/981-4361, ⓦwww.oldmazatlaninn.com. Hidden gem, a couple of blocks from the seafront (Olas Altas). The 21 rooms here were renovated in a bright, funky style in 2007, with stone floors, lots of exposed brick, cable TV, wi-fi and balconies looking over the city and the beach; there's also a tiny pool and rooftop patio, and the weekly rates are a great deal (from US$452). ❺

Royal Dutch Casa de Santa María Constitución 627 ⓣ669/981-4396, ⓦwww.royaldutchcasadesantamaria.com. Charming B&B with friendly and helpful Dutch management. Rates include a full breakfast, coffee and tea, as well as afternoon tea and pastries. Reserve at least two weeks in advance, as they are almost always full. ❺

La Siesta Olas Altas 11, between Ángel Flores and Escobedo ⓣ669/981-2640, ⓦwww.lasiesta.com.mx. Lovely old hotel with private balconies and great sea views (worth the extra money); drawbacks are small rooms and noise from *El Shrimp Bucket* restaurant next door. Prices drop to M$390 April–July, and Aug–Dec. ❹

Near the bus station

Emperador Panuco, right opposite the bus station ⓣ669/982-6288, ⓔemperadorhotel@hotmail.com. Convenience and the budget price are the main attractions here, though rooms are clean and comfortable, with TV and a/c. ❸

Hotel Sands Arenas Av del Mar 1910 ⓣ669/982-0000, ⓦwww.sandsarenas.com. Facing the beach, two blocks down from the bus station. Comfortable, US-style motel with pool, slide and sea views; good value off-season, when prices drop by over fifty percent. ❺

Zona Dorada and Nuevo Mazatlán

Captain Moe's Bed & Breakfast Río Bravo 403 ⓣ1-866/252-6364, ⓦwww.captmoe.com. Rare B&B in the Zona Dorada, three blocks from the beach, with simple but cosy rooms, all with tiled floors, fridge, free wi-fi and bathroom. You also get access to a courtyard kitchen and free phone calls to the US, Canada, Ireland and the UK. ❺

Crowne Plaza Resort Mazatlán Sábalo Cerritos 3110, Marina Mazatlán ⓣ669/988-0324, ⓦwww.mazatlanapartments.com. This US$45-million hotel was opened in 2009 by President Calderón himself, and though it's a long trek from the main part of town, the boutique suites here, dressed all in white with touches of red, are truly exceptional, and come with ocean views, jacuzzis and plenty of extras. ❽

Inn at Mazatlán Camarón Sábalo 6291 ⓣ669/913-5500, ⓦwww.innatmaz.com. This classy hotel–time-share complex oozes chic (or at least the Mazatlán equivalent thereof). Larger apartment units are excellent value for families or small groups. ❼

Motel Marley Gaviotas 226 ⓣ669/913-5533, ⓦwww.travelbymexico.com/sina/marley. Comfortable units in small-scale place with great position right on the sand, and a pool. Still pricey, but you won't find a place on the water for much less. ❻

Playa Mazatlán Gaviotas 202 ⓣ669/989-0555, ⓦwww.hotelplayamazatlan.com. Vast 1950s beachside resort – if you want the full Mazatlán experience in the heart of the action, this is your best choice, with a huge programme of activities and great pool, though rooms are fairly standard three-star fare. ❼

Puerto Bonito Emerald Bay Ernesto Coppel Compaña s/n, Nuevo Mazatlán ⓣ669/989-0525, ⓦwww.pueblobonitoemeraldbay.com. For unabashed luxury, you can't do much better than this posh condo resort. Each suite comes with a jaw-dropping ocean view and balcony or terrace, some with outdoor jacuzzis. Round-trip airport transfers are US$19, and rates come down by a third off-season, but this is a long taxi ride from the centre of town. ❾

The town and around

As befits a proper Mexican town, Mazatlán's **Plaza República** is very much the commercial heart of the city and the *centro histórico*, harbouring the cathedral, post office, dour modern government offices, main bank branches and travel agencies. Always animated, it's especially lively on Sunday evening from 6 to 8pm, when there's a free *folklórico* show with singing and dancing. The twin-towered **Catedral de la Inmaculada Concepción** is the only real building of note, completed in

1899 in an eclectic style incorporating neo-Gothic, Spanish and Romanesque elements, with a particularly grand interior and main altar.

Take time to explore the **Mercado Pino Suárez**, two blocks north on Juárez, and the city's newest museum, a block west from the market, the enlightening **Museo Casa de los Pérez Meza** (Tues–Sat 10am–6pm; M$25; ⓣ669/981-7987) at Melchor Ocampo 510. Opened in 2009 by legendary diva Elisa Pérez Meza, the museum honours the music of Sinaloa, particularly the state's *musica banda,* which was pioneered by her equally famous father, El Trovador del Campo himself, from the 1930s. The museum houses a small collection of memorabilia, a video display, a pleasant courtyard café and a performance space (where Elisa sometimes sings).

Plaza Machado, a few blocks southwest of the main plaza, is by far the most popular of the old town squares. It's surrounded by fine nineteenth-century buildings, notably the **Centro Municipal de las Artes** and adjacent **Teatro Angela Peralta**, which opened in 1874 – check ⓦwww.culturamazatlan.com for what's on. The theatre is named after the "Mexican Nightingale", who died in the art centre next door in 1882 (it was a hotel at the time). Incidentally, the same building served as the workshop for the "inventor" of the *pulmonía* in 1965.

Just off the plaza on Constitución is the **Casa Machado**, a captivating museum set in a house dating from 1846 and depicting life in nineteenth-century Mazatlán (daily 10am–6pm; M$20). Other attractions include the small **Museo Arqueológico**, Sixto Osuna 76 (Tues–Sun 10am–1pm & 4–7pm; M$31), just a couple of blocks towards Olas Altas, which is primarily notable for having English labelling – the museum charts the pre-Hispanic cultures of Sonora state, with highlights including beautifully crafted **Aztatlán pottery** (750–1200 AD) and a collection of figurines, pots and statues, ending with the **Jorobado de la Nautical**, a strange figure of a hunchback dug up by accident and thought to have magic powers. Across the street is the curious little **Museo de Arte** (Tues–Sat 10am–2pm & 4–7pm, Sun 10am–2pm; free) set around a pretty courtyard, with a permanent collection of modern work from the late 1970s on, and temporary exhibits of contemporary work. The *centro histórico* has become a magnet for Mexican and international artists in recent years; you can get a taster of the scene on the **First Friday Art Walks** (ⓦartwalkmazatlan.com), held every first Friday of the month (Nov–May 4–8pm; free), when 21 galleries and over 35 artists open their doors for self-guided tours (pick up maps at hotels or at the website). You can also spend an enjoyable hour or so at the **El Acuario Mazatlán** (daily 9.30am–5.30pm; M$75; ⓦwww.acuariomazatlan.gob.mx), the city aquarium at Av de los Deportes 111, just off Avenida del Mar halfway between the *centro histórico* and the Zona Dorada.

There are scintillating **views** of town from the top of the **Cerro del Vigía** or **Cerro de la Nevería**; if you're not feeling very energetic, you can take a *pulmonía* or taxi up the latter. Likewise, the top of the **Faro de Crestón** at the southern edge of town is a good vantage point, though you'll have to walk up – the views from the *Sky Room* bar in the *Best Western* are just as good (see p.173).

The beaches: Playa Olas Altas, the Zona Dorada and Isla de la Piedra

Right in the *centro histórico*, **Playa Olas Altas** is where Mazatlan's transformation into a resort began in the 1920s, though the faded tiles and peeling paint of the *Belmar Hotel* (which opened in 1924) are in dire need of a makeover. The malecón here is still a great place to watch the sun go down, but not the best place to swim – it's rather rocky and the waves tend to be powerful (*olas altas* means "high waves"). Indeed, this is a decent place to **surf** (though not for beginners) – you can rent boards at *Looney Bean* (see p.173).

Following the seafront drive from here around the jagged coast under the Cerro de la Nevería brings you to the **Mirador** – an outcrop from which local daredevil youths or *clavadistas* plunge into the sea. At a little over 10m, it's nowhere near as spectacular as the high-diving in Acapulco, but is exciting and dangerous nonetheless. You'll see them performing whenever there are enough tourists to raise a collection, generally starting at 10am or 11am – especially during the summer and Semana Santa – and again in the late afternoon (around 5pm) when the tour buses roll through. You'll also find an arts and craft market here most days (though it's mostly touristy stuff), along with several popular *raspados* (shaved ice flavoured with syrup) stalls, especially in summer when the evenings are very busy.

From here the paved **malecón** runs for 10km to the *Fiestaland* complex (see opposite) in the Zona Dorada via the long sweep of **Playa Norte** – it's worth skipping this and walking (or taking the bus) all the way to the **Zona Dorada** around **Sábalo**, where the first of the big hotels went up and the sands improve greatly. The beaches right in front of the hotels are clean and sheltered by little offshore islands, while further on they're wilder but emptier. The more populous area does have its advantages – the beach never gets too crowded (most people stay by their pools and bars) and there's always a lot going on: water-skiing, sailing, parasailing, you name it. Among the dozens of artesanía markets and shopping malls here, **Sea Shell City**, on Rodolfo Loaiza in the heart of the Zona, stands out as the kitschiest of all – a two-storey emporium of seashells that describes itself as a museum and is definitely worth a look.

Buses (marked "Sábalo") leave from Mercado Pino Suárez on the Juárez side, and run up Avenida del Mar and right through the Zona to the last hotel, where they turn around. Those marked "Cerritos" can be picked up on Avenida del Mar at *Fiestaland* in the Zona Dorada and run north up along Camarón Sábalo. If your goal is to reach a beautifully serene beach, stay on the bus in this direction to either Playa Cerritos or Playa Bruja. This is at the heart of the new mega resorts and development of **Nuevo Mazatlán**, but the beaches remain fairly free of crowds and there are plenty of restaurants and places for a post-beach drink.

South of the town centre, you can take a short and inexpensive boat trip (every 10min; 5am–7pm; M$20) from the beach next to the ferry dock to the **Isla de la Piedra** (or Stone Island), actually a long peninsula with a Caribbean feel and a very good palm-fringed beach that stretches for miles and is excellent for swimming. It is possible to sleep out or sling a hammock on the terrace of one of the small restaurants – ask the owner first. Once a very basic community, the Isla is now included in many tour itineraries and can become crowded, especially on Sunday afternoons, when locals congregate for live music and dancing.

Eating, drinking and nightlife

As a rule, Mazatlán's more authentic and lower-priced **restaurants** are in the *centro histórico*. For rock-bottom prices, seek out the basic restaurants on the upper floor of the **Mercado Pino Suárez** on the corner of Melchor Ocampo and Juárez. You can come across bargains in the Zona, too, as long as you don't mind the menu being in English and the prices in dollars. The sheer number of tourists there means lots of competition and **special offers**; breakfast deals are often the best of all. **Plaza Machado** is the most romantic place to hang out and watch the crowds, but there are more clubs and bars in Zona Dorada. For a rare slice of Mazatlán history, stop by *Panadería La Espiga Dorada* at Constitución 217, a fabulous old bakery selling all sorts of traditional cakes and breads.

Centro histórico

Altazar Ars Café Constitución, on Plaza Machado. Serves breakfast, burgers, tacos and the best coffee in town. At night turns into a rock and blues club/bar, with live music every evening except Sunday.

Looney Bean Olas Altas 166-G, a block down from *El Shrimp Bucket* ⓦ www.looneybean.com. Friendly outpost of the Californian artisan coffee chain and internet café, offering fine americanos, espressos and capuchinos from M$12 (limited seating).
Mercado Pino Suárez Juárez and Valle. *Jugo* stalls downstairs, as well as the respected *El Tigre* stall (tostadas M$10, *comida* M$30 and *ceviche* M$10–12); most cafés are in the upstairs gallery overlooking Juárez, serving breakfasts and cheap *comidas* (M$20) – follow the crowds as always, though *Restaurante Nancy* is usually a good bet.
Pastelería Panamá Juárez and Canizales, on the corner opposite the cathedral ⓣ 669/980-2333. Diner-style restaurant/cafetería, good for breakfast but not cheap (dishes M$80–100). You can also take away a host of delectable pastries from the bakery and munch them on the plaza.
Puerto Viejo Olas Altas 25 ⓣ 669/982-1886. Favourite with expats and locals alike for seafood, while the congenial location on the seafront makes it perfect for a few evening beers. Red snapper, prawn and calamari for M$70, *comida* from M$48.
El Shrimp Bucket Olas Altas 11, between Ángel Flores and Escobedo ⓣ 669/981-6350. One of the oldest and best-known restaurants in Mazatlán (since 1963) and apparently the original in the *Carlos 'n' Charlie's* chain. Now in bigger, plusher premises, it still has plenty of atmosphere and decent if pricey fish tacos, mahi-mahi, marlin stew and plenty of prawns; the best deal is the M$150 all-you-can-eat menu (Fri & Sat 2–7pm).
Topolo & Habaneros Wine Bar Constitución 629, on the corner of Juárez ⓣ 669/136-0660, ⓦ www.habanerosmazatlan.com. Popular restaurant that offers slightly upmarket Mexican fare (like *poblano* peppers stuffed with cheese) while the wine bar has a happy hour 1–5pm daily. Open Mon–Sat 1–11pm.
El Túnel Carnaval 1207, opposite the Teatro Angela Peralta (no phone). Perhaps the best Mexican food in all of Mazatlán, patronized by locals and tourists alike since 1945. Great Sinaloa specialities such as *asado a la plaza*, *pozole* and home-made gorditas, but no beer (although you can bring your own). Open from 6pm, closed Wed.

Zona Dorada

Los Arcos Camarón Sábalo 1019, across from the *Holiday Inn* ⓣ 669/913-9577. Locals flock to this relaxed modern restaurant, close to the beach, for some of the best seafood in the city and especially good shrimps.
Arre LuLú De las Garzas 18 ⓣ 669/916-7131. A not so crowded alternative for seafood and cheap drinks; it also offers a traditional Mexican menu. You can get a complete breakfast of eggs, beans, tortillas, juice and coffee for under M$50.
El Capitano off Gaviotas, right on the beach ⓣ 669/913-1191. Large, open-air seafood restaurant overlooking the ocean. Serves shrimp, lobster and seafood platters at low prices (around M$40–50 per entrée) – popular with foreign students.
Casa Loma Gaviotas 104 ⓣ 669/983-5398, ⓦ www.restaurantcasaloma.com. For that perfect romantic – and expensive – evening, this secluded restaurant in a colonial setting has far more atmosphere than the big hotels. Reservations are recommended. Dishes average M$150–220. Closed late Aug to Sept.
Gus y Gus Camarón Sábalo 1730 (across from *Costa De Oro hotel*) ⓣ 669/914-4501, ⓦ www.gusygus.com. Great little open-air restaurant, serving especially good chicken fajitas (M$90), shrimp *ceviche* (M$85) and marlin tacos (M$59); most main dishes run M$95–170. If you like classic rock you'll love the house band, which entertains a mostly tourist crowd nightly.
Pancho's Gaviotas 408 ⓣ 669/914-0911 This is another tourist favourite, with an attractive wood and tile dining room and excellent fresh seafood – think stuffed fish fillets (M$150), coconut shrimp (M$192) and frog legs (M$126). The zesty margaritas make it ideal for sunset drinks.

Bars and clubs

Café Pacífico Constitución 501, on Plaza Machado, *centro histórico*. Mexican and European mix of styles in a pub with a selection of beers and liquors, snacks, sandwiches and coffee. A relaxing place to drink without the macho overtones of many Mexican bars. Open until 2am.
Edgar's Bar Serdán and Escobedo, *centro histórico* ⓣ 669/982-7218. Dating from 1949, this venerable cantina now proclaims "Ladies welcome" in English at the door; inside it's still a slice of traditional Mazatlán, with old photos on the walls, ancient patrons and live music at night.
Fiestaland Av del Mar and Buelna, at the far end of the coastal road, Zona Dorada ⓣ 669/984-1666. This bizarre, all-white castle-like structure is a conglomeration of pricey nightclubs, discos and bars, of which *Bora Bora* and *Valentino* – both clubs – are the most popular.
No Name Café Rodolfo T. Loaiza 417, a few steps down from Sea Shell City, Zona Dorada. This sports-themed restaurant, managed by a Chicago Cubs fan, does breakfast, beer, spare ribs and parties. Over thirty big-screen TVs show the day's action.
Sky Room *Best Western Hotel Posada Freeman*, Olas Altas 79 (see p.169). Worth a visit for the spectacular views across the old town

Moving on from Mazatlán

Buses

Numerous **bus** companies operate from the main bus terminal, most owned by Grupo Estrella Blanca (☎1-800/507-5500), including Futura, Transportes Chihuahuenses, Pacifico, Norte de Sonora and Elite, but also Turistar and TAP. All have *de paso* services roughly hourly in both directions, beginning at 6.30am, and frequent local buses to **Los Mochis** (M$340; 6hr), **Tepic** (M$210; 4hr 30min), **Guadalajara** (M$410; 8hr) and **Durango** (M$315; 7hr). There are a few direct services to Puerto Vallarta (M$400; 7hr), but companies like TAP also offer more frequent services via a change in Tepic (usually the wait is 30min) – they can reserve seats all the way. For San Blas and the nearby beaches you'll need to take a bus to Tepic and change. There are also three or four long-distance services to **Mexico City** (M$720; 18hr) and **Tijuana** (M$1114; 26hr). To reach the bus station from downtown, take a "Sábalo" bus along the beachfront from Juárez near the market, then walk 300m along Espinoza. Taxis should be no more than M$50.

Ferries

Baja Ferries (Ⓦwww.bajaferries.com) runs services to **La Paz** (Mon–Sat 5pm; 12hr; schedule subject to change) from the port at Playa Sur, 1km southeast of the *centro histórico*; catch the "Playa Sur" bus from Juárez. Information and **tickets** are available from their offices (☎669/985-0470) at the port: a *salón* class ticket (available on all boats) qualifies you for a reclining seat (M$1190), a *turista*-class ticket gets you a space in a four-berth cabin (M$760 extra), *cabina* (M$900 extra) in a two-berth cabin; a small car will cost around M$2440, but bicycles go free. Prices include breakfast and dinner, though the food onboard isn't great; there are signs prohibiting bringing your own, though no one checks or seems to care. Travel agents in Mazatlán should also be able to arrange tickets.

Planes

Mazatlán's **airport** (☎669/982-2399) is 20km south of the city and only reachable by expensive taxi (around M$250). Flights are run by Aéreo Calafia (☎669/984-4300), Aéreo Servicio Guerrero (☎669/112-0677), Aeroméxico (p.31), Alaska Airlines (p.31), Continental (p.32), Frontier, Mexicana (☎669/913-0770), Viva Aerobus (p.36), Volaris (p.36) and WestJet.

and lower Mazatlán, the cruise ships and islands, especially at night. Drinks are reasonable (M$35 for shorts) considering, and you'll often have the place to yourself.

Twisted Mama's La Laguna 500, near Garzas, Zona Dorada ☎669/112-0255. This Canadian-owned bar and restaurant has garnered a huge following, mainly due to its party atmosphere, phenomenal margaritas – try the watermelon, mint and cucumber – and the excellent live bands. The fish and chips isn't bad either.

Listings

Banks and exchange Citibank, Camarón Sábalo 1312, and Banamex, on Juárez at Ángel Flores by the main plaza, which has the longest hours (9am–2pm) and good exchange rates. Most places in the Zona accept dollars though often at a poor rate, so you may want to make use of Mazatlán's numerous casas de cambio.

Bookshops Mazatlan Book & Coffee Company, Sábalo 610 (opposite *Costa de Oro Hotel* and behind Banco Santander) ☎669/916-7899, Mon–Sat 10am–6pm for maps, dictionaries, books for sale or exchange, plus gourmet coffee.

Car rental Dozens of outlets, including: Budget, Camarón Sábalo 402 ☎669/913-2000; Express, Camarón Sábalo 610 ☎669/913-0800; and Hertz, Camarón Sábalo 314 ☎669/913-6060.

Consulates Canada, Playa Gaviotas 202, opposite *Hotel Playa Mazatlán* ☎669/913-7320;

US (representative only), Playa Gaviotas 202 ⓣ669/916-5889.

Internet access The cheapest is located in the *centro histórico*. Try Cyber El Globo, Canizales 815 (10am–10pm; M$10/hr), or On Line Café, Sixto Osuna 115, (8am–7.30pm; M$10/hr). See also the *Looney Bean* café. You will find many internet places on the main drag in the Zona Dorada, though most are pricey, up to four times the cost of those in the old town (M$40–80/hr).

Laundry Lavandería La Blanca, Sábalo 357 and others at regular intervals throughout the Zona.

Emergencies ⓣ060.

Hospital Balboa Hospital at Sábalo 4480 has a 24hr walk-in clinic with English-speaking doctors (ⓣ669/916-5533 or 669/916-7933, ⓦwww.hospitalsinmexico.com).

Police ⓣ060 for emergency assistance; traffic police ⓣ669/983-2616.

Post office Juárez and 21 de Marzo (Mon–Fri 8am–6pm, Sat 9am–1pm; ⓣ669/981-2121).

Spanish courses Centro de Idiomas (Callejón Aurora 203 Pte ⓣ669/985-5606, ⓦwww.spanishlink.org) is a well-established, award-winning Spanish language school. They offer reasonably priced courses in conversational Spanish, and can arrange homestays with Mexican families.

Tours and activities Any major hotel will be able to arrange a host of tours – whether related to nature, culture or adventure – around the city and to the outlying islands or villages. The major operators include Ole (ⓣ669/916-6288, ⓦwww.oletours.com), Vista (ⓣ669/986-8610, ⓦwww.vistatours.com.mx) and Pronatours (ⓣ669/916-6287, ⓦwww.elcid.com/pronatours/). Jet skis, catamarans and boats can usually be rented on the beach with no prior arrangement necessary. Mazatlán Surf Center, Sábalo near Gaviotas, will rent you a surfboard for M$250/day and offer 2hr lessons from M$650 (ⓣ669/913-1821, ⓦwww.mazatlansurfcenter.com).

Tepic

Around 280km south of Mazatlán, the first town of any size is **TEPIC**, capital of the state of Nayarit. Despite its antiquity – the city was founded by Hernán Cortés's brother, Francisco, in 1544 – there's not a great deal to see here. It's appealing enough in a quietly provincial way, but for most travellers it's no more than a convenient **stopover** along the route to Guadalajara, or a place to switch buses for **San Blas** (see p.176) and the coast (there are no direct buses from Mazatlán to San Blas).

The eighteenth-century **cathedral**, on the Plaza Principal, is worth a quick look, as is the small **Museo Regional de Nayarit** (Mon–Fri 9am–7pm, Sat 9am–3pm; M$37; ⓣ311/212-1900), at the corner of México and Zapata, south from the plaza, with an absorbing collection of local pre-Columbian and Huichol artefacts. The **Museo de Los Cuatro Pueblos** (Mon–Fri 9am–2pm & 4pm–7pm, Sat 10am–2pm; free), at the corner of Hidalgo and Zacatecas, has anthropological displays documenting the cultures of Nayarit's indigenous peoples. You could also check out the **Museo Amado Nervo** at Zacatecas 284 Nte (Mon–Fri 9am–2pm, Sat 10am–2pm; free; ⓣ311/212-2916), which commemorates the life and works of one of Mexico's most famous poets, in the house where he was born in 1870. Plenty of places sell **Huichol artesanías** (see box, p.176), including vibrant yarn paintings and bead statues; alternatively, you can buy them directly from Huichol artists in the main plaza.

Practicalities

Tepic's **Central Camionera** lies a few kilometres east of the centre on Avenida Insurgentes Sur, but local buses (M$5) shuttle in and out from the main road outside – to reach the centre, cross the street and catch the first bus marked "Centro". **Taxis** should be around M$30–40. TAP runs comfortable first-class buses to Mazatlán (M$209; 4hr 30min), Guadalajara (M$205; 3hr 30min), Los Mochis (M$545; 10hr 30min), Mexico City (M$640; 10hr), Tijuana (M$1110; 30hr) and Puerto Vallarta (M$170; 3hr). Transportes Norte de Sonora runs hourly

The Huichol

The **Huichol**, or Wixárika, are the most intensely mystical of Mexico's indigenous peoples. Dwelling in isolated mountain settlements around the borders of Nayarit, Jalisco, Zacatecas and Durango, they practise an extant form of **pre-Columbian shamanism**, having accepted only token elements of Spanish Catholicism.

For the Huichol, religion and ritual are central elements of daily life. The cultivation of maize, particularly, is bound up with sacred rites and esoteric meaning. **Animism** – the belief that all objects are alive and imbued with spirit – is key to their enigmatic worldview: rocks, trees, rivers and sky all have souls and there are as many gods as there are things in the world.

Peyote, a hallucinogenic cactus, is the most important and powerful god in their vast pantheon. Gathering and ingesting this plant is a major part of the ceremonial calendar, which includes an annual cross-country pilgrimage to the sacred desert around Real de Catorce to acquire supplies (see p.236). Grandfather Peyote is the teacher and guardian of the Huichol. He delivers sacred visions, heals the sick and guides the community.

Huichol artesanías are particularly striking and include vivid **"yarn paintings"** that are created by pressing lengths of yarn into wax. They represent peyote visions and are filled with vibrantly rendered snakes, birds, deer and other sacred animals, as well as gourd bowls and other ritually significant objects. Circular motifs usually symbolize peyote itself, or its flower. You can buy these paintings in Tepic and elsewhere.

second-class buses to **San Blas** (M$42; 1hr) and **Santiago Ixcuintla** (M$40; 1hr 30min). For **Chacala**, take the Vallarta bus and get off at Las Varas – you can take a *colectivo* from there for around M$20.

The main **state tourism office** is inconveniently located in the Ex-Convento de la Cruz, at the corner of Calz del Ejercito and México (Mon–Fri 9am–5pm; ⓣ311/214-8071, ⓦwww.visitnayarit.com), although there are other branches in town, including the city tourist office on the corner of Amado Nervo and Puebla (daily 8am–8pm; ⓣ311/212-8037) and inside the bus station. **Banks** are situated on and around the main plaza.

If you have to **stay the night** try the cheap but clean *Cibrian*, Amado Nervo 163 Pte (ⓣ311/212-8698; ❸), or the relatively luxurious *Fray Junipero Serra*, Lerdo 23 Pte (ⓣ311/212-2211, ⓦwww.frayjunipero.com.mx; ❺), right on the plaza, and the much more atmospheric *Hotel Real de Don Juan* (ⓣ311/216-1888, ⓦwww.realdedonjuan.com; ❼) at México and Juárez.

As for **food**, there's plenty of choice around the plaza and on México: *Pat Pac's*, upstairs at México Nte and Morelos, is good, popular and reasonably priced, offering an excellent breakfast buffet and Mexican menu; *Café Diligencias* (ⓣ311/212-1535) México 29 Sur, is a good place to linger over a coffee; while *El Trigal* (ⓣ311/216-4004), corner of Zapata and Veracruz, serves decent vegetarian fare. For something smarter, try *Emiliano Comida y Vino* at Zapata 91 Ote (ⓣ311/216-2010), which offers fine Mexican dining and an excellent wine list.

San Blas and around

West of Tepic lies the coastal plain: sultry, marshy and flat, dotted with palm trees and half-submerged under lagoons teeming with wildlife. You have to travel through this to reach **SAN BLAS**, as godforsaken a little town as you could hope to see – at least on first impression. It was an important port in the days of the

Spanish trade with the Philippines (until Acapulco took over), wealthy enough to need a fortress to ward off the depredations of English piracy, but though it still boasts an enviable natural harbour and a sizeable deep-sea fishing fleet, almost no physical relic of the town's glory days remains.

Life in San Blas is extremely slow. The positive side of this is an enjoyably laid-back travellers' scene, with plenty of people who seem to have turned up years ago and never quite summoned the energy to leave. For such a small town, though, San Blas manages to absorb its many visitors – who come mainly in winter – without feeling overrun, submissive or resentful. During the summer it's virtually deserted, but in January and February the town is a magnet for **bird watchers**, and in February the city also hosts its biggest festival in honour of San Blas (St Blaise). Do not come here without insect repellent or you will be eaten alive: legions of ferocious sand flies (*jejénes*) plague the beaches mornings and late afternoon, and the mosquitoes descend en masse at dusk.

Arrival and information

The majority of the **buses** (second-class only) serving San Blas arrive from Tepic (M$42; 1hr), 65km east (last bus around 7.30pm). Taxis charge around M$500 for the trip. There are four daily services to/from Puerto Vallarta (M$110; 3hr). Taxis from Puerto Vallarta airport will charge around M$1200 (around M$1000 coming back). Note that Vallarta is one hour ahead of San Blas. There's also a daily bus to

Guadalajara (M$180; 5hr) via Tepic, and a couple of afternoon buses to Santiago Ixcuintla (M$35; 1hr).

The **bus station** is on Sinaloa at Canalizo at the northeast corner of the main plaza, right in the centre of town. Here Juárez crosses Heroico Batallón de San Blas, which runs 1km south to the town beach, **Playa El Barrego**. The **tourist office** (Mon–Fri 9am–3pm; ⓣ323/285-0221) is located inside the Palacio Municipal on the main plaza, with a smaller branch open similar hours at Playa El Borrego, across from *Stoner's Surf Camp*. The best source of information, though, is ⓦwww.visitsanblas.com, run by local expat Pat Cordes.

Accommodation

Part of the appeal of San Blas is that there's plenty of choice of budget **accommodation**. Most places are on Juárez or Heroico Batallón. The town is especially well geared to small, **self-catering** groups: "bungalows" and "suites" are apartments with up to six beds, a small kitchen and usually (though you should check) some cooking equipment. There's also free camping on Playa El Barrego, but the bugs and the availability of good, cheap accommodation in town make this less than appealing.

Bungalows La Quinta California Matanchén 3, Palmar de Los Cocos ⓣ323/285-0310, ⓦwww.quintacalifornia.com. Friendly management and bargain two-bedroom apartments set around a leafy, tranquil courtyard. Short walk from the beach, behind *El Herradero Cantina*, amongst the trees (take Las Islitas, off Batallón). ❸

La Casa de las Cocadas Juárez 145, at the corner of Comofort ⓣ323/285-0960, ⓦwww.etcbeach.com/casa-cocadas. The nicest place to stay in town, close to the river in a beautifully renovated old building; ten simple but tastefully decorated rooms with earthy, hand-crafted furnishings, some with balconies. ❺

Casa María Canalizo 67 ⓣ323/285-1057, ⓦcasamaria.sanblasmexico.com. Long-established and well-known cheapie with comfortable, clean rooms (with bathroom and cable TV) surrounding a courtyard filled with caged birds; shared kitchen and free washing machine. ❸ (extra M$100 for a/c)

Casa Roxanna Bungalows El Rey 1 ⓣ323/285-0573, ⓦwww.casaroxanna.com. Exceptional value with immaculate rooms and good kitchenettes, all with wi-fi, cable TV and use of pool and laundry – the pick of the self-catering apartments in town. ❹

Casa de Valorien Bahía de Matanchén, near Santa Cruz ⓣ327/103-6876, ⓦwww.casadevalorien.com. Excellent B&B managed by friendly hosts Janice and Valorien, occupying a secluded spot on the bay with stairs down to the beach below (it's several km south of San Blas, but easy to reach by bus or taxi). Three bright and cosy rooms and fabulous gourmet dining. ❺

Garza Canela Paredes 106, follow signs from Batallón ⓣ323/285-0112, ⓦwww.garzacanela.com. Luxurious a/c rooms, pool, garden, and some kitchenettes. Rates include breakfast, and the poshest restaurant in town, *El Delfin*, is on site. Significant discounts during low season. ❺

Hotel Bucanero Juárez 75 ⓣ323/285-0101. Good, clean budget rooms surrounding an airy courtyard and fountain. A good spot if you are looking for a hotel within a stone's throw of the action; a/c available for an additional charge. ❸

Hotel Hacienda Flamingos Juárez 105 ⓣ323/285-0485, ⓦwww.sanblas.com.mx. Hotel set in a gorgeous old mansion built in 1883 with a wonderful garden courtyard with pool and ping-pong table – the building has a lot more character than the rooms, which are sleek and classy but relatively standard modern fare. ❺

Posada del Rey Campeche 10, not far from the water ⓣ323/285-0123. Modern, plain and comfortable mid-range option with a/c and fans. Tiny pool and bar with views to the water. ❺

El Ranchero Batallón at Michoacán ⓣ323/285-0892. Friendly in the extreme; rooms with or without bath include use of kitchen; beds in communal rooms at peak times. Having become a popular budget choice, it's often full in winter, and can be a bit noisy. ❷

The town and around

Beyond lying on the pristine **beaches** to the south of San Blas, **bird watching** and taking an beguiling jungle-boat trip to **La Tovara springs** (see opposite for both), most visitors seem content simply to relax or amble about town. A more focused hour can be spent at **Las Ruinas de la Contaduría**, the remains of a late eighteenth-century fort which, with the vaulted remains of a chapel, **La Iglesia de Nuestra Señora del Rosario**, crown the Cerro de San Basilio near the river, a kilometre along Juárez towards Tepic; the ruins are said to have inspired Henry Wadsworth Longfellow's poem, *The Bells of San Blas*, though the poet never came here. From the top you get sensational views over the town to the ocean, where, according to Huichol legend, the small white island on the horizon is said to represent peyote.

San Blas is also an excellent place for both **fishing** and **whale-watching** trips, the latter in the winter months. It is inexpensive as far as sport fishing goes, and M$1500–2000 will get you a five- to seven-person boat for the day, allowing you to trawl for yellowfin tuna, barracuda and others. There are a number of guides in town who'll take you out, but one of the best around is Ruben Tiscareno (Guadalupe Victoria 94; ⓣ323/285-0420). He charges around M$2000 for fishing (three or four people), M$1500 (six people) for whale watching, and M$800 (up to eight people) for bird watching in the estuary.

La Tovara and jungle boat trips

The **lagoons and creeks** behind San Blas are almost unbelievably rich in **bird life** – white herons and egrets are ubiquitous, as are hundreds of other species that no one seems able to name (any bird here is described as a *garza* – a heron). The best way to catch a glimpse is to get on one of the three-hour boat trips into the jungle, the launch negotiating channels tunnelled through dense mangrove, past sunbaking turtles and flighty herons. The best time to go is at dawn, before other trips have disturbed the animals; you might even glimpse a caiman (alligator) along the way. Most trips head for **La Tovara**, a cool freshwater spring that fills a beautiful clear pool perfect for swimming and pirouetting off the rope swing – if you're not put off by the presence of alligators, that is. Eat at the fairly pricey palapa restaurant or bring your own picnic.

Trips leave from the river bridge 1km inland from the main plaza along Juárez: get a group together for the best prices. Rates are fair and start at around M$400 for four, M$100 per extra person for three hours; it's around M$100 extra person for a side trip to the local **crocodile farm**. You may also want to consider negotiating something longer, giving more time for swimming and wildlife spotting en route.

The beaches

As well as the fine beaches right in town (**Playa El Borrego**) and **Isla de Rey**, just offshore (M$5 by boat), there are others some 7km away around the **Bahía de Matanchén**, a vast, sweeping crescent of a bay entirely surrounded by fine soft sands. At the near end, the tiny community of **Matanchén** is the launching point for the long stretch of **Playa Las Islitas** (via dirt road), which has numerous palapa restaurants on the beach that serve up grilled fish and cold beers. At the far end of the bay lies the village **Aticama** (with more basic shops and places to eat), the disappointing **Playa Los Cocos**, where erosion is steadily eating away at what was once a pristine beach, and the better **Playa La Miramar** beyond. In between, acres of sand are fragmented only by flocks of pelicans and the occasional crab. There are plenty of spots where you can camp if you have the gear and lots of repellent. The waves here, which rise offshore beyond Miramar and run in, past the point, to the depths of the bay, are in the *Guinness Book of Records* as the longest in the world: it's very rare that they are high enough for surfers to ride them all the way in, but there's plenty of lesser **surfing** potential – surfboards and boogie boards can be rented at **Stoner's Surf Camp** (ⓦwww.stonerssurfcamp.com) at Playa El Borrego for M$20–50/hr, or M$80–150/day. You can also **stay** in basic cabins here for M$250, or camp for M$50.

Major fiestas

January

Ortiz Tirado Music Festival (last week of Jan). Thousands descend upon Álamos (see p.148) for a week-long celebration in honour of Dr Alfonso Ortiz Tirado. Concerts, parades, cultural events and plenty of merry-making.

February

Día de San Blas (first week of Feb). The *feria* in San Blas (see p.176) starts on January 30 and ends a week or so later. Parades, fireworks and ceremonies.

Carnaval (week before Lent; variable Feb–March). Celebrated with particular gusto in Mazatlán (see p.167).

May

Día de la Santa Cruz (May 3). Celebrated in Santiago Ixcuintla (see p.181), north of Tepic, with traditional dances.

September

Independence Day (Sept 16). Celebrated everywhere.

December

Día de la Inmaculada Concepción (Dec 8). Celebrated by the pilgrims who converge on Álamos (see p.148) and Mazatlán (see p.167), with parades, music and dancing.

You can walk from San Blas to Matanchén, just about, on the roads through the lagoons – it's impossible to penetrate along the coast, which would be much shorter. Considering the sweltering temperatures in this area, it's far easier to make the trip on one of the **buses** ("El Llano") that leave several times daily from the bus station; these go along the **Bahía de Matanchén**, through **Matanchén village** (where you get off for Las Islitas) Aticama, Los Cocos and on to Santa Cruz (M$10). Coming back, just flag down the first bus. You can also **take a local taxi** (bargain fiercely – it should be M$100 to Los Cocos).

Eating and drinking

Seafood is big business in San Blas and you can buy it at beachfront palapas and street stands near the Tovara *embarcaderos* or Playa El Borrego, as well as at the established **restaurants** in town. There's also plenty of fruit and other healthy offerings to cater for the tourists. At the beach most places close around sunset, and if you want to eat later you'll have to walk into town – a flashlight to guide your way is a worthwhile investment.

Cha Cha's (aka El Cocodrilo) Juárez 1 ☎323/285-004. A San Blas fixture with a great location on the plaza. Travellers and locals alike come for the excellent, if a bit pricey, seafood, and to relax and drink long after the activity in the plaza has died down.

La Familia Batallón 62. Reasonably priced and unpretentious place serving steaks and seafood, with TV showing US movies. Family-run, as the name suggests. Closed Sun.

La Isla Mercado at Paredes, two blocks from the plaza ☎323/285-0407. A must, if only to admire the astonishingly kitschy decor: draped fishing nets festooned with shell pictures, shell mobiles and shell lampshades. Moderately priced meat and great seafood. Also known as *Chief Tony's*.

Mike's Place Juárez 36 above *McDonald's*. Quiet drinking midweek but livens up on Friday and Saturday with dancing, live music and anything from Latin to classic rock.

Restaurant McDonald Juárez 36 ☎323/285-0432. No relation to Ronald's place, this friendly restaurant just off the main plaza serves excellent, good-value meals (M$50–100). Breakfasts are particularly tasty; you'll often find a crowd of expats here to enjoy them.

San Blas Social Club Juárez at Canalizo, near the plaza. Popular café, bar and erstwhile jazz club, with live music Friday and Saturday, hearty pub food (check out the steak and fries specials on Tuesday nights; M$75; Nov–May).

Listings

Banks and exchange The Banamex on Juárez just east of the plaza (Mon–Fri 9am–2pm) has an ATM, but does not change foreign currency (including US$s) and is plagued by long queues, poor rates and an occasional lack of funds. Change money before you get here.

Internet access You'll find plenty of internet cafés in town. Try *Café Net San Blas*, on Juárez and Batallón (daily 9am–10pm; M$10/hr), around the corner from the *McDonald* restaurant; lots of place have wi-fi.

Post office A block northeast of the bus station at Sonora and Echevarría.

Around San Blas: Santiago Ixcuintla and Mexcaltitán

North of San Blas, from Hwy-15 you can take the turn-off for **SANTIAGO IXCUINTLA**, a market town where the only real interest lies in the **Centro Cultural Huichol** (Mon–Sat 9am–2pm & 4–8pm; free; ⓣ323/235-1171), approximately 1.5km from the central plaza towards Mexcaltitán at 20 de Noviembre and Constitución. This cooperative venture, aimed at supporting Huichol people and preserving their traditions, raises money by selling quality Huichol art and offering various classes; the centre is most active between November and May.

North of Santiago, located on a lily-strewn lagoon and supporting only a few hundred habitants, is the extraordinary islet of **MEXCALTITÁN** – "House of the Mexicans" in Náhautl, which looks something like a very tiny version of Tenochtitlán, the Aztec capital before the Spaniards arrived. Indeed, the place is one candidate for the legendary Aztec homeland Aztlán, from which the tribe set out on their exodus to the Valley of México; the small **Museo del Origen** on the plaza (Tues–Sun 9am–2pm & 4pm–7pm; M$5) addresses that hypothesis with a

▲ Rowing across the lagoon, Mexcaltitán

collection of archeological relics. Mexcaltitán sees very little tourism, but you should be able to find a guide to paddle you around the island (M$600/day) and accommodation at the single **hotel**, *Ruta Azteca* (☎323/235-6020; ❸), offering four bare-bones rooms near the church. There's a handful of inexpensive **restaurants**, most specializing in seafood and **shrimp** – try *El Camarón* on the plaza, or *Restaurante Albera*, on the east side of the island. If you're in the area around the end of June you should definitely try to visit the island fiesta, on June 28 and 29, when there are canoe races on the lagoons and rivers; be sure to make a reservation, too. To reach Mexcaltitán from Santiago, catch a *combi* from the station on Juárez, one block from the plaza (M$20) to La Batanga (taxis are around M$150). The journey takes about 45 minutes and is followed by a fifteen-minute boat ride from La Batanga across the lagoon (M$10).

Travel details

Buses

Services on the main highways south from Nogales are excellent, with constant fast traffic and regular express services, if you want them, from the border all the way to Mexico City. Be warned, though, that it can be hard to get a seat on *de paso* buses along the way, especially in Hermosillo, Culiacán and Los Mochis. Second-class buses usually cover the same routes, running ten to twenty percent slower.

Álamos to: Navojoa (hourly; 1hr); Phoenix (1 daily; 13hr).

Guaymas to: Hermosillo (every 30min; 2hr); Los Mochis (every 30min; 5hr); Mexicali (every 30min; 11hr); Navojoa (every 30min; 3hr); Nogales (hourly; 5hr 30min); Tijuana (every 30min; 14hr).

Hermosillo to: Bahía de Kino (13 daily; 2hr); Guaymas (every 30min; 2hr); Mexicali (every 30min; 9–10hr); Nogales (hourly; 4hr); Tijuana (every 30min; 12–13hr).

Los Mochis to: El Fuerte (hourly; 2hr); Guaymas (every 30min; 7hr); Mazatlán (every 30min; 7hr); Navojoa (every 30min; 2–3hr); Tijuana (every 30min; 19hr); Topolobampo (every 15min; 40min).

Mazatlán to: Culiacán (every 30min; 2hr 30min); Durango (12 daily; 6hr); Guadalajara (every 30min; 8hr); Los Mochis (every 30min; 7hr); Tepic (every 30min; 4hr); Tijuana (every 30min; 26hr).

Navojoa to: Álamos (hourly; 1hr); Ciudad Obregón (every 30min; 1hr 30min); Guaymas (every 30min; 3hr); Los Mochis (every 30min; 2–3hr); Tijuana (every 30min; 17hr).

Nogales to: Guaymas (hourly; 5hr 30min); Guadalajara (hourly; 25hr); Hermosillo (hourly; 3hr); Mexico City (hourly; 32hr); Puerto Peñasco (4 daily; 5hr).

San Blas to: Guadalajara (1 daily; 7hr); Puerto Vallarta (4 daily; 3–4hr); Santiago Ixcuintla (3 daily; 1hr); Tepic (hourly; 1hr 30min).

Tepic to: Guadalajara (every 30min; 5hr); Mazatlán (every 30min; 4hr); Puerto Vallarta (hourly; 3–4hr); San Blas (hourly; 1hr 30min); Tijuana (every 30min; 30hr).

Trains

Los Mochis to: El Fuerte (2 daily at 6am & 7am; 2hr 55min); Creel (2 daily at 6am & 7am; 10hr 10min); Chihuahua (2 daily at 6am & 7am; 15hr 30min).

Chihuahua to: El Fuerte (2 daily at 6am & 7am; 12hr 40min); Creel (2 daily at 6am & 7am; 5hr 25min); Los Mochis (2 daily at 6am & 7am; 15hr 30min).

Flights

Almost every town of any size has an airport, with flights, not necessarily direct, to Mexico City. Busiest are Hermosillo, with half a dozen flights a day to the capital by a variety of routings, and Mazatlán.

Mazatlán to: Denver (3 weekly); La Paz (1 daily); Los Angeles (3 daily); Mexico City (4 daily); Tijuana (2 daily).

Ferries

Purchase tickets as far in advance as possible, thereby avoiding long queues during the busy summer months. All services are subject to change, so always check the schedule in advance.

Guaymas to: Santa Rosalía (8pm Mon, Tues, Thurs & Sat; 7hr).

Mazatlán to: La Paz (5pm Mon–Sat; 12hr).

Topolobampo (Los Mochis) to: La Paz (daily 5pm; 6hr).

3

The north

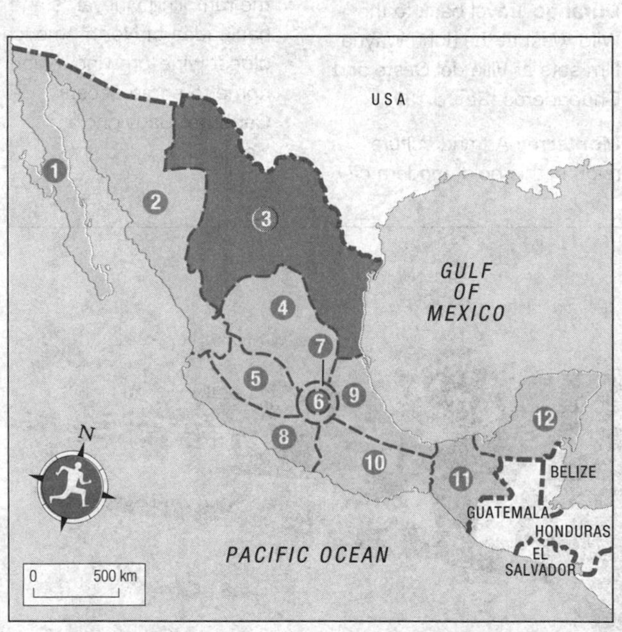
USA
GULF OF MEXICO
PACIFIC OCEAN
BELIZE
GUATEMALA
HONDURAS
EL SALVADOR
N
0 500 km
1
2
3
4
5
6
7
8
9
10
11
12

CHAPTER 3 Highlights

* **Paquimé** The enigmatic ruins at Casas Grandes are remnants of the most significant Pre-Columbian culture in northern Mexico. See p.190

* **Chihuahua** Lively colonial city sprinkled with grandiose nineteenth-century mansions, including the home of Pancho Villa. See p.192

* **Durango** Travel back to the Wild West at the John Wayne film sets at Villa del Oeste and Chupaderos. See p.199

* **Monterrey** Art and culture reign in this bold, modern city, where superb museums and the bohemian Barrio Antiguo await. See p.215

* **Cabrito asado** Succulent roast goat is a specialty of Mexican cowboy country, best experienced at restaurants such as *El Rey del Cabrito* in Monterrey. See p.224

* **Valle de Parras** Explore the rambling vineyards and haciendas of North America's oldest wine-growing region, home to some decent Cabernet Sauvignon. See p.228

▲ Casas Grandes, Paquimé

3 The north

Rich in legends of the country's revolutionary past, Mexico's **north** has a modern history dominated by its relationship with the United States, just across the Río Bravo. Indeed, though much of the region is harsh, barren and sparsely inhabited, far less visited than the country's tourist-saturated southern states, cross-border trade – as much about the daily movement of people as goods – means it's one of the richest and most dynamic parts of Mexico. It's not all business, though. Rugged and untamed, the north is home to deserts, mountains, seedy frontier towns and modern cities, as well as a proud and hospitable people deeply rooted in ranching culture, perhaps best symbolized by folk hero **Pancho Villa** (see box, p.196).

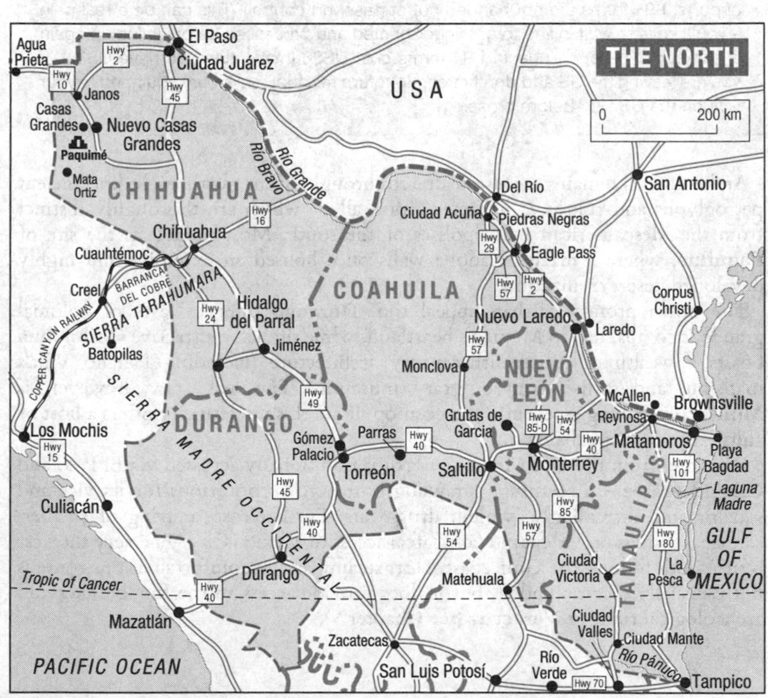

Crossing the US border

Thanks to heightened security on both sides of the US/Mexican border, procedures have become fairly standardized at every crossing – the major differences relate to volume of traffic (with Tijuana and Juárez invariably the busiest), though you can expect rush-hour traffic to be bad everywhere, and that going into the US will usually take longer than crossing into Mexico (especially if driving).

If **crossing into Mexico** by **bus**, you'll stop first at Migración where non-Mexicans must get off to fill out the FMT immigration form (sometimes known in English as the "tourist card"). Entry into Mexico costs US$22 or peso-equivalent (you can skip this if staying within 35km of the border; see Basics p.59). After Migración, the bus will stop for a thorough customs search and everyone must get off and take their bags through a screening area: in practice this is usually fast and efficient. If **walking** across the border, the procedure is more or less the same, though you'll have to actually go into the Migración office and ask for the FMT – they are not handed out automatically. If walking or driving, note that bridges across the Río Grande have tolls (usually US$3/M$45 for cars). If you're **driving** and need an FMT, aim for the "Items to Declare" lanes, tell the inspectors you need your card and park in the adjacent lot.

Entering the US can be a lot more time-consuming, and even US citizens now require a passport to enter. Everyone else needs a visa or visa-waiver to enter the US (see p.60). If you fly into the US, cross the land border into Mexico and intend to return the same way, keep your original **I-94 or I-94W** in your passport, to avoid having to apply again when you re-enter the US (assuming the form is still valid of course). If you do not have either form, you'll need to visit the US Immigration offices at the border – these are separate areas before the actual passport control (unlike airports, I-94 forms are not handed out at passport control). This can be a real pain – you'll have to wait in line to get finger-printed and processed before lining up again at the actual passport check. I-94 forms cost US$6 (make sure you have US$s). If you are leaving the US and don't intend to return this trip, make sure you hand in your I-94 on the US side before crossing.

Archeological remains are also scattered throughout the north, including ancient petroglyphs and ruined Chichimec cities, all of which are thoroughly distinct from the Mesoamerican metropolises of the south. Most notable is the site of **Paquimé**, where a maze of adobe walls once housed an extensive and highly developed desert civilization.

The north promises urban appeal too. **Durango** offers a taste of colonial grandeur comparable to Mexico's heartland, while similarly attractive **Chihuahua** boasts a wealth of nineteenth-century architecture (including Pancho Villa's mansion) and stylish contemporary museums. The real draw, however, is **Monterrey**. Young, energetic and cosmopolitan, this modern city offers a host of cultural and artistic diversions.

Overland from the US, Mexico's north is traditionally accessed via El Paso and **Ciudad Juárez** – a seething, sprawling border town notorious for its vice and squalor and, increasingly, violent drug wars. Further east, a string of smaller, calmer crossings provide rapid (and safer) access to Mexico City. The very shortest route south follows the Gulf coast. Hot, steamy and uncomfortable, this route is not especially recommended, but it does provide access to the fine beaches and archeological ruins of **Veracruz** (see Chapter 9).

The central corridor

Ciudad Juárez, the behemoth point of entry into Mexico's central corridor, offers little to detain most people heading south. If you have time, an excursion to the ruins at **Paquimé**, near Nuevo Casas Grandes, is worth the four-hour ride from the border – and if you have a car, there are several other enticing destinations nearby. History lovers will also enjoy **Chihuahua**, the home of Pancho Villa and a relatively affluent city that has invested a lot in its heritage, museums and art.

Ciudad Juárez

Sprawling **CIUDAD JUÁREZ**, just across the border from El Paso, Texas, is possibly Mexico's nastiest border town. Vast, dirty and riddled with visible social problems at the best of times, it's spiralling drug-gang violence led to the Mexican army being deployed to patrol its bullet-spattered streets in 2008 – around 2660 people were murdered here in 2009. This followed the already notorious rape and murder of over four hundred women since 1993, "las muertas de Juárez" portrayed in the depressing Jennifer Lopez movie *Bordertown* (2007) and Roberto Bolaño's seminal novel *2666*. There's an element of paranoia to this of course; Juárez is a city of two million people that, by and large, functions like anywhere else in Mexico, and tourists are very rarely targeted by drug gangs. The troops had improved the security situation by early 2010, but it's still a good idea to pass

The Mexican drug wars

Ciudad Juárez has become one of the most violent epicentres of the escalating **Mexican drug wars** – a violent struggle between rival cartels to control the flow of narcotics into the US, and increasingly, between these gangs and the Mexican government. The violence made prime-time news in the US in 2009 (after almost six thousand people were killed in 2008), and led to a stream of travel warnings relating to cities along the US–Mexico border (though many pundits believe this was an over reaction).

Mexican gangs began to take over the US cocaine trade from the Colombians in the 1990s, and were originally drawn into roughly two rival camps led by the **Gulf cartel**, based in Matamoros, and the **Sinaloa cartel** with its ally the **Juárez cartel** (Gulf ally the Tijuana cartel has been dramatically weakened in recent years). Since 2007 however, the Juárez cartel has been locked into a vicious turf war with the Sinaloa cartel, for control of Ciudad Juárez, and the Gulf cartel is now run by a terrifying group of ex-soldiers known as **Los Zetas**, whose notoriously violent tactics have led to their dominance of the drug trade. In 2006, President Felipe Calderón ended decades of government inaction by sending federal troops to the state of Michoacán to end drug violence there (spurring a violent response from local drug lords, "La Familia"), and he's continued to take an aggressive stance on tackling the cartels, many of which have infiltrated local police departments; in 2009 the notorious **Beltrán-Leyva cartel** (allies of Los Zetas) was severely weakened after its key leaders were killed or captured.

Despite the sensational headlines, it's important to remember that most of Mexico remains peaceful; as a visitor you should be safe (tourists are rarely targeted), though it obviously makes sense to avoid the major trouble spots if you can, particularly along the US border. If driving a car from the US, check the current situation with US authorities before you go (see p.60).

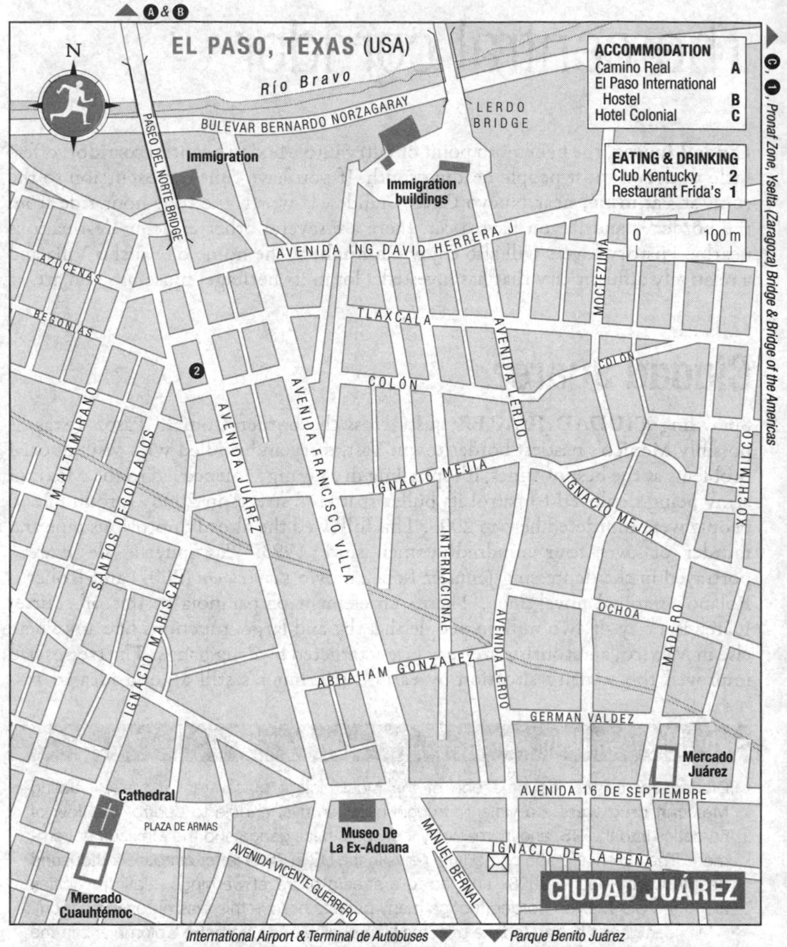

through Juárez as quickly as possible – you won't miss much. In five hours you can reach Chihuahua (373km) or, rather closer, Nuevo Casas Grandes, the base for excursions to the archeological site at Casas Grandes.

Arrival and information

Two downtown toll bridges serve one-way traffic in and out of Ciudad Juárez from neighbouring **El Paso**, Texas. Northbound vehicles cross the **Paseo del Norte Bridge** from Juárez, while southbound vehicles use the **Stanton St/ Lerdo Bridge** (tolls: cars US$2.50; pedestrians US$0.50). If you're on foot you can enter on either bridge (Paseo del Norte is best); coming back you must use the Paseo del Norte crossing (cars M$20, by foot M$3). If you're planning to venture deeper into Mexico, be sure to visit one of the immigration offices (see p.59 for border formalities). Additionally, there are two bridges that serve two-way traffic. The **Bridge of the Americas** (free) lies 4km east of the city centre on the edge of the **Zona Pronaf**, an area of sheltered tourist development a world away from the sleazy machinations of downtown Juárez. East of here lies the **Yselta (Zaragoza) Bridge** (same tolls), well connected to the main highways and good for a speedy escape. All are open 24 hours.

Once across either of the two downtown bridges, **taxis** to the main bus terminal should be around M$100, or M$250 to the airport; alternatively, you can catch a local bus from the corner of Guerrero and Villa near the market for M$5. The city's **Terminal de Autobuses** (Ⓣ656/613-6037) lies 5km from the centre at Flores and Borunda, and has services to both US and Mexican cities. You can take a direct bus to the terminal from the El Paso Greyhound station with Autobuses Americanos for US$6, or a taxi from El Paso airport for US$48 (it's US$42 to downtown Juárez). To get to the border from the bus terminal, take a taxi (M$100) or any local bus marked "Centro".

Arriving at the **Aeropuerto Internacional Abraham González**, 14km south of the border, you'll find ATMs and all the major car rental firms, including Budget (Ⓣ656/633-0954). Taxis into town or to the border should be around M$250. Taxis to and from El Paso airport are a hefty US$60/M$600. Aeroméxico runs a free shuttle bus to the *Camino Real Hotel* in El Paso (6 times daily) for its passengers; Viva Aerobus charges its passengers US$10 for rides to El Paso (to Civic Center Plaza).

The Ciudad Juárez **tourist office** is inconveniently located in the **Pronaf zone** at Av de las Américas 2551, just across the Bridge of the Americas (Mon–Fri 9am–5pm, Sat & Sun 10am–2pm; Ⓣ656/611-3174, Ⓦwww.visitajuarez.com).

Accommodation

None of the hotels in Ciudad Juárez is particularly good value and there's little point in **staying the night** – most business visitors stay in the comfortable chain motels on the outskirts of town, which are little use without a car. The best choice close to the border is *Hotel Colonial* at Abraham Lincoln 1355 (Ⓣ656/613-5050, Ⓦwww.hotelescolonial.com; ❹) in the Pronaf zone around 1km south of the Bridge of the Americas. You might be tempted to stay in El Paso instead, where the best **budget** choice is the *El Paso International Hostel*, 311 E Franklin St (Ⓣ915/532-3661, Ⓦwww.elpasohostel.com; dorms US$24.95). The *Camino Real* is the obvious luxury option in El Paso, a short walk from the border at 101 South El Paso St (Ⓣ915/534-3000, Ⓦwww.caminoreal.com; ❼).

Eating and drinking

Places to eat are plentiful around the centre and border area, although new arrivals should probably take it easy on the street food. **El Paso** offers better value, however, and if you've been in Mexico some time, you may well want to rush across the border to the swanky *Camino Real* or the burger joints near the Greyhound station. One of the best places to eat in Juárez is *Restaurant Frida's* (daily 2pm–2am; Ⓣ656/639-0148), Paseo Triunfo de la República 2525, in the Zona Pronaf, a beautifully decorated space dedicated to Frida Kahlo, that knocks out reasonably good Mexican dishes for around M$120–250. The classic place for a **drink** is *Club Kentucky* at Juárez 629 (Ⓣ656/632-6113), open since 1920 and one of numerous Mexican cantinas to claim the invention of the margarita.

Listings

Banks and exchange It's easy enough to change money at casas de cambio and tourist shops along Juárez and 16 de Septiembre; most banks are also on 16 de Septiembre, and you'll find ATMs at nearly all of them. Most places accept dollars, but make sure you know the current exchange rate.

Moving on from Ciudad Juárez

Ciudad Juárez is something of transport hub, and its **Terminal de Autobuses** is busy with long-distance buses that connect cities in the north and centre of the country. The major lines are Omnibus (⊕01-800/011-6336, ⊛www.odm.com.mx) and various companies under the Estrella Blanca umbrella (⊕01-800/507-5500, ⊛www.estrella blanca.com.mx). You should be able to pick up a first-class ride to any major city north of Mexico City. Destinations include: **Casas Grandes** (every 1–2hr; 4hr), **Chihuahua** (hourly; 5hr), **Monterrey** (11 daily; 18hr), **San Luis Potosí** (every 1–2hr; 20hr), **Zacatecas** (hourly; 16hr) and **Mexico City** (every 1–2hr). Second-class and *de paso* services are also prolific, and serve Baja California as well as all of the above.

International bus services are handled by Autobuses Americanos (⊕656/610-8529). It runs an hourly shuttle bus to **El Paso Greyhound Bus Station** (1hr 45min; US$6 or peso-equivalent), from where Greyhound buses shoot off west (Phoenix and LA) and east (Dallas, San Antonio). Autobuses Americanos also serves US destinations direct from Juárez, including Los Angeles (4 daily), Dallas (2 daily), Phoenix (3 daily) and Santa Fe (4 daily). Heading to the US you can also take a taxi to the border (M$100) and walk across the bridge onto Santa Fe, a shabby street of budget stores that seems like an extension of Juárez. It's a short walk straight along here to the *Camino Real* hotel (see p.189), or you can grab an El Paso taxi, which are metered; you should get to **El Paso airport** for around US$20 (this is much cheaper than taking a taxi across the border). El Paso airport has cheaper connections to the rest of the US than Juárez airport, though you'll usually have to change planes in Houston or Phoenix.

Flights from Aeropuerto Internacional Abraham González (⊕625/633-0734) serve Mexican destinations including Chihuahua, Guadalajara, Hermosillo, Monterrey, Tijuana and Mexico City via Aeroméxico. InterJet operates budget flights to Mexico City and Viva Aerobus serves Monterrey. Taxis charge M$250 for trips between downtown and the airport. For further information, see Travel details, p.230.

Car rental Alamo, Paseo Triunfo de la República 2412 ⊕656/611-1010; Budget, Paseo de la Victoria 2527 ⊕656/648-1757.

Consulate US, López Mateos 924 Nte ⊕656/611-3000.

Internet access The public library across the border in El Paso (Mon–Thurs 9am–8pm, Fri 11am–6pm, Sat 9am–6pm, Sun 1–5pm; ⊕915/543-5401) has free internet access. Walk north past the *Camino Real* hotel for about two blocks; it's on the corner of Franklin and Oregon.

Post office At the corner of Lerdo and Peña, one block south of 16 de Septiembre.

Paquimé and around

The curious ruins of **Paquimé** (Tues–Sun 10am–5pm; M$49) are the most significant, and certainly the most thought-provoking, remains of a sophisticated civilization in northern Mexico. Originally home to an agricultural community and comprising simple adobe houses (similar to those found in Arizona and New Mexico), it became heavily influenced by Mesoamerican, probably Toltec, culture. Whether this was the result of conquest or, more likely, trade, is uncertain, but from around 1000 to 1200 AD, Paquimé flourished. **Pyramids** and **ball-courts** were constructed, and the surrounding land was irrigated by an advanced system of **canals**. At the same time local craftsmen were trading with points both south and north, producing a wide variety of elaborate ornaments and pottery. Among the finds at the site (many of them are now in the Museum of Anthropology in Mexico City), have been cages that held exotic imported birds, whose feathers were used in making ornaments; necklaces made from turquoise, semiprecious stones and shells obtained from the Sea of Cortés; and other objects of copper, bone, jade and mother-of-pearl.

Much must have been destroyed when the site was attacked, burned and abandoned around 1340 – either by a marauding nomadic tribe, such as the Apache, or in the course of a more local rebellion. Either way, Paquimé was not inhabited again, its people leaving their already depleted trade for the greater safety of the sierras. When excavation began in the late 1950s, there were only a few low hills and banks where walls had been, but by piecing together evidence archeologists have partly reconstructed the adobe houses – the largest of which have as many as fifty interconnecting rooms around an open courtyard or **ceremonial centre**. The foundations of the houses, which were originally two or three storeys high, have been reconstructed to waist-height, with an occasional standing wall giving some idea of scale.

To fully appreciate the sophistication of this civilization, first visit the **Museo de las Culturas del Norte** (same hours; free with main site entry), a beautifully laid-out, if thinly stocked museum, architecturally designed to mimic the ruins of the defence towers that once stood on the site. Inside you'll find a large model of how Paquimé must have looked, interactive touch-screen consoles with commentary in Spanish and English and intelligent displays of artefacts. Modern examples of finds from the surrounding area – drums, dolls in native costume, ceramics and ceremonial masks – compete with Paquimé objects, notably striking pottery, often anthropomorphic vessels decorated in geometric patterns of red, black and brown on a white or cream background.

Practicalities

To **reach the site** you have to travel 260km south of Ciudad Juárez to **Nuevo Casas Grandes**. Travelling from Chihuahua is also an option, as buses for the four-hour journey (around 300km) depart regularly. Once in Nuevo Casas Grandes (buses arrive outside the adjoining Estrella Blanca and Omnibus offices on Obregón), take one of the frequent yellow buses ("Casas Grandes/Col Juárez") from the corner of Constitución and 16 de Septiembre to the plaza in the smaller village of **CASAS GRANDES** (about 15min; M$6), from where the site is signposted – it's a ten-minute walk. Taxis charge around M$100 from Nuevo Casas Grandes. If you leave Ciudad Juárez very early you can visit the site and continue to Chihuahua in the same day, but if you need **accommodation**, there are a few inviting options in Casas Grandes; *Las Guacamayas B&B* (Ⓣ636/692-4144, Ⓦwww.mataortizollas.com; ❺) is closest to the ruins, offering cosy adobe rooms (in part modelled on Paquimé), wi-fi and breakfast. You can also stay at the *Pueblo Viejo Courtyards* (Ⓣ636/692-4402), Av Victoria 420, artfully restored adobe houses near the main plaza, adorned with local antiques (wi-fi but no TV) – one of the best houses is *La Casa del Nopal*. Rates are usually M$1500 per week for one bedroom with bath, or M$2500 per week for a suite with a kitchen and a dining room (call for nightly rates).

Dining in Casas Grandes is surprisingly good. *El Mesón del Kiote* (Ⓣ636/692-4037) on Juárez near the PEMEX station, heading back towards Nuevo Casas Grandes, offers delicious local food and freshwater fish, generous margaritas and addictive guava pie. *La Finca de Don Cruz* (Ⓣ636/692-4343) is also on Juárez, five blocks from the plaza in the direction of Mata Ortiz. It's popular with tour groups, but still serves fabulous northern Mexican cuisine. For something quick and cheap *Mar y Sol* on the plaza knocks out decent burritos, tacos, hamburgers and ice creams. If you need **internet** access, try Internet Espacio (Mon–Sat 9am–8pm; M$15/hr; Ⓣ636/692-4143) on López Mateos.

Nuevo Casas Grandes itself is small and not especially interesting. If you get stuck here, aim to stay at the amicable *Hotel Piñón*, Juárez 605 Nte (Ⓣ636/694-0655, Ⓔmotelpinon@prodigy.net.mx; ④), which has a pool and even a small museum of Paquimé clay pots. *El Pollo Feliz* serves excellent roast chicken on 5 de Mayo, four blocks from the main plaza, while the *Panadería La Guadalupana*, one block west of the *Piñón*, is a venerable bakery serving cheap *pan dulce*.

Mata Ortiz

If you've trekked out all the way to Casa Grandes, you should also check out **MATA ORTIZ**, some 27km south of Nuevo Casas Grandes, a flourishing artisanal pottery community inhabited by artists from all over the world. It's a tranquil, appealing little village of adobe houses, and the best thing to do is just wander the streets soaking up the atmosphere and visiting any galleries you like the look of – most artists will be happy to introduce their work and sell you some pieces. Some of the best include **Jorge Quintana**'s gallery at the *Adobe Inn*, just before the train tracks (for fine pottery and Oaxaca textiles); **Juan Quezada**'s gallery across from the old train station; and **Mauro Quezada**'s gallery (from Juan Quezada's house, take the street toward the river to the end and turn right). If you fancy staying, Jorge Quintana actually runs the comfortable *Adobe Inn* (which also serves food; Ⓣ36/661-7135; ⑤).

Taxis will take you to Mata Ortiz for M$350, or M$500 return from Nuevo Casas Grandes – knock off about M$100 from Casa Grandes (there are no buses).

Chihuahua

The capital of the largest state in the republic, **CHIHUAHUA** was the favourite home of Revolutionary hero **Pancho Villa**. It's also been the scene of some crucial episodes in Mexico's history, not least the execution of **Miguel Hidalgo** (see p.195) in 1811. Today it's a sprawling, workaday city of 775,000, but the colonial centre boasts several fine museums and is sprinkled with grandiose nineteenth-century mansions, built when silver brought wealth to the region's landowning class. This is also *vaquero* heartland and one of the best places in the country to look for **cowboy boots**: you're spoilt for choice in the centre, especially in the blocks bounded by Calle 4, Juárez, Victoria and Ocampo. Incidentally, you're unlikely to see many of the little bug-eyed dogs here, said to have been discovered in the state in the 1850s – though in the summer months you will see over thirty multicoloured chihuahua sculptures scattered around town as part of the annual "Dog Parade".

Arrival, information and city transport

Transport in and out of Chihuahua is not well coordinated. The **Terminal Central de Autobuses** (with guardería 9am–11pm) is 10km east of the centre, near the airport on Juan Pablo II; local buses (M$6) run from right outside to and from downtown, and there are plenty of taxis, though they will insist on a hefty M$100 fee – you'll find plenty of taxis willing to take you back for M$70. Note that most buses from **Creel** will drop you in the centre of town (near the plaza) before heading out to the bus terminal – check when you get on. From Chihuahua's **General Roberto Fierro Villalobos International Airport** (Juan Pablo II km 14) a fixed-fare system operates – buy your voucher as you leave the terminal (around M$200 for downtown). Arriving by **train** from the Copper Canyon at the CHP station (Ⓣ614/439-7200), you're 2km southeast of

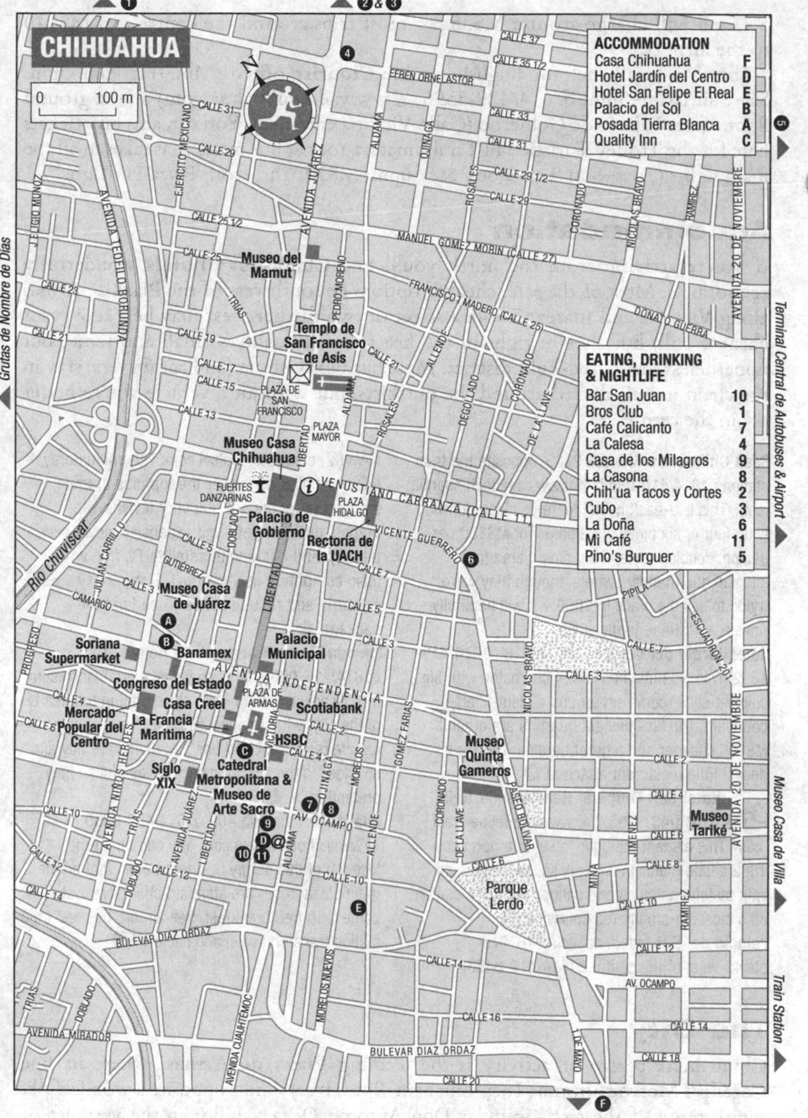

the centre at Mendez and Calle 24. You can take a bus into the centre, but you'll probably want to take a taxi (around M$40).

Central Chihuahua is compact enough for you to **get around** everywhere on foot, but bear in mind that addresses can initially be confusing. Even-numbered cross streets lie to the south of the central Plaza de Armas and odd numbers to the north, with shop or hotel numbers taking their initial digit from the associated street; thus, Allende 702 is between calles 7 and 9 north of the centre, but Allende 607 will be south of the centre between calles 6 and 8. **Taxi** ranks can be found on Plaza de Armas (next to Casa Creel) and next to the *Hotel Palacio del*

Sol, and will charge around M$35 for most trips around the centre and M$140 to the airport.

There's a small, helpful English-speaking **tourist office** (Mon–Fri 9am–5pm, Sat–Sun 10am–5pm; ⓣ614/429-3596, ⓦwww.ah-chihuahua.com) on the ground floor of the Palacio de Gobierno (Calle Victoria entrance). You can also buy tickets here for the Trolley Turístico El Tarahumara, a tourist bus route that takes in all the main sights (Tues–Sun 9am–noon & 3–6pm; M$30; 1hr) from Plaza Hidalgo.

Accommodation

If you're arriving from the north you'll find Chihuahua's **hotels** wonderfully economical. Most of the safe, cheaper options lie southwest of the Plaza de Armas along Victoria and Juárez. Those a street or two further west may be a few pesos cheaper still, but they're right in the heart of Chihuahua's small and tame, but nonetheless seedy, red-light district. Most business visitors (and car drivers) stay in the chain motels dotted around the outskirts, but without a vehicle you're better off in the centre.

Casa Chihuahua Mendez 2203, opposite the train station ⓣ614/410-0843, ⓦwww.casadechihuahua.com. This laid-back hostel features clean dorms (with four or six pinewood bunks) for M$150 per person, double rooms, a big dining area (no kitchen) and friendly owners, though they were trying to sell the place in 2009 – it will hopefully remain a hostel regardless. ③

Hotel Jardín del Centro Victoria 818 ⓣ614/415-1832. This old hotel has lots of character, with big colonial-style rooms set around a plant-filled courtyard. The less elegant quarters are around M$100 cheaper and a great bargain. There's a decent little restaurant attached. ④

Hotel San Felipe El Real Allende 1055 ⓣ614/437-2037, ⓦwww.sanfelipeelreal.com. This elegant boutique is set in a gorgeous 1882 adobe mansion with six suites decked out with tasteful antiques and canopy beds, it's centred on a blossom-smothered courtyard. ⑥

Palacio del Sol Independencia 116, five blocks west of the centre ⓣ614/412-3456, ⓦwww.hotelpalaciodelsol.com. This multistorey luxury hotel is no longer the top digs in town, though the rooms are still very lavish, with drapes, thick carpets and expansive views over the city, and come with satellite TV, free wi-fi (also computers in the lobby). Gym, pricey cafeteria and restaurant/bar round out the package. ⑥

Posada Tierra Blanca Niños Héroes 102 ⓣ614/415-0000, ⓦwww.posadatierrablanca.com.mx. Spacious, motel-style place right in the heart of the city, with an open-air pool, gymnasium, on-site restaurant and bar. The rooms are tidy and spacious, although not nearly as tasteful as they pretend to be. ⑤

Quality Inn Victoria 409 ⓣ614/439-9000, ⓦwww.choicehotels.com. You can't beat the location of this comfy business hotel, right on the main plaza; room are standard chain fare, but come with free breakfast, free airport, bus and train station transfers, wi-fi and cable TV. ⑤

The City

Chihuahua's centre of activity is the teeming **Plaza de Armas**, where its fine **Catedral Metropolitana** (Tues–Sun 6am–9pm; free) stands opposite a wonderfully camp statue of the city's founder Don Antonio Deza y Ulloa in the very act of pointing to the ground, as if to say, "Right lads, we'll build it here." The Baroque, twin-towered edifice was begun in 1725 but took more than one hundred years to complete: work well worth it, though, since the interior detail is the equal of the ornate facade. Look inside for the shrine to **Pedro Maldonado** (born here in 1892), who was beaten to death by soldiers of Mexico's anti-Catholic government in 1937. Now known as San Pedro de Jesús Maldonado Lucero, he became Chihuahua's first saint in 2000. In a modernized crypt beneath the cathedral (enter via the separate entrance on Victoria), the small **Museo de Arte Sacro** (Mon–Fri 10am–2pm & 4–6pm; M$10) displays some fine examples of Baroque Mexican religious art from the eighteenth century, notably a selection of sombre paintings of saints by Francisco Martínez and a collection of dark and forbidding images in which Christ is pushed, pulled, stabbed and punched; there are also a few works by Miguel Cabrera and memorabilia of Pope John Paul's visit in 1990.

From the plaza you can stroll north along pedestrianized Libertad, lined with chain stores and cheap snacks stalls, to Museo Casa Chihuahua and Plaza Mayor (see below), though aficionados of Mexican history should detour to the **Museo Casa de Juárez** (Tues–Sun 9am–7pm; M$10; ⓣ614/410-4258) at Juárez and Calle 5, also known as the Museo de la Lealtad Republicana ("Museum of Republican Loyalty"). This is essentially a monument to **Benito Juárez** and the turbulent years of the French Intervention; forced out of Mexico City by the French, President Juárez spent three years here from 1864, when this house was the epicentre of the independent national government. Today his former offices and personal chambers have been furnished in period style, and many of his letters and personal affects are on display, including his battered horse-drawn carriage. Other rooms put the whole period in context, though you'll need to read Spanish to make the most of this.

Museo Casa Chihuahua and around

At the north end of Libertad you'll see the **Museo Casa Chihuahua** (Wed–Mon 10am–6pm; M$40, free Sun), the former Palacio Federal and now a thoroughly absorbing museum. Built in 1910, the current structure replaced an eighteenth-century Jesuit college, which was converted to a military hospital after the expulsion of the Jesuits from Mexico in 1767. Padre Miguel Hidalgo y Costilla and Ignacio Allende, the inspiration and early leaders of the Mexican War of Independence, were imprisoned here in 1811, before being executed across the road (see below). Only one stone tower was preserved from the older structure, containing the **Calabozo de Hidalgo**, "Hidalgo's dungeon", where the rebels are said to have been held. Hidalgo's cell now forms the centrepiece of the lower-level Museo del Sitio, a series of multimedia exhibits charting the history of the building from the early Spanish missions to its rebirth as a museum. Upstairs, the Museo Patrinomio is an innovative series of galleries introducing the state of Chihuahua, divided thematically between deserts, plains and mountains, and featuring sections on art, history, traditional dress and popular culture: look out for the display on Hollywood star **Anthony Quinn**, who was born in the city in 1915, and enlightening sections on the Mormons and Menonnites.

Across the road is the stately **Palacio de Gobierno**, completed in 1892 on the other side of the former Jesuit college and containing two small museums worth a quick peek. The **Galería de Armas** (Tues–Sun 9am–5pm; free) houses an assortment of weapons from the Independence struggle, including the extraordinary 3m-long "Rifle de Avancarga", while the **Museo de Hidalgo** (same hours) commemorates the great man himself with a replica of the sacristy in Dolores where it all began; dioramas represent the Dolores church, the Querétaro Conspiracy and the attack on Guanajuato (Spanish labels only). Beyond here the main courtyard is an enthralling space lined with bold **murals** of scenes from Mexico's colonial past painted by Aarón Piña Mora in the 1960s – Hidalgo and Allende were executed here, their severed heads sent for public display in Guanajuato. The site of the deed is marked with a small shrine ("the nation's altar") on the ground floor.

Head out past the tourist information desk (see opposite) onto Plaza Hidalgo and you should see the poignant temporary monument to the **Creel Massacre** (see p.162), though this may have been dismantled by 2010. To the north lies the modern expanse of **Plaza Mayor**, with its grand monument to freedom, the Ángel de la Libertad, erected in 2003. At the north end, the **Templo de San**

Francisco de Asís is considered the oldest building in the city (dating from 1726), and though fairly plain inside has increased importance due to another Hidalgo connection. The attached Capilla de San Antonio is where the hero's headless torso was initially buried in 1811, before being exhumed and triumphantly entombed in Mexico City in 1823.

Museo Casa de Villa and around

Chihuahua's premier sight, the **Museo Casa de Villa**, or more formally the **Museo de la Revolución Mexicana**, is 2km east of the centre at Calle 10 no. 3010 (Tues–Sat 9am–7pm, Sun 10am–4pm; M$10; ⓣ614/416-2958). This enormous mansion was built by Villa (see box below) in the early twentieth-century (though he only spent time here in 1914, when governor of the state) and inhabited, until her death in 1981, by Villa's "official" widow Doña Luz Corral (there were allegedly many others); it has now been taken over by the Mexican army. The collection is a fascinating mix of weapons, war plans and personal mementos, including the bullet-riddled Dodge in which Villa was assassinated in 1923. Look out for Villa's incredibly elaborate saddles and a grimly comical poster of 1915, urging "gringos" to head south and ride with Villa for "gold and glory". Quite apart from the campaign memories, the superbly preserved old bedrooms and bathrooms, richly decorated with florid murals and Spanish floor tiles, give an interesting insight into wealthy Mexican life in the early 1900s.

To get there, walk along Ocampo, or take a bus (marked "Ocampo") two blocks past the huge Iglesia del Sagrado Corazón de Jesús, then turn left along Mendez for two more blocks. You may well want to break the journey at the extraordinarily elaborate **Museo Quinta Gameros** (Tues–Sun 11am–2pm & 4–7pm; M$20, Wed M$10; ⓣ614/416-6684), at the junction of Calle 4 and Paseo Bolivar.

Pancho Villa

Few Mexican folk heroes command so much reverence as Francisco "Pancho" Villa, the ruthless *bandito* and cattle rustler turned revolutionary, though facts about his life remain surprisingly obscure. Born in San Juan del Río, Durango, around 1878 (sources differ), to a simple peasant family, he became an outlaw whilst still a teenager and seems to have developed a loyal group of followers. Though he had virtually no formal education, Villa was not the average bandit; quick-witted and ambitious, in 1910 he decided to support the revolt of Francisco Madero (p.862) against the Díaz regime. As commander of the formidable División del Norte, Villa became a key player in the **Mexican Revolution**. He became a bitter enemy of Victoriano Huerta after Madero was executed in 1913, helping to oust the dictator the following year and briefly becoming governor of Chihuahua after hard-fought victories at Chihuahua, Ciudad Juárez, Tierra Blanca and Ojinaga. When Villa fell out with the new president, Carranza, fighting continued and even spilled across the border (leading to a failed US expedition to capture the rebel). With the death of Carranza in 1920 Villa finally laid down his guns, dividing time between Hidalgo del Parral and Chihuahua. Violence continued to haunt him however, and he was assassinated in Parral in 1923 – it was never determined who ordered the killing.

In Mexico, Villa remains a national hero, a Robin Hood-like figure who not only defeated the Mexican regime, but was also the only foreigner to attack the US (since the War of 1812) and survive. North of the border his image was enhanced by lurid US media reports – indeed, his sombrero and cartridge belts have become the stereotypical accessories of Mexican movie *banditos* ever since. Villa himself courted **Hollywood** and even starred in a film incorporating actual scenes of the Battle of Ojinaga in 1914 (portrayed by Antonio Banderas in *And Starring Pancho Villa As Himself*).

Just the sort of ostentatious display of wealth that Villa and his associates were hoping to stamp out in their battle against the landed elite, the *belle époque* showcase was built for successful mine owner Don Manuel Gameros as an exact replica of a posh Parisian home – completed in 1910, just in time for the Revolution. The hapless Gameros fled the country and his mansion became the home of Venustiano Carranza (the Gameros family did reclaim the house in the 1920s). The interior is sumptuously decorated, with magnificent Art Nouveau stained glass and ornate woodwork, and, curiously, scenes from *Little Red Riding Hood* painted on the children's bedroom wall. History buffs should also make a stop at the **Museo Tariké** (Mon–Fri 9am–6pm, Sat & Sun 10am–4pm: M$10) at Calle 4 no. 2610 (just west of 20 de Noviembre), which has a small but engaging summary of all the major events in the city's history, from the early settlements of Cochos Indians and the foundation of the Spanish town in 1709, to the 1910 Revolution and Pancho Villa.

Las Grutas de Nombre de Dios

The remarkable five-million-year-old cave system known as the **Grutas de Nombre de Dios** (Tues–Sun 9am–4pm; M$50; tours 1hr; ⓣ614/432-0518) is just fifteen minutes' ride from downtown, accessible by guided tours only. You'll be taken through seventeen caverns on a 1.3km trail studded with astonishing features such as the "Tower of Pisa" and the "Grand Canyon", a maze of crumpled rocks and dripping stalactites. Take a taxi for M$70 or a "Nombre de Dios" bus (M$6) from Calle 4 and Niños Héroes.

Eating, drinking and nightlife

There's no shortage of good **places to eat** in Chihuahua, from basic cafés around the **Mercado Popular del Centro** (west of Juárez between calles 4 and 6) and taco stalls to fancier steak houses and American burger restaurants around the main plazas.

For traditional, back-slapping cantina **drinking**, pick one of the swing-door places at the southern end of Juárez, though take care. If you're after something a little more upmarket, rub shoulders with Chihuahua's more moneyed set at the bars and clubs of the **Zona Dorada** along Juárez's northern reaches, close to its junction with Colón.

Restaurants

Café Calicanto Aldama 411 ⓣ614/410-4452. Popular restaurant with live Mexican music Tues–Sun. They serve meat-filled Chihuahuan specialities for around M$70. There's also an interesting vegetarian menu and various alcoholic coffees. Try the *beso de Santa*: coffee, milk, cognac, cinnamon and vanilla.

La Calesa Juárez 3300, at Colón ⓣ614/416-0222, ⓦwww.lacalesa.com.mx. One of Chihuahua's fanciest restaurants, all dark wood panels, crisp linen tablecloths, sparkling wine glasses and waistcoated waiters. Northern-style steaks are the house speciality. Expect to pay M$90 for *chiles rellenos de camarón* and up to M$200 for a massive plate of succulent *mariscos*. Bookings recommended at weekends.

Casa de los Milagros Victoria 810, opposite *Hotel Reforma* ⓣ614/437-0693. Casual restaurant and bar comprising a beautiful colonial courtyard with fountain, surrounded by numerous small rooms. Here, Chihuahua's well-groomed meet for margaritas (M$30), one of 25 brands of tequila (M$10–50 a shot), real coffee and light snacks such as *quesadilla de flor de calabaza* (squash flower; M$40), burgers and salads.

La Casona at Aldama and Ocampo ⓣ614/410-0063, ⓦwww.casona.com.mx. If you fancy a splurge make sure you visit this sumptuous restaurant, housed inside the main courtyard of the Casa de Don Luis Terrazas, completed in 1893 for one of the state's richest landowners. A meal of fine contemporary Mexican cuisine or Argentine steaks will cost around M$450 per person.

Chih'ua Tacos y Cortes Universidad 2902; Plaza Vallarta; Walmart, Periferico de la Juventud 6501 at Av 2200; Plaza las Haciendas;

Ⓦwww.chihuatacos.com. This much loved local *tacquería* started life as a humble stall but has morphed into a major Mexican franchise; it's worth the short taxi ride to one of its modern outlets in the city to try its huge taco plates and delicious *tortas*.
La Doña Bolivar 722, at Coronado ⓣ614/410-9025. Modern, hip coffee shop, with contemporary international cuisine, live music (jazz Fri, *trova* Sat) and happy hour Tues (6–11pm). Mon–Sat 8am–midnight, Sun 9am–5pm.
Mi Café Victoria 1000, opposite the *Hotel San Juan*. Reliable American-style diner with prices and quality both a little above average. The M$40 breakfast menu is in English and Spanish and extends from *norteño* and *ranchero* dishes to hotcakes and syrup. Come here later for burgers, sandwiches and steak and seafood mains. Free wi-fi. Daily 7.30am–10.30pm.
Pino's Burguer Carbonel and Americas; Calle 32 no. 704; ⓣ614/411-7951. With the best burgers in town, this local chain is worth making an effort to reach – it has two branches in the north of the city.

Bars and clubs

Bar San Juan Victoria 823. This hotel bar is a classic place for a beer, with old-fashioned jukebox and plenty of *tranquilo* regulars nipping in for a drink in the afternoon. Open noon–2am.
Bros Club Plaza San Agustín ⓣ614/414-7750. This bar and club was opened by popular Mexican comedian Omar Chaparro in 2005, and though the buzz has faded somewhat, it's still a lot of fun and a good place to hear live acts as well as the best DJs in the city.
Cubo Juárez 3114 ⓣ614/410-6865. One of the most popular clubs in the Zona Dorada, always packed at the weekends for the live music, hardcore house and electronica – cover is usually M$50.

Listings

Banks Most banks are centrally located, and nearly all have ATMs, with branches on Victoria and Libertad around the Plaza de Armas.
Buses The Terminal Central de Autobuses (see p.192) has representatives from Estrella Blanca, Grupo Senda, Elite, Turistar and Omnibus de México, plus Autobuses Americanos for buses to Denver, Los Angeles, Phoenix, Dallas and a few other US cities. Between the bus companies there are hourly buses to Juárez, frequent buses to Creel and a handful of buses for the five-hour jaunt to Nuevo Casas Grandes. The buses south are equally frequent, with hourly buses to Parral, at least ten buses daily to Durango, and services every other hour to Mexico City and Guadalajara.
Hospital Clínica del Centro at Ojinaga 816 (ⓣ614/439-8100).
Internet access You'll find a few terminals inside *Mi Café*, Victoria and C 6 (M$15/hr), and many more at Copy Graphix on Aldama (between Calle 10 and Ocampo), open Mon–Fri 9am–1.30pm & 3.30–7pm, Sat 8.30am–4pm (M$10/hr).
Police ⓣ060; tourist police ⓣ01800/201-5589.
Post office Libertad 1700, behind the church (Mon–Fri 8am–5pm, Sat 9am–1pm).
Travel agent Rojo y Casavantes, Guerrero 1207, at Allende ⓣ614/439-5858, Ⓦwww.rojoycasavantes.com (Mon–Fri 9am–7pm, Sat 9am–1pm).

South to Durango

Below Chihuahua sprawls a vast plain, mostly agricultural, largely uninteresting and broken only occasionally by an outstretched leg of the Sierra Madre Occidental. At **Jiménez** the road divides; Hwy-49 heads straight down through Gómez Palacio and Torreón, while Hwy-45 curves westwards to Durango.

On the longer route, **Durango** is the first of the Spanish colonial towns that distinguish Mexico's heartland, and it's certainly the most attractive city between here and the US border. That said, it's a good eight to ten hours on the bus from Chihuahua, so you might consider breaking the journey in **Hidalgo del Parral**.

Parral

PARRAL, or "Hidalgo del Parral" as it's officially known, has a certain provincial and aesthetic charm. The town is fixed in Mexican consciousness as the place where

Pancho Villa (see p.196) met his demise under a spectacular hail of hot lead in 1923. The **Museo Francisco Villa** at Juárez 11 and Barrera (Tues–Sun 10am–5pm; M$10; ⓣ627/522-5282), close to the spot where Villa's bullet-ridden vehicle came to a halt, commemorates the assassinated hero with displays of revolutionary effects, antique weapons, a small shrine and plenty of enigmatic old photos.

The town's history goes much further than this, however, having been established in the early seventeenth century as a silver-mining centre. The ramshackle spectre of the **Mina La Prieta** (Tues–Sun 10am–5pm; M$25; ⓣ627/525-4400), founded in 1629, overlooks Parral from a hill on the edge of town. It closed in 1975 but you can take a short tour of some of the mine workings, 100m down by elevator, left almost as they were over thirty years before. At the mine head there's the **Museo Regional de Minería** (Tues–Sun 10am–5pm; M$10), containing heaps of old mining equipment.

Mineral profits helped build some of the town's more impressive edifices, including the **Palacio Alvarado** (Tues–Sun 10am–5pm; M$20; ⓣ627/522-0290) on Riva Palacio, a restored mansion of 1903 commemorating local mining magnate Don Pedro Alvarado. He was reputedly a close friend and business associate of Pancho Villa, which might explain why Villa was buried in the Alvarado funerary wagon, now parked inside the building. You'll find some excellent photos in this museum that chart the town's development.

Parral is also home to several striking churches. The **Templo de San José** on Plaza Principal (not the cathedral on the Jardín Plaza de Guadalupe) is one of the oldest (dating from the 1670s) and most interesting; it houses the remains of the town's founder, Don Juan Rangel de Viesma. Also worth a look is the **Iglesia de la Virgen del Rayo**, a few minutes' walk over the river. Legend has it this was constructed by an Indian on the proceeds of the gold mine he had discovered and worked in secret; the authorities tortured him to death in an attempt to find the mine, but its location died with him.

Practicalities

Parral's compact colonial heart is around twenty minutes' walk from the main **bus terminal** (daytime luggage storage) – turn left, then left again onto Independencia – or take a bus or taxi (M$30) from just outside. There are buses almost hourly to Durango and Chihuahua, as well as frequent services to Juárez. The cheapest acceptable **hotel** in the centre is the basic but clean *Hotel Chihuahua* at Colón 1 (ⓣ627/522-1513; ❸). More comfortable, *Hotel Acosta*, near the main plaza on Agustín Barbachano 3 (ⓣ627/522-0221; ❸), is a pleasant old establishment with excellent rooms that overlook the city, a rooftop terrace and 1950s atmosphere. For a touch of luxury only a stone's throw from the bus station, stroll to the *Hotel Los Arcos*, Pedro de Lille 5 (ⓣ627/523-0597; ❹), where rooms faces a modern, plant-filled courtyard and come with satellite TV; there's also a restaurant. For **eating**, in the centre just off the plaza the bright and cheery 24-hour *Restaurant Morelos*, Plazuela Morelos 22, serves *pozole de puerco* for M$55 and excellent *enchiladas suizas*, made with chicken, guacamole and green chile. The popular *Chagos* (ⓣ627/522-2873) makes a good dinner spot, with filling, though slightly pricey, steaks; it's at Plazuela Morelos 1. If you need a **bank**, a branch of Bancomer lies on the corner of Barbachano and Coronado, at the Plaza Principal. For **internet** try SMAC-Line at Mercaderes 80 (Mon–Fri 9am–2pm & 4–7.30pm, Sat 9.30am–7.30pm; M$10/hr).

Durango

Although the Sierra Madre still looms on the western horizon, the country around **DURANGO** itself is flat. Just two low hills mark out the city from the plain: the **Cerro del Mercado**, a giant lump of iron ore that testifies to the area's

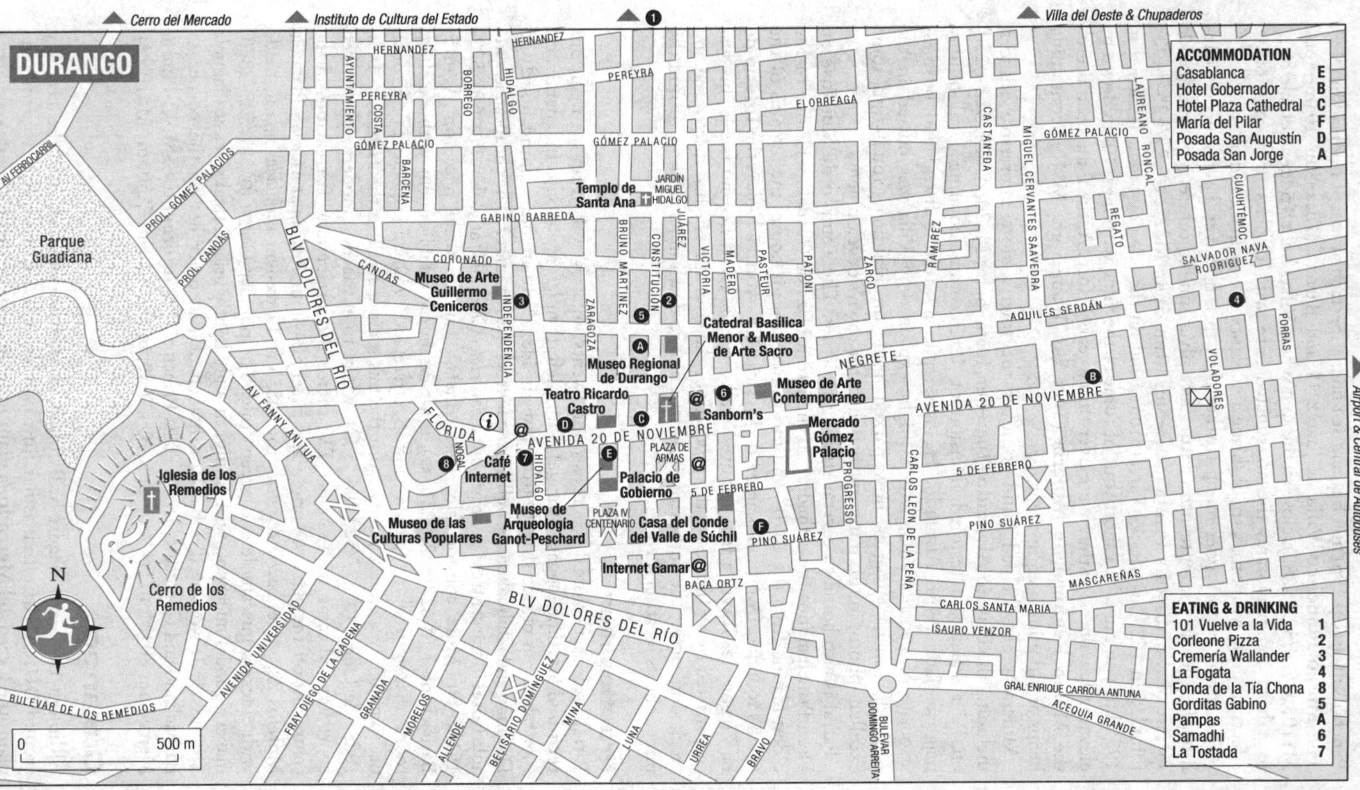
DURANGO
Cerro del Mercado
Instituto de Cultura del Estado
Villa del Oeste & Chupaderos
Airport & Central de Autobuses
Zoo (1km)
ACCOMMODATION
Casablanca E
Hotel Gobernador B
Hotel Plaza Cathedral C
María del Pilar F
Posada San Augustín D
Posada San Jorge A
EATING & DRINKING
101 Vuelve a la Vida 1
Corleone Pizza 2
Cremería Wallander 3
La Fogata 4
Fonda de la Tía Chona 8
Gorditas Gabino 5
Pampas A
Samadhi 6
La Tostada 7
Templo de Santa Ana
Jardín Miguel Hidalgo
Museo de Arte Guillermo Ceniceros
Catedral Basílica Menor & Museo de Arte Sacro
Museo Regional de Durango
Teatro Ricardo Castro
Museo de Arte Contemporáneo
Sanborn's
Mercado Gómez Palacio
Plaza de Armas
Palacio de Gobierno
Café Internet
Museo de Arqueología Ganot-Peschard
Museo de las Culturas Populares
Plaza IV Centenario
Casa del Conde del Valle de Súchil
Internet Gamar
Iglesia de los Remedios
Cerro de los Remedios
Parque Guadiana
Avenida 20 de Noviembre
Blv Dolores del Río
Av Fanny Anitua
Avenida Universidad
Bulevar de los Remedios
Bulevar Domingo Arreita
Gral Enrique Carrola Antuna
Acequia Grande
Av Ferrocarril
Prol. Gómez Palacios
Prol. Canoas
0 500 m
N

mineral wealth, rises squat and black to the north, while to the west a climb up the **Cerro de los Remedios** provides a wonderful panorama over the whole city. Officially named Victoria de Durango, the city, with its nearly 550,000 inhabitants, sits between these two hills in the Valle del Guadiana. Highways 45 and 40 intersect here, making it an important transport junction between the coast and the interior cities of Torréon, Saltillo and Monterrey, but the town is worth a visit of a day or two in its own right, with beautiful colonial architecture and evocative film sets where the likes of John Wayne made movies in the 1960s. The people, too, are a charismatic and gregarious bunch whose hospitality comes as a charming respite from the north.

Durango's **fiesta**, on July 8, celebrates the city's foundation on that day in 1563 by Francisco de Ibarra. Festivities commence several days before and run right through till the fiesta of the Virgen del Refugio on July 22 – well worth going out of your way for, though rooms are booked solid.

Arrival and information

Buses arrive at the **Central de Autobuses** (guardería, 7am–11pm) over 4km east of downtown; to get to the centre, take one of the off-white buses (M$5) marked "Centro" or "ISSSTE" from in front of the station. These will drop you right at the Plaza de Armas near the cathedral. **Taxis** are metered and should be around M$25. Facing the cathedral, turn left along 20 de Noviembre (as it runs into Florida) just past Independencia to reach the second-floor **tourist office**, Florida 1106 Pte (Mon–Fri 8am–8pm; ⓣ618/811-9677, ⓦwww.durangoturismo.com).

Accommodation

There's no shortage of **rooms** in Durango, though you should book ahead if you want to visit during the fiesta. Most of the cheaper places are pretty grim; if price is your only concern, try around the market, though even here the better places charge heavily. If you're willing to spend a little more, Durango has a couple of very fine places worth splashing out on, and there are the usual motel chains on the outskirts along Blv Francisco Villa if you're driving.

Casablanca 20 de Noviembre 811 Pte, at Zaragoza ⓣ618/811-3599, ⓦwww.hotelcasablancadurango.com.mx. Big, old-fashioned colonial hotel. Spacious, comfortable and reasonably good value, if unexciting. ❺

Hotel Gobernador 20 de Noviembre 257 Ote ⓣ618/813-1919, ⓦwww.hotelgobernador.com.mx. The best hotel in town is a luxurious monolith surrounded by verdant gardens; the spacious rooms come with marble-clad bathrooms and wall-mounted LCD TVs, and there's a pool, gym and all the business-related extras. ❼

Hotel Plaza Cathedral Constitución 216, beside the cathedral ⓣ618/813-2480. Great value for such a charming, historic and centrally located hotel. Most of the rooms aren't as spacious as the grandiose stone corridors might suggest, but it's still the best budget option considering its position right next to the cathedral. ❸

María del Pilar Pino Suárez 410 ⓣ618/811-5471. The rooms inside this pink building are all clean and tidy, come with private bath and phone and are a pretty good deal for your money. The management keeps a good stock of maps and other tourist information in the lobby. ❷

Posada San Augustin 20 de Noviembre 906 Pte, at Hidalgo ⓣ618/837-2000, ⓦwww.posadasanagustin.com. Excellent mid-range option, with simple but cosy a/c rooms with cable TV, set around a courtyard in a graceful nineteenth-century building – tends to be quieter than the *San Jorge*. ❹

Posada San Jorge Constitución 102 Sur, at Serdán ⓣ618/813-3257, ⓦwww.hotelposadasanjorge.com.mx. The best of the mid-range places, a gorgeous eighteenth-century colonial house and former treasury, with a two-storey courtyard alive with the song of caged birds and chatter from the attached Brazilian restaurant. Rooms, all with cable TV, are individually decorated in rustic fashion, with tiled floors, wood beams, bold paintwork and potted cacti. Prices drop by about M$200 off-season. ❺

The Town

Almost all the monuments in downtown Durango are clustered in a few streets around the **Plaza de Armas** and the huge covered market nearby. On the plaza itself is the **Catedral Basílica Menor** (daily 7.30am–1.30pm & 4–9pm; free) its two robust domed towers dwarfing the narrow facade. It's a typical Mexican church in every way: externally imposing, weighty and Baroque, with a magnificent setting overlooking the plaza, but the interior is ultimately disappointing – dim and uninspired by comparison. Much better is the opulent collection of religious art and historical artefacts within the cathedral's **Museo de Art Sacro** (Tues–Fri 10am–1.30pm & 4–7pm, Sat & Sun 9am–2pm; M$15); enter on Negrete, behind the cathedral.

South of the cathedral

Following 20 de Noviembre down from the cathedral (stretching away to the left as you face it) brings you to the grandiose Porfiriano **Teatro Ricardo Castro** (daily 9am–3pm; free), completed in 1924, with its elegant interior of marble floors and crystal chandeliers. Turn south onto Zaragoza near here for the **Museo de Arqueología Ganot-Peschard** (Tues–Fri 9am–6.30pm, Sat & Sun 11am–6pm; M$5; ⓣ618/813-1047) at no. 315, which has a fine display of pre-Columbian finds from Durango state (Spanish captions only). Keep walking south and you'll come out at 5 de Febrero and **Plaza IV Centenario**, its north side dominated by the porticoed facade of the **Palacio de Gobierno** (daily 9am–6pm; free). Originally the eighteenth-century mansion of Spanish mining magnate Juan José Zambrano, it was taken over by the local government after the War of Independence. Local artist Francisco Montoya de la Cruz decorated the stairwells and walls of the two-storey, arcaded patio inside in 1950 with bold murals depicting the state's history.

If you walk west along 5 de Febrero, just beyond Independencia, you'll find the **Museo de las Culturas Populares** at no. 1107 (Tues–Fri 9am–6pm, Sat 10–6pm, Sun noon–7pm; M$5; ⓣ618/825-8827), with rooms dedicated to local, native styles of weaving, ceramics, basketware and mask-making. Enthusiastic guides explain all, and there are often interesting temporary exhibitions.

▲ Catedral Basílica Menor, Durango

Heading back along 5 de Febrero in the other direction leads to the **Casa del Conde del Valle de Súchil** at Madero, the most elaborate of the town's Spanish-style mansions. Built in the eighteenth century by the Conde de Súchil, sometime Spanish governor of Durango, its exuberantly carved columns and wealth of extravagant detail are quite undamaged by time. History has given the mansion some strange functions, though: it was the seat of the local Inquisition for some time, while nowadays it's owned by a bank, having had a brief spell as an upmarket shopping mall. A little further along 5 de Febrero, you reach the back of the **Mercado Gómez Palacio**. It covers a whole block on two storeys and sells just about everything anyone could want, from medicinal herbs to farm equipment to food; it also holds a couple of *bodegas* upstairs that serve beer to a primarily local crowd.

North of the cathedral

Back at the main plaza, you can stroll up Constitución, a lively shopping street with several small restaurants, perhaps taking a detour at Serdán and walking over to the **Museo Regional de Durango** at Victoria 100 Sur (Tues–Sat 9am–3.45pm, Sun 10–3pm; M$10). The captivating former residence of ex-Governor Francisco Gómez Palacio, completed in 1890, houses another small exhibition on local history, and a more engaging collection of Miguel Cabrera paintings.

Further up Constitución lies the **Jardín Miguel Hidalgo** and Templo de Santa Ana, much more peaceful than the main plaza for an evening *paseo*. From here you can make a loop back to the tourist office via the **Museo de Arte Guillermo Ceniceros** (Tues–Sun 9am–6pm; free; ⓣ618/825-0027) at Independencia 135 Nte, a vibrant showcase for local Durango artists, including Guillermo Ceniceros himself. Alternatively, take a taxi to the **Instituto de Cultura del Estado de Durango** (ICED) at 16 de Septiembre 130 (Tues–Fri 9am–6pm, Sat & Sun 10am–6pm; free). Housed in another series of grand Porfiriano buildings, Durango's premier cultural space contains several small but enlightening exhibits on the history and culture of the state, including an art gallery and the **Museo del Cine Rafael Trujillo**, dedicated to the famous Durango film-maker and absorbing many of the film-related exhibits from the former Museo del Cine. By 2010 there should also be a Museo de la Revolución on site.

Cerro de los Remedios

If you have kids in tow, or just fancy a break from bus diesel fumes, make for the prominent Cerro de los Remedios, 2km west of the city centre, or more particularly, **Parque Guadiana** on its northwestern flanks – take a bus marked "Remedios/Parque Guadiana" from outside the cathedral (M$5) – a vast area of fragrant eucalyptus and shady willows, dotted with fountains and kids' playgrounds. Durango's latest pride and joy adjoins the park on Parque Sahuatoba Blv: the **Museo Interactivo Bebeleche** (ⓦwww.bebeleche.org.mx), a lavish hands-on museum and learning centre targeted at children – it should be open by 2010, but check the website or tourist office for the latest.

Eating, drinking and nightlife

It isn't difficult to find great **places to eat** in Durango, among them – and for no apparent reason – a proliferation of Italian restaurants. Your cheapest eating options are the stalls upstairs in the **market**, some of which serve excellent food. Apart from on Sunday evenings, when the streets around the plaza are blocked off for the weekly free **entertainment** – mainly *norteña* and *ranchera* bands – nightlife revolves around the restaurants. For **live music**, try *Tres Durangos* at Negrete 308 (ⓣ618/811-1747).

101 Vuelve a la Vida Felipe Pescador at Cuauhtémoc ⓣ618/818-9027. If you fancy seafood, it's worth hopping in a taxi (5min) for this popular, no-frills place, serving excellent shellfish and fresh seafood platters, as well as a host of cheap beers and cocktails.

Corleone Pizza Constitución 114 Nte, at Serdán ⓣ618/811-6900. One of the best Italian joints in the city, this buzzing family restaurant is best known for its pizzas (from M$50) and an admirable range of cocktails.

Cremería Wallander Independencia 128 Nte ⓣ618/811-7705. Tempting store loaded with locally made cheeses, baked goods, cookies, cakes and huge tortas for lunch (M$25–50).

La Fogata Cuauhtémoc 200 Sur at Negrete ⓣ618/817-0347. This moderately priced, elegant restaurant is the choice of Durango's movers and shakers, serving international and Mexican food but best known for its succulent steaks.

Fonda de la Tía Chona Nogal 110 ⓣ618/812-7748. A Durango dinner favourite, the ageing, ornate interior is often packed with *Durangueños*. It serves excellent traditional Durango cuisine (try their *caldillo durangueño*, beef stew) at reasonable prices (M$50–150).

Gorditas Gabino Constitución 100 Nte ⓣ618/813-0121. Bright, clean, economical restaurant serving steaks, tacos, burritos and burgers. They do a pretty decent *enchiladas rojas* for a few pesos, and the trademark gorditas (deep-fried corn meal with sausage) are fabulous.

Pampas Constitución 102 Sur, in the *San Jorge* hotel ⓣ618/827-6121, ⓦwww.pampasdurango.com. Its menu largely comprises Brazilian cuts of juicy grilled steak and meats, in something resembling *churrascuria*-style eating.

Samadhi Negrete 403 Pte ⓣ618/811-6227. Small, brightly coloured joint, which serves a bargain veggie *comida* for M$35–55, yogurt, salads and vegetable-filled enchiladas.

La Tostada Florida 1125 ⓣ618/811-4577. This pleasant, clean restaurant is popular with the locals. It serves Mexican staples and good breakfasts too, all for under M$50.

Listings

Banks There's a convenient branch of Bancomer right by the plaza at the corner of 20 de Noviembre and Constitución, in addition to several other banks nearby.

Buses Durango's bus station is well connected to points both north and south, with multiple services a day to destinations including Aguascalientes, Ciudad Juárez, Mazatlán, Mexico City, Monterrey, Parral and Zacatecas.

Internet access Durango usually has several inexpensive internet cafés, though as always, places seem to go in and out of business fast. Try Ofinet on Victoria (Mon–Sat 9.30am–9pm; M$10/hr).

Post office Some twelve blocks east of the cathedral, at 20 de Noviembre 500-B Ote (Mon–Fri 8am–6pm, Sat 9am–noon).

Around Durango: movie sets

The full title of Durango's tourist office is the **Dirección de Turismo y Cinematografía del Estado de Durango**. Until fairly recently it spent much of its time organizing the vast number of **film** units that came to the area to take advantage of its remarkably constant, clear, high-altitude light, its desert and mountain scenery. Westerns were the speciality: John Wayne made seven films here, and in the 1990s comedian John Candy actually died in Durango whilst filming his last movie. Although only half a dozen movies have been shot here over the last decade (*Bandidas* in 2004 was the last one), you can still see the remains of the permanent sets at Villa del Oeste and Chupaderos. The main road from Parral runs within a few hundred metres of these movie towns, so it's easy enough to get there by bus (around M$15), though flagging one down when you leave can take much longer – alternatively you can take the special bus to Villa del Oeste on Saturday and Sunday from Plaza de Armas in Durango (M$30, includes admission), forty minutes before each show.

Villa del Oeste (Tues–Fri noon–7pm, Sat & Sun 11am–7pm; M$10, weekends M$25; ⓣ618/112-2882), lies 12km north of Durango, a kind of small theme park comprising the hundred-metre-long street of Bandido, which looks straight out of the Wild West until you realize the saloons and shops have been refashioned into a themed restaurant, music hall and a bar and grill. During the week it's fairly quiet, but on weekends there's a kitschy but enjoyable show featuring gun-slinging cowboys and cabaret girls (Sat 2.30 & 4.30pm; Sun 1.30, 3.30 & 5.30pm; free with park entry).

If all this sounds too cheesy, take a Parral-bound bus to the dusty village of **CHUPADEROS**, 2km further north, where the villagers have pretty much taken over a former set: the church and "Prairie Lands Hotel" are lived in and one house is a grocery store. A good way to link the two towns is to catch the bus out to Chupaderos, then follow the track past the lived-in church, across the train tracks and through scrubby, cactus-strewn desert 2km to a kind of back entrance to Bandido in Villa del Oeste, where you may or may not be charged entry. It is a particularly nice walk in the late afternoon, past the heat of the day.

On **leaving Durango** you face a simple choice: **west** to the Pacific at Mazatlán, over an incredible road through the Sierra Madre, which is itself a worthwhile journey; **east** towards Torreón, Saltillo and Monterrey; or **south** to Zacatecas (see p.248), among the finest of Mexico's colonial cities.

The northeast

Most travellers simply pass through the **northeast** after crossing the US border, hot-footing it straight to the Bajío (Chapter 4) or even Veracruz (Chapter 9), but they miss out on some iconic Mexican food, music and a smattering of absorbing sights – besides, you're talking at least twelve hours on the bus.

The northeast **border towns** themselves attract a steady stream of day-trippers from the US, though like elsewhere this trade was severely disrupted in 2009, and anyway, with a couple of exceptions there's little to keep you from heading south as quickly as possible. It would certainly be a pity to miss **Monterrey**, Mexico's industrial dynamo and home to some of the nation's best museums and its most famous brewery. Neighbouring **Saltillo** is a pleasant place to break a long journey, while the adventurous can assess the growing quality of **Parras** wines.

The Lower Río Bravo Valley: Ciudad Acuña to Matamoros

The **Río Bravo**, known to Americans as the **Río Grande**, forms the border between Texas and Mexico, a distance of more than 1500km. The country through which it flows is arid semi-desert, and the towns along the lower section of the river are heavily industrialized and suffer from appalling environmental pollution. This is the **maquiladora** zone, where foreign-owned assembly plants produce consumer goods, most of them for export to the US. There are few attractions for tourists, however, and most visitors are here only for cheap bric-a-brac shopping, tasty **snacks** or simply passing through on their way south.

Ciudad Acuña

The smallest of the border towns, **CIUDAD ACUÑA** is quiet, relaxed and intensely hot. Its dusty, iconic Tex-Mex streets have proved a magnet for film-makers: Robert Rodriguez's cult Mexican thriller *El Mariachi* (1992) and its sequel, *Desperado* (1995), were shot here (*Mariachi* lead actor Carlos Gallardo was actually born in the town). Contrary to the images portrayed on the silver screen however, Acuña is one of the least violent towns on the border, noted more for its classic **diners** and, (somewhat bizarrely), dove-hunting than gunfights.

Practicalities

Arriving over the bridge from **Del Rio** (pedestrians US$0.75; cars US$2.50), Texas, there's a map of the town in the modern customs building, together with some limited tourist information. A fully fledged **tourist information** office is at Lerdo 110 where it meets Hidalgo (Mon–Fri 9am–5pm; ⓣ877/772-1600). The main **bus station**, at the corner of Matamoros and Ocampo, is just five blocks from the border and one from the plaza. Of the **banks**, Bancomer, Madero 360, off Juárez, has a 24-hour ATM, as does Scotiabank at the corner of Guerrero and Madero. The **post office** is at Hidalgo 320, past Juárez. You'll pass several **hotels** as you walk down Hidalgo from the border: none is especially good value, but if you want to stay near the gaudy heart of town, try the *Hotel Villa Real*, Bravo 643 (ⓣ877/772-7949, ⓦwww.hvillareal.com; ❻), which is five blocks from the border and equipped with all the standard chain-hotel comforts.

The biggest **bars** and **restaurants** in Acuña – the ones which cater to dollar-toting border-crossers – are located around Hidalgo and Madero. Everyone seems to end up at Texan-favourite *Ma Crosby's*, Hidalgo 195 Ote (ⓣ877-772-2020), at Matamoros and Hidalgo, a restaurant/bar since the 1920s serving all sorts of easy-to-eat Mexican food – the menu is in English and the prices in US$s, but it's worth going just to see what all the fuss is about. For cheaper cakes and buns head a few blocks down Hidalgo to the venerable *Panadería Chapa*, where you can stuff yourself for a few pesos. The other obligatory stop for all visitors here is the *Corona Club* at Hidalgo 200, the bar that featured in *Desperado* and now smothered in signed US$ bills rather than bullet holes.

Onward transport is more frequent from towns further south, and it may be easier to head to Piedras Negras, ninety minutes away, and change **buses** there; however, there are a few daily services from Acuña to **Saltillo** (7hr) and **Monterrey** (8hr) via Monclova, and a couple to Mexico City.

Piedras Negras

Quaint, friendly and hassle-free, with the most laid-back immigration officers you're likely to encounter anywhere in Mexico, **PIEDRAS NEGRAS** is the ideal border town. It's also the unlikely place where **nachos**, the ubiquitous Tex-Mex snack food, were "invented" in the 1940s. The unpretentious main plaza is directly opposite the international bridge, and hotels and restaurants aren't far away. Nonetheless, there's no reason to stay longer than it takes than grab a meal and catch the first bus south.

Practicalities

Piedras Negras's extremely helpful **tourist office** (Mon–Fri 9am–5pm; ⓣ878/782-8424, ⓦwww.ocvpiedrasnegras.com), by the main square as you enter Mexico from **Eagle Pass**, Texas (border bridge toll: pedestrians US$0.50, cars US$2.50), has free maps of the town and Eagle Pass on the other side, as well as of other cities in Coahuila. From the customs post, Allende runs straight ahead

The king of nachos

Contrary to popular belief, that addictive combination of crispy tortilla chips and melted cheese – a staple snack all over the US and beyond – is not traditional Mexican food. Nachos were actually dreamt up in 1943 in **Piedras Negras** by Ignacio "Nacho" Anaya, allegedly whilst trying to feed a group of US army wives after hours. He was forced to cook up whatever he had left in the kitchen: essentially toasted tortillas, cheese and jalapeño peppers. The idea caught on, especially in Texas, but it wasn't until the 1970s that "nachos" became popular throughout the US (it's never had quite the same appeal in Mexico). When Anaya died in 1975 a bronze plaque in his memory was erected in Piedras Negras, and the town hosts an **International Nacho Festival** around October 21 each year. The two-day event features live music, art and a goofy attempt to make the world's biggest nacho.

The original nacho restaurant no longer exists, but Anaya went on to work at the *Moderno Restaurant*, Morelos 407-A (Ⓣ878/782-0098), which still uses the original "recipe". Here you can order the classic nachos (cheese and jalapeño only), or the special nachos prepared with fresh jumbo shrimp.

towards the **bus station** (Ⓣ878/782-7484) – a taxi should be around M$25. You'll find frequent first- and second-class departures to all the major points south including **Mexico City** (17hr), **Monterrey** (5hr) and **Saltillo** (7hr). If you're headed **Stateside**, cross the border to Eagle Pass and walk 200m north to the Greyhound station, which has three direct departures to San Antonio daily (3hr–3hr 20min; US$30). Bancomer (Mon–Sat 9am–5pm), one block from the main plaza on Morelos and Abasolo, has a 24-hour ATM.

If you get stuck here, the best deal by far is the comfortable *Autel Río*, Padre de las Casas 121 Nte, at Teran (Ⓣ878/782-7064; ④), with cable TV in every room, a swimming pool and plenty of parking space; they also offer guests free internet access and a light breakfast in the lobby.

For a great introduction to cheap Mexican **food**, head straight for the *taquerías* around the market, or head to the *Moderno* (see box above).

Nuevo Laredo

The giant of the eastern border towns, **NUEVO LAREDO** is alive with the imagery and commercialism of the frontier. It doubles as the transport hub for the whole area, with dozens of departures to Mexico City and all major towns in the north. Cross-border traffic, legal and illegal, is king here, and both bridges from the Texan town of **Laredo** are usually crowded with pedestrians and vehicles 24 hours a day. The Mexican side greets you with insurance offices and sleazy *cantinas*; traditionally the town has drawn visitors because of its bars, souvenir shops and cheap "prescription" drugs. Yet like everywhere else on the border, tourism virtually collapsed in 2009. Even though a heavy police presence and an apparent truce between cartels have seen drug-related violence in the city tail off since 2008 (it had seen some of the worst in Mexico), there's little point in staying.

Coming from **Laredo**, Texas, it's best simply to move on as fast as possible. If you want to have a quick look around head up Guerrero, past the curio shops and dozens of casas de cambio, and you'll find everything you're likely to need within seven or eight blocks of the border. Walk past the first square, **Plaza Juárez**, home to the cathedral, and head for the main square, the palm-shaded **Plaza Hidalgo**, easily the most pleasant spot in the city. If you need to kill a couple of hours, the pride and joy of Nuevo Laredo is the **Estación Palabra Gabriel García Márquez** (Mon & Wed–Sat 10am–7pm, Sun noon–5pm; free; Ⓦwww.estacionpalabra.com), a smart new literary centre named, rather tenuously, to commemorate the arrival in Mexico of the famous Colombian writer here in 1961. The centre contains a small bookshop, library, temporary art exhibits and a tranquil reading room; it's in the old train station at César López de Lara 1020, 2km southwest of the border.

Practicalities

If you're entering or leaving Mexico on foot, you'll take Puente Internacional No. 1; there's a small toll, payable in dollars or pesos if you're heading north, but in US currency only (US$0.75) when Mexico-bound – cars pay US$3 (coming back it's around US$0.35 on foot and US$3 for cars, or peso-equivalent). The bridge becomes the main drag, Ave Guerrero, on the Mexican side, but drivers can also use the nearby Puente Internacional No. 2 (same tolls), and bypass downtown. Despite the crush, immigration usually proceeds smoothly, though expect long queues crossing to the US in the mornings and on Sunday evenings.

Nuevo Laredo's huge **Central de Autobuses** (24hr guardería) is around 5km south of town at Refugio Romo 4731 and Melgar (used mostly by the Senda and Estrella Blanca companies), but battered city buses (marked "Puente"/"Centro") run frequently between here, the border crossings and Plaza Hidalgo (M$5); it's about a 25-minute journey. Buses back (marked "Carretera") leave from outside the Palacio Municipal – which houses the **post office** – tucked around the back on Camargo. **Taxis** should be around M$50, though drivers may ask for a lot more. More convenient is the **Nueva Terminal de Autobuses** (Ⓣ867/719-3884) at César López de Lara 3228 and Oaxaca, which is used by Autobuses del Noreste and Ómnibus de México (including Turistar Ejecutivo). Both terminals are served by buses from Monterrey (3hr) and Mexico City (15hr) day and night. Other buses come and go from Saltillo, Ciudad Victoria, Guadalajara and Zacatecas and Tampico. The Greyhound bus station in Laredo has frequent connections to San Antonio (2hr 30min; US$30).

Quetzalcóatl International Airport is 14km and a long taxi ride (about M$200) out of town. There's actually nothing international about it, as the only (very expensive) flights available are between here and Mexico City (on Mexicana). **Laredo International Airport** across the border has connections to Houston and Dallas – taxis charge US$40 back and forth from the Mexican side of the border.

The **tourist office** (Mon–Fri 9am–5pm; Ⓣ867/713-7008, Ⓦwww.turismonuevolaredo.gob.mx) is about three blocks from the border in the old Banco Longoria building at Matamoros 309, one block west of Guerrero. Bancomer and Santander **banks**, both with ATMs, are around the corner at the junction of Reforma and Canales.

If for some reason you get stuck here it's best to opt for the safer chain **hotels** that surround the centre: the *Crowne Plaza* (Ⓣ867/711-6200, Ⓦwww.crowneplaza.com/nuevolaredo; ❺) at Reforma 3500, around 6km south of the border, is one of the newer, better options and internet room rates are reasonable. The *Fiesta Inn* (Ⓣ867/711-4444, Ⓦwww.fiestainn.com; ❺) at Reforma 5530 is a similarly safe and comfy choice.

There are plenty of decent places to **eat** around town, though many have closed since the downturn. Try the local *cabrito* (smoked young goat) if you get a chance; *El Principal* at Guerrero 624 and Dr. Mier (Ⓣ867/712-1301) and *El Rincón del Viejo* (Ⓣ867/712-2523) at Dr. Mier 4835 are always good value (reckon on M$50–150 per dish).

Reynosa

A very easy border crossing and excellent transport connections combine to make **REYNOSA** a favourite point to enter Mexico. A sprawling industrial city filled with car repair shops and PEMEX plants, it holds little to detain you, but the centre is compact, people are generally friendly and coming and going is simple.

Practicalities

Crossing the international bridge over the Río Bravo from **McAllen**, Texas (US$0.50 pedestrian toll, US$2.25 for cars), don't forget to call in at the *migración* office (assuming you're headed south) and perhaps the small **tourist office** (Mon–Fri 9am–5pm; ⓣ899/922-5186, ⓦwww.tamaulipas.gob.mx), though don't expect too much information. The **bus station** is probably your first priority, and though **buses** (M$5) do run into the centre and out again to the Central Camionera, it's easier simply to take a **taxi** (around M$30) or tackle the twenty-minute walk. Immediately off the bridge, head straight on along Lerdo de Tejada, which soon becomes Zaragoza, to the Plaza Principal, about five blocks down, where you'll find a couple of **banks** with ATMs. From here the bus station can be reached by following Hidalgo, the pedestrianized main street, for a few blocks and then turning left into Colón.

Hotels here aren't great value for your money, and, as always, it makes sense to head south as fast as possible; Monterrey is only three hours by bus. If you have to stay, the *Grand Premier Hotel*, Colón 1304 (ⓣ899/922-4850; ⑤) is a safe, comfortable choice in town, but otherwise head to the modern chain hotels on the outskirts via Hwy-40 to Monterrey (Blv Hidalgo): the *Holiday Inn Industrial Poniente* at Hidalgo and Avenida Encino (ⓣ899/909-0170, ⓦwww.holidayinn.com; ⑦) is a solid, high-class option.

There are a number of inexpensive **food stalls** and a Gigante supermarket by the bus station, as well as the well-stocked **Mercado Zaragoza** on Hidalgo, one block south of the Plaza Principal. For a proper meal, you can't beat *La Mansión del Prado*, at Emilio Portes Gil and Mendez (ⓣ899/922-9914; closed Sun), which serves huge steaks, and great seafood.

Moving on, the Valley Transit Co operates buses between Reynosa bus station and the Greyhound station in McAllen, Texas (where there are frequent departures to San Antonio), roughly every thirty minutes between 5.30am and 8.30pm (US$2 or peso-equivalent). The nine-kilometre journey takes about forty minutes, including immigration. Buses to the rest of Mexico include services to Matamoros (1hr) and Ciudad Victoria (4hr 30min); Tampico (7hr) and Veracruz (16hr) on the Gulf coast; and Monterrey (3hr), Mexico City (13hr) and Zacatecas (10hr).

Matamoros

MATAMOROS, across the Río Grande from the southernmost point of Texas, at **Brownsville**, is a buzzing little town with more history than the settlements strung out to its west. What began in the mid-eighteenth century as a cattle-ranching colony eventually became known – with the introduction of the port of Bagdad – as "La Puerta México", and in the nineteenth century Matamoros (along with Veracruz) became the main port of entry for foreign immigrants. At the turn of the nineteenth century, rail lines from both sides of the border were directed through Matamoros, and again the city found itself as the necessary link in the trade crossroads. And since the passage of **NAFTA** in 1994, Matamoros has established itself as an important point for trade.

Arrival and information

Having paid your toll (US$0.50 or M$5 for pedestrians, cars pay US$2.25 and U$2.10 or M$24 coming back), walked across the Puente Nuevo (24hr) and dealt with immigration, you'll be wanting the casa de cambio at the border before boarding the fixed-price *peseros* (M$5) known here as "maxi taxis", which run

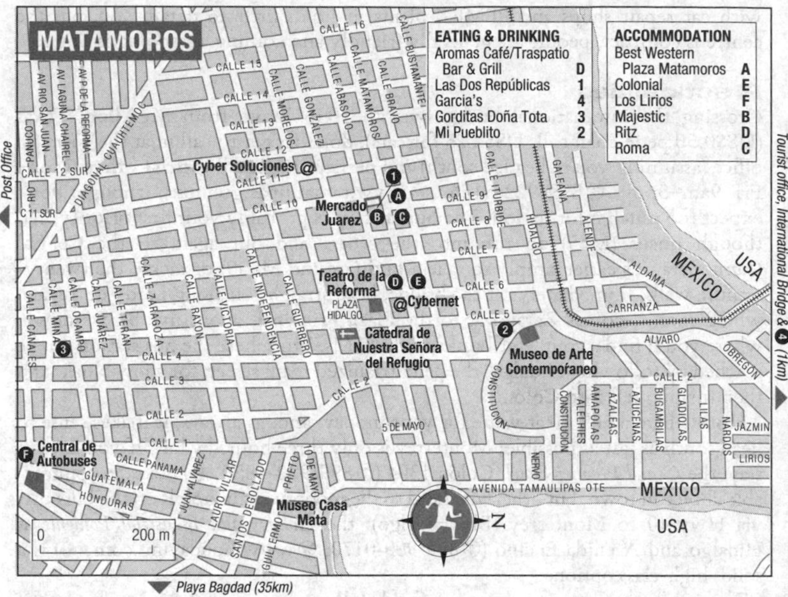

frequently along Obregón to the centre and the **Central de Autobuses** (☎871/812-2777; restaurant and guardería 6.30am–10.30pm), a long way south on Canales (look for "Centro" for Plaza Allende, "Puente Internacional" for the border or "Central" for the bus station). If heading into the Mexican interior, don't forget to have your tourist card stamped at the border. **Taxis** at the border will ask for US$6–8 (M$80) for trips in town and M$100 or more for the bus station – locals rarely pay more than M$50.

The Matamoros **tourist office** (Mon–Fri 9am–6pm, Sat 9am–3pm; ☎868/812-0212, Ⓦwww.ocvmatamoros.com.mx), right at the Mexican border post, is worthwhile for the latest Matamoros info, or for any destinations further south. Ask about the **free buses** that depart from near here to Mercado Juárez.

Accommodation

Staying in Matamoros is no problem. There are hotels in all price categories, including several good budget choices on Abasolo, the pedestrianized street between calles 6 and 11, a block north of Plaza Hidalgo. There are also a number of **more expensive** hotels in the same area; if you're in a large group, it can be worthwhile asking for a suite.

Best Western Plaza Matamoros Bravo 1421 and C 9 ☎868/816-1696, Ⓦwww.bestwestern.com/mx/hotelplazamatamoros. If you're looking for a bit of comfort in the centre, this is the best choice; it's average chain hotel fare by US standards, but it's clean and safe, and the free breakfast is good – you also get free transport within the city. Restaurant, parking and rooms with a/c, free internet and cable TV. ❺

Colonial corner of C 6 and Matamoros 603 ☎868/816-6606, Ⓦwww.hcolonial.com. This is the best mid-range choice. The colourful and clean Mexican-style rooms have Spanish tile floors (some with small balconies), though this is colonial-style rather than truly historic. ❺

Los Lirios Aguilar 9 and C 1 ☎868/813-4406. Great budget choice, with spacious, clean rooms and simple showers, very close to the bus station. ❸

Majestic Abasolo 131 ☎868/813-3680. Best value among the budget hotels; the staff are friendly and rooms are clean, large and have ample hot water. ❷

Ritz Matamoros 612 at C 7 ⓣ868/812-1190, ⓦwww.ritzhotel.org. Comfortable hotel with slightly old-fashioned rooms, but whose rates include buffet breakfast. There's a suite available for six people, plus plenty of safe parking, cable TV, and it's about M$100 cheaper at weekends. ❺

Roma at C 9 and Bravo 1420 ⓣ868/813-6176, ⓦwww.hotelfroma.com. Not as nice as the Best Western across the street, but it's at least M$200 cheaper and perfectly adequate considering the central location. Rooms are a bit plain, but come with free wi-fi and basic cable. ❺

The Town

Matamoros's busy but compact *centro histórico*, focused on plazas Hidalgo and Allende and the **Mercado Juárez**, on calles 9 and 10, is a fairly stereotypical Mexican city centre. You'll find the rather dour-looking **Catedral de Nuestra Señora del Refugio** on Hidalgo, originally completed in 1833 but best known today for its valuable reproduction of Michelangelo's *La Pietà* inside, carved from Carrera marble in Italy in 2005.

If you've got an hour to kill, pop along to the **Museo Casa Mata**, Santos Degollado at Guatemala (Tues–Sat 8am–4pm, Sun 8am–2pm; free), which houses a collection of memorabilia from the Revolution and a selection of Huastec ceramics in a fort begun in 1845 to repel invaders from north of the border. When Zachary Taylor stormed in the following year, however, the building was still unfinished. Near the centre at the northeast corner of Abasolo and Calle 6, is the historic **Teatro de la Reforma** (ⓣ868/812-5120) originally completed in 1865, but replaced by a modern building in the 1950s. In 1992 the theatre was meticulously restored to its original style at the request of the town mayor, and now hosts drama and ballet performances and various local entertainment. You might also check out the **Museo de Arte Contemporáneo de Tamaulipas** (Tues–Sat 10am–2pm & 3–6pm; M$15, free Wed; ⓣ868/813-1499, ⓦwww.mact.tamaulipas.gob.mx), at Constitución and Quinta, just off Obregón, an exuberant Modernist structure that shows revolving exhibitions from some of the best contemporary Mexican multimedia artists.

Playa Bagdad

Playa Bagdad, Matamoros's pleasant beach 35km east of town, was named after the US port of Bagdad, which stood at the mouth of the Río Grande and was at one point the only port supplying the Confederates during the Civil War. Clean (though watch out for broken glass) and pounded by invigorating surf, it offers the chance for a first (or last) dip in the surf off Mexico's Gulf coast, and is very popular at weekends with Mexican families, who gather in the shade of the palapas that stretch for miles along the sand. There are lots of **seafood restaurants**, but few actually seem to offer much worth eating, so most locals bring picnics or cook on the public barbecues. You'll need half a day to make a worthwhile trip out to the beach, though you can **camp** for free in the sandhills. To get there, take a *combi* (M$25) marked "Playa" from the Plaza Allende, which drops you off in the car park by the Administración. It takes about an hour, and the office has showers (small charge) and lockers where you can safely store your clothes while you swim.

Eating and drinking

Although most **restaurants** in Matamoros are fairly expensive – lots cater to cross-border trade – there are plenty of places for cheap, filling meals lining Calle 10 just off Plaza Allende, Calle 9 between Matamoros and Bravo, and a few *taquería* stands on the pedestrian *peotonál*, Abasolo.

Aromas Café/Traspatio Bar & Grill Calle 6 no. 181 ⓣ868/812-6232. The most fashionable place to sip coffee in town, with a decent restaurant (mains M$75–150) and terrace downstairs, and a funky bar area featuring live music and DJs at the weekend.

Las Dos Repúblicas C 9 between Abasolo and Matamoros ⓣ868/816-6894. Inviting colonial-style restaurant open since 1934, dishing up mammoth plates of tortillas, tacos, quesadillas and the like until around 7pm; everything on the menu costs about M$40. Yet another place that claims to have invented the margarita (in 1935).

Garcia's Obregón 82 ⓣ868/812-3929, ⓦwww.garcia-s.com. It doesn't get more touristy than this, but it's worth coming to *Garcia's* once for the archetypal border experience, literally a few metres from the bridge to scoop up as many day-trippers as possible. You can shop, eat reasonable international dishes in the restaurant and drink in the cabaret-like bar (which has live bands).

Gorditas Doña Tota Mina 15 at C 5 ⓣ868/816-6283. The Ciudad Victoria chain has several popular branches here (this is the closest to downtown), a good introduction to Mexico's addictive gorditas, from pork with salsa, to beans and cheese fillings – or a last chance to scoff as many as possible. Around M$10–12.

Mi Pueblito C 5 and Constitución, opposite MACT ⓣ868/816-0586, ⓦwww.mi-pueblito.com. Popular family restaurant in a giant faux palapa, with big Mexican breakfasts (from M$45) and all the classics for lunch and dinner (average M$80–110) – the bar is also a good place to grab a drink, best-known for its stock of two hundred tequilas.

Listings

Banks and exchange There are branches of Bancomer at the corner of Matamoros and C 5, on the plaza itself, and Santander (all operate Mon–Fri 9am–3pm). There are decent currency exchange facilities in the centre: head for Banorte, on Morelos between C 6 and C 7.

Buses The Central de Autobuses is well served by buses to the US and to the interior of Mexico. Americanos runs 6 daily buses (US$13 or peso-equivalent; 1hr 15min) between Matamoros and the Greyhound station in Brownsville (US ⓣ956/546-7171); it also runs four daily buses direct to San Antonio (7hr), two daily to Houston (8hr) and 2 daily to Dallas (13hr). Heading into Mexico there are numerous buses to Ciudad Victoria (4hr), Veracruz (16hr), Mexico City (14hr), Monterrey (5hr), Tampico (7hr) and Zacatecas (12hr). Less frequent services run to Mexicali, Guadalajara, Durango and Mazatlán.

Internet access There are a few places off lower Abasolo and around Plaza Hidalgo, most charging M$15/hr, though cafes open and close frequently. Try Cybernet at Matamoros between C 5 and C 6 (Mon–Sat 10am–10pm, Sun 2–6pm; M$15/hr) or Cyber Soluciones, C 11 at Morelos (Mon–Sat 9am–9pm, Sun 10am–9pm; M$15/hr).

Post office C 11 and Río Bravo (Mon–Fri 9am–3pm).

The coastal route

The eastern seaboard has so little to recommend it that even if you've crossed the border at Matamoros, you'd be well advised to follow the border road west to **Reynosa** and then cut down to Monterrey (see p.215). Unless you're determined to go straight down through Veracruz to the Yucatán by the shortest route, avoiding Mexico City altogether, there seems little point in following the coast. Here in the northeast there's plenty of sandy beachfront, but access is difficult, beaches tend to be windswept and scrubby, and much of the area is marred by oil refineries. Several small-scale resorts have grown up here (such as La Pesca and the villages around Laguna Madre), but these tend to be popular with nearby city-dwellers and have little to offer compared with the beaches further south. It's also very, very hot.

At the time of the Spanish Conquest this area of the Gulf coast was inhabited by the **Huastecs**, who gave their name to the region around Tampico and the eastern flanks of the Sierra Madre Oriental. Huastec settlement can be dated back some 3000 years; their language differs substantially from the surrounding native tongues, but has close links with the Maya of Yucatán. **Quetzalcoatl**, the feathered serpent god of Mexico, was probably of Huastec origin. At their most powerful between 800 and 1200 AD, the Huastecs were still at war with the Aztecs when the Spaniards arrived in the sixteenth century, finding them willing allies. After a successful campaign against Tenochtitlán, the Aztec capital, the Spaniards, first under Cortés and later the notorious Nuño de Guzmán, turned on the independent-minded Huastecs, decimating and enslaving their former allies.

Ciudad Victoria

CIUDAD VICTORIA, capital of the state of Tamaulipas, is little more than a place to stop over for a night. It's not unattractive but neither is it interesting, and while the surrounding hill country is a paradise for hunters and fishing enthusiasts, with a huge artificial lake called the **Presa Vicente Guerrero**, others will find little to detain them. The **bus station** (guardería daily 7am–10.30pm; M$5/hr) is a couple of kilometres east of the centre; take any city bus (M$5) labelled "Centro" or a taxi for M$40–50. Most of the town's facilities are concentrated around Plaza Hidalgo, but aside from the rather bland church, there isn't a whole lot going on. You've got several **hotels** to choose from here, including the excellent *Los Monteros*, Hidalgo 962 (Ⓣ834/312-0300, Ⓦwww.paginasprodigy.com/losmonteros; ❸), a lovely old colonial building with large rooms that are much cheaper than you might expect, and *Hostal de Escandón*, Juárez 143 at Hidalgo (Ⓣ834/312-9004; ❷), which offers good, clean rooms and meals for M$20 or so. If you're looking for more comfort, you'll have to hit the chain hotels beyond the centre – the smart *Holiday Inn Express* (Ⓣ834/318-6000, Ⓦwww.ichotelsgroup.com; ❼) at Adolfo Lopez Mateos 909 is the business traveller's choice.

When it comes to **eating**, you'd be remiss not to visit a branch of *Doña Tota Gorditas*, as the much-loved chain was founded here by Carlota Murillo (Doña Tota herself) in 1952, with her signature pork stew in salsa, beans and cheese, and pork with *mole gorditas*. The two central restaurants are at Juárez Ote 205 (Ⓣ834/312-7316) and Hidalgo 10 (Ⓣ834/312-6739). *Restaurant Los Candiles*, in *Hotel Sierra Gorda*, serves pricier Mexican fare, breakfasts and comida corrida at lunch.

Tampico

Along the 200km of road southeast from Ciudad Victoria to **TAMPICO**, one of Mexico's busiest ports, the vegetation becomes increasingly lush, green and tropical – the Tropic of Cancer passes just south of Ciudad Victoria and the Río Pánuco, forms the border with the steamy Gulf state of Veracruz. Today, the older parts of town have a slightly dilapidated feel, with peeling, ramshackle clapboard houses contrasting with the affluent but characterless US mall-style development on the outskirts. However, in a bid to attract more tourists, the downtown area has been spruced up with a host of thoughtful restoration projects, and the graceful New Orleans-style cast-iron buildings add a vaguely sophisticated charm to the main plazas.

As a treasure port in the Spanish empire, Tampico suffered numerous pirate raids and was destroyed in 1684. Rebuilding didn't begin in earnest until 1823, the date of the cathedral's foundation, and in 1828 Spain landed troops in Tampico in a vain and short-lived attempt to reconquer its New World empire. The discovery of oil in 1901 sparked Tampico's rise to prominence as the world's biggest oil port in the early years of the twentieth century. Tampico's oil boom lasted into the 1920s, with many of the city's finer buildings constructed during this period of rapid economic growth.

Arrival and information

Tampico's modern **bus station** (guardería 6am–midnight) is in an unattractive area some 10km north of the city, though waiting for buses here can be one of northern Mexico's little pleasures, as the waiting hall offers comfortable couches.

To get downtown, take a bus, a rattling *colectivo* or one of the shared *perimetral* taxis (all M$5). Buses back to the terminal leave from Plaza de Armas, at the corner of Olmos and Carranza. Arriving at Tampico's **Francisco Javier Mina airport**, some 15km north of the city, you'll have to take a taxi (around M$65 for a *colectivo*).

You'll find **tourist information booths** on both plazas, though these seem to be open quite irregularly. If you need a map, you could try asking in one of the swankier hotels (the main **tourist office** is northwest of the centre at Hidalgo 2703 and a real pain to get to; ⓣ833/217-8940, ⓦwww.tampico.gob.mx). The **post office** at Madero 309 is easy to find, upstairs in the Correos building on the north side of the Plaza de la Libertad, and there are **banks** on the Plaza de Armas and all through the central area. Numerous **internet** cafés line 20 de Noviembre near the plaza: try SCACT, Obregón 116 (daily 9am–11pm), or Canarias Cybercafe, Carranza 214 (daily 8am–9pm), both charging M$10 per hour.

Accommodation

One thing you can say for Tampico is that there's no shortage of **hotels**, though most are either expensive or very sleazy. Downtown, many of the cheaper hotels around the docks, train station and market area operate partly as brothels.

Best Western Gran Hotel Sevilla Héroes del Cañonero 304, at the southwest end of the Plaza de la Libertad ⓣ833/214-2833, ⓦwww.bestwestern.com. Some of the sleek, wooden-floored rooms have great plaza views. ❻

Hotel Inglaterra Díaz Mirón 116 ⓣ833/219-2857, ⓦwww.hotelinglaterra.com.mx. On the Plaza de Armas, this is one of the most luxurious central options with compact but stylish modern rooms, a restaurant and a small pool. ❻

Hotel Santa Helena Rosalio Bustamante 303 ⓣ833/213-3507. The rooms here have a/c and TV, and there's a good, if pricey, restaurant. ❹

Impala Díaz Mirón 220 Pte ⓣ833/212-0990, ⓦwww.impalatampico.com. This aged hotel has been renovated many times over the years and remains exceptionally clean, even elegant; the huge buffet breakfast is included. ❺

Posada del Rey Madero 218 Ote ⓣ833/214-1024, ⓦwww.hotelposadadelrey.com.mx. Comfortable lodgings on the Plaza de la Libertad. The spacious rooms overlook the square; they can be a bit noisy. ❹

Regis Madero 605 Ote ⓣ833/212-0290. The rooms at the *Regis*, a 5min walk from the plaza, are plain and high-ceilinged. There's a Chinese restaurant attached. ❸

The town and around

Downtown, the city's dual nature is instantly apparent. Within a hundred metres of each other are two plazas: the grandiose **Plaza de Armas** – rich and formal, it is ringed by government buildings, the impressive **Catedral Inmaculada Concepción** (built in the 1930s with money donated by American oil tycoon Edward Doheny) and the smart hotels; and the **Plaza de la Libertad**, which is raucous, rowdy – there's usually some form of music played from the bandstand each evening – and peopled by wandering salesmen. Ringed by triple-decker wrought-iron verandas, it has been spruced up in recent years to form an attractive square, almost New Orleans in flavour.

Also worth a look is the spanking new **Espacio Cultural Metropolitano** or **METRO Tampico** (ⓣ833/126-0888, ⓦmetro.tamaulipas.gob.mx), home to two theatres, El Teatro Metropolitano and Teatro Experimental, highly regarded art galleries (Tues–Sun 10am–6pm; M$30, free Tues) featuring temporary exhibits and the **Museo de la Cultura Huasteca** (Tues–Sun 10am–6pm; free), which provides an absorbing introduction to Huastec culture through original artefacts and engaging displays. It's a bit of a hike to reach it (it overlooks Laguna del Carpintero, 2km north of downtown), so catch a

"Central Camionera" bus from Olmos and ask to get off at the Parque Metropolitano – taxis should be M$30–40. It's easy to find on foot; just walk north on Olmos from Plaza de Armas till you hit the lake, then stroll (anti-clockwise) around the edge till you see it.

Eating and drinking

There are more than enough good **places to eat** to keep you happy for the day or so you might spend here. The town's gastronomical market, a block south of the Plaza de la Libertad, has numerous food stalls selling delicious seafood, especially crab. You'll find the larger, modern restaurants in the Zona Dorada, along Avenida Hidalgo.

Elite Restaurante and Helados Díaz Mirón 211 Ote ⓣ833/212-0364. A quiet haven in this noisy town, *Elite* does ice cream and good Mexican staples for under M$50.

Jardín Corona Hidalgo 1915 ⓣ833/213-6710, ⓦwww.jardin-corona.com. Plush Argentinian seafood and steak restaurant, worth the taxi ride for the huge plates of shrimp, crab and fresh fish, as well as fabulous *bife de chorizo*. Reckon on spending at least M$300 per head for a good meal. Live Latino sounds every Fri & Sat.

Naturaleza Aduana 107 Nte ⓣ833/212-4979. Come here for buffet breakfasts and comida corrida lunches (8am–8.30pm). The same owners run the large health-food store next door.

Super Cream Hidalgo 4713 ⓣ833/226-9058. A quick and economical diner-style joint that serves fairly decent Mexican staples and ice cream.

La Troya Madero 218, in the *Posada del Rey* ⓣ833/214-1024. The best dining in town, if only for its location. The menu consists of strong Spanish and seafood dishes (M$100–200).

The road to San Luis Potosí

It is a seven-hour run from Tampico to San Luis Potosí (see p.240) – ideal for a sleep-over on a night bus you might think, but there are a couple of places along the way you could consider breaking the journey for. The town of **Río Verde**, surrounded by lush fields of maize, coffee and citrus fruit, is ringed by thermal springs and has the benefit of a small lake fed by one of them, the **Laguna de la Media Luna**. The lake is popular with snorkellers and divers, attracted by depths of up 36m (visibility of up to 30m) and numerous freshwater fish and turtles. The lake is 1000 metres above sea level, so divers need to make the necessary adjustments for altitude.

Still further east, the highway comes to **Ciudad Valles**, a busy commercial town some 140km from Tampico and the coast. The frequent **buses** to San Luis Potosí, Mexico City and Monterrey will set you back about M$350 to M$400.

Monterrey and around

The third-largest city in Mexico (with four million in the metro area), and capital of Nuevo León, **MONTERREY** is a dynamic, hard-partying showcase for contemporary Mexico, though the heavy industry that made its wealth has far less importance these days – the biggest steel works closed in 1986. While the vast network of factories, the traffic, urban sprawl, pollution and ostentatious wealth that characterize the city are relatively recent developments, the older parts retain an air of colonial elegance. The city's setting, too, is one of great natural beauty – ringed by jagged mountain peaks, the Cerro de la Silla, or "Saddle Mountain", dominates the landscape. But what makes Monterrey really outstanding is the abundance of modern architecture and the bold statuary sprouting everywhere, expressions of Mexico at its most confident.

Festive Monterrey

In addition to the national and religious holidays, Monterrey has a number of exuberant local festivals.

Festival Internacional de Titeres (mid-July). This puppet festival is particularly appealing to kids, with Mexican and international puppeteers holding shows in the city.

Festival Internacional de Cine de Monterrey (end of Aug) ⓦwww.monterreyfilmfestival.com. The Monterrey film festival is one of Latin America's largest, showcasing the best Mexican, Latin American and international films, as well as organizing lectures and other free events.

Festival Internacional de Santa Lucía (Sept/Oct) ⓦwww.festivalsantalucia.org.mx. Massive celebration of performing arts, with international dance, music and theatre (this replaced the former Festival Cultural Barrio Antiguo).

Festival Internacional de Danza Extremadura-Lenguaje Contemporáneo (end of Oct) ⓦwww.festivalextremadura.org. Scintillating dance festival with a heavy emphasis on local and Mexican troupes (contemporary), as well as some international guests.

Arrival and information

Monterrey is the transport hub of the northeast, with excellent national and international connections. Flights from the rest of Mexico and from several points in the US (served by Continental, Delta and Northwest) arrive at **Aeropuerto Internacional Mariano Escobedo** (ⓣ81/8345-4434), 6km or so northeast of the city, only accessible by taxi for around M$220 – fares are set according to a zone system, so buy a ticket at the terminal before you exit.

Scores of **buses** pull into the enormous Central de Autobuses, northwest of the centre on Colón, complete with its own shopping centre, 24-hour guardería on the west side (M$5/hr) and an internet café (M$15/hr). To get from the **bus station** to the central Macroplaza, turn left towards the Cuauhtémoc metro station (see opposite) and take Line 2, or pick up a #1, #7, #17 or #18 bus heading down Pino Suárez and get off at a suitable intersection: Ocampo, Zaragoza or Juárez, for example. You can also get just about anywhere by **taxi**; buy a ticket at the booth before leaving the terminal. Taxis here also run on a zone system which starts at M$30 – the area around the Macroplaza is M$40 and the Obispado M$45, while trips to the airport cost the maximum M$200.

There's usually someone who can speak English at the helpful Infotur **tourist office**, Washington 648 Ote, inside the Antiguo Palacio Federal (daily 9am–6pm; ⓣ81/8152-3333, ⓦwww.nl.gob.mx). They offer a wide variety of maps and leaflets – including the handy quarterly *Explore Monterrey* – and information on hotel prices and local travel agencies. For tourist information when dialling from outside Nuevo León, call ⓣ01-800/832-2200.

City transport

The easiest way to get around Monterrey is by **taxi**, though traffic can be bad at the usual rush-hour times. Most taxis you hail in the street should use meters, which start at M$7.90 – trips anywhere in the city will rarely top M$50. Taxis waiting at hotels tend to follow the zone system enforced at the bus station and airport, but these rates are only slightly more expensive.

Though limited in scope, the fastest way to get around the city – and certainly between downtown and the bus station – is to take the clean and efficient **Metrorrey** system, which runs on two lines: Line 1 is elevated and runs east–west above Colón (you see it as soon as you emerge from the bus station); and Line 2 runs underground from Sendero in the north of the city to the Macroplaza (at the station General I. Zaragoza), connecting with Line 1 at the Cuauhtémoc stop, right by the bus station. It's simple to use: tickets cost M$4.50 per journey and are available singly or as a multi-journey card (at a small saving) from the coin-operated ticket machines. The system runs from around 5am until midnight.

Another touristy option is the **Paseo Cultural en Tranvía** (Cultural Trolley Tour; daily: spring & summer 4–10pm; autumn and winter 2–8pm; M$20), which makes a 45-minute loop from Macroplaza taking in seven stops (including MARCO), every thirty minutes, though the limited hours make this somewhat restrictive.

The streets of Monterrey are almost solid with **buses**, following routes that appear incomprehensible at first sight. The city authorities have taken steps to resolve the confusion by numbering all the stops (*paradas*), having the fares written on the windscreen and occasionally providing the tourist office with **route plans**,

EATING & DRINKING

La Casa del Maíz	21
El Coliseo	2
La Fonda del Rey	11
El Gaucho	7
Gorditas Doña Tota	1 & 13
El Infinito	23
Madre Oaxaca	22
Las Monjitas	16 & 17
Nuequén	3
Restaurante Vegetariano Superbom	20
El Rey del Cabrito	24
Tacos del Julio	8

NIGHTLIFE

At Loft	18
Bar 1900	I
Café Iguana	15
Café Paraíso	19
Groovy Bar	14
Manaus	5
Mumbar	G
Nassau	6
Sierra Madre Brewing Company	9
La Tumba	10
Uma Bar	12
El Zócalo	4

but it still takes a fair amount of confidence to plunge into the system. Useful routes include #1, #17 and #18, which run north–south through town and out to the northern sights – the standard fare is M$8.50 within the city.

Accommodation

Accommodation in Monterrey is targeted at business travellers, but there are a few **budget hotels** near the bus station and outside the centre. Further **downtown**, rooms are of a different class altogether, in modern hotels, all with air-conditioning and many with pools. The most atmospheric place to stay is the **Barrio Antiguo** but options here are lacking; most downtown hotels are located within the **Zona Rosa**, the modern commercial district west of the Macroplaza. All the major US chains are well represented in Monterrey, though the best properties lie far from the centre.

La Casa del Barrio Montemayor 1221 ⓣ81/8344-1800, ⓦwww.lacasadelbarrio.com.mx. Fabulous budget option in the heart of the Barrio Antiguo, with friendly, helpful owners who can help with all sorts of adventure tours Dorms (four or six beds; M$180) and comfy single or double rooms, some en suite. Wi-fi and internet access, laundry and kitchen included. ❸–❹

Fastos Colón 956 Pte, right opposite the bus station ⓣ81/8372-3250, US ⓣ1-800/839-2400, ⓕ81/8372-6100. Comfortable, modern hotel with large rooms all featuring a/c and satellite TV, and internet access in the lobby. Perfect for those passing through on early/late buses. ❺

Fundador Montemayor 802 ⓣ81/8342-0121, ⓦwww.travelbymexico.com/leon/fundador. Colonial tiles and wood panelling feature at one of the best-value downtown hotels. Located in a rare spot in the Barrio Antiguo, with clean and comfortable, if boring, a/c rooms, all with local TV. There's a fancy restaurant in the same building. ❸

Gran Hotel Ancira Hidalgo and Escobedo, on Plaza Hidalgo ⓣ81/8150-7000, US ⓣ1-800/333-3333, ⓦwww.hotel-ancira.com. Built as a grand hotel in 1912 and full of Art Nouveau elegance, including a winding marble staircase and posh restaurant replete with gilded birdcages, this is an outstanding upmarket option; owned and operated by Radisson. Rooms are spacious and come with cable TV and free internet. Deals on the web can make this surprisingly reasonable. ❺

El Gran Paso Inn Zaragoza 130 Nte ⓣ81/8340-0690, ⓦwww.elpasoautel.com. Basic mid-range option with winter rates and comfortable, if uninteresting rooms with cable TV and bath. It also has parking, a restaurant and a pool. ❺

Hotel Virreyes Amado Nervo 902 Nte ⓣ81/8374-6610. Another bus-station option that has clean and basic lodgings with fan and bathroom, but not much else. ❸

Monterroco San Francisco 205 ⓣ81/1365-4690, ⓦwww.monterroco.com. Attractive hostel set in an attractive colonial house 2km west of downtown. Dorm rooms (with four, six or eight beds; M$145) have lockers, shared bathrooms and free wi-fi, and there's a computer for internet. Guests also have access to a barbecue terrace, a small pool, LCD TV, laundry and kitchen. Private en-suite rooms also available. ❸

Quinta Real Diego Rivera 500, Valle Ote ⓣ81/8368-1000, ⓦwww.quintareal.com. Generally regarded as Monterrey's top hotel, this opulent pile is a luxurious amalgam of modern comfort and colonial style; it's a 15min ride from downtown in the hip Valle area. The spacious suites come with marble-covered bathrooms and living room; some have balconies. ❾

Royalty Hidalgo 402 Ote ⓣ81/8340-9800, US ⓣ1-800/830-9300, ⓦwww.hotelroyalty.com.mx. Straightforward, middle-of-the-road business-style hotel with a/c rooms, cable TV, gym, jacuzzi and a tiny pool. ❺

Safi Royal Luxury Pino Suárez 444 ⓣ81/8399-7000, ⓦwww.safihotel.com. Luxurious five-star hotel with expansive marble floors, elegant staircases and garden. The rooms are spacious, and there's a restaurant attached. ❻

The City

Most visitors' first impressions of Monterrey are unfavourable – the highway roars through shabby shantytown suburbs and grimy manufacturing outskirts – but the **city centre** is quite a different thing. Here, colonial relics are overshadowed by the office buildings and expensive shopping streets of the **Zona Rosa**, and by some extraordinary modern architecture – the local penchant for planting buildings in the ground at bizarre angles is exemplified above all by the **Planetario Alfa** and the **Instituto Tecnológico**. The city in general rewards a day of wandering, but there are three places specifically worth going out of your way to visit – the old **Obispado** (bishop's palace), on a hill overlooking the centre, the giant **Cervecería Cuauhtémoc** to the north and the magnificent **Museo de Arte Contemporáneo** (MARCO).

Of Monterrey's two main **markets** – Juárez and Colón – the latter, on Avenida de la Constitución, south of the Macroplaza, is more tourist-oriented, specializing in local artesanía. Incidentally, the best of Monterrey's **flea markets** (*pulgas*; literally, fleas) is also held on Constitución: market days are irregular, but ask any local for details.

The Macroplaza and around

At the heart of Monterrey, if not the physical centre, is the **Macroplaza** (officially the Plaza Zaragoza, and sometimes known as the "Gran Plaza"), which was created by demolishing six blocks of the city centre. It links the intensely Modernist **Palacio Municipal**, built on stilts at the southern end of the square in 1973, to the beautiful red-stone **Palacio de Gobierno** on what used to be Plaza 5 de Mayo. The result is undeniably stunning, with numerous lovely fountains, an abundance of striking statuary, quiet parks and shady patios, edged by the **Catedral Metropolitana**, museums including the impressive **Museo de Arte Contemporáneo** and state administration buildings – you'll see plenty of squawking red-crowned Amazon parrots in the gardens here, the thriving descendants of escaped pet birds. There are also frequent concerts, dances and other entertainments laid on; in the evenings people gravitate here to stroll, and to admire the laser beam that flashes out from the top of the 70m-tall, graceful slab of orange concrete known as the **Faro del Comercio**, designed by the lauded Mexican architect Luis Barragán in 1984.

West of the Macroplaza are the smart shops, multinational offices and swanky hotels of the Zona Rosa, centred on little **Plaza Hidalgo** – a much more traditional, shady place, with old colonial buildings set around a statue of Miguel Hidalgo. Pedestrianized shopping streets fan out behind, crowded with window-gazing locals.

In between Plaza Hidalgo and the Macroplaza, in the old City Hall, you'll find the **Museo Metropolitano** (Tues–Sun 10am–6pm; free) with a small exhibit introducing the city's history, beginning with its foundation in 1596 by Diego de Montemayor – labels are in Spanish only, but the lovely inner courtyard is worth a look in any case.

Museo de Arte Contemporáneo

At the southern end of the Macroplaza lies the wonderful **Museo de Arte Contemporáneo**, or **MARCO**, at the junction of the plaza and Ocampo (Tues–Sun 10am–6pm, Wed until 8pm; M$60, free Wed; Ⓦwww.marco.org.mx). Vistors are greeted by Juan Soriano's *La Paloma*, an immense sculpture of an obese black dove whose curvaceous lines stand in dramatic contrast to the angular terracotta lines of the museum building. It was designed in 1991 by Mexico's leading architect, **Ricardo Legorreta**, whose highly individual buildings share common themes: visitors from the southwest of the US may recognize the style from various structures dotted around Texas, Arizona and New Mexico. Inside, none of the floors and walls seems to intersect at the same angle. The vast, at times whimsical, open plan centres on an atrium with a serene pool into which a pipe periodically gushes water: at the sound of the pump gurgling to life, you find yourself drawn to watch the ripple patterns subside. You might imagine that such a courageous building would overwhelm its contents, but if anything the opposite is true. Apart from a couple of monumental sculptures tucked away in courtyards, there is no permanent collection, but the standards maintained by the temporary

▲ Lagrimas Negras: an exhibition of Betsabeé Romero's work, MARCO

exhibits are phenomenally high. A key factor in this is undoubtedly the bias towards Latin American (particularly Mexican) artists, who are currently producing some of the world's most innovative and inspiring works; the exuberant paintings of Víctor Rodríguez, the tyre-inspired installations of Betsabeé Romero and the surrealism of Cuban painter Wifredo Lam have all featured in the past. The quality art bookshop and fancy *Restaurant Marca* (Mexican buffets Tues–Fri & Sun 1–4pm; ⓣ81/8262-4500 ext 262) are both worth visiting.

Catedral Metropolitana de Nuestra Señora de Monterrey

The relatively modest eighteenth-century **Catedral Metropolitana de Nuestra Señora de Monterrey** (Mon–Fri 7.30am–8pm, Sat 9am–8pm, Sun 8am–8pm; free), is located opposite MARCO. It's a beautifully maintained Baroque structure with its one highly ornate multilevel tower completed in 1899. Highlights inside include the vivid murals at the altar, completed by Ángel Zarraga in the 1940s. The palatial edifice just to the north is the **Casino Monterrey**, a posh entertainment centre for government types and strictly off-limits.

Museo del Palacio de Gobierno

At the northern end of the Macroplaza, the **Museo del Palacio de Gobierno** (Tues–Fri 10am–7pm, Sat & Sun 10am–8pm; free; ⓣ81/2033-9900, ⓦwww.museodelpalaciodegobierno.org.mx) is a typically futuristic Monterrey museum and especially good for non-Spanish speakers: English information cards are on hand throughout. The state government building was completed in 1908 as a magnificent example of late Neoclassical style, and the museum uses this to hypnotic effect. Rooms are dimly lit and suffused with ambient music, with historic artefacts enhanced with video, images, computer screens and small, easily digested stories. The exhibits chart the history of Nuevo León state, focusing on the themes of government and law – displays piece together the transition from colony to federal state, examine the evolving role of the governor over time and end as a sort of shrine to Mexican democracy, covering the development of a Mexican constitution, elections and a free press. There are also rooms dedicated to the region's commercial development (think goats, sugar cane and oranges), and how transport and communications helped create modern Monterrey. The original *Galería de Gobernadores* is also preserved in gilded splendour – the state legislature held sessions here until 1985, when the new Congreso del Estado building further down the plaza took over (the governor of Nuevo León still maintains offices in the old building).

Barrio Antiguo

The oldest and most enticing part of downtown survives to the east of the Macroplaza, where the **Barrio Antiguo** is an increasingly gentrified district populated by chi-chi galleries, appealingly laid-back cafés and, once the sun has gone down, the city's best nightlife. The city authorities are even playing ball, installing old-fashioned street lamps and taking measures to calm the traffic. There's usually a host of artistic goings-on here: check out the **Museo Estatal Culturas Populares** (Tues–Sun 10am–6pm; ⓣ81/8344-5311) in the Casa del Campesino at Absalo 1024 Ote, at Mina, or the bulletin boards posted in many of the local cafés and bars. There's also **La Casa de los Titeres** at Jardón 968 (Mon–Fri 9am–1pm & 2–6pm, Sun 3–7pm; M$30; ⓦwww.baulteatro.com), a small museum with an extensive and rather odd collection of puppets displayed behind glass. At 5pm on Sundays the owners put on a puppet show (M$80, kids M$50) based on anything from *Little Red Riding Hood* to García Lorca, which usually attracts a fair-sized crowd.

Paseo Santa Lucía

Just to the east of the Macroplaza and north of the Barrio Antiguo lies one of the city's newest and most impressive clusters of attractions, linked together by the **Paseo Santa Lucía**.

Museo de Historia Mexicana

The **Museo de Historia Mexicana**, Dr. Coss 445 Sur (Tues–Fri 10am–7pm, Sat & Sun 10am–8pm; M$40, free Tues & Sun; ⓦwww.3museos.com), is another bold architectural statement with temporary and permanent displays on **Mexican national history**, with everything presented in a fairly unconventional manner. The permanent exhibits are upstairs in a vast, open-plan hall centred on the Área Tierra, a dimly lit contemplative space surrounded by mock rainforest. The rest is split simply into four galleries, with minimal labelling, an extensive array of traditional costumes, interactive computer consoles and carefully selected exhibits. The highlights of the Mexico Antiguo section are the scale models of ancient cities such as Palenque, Monte Albán and Teotihuacán, while the Virreinato (The Viceroyalty) area covers the colonial period with a vast golden *retablo* the main centrepiece (a 1960s copy of a 1670 original). The nineteenth-century and Mexico Moderno galleries complete the picture, but this is very much an impressionistic museum – don't expect lots of dates and details. Nevertheless, if you don't read Spanish you might find the monolingual captions a tad frustrating.

Museo del Noreste

A covered walkway connects the Museo de Historia to Monterrey's latest star attraction, the **Museo del Noreste**, or just MUNE (Tues–Fri 10am–7pm, Sat & Sun 10am–8pm; M$40, free Tues & Sun); entry is free with your Museo de Historia ticket. As you'd expect by now, this is not your average history museum – though it covers the **history of northeast Mexico** chronologically, from pre-colonial times through to the present, it uses a similar multimedia approach and is deeply thought-provoking. For starters, the exhibits begin with modern times and work backwards. More significantly, the "northeast" here includes the

US state of Texas, and virtually every exhibit is approached through the prism of cross-border relations; the idea that the fate of both sides has been fundamentally entwined for hundreds of years makes sense, but the focus on Mexico's cultural impact on Texas, and the suggestion that it has a paramount role in its future (by 2025 half of the Texan population will be of "Mexican origin") would be viewed as highly controversial by many Americans. The museum also presents a fresh look at the much neglected Indian tribes of the region, takes an unusually positive view of the Díaz regime and systemically lays out the tortured history of how the current US/Mexican border came to be. Labels are in Spanish and English.

Once you've exhausted every angle of Mexican history head below the museum plaza to the **Paseo Santa Lucía** proper, a landscaped canal-side path replete with waterfalls, gardens and snack stalls that leads 2.5km east to the Parque Fundidora – it's a sweaty but tranquil thirty-minute walk, or a leisurely cruise in one of the boats that regularly plies between the two sites (daily 10am–10pm; M$40). Tickets are good for return trips the whole day.

Parque Fundidora

Paseo Santa Lucía ends at the serene **Parque Fundidora** (Ⓦwww.parquefundidora.org), a surreal landscape of green parkland, industrial chimneys and former steel-processing plants, which have been converted into art halls, stadiums and museums. Get a map (free) at the park entrance, from where it's another fifteen minutes to the end of the canal and boat dock, marked by a waterfall set in a giant steel cauldron. If time is short, head straight to the **Museo del Acero Horno-3** (Tues–Thurs & Sun 10am–6pm, Fri & Sat 11am–7pm; M$90; Ⓣ81/8126-1100, Ⓦwww.horno3.org) a remarkable museum created out of the guts of a jagged steel mill dominating much of the park and the city. Inside are galleries tracing the history of the steel industry in Monterrey, as well as the steel-manufacturing process itself – the highlight is the Show del Torne, which reproduces the dazzling spectacle of steel-making. You can also visit the forty-metre viewing platform and the restaurant *El Lingote* (Tues–Sun 1pm–midnight). Elsewhere in the park, the **Centro de la Artes** is a series of three warehouses displaying temporary art exhibits, usually with a local focus, and there's a theme park for kids honouring Sesame Street – **Plaza Sésamo**. Catch the metro (Line 1) to Parque Fundidora – the park lies south of the station across Madero.

El Obispado

The elegant and beautifully renovated **Obispado**, the old bishop's palace, tops Chepe Vera hill to the west of the centre like a golden temple, but lies well within the bounds of the city. Its commanding position – affording magnificent views when haze and smog allow – has made it an essential target for Monterrey's many invaders. Completed in 1787, it has served as a barracks, a military hospital and a fortress: among its more dramatic exploits, the Obispado managed to hold out for two days after the rest of the city had fallen to US general Zachary Taylor in 1846. After so much history elsewhere in the city, you might baulk at the **Museo Regional de Nuevo León** inside (Tues–Sun 10am–7pm; M$41; Ⓣ81/8123-0644) – essentially another journey through the past of Nuevo León, with an emphasis on religious and secular art, arms from the War of Independence, revolutionary pamphlets and old carriages – but the collection has an oddly appealing charm and is evocatively set in the original stone chambers with timber ceilings. Labels are in Spanish only.

You get to the Obispado along Padre Mier, passing on the way the monumental modern church of **La Purísima**. Take the R4 bus, alighting where it turns off Padre Mier, then continue to the top of the steps at the end of Padre Mier and turn left; it's a ten-minute walk in all. Return to the centre using any bus heading east on Hidalgo.

North of the centre

If you're thirsty after all this, head out to the massive premises of **Cervecería Cuauhtémoc Moctezuma** (Cuauhtémoc Brewery), established in 1890. This is where they make the wonderful Bohemia, Indio and Tecate beers you'll find throughout Mexico (as well as the rather bland Carta Blanca and export Sol), and somehow it seems much more representative of Monterrey than any of the city's prouder buildings. Free guided tours of the brewery run almost hourly throughout the day from the office next to the **Jardín Cerveza** (beer garden; daily 10am–6pm), at Alfonso Reyes 2202 Nte, 1km north of the bus station. You can claim one free glass of beer (usually Carta Blanca) here, or buy the better draft beers on offer. The comprehensive **tours** (Mon–Fri 9am–5pm, Sat 9am–2pm; free; 1hr–1hr 30min) are usually given in Spanish, and you need to make a reservation if you require an English-speaking guide (Ⓣ81/8328-5355) – reservations are recommended in any case. Note that male visitors cannot wear shorts, sandals or short-sleeved shirts, and you cannot take photos. Founded by the brewery in 1973 just behind the beer garden, the **Salón de la Fama** (Mon–Fri 9.30am–6pm, Sat & Sun 10.30am–6pm; free), the Sporting Hall of Fame, commemorates the heroes of Mexican baseball. To get to the site take Line 2 to General Anaya station, and walk 300m south.

For decades, glass production has been one of Monterrey's industrial strengths (for one thing, it has to provide all the beer bottles to the brewery), and to tap into the long history of Mexican glassware, pop along to the **Museo del Vidrio**, at the corner of Zaragoza and Magallanes 517 (Tues–Sun 10am–7pm; M$15, free Sun; Ⓦwww.museodelvidrio.com). A small but select display of pieces over the centuries and a mock-up of a nineteenth-century apothecary's only act as a prelude to the attic, where modern, mostly cold-worked glass sculpture is shown to advantage; Raquel Stolarski's *Homage to Marilyn* is particularly fine. To get there, take Line 1 to Del Golfo station, walk two blocks west and then two blocks north up Zaragoza.

Club de Fútbol Monterrey

Monterrey is known throughout Mexico for having fanatical sports supporters, and watching a home game of the **Club de Fútbol Monterrey** (Ⓦwww.rayados.com) is a good introduction to the frenetic world of Mexican football (soccer). For a real spectacle attend any match against UNAL Tigres, Monterrey's fierce rivals – known as the Clásico Regiomontano, this is the second most important derby in Mexico (behind the Superclásico between Guadalajara and América). Until 2011 the team (known as Rayados or "the striped ones" because of their uniform) will play at the Estadio Tecnológico on Junco de la Vega, 2km southeast of downtown, before moving to the new Estadio de Fútbol Monterrey at the Parque La Pastora in Guadelupe, an eastern suburb of the city. Buy tickets at the stadium or via online vendors such as Ⓦwww.ticketmaster.com.mx (tickets from M$130).

You can also see **bullfights** at the Plaza de Toros Monumental, Alfonso Reyes 2401 (Ⓣ81/8374-0450, Ⓦwww.monumentallorenzogarza.com) and **lucha libre** at the Arena Coliseo (Ⓣ81/8375-5001, Ⓦwww.arenacoliseo.com) near the bus station at Colón 1050 (Mon, Tues, Fri and Sun).

Planetario Alfa

Like some vision from H.G. Wells's *The War of the Worlds*, the cylindrical form of the **Planetario Alfa**, Roberto Garza Sada 1000, 8km south of the city centre (Tues–Fri 3.30–8pm, Sat & Sun 11.30am–8pm; museum only M$45, museum and film M$80, film only M$50; Ⓦwww.planetarioalfa.org.mx), rises out of the ground at a rakish angle, providing an unusual venue for Omnimax films (hourly). If you've never seen one of these super-wide-vision movies before, or have kids to entertain, it may be worth the trip out here. Otherwise, the few science demonstrations and hands-on experiments aren't really worth the bother. If you do come, don't miss Rufino Tamayo's stained-glass opus, outside the main complex, in the Universe Pavilion. The best way to get here is on the **free shuttle bus**, which leaves from a dedicated stop at the western end of the Alameda on Washington. Check times on the website: it currently departs 3.10pm, 4.10pm, 5.10pm and 8.10pm weekdays and every hour from 11.10am to 8.10pm at the weekends.

Eating and drinking

Monterrey's traditional **restaurants** cater to hearty, meat-eating *norteños*, with *cabrito al pastor* or the regional speciality *cabrito asado* (whole roast baby goat) given pride of place in window displays. In the **centre** there are dozens of places around the Macroplaza and Barrio Antiguo, all convenient for downtown hotels, but if you're prepared to drive or take taxis, the up-and-coming area known as **Zona Valle** (south of the centre in the affluent suburb of San Pedro Garza García and along Lázaro Cárdenas), and southeast Monterrey (along Garza Sada) are where you'll find the latest trend-setters and a range of international cuisines. For fresh produce and cheap snacks you could do worse than join the locals at the **Mercado Juárez**, north of the Macroplaza on Aramberri.

La Casa del Maíz Abasolo 870-B Ote, at Dr. Coss ⓣ81/8340-4332. Airy, modern place taking its decorative cues from MARCO down the street, and serving unusual Mexican dishes, either with or without meat. Try the *memelas la maica*, a kind of thick tortilla topped with a richly seasoned spinach and cheese salsa. Opens at 6pm Mon–Thurs, and 1pm Fri–Sun. Have a drink after at the funky *Café 13 Lunas* at no. 876 next door.

El Coliseo Colón 235. Clean and cheerful 24hr place near the bus station, serving regular Mexican staples and seafood at low prices; quesadillas (M$25), bean tacos (M$20) and passable café con leche (M$7) – set meals from M$52.

La Fonda del Rey Matamoros 816 Ote. Bright and cheery cantina that does decent and economical Mexican staples for breakfast and lunch. Mon–Fri 9am–5pm.

El Gaucho Gómez Morín 300–1120 ⓣ81/8378-1511, ⓦwww.gauchoargentino.com.mx. One of the best Valle restaurants, worth the taxi ride for the finest steaks in the city – prime slabs of Argentine beef for around M$300.

Gorditas Doña Tota Plaza México, Morelos 359; Escobedo 519 at Allende; Pino Suárez 1202 at Colón. This chain, founded in Ciudad Victoria in 1952 (see p.213), serves up delicious little gorditas for just M$8–9 and has many outlets throughout the city – the first two are best for downtown, while the latter is handy for the bus station. Open daily 8am–9pm.

El Infinito Jardón 904 Ote ⓣ81/8989-5252. A surprising little find, with sofas and a small lending library (some English books), serving some of Monterrey's best espressos and lattes, and a posh menu offering salmon (M$165), specials like stewed chicken with almonds (M$139) and plenty of pizza (from M$89) and pasta (from M$99). A few times a month they have live acoustic music.

Madre Oaxaca Jardón 814 Ote ⓣ81/8345-1459. The speciality of this beautiful upmarket restaurant is Oaxacan cooking, the most delicious of Mexico's regional cuisines. Check this place out, especially if you can't get down south (mains from M$120).

Las Monjitas Morelos 240 Ote ⓣ81/8344-6713. Waitresses dressed as nuns dish up Mexican steaks and a selection of quality *antojitos*, including such house specialities as the *Father Chicken*, *The Sinner* and *Juan Pablo II*; the last is an artery-hardening combination of salami, pork, bacon, peppers, grilled cheese and guacamole. Beautiful *azulejos* on the walls and a stunningly kitsch Spanish façade make the slightly elevated prices worthwhile. There's a second, more down-to-earth branch a couple of blocks along at Escobedo Sur 903, offering lunch specials for M$50. Open daily 8am–11pm.

Nuequén Dr. Coss 659 ⓣ81/8343-6726. Renowned upmarket restaurant that specializes in Argentine cuisine, though they also have good Mexican and Italian dishes on the menu; signature steaks M$120–240, while tasty empanadas are M$33. Open from 1pm. Closed Mon.

Restaurante Vegetariano Superbom Galeana 1018, between Hidalgo and Ocampo. Excellent vegetarian *comidas* (M$45), and an all-you-can-eat buffet (M$75) from noon until 5pm; mornings the food is à la carte. Closed Sat.

El Rey del Cabrito Dr. Coss and Constitución 817 Ote ⓣ8345-3232. The best place in town for *cabrito* is this slightly other-worldly restaurant, adorned with stuffed lions, an incongruous statue of Hindu elephant god Ganesha and even Egyptian hieroglyphs. The main event is a sizzling, succulent treat (from M$200) and you can also try their charcoal-grilled beef – all best experienced in a group.

Tacos del Julio Vasconcelos 100, at Juárez, and Río Orinoco 115, Zona Valle (San Pedro) ☎81/8338-2033, ⓦwww.tacosdeljulio.com. Popular Monterrey chain since 1993 that has spread north of the border thanks to its high-quality tacos and plates of five *taquitos* stuffed with all manner of tasty fillings; try the *volcanes*, with steak and cheese (M$45).

Nightlife

After dark, the place to head is the **Barrio Antiguo**, five square blocks of cobbled streets bounded by Dr. Coss, Matamoros and Constitución. On Thursday, Friday and Saturday evenings (9pm–2am), the police block off the junctions, leaving the streets – especially Padre Mier and Madero – to hordes of bright young things surging back and forth in search of the best vibe. Alternatively, take a taxi to the Zona Valle and San Pedro Garza García where the latest mega clubs and bars play host to a smart, affluent set and real-ale drinkers can indulge at the *Sierra Madre Brewing Company* at José Vasconcelos 564 (☎81/8348-4826).

At Loft Morelos 870 ☎81/8342-7031. This is the place to come if you're in the mood for hip-hop or rap. The grand, plant- and flower-smothered house is hard to miss.

Bar 1900 *Gran Hotel Ancira*, Hidalgo and Escobedo, on Plaza Hidalgo ☎81/8150-7000. Colonial-style bar with cosy booths or bar stools, wood floors, and decorated with bold Art Nouveau murals – live music most nights and a decent range of bottled beers, wines and spirits.

Café Iguana Montemayor 927 ☎81/8343-0822 ⓦwww.cafeiguana.com.mx. Monterrey's best rock club (though their DJs play techno and electronica most Thurs & Fri nights). Live rock bands usually perform on Saturdays. Cover is either free or rarely tops M$50.

Café Paraíso Morelos 958 Ote. Multi-roomed café and bar with local artwork on the walls, serving a fabulous range of coffees, delicious and huge tortas with fries (M$40) and fairly pricey drinks, though beers are two-for-one (M$30) round-the-clock.

Groovy Bar Padre Mier 850, between Dr. Coss and Montemayor ☎81/8343-7077. Psychedelic murals of Hendrix and the Beatles adorn this student favourite, a no-frills bar with a vaguely 1960s theme, live acts and DJs – usually no cover.

Manaus Padre Mier 1094 ☎81/8989-1920, ⓦwww.manaus.com.mx. For a full-on Latino club experience *Manaus* is hard to beat, with a blend of all the latest Mexican, Latin and US sounds, and a buzzing crowd. Thurs–Sat only.

Mumbar Padre Mier 943, between Mina and Montemayor ☎81/8218-4829, ⓦwww.mumbar.com.mx. The combination of Cuban food, Latin house and live music is hard to resist (the music begins after 10pm), though they only open Thurs, Fri and Sat. Men pay M$70 (Fri) and M$150 (Sat) – ladies are free. Beers are M$5.

Nassau Padre Mier 1106 Ote. Fun, popular club with three different floors, featuring alternative vibes on the first, and pop and dance on the subsequent levels. There's also a loft space to chill out in.

La Tumba Padre Mier 827 Ote ☎81/8345-6860, ⓦwww.latumba.com. The main draw at this large, semi-outdoor bar is live acoustic music Thurs–Sat. Expect to hear anything from blues to jazz to rock. Open 5pm–2am. Cover M$20–50.

Uma Bar Dr. Coss 837 ☎81/8343-9372, ⓦwww.umabar.com.mx. This dimly lit, super fashionable lounge bar has a Asian theme with murals, oil lamps and rugs, and showcases rock, house and pop. It's a good place to come for a quality cocktail.

El Zócalo Padre Mier 1043. This small courtyard just off the street is home to a gaggle of bars and clubs always heaving at the weekends – try *La Kintada*, *Next* or *Club 22*.

Listings

American Express American Express, Lázaro Cárdenas 1000, Del Valle ☎81/8133-0701 (daily 10am–7pm), holds clients' mail, and replaces and cashes travellers' cheques.

Banks and exchange You can change money at any of the several casas de cambio on Ocampo between Zaragoza and Juárez (Mon–Fri 9am–1pm & 3–6pm, Sat 9am–12.30pm), and change travellers' cheques at banks (almost all with ATMs), most of which are on Padre Mier, right downtown.

Moving on from Monterrey

You'll have no trouble getting a **bus** out of Monterrey at almost any time of day or night, to points all around the country. Chihuahua (10hr), Ciudad Victoria (4hr), Durango (8hr), Matamoros (5hr), Mazatlán (16hr), Mexico City (11hr), Saltillo (1hr 45min), San Luis Potosí (7hr) and Tampico (7hr) are some of the major destinations served by the three big players: Grupo Senda, Omnibus and Estrella Blanca. Monterrey is also a good place to pick up transport into **Texas**: Transportes del Norte has direct connections with the Greyhound system with transfers in Nuevo Laredo (3hr; M$220); Americanos runs direct to San Antonio (7hr; M$350), Houston (10hr; M$460), Dallas (12hr; M$570), Austin (M$475) and Chicago (28hr; M$2100). Turimex also runs direct to San Antonio (6hr; US$48).

Monterrey's international **airport**, General Mariano Escobedo, is similarly well connected, with some three hundred **flights** a day. A plethora of lines use it as a hub, including Aeroméxico and budget carrier Viva Aerobus. Destinations include Mexico City, Guadalajara, Toluca, Cancún, Tijuana, Veracruz and Chihuahua. US destinations form around a fifth of all outbound destinations and include Houston, Dallas, Las Vegas and Chicago, among others.

For further information, see Travel details, p.230.

Books Sanborn's, on Morelos near the Macroplaza (daily 9am–10pm), holds a rather poor selection of English-language novels, though it does sell numerous magazines and some guides. You might find some English titles in Librería Iztaccihuatl, Morelos 437 (Mon–Fri 9am–8.30pm, Sat 10am–8pm, Sun 11am–3pm), Librería Cosmos, Escobedo 821, and Librería de Cristal just off Morelos at Parras Ballesteros 802.

Car rental If you fancy renting wheels to get out to the sights immediately around Monterrey, or to explore the mountains, head to the airport or Plaza Hidalgo where all the main agencies have offices. Payless, Escodebo 1011 Sur (Ⓣ81/8369-8569) has the best deal at M$300/day (without insurance). Others include Hertz at the *Sheraton*, Hidalgo 310 (Ⓣ999/911-8040), and Budget, Hidalgo 433 Ote (Ⓣ81/8340-4100).

Consulates Australia, Parque Corporativo, Equus Torre Sur, Ricardo Margain 444, San Pedro Garza García Ⓣ81/8158-0791; Canada, Gómez Morín 955, Suite 404 (Mon–Fri 9am–1.30pm & 2.30–5.30pm; Ⓣ81/8378-0240); South Africa, Blv Díaz Ordaz 200, Colonia Santa María (Ⓣ81/8335-5949); US, Constitución 411 Pte (Mon–Fri 8am–2pm; Ⓣ81/8047-3100, Ⓦmonterrey.usconsulate.gov).

Emergencies Angeles Verdes (Ⓣ81/8115-0074); Cruz Roja (Ⓣ81/8342-1212); Cruz Verde (Ⓣ81/8371-5050); police (Ⓣ066 or 81/8343-0173); Hospital Muguerza, Hidalgo 2525 (Ⓣ81/8399-3400).

Internet access As always, internet cafés open and close frequently here; the café at the Central de Autobuses is fairly dependable (see p.216). Facilities downtown include Internet Zone, Carranza 919, which has a card system letting you log in and out whenever you like, or Viajes alto.com at Escobedo 831 – both just off the Morelos shopping zone.

Laundry Antillón 237, between Matamoros and Sanchez.

Post office In the Palacio Federal, Washington 648, at the north end of the Macroplaza (Mon–Fri 8am–7pm, Sat 9am–1pm).

Around Monterrey

After a day or two the bustle of Monterrey can get to you, but you can escape to the surprisingly wild and scenic surrounding countryside. Without your own vehicle or taxi, however, getting around the sights in the vicinity can be awkward. An exception is a trip to the subterranean caverns of **Parque Grutas de García** (daily 9am-5pm; M$60; Ⓣ81/8347-1533), which, despite some impressive stalactites and stalagmites and an underground lake, have lost some of their appeal through overdevelopment. Only 46km west of Monterrey near the village of **VILLA GARCÍA**, they are a popular outing from Monterrey, especially at weekends, when hundreds cram onto the funicular tram from the village; you can walk from the end of the tram line to the caverns in about thirty minutes. Buses run several times daily to Villa García (M$12; 1hr) from outside the Central de Autobuses; from there you'll need to take a taxi (M$60) for the remaining 9km.

The trip to the **Parque Ecoturístico Cascada Cola de Caballo** (Horsetail Falls; Tues–Sun 9am–7pm; M$30), 40km south of Monterrey on Hwy-85, is only really worthwhile after the rains, when the falls gush down a 25m cliff-face in spectacular fashion. The falls are a six hundred metres hike from the car park, but you can also hire horses (M$30) or horse-drawn carriages (M$20). The falls are near the village of **SANTIAGO**, heavily promoted as a "Pubelo Mágico", with a pretty 1745 church and quaint restaurants – assuming the tour buses are not around. To get here by bus, take a Lineas Amarillas service from the main bus station to **El Cercado** (M$20), where *colectivos* (M$15) wait to take you to the falls. **Taxis** charge around M$650 for round trips (3–4hr) to either the Grutas de García or Cola de Caballo from downtown Monterrey.

Saltillo and around

Capital of the state of Coahuila, **SALTILLO** is the place to head for if you can't take the hustle of Monterrey. Lying just 85km to the southwest, down fast Hwy-54 that cuts through the Sierra Madre Oriental and a high desert of yucca and Joshua trees, it's infinitely quieter, much smaller than Monterrey and, at 1600m above sea level, feels refreshingly cool and airy.

There's not a great deal to do here, but it's still a lovely place to stroll around, admire some beautiful buildings and soak up the colonial ambience. Two contrasting, and almost adjoining, squares grace the centre of town: the **Plaza Acuña**, surrounded by crowded shopping streets, marks the rowdy heart of the modern city, while the old **Plaza de Armas** is formal, tranquil, illuminated at night and sometimes hosts music performances. Facing the **Museo del Palacio** (Tues–Sun 10am–6pm; free), which has a mildly interesting historical display, across the Plaza de Armas, the magnificent eighteenth-century **Catedral de Santiago** (daily 9am–1pm & 4–7.30pm) is one of the most beautiful churches in northern Mexico, with an elaborately carved churrigueresque facade and doorways, an enormous bell tower and a smaller clock tower. On the south side of the square the **Instituto Coahuilense de Cultura** (Tues–Fri 10am–7pm; free) often hosts diverting temporary exhibits by Coahuila artists.

The town's oldest streets fan out from the square, with some fine old private houses. One historical building worth seeking out is the carefully preserved old **Ayuntamiento** (town hall) on the corner of Aldama and Hidalgo. The walls of the courtyard and the staircase are adorned with murals depicting the history of the town from prehistoric times to the 1950s. Calle Victoria spurs west off the square, passing a few hundred metres of the city's major shops and cinemas, on the way to the **Alameda**, a shaded, tree-lined park, peopled with students looking for a peaceful spot to work – there are several language schools in Saltillo, as well as a university and technical institute; in summer especially, numbers of American students come here to study Spanish.

Saltillo is famous for its **sarapes** (multicoloured woollen shawls), and there are several small shops where (at least on weekdays) you can watch the manufacturing process. The best is tucked at the back of the artesanía shop El Sarape de Saltillo, Hidalgo 305 Sur (Mon–Sat 9am–1pm & 3–7pm). Sadly, the old ways are vanishing fast, and most now use artificial fibres and chemical dyes: many of those in the market are mass-produced in virulent clashing colours.

Birders should head to **Museo de las Aves de México**, at the intersection of Hidalgo and Bolívar (Tues–Sat 10am–6pm, Sun 11am–7pm; M$10; Ⓦwww.museodelasaves.org), where you'll find a large collection of stuffed birds on exhibit throughout various themed rooms. About 3km out of town, the impressive **Museo del Desierto** at Pérez Treviño 3745 in Parque Las Maravillas (Tues–Sun 10am–5pm; M$65, kids M$35; Ⓣ844/986-9000, Ⓦwww.museodeldesierto.org) charts the development and history of deserts, and displays plenty of child-pleasing dinosaur fossils, though labelling is in Spanish only.

Practicalities

City bus #9 (M$5) runs between Saltillo's main **bus station**, 3km southwest of the centre, the cathedral on the Plaza de Armas, and onwards a couple more stops to the Plaza Acuña, right at the heart of things (to get back, catch it on Aldama near Zaragoza). The local **Oficina de Convenciones y Visitantes** is inconveniently located at Carranza 8520 (Mon–Fri 9am–5pm; Ⓣ844/432-3690, Ⓦwww.ocvsaltillo.com), but there is usually an information kiosk on the Plaza de Armas (daily 10am–5pm). The **post office** is at Victoria 453, and there are long-distance **phones** and **banks** with ATMs all over the centre of town. At Padre Flores 159, Cyberbase has **internet** access for M$10/hr (Mon–Fri 8am–10pm, Sat 10am–10pm).

Most of the better-value **hotels** are in the side streets immediately around Plaza Acuña, but have a tendency to fill up each night. The *Hotel Bristol*, Aldama 405 Pte (Ⓣ844/154-0134; ❸), is basic but a clean budget place, with cable TV and a little historic character. If you can spend a little more and want to savour some colonial splendour, check out the *Hotel Urdiñola*, Victoria 251 (Ⓣ844/414-0940, Ⓦwww.ahg.com.mx; ❸), with its tiled open lobby dominated by a wide staircase flanked by suits of armour, and fountains trickling amidst the greenery of the courtyard. For a bit more luxury, try the *Hotel Colonial Alameda* at Obregón 222 (Ⓣ844/410-0088), Ⓦwww.hotelcolonialalameda.com; ❺), which is great value considering the lavish rooms and gorgeous colonial property.

Restaurants in Saltillo tend to close early, and the ones in the centre mainly cater for office workers and students. There are plenty of cheap places to eat around the **Mercado Juárez**, beside the Plaza Acuña, which is a decent market in its own right – tourists are treated fairly and not constantly pressed to buy.

One of the best options on Plaza Acuña is *Tacos El Pastor* (at the corner of Aldama and Padre Flores), where sets of four tasty tacos (the bistec is best) start at around M$28, and the salsas are always fresh. Try Saltillo's famous *pan de pulque*, bread made of wheat, egg, cinnamon and unrefined cactus juice, at *Panadería Mena Pan de Pulque*, Madero 1350, three long blocks west of Carranza. (four buns for M$20). For high-quality sit-down meals, take a taxi out to *El Mesón Principal* (Ⓣ844/415-0015, Ⓦwww.mesonprincipal.com) at Carranza and Avenida Egipto, which specializes in sizzling *cabrito al pastor* (barbecued baby goat), and mouth-watering *fritada* (grilled steak platter). You should also check out acclaimed restaurant *La Canasta* at Carranza 2485 (Ⓣ844/415-8840), which opens till midnight and serves fine international and Mexican cuisine, steaks and their specialities, *arroz huerfano* ("orphan" rice with ham, nuts and bacon) and lemon pie; M$150–300 for mains.

Valle de Parras

Around 160km west of Saltillo, the **Valle de Parras** is the oldest **wine-growing** region in Mexico. Dismissed as poor quality for years, the region's Cabernet Sauvignons in particular, which account for around seventy percent of production,

Major fiestas

February

Carnaval (week before Lent; variable Feb–March) is at its best in the Caribbean and New Orleans-like atmosphere of Tampico – also in Ciudad Victoria and Monterrey.

March

Festival de San José (March 19). Celebrated in Ciudad Victoria.

Birth of Benito Juárez (March 21). Ceremonies to commemorate Juárez's birth in Matamoros.

July

Día de Nuestra Señora del Refugio (July 4). Marked by dancing and pilgrimages in Matamoros.

August

Feria de la Uva (Aug 9). Exuberant festivities in Parras, between Saltillo and Torreón.

Feria de Saltillo (around Aug 13). Saltillo begins its annual festival, featuring agricultural and art exhibitions, music and dance performances, and plenty of the local *sarapes* (shawls).

September

Feria de Nuevo Laredo (Sept). Major festival on the border at Nuevo Laredo.

Independence Day (Sept 16). Festivities everywhere, but the biggest in Monterrey.

October

Fiesta de Amistad (late Oct). Joint week-long celebrations between the border town of Ciudad Acuña and its Texan neighbour Del Rio. Bullfights, pageants and a parade, which starts in one country and ends in the other.

November

Día de San Martín de Porres (Nov 3). Fiesta with native dances in Tampico.

Feria de la Cultura Barrio Antiguo (Nov 15–25). One of Monterrey's leading festivals; throngs of people come for music and food when the city's many cafés open to the street.

December

Día de la Virgen de Guadalupe (Dec 12). Big celebrations everywhere, especially in Guadalupe de Bravos; El Palmito (Durango), between Durango and Parral; Ciudad Anahuac (Nuevo León) in the north of the state; and Abasolo, near Monterrey. Monterrey itself attracts many pilgrims at this time.

are finally garnering a following in international markets. The area is anchored by the pleasant colonial market town of **PARRAS DE LA FUENTE**, served by regular second-class bus from Saltillo (M$85; 2hr 30min). Once here you can walk everywhere in town, though you'll need to take a taxi to **Las Bodegas de Casa Madero** and **Hacienda Casa Grande** (daily 8am–5.30pm; free; Ⓣ84/2422-0055, Ⓦwww.madero.com.mx), 8km north of town; this is the largest and oldest producer, with roots going back to the Americas' first winery, established here in 1597 by the Spaniards. You can take free thirty-minute tours of the facilities and museum, buy and taste the wine, and admire the colonial hacienda on site. Just 2km west of town at Ramos Arizpe 131, the **Antigua Bodega de Perote** (Ⓣ84/2422-1698, Ⓦwww.antiguahaciendadeperote.com) produces fine wines as well as brandy and sotol, the local spirit. It's also an inviting **hotel** (M$425). Established by Italians in 1891 back in downtown Parras, **Las Bodegas El Vesubio** is a smaller operation at Madero 36 – the shop is open daily (Mon–Fri 9am–1pm & 2–7pm, Sat & Sun 9am–7pm). The best **place to stay** in town is the colonial *Hostal el Farol* at Arizpe 301 (Ⓣ84/2422-1113, Ⓦwww.hostalelfarol.com; ❻).

Travel details

Buses

Chihuahua to: Ciudad Juárez (at least hourly; 5hr); Creel (every 1–2hr; 4hr); Mexico City (every 2hr; 18hr); Nuevo Casas Grandes (11 daily; 4hr 30min); Zacatecas (hourly; 12hr).
Ciudad Acuña to: Monterrey (4 daily; 8hr); Piedras Negras (hourly; 1hr 30min); Saltillo (8 daily; 7hr).
Ciudad Juárez to: Chihuahua (at least hourly; 5hr); Durango (at least hourly; 16hr); Mexico City (every 1–2hr; 24hr); Nuevo Casas Grandes (every 1–2hr; 4hr); Parral (at least hourly; 10hr); Torreón (at least hourly; 12hr); Zacatecas (hourly; 16hr).
Ciudad Victoria to: Matamoros (hourly; 4–5hr); Monterrey (hourly; 4hr); Reynosa (9 daily; 4–5hr); Tampico (hourly or better; 3hr).
Creel to: Batopilas (1 daily; 6hr); Chihuahua (14 daily; 4–5hr); Divisadero (7 daily; 1hr); Guachochi (2 daily; 3hr).
Durango to: Aguascalientes (20 daily; 6hr); Ciudad Juárez (at least hourly; 12–14hr); Mazatlán (9 daily; 7hr); Mexico City (14 daily; 12–13hr); Monterrey (every 1–2hr; 9hr); Parral (9 daily; 6hr); Torreón (every 1–2hr; 4hr 30min); Zacatecas (roughly hourly; 4hr 30min).
Guachochi to: Chihuahua (5 daily; 7–9hr); Creel (2 daily; 3hr); Parral (6 daily; 4hr).
Matamoros to: Chicago (2 daily; 36hr); Ciudad Victoria (hourly; 4–5hr); Dallas (8 daily; 12hr); Houston (11 daily; 5hr); Monterrey (hourly; 4hr); Reynosa (every 45min; 2hr); San Antonio (8 daily; 6hr); Tampico (hourly; 7–8hr).
Monterrey to: Ciudad Victoria (hourly; 4hr); Dallas (4 daily; 12hr); Guadalajara (15 daily; 12hr); Houston (4 daily; 10hr); Matamoros (hourly; 4hr); Matehuala (hourly; 4–5hr); Mexico City (hourly; 12hr); Nuevo Laredo (every 30min; 3hr); Piedras Negras (12 daily; 5–7hr); Reynosa (every 30min; 3hr); Saltillo (constantly; 1hr 30min); San Antonio (5 daily; 7hr); San Luis Potosí (hourly; 7hr); Tampico (hourly; 7–8hr); Zacatecas (hourly; 7hr–7hr 30min).
Nuevo Casas Grandes to: Chihuahua (hourly; 4hr 30min); Ciudad Juárez (every 1–2hr; 4hr).
Nuevo Laredo to: Acapulco (2 daily; 20hr); Austin (14 daily; 7hr); Chicago (2 daily; 36hr); Dallas (14 daily; 9hr); Guadalajara (5 daily; 14hr); Houston (9 daily; 7hr); Mexico City (10 daily; 15hr); Monterrey (every 30min; 3hr); Piedras Negras (8 daily; 3hr); Reynosa (8 daily; 4hr); Saltillo (8 daily; 4–5hr); San Antonio (hourly; 4hr); San Luis Potosí (14 daily; 12hr); Tampico (2 daily; 10hr); Zacatecas (6 daily; 8hr).
Parral to: Chihuahua (roughly hourly; 4hr); Durango (11 daily; 6hr); Guachochi (6 daily; 3hr 30min).
Piedras Negras to: Ciudad Acuña (hourly; 1hr 30min); Mexico City (3 daily; 18hr); Monterrey (8 daily; 5–7hr); Nuevo Laredo (10 daily; 3hr); Saltillo (12 daily; 7hr).
Reynosa to: Ciudad Victoria (9 daily; 4–5hr); Matamoros (every 45min; 2hr); Mexico City (6 daily; 14–16hr); Monterrey (every 30min; 3hr); Nuevo Laredo (9 daily; 4hr); San Luis Potosí (11 daily; 9–10hr); Tampico (hourly; 7hr); Zacatecas (10 daily; 9hr).
Saltillo to: Ciudad Acuña (14 daily; 7hr); Guadalajara (13 daily; 10hr); Parras (9 daily; 2hr 30min); Mazatlán (4 daily; 12hr); Mexico City (every 1–2hr; 12hr); Monterrey (constantly; 1hr 30min); Nuevo Laredo (every 1–2hr; 4–5hr); Piedras Negras (15 daily; 7hr).
Tampico to: Ciudad Victoria (hourly or better; 3hr); Matamoros (hourly; 7–8hr); Mexico City (every 1–2hr; 8hr); Monterrey (hourly; 7–8hr); Nuevo Laredo (2 daily; 10hr); San Luis Potosí (11 daily; 7hr); Veracruz (8 daily; 9hr).

Trains

The Copper Canyon railway (see p.192) is the big attraction in this region – the last remaining passenger train in Mexico.

Flights

There are frequent flights from most of the major cities to the capital – Chihuahua, Monterrey and Tampico all have several a day. From Monterrey you can also fly to Guadalajara and Acapulco, and there are international services to Dallas, Houston, San Antonio and Chicago. From Ciudad Juárez and Nuevo Laredo you can get to the capital and Guadalajara.

The Bajío

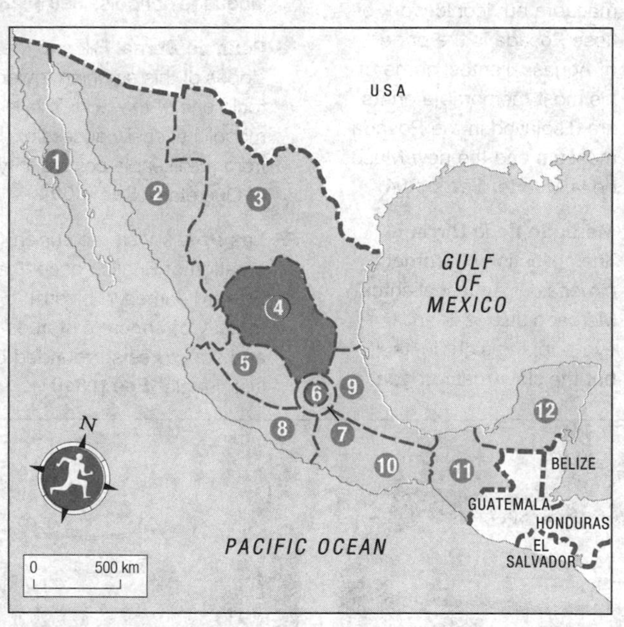
USA
GULF
OF
MEXICO
PACIFIC OCEAN
BELIZE
GUATEMALA
HONDURAS
EL
SALVADOR
N
0
500 km
1
2
3
4
5
6
7
8
9
10
11
12

CHAPTER 4 Highlights

✱ Real de Catorce Artfully restored colonial hotels, fine Italian meals and haunting desert scenery make this semi-ghost-town perfect for relaxing, extended stays. **See p.236**

✱ Zacatecas Glorious former silver town located high up in the northern deserts. **See p.248**

✱ Posada pilgrimage The macabre but iconic work of José Posada is the pride of Aguascalientes; some of his most memorable prints are displayed in the Posada museum and the new Museo de la Muerte. **See p.264**

✱ Mercado de la Birria The collection of aromatic *birrierías* at Aguascalientes' Mercado Juárez is an eye-popping sight in itself, but the slow-roasted goat meat, served in a spicy broth, is the real star. **See p.266**

✱ Guanajuato Captivating university town set dramatically over the steep slopes of a ravine. **See p.268**

✱ San Miguel de Allende Gorgeous colonial town with some of the most enticing boutique hotels in Mexico, an appealing, languid lifestyle and highly regarded Spanish language schools. **See p.284**

✱ Peña de Bernal Hike up the slopes of this stunning tower of rock, one of the world's tallest monoliths, easily accessible from the likeable colonial city of Querétaro. **See p.304**

✱ Las Pozas Visit the surreal creation of English eccentric Edward James, a bizarre fantasy of concrete statues and structures surrounded by lush jungle. **See p.310**

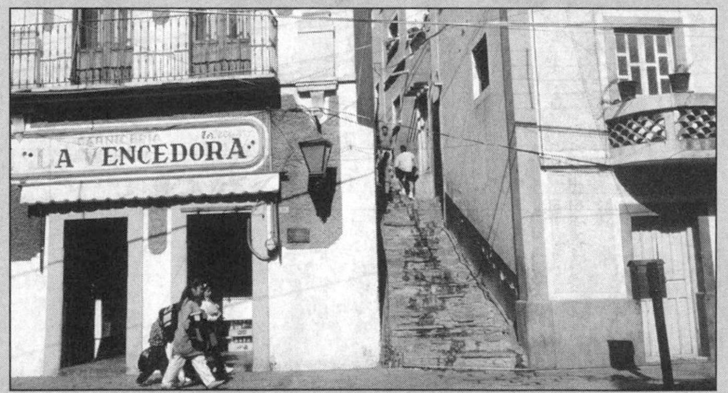

▲ Guanajuato

4

The Bajío

Scattered with enchanting colonial towns and rugged, dust-blown hills, the fertile valleys of the **Bajío** spread across Mexico's central highlands almost from coast to coast and as far south as the capital. This has long been the most heavily populated part of the country, providing much of the silver and grain that supported Mexico throughout the years of Spanish rule. Indeed, the legacy of **Spanish architecture** remains at its most impressive here, in meticulously crafted towns that – at their cores at least – have changed little over the centuries.

The Bajío grew rich on just one thing – **silver** – but in time the region also grew restive under the heavy-handed rule of Spain. The wealthy Creole (Spanish-blooded but Mexican-born) bourgeoisie were free to exploit the land and its people, but didn't control their own destinies; lucrative government posts and high positions in the Church were reserved exclusively for those actually born in Spain, while the indigenous peoples and poor *mestizos* were condemned either to landless poverty or to near-fatal labour. Unsurprisingly, then, the Bajío was ripe for revolution. This land is *La Cuna de la Independencia* (the **Cradle of Independence**), where every town seems to claim a role in the break with Spain. In Querétaro the plotters held many of their early meetings, and from here they were warned that their plans had been discovered; and in Dolores Hidalgo the famous *Grito* was first voiced by Father Hidalgo, proclaiming an independent Mexico.

Approaching the Bajío from the north you cross several hundred kilometres of desert landscape punctuated only by the occasional ranch, or defunct mining towns, such as the wonderfully strange semi-ghost-town of **Real de Catorce**, where decades of abandonment are gradually being reversed. Only then do you reach the colonial cities of **Zacatecas** and **San Luis Potosí** – both eponymous state capitals – that mark a radical change in landscape and architecture. San Luis, a large modern metropolis, has its share of monuments, but Zacatecas is far more exciting, an oasis of culture and sophistication built with the bounty of the silver mines that riddle the landscape hereabouts. Further south and crazily ranged up the sides of a ravine, **Guanajuato** is quite simply one of the country's richest and most scenic colonial towns, with one of its finest Baroque churches, a thriving student life and, for good measure, a ghoulish museum of mummies. The beguiling hillside town of **San Miguel de Allende** also has its advocates, as much for its wonderful setting as for the comforts of home, ensured by a large population of foreign artists, gringo retirees and language students. **Dolores Hidalgo**, in particular, is a point of pilgrimage for anyone with the least interest in Mexico's independence movement, as is, to a lesser extent, **Querétaro**, a large and industrial city that preserves an underrated colonial quarter at its heart. Querétaro also serves as a good base for exploring the **Sierra Gorda**, particularly the concrete fantasy sculptures of **Las Pozas** near Xilitla.

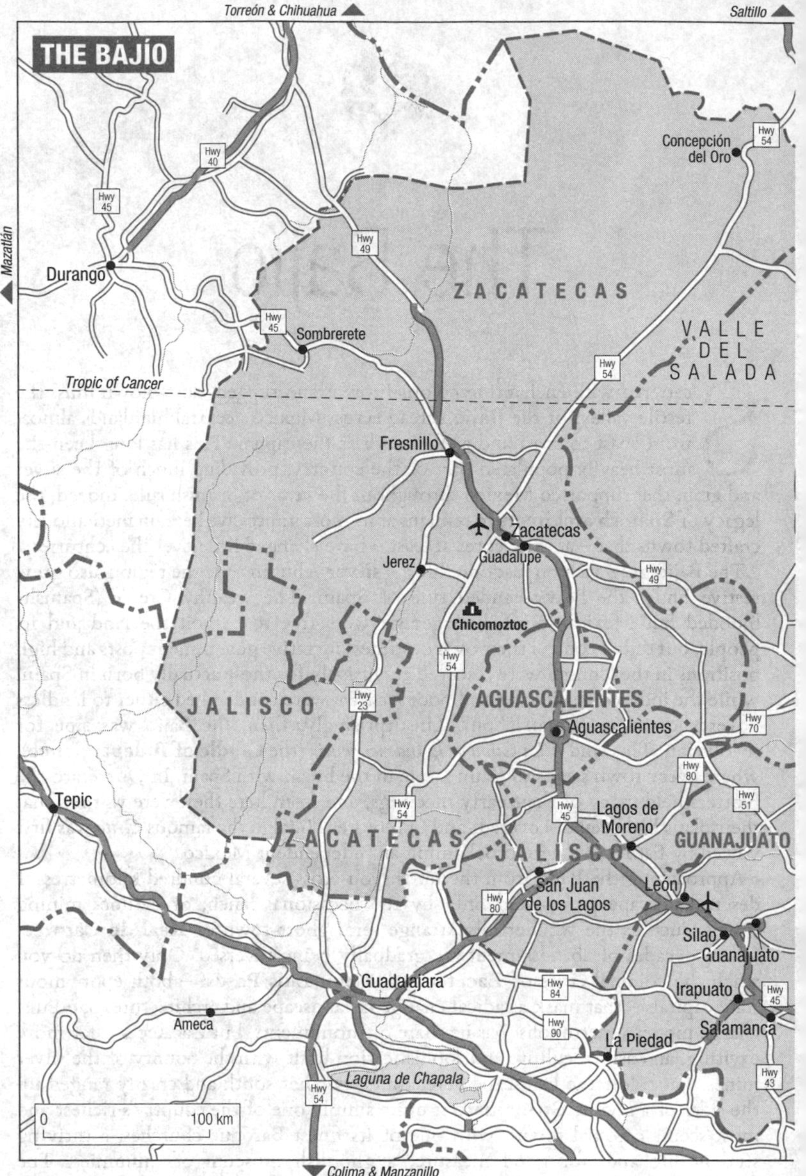

Matehuala and Real de Catorce

Matehuala is the only major town along the highway that links Saltillo, around 260km to the north, and San Luis Potosí, around 200km south. Between the two runs the relatively fast Hwy-57, so there's little need to stop here except to use it as a staging post for the alluring former mining town of **Real de Catorce**.

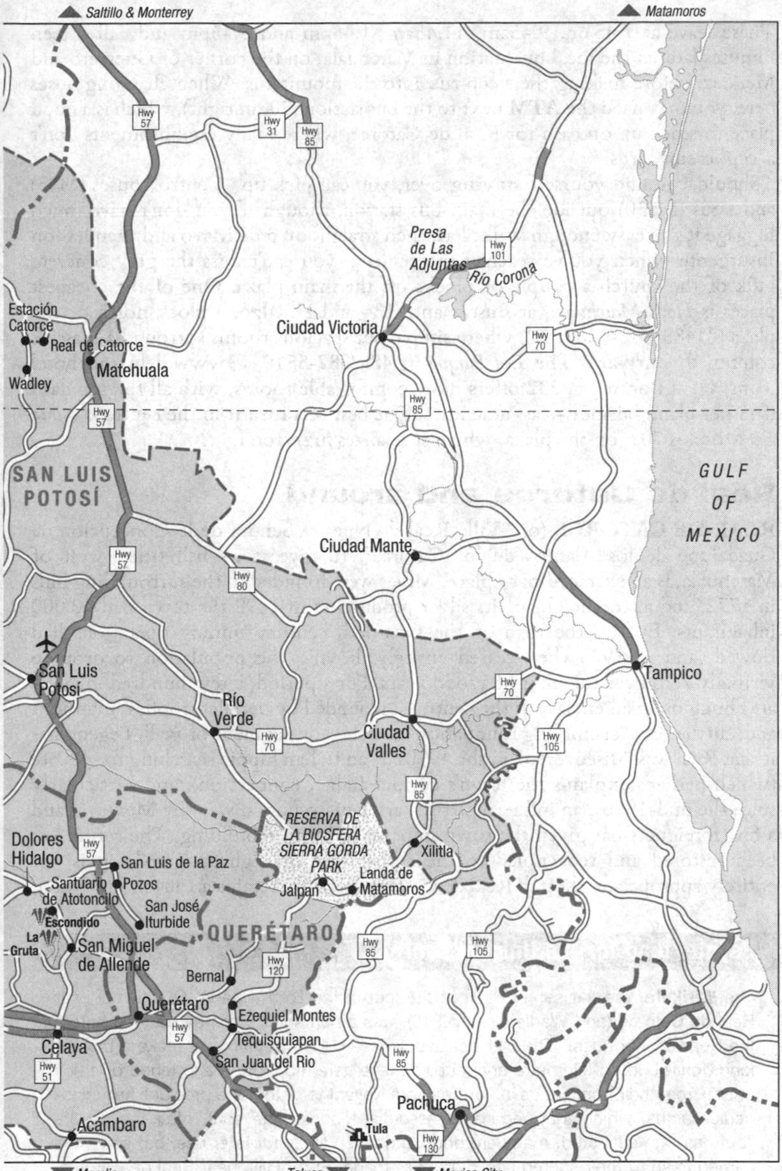

Matehuala

A typically lively northern commercial town, **MATEHUALA** holds little interest unless you happen to coincide with the **Fiesta de Cristo de Matehuala** (Jan 6–15), ten days of religious ceremonies, dancing, fireworks and general celebrations.

At other times you may only see the main **bus station**, just off the highway on 5 de Mayo, 2km south of the centre, which has buses to Catorce (2hr; M$47).

These leave at 7.45am, 9.45am, 11.45am, 1.45pm and 5.45pm and call fifteen minutes later at the local bus station in Matehuala, on the corner of Guerrero and Mendez, before making the steep run into the mountains. When changing buses here, you may need the **ATM** next to the bus station (200m right), which is a good place to stock up on cash for Real de Catorce, where many establishments don't accept credit cards.

Should you find yourself **staying** over, you can pick up "Centro" buses (M$5) and taxis (M$30) outside the main bus station, though if you don't have much luggage it's an easy enough walk: left, then straight up 5 de Mayo and then left on Insurgentes when you've reached the centre – you can't miss the grey concrete bulk of the church a couple of blocks off the main plaza. One of the cheapest places is *Hotel Matehuala*, at Bustamante 134 and Hidalgo, a block north of the plaza (Ⓣ488/882-0680; ❸), where simple but spacious rooms surround a massive columned courtyard. The *Del Parque* (Ⓣ488/882-5510, Ⓦwww.delparquehotel.com; ❺) at Bocanegra 232 offers more comfortable rooms, with all the standard if rather bland business-class amenities. The best **restaurant** in the centre is *Santa Fe*, Morelos 709, on the plaza, which specializes in seafood.

Real de Catorce and around

REAL DE CATORCE (or "Villa Real de Nuestra Señora de la Concepción de Guadalupe de los Alamos de los Catorce", to give it its full title), west of Matehuala, is an extraordinary place. Mines were founded in the surrounding hills in 1772, and at the height of its silver production in 1898 the town had 40,000 inhabitants. But by the turn of the twentieth century mining operations had slowed, and in 1905 they ceased entirely, leaving the population to drop to virtually zero over the next fifty-odd years. For a period, a few hundred inhabitants hung on in an enclave at the centre, surrounded by derelict, roofless mansions and, further out, crumbling foundations and the odd segment of wall. Legend has it that Real was "discovered" in the 1970s by an Italian hippie searching for peyote (which perhaps explains the town's curious Italian connection), and particularly since the mid-1990s, an influx of artists, artesanía vendors, wealthy Mexicans and a few foreigners has given the town impetus to begin rebuilding. The centre has been restored and reoccupied to the extent that the "ghost-town" tag is not entirely appropriate, though Real de Catorce certainly retains an air of desolation,

Peyote: food for the Huichol soul

The **Wirikuta**, the flat semi-desert at the foot of the Sierra Madre Occidental near Real de Catorce (and Wadley, see p.240), was a rich source of **peyote** long before the Spanish Conquest. The Huichol people (see p.176) traditionally make a month-long, four-hundred-kilometre annual pilgrimage here (now often shortened by truck or car) from their homelands in northeastern Nayarit to gather the precious hallucinogenic cactus, which they regard as essential food for the soul. After the peyote "buttons" are collected, many are dried and taken away for later use, but some are carried fresh to their sacred site, Cerro Quemada (Burnt Hill), near Real de Catorce, for ceremonies.

Tales of achieving higher consciousness under the influence of peyote have long drawn foreigners, many of them converts of the books of **Carlos Casteneda**. Indeed, Real de Catorce only made it onto the tourist itinerary after it became a waystation on the hippy-druggy trail in the 1970s. New Agers continue to visit, but the hills round about have been picked clean and there are fears that over-harvesting may threaten the continued Huichol tradition.

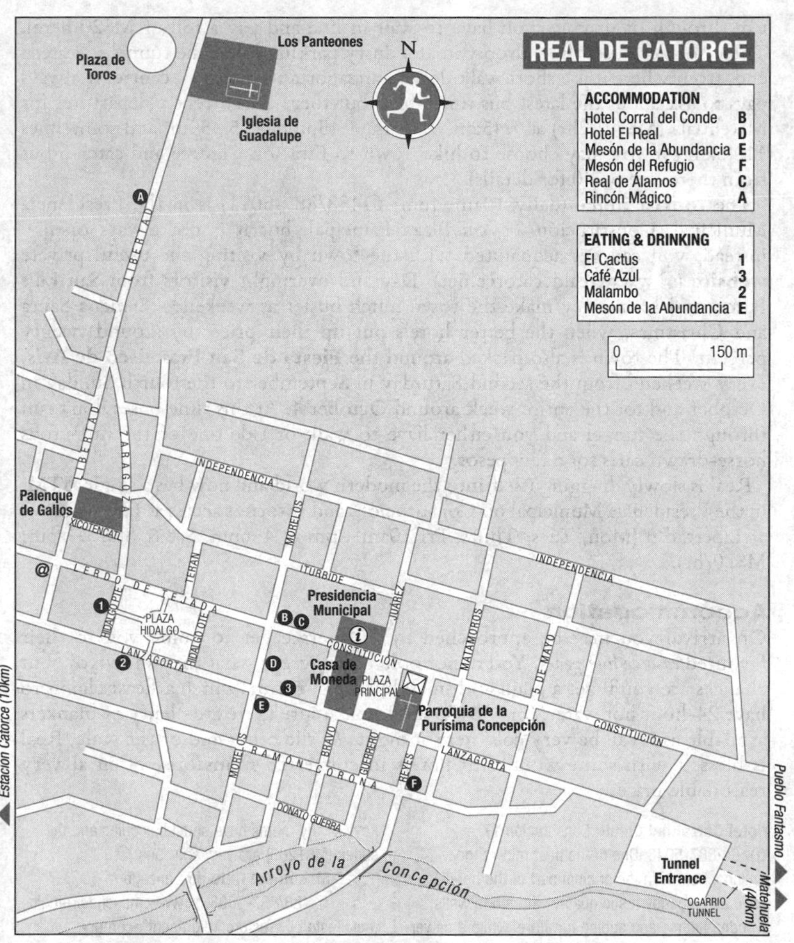

especially in the outskirts; the occasional pick-up shoulders its way through the narrow cobbled streets, but most of the traffic is horses and donkeys. There's not much in the way of sights to visit: simply wandering around, kicking up the dust and climbing into the hills are big and worthwhile pastimes here.

The population now stands at around 1500, the foreign contingent coexisting amiably with locals who increasingly depend on the tourist industry (the town was made a "Pueblo Mágico" in 2001). Lovers of high kitsch will also be pleased to find whole rows of stalls selling tacky icons and religious paraphernalia. Every year or so a new restaurant or hotel opens up, and the town has become another popular Hollywood location, featuring in movies such as *Bandidas* (2006) and the decidedly mediocre *The Mexican* (2001).

Arrival and information

Most people arrive from Matehuala by **bus**. The bigger buses can't get through the Ogarrio tunnel, so you'll probably have to change buses at the eastern end for the run through (if driving, you have to wait in line and pay a toll of M$20 here). These smaller buses (free) drop you at a dusty parking lot at the tunnel's western end, from where it is a short walk down Lanzagorta to the town centre. It always pays to ask about the latest bus timetables, but there are currently departures for Matehuala (M$47; 2hr) at 7.45am, 9.45am, 1.45pm and 5.45pm, and sometimes 11.45am (or you may choose to hike down to Estación Catorce and catch a bus from there: see p.240 for details).

The **tourist office** (daily 10am–4pm; ⓣ488/887-5071) is in the Presidencia Municipal, Constitución 27, on Plaza Principal, but it is not always open – instead, you can get acquainted with the town by visiting the useful private **website** (ⓦwww.realdecatorce.net). Day and overnight visitors from San Luis Potosí and Monterrey make the town much busier at weekends, Semana Santa and Christmas, when the better hotels put up their prices by around twenty percent. The town is also packed around the **Fiesta de San Francisco de Asís**, every weekend from the second Saturday in September to the fourth Sunday in October and for the entire week around October 4. At this time buses don't run through the tunnel and you either have to walk or ride one of the numerous horse-drawn carts for a few pesos.

Real is slowly dragging itself into the modern world and now has a single **ATM**, in the Presidencia Municipal on Constitución, and **internet** access at El Quemado, at Libertad 5 (Mon, Tues, Thurs, Fri 10am–2pm & 4–6pm, Sat & Sun 2–8pm; M$20/hr).

Accommodation

On arrival you may be approached by villagers eager to guide you to their favoured *casa de huéspedes*. You're not obliged to accept what they show you, but chances are you'll get a plain and small but clean **room**, which at least claims to have 24-hour hot water, for M$100–180: make sure there are plenty of blankets available as it can be very cold here at night. At the other end of the scale, Real is blessed with some wonderful hotels in converted **mansions**, often at very reasonable prices.

Hotel Corral del Conde Constitución 17 ⓣ488/887-5048. One of the best mid-range options. Rooms in the original part of the hotel have an elegantly rustic quality with stone walls, wooden beams and ageing furniture, while a newer section across the road has more modern but equally comfortable rooms. They don't take reservations. ❺

Hotel El Real Morelos 20, behind the Casa de Moneda ⓣ488/887-5058, ⓦwww.hotelelreal.com. A charmingly converted old house with clean, airy rooms featuring native decoration, TVs (including videos and a video library), fireplaces and views galore. It's reputed to be haunted. ❺

Mesón de la Abundancia Lanzagorta 11 ⓣ488/887-5044, ⓦwww.mesonabundancia.com. Located on the corner of Morelos, this friendly hotel was rebuilt from the 1860s ruins of the old town Treasury, and is full of masks, huge stone-built rooms with beamed ceilings, rug-covered brick floors and ancient doors with their original hefty keys. Many rooms have small balconies and the suites (M$1200) are very spacious. ❺

Mesón del Refugio Lanzagorta 55 ⓣ488/887-5068, ⓦwww.mesondelrefugio.net. Tastefully restored eighteenth-century mansion, completely renovated in a chic, modern style with a glass-covered courtyard and cosy rooms with internet, satellite TV, heating, telephone and restaurant serving breakfast. ❺

Real de Álamos Constitución 21 ⓣ488/887-5009. One of the better budget hostels, just west of the Palacio Municipal, with comfortable enough concrete-walled rooms and low prices for singles (M$150). ❸

Rincón Mágico Zaragoza 10, at Libertad ⓣ488/887-5113. Nicely placed between the slightly scruffy *hospedajes* but half the price of the swanky joints, this small hotel has comfy rooms, some better than others and some with views down the plains. A restaurant/bar operates at weekends. ❸

The Town

Real de Catorce is built in a high mountain valley at the end of a beautifully constructed 25-kilometre cobbled road through semi-desert dotted with agave and stunted Joshua trees. The final 2.3km is through the **Ogarrio tunnel** (named after the founder's home town in Spain), opened in 1901, which is only broad enough for one vehicle at a time. As you drive through, the odd mineshaft leads off into the mountain to either side – by one there's a little shrine, the **Capilla de Nuestra Señora de los Dolores**, to miners who died at work.

In the town, the austere, shuttered stone buildings blend with the bare rocky crags that enclose them. The single main street, **Lanzagorta**, runs past the 1817 **Parroquia de la Purísima Concepción** (daily 7am–7pm) with its square, shaded plaza and unusual removable wooden floorboards (for cleaning), and on down to the **Plaza Hidalgo** (aka Plaza de Armas), with its central bandstand. It's the church that attracts most Mexicans to Real, or rather the miraculous figure of St Francis of Assisi (known as Panchito, Pancho being a diminutive of Francisco) housed here. You'll soon spot the shrine by the penitents kneeling before it, but take time to head through the door to the left of the altar, where the walls are covered with hundreds of handmade *retablos* giving thanks for cures or miraculous escapes effected by the saint. They're a wonderful form of naive folk art, the older ones painted on tin plate, newer examples on paper or card or even photographs, depicting events that range from amazing to mundane – last-second rescues from the paths of oncoming trains, or simply the return of a stolen vehicle – all signed and dated with thanks to Panchito for his timely intervention.

Across the square, the **Casa de Moneda** (Wed–Sun 10am–3pm; M$10) is a magnificent old mansion with two storeys on one side and three on the other, thanks to the sloping site it was built on. This is where Real's silver was minted into coin, though Emperor Maximilian closed it just 14 months after it was completed in 1865. After a meticulous restoration it now serves as an art gallery and cultural centre, with temporary exhibitions from all over Mexico. Heading north out of town along Zaragoza, duck a few metres up Xicotencatl to the Roman-looking **Palenque de Gallos** of 1863 (daily 9am–5pm; free), where cockfights were once held, then continue out along Zaragoza and Libertad to the ruinous Plaza de Toros, opposite **Los Panteones** (daily except Tues 9am–5pm, though hours depend on the gatekeeper's mood; free) where Real's dead lie covered by rough piles of dirt all around the decaying 1779 church. Peek inside to see its still-vibrant frescoes, which are going mouldy around the edges – just as they should be in a town like Real.

Eating and drinking

Eating cheaply in Real de Catorce is easy, with numerous stalls and shops selling gorditas and tortas, mostly along Lanzagorta. Many of the best eateries in town are **Italian**-oriented restaurants, a legacy of the influx of Italian expats since the 1980s.

El Cactus Plaza Hidalgo ☎488/887-5056. Owned by an Italian chef and his Mexican wife, *Cactus* serves fine cannelloni and great tortas (M$50–100), as well as stocking a huge range of fancy teas.

Café Azul Lanzagorta 27, next to *Mesón de la Abundancia* ☎488/887-5131. Relaxed Swiss-run café serving good coffee, home-made cakes and sweet and savoury crepes (M$50). Closed Wed.

Malambo Lanzagorta between Allende and Zaragoza. Lovely, if pricey, restaurant with some outdoor seating around a tinkling fountain. The pizzas are good, but their signature light and flaky empanadas, served with a fresh salad (M$95), are excellent. For dessert don't miss the piping-hot apple and chocolate dumpling.

Mesón de la Abundancia (see opposite) ☎488/887-5044. The pick of the bunch. The Mexican and Italian food is superbly cooked and presented, and worth every peso: expect to pay M$200 for a full meal including a slice of torte and espresso. Credit cards accepted.

Estación Catorce and Wadley

The town's sights are soon exhausted, but you could spend days exploring the surrounding mountains, visiting ruins, or heading downhill to the *altiplano* (high plain) of the desert below. One of the most relaxing ways to go is on **horseback**: horses are usually available around Plaza Hidalgo and in front of the *Mesón de la Abundancia*, from where **guides** will take you out across the hills, perhaps visiting the Huichol ceremonial site of Cerro Quemado, though this can seem unpleasantly voyeuristic if any Huichol are around. Midweek tours cost around M$150–180 for three or four hours; prices are higher on weekends; better deals can be struck by rounding up a ready-to-go group, and then haggling hard. For **short hikes**, the best nearby destination is the **Pueblo Fantasmo** "Ghost Town", extensive mine ruins reached in an hour or so by following the winding track uphill just to the left of the Ogarrio tunnel entrance as you face it.

The most rewarding unguided **longer hike** (12km one way; 3hr down, 4hr return; 850m ascent on the way back) leads downhill from Plaza Hidalgo (with the stables on your left), then forks right after 50m and follows a 4WD track towards the small dusty trackside town of Estación Catorce. You'll soon find yourself walking among mine ruins – you'll pass a dam built to provide water and power for the mines, and even a tall chimney from one of the smelters. After about an hour you get to the small village of **Los Catorces**, and beyond its cemetery, a second settlement known as **Santa Cruz de Carretas** (about 2hr from Real).

At this point, you've already experienced the best of the hike, but it is possible to continue to **ESTACIÓN CATORCE**, an hour further on. If the idea of hiking back seems too daunting, try flagging down the occasional vehicle, and be prepared to pay for your ride. Estación Catorce itself is not a place to linger, though if you get stuck, there are a couple of fleapit hotels and places to eat, located where **buses** depart, on the scruffy square by the rail tracks. Apart from local services to Wadley (at 10.30am, 4pm & perhaps a couple of others; 20min) all buses head north from here to Saltillo (8am, 2pm & 6pm; 4hr) or south to San Luis Potosí via Matehuala (6am, 7.30am & 2pm; 4hr).

Around 10km south of Estación Catorce along the asphalt road lies **WADLEY** (or Estación Wadley), a small, dusty village that at first acquaintance seems even less appealing. It has, however, garnered a devoted following, chiefly for its proximity to a section of desert known to the Huichol as Wirikuta (p.236), renowned for its abundant **peyote** (as explored in the 2008 experimental Indie flick *Wadley*). Most people rent a room for a few days, usually with a kitchen as restaurants here are very limited: ask around and you should find somewhere for around M$100 per night, especially if you are staying a few days (most people end up with *Don Tomas*). Officially at least, "eating" peyote is frowned upon and there have been several police crackdowns in recent years – aficionados usually sample peyote where they find it in the desert (sometimes camping the night). Don't bring any back with you.

San Luis Potosí

Situated to the north of the Bajío's fertile heartland, the sprawling industrial city of **SAN LUIS POTOSÍ** boasts a rich colonial centre crammed with solid stone buildings reminiscent of a classical Spanish town, and it's an easy (flat), likeable place to explore. The city was founded as a Franciscan mission in 1592, but it wasn't long before the Spanish discovered significant deposits of gold and silver in the country round about and began to develop the area in earnest. They added the name Potosí (after the fabulously productive mines in Bolivia) in the expectation

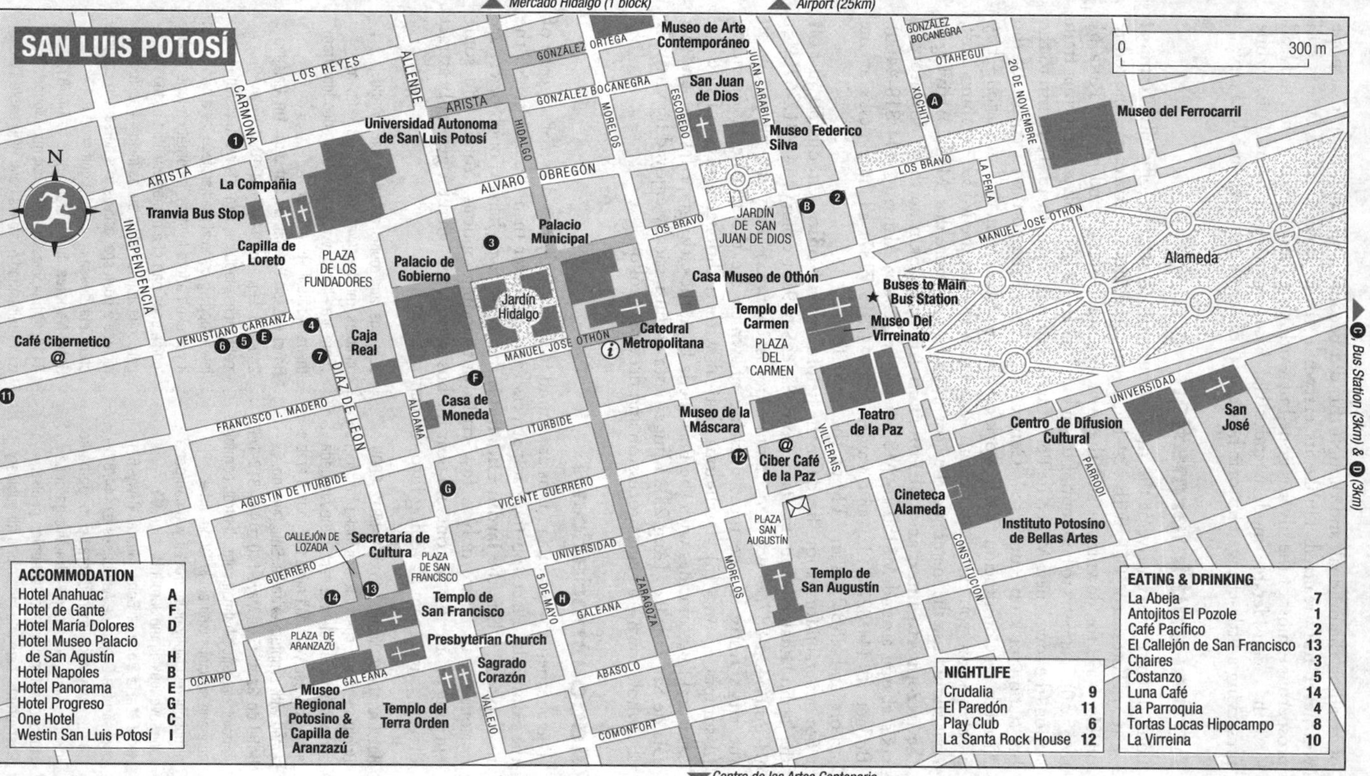
SAN LUIS POTOSÍ
Mercado Hidalgo (1 block)
Airport (25km)
C, Bus Station (3km) & D (3km)
Centro de las Artes Centenario
8 (100m), Zona Rosa (500m), Parques Tangamanga (2km), 9 & 10
0
300 m
N
Museo de Arte Contemporáneo
San Juan de Dios
Museo Federico Silva
Museo del Ferrocarril
Universidad Autonoma de San Luis Potosí
La Compañia
Tranvia Bus Stop
Capilla de Loreto
PLAZA DE LOS FUNDADORES
Palacio de Gobierno
Palacio Municipal
Jardín Hidalgo
Catedral Metropolitana
JARDÍN DE SAN JUAN DE DIOS
Casa Museo de Othón
Templo del Carmen
PLAZA DEL CARMEN
Buses to Main Bus Station
Museo Del Virreinato
Alameda
Café Cibernetico
Caja Real
Casa de Moneda
Museo de la Máscara
Ciber Café de la Paz
Teatro de la Paz
Centro de Difusion Cultural
San José
Cineteca Alameda
Instituto Potosíno de Bellas Artes
PLAZA SAN AUGUSTÍN
Templo de San Augustín
CALLEJÓN DE LOZADA
Secretaría de Cultura
PLAZA DE SAN FRANCISCO
Templo de San Francisco
Presbyterian Church
PLAZA DE ARANZAZÚ
Sagrado Corazón
Museo Regional Potosino & Capilla de Aranzazú
Templo del Terra Orden
LOS REYES
CARMONA
ALLENDE
ARISTA
GONZALEZ ORTEGA
GONZALEZ BOCANEGRA
HIDALGO
MORELOS
ESCOBEDO
JUAN SARABIA
XOCHITL
OTAHEGUI
20 DE NOVIEMBRE
LOS BRAVO
LA PERLA
MANUEL JOSE OTHÓN
ALVARO OBREGÓN
INDEPENDENCIA
VENUSTIANO CARRANZA
DIAZ DE LEON
FRANCISCO I. MADERO
ALDAMA
ITURBIDE
AGUSTIN DE ITURBIDE
VICENTE GUERRERO
VILLERAIS
UNIVERSIDAD
PARRODI
CONSTITUCION
GUERRERO
5 DE MAYO
GALEANA
ZARAGOZA
ABASOLO
COMONFORT
OCAMPO
VALLEJO
ACCOMMODATION
Hotel Anahuac A
Hotel de Gante F
Hotel María Dolores D
Hotel Museo Palacio de San Agustín H
Hotel Napoles B
Hotel Panorama E
Hotel Progreso G
One Hotel C
Westin San Luis Potosí I
NIGHTLIFE
Crudalia 9
El Paredón 11
Play Club 6
La Santa Rock House 12
EATING & DRINKING
La Abeja 7
Antojitos El Pozole 1
Café Pacífico 2
El Callejón de San Francisco 13
Chaires 3
Costanzo 5
Luna Café 14
La Parroquia 4
Tortas Locas Hipocampo 8
La Virreina 10

of rivalling the original, and though this did become a wealthy town, that hope was never fully realized. Unlike its erstwhile rivals, however, San Luis is still prosperous – most of the silver is gone but working mines churn out zinc and lead – with a considerable modern industrial base. As a result, San Luis, while preserving a little-changed historic heart, is also a large and lively modern city.

Arrival and information

Long-distance buses arrive at the main suburban **bus station** (officially Terminal Terrestre Potosina or TTP, with a 24-hour guardería), around 3km east of the centre on Hwy-57; for downtown and the Alameda walk outside and board "Ruta 6" (M$5.50). It appears to head out of town but doubles back: get off at the former train station (the town's new Museo de Ferrocarril) and walk from there. To return to the bus station, pick up Ruta 6 for "Central TTP" from the northwest corner of the Alameda on Constitución. **Taxis** work on a zone system from the bus station – buy a ticket before you exit the terminal. Rides into the city are M$39 – coming back, taxis should use the meter and the cost should be no more than M$30. Arriving at the **Aeropuerto Internacional Ponciano Arriaga** (25km north of downtown), taxis charge around M$150 to M$200 to the centre; Alamo (Ⓣ444/818-4400), Budget (Ⓣ444/822-2482) and Payless (Ⓣ444/816-7787) all have desks at the airport, and HSBC has an ATM on the lower level.

For general information, head for the helpful **tourist office**, Othón 130, just off the Jardín Hidalgo (Mon–Fri 9am–9pm, Sat & Sun 9am–5pm; Ⓣ444/812-6769 or 01-800/3433-887, Ⓦwww.visitasanluispotosi.com.mx). They can fill you in on the city's **festivals**, the most exciting of which are the Día de la Asunción (Assumption; Aug 15), a religious festival with traditional dances outside the cathedral that coincides with the Feria de la Uva, the city's grape festival, and the Día de San Luis Rey (Aug 25), a huge fiesta enthusiastically enjoyed by virtually the whole town – a giant procession and fireworks follow.

Accommodation

The cheapest **rooms** in San Luis are found in the slightly run-down area north of the **Alameda**. Places on the back streets can be quieter than those closer to the main plazas, where the **Jardín Hidalgo** is the focus. Even here, though prices are reasonable, there are only a few truly outstanding options. You'll find some enticing choices further out and near the bus station, though these generally attract drivers as it's a pain travelling into the centre from here.

Hotel Anahuac Xochitl 140 Ⓣ444/812-6505. Bright, clean and cheery rooms make this friendly and comfortable hotel the best in the Alameda area, provided you don't mind the photos emblazoned with scripture extracts. Safe parking. ❸

Hotel de Gante 5 de Mayo 140 Ⓣ444/812-1492, Ⓔhotel_degante@hotmail.com. Central, comfortable and spacious with cable TV but little atmosphere; chiefly of interest if you can get a room overlooking the Jardín Hidalgo. ❹

Hotel María Dolores Benito Juárez (Hwy-57), opposite the Central de Autobuses Ⓣ444/822-1882, Ⓦwww.hotelmariadolores.com. Upmarket low-rise hotel, set around attractive gardens studded with palms and swimming pools. Restaurants, bars and nightclubs fill ancillary buildings, and rooms, all with cable TV and minibars, mostly have direct access to lawns. There are almost always sizeable reductions from the rack rate if you ask. ❹

Hotel Museo Palacio de San Agustín Galeana 240 at 5 de Mayo Ⓣ444/144-1900, Ⓦwww.palaciodesanagustin.com. It's worth visiting this jaw-dropping colonial masterpiece for a drink even if you can't afford to stay; the ornate interior and lobby, once part of a monastery, hint at the gorgeous antique-filled suites inside. Facilities include a posh spa, access to a horse and carriage, chauffeur-driven cars and a golf course. ❾

Hotel Napoles Juan Sarabiá 120 Ⓣ444/812-8418, Ⓔhnapoles@prodigy.net.mx. Modern and well-maintained business hotel with cable TV and phone in the carpeted rooms, and parking. One of the best in this price range. ❹

Hotel Panorama Venustiano Carranza 315, just west of Plaza Fundadores ⓣ444/812-1777 or 01-800/480-0100, ⓦwww.hotelpanorama.com.mx. Slick, upmarket business hotel, though the rooms are fairly compact and a little overpriced; the floor-to-ceiling windows are great, but the bathrooms are tiny and some of the rooms are showing their age. You do get free internet and free transport to the airport, and it's the best hotel in the centre. ❺

Hotel Progreso Aldama 415, at Iturbide ⓣ444/812-0366. Solid budget option downtown, this old but well-maintained property displays some unusual details such as rare ceramic tiles. Rooms are plain, but with TVs. Ask for a streetside room, as some internal rooms are a bit poky, with poor ventilation. Breakfast available. ❸

One Hotel Benito Juárez 140, near the Central de Autobuses ⓣ444/100-9400, ⓦwww.onehotels.com. This modern chain offers superb value, with compact, minimalist rooms equipped with blond-wood furnishings, wi-fi, flat-screen TVs and desks targeted at business travellers – cheap rates online and, mercifully, no smoking allowed anywhere in the hotel. ❹

Westin San Luis Potosí Real de Lomas 1000 ⓣ444/825-0125, ⓦwww.starwoodhotels.com. Not your average luxury chain, but an opulent hacienda 8km from downtown, featuring lavish suites and five-star service; outdoor pool, free airport transfers and gym are some of the extras. ❼

The City

The ravishing historic centre of San Luis Potosí is set on a tidy grid of largely pedestrianized streets around a series of little colonial plazas. Chief among these is the **Jardín Hidalgo**, the old Plaza de Armas, surrounded by state and city government offices and overlooked by the cathedral. From the northeast corner of the plaza, pedestrianized Hidalgo and the streets around it comprise the city's main shopping area; the department stores near the plaza give way to smaller, simpler shops as you approach the **Mercado Hidalgo**, a good place for souvenirs and fresh produce. Further north, the street stalls and stores become increasingly basic until you reach the **Mercado República**, another, much larger produce and clothing market, beyond the main road that delineates the edge of the centre.

Jardín Hidalgo and around

Though not the most elegant of the city's churches, the **Catedral Metropolitana** (daily 7.30am–2pm & 4.30–8.30pm) is nonetheless an impressive piece of architecture and dominates the east side of the **Jardín Hidalgo**. It was built in the early eighteenth century, but successive generations have ensured that little remains of the original – note the odd mismatching colours of the two towers and the ornate, swirling, carved pillars on the facade. Check out the nineteenth-century interior, which is fittingly opulent for such a wealthy city. Facing the cathedral across the square is the long facade of the **Palacio de Gobierno**, with its balustraded roof. This, too, has been substantially refurbished since its initial completion in 1789, but at least alterations have preserved the harmony of its clean Neoclassical lines. At the time of writing a massive renovation was almost complete; by the end of 2010 you should be able to visit the **Sala Juárez** inside, a suite of rooms occupied by Benito Juárez when San Luis became his temporary capital in 1863 (head up either set of stairs and turn left). French troops supporting Emperor Maximilian soon drove him out, but Juárez returned in 1866, and in this building confirmed the death sentence passed on Maximilian. Just behind the cathedral lies the **Casa Museo de Othón**, Othón 225 (Tues–Fri 10am–2pm & 4–6pm, Sat & Sun 10am–2pm; M$5), a pretty and well-tended museum, though a rather lifeless tribute to Manuel José Othón, San Luis's most famous poet (who was born here in 1858), mainly comprising some of his furniture.

Plaza del Carmen and around

Moving east along Othón, the **Templo del Carmen** (daily 7am–1.30pm & 4–9pm), on **Plaza del Carmen**, is the most beautiful and harmonious of all San Luis's churches, dating from 1764. Exuberantly decorated with a multicoloured tiled dome and elaborate Baroque facade, it has an equally flashy interior: in particular, a fantastically intricate nineteenth-century *retablo* attributed to eccentric artist and polymath Francisco Tresguerras. Next door to the church is the moderately interesting **Museo del Virreinato** (Tues–Fri 10am–7pm, Sat 10am–5pm, Sun 11am–5pm; M$10), a huge collection of artwork and artefacts from the Spanish colonial era.

A few steps south is the bulky, columned **Teatro de la Paz** (ticket office daily 10am–2pm & 4–8pm), built in 1889 under Porfirio Díaz and typical of the grandiose public buildings of that era, though its modern interior fails to live up to the extravagance of the exterior (open for performances only). Directly opposite the theatre, you'll find the compulsive and fascinating **Museo Nacional de la Máscara**, Villerias 2 (Mon & Wed–Fri 10am–6pm, Sat 10am–5pm, Sun 10am–2pm; entry M$15–20, free Sun), with exhibits on everything from pre-Hispanic masks to costumes that are still worn for fiestas and traditional dances – by 2010 the museum should be open after a long and painstaking restoration that has seen its home in the former Palacio Federal, built in 1897, finished off like a mini-palace (check with the tourist office for the latest news). Highlights should include the so-called "giants of San Luis", eight enormous models representing four royal couples (from Africa, Europe, Asia and America), which are flaunted in the streets during the festival of Corpus Christi in May, and an ancient funerary mask made from a skull, inlaid with a mosaic of turquoise and black stone. South of the museum, another magnificent original Baroque exterior, that of the **Templo de San Agustín**, faces out onto Plaza San Agustín – the elegant Neoclassical exterior, reconstructed in the 1840s, is often decorated with flowers.

Museo Federico Silva and the Museo de Arte Contemporáneo

If you trace your steps back to the Plaza del Carmen and this time head north, you'll come to one of San Luis Potosí's highlights, the **Museo Federico Silva**, Jardín de San Juan de Dios (Mon–Sat 10am–6pm, closed Tues, Sun 10am–2pm; M$30; Ⓣ444/812-3848, Ⓦwww.museofedericosilva.org), which focuses on the works of Federico Silva, one of Mexico's most exalted sculptors (born in Mexico City in 1923). The museum is housed in a Neoclassical school building completed in 1907, its open spaces a lovely synthesis of the classic and the contemporary, much like the works of Silva (now in his eighties) who creates modern interpretations of Mexico's pre-Hispanic forms. His blockish volcanic stone and steel forms dominate the galleries: some are vaguely human and others geometric abstractions, but all are beautifully lit. Don't miss *Scriptum*, a huge block of stone (adorned with four simple carved circles) entirely filling a kind of crypt, below the ground floor, as if it were secreted deep within some Aztec pyramid.

If this whets your appetite for contemporary Mexican art, walk two blocks northwest to the spanking new **Museo de Arte Contemporáneo** (Tues–Sun 10am–6pm), which should be open by 2010 in the handsome old post office (which dates from the 1860s), as a slick showcase for up-and-coming local and national artists.

Plaza de los Fundadores

Immediately west of Jardín Hidalgo, the paved **Plaza de los Fundadores** is a much larger and more formal open space, commemorating the foundation of the city near this spot in 1592. The plaza is dominated by the enormous Neoclassical **Edificio Central de la Universidad**, the main state university building, and two small adjacent churches, the **Capilla de Loreto** (usually locked) and **La Compañía** (usually open), while the fine arcaded portals of the square continue around the corner into Avenida Venustiano Carranza.

There's more interest a block south along Aldama, where you can admire the ornate Baroque facade of the **Caja Real**, the old mint dating from 1763 – one of the finest colonial mansions in San Luis. It is now owned by the university, which sometimes holds temporary exhibitions here.

Plaza de San Francisco

Continuing south along Aldama you come to the quiet **Plaza de San Francisco**, a lovely, shaded area redolent of the city's colonial history. It's named after the Franciscan convent whose church, the eighteenth-century **Templo de San Francisco**, towers over the plaza's west side and features a magnificent crystal chandelier in the shape of a sailing ship, hanging over the nave. The convent itself now houses the **Museo Regional Potosino** (Tues–Sat 10am–7pm, Sun 10am–5pm; M$37, free Sun), an absorbing collection of pre-Hispanic sculpture and other archeological finds, displays of local Indian culture and traditions and articles relating to the history of the state of San Luis Potosí. In addition to a fine cloister, there's access, upstairs, to the lavish Baroque chapel, **Capilla de Aranzazú** – said to be the only chapel in Latin America located on an upper floor – with exceedingly rich and enthusiastically restored churrigueresque decoration. Inside and through the side chapels lies a miscellaneous collection of religious paintings and artefacts. You'll find the entrance to the museum behind the church at the **Plaza de Aranzazú**, another pleasant open space which hosts a small arts and crafts market on Saturdays.

At the southern end of the Plaza de San Francisco, two more tiny and elaborate churches, **Sagrado Corazón** (which dates from 1731) and the even older **Templo del Tercera Orden** (established in 1698) stand side by side, with the small, plain 1894 National Presbyterian Church, terribly incongruous amid all this Baroque grandeur, facing them across Galeana.

Centro de las Artes Centenario

The most prestigious of a spate of new cultural projects opened in San Luis Potosí in 2009/2010, the **Centro de las Artes Centenario** (Mon–Fri 10am–2pm & 5–8pm, Sat & Sun 11am–5pm; M$10; ⓣ444/137-4100, ⓦwww.centrodelasartesslp.gob.mx) is an exciting transformation of an unusual historic building, with every corner of the former state prison, built in the 1890s, renovated, modified or filled with art. Temporary exhibitions here showcase local and visiting artists, while the **Museo del Sitio** charts the history of the prison and delves into the themes of "culture and democracy". There's also a library and space for a variety of shows and events – check the website for the schedule. The centre is at Calzada de Guadalupe 705, around 1km south of Jardín Colón (which is at the southern end of Zaragoza).

Parque Tangamanga I

If urban life is getting you down, catch the "Ruta 32" or "Parques del Sur" from the Alameda to the green expanse of the **Parque Tangamanga I** (open daily 5.30am–7pm, till 11pm on Mon; free; ⓦwww.parquestangamanga.gob.mx), around 2km west of the Jardín Hidalgo, with the main entrance on Salvador Nava Martinez. Founded in the early 1980s, the park still lacks maturity, and there are great stretches that remain undeveloped, but it makes a pleasant weekend outing nonetheless. It's a vast space of around 3.5 square kilometres and offers picnic spots, fitness circuits and a couple of small lakes. Joggers, soccer players and cyclists come here, and you can rent **bikes** for M$50 an hour from a kiosk (Tues–Sun). The park also has the added attraction of the innovative **Museo Laberinto de las Ciencias y la Artes** (Tues–Fri 9am–4pm, Sat & Sun 10am–7pm; M$30; ⓣ444/102-7800, ⓦwww.museolaberinto.com) on Cordero at the southern end, the city's latest high-tech museum containing hands-on science displays, 3D cinema (shows every hour) and exhibitions primarily aimed at kids, though the building itself is certainly worth a look. There's also the **Museo de Arte Popular** (Tues–Fri 10am–2pm & 4–6pm, Sat 10am–2pm; M$3), a showcase museum-shop of local crafts, at the bottom of Tatanacho opposite the main park entrance.

Eating and drinking

The centre of San Luis has several **cafés** and simple **restaurants** offering good-value *menus del día*. Local specialities to look out for include deep-fried enchiladas and tacos or *enchiladas Potosinos* (or *Huastecas*), dripping with salsa and cheese, and *cecina*, a thin cut of marinated and dried steak. The **Mercado Hidalgo** is home to a host of food stalls that serve both snacks as well as a host of regular Mexican dishes for around M$20 or less – you'll find them upstairs overlooking the main market. *Comedor Lucy* is a safe choice, but they're all pretty similar.

Central San Luis

La Abeja Díaz de León 104, off Plaza Fundadores. Bright takeout shop (with a couple of tables) serving natural yogurts, fruit smoothies (M$40–50), health foods and vitamins.

Antojitos El Pozole Carmona 205 at Arista ⓣ444/814-9900. Justly popular local chain established in 1985, famous for its *pozole* (thick stew of chunky bits of chicken, corn and spices): order *pozole rojo* or *blanco* (both M$58 for a filling bowl). The *tacos rojos* (M$50 for six) and *quesadillas de papa* (M$46 for five) are also worth trying. This branch is most central, in what feels a bit like someone's house with several small rooms. Tues–Sun noon–11.30pm.

Café Pacífico Los Bravo and Constitución, with another location around the corner. Come here for a potent mix of gossip, action and tasty Mexican food at moderate prices in a diner-like setting. Open 24hr, this very popular café-restaurant even has a nonsmoking section; the weekend brunch buffets (9–11am) are good value.

El Callejón de San Francisco Callejón de Lozada 1 ⓣ444/812-4508. Enchanting, quiet beam-and-stone restaurant, with an enticing rooftop terrace. *Antojitos* such as chicken fajitas and *tacos Potosinos* (both around M$80) compete for attention with succulent *arranchera* steaks (M$110). Reservations advised for dinner, especially at weekends; Mon–Fri 6pm–midnight, Sat 2pm–midnight. Closed Mon.

Chaires Jardín Hidalgo. Right on the plaza, *Chaires* is alive with families, friends and canoodling couples sipping java and tucking into elaborate pastries (M$13–20).

Costanzo Carranza 325, at Plaza Fundadores. A confection chain, with all manner of tempting chocolates and sweet things in shiny paper. Chocolates are priced per 100g, with even the most decadent costing around M$20. Mon–Sat 10am–8.30pm, Sun 11am–7pm.

Luna Café Universidad 155. Slightly more upscale than *Los Frailes* next door, offering gourmet coffees and cocktails. Daily 5pm–midnight.

La Parroquia Carranza 303 at Plaza Fundadores ⓣ444/812-6681. Comfortable middle-of-the-road diner featuring comfy booths, where crusty rolls replace the traditional stack of tortillas. Excellent breakfasts (M$80–90) and comida corrida (dishes M$50–80) – a firm favourite with local office workers. Daily 7am–midnight.

La Avenida

Tortas Locas Hipocampo Carranza 725, at top end of Avenida. Casual local hangout with fresh tortas (M$20–42), *aguas frescas* and rare sidewalk seating. Exceptionally clean.

La Virreina Carranza 830 ⓣ444/812-3750, ⓦwww.lavirreina.com.mx. Established in 1959, this upmarket restaurant has remained a fixture on Avenida, serving top-notch Mexican and international dishes in a refined, colonial dining room (enhanced with paintings from the "Viceroyalty" period and an early 1900s Steinway piano). Mains average M$150–250. Closed Mon.

Moving on from San Luis Potosí

To get to the **bus station** (Terminal Terrestre Potosina or TTP), take a Ruta 6 bus (M$5.50) for "Central TTP" from the northwest corner of the Alameda on Constitución. Taxis should use the meter and should cost no more than M$30. Buses cover every conceivable route, with departures for Mexico City (5hr) and Monterrey (7hr) every few minutes, and for Guadalajara (5hr), Tampico (7hr) and the US border at least hourly. Flecha Amarilla has excellent second-class services to Dolores Hidalgo (14 daily; 4hr 30min), San Miguel de Allende (every couple of hours; 5hr) and Guanajuato (slightly less frequently; 5hr). Northbound, there are very frequent services to Matehuala (2hr 30min), where you change for buses to Real de Catorce.

Taxis charge around M$200 for the trip to Aeropuerto Internacional Ponciano Arriaga (25km north of downtown). Domestic flights connect with Mexico City and Monterrey, and there are also daily departures to Dallas, Houston and San Antonio.

For further information, see Travel details, p.311.

Nightlife

San Luis has a vibrant **nightlife**, with numerous **clubs** staying open until the early hours at the weekend (note that most clubs and bars are cash only). The section of Carranza (affectionately known as **La Avenida**), starting half a kilometre west of Plaza Fundadores, has traditionally been the place to go – since the recession of 2008/2009 however, this area has been hit hard, with plenty of 'for rent' signs lining the street. The places listed below are still worth a look, but check at your hotel before heading out. Otherwise, stick to the smaller but more central collection of bars along Universidad, north of the Templo de Francisco. For movies, check out the wonderfully restored **Cineteca Alameda**, facing the Alameda at Constitución and Universidad (Ⓦ www.cinetecaalameda.blogspot.com).

Crudalia Carranza 1065-A Ⓣ 444/833-4750, Ⓦ www.crudalia.com. This much-loved chain is a popular student hangout with cheap beers and plastic tables and chairs outside.

El Paredón Carranza 473 Ⓣ 444/812-5555. This themed Mexican sports bar features a huge gold statue of Pancho Villa at the door (it's named after a famous Villa victory) – a good place to get an early evening beer.

Play Club Carranza 333 Ⓣ 444/812-5692. San Luis's hottest nightspot and concert hall. The meat market begins after midnight – cover varies.

La Santa Rock House Escobedo 125 Ⓣ 444/812-4533, Ⓦ www.lasantarockhouse.com. This relaxed bar is the best place for live rock at the weekends (cover M$15), usually starting at 10pm. Most drinks range M$18–30. Thurs–Sat 9pm–4am.

Listings

Banks and exchange There are banks with ATMs and several casas de cambio all around the main plazas, including Banamex at Allende and Obregón.

Books and newspapers The newsstands on Los Bravo, just off the Jardín Hidalgo, usually have a few English-language publications, and it might be worth trying Librerías Gonvil, Carranza 500 at Bolivar, which has a tiny selection of English-language books (mostly classics).

Emergencies For general emergencies dial Ⓣ 066. For medical emergencies, the handiest clinic is Beneficencia Española, Carranza 1090 (Ⓣ 444/811-5694), or just call the Cruz Roja on Ⓣ 444/815-3635.

Laundry Lavandería La Gotita, 5 de Mayo 870-A (Ⓣ 444/814-2783), at Hernandez. M$30/load. Mon–Fri 10am–8pm, Sat 10am–3pm.

Internet access Several places, including Café Cibernetico, Carranza 416 (daily 10am–9pm; M$15/hr).

Pharmacy Farmacia La Perla, Los Bravo 240 at Escobedo (Ⓣ 444/812-5922) and Farmacia Guadalajara, at Carranza 100, are always open.

Post office Universidad 526 (Mon–Fri 8am–3pm).

Zacatecas

Almost 2500m up and crammed into a narrow gully between two hills, elegant **ZACATECAS** is overflowing with ornate colonial architecture and absorbing museums, ranking alongside Guanajuato as one of the Bajío's finest destinations – the obvious wealth projected by its fine stone buildings makes this another city that seems plucked straight out of classical Spain. It remains much as the British Admiralty's *Handbook of Mexico* described it in 1905: "irregular", its streets "very narrow, steep, and frequently interrupted by stone steps" and "much exposed to winds blowing through the gorge". Those same winds still gust bitterly cold in winter, and even though many of the once-cobbled streets are now paved and choked with traffic, the town is otherwise little changed.

Some history

It didn't take the conquistadors long to discover the enormous lodes of **silver** in the hills of Mexico's central highlands, and, after some initial skirmishes with the Zacateco Indians, the city of Zacatecas was founded in 1546. For the next three centuries its mines disgorged fabulous wealth, enriching both the city and the Spanish Crown; in 1728 the mines here were producing one-fifth of all Mexico's silver. The end of the boom, when it came, was brought about more by the political uncertainties of the nineteenth century than by the exhaustion of the mines, some of which still operate today. Throughout nearly a century of war, Zacatecas itself became an important prize: there were major battles here in 1871, when Benito Juárez successfully put down local rebels, and in 1914 when Pancho Villa's **División del Norte** captured the city, completely annihilating its 12,000-strong garrison – known as the *Toma de Zacatecas* (Taking of Zacatecas), it was the bloodiest battle of the Revolution, with the military forces counting approximately 7,000 dead and many more civilian casualties. The loss of Zacatecas broke the back of the Huerta regime (see p.862).

Today Zacatecas is booming once more, its business and light industry boosted by the increasing flow of traffic between Mexico and the US. The town's prosperity has ensured a strong vein of civic pride, and many of the old colonial buildings have been lovingly restored. The granting of **UNESCO World Heritage status** to the historic centre has helped maintain its rich and sophisticated air, and forced new growth south of town on the road towards Guadalupe. Lack of parking downtown has even pushed university and government departments out to the modern developments, which are lent an increasingly Americanized feel by the presence of a Wal-Mart, multiplex cinemas and dozens of fast-food franchises.

Arrival and information

Situated at one of northern Mexico's crucial crossroads, Zacatecas's modern **Central de Autobuses** is a hive of activity both day and night, four kilometres south of the centre (24-hour guardería M$5/hr). To get into town take "Ruta 8" **bus** (every few minutes 7am–9pm; M$4.50) or a **taxi** – the fare is a standard M$30. If you take the bus get off at the Jardín Independencia – it's within reasonable walking distance of most of the accommodation. To return to the bus terminal, take "Ruta 8" (marked "Central Camionera"), which runs frequently along Villalpando and then down González Ortega. From the **Aeropuerto Internacional de Zacatecas**, 27km north of town, take a taxi into the centre for M$200. Once in town you should be able to get around

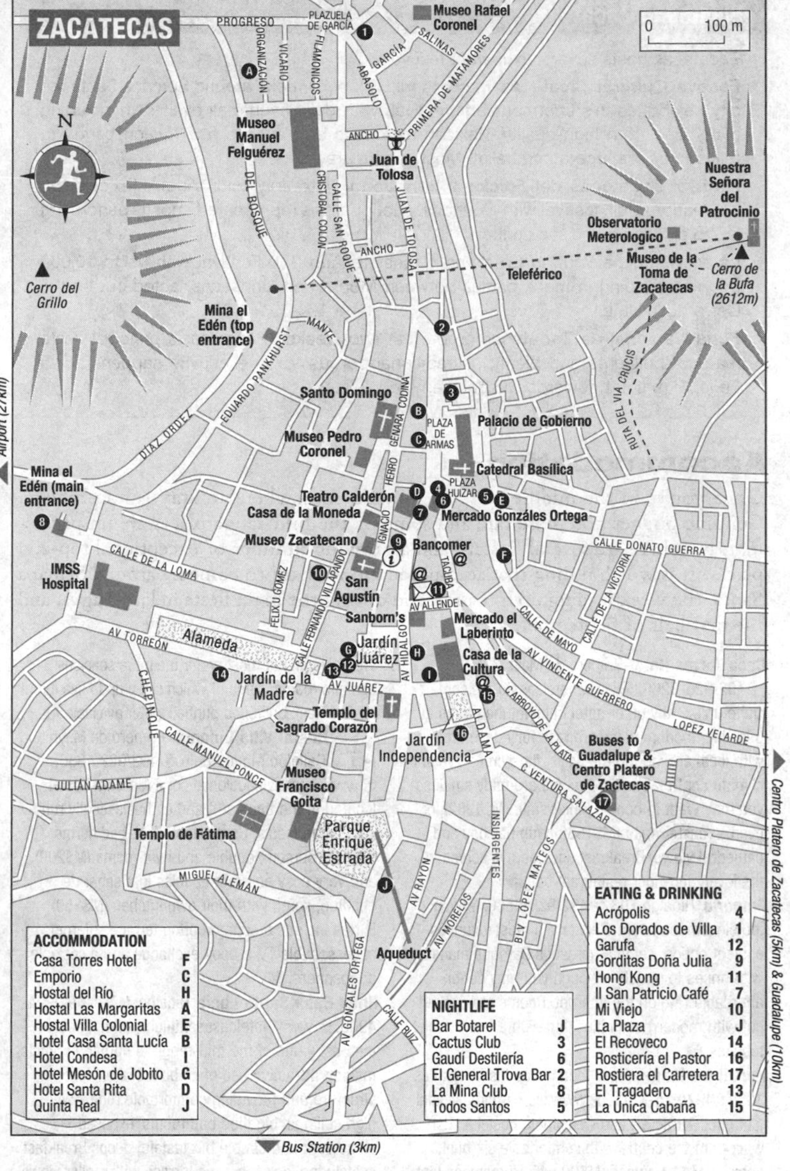

on foot, though **taxis** are easy to find at the Jardín Independencia – they don't use meters, so negotiate the price in advance (M$30 should cover most destinations).

Barely marked, the **tourist office** is at Hidalgo 401 (daily 9am–9pm; ⓣ492/924-4047 or 01-800/712-4078, ⓦwww.turismozacatecas.gob.mx); it can provide a smattering of leaflets and informative, friendly advice.

Fiestas in Zacatecas

Zacatecas hosts several exuberant festivals:

Festival Cultural Zacatecas (March/April). For two weeks around Semana Santa the city celebrates this enormous arts festival, with daily events all over town including everything from high-quality Mexican rock acts and even a few foreign bands to folkloric dance, opera and ballet. Most events are free.

Festival Zacatecas del Folclor International (late July–early Aug). Mexico's top international folk festival with around fifty nationalities represented, mostly performing in the plazas around the centre.

La Morisma de Bracho (weekend closest to Aug 27). Festival with up to 10,000 people engaging in mock battles between Moors and Christians, acted out on the Cerro de la Bufa.

Feria Nacional de Zacatecas (Sept, first two weeks). Zacatecas's principal fiesta features bullfights and plenty of traditional carousing. The activity happens at La Feria, 3km south towards Guadalupe.

Accommodation

Once you're in the middle of town, finding somewhere **to stay** is no problem. Genuine budget hotels are rare and some of the mid-range places are unspectacular, but there are several hostels, and a growing number of exceptional top-end places. It is worth noting that accommodation is hard to come by around Semana Santa, the week leading up to Easter, and during the main fiesta in late August and the first half of September.

Casa Torres Hotel Primero de Mayo 325 ⓣ492/925-3266, ⓦwww.hotelcasatorres.com. Quite unlike any other hotel in town, the rooms at this chic, modern place are tastefully decorated, with local artwork on the walls, flat-screen TVs and climate control. Standard rooms are fairly small so you may want to book a junior suite (M$1282), or even a master suite (M$1538) with balcony and cathedral views. Breakfast (included) is served in the lovely top-floor restaurant/bar. ❺

Emporio Hidalgo 703 ⓣ492/925-6500, ⓦwww.hotelesemporio.com. Zacateca's most luxurious, opulent option, set in a gorgeous Baroque mansion, with prices to match – though you may get an affordable rate on the internet. Rooms are decked out with modern amenities, but with a few colonial touches. ❽

Hostal las Margaritas Segunda de las Margaritas 105 ⓣ492/925-1711, ⓦwww.lasmargaritashostal.com.mx. Attractive and welcoming hostel a short walk from the centre with comfortable six-bunk dorms (M$110/person; M$90 with HI membership), doubles and twins. There's an inviting rooftop terrace with a kitchen, a pool table downstairs, internet access and laundry facilities. ❷

Hostal del Río Hidalgo 116 ⓣ492/924-0035. Rambling colonial place full of character and right in the heart of things. All rooms are whitewashed and come with simple decor and TV. The basement rooms are cheaper, but most prefer the more spacious upstairs rooms, some of which sleep up to five (great for families). Unlimited purified water available. ❸

Hostal Villa Colonial Primero de Mayo and Callejón Mono Prieto ⓣ492/922-1980, ⓦwww.hostalvillacolonial.com. A dream hostel located in the thick of it and enthusiastically run by Zacatecan locals. Comfortable four-bed dorms (M$100/person), double and twin rooms (M$200) and very cosy en-suite doubles in a separate building, some with their own kitchen (M$250). Extras include a sunny rooftop terrace, internet access, cable TV, a book exchange and a sociable atmosphere. ❷

Hotel Casa Santa Lucía Hidalgo 717 ⓣ492/924-4900, ⓦwww.hotelcasasantalucia.com. Perhaps the best value of the mid-range to upmarket hotels, making attractive use of its beautiful ancient structure and providing comfortable rooms with high ceilings, big tiled bathrooms, exposed stonework and simple but tasteful decor. Breakfast is included, and there's a terrace with stellar views of the cathedral and La Bufa. ❺

Hotel Condesa Juárez 102 ⓣ492/922-1160, ⓦwww.hotelcondesa.com.mx. Modern hotel in a central location amid the action of the Jardín Independencia. The huge lobby exhibits old photos and the compact but modern rooms come with cable TV and cherrywood furniture; some have bathtubs (M$700). Ask for a room with a view of the jardín. There's also a lovely café and serviceable hotel bar. 4

Hotel Mesón de Jobito Jardín Juárez 143 ⓣ492/924-1722, reservations ⓣ01-800/021-0040, ⓦwww.mesondejobito.com.mx. An entire alley off the city's most enchanting colonial square has been converted into this superb luxury hotel. Pretty, plush and private, all rooms come with a/c, and some with jacuzzis. There are two formal restaurants, and a bar with live music – just what you'd expect in a top hotel. 8

Hotel Santa Rita Hidalgo 507 ⓣ492/925-1194, ⓦwww.hotelsantarita.com. Incredibly stylish hotel, featuring an intelligent refit of an old colonial house, replete with contemporary art; suites come with street or patio views and terraces, free wi-fi and polished wood floors. 8

Quinta Real González Ortega, by the aqueduct ⓣ492/922-9104 or 01-800/457-4000, ⓦwww.quintareal.com. Gorgeous and outrageously luxurious hotel in the shadow of the colonial aqueduct that has beautifully incorporated what was once Zacatecas's bullring. Every comfort is taken to the extreme degree (there's even a "pillow menu"), and this is certainly a place worth saving up for, not to mention one of the most distinctive properties in the Americas. 9

The City

Zacatecas is dominated by the **Cerro de la Bufa** (2612m), with its extraordinary rock cockscomb crowning the ridge some 237m above the Plaza de Armas; at night it's illuminated, with a giant cross on top. A modern Swiss cable car connects the summit with the slopes of the Cerro del Grillo – an exhilarating ride straight over the heart of the old town. From here, the city's sprawl isn't particularly inviting, but it's when you get down there, among the narrow streets, twisting alleys, colonial fountains, carved doorways and ornate churches, that the city's real splendour is revealed. The highlight is undoubtedly the ornate **cathedral**, from which all other main sights are within walking distance. Just a few paces from the market and from the important junction of Juárez and Hidalgo, the **Jardín Independencia** is in effect the city's main plaza, where people gather in the evenings and wait for buses – the **Casa Municipal de Cultura** (ⓦwww.cultuzac.blogspot.com) nearby hosts art and cultural events. West of the Jardín Independencia is the **Alameda**, a thin strip of stone benches, splashing fountains and a bandstand that makes a cool retreat from the heat of the day. Adjacent, you'll find the charming oasis **Jardín de la Madre**, distinguishable by its fountain featuring a beatific maternal figure and well-tended flora.

The cathedral and around

Zacatecas's flamboyant **Catedral Basílica** (daily 7am–1pm & 3–9pm) is the outstanding relic of the city's years of colonial glory: built in the pink sandstone typical of the region, it represents one of the latest, and arguably the finest, examples of Mexican Baroque architecture. It was completed in 1752, its facade carved with a wild exuberance unequalled anywhere in the country. The interior, they say, was once at least its equal – furnished in gold and silver, with rich wall hangings and a great collection of paintings – but as everywhere, it was despoiled or the riches removed for "safekeeping", first at the time of Juárez's reforms and later during the Revolution; only the structure itself, with its bulky Doric columns and airy vaulting, remains to be admired. Look out for the chapel on the left as you enter, dedicated to local priest and martyr **San Mateo Correa Magallanes** (1866–1927), murdered during the anti-Roman Catholic persecutions of the 1920s and canonized in 2001. On each side of the cathedral there's a compact plaza: to the south a tiny paved *plazuela*, **Plaza Huizar**, which often hosts lively street theatre and impromptu musical performances, and to the north the formal **Plaza de Armas**, surrounded by more colonial buildings.

On the east side of the latter plaza, the **Palacio de Gobierno** (Mon–Fri 9am–8pm; free) was built as the residence of the Conde Santiago de la Laguna in 1727 and subsequently bought by the state government. In keeping with local fashion, a modernist mural depicting the city's history – completed in 1970 by Antonio Rodríguez – embellishes the staircase of the interior courtyard. Opposite, along with what is now the *Hotel Emporio*, lies the Palacio de Justicia, known locally as the **Casa de la Mala Noche**. According to legend, its builder, Manuel de Rétegui, was a mine-owner down to his last peso, which he gave away to a starving widow to feed her family. He then spent a long night of despair in the house ("*la mala noche*"), contemplating bankruptcy and suicide, until at dawn his foreman hammered on the door with the miraculous news that a huge vein of silver had been struck, and they were all to be rich.

On the south side of the cathedral, the **Mercado González Ortega** is a strikingly attractive market building, opened in 1889. It takes advantage of its sloping position to have two fronts: the upper level opening onto Hidalgo, the lower floor with entrances on Tacuba. Converted into a fancy little shopping mall, it's now filled with tourist shops and smart boutiques, as well as a superb wine store. On Hidalgo opposite the mercado, the **Teatro Calderón** is a grandiose Italianate theatre completed in 1891. At the southern end of the mercado, broad steps help turn the little **Plazuela Goitia** into a popular place for street theatre.

Santo Domingo

Climbing up from the west side of Plaza de Armas towards the Cerro del Grillo are streets lined with more mansions – some restored, some badly in need of it, but all deserted by the mining moguls who built them. The church of **Santo Domingo** (daily 7am–1pm & 5–8pm) stands raised on a platform above the plaza of the same name, just uphill from the Plaza de Armas – its hefty, buttressed bulk a stern contrast to the lightness of the cathedral, though it was built at much the same time. In the gloom of the interior you can just make out the gilded churrigueresque *retablos* in the chapels.

Museo Pedro Coronel

The **Museo Pedro Coronel** (Fri–Wed 10am–5pm; M$30; ⓣ492/922-8021), occupies what was originally a Jesuit monastery next to Santo Domingo church. Pedro Coronel Rivera was a local artist, brother of Rafael Coronel (see p.254),

▲ Plaza de Armas, Zacatecas

who managed to gather an art collection that reads like a *Who's Who* of modern art: you'll find paintings here by Picasso, Kandinsky, Braque, Chagall, Dalí and Miró, among others, as well as lithographs by Calder and Moore, architectural drawings by Piranesi, Hogarth engravings and a separate room of Pedro's own paintings and sculptures. It's undeniably an amazing collection, but it's not as good as the roll call makes it sound; with the exception of a few of the Mirós, these are mostly minor works. Some of the peripheral collections are more interesting, in particular the West African and Oriental art, and the Mexican masks – some are the haunting death masks traditionally used in the re-staging of battles between the Spanish and the Moors. The building itself served as a hospital, a barracks and a prison before becoming a museum, and one of the grimmer dungeons is also preserved as an exhibit.

Museo Zacatecano and around

Heading south along Ignacio Hierro you'll find the **Casa de la Moneda**, Zacatecas's mint in the days when every silver-producing town in Mexico struck its own coins; undergoing an ambitious restoration at the time of writing, it should be open sometime in late 2010.

Further along you come to the **Museo Zacatecano**, Dr. Hierro 301 (Wed–Mon 10am–5pm; M$20; ⓣ492/922-6580), where some superb and wonderfully natural 1940s photos of the Huichol people lead to a room chock-full of some two hundred Huichol embroideries that incorporate an amazing range of geometric designs, as well as maize symbols, deer and butterflies, all executed in black, red and green (for death, life and prosperity respectively). It should come as no surprise that peyote features in a big way. Nothing is labelled, but one of the attendants may well give you an unbidden guided tour. Most of the rest of the museum is given to a display of religious iconography: a couple of hundred wonderful hand-painted *retablos*, including a couple of sixteenth-century examples, depicting just about every saint, martyr and apostle going.

Across the street lies **San Agustín**, an early eighteenth-century church that, after the Reform Laws, was converted into a casino, while the adjoining monastery became a hotel. It has been under restoration, on and off, for decades, and is currently undergoing a final push; it's already being used as a cultural centre (check events in the *Agenda Cultural* magazine on-line at ⓦwww.zacatecas.gob.mx) and you can normally have a peek inside the cavernous interior. Don't miss the fabulously ornate plateresque side door, a smaller version of the cathedral facade.

Museo de Arte Abstract Manuel Felguérez

Moving north along Juan de Tolosa, cut up a signposted alley to reach the **Museo de Arte Abstract Manuel Felguérez** (Wed–Mon 10am–5pm; M$30; ⓣ492/924-3705) at Colón and Seminario, an extensive gallery imaginatively converted from a prison and its associated church. In places the cells have been turned into mini-galleries where the intimacy of the space draws you into the works. Elsewhere several levels of cells have been ripped out to leave huge rooms with floor-to-ceiling paintings, sculptures and installations viewed from steel walkways that gradually take you higher. Half of what's on show is by **Manuel Felguérez**, a native of Zacatecas state and an approximate contemporary of the Coronel brothers (see opposite). Within the field of abstract art he is almost as highly regarded, though it can take some effort to fully appreciate his work, particularly that of the early 1980s when he developed an obsession with male reproductive anatomy. He is perhaps most successful in his sculpture, notably the 1995 *El Arco del Día*, a huge bronze tripod that looks like it has just landed in a side chapel off the church. Nearby, his huge canvas entitled *Retablo de los Mártires* is also particularly striking. Elsewhere within the museum there is work by the **Coronel brothers** and several other of Felguérez's Mexican contemporaries, as well as an excellent art bookshop, though almost everything is in Spanish.

Museo Rafael Coronel

Pedro Coronel may have amassed a spectacular art collection, but his brother Rafael has a far more beautiful museum, the centrepiece of which is a huge collection of traditional masks, possibly the finest in Mexico. The wonderful **Museo Rafael Coronel** (Thurs–Mon 10am–5pm; M$30; ⓣ492/922-8116) occupies the ex-Convento de San Francisco on the north side of town on Callejón de San Francisco. Founded in 1593 as a Franciscan mission (the facade is said to be the oldest in the city), it was rebuilt in the seventeenth century, only to begin deteriorating after the Franciscans were expelled in 1857 and finally suffer destruction during Villa's assault. The building and gardens have now been partially but beautifully restored, and the museum brilliantly integrated with the ruins. There are more than four thousand masks on display, which makes taking it all in a bit overwhelming. The masks trace the art's development in what is now Mexico from some very ancient, pre-Columbian examples to contemporary masks: often there are twenty or more variations on the same theme, and one little room is entirely full of the visages of Moors and Christians from the La Morisma festival (see p.250). As well as the masks, you can see Coronel's impressive collections of ceramics and puppets, the town's original charter granted by Philip II in 1593 and sketches and drawings connected with Coronel's wife Ruth Rivera, architect and daughter of Diego. There's also a bookshop and a smart café. If you don't fancy the pleasant walk to or from town, several bus routes, including #5, #8 and #9, pass close by.

The aqueduct and Museo Francisco Goitia

In the other direction towards the south of the city, you can follow the line of the **aqueduct** that used to carry water to this area. Not much of it remains, but what does can be inspected at closer quarters from the little **Parque Enrique Estrada** on González Ortega – the continuation of Hidalgo up the hill from the centre. At the back of the park, in what was once the governor's residence at **Enrique Estrada 102**, stands a third local artist's museum, the **Museo Francisco Goitia** (Tues–Sun 10am–5pm; M$30; ⓣ492/922-0211, ⓦwww.museofranciscogoitia.com). Goitia was one of Mexico's leading painters early in the twentieth century, and this enjoyable little museum houses a permanent exhibition of his work and that of more modern local artists (including Pedro Coronel), as well as hit-or-miss temporary displays and travelling art shows.

Mina El Edén

The **Mina El Edén**, or Eden Mine (daily 10am–6pm; M$70, kids under 12 and seniors M$35), is perhaps the most curious and unusual of all Zacatecas's attractions. The main entrance to the old mine, from where you can explore some of the sixteenth-century shafts in the heart of the Cerro del Grillo, is in the west of the city, up a road behind the modern IMSS Hospital General de Zona No. 1. This super-rich mine produced the silver that gave Zacatecas its wealth, and though little is dug up around the town today, Fresnillo, 60km to the north, has the world's largest silver mine, which sometimes produces seven tons of the precious metal a day.

The forty-minute guided tour (roughly every 15min; generally in frenetic Spanish, but ask if a bilingual guide is available) – which takes in only a fraction of the workings – involves a small train ride 500m into the mountain. Here a well-presented **museum** displays rocks from around the world (though mostly

Mexico), including impressive geodes and fossilized ammonites and trilobites. You're then taken on a fairly sanitized look at the mine workings – subterranean pools, chasms crossed on steel bridges and scattered machinery, all complete with colourfully lit mannequins dressed as miners. Enthusiastic guides tell of the thousands of miners that died during the mine's four hundred years of operation. The high number of fatalities seems perfectly possible when you see level upon level of old galleries falling away for some 320m beneath you, inaccessible since the mine flooded when production stopped in 1966. The entire hill is honeycombed with tunnels, and in one of them a lift has been installed that takes you up to the slopes of the Cerro del Grillo, about 200m from the lower station of the cable car (you can also enter the mine from this end, though you may have a longer wait for a guide). It is also worth returning in the evening to dance the night away at *La Mina Club* (see p.257).

To **reach the mine**, take bus #7 from the Hidalgo and Juárez to the hospital, or walk, taking in a pleasant stroll along the Alameda followed by a brief climb.

The Teleférico and Cerro de la Bufa

The lower station of the **Teleférico** (cable car; daily 10am–6pm; M$27 each way; Thurs–Sat also 7pm–midnight, M$40 each way; services can be disrupted by strong winds) is on the slopes of the Cerro del Grillo, near the back entrance to El Edén. It's an easy climb up from San Agustín, or you can take bus #7 right to the door. Out from the station you pass right over the city centre – the views down on the houses are extraordinary. Most people come back the same way, but walking down on the paved Ruta del Via Crucis is no great strain.

From the **Cerro de la Bufa** station it's a brisk uphill walk to the pristine **Templo de Nuestra Señora del Patrocinio**, an eighteenth-century chapel with an image of the Virgin said to perform healing miracles. The main viewpoints are here, offering a jaw-dropping panorama of Zacatecas and its surroundings, though this is not the actual summit: only one of the three peaks is accessible, El Chico (the smallest), topped by the **Observatorio Meterologico**, another short walk uphill from the chapel. The observatory dates back to 1906, and though you can't go insides the mesmerizing views are worth the climb.

Back down next to the chapel, the **Museo de la Toma de Zacatecas** (daily 10am–5pm; M$20) honours Pancho Villa's spectacular victory here in 1914, also commemorated with a dramatic equestrian statue of the general outside. The museum is primarily a collection of black-and-white period photos – some showing harrowing scenes of piled-up dead bodies – and some old weapons and uniforms, and unless you read Spanish or have an interest in the Revolution, easily skipped. Similarly, the final room dedicated to Ángela Ramos aka "Juana Gallo" (immortalized in the eponymous 1961 Mexican movie) just contains black-and-white photos of the peasant heroine; she is supposed to have joined the rebels at Zacatecas after her father and fiancé were murdered. Behind the Villa statue two paths skirt around the base of La Bufa to the **Mausoleo de los Hombres Ilustres**, where *Zacatecanos* who have made their mark on history have been buried since the 1940s, or at least have their memorials – unless you are a student of Mexican history, you're unlikely to have heard of any of them.

Eating and drinking

For a relatively small town, Zacatecas has a surprising number of exceptional **restaurants**, pretty much all located in a small area around the centre. For inexpensive tacos, tostadas and burgers, head away from the centre towards Ventura Sálazar, which is lined with places serving quick snacks – at the end of Sálazar, on the other side of López Mateos at no. 412, *Rostiera El Carretera* offers succulent whole roasted chickens for just M$70. Other reliable hunting grounds are the compact **Mercado El Laberinto**, just north of the Jardín Independencia, and **Calle Aldama** in the mornings, for stalls selling tamales and *atoles*.

While in Zacatecas, you should sample *tuna*, the succulent green or purple fruit of the prickly pear cactus. In season they're sold everywhere, ready-peeled and by the bucketload. Look out, too, for donkeys saddled with earthenware jars from which you can buy *aguamiel* (literally, honey water), the juice of the maguey cactus, which can be fermented to produce *pulque* (see p.52).

Acrópolis Hidalgo, at Mercado González Ortega ☎492/922-1284. Very popular café, established in 1943, serving all the usual appetizing Mexican breakfasts (M$68–85) from 8.30am, as well as ice cream (M$45), fruit juices, good coffee (from M$15) and main meals (tortas from M$40) until 10pm. English menus are available.

Los Dorados de Villa Plazuela de García 1314 ☎492/922-5722. Cosy little restaurant a short walk from the centre with lovely tiled walls and exotic birds. Look out for pictures of "Los Dorados", the young followers of Pancho Villa. The excellent traditional menu mostly comprises *moles* and enchiladas that keep people coming back for more. Mains average M$40–60. Reserve in advance. Open daily from 3pm.

Garufa Jardín Juárez 135 ☎492/924-2910, Ⓦwww.garufa.com.mx. Argentine restaurant chain specializing in gargantuan and super-succulent steaks imported from the pampas (M$160–250), along with much cheaper salads and pasta dishes, all of which are served in attractive rustic surroundings.

Gorditas Doña Julia Hidalgo 409 (no phone). A one-trick pony, only serving gorditas (M$10 each) stuffed with either various cuts of meat, refried beans, shredded nopal cactus in a hot salsa or *mole* and rice, either to go or to eat in this cheerfully bright, open-fronted restaurant.

Hong Kong Allende 117 ☎492/924-2786. Attractive Cantonese-style restaurant and bar upstairs in the colonial surroundings of the bishop's former residence. All the expected foo yung, chow mein and fried rice dishes are here, mostly around M$50.

Il San Patricio Café Hidalgo 403 ☎492/922-4399. The best (Italian) coffee in town, and only a little more expensive than places selling far inferior brews. The extra couple of pesos are further justified by the peaceful courtyard setting, a choice of delicious cakes and a number of magazines to browse, some in English – blink and you'll miss the tiny sign, just next to the tourist office.

Mi Viejo Fernando Villalpando 319 (no phone). Intimate little café away from the bustle of town, with a great selection of coffees and sweet and savoury crepes, mostly around M$40–50. Tues–Sun 5–10pm.

La Plaza inside the *Quinta Real* (see p.251), ☎492/922-9104. Pick of the bunch for an expensive, formal meal, if only for the setting overlooking the former bullring on a series of indoor terraces. Expect to spend around M$500 per person for a full meal of nopal stuffed with shrimp, chicken in a tamarind sauce, dessert, coffee and something from the wine list – which includes a good Mexican selection.

El Recoveco Torreón 513 ☎492/924-2013. One of the better bargains, with an all-you-can-eat buffet of over thirty dishes for M$62 (lunch) and M$72 (dinner). Specials include the *enchiladas zacatecanas* (pork in a spicy sauce) and the *asado de boda* (a bit like a pork *mole*). Open daily 8.30am–7pm. Second branch at Jardín Juárez 38 (daily 2–7pm).

Rosticería el Pastor Independencia 214 (no phone). The scent of wood-roasted chicken wafts to the street from this inexpensive, family-friendly joint. M$60 buys you a generous chicken dinner with all the fixings. Daily 8am–8.30pm.

El Tragadero Juárez 232, by the Alameda ☎492/922-4332. Inexpensive and reliable traditional Mexican restaurant with delicious and piquant *enchiladas zacatecanas* for M$40, with chicken M$45. Tues–Sun 9am–8.30pm.

La Única Cabaña Independencia at Juárez ☎492/922-5775. Always alive with activity, this is one of the town's cheapest and most popular taco restaurants. Good, basic food served with a wide selection of salsas and beer at bargain prices in clean surroundings. Tacos are M$6–8, and a full chicken dinner costs M$90. Wonderfully fruity and thirst-quenching *aguas* are also sold to go. Try the sprightly *chía* flavour (a local herb).

Nightlife and entertainment

Nightlife in Zacatecas, especially at weekends while the university is in session, is a boisterous affair, with much of the early-evening action happening on the streets – there always seems to be some procession or a band playing, usually in the small plazas at either end of the Mercado González Ortega. On Friday and Saturday evenings (and sometimes Thurs and even Sun) you may well encounter a **callejóneada** (see p.280) during which musicians – usually with several big drums and a brass section – promenade around the back alleys followed by whoever wants to tag along. There's often a donkey bearing carafes of tequila, and you may be offered some, though it is as well to come equipped with your own tipple. Tag on as you hear the procession go by, or head to the Plaza de Armas around 9pm to catch the start. Either way, a *callejóneada* is great start to an evening on the town, when you can visit some of the numerous bars and clubs that dot the downtown landscape.

Bar Botarel in the *Quinta Real* (see p.251). Stylish cellar bar built under the seating of what used to be the bullring. Arrive soon after 6pm to get one of the intimate booths, from where you can look out at the plaza and the rest of the hotel. Prices are almost twice what you pay in other places, but nowhere else has the same sense of romance. Live music Fri and Sat until midnight. Daily 6pm–1am.

Cactus Club Hidalgo 634 ⓣ492/922-0509. Lively and popular nightclub with pool and table football upstairs. Small cover charge for men on Fri and for all on Sat, but free on Wed when they have two-for-one drinks specials. Mon–Sat 8.30pm–3am.

Gaudí Destilería Tacuba, at the bottom portion of the Mercado González Ortega ⓣ492/922-1433. Fashionable dance club that's packed at weekends, and particularly Thurs nights, when entry is free and beers only M$10. Normal cover M$20–30. Thurs–Sat 10pm–3am.

El General Trova Bar Hidalgo 804. Very agreeable, mostly acoustic venue and bar where local musicians play every night except Mon (7pm–2.30am). Great views from the upstairs bar.

La Mina Club main entrance to Mina El Edén (see p.254) ⓣ492/922-3002. Zacatecas's major club, right in the heart of the mountain and accessed on the same train used in the mine tour. From 11pm it is pumping with Latin numbers, US and European dance tunes, but mostly cheesy electronic techno music. If you don't enjoy being trapped in an enclosed space, *La Mina* is not for you. Thurs–Sat 10pm–3am, reservations essential Fri and Sat; M$100 entry.

Todos Santos Aguascalientes 235 ⓣ492/925-4683. Tucked into a tastefully decorated cellar, this is a modern take on the traditional cantina, but far more chic. There's usually an engaging mix of locals and visitors (women are certainly welcome), and entertainment is provided by roving minstrels.

Listings

American Express Viajes Mazzocco, López Portillo 746, Plaza Commercial Zacatecas 2000 (Mon–Fri 9am–7pm, Sat & Sun 9am–2pm; ⓣ492/922-0859, ⓦwww.viajesmazzocco.com). It holds mail, cash, replaces travellers' cheques and organizes city tours.

Banks and exchange Plenty of banks are situated along Hidalgo between Juárez and Allende, all with 24hr ATMs and offering currency exchange (Mon–Fri 9am–1pm).

Books and newspapers The best (though still limited) source of English-language magazines is Sanborn's, Hidalgo 212 – it's hard to find English-language books anywhere in Zacatecas.

Emergencies For general emergencies call ⓣ066. For tourist emergencies call ⓣ492/922-0180. Cruz Rojo (ⓣ492/922-3005) handles medical emergencies.

Internet access Numerous businesses around town, mostly competitively priced at M$10–15/hr. Try Cyber Central, Hidalgo 304 (daily 10am–9pm).

Laundry Lavandería El Ángel, Aguascalientes 233 (daily 8am–8pm), has a minimum 3kg load (M$15 per kg).

Pharmacy Farmacia Guadalajara at López Mateos 305 is 24hr; a more central branch is at Hidalgo and Juárez (Mon–Fri 8am–4pm, Sat 9am–1pm).

Post office Allende 111 (Mon–Fri 8am–4pm, Sat 9am–1pm).

Spanish courses Founded in 1973, Fenix Language Institute, Ledezma 210 (ⓣ492/922-1643, ⓦwww.fenixlanguageinstitute.com) has highly regarded courses for around US$150/week or US$20/hr for private classes.

Travel agencies and tours Several local agencies handle general travel requirements and offer tours of the city and to surrounding attractions: try Viajes Mazzocco (see "American Express"); and Operadora Zacatecas, Hidalgo 630 (ⓣ492/924-0050 or 01-800/714-4150), opposite the *Hotel Casa Santa Lucía*. All the bigger hotels stock leaflets detailing tours to Guadalupe (M$200) and to Chicomoztoc (M$250), among other destinations.

Moving on from Zacatecas

To get to Zacatecas's **Central de Autobuses** take a "Ruta 8" **bus** (every few minutes 7am–9pm; M$4.50), marked "Central Camionera", which run frequently along Villalpando and then down González Ortega. Taxis should be M$30. There are frequent long-distance bus services to all parts of northern Mexico, including hourly buses to Durango (5hr) and Chihuahua (13hr), some of which push on through to the border at Ciudad Juárez (18hr). There are direct buses running to Monterrey (7hr) hourly and a couple daily to Mazatlán (10hr); you could also catch the first bus to Durango and get a connection to Mazatlán from there. Heading south, there are frequent buses to Mexico City (8hr), either via Aguascalientes (2hr) and León (3–4hr) or through San Luis Potosí (3hr). If you're headed to Real de Catorce, you'll need to change at San Luis Potosí and then Matehuala: make an early start to be sure of getting there in a day.

Taxis to the **Aeropuerto Internacional de Zacatecas** should be around M$200. Direct flights link the city to Chicago and Los Angeles, but for domestic destinations you'll need to change in Mexico City.

For further information, see Travel details, p.311.

Around Zacatecas

It's well worth basing yourself in Zacatecas to explore the immediate surroundings, not least the **Centro Platero de Zacatecas**, where the local tradition of silver-working reaches its highest expression. Those with no interest in buying should definitely continue to **Guadalupe** – virtually a suburb of Zacatecas – to see the Convento de Guadalupe, a rich, sumptuously decorated monastery, rare in that it has survived the centuries more or less unscathed, and for that reason one of the most important such buildings in Mexico. Further out, the ruins of the great desert fortress town **Chicomoztoc** are by contrast quite unadorned, but enormously impressive nonetheless. You'll need to allow the best part of a day for either Chicomoztoc, or the picturesque town of **Jerez**, a pleasant day out of town anytime but essential for the cowboy festival on Easter Saturday. You can venture out to any of these places independently, though several travel agents in Zacatecas offer tours (see p.257).

The Centro Platero de Zacatecas

Galleries in Zacatecas sell stacks of jewellery, but the quality is often low and the designs unimaginative and poorly executed. If you are serious about buying silver, or just want to see artisans at work, devote a couple of hours to visiting the **Centro Platero de Zacatecas** (Mon–Fri 9am–6pm, Sat 10am–3pm; free), located about 5km south of the centre in the former Hacienda de Bernárdez. "Ruta 11" from López Mateos runs to the gate (M$4.50), where you can ask directions and walk the last kilometre; alternatively take a taxi to the door for M$40–50.

Within the ex-hacienda, students and recent graduates of the on-site silversmith school maintain a series of small workshops where you can see them creating original designs, many influenced by pre-Columbian images, or iconography associated with Zacatecas. Of course, everything is for sale, often at very reasonable prices, though the very best work commands a high price tag.

Guadalupe

Local buses run out to **GUADALUPE**, 7km southeast of Zacatecas's centre, every few minutes from López Mateos (M$4.50) – taxis should take you for M$35–40. Once there, you can't miss the enormous bulk of the **Templo y Convento de Guadalupe**, with its dome and asymmetric twin towers. A flagged, tree-studded courtyard provides access to both the church and the monastery, preserved as the **Museo de Guadalupe** (daily 9am–6pm; M$41, free Sun). The monastery, founded in 1707, is a vast and confusing warren of a place, with seemingly endless rows of cells opening off courtyards, stairways leading nowhere and mile-long corridors lined with portraits of monks and vast tableaux from the life of St Francis. There are guided tours in Spanish, but it's more enjoyable to wander alone, at your own pace, possibly tagging onto a group for a few minutes when your paths cross. The museum is divided into two main sections: the **Museo de Sitio** and the **Pinacoteca**, a richly stocked **art gallery**. Oil paintings cover every wall of the gallery's 27 rooms of rough tiled floors and whitewashed walls, mostly with a religious theme: Cristóbal de Villalpando, Antonio de Torres, Gabriel José de Ovalle, Miguel Cabrera, Luis Juárez and Juan Correa all feature. Look particularly for the mid-eighteenth-century *Passion of Christ* series of oils by Zacatecan artist de Ovalle, who acknowledged the source of wealth of his patrons by featuring silver ornament and vessels in some of the paintings, and *La Anunciación* by Villalpando, one of Mexico's most important painters of the early eighteenth century.

Highlights of the the Museo de Sitio are the **Biblioteca Conventual**, the historic library, and the **Coro Alto**, the raised choir at the back of the church, with its beautifully carved and painted wooden choir stalls. The **Capilla de Nápoles**, built in 1856, whose Neoclassical domed roof is coated in elaborately filigreed gold leaf, is only open on special occassions.

Chicomoztoc

The ruins of **CHICOMOZTOC** (daily 9am–5.30pm; M$37), also known as La Zona Arqueológica de La Quemada, lie some 52km south from Zacatecas on the road to Villanueva and Guadalajara. The scale of the complex isn't apparent until you're inside – from the road you can vaguely see signs of construction, but the whole thing, even the huge restored pyramid, blends so totally into the mountain behind as to be almost invisible. No two archeologists seem to agree on the nature of the site, its functions or inhabitants, even to the extent that many doubt it was a fortress, despite its superb natural defensive position and hefty surrounding walls. Most likely it was a frontier post on the outskirts of some pre-Aztec sphere of domination – probably the Toltecs – charged with keeping at bay the southward depredations of the Chichimeca. Alternatively, it could simply be the work of a local ruling class, having exacted enough tribute to build themselves these palaces and needing the defences to keep their own subjects out. Huichol legend seems to support the second theory: there was an evil priest, the story runs, who lived on a rock surrounded by walls and covered with buildings, with eagles and jaguars under his command to oppress the population. The people appealed to their gods, who destroyed the priest and his followers with "great heat", warning the people not to go near the rock again. Chicomoztoc was in fact destroyed by fire around 1300 AD and was never reoccupied; even today, the Huichol, in their annual pilgrimage from the Sierra Madre in the west to collect peyote around Real de Catorce to the east, take a long detour to bypass this area.

In addition to the reconstructed temple here, you'll see a large hall with eleven pillars still standing, a ball-court, an extensive (if barely visible from the ground) system of roads heading out into the valley and many lesser, ruinous structures all listed for eventual reconstruction. Much of the restoration work is based on drawings produced over the course of ten years from 1825 by a German mining engineer, Carlos de Burghes. Copies are on display in the superb **Museo de La Quemada** (daily 10am–4pm; M$10; ☎492/922-0403), at the site, which makes a masterful job of bringing the place alive with a select display of artefacts, a detailed area model and several explanatory videos (in Spanish only).

Most visitors get to the site by car (it's a 30min drive along Hwy 54) or **taxi** (M$250 round trip), but **getting to Chicomoztoc** is also easy enough by public transport, with Villanueva-bound buses (M$30) leaving every thirty minutes or so from López Mateos in Zacatecas. They're usually happy to drop you at the start of the two-kilometre access road (ask for "las ruinas"); the ride to this point takes about an hour, from where you've got a 25-minute walk to the entrance. To get back, hike to the highway and either flag down the first bus you see, or try to hitchhike while you're waiting.

Jerez

For an enjoyable day out of Zacatecas consider a ride out to **Jerez** (formally Jerez de García Salinas), another "Pueblo Mágico" 50km southwest of the city, which is particularly lively on Sundays (market day). It is a pleasant colonial country town gradually being populated by Canadian and US retirees, who appreciate the slower pace and lower altitude that translates into a warmer year-round climate. If you can, time your visit to coincide with the annual ten-day **Spring Festival**, celebrated around Easter with *charreadas* (rodeos), bullfights, bands and much tequila drinking. The climax is the Easter Saturday procession when they burn an effigy of Judas. Festivities around the **Día de la Virgen de la Soledad** (Sept 8–15) are also worthwhile with an opportunity to catch the Danzas de los Matlachines.

At other times you can simply wander the pleasant colonial centre, visiting the Porfiriano-era **Teatro Hinojosa**, on Jardín Hidalgo, and the attractive church of **Inmaculada Concepción** just nearby. Buses (M$30) to Jerez leave hourly from Zacatecas's Central de Autobuses, and take about an hour.

Aguascalientes

The flourishing industrial town of **AGUASCALIENTES**, 128km south of Zacatecas, is an important and booming provincial capital with some fine colonial monuments in among its newer buildings. A couple of engrossing **museums**, including the tribute to José Posada, make this an intriguing place to stop over for a day or two, especially when you take into account the town's reputation for some of the finest **fiestas** in Mexico – rarely a week goes by without celebration, or at least a band playing in one of the plazas at the weekend – and for its tempting array of street **food**, particularly the sumptuous **birria** (roast goat or mutton stew)

Arrival, orientation and information

The **Central de Autobuses** is around 2km south of the centre on the city's ring road (Avenida de la Convención), from where there's a frequent bus service into the **Plaza de la Patria** ("Centro"), at the heart of town. To get back to the bus station from the centre, catch a bus marked "Central" from along Galeana at Insurgentes, just opposite the Plaza Patria shopping mall (all city buses charge M$5). **Taxis** use meters in Aguascalientes (which start at M$10); from the bus station to Plaza Patria should only be around M$20, though some drivers may optimistically try and set a higher price if they can – insist on the meter.

All the important public buildings as well as the cathedral, government offices, fancier hotels and a handful of banks are located in the **Plaza de la Patria**; many of the streets around here are pedestrianized, and most things you'll want to see are in easy walking distance.

The **tourist office** is also in the plaza, on the ground floor of the Palacio de Gobierno (Mon–Fri 9am–8pm, Sat & Sun 10am–6pm; ⓣ449/910-0051,

Ⓦwww.aguascalientes.gob.mx). The staff can give you information on the city's **festivals**, including the nearly two-centuries-old **Feria de San Marcos** (Ⓦwww.feriadesanmarcos.com), famous throughout Mexico. Celebrated in the Jardín San Marcos from mid-April to mid-May, events include everything from bullfights and live music to film festivals and rides for kids (many of the events are free).

Accommodation

Budget accommodation in Aguascalientes is located mostly around the market area, while some of the **hotels** on and around the Plaza de la Patria offer real luxury. During the *ferias* (mid-April to mid-May and the week around Nov 1), rooms are almost impossible to obtain at short notice and are likely to cost at least fifty percent more.

Hacienda del Roble 5 de Mayo 540 ⓣ449/915-3994. One of the best-value places in town; big, clean and relaxed, with friendly management; rooms have cable TV, and there's plenty of parking. ❹

Hotel Maser Juan de Montoro 303 ⓣ449/915-9662. Attractive and well-cared-for budget hotel with airy rooms around a central courtyard, and parking available. Rooms with TV cost M$30 more. ❸

Hotel Rosales Guadalupe Victória 104 ⓣ449/915-2165. A bargain for the location, right by the north side of the plaza, with pleasantly furnished rooms around a central courtyard and 24hr hot water. ❸

Hotel Señorial Colón 104, south side of Plaza Principal ⓣ449/915-1630. Simple carpeted rooms, but decent value for its location, particularly the corner rooms overlooking the plaza. ❸

Lukas Hostel Gómez Farías 541, a short walk north of Mercado Terán ⓣ449/917-9123, ⓦwww.lukashostel.com. The city's only hostel is a great choice, with friendly owners, basic en-suite singles and doubles, and clean six-bed dorms for men and women (M$100). You also get free wi-fi, free laundry, tea and coffee, and use of kitchen. ❸

Mexico Plaza Hotel Boutique Luis Donaldo Colosio 617 ⓣ1-800/343-4444, ⓦwww.mexicoplaza.com.mx. This is a fabulous option, part of a chain of plush boutique hotels, all glass, dark wood, and designer furniture; it's a bit pricey, though, and located in the northern suburbs. ❼

Quality Inn Nieto 102, on Plaza Principal ⓣ449/994-6670, ⓦwww.choicehotelsmexico.com. The former *Hotel Río Grande* has become a standard business chain hotel, offering bags of comfort and superb location, though little soul. Some rooms have views over the plaza, and all have cable TV with lots of US channels. Free wi-fi and breakfast; this is the best mid-range choice in town. ❺

Quinta Real Aguascalientes Aguascalientes Sur 601 ⓣ449/978-5818, ⓦwww.quintareal.com. Still the most luxurious hotel in the city, set in dazzling modern premises designed to look like a colonial monastery, with spacious suites and all the extras: pool, lush gardens and terrace bar. It's on the southern edge of the city, though – you'll need to take a lot of taxis. ❾

The City

Below the entire centre of Aguascalientes lies a series of mysterious and poorly understood tunnels and catacombs carved out by an unknown pre-Columbian civilization (sadly off-limits to the public). The Spanish initially referred to the place as La Ciudad Perforada (the Perforated City), then proceeded to build the current cluster of colonial buildings from the seventeenth century. These are arranged around the **Plaza de la Patria**, with its cathedral, and the **Palacio de Gobierno**, with its impressive murals. Fanning out from there are a few worthwhile museums, chief among them the **Museo José Guadalupe Posada**, dedicated to Mexico's most famous engraver.

The Plaza de la Patria and around

The **Plaza de la Patria** is the traditional heart of Aguascalientes, an enormous area centred around the **Exedra**, an amphitheatre-shaped space for performances, overlooked by a column topped with a Mexican eagle (which symbolizes the geographical centre of Mexico). Chief of the buildings here is the **Palacio de Gobierno** (daily 8am–8pm; free), an entrancing Baroque mansion constructed in 1665 as a private residence (it became city hall in 1856). Built from reddish volcanic rock, it contains an arcaded courtyard with a grand central staircase, decorated with four marvellous **murals** by the Chilean Oswaldo Barra Cunningham, who learnt his trade from Diego Rivera. The first of the murals, at the back on the ground floor, was painted in 1961, with others created in subsequent years: the most recent (from 1992) are at the front of the building.

Next door, the eighteenth-century **Palacio Municipal** is stately but rather bland in comparison, while down the other side of the plaza, the eighteenth-century **Catedral Basílica de Nuestra Señora de la Asunción** (daily 7am–2pm & 4–9pm) has been refurbished to reveal its full glory, in an ostentatious welter of gold, polished marble and several paintings by Miguel Cabrera. The altar is particularly magnificent, but don't miss the side chapel next to it, with a captivating all-turquoise interior. Look out also for the small plaque honouring Montoro Rodríguez, who founded the city in 1575, whose remains are said to be buried somewhere under the floor. The **Pinacoteca Religiosa** (same hours), in an annex, is well worth a look for its collection of eighteenth-century religious paintings, notably more work by Cabrera.

Just across the street on the south side of the cathedral is the **Teatro Morelos** (ⓣ449/915-1941, ⓦwww.aguascalientes.gob.mx), built in 1882 and notable as the location for the famous convention between Zapata, Villa and Carranza in

1914, commemorated with a large plaque opposite. Call or check the city website for the current programme.

Avenida Carranza leads down beside the cathedral to the **Casa de la Cultura** (daily 7am–9pm; free), a delightful seventeenth-century mansion given over to music and dance classes and the occasional exhibition in the **Galería de la Ciudad** at the entrance. The notice board here is an excellent place to find out what's on around town, and in the patio there's a small café (see "Eating and drinking", p.265) – a tranquil spot to have a drink. A little further down, at Carranza 118, the **Museo Regional de Historia** (Tues–Sun 10am–7pm; M$37; ⓣ449/916-5228) chronicles local history (Spanish captions only) in an elegant mansion built in 1901; exhibits range from a fossilized mammoth tusk and prehistoric arrow heads to Spanish colonial artefacts. Highlights include some remarkable pieces of pre-Columbian pottery and jewellery; the white shell necklace is especially striking.

Escape from the sun by heading west on Carranza to the shady **Jardín de San Marcos** (daily 6am–10.30pm) a long, beautifully manicured park that runs down to the eighteenth-century **Templo de San Marcos** (daily 7am–2pm & 4–9pm). Turning left here you're on the pedestrianized **Andador Pani**, which cuts through to López Mateos, its modern buildings a complete contrast to what went before. On your left is the **Casino de la Feria** with its giant *palenque*, where cockfights are staged during the fair. Once very much the face of modern Aguascalientes, the boulevard still packs in the crowds at weekends with its bars and restaurants, and leads south to the rather drab Expoplaza, essentially a large shopping mall. Heading back to the centre, follow **Calle Nieto** which is lined with boutiques selling one of the city's most recognized crafts: **lace**.

Museo José Guadalupe Posada and around

Though it only occupies a couple of rooms in a small building about 1km south of the centre, the **Museo José Guadalupe Posada** (Tues–Sun 11am–6pm; M$10; ⓣ449/915-4556) is one of the main reasons to visit Aguascalientes. Indeed, the town is almost a place of pilgrimage for devotees of this influential printmaker,

▲ Murals by Oswaldo Barra Cunningham, Palacio de Gobierno, Aguascalientes

Posada – the most Mexican artist

The frequently macabre work of **José Guadalupe Posada** will be familiar even if his name is not: Diego Rivera was not so wrong when he described the prolific Posada as "so outstanding that one day even his name will be forgotten". He was born a baker's son in Aguascalientes in 1852, and was later apprenticed to a lithographer. In 1888 he moved to the capital (having meanwhile lived in León for some time), and started to create in earnest the thousands of prints for which he soon became known. He mainly worked for the editor and printer Vanegas Arroyo, and his images appeared on posters and in satirical broadsheets that flourished despite – or more likely because of – the censorship of the **Porfiriano era**. Some of Posada's work was political, attacking corrupt politicians, complacent clergy or foreign intervention, but much was simply recording the news (especially disasters, which so obsess the Mexican press to this day), lampooning popular figures or observing everyday life with a gleefully macabre eye. Later, the events and figures of the Revolution, grotesquely caricatured, came to dominate his work.

Technically, Posada moved on from lithography to **engraving** in type metal (producing the characteristic hatched effect seen in much of his work) and finally to zinc etching, an extremely rapid method involving drawing directly onto a zinc printing plate with acid-resistant ink, and then dipping it in acid until the untouched areas corrode. Although the *calaveras*, the often elegantly clad skeletons that inhabit much of his work, are his best-known creations, the Aguascalientes museum devoted to him covers the full range of his designs. They all bear a peculiar mix of Catholicism, pre-Columbian tradition, preoccupation with death and black humour that can only be Mexican – and that profoundly affected all later Mexican art. Rivera and Orozco are just two of the greats who publicly acknowledged their debt to Posada, who died in 1913.

who is best known for his political satire and criticism of the Catholic Church (see box above). Rooms on three sides of a courtyard contain scores of nicely pressed lithographs, along with the original plates, contemporary photos and biographical information in Spanish.

The museum occupies the former priest's house of the adjacent **Templo del Señor del Encino** (daily 7am–1pm & 5–7pm), another elegant eighteenth-century church of pinkish sandstone. Amid the riotously gilded interior are vast paintings depicting the Stations of the Cross, completed by the Lopez brothers in 1798, and the miraculous and much-venerated "black Christ" of Encino – also depicted in stained glass above the main door – with strangely thick, long black hair. To get there, head east from the main plaza and take the first right, Díaz de León, south for about seven blocks. In front of the church and museum there's a pleasant, quiet square, at the heart of the peaceful old neighbourhood of Triana.

Museo de Arte Contemporáneo and Museo Nacional de la Muerte

A few blocks northeast of the Plaza de la Patria at the corner of Morelos and Primo Verdad, the **Museo de Arte Contemporáneo** (Tues–Sun 11am–6pm; M$10, free Sun; ⓣ449/918-6901) is home to some of the most exciting and provocative art from the region, with exhibitions that change every two months. Call or check ⓦwww.aguascalientes.gob.mx for what's on. There's also a permanent collection of work by **Enrique Guzmán**, the talented but troubled painter born here in 1952, who took his own life at the age of 34. One block north along Morelos, in a graceful old university building next to Templo de San Diego, the **Museo Nacional de la Muerte** (Tues–Sun 10.30am–6.30pm; M$20; ⓣ449/139-3258, ⓦmuseonacionaldelamuerte.uaa.mx) casts a macabre eye over Mexico's obsession with death rituals and images of death over the centuries, though it's not as grim as it sounds. The exhibits start with Mesoamerican traditions, with plenty of ancient statuary and a massive collection of model skulls, though these are so colourfully painted, bejewelled and stylized they seem more like kids' toys than religious totems. Especially striking are the abacus with tiny skulls and the "tree of death" sculptures. Labels are in Spanish only but this is really a visual experience. The museum ends with a stylish art gallery, all red-tinted, which houses an eclectic collection of death-related art from the nineteenth century on, including work by Posada and his predecessor, Manuel Manilla. Afterwards, raise your spirits in the tranquil courtyard café, in the shadow of San Diego's main dome.

Museo de Aguascalientes and around

A couple of blocks further east you'll reach the over-the-top **Templo de San Antonio** (Mon–Sat 6.30–10am, 11.30am–12.30pm & 6–9pm, Sun 6.30am–noon & 5.30–9pm), completed around 1908 and featuring a muddled facade with some vaguely discernible Neoclassical elements. Inside, murals by local architect Refugio Reyes provide a blaze of colour. Opposite is the imposing **Museo de Aguascalientes** (Tues–Sun 11am–6pm; M$10, free Sun; ⓣ449/915-9043), a bold Neoclassical palace constructed in 1903. Its art collection, mostly modern, is mainly of interest for its works by Saturnino Herrán, a local who was a contemporary and friend of Diego Rivera but who died young and never really achieved much recognition. Note his large stained-glass panel, and also rooms full of charcoal drawings, block prints and paintings by Gabriel Fernández Ledesma, another local son of some note.

The Baños Termales de Ojocaliente

You'll need to travel some 4km east from here to experience the **hot springs** that gave the city its name. The **Baños Termales de Ojocaliente** (daily 7am–7pm; main pool M$30; ⓣ449/979-0721) is really just a outdoor swimming pool complex outside town on the road to San Luis Potosí (Av Technológico 102) – the private baths are much hotter (from M$120/hr). A visit is only worthwhile if you're desperate for a soak: to get there, take "Ruta 12" along López Mateos (M$5).

Eating and drinking

Central Aguascalientes is jam-packed with cheap, tasty **food** stalls and canteens selling local specialities and snacks, though smarter restaurants are a bit thin on the ground. *Birria* (barbecued goat or mutton, shredded and served with a bowl of piquant broth, then eaten with a tortilla) and *lechón al horno* (roast pig) are specialities, along with *atole* (sweet corn-and chocolate-based drink), and desserts with guava (*guayaba*) – get a taster of the latter at *La Casa de las Guayabas* at Nieto 117, just behind the main plaza. The city has three lively markets near the centre, all excellent places to eat (see p.266), though **Mercado Terán** is better known for fresh fruit, piles of chiles, meat and produce – you can also check out the drink stalls here.

Fancier places line **López Mateos**, especially just west of the centre towards the Paseo de la Feria. While you're in town you should try some of the local **wine** (not always easy except in the more expensive restaurants) or at least the **brandy**: San Marcos is the best known, made here and sold all over the republic.

Los Antojos de Carranza Carranza 301 ⓣ449/994-1977. Plenty of traditional, well-presented Mexican dishes, most M$50–60 (roast meats M$80–100), but more a place to stop in for a beer (M$25), local brandy (M$50) and all manner of *botanas*. Also does decent breakfasts from M$50.

Los Arquitos Café Inside the Casa de la Cultura, Carranza 101 ⓣ449/910-2010. Serene spot for top-quality quiche, salads and that Mexican rarity, a strong espresso. Mon 4–9pm, Tues–Fri 10am–1pm & 4–9pm.

Lechón Pascualito Díaz de León 101. This no-frills local shop has been knocking out *lechón* since 1956 – owners carefully roast, dice, then serve the meat in mouth-watering tacos (M$20). Mon–Fri 9am–10pm.

Mercado Juárez aka Mercado de la Birria, Victoria and Unión. If you love street food you're in for a treat here, as this market is effectively a whole alley of cheap *birrierias* (*birria* stalls), with aromatic goat meat roasted right in front of you. Pick the place with the most patrons. Big plates from M$30, small M$18.

Mercado Morelos Morelos and Obregón. This is a giant food court loaded with tempting snack stalls; the star here is *Ruben's Tacos*, where glorious *carne asada* and *bistek* are stuffed into tortillas as you sit at the counter and spoon on the salsa (around M$20).

Mitla Restaurante Madero 222 ⓣ449/916-6157. Popular, old-fashioned Mexican restaurant that has been operating since 1938, with white-jacketed waiters serving a good selection of national and local dishes, including seafood and very reasonable comidas corridas (M$50–80). There's also an impressive M$75 breakfast buffet, and M$25 daily specials.

La Saturnina Carranza 110 ⓣ449/994-0449. Lovely and colourful courtyard café that's great for breakfast, lunch or just coffee and cake; try the *café de olla* (cinnamon-infused coffee; M$18), a city speciality, and the justly lauded *chiles rellenos* (M$71) and local-style tacos (M$53).

Tacos Perrones Nieto 445. Amiable staff and an early start make this great place to try *tacos perrones* "Rosarito-style" (M$25), tacos stuffed with fine *arrachera* steak and smothered in guacamole and beans.

Listings

Banks and exchange Banamex and Bancomer are on 5 de Mayo on the north side of Plaza de la Patria, both with 24hr ATMs.

Buses Aguascalientes is situated on Hwy-45 between Zacatecas (2hr) and León (2hr), and there are hourly buses in either direction, many continuing as far as Chihuahua (15hr) and Mexico City (6hr) (via Irapuato and Querétaro). There are also slower services to Guadalajara (3hr) and San Luis Potosí (3hr). For Guanajuato (1 daily; 3hr), it's quicker to take a bus to León first and get a connection there.

Internet access Very few places in the centre, but try *Web@Coffee Club* inside the Plaza Patria shopping mall (daily 10am–8pm; M$10/hr).

Pharmacy Plenty in the centre – try Farmacia Sánchez (24hr), Madero 213, 1 block from Plaza de la Patria.

Post office The main post office (Mon–Fri 8am–6pm, Sat 9am–1pm) is at Hospitalidad 108, a block north of the plaza and reached by following Morelos and then turning right.

Around Aguascalientes: Lagos de Moreno

Just 70km southeast of Aguascalientes in Jalisco state, **LAGOS DE MORENO** lies at the intersection of the old road from Mexico City to Ciudad Juárez and Hwy-80 (which runs from Guadalajara to San Luis Potosí and the northeast). Though the town has always been a major staging post, surprisingly few tourists stop here now and, despite the heavy traffic rumbling around its fringes, it's a quiet and rather graceful little town, with colonial streets climbing steeply from a small river to a hilltop monastery.

Cross the bridge by the bus station and head to your left along the stream, away from the choking fumes of the main road, and it's hard to believe you're in the same place. Whether you plan to stay a couple of hours or a few days, you'll want to head for the central **Jardín de los Constituyentes** and the impressive twin towers of the Baroque **Parroquia de la Asunción** (completed 1742): in the streets around it are a smattering of colonial mansions and official buildings, including a forbidding-looking jail that's still in use. The **Teatro José Rosas Moreno**, on the north side of the plaza behind the church, which opened in 1907 to stage opera performances, is worth a look for the beautiful mural on the dome depicting the Revolution and Independence, with local hero José Rosas Moreno, a famous writer of tales and fables, as the centrepiece. Once you've seen the centre, you might want to embark on the long climb up to the **Templo del Calvario**, a hillside church ten blocks to the north. The monastery is inhabited by monks, so you can't visit, and the church itself is tumbling down, but it's worth the trek for the **view**, especially at sunset.

There are several reasonable **hotels** near the main plaza. On the square itself, the red-painted and cavernous *Hotel París*, González León 339 (Ⓣ474/742-0200; ❷) has some basic but comfortable doubles and slightly more expensive, newer rooms (❸). The slightly posher *Hotel Colonial*, Hidalgo 279 (Ⓣ474/742-0142; ❹), has pretty public areas and its own restaurant though the rooms are only average. For more comfort try *Hotel Lagos* at Juárez 350 (Ⓣ474/741-2020, Ⓦwww.lagosinn.com; ❺), a modern, attractive four-star with spacious rooms set around a tranquil atrium. The plaza also boasts a few good **bars** and **places to eat** – *Las Palomas* at Hidalgo 242 is usually a reliable choice.

Getting to and from Lagos de Moreno could hardly be easier: there are **buses** at least every thirty minutes from Guadalajara (4hr), León (1hr 15min), Aguascalientes (1hr 30min), Zacatecas (4hr) and Mexico City (6hr).

San Juan de los Lagos

Some 45km southwest of Lagos de Moreno, on the road to Guadalajara, the old highway runs through **SAN JUAN DE LOS LAGOS**. From its outskirts, San Juan seems like just another dusty little town; in the centre, though, you'll find an enormous bus station surrounded by scores of hotels. This is thanks to the vast **Catedral Basílica de Nuestra Señora de San Juan de los Lagos** and the miraculous 38cm-tall **image of the Virgin** that it contains, making it the second most important pilgrimage centre in Mexico; crafted in the sixteenth century, the statue is said to have performed its first miracle in 1623 (bringing to life a dead girl) and it's been venerated ever since. The site's busiest dates are February 2 (**Día de la Candelaria**) and December 8 (**Fiesta de la Inmaculada Concepción**), when the place is crammed with penitents, pilgrims, those seeking miraculous cures and others who are just there to enjoy the atmosphere. The celebrations build up for a couple of weeks beforehand, and spill over to several lesser events throughout the year, notably the first fortnight of August and the entire Christmas period. There's little chance of finding a room at these times and little point in staying long at any other, so it's best to treat San Juan de los Lagos as a day trip from – or stopover between – Lagos de Moreno and Guadalajara (less than an hour from the former, around three hours from Guadalajara).

León

Heading south from Aguascalientes, most buses bypass Lagos de Moreno and head straight for **LEÓN**, a teeming, industrial city with a long history of excellence in **leatherwork**. This tradition is reflected in the scores of shoe factories and, in the centre, hundreds of shoe shops: it's a good place to buy hand-tooled cowboy boots, jackets, belts or just about anything else made of leather, but there's little else to see.

The area around the bus station (known as the **Zona Piel**; Ⓦwww.zonapielleon.com.mx), about 3km from the city centre, has the highest concentration of leather and shoe shops, most of which have very reasonable prices, although there are also some higher-class and more expensive boutiques. If you're changing buses in León it's well worth taking an hour to wander round the station's immediate vicinity; walk south three blocks along Hilario Medina to Plaza Piel and Plaza del Zapato (Ⓦwww.plazadelzapato.com), opposite at López Mateos 1601 Ote, two malls with the best concentration of stores. You can also try the Centro de Calzado

CTM (Ⓦwww.plazadelcalzadoctm.com), two blocks west on Taxco between Luz and Salina Cruz.

If you have time to explore the town proper, stash your bag at the bus station's guardería and head for the partly pedestrianized Centro Histórico. The linked **Plaza de los Fundadores** and **Plaza de los Martíres** are spacious, tranquil and elegant, with the fine eighteenth-century **Basílica-Catedral Metropolitana de Nuestra Madre Santísima de la Luz** built by the Jesuits, and a typically colonial Palacio Municipal. Little else survived a disastrous flood in 1883, but the plaza is surrounded by broad boulevards lined with shops, and there are a couple of other churches that deserve a look: the Baroque **Templo de los Angeles** and the extraordinary marble **Templo Expiatorio**, 500m southeast on Madero, which was started in 1921 and has been worked on ever since (it is expected to be complete in 2010). The latter is particularly impressive, with its high-relief copper doors revealing a white Gothic interior illuminated by modern stained glass. You can also visit the crypt (Fri, Sat & Sun 10am & 1pm; M$5). The city's main festival is the **Feria de León** (Jan 10–20), a big agricultural and industrial fair that finishes with religious festivities on the Día de San Sebastián.

Practicalities

To get into town from the **Central de Autobuses**, walk left out of the station along Hilario Medina, pick up a local bus marked "Centro" (M$4) headed to the right along López Mateos and get off at the "Centro Histórico" stop (heading back, take a bus marked "Central" along López Mateos). **Taxis** should be around M$50.

León also has the region's main **airport**, the nearest to both Guanajuato and San Miguel de Allende, with flights from all over Mexico and Houston, Dallas, LA, Chicago and more. On arrival, many just rent a car or grab a cab direct to their destination (around M$250 to León), but second-class buses also ply the highway between León and Guanajuato; wave madly and you may be able to flag one down (around M$30).

Should you need a place to stay here, you'll find numerous mid-range options and a number of cheapish **hotels** in the streets immediately around the plaza: try the basic, clean TV- and fan-equipped *Fundadores*, Ortiz de Domínguez 218 (Ⓣ477/716-1727; ❷), or the far more comfy *Howard Johnson Hotel Condesa*, Portal Bravo 14, overlooking the plaza (Ⓣ477/788-3929, Ⓦwww.hjleon.com; ❺), which offers reasonably priced four-star luxury.

Guanajuato

Shoe-horned into a narrow ravine, **GUANAJUATO** was for centuries the wealthiest city in Mexico, its mines pouring out silver and gold in prodigious quantities. Today it presents an astonishing sight: upon emerging from the surrounding hills you come on the town quite suddenly, a riot of colonial architecture, tumbling down hills so steep that at times it seems the roof of one building is suspended from the floor of the last. Declared a UNESCO World Heritage Zone in 1988, Guanajuato is protective of its image: there are no traffic lights or neon signs here, and the topography ensures that there's no room for new buildings. As a result, it's another town that has drawn the attention of North American expats, and *Starbucks* and *Domino's* have – somewhat discreetly – arrived in the old centre.

Today the city has plenty of life in its narrow streets (especially during term time), many outstanding places to eat and drink, and lots to see. There's an old-fashioned, backwater feel to the city, reinforced by the students' habit of going serenading in black capes, the brass bands playing in the plazas and the town's general refusal to make any special effort to accommodate the flood of tourists – who thankfully never really manage to disturb the daily ebb and flow.

Arrival and information

Guanajuato has two centres: the western end of town is somewhat rougher, focused on the plaza outside the **Mercado Hidalgo**, where there is always plenty of action in the bars and cheap cafés; to the east, where Juárez becomes Sopeña, the city is calmer, focusing on the **Jardín de la Unión**, with its shaded restaurants, happy tourists and neatly clipped trees. The **bus station** lies 6km west of the city. Regular local buses ("Centro–Central") shuttle into town in about fifteen minutes (M$5), usually stopping outside the Mercado Hidalgo and the Jardín de la Reforma. **Taxis** charge around M$35–40 for trips into the city (meters are not used); you shouldn't pay more than M$40 for any journeys in town (if in doubt ask the tourist office for the latest rates).

The **Aeropuerto Internacional de Guanajuato** is actually 30km west of Guanajuato at Silao (closer to León; see opposite); taxis direct to Guanajuato should cost around M$300, but if you're prepared to take a taxi to the bus station in Silao (M$120) you can take a regular second-class bus from there for just M$20.

Drivers will find Guanajuato's labyrinth of tunnels and prescriptive one-way streets confusing at first; you'll make your life easier by parking your vehicle and walking most places. The exception is a drive around the encircling Carretera Panorámica, which, as you would expect, has panoramic views of the district.

It's worth checking out the basic **information desk** at the offices of the tourism department, Plaza de la Paz 14 (Mon–Fri 9am–7.30pm, Sat 10am–5pm, Sun 10am–2pm; ⓣ473/732-1574 or 01-800/714-1086, ⓦwww.vamosaguanajuato.com), where you'll usually find English speakers; there are also lots of private **information booths** throughout town offering tours and hotel reservations. You might also check out ⓦwww.guanajuatocapital.com, another useful website with information on the city. Guanajuato plays host to some boisterous **festivals**, including the huge **Cervantino Festival** (see box, p.279), as well as the **Fiestas de San Juan y Presa de la Olla** (June 24), when fireworks, fairground rides and the crowning of the "Reina de las Fiestas" (Queen of the Festivals; elected by a special commission comprising the mayor, city council and various city social clubs) take place on the saint's day at the Presa de la Olla, and the **Apertura de la Presa de la Olla** (first Mon in July), the traditional opening of the dam's floodgates to sluice out and clean the city's riverbed (along with local dances and serenading).

Accommodation

Guanajuato has an excellent selection of rooms at a wide range of prices. In the last couple of years there has been an explosion of **hostels** (though many seem to go in and out of business), and top-end places continually raise their standards. Rooms can be hard to come by during certain times of the year, especially on Mexican public holidays, at Christmas, Semana Santa and during the **Festival Internacional Cervantino** (two and a half weeks in Oct; see box, p.279). If your trip coincides with one of these holidays, it's worth trying to book a room several weeks, if not months, in advance. If you can get a room on such occasions, you'll pay a thirty-to-fifty percent premium on the rates quoted here, which are already fairly high by Mexican standards. By far the best place to stay in the centre of town is around the **Jardín de la Unión**, even if plaza-view rooms come with a sizeable premium and, at weekends, mariachi accompaniment until well past midnight.

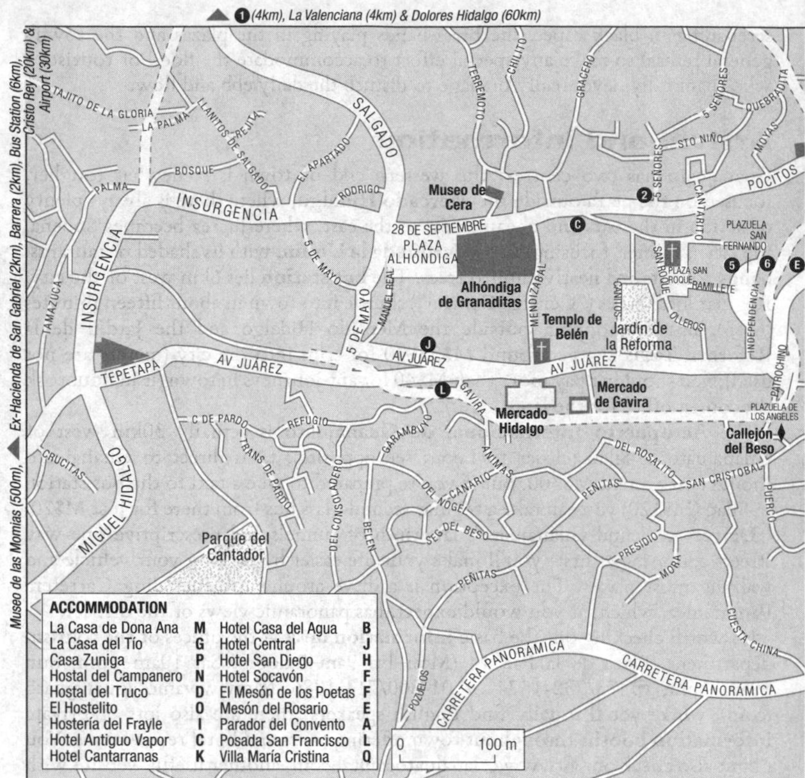

Near the Mercado Hidalgo

Hotel Antiguo Vapor Galarza 5 ⓣ473/732-3211, ⓦwww.hotelavapor.com. Set in a beautifully converted eighteenth-century house, this smart hotel has a boutique feel, combing modern luxury with exposed brick, wrought iron and wood furniture; breakfast included. 7

Hotel Central Juárez 111 ⓣ473/732-0080. The best of the cheap hotels around the Jardín Reforma, comprising simple rooms with TV and bathroom. 3

Hotel Socavón Alhóndiga 41-A ⓣ473/732-4885, ⓦwww.hotelsocavon.com.mx. A dark tunnel opens into the sunny courtyard of this small, friendly place that's well cared for. Attractive brick-ceilinged rooms all come with TV. A short walk from the centre but worth it – there's a decent Mexican restaurant (*La Fonda del Minero*) and parking on site. 5

Mesón del Rosario Juárez 31 ⓣ473/732-3284. Great location in the heart of town (mid-way between the mercado and jardín), set in a colonial mansion built in 1784 with small but clean rooms decked out in period style, tile-clad bathrooms and local TV – good value. 4

Jardín de la Unión and around

La Casa de Dona Ana Callejón Calixto 42 (en route to the Pípila) ⓣ473/732-5789, ⓦwww.lacasadedonaana.com. This marvellous place offers two rental houses (US$375 per week) and three rental suites (U$275 per week), perfect for long-stays or groups, and B&B rooms adorned with rugs and wall hangings in a two-storey colonial house built around a central patio. 5

La Casa del Tío Cantarranas 47 ⓣ473/733-9728, ⓦwww.lacasadeltiohostel.com. Comfortable hostel with relatively spacious dorms (M$110) and private rooms with bath, a small kitchen (free tea and coffee) and a charming roof terrace festooned with cacti. 15min free internet access daily. 1

Casa Zuniga Callejón de Pochote 38 ⓣ473/732-8546, ⓦwww.casazuniga.net. Welcoming modern B&B on the slopes right next to the funicular and near the Pípila, with cosy,

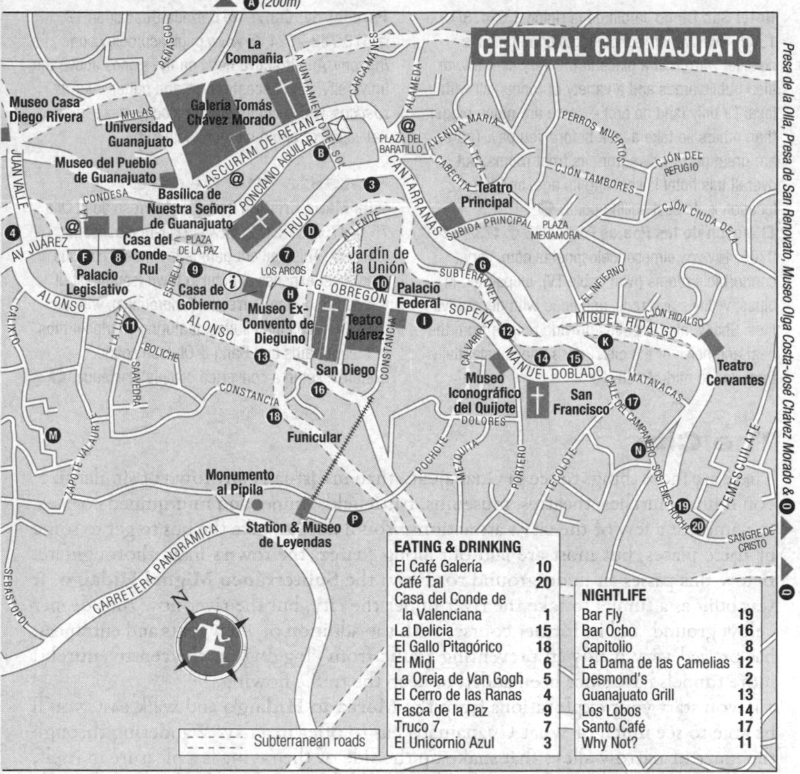

colonial-style rooms, friendly hosts Rick and Carmen Zuniga, lip-smacking steak and eggs for breakfast and fabulous views from the terrace. ❺

Hostal del Campanero Campanero 19 ⓣ473/734-5665, ⓔhostaldelcampanero@hotmail.com. Good-value hostel with dorms (M$170), private single rooms (M$250) and doubles (M$480). There's no real kitchen but a continental breakfast is served, and you get 15min free internet access. ❹

Hostal del Truco Truco 4 ⓣ473/734-7030. Renovated colonial mansion with cheap, clean dorms (M$110) just off the main plaza. It has free internet, lockers, luggage store and self-catering barbecue. ❶

El Hostelito Sangre de Cristo 9 (south of the centre) ⓣ473/732-5483, ⓔhostalitogto@hotmail.com. Popular hostel despite the walk into town, with clean dorms (M$200) and private rooms (with bath), congenial staff, a decent kitchen, cable TV and breakfast included. ❸

Hostería del Frayle Sopeña 3 ⓣ473/732-1179, ⓦwww.hosteriadelfrayle.com. This is the best option near the jardín, located in a lovely colonial-style building right in the heart of things with bougainvillea-draped courtyards, spacious common areas and rooms that feature artfully tiled bathrooms. Room quality varies, so look at a few first. Can be noisy, of course. ❺

Hotel Cantarranas Cantarranas 50, half a block from the Teatro Principal ⓣ473/732-5241, ⓦwww.hostalcantarranasgtocapital.com. Friendly and clean little place tucked away in the back streets. It doesn't look like much from the outside, but features a wonderful rooftop terrace with views of the Pípila (see p.274). Rooms have king-sized beds, and the suites all come with a kitchen stocked with utensils. There's even a three-room suite sleeping six. ❹

Hotel Casa del Agua Plazuela de la Compañía 4 ⓣ473/734-1974, ⓦwww.hotelcasadelagua.com.mx. Elegant seventeenth-century building converted into a chic hotel on contemporary lines. There are just fifteen light and airy rooms, all very nicely appointed with spa bath and cable TV. ❻

Hotel San Diego Jardín de la Unión 1 ⓣ473/732-1300, ⓦwww.hotelsandiegogto.com.mx. Fine colonial warren of a place in the very centre with tiled public areas and a variety of rooms, all with local TV only (and no a/c) – some are much bigger than others so take a look before you pay. There are great plaza views from its front rooms, but overall this hotel is showing its age, and the location is its best selling point. ❺

El Mesón de los Poetas Positos 35 ⓣ473/732-0705, ⓦwww.elmesondelospoetas.com. Very comfortable rooms (with cable TV), all painted in blues, yellows and reds, and lined with decorative tiles. Shady interior patios provide respite from the heat and noise of the city. Prices rise substantially from Jan to mid-March. ❻

Parador del Convento Calzada Guadalupe 17 ⓣ473/732-2524, ⓦwww.paginasprodigy.com/hpconv. An attractive hotel on the slopes above the university, with decent rooms and better *cuartos rústicos*, which come with a balcony, more imaginative decor and a lot more space. ❹

Outside the centre

Villa María Cristina Paseo de la Presa de la Olla 76 ⓣ473/731-2182, ⓦwww.villamariacristina.com.mx. This opulent gem is the most luxurious (and most expensive) hotel in town (southeast of the centre on the Carretera Panorámica), with just thirteen enchanting suites, featuring whirlpool tubs or steam baths and Bang & Olufsen sound systems, set in a converted colonial hacienda. ❾

The City

There are more things to see in Guanajuato than in virtually any town of similar size: you'll find churches, theatres, museums, battlefields, mines and mummified corpses, to name but a few of the city's attractions. You'll need to take the bus to get to some of these places, but most are laid out along Juárez, the town's main thoroughfare. Below this passes an underground roadway: the **Subterráneo Miguel Hidalgo**. It was built as a tunnel to take the river under the city, but the river now runs deeper below ground, and its former course, with the addition of a few exits and entrances, has proved very handy in preventing traffic from clogging up the centre entirely; more tunnels have since been added to keep the traffic flowing.

If you start your explorations from the **Mercado Hidalgo** and walk east, you'll be able to see much of what Guanajuato has to offer in a day. Wandering through the maze of narrow alleys that snake up the side of the ravine is a pleasure in itself, if only to spot their quirky names like Salto del Mono (Monkey's Leap) or Calle de las Cantarranas (Street of the Singing Frogs). Incidentally, references to **frogs** crop up everywhere around town – in sculpture, artesanías and T-shirts. The valley once had so many of the amphibians that the original name of the city was Quanax-huato, meaning "Place of Frogs".

Mercado Hidalgo and around

The first building of note as you head east up Juárez from where buses stop is the **Mercado Hidalgo** (most stalls open daily 9am–9pm) a huge iron-framed construction of 1910 reminiscent of British Victorian train stations and crammed with every imaginable sort of goods. East of the market, to the left and through the **Jardín de la Reforma**, with its fountain and arch, you get to the lovely, quiet **Plaza San Roque**. A small, irregular, flagged space, the plaza has a distinctly medieval feel, heightened by the raised facade of the crumbling church of **San Roque** that towers above. It's a perfect setting for the city's lively annual **Cervantes Festival** (see box, p.279). The Callejón de los Olleros leads back down to Juárez, or you can cut straight through to the livelier **Plazuela San Fernando**, with its stalls and restaurants. Return to Juárez from here and you emerge more or less opposite the **Plazuela de los Angeles**. In itself this is little more than a slight broadening of the street, but from here steps lead up to some of Guanajuato's steepest, narrowest alleys. Just off the plazuela is the **Callejón del Beso** (20m up Callejón del Patrimonio and turn left), so called because at only a little over half a metre wide, it is slim enough for residents to lean out of the upper-storey balconies and exchange kisses across the street – naturally enough there's a *Canterbury Tales*-style legend of star-crossed lovers associated with it. To learn more, join one of the *callejóneadas* (see p.280) that pass this way, or engage the services of one of the small children who hang around eager to tell a tale.

Plaza de la Paz and around

The **Plaza de la Paz** lies east of the Jardín de la Reforma, beyond a number of banks on Juárez. The plaza boasts some of the town's finest **colonial buildings**, notably the **Palacio Legislativo** (completed in 1900 and still in use today), and the adjacent late eighteenth-century **Casa del Conde Rul y Valenciana** (built by the owners of the richest mine in the country; Don Diego Rul was killed fighting rebels in 1814). The latter was designed by Eduardo Tresguerras, undoubtedly the finest Mexican architect of his time, and played host briefly to Baron Alexander von Humboldt in 1803, the German naturalist and writer, an event commemorated by a plaque. Today it serves as the regional courthouse.

On the far side of the plaza stands the honey-coloured **Basílica de Nuestra Señora de Guanajuato** (daily 8am–9pm), a Baroque parish church that was completed in 1796 and houses an ancient image of the Virgin, patroness of the city. This wooden statue, which now sits amidst silver and jewels, is said to have been given to Guanajuato in 1557 by Philip II, in gratitude for the wealth that was pouring from here into Spanish royal coffers. The **Casa de Gobierno** (closed to the public), a short way down towards the Jardín de la Unión (see below), is another fine mansion, this time with a plaque recording that Benito Juárez lived here in 1858, when Guanajuato was briefly his provisional capital.

Around the Jardín de la Unión

From the Plaza de la Paz, you can cut up to the university, but just a short distance further east on the main street (Juárez has become Obregón at this point) is the **Jardín de la Unión**, Guanajuato's main plaza. It's a delightful little square – or rather triangle – set back from the street, shaded with trees, surrounded by cafés and with a bandstand in the centre from which the town band regularly plays in the early evening. This is the best time to sit and linger over a drink, enjoying the passing spectacle of the evening *paseo*.

Facing the Jardín across Obregón stands the Baroque church of **San Diego**, inside which are several old paintings and interesting chapels. One altar in particular is dedicated to the infant Jesus and mawkishly filled with toys and children's tiny shoes left as offerings. A side entrance leads to the **Museo Ex-Convento Dieguino** (daily 10am–6pm; M$6), which is gradually being developed as gallery space amongst the stone foundations of the church – the small display of archeological finds here, and the renovated crypt space itself is interesting, but unless an exhibition is on show, there's not much else to see. Next door to the church is the imposing Neoclassical frontage of the **Teatro Juárez** (Tues–Sun 9am–1.45pm & 5–7.45pm; M$35, cameras M$30), all Doric columns and allegorical statuary. The interior of the theatre is fabulously plush, decked out in red velvet and gilt, with chandeliers and a Moorish proscenium. Built at the end of the nineteenth century, it was opened in 1903 by the dictator Porfirio Díaz himself.

Beyond the Jardín, Obregón becomes Sopeña, lined by fancy boutiques, restaurants and bars as far as the pretty pink church of San Francisco, which marks the Plaza San Francisco. Here, too, is the **Museo Iconográfico del Quijote** (Tues–Sat 10am–6.30pm, Sun 10am–2.30pm; M$20, students free), an extraordinary little collection devoted entirely to Don Quixote, testament to the influence of Cervantes' seminal novel on subsequent generations of artists. The museum contains mainly paintings of the don – including some by Pedro and Rafael

Learning Spanish in Guanajuato

Guanajuato has become a popular place to spend a couple of weeks learning Spanish – the only potential problem here is that there are so many other English speakers around you may get less Spanish practice than you had hoped. One way to avoid this is to **stay with a local family** (typically around M$250–300 a day), sharing meals with them and getting plenty of opportunity to try out your new language skills; invariably, schools can arrange this. Classes with up to five students usually **cost** around M$60 an hour, and a little less if you're doing more hours per day. One-to-one tuition is around M$150 an hour. The 2009 swine flu/recession hit this sector hard, however (the highly regarded Academia Falcon closed after 50 years), and many schools were empty, so check the latest before you go. The best choice at the time of writing was **Escuela Mexicana** Potrero 12 (ⓣ473/732-5005, ⓦwww.escuelamexicana.com) in the heart of town offering everything from one-week beginners' courses to extensive advanced classes and an array of specialist courses in such subjects as culture, literature, politics and Mexican cooking. Their intensive "Spanish for Travellers" requires four hours of coursework a day and one or two weeks' commitment (US$180–270 per week, plus US$35 registration).

Coronel – but also a Dalí print, a Posada engraving of the hero as a *calavera*, an imposing sculpture by Federico Silva, murals, tapestries, sculptures, busts, miniatures, medals, plates, glassware, chess sets, playing cards, pipes and cutlery – you name it, it's here. There's also a mural-smothered shrine to the maestro himself, containing a statue of Cervantes.

Pípila

The **Monumento al Pípila**, a bulky statue on the hillside almost directly above the Jardín de la Unión, affords fantastic views of Guanajuato. From the viewpoint at its base you seem to be standing directly on top of the church of San Diego. It's an especially magical spot for the 45 minutes or so during which the sun sets behind the hills and the electric lights start to come on in town. The steep climb takes about twenty minutes going up and ten minutes coming down. There are several possible routes up through the alleys – look for signs saying "al Pípila" – including up the Callejón del Calvario, to the right off Sopeña just beyond the Teatro Juárez; from the Plazuela San Francisco; or climbing to the left from the Callejón del Beso. The signs run out, but if you keep climbing as steeply as possible you're unlikely to get lost and the paved trail is fairly easy to follow. There's also a bus ("Pípila") that takes you round the scenic Carretera Panorámica, and the **funicular** (Mon–Fri 8am–9.45pm, Sat 9am–9.45pm, Sun 10am–9pm; M$15 each way), a kind of cliff railway that whisks you up the steep valley side from behind the church of San Diego – for M$40 you also gain entry to the kitchsy **Museo de Leyendas** (Mon–Fri 9am–6.30pm, Sat 10am–7pm, Sun noon–7pm; M$35) at the summit station (animatronic figures highlight the many legends of the city), but unless you have bored kids in tow this is definitely worth skipping. Pípila was Guanajuato's own Independence hero (see opposite), and at the top you'll always find crowds of Mexican tourists trawling the food stalls here for snacks to munch while enjoying the views.

Around the Universidad Guanajuato

At the back of the Jardín de la Unión and a little to the north, the **Plaza del Baratillo** is a small, bustling space usually alive with students hanging out or busy at the internet cafés. From here the Teatro Principal is down to the right, while if you follow the curve on round to the left you find the church of **La Compañía** (daily 7.30am–9:30pm). The highly decorated monumental Baroque church is just about all that's left of a Jesuit seminary founded in 1734; step inside to admire the unusually light interior afforded by the clear glass in the dome, added in 1884 and inspired by St Peter's in Rome. At the back in the sacristy is a small museum or *pinacoteca* (Mon–Sat 10am–5pm, Sun 10am–2pm; M$10) with a few seventeenth- to nineteenth-century oils, including four images of saints by Miguel Cabrera.

The seminary was an educational establishment that eventually metamorphosed into the **Universidad Guanajuato**, now one of the most prestigious in Mexico. The university building is in fact quite modern – only finished in 1955 – but is designed to blend in with the town, which, for all its size, it does surprisingly effectively. There's not a great deal of interest inside, but you could check out the temporary art exhibits in the **Galería Tomás Chávez Morado** (daily 10am–6pm; free) at the bottom of the main entrance at Lascurain de Retana 5.

Next door to the university building, the **Museo del Pueblo de Guanajuato** (Tues–Sat 10am–6.30pm, Sun 10am–2.30pm; M$15) is a collection of local art and sundry oddities, housed in the eighteenth-century home of the Marqués de San Juan de Rayas. It's an arresting building with a delightful little Baroque chapel (added in 1776), where much of the decoration has been replaced by modern murals painted by one of the standard-bearers of the Mexican muralist tradition, José Chávez Morado (who died in Guanajuato in 2002).

Museo Casa Diego Rivera

Positos leads west from the front of the university to the absorbing **Museo Casa Diego Rivera**, Positos 47 (Tues–Sat 10am–7.30pm, Sun 10am–3pm; M$15), the home where Guanajuato's most famous son was born in 1886. For most of his life Rivera, an ardent revolutionary sympathizer and Marxist (see p.400), went unrecognized by his conservative home town, but with international recognition of his work came this museum, in the house where he was raised until he was 6. Until 1904, the Rivera family only occupied the lower floor, which is now furnished in nineteenth-century style, though only the beds and a cot actually belonged to them. The place is far bigger than it looks from the outside, and the extensive upper floors contain many of Rivera's works, especially early ones, in a huge variety of styles – Cubist, Pointillist, Impressionist – showing the influences he absorbed during his years in France and Spain. Although there are no major works on display, the many sketches and small paintings are well worth a look, particularly those showing his fascination with all things pre-Columbian.

The Alhóndiga

The **Alhóndiga de Granaditas** (Tues–Sat 10am–5.45pm, Sun 10am–2.45pm; M$49), the most important of all Guanajuato's monuments, lies west of the Museo Diego Rivera, more or less above the market. Originally a granary, later a prison and now an absorbing regional museum, this was the scene of the first real battle and some of the bloodiest butchery in the War of Independence. Just thirteen days after the cry of Independence went up in Dolores Hidalgo, Father Hidalgo approached Guanajuato at the head of his insurgent force – mostly peons armed with nothing more than staves and sickles. The Spanish, outnumbered but well supplied with firearms, shut themselves up in the Alhóndiga, a redoubtable fortress. The almost certainly apocryphal story goes that Hidalgo's troops could make no impact until a young miner, nicknamed **El Pípila** ("the Turkeycock"), volunteered to set fire to the wooden doors – with a slab of stone tied to his back as a shield, he managed to crawl to the gates and start them burning, dying in the effort. The rebels, their path cleared, broke in and massacred the defenders wholesale. It was a short-lived victory – Hidalgo was later forced to abandon Guanajuato, leaving its inhabitants to face Spanish reprisals, and was eventually tracked down by the royalists and executed in Chihuahua. His head and the heads of his three chief co-conspirators, Allende, Aldama and Jiménez, were suspended from the four corners of the Alhóndiga as a warning to anyone tempted to follow their example, and there they stayed for over ten years, until Mexico finally did become independent. The hooks from which they hung are still there on the outside walls.

Inside, there's a memorial hall devoted to the Martyrs of Independence and the **museum** itself, upstairs. On the staircases are **murals** by local artist José Chávez Morado (see opposite) depicting scenes from the War of Independence and the Revolution, as well as native folklore and traditions. The museum's exhibits, mostly labelled in Spanish, span local history from pre-Hispanic times to the Revolution: the most interesting sections cover the Independence battle and everyday life in the colonial period. One of the iron cages in which the rebels' heads were displayed is present, as are lots of weapons and flags and a study of Guanajuato's mining industry in the 1890s, the city's last golden age. There's also plenty of art, especially a wonderful series of portraits by Hermenegildo Bustos (1832–1907), the celebrated artist born near León; and don't miss the small artesanías section by the side door, which displays a bit of everything from fabrics and clothes to saddles and metalwork.

Museo de las Momias

Halfway up the hill going west along Juárez from the Alhóndiga, the ghoulish **Museo de las Momias** (daily 9am–6pm; M$50), holds a very different sort of attraction. Here, lined up against the wall in a series of glass cases, are more than a hundred mummified human corpses exhumed from the local public cemetery. All the bodies were originally laid out in crypts, but if after five years the relatives were unable or unwilling to make the perpetuity payment, the remains were usually removed. Over time many were found to have been naturally preserved, and for years the cemetery became an unofficial tourist attraction. The damage done to the site prompted the government to step in, and now the "interesting" bodies are on display here – others, not properly mummified or too dull for public titillation, have been burned or transferred to a common grave. Some of the wasted, leathery bodies are more than a century old (including a smartly dressed mummy from the 1860s said to have been a French doctor) while others are relatively recent fatalities. The burial clothes hang off the corpses almost indecently – some are completely naked – and the labels (in English) delight in pointing out their most horrendous features: one twisted mummy, its mouth opened in a silent scream, is the "woman who was buried alive"; another, a woman who died in childbirth, is displayed beside "the smallest mummy in the world". Some of the labelling is written in the first person, adding another disturbing twist. It's all absolutely grotesque, but not without a degree of macabre fascination. You can continue into the **Salón del Culto a la Muerte** (same hours; M$10; buy ticket at main entrance), a house-of-horrors-style extension, with an array of holographic images, jangly motorized skeletons, a rusty old chastity belt and yet more mummies. Fans of kitsch will be delighted with the hawkers outside selling mummy models and mummy-shaped shards of rock. To get to the museum, either catch a bus ("Panteón" or "Momias") anywhere along Alonso or Juárez, or walk about 500m west of the Mercado Hidalgo along Juárez, then left onto Calzada del Panteón.

Presa de la Olla and the Museo Olga Costa-José Chávez Morado

East of the centre of town, Sangre de Cristo (later Paseo de la Presa) runs gradually uphill for a couple of kilometres through some of Guanajuato's fancier residential districts before ending up at the **Presa de la Olla** and the Presa San Renovato, two dams with small and rather unimpressive reservoirs. Off Sangre de Cristo, Pastita runs northeast past a decayed section of an old aqueduct to the **Museo Olga Costa-José Chávez Morado** (Tues–Sat 10am–7pm, Sun 10am–3pm; M$15). The museum was formerly the Hacienda de Guadalupe and is where Mexican muralist **José Chávez Morado** (1909–2002) and his German painter wife (Olga Costa) spent much of their married life. He moved out and donated the building to the city of Guanajuato on his wife's death in 1993. The house has been left largely as it was when they lived here, an eclectic mix of styles explained (in Spanish) by the guide: eighteenth-century majolica ceramics, seventeenth-century French chairs, Dutch porcelain, Iranian wall hangings and a fine collection of ex-votos. There's little of their work on show, but notice Morado's blue and white lamp, and his stained-glass windows – all blotches in red, yellow, blue and black – on the way up to the studio, now given over to temporary exhibitions. The museum is less than thirty minutes' walk from the Jardín de la Unión, or you can flag down any bus marked "Pastita" at the eastern end of town.

Ex-Hacienda de San Gabriel de Barrera

If the crush of Guanajuato gets too much for you, head 2km west (either by foot or take any bus going to the Central de Autobuses) to the **Ex-Hacienda de San Gabriel de Barrera** (daily 9am–6pm; M$22), a colonial home now transformed into a alluring little museum. The beautifully restored **gardens** of the hacienda range through a bizarre selection of international styles – including English, Italian, Roman, Arabic and Mexican – and make a wonderful setting for the house, which has been renovated with a colonial look. Cool rooms evoke daily life among the wealthy silver barons of nineteenth-century Guanajuato and include numerous fine pieces of furniture dating back several centuries: grand and opulent on the ground floor, rich in domestic detail upstairs. It's an enlightening place to wander at your leisure and brings home the sheer wealth of colonial Guanajuato.

La Valenciana

From close by the Alhóndiga on Calle Alhóndiga, buses ("Valenciana"; infrequent enough to make a short M$30 taxi ride a worthwhile investment) wind their way 4km uphill to the mines and church in **La Valenciana**. Near the top of the pass here, overlooking Guanajuato where the road to Dolores Hidalgo and San Miguel heads off north, you'll see the elaborate facade of the extraordinarily sumptuous **Templo de San Cayetano de Valenciana** with its one completed tower. Built between 1765 and 1788, it's the ultimate expression of Mexico's churrigueresque style, with a profusion of intricate adornment covering every surface – even the mortar, they say, is mixed with silver ore. Inside, notice the enormous gilded *retablos* around the main altar and in each arm of the cross, and the delicate filigree of the roof vaulting, especially around the dome above the crossing.

The church was constructed for its owner, the Conde de Rul y Valenciana, who also owned La Valenciana **silver mine** – for hundreds of years the richest in Mexico, tapping Guanajuato's celebrated Veta Madre (Mother Lode). The mine still operates on a vastly reduced level, but exploitation continues apace with a clutch of ways to lure tourists to the associated silver shops, rock-sellers and restaurants. Behind the church, the original mine entrance now operates as the **Bocamina San Cayetano** (daily 10am–6pm; M$25), one of 23 interconnecting pits in the region and named after the patron saint of miners. Donning a hard hat fails to lend credibility to a brief tour of the upper 60m of tunnels, which end at a shrine to the mine's patron. Better organized is the **Bocamina San Ramón** (daily 10am–7pm; M$30; Ⓣ473/732-3551, Ⓦwww.bocaminasanramon.com), just beyond the church on the main road, which has small museum in a lavish hacienda (once owned by one of the mine foremen), and another tour into the first section of an ancillary mine shaft (48m deep and 50m long), part of which has been converted into a bar and restaurant. If you're really interested in the city's mining history, check out the **Mina Experimental El Nopal**, run by the university at the ex-Hacienda San Matías, and part of most organized "mining tours" of the city (see p.281).

Cerro de Cubilete and the statue of Cristo Rey

If you approached Guanajuato from León, you'll already have seen the huge statue of **Cristo Rey** crowning the 2661-metre **Cerro de Cubilete**, 20km west of the city. Variously claimed to occupy the geographical centre of the republic or just the state of Guanajuato, it seems a neat coincidence that it should be on the highest hill for miles. Nevertheless, the complex of chapels and pilgrims' dormitories is without question magnificently sited, with long views across the plains. At its heart is a twenty-metre bronze statue – erected in 1950 and ranking as the world's second largest image of Christ, just behind Rio de Janeiro's – standing on a golden globe flanked by cherubs, one holding a crown of thorns, the other the golden crown of the "King of Kings".

The easiest way to get up here is on one of the M$150 **tours** advertised all around Guanajuato, though you can do the same for less than half the price by nipping out to the Central de Autobuses and picking up one of ten daily Autobuses Vasallo de Cristo, which run up there in around thirty minutes – these also go through Valenciana.

Eating and drinking

Finding something good to eat in Guanajuato is easy – it's nearly impossible to walk more than a few yards down Juárez without passing some kind of café or restaurant. The **university area**, too, has plenty of choice and **Plaza Baratillos** is the place to come for cheap tamale stalls in the morning. Rather more adventurous, and cheaper still, are the stalls in the **Mercado de Gavira** (the modern annex of the **Mercado Hidalgo**: two floors of delights and horrors. You're advised to take a careful look at what's on offer before succumbing to the frantic beckoning of the stallholders – some stalls are distinctly cleaner and more appetizing than others, but you'll pay around M$25–30 for a filling meal. Up around the **Jardín de la Unión**, the pricey outdoor restaurants are well worth visiting; in fact many people seldom stray from the excellent range of places all within five minutes' walk of each other along **Sopeña** and the surrounding streets.

El Café Galería Sopeña 10, right by the Teatro Juárez ⓣ473/732-2566. Fashionable hangout with eating inside and a very popular outdoor terrace across the road where the service can be slow. Prices are pretty reasonable (M$35 eggs, M$14 coffee) and a bucket of beers costs M$100.

Café Tal Temezcuitate 4 ⓣ473/732-6212. Great little café that roasts its own beans and consequently has some of the best coffee in town (from M$12). They also have good fruit and yogurt breakfasts, a variety of teas and free wi-fi.

Casa del Conde de la Valenciana at La Valenciana, 4km from town (see p.277) ⓣ473/732-2550. Beautifully set restaurant in the courtyard of a former hacienda with vines growing up the walls. The Mexican food is nicely prepared and presented, and you should leave room for the ice creams served scooped out of the fruits they are flavoured with. Roughly M$200 for a full meal. Mon–Sat 1–8pm.

El Cerro de las Ranas Juan Valle 7. The slightly sterile atmosphere here won't encourage you to linger, but the food is top value, especially the comida corrida (M$40), and comes with a bottomless jug of *agua fresca*.

La Delicia Plaza de San Francisco 12. Eat-in *pastelería* with window seats that catch the afternoon sun and menu that includes hot chocolate, coffees and *rebanadas*.

El Gallo Pitagórico Constancia 10 ⓣ473/732-9489. One of Guanajuato's most popular restaurants, with a predominantly Italian menu, eclectic decor and a fabulous location high on the valley slopes right behind the San Diego church. Dine on prosciutto and melon followed by a tasty putanesca as the sounds of the Jardín de la Unión waft up through the open windows. Around M$90 for pastas and M$120 for *secondis*. Daily 2–11pm.

El Midi Plazuela de San Fernando 41 (no phone). A refreshing change from endless Mexican and Italian dining, this southern French place serves an enticing array of dishes from the Midi – among them quiches, terrines, salads and olive loaf – all self-served from a cold buffet and charged by weight (M$13/100g). Unless you're a glutton it works out very reasonably, and the coffee and desserts are mouth-watering. Closed Sat.

La Oreja de Van Gogh Plazuela de San Fernando 24 ⓣ473/732-0301. Choose a starry night to sit outside at this relaxed restaurant on a tranquil square away from the bustle of the Jardín de la Unión. Try the thick chicken stew served in a *molcajete* (M$115) or an *arrachera* steak (M$120). There's live acoustic music most nights.

Tasca de la Paz Plaza de la Paz 28 ⓣ473/734-2225. Smart Spanish restaurant with outdoor tables, serving European delights such as *paella*, chicken in white wine and *jamón serrano*. Expect to pay around M$50 for tapas and M$120 for main dishes.

Truco 7 Truco 7 ⓣ473/732-8374. Beautiful little old-school café with a young, convivial atmosphere, comfy chairs and art covering the walls. Great, moderately priced breakfasts, *comidas*, salads, steaks and wonderful garlic soup with an egg poached in it. Ask for your cappuccino *sin miel* to avoid getting a dollop of corn syrup in it. Mains average M$35–50.

El Unicornio Azul Plaza del Baratillo 2 ⓣ473/732-0700. Tiny vegetarian restaurant selling whole-wheat breads to go and soya burgers (M$22) and juices (M$15–20) to have inside.

Nightlife and entertainment

Home to a superb host of cafés and bars, Guanajuato is the perfect town in which to sit around and knock back a coffee or a bottle or beer or two. Things are especially busy at weekends, when refugees from the bigger cities, including Mexico City and León, come here to enjoy themselves. Most of the better places are close to the Jardín de la Union and the university, while the rougher **bars** and **clubs** are down on Juárez around Mercado Hidalgo, where the cantinas are generally reserved for men and prostitutes.

Festival Internacional Cervantino

Usually referred to simply as the **Cervantino**, this two-and-a-half week festival (early to mid-Oct; ⓣ473/731-1150 or 731-1161, ⓦwww.festivalcervantino.gob.mx) is a celebration of all things to do with sixteenth-century Spanish author **Miguel de Cervantes**, though it is primarily about his most famous character and hapless romantic, Don Quixote. The festival features performances by international and Mexican musicians, dancers, theatre groups and street-performers, and each year a different region or country is picked to be the focus. The festival has its foundations in the 1950s, when students performed **entremeses** – swashbuckling one-act plays from classical Spanish theatre – outdoors in places such as Plaza San Roque. These still take place here, and you don't need good Spanish to work out what's going on, as they're highly visual and very entertaining; some performances are free, but tickets to most plays cost around M$250 (ⓦwww.ticketmaster.com.mx). Groups of students will quite often put on impromptu performances outside festival times, so it's worth wandering up here in the early evening just to see if anything is happening, especially on Saturday nights. The Cervantino is now far larger, and during the festival the town, and just about every imaginable performance space, is alive with music and cultural events – opera, dance, literature readings, music performances. You'll have to pay to get into many events, but there is almost always something free happening in the Plaza Alhóndiga. It is a great time to be here, though you'll need to book accommodation months in advance; note also that the streets are usually jam-packed with revellers, though since 2007 the sale of alcohol has been regulated at the festival (and it's illegal to drink on the street).

An excellent way to pass an hour or so is to follow one of the organized **callejóneadas** – walking tours that wind through the sidestreets and back alleys following a student minstrel group known as *estudiantinas*. *Callejóneadas* are aimed at Mexicans, so without fluent Spanish and some local knowledge you'll miss most of the jokes and risqué tales, but they're great fun all the same. It is possible to buy your own beer or wine and just tag along, but for the full experience you'll need a ticket. These can be bought (for around M$100) from any of the information booths, at Juárez 210, or from the *estudiantinas* who hang around the Jardín de la Unión from around 6.30pm. They entitle you to a *porrón* (a kind of ceramic drinking vessel), which is topped up as you promenade. In high season, there's something happening most nights of the week, but at other times of the year Tuesday, Thursday, Friday and Saturday are your best bets, and the event usually kicks off around 8.30pm.

Bars and clubs

Bar Fly Sóstenes Rocha 30 (on the corner). Tiny, sociable second-floor bar with folk, jazz or acoustic music most nights from 9pm, and seldom any cover. Wed–Sat 7pm–2am.

Bar Ocho Constancia 8. Youthful bar set up with sofas for intimate conversation, and a pool table upstairs – it also serves decent burgers and bar food. A good place to wind down after the clubs. The name is a play on the word *borracho*, Spanish for "drunk". Daily from around 3pm to 3am.

Capitolio Plaza de la Paz 62. One of the town's premier clubs for tourists, students and locals; there's a spacious dance area, two bars and a smaller hip-hop room at the back. Music varies from the usual salsa, Latino and US pop dance hits, to more serious reggaeton, rock and techno. Open Wed–Sat from 10.30pm to around 4.30am. Usually M$50 cover.

La Dama de las Camelias Sopeña 34, opposite Museo Iconográfico ⓣ473/732-7587. Great bar imaginatively decorated with evening dresses, high-heeled shoes and smashed mirror fragments. *La Dama* stays open from 8pm to 4am and offers dancing most nights and great salsa late on Fri. Closed Sun.

Desmond's Positos 79. Intimate Irish pub and restaurant run by a long-time resident Irishman. Guinness is available, of course, and there's a different music style each evening, including Trad Irish on Wed. Open daily 2pm–midnight.

Guanajuato Grill Alonso 4 ⓣ473/732-0285. Guanajuato's other main club is bigger than *Capitolio* and tends to be packed with local teenagers dancing to hardcore house and techno.

Los Lobos Manuel Doblado 2. Dim and often crowded bar that resounds nightly to thumping rock classics. Cheap-ish beer.

Santo Café Campanero 4. Reached by a small bridge over a pedestrian alley, this quiet restaurant, café and bar is a favourite of intellectuals looking to wax philosophical over a drink; there's also free wi-fi.

Why Not? Alonso 34 Altos. This is the late-night/early-morning hangout of choice (usually open till 4am), very popular with foreign students, with a pool table and a mix of ska, reggae, hip-hop and rock.

Moving on from Guanajuato

To get to the Central de Autobuses take a local bus ("Centro–Central"; M$5) from Mercado Hidalgo and Juárez. Taxis charge around M$40. There are regular services to Dolores Hidalgo (1hr 30min), Guadalajara (4hr), Mexico City (5hr), San Luis Potosí (5hr) and Aguascalientes (3hr), and almost constant departures for León (1hr). There are relatively few first-class buses direct to San Miguel de Allende (ETN runs a couple; 1hr 30min), but there are plenty of second-class departures; if you have any problem getting anywhere else, head for León (see p.267), which is on the main north–south highway and has much more frequent services. Viajes Frausto, Obregón 10, close to the Jardín de la Unión (ⓣ473/732-3580), has the timetables, fares and booking facilities for all first-class companies operating from the bus station.

Taxis to the Aeropuerto Internacional de Guanajuato (closer to León; see p.267) should cost around M$300. Flights from here connect with Mexico City, Monterrey and Tijuana, as well as **Chicago, Dallas, Houston and Los Angeles**.

For further information, see Travel details, p.311.

Listings

American Express Viajes Georama, Plaza de la Paz 34, operates as a travel agency (Mon–Fri 9am–8pm, Sat 10am–2pm; ⓣ473/732-5101, ⓔviajes_georama@hotmail.com), and also has all the usual Amex services.
Banks and exchange Banks can be found along Juárez: Bancomer at no. 9, Banamex on Plazuela de San Fernando and a convenient branch of Banorte between Plaza de la Paz and the Jardín Unión.
Emergencies Police ⓣ473/732-0266; Cruz Roja ⓣ473/732-0487; for emergency medical attention visit Centro de Salud Urbano de Guanajuato, Pardo 5 (ⓣ473/732-1467).
Internet access Numerous places around town, especially around Plaza Baratillo where M$10/hr is the norm. For those with lap-tops and PDAs, there's free wi-fi at several cafés around the Jardín de la Unión. El Tapatío on Lascurain de Retana is just M$8/hr; Antigua Café on Juárez is M$6/hr.
Laundry Lavandería del Centro, Sopeña 26 (Mon–Sat 9am–8.30pm; ⓣ473/732-0436). M$50/3–5kg.
Pharmacy El Fénix, Juárez 106, near Plazuela de Los Angeles (Mon–Sat 8am–10pm, Sun 9am–9pm).
Post office Ayuntamiento 25, opposite the Templo de la Compañía (Mon–Fri 9am–5pm, Sat 9am–1pm).
Taxis Linea Dorada ⓣ473/732-9172.
Tours Transportes Turísticos de Guanajuato, Bajos de la Basilíca 2 (ⓣ473/732-2134), across from the tourist office, offers a range of tours (and can provide English-speaking guides). City tours start at M$100 pesos (4hr), excluding entrance fees. Daily 8.30am–9pm.

Dolores Hidalgo and around

Fifty kilometres or so from both Guanajuato and San Miguel de Allende, **DOLORES HIDALGO** is as ancient and as historically rich as either of its southern neighbours. This was Father Hidalgo's parish, and it was from the church in the main plaza here that the historic **Grito de la Independencia** ("Cry of Independence") was first issued in 1810 (see box, p.282). The town celebrates the event annually with the **Fiestas de Septiembre**, ten days of cultural and sporting events, music and fireworks, culminating with the *Grito* around dawn on the sixteenth.

Perhaps because of its less spectacular location or maybe because there is no university or major language school, Dolores hasn't seen a fraction of the tourist development that has overtaken other places in the Bajío (despite becoming yet another "Pueblo Mágico" in 2002). It's a good bet, though, for a one-night stopover, and if you can't find accommodation in Guanajuato or San Miguel, this is certainly the place to head; you'll get a better room here for appreciably less. True, there is less to see, but it's an elegant little town and thoroughly Mexican; it's busy, too, as it sits on a traditionally important crossroads on the silver route from Zacatecas.

Just a couple of blocks from the bus station as you walk along Hidalgo towards the central plaza, the **Casa Hidalgo** (Tues–Sat 10am–5.45pm, Sun 9am–4.45pm; M$31, free Sun), the great man's home between 1804 and 1810, was rebuilt after the Spanish destroyed it and has been converted into a museum devoted to his life, very much a point of pilgrimage for Mexicans on day trips. It's a bit heavy on written tributes from various groups to the "Father of Independence" and on copies of other correspondence he either sent or received – but it's edifying nonetheless and includes a few highlights such as his letter of excommunication from the Inquisition less than a month after the *Grito*. Continuing in the same direction, you come to a beautifully laid-out plaza, overlooked by the exuberant facade of the famous church, the **Parroquia de Nuestra Señora de los Dolores**, where a left turn takes you to the **Museo de la Independencia Nacional**, Zacatecas 6 (daily 9am–5pm; M$15, free Sun). Inside, vibrant, graphic murals depict significant scenes from Mexican history from the Aztec perception of the world through to the many indigenous rebellions against Spain and the life of Hidalgo. Don't miss the glass cabinets filled with record sleeves and cowboy boots

The Grito de la Independencia

On the night of September 15, 1810, **Padre Miguel Hidalgo y Costilla** and some of his fellow leaders of the Independence movement, warned by messengers from Querétaro that their intention to raise a rebellion against Spanish rule had been discovered, decided to bring their plans forward. At dawn on September 16, Hidalgo, tolling the church bell, called his parishioners together and addressed them from the balcony of the church with an impassioned speech ending in the **Grito de la Independencia**, "¡Mexicanos, Viva México!" This cry is now repeated every year by the president in Mexico City and by politicians all over the country at midnight on September 15, as the starting point for Independence Day celebrations. September 16 remains the one day of the year when the bell in Dolores Hidalgo's parish church is rung; however, the bell in place today is a copy of the original, which was either melted down for munitions or hangs in the Palacio Nacional in Mexico City, depending on which story you believe.

that pay homage to the greatest *ranchera* singer of all time, José Alfredo Jimenez, another of Dolores's native sons, who died in 1973.

Practicalities

Dolores is connected to both San Miguel Allende (45min) and Guanajuato (1hr 30min) by regular, rapid second-class **buses** to and from the Flecha Amarilla terminal, on Hidalgo beside the river. Herradura de Plata also has a terminal a block away at the corner of Chiapas and Yucatán, from where buses run every thirty minutes south to San Miguel de Allende and Mexico City. There's little need to visit Dolores's small **tourist office** (daily 10am–4pm; ⓣ418/182-1164, ⓦwww.dolores-hidalgo.com.mx), on the main plaza by the church, but they can give advice on where to buy the town's famous **ceramics**.

Finding a room is seldom a problem except during the week leading up to September 16, when the town is packed. The cheapest of the local **hotels** is *Posada Dolores*, Yucatán 8, past the Independence Museum and then left (ⓣ418/182-0642), easily missed behind a small doorway, with basic, dingy rooms downstairs (❶) and better rooms upstairs, with TV (❷). The best budget accommodation in town is *Hotel CasaMia*, San Luis Potosí 9-B at Oaxaca (ⓣ418/182-2560, ⓦwww.hotelcasamia.com.mx; ❸), , which offers simple but modern, spotless double rooms with tiled floors, bathroom, cable TV and fan. Slightly more upscale places are all good value: try *Posada Cocomacan*, Plaza Principal 4 (ⓣ418/182-6086, ⓦwww.posadacocomacan.com.mx; ❹), with its cool interior, cable TV and some rooms overlooking the plaza.

You can also **eat** well around the plaza, notably at artsy *La Taberna*, where most dishes are less than M$20, and colonial-style *El Carruaje*, which does a tasty *menu del día* (M$75) and weekend buffets (M$60–100) and has live music in the evenings. Dolores Hidalgo is also home to the country's most unusual **ice-cream** flavours: Mexicans come in droves to the Plaza Principal to lick scoops of creamy alfalfa, *mole*, *cerveza*, shrimp and avocado (fortunately most vendors let you sample before you commit to a full cone).

East of Dolores: Pozos and San José Iturbide

The intriguing half-deserted settlement of **Pozos** and historic town of **San José Iturbide** make easy and absorbing excursions from Dolores. Both can be reached from **San Luis de la Paz**, 40km northeast of Dolores: frequent bus services connect the three towns, as well as south to Querétaro or San Miguel de Allende. Taxis from San Miguel will charge around M$750 for a round trip (up to six people) to Pozos.

Pozos

Just 14km south of San Luis, the road to San José passes through what was once a rich and flourishing mining community called Real de Pozos. Now just known as **POZOS** (and officially, Mineral de Pozos), it is often referred to as a ghost-town, though in reality it is far from dead, with around 3,500 people living in the streets clustered around the gaping maw of half a church.

While you shouldn't expect swinging doors flapping in the breeze and tumbleweed gusting through the streets, you will find vast areas of collapsed masonry inhabited only by the odd burro. In the last decade or so the village has undergone a bit of a revival and is fast becoming a sub-colony of San Miguel de Allende, with foreigners buying up property; the town has five restaurants, three hotels, around ten art galleries and numerous North American artists (many of whom are part-timers). Yet crumbling ruins still outnumber the development – for now at least – and the town's edges, fringed with desert, mine workings and abandoned haciendas, remain an enchanting, if potentially dangerous, place. Many tunnels are unmarked and if hiking, take extra care. Check ⓦwww.mineraldepozos.com for the latest information.

If the prospect of moody walks isn't enough to entice you to **stay**, you might just be tempted by *Casa Mexicana*, Juárez 2 on the Plaza Principal (ⓣ442/293-0014, ⓦwww.casamexicanahotel.com; ❺), a five-bedroom B&B with exquisite and highly individual rooms set around a blossom-filled garden, and with an on-site art gallery. Expertly prepared meals are also served to non-guests, or you could just drop in for a margarita. Your other choice is the cleverly restored *Posada de la Minas*, a colonial mansion one block from the plaza at Manuel Doblado 1 (ⓣ442/293-0213, ⓦwww.posadadelasminas.com; ❻) with inviting rooms and suites ranging from M$650 to M$1110. The third hotel, *Casa Montana*, at Plaza Principal 4, is expected to reopen under new ownership in 2010. In addition to the B&B restaurants, one of the best places to **eat** is *Los Famosas de Pozos*, Hidalgo 10B (daily 11am–8pm; ⓣ442/293-0112) which serves Mexican and American food, and home-made pies and ice cream (it's also an art gallery). *La Pila Seca* at Aldama 8 does big breakfasts from M$40, while tiny *El Portal* on the plaza does cheap snacks and burgers.

San José Iturbide

Further south and 50km from San Luis, **SAN JOSÉ ITURBIDE** is an immaculate town centred on a tidy plaza, chiefly distinguished by its behemoth Neoclassical **church**, dedicated to Agustín de Iturbide, a local opportunist who started the War of Independence as a general loyal to Spain – inflicting major defeats on Morelos – only to change sides later. Having helped secure Mexico's Independence without any concomitant reform, he briefly declared himself emperor in 1822. The plaque reads, accurately enough, "from one of the few towns which have not forgotten you".

There's little reason to stay, but if you just fancy a night in a small ordinary Mexican town with good **accommodation**, then try the excellent *Hotel Los Arcos*, Plaza Principal 10, right by the church (ⓣ419/198-0330, ⓔhotellosarcos@sanjoseiturbide.com; ❹), with large, modern, carpeted rooms. There's also the convenient, comfortable but basic *Hotel Unión*, Callejón Olivera 10, two blocks along Allende (ⓣ419/198-0071; ❹). The best meals in town are in the **restaurant** at *Los Arcos*, and at *El Diezmo* (ⓣ419/198-0645) another hotel at Nicolas Campa 16, which has wonderful views of the church.

San Miguel de Allende

Set on a steep hillside overlooking the Río Laja and dominated by red rooftops and domed churches, **SAN MIGUEL DE ALLENDE** might seem little different from any other quaint colonial town. Its distinct character, though, is soon apparent: San Miguel's primary function today is as a picture-perfect version of Mexico for tourists (a *Starbucks* even graces the plaza), and it's home to hundreds of artists and writers, as well as flocks of foreign students drawn to the town's several language and arts schools. More visibly – like Álamos (p.148) and several towns in Baja California – it has attracted a large population of US and Canadian **expats** (mostly retirees) and property prices here are on a par with San Francisco. The influx can be, in part, attributed to Tony Cohan's popular book *On Mexican Time*, which tells the story of a writer and his artist wife who abandon smog-ridden Los Angeles for a quieter life in San Miguel, where they restore an old house, learn the local lifestyle and are slowly seduced by the colonial city's unique charm. Now something like ten percent of the population are foreigners, some ten thousand of whom live in the vicinity more or less permanently, generally in peaceful co-existence with the locals.

Yet despite all this, San Miguel retains an undeniable charm; the colonial centre remains wonderfully preserved architecturally, and still serves as the spiritual centre of the Mexican community – get up at dawn and its cobbled, hilly streets are hauntingly beautiful and quite unlike anything else in the Baíjo. There are few major sights, but the whole town (which has been a national monument since 1926, hence no new buildings, no flashing signs and no traffic lights) is crowded with old seigneurial mansions and curious churches. For all its popularity (and there are often more Mexican tourists here than foreigners), the town is a pleasant place to rest up for a while in comfort – assuming you have plenty of cash.

The town was founded in 1542 by a Franciscan friar, Juan de San Miguel, and as "San Miguel El Grande" became an important supply centre for the big mining towns, and a stopover on the main silver route from Zacatecas. The name was later changed to honour **Ignacio Allende**, a native who became Hidalgo's chief lieutenant during the 1810 Revolution. What got it started as a magnet for foreigners, though, was the foundation in 1938 of the Escuela Universitaria de Bellas Artes by Peruvian artist Felipe Cossio del Pomar, an arts foundation that enjoyed an enormous boost after World War II when returning American GIs found that their education grants could be stretched much further in Mexico; Pomar re-located the school in 1950 as today's well-respected Instituto Allende.

The country hereabouts is still ranching territory, though even this is increasingly being taken over by tourist activities: attractions include hot springs, a nearby golf course, horseriding at a couple of dude ranches and mountain-biking.

Arrival and information

San Miguel has surprisingly poor long-distance bus connections, but this is still the easiest way to arrive, perhaps expedited by a change at Guanajuato or Querétaro (which have frequent services to San Miguel). The **bus station** (with small guardería) is about 2km west of the centre, from where there are **taxis** (M$30–35 into the centre; fix the price first as there are no meters), and regular local buses (marked "Centro–Central"; M$5) that run into town along Canal. San Miguel's closest **airport** is near León (see p.267), from where English-speaking Viajes San Miguel, Sollano 4 (Mon–Fri 9am–2.30pm & 4.30–7pm, Sat 10am–2pm; ⓣ415/152-2537, ⓦwww.viajessanmiguel.com), runs a shuttle van (reserve in advance) meeting most flights for US$30 or peso-equivalent. It also runs a US$70 shuttle service to the airport in Mexico City.

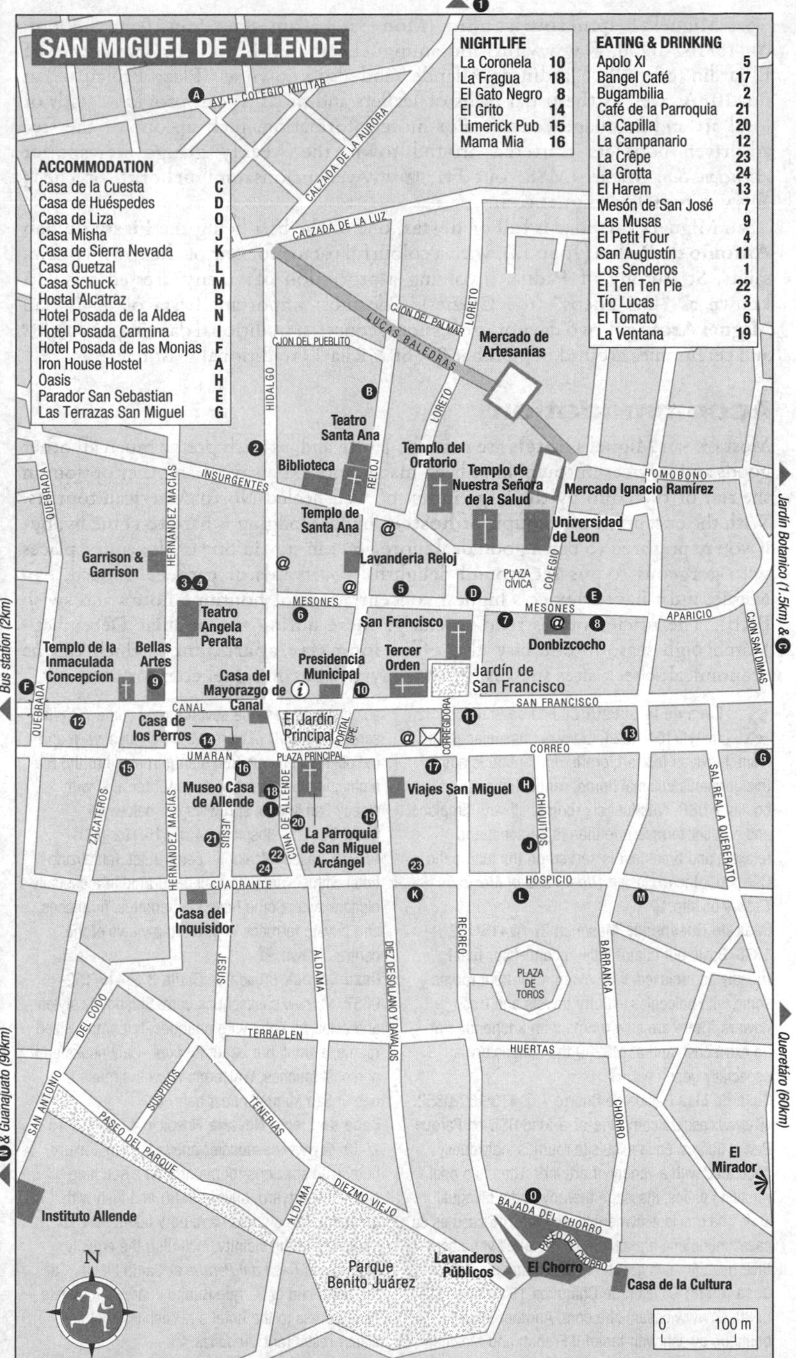
SAN MIGUEL DE ALLENDE
NIGHTLIFE
La Coronela 10
La Fragua 18
El Gato Negro 8
El Grito 14
Limerick Pub 15
Mama Mia 16
EATING & DRINKING
Apolo XI 5
Bangel Café 17
Bugambilia 2
Café de la Parroquia 21
La Capilla 20
La Campanario 12
La Crêpe 23
La Grotta 24
El Harem 13
Mesón de San José 7
Las Musas 9
El Petit Four 4
San Augustín 11
Los Senderos 1
El Ten Ten Pie 22
Tío Lucas 3
El Tomato 6
La Ventana 19
ACCOMMODATION
Casa de la Cuesta C
Casa de Huéspedes D
Casa de Liza O
Casa Misha J
Casa de Sierra Nevada K
Casa Quetzal L
Casa Schuck M
Hostal Alcatraz B
Hotel Posada de la Aldea N
Hotel Posada Carmina I
Hotel Posada de las Monjas F
Iron House Hostel A
Oasis H
Parador San Sebastian E
Las Terrazas San Miguel G
Mercado de Artesanías
Teatro Santa Ana
Biblioteca
Templo del Oratorio
Templo de Nuestra Señora de la Salud
Mercado Ignacio Ramírez
Templo de Santa Ana
Universidad de Leon
Garrison & Garrison
Lavanderia Reloj
Teatro Angela Peralta
San Francisco
Donbizcocho
Templo de la Inmaculada Concepcion
Bellas Artes
Presidencia Municipal
Tercer Orden
Jardín de San Francisco
Casa del Mayorazgo de Canal
Casa de los Perros
El Jardín Principal
Museo Casa de Allende
Viajes San Miguel
La Parroquia de San Miguel Arcángel
Casa del Inquisidor
Plaza de Toros
Plaza Cívica
Plaza Principal
El Mirador
Instituto Allende
Parque Benito Juárez
Lavanderos Públicos
El Chorro
Casa de la Cultura
Av. H. Colegio Militar
Calzada de la Aurora
Calzada de la Luz
Lucas Baledras
Cjon del Palmar
Cjon del Pueblito
Loreto
Hidalgo
Reloj
Insurgentes
Homobono
Quebrada
Hernandez Macias
Mesones
Colegio
Aparicio
Cjon San Dimas
Canal
San Francisco
Portal Gpe
Corregidora
Umaran
Correo
Sal Real a Queretaro
Zacateros
Jesus
Cuna de Allende
Chiquitos
Cuadrante
Hospicio
Recreo
Aldama
Diez de Sollano y Davalos
Barranca
Terraplen
Huertas
Del Codo
San Antonio
Suspiros
Tenerias
Paseo del Parque
Diezmo Viejo
Chorro
Bajada del Chorro
Paseo del Chorro
Bus station (2km)
Jardín Botanico (1.5km) & C
Querétaro (60km)
N & Guanajuato (90km)
0 100 m
N

San Miguel's helpful **tourist office** (Mon–Sat 8.30am–8pm, Sun 10am–5.30pm; Ⓣ415/152-0900, Ⓦwww.turismosanmiguel.com.mx) is on the north corner of El Jardín (officially "Jardín de Allende" and also known as "Plaza Principal") at no. 10. As well as the usual racks of leaflets and maps, it can provide details of local art and language courses. For more information, pick up one of the free ad-driven booklets scattered around town, the weekly gringo **newspaper** *Atención San Miguel* (M$8; out Fri; Ⓦwww.atencionsanmiguel.org), or check Ⓦwww.portalsanmiguel.com.

San Miguel's calendar is full of **fiestas**, one of the best being the **Fiesta de San Antonio de Padua** (June 13), with a colourful parade for one of the town's patron saints, St Antony of Padua, involving a procession of crazily dressed revellers known as "Los Locos" (the Crazies). The most important fiesta of all is **San Miguel Arcángel** two days of processions, concerts, traditional dancing, bullfights and ceremonies around September 29, St Michael's traditional feast day.

Accommodation

Most of San Miguel's **hotels** are near the Jardín and, as with pretty much all other goods and services in town, have been made more expensive than other options in the rest of the Bajío by the large influx of well-heeled North American tourists. With the exception of a couple of **hostels**, budget lodging is hard to come by, but if you're prepared to pay a good deal more you can stay in one of dozens of places with gorgeous rooms set around delightful courtyards or gardens. Indeed, San Miguel must have Mexico's highest concentrations of boutique hotels and swish B&Bs. The pricier places tend to charge more during the popular December–March high season. The city also offers **long-stay apartments**, which can be economical; check sites such as Ⓦwww.myrentalinsanmiguel.com for ideas.

Casa de la Cuesta Cuesta de San José 32 Ⓣ415/154-4324, Ⓦwww.casadelacuesta.com. Mexican folk-art, crafts and antiques adorn this gorgeous colonial home, renovated as a boutique B&B. With just six rooms, all with fireplace and outdoor terrace attention is personal and relaxed, and breakfast is served on the lush patio. Check out the exclusive *Other Face of Mexico Gallery* on site. ❾

Casa de Huéspedes Mesones 27 Ⓣ415/152-1378. Basic but quaint little second-floor hotel: friendly and relaxed, with clean, well-kept rooms – some with balconies – fluffy towels and fresh flowers. There are also rooms with kitchenette at no extra cost, and at M$200 the singles are an especially good deal. ❸

Casa de Liza Bajada de Chorro 7 Ⓣ415/152-0352, Ⓦwww.casaliza.com. One-of-a-kind B&B on Parque Benito Juárez. Each exquisite room is individually decorated with a variety of artwork. There's a pool, rambling patios, massage therapy and a bilingual staff. The gracious owners live by the "mi casa es su casa" motto and are all too happy to tell you about their most famous guest: Antonio Banderas. ❻

Casa Misha Callejón de Chiquitos 15 Ⓣ415/152-0580, Ⓦwww.casamisha.com. Another luxury boutique awash with tasteful French and Mexican colonial antiques; the seven rooms come with flat-screen TVs, DVD players, MP3 hookups, wi-fi and patios that spill out onto lush gardens, but the real highlight is breakfast on the roof terrace, with sleepy San Miguel sprawled out below. ❾

Casa Quetzal Hospicio 34 Ⓣ415/152-0501, Ⓦwww.casaquetzalhotel.com. Quiet, tantalizing hotel with seven suites, all decorated in a casually elegant style. Some have kitchenettes, fireplaces and private terraces with rooftop views of the centre of town. ❼

Casa Schuck Bajada de Garita 3 Ⓣ415/152-0657, Ⓦwww.casaschuck.com. Splendidly styled and colourful hotel with antiques, ten amply sized rooms, a small but beautiful pool, leafy nooks and personal touches. Welcoming owners make this one of San Miguel's best bets. ❾

Casa de Sierra Nevada Hospicio 42 Ⓣ415/152-7040, Ⓦwww.casadesierranevada.com. Luxury hotel with spacious rooms around a soothing colonial courtyard, built in 1580 and lush with greenery. The owners have now taken over six mansions in the vicinity, including the equally sumptuous *Casa del Parque* at Santa Elena 2, at the north end of Parque Benito Juárez. All guests have access to the hotel's refreshing pool and classy restaurant, *Andanza*. ❾

Hostal Alcatraz Relox 54 ⓣ415/152-8543, ⓦwww.geocities.com/alcatrazhostel/. Central and welcoming hostel with all the expected amenities, including kitchen, luggage storage, internet access (free) and wi-fi. Dorms M$110/person. ❶

Hotel Posada de la Aldea Ancha de San Antonio 15 ⓣ415/152-1022, ⓦwww.naftaconnect.com/hotellaaldea. Clean and comfortable a/c rooms all have modern amenities in this enormous hotel popular with Mexican tourists. There's a pool, tennis courts and parking, but its main virtue is being opposite the Instituto Allende and it's (relatively) reasonable rates. ❺

Hotel Posada Carmina Cuna de Allende 7, a few metres south of the Jardín ⓣ415/152-0458, ⓦwww.posadacarmina.com. Large rooms with brick floors, high ceilings and white walls are set amid yet more colonial splendour around an congenial restaurant (*La Felguera*, open till 5pm); there are cheaper but still very comfy, remodelled rooms in an adjacent wing – all come with flat-screen satellite TVs and free wi-fi (though signal is weak beyond the courtyard). You can't beat its location, one block from the Jardín, and the staff are friendly and very helpful. ❻

Hotel Posada de las Monjas Canal 37 ⓣ415/152-0171, ⓦwww.posadalasmonjas.com. Decent mid-range choice, with simple but adequate motel-like rooms (no TVs) set in the rambling remains of an old monastery – some are small and cell-like, though, so look before paying (the best rooms look over the roof terrace); also has parking, restaurant and laundry. ❹

Iron House Hostel Colegio Militar 17-D ⓣ415/154 -6108, ⓦwww.geocities.com/hostelsma. Small, friendly hostel about a 10min walk north of town in a quiet suburb. There are dorms, private rooms, a decent kitchen and free internet access (with wi-fi). Owner Ricardo is usually up for joining his guests for a night on the town, and on Tues and Wed (7–9pm) leads free salsa lessons at *Mama Mia*. English spoken but Spanish encouraged. Dorms M$100/person. ❸

Oasis Callejón de Chiquitos 1-A ⓣ415/154-9850, ⓦwww.oasissanmiguel.com. Congenial hosts preside over this expensive but enticing four-suite boutique, with lavish rooms embellished with Mudéjar daybeds, four-posters, fireplaces, flat screen TVs and DVD players. The gourmet breakfasts are an event, and the complimentary tea and pastries served throughout the day add a refined touch. ❾

Parador San Sebastian Mesones 7 ⓣ415/152-7084. Cool and tranquil, with simple rooms around a colonial courtyard. Ask for one of the larger rooms at no extra cost – a huge bargain. ❸

Las Terrazas San Miguel Santo Domingo 3 ⓣ415/152-5028, ⓦwww.terrazassanmiguel.com. These four luxurious *casas* on the hillside, four blocks from the plaza, come with kitchen, cable TV, bathrooms, wi-fi and private terraces; breakfast and a bottle of wine on arrival are included. Fabulous option for families or groups. ❽

The Town

Head first to **El Jardín Principal**, San Miguel's main plaza, which is within walking distance of almost everything you'll want to see and the main focus of activity in town – on Sundays traditional Mexican bands play live music throughout the afternoon. The **Instituto Allende**, south of the centre and a fairly easy walk from here, is an alternative hub, and an especially useful source of information for anyone who wants to stay in San Miguel longer than a couple of days.

Wherever you go in town, it seems that any place that's not a café or restaurant is operating as some kind of gallery or **artesanía** shop. The stores offer a bewildering array of top-notch goods from all over Mexico – prices are correspondingly high, some even bordering on extortionate. There are really too many quality places to be very specific, but as a starting point, try Canal, Umarán and Zacateros streets immediately south and west of the Jardín.

El Jardín

The most famous of the city's landmarks, **La Parroquia de San Miguel Arcángel** (daily 6am–9pm) – the parish church – takes up one side of the Jardín. This gloriously over-the-top structure, with a towering pseudo-Gothic facade bristling with turrets and spires, was rebuilt in 1880 by a self-taught Indian stonemason Zeferino Gutiérrez. Gutiérrez supposedly learned about architecture by studying postcards of great French cathedrals and then drew diagrams in the dust to explain to his workers what he wanted, and the church does seem to reflect the French penchant for neo-Gothic architecture at that time. Inside, the patterned tilework of the floor, the *azulejos* along the walls and the pure semicircular vaulting along the nave exhibit distinct Moorish influences. Look out for the *Cristo de la Conquista*, a revered sixteenth-century image of Christ, and the small shrine to San Judas Tadeo, littered with small photos and votive offerings. Ex-president Anastasio Bustamante (1790–1853) spent his last days in San Miguel, and is buried in the crypt.

Opposite the church is a block containing the former **Presidencia Municipal** (site of Mexico's first independent city council in 1810), and the **Galería San Miguel**, one of the most prestigious of the many galleries showing local artists' work. The remaining two sides of the square are lined with covered *portales*, under whose arches vendors of drinks and trinkets shelter from the sun, with a row of shops behind them. On the Jardín, too, are some of San Miguel's most distinguished mansions, all of them – like almost every home in San Miguel – built in the Spanish style. The **Casa de Don Ignacio de Allende**, on the corner of Allende and Umarán, was the birthplace of the Independence hero: a plaque notes *Hic natus ubique notus* – "here was born he who is famous everywhere". The house now operates as the **Museo Histórico de San Miguel de Allende** (Tues–Sun 9am–5pm; M$37, free Sun), completely renovated in 2009, with a five-minute introductory video and a ground floor of fossils, pots and diagrams exploring Mexico's pre-Hispanic and colonial past, naturally concentrating on the San Miguel area and the great man himself. The second floor has been restored in period style, to reflect the lives of wealthy townsfolk in the eighteenth century, with an oratory, kitchen and various living rooms ending with a small exhibit on the start of the 1810 uprising.

Around the next corner, at Canal 4, you can see the **Casa del Mayorazgo de la Canal** (now a Banamex) with an elaborately carved doorway and elegant wrought-iron grilles over the windows. Near here, too, just half a block down Umarán at no. 4, is the Casa del Insurgente, former home of revolutionary hero Juan de Mafuele, but better known as the **Casa de los Perros**, for its central balcony supported by little stone dogs.

East and north of El Jardín

Leave the Jardín to the east and head uphill on San Francisco to where the streets seem less affected by outsiders – Spanish or *norteamericano*. The architecture is still colonial, but the life that continues around the battered buildings seems cast in a more ancient mould. A block along San Francisco, the elaborate churrigueresque facade of the church of **San Francisco** contrasts sharply with its Neoclassical towers (added in 1799 by Francisco Tresguerras), tiled dome and plain interior, and quite overshadows the modest simplicity of its smaller neighbour, seventeenth-century **Tercer Orden** (usually closed).

Behind and to the north, San Miguel's old market area has been refurbished to create the Plaza Cívica (formerly the Plaza de la Soledad), complete with a huge equestrian statue of Allende – you'll usually see clumps of students near here, outside the Ex-Convento de San Franciso de Salas, now part of the Universidad de León. Next door, the **Templo de Nuesta Señora de la Salud**, with its unusual concave facade topped by a scallop-shell pediment, was completed in the eighteenth century as the college chapel. Further to the left sits the **Templo del Oratorio de San Felipe Neri** (daily 6.30am–1pm & 5.30–8.30pm), its Baroque facade showing signs of native influence – presumably the legacy of indigenous labourers – but the main interest lies inside in a series of oil paintings, among them a group of 33 depicting the life of St Philip Neri, and an image to the right of the altar of the Virgen de Guadalupe attributed to Miguel Cabrera. The main altar itself is another creation of Zeferino Gutiérrez. One of its chapels inside, the gilded **Santa Casa de Loreto** (daily 7–9am & 6–8pm), is a copy of the Santa Casa di Loreto in Italy, and was put up by the Conde Manuel de la Canal in 1735.

The **Mercado Ignacio Ramirez** lies north of here and has managed to remain almost entirely traditional, with fruit, vegetables, medicinal herbs, pots and pans all on display, though little exists specifically for tourists among the cramped tables with their low canvas awnings. Official market day is Sunday, but no one seems to have told the locals, and it's pretty busy all week. Behind the regular market along **Andador Lucas Balderas** lies the **Mercado de Artesanías**, crammed with the sort of handicrafts you see all over Mexico (folk art, pottery, colourful textiles, cut glass, papier-mâché and silver jewellery), though little of what's here seems especially good value. You'll find much more exciting goods in the many crafts shops around town.

From the Oratorio de San Felipe Neri you can head west along Insurgentes to the **Biblioteca Pública**, Insurgentes 25 (Mon–Fri 10am–7pm, Sat 10am–2pm; ⓣ415/152-0293, ⓦwww.bibliotecasma.com), which lends a substantial collection of books in English (see "Listings", p.293, for more details). They also sell a number of cheap secondhand books on Thursdays – either duplicates or those deemed too lightweight for preservation in the library. Inside the library, the *Café Santa Ana* offers a quiet space to sit down and read, while on Sundays you can join the popular **House and Garden Tour** (buy tickets between 11am and noon; M$200; 2hr), which takes you inside two or three historic private homes each week. You should also enquire here about the programme at the library's **Teatro Santa Ana**, which shows movies and plays.

Bellas Artes

The Centro Cultural Ignacio Ramírez "El Nigromante" (also known as **Bellas Artes**; daily 9am–7pm; free; ⓣ415/152-0289) is at Hernández Macías 75, just one block downhill from the Jardín. Housed in the romantic cloistered courtyard of the 1765 **Convento de la Concepción**, it's an arts institute run by the state fine-arts organization (replacing the original school established by Felipe Cossio del Pomar here in 1938), concentrating on music and dance, but to a lesser extent teaching visual arts, too. Mexicans can take courses here for virtually nothing; foreigners pay rather more (prices vary, but reckon on around M$50 for most classes). Around the courtyard there are various exhibitions, and several murals, including an entire room covered in vivid, abstract designs by **Davíd Alfaro Siqueiros** from the 1940s. Dedicated to the life of Ignacio Allende, the mural was left unfinished after Siqueiros fell out with the school's owner. There's also the lovely *Las Musas* café (see p.292). The **Templo de la Immaculada Concepción**, part of the complex, is nice, too, and notable mainly for its tall dome raised on a drum, again said to be the work of the untrained Zeferino Gutiérrez in 1891, this time modelled on Les Invalides in Paris (no doubt via postcard).

Instituto Allende and around

The **Instituto Allende** (ⓣ415/152-0190, ⓦwww.instituto-allende.edu.mx) lies down at the bottom of the hill at San Antonio 22, following Hernández Macías south from La Concepción. On the way, at the corner of Cuadrante, you pass the **Casa del Inquisidor**, Cuadrante 36, an eighteenth-century mansion with a particularly fine facade (you can't go inside), and opposite, the old building that served as a jail for the Inquisition. The Instituto itself, on the edges of the old town, occupies a former 1730s hacienda of the Condes de la Canal – it was established here in 1950 by Felipe Cossio

▲ San Miguel de Allende

del Pomar and was later accredited by the University of Guanajuato. It offers courses in all kinds of arts, from painting to sculpture to photography, in crafts like silverwork and weaving, and Spanish-language instruction at every level (see p.294), all within verdant, park-like grounds. There's a café down here, too, and an office dealing with long-term accommodation.

El Chorro

Ten minutes' walk immediately south of town, shaded **Parque Benito Juárez** was created out of the fruit orchards that belonged to many of the city's old families. The homes round about are still some of the fanciest in town. From here it's an uphill walk to **El Chorro**, the little hill whose springs supply the city with water, and the site of the town originally founded by Juan de San Miguel. Here you'll find the **Lavanderos Públicos**, a series of twenty old-fashioned tubs where some locals still come to do their washing (and gossip). From the *lavandería* the Paseo del Chorro winds uphill to a series of seven former public bathhouses, which now form part of the **Casa de la Cultura** (Mon–Fri 9am–8pm, Sat 4–8pm; ⓦwww.casadelacultura.spaces.live.com), another popular location for classes, events and shows (check the website). To get the best views over town you'll have to climb higher (follow Bajada de Charro) to **El Mirador**, the viewing point on the road to Querétaro, where there's a little belvedere, a small café and San Miguel spread out below, with the broad plain and a ridge of mountains behind.

Jardín Botánico

When you've had your fill of swanky cafés and artesanía shopping, consider spending a few hours at the **Jardín Botánico**, 1.5km northeast of town (daily dawn–dusk; M$30; ⓦwww.elcharco.org.mx). Officially known as **El Charco del Ingenio**, it sprawls over the hill above town, just behind a suburb of some of San Miguel's finest new homes, almost all colonial in execution but with every amenity. The garden itself resembles almost any patch of northern Mexico desert (it is meant to), but comes heavily planted with various types of cactus, which has made it incomparably richer botanically than the surrounding desert. Around 10km of grassy paths wind through, some accessible to mountain bikes. If you're here around a full moon, check the website for details of the *temazcales*, ritual herb steam baths built within the garden, and open to the public (around M$250, reservations required; ⓣ415/154-8838).

To **get to** the Jardín Botánico, follow Homobono east from the market, walking steeply uphill taking the left turn when it forks. After ten minutes or so you reach one of the pedestrian entrances. **Taxis** are M$25.

Eating and drinking

Eating in San Miguel can be an expensive business; even local staples such as cappuccinos and margaritas are likely to cost half as much again as they would in, say, Querétaro and to find a decent supermarket or grocery store you'll have to take a taxi or bus to the outskirts. The **mercado** (see p.289) has the usual budget choices (tortas, tacos, *jugos* and the like), but nothing special. Still, San Miguel's **restaurants** can be a tremendous relief for long-term travellers, with loads of stuff you may not have tasted for weeks and a surprising array of **vegetarian** options. The plentiful **cafés** are alive with students and expats who often seem to do little but hang out in such places all day – which is not a bad idea. The food quality is excellent, and with delicate gringo stomachs in mind, many places prominently advertise their assiduous use of sanitized water.

Apolo XI Mesones 43 ⓣ415/154-6252. Head upstairs here for ultra-casual, cheap *carnitas* (sold by the kilo) served on an open-air terrace. The hot and vinegary house pickles will curl your toes.

Bugambilia Hidalgo 42 ⓣ415/152-0127. Longstanding, charming courtyard restaurant. Tuck into beautifully prepared Mexican dishes such as warm goat's cheese topped with toasted almonds, followed by chicken in tamarind or mole sauce, or *chiles en nogada* – expect to pay around M$500 for two, cheaper than most of the city's posh restaurants. There's usually live acoustic guitar music. Daily 1–10pm.

Café de la Parroquia Jesús 11 ⓣ415/152-3161. A great little place with seats inside or in the courtyard, justly popular with expats for breakfasts of hotcakes or yogurt and fruit (around M$40). Good Mexican food served as well – tamales, *chilaquiles* and the like for M$50–80 – and coffee all day long. Becomes dinner spot *La Brasserie* at night. Tues–Sat 8am–4pm, Sun 8am–2pm.

La Campanario Canal 34 ⓣ415/152-0775. Another upmarket place noted for its fresh seafood: red snapper and trout are usually solid choices, but lobster and shrimp also feature heavily and the sauces are all exquisite. Eat within a converted colonial hacienda, or preferably on the stunning rooftop terrace, which overlooks the Concepción church. Open 1–11pm, closed Thurs.

La Capilla Cuna de Allende 10, steps from the Jardín ⓣ415/152-0698. San Miguel's most spectacular dining experience. Housed in what

San Miguel's cultural calendar

Film and music **festivals** pepper the year in San Miguel, kicking off with the Festival Internacional de Cine Expresión en Corto (third week of July; ⓦwww.expresionencorto.com), a week-long short-film festival that's rapidly gaining worldwide recognition. The quarter-century-old Festival de Música de Cámara (Chamber Music Festival; first two weeks in Aug; ⓣ415/154-8722, ⓦwww.chambermusicfestival.com) features a range of performances by internationally acclaimed musicians. The Festival Internacional de Jazz & Blues (last week of Nov/first week Dec; ⓦwww.sanmigueljazz.com) includes two shows nightly by international performers at various locations in town from M$250 up. At other times, check out the programme at the Teatro Ángela Peralta at Mesones 82 (ⓣ415/152-2200), which typically hosts ballet, theatre and occasional performances of classical music throughout the year.

was once part of the town's main chapel, this lovingly restored two-storey restaurant has a thoughtful menu featuring international and local specialities made with seasonal ingredients, such as pumpkin soup and roast duck, with rooftop dining under the cathedral spires. It's not cheap (main dishes range M$200–330) but it's worth every peso. Reservations recommended. Closed Tues.

La Crêpe Hospicio 37 ⓣ415/154-9435. The delicious crepes prepared at this small café with a laid-back patio have a fanatical following and rightly so; there's a huge variety of sweet or savoury fillings (try the Bombay curry or *ratatouille*), and the crepes are as delicate as anything you get in France. It also serves a variety of soups, salads and fish. Mon, Tues & Thurs–Sat 1–10pm, Sun 11–4pm.

La Grotta Cuadrante 5 ⓣ415/152-4119. Terrific pasta and pizza joint, now expanded to a cosy room with red-washed walls and kitchen pans hanging from the ceiling. The home-made pasta dishes (M$95) are tasty but no match for the crispy pizza and calzone. Also fresh salads and a small selection of *secondi piatti*.

El Harem Murillo 7 at Correo. Lebanese restaurant serving hummus with pita bread (M$35), lamb brochettes (M$75) and stuffed vine leaves. Only one table on the ground floor, but the upstairs patio offers more room and great views. Coffee-ground "readings" a bonus. Closed Tues.

Mesón de San José Mesones 38 ⓣ415/152-3848. Another top-notch patio restaurant serving quality Mexican breakfasts (from M$50) and lunch for M$75–100, including several cheaper vegetarian choices such as pastas and cheese enchiladas (M$50–70). Mon–Sat 9am–5pm, Sun 8am–4pm.

Las Musas in the Bellas Artes complex. Thoughtfully sited café away from the traffic noise, where students take a break over coffee (M$20), sandwiches, ice cream and croissants (pastries from M$28).

El Petit Four Mesones 99 ⓣ415/154-4010. Delightful little French *patisserie* with a few tables where you can tuck into a *pain au chocolat* or a slice of *tarte aux pommes* with your espresso. Superb raspberry tarts. Closed Mon.

San Augustín San Francisco 21 ⓣ415/154-9102. Owned by a retired Mexico City *telenovela* star, this tempting café is especially known for its sugary, fried *churros* eaten with hot chocolate – either sweet Spanish, semi-sweet French or Mexican, flavoured with cinnamon (M$35). Get a table with a view of the San Francisco church.

Los Senderos Carretera San Miguel Allende–Dolores (2.5km from downtown) ⓣ415/155-9571, ⓦwww.los-senderos.com. The taxi journey out here is rewarded by a delicious organic menu featuring items such as roast beef sandwiches (M$160), coconut shrimp (M$140) and weekend brunch from M$120. Wed–Sun lunch, dinner by reservation only.

El Ten Ten Pie Cuna de Allende 21 ⓣ415/152-7189. Small café with walls covered in the work of local artists, serving good Mexican staples from M$50 and an extensive M$80 comida – expats like to sip drinks on the street-side patio opposite.

Tío Lucas Mesones 103 ⓣ415/152-4996. Some of the most succulent steak in town – a New York strip, or beef medallions baked in red wine and served with peppers and Roquefort (M$180–260) – comes in generous portions and is served on a verdant patio to the strains of quality live jazz most nights. The chicken and seafood dishes are equally memorable, and they serve excellent margaritas.

El Tomato Mesones 62, east of Hidalgo ⓣ415/154-6390. Mostly healthy, mostly vegetarian place for lunch and dinner, with soya- and spinach-based burgers, exotic salad concoctions and a M$80 three-course menu. Closed Tues.

La Ventana Sollano 11 ⓣ415/154-7728. Your best bet in town for a caffeine fix, this quiet coffee shop features dark roasts from Chiapas and all manner of java concoctions. Drinks also available to go from a street-front window for M$12.

Nightlife

Nightlife in San Miguel can be expensive. Prices are fairly high but the main culprit is the sheer range of things to do – a refreshing change in itself. Your best bet is to gather with everyone else in the Jardín to take the air, stroll around and check out what's going on.

La Coronela San Francisco 2 ⓣ415/152-2746. Dependable upmarket cantina decorated with old Mexican cinema posters, featuring two-for-one beers on Mon and Tues. Daily noon–1am.

La Fragua Cuna de Allende 3, just off the Jardín ⓣ415/152-1144. Popular local stand-by, set beneath stone arches and a bar stacked with bottles; features a decent food menu, an expansive cocktail lounge and live music most nights of the week (jazz on Fri). Happy hour runs 4–6pm during the week; at weekends you get half-price margaritas at this time. Tues–Sun noon–2am.

El Gato Negro Mesones 10. Tiny and hip swinging-door cantina (women welcome) absolutely plastered in photos of Marilyn Monroe – plus a couple of Jim Morrison and John Lennon. The drinks are cheap, and there's no cover. There's also an old-fashioned *pissoire*.

El Grito Umarán 15 ⓣ415/152-0048. Currently the top club in town, though things do change surprisingly fast. For now, this remains the place to be seen for fashionable locals, if they're willing to pay; cover is usually at least M$150. The cavernous interior is decked out with colonial chandeliers, stone work and sculpture, while the DJs spin the usual mix of house and Latino sounds. Open Fri & Sat 10pm–4am.

Limerick Pub Umarán 24 ⓣ415/154-8642. Enthusiastic Irish-themed pub, replete with pool table, dartboard, board games and Guinness, popular with locals and expats alike. It's also a fun place to watch live sports events. Daily 1pm–2am.

Mama Mia Umarán 8 ⓣ415/152-2063. Probably the most happening nightspot in town, with restaurant, sensational terrace bar with enthralling views over the rooftops and the adjacent after-hours *Mama's Bar*. You can count on good DJs, live bands and live salsa on Fri and Sat nights (midnight–3am). There are also free salsa classes on Wed nights (7pm). Open Wed–Sat from 10pm.

Listings

American Express Viajes Vertiz, Hidalgo 1, just north of El Jardín (Mon–Fri 9am–2pm & 4–6.30pm, Sat 10am–2pm; ⓣ415/152-1856, ⓦwww.viajesvertiz.com), will hold mail, reissue stolen or lost cheques, and cash them if they have enough money.

Banks and exchange Banamex, at the northwest corner of El Jardín on Canal, and Banorte, half a block east of Banamex along San Francisco; most banks have ATMs.

Bike rental See box below.

Books The best bookshop is the US-expat-owned Garrison & Garrison at Macías 59 (Mon–Sat 10am–6pm, Sun 2–6pm); it sells a thoughtful range of new and secondhand English-language books, as well as organic brownies for M$19 and coffee. Airport novels and weightier fiction, along with hardbacks, magazines and art supplies are all stocked by El Colibrí, Sollano 30 (Mon–Sat 10am–3pm & 4–7pm), a block or so south of El Jardín.

Consulates US, Hernández Macías 72, opposite Bellas Artes (Mon–Fri 9am–1pm; ⓣ415/152-2357).

Tours and activities in and around San Miguel de Allende

Bici-Burro Hospicio 1 ⓣ415/152-1526, ⓦwww.bici-burro.com. A range of van, hiking and bike tours (M$800–1400), most frequently to the Santuario de Atotonilco (38km; 5–6hr), or to Pozos (7hr). They'll also rent you a good hardtail machine for around M$500 a day and point you in the right direction.

Coyote Canyon Horseback Adventures ⓣ415/154-4193, ⓦwww.coyotecanyonadventures.com. Group and private riding trips, lessons and even moonlit excursions at a variety of levels at their ranch 16km southwest of town. All trips give a great introduction into charro life; they run half-day outings (US$85) as well as full-day (US$135) and overnight excursions (US$190). Full-day trips might also include hiking, mountain-biking (US$65) and hot-air ballooning (US$200).

Historic Walking Tour (Mon, Wed & Fri 10am; M$150; ⓣ415/152-7796). Meet in the Jardín across from the Parroquia at 9.45am for a gentle stroll around town and a good deal of education. All the proceeds go towards medical care for underprivileged children. Private tours at any time are M$800 (1–5 people) and M$200 each for more than five people.

The tourist office can also supply lists of **local guides**: Ricardo Salgado González (ⓣ415/111-3817, ⓔricardosalgado@turismosanmiguel.com.mx) leads illuminating walking tours (US$10/2hr) and bus tours (US$20) of San Miguel, and also goes to Dolores (US$30; 4hr) and Pozos (US$30; 5hr). For the **House and Garden Tour** see p.289.

Emergencies General emergencies ⓣ415/152-0911; Cruz Roja ⓣ415/152-1616; police ⓣ415/152-0022.

Internet access Try the Don Bizcoche bakery at Mesones 16 where there are many terminals (Mon–Sat 6am–9pm, Sun 6am–6pm; M$15/hr or M$0.20/min). Madre Tierra at Correo 12 charges M$10 for 10min, while La Guarderia.net at Reloj 46 charges M$5 for 20min.

Laundry Lavandería El Reloj at Reloj 34-A charges around M$25/2kg (Mon–Fri 8am–8pm, Sat 8am–5pm); Lavamagico, Pila Seca 5 (Mon–Sat 8am–8pm), offers a same-day service (M$45 for up to 4kg) if dropped off before noon.

Library The Biblioteca Pública, Insurgentes 25, allows visitors to borrow books after obtaining a library card (two passport photocopies and M$100; valid one year) and leaving a M$100 deposit.

Pharmacy Farmacia Agundis, Canal 26 (daily 9.30am–1am). English spoken.

Post office and couriers Correo 16 (Mon–Fri 8am–4pm, Sat 8am–noon). There are numerous express postal services, including DHL, at Correo 21 and opposite the post office.

Around San Miguel

One of the easiest and most enjoyable outings from San Miguel is to spend a good part of the day at one of the local **hot springs**, where the warm thermal waters are ideal for soaking your bones. There are numerous hotels and mini-resorts with geothermal pools all around the area, but the best and easiest to reach are clustered around 9km to the northwest of town on the road to Dolores Hidalgo. The most popular (certainly with San Miguel's wintering Americans) is **La Gruta** (daily 8am–5pm; M$90) right by the highway at km 9.5 with a series of outdoor mineral pools at different temperatures all surrounded by lawns and banana trees. There's even a little grotto you can swim into with an artificial waterfall, and a small and reasonably priced restaurant on site with snacks and M$45 fajitas. Around 500m before La Gruta, a side road leads just over a kilometre to **Escondido** (daily 8am–5.30pm; M$90; ⓣ415/185-2020, ⓦwww.escondidoplace.com), an equally appealing proposition, with small lily-filled lakes all around, cool outdoor pools

Learning Spanish in San Miguel de Allende

For many people, the reason to come to San Miguel is to learn Spanish. Notice boards around town advertise private lessons, but most people end up taking one of the courses run by the main **language schools**, each of which offers a range of courses taught by professional Mexican teachers. Instruction is almost entirely in Spanish, with the focus on practical usage rather than academic theory. The best known is the Instituto Allende, though the others compete admirably on both price and quality. Students usually stay with a local family (US$22–28 a day for full board) to consolidate the instruction.

Academia Hispano Americana Mesones 4 (ⓣ415/152-0349, ⓦwww.ahaspeakspanish.com). Respected school running four-week Spanish immersion sessions (6hr/day; US$665) and more relaxed semi-intensive programmes (4hr/day; US$160/week), plus extension courses in Mexican history, literature and folklore.

Instituto Allende Ancha de San Antonio 20 (ⓣ415/152-0190, ⓦwww.instituto-allende.edu.mx). The most prestigious of the schools, the Instituto conducts university-credited four-week courses (starting the first Mon of each month), offering everything from one to four hours a day (from US$90/2 weeks) throughout the year at all levels. There are also intensive one-to-one classes (US$14/hr), less demanding monthly courses and special subject courses in topics such as Mexican history, ceramics, paper-making and photography, among others.

Instituto Habla Hispana Calzada de la Luz 25 (ⓣ415/152-1535, ⓦwww.mexicospanish.com). Runs month-long courses for US$560 with around twenty contact hours per week; alternatively, you can just do a week for US$170. They'll also organize homestays for around US$21 a day for a double, and US$26 for a private room.

and a series of small indoor ones linked by little tunnels and cascades. It can be quiet here midweek, but comes alive at weekends. Second-class **buses** to Dolores Hidalgo from San Miguel's bus station will all drop off on the highway near both sets of pools (M$6); you can also take a "Santuario" bus from Calzada de la Luz and Reloj (M$7). To get back just flag down any bus you see. **Taxis** will charge around M$120 each way.

A day at the hot springs can be conveniently combined with a worthwhile outing to **SANTUARIO DE ATOTONILCO** (easily confused with the larger Atotonilco el Grande in Jalisco state), 5km further in the same direction, then 3km down a side road. This is a dusty, rural indigenous community whose church has come to be a centre of pilgrimage for two reasons – it was founded by Padre Felipe Neri in 1740, who was later canonized, and it was from here that Padre Hidalgo, marching from Dolores to San Miguel, took the banner of the Virgin of Guadalupe that became the flag of the Mexicans in the War of Independence. His comrade-in-arms Allende was married here in 1802. The six chapels of the church, liberally plastered with murals and freely interspersed with poems, biblical passages and painted statues, demonstrate every kind of Mexican popular art, from the naive to the highly sophisticated. The interiors, smothered with multicoloured frescoes and fine carvings, look resplendent after a comprehensive restoration, and the shrine was declared a UNESCO World Heritage site in 2008. Direct **buses** ("Santuario"; M$7) leave every hour from Calzada de la Paz in San Miguel (45min) and spend ten to fifteen minutes in Atotonilco, giving you just enough time for a quick look before the run back, when you can get dropped off at the hot springs. Taxis will charge at least M$120 one way.

Querétaro and around

Most people seem to hammer straight past **QUERÉTARO** on the highway to Mexico City, catching sight only of the expanding industrial outskirts and the huge modern bus station. Yet of all the colonial cities in the Bajío, this is perhaps the most surprising, with a tranquil historical core that boasts magnificent mansions and some of the country's finest ecclesiastical architecture. Little more than two hours from Mexico City, and at the junction of every major road and rail route from the north, it's also a wealthy and booming city, one of the fastest-growing in the republic thanks to industrial decentralization and its close proximity to the capital. This vibrancy, along with a series of pretty plazas linked by narrow alleys lined with restaurants and bars, makes Querétaro an alluring place to spend a couple of days. There are points of interest, too, in the surrounding hills of the Sierra Gorda, notably the small towns of **Bernal** and **Tequisquiapan**, and much more distant charms of Edward James's jungle "sculpture garden" at **Xilitla**.

Some history

There's a history as rich and deep here as anywhere in the republic, starting before the Conquest when Querétaro ("rocky place") was an Otomí town subject to the **Aztecs**; many Otomí still live in the surrounding area. In 1531 the Spaniards took control without much struggle and under them the town grew steadily into a major city and provincial capital before becoming, in the nineteenth century, the setting for some of the most dramatic events of Mexican history. It was here, meeting under the guise of Literary Associations,

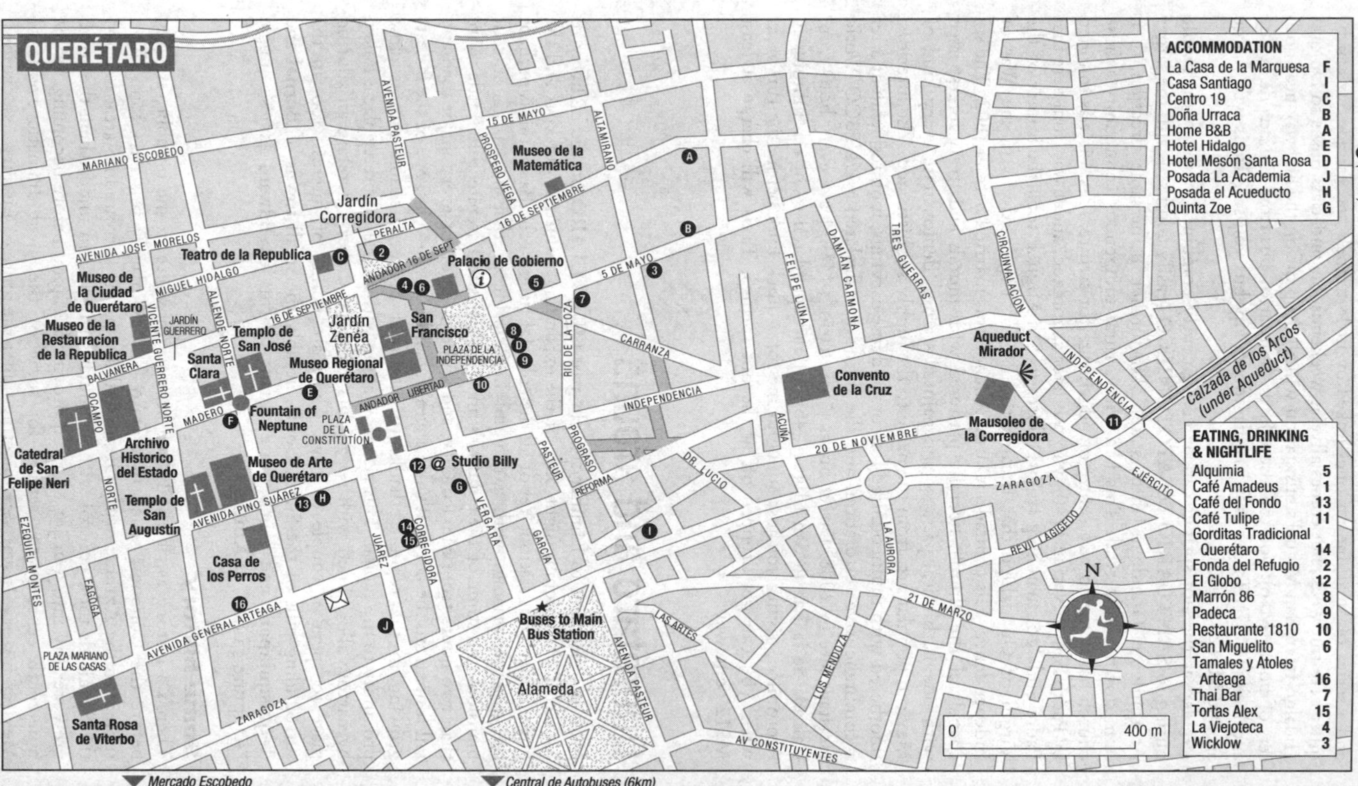
QUERÉTARO
ACCOMMODATION
La Casa de la Marquesa F
Casa Santiago I
Centro 19 C
Doña Urraca B
Home B&B A
Hotel Hidalgo E
Hotel Mesón Santa Rosa D
Posada La Academia J
Posada el Acueducto H
Quinta Zoe G
EATING, DRINKING & NIGHTLIFE
Alquimia 5
Café Amadeus 1
Café del Fondo 13
Café Tulipe 11
Gorditas Tradicional Querétaro 14
Fonda del Refugio 2
El Globo 12
Marrón 86 8
Padeca 9
Restaurante 1810 10
San Miguelito 6
Tamales y Atoles Arteaga 16
Thai Bar 7
Tortas Alex 15
La Viejoteca 4
Wicklow 3
1 (200m) & Bernal
Cerro de las Campañas (1km) & Museo la Magia del Pasado
Mercado Escobedo
Central de Autobuses (6km)
Museo de la Matemática
Jardín Corregidora
Teatro de la Republica
Palacio de Gobierno
Museo de la Ciudad de Querétaro
Museo de la Restauracion de la Republica
Jardín Guerrero
Templo de San José
Jardín Zenéa
San Francisco
Plaza de la Independencia
Santa Clara
Museo Regional de Querétaro
Fountain of Neptune
Plaza de la Constitución
Catedral de San Felipe Neri
Archivo Historico del Estado
Museo de Arte de Querétaro
Studio Billy
Templo de San Augustín
Casa de los Perros
Buses to Main Bus Station
Alameda
Santa Rosa de Viterbo
Convento de la Cruz
Aqueduct Mirador
Mausoleo de la Corregidora
Calzada de los Arcos (under Aqueduct)
15 de Mayo
Mariano Escobedo
Avenida Pasteur
Prospero Vega
Altamirano
16 de Septiembre
Peralta
Andador 16 de Sept
Avenida Jose Morelos
Miguel Hidalgo
Allende Norte
Vicente Guerrero Norte
5 de Mayo
Felipe Luna
Damián Carmona
Tres Guerras
Circunvalación
Rio de la Loza
Carranza
Independencia
Andador Libertad
Balvanera
Ocampo
Madero
Norte
Avenida Pino Suárez
Ezequiel Montes
Fagoga
Juárez
Corregidora
Vergara
Garcia
Pasteur
Prograso
Reforma
Dr. Lucio
Acuña
20 de Noviembre
Zaragoza
Ejército
Revil Lagigedo
La Aurora
21 de Marzo
Las Artes
Los Mendoza
Av Constituyentes
Avenida General Arteaga
Plaza Mariano de las Casas
N
0
400 m

that the **Independence** conspirators (or "reformers") laid their earliest plans. In 1810 one of their number, María Josefa Ortiz de Dominguez, wife of the town's Corregidor (or governor – she is known always as "La Corregidora"), found that her husband had learned of the movement's intentions. Although locked in her room, La Corregidora managed to get a message out warning the revolutionaries, thus precipitating an unexpectedly early start to the struggle for independence.

Later in the century, less exalted events took place. The **Treaty of Guadalupe Hidalgo**, which ended the Mexican–American War by handing over almost half of Mexico's territory – Texas, New Mexico, California and more – to the US, was signed in Querétaro in 1848, and, in 1867, Emperor Maximilian made his last stand here. Once defeated, he was tried by a court meeting in the theatre and finally faced a firing squad on the hill, the Cerro de las Campañas, just to the north of town. The same theatre hosted an important assembly of Revolutionary politicians in 1916, leading eventually to the signing here of the 1917 Constitution, which is still in force today.

Arrival, orientation and information

Querétaro's massive **Central de Autobuses** lies 6km south of town and is one of the busiest in this part of Mexico, with three separate buildings: Sala A for long-distance and first-class companies, and salas B and C for shorter runs and second-class companies. Fixed-price **taxis** (buy a ticket from the kiosk) run from outside all terminals (downtown is zone C; M$37), and an endless shuttle of **local buses** ("Ruta 8" is the most convenient) runs to the centre from the end of Sala B. Buses generally don't enter the historic centre, so get off at Zaragoza, by the Alameda, and walk from there. This is also the spot to pick up services back to the bus station: #36 and others. All city buses are M$5. Taxis don't use meters in Querétaro so fix the price in advance – the bus station should be M$30 from downtown.

For all its sprawl, Querétaro is easy to find your way around once you get to the centre, since the core remains confined to the grid laid down by the Spanish: all the tiny plazas are interconnected by pedestrian walkways known as *andadores*. The main focus is the central plaza, the **Jardín Zenéa**, with its typical triumvirate of bandstand, clipped trees and bootshines. To the west lies the commercial centre with the bulk of the shops, but you'll probably spend much of your time to the east among the gift shops, restaurants and bars leading to the Plaza de la Independencia.

The **tourist office**, Pasteur 4 Nte (daily 9am–8pm; Ⓣ442/238-5067, Ⓦwww.queretaro.travel), offers free maps and basic advice. If you're short of time hour-long **trolley tours** (Mon–Fri 11-6pm, every hr; M$60; Sat & Sun 11am–9pm; M$70; Ⓣ442/148-9176, Ⓦwww.tranviaturistico.com), which start outside the Museo Regional and visit the main sights, might help you get your bearings, though commentary is usually given in Spanish only.

Accommodation

For **hotels**, head straight for the Jardín Zenéa and the streets in its immediate vicinity. Streetside rooms may be noisy, but there's a fair selection of places in this area, several of them particularly gorgeous (and expensive). There are also several budget places, though after a spate of closures, no **hostels** at the time of writing. Querétaro has improved in the mid-range, with several boutique-type places in the centre offering terrific value – booking ahead is crucial.

La Casa de la Marquesa Madero 41 ⓣ442/212-0092, ⓦwww.lacasadelamarquesa.com. Enchanting hotel housed in a 1756 mansion with a gorgeous Moorish courtyard. The antique-furnished Imperial suites (M$3500) are magnificent, though they also have slightly less luxurious rooms (M$1800–2100) in a separate building across the road. Breakfast included. 8

Casa Santiago 20 de Noviembre 22 ⓣ442/212-6352, ⓦwww.casantiago.mexico.googlepages.com. This initimate B&B has garnered a loyal following; tranquil, spacious rooms near the centre, an interior decked out with local art, a helpful owner and soothing roof terrace keep them coming back. Free wi-fi. 5

Centro 19 Corregidora 19, at Ángela Peralta ⓣ442/212-1234, ⓦwww.centro19hotel.com. Considering the quality, location and price, this is a fabulous option; no wonder its rooms – modern, compact and stylish – are almost always booked solid. Free wi-fi, parking and cable TV. 5

Doña Urraca 5 de Mayo 117 ⓣ442/238-5400 or 01-800/021-7116, ⓦwww.donaurraca.com.mx. The modern alternative to the *Casa de la Marquesa*, this is one of the city's swankiest hotels and comes complete with heated outdoor pool and spa. Rooms are named for birds and feature stone, wood and gorgeous natural-fibre linens. Packages including massage and spa treatments are surprisingly reasonable. 9

Home B&B 16 de Septiembre 104 ⓣ442/183-9139, ⓦwww.queretarobandb.com. This welcoming B&B is excellent value, with simple, clean and cosy rooms, home-cooked gourmet breakfasts, wi-fi and a roof terrace. Also rents the comfortably furnished five-bedroom house next door for US$190. 4

Hotel Hidalgo Madero 11 Pte, just off Jardín Zenéa ⓣ442/212-0081, ⓦwww.hotelhidalgo.com.mx. Basic but clean modern rooms set around an open colonial era courtyard, all with bath and cable TV – claims to be the first hotel in the city, opening in 1825. Some of the larger rooms with balconies go for M$60 more. Solid mid-range option. 4

Hotel Mesón Santa Rosa Pasteur 17 Sur ⓣ442/224-2623, ⓦwww.hotelmesonsantarosa.com. Superb luxury hotel, very quiet and beautiful, in an old colonial mansion on the Jardín Independencia, with a great restaurant to boot. 7

Posada La Academia Pino Suárez 3 ⓣ442/224-2739. The neat, basic rooms here are nothing special, though they are the cheapest in town and some have TVs and bathrooms. M$150 shared bathroom, with TV. 3

Posada el Acueducto Juárez 64 Sur, at Arteaga ⓣ442/224-1289. Cheerily painted and well-cared-for budget hotel, right in the centre, with modern a/c rooms, all with cable TV. The large suites (M$500) are particularly nice. 3

Quinta Zoe Vergara 22 ⓣ442/212-3187, ⓦwww.quintazoe.com. This Spanish colonial inn is another great deal, with internet rates sometimes as low as US$55; four simple but tastefully decorated rooms, all with bathrooms adorned with colourful tiling, in an eighteenth-century mansion in the centre of town. Cable TV and free calls to Mexico and North America. 5

The City

Querétaro's underrated colonial centre is particularly magical at the weekends, when festive crowds and markets throng the streets, and church bells echo across the plazas. The church of **San Francisco**, dominating the **Jardín Zenéa**, Querétaro's main square, was one of the earliest founded in the city. Its eye-popping facade incorporates a dome covered in *azulejos* – coloured tiles imported from Spain around 1540 – but for the most part San Francisco was rebuilt in the seventeenth and eighteenth centuries. Take a look at the similarly opulent interior for an introduction to the city's remarkable treasure trove of religious art. Adjoining the church, in what used to be the Grande Convento de San Francisco, is the **Museo Regional de Querétaro** (Tues–Sun 10am–7pm; M$41). The building alone is reason enough to visit, though the displays inside are well worth an hour or two. Built around two large tangerine-coloured cloisters, the museum is being sensitively refurbished, with wooden floors, cream stone walls and a host of engaging chronologically arranged exhibits charting the history of Querétaro state, beginning with a large section on prehistoric culture and the region's indigenous tribes. Displays upstairs focus on the spiritual history of the state under the Spanish missionaries, and currently end at the Spanish colonial period (1521–1821), here presented thematically through society, economy, government and a section on the Sierra Gorda town of Cadereyta. Once the renovation is complete, you should also be able to view such venerable relics as the keyhole through which La Corregidora passed on her news and the table on which the Treaty of Guadalupe Hidalgo was signed. As impressive as the museum is, you really need to read Spanish to make the most of it.

South of the museum lies the **Plaza de la Constitución**, formerly a market square now transformed into an attractive modern plaza with a central fountain that mimics the domed roof of the building on its south side. There's more to see a couple of blocks north of the Jardín Zenéa at the **Teatro de la República**, which sits at the junction of Juárez and Peralta (Tues–Sun 10am–3pm & 5–8pm; free; ⓣ442/212-0339). Opened in 1852, this grand theatre has played a vital role in Mexican history: a court met here to decide the fate of Emperor Maximilian in 1867, and in 1917 the Mexican Constitution was agreed upon inside. A small exhibition celebrates the latter event upstairs (above the lobby), though the main reason to walk up here is to take a peek at the theatre itself, a magnificent space with four levels of enclosed balcony seating. Today the theatre is home to the Querétaro Philharmonic Orchestra and hosts several concerts through the year – call or ask at the tourist office for the latest programme.

Around the Plaza de la Independencia

The little pedestrianized alleys that lead up to the east of the Jardín are some of the city's most interesting, crammed with ancient houses, little restaurants, art galleries and shops selling junky antiques and the opals and other semiprecious stones for which the area is famous. If you decide to buy, double-check the stones for authenticity. The first of several little plazas and almost part of the Jardín Zenéa is the **Jardín Corregidora**, with an imposing statue of La Corregidora and several restaurants and bars where you can sit outside. Further south, the pedestrianized Andador Libertad runs past art galleries and boutiques from the Plaza de la Constitución to the **Plaza de la Independencia**, or Plaza de Armas, a very refined, arcaded open space. In the middle of the plaza stands a statue of Don Juan Antonio de Urrutia y Arana, the man who built Querétaro's all-important aqueduct (see p.302), providing the city with drinking water. Around the square is the **Casa de la Corregidora**, now the Palacio de Gobierno (Mon–Fri 8am–9pm, Sat 8am–6pm; free). It was here, on September 14, 1810, that La Corregidora was locked up (in her own house) while her husband made plans to arrest the conspirators. She managed to get a message to Ignacio Perez, who carried it to Independence movement leaders Allende and Hidalgo in the towns of San Miguel and Dolores. The palacio sometimes holds special events, but there's not a great deal to see inside.

Avenida Morelos and around

While the city's more exciting restaurants and bars remain around the eastern plazas, the commercial centre of Querétaro lies west of Jardín Zenéa, on and around **Avenida Morelos**. This is where you'll find most of the shops, on formal streets lined with stately mansions. At the corner of Madero and Allende, the little Jardín de Santa Clara features a famous **Fountain of Neptune**, designed by **Francisco Eduardo Tresguerras** in 1797. Tresguerras (1765–1833) is rightly regarded as one of Mexico's greatest architects – he was also a sculptor, painter and poet – and was almost single-handedly responsible for developing a native Mexican architectural style diverging from (though still close to) its Spanish roots. His work, seen throughout central Mexico, is particularly evident here and in nearby Celaya, his birthplace. Beside the fountain rises the deceptively simple church of **Santa Clara**, once attached to one of the country's richest monasteries,

▲ Fountain, Querétaro

dating back to 1633. Inside it's a riot of Baroque excess, with gilded cherubs and angels swarming all over the profusely decorated *retablos* (gold-painted wooden altarpieces), virtually lining the length of the nave, created in the 1770s.

Carry on west down Madero through Jardín Guerrero and you get to the **Archivo Histórico del Estado**, a stately 1860s building, and the **Catedral de San Felipe Neri**, which was completed in 1805 but only given cathedral status in 1931. The facade is a wonderful blend of pink sandstone and soaring Corinthian columns (one looks like carrot top), but by Querétaro's standards, the interior is relatively plain. Cut north along Guerrero, however, and you'll come to the **Museo de la Restauración de la República**, Guerrero 23 Nte (Mon–Fri 9am–5pm, Sat & Sun 10am–5pm; free). An ex-Capuchin convent founded in 1721 (though most of what you see was added in the nineteenth century), its small and well-presented series of rooms and courtyards is dedicated to the history of the French Intervention (1863–67) and the restoration of the Republic under Benito Juárez, highlighted with period weaponary, old prints, scale models and other bits and pieces. A room is also dedicated to Maximilian himself, who was imprisoned here in 1867 before being shot – again, though, you need to read Spanish to get the most out of the museum.

Next door at no. 27 and occupying the same ex-convent premises, the **Museo de la Ciudad de Querétaro** (Tues–Sun 11am–7pm; M$5), fills a warren of rooms and galleries with temporary exhibitions, predominantly contemporary installation art, painting, sculpture and photography.

Museo de Arte de Querétaro and around

A couple of blocks south of the Museo de la Ciudad lies the **Museo de Arte de Querétaro**, Allende 14 Sur (Tues–Sun 10am–6pm; M$30, free Tues) occupying the former Palacio Federal next to the church of **San Agustín** (another example of Baroque splendor and itself worth a look inside – check out the gargoyles with water spouts on the roof). Originally an Augustinian monastery completed in 1728 (it was also a prison and a post office before becoming the federal offices in 1889), the museum is one the most ornate buildings in town. In the cloister, every surface of the two storeys of portals is carved with grotesque figures, no two quite alike, and with abstract designs. The sculptures, often attributed to Tresguerras though almost certainly not by him, are full of religious symbolism, which you should try to get someone to explain to you. The large figures supporting the arches, for example, all hold their fingers in different positions: three held up to represent the Trinity, four for the Evangelists and so on. The contents of the museum are small but absorbing, with galleries devoted to mediocre seventeenth-century European painting (mostly anonymous artists) and nineteenth-century Mexican art downstairs, along with temporary exhibition spaces usually featuring much better contemporary work. The collection of Mexican painting upstairs is mostly from the seventeenth and eighteenth centuries, focusing on Mannerism and Baroque styles, with the highlight a room full of works attributed to Manuel Cabrera.

The church of **Santa Rosa de Viterbo** sits further out in this direction, at the junction of Arteaga and Montes, but is well worth the short walk. Its magnificent interior rivals Santa Clara for richness of decoration, plastered with art work, murals and vast gold *retablos*, but here there is no false modesty on the outside either. Two enormous flying buttresses support the octagonal cupola (remodelled by Tresguerras) and a blue and white tiled dome. The tower, too, is Tresguerras's work, holding what is said to be the first four-sided public clock erected on the American continent.

Convento de la Cruz

There's more to see a short walk east from the centre at the **Convento de la Cruz** (Tues–Sat 9am–2pm & 4–6pm, Sun 9am–4pm; half-hour guided tours in English on request; small donation requested), built on the site of the battle between the Spaniards and the Otomí in which the conquistadors gained control of Querétaro. According to legend, the fighting was cut short by the miraculous appearance of Spanish patron saint St James (Santiago – the city's full name is Santiago de Querétaro – who coincidentally was also claimed to have helped vanquish the Moors), and a dazzling cross in the sky, which persuaded the Indians to accept defeat and become Christians. The **Capilla del Calvarito**, next door to the monastery entrance, marks the spot where the first Mass was celebrated after the battle. The monastery itself was founded in 1683 by the Franciscans as a college (Colegio Apostólico de Propaganda Fide) and grew over the years into an important centre for the training of missionaries, with a massive library and rich collection of relics. Because of its hilltop position and hefty construction, the monastery was also frequently used as a fortress. Functioning as one of the last

Spanish redoubts in the War of Independence, it was Maximilian's headquarters for the last few weeks of his reign and he was subsequently imprisoned here to await execution (before being moved to the convent on Guerrero, see p.300). The convent's greatest source of pride is the **Árbol de la Cruz**, a tree in the garden whose thorns sprout in the shape of little crosses. The tree grew, so the story goes, from a walking stick left behind by a mysterious saintly traveller who slept here one night. It certainly does produce thorns in the form of crosses, and the monks, who appear very excited by the phenomenon, point out that an additional five percent of the thorns grow with extra spikes to mark the spots where nails were driven through Christ's hands and feet; look for the framed collection in the entrance foyer.

Come up to the monastery in the late afternoon, then wander 200m further east along Ejército Republicano to the **Mausoleo de la Corregidora** (daily 9am–5pm; free), where the heroine's remains, along with those of her husband, are surrounded by statues of other illustrious *Querétanos*. Across the road a *mirador* provides a spell-binding sunset view of the city's 1.3-kilometre-long **aqueduct**, a graceful series of 74 arches up to 23m high, built between 1726 and 1738 to bring water into the city from springs nearly 9km away. Spotlit at night, it looks magnificent, especially as you drive into town. *Café Tulipe* and *Café Amadeus* (see opposite) are both a short stroll down the hill from here.

Cerro de las Campañas

One kilometre west of the centre via Morelos or Hidalgo, the gentle eminence of the **Cerro de las Campañas** ("Hill of Bells") commands wide, if less than scenic, views over Querétaro and its industrial outskirts. Maximilian and his two generals, Miguel Miramón and Tomás Mejía, faced the firing squad here (a small chapel, built in 1900 by Porfirio Díaz near the entrance, marks the spot). The hill is dominated by a vast stone statue of the victor of that particular war, Benito Juárez, glaring down over the town. Beyond the statue is the mildly entertaining **Museo La Magia del Pasado** (Tues–Sun 9am–5pm; M$15, free for kids under 15; ⓣ442/215-9031) with lots of interactive exhibits on Querétaro's history targeted primarily at kids; the main focus is the Republican attack of 1867 that led to Maximilian's capture. In order to reach the summit, avoid the parts of the new university campus sprawling up one slope; follow Hidalgo west, turn right onto Tecnológico and then left after 400m onto Justo Sierra where there's the entrance to the neatly tended Parque Municipal del Cerro de las Campañas (daily 6am–6pm; M$1).

Eating, drinking and nightlife

There's plenty of good food in Querétaro, and some delightful places to sit outside amid the alleys and plazas east of the **Jardín Zenéa**. Try to sample a couple of **local specialities**, particularly a hearty lentil soup laced with chunks of dried fruit (usually just called "sopa regional"): it sounds odd but is delicious, though vegetarians won't appreciate the pork-broth base. Also try *enchiladas Queretanas*, tortillas fried in a chile sauce and stuffed with onions and cheese.

Sunday **buffets** are big business here, and a host of places run Mexican-style brunches, usually great value at M$80–120. If you want to get together something of your own, head for the **Mercado Escobedo**, sprawled across several blocks just off Calzada Zaragoza, not far from the Alameda.

Evening **entertainment** tends to involve a couple of beers in one of the restaurants or an hour or two lingering in one of the cafés. For a livelier scene, head to the bars along 5 de Mayo and see where the night takes you. The bigger **clubs** are all out in the suburbs and fashions change rapidly, so ask around and follow the crowd (probably by taxi). Many have some sort of live music at weekends and charge M$50–100 to get in.

Restaurants and cafés

Café Amadeus Zaragoza 306 (Calzada de los Arcos), halfway along the aqueduct ⓣ442/213-6403. Munch on scrumptious tortes or fine breakfasts and *antojitos* (from M$60) all to the strains of Mozart.

Café del Fondo Pino Suárez 9 ⓣ442/212-0905. This airy multi-roomed café serves bargain breakfasts from 7.30am; fresh juice, espresso and a plate of eggs, enchiladas or hotcakes for under M$25. There are also more substantial dishes available throughout the day, and good coffee and cakes until around 10.30pm. One room is often devoted to boardgames, most frequently chess.

Café Tulipe Calzada de los Arcos 3, near the west end of the aqueduct ⓣ442/213-6391. A definite favourite for its predominantly Mexican but French-tinged menu – filet mignon for M$110 – plus delectable desserts. The delicious fondue and *caldo conde* (a black bean, cream and herb soup) are especially good.

Fonda del Refugio Jardín Corregidora 26, behind the statue ⓣ442/212-0755. One of several decent places surrounding this attractive plaza. They serve food (including a popular Sunday buffet), but this is primarily a place to sit outside, drink and watch the world go by.

El Globo Corregidora 41. About the best *pastelería* in town, with lots of French pastries – croissants, *pain au chocolat* and so on – big sticky cakes and even their own brand of ice cream, all to take out.

Gorditas Tradicional Querétaro Corregidora 102. Watch the venerable old ladies at this small shop prepare hearty gorditas to eat or take away (M$8–12). Tends to open later into the evening than its equally popular neighbour, *Tortas Alex*.

Marrón 86 Pasteur 9, Plaza de la Independencia ⓣ442/214-3994. Prime real estate under the colonnades on the Plaza de Armas. Good for pasta dishes, stuffed baguettes and salads, but the coffee is really the highlight.

Padeca *Hotel Mesón de Santa Rosa*, Pasteur 17 Sur, Plaza de la Independencia ⓣ442/224-2623. Quality restaurant serving predominantly Italian dishes (gnocchi M$95, steaks M$150) – in a tranquil garden setting in the courtyard of the hotel.

Restaurante 1810 Andador Libertad 65 ⓣ442/214-3324, ⓦwww.restaurante1810.com.mx. Outstanding sidewalk restaurant that does regional specialities to perfection. You'll have to take your chances with the live entertainment – sometimes relaxing jazz, though often cheesy crooners. Expect to pay M$60 for Mexican staples, M$80–150 for meat and fish dishes. Mon–Sat 8am–midnight, Sun 8am–10pm.

San Miguelito Andador 5 de Mayo 39 ⓣ442/224-2760. This unique spot has a justly earned reputation as one of the city's best restaurants, and you're guaranteed an impressive selection of delicious regional, national and international dishes in eclectic surroundings – it's set inside the courtyard of the *Casona de los Cincos Patios*. Try the chicken in chipotle sauce or one of their fine steaks. Mains around M$110. Tues–Sat 1–11pm, Sun 1–5pm.

Tamales y Atoles Arteaga Arteaga 48. This local secret, on a stretch of street with several tamale specialists, knocks out steaming hot tamales as you wait: choose from regular (*salsa verde con carne* or *rajas con queso*) for M$9, or *Tamales Oaxaqueños* (like *mole con pollo*) for M$13. Open daily 8–11am & 6–10pm.

Bars

Alquimia 5 de Mayo 71. Sophisticated, dimly lit bodega with bottles racked up behind the bar and the doors thrown open to the street. Perfect for a quiet beer or one of their delicious cocktails. Tues–Sat 8pm–2.30am.

Thai Bar 5 de Mayo 56. Somewhat misnamed, this chic spot is primarily a bar populated by sophisticated *Querétanos*, though it does serve passable Thai food and sushi. Closed Mon.

La Viejoteca Andador 5 de Mayo 39. Fabulous bar set in an old apothecary shop, with a large high-ceilinged room and bar backed with old medicine bottles, pots and dusty wooden shelves – even the ironwork stools look like Victorian antiques. Packed most evenings and often has live music. Expect a M$60 cover towards the weekend and M$40 for bottled beers – it also does taco plates for around M$100. Operates as a café 10am–6pm, and a bar from 7pm till late.

Wicklow 5 de Mayo 86 ⓣ442/307-6063, ⓦwww.wicklow.com.mx. Every aspiring international city seems to have at least one Irish pub, and Querétaro is no exception, *Wicklow*'s green-washed exterior hinting at all the usual themes inside – Guinness, stews and plenty of good craic.

Moving on from Querétaro

To get to the Central de Autobuses take a local bus from Zaragoza, by the Alameda (M$5). Taxis should be around M$30 from downtown. There are regular first-class services to Guadalajara (4–5hr), Mexico City (3–4hr) and San Luis Potosí (2hr 30min), and three buses direct to San Miguel de Allende (1hr 15min) and Guanajuato (3hr) – second-class departures are a lot more frequent. Querétaro's Aeropuerto Internacional is 8km northeast of the centre (M$300 by taxi), and hosts regular flights to Houston, Guadalajara and Monterrey.

For further information, see Travel details, p.311.

Listings

American Express Turismo Beverly Querétaro, Tecnológico 118 (Mon–Fri 9am–2pm & 4–6pm, Sat 9am–noon; ⓣ442/216-1511), has all the usual services. It's around 2km southwest of the centre, reached by buses running west along Zaragoza to Tecnológico, then 200m south.

Banks and exchange There are several banks around the Jardín Zenéa that will change currency (Mon–Fri 9am–3pm), and a couple of casas de cambio south along Juárez.

Books and newspapers Querétaro has plenty of bookshops, but you'll be lucky to find anything in English. International weeklies can usually be found at the newspaper stands around the Jardín Zenéa and the Plaza de la Independencia. Beyond that, Sanborn's, on Constituyentes, 2km southeast of the centre, has a wide range of magazines.

Emergencies For general emergencies call ⓣ066; Cruz Roja ⓣ442/229-0505.

Internet access There are several internet places in the centre mostly costing M$10–12/hr, including Studio Billy (a tattoo shop) on Independencia between Vergara and Corregidora (M$10/hr).

Laundry Lavandería Verónica, Hidalgo 153 at Ignacio Pérez (Mon–Fri 9am–2.30pm & 4.30–8pm, Sat 9am–3pm), lies about 1km west of the centre.

Pharmacy There are dozens of pharmacies around the centre, including the large Farmacia Guadalajara at Madero 32, just west of the Jardín Zenéa.

Post office Arteaga 5 (Mon–Fri 8am–6pm, Sat 9am–1pm).

Spanish schools Ole Centre for Spanish Language and Culture, Mariano Escobedo 32 (ⓣ442/234-4023, ⓦwww.ole.edu.mx). Good-value Spanish courses in a town where you won't get too distracted talking English to all the foreign visitors. Classes start at US$157/week for 15hr, or US$15/hr for individual lessons.

Around Querétaro

From Querétaro you can race straight to Mexico City on Hwy-57, and if you are not reliant on public transport, then there are a couple of places that might be visited en route: the ancient Toltec capital of Tula, and Tepotzotlán, with its magnificent Baroque architecture, both of which are covered in Chapter 5. But before charging south, consider exploring the towns around Querétaro, particularly **Bernal**, **Tequisquiapan** and **San Juan del Río**, where you could easily spend a pleasant few days exploring.

Bernal

The pretty village of **BERNAL**, 45km east of Querétaro, hunkers under the skirts of the soaring Peña de Bernal, a 350-metre-high chunk of volcanic rock that towers over the plains and is claimed to be the fourth tallest monolith in the world – after Australia's Mount Augustus, the Rock of Gibraltar and Rio's Sugarloaf. By wandering towards the peak you'll soon pick up a rough but clearly marked path about two-thirds of the way to the top (the ascent takes up to an hour, half that to get down), where there's a small shrine and long views stretching out below. Only appropriately equipped rock climbers should continue up the metal rungs to the summit, passing a memorial plaque to an earlier adventurer along the way.

At weekends, half of Querétaro seems to come out here, making for a festive atmosphere, but midweek it is an altogether more peaceful place: the mountain is likely to be deserted and you'll be just about the only thing disturbing the serenity of the village plaza with its charming little church and terracotta-washed buildings, sumptuous in the afternoon light. Be forewarned, however, that many businesses are only open at the weekends and many more shut for the month of May.

Practicalities

The centre is ringed by narrow streets full of shops selling handicrafts, and there's even a small **tourist office** on Hidalgo (usually open Thurs–Tues 10am–5pm; ⓣ441/296-4126), which runs west from the plaza, though there isn't much they can tell you that you can't discover for yourself in ten minutes. Also on Hidalgo is one of the best **places to eat**, in the shaded courtyard of *Mesón de la Roca*, at no. 5 (ⓣ441/296 4163), serving moderately priced and well-presented Mexican dishes along with a M$80 comida corrida and, for the daring, grasshopper tacos (M$75). There are also several cheap *comedores*, and at weekends perhaps a dozen restaurants to choose from. Flecha Amarilla provide hourly **buses** from Querétaro's bus station (M$25; 1hr) which drop you on the highway five minutes' walk from Bernal centre; it's worth remembering that the last bus back passes at around 6pm. It is also possible to continue to Tequisquiapan by taking a bus (M$15; 30min) to the small town of Ezequiel Montes and changing there.

If you get stuck, or just fancy a night here (not a bad thing), there are tantalizing views of the rock from the comfy **rooms** at *Parador Vernal*, Lázaro Cárdenas 1, on the eastern edge of town (ⓣ441/296-4058, ⓦwww.paradorvernal.com.mx; ⑤).

Tequisquiapan

Some 20km north of San Juan, along a road lined with factories and workshops, **TEQUISQUIAPAN** ("Tequis" to locals), is a former Otomí village that developed in viceregal times primarily on account of its warm springs. Exclusive villas, all with beautifully tended walled gardens, are set around the central Plaza Santa María, itself ringed by arched *portales* on three sides and the church on the fourth, painted in soft tones of orange, red and azure. It is very popular with wealthy *chilangos* (residents of Mexico City) up from the capital, but has never really caught on with *extranjeros*. Although perfect as a weekend escape from the city, there's little to do other than bathe in your hotel pool, dine in one of many restaurants around the plaza and nose around the boutiques, some of which are cheap, many expensive and almost all of the highest standard. Like San Juan del Río, further south, Tequisquiapan has a big **crafts market** – especially active on Sundays – one block from the main plaza.

It is worth trying to time a visit to Tequisquiapan with one of the town's many **festivals**, including the **Feria del Toro de Lidia** (middle week of March), which features bullfights, and the **Feria Internacional del Queso y del Vino** (late May and early June), a major wine and cheese festival. There's plenty of free food and drink and no shortage of other entertainment, including music and dancing. If you miss the festival and still have a taste for wine, **Freixenet**, the Spanish producer of *cava* (Spanish champagne), has an outpost about 20km north at Carretera San Juan del Río–Cadereyta km 40.5 (tours Mon–Fri noon, 1.30pm & 3pm, Sat & Sun 11am–4pm hourly; ⓣ414/277-0147, ⓦwww.freixenetmexico.com.mx), with free twenty-minute tours and tasting.

Practicalities

Free town maps are available from the **tourist office** (Mon–Fri 9am–7pm, Sat & Sun 10am–8pm; ⓣ414/273-0295, ⓦwww.tequis.info) on the main square. When the attraction of artesanía shopping begins to pall you'll probably want to press on, but if you decide to stay you can choose from the thirty-odd **hotels** packed into the tiny town, most ranged around bougainvillea-draped courtyards, many with pools fed by springs. About the cheapest place in town is *Posada San Francisco*, Moctezuma 2 (Ⓣ414/273-0231; ❹), featuring comfortable rooms decorated with artesanías and with access to a lush garden. Ask for one overlooking the pool. It's a small step up to *Hotel La Plaza*, on the plaza at Juárez 10 (Ⓣ414/273-0005, Ⓦwww.tequisquiapancom.mx/la_plaza; ❺), very relaxed, with its own pool and some very attractive suites (M$1057). Newer, but with a lot more character, *Hostal del Viejo*, Morelos 4 at Salvador Michaus (Ⓣ414/596-7148, Ⓦwww.hostaldelviejo.com.mx; ❻), has seven spacious rooms – some compact doubles (M$850) and much larger master suites (M$1250) – in a converted colonial mansion, all set around a courtyard with a small pool. Prices almost halve during the week.

For budget **eating** you can grab a M$30 *comida* at a cluster of *fondas* at the back of the market just off the east side of the main square. **Restaurants** abound, though many only really come to life at the weekend. The town is so small that you can walk around them all in ten minutes and see what appeals to you, though it is worth strolling along Salvador Michaus to *La Bicicleta* (daily 1.30–10pm; Ⓣ414/273-1510) which serves succulent barbecue steaks and roast goat, all at low to moderate prices.

Flecha Azul **buses** from Querétaro (Sala C; every 30min 6.30am–9pm; M$35; 1hr) run direct to Tequisquiapan, and there's also a bus every half-hour from San Juan del Río (see below). From the bus station, turn right and walk the ten minutes into the plaza, passing an ugly concrete tripod said to mark the geographical centre of the country.

San Juan del Río

Though **SAN JUAN DEL RÍO**, 50km south of Querétaro, looks insignificant from the highway, it is in fact a major market centre, and a popular weekend outing from both Querétaro and the capital. Among the goods sold here are **gemstones** – mostly local opals, but also imported jewels, which are polished and set in town – as well as baskets, wine and cheese. Once again, if you're going to buy gems, be very careful: it's easy to get ripped off. Other purchases are safer, though not particularly cheap on the whole. The best-known local wine is Hidalgo, a brand sold all over the country and usually reliable.

The Mercado Reforma and the twin central squares of the Jardín Independencia and Plaza de los Fundadores are a couple of long blocks north of **Avenida Juárez**, up Hidalgo, but there is more interest a couple of blocks south of Juárez at **Museo de la Muerte**, 2 de Abril 42 (Tues–Sun 10am–6pm; free), where the former cemetery, on a hill overlooking town behind the church of Santa Veracruz, conveys the different ways Mexicans express their connectedness with the dead. The fairly cursory displays of pre-Hispanic and Catholic rituals and beliefs won't detain you long. At weekends, a tourist trolley, the **Tranvia Turístico** (Sat & Sun noon, 1pm, 2pm & 3pm; M$40) makes a circuit of all the main sights in the area.

Practicalities

Direct buses from Querétaro (Flecha Azul from Sala B, among others; every 20min; around M$25) take forty minutes to get to San Juan del Río's **bus station**, a couple of kilometres south of town. A local bus will run you up Hidalgo (M$5) and drop you on a broad section of Avenida Juárez, where there's a central fountain, manicured trees and an attractive arcade on one side. Here you'll find an occasionally open **tourist kiosk** (check Ⓦwww.sanjuanense.com for current information).

If you decide that you'd like to stay a while to enjoy San Juan's unhurried atmosphere, take your choice of several good **hotels**, on or just off Juárez: the best value is *Layseca*, very central at Juárez 9 Ote (Ⓣ427/272-0110,

Edward James

Born in 1907 to a second-rank British aristocratic mother and American railroad millionaire father, **Edward James** may well have also been an illegitimate descendant of King Edward VII. He grew up cosseted by an Eton and Oxford education, and with no lack of money set about a life as a poet and artist. Meeting with only limited success, he turned his attentions to becoming a patron of the arts, partly in an attempt to prolong his waning marriage to a Hungarian dancer, Tilly Losch. Despite his bankrolling ballets that served as vehicles for her talent (notably those by George Balanchine's first company), she eventually left him, whereupon he retreated from London society to Europe. Here he befriended Salvador Dalí, and agreed to buy his entire output for the whole of 1938. As James increasingly aligned himself with the Surrealists, Picasso and Magritte also benefited from his patronage. Indeed, Picasso is reputed to have described James as "crazier than all the Surrealists put together. They pretend, but he is the real thing." During World War II, James moved to the US, where he partly funded LA's Watts Towers and made his first visit south of the border. After falling in love with Xilitla, he moved here in the late 1940s and experimented with growing orchids (which all died in a freak snowstorm in 1962) and running a small zoo. In his later years he was often seen with a parrot or two in tow as he went about building his concrete fantasy world. Aided by local collaborator and long-time companion **Plutarco Gastelum Esquer** and up to 150 workers, James fashioned **Las Pozas** (see p.310) continually revising and developing, but never really finishing anything. By the time he died in 1984, he had created 36 sculptures, spread over more than 20 acres of jungle. He left his estate to Esquer and his family, though without making any provision for the upkeep of his work.

Ⓔ hotellayseca@prodigy.net.mx; ❹), an old colonial house with nicely decorated rooms set around an appealing open courtyard. In summer you might appreciate the pool at the friendly, pleasant and comfortable *Portal Royalty*, Juárez 20 Ote (Ⓣ 427/672-0038; ❺). For something to eat, choose from several **restaurants** along Juárez, many with outdoor seating. There's tasty seafood at *Plaza del Mariscos*, at Juárez 1 and Hidalgo (Ⓣ 427/272-7200), and a M$48 *menu del día* and good coffee, burgers and salads at the fun *Café con Rock*, Plaza Independencia 61 (daily 1–11pm; Ⓣ 427/272-3323).

The Sierra Gorda and Xilitla

You'll need to set aside a couple of days to explore the hill country to the northeast of Querétaro, particularly if you're headed for the wonderful tropical fantasy world of **Las Pozas** at Xilitla. This is the **Sierra Gorda**, a remote and mountainous region where roads are winding and travel slow; much of the region is now protected within the Reserva de la Biosfera Sierra Gorda (Ⓦ www.sierragorda.net). There are bus services to most places and several companies run tours, but this is an ideal region to explore by car, motorbike or even bicycle, though you'll need to be fit.

Apart from Las Pozas, the region's main attractions are the **Sierra Gorda missions**, five communities (each with an elaborate church) from the final phase of Mexico's Christianization in the mid-eighteenth century. The missions were founded by Spanish Franciscan **Frey Junípero Serra**, who'll be familiar to Californians – once his work in Mexico was complete, he continued evangelizing in the new missions there. He spent nine years in the Sierra Gorda working with, and gaining the trust of, the indigenous people. It is this rare synthesis of missionary and native creative efforts that earned the district UNESCO World Heritage status in 2003.

Fiestas

The Bajío is one of the most active regions in Mexico when it comes to celebrations. The state of Guanajuato is especially rich in fiestas: the list below is by no means comprehensive and local tourist offices (and the state websites) will have further details.

January

Fiesta de Cristo de Matehuala (Jan 6–15). Feria in Matehuala (see p.235).

Feria de León (Jan 10–20). Agricultural and industrial fair in León (see p.267).

Día de San Sebastián (Jan 20). The climax of ten days of pilgrimages in San Luis Potosí and León (see p.267).

Natalicio del General Allende (Jan 21). Parades and celebrations in San Miguel de Allende (see p.284).

February

Día de la Candelaria (Feb 2). Major religious festival in San Juan de los Lagos (see p.267).

March

St Patrick's Day (March 17). Now in San Miguel de Allende (see p.284).

Batalla de las Flores (Fri before Good Friday). Altar-building in Guanajuato (see p.268).

Semana Santa (Holy Week). Observed with a huge procession almost everywhere. See especially San Miguel de Allende, San Luis Potosí and Guanajuato (see p.268).

Zacatecas en la Cultura (two weeks around Semana Santa). Enormous citywide celebrations of all strands of culture in Zacatecas (see p.248).

Feria del Toro de Lidia (middle week of March). Bullfights in Tequisquiapan (see p.305).

Peregrinatión (two Sun before Easter). Religious procession in San Miguel de Allende (see p.284).

April

Feria de San Marcos (mid-April to mid-May). Huge, month-long fair in Aguascalientes (see p.260).

Peregrinatión (second Sun before Easter). Culmination of a week's celebration in San Miguel de Allende, with an overnight pilgrimage following an image of Our Lord of the Column from Atotonilco to the church of San Juan de Dios in San Miguel. The procession is greeted at dawn with rejoicing and fireworks (see p.284).

May

Internacional Feria de Queso y Vino (late May–early June). Tequisquiapan (see p.305).

Día de María Auxiliadora (May 24). Fiesta lasting until the next Sun at Empalme Escobeda, 25km south of San Miguel de Allende, with traditional dances including that of Los Apaches, one of the few in which women take part.

June

Fiesta de San Antonio de Padua (June 13). "The Crazies" are out in San Miguel de Allende (see p.284).

Fiestas de San Juan y Presa de la Olla (June 24). This Guanajuato family festival kicks off with the coronation of a festival queen, and features concerts by Mexican pop stars, a food festival, craft displays and activities aimed at kids (see p.268).

July

Apertura de la Presa de la Olla (first Mon in July). Festivities and dancing in Guanajuato (see p.268).

Festival del Día de Santiago (July 25). Stylized battles just outside Aguascalientes (see p.260).

International Folk Festival (late July–early Aug). Mexico's top folk festival in Zacatecas, with around fifty nationalities represented (see p.248).

August

Festival de Música de Cámara (first two weeks of Aug). Chamber music festival in San Miguel de Allende (see p.284).

Día de la Asunción (Assumption; Aug 15). Religious and grape festivals in San Luis Potosí and Aguascalientes (see p.260).

Día de San Luis Rey (Aug 25). Festivities in San Luis Potosí (see p.240).

La Morisma (weekend closest to Aug 27). Massive mock battle between Moors and Christians in Zacatecas (see p.248).

September

Día de la Virgen de Remedios (Sept 1). Lively fiesta in Comonfort, 25km south of San Miguel de Allende (see p.284).

Feria de Zacatecas (first two weeks of Sept). Zacatecas's principal fiesta (see p.248).

Fiesta de San Francisco de Asís (second Sat in Sept to fourth Sun in Oct). Weekly pilgrimages to Real de Catorce. (see p.236)

Día de la Virgen de la Soledad (Sept 8–15). Festival in Jerez (see p.260).

Independence Day (Sept 16). Celebrations everywhere, particularly in Dolores Hidalgo and San Miguel de Allende (see p.284).

San Miguel Arcángel (Sept 29). San Miguel de Allende's most important festivities (see p.284).

October

Fiesta de San Francisco de Asís (Oct 4). Final massive pilgrimage in Real de Catorce (see p.236).

Festival Internacional Cervantino (early to mid-Oct). Huge cultural and arts festival in Guanajuato (see p.238).

November

Día de los Muertos (Day of the Dead; Nov 2). Celebrated everywhere (see p.54).

Fiesta de las Iluminaciones (Nov 7–14). Religious festivities in Guanajuato (see p.268).

Festival Internacional de Jazz & Blues (last weekend in Nov). In San Miguel de Allende (see p.284).

December

Día de la Inmaculada Concepción (Dec 8). A religious festival with a feria and traditional dancing in Dolores Hidalgo and San Juan de los Lagos (see p.267).

Christmas Posadas (Dec 16–25). These traditional parades are widely performed. Particularly good in Querétaro on Dec 23 when there's a giant procession with bands and carnival floats (see p.295).

Jalpan

The main route from Querétaro towards Xilitla is Hwy-120, picked up at the small town of Ezequiel Montes. From there it twists its way through the mountains, climbing a couple of passes. The only major town along the way is **JALPAN**, in the heart of the Sierra Gorda, 120km northeast of Querétaro. Now the largest of the missions, it is an attractive colonial place centred on its church. This was the first such church in the area and its Baroque facade became a template for the others to follow. On either side of its central panel are the Virgins of Pilar and Guadalupe, the patrons of Spain and Mexico. For more background on the missions and the indigenous people who built them, call at the **Museo Historic de Sierra Gorda**, on the square at Junípero Serra 1 (daily 10am–3pm & 5–7pm; M$10). Next door is the inviting *Hotel Misión Jalpán* (Ⓣ441/296-0165, Ⓦwww.hotelesmision.com.mx; ➎), and across the plaza you can **stay** at the *Hotel María del Carmen*, Independencia 8 (Ⓣ441/296-0328; ➌). The **bus station** is 1km northeast of town.

The other four missions – Landa, Tilaco, Tacoyol and Concá – are harder to visit without your own transport.

Xilitla and Las Pozas

Travelling through the Sierra Gorda is a joy in itself, but really doesn't prepare you for the picturesque small town of **Xilitla**, sprawled over the eastern foothills some 320km northeast of Querétaro. Hemmed in by limestone cliffs, it's set in a dramatic location, and at 600m, it's warmer than the rest of the Bajío, with a lusher feel. There are tremendous views over the surrounding temperate rainforest, which is thick with waterfalls, birdlife and flowers, particularly wild orchids. It is mainly of interest as a place to relax, though you might devote a few minutes to admiring the beautifully preserved interior of the sixteenth-century **Ex-Convento de San Agustín**, which overlooks the central plaza, Jardín Hidalgo.

The real justification for the lengthy journey to Xilitla is to visit **Las Pozas** (roughly 9am–6pm; M$30; Ⓦwww.xilitla.org), some 2.5km east of town along a dirt road: head down Ocampo on the north side of the square, turn left and follow the signs. It is a pleasant walk downhill on the way there, or you can grab a taxi for around M$60. Having lived here since 1947, English eccentric **Edward James** (see box, p.307) spent the 1960s and 1970s creating a surreal jungle fantasy on the site, full of outlandish concrete statues and structures. Sprouting beside nine pools ("pozas") of a cascading jungle river you'll find a spiral staircase that winds up until it disappears to nothing, stone hands almost 2m high, thick columns with no purpose, a mosaic snake and buildings such as the "House With Three Stories That Might be Five" and "The House Destined To Be a Cinema". Only one is in any sense liveable, a hideaway apartment four storeys up where James spent much of his time. With so little complete, there are all sorts of unprotected precipices: take care. In 2007, the Fondo Xilitla consortium (which includes CEMEX and the San Luis Potosí state government) bought the site for US$2.2 million, with the aim of turning it into a world-class attraction; plans are still at an early stage (and any development is likely to be slow-moving), but check the website for the latest.

For now at least you can see everything in an hour or so, but plan to spend the better part of a day here bathing in the pools and just chilling out; the restaurant is usually open Wed–Sun. You can also take a guided tour (in English M$250; 1hr 15min), which can be a good way to get to grips with what's on display.

Back in town, call at the **Museo Edward James**, behind the *Posada El Castillo* (nominally daily 10am–6pm, but actually open when they feel like it; M$30), which showcases James's life and particularly his work here. Photos of the construction are particularly worth perusing.

Practicalities

Getting to Xilitla can be time-consuming. Eight twisting hours through the Sierra Gorda from Querétaro (7 buses daily), it's perhaps most easily accessed by bus from the unexciting but sizeable town of Ciudad Valles, on the highway between San Luis Potosí and Tampico (hourly 4am–5pm; M$55; 1hr 30min), some 60km north. There are also one or two services direct from Tampico (M$250; 4hr) and San Luis Potosí (M$400; 6hr): all pull up outside one of two bus company offices close to Jardín Hidalgo. There's no tourist office, but everything else (including several **banks** with ATMs and the **post office**) is easy to find on the streets nearby. Here, too, you'll find several serviceable restaurants such as *Cayo's* (Ⓣ489/365-0044), two blocks from the plaza at Alvarado 117, with good basic Mexican food (try the cheese-filled *enchiladas huastecas*) and superb views across the palms. You'll also find plenty of taco stands and simple, clean accommodation around the plaza.

The **place to stay** in Xilitla is *Posada El Castillo*, Ocampo 105, half a block down from the plaza (Ⓣ489/365-0038, Ⓦwww.junglegossip.com/castillo.html; no credit cards; ❺), in the house where James lived when he wasn't ensconced in his hut or apartment at Las Pozas. His spirit still inhabits the eight highly individual guestrooms, harmoniously blending Mexican, English and Moorish styles. There's a lovely pool, meals are served and the hosts not only speak English but also have produced a documentary on James's life and work, which they screen for guests. If your budget can't stretch this far, stay at *Hotel Dolores*, Matamoros 211 (Ⓣ489/365-0178, Ⓦwww.hoteldoloresxilitla.com; ❹), a modern and very clean hotel featuring elegant rooms with TV and fan, some also with air-conditioning and fine mountain views (M$500). To get there, follow Hidalgo east from the main square for one long block, head straight across the road and down a long flight of stairs. At the bottom of the steps turn left. The cheapest rooms are at *Hotel Casa María Mercado*, Guerrero 103, tucked in behind the market (Ⓣ489/365-0049; ❷). They're all decent, clean and ranged around a modern central courtyard. Those on the top floor have more air and limited views.

Travel details

Buses

Aguascalientes to: Guadalajara (roughly hourly; 6hr); Guanajuato (5 daily; 4hr); León (every 30min; 2hr); Matehuala (at least hourly; 2hr); Mexico City (hourly; 7hr); Querétaro (hourly; 6hr); San Luis Potosí (hourly; 3hr); San Miguel de Allende (4 daily; 4hr 30min); Zacatecas (every 30min; 2hr).
Ciudad Valles to: Tampico (12 daily; 2hr 30min); San Luis Potosí (hourly; 4hr 30min); Xilitla (hourly 4am–5pm; 1hr 30min).
Dolores Hidalgo to: Guanajuato (every 20min; 1hr); León (every 20min; 2hr 45min); Mexico City (every 40min; 5hr); Querétaro (every 40min; 2hr 30min); San Luis de la Paz (every 20min; 1hr); San Luis Potosí (10 daily; 2hr 30min); San Miguel de Allende (every 20min; 50min).
Guanajuato to: Aguascalientes (4 daily; 4hr); Dolores Hidalgo (every 20min; 1hr); Guadalajara (5 daily; 6hr); León (constantly; 40min); Mexico City (7 daily; 4hr); Querétaro (8 daily; 3hr); San Luis de la Paz (5 daily; 2hr 30min); San Luis Potosí (10 daily; 3hr); San Miguel de Allende (10 daily; 1hr 30min).
Lagos de Moreno to: Aguascalientes (every 30min; 1hr 30min); Guanajuato (roughly hourly; 1hr 30min); Leon (every 15min; 1hr).
León to: Aguascalientes (hourly; 1hr); Guadalajara (hourly; 4hr); Guanajuato (constantly; 40min); Mexico City (hourly; 5hr); Querétaro (hourly; 2hr); Zacatecas (hourly; 4hr).
Matehuala to: Real de Catorce (4–5 daily; 2hr); Saltillo (hourly or better; 3hr); San Luis Potosí (every 30min; 2hr); Wadley (4 daily; 1hr 45min).
Pozos to: San José Iturbide (every 30min; 40min); San Luis de la Paz (every 30min; 20min).
Querétaro to: Aguascalientes (hourly; 5hr); Bernal (hourly; 1hr); Dolores Hidalgo (every 40min; 2hr); Guadalajara (hourly; 6hr); Guanajuato (6 daily; 3hr);

León (hourly; 2hr); Jalpan (hourly; 5hr); Mexico City (every 10min; 3hr); Morelia (every 30–60min; 3hr); San Juan del Río (every 15min; 45min); San Luis Potosí (hourly; 2hr); San Miguel de Allende (every 40min; 1hr 15min); Tequisquiapan (every 30min; 1hr); Tula (9 daily; 2hr 30min); Xilitla (3 daily; 7hr); Zacatecas (hourly; 5hr).

San José Iturbide to: Pozos (every 30min; 40min); Querétaro (every few min; 1hr 10min); San Luis de la Paz (every 30min; 1hr).

San Juan del Río to: Mexico City (every 15min; 3hr 15min); Querétaro (every 15min; 45min); Tequisquiapan (every 20min; 30min); Tula (9 daily; 1hr 30min).

San Luis de la Paz to: Dolores Hidalgo (every 20min; 1hr); Guanajuato (10 daily; 2hr 30min); Pozos (every 30min; 20min); San José Iturbide (every 30min; 1hr).

San Luis Potosí to: Aguascalientes (hourly; 2hr 30min); Dolores Hidalgo (13 daily; 2hr 30min); Guadalajara (hourly; 5hr); Guanajuato (10 daily; 3hr); Matehuala (every 30min; 2hr 30min); Mexico City (frequently; 5hr); Monterrey (hourly; 7hr); Nuevo Laredo (6 daily; 10hr); Querétaro (hourly; 2hr 30min); San Miguel de Allende (8 daily; 3hr); Tampico (4 daily; 7hr); Wadley (3 daily; 4hr); Zacatecas (10 daily; 3hr).

San Miguel de Allende to: Aguascalientes (2 daily; 4hr); Dolores Hidalgo (every 15min; 50min); Guanajuato (10 daily; 1hr 30min); Mexico City (every 40min; 4hr); Querétaro (every 40min; 1hr 15min); San Luis Potosí (8 daily; 3hr).

Tequisquiapan to: Mexico City (every 40min; 3hr 45min); Querétaro (every 30min; 1hr); San Juan del Río (every 20min; 30min).

Xilitla to: Ciudad Valles (hourly; 1hr 30min); Jalpan (every 30min; 2hr); Querétaro (8 daily; 7hr); San Luis Potosí (3 daily; 6–7hr); Tampico (7 daily; 4–5hr).

Zacatecas to: Aguascalientes (every 30min; 2hr); Chihuahua (hourly; 12hr); Ciudad Juárez (hourly; 16hr); Durango (hourly; 4hr); Guadalajara (hourly; 5hr); Jerez (hourly; 1hr); León (hourly; 4–5hr); Mazatlán (2 daily; 10hr); Mexico City (roughly hourly; 8hr); Monterrey (roughly hourly; 7hr); Nuevo Laredo (5 daily; 8hr); Puerto Vallarta (1 daily; 10hr); Querétaro (hourly; 6hr); San Luis Potosí (10 daily; 3hr); Tijuana (4 daily; 36hr); Torreón (roughly hourly; 6hr).

Flights

Guanajuato/León to: Chicago (1 daily; 5hr); Dallas (3 daily; 2hr); Houston (4 daily; 2hr); Los Angeles (4 weekly; 3hr); Mexico City (9 daily; 1hr); Monterrey (3–4 daily; 1hr 10min); Tijuana (2 daily; 2hr).

San Luis Potosí to: Dallas (1 daily; 1hr 45min); Houston (1 daily; 1hr 45min); Mexico City (7 daily; 1hr 10min); Monterrey (1 daily; 1hr 10min); San Antonio (1 weekly; 1hr 15min).

Zacatecas to: Chicago (1 daily; 4hr 25min); Los Angeles (3 weekly; 3hr); Mexico City (8 daily; 1hr 30min).

5

Northern Jalisco and Michoacán

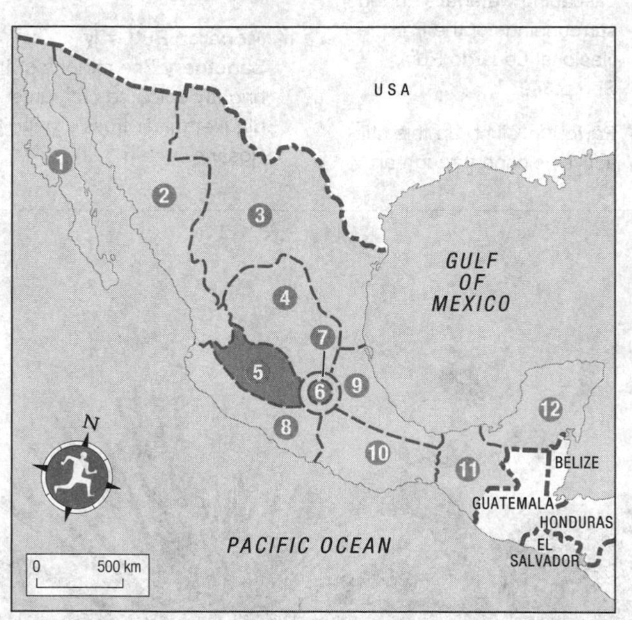

CHAPTER 5

Highlights

* **Guadalajara** Experience the drama of mariachi music in Mexico's most "Mexican" city, the capital of Jalisco. See p.317

* **Tequila** Visit a tequila distillery and, more importantly, sample the legendary spirit in a café on the town's plaza. See p.340

* **Uruapan** Take in the cascading waterfalls and lush surroundings of the Parque Nacional Eduardo Ruíz. See p.349

* **Paricutín** Climb up this still-active volcano through an unearthly landscape. See p.354

* **Pátzcuaro** One of the best places in Mexico for seeing the spectacular and moving Day of the Dead celebrations. See p.355

* **Morelia** Enjoy dulces, wine and classical music in one of the cafés overlooking historic Morelia's central plaza. See p.365

* **Monarch Butterfly Sanctuary** See millions of the brightly coloured creatures blanket the fir trees around El Rosario. See p.372

▲ Harvesting agave plants for tequila

5

Northern Jalisco and Michoacán

Separated from the country's colonial heartland by the craggy peaks of the Sierra Madre, the stretch of land from Guadalajara to Mexico City through the semitropical states of **Jalisco** and **Michoacán** has an unhurried ease that marks it out from the rest of the country. Containing a complex landscape of lofty plains and rugged sierras, the area is blessed with supremely fertile farms, fresh pine woods, cool pastures and lush tropical forest.

Something of a backwater until well into the eighteenth century, the high valleys of Michoacán and Jalisco were left to develop their own strong regional traditions and solid farming economy. Wherever you go, you'll find a wealth of local commercial goods, both agricultural and traditionally manufactured items, from avocados to tequila, glassware to guitars. Relative isolation has also made the region a bastion of conservatism – in the years following the Revolution, the Catholic *Cristero* counter-revolutionary guerrilla movement enjoyed its strongest support here. Nor has the region been unaffected by the country's **drug wars**, as gangs struggle for control of the country's trade in illegal substances. This was gruesomely illustrated in 2006 in otherwise peaceful Uruapan, when mobsters invaded a nightclub and rolled five freshly severed heads onto the dancefloor, and during Independence Day celebrations in 2008, when they threw grenades into the crowd in Morelia's main square, killing eight people. The drug lords aren't interested in law-abiding tourists, so there is no cause for alarm, though you may notice an increase in highway police checks.

Easygoing **Guadalajara**, Mexico's second city is packed with elegant buildings and surrounded by scenic countryside. Outside the city, the land is spectacularly green and mountainous, studded with volcanoes and lakes, most famously **Laguna de Chapala**. There are also some superb colonial relics, especially in the forms of **Morelia** and **Fatzcuaro**, although its the latter's majestic setting and still powerful Indian traditions that first call your attention.

Aside from this, Jalisco and Michoacán are among the most serene states in the country: relaxing, easy to get about and free of urban hassle. Add the fact that Jalisco is the home of **mariachi** and **tequila** and you've got a region where you could easily spend a couple of weeks exploring without even beginning to see everything. Overall, tourist numbers are pretty low except for in Pátzcuaro around the Day of the Dead, and winter weekends at the **Monarch Butterfly Sanctuary**.

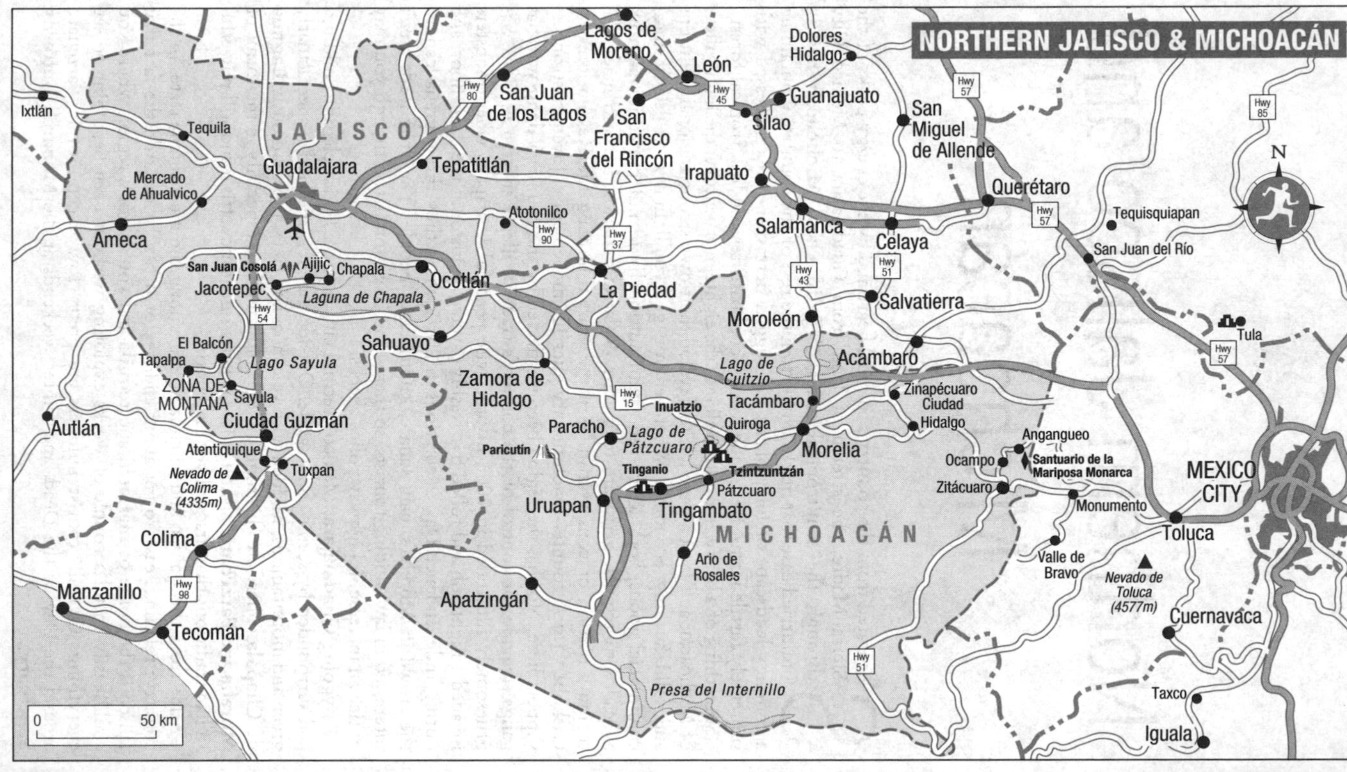
NORTHERN JALISCO & MICHOACÁN
N
JALISCO
MICHOACÁN
Ixtlán
Tequila
Mercado de Ahualvico
Ameca
Guadalajara
Tepatitlán
San Juan de los Lagos
Lagos de Moreno
León
San Francisco del Rincón
Silao
Guanajuato
Dolores Hidalgo
San Miguel de Allende
Irapuato
Querétaro
Tequisquiapan
San Juan del Río
Salamanca
Celaya
Salvatierra
Moroleón
Acámbaro
La Piedad
Atotonilco
Ocotlán
San Juan Cosolá
Ajijic
Chapala
Jacotepec
Laguna de Chapala
Sahuayo
El Balcón
Tapalpa
Lago Sayula
ZONA DE MONTAÑA
Sayula
Autlán
Ciudad Guzmán
Atentiquique
Tuxpan
Nevado de Colima (4335m)
Colima
Manzanillo
Tecomán
Zamora de Hidalgo
Paricutín
Paracho
Lago de Pátzcuaro
Inuatzio
Quiroga
Tinganio
Tzintzuntzán
Pátzcuaro
Uruapan
Tingambato
Ario de Rosales
Apatzingán
Presa del Internillo
Lago de Cuitzio
Tacámbaro
Morelia
Zinapécuaro
Ciudad Hidalgo
Angangueo
Ocampo
Santuario de la Mariposa Monarca
Zitácuaro
Monumento
Valle de Bravo
Nevado de Toluca (4577m)
Toluca
MEXICO CITY
Cuernavaca
Taxco
Iguala
Tula
Hwy 80
Hwy 45
Hwy 57
Hwy 85
Hwy 90
Hwy 37
Hwy 43
Hwy 51
Hwy 54
Hwy 15
Hwy 98
0
50 km

Guadalajara and northern Jalisco

Guadalajara dominates the state of Jalisco as its capital and main attraction, but outside the capital, the state is green, lush and mountainous. **Tequila** offers fine liquor, **Laguna de Chapala** has tranquil scenery, and mountain villages such as Tapalpa have fresh air and a more sedate pace of life.

Guadalajara

The second city of the Mexican Republic, **GUADALAJARA** is considered the most "Mexican" of the country's big cities. Being less frenetic than the capital, however, doesn't make it peaceful, and Guadalajara is huge and sprawling. Its conversion to a sleek metropolis has resulted in a hike in prices and some sacrifice of Mexican mellowness in favour of a US-style business ethic, but it's still an enjoyable place to visit, with the edge on Mexico's other big cities for trees, flowers, cleanliness and friendliness. It also remains a great place to see something of traditional and modern Mexico, as it offers everything from museums, galleries and colonial architecture to magnificent revolutionary murals by José Clemente Orozco to a nightlife scene enlivened by a large student population.

Parks, little squares and open spaces dot the city. Right downtown, around the cathedral, is a series of plazas unchanged since the days of the Spanish colonization. This small colonial heart of Guadalajara can still, especially at weekends, recall an old-world atmosphere and provincial elegance. The centre is further brightened by the **Plaza Tapatía**, which opens out the city's historical core to pedestrians, mariachi bands and street theatre. Around this relatively unruffled nucleus revolve raucous and crowded streets typical of modern Mexico, while further out still, in the wide boulevards of the new suburbs, you'll find smart hotels, shopping malls and office buildings.

Some history

Guadalajara was founded in 1532, one of the fruits of the vicious campaign of **Nuño de Guzmán** at the time of the Conquest – his cruelty and corruption were such that he appalled even the Spanish authorities, who threw him into prison in Madrid, where he died. The city, named after Guzmán's birthplace, thrived, was officially recognized by Charles V in 1542 and rapidly became one of the colony's most Spanish cities – in part because so much of the indigenous population had been killed or had fled during the Conquest. Isolated from the great mining industry of the Bajío, Guadalajara evolved into a regional centre for trade and agriculture. The tight reins of colonial rule restrained the city's development, and it wasn't until the end of the eighteenth century, as the colonial monopolies began to crumble, that things really took off. Between 1760 and 1803 the city's population tripled, reaching some 35,000; a new university was established; and the city became famous for the export of wheat, hides, cotton and wool.

When Spain's colonial empire finally fell apart, Guadalajara supported Hidalgo's independence movement and briefly served as the capital of the nation. By the

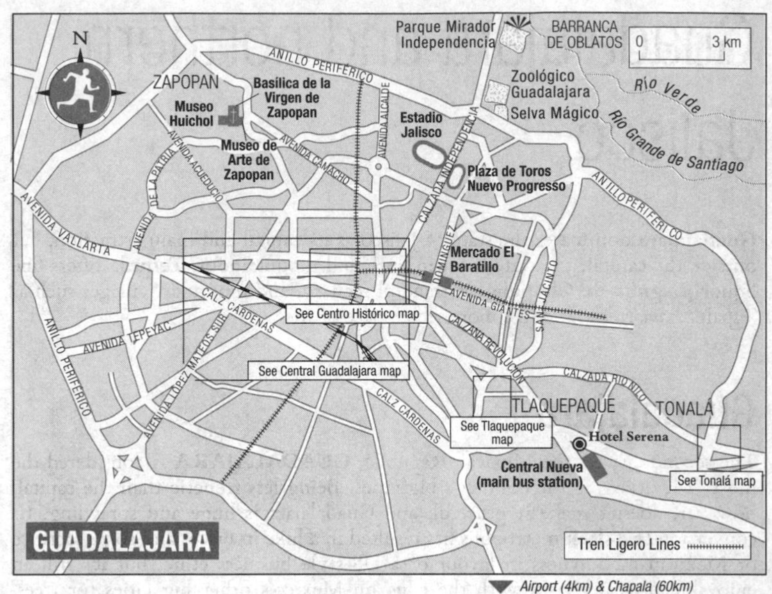

beginning of the twentieth century it was already the second largest city in the Republic, and in the 1920s the completion of the rail link with California provided a further spur for development. More recently, the exodus from Mexico City and attempts at industrial decentralization have continued to swell the urban area's population, which now tops four million.

Arrival

Guadalajara's **airport** is some 17km southeast of the city on the road to Chapala. Facilities include money exchange and car rental, and there's also the usual system of fixed-price taxis and vans to take you downtown (around M$220 for a car with up to four people – vouchers are sold inside the terminal and the ride takes 45min–1hr). The cheap way of getting into town (M$5–10) is to head out of the terminal and right, continue for about 200m to the next junction, and take a red and white Chapala bus from the stop in front of the PEMEX station to the Central Vieja (see opposite). City bus #176 to the city centre also passes here, but does not usually stop to pick up passengers.

Some 10km out in the city's southeastern suburbs, Guadalajara's **Central Nueva** (aka Camionera Nueva), is one of Mexico's largest bus terminals, comprising seven buildings strung out in a wide arc, with its own shopping centre (Nueva Central Plaza) and hotel (the *Serena*; see p.323. Each building serves a different area, but since they're organized by bus company rather than route, it's not quite that simple – there are buses to Mexico City from just about every building, for example. Bus company staff are usually happy to tell you which company, and therefore which building, suits your needs. #616 ("Centro") and the slightly dearer (but faster) turquoise TUR bus stop outside each terminal, #644B or #275 from Avenida Revolución, the main road behind terminal 1 (which takes a more direct route than #616); all these take you to Avenida 16 de Septiembre, within walking distance of the cathedral if not right past it. The last city buses between the terminal and the centre leave at around 10pm. A taxi downtown costs around M$95. For details of how to reach the terminal from the centre see the box on p.334; for details of intercity services from the terminal, see p.339.

Some second-class buses from local destinations, including Tequila, Tapalpa, Ciudad Guzmán and the villages on the shores of Laguna de Chapala, as well as the airport service, use the **Central Vieja** (aka Camionera Vieja), the old downtown terminal, surrounded by cheap hotels. If you're coming from somewhere only an hour or two away, it can be worth the slightly less comfortable second-class journey for the convenience of this much more central point of arrival. The two bus stations are connected by the #616 bus.

The **train station**, a couple of kilometres south of the centre at the bottom of Calzada Independencia is used only for the touristy Tequila Express (see box, p.340).

Orientation

The centre of the old city is a relatively compact grid around the junction of **Morelos** and **16 de Septiembre**, by the huge bulk of the **cathedral**; east of here Morelos leads to the **Plaza Tapatía** and the **Mercado Libertad**, while to the west are busy shopping streets. **Juárez**, a couple of blocks south, is actually the main east–west thoroughfare in the centre, heading out to the west past the **university** (where it becomes Vallarta), and crossing avenidas **Chapultepec** and **Américas** in an upmarket residential area. Further west still, it crosses **López Mateos**, a main through route, which heads south past the **Plaza del Sol**, a shopping centre surrounded by big hotels, restaurants and much of Guadalajara's best, but most expensive, nightlife, and eventually heads out of the city as the main road towards Colima and the coast.

The main north–south arteries in the centre are the **Calzada del Federalismo**, along which the Tren Ligero, the city's metro, runs, and **Calzada Independencia**, which runs from the train station past the **Parque Agua Azul**, the old bus station, the market and Plaza Tapatía, and eventually out of the city to the **Parque Mirador**. Finally, **Revolución** leads off Independencia towards the southeast, to Tlaquepaque, the new bus station and Tonalá. If you fancy taking a **city tour** to get your bearings, try Panoramex (Ⓣ33/3647-8363, Ⓦwww.panoramex.com.mx), which offers a five-hour tour in Spanish and English for M$300 and day trips with English-speaking guides to Chapala and Ajijic, or to the Cuervo distillery in Tequila, for the same price.

Information

There is a **tourist information office** (Mon–Fri 9.30am–2.30pm) just inside the main entrance of the Palacio de Gobierno on Plaza de Armas, and tourist information booths (Mon–Fri 8.30am–1.55pm & 2.30–7.55pm, Sat & Sun 9.30am–2.55pm) at the main bus station, the airport, Plaza de Guadalajara (the square in front of the cathedral), Plaza de la Liberación, Morelos with Independencia, Plaza Tapatía, and

Useful bus routes

All of these also run in the opposite direction: the #600 numbers are minibuses.

#60 Calzada Independencia–soccer stadium and bullring–Central Vieja

#176 Centro–airport

#275 Tonalá–Central Nueva –Tlaquepaque–Centro (16 Septiembre)–Zapopan

#616 Centro (Jardín de San Francisco)–Central Vieja–Central Nueva

#629 Centro–Morelos (westbound)/Pedro Moreno (eastbound)–Minerva Circle

#706 TUR Tonalá–Central Nueva –Tlaquepaque–Centro (16 Septiembre)–Zapopan

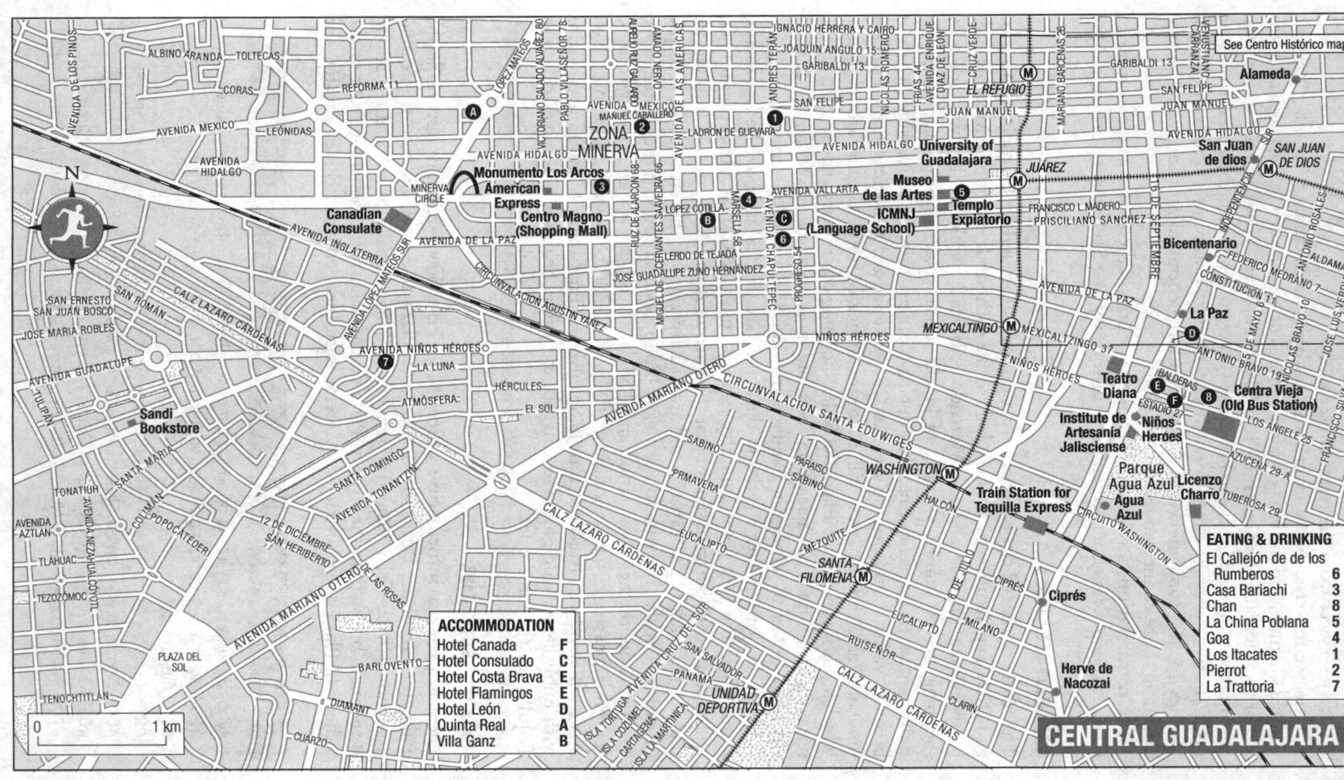
CENTRAL GUADALAJARA
See Centro Histórico map
Alameda
San Juan de dios
Bicentenario
La Paz
Centra Vieja (Old Bus Station)
Teatro Diana
Institute de Artesanía Jalisciense
Niños Heroes
Parque Agua Azul
Agua Azul
Licenzo Charro
Train Station for Tequilla Express
Ciprés
Herve de Nacozai
University of Guadalajara
Museo de las Artes
Templo Expiatorio
ICMNJ (Language School)
Monumento Los Arcos
American Express
Centro Magno (Shopping Mall)
Canadian Consulate
Sandi Bookstore
ZONA MINERVA
EATING & DRINKING
El Callejón de de los Rumberos 6
Casa Bariachi 3
Chan 8
La China Poblana 5
Goa 4
Los Itacates 1
Pierrot 2
La Trattoria 7
ACCOMMODATION
Hotel Canada F
Hotel Consulado C
Hotel Costa Brava E
Hotel Flamingos E
Hotel León D
Quinta Real A
Villa Ganz B
0 1 km
N

Jardín de San Francisco, or you can call the state tourism office on ⓣ33/3668-1600 or 3668-1601, or toll-free from elsewhere in the country on ⓣ01-800/363-2200. Guadalajara's city council has a very good tourist information website at ⓦvive.guadalajara.gob.mx, and the city's Visitors and Conventions Office has one at ⓦwww.gdlmidestino.com.

The best source of **listings** information is the *Acid* magazine section that comes with Friday's edition of Guadalajara's main newspaper, *Público*. The cooler cafes often have a copy lying around. For something in English, opt for the weekly *Guadalajara Reporter* (ⓦwww.guadalajarareporter.com), which reflects the concerns of the expat community in town and around Laguna de Chapala.

For details of **banks**, foreign exchange, **post offices**, **telephones** and much more, see "Listings", p.338.

City transport

Getting around town is not too difficult once you've got the hang of the transport system. Most city-centre attractions are within walking distance of each other, and almost all buses are funnelled through the centre on a few main roads, with destinations on the windscreen. The sheer number of buses and the speed at which they move can make things slightly more difficult, however, especially at peak hours when you may have to fight to get on; if possible, get a local to show you exactly where your bus stops. Most bus rides cost M$5, but the turquoise, air-conditioned TUR express buses cost M$9.50. Along Calzada Independencia, the **Macrobús** (ⓦwww.macrobus.com), with its own dedicated lanes, and stations with platforms, costs M$5 per journey.

The **Tren Ligero** (metro system), with one north–south and one east–west line, is designed for local commuters. You may not use it at all, though it can be handy for quick east–west travel across the centre. To ride, buy a one-journey token (M$5) from a machine on the platform.

Taxis are also reliable if you're in a hurry, and for a group they aren't usually too expensive as long as you establish a price at the outset; many downtown taxi ranks post a list of fixed prices. From the centre to the Plaza del Sol, Central Nueva or Zapopan should cost around M$80; it'll be around M$50 to Tlaquepaque and M$170 to the airport. Fares are generally 25 percent higher after 10pm and before 6am.

The best way to get around, however, is **on foot** – Guadalajara's streets are even more pleasant if you appreciate them slowly.

Accommodation

With a range of hotels to suit all budgets (as well as a couple of **hostels**) right in the *centro histórico*, there is little reason to stay elsewhere in the city. In this area you'll be able to walk to everything in the centre and have easy access to buses out to the outlying suburbs.

If you're looking for a budget option and the central places are all full, consider some of the **cheap hotels** around the old bus station or in the streets south of the Mercado Libertad. Both areas are noisy and none too appealing, though the hotels we've listed are fine.

Most of the more **expensive** business hotels tend to be a long way out to the west of the city, though you're almost certainly better off in the **luxury B&B-style places** downtown or in Tlaquepaque.

There's also Avenida López Mateos, 2km to the west of the centre, which is Guadalajara's **motel** row. This can be handy if you're driving and don't want to tackle the city. Finally, if you arrive late at night at the **Central Nueva** and all you want to do is sleep, try *Hotel Serena* (see p.323).

In the centre

Don Quixote Hotel Héroes 91 ⓣ33/3658-1299, ⓦwww.hoteldonquijoteplaza.com.mx. Friendly, small hotel with rooms around a colonial-style courtyard. A little more characterful than most of the hotels in this price bracket. ❹

AP Hostel Guadalajara Centro Maestranza 147 ⓣ33/3562-7520, ⓦwww.hostelguadalajara.com. Very central and modern hostel (though in an old building) full of backpackers and language students, with internet access, laundry and cooking facilities, free bicycle hire, private lockers and friendly staff who regularly organize nights out to interesting bars. A light breakfast is included and if you pay in advance you get four nights for the price of three. Dorms M$165, ISIC cardholders M$145, IYH members M$125. ❸

Hostel de María Nueva Galicia 924 ⓣ33/3614-6230, ⓔhostaldemaria@prodigy.net.mx. Peaceful hostel in a quiet neighbourhood near the cathedral. Mostly six-bunk dorms (M$165/person, HI members M$155) plus a couple of private rooms. Free internet access and a continental breakfast included. ❹

Hotel de Mendoza Carranza 16, at Hidalgo ⓣ33/3942-5151, ⓦwww.demendoza.com.mx. Attractive establishment in a refurbished colonial convent. Rooms come with all amenities (including a safe) and access to the nicest pool in the centre. A great location makes this an ideal base for sightseeing. ❽

Hotel Fénix Corona 160 ⓣ33/3614-5714, ⓦwww.holahoteles.com.mx. Large, modern, four-star hotel with impeccable rooms right in the centre. Go for one on the upper floors with views of the cathedral. Promotional rates are usually available, sometimes including breakfast. Wheelchair-accessible. ❼

Hotel Francés Maestranza 35 (just off the plaza behind the cathedral) ⓣ33/3613-1190 or 01-800/718 -5309, ⓦwww.hotelfrances.com. Guadalajara's most appealing upmarket hotel, in a beautiful colonial building, founded as an inn in 1610 (its elevator is said to be the second ever installed in the city), though the rooms are a little drab and you might want to upgrade to a junior suite (M$819). Even if you're not staying, try to stop by for a superb margarita in the lobby bar. ❺

Hotel Hamilton Madero 381 ⓣ33/3641-6726. Clean and friendly, the *Hamilton* is very cheap and consequently a popular spot with backpackers and young Mexican couples. Rooms have private bath, and TV costs a few pesos extra. ❷

Hotel Jorge Alejandro Hidalgo 656 ⓣ33/3614-0532, ⓦwww.hotel-jorgealejandro.com. Spotless rooms in a central hotel. Most rooms are carpeted, and there's internet access and parking. Larger rooms are good for families or groups. ❸

Hotel Posada San Pablo Madero 429 ⓣ33/3614-2811. Spotless rooms around a covered courtyard, but only the upstairs rooms with shared bathrooms have outside windows. Ring the bell at the front door for entrance. ❸

Hotel Santiago de Compostela Colón 272 ⓣ33/3613-8880, or 01-800/365-5300, ⓦwww.hotelsantiagodecompostelagdl.com. Attractive hotel set around an enclosed courtyard decorated with Turkish rugs. Rooms are well appointed with a/c, carpets and cable TV, though the streetside ones can be noisy. All have a deep tiled bath but you may just prefer to use the lovely rooftop pool. ❺

Posada Regis Corona 171 ⓣ33/3613-3026, ⓦwww.posadaregis.com. Appealing ramshackle old building locked away from the world behind an iron gate, and with high-ceilinged rooms around a peaceful, covered courtyard. They also have small rooms on the roof (M$200/person) that are ideal for one but acceptable for two. ❹

San Rafael Inn López Cotilla 619 ⓣ33/3614-9146, ⓦsanrafael1.tripod.com. A pleasant, friendly little place in a prettily decorated old house. For those on a budget, they have a few cheap rooms with shared bath (❷), but these need to be reserved well ahead. Some rooms are brighter than others, and internet access is available. ❸

Around the Mercado Libertad

Hotel Ana-Isabel Javier Mina 164 ⓣ33/3617-7920. Simple but clean tiled rooms with TVs and parking nearby. Apart from one room, windows face inward, which can make the rooms rather dark (those on the top floor less so). Go for the quieter rooms at the back if possible. ❸

Hotel Chapala José María Mercado 84 ⓣ33/3617-7159, ⓕ3617-3410. Around the corner from the *Ana-Isabel*, with small but neat rooms, all equipped with a TV and ceiling fan. You pay slightly less for rooms on the second floor than for those on the first. ❷

Hotel Maya López Cotilla 39 ⓣ33/3614-5454. Decorated in vibrant pink and verging on the kitsch, the rooms are bare but decent with TV and parking. It is a noisy area but a short walk to the centre. ❸

South of the centre: Calzada Independencia and the Central Vieja

Hotel Canada Estadio 77 ⓣ33/3619-4014, ⓕ3619-3110. One of dozens of hotels surrounding the old bus station, this large place is pretty good value with the bonus of the excellent *Restaurante*

Ottawa and some slightly nicer "suites" (M$350). Not to be confused with the *Gran Hotel Canada* nearby. ❸

Hotel Costa Brava Independencia 739 Sur ⓣ33/3619-2324 or 3619-2327. Friendly, new hotel. All rooms have TV. Those facing the road are slightly fancier, but the inward-facing rooms are quieter. ❷

Hotel Flamingos Independencia 725 Sur ⓣ33/3619-8764. Though the hotel is in a slightly run-down 1970s concrete building, the rooms are clean and fresh, and there's even a penthouse suite. ❷

Hotel León Independencia 557 Sur ⓣ33/3619-6141 (also shown on the map on p.320). Very cheap and basic, but clean and perfectly serviceable. Rooms have bathrooms and 24hr hot water. A bargain. ❶

West of the centre: López Cotilla and the Zona Minerva

Hotel Consulado López Cotilla 1405 ⓣ33/3563-6465, ⓦwww.hotelconsuladogdl.com.mx. With its chic modern entrance and minimal leather sofas this place is unlike almost everywhere else in town, though the comfortable rooms don't quite follow the style. There's free internet, off-street parking and several good restaurants nearby. ❹

Quinta Real México 2727 ⓣ01-800/500-4000 or 33/3669-0600, toll-free from the US ⓣ1-866/621-9288, ⓦwww.quintareal.com. Gorgeous luxury hotel that's also well set up for business guests. The grounds are spacious and immaculately tended, with a pool, and the suites come with neocolonial styling and every amenity. Breakfast included. ❾

Villa Ganz López Cotilla 1739 ⓣ33/3120-1416, ⓦwww.villaganz.com. A gorgeous boutique hotel with nine impeccably decorated suites and most luxuries on hand; no pool but free use of a nearby gym. Common areas are so delightful you'll never want to step outside, though it is only a short walk to some great bars and restaurants. Rates start at US$245 and include continental breakfast and "welcome cocktail". ❾

Near the Central Nueva

Hotel Serena Central Nueva, beside Sala 1 (see map, p.318) ⓣ33/3600-0910. Conveniently located by the Central Nueva, this hotel is modern and soulless, and not the cleanest place in town, but has two pools, a restaurant and 24hr room service, and the rooms are reasonably quiet. ❹

Tlaquepaque

AP Casa Campos B&B Francisco Miranda 30-A. ⓣ33/3838-5296, ⓦwww.hotelcasacampos.com. One of the most charming places in town to lay your head, this beautifully remodelled colonial house comes with modern fittings, an understated elegance and a family of palm-size marmoset monkeys that have free range of the garden. Rates include breakfast in the adjacent sleek modern restaurant *Sandwich & Friends*. Reserve well ahead, especially in winter. ❽

Hacienda retreats

For a completely different perspective on Jalisco, consider staying at one of the numerous well-preserved **haciendas** within an hour's drive of Guadalajara. They are easy, if somewhat pricey, overnight escapes which offer a change of pace from the bustling city. Haciendas are ideal for those on shorter trips who want quickly and comfortably to experience a bit of the countryside, and learn a little about a different side of *Tapatío* lifestyle. The tourist office of Guadalajara (ⓣ33/3668-1600, ⓦwww.visita.jalisco.gob.mx) can provide information on these and other rural homes and relaxing retreats. You can also go directly to ⓦwww.haciendasycasonas.com, which has links to more than twenty such places.

One particularly fine example is *Hacienda El Carmen*, 35km west of the city, Km 58 Carretera Gdl-Tala-Etzatlán (ⓣ33/3633-1771 or 01-800/561-4053, ⓦwww.haciendaelcarmen.com.mx; ❽, which originated as a family-owned estate, became a convent in 1722 and retains a traditional feel in its current incarnation as a luxury hotel. Colonial-style accommodation encircles a patio garden, full spa and Aztec sweat lodge. There's also horseriding and mountain-biking on country roads, and nearby you'll find the archeological ruins of Guachimontones (Teuchitlán, 300–900 AD).

Other top haciendas in the area include: *Hostal Casona de Manzano* (ⓣ343/432-1141, ⓦwww.casonademanzano.com; ❼), *La Casa de Los Patios* (ⓣ342/422-0112, ⓦwww.lacasadelospatios.com; ❺) and *Hotel-Restaurante Mis Amores* (ⓣ376/766-4640, ⓦwww.misamores.com; ❻).

La Casa del Retoño Matamoros 182 ☎33/3635-7636, Ⓦwww.lacasadelretono.com.mx. Neatly set away from the commercial bustle of Tlaquepaque, this modern B&B has eight cheery artesanía-decorated rooms and a sunny terrace and garden where you can eat your Continental breakfast. ❺

Donde el Indio Duerme Independencia 74 ☎33/3535-2189, Ⓦwww.indiosleep.com. More basic than everything else hereabouts; simple, clean rooms at good prices (newer rooms cost slightly more). ❷

La Villa del Ensueño Florida 305 ☎33/3635-8792, Ⓦwww.villadelensueno.com. This "Villa of Dreams" is a delightful boutique hotel with spacious rooms all tastefully decorated and with lovely tiled bathrooms. A pool and quiet little spaces to hang out in make it a great place to come back to between shopping forays. Rates include a buffet breakfast. ❼

The City

Any tour of Guadalajara inevitably starts at the **cathedral**. With the Sagrario, or sacristy, next door, it takes up an entire block at the very heart of the **colonial centre**, which is bordered by four plazas that form the shape of a Latin cross. The

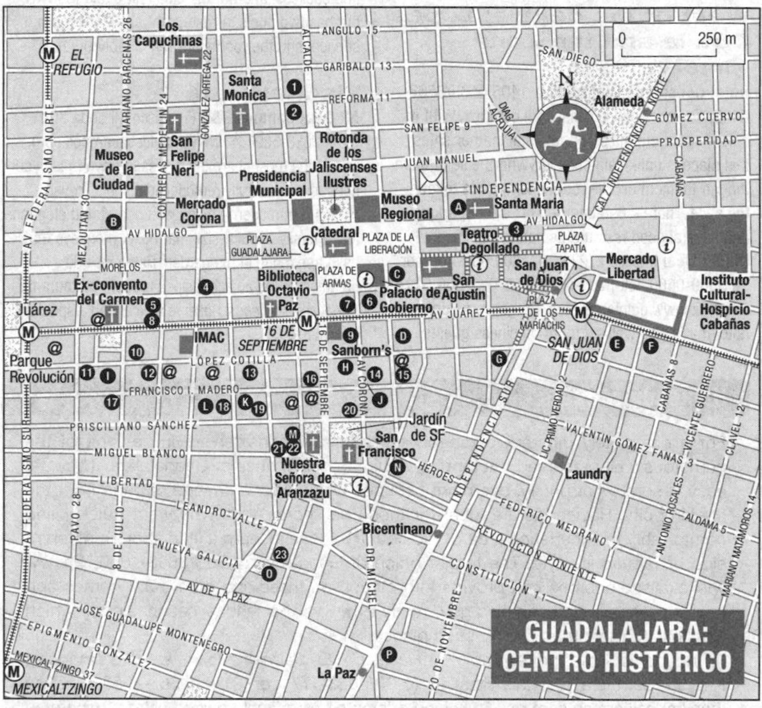

ACCOMMODATION

Don Quixote Hotel	N	Hotel León	P
Hostel de Maria	O	Hotel Santiago de Compostela	M
Hostel Guadalajara	D	Posada Regis	J
Hotel Ana-Isabel	F	Posada San Pablo	L
Hotel Chapala	E	San Rafael Inn	I
Hotel de Mendoza	A		
Hotel Fénix	H		
Hotel Francés	C		
Hotel Hamilton	K		
Hotel Jorge Alejandro	B		
Hotel Maya	G		

EATING, DRINKING & NIGHTLIFE

Alta Fibra	19	Café Madoka	5	Mariscos Galeana	13
Antigues del Carmen	11	Café Madrid	7	El Mutualismo	17
El Baron	14	Café Red	18	Pastelería Luvier	16
Birriera Las Nueve Esquinas	23	Café O Le	4	La Prisciliana	21
		La Chata	9	La Rinconada	3
		Chong Wah	8	El Tacazo	6
		El Dispertador	1 & 2	Taquería Los Faroles	20
		La Fonda de San Miguel	4	El Teu Lloc	10
		Hotel Francés	C	Villa Madrid	12
		Lido	22		
		La Maestranza	15		

traffic, noise and bustle of the busiest commercial areas of downtown Guadalajara surround the plazas: to the east the crowds spill over into Plaza Tapatía, with its upmarket shops, and to the complete contrast of the old market beyond that; less modern shopping streets to the west are also busy.

Venture a little further out and the atmosphere changes again. Guadalajara's rapid expansion has swallowed up numerous communities: once-distinct villages are now barely distinguishable from the city all around. Heading **west**, the university area blends into chic suburbs and some of the city's most expensive real estate. **East**, Tlaquepaque and Tonalá are the source of some of the area's finest handicrafts. And finally to the **north**, Zapopan has a huge, much revered church and a museum of indigenous traditions, while the Barranca de Oblatos offers stunning canyon views and weekend picnic spots.

The cathedral and around

With its pointed, tiled twin towers, Guadalajara's cathedral (daily 8am–8pm; free) is a bizarre but successful mixture of styles. Building work began in 1561 and didn't finish for over a century – since then, extensive modifications, which effectively disguise the fact that there was probably never a plan behind the original design, have included a Neoclassical facade and new twin yellow-tiled towers (the originals collapsed in an 1818 earthquake). The richly decorated interior is best seen in the evening, when they turn on the lights. The picture of the Virgin in the sacristy is attributed to the Spanish Baroque artist **Murillo**.

Flanking the cathedral is a series of bustling plazas – Plaza Guadalajara, Rotonda de los Jaliscenses Ilustres, Plaza de la Liberación and Plaza de Armas. At weekends and on warm evenings these plazas are packed, the crowds entertained by an array of street performers and wandering musicians; there are frequently bands playing during the day, too. The Plaza Guadalajara, formerly known as the Plaza de los Laureles for all its topiaried laurel trees, faces the main west entrance of the cathedral. It is bordered to the north by the porticoed **Presidencia Municipal** (only built in 1952, though you wouldn't know it). On the north side of the cathedral lies the **Rotonda de los Jaliscenses Ilustres**. This Neoclassical circle of seventeen Doric columns is the latest architectural expression of Jaliscan pride and commemorates the state's heroes. Around the cathedral and departing regularly from in front of the Museo Regional, Mercado de San Juan de Dios and the Jardín de San Francisco are *calandrias*, or elegant **horse-drawn covered carriages**. Most drivers are knowledgeable (and entertaining) city guides and charge around M$200 (for 1–4 people) for a 45-minute tour.

Museo Regional

Just north of the cathedral, the **Museo Regional** (Tues–Sat 9am–5.30pm, Sun 9am–4.30pm; M$41, free Sun) is housed in an eighteenth-century colonial mansion. Over time it's been a religious seminary, a barracks and a school; it's now a supremely elegant setting for an extensive and diverse collection. Downstairs, exhibits start with a section devoted to regional **archeology** and range from stone tools and the skeleton of a mammoth to the finest achievements of western Mexican pottery and metalworking. The peoples of the west developed quite separately from those in southern and central Mexico, and there is considerable evidence that they had more contact with South and Central American cultures than with those who would now be regarded as their compatriots. The deep **shaft tombs** displayed here are unique in Mexico, but were common down the Pacific coast in Peru and Ecuador. In the centuries before the Conquest, the Tarascan kingdom, based around Pátzcuaro (see p.355), almost came to rival the strength of the Aztecs – partly due to their more extensive knowledge and use of metals. The

Aztecs tried, and failed, to extend their influence over Tarascan territory; it wasn't until after Cortés's destruction of Tenochtitlán that the Tarascans submitted relatively peacefully to the conquistadors.

Upstairs, along with rooms devoted to the state's **modern history** and ethnography, is a sizeable gallery of colonial and modern art. Most remarkable here is the large collection of **nineteenth-century portraiture**, a local tradition that captures relatively ordinary Mexicans in a charmingly naive style.

▲ Miguel Hidalgo mural by José Clemente Orozco, Palacio de Gobierno, Guadalajara

Plaza de Armas and the Palacio de Gobierno

On the south side of the cathedral, the **Plaza de Armas** centres on an elaborate *belle époque* rotunda – a present from the people of France – where there's music (often the state band) Tuesday to Friday and Sunday evenings at 6.30pm. Dominating the eastern side of the square is the **Palacio de Gobierno** (daily 9am–7pm; free), recognizable by its Baroque facade with a clock surrounded by elements from the Aztec calendar. Here Padre Miguel Hidalgo y Costilla (the "father of Mexican Independence") proclaimed the abolition of slavery in 1810, and, in 1858, Benito Juárez was saved from the firing squad by the cry of "*Los valientes no asesinan*" – "the brave don't murder." But the overwhelming reason to enter the arcaded courtyard is to see the first of the great **Orozco murals**.

The main mural dates from 1937 and is typical of Orozco's work (see box, p.328) – Hidalgo blasts triumphantly through the middle, brandishing his sword against a background of red flags and the fires of battle. Curving around the sides of the staircase, scenes depict the Mexican people's oppression and struggle for liberty, from a pre-Conquest Eden to post-revolutionary emancipation. Upstairs in the domed Congress Hall a smaller Orozco mural (his last, painted just before his death in 1949) also depicts Hidalgo, this time as *El Cura de Dolores* (the priest from Dolores), legislator and liberator of slaves.

Plaza de la Liberación

Back around the cathedral, the largest of the four squares is the **Plaza de la Liberación**, which lies between the cathedral and the **Teatro Degollado**, to the east. Modelled on La Scala in Milan, the theatre was built in the mid-nineteenth century and inaugurated in 1866 during the brief reign of Maximilian (see p.860). It's an imposing, domed Neoclassical building with a Corinthian portico; look on the portico's pediment for a frieze depicting the Greek Muses. A programme of drama and concerts is still staged here, mostly in October during the fiesta, though also sporadically throughout the rest of the year. The impressively restored **interior** (viewing Tues–Sun noon–2pm except when the theatre is in use; free) is notable for its frescoed ceiling, which illustrates scenes from the fourth canto of Dante's *Divine Comedy*.

On either side of the theatre are two small churches, **Santa María** and **San Agustín**, the only remains of a monastery that once stood here. San Agustín has a fine Baroque facade; relatively plain Santa María is one of the oldest churches in the city, built in the seventeenth century on the site of Guadalajara's first cathedral.

East along the Plaza Tapatía: the Hospicio Cabañas

Behind the theatre is the beginning of the **Plaza Tapatía**, with its view all the way down to the Hospicio Cabañas, home to another set of Orozco's murals. The plaza was constructed in the late nineteenth century by demolishing some of the city's oldest neighbourhoods, but manages to look as if it has always been there. It takes its name from *tapatío* – an adjective used to describe anything typical of Guadalajara, supposedly derived from the capes worn by Spanish grandees (Guadalajarans themselves are often referred to as *Tapatíos*).

At its eastern end, the plaza opens out to a broad paved area full of wacky anthropomorphic **bronze sculptures**, the work of Guadalajara native **Alejandro Colunga**. Stretched, squashed and generally distorted human figures form chairs, their patinas rubbed shiny by thousands of tired shoppers and tourists.

Beyond the sculptures, the **Instituto Cultural-Hospicio Cabañas** (Tues–Sat 10am–6pm, Sun 10am–3pm; M$70, free Tues, M$30 to bring in a camera) was founded as an orphanage by Bishop Juan Cabañas y Crespo in 1805 and took nearly fifty years to complete. Designed by Spanish architect Manuel Tolsá, the

José Clemente Orozco

José Clemente Orozco (1883–1949) was a member, along with Diego Rivera and David Siqueiros, of the triumvirate of brilliant artists who emerged from the Revolution and transformed Mexican painting into an enormously powerful and populist political statement, especially through the medium of the **giant mural**. Their chief patron was the state – hence the predominance of their work in official buildings and educational establishments – and their aim was to create a national art that drew on native traditions. Almost all their work is consciously educative, rewriting – or, perhaps better, rediscovering – Mexican history in the light of the Revolution, casting the imperialists as villains and drawing heavily on pre-Hispanic themes. Orozco, a native of Jalisco (he was born in Zapotlan, now Ciudad Guzmán), was perhaps the least overtly political of the three; certainly, his later work, the greatest of which is here in Guadalajara, often seems ambiguous. As a child he moved to Guadalajara and then to Mexico City, where he was influenced by renowned engraver **José Guadalupe Posada** (see box, p.264) and where he painted murals from 1922 to 1927. His best works from this period are the series including *The Destruction of the Old Order* which he painted at the Antiguo Colegio de San Ildefonso in Mexico City (see p.403). Then followed seven years in the US, where his works included his mammoth *The Epic of American Civilization* at Dartmouth College in Hanover, New Hampshire, but it was on his return that his powers as an artist reached their peak, in the late 1930s and 1940s, above all in his works at Guadalajara's Hospicio Cabañas and the University of Guadalajara (see p.327 & p.330).

Hospicio is a huge, beautiful and tranquil building, with 23 separate patios surrounded by schools of art, music and dance; an art cinema/theatre; various government offices; and a small cafeteria. The chapel, the **Capilla Tolsá**, is a plain and ancient-looking structure in the form of a cross, situated in the central patio right at the heart of the building. Orozco's **murals**, in keeping with their setting, are more spiritual than those in the government palace, but you certainly couldn't call them Christian: the conquistadors are depicted as the Horsemen of the Apocalypse, trampling the native population beneath them. The Man of Fire – who leads the people from their dehumanizing, mechanized oppression – has a symbolic role as liberator, which is clearly the same as that of Hidalgo in the palace murals. In this case, he is a strange synthesis of Christian and Mexican deities, a Christ-Quetzalcoatl figure. There are benches on which you can lie back to appreciate the murals, and also a small museum dedicated to Orozco, with sketches, cartoons and details of the artist's life.

Almost alongside the Hospicio is the vast **Mercado Libertad** (locally known as Mercado San Juan de Dios), which Guadalajarans claim is the world's largest indoor market. Although the building is modern, much of what's inside is thoroughly traditional, and it's one of the few places in the city where you can still haggle over prices. Beyond the touristy souvenir stalls, you'll find *curanderas* offering herbal remedies, dried iguanas (for witches' brews) and the renowned Paracho guitars. There are also countless stalls selling all manner of regional food and vast piles of colourful fruit, vegetables, chocolate and spices and traditional leather goods from saddles to clumpy working boots. The market is huge, chaotic and engrossing, but before you buy crafts here, it's worth paying a visit to the **Instituto de la Artesanía** in the Parque Agua Azul (see opposite), or to the expensive boutiques in Tlaquepaque (see p.331), to get some idea of the potential quality and value of the goods.

Immediately southwest of the Mercado is the **Plaza de los Mariachis**, a place to return after dark to hear Guadalajara's finest musicians (see p.337).

South of the Plaza de Armas: Parque Agua Azul

South of the Plaza de Armas, the churches of **San Francisco** and **Nuestra Señora de Aranzazu** face each other across 16 de Septiembre. San Francisco lies on the site of what was probably Guadalajara's first religious foundation, a Franciscan monastery established in the years just after the Conquest. The present church was begun in 1684 and has a beautiful Baroque facade. Aranzazu, by contrast, is entirely plain on the outside, but conceals a fabulously elaborate interior, with three wildly exuberant, heavily carved and gilded churrigueresque retables. The **Jardín de San Francisco**, which would be pleasantly peaceful were it not for the number of local buses rattling by, lies across from the two churches.

Several buses (marked "Parque Agua Azul") run down from past the Jardín de San Francisco to the **Parque Agua Azul** (Tues–Sun 10am–6pm; M$5). You couldn't really describe the park as peaceful: there's always some kind of activity going on and the green areas are permanently packed with kids enjoying the zoo and playgrounds. An outdoor concert shell (*la concha*) hosts popular free performances on Sundays, and weekends see football games and crowds. Nonetheless, by Guadalajara standards, it's a haven of calm, especially during the week, and the entrance fee includes attractions such as a dome full of butterflies; exotic caged birds, including magnificent toucans; a palm house, also full of tropical birds; and a strange, glass-pyramid orchid house.

Perhaps the area's greatest attraction (and accessed from outside the park) is the **Instituto de la Artesanía Jalisciense**, Calzado González Gallo 20 (Mon–Sat 10am–6pm, Sun 10am–4pm; free), a showcase for regional crafts that is as much a museum as a shop. Its collection is ambitious, with examples of all sorts of local crafts – furniture, ceramics, toys, glassware, clothing – of the highest quality. Many of the items are expensive, but are worth it when you consider the fine worksmanship.

West of the Plaza de Armas

The area to the west of the cathedral is a great part of the city for aimless meandering. There has been far less modernization in this direction, and the busy shopping streets, many of them closed to traffic, turn up fascinating glimpses of traditional Mexican life and plenty of odd moments of interest. The small, general **Mercado Corona** is at Santa Monica and Hidalgo. A little further out, the university area is quieter than the centre, the streets broader, and there's also a younger atmosphere, with plenty of good restaurants and cafés. Still further in the same direction are expensive residential areas, interesting in their own way for the contrast to crowded downtown.

The "Ex-Templo de la Compañía", or the **Biblioteca IberoAmericana Octavio Paz** (Mon–Fri 9am–9pm, Sat 9am–5pm; free) – lies just west of the Plaza de Armas at the junction of Pedro Moreno and Colón. Originally a church, the building later became a university lecture hall, during which time the nineteenth-century Neoclassical facade was added and it was decorated with **murals** by **David Siqueiros** and **Amado de la Cueva**. Currently a library, it has dramatic crimson-hued murals depicting workers, peasants and miners in a heroic-socialist style; they are open to visitors and make an interesting contrast to Orozco's work. Outside there's an attractive little plaza, and the pedestrianized streets make a pleasant escape from the traffic, if not the crowds.

Immediately to the north of the *biblioteca* are several examples of the beautiful, little-known Baroque churches that stud Guadalajara. The closest is the **Templo de Santa Monica**, on Santa Monica between San Felípe and Reforma, with fabulously rich doorways and an elegant, stone interior. The nearby **Templo de San Felípe Neri**, San Felípe at Contreras Medellin, is a few years younger – dating from the second half of the eighteenth century – and more sumptuously decorated, with a superb facade and lovely tower. Both of these churches have extravagant rain-spouts, which take the form of dragons on San Felípe. A block along Gonzales Ortega, at the corner of Garibaldi, the **Templo de las Capuchinas** is, conversely, plain and fortress-like; inside, though, it's more interesting, with paintings and a lovely vaulted brick roof. Back south towards Juárez and the main drag, the **Museo de la Ciudad**, Independencia 684 (Tues–Sat 10am–5.30pm, Sun 10am–2pm; M$8.50), housed in a former convent, showcases the city's history through photos and artefacts.

Back on the main route west, at Juárez and 8 de Julio, the **Ex-Convento del Carmen** was one of the city's richest monasteries, but its wealth has largely been stripped, leaving an austere, white building of elegant simplicity. Modern art exhibitions, dance events and concerts are regularly staged here (a programme of forthcoming events is posted outside the entrance).

The University and the Zona Minerva

The **University** is a fifteen-minute walk west along Juárez from the centre, but if you're heading any further this direction, you may want to take a bus or taxi (anything heading for the Plaza del Sol should pass all the areas below, or look for "Par Vial").

The Parque Revolución, immediately west of Federalismo (and the north–south Tren Ligero line), marks the start of the campus of the **Universidad de Guadalajara**. A couple of hundred metres on you can see more of **Orozco**'s major murals, among the first he painted in Guadalajara, in the University's **Rectoría General** at Juárez 975 (Mon–Fri 8am–8pm; free). Head for the main hall (*paraninfo*) to see the frescoed dome and front wall. Again, the theme of the works fits the setting: the dome shows the glories and benefits of learning, while the wall shows the oppressed masses crying out for books and education, which are being denied them by fat capitalists and the military. Round the back of the same building, the **Museo de las Artes**, López Cotilla 930 (Tues–Fri 10am–6pm, Sat & Sun 10am–4pm; prices depend on what's on) houses temporary art exhibitions. Immediately south of the museum is the **Templo Expiatorio**, a modern neo-Gothic church modelled on Orvieto cathedral in Italy and featuring some innovative stained glass and an attractive altarpiece.

Beyond the university, Juárez changes its name to Vallarta, and the character of the street changes rapidly, too. Within ten blocks, around the major junction of Vallarta and Chapultepec, you find yourself in what could be a different city. The **Zona Minerva** – far quieter than the blocks to the east – is a place of broad avenues, expensive shops and pleasant restaurants. The best are a couple of blocks south along López Cotilla, an altogether more pleasant place to stroll than busy Vallarta.

Further west along Vallarta, the vast **Centro Magno** shopping centre has upscale shops and international fast-food restaurants, and makes an air-conditioned respite on a hot day. Opposite is an American Express office and the offices for a number of airlines, including American, Aero California and Mexicana. Beyond Centro Magno, Vallarta crosses the major artery of López Mateos at the **Minerva Circle**, an intersection marked by a double triumphal arch. This Neoclassical **Monumento Los Arcos** (daily 8am–7pm; free) contains a colourful mural and stairs up to the roof, which has good views.

Most buses turn left at the Minerva Circle down López Mateos Sur towards the **Plaza del Sol**, a vast commercial development said to be one of the largest in Latin America. There's an enormous shopping centre, as well as administrative offices, and inside there's a couple of good cafés, an ice-cream parlour and, in the evenings, several nightclubs. Also on López Mateos are numerous big hotels and themed restaurants – all very much the modern face of suburban Mexico.

San Pedro Tlaquepaque

TLAQUEPAQUE (officially San Pedro Tlaquepaque) is famous for its artesanías and its **mariachi** bands. Once a separate town some 5km southeast of the centre, it has long since been absorbed by urban sprawl, and most of its traditional crafts taken over by chi-chi designer-furniture and jewellery stores, but you can still find crafts – such as ceramics, glass, jewellery and textiles. Prices are high, but so are standards, and there are usually some moderately priced ceramics and glassware.

Tlaquepaque centres around a pleasantly laid-back main square complete with bandstand, on whose north side is the blockish church of **San Pedro**. To the west of the square, the three-domed **Nuestra Virgen de la Soledad** is an almost equally distinctive landmark. Along the square's south side runs Independencia. At the plaza's southeast corner you'll find **El Parian**, an enclosed plaza that is, in effect, the biggest bar that you've ever seen – actually a dozen or so separate establishments, but since everyone sits outside, the tables tend to overlap and strolling serenaders wander around at random, it all feels like one enormous place. Food, drink and prices are good, but check the bill for added service charges. At the weekend, particularly Sunday afternoons, you'll see mariachi at its best here, and locals add their own vocal renditions to the musicians' backing. On weekdays it can be disappointingly quiet (or pleasantly peaceful, depending on your fondness for mariachi).

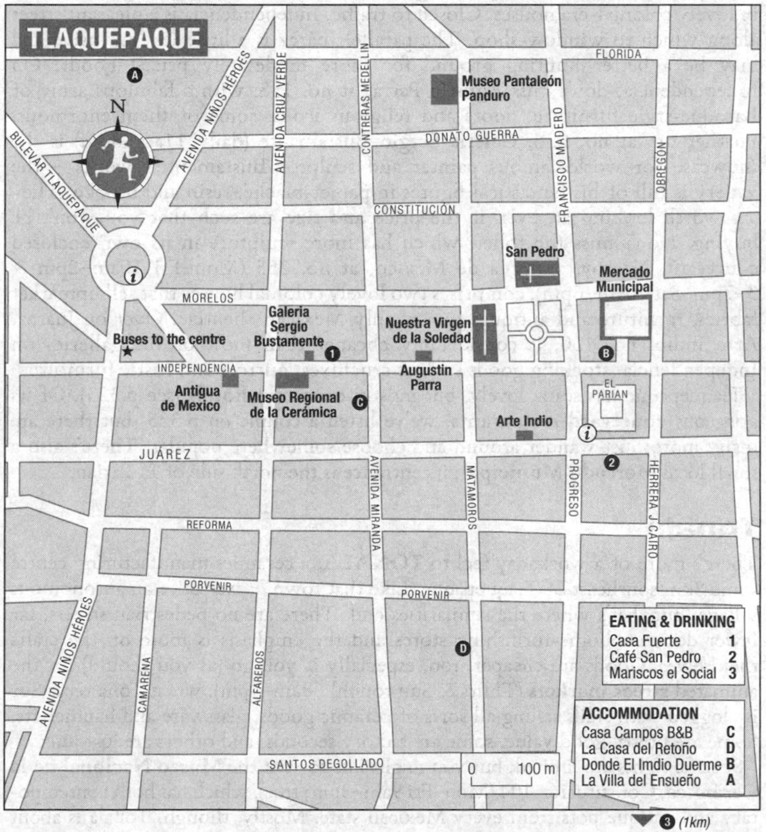

For an insight into just how wonderful the local ceramics can be, visit the **Museo Pantaleón Panduro**, Princiliano Sánchez at Flórida (Tues–Sat 10am–6pm, Sun 10am–5pm; free), which was named after the father of Jaliscan ceramicists. Here you can see exemplary prize-winning pieces from the museum's annual ceramics competition (held each June). To learn something of the techniques used, visit the small **Museo Regional de la Cerámica**, Independencia 237 (Mon–Sat 10am–6pm, Sun 10am–3pm; free), which has displays of pottery not only from Tlaquepaque but from all over the state, especially Tonalá (see below). Beyond the individual works of some of the finest craftsmen, there's a traditional kitchen on display, complete with all its plates, pots and pans, and the building is a fine old mansion in its own right. Of course, there is also a shop.

Practicalities

The #275 or TUR **bus** from the centre (16 de Septiembre) will drop you on Niños Héroes at the western end of Independencia, Tlaquepaque's main street, just after you've passed under a brick pedestrian bridge and round a traffic circle. From here, simply walk up Independencia toward El Parian. There's a **tourist information kiosk** (Mon–Fri 9.45am–8pm, Sat & Sun 10am–8pm) at the corner of Juárez and Progresso, by El Parian. Nearby, several banks have **ATMs** in case you've been carried away by the shopping experience.

Tlaquepaque's fancier **shops** and galleries lie near the Museo Regional, many in lovely colonial-era houses. Closed to traffic, Independencia is a pleasant street along which to window-shop. The parallel Juárez is a little less exclusive and may be a better hunting ground for more moderately priced goods. On Independencia, don't miss Agustín Parra, at no. 158, with a fabulous array of Baroque-style furniture, doors and religious icons, some of them enormous. Further up, at no. 238, Galeria Sergio Bustamante (daily 11am–8pm) is the showcase for world-famous painter and sculptor Bustamente's works – the gallery is full of his fantastical figures in papier-mâché, resin and bronze. They are worth looking at, even if the price and size are such that you won't be buying. Don't miss the toilet, which has more sculpture in its own enclosed courtyard. Nearby, Antigua de México, at no. 255 (Mon–Fri 10am–2pm & 3–7pm, Sat 10am–6pm), comprises two lovely colonial houses that sell upmarket fabrics, furniture and antiques to a mainly Mexican clientele. Over on Juárez, Arte Indio, no. 130, is considerably cheaper than most of the galleries on Independencia, stocking goods such as crucifixes, mirrors and rustic furniture.

Tlaquepaque has some lovely, but mostly expensive **hotels** (see p.323). Of its gorgeous **courtyard restaurants**, we've listed a couple on p.335, but there are many more; just wander around and choose somewhere popular. There's also a small local **Mercado Municipal**; its entrance is the north side of El Parian.

Tonalá

There's more of a workaday feel to **TONALÁ**, a ceramics manufacturing centre some 8km southeast of Tlaquepaque. Like that town, it was once an autonomous village, but that's where the similarities end. There are no pedestrian streets, far fewer designer home-furnishing stores and the emphasis is more on the crafts themselves. Goods are cheaper, too, especially if you go (as you should) for the animated **street markets** (Thurs & Sun roughly 8am–4pm), when Tonaltecas Sur is clogged with stalls selling all sorts of ceramic goods, glassware and handicrafts. Some are pretty good value, some are factory seconds, and others are just junk.

Specific sights are limited, but you might like to visit the **Museo Nacional de la Cerámica**, Constitución 104 (Mon–Fri 9am–3pm; free), which has both contemporary and antique pots from every Mexican state. Mostly, though, Tonalá is about strolling and browsing, but if you've more than a passing interest in ceramics it is worth making for some specific **shops**. Start with **Mis Amores**, Tonaltecas Sur 80, which has all sorts of ceramics, papier-mâché and sheetmetal work including designs based on the works of Posada (see box, p.264), such as *La Catrina*, his famous skeleton woman with a huge floral hat. Close to Tonalá's central plaza, visit **Galeria José Bernabe**, Hidalgo 83, the place to come for superb and highly regarded *petatillo*, an intricate ceramic form with painted animals and flowers on a cross-hatched background. A few blocks further north at **Artesanía Erandi**, López Cotilla 118, you can head out the back of the shop to see artisans hand-painting plates. The plates are made at the factory virtually across the road, and they export all over the world. Moving west, you may need to knock on the door to gain access to **La Casa de Salvador Vásquez Carmona**, López Cotilla 328, which looks like a simple private residence, and gives no indication of being a shop or workshop. However, around the rear patio, Carmona shapes pots and bowls, hand-fires them, then paints the finished article. He'll show you his gallery complete with finished pots that have graced the covers of magazines and design glossies.

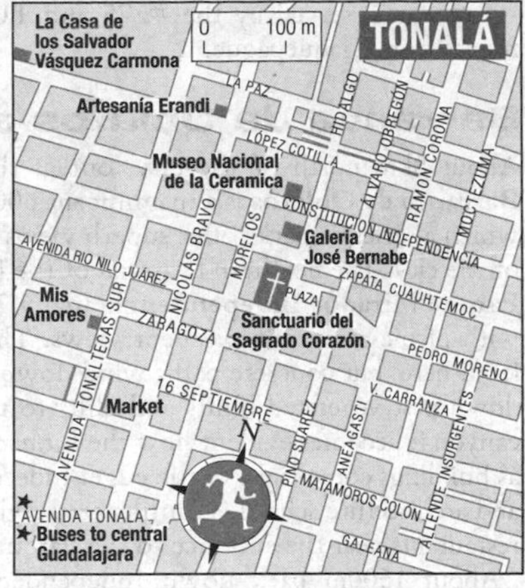

To get to Tonalá from the centre of town, take a #275 or TUR bus heading south on 16 de Septiembre. Get off at the corner of Avenida Tonalá and Tonaltecas Sur.

Zapopan

ZAPOPAN, some 7km northwest of the city centre, is the site of the **Basílica de la Virgen de Zapopan**, one of the most important churches in the city, much revered by the Huichol people. Pope John Paul II gave a Mass in the giant **Plaza de las Américas** in front of the church during a visit to Mexico in 1979; a statue commemorates the event. The Baroque temple houses a miraculous image of the Virgin: the 25cm-high figure was dedicated to the local Indians by a Franciscan missionary, Antonio de Segovia, after he had intervened in a battle between them and the conquistadors. Since then, it has been constantly venerated and is still the object of pilgrimages, especially on October 12, when several hundred thousand people gather early in the morning to march the Virgin back to the Basílica after an annual six-month tour of all the churches in Guadalajara.

Beside the church, the small **Museo Huichol Wixarica de Zapopan** (Mon–Sat 9.30am–1.15pm & 3–5.45pm; M$10), an ethnographic museum, exhibits clothes and objects relating to Huichol traditions, as well as a photographic display of their modern way of life. They also sell Huichol crafts, including psychedelic yarn paintings (*cuadros de estambre*) and beadwork.

Just east of the Plaza de las Américas, the **Museo de Arte de Zapopan**, Andador 20 de Noviembre 166 (ⓦwww.mazmuseo.com; Tues–Sun 10am–6pm; M$12, Sun M$6, free Tues) is Guadalajara's best contemporary art gallery. Changing exhibitions cherry-pick the best talent from Mexico and abroad – painting, sculpture, photography, video installations, you name it.

Zapopan is served by the #275 and TUR **buses** at the opposite end of their routes from Tlaquepaque.

Barranca de Oblatos and the zoo

About 8km north of the city, out at the end of Calzada Independencia, the **Barranca de Oblatos** is a magnificent 600-metre-deep canyon, along the edge of which a series of parks offer superb views and a welcome break from the confines of the city. The northern terminal of the Independencia Macrobús route is by the **Parque Mirador Independencia** (daily 7am–7pm; M$3), a popular family spot with picnic areas and excellent views. There is no access down into the canyon from here, but concrete paths wind down to the brink, where you can look gaze down past vegetated bluffs and cliffs to the river far below. Looking along the canyon it becomes evident how the *barranca* limits the city's northward expansion, as buildings come right to the edge. Indeed, a new building at the adjacent design and architecture school is cantilevered right over the void. Several good cafés and restaurants near the entrance to the Parque Mirador cater to student budgets.

About 1500m back down Independencia towards the city (Macrobús stop Zoológico) is the **Zoológico Guadalajara** (Wed–Sun 10am–5.30pm; M$51), which has superb canyon views from its northern end, along with a relatively well-kept selection of Mexican and international wildlife. Opened in 1988, the modern zoo also features an ecological centre that works to preserve a range of endangered species through education and reproduction initiatives. World-renowned artist Sergio Bustamante created the monkey sculptures that greet visitors at the zoo's entrance. Assorted entry packages also give access to a train ride through the zoo and a twenty-minute Masai Mara truck "safari" through an open area populated with African beasts.

The adjacent **Selva Mágica** (Tues–Sun 10am–6pm; entry packages M$80–150) offers all manner of amusement park rides.

Eating and drinking

Tapatíos take their food seriously. Guadalajara boasts hundreds of **places to eat**, ranging from elegant restaurants to unpretentious cafés, and from *loncherías* (cafés with an emphasis on short orders) to *neverías* (with ice cream and fresh-fruit drinks). Don't pass up the **street vendors** either – their fresh tacos and bags of spiced fruit are delicious and make a cheap, healthy snack.

For basic meals, the mezzanine of the **Mercado Libertad** has seemingly hundreds of little stands, each displaying their own specialities. There's a more limited, but handier, selection at the **Mercado Corona**.

In the centre, your best choice is west of the cathedral, where traditional cafés and restaurants line **Juárez**. Though there are plenty of more **expensive** places round the centre, they tend to be rather dull: in the evenings, locals are far more likely to be found out in the suburbs. A good and relatively close hunting ground is **López Cotilla**, a few blocks west of the university.

Downtown

Alta Fibra Sanchez 370, between Ocampo and Galeana. As the name suggests, *Alta Fibra* specializes in high-fibre foods; the menu isn't strictly vegetarian, but is low fat. Excellent-value comida corrida (M$39), and a range of other bargain dishes. There's also a wholemeal bakery next door. Closed Sun.

Birrieria Las Nueve Esquinas Colón 384. Peacefully set on a quiet plaza, this little restaurant serves up traditional Mexican mutton dishes and does excellent *birria de chivo* (goat stew; M$67 or M$89).

Café Madoka Gonzalez Martínez 78. Big, traditional café, operating since 1959 and serving tasty breakfasts (especially the *chilaquiles al pollo*), soups and *antojitos* (mostly around M$55). You can also just play dominoes and sip a coffee; try the "Café Madoka Especial", served with a dollop of vanilla ice cream.

Café Madrid Juárez 264 near Corona. A smallish 1950s-style diner and coffee bar, good for moderately priced breakfasts, comidas corridas (M$49) and sandwiches (8am–10pm).

Cafe Red Ocampo 216. Cool little café – there's a wall of images of Frida Kahlo. It's a nice spot to relax with a magazine and a coffee, grab lunch (baguettes M$45–55, salads M$45–50) or a cheap beer (M$10). Open afternoons and evenings until 11pm. Closed Sun.

Caffe O Le Donata Guerra 23. Intimate city café with good lattes and complex infusions (such as cherry, banana and Jamaica blossom), but nothing to eat bar the occasional biscuit.

Chan Los Ángeles 131 (see map, p.320). Very handy cheap diner by the Central Vieja, offering fish and meat dishes, and great-value breakfasts and comidas corridas (both M$38).

La Chata Corona 126. Excellent medium-priced Mexican dishes, including *mole* and *platillo jalisciense* (chicken with side snacks; M$72). Hugely popular with local families since 1942, so expect to queue, especially at mealtimes. Extensive breakfasts go for M$68–74.

Chong Wah Juárez 558. Moderately priced Cantonese food to eat in or take away. Though there are now a fair few Chinese restaurants around town, this remains the best, and their buffet lunch (M$55) is also the finest in town.

El Despertador Reforma 319 and Alcalde 287. If you care about your coffee, this is absolutely the best in town: espresso, Americano or permutations thereof, served at a tiny three-seat counter on Reforma (8.30am–7pm) or in a peaceful little garden off Alcalde (4–10pm). They also do teas and infusions, but it's the coffee that makes this place live up to its name ("the waker-upper").

La Fonda de San Miguel Donata Guerra 25 ⓣ33/3613-0793, ⓦwww.lafondadesanmiguel.com., A delightful restaurant in the courtyard of a former convent in the centro histórico. The tinkling fountain and caged birds are replaced at night (though it closes at 6pm on Sun & Mon) by a constellation of pinprick lampshades creatively imitating the night sky. Try the excellent *sopa de tortilla* (M$41), perhaps followed by the "*Molcajete San Miguel*" (M$113), a big stone mortar filled with a steaming stew of chicken, mushrooms, onions and cheese.

Lido Colón 294, at San Miguel Blanco. Spanish-style bar and restaurant, serving good, moderately priced Mexican *moles*, sandwiches, snacks and a M$60 set menu. Open 24hr.

Mariscos Galeana Galeana 154, at López Cotilla. Seafood restaurant with prawn and octopus (M$55–90), among other delicious dishes.

Pastelería Luvier Colón 183. One of the best of many *panaderías* and *pastelerias* in the centre.

La Rinconada Morelos 86, at Callejón del Diable, Plaza Tapatía ⓣ33/3613-9914. In a glorious colonial setting, this moderately expensive restaurant serves seafood dishes (salmon with fine herbs or pimiento verde for M$110), US-style steaks (from M$170) and Mexican specialities. Their lunch buffet (M$66) is good value.

El Tacazo Juárez 246. Fast, flavourful tacos; popular and cheap, though choices such as *lengua* (tongue) and *cabeza* (head) are not for the timid.

Taquería Los Faroles Corona 250. Popular taco and torta joint serving a wide range of tacos until midnight daily. It's a good place to have your first taste of *torta ahogada* (M$24), washed down with horchata.

Villa Madrid López Cotilla 551 at Gonzalez Martínez. Great *licuados*, fruit salads and yogurt, as well as sandwiches and salads.

University and further out

La China Poblana Juárez 887. Reasonably priced, traditional Puebla dishes, including *mole* and *chiles en nogada*.

Goa López Cotilla 1520 ⓣ33/3615-6173. Guadalajara's only Indian restaurant, intimately lit and with Bollywood on the screen. Serves a range of excellent dishes, several straight out of the tandoor. Mains are mostly M$80–90 though prawn dishes are more like M$130. Closed Mon.

Los Itacates Chapultepec Nte 110, at Sierra ⓣ33/3825-1106. Traditional Mexican food (mains around M$60–75), with *chiles en nogada* served in season (July–Oct) only.

Pierrot Justo Sierra 2355 ⓣ33/3630-2087. The city's finest French restaurant, in gracious surroundings and with attentive but never intrusive service. The filet mignon in mushroom sauce and the chocolate mousse are both spectacular. Closed Sun.

La Trattoria Niños Héroes 3051 ⓣ33/3122-1817. The lively Italian restaurant is one of Guadalajara's best. *Segundi piatti* such as saltimbocca and devilled prawns go for around M$125. Evening reservations recommended.

Tlaquepaque

Café San Pedro Juárez 81 (see map, p.331). Tlaquepaque's best coffee, with seating under the *portales* and a great range of teas and cakes.

Casa Fuerte Independencia 224 (see map, p.331) ⓣ33/3635-9015, ⓦwww.casafuerte.com. Pleasant courtyard restaurant in a majestic mansion. Enjoy the live accompaniment, often mariachi, while you sample the likes of tamarind shrimp or salmon in caper butter.

Gastronomía Jalisciense: Tapatío specialities

While in Guadalajara, you shouldn't miss out on some of Jalisco's culinary specialities. The most celebrated is **birria**, stewed beef or mutton in a spicy, but not particularly hot, sauce, and served with tortillas or in tacos from street stalls, bars and in markets. **Roast goat** is another favourite, often seen in the markets along with a goat's skull (just in case you don't know what *chivo* means). **Pozole**, a stew of pork and hominy (ground maize) is also popular, and typically found as a restaurant special on Thursdays. Rarely seen much beyond the city limits, there's also **torta ahogada** (literally "drowned sandwich"), a bread roll stuffed with a filling of your choice (traditionally pork) then drenched with a thin, spicy salsa that soaks right through the bread. It's a bit messy, but extremely delicious. And then, of course, there's **tequila**, discussed more fully on p.341.

Mariscos el Social Delicias 117 (1km south and 400m east of the main square; arrowed off the map on p.331). Locally – and deservedly – renowned seafood diner, where a big cup of juicy king prawns and octopus (M$87) is helped down by zingy, fresh raw salsa and ice-cold beer. They also do excellent cocteles, ceviche and seafood soup.

Nightlife

Traditionally the downtown area hasn't been that lively, but things are picking up, particularly southwest of the cathedral (along López Madero, Madero and Sanchez) and in the **Nueve Esquinas** quarter, three blocks further south, where Colon and Galeana meet. Most of the fashionable, younger-crowd *Tapatíos* tend to hang out in the distant moneyed suburbs – the **Plaza del Sol complex**, for example, houses a couple of clubs, as do many of the big hotels out that way. Any of them will knock a sizeable hole in your wallet. There are more clubs where Juárez becomes **Avenida Vallarta** (most of which enforce the "no jeans or sneakers" policy typical at Mexican nightspots). **Avenida López Mateos** has a number of trendy pubs with live music and a younger crowd. Some have open bars on certain nights of the week in exchange for a cover charge of around M$100 for men, usually M$50 or less for women.

Guadalajara has a reputation for being one of Mexico's gayest cities, and while that doesn't mean public displays of affection are widely accepted, there's greater freedom in the dozen or so bars and clubs that advertise their orientation with rainbow flags. Guadalajara's **gay quarter** is centred on the junction of Ocampo and Sanchez, about five blocks southwest of the cathedral. *La Prisciliana* (see opposite) is a good place to start, and Spanish-speakers can check out what's going on at Ⓦwww.gaygdl.com.

Antigues del Carmen Jacobo Galvez 45-B, at Juárez with Pavo Ⓣ33/3658-2266. Decent restaurant that spills out onto a shaded plaza (Jardín del Carmen), where you can eat, drink or dance to live or recorded light Latino sounds. No cover charge, but food and drink prices have an entertainment component built in. Alternatively, you can just hang out under the trees and listen for free.

El Barón upstairs at Corona 181. Traditional restaurant-bar with Latin music. There are usually live performances at 9.30pm, 11.30pm and 2.30am. Daily 8.30pm–4am.

El Callejón de los Rumberos Chapultepec Sur 287, at Lerdó de Tejeda, Ⓦwww.elcallejondelosrumberos.com. Cuban-style dance bar featuring salsa and other Latin sounds Mon–Thurs 6.30–11pm, with a cover charge on Mon & Tues.

Casa Bariachi Vallarta 2221 (see map, p.320). Loud and colourful restaurant-bar decorated with giant piñatas and full of mariachi bands. Closed Sun.

Hotel Francés Maestranza 35. Piano-bar-style establishment in the courtyard of one of the centre's grander hotels. Come in the early evening (before 8pm) for happy-hour drinks. On Friday there are mariachis, folk dancers and a *charreo* lassooist.

La Maestranza Maestranza 179. Fairly straightforward drinking bar made all the more appealing by walls completely plastered with bullfight promo posters (plus a few bull's heads above the bar). DJs at weekends and moderately priced drinks.

La Moresca López Cotilla 1835, at De Cervantes Savedra. Lively late-closing restaurant and bar that makes a good spot for a bottle of house wine and a *bruschetta*.

El Mutualismo Madero 553. On Thurs, Fri and Sat nights this cavernous venue (normally a cantina) gets taken over by a band (usually Cuban, sometimes rock) and everyone hits the dancefloor. Ceiling fans and wide-open windows give a suitably Cuban dancehall feel. M$10 cover.

La Prisciliana Sanchez 296. Dark and chilled-out gay bar (non-gays welcome) with casual drinking to Latin dance beats. A good place to kick the night off – then follow the crowds.

El Teu Lloc López Cotilla 570. The emphasis here is on drinking, but they also do very good pizza (M$60–84) and stuffed baguettes (M$60–78). There's a different house band every night, mostly acoustic, Latin, jazz and world music. Bands start around 9pm; things usually close down by midnight, so it's a good place to begin your night out.

Entertainment

There's an impressive range of traditional Mexican and classical concerts, contemporary gigs, classic and modern film, theatre and opera performances and art exhibitions in town – you can see some kind of performance most nights of the week. Anyone on a tight budget should check out the **Plaza de Armas**, where there's usually something free happening. One thing no visitor to Guadalajara should miss is hearing mariachi in its hometown, specifically at the **Plaza de los Mariachis**.

Going to the **cinema** in Guadalajara is not particularly convenient, as suburban multiplexes have killed downtown movies. The big shopping centres such as Centro Magno and Plaza del Sol have the latest blockbusters, and we've also listed a couple of more convenient alternatives.

Several entertaining **festivals** take place throughout the year including: the highly animated **Día de San Pedro** in Tlaquepaque (June 29), with mariachi, dancing and processions; and the **Día de la Virgen de Zapopan** (Oct 12), an all-night fiesta capped with a massive early-morning procession that starts before dawn at the cathedral and finishes in Zapopan. Crowds and assorted food vendors start arriving the evening before, when there all sorts of music and the *portales* are choked with people bedding down for the 4am start.

In the autumn, everything cranks up to fever pitch for the Fiestas de Octubre (ⓦwww.fiestasdeoctubre.com.mx), a month-long celebration when downtown Guadalajara comes alive with all manner of outdoor performances and bands, often free. Daily events include *charreadas* (rodeos), processions and fireworks, as well as all kinds of free entertainment – modern Mexican music performances are put on from noon till 10pm in the fairgrounds of the Benito Juárez auditorium.

Live music

Instituto Cultural Mexicano Norteamericano de Jalisco (ICMNJ) Enrique Díaz de León 300 ⓣ33/3825-5838, ⓦwww.institutocultural.com.mx. Hosts classical music concerts and recitals all year.

Plaza de Armas Regular free performances of Jaliscan music in the rotunda just south of the cathedral (Tues–Fri & Sun 6.30pm).

Plaza Fundadores An open area behind the Teatro Degollado that sometimes sees music or drama performances at weekends; often free.

Plaza de los Mariachis Guadalajara is the home of mariachi, and you shouldn't leave town without experiencing it. You needn't spend anything at all in the Plaza de los Mariachis, a short pedestrianized street by the Mercado Libertad and the church of San Juan de Dios, where mariachi bands stroll between bars, playing to anyone prepared to cough up for a song. Players start arriving in the late afternoon but it's best after dark, when there are usually several bands. If they play for you personally, you'll have to negotiate a price before they start, probably around M$100 for one or two songs, but only M$200 for five. You'll also find mariachi bands in Tlaquepaque.

Teatro Degollado This magnificent theatre in central Guadalajara hosts a regular programme of theatre and dance. Pick up details of events from the tourist office or from Ticketmaster (ⓣ33/3818-3800, desk in Fabricas de Francia department store at Juárez 272).

Teatro Diana 16 de Septiembre 710 ⓣ33/3614-7072, ⓦwww.teatrodiana.com. Large, modern theatre hosting shows, musicals and plays.

Cinema

Cineclub Alianza Alianza Francesa, López Cotilla 1199 ⓣ33/3825-2140, ⓦwww.alianzafrancesa.org.mx/guadalajara. Occasional French films usually subtitled in Spanish.

Cinépolis Centro Magno Vallarta 2425 ⓣ33/3630-3940, ⓦwww.cinepolis.com.mx. The most convenient multiplex, around 3km west of downtown. Most movies dubbed into Spanish.

Ex-Convento del Carmen Juárez 638 ⓣ33/358-7825, ⓦwww.centroaudiovisualcom. Alternative and classic movies, plus the occasional festival. Films usually shown in their original language. Tickets usually M$25.

Sport

Jaliscans pride themselves on their equestrian skills, notably in the regular *charreadas* (**rodeos**) held every Sunday (from noon) at the Licenzo Charro de Jalisco, Dr Michel 577 near the Parque Agua Azul. For details call ⓣ33/3619-6876 or just turn up; tickets are usually M$30.

Bullfights are considered to be a sport for connoisseurs, and the cognoscenti watch the *corrida* at the city's largest bullring, the Plaza de Toros Nuevo Progreso (ⓣ33/3637-9982, ⓦwww.plazanuevoprogreso.com.mx), almost 4km northeast of the centre along Calzada Independencia. Fights occur several times in October, then on irregular Sundays until March (4.30pm; tickets M$50–300).

Almost opposite the bullring is the enormous Estadio Jalisco, where *Tapatíos* go to watch their favourite sport, **football**. It was a venue for matches at both the 1970 and 1986 World Cups, but is primarily the stadium for FC Guadalajara (Las Chivas; ⓦwww.chivascampeon.com) who play their home matches here (usually Sat night and Sun afternoon), though they have a new stadium under construction further out of town. Tickets start from as little as M$60, though for around M$250 you can get a really good seat. Of the city's two other top-division teams, Atlas (ⓦwww.atlas.com.mx) also play here, while Tecos have their own stadium (Estadio Tres de Marzo) in Zapopan.

Buses #60 and the Macrobús (Monumental station) run up Calzada Independencia to the bullring and football stadium.

Listings

Airlines and flights Several offices at Vallarta 2440, opposite Centro Magno, 3km west of downtown. Aerocalifornia, Vallarta 2440 (ⓣ33/3616-2525); Aeromar, Vallarta 2440 (ⓣ33/3616-3005); American, Vallarta 2440 (ⓣ33/3616-4090); Azteca, Vallarta 2440 (ⓣ33/3630-4615); Continental, Astral Plaza Galerias (ⓣ33/3647-4251); Delta, López Cotilla 1701 (ⓣ33/3615-2850); Mexicana, Mariano Otero 2353 (ⓣ33/3112-0011); United, Vallarta 2440 (ⓣ33/3813-4002).

American Express Vallarta 2440, opposite Centro Magno ⓣ33/3818-2319 (Mon–Fri 9am–6pm, Sat 9am–1pm).

Banks and exchange There are numerous banks (all with ATMs) throughout the centre, including a cluster around Corona and Juárez. Virtually identical rates, faster service and longer hours are available in the dense cluster of casas de cambio around the corner of Maestranza and López Cotilla. After hours, the bigger hotels will usually change money at a considerably worse rate. Alternatively, try American Express (see above) or Thomas Cook, Vallarta 2440, locale D-1 ⓣ33/3818-2323.

Books You're better off looking for English-language books & magazines in Chapala and Ajijic (see p.343 & p.344), but you will find limited supplies at Sanborn's, Juárez between 16 de Septiembre and Corona, and at Vallarta 1600. Downtown, try Librería Gonvill, López Costilla and Guerra, which has a few novels. Way out west in Colonia Chapalita, Sandi Bookstore, Tepeyac 718 (ⓣ33/3121-0863, ⓦwww.sandibooks.com), has a stack of books in English, including travel guides.

Car rental Agents can be found at the airport, and there's a slew on Niños Héroes at Manzano (not far from the Parque Agua Azul); firms include Budget, Guadalajara Chapala 9880 (ⓣ33/3613-0027); Europcar, Mariano Otero 1170 (ⓣ33/3122-6979);

National, Niños Héroes 961-C (ⓣ33/3614-7175; Quick, Niños Héroes 954 (ⓣ33/3614-6052); and Alamo, Niños Héroes 982 (ⓣ33/3613-5560).
Consulates Australia, López Cotilla 2018 (ⓣ33/3615-7418); Canada, *Hotel Fiesta Americana*, Local 30, Aurelio Aceves 225, Colonia Vallarta Pte (ⓣ33/3616-5642); Guatemala, Mango 1440, Colonía Jardines de la Victoria (ⓣ33/3811-1503); Honduras, Regidores 1114, Colonía Chapultepec (ⓣ33/3817-4998); South Africa, Mexicaltinzgo 1665 2nd floor, Colonia Moderna (ⓣ33/3825 8086); US, Progreso 175, Colonía Americana (ⓣ33/3268-2100).
Emergencies The general emergency number is ⓣ066. There's a police station at Roberto Michel 384, southeast of Parque Agua Azul (ⓣ33/3619-2283), or you can report a crime or accident at the Procuraduría de Justicia (Justice Department), 5100 Cruz del Sur, Las Aguilas, 6km southeast of the centre (ⓣ33/3634-5913).
Internet access There are several internet cafés in central Guadalajara, with prices generally M$10–15/hr. Places marked on our map are at: Colón 230 (Miami.Net, open 24/7), Maestranza 175-A (closed Sun), López Cotilla 491 and 531, Juárez 642 and 675. *El Despertador* (see p.335) has an internet café at Alcalde 287.
Laundry The closest laundry to the centre is at Aldama 129, off Independencia in a slightly rough area a few blocks south of the Mercado Libertad (Mon–Sat 9am–7pm).
Markets and shopping The giant Mercado Libertad may be the biggest of Guadalajara's markets, but every city *barrio* has its own. They include the very touristy Mercado Corona near the cathedral, and craft markets and upscale boutiques in Tlaquepaque and Tonalá. The flea market El Baratillo (Sun) is vast, sometimes stretching a mile or more along Javier Mina, starting a dozen blocks east of the Mercado Libertad. The city is also big on nutritionists, and health-food/aromatherapy stores; head for López Cortilla if you're after some echinacea, green tea or muscle-building protein powder.
Pharmacy Farmacia Guadalajara, with several locations in the centre including Moreno 160 near Plaza Tapatía (open 24hr). There's another branch at López Cotilla 423 at Galeana (daily 7am–10pm).
Phones Casetas are thin on the ground, though there's one at Colón 228. One or two of the internet places (such as the one at Maestranza 175-A) do cheap VOIP calls.
Post office Venustiano Carranza 16 at the junction with Independencia (Mon–Fri 8am–7pm, Sat 8am–4pm).
Spanish courses Guadalajara makes a pretty decent place to learn Spanish, with several schools handily sited close to downtown. One of the most popular is IMAC, Donata Guerra 180 at Madero (ⓣ33/3613-1080, ⓦwww.spanish-school.com.mx/guadalajara) with a flexible schedule allowing short or long courses as well as special-interest

Moving on from Guadalajara

If you're heading to destinations within about 150km of Guadalajara, chances are you're best off heading to the **Central Vieja** (see p.319). Here you'll find **second-class bus** services to places such as Chapala, Ajijic, Tequila and Tapalpa. A few first-class services to these same destinations also leave from here, so it is worth looking around to see who offers the best deal.

All **long-distance buses** leave from the **Central Nueva**, way out in suburbia (see p.318). To get there from the centre, pick up the #616, #644B, #275, the faster TUR bus, or anything marked "Central Nueva" heading south along 16 de Septiembre. The more popular destinations seem to have buses from just about every building. In general, salas 1 and 2 serve destinations in **Jalisco**, Colima and **Michoacán**, plus **Pátzcuaro** and many of the premium services to Mexico City; Mexico City via **Morelia**; and many towns in the Bajío. Salas 3 and 4 have buses to the north and northwest, with services to Puerta Vallarta; the US border; and up the Pacific coast, plus points en route. Sala 5 is for eastbound services towards San Luis Potosí and Tampico, as well as some more local services; Sala 6 serves the Bajío, the northeast and many local second-class buses; and Sala 7 serves the north and northeast again, as well as Mexico City.

From the airport (see p.318) there are constant **flights** to Mexico City, as well as departures to most other Mexican cities and direct connections to many US, Canadian and Central American destinations.

For more detailed journey times and durations, see Travel details on p.375.

classes in ceramics, guitar and flamenco, among other options, and homestay opportunities. Others worth considering are Guadalajara University's CEPE, Tomás V Gómez 125 (Ⓣ33/3616-4399, Ⓦwww.cepe.udg.mx) and the Instituto Cultural Mexicano Norteamericano de Jalisco Díaz de León Sur 300 (Ⓣ33/3825-5838, Ⓦwww.institutocultural.com.mx).

Travel agents There are plenty of travel agents around the centre, including in the lobbies of all the big hotels, or head for American Express or Thomas Cook (see "Banks and exchange").

Tequila and around

The approach to **TEQUILA**, some 50km northwest of Guadalajara, is through great fields of spiky cactus-like blue agave. It's from these rugged plants that the quintessentially Mexican liquor has been produced here since the sixteenth century, with the *indígenas* fermenting its precursor for at least 1500 years before that, a legacy which earned Tequila and its surroundings UNESCO World Heritage status in 2006.

The town itself is a pretty enough little place, with its fine church and smattering of bourgeois mansions, but most tourists come to visit the distilleries. The slickest operation in town is run by José Cuervo, in their La Rojeña factory, north of the main square, parts of which date back to 1758. Here **Mundo Cuervo** (Ⓣ01-800/006-8630, Ⓦwww.mundocuervo.com), offers **tours** every hour (daily 10am–5pm, tours in English are at 1pm and 3pm, but these times change so it's best to check in advance). The basic tour (45min; M$100), makes a quick turn through the factory, where you can taste the raw distillate, then continues to the barrel storage area, where you can try a little of the finished product. Extended tours (M$200–250) take in all this, give you a chance to sit down and learn how to appreciate the qualities of the various tequilas and include a margarita and a visit to the old storage cellars – it's worth the few extra pesos. At the weekend there are even more extended "VIP" tours (M$300–380). If you're interested in something a little less stage-managed but still informative, Sauza's **La Perseverancia** distillery, Mora 80, also offers tours (Mon–Fri 11am, 12.30pm, 3pm & 4pm, Sat 11am & 12.30pm; M$70; usually bilingual). To get there, head five blocks west of the plaza along Ramon Corona.

Across the street from the main entrance to Mundo Cuervo is the small but proud **Museo Nacional del Tequila** (daily 9am–4pm; M$15), where you can learn about the history of the popular drink and its crucial role in the town's development. They have a fine collection of tequila bottles (both ornate and primitive) and agave art.

The Tequila Express

One of the best ways to experience the Tequila region is to travel on the **Tequila Express** (Ⓦwww.tequilaexpress.com.mx), one of only three train rides left in Mexico (the others being the longer Copper Canyon run – see p.157 – and a suburban line in Mexico City). It is undoubtedly touristy, but gives you ample chance to learn something of the process and see how the agave is harvested, and includes lunch accompanied by mariachi music and no shortage of samples. The train doesn't actually take you to the town of Tequila; rather it travels at a stately pace through blue agave fields and stops 15km short at the town of Amatitán, home of Herradura's Hacienda San José del Refugio (see p.341).

The Tequila Express is packaged as an all-in-one **day tour** (Sat, Sun and holidays 10am; M$950, kids 5–12 M$550, infants free). Tickets should be bought a few days in advance from the Chamber of Commerce cashier department, Vallarta 4095 at Niño Obrero (Ⓣ33/3880-9099), or from their downtown office at Morelos 395 (Ⓣ33/3614-3145), or through Ticketmaster (Ⓣ33/3880-9099; booking fee charged).

When you enter town you may be approached by people trying to get you to visit less-well-known **out-of-town distilleries** such as La Cofradia (Ⓦwww.tequilacofradia.com). These trips can be a bit hit-or-miss, but when they're good, they can be wonderful experiences with far fewer people and a more personal touch. The factories are typically amidst the agave fields so you may also see something of the harvesting. Trips cost around M$60 and include a minibus ride out there. The serene **Herradura distillery** (Hacienda San José del Refugio Ⓣ01-800/710-9868, Ⓦwww.herradura.com: 90min tours Mon–Fri 9am, 10am, 11am, noon, 1pm, 2pm & 3pm, Sat 9am, 10am & 11pm; M$100; in English by advance arrangement) in the small town of **Amatitán**, 15km southeast of Tequila on the main road from Guadalajara, deserves a stop. Again, groups tend to be smaller, the firm uses strictly traditional methods, and their tequila is considered by connoisseurs to be among the best (the real ale of tequilas, if you like).

Tequila practicalities

It's easy enough **to get to Tequila** on regular **buses** from Guadalajara's Central Vieja bus station (Sala B; every 20min; 1hr 45min), or save a little time by picking up the same bus outside the Periférico Sur station, the southern terminus of the Tren Ligero line 1. Unfortunately, the bus is pretty slow and it can be rather uncomfortable to return to Guadalajara after a few too many tequila samples. A good alternative is to go on an **organized tour** such as the Tequila Express train (see box opposite), the Panoramex tour (see p.319), or Mundo Cuervo's own tour, which leaves from the *Hotel Roma*, Juárez 170, daily at 9.30am, for a six-hour day-trip (M$300).

Making tequila

Visitors to Tequila are often surprised to hear that the town's eponymous spirit is more complex than its reputation lets on. As with alcoholic beverages considered more sophisticated, like champagne, **tequila** is subject to strictly enforced appellation rules: true tequila must be made from at least 51 percent **Weber blue agave** grown in the *Zona Protegida por la Denomination de Origen* – essentially all of Jalisco plus parts of Nayarit, Michoacán, Guanajuato and Tamaulipas. The balance can be made up with alcohol from sugar or corn, but a good tequila will be one hundred percent agave, which gives more intense and flamboyant flavours, and will be stated on the label.

The agave takes seven to ten years to reach an economically harvestable size. The plant is then killed and the spiky leaves cut off, leaving the heart, known as the **piña** for its resemblance to an oversized pineapple. On distillery tours you can see the hearts as they're unloaded from trucks and shoved into ovens, where they're baked for a day or so. On emerging from the ovens, the warm and slightly caramelized *piñas* are crushed and the sweet juice fermented, then distilled.

Tequila isn't a drink that takes well to extended **ageing**, but some time in a barrel definitely benefits the flavour and smoothness. The simplest style of tequila, known as *blanco* or *plata* (white or silver), is clear, and sits just fifteen days in stainless steel tanks. The *reposado* (rested) spends at least two months in toasted, new white-oak barrels. The degree to which the barrels are **toasted** greatly affects the resulting flavours; a light toast gives spicy notes; a medium toast brings out vanilla and honey flavours; and a deep charring gives chocolate, smoke and roast almond overtones. If left for over a year the tequila becomes *añejo* (old), and typically takes on a darker colour. A fourth style, *joven* (young), is a mix of *blanco* with either *reposado* or *añejo*. While the nuances of tequila are slowly being explored by a select few, the benefits of oak ageing aren't appreciated by all – many still prefer the supple vegetative freshness of a good *blanco*.

Regular buses drop off passengers on the edge of Tequila, from where it is a one-kilometre walk along Sixto Gorjón to the main plaza and Mundo Cuervo. Unless you work in the spirits business and are on a buying trip, there's little need to spend more than an afternoon in Tequila, but you can **stay** at the comfortable *Hotel Plaza Jardín*, José Cuervo 13 (Ⓣ374/742-0061, Ⓦwww.hotelplazajardin.com; ❹) right on the main plaza, which has air-conditioned rooms, a nice rooftop terrace and its own restaurant and bar. A cheaper alternative is *Hotel Posada del Agave*, Sixto Gorjón 83 (Ⓣ374/742-0774; ❸), whose lime-green rooms are equipped with ceiling fans. More likely you'll just want a **meal**, best at *La Fonda Cholula*, a bright colourful place to eat right opposite Mundo Cuervo. They have nice shady rooftop seating and serve respectable *chiles en nogada* for M$100.

Visiting Tequila is particularly fun during one of its **fiestas**: the town celebrates the **Día de la Santa Cruz** (May 3) with mariachi and plenty of imbibing; and **La Señora de la Salud** (Dec 8), with rodeos, cockfights, fireworks and more drinking. **World Tequila Day** (May 27) is celebrated with parades and drinking, but in Amatitán rather than Tequila itself (arguably, Amatitán was the original centre of "mezcal wine" production before the arrival of the railway made Tequila its distribution centre and gave the liquor its modern name).

Laguna de Chapala and around

At around 35km wide and 120km long, **Laguna de Chapala**, just over 50km south of Guadalajara, is the largest lake in Mexico. Its northern shore has long been a favourite retreat for *Tapatíos*, especially since the early years of the twentieth century when dictator Porfirio Díaz regularly spent his holidays here. Expats from north of the border, particularly Canadians, have also been appreciative of the lake scenery and even year-round temperatures. It is said that there are now around 30,000 such people living in and around Guadalajara, a sizeable proportion of whom have settled on the lakeside – particularly in **Chapala** and in the smaller village of **Ajijic**. Most of these snowbirds are retirees – during the 1990s, Laguna de Chapala was spoken of locally as being in the "gay 90s", the joke being that anyone who lived there was either gay or over 90, but some are writers or artists *manqués*, hoping for inspiration, like Ken Kesey, or **D.H. Lawrence**, who wrote the first draft of *The Plumed Serpent* here.

This mass expat presence has rendered the area rather expensive and in many respects somewhat sanitized and stratified – you'll see numerous real estate offices trying to sell lots in newly created gated communities, and as you'd imagine, English is spoken widely. There are even a couple of English-language magazines produced here: the *Lake Chapala Review* and the *El Ojo del Lago*. None of this, though, can detract from the allure of the deep-red sunsets over the lake.

The lake averages only eight metres deep, and during the 1980s and 1990s the **lake level** dropped when the government used its feeder rivers as a fresh-water supply for Guadalajara and Mexico City; the lake receded so far that shoreline property was 2km from the water's edge. Levels have now improved thanks to heavier rainfall and the work of the 20,000-strong group Amigos del Lago de Chapala (Ⓦwww.amigosdelago.org), but agricultural runoff has raised nitrate pollution to unsustainable levels and encouraged the growth of choking **water hyacinth**. The *charales*, the fish for which the lake was once famed, are virtually gone.

Nonetheless, the lake remains popular, and on **weekends** and holidays day-trippers from the city help to create a party atmosphere. Panoramex (see p.319) runs a day trip to Chapala and Ajijic from Guadalajara (M$300). **Peak season** is November to April, which coincides with the arrival of seasonal snowbirds.

Chapala

CHAPALA (Ⓦwww.chapala.com) on the northern shore of the lake, is a sleepy community with a quiet charm and relaxed pace, but it becomes positively festive on sunny weekends, when thousands come to eat, swim or take a boat ride out to one of the lake's islands. Shoreline restaurants all offer the local speciality, *pescado blanco*, famous despite its almost total lack of flavour and lake-bottom origins, and street vendors sell cardboard plates of tiny fried fish from the lake, known as *charales*. Head to the left along the promenade, past streets of shuttered nineteenth-century villas, and you'll find a small **crafts market**. There's even a flat *ciclopista* (cycle path) running along the lakeside between Chapala and Ajijic for easy cycling and walking, with nice views of the lake; on a hot day it beats taking the bus.

If you're in the mood for a longer walk, you might consider heading up to the cross on the top of the hill overlooking the town: there's a path starting on López Cotilla between no. 316 and no. 318, across the street from *Hotel Candilejas* (see below).

Practicalities

Buses leave the old bus station in Guadalajara for Chapala throughout the day (Sala A; every 30min; 6am–9pm). Be sure to get on one of the *directo* services, or you'll stop at every little village along the way. From Chapala, regular services run on to Ajijic (10min), San Juan Cosalá (15min) and Jacotepec (25min). From the bus station, the main street, Madero, stretches six blocks down to the lakeside, where Ramon Corona leads off to the left. The main square is halfway down Madero, where López Cotillo crosses it (take a left here to reach Juárez and then Zaragoza, both parallel with Madero). Hidalgo, the road to Ajijic, branches off Madero to the right just beyond the main square.

There is a **tourist information booth** at the junction of Madero and Ramon Corona, but it doesn't seem to have any regular hours. A gaggle of banks with **ATMs** gather around the junction of Madero and Hidalgo, and there's a **caseta telefónica** at Encarnacion Rosas, just off the main square, and across Madero at no. 230-B, a **bookshop** stocking the *Miami Herald*'s Mexico edition, *USA Today*, a good number of international magazines and a few novels in English. The **post office** is 200m down Hidalgo on the left, and there's a **laundry** on the corner of Zaragoza and López Cotilla. If you decide you want to spend more than a day here, Chapala does have some decent **places to stay**. At the *Hotel Candilejas,* López Cotilla 363 (Ⓣ376/765-2279; ❸), just off the main square, with tiled floors and arched brick ceilings, guests are treated like members of the family. For more mod cons but less olde worlde charm, the *Hotel Montecarlo*, Hidalgo 296 (Ⓣ376/765-2120, Ⓦwww.hoteles.udg.mx; ❺), 1km from the junction with Madero, offers tennis courts, a pool, lake views and airy rooms. The nicest option in town is *Quinta Quetzalcoatl*, Zaragoza 307 (Ⓣ376/765-3653, Ⓦwww.accommodationslakechapala.com; no kids; breakfast included ❻), where D.H. Lawrence wrote *The Plumed Serpent*. There's a wide assortment of gorgeous rooms, each with its own private terrace, set in a lovely garden with a small pool; in winter particularly, you should book well ahead.

For **places to eat**, *Café Paris*, Madero 421, has good breakfasts and reasonably priced *comidas*, as well as great booths for people-watching. Under the *portales* of the main square, *Chapala's Fonda*, Paseo de los Ausentes 621, dishes out tasty *chilaquiles*, breakfasts, soups and *antojitos*. *Restaurant Superior*, Madero 415, does reasonably priced breakfasts, and fish and meat dishes, including fish fillet stuffed with crab. For a larger meal, try *Cazadores*, Ramon Corona 8 (Ⓣ376/765-2162; closed Mon), which has been serving hearty, and somewhat pricey, surf-and-turf dinners amidst the faded elegance of a grand mansion since 1956. In addition to all these, there is also a row of fish restaurants competing for custom along the lakefront – most of the fish served is brought in from elsewhere, due to the lake's depleted stock and contamination.

Ajijic

With its narrow cobbled streets, **AJIJIC**, 7km west of Chapala, is smaller, quieter and more self-consciously arty. It may be a wonderful place to paint or retire, with a thriving expat social and cultural life, but as a visitor you're likely to exhaust its charms in a couple of hours – long enough to wander by the lake, visit the art galleries, have a meal and perhaps check out the **Casa de Cultura**, on the north side of the plaza, which hosts musical performances and art exhibitions.

Practicalities

The **bus** drops you either in the centre or on the Carretera Chapala, from where Colón runs six blocks southward to the lake, with the main square halfway along it. Many of the best places to stay and eat are within a couple of blocks of here. There's a high standard of **accommodation** in town, as well as **apartments** and **houses** to rent for longer stays; check out the notice boards in shops and galleries. One of the best picks in town is *Mis Amores*, Hidalgo 22 (Ⓣ376/766-4640, Ⓦwww.misamores.com; ❻), Ajijic's answer to a contemporary boutique hotel, with tasteful decor, individual terraces shaded by banana trees and a warm proprietor; advance booking is advisable. *La Nueva Posada*, Donato Guerra 9 (Ⓣ376/766-1444, Ⓦhotelnuevaposada-ajijic.com; breakfast included ❼), by the lake three blocks east of Colón, is an eclectically decorated, welcoming place with lovely gardens, a small pool and distant water views. The main building feels like a grand hotel; you can also opt for one of the separate villas. There's an excellent restaurant where breakfast (included) is served. *Hotel Italo*, off the main square at Guadalipe Victoria 10 (Ⓣ376/766-2221; ❸), is a decent bet even though the bells of the church next door ring every hour – light sleepers will want to try elsewhere.

If you are **eating** on a tight budget, head for the makeshift family-run *sopes* stands around the plaza, where you can dine heartily for M$35. Many of the better restaurants cater to expat tastes, serving loads of salads and juices. One of the better examples is *The Secret Garden*, Hidalgo 12, with a relaxed and shady garden setting that's perfect for espresso and a muffin, or something from their healthy-leaning menu – stuffed white or whole-wheat baguettes, garden burger and salad, or vegetable lasagna. The restaurant in the *Hotel Italo* serves authentic pizza (large for M$100–120) and pasta, though you'll do well to go for the imaginative daily specials. For something special, visit *Nueva Posada* in the hotel of the same name, a lovely restaurant with lake views, where you can sit down to *sopa Azteca* followed by pork chops with jalapeño and mint jelly (M$120) or grilled salmon with Grand Marnier and balsamic glaze (M$130), all done to perfection.

San Juan Cosalá

Buses continue five kilometres west of Ajijic along Carratera Chapala towards **SAN JUAN COSALÁ**. On the lakeshore, 1km east of the village, you come upon a string of lakeside resorts around a spa belonging to the *Hotel Balneario* (M$60) and pool (M$140, but free for *Hotel Balneario* and *Villa Bordeaux* guests), which offer visitors a chance to bask in natural thermal waters said to have healing properties. The *Hotel Balneario* (Ⓣ376/761-0222, Ⓦwww.hotelspacosala.com; ❻), right beside the pool, is the cheapest and most popular. The rooms are nothing special for the price, but the same applies to neighbouring establishments. Perhaps the best value is the adjacent and very slightly pricier *Villa Bordeaux* (Ⓣ376/761-0494, Ⓦwww.hotelspacosala.com; ⑥), a more upmarket hacienda-style hotel featuring a thermal pool, sauna, steam room and rooms each with a terrace overlooking the pool to the lake. Both places offer a range of massages priced M$125–570 and lasting twenty to ninety minutes depending on the treatment you choose.

South towards the coast

Some of the most delightful subalpine scenery in Mexico lies southwest of Laguna de Chapala, on the road to Colima. You'll miss much of it if you stick to the speedy toll road (Hwy-54), though even that has its exciting moments as it passes the Zona de Montaña: the following places are all reached from the far slower, far more attractive, if bumpier, old road plied by second-class buses.

Tapalpa

The town of **TAPALPA**, 130km southwest of Guadalajara, makes an ideal base for a few days of relaxation amid upland pastures and pine forests. It is reached via a steep, winding road off the old highway, which climbs continuously until it crests a 2300-metre ridge at El Balcón. If you're driving, stop here to check out the view back down the valley and to feel the near-constant steady breeze, a phenomenon that drew World Cup paragliding events in 2002 and 2004.

Pretty little Tapalpa, 10km further on, lies amid magnificent surroundings – ranch country and tree-clad hills that are often covered in a gentle mist. With a population of only around 16,000, there's a village feel to it, especially around the plaza. Here you'll find eighteenth-century wooden-balconied houses, encircling *portales* and two impressive **churches** – the larger with an unusually plain brick interior. On the outskirts, clusters of cabañas dot the woods luring upwardly mobile *Tapatíos*, and a fair bit of desirable real estate has sprung up in recent years.

There's good **walking** in almost any direction from Tapalpa, with plenty of wildlife, especially birds, to spot; black vultures (urubu birds) are often seen soaring on the thermals. You can also hire **horses** (look for the signs) for the popular ride to the local waterfall. One especially pleasant hike is to **Las Piedrotas** (10km return; 2hr), which follows a decent but little used road towards Chiquilistlán (marked as you enter Tapalpa). It passes the romantic ruins of a *fábrica* – an old water-driven paper mill – and climbs towards a gorgeous valley of pasturelands, studded with wild flowers and huge boulders. If you don't fancy walking both ways, get a taxi to drop you off (around M$70) and walk back.

Tapalpa is very much on the Guadalajara weekender circuit, so try to visit midweek when its old-world charm is little affected (although hotels remain rather pricey). It's very cold in winter, and even the summer nights can become chilly. Locals brew their own mescal in the village, which may help warm you.

Practicalities

Second-class **buses** run from Guadalajara's old bus station (Sala B; approximately every 90min; 3hr) to Tapalpa where they stop outside the ticket office at Ignacio López 10, two blocks south of the plaza. Four daily services go direct to Sayula (1hr) and Ciudad Guzmán (2hr), but many more pass by the junction of the main road (El Crucero, 32km away); it's easy enough to catch a Guadalajara-bound bus, or even hitch, down there, but if you do hitch, go during the day and leave yourself plenty of time. Locals consider the route dangerous after dark.

For most things, head for Tapalpa's main plaza, where several of the old buildings have been refurbished as restaurants and hotels; there's even a **bank** with ATM at Matamoros 1 in the southeast corner of the plaza, and a **tourist office**, on the north side (daily 9am–5pm; ⓣ343/432-0493, ⓦwww.tapalpaturistico.com). For the **internet** and good coffee, head to @ Rova, a cybercafé and *pastelería* at Matamoros 7, in the little courtyard on the south side of the plaza.

During the week you may be one of the few visitors, but all **rooms** are often taken at weekends and around the **fiesta** for the Día de la Virgen de Guadalupe (Dec 12), when Tapalpa attracts pilgrims from a wide area. *La Casa de Maty*, Matamoros 69 (ⓣ343/432-0189, ⓦwww.lacasadematy.com.mx; ❻), on the south side of the plaza, is the pick of the pricier places to stay in town; its comfortable, rustic rooms are set around a beautiful plant-filled courtyard with a fountain. At the *Villa de San José*, Cerrada Ignacio López 91 (ⓣ343/432-0451, ⓦwww.hotelvilladesanjose.com; ❺), one block southeast of the plaza, you'll find country-style charm in rooms with warm wooden floors. Rates include continental breakfast. The cheapest place in town is *Posada La Hacienda*, Raúl Quintero 120 (ⓣ343/432-0193, ⓦwww.posadalahacienda.com; ❸), half a block southeast of the plaza. The good-value rooms are spacious, and some have views of the surrounding countryside.

Numerous **restaurants** around the main plaza serve plain country food. Look out for places serving *poche*, a local wine made from an unusual concoction of pomegranate, peanuts, coffee and guava. It's also a good place to try *queso fundido*, as the farms hereabout produce good cheese – *Los Girasoles*, Obregón 110 (ⓣ343/432-0458), a lovely little place just off the southwest corner of the plaza, serves it with added ingredients such as chorizo or mushrooms. The balcony at *Paulinos*, on the north side of the plaza, is a nice spot to watch the town come awake over *huevos rancheros*, while *La Villa*, Raúl Quintero 93, is perfect for a sundowner.

Sayula

Beyond the turn-off for Tapalpa, the old main road continues 12km south to **SAYULA** (the name chosen by D.H. Lawrence for the town on Laguna de Chapala in *The Plumed Serpent*) and then to the sizeable city of Ciudad Guzmán. Sayula was once fought over by indigenous tribes eager to control the production of salt from the nearby lake – but there's little to see, apart from a thriving market and some old convents that have been converted into basic **hotels**. If you're in the region around December 8, though, be sure to call in for the Día de la Inmaculada Concepción, a **fiesta** with traditional dances including the Danza de la Conquista, which partly re-enacts the Spanish Conquest. The **bus** stops at Portal Rayon 31, on Indpendencia, a block and a half from the pretty central plaza. Here you'll find *Hotel la Fortaleza,* Portal Galeana 5 (ⓣ342/422-0633; ❷), with large, dark rooms around an attractive and pleasantly run-down courtyard. About five blocks towards the highway, *Hotel Meson del Anima*, Avila Camacho 171 Ote (ⓣ342/422-0600; ❷), has some nicer rooms, and even a pool but less character.

Ciudad Guzmán

The birthplace of José Clemente Orozco, **CIUDAD GUZMÁN** is a busy little city thoroughly steeped in local culture, with attractive colonnaded streets in the centre, though there seems little reason to stop except to break a journey. If you do visit, don't miss the pleasant **Museo de las Culturas de Occidente**, Dr. Angel Gonzalez 21 (Tues–Sun 9.30am–5.30pm; M$31), off Reforma, a block west of the plaza. It's just one room, but there are some lovely clay figures and animals in the collection of local archeology, and often an interesting temporary display that may include early works by **Orozco**. The centre of the town's main plaza is a bandstand with a replica of Orozco's *Man of Fire* mural from Guadalajara (see p.328).

Buses stop at the new Central de Autobuses around 2km west of the town centre; it has good connections to Guadalajara and the coast. Local buses (#5a & #6b) stop outside and run to the plaza along Madero y Carranza, which becomes Reforma. As ever, almost everything of interest is on or around the plaza, where you'll find banks, phones and **places to stay**. The pick of places is *Hotel Zapotlán*, Federico del Toro 61, along the west side of the plaza (Ⓣ341/412-0040; ❸), which has a beautiful courtyard with palms and creepers, comfy rooms and continental breakfast. Rooms come with ceiling fans, which are very low in some rooms; watch your head. A block to the north, the *Hotel Flamingos*, Federico del Toro 133 (Ⓣ341/412-0103; ❷), has less character but is clean and quiet.

Back on the plaza are a few *taquerías* and a couple of **restaurants**, including the decent, reasonably priced *Juanito*, at Portal Morelos 65, a few doors from the *Hotel Zapotlán*. One block to the south, the attractive *Los Portales*, at Refugio Barragán del Toscano 32, has delicious, reasonably priced breakfasts and Mexican main dishes in a Moorish-style courtyard. There are also good value tortas and *licuados* at *El Buen Sazon*, Reforma 22. You can have an inexpensive and healthy breakfast with cereal and fresh juice at the stands behind the church in the main square. The salty local cheeses are a treat and can be bought at the daily **market** near the stalls.

The road from Ciudad Guzmán to Colima

Between Ciudad Guzmán and Colima, the drive becomes truly spectacular, through country dominated by the **Nevado de Colima** – at 4335m the loftiest and most impressive peak in the west, which is snowcapped in winter. The main highway slashes straight through the mountains via deep cuts and soaring concrete bridges, while the old one snakes above and beneath it as it switchbacks its way through the hills. Both have great views of the Nevado on a clear day. If you're on the old road, close your windows as you pass through **Atenquique**, a lovely hidden valley some 25km from Ciudad Guzmán, which is enveloped in a pall of fumes from a vast paper works. Not far from here, off the road and served by two buses an hour from Ciudad Guzmán, **Tuxpan** – not to be confused with Tuxpán in Veracruz (see p.600), where the exiled Fidel Castro plotted, organized and set off for the Cuban revolution - is a beautiful, ancient little town. It's especially fun during its frequent, colourful **fiestas**, including the Día de San Sebastian (Jan 20), with its traditional dances; the Día del Señor de la Misericordia (last Sun in May), in honour of this miraculous and highly venerated image; and the Día de Santiago Apóstol (July 25), which is celebrated with fireworks.

Northern Michoacán

To the southeast of Jalisco, **Michoacán** state is one of the most beautiful and diverse in all Mexico, spreading as it does from a very narrow coastal plain with several tiny beach villages, up to where the Sierra Madre Occidental reaches eastwards into range after range of wooded volcanic heights.

However, despite its beauty and charms, Michoacán remains a region that people travel through rather than to. Morelia, Pátzcuaro, Uruapan and other towns lie conveniently near the major route from Guadalajara to Mexico City. The state tourism department's **website** is Ⓦwww.turismomichoacan.gob.mx, and there's more online information at Ⓦwww.michoacan-travel.com.

Guadalajara to Uruapan

From Guadalajara, the most direct route to Mexico City heads through the major junction of La Piedad and continues east towards Irapuato. If you can afford to dawdle a while, though, it's infinitely more rewarding to follow the slower, southern road through Zamora and Morelia, spending a couple of days in Uruapan and Pátzcuaro. From Uruapan, Hwy 37 slices south through the mountains to the Pacific coast at Lázaro Cárdenas (see p.547).

Leaving Guadalajara, you skirt the northeastern edge of Laguna de Chapala before turning south, heading into Michoacán and reaching **ZAMORA DE HIDALGO**, some 200km away. Zamora has little intrinsic interest. However, if you're planning to head straight down to Uruapan you may want to change buses here – you can catch a direct bus from Guadalajara to Zamora, where there's a frequent service to Uruapan. Although not much to go out of your way for, the town boasts several small restaurants and a market very close to the bus station. The old cathedral, unusually Gothic in style, is ruined and often closed, but you can while away some time on the pleasant grassy plaza in front.

Vasco de Quiroga – the noble conquistador

When the Spaniards arrived in Michoacán in 1519, they found the region dominated by the **Purépechan** people – whom they named **Tarascans** – whose chief town, Tzintzuntzán, lay on the shores of Lago de Pátzcuaro. The Tarascan civilization, a serious rival to the Aztecs before the Conquest, had a widespread reputation for excellence in the arts, especially metalworking and feathered ornaments. Though the Tarascans submitted peaceably to the Spaniards in 1522 and their leader converted to Christianity, they did not avoid the massacres and mass torture that **Nuño de Guzmán** meted out in his attempts fully to pacify the region. Guzmán's methods were overly brutal, even by colonial standards, and an elderly Spanish nobleman-turned-priest, **Vasco de Quiroga**, was appointed bishop to the area in an attempt to restore harmony. He succeeded beyond all expectations, securing his reputation as a champion of the native peoples – a reputation that persists today. He coaxed the native population down from the mountains to which they had fled, established self-sufficient agricultural settlements and set up missions to teach practical skills as well as religion. The effects of his actions have survived in a very visible way for, despite some blurring in objects produced for the tourist trade, each village still has its own craft speciality: lacquerware in Uruapan, guitars in Paracho, copper goods in Santa Clara del Cobre, to name but a few.

Vasco de Quiroga also left behind him a deeply religious state. Michoacán was a stronghold of the reactionary **Cristero** movement, which fought a bitter war in defence of the Church after the Revolution. Perhaps, too, the ideals of Zapata and Villa had less appeal here as Quiroga's early championing of native peoples' rights against their new overlords meant that the hacienda system never entirely took over Michoacán. Unlike most of the country, the state boasted a substantial peasantry with land it could call its own and therefore it didn't relate to calls for land and labour reform.

If you're driving, there's no need to stop between Zamora and Uruapan, though you may want to pause a while in the village of **PARACHO**, 50km south of Zamora, which has been famous for the manufacture of **guitars** and other stringed instruments since Quiroga's time. Every building seems to house a workshop, a guitar shop or both. The guitars vary enormously in price and quality – many are not meant to be anything more than ornamental, but others are serious, handcrafted musical instruments. Though you'll find them on display and for sale in the markets and artesanía museums in Uruapan or Pátzcuaro, if you're really looking to buy, you should do it here at the source. Paracho also hosts a couple of fascinating **fiestas**. On Corpus Christi (the Thurs after Trinity, usually late May/early June) you can witness the **Danza de los Viejitos** (see box, p.351). August 8 sees an even more ancient ceremony, whose roots go back to well before the Spanish era: an ox is sacrificed and its meat used to make a complicated ritual dish (*shuripe*) that is then shared out among the celebrants. This coincides with the music, dance and general jollity of the **Feria Nacional de Guitarra**, the National Guitar Fair.

Uruapan and around

URUAPAN, they say, means "the place where flowers bloom" in the Tarascan language, though *Appleton's Guide* for 1884 tells a different story: "The word Uruapan comes from *Urani*, which means in the Tarasc language 'a chocolate cup', because the Indians in this region devote themselves to manufacture and painting of these objects." Demand for chocolate cups, presumably, has fallen since then, but whatever the truth, the modern version is certainly appropriate: Uruapan, lower (at around 1600m) and warmer than most of its neighbours, enjoys a steamy subtropical climate and is surrounded by thick forests and lush parks.

It's a prosperous and growing town, too, with a thriving commerce based on the richness of its agriculture (particularly a vast export market in **avocados** and **macadamia nuts**) and on new light industry. To some extent these businesses have come to overshadow the old attractions, creating ugly new development and displacing traditional crafts, but Uruapan remains a lively place with a fine market, an abiding reputation for **lacquerware** and fascinating surroundings – especially the giant waterfall and "new" volcano of Paricutín (see p.354).

Arrival and information

Most visitors arrive at Uruapan's modern **bus station**, the Central de Autobuses, 3km northeast of the centre; a local bus (marked "Centro") from right outside will take you down to the Plaza Morelos, the plaza in the heart of town, or back again from there. There's also a domestic **airport** with daily connections from Mexico City.

Uruapan's **tourist office** (Casa Regional del Turista), Independencia 15 (daily 8.30am–7pm; ⓣ452/524-0667, not only gives away a good **map** of town but also showcases and sells local crafts, and has information on the wealth of local **festivals**. The most exciting and interesting of these are: Año Nuevo (Jan 1), when the Danza de los Viejitos is performed; Palm Sunday (the Sun before Easter), the culmination of a week's celebration when the *indígenas* collect palms from the hills and make ornaments from the leaves; Día de María Magdalena (July 22), when there's a processions of animals through the streets; Día de San Francisco (Oct 4), one of the year's biggest saint's day celebrations; and the Feria de Aguacate (Nov/Dec), a three-week avocado fair with agricultural exhibits and artesanía displays.

Numerous **banks** with ATMs lie along Cupatitzio, a block or so south of the plaza, and there are **casas de cambio** (for US dollars only) at Portal Degollado 15 in the northeast corner of the plaza and at Carranza 14-D, just west of Juan Ayala. There's a **caseta telefónica** at Manuel Ocaranza 3, just south of the plaza, plus a

couple on the west side of the plaza, and very cheap VOIP calls, especially beyond North America, in the **internet** café at Caranza 34-B (by *Casa Chikita*; Mon–Sat 9am–9pm; internet M$9/hr), though the cheapest web surfing is at Independencia 33 (Mon–Sat 11am–10pm, Sun 11am–5pm; M$5/hr).

Accommodation

Uruapan lures visitors with its proximity to breathtaking natural beauty, which makes **camping** is an excellent idea if you plan to stay in the area. *Campamento Regional* (☎452/523-2309), on the edge of the Parque Nacional Eduardo Ruíz, 3km northwest of downtown, has sites or cabañas for M$100 per person, including access to a cooking area, or rooms sleeping up to eight with full kitchen and bath for M$150–200 per person. The town also seems to have more than its fair share of **hotels**, most of them conveniently sited around – or at least within walking distance of – Plaza Morelos.

Casa Chikita Carranza 32-A ☎452/524-4174, Ⓦwww.casachikita.com. This appealing B&B in a nineteenth-century colonial house, set around a central courtyard, has lovely, high-ceilinged rooms. Continental breakfast included. ❺

Gran Hotel Acosta Filomena Mata 325 ☎452/523-4564. Opposite the bus station, this is hardly an ideal spot, but if you're passing through it does offer clean, simple, reasonably priced rooms. ❷

Hotel Capri Portal Degollado 10, at the eastern end of the plaza ☎452/524-2186. The action of

The Dance of the Little Old Men

The **Danza de los Viejitos**, or the **Dance of the Little Old Men**, is the most famous of Michoacán's traditional dances. It is also one of its most picturesque, with the performers (usually children), dressed in baggy white cotton and masked as old men, alternating between parodying the tottering steps of the *viejitos* they represent and breaking into complex routines. Naturally enough, there's a lot of music, too. You'll see the dance performed at festive occasions all over Michoacán, but the finest expression is in Paracho (see p.349).

the plaza often spills over into the lobby of this very basic hotel featuring fairly scruffy rooms with bath. It is, however, a much better bet than other hotels on the same block. ❶

Hotel Concordia Portal Carillo 8 ⓣ452/523-0400 or 01-800/420-0400, ⓦwww.hotelconcordia.com.mx. Modern, clean and efficient: all rooms are pleasantly decorated, and have TV and phone. There's parking and a good breakfast buffet (extra M$65), but it is less characterful than the cheaper *Regis*. ❺

Hotel Continental Nicolas Bravo 34 ⓣ452/523-5028 or 01-800/714-2228, ⓦwww.continentaluruapan.com. Relatively quiet hotel with modern, clean rooms (the best ones are in the new wing), with TV and phone, parking facilities and a restaurant. ❺

Hotel del Centro Aldama 3 (no phone). Simple rooms with bathrooms and hot water at bargain prices, arranged around two sunny courtyards; nothing fancy, but friendly and cheap. ❶

Hotel del Parque Independencia 124, near the Parque Nacional ⓣ452/524-3845. Best of the cheapies: clean and friendly, with large rooms (those at the front are nicest but a bit noisy), en-suite bathrooms and parking facilities. ❷

Hotel Real de Uruapan Nicolas Bravo 110 ⓣ452/527-5900 or 01-800/000-7325, ⓦwww.realdeuruapan.com.mx. Nine-storey international-style hotel with carpeted rooms, each with TV and phone. The executive rooms on the upper floors get the best views over the town. ❺

Hotel Regis Portal Carillo 12 ⓣ452/523-5844. Friendly place in a central location featuring characterful rooms with the accompaniment of twittering caged birds. Parking is available and some rooms overlook the plaza (though that makes them noisy). ❹

Mansión del Cupatitzio at the northern end of the Parque Nacional Eduardo Ruíz ⓣ452/523-2100 or 01-800/504-8793, ⓦwww.mansiondelcupatitzio.com. Uruapan's finest hotel, with superb service, a pool, a terrace restaurant and beautiful grounds full of plants and flowers. The hotel is conveniently adjacent to the entrance to the national park. Wheelchair accessible with an adapted room. ❼

Posada Morelos Morelos 30 ⓣ452/523-2302. Secure, family-run hotel set around a pleasant courtyard. Clean and reasonably priced singles plus rooms for groups. There are also rooms without baths (❷) for anyone really on a budget. Avoid rooms near the noisy street. ❸

Plaza Morelos and around

The animated **Plaza Morelos**, a long strip of tree-shaded open space, is in every sense the heart of Uruapan. It's surrounded by everything of importance: shops, market, banks, principal churches and many of the hotels. This is the place to head first, either to find a place to stay or simply to get a feel for the place. The **Casa de la Cultura** (daily 8.30am–8.30pm; free), in the northwest of the plaza, hosts regular cultural events, exhibitions, concerts and dance performances. There's a bulletin board of upcoming events in the entrance.

Also on the plaza is the town's only overt tourist attraction, **La Huatapera**. One of the oldest surviving buildings in Uruapan, it has been exquisitely restored to house the **Museo de las Cuatro Pueblos Indígenas** (Tues–Sun 9.30am–1.30pm & 3.30–6pm; free), a small display of arts and crafts from the state's four indigenous peoples: the Purépecha, the Nahua, the Otomí and the Mazahua. Look out for particularly fine Purépecha lacquerware gourds, and a Nahua harp with its lute-like acoustic box, as well as beaten copperware from Santa Clara del Cobre (see p.364). The small courtyard and adjoining chapel were built by Juan de San

Miguel, the Franciscan friar who founded the town itself, and were later adopted by Bishop Quiroga as a hospital and training centre. The carvings around the windows bear a marked Arab influence, as they were crafted by Christianized Moorish artisans from Spain (Mudéjares).

The wares shown in the museum are of the highest quality, and are worth close inspection if you plan to go out hunting for bargains in the market or in the shops around the park. The art of making lacquer is complex and time-consuming, involving the application of layer upon layer of different colours, with the design cut into the background. All too many of the goods produced for tourists are simply given a couple of coats (one for the black background with a design then painted on top), which is far quicker and cheaper but results in an inferior product.

Meracado de Antojitos

On the west side of the museum, an alley runs down to the **Mercado de Antojitos**, a large open **market** section just half a block north of the plaza, where women serve up meals for stallholders and visitors alike at a series of long, open-air tables. Here you'll find the cheapest, and very often the freshest and best, food in town – this is a great place to sample the salty regional cheese, *adobada*. The rest of the market, with herb and fruit stalls but mostly clothes, shoes and CDs, sprawls along Corregidora and Constitución. Despite the variety of wares, for **native crafts** like pottery or wood furniture you're far better looking at the smattering of shops along **Independencia**, which leads up from the plaza to the Parque Nacional. At the top of this street are several small places where you can watch the artisans at work – some establishments are no more than a single room with a display of finished goods on one side and a worktable on the other, while others are more sophisticated operations. Opposite the entrance to the park is a little "craft market", mostly selling very poor souvenirs.

Río Cupatitzio and the Parque Nacional Eduardo Ruíz

Just fifty acres on the northwestern edge of downtown and 1km from the plaza, the **Parque Nacional Eduardo Ruíz** (or Parque Nacional Barranca Cupatitzio; daily 8am–6pm; M$12), is far more compact than national parks you may be used to elsewhere, but this luxuriant and tropical city park is one of Uruapan's proudest assets. The Río Cupatitzio flows through in a little gorge, via a series of man-made cascades and fountains. The river springs from a rock known as *La Rodilla del Diablo* ("the Devil's knee"); according to legend, water gushed forth after the Devil knelt here in submission before the unswerving Christian faith of the drought-ridden population. Alternatively, it is said that the Devil met the Virgin Mary while out strolling in the park, and dropped to his knees in respect. *Cupatitzio* means "where the waters meet", though it's invariably translated as "the river that sings" – another appropriate, if not entirely accurate, tag.

Locals come here to stroll the cobbled footpaths betweens stands of banana plants, gaze at the cascades (particularly good during or just after rain), catch trout and eat at assorted restaurants and taco stands. There are two entrances, one at the end of Independencia (take a bus along here if you don't feel like walking), and one up by the *Mansión del Cupatitzio* hotel.

Some 12km south of Uruapan, the river crashes over the waterfall of **La Tzaráracua**, an impressive 25-metre plunge amid beautiful forest scenery. This is also a popular outing with locals, especially at weekends, and hence fairly easy to get to – take one of the buses (marked "Tzaráracua") from the south side of the plaza at Cupatitzio (hourly), or share a taxi. If it seems too crowded here, make for the smaller falls, **Tzararacuita**, about 1km further downstream.

▲ Waterfall, Parque Nacional Eduardo Ruíz

Eating and drinking

There are plenty of decent places to eat in town, though little that's truly spectacular. The best place to sample local delights at low prices is the **Mercado de Antojitos** (see opposite).

Café Oriental Portal Matamoros 16. Snacks, cakes, pies, breakfasts and a M$60 comida corrida, and if you want to wash it down with a strong coffee, there's a branch of *La Lucha* (see below) next door.

Café Tradicional de Uruapan Carranza 5. This Uruapan classic serves great breakfasts, superb local coffee, ice cream, cakes, *antojitos* and a decent range of herbal and fruit teas (including an intriguing piña colada). Airy window seating, but the interior is a bit darker. Definitely a place to relax, usually until 11pm.

La Casa Revolución 3. Charming courtyard café-cum-cocktail lounge that's good for a coffee during the day or a tequila in the evening, when it becomes a bit of a hangout.

Comida Económica Mary Independencia 59. Wholesome home-style cooking at low prices. Perfect for breakfast and comidas corridas (M$40), though go elsewhere for your coffee.

Cox-Hanal Carranza 31-A. Tacos, Yucatan-style *antojitos*, and beers, all at low prices and in clean surroundings, though opening hours are a little unpredictable.

Hotel Real de Uruapan Nicolas Bravo 110. Top-floor restaurant with a beautiful view. Reasonably priced evening meals. Expect the likes of avocado soup (M$35) followed by steak (M$98–110) or shrimp in garlic and chile (M$125).

La Lucha Garcia Ortiz 22. A small café that's been going since the Revolution. They serve only basic coffee and cakes, but it's a good place to sample the full-flavoured local caffeine brews. There's also a small and rather cramped branch at Portal Matamoros 16, on the south side of the plaza.

La Pergola Portal Carrillo 4, on the south side of the plaza. Popular restaurant serving a selection of regional and national dishes (M$48–110), a good comida corrida (M$65) and local coffee.

La Terraza de la Trucha at the upper entrance to the Parque Nacional Eduardo Ruíz. Simply a delight. Enjoy avocado cocktail (M$25), grilled *trucha* (trout; M$75–90) and heavenly *aguas frescas* while surveying the park's waterfalls and giant banana trees. Daily 9am–6pm.

Paricutín

An ideal day trip from Uruapan, the "new" **volcano of Paricutín**, about 40km northwest of town, gives you an unusual taste of the surrounding countryside. On February 20, 1943, a Purépecha peasant working in his fields noticed the earth rumble and then smoke. The ground soon cracked and lava began to flow to the surface. Over a period of several years, it engulfed the village of Paricutín and several other hamlets, forcing the evacuation of some seven thousand inhabitants. The volcano was active for eight years, producing a cone some 400m high and devastating an area of around twenty square kilometres. Now there are vast fields of lava (mostly cooled, though there are still a few hot spots), black and powdery, cracked into harsh jags, along with the dead cone and crater. Most bizarrely, a church tower – all that remains of the buried hamlet of San Juan Parangaricutiro – pokes its head through the surface. The volcano wasn't all bad news, though: during its active life the volcano spread a fine layer of dust – effectively a fertilizer – on the fields that escaped the full lava flow, and drew tourists from around the world. It is still popular, especially on Sundays, when the upwardly mobile from Uruapan come out to play.

The volcano is visited from the small and very traditional Purépecha village of **Angahuan**, where the women still wear heavily pleated satin skirts with an embroidered apron and a shawl. On the **plaza**, the **church** warrants a second glance. Built in the sixteenth century, its doorway was carved in the largely Arab Mudéjar style by Andalusian artisans (Andalusia was the centre of fine arts in the Arab world until the fall of Granada in 1492). The cross in the courtyard, on the other hand, is most definitely Mexican, complete with serpents, a skull and other pre-Hispanic motifs. In the street to the right of the church (as you look at it), across from the side gate of the courtyard, a door lintel has been turned into a kind of lava frieze of the volcano and church tower.

Practicalities

To see much of Paricutín you really need to set aside a day. You'll want to leave Uruapan early (say 7am or 8am) so you get as much of the hiking as possible done in the cool of the day and catch the ruined church in the morning light. You'll also need to take **food and drink** as there is very little available in Angahuan.

By **car**, simply take the main road to Los Reyes and look for signs to Angahuan – there are many. By **bus**, hop aboard the Autotransportes Galeana/Ruta Paraíso service toward Los Reyes or Zicuicho from the Central de Autobuses in Uruapan (half-hourly 5.30am–7pm; about 1hr 20min; M$18). Alternatively, walk up to the Glorieta roundabout at the junction of Calzada de San Miguel and Calzada Juarez and flag down the bus there. The bus climbs about 700m from Uruapan up through pines then drops you on the highway outside the village.

When you get off the bus in Angahuan you'll be besieged by boys and men offering to **guide** you or take you on **horseback**; it's not a bad idea to hire a guide, as the paths through the lava are numerous and can be difficult to follow. **Prices** fluctuate with demand, but you can probably expect to pay around M$250 for a guide for the day, plus another M$250 for each horse (one for the guide plus one for each tourist). A return trip to the cone of the volcano will take about eight hours on either foot or horseback. If you just want to see the ruined church, a couple of hours will suffice (and rates for guides and horses will be rather cheaper). The horse trail is easier than the walking trail, though it finishes at the base of the main cone, leaving you to tackle the final steep climb on your own.

It is a ten-minute walk from the bus stop to the plaza and church. From the plaza, turn right down Juárez for about 200m to an ornately carved wooden house on the left. Veer left here (not signposted) and head straight on for a kilometre to reach the **Centro Turístico de Angahuan** (daily 7am–8pm; M$10), which offers superb views of the volcano from its *mirador*, has a small museum on the creation of the volcano and local Purépecha culture and includes a decent restaurant. You can also **stay** here in concrete block cabañas (Ⓣ452/523-3934), each with an open fire. Most are set up for six (M$730) but there are some designed for four (M$520). There's also tent **camping** for M$50 per person.

Tinganio

The small but pretty and well-restored pre-Hispanic ruin of **TINGANIO** (daily 10am–5pm; M$40) is roughly halfway between Uruapan and Pátzcuaro in a town that is now called **Tingambato**. The site was first inhabited around 450–600 AD and greatly expanded between 650 and 900 AD. Though the structures draw on several architectural styles, that of Teotihuacán is particularly evident, especially in the pyramid that dominates the religious area, overlooking a plaza with a cruciform altar. The adjacent ball-court shows Toltec design influence. Beyond the ball-court, an unexcavated pyramid lies under a grove of avocado trees. In the residential area just to the north, a sunken plaza with two altars and five stairways, each to a separate residence, is very much in the style of Teotihuacán, but the tomb under the largest residence (which the caretaker will open on request) has a false dome suggestive of Maya influence. Surrounded by beautiful countryside, the site is best appreciated from atop the pyramid. Except on Sundays, you are not likely to see many foreigners here. If you're going by car, take the *cuota* highway from Uruapan towards Pátzcuaro and take the Zirahuén exit and follow the *libre* road past Ajuno to Tingambato. It lies approximately 30km west of Pátzcuaro: buses between Uruapan and Pátzcuaro pass right by.

Pátzcuaro and around

PÁTZCUARO is almost exactly halfway between Uruapan and Morelia, some 60km from both, yet strikingly different from either – far more colonial than Uruapan and infinitely more Indian than Morelia, boasting both fine architecture and a rich indigenous culture. Sitting on **Lago de Pátzcuaro** (see p.360), Mexico's most beautiful lake, it hosts the country's most spectatcular Day of the Dead celebrations (see box, p.363).

Arrival and information

Buses into town may stop at "estación" (the old train station), by the harbour (handy for *Hotel Posada de Don Vasco* and *Villa Pátzcuaro*), but for the town centre you'll want the **Central** (bus station). Located 2km south of town, this is a fifteen-minute walk from the centre (cross the main road, head right and turn left down Federico Tena) or a brief bus ride (take services marked "Centro" or "Col Popular"). Long-distance buses between Morelia and Uruapan will drop you on the main highway about 10km distant: be sure to get a bus going specifically to Pátzcuaro. Buses back to the bus station ("Central") can be picked up in Plaza Bocanegra or along Federico Tena. Although the outskirts of Pátzcuaro straggle about three kilometres or so down to the lakeshore, the centre of town is very small indeed, focusing on the two main squares, **Plaza Vasco de Quiroga** (or Plaza Grande) and **Plaza Bocanegra** (Plaza Chica).

The **tourist office** (Mon–Sat 9am–8pm, Sun 9am–3pm & 5–8pm; ⓣ434/344-3486) is on the west side of Plaza Quiroga at no. 1. The staff can give you information on the town's **festivals**, principally Año Nuevo (Jan 1), when the Danza de los Viejitos (Dance of the Little Old Men) is performed; the Day of the Dead (see p.363); and La Señora de la Salud (Dec 8), a saint's day event attended by many Tarascan pilgrims: you'll witness the worshippers in an intense, almost hypnotic fervour. The

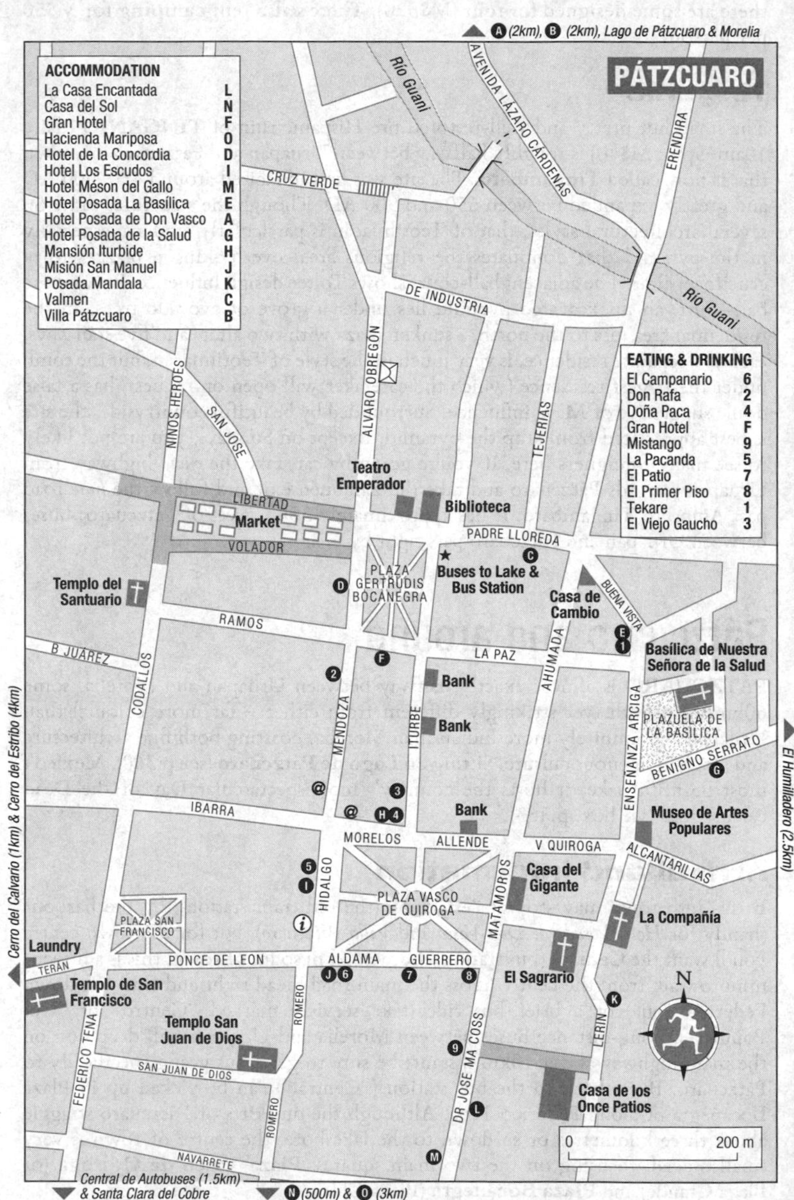

scrubby park outside the basilica becomes a fairground and there are all manner of Tarascan dances.

Accommodation

With the recent arrival of a small **hostel** and the ever-expanding selection of top end **B&Bs** and hotels, Pátzcuaro offers an excellent range of places to stay. Prices are a little higher then elsewhere in the state, but if you are prepared to pay a little more you'll get a lot more elegance. Most establishments are on one or other of the plazas, with the ritzier ones surrounding Plaza Vasco de Quiroga and a selection of simpler places around the Plaza Bocanegra.

Rates generally spike at Christmas/New Year, Semana Santa and Easter. The same is true around the **Day of the Dead** (first two days of Nov), when there's little chance of getting a room unless you book at least a couple of months ahead (more like six to twelve months for some of the posher places).

Casa del Sol Michoacán 43, Colonia San Lazarao ⓣ434/342 0975, ⓔcasadelsolpatzcuaro@yahoo.cm.mx. Family homestay in a workaday *barrio* very near the bus station (instead of turning left down Federico Tena, take the next left and climb it to the top, and it's almost opposite you), and ten minutes from the centre (Michoacán is a continuation of Romero). Very friendly and by far the cheapest deal in town, especially for single travellers. ❷

La Casa Encantada Dr Coss 15 ⓣ434/342-3492, ⓦwww.lacasaencantada.com. Gorgeous and intimate American-owned B&B in the heart of town. Beautiful touches in the furnishings, and delicious breakfasts raise it above the ordinary. ❼

Gran Hotel Plaza Bocanegra 6 ⓣ434/342-0443, ⓦwww.granhotelpatzcuaro.com.mx. Smallish rooms but bright and breezy and each with TV and phone in a friendly hotel right on the plaza. ❺

Hacienda Mariposa km 3.5 Carretera Pátzcuaro–Santa Clara del Cobre ⓣ443/333-0762, ⓦwww.haciendamariposas.com. This comfortable, upscale oasis, south of town off the Santa Clara del Cobre road, offers pony treks, ecotours and superb cuisine in serene wooded surroundings. ❻

Hotel de la Concordia Plaza Bocanegra 31, ⓣ434/342-0003. Well-maintained, clean rooms, with secure parking and TV. Discounts often available midweek and off-season. ❹

Hotel Los Escudos Plaza Quiroga 73 ⓣ434/342-1290, ⓦwww.losescudospatzcuaro.com. Beautiful colonial building with rooms around two flower-filled courtyards; all are carpeted and have TV, some have fireplaces too. Ask for a room in the original hotel and not the extension next door. Good value. ❹

Hotel Mesón del Gallo Dr Coss 20 ⓣ434/342-1474, ⓦwww.mexonline.com/mesondelgallo.htm. One of the town's oldest hotels. Attractive, rustic common spaces, decent rooms and an excellent restaurant. ❹

Hotel Posada La Basílica Arciga 6, opposite the basilica ⓣ434/342-1108, ⓦwww.posadalabasilica.com. Delightful rooms, some with fireplaces, in an eighteenth-century building with superb views of the town. All the expected amenities, including fireplaces, cable TV, phones and wi-fi. Breakfast included. ❼

Hotel Posada de Don Vasco Lázaro Cárdenas 450, 2km north of town ⓣ434/342-0227, ⓦwww.bestwestern.com. This tastefully decorated hotel was built in 1938. Now a Best Western, it boasts a swimming pool, tennis court and gardens filled with fruit trees. All rooms are well appointed, though it's worth paying a bit extra for a "Colonial" room, with nicer decor and bathtub. ❽

Hotel Posada de la Salud Serrato 9 ⓣ434/342-0058, ⓔposadadelasalud@hotmail.com. Behind the basilica, a short walk from the centre. Beautiful little hotel, peaceful and spotless and run by two sisters; some rooms have fireplaces, and there's a small garden. Among the best value in town. ❸

Mansión Iturbe Plaza Quiroga 59 ⓣ434/342-0368, US & Canada ⓣ1-866/678-6102, ⓦwww.mansioniturbe.com. Once a muleteer's house, this small luxury inn and architectural jewel is run by a mother–daughter team. There's a library, superb dining and attractive bedrooms with soaring ceilings and down duvets. Breakfast included. ❻

Misión San Manuel Plaza Quiroga 12 ⓣ434/342-1050, ⓔmaisonmanuel5@hotmail.com. The great colonial front on this ex-convent hides a charming and beautifully maintained interior. Comfortable rooms, several with fireplaces. ❹

Posada Mandala Lerin 14 ⓣ434/342-4176, ⓦwww.paginasprodigy.com/posadamandala. This friendly and excellent-value guesthouse near the

Casa de los Once Patios has a range of rooms at different prices, free tea and coffee, use of a kitchen, a little library and exquisite rooftop views. ❸

Valmen Padre Lloreda 34 ⓣ434/342-1161, ⓦwww.hotelvalmen.com. Large, clean, tiled rooms with TV and bathroom, all around a plant-filled courtyard. A good budget option, though the candy-green walls in the public areas won't be to everyone's taste. ❸

Villa Pátzcuaro Lázaro Cárdenas, 2km north of town ⓣ434/342-0767, ⓦwww.villapatzcuaro.com. Great little hotel and RV park in spacious grounds with a small pool. Tent and RV campers (M$70 per person) have access to a kitchen. Tasteful rustic-style rooms are imaginatively decorated and very clean and come with breakfast. There are also a couple of self-contained houses for longer stays. Frequent buses from Plaza Bocanegra pass right outside. ❹

The Town

More than anywhere in the state, Pátzcuaro owes its position to **Bishop Vasco de Quiroga** (see box, p.348), whose affection for the area's indigenous peoples led him to settle in the Purépechan heartland on the shores of Lago de Pátzcuaro. It was he who decided, in the face of considerable opposition from the Spaniards in Morelia (then known as Valladolid), to build the cathedral here, where it would be centrally located. Although subsequent bishops moved the seat of power back to Morelia, the foundation had been laid for the community's continued success. Pátzcuaro enjoyed a building boom in the sixteenth century and has been of secondary industrial and political importance ever since. Throughout the centre are old mansions with balconies and coats of arms, barely touched since those early years. Today, quaint Pátzcuaro has developed into an upmarket and artistically inclined town with numerous boutiques. You can spend hours wandering around the beautiful – and expensive – arts, crafts and antique shops, aimed mainly at visitors from Mexico City and abroad.

The plazas

Nothing much worth seeing in Pátzcuaro lies more than a few minutes' walk from **Plaza Gertrudis Bocanegra**, named after a local Independence heroine, and **Plaza Vasco de Quiroga**. The finest of Pátzcuaro's mansions are on the latter, especially the seventeenth-century **Casa del Gigante**, with its hefty pillars and crudely carved figures. Another nearby mansion is said to have been inhabited by Prince Huitzimengari, son of the last Tarascan king. Both are privately owned, however, and not open to visitors. There are more luxurious houses on the Plaza Bocanegra, but the most striking thing around here is the **Biblioteca** (Mon–Fri 9am–7pm, Sat 10am–1pm), with its rough-hewn wooden barrel ceiling. The former sixteenth-century church of San Agustín, it has been converted into a library and decorated with **murals** by **Juan O'Gorman** depicting the history of Michoacán, especially Nuño de Guzman burning alive the leader of the Tarascans. O'Gorman (1905–82) possessed a prodigious talent, and is one of the muralists who inherited the mantle of Rivera and Orozco: his best-known work is the decoration of the interior of Chapultepec Castle in Mexico City (see p.419).

The Basilica and El Humilladero

East of the Plaza Bocanegra, Quiroga's cathedral – **the Basílica de Nuestra Señora de la Salud**, or **Colegiata** – was intended by Quiroga to be Pátzcuaro's masterpiece, with space for 30,000 worshippers. A massive structure for such a small town, it was never completed, and the existing basilica, finished in the nineteenth century, is only the nave of the original design. Even so, it is often full, for local people continue to revere Quiroga: the first chapel on the left as you walk in the main entrance is the **Mausoleo de Don Vasco**, the doors typically closed and adorned with notes of thanks for his miraculous interventions. The church also possesses a miraculous healing image of the Virgin, crafted in a traditional

Tarascan method out of *pasta de caña*, a gum-like modelling paste made principally from maize. Services here are extraordinary, especially for the town's patron saint, the Virgin de la Salud, on December 8.

A twenty-minute walk east along Serrato is **El Humilladero** ("the place of humiliation"), probably the oldest church in Pátzcuaro. It stands on the site where the last Tarascan king, Tanganxoan II, accepted Spanish authority – hence the humbling name. Such a tag may seem appropriate with hindsight, though a more charitable view suggests that Tanganxoan was simply hoping to save his people from the slaughter that had accompanied resistance to the Spaniards elsewhere. The church itself, pretty enough, is often closed, so there's little to see.

Museo de Artes Populares

The **Museo de Artes Populares**, at the corner of Quiroga and Lerin, south of the basilica (Tues–Fri 9am–6pm, Sat & Sun 9am–4.30pm; M$37), occupies the ancient Colegio de San Nicolas. Founded by Quiroga in 1540, the college is now devoted to a superb collection of regional handicrafts: local lacquerware and pottery; copperware from Santa Clara del Cobre; and traditional masks and religious objects made from *pasta de caña*, which, apart from being easy to work with, is also very light, and hence easily carried in processions. Some of the objects on display are ancient, others the best examples of modern work, and all are set in a very beautiful building. Almost opposite, the church of **La Compañía** was built by Quiroga in 1546 and later taken over by the Jesuits.

Casa de los Once Patios

A short walk south of the art museum on Lerin, the **Casa de los Once Patios** (daily 10am–7pm, though individual stores may keep their own hours) is an eighteenth-century convent converted into a crafts showhouse, full of workshops and moderate to expensive boutiques. As its name suggests, the complex is set around a series of tiny courtyards, and it's a fascinating place to stroll through even if you can't afford the goods. You can watch restored treadle looms at work, admire the intricacy with which the best lacquerware is created and wander at liberty through the warren of rooms and corridors.

Cerro del Estribo

The best views of Lago de Pátzcuaro are found east of town along the road to the Cerro del Estribo: head out along Terán past the Templo San Francisco. It is about a kilometre from here to the **Cerro del Calvario**, a tiny hill topped by the little **chapel of El Calvario**. You won't be able to see much from the chapel, so take the road to the right just before you reach it and continue on along a cobbled, cypress-lined avenue. You'll climb over 200m in the next 3km to a viewpoint with great vistas over Lago de Pátzcuaro and Janitzio. You can get a taxi out here from town, or if you're walking and don't fancy the road, look out for a parallel horse trail on the right.

From the viewpoint, 417 steps lead straight up to the very summit of **Cerro del Estribo** (Stirrup Hill), though the views are no better.

Eating and drinking

Most of Pátzcuaro's hotels have their own **restaurants**, with fairly standard menus throughout: lots of reasonably priced, if unexciting, comidas corridas. Most of the establishments ringing Plaza Quiroga rely too heavily on their (admittedly excellent) location and the food is neither exceptional nor great value; they're better for a snack or coffee. Most of the more interesting places are tucked down side streets. Cheap eats are hard to find, but there are a few food stalls in the

market, which is at its most colourful and animated on Friday, when the *indígenas* come in from the country to trade and barter their surplus. Most evenings you can also get basic food from the stalls in the Plaza Bocanegra.

One feature of virtually all menus in town is *pescado blanco*, a rather flabby whitefish from the lake, and *sopa tarasca* – a tomato-based soup with chile and bits of tortilla. For the best **fish**, head to the lake, where a line of restaurants faces the landing jetty. A dish of *pescado blanco* will set you back M$90–100; cheaper set menus offer fish, but not from the lake.

Pátzcuaro isn't really a late-night kind of place. Most of the restaurants close up by around 9pm, and even the few **bars** close fairly early.

El Campanario Plaza Quiroga 12. Reasonably lively bar on the Plaza Quiroga, often with either a DJ or a couple of musicians playing in the corner.

Don Rafa Mendoza 30. A pleasant room decorated with old photos of Pátzcuaro makes a comfortable setting for very tasty three-course *menu del día* (M$60). Delicious fresh salsa on every table, and attentive service.

Doña Paca Plaza Quiroga 59, attached to the *Mansión Iturbe* hotel ⓣ434/342-0368. Come here for comfortable and elegant dining and a menu of reasonably priced regional dishes, including creative salads of local ingredients, triangular Purépechan tamales (*corundas*), hearty Tarascan soup, *churipo de carne* (beef stew) and fish with coriander sauce. Open for breakfast daily, lunch Tues–Sat.

Gran Hotel Plaza Bocanegra 6. The streetside tables here catch the morning sun, making it one of the best spots in town for a hearty breakfast (M$50–60).

Mistongo Dr Coss 4. Inviting restaurant with pared-down traditional Mexican decor, serving the likes of *sopa tarasca* (M$40), fajitas (M$90) and smoked pork with plum chutney (M$120). Closed Mon.

La Pacanda Portal Hidalgo, Plaza Quiroga. Just a couple of wooden carts with metal tubs on ice serving superb ice cream and sorbets since 1905. Try interesting flavours like tequila, mandarin and tamarind.

El Patio Plaza Quiroga 19. Quite a chic little restaurant offering good coffee, reasonably priced breakfasts, *antojitos*, steaks, sandwiches and, of course, fish.

El Primer Piso Plaza Quiroga 29, ⓣ434/342-0122. This gourmet place serves a mixture of Tarascan, French and Italian flavours at tables upstairs overlooking the square. Expect the likes of palmetto and artichoke-heart salad (M$70) followed by fillet Roquefort (M$128) or chicken *nogada* (M$108).

Tekare Arciga 6, inside the *Hotel Posada La Basílica* ⓣ434/342-1108. Try the house speciality, *kurucha urapiti* (battered whitefish with chiles). Great views of the town and beyond to the lake.

El Viejo Gaucho Iturbide 10 ⓣ434/342-0368. Relaxed restaurant with a loosely Argentine-influenced menu of steaks and burgers. There's also a separate bar where live music (cover around M$25) is performed most evenings from around 8pm.

Listings

Banks and exchange There's a bank on the north side of Plaza Quiroga and a couple more on Iturbe between the two plazas (all with ATMs). At the corner of Buena Vista and Ahumada near the *Hotel Valmen* there's a casa de cambio.

Internet access Numerous places all charging around M$12/hr. Try Meg@net at Mendoza 8 and Plaza Quiroga 67.

Laundry Lavanderia San Francisco, Terán 16, is in front of the Templo San Francisco (Mon–Sat 9am–9pm).

Post office Obregón 13 (Mon–Fri 8am–4pm, Sat 9am–1pm).

Spanish courses The Centro de Lenguas y Ecoturismo de Pátzcuaro, Navarette 50 (ⓣ434/342-4764, ⓦwww.celep.com.mx), offers well-regarded language classes. Homestays also available.

Telephones You can phone and fax from several casetas on the east side of Plaza Bocanegra, or at cardphones under Portal Hidalgo on the west side of Plaza Quiroga.

Lago de Pátzcuaro and Janitzio

Apart from the beautiful town itself, Pátzcuaro's other great attraction is **Lago de Pátzcuaro**. It's around 4km (less than an hour's **walk**) down to the jetty (follow the "embarcadero" signs), while **buses** and minibuses leave from the Plaza Bocanegra. Those marked "Lago" will drop you right by the boats. The lake itself was once a major thoroughfare, but that role has declined since the completion of roads linking the lakeside villages a few years back. Most locals now take the bus rather than paddle around the water in canoes, but there is still a fair amount of traffic and regular trips out to the closest island, **Janitzio** (see p.362).

There isn't a great deal to see or do on the other islands in the lake, with the exception of **Isla Yunuén**, where you can stay in the rustic *Cabañas de Yunuén* (Ⓣ434/342-4473; ④), each with a small kitchen and TV. A boat makes trips to the island from the Muelle General (main dock area) in Pátzcuaro (M$75 round trip).

The lake's other draw is the chance to see and photograph the famous **butterfly nets** wielded by indigenous fishermen in tiny dug-out canoes. It is a long time since this was considered a viable means of gaining food, but a handful of nets are maintained to catch tourists. Occasionally a group of locals lurking in readiness on the far side of Janitzio will paddle into camera range when a sufficiently large collection of money has been taken.

▲ Butterfly nets, Lago de Pátzcuaro

Janitzio

From a distance, the island of **Janitzio** looks quaint, but as you get closer it appears almost squalid. With fishing becoming ever less viable and with no land flat enough for agriculture, the conical, car-free island has found itself relying increasingly on the tourism industry – you'll be besieged by souvenir hawkers from the moment you arrive. Still, it is worth the journey if only for the opportunity to spend some time on the lake and for the expansive views from the top of the island. From the dock, head straight up one of the many alleys that climb steeply between assorted **fish restaurants** (generally better away from the dock) and tacky souvenir stalls to the summit, which are crowned by an ugly 49-metre-**statue of Morelos**. Ascend the spiral staircase inside (typically daily 8am–7pm; M$7), past murals depicting Morelos's life and the struggle for independence, to the viewpoint right by his upraised, clenched fist. If heights make you queasy, there's a pleasant path that encircles the island running around the lakeshore. It takes about thirty minutes to make a full circuit.

Fares to the island from Pátzcuaro's Muelle General (main dock area) are fixed (M$40 round trip; get your ticket before you board). Seventy-seat *lanchas* make the stately, if noisy, half-hour crossing (daily 7am–7pm; every 15min).

Around Lago de Pátzcuaro

No visit to Pátzcuaro is complete without an excursion to the small lakeside villages, which, thanks to Vasco de Quiroga, each specialize in a different **artesanía**. **Getting around** the villages is fairly easy. Buses to Tzintzuntzán and Quiroga leave from the Central de Autobuses but can also be picked up on the highway close to the *embarcadero*. You can also take a *colectivo* from the Plaza Bocanegra to Ihuatzio, and another from there to Tzintzuntzán. Buses and *colectivos* then continue frequently to Quiroga.

Ihuatzio

While they're no match for the ruins at Tzintzuntzán, further around the lake (see opposite), the older, pre-Tarascan ruins of **IHUATZIO** (daily 10am–6pm; M$37) are interesting in their own right and worth a peek if you have the time. Located around 12km north of Pátzcuaro, 4km off the Pátzcuaro–Quiroga road on a remote track that traverses a cow pasture, Ihuatzio was strategically placed near the shores of Lago de Pátzcuaro and used for water defence and enemy lookout. The ruins are essentially divided into two sections, one older than the other: the first (900–1200 AD) is thought to have been constructed by the Náhuatl, and the second dates from 1200–1530 AD, during the Tarascan occupation. Two fifteen-metre-high **squared-off pyramids**, once considered a sort of Plaza de Armas, are the main features of the site open to the public.

Buses to Ihuatzio leave from the Plaza Bocanegra in Pátzcuaro every few minutes (M$7). You'll be dropped at the end of a cobblestone road and will have to walk 1500m to the site's entrance. On the walk, look for three vegetated hummocks which are the unexcavated ruins of *yácatas* (see below). To continue to Tzintzuntzán, hop on one of the frequent Quiroga-bound *colectivos* from the road where you were dropped off.

Tzintzuntzán

The remains of **TZINTZUNTZÁN** (daily 10am–6pm; M$41), ancient capital of the Tarascans, lie 15km north of Pátzcuaro on the road to Quiroga. The site was established around the end of the fourteenth century, when the capital was moved from Pátzcuaro, and by the time of the Conquest the Spaniards estimated that there were as many as 40,000 people living here, with dominion over all of what is now Michoacán and large parts of the modern states of Jalisco and Colima. Homes and markets, as well as the palaces of the rulers, lay around the raised **ceremonial centre**, but all that can be seen today is the artificial terrace that supported the great religious buildings (*yácatas*), and the partly restored ruins of these temples.

Even if you do no more than pass by on the road, you can't fail to be struck by the scale of these buildings and by their semi-circular design, a startling contrast to the rigid, right-angled formality adhered to by almost every other major pre-Hispanic culture in Mexico. Climb up to the terrace and you'll find five *yácatas*, of which four have been partly rebuilt. Each was originally some 15m high,

The Day of the Dead around Lago de Pátzcuaro

The **Day of the Dead** (Nov 1, and through the night into the next day) is celebrated in spectacular fashion throughout Mexico, but nowhere more so than on Lago de Pátzcuaro, particularly the island of **Janitzio**. On this night, the locals conduct what is an essentially private meditation, carrying offerings of fruit and flowers to the cemetery and maintaining a vigil over the graves of their ancestors until dawn, chanting by candle-light. Death is considered a continuation of life, and this is the time when the souls of *muertitos* (deceased loved ones) return to the land of the living. It's a spectacular and moving sight, especially early in the evening as indigenous people from the surrounding area converge on the island in their canoes, with a single candle burning in each bow.

Impressive and solemn though the occasion is, over the years the occasion has become somewhat marred by its sheer press of **spectators**, both Mexican and foreign. Thousands head over to tiny Janitzio, and from around 10pm on Oct 1 until around 3am the following morning you can hardly move, especially in the cemetery where the vigil takes place amid a riot of marigolds and candles. If you can manage it, stay up all night and return to the cemetery around 5am when it is quiet and the first hint of dawn lightens the eastern sky. Alternatively, head to one of the other lakeside communities marking the Day of the Dead – Tzurumutaro, Ihuatzio, Cucuchucho or Tzintzuntzán. There's no guarantee of a quiet and respectful vigil, but crowds will be smaller and the cemeteries no less amazing.

tapering in steps from a broad base to a walkway along the top less than 2m wide. Devoid of ornamentation, the *yácatas* are in fact piles of flat rocks, held in by retaining walls and then faced in smooth, close-fitting volcanic stone. The terrace, which was originally approached up a broad ceremonial ramp or stairway on the side furthest from the water, affords magnificent views across the lake and the present-day village of Tzintzuntzán. Tzintzuntzán means "place of the hummingbirds"; you're unlikely to see one nowadays, but the theory is that there were plenty of them around until the Tarascans – who used the feathers to make ornaments – hunted them to the point of extinction. The ruins are around 1km from the village and are signposted "Zona Arqueológica" up a side road.

Down in the **village**, which has a reputation for producing and selling some of the region's best ceramics, you'll find what's left of the enormous **Franciscan Monastery** founded around 1530 to convert the Tarascans. Much of this has been demolished, and the rest substantially rebuilt, but there remains a fine Baroque **Templo de San Francisco** and a huge atrium where the indigenous people would gather for sermons. Vasco de Quiroga originally intended to base his diocese here, but eventually decided that Pátzcuaro had the better location and a more constant supply of water. He did leave one unusual legacy, though: the **olive trees** planted around the monastery are probably the oldest in Mexico, since settlers were banned from cultivating olives in order to protect the farmers back in Spain. The broad, veined trunks certainly look their age, and several only have a few living branches sprouting from apparently dead trees.

Tzintzuntzán has several good **fiestas**. Carnaval here takes the form of a week-long party called La Fiesta del Señor del Rescate, celebrating a miracle in which, during a nineteenth-century measles epidemic, the sexton of the church discovered an old painting of Christ hidden away in the crypt, and made a vow that if prayers to this image would rescue the town, he would pay for a huge party in celebration; the prayers duly worked, and the party is held every year to this day. Unfortunately the miraculous image itself was destroyed by fire in 1944. Also big here is Semana Santa (the week before Easter Sunday), when the Thursday sees the ceremony of Washing the Apostles' Feet, followed on Good Friday by further scenes from Christ's Passion acted out around town.

Quiroga

QUIROGA, 8km northeast of Tzintzuntzán and around 25km from Pátzcuaro, is another village packed with craft markets, though the only genuinely local products seem to be painted wooden objects and furniture. This said, there's plenty of other good wares – leather and woollen goods in particular – in the daily handicrafts **market** which spreads on side streets in all directions from the main plaza.

Make an effort to come to Quiroga if you're in the area around the first Sunday in July, when the town celebrates the **Día de la Preciosa Sangre de Cristo** with a huge fiesta and a beautiful torch-lit procession behind a paraded image of Christ.

Santa Clara del Cobre

Approximately 25km south of Pátzcuaro, via a country road over a pine-draped pass, lies **Santa Clara del Cobre**, long celebrated for the **copper crafts** on which it continues to thrive. There are no fewer than two hundred family-run studios (*talleres*) and shops, many of which line the quaint town's arcades and side streets selling everything from cheap bracelets and thimbles to hammered sinks and sparkling *carnitas* cauldrons.

Much more of the metal is on display at the town's **Museo del Cobre**, Morelos 263 at Pino Suárez (Tues–Sat 10am–3pm & 5–7pm, Sun 10am–4pm; M$5), which exhibits a small but impressive collection of decorative and utilitarian copper crafts. Sadly, only a handful of these intricate old designs are still being incorporated into the production of modern goods. The annual **Feria Nacional del Cobre** (Copper Fair), combined with the **Fiesta de la Virgen del Sagrario**, is held in Santa Clara del Cobre from August 6 to 17. Festivities include exhibits and sales of hand-worked copper, music and dance.

While the town is a quick day trip from Pátzcuaro, you may be moved to spend the night – if not to shop then to enjoy the clear vistas and mountain air. *Hotel Oasis* (Ⓣ434/343-0040, Ⓔade_zc@hotmail.com; ❸) is serviceable and centrally located on the main plaza. Be sure to ask for a room with mountain views. Restaurant *El Portal*, Portal Matamoros 18, overlooks the main plaza and serves good breakfasts (M$40–60) and comidas corridas (M$65–70) along with fish dishes (M$70–90). Driving time to Santa Clara del Cobre from Pátzcuaro is about twenty minutes (follow signs for Opopeo); taxis cost M$80, and buses and *combis* (M$7) leave frequently from the main road opposite the top of Federico Tena for the thirty-minute trip.

Morelia

The state capital, **MORELIA**, is in many ways unrepresentative of Michoacán. It looks Spanish and, despite a large indigenous population, it feels Spanish – with its broad streets lined with seventeenth-century mansions and outdoor cafés sheltered by arcaded plazas, you might easily be in Salamanca or Valladolid. Indeed, the city's name was Valladolid until 1828, when it was changed to honour local-born Independence hero José María Morelos.

Morelia has always been a city of Spaniards. It was one of the first they founded after the Conquest – two Franciscan friars, Juan de San Miguel and Antonio de Lisboa, settled here among the native inhabitants in 1530 and first laid claim to the city. Ten years later, they were visited by the first viceroy of New Spain, Antonio de Mendóza, who was so taken by the site that he ordered a town to be built, naming it after his birthplace and sending fifty Spanish families to settle it. From the beginning, there was fierce rivalry between the colonists and the older culture's town of Pátzcuaro. During the lifetime of **Vasco de Quiroga**, Pátzcuaro had the upper hand, but later the bishopric was moved here, a university founded, and by the end of the sixteenth century there was no doubt that Valladolid was predominant.

Though there are specific things to look for and to visit in present-day Morelia, the city as a whole outweighs them: it was declared a UNESCO World Heritage site in 1991 and city ordinances decree that all new construction must perfectly match the old, such that it preserves a remarkable unity of style. Nearly everything is built of the same faintly pinkish-grey stone (trachyte), which, being soft, is not only easily carved and embellished but weathers quickly, giving even relatively recent constructions a battered, ancient look. Best of all are the plazas dotted with little cafés where you can while away an hour or two.

Arrival and information

Morelia's modern **bus station** is around 3km northwest of the centre on the city's ring road. You can catch a cab into town (fixed-price tickets sold inside the terminal; M$35 to the cathedral) or walk out onto the main road and wait for a Roja 1 *colectivo* (look for a white minibus with a red band). To return to the bus station, catch the same *colectivo* from along Ocampo. At the bus station, Sala A is predominantly first class, salas B and C are for second-class and local services. Once in town, plenty of **local buses** ply Madero, though getting around town is easy enough on foot.

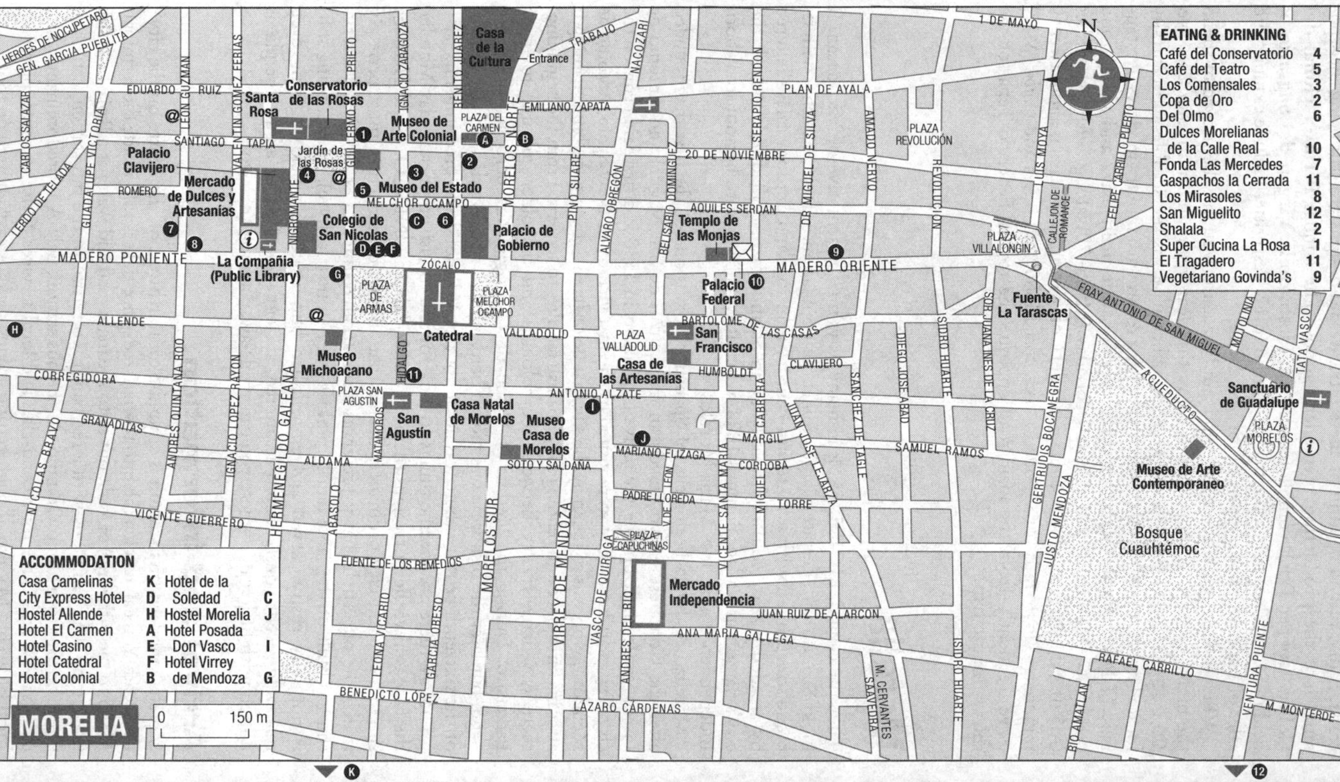
MORELIA
0 150 m
EATING & DRINKING
Café del Conservatorio 4
Café del Teatro 5
Los Comensales 3
Copa de Oro 2
Del Olmo 6
Dulces Morelianas de la Calle Real 10
Fonda Las Mercedes 7
Gaspachos la Cerrada 11
Los Mirasoles 8
San Miguelito 12
Shalala 2
Super Cucina La Rosa 1
El Tragadero 11
Vegetariano Govinda's 9
ACCOMMODATION
Casa Camelinas K
City Express Hotel D
Hostel Allende H
Hotel El Carmen A
Hotel Casino E
Hotel Catedral F
Hotel Colonial B
Hotel de la Soledad C
Hostel Morelia J
Hotel Posada Don Vasco I
Hotel Virrey de Mendoza G
Casa de la Cultura
Entrance
Conservatorio de las Rosas
Santa Rosa
Museo de Arte Colonial
Plaza del Carmen
Jardín de las Rosas
Museo del Estado
Palacio Clavijero
Mercado de Dulces y Artesanías
Colegio de San Nicolas
Palacio de Gobierno
La Compañia (Public Library)
Zócalo
Plaza de Armas
Plaza Melchor Ocampo
Catedral
Museo Michoacano
Plaza San Agustin
San Agustín
Casa Natal de Morelos
Museo Casa de Morelos
Templo de las Monjas
Palacio Federal
Plaza Valladolid
San Francisco
Casa de las Artesanías
Plaza Revolución
Plaza Villalongín
Fuente La Tarascas
Sanctuario de Guadalupe
Plaza Morelos
Museo de Arte Contemporaneo
Bosque Cuauhtémoc
Mercado Independencia
Plaza Capuchinas
Central Camionera
Madero Poniente
Madero Oriente
Morelos Norte
Morelos Sur
Fray Antonio de San Miguel
Acueducto
N

There's a **tourist information** kiosk at the south end of the Mercado de Dulces on Gomea Ferias (daily 9am–8pm; ⓣ443/317-8039, or toll-free from elsewhere in the country on ⓣ01-800-830 5363, ⓦwww.visitmorelia.com), and the state tourist office is east of the centre at Tata Vasco 80 (Mon–Fri 9am–2pm & 4–6pm; ⓣ443/317-8052, or toll-free from elsewhere in the country on ⓣ01-800/450-2300, ⓦwww.turismomichoacán.gob.mx). Try to get here for the **Festival Internacional de Guitarra** (held in March or April, ⓦwww.figmorelia.com.mx), a fantastic gathering of musicians from around the world; Expo Feria (dates vary in April/May), the Michoacán Expo Fair celebrating the arts and industry of the region; Morelos's birthday (Sept 30), celebrated with civic events, fairs, dances and fireworks; or the Festival Internacional de Música (second and third week in Nov, ⓦwww.festivalmorelia.com.mx), an international festival with concerts, recitals, operas and conferences.

Accommodation

With a couple of **hostels**, some reasonable mid-range **hotels** and a choice of excellent high-end places around the central squares you can't go far wrong. Prices are fairly consistent all year, though the better places may bump up their rates twenty percent or so around the Day of the Dead, when it's also a good idea to book ahead.

Casa Camelinas Jacarandas 172. Colonia Nueva Jacarandas ⓣ443/324-5194, US ⓣ1-707/942-4822, ⓦwww.mexonline.com/casacam1.htm. Friendly B&B 1.5km south of the centre (a short taxi or *combi* ride – take the orange #3 from Morelos Sur by the cathedral), with light, spacious rooms with private bath and decorated with work by local artisans. Book ahead as there aren't many surrounding options if it's full. 5

City Express Hotel Portal Hidalgo 245, on the Plaza de Armas ⓣ443/310-8400 or 01-800/248-9397, ⓦwww.cityexpress.com.mx. Great position under the colonial arches, and very modern if rather soulless. There's free wi-fi and a gym, but only eight of its sixty rooms have outside windows. 5

Hostel Allende Allende 843 ⓣ443/312-2246. Excellent hostel with rooms around a leafy courtyard that's great for relaxing. Single-sex dorms (M$140; M$126 for HI and ISIC cardholders) are vastly outnumbered by private rooms, all with private bath. There's a small kitchen, free wi-fi and 24hr check-in. 2

Hostel Morelia Mariano Elízaga 57 ⓣ443/312-1062. Dorm-only hostel (M$180; HI member M$170) with a small kitchen and communal area with hammock, and free internet access.

Hotel El Carmen Eduardo Ruíz 63 ⓣ443/312-1725, ⓔhotel_elcarmen@hotmail.com. Friendly hotel on a pretty square, with clean rooms, mostly with TV and bathroom. Some are a little small, while the better ones overlook the Plaza del Carmen. 3

Hotel Casino Portal Hidalgo 229 ⓣ443/313-1328 or 01-800/450 2100, ⓦwww.hotelcasino.com.mx. Best Western hotel on the Plaza de Armas set around a covered courtyard. Rooms lack character but maintain high standards with all the usual amenities. 6

Hotel Catedral Ignacio Zaragoza 37 ⓣ443/313-0406 or 01-800/714-1518, ⓦwww.hotelcatedralmorelia.com. Rooms around a restaurant in a covered colonial courtyard. A room with a cathedral view costs slightly more than one without. 6

Hotel Colonial 20 de Noviembre 15 ⓣ443/312-1897. One of the cheaper places in the centre with a wide range of rooms, all with bathrooms (hot water all day) and free wi-fi. The nicest rooms face the street. 4

Hotel de la Soledad Ignacio Zaragoza 90 ⓣ443/312-1888, ⓦwww.hoteldelasoledad.com. This spectacular colonial building, just off the Plaza de Armas, is the city's oldest inn. Breezy rooms are set around a beautiful open courtyard or a slightly less attractive back courtyard. 9

Hotel Posada Don Vasco Vasco de Quiroga 232 ⓣ443 /312-1484, ⓔposada_don_vasco@hotmail.com. Reasonably priced colonial-style hotel is one of the best deals downtown. Some rooms are dull and modern and others a bit poky, so have a look around. Services include cable TV, free wi-fi and free phone calls to Mexican landlines. 3

Hotel Virrey de Mendoza Madero 310 Pte ⓣ443/312-0045 or 01-800/450-2000, US ⓣ1-866/299-7492, Canada ⓣ1-877/889-2161, ⓦwww.hotelvirrey.com. Fantastic colonial grandeur: even if you can't afford to stay it's worth dropping by to take a look or have a drink in the courtyard. The rooms aren't as impressive as the lobby, but it is a lovely spot just the same for its history, majestic public spaces and fine service. 9

The Town

Everything you're likely to want to see is within easy walking distance of the **Plaza de Armas**, the heart of the colonial centre. **Avenida Francisco Madero**, which runs along the north side of Plaza de Armas and the cathedral, is very much the main street, with most of the important public buildings and major shops strung out along it.

Around the cathedral

At the heart of the city, Morelia's massive **cathedral** boasts two soaring towers that are said to be the tallest in Mexico. Begun in 1640 in the relatively plain Herrerian style, the towers and dome were not completed for some hundred years, by which time the Baroque had arrived with a vengeance; nevertheless, the parts harmonize remarkably, and for all the cathedral's size and richness of decoration, perfect proportions prevent it from becoming overpowering. The interior, refitted towards the end of the nineteenth century, after most of its silver ornamentation had been removed to pay for the wars, is simple. A few early colonial religious paintings are preserved in the choir and the sacristy.

Flanking the cathedral, the **Plaza de Armas** (or de los Martíres) is the place to sit around and revel in the city's leisurely pace – relax with a coffee and a morning paper (you can buy a few international newspapers from the stands here) in the cafés under its elegant arcaded *portales*. On the southwestern edge of the plaza, at the corner of Allende and Abasolo, the **Museo Michoacano** (Tues–Sun 9am–4.30pm; M$37, free Sun) occupies a palatial eighteenth-century mansion. Emperor Maximilian lodged here on his visits to Morelia, and it now houses a collection that reflects the state's diversity and rich history: the rooms devoted to archeology are, of course, dominated by the **Tarascan culture**, including pottery and small sculptures from Tzintzuntzán, but also display much earlier objects, notably some obsidian figurines. Out in the patio are two magnificent old carriages, while upstairs the colonial epoch is represented in a large group of religious paintings and sculptures and a collection of old books and manuscripts.

A smaller square, the **Plaza Melchor Ocampo**, flanks the cathedral on the other side. Facing it, the **Palacio de Gobierno** was formerly a seminary – Independence hero Morelos and his nemesis Agustín Iturbide studied here, as did Ocampo, a nineteenth-century liberal supporter of Benito Juárez. It's of interest now for Alfredo Zalce's **murals** adorning the stairway and upper level of the patio: practically the whole of Mexican history, and each of its heroes, is depicted.

Immediately east along Madero are several **banks** that are among the most remarkable examples of active conservation you'll see anywhere: old mansions that have been refurbished in traditional style, and somehow manage to combine reasonably efficient operation with an ambience that is wholly in keeping with the setting.

West and north of the plaza

One block west of the Plaza de Armas, the **Colegio de San Nicolas** is part of the University of Michoacán. Founded at Pátzcuaro in 1540 by Vasco de Quiroga, and moved here in 1580, the college is the second oldest in Mexico and hence in all the Americas – it now houses administrative offices and various technical faculties. To the side, across Nigromante in what was originally the Jesuit church of **La Compañía**, is the public library, while next to this is the beautiful **Palacio Clavijero**, now converted into government offices. Alongside the Palacio, down Gomez Farias, enclosed *portales* are home to the **Mercado de Dulces y Artesanías**, groaning with the sweets for which the city is famed, along with stalls selling leather jackets, guitars and other handicrafts, though little of much quality.

At the north end of Nigromante, on another charming little plaza – the Jardín de las Rosas – you'll come across the Baroque church of **Santa Rosa** and, beside it, the **Conservatorio de las Rosas**, a music academy founded in the eighteenth century. From time to time it hosts concerts of classical music – the tourist office should have details.

Also here, at Guillermo Prieto 176, near the corner of Santiago Tapia, is the **Museo del Estado** (Mon–Fri 9am–2pm & 4–8pm, Sat & Sun 10am–6pm; free). Inside this eighteenth-century former home, the complete furniture and fittings of a traditional *farmacia* have been reconstructed, after which you move, somewhat incongruously, to the prehistory and archeology collections. This is mostly minor stuff, though there are some intriguing ceramic figurines and some fine, unusual Tarascan jewellery, including gold and turquoise pieces, and necklaces strung with tiny crystal skulls. Upstairs, there's one room of colonial history and various ethnological exhibits illustrating traditional local dress and lifestyles – a butterfly fishing net from Pátzcuaro plus displays on copper working and guitar manufacture.

East of here, or north from the cathedral on Juárez, is the **Museo de Arte Colonial** (Mon–Fri 9am–8pm, Sat & Sun 9am–7pm; free). Its collection of colonial art is almost entirely regional, and not of great interest, though there is an expansive display of rather gory crucifixes. Of greater interest on the north side of the plaza, entered from Morelos, the beautiful old Convento del Carmen now houses the **Casa de la Cultura** (daily 10am–8pm, later if there's something special on; free). It's an enormous complex, worth exploring in its own right, with a theatre, café, space for temporary exhibitions and classes scattered around the former monastic buildings.

South of the plaza

Two blocks southeast of the cathedral, on Morelos Sur, the **Museo Casa de Morelos** (daily 9am–7pm; M$31, free Sun) is the relatively modest eighteenth-century house in which Independence hero José María Morelos y Pavón lived from 1801 (see box, p.370). It's now a museum devoted to his life and the War of Independence. Nearby, at the corner of Corregidora (the continuation of Alzate) and García Obeso, you can see the house where the hero was born, the **Casa Natal de Morelos** (Mon–Fri 9am–8pm, Sat & Sun 9am–7pm; free), which now houses a library and a few desultory domestic objects. This in turn is virtually next door to the church of **San Agustín**, from where pedestrianized Hidalgo runs up one block to the Plaza de Armas.

Walk a couple of blocks in the other direction – or take Valladolid directly from the Plaza Ocampo – to find Plaza Valladolid and the church of **San Francisco**. Its former monastery, next door, has been turned into the **Casa de las Artesanías** (Mon–Sat 9am–8pm, Sun 9am–3.30pm; free; ⓦwww.casadelasartesanias.gob.mx), possibly the most comprehensive collection of Michoacán's crafts anywhere, almost all of which are for sale. The best and most obviously commercial items are downstairs, while on the upper floor are a series of rooms devoted to the products of particular villages, often with craftspeople demonstrating their techniques (these are staffed by villagers and hence not always open), and a collection of historic items that you can't buy.

Around the aqueduct

One of the most attractive parts of town to while away a few hours lies about fifteen minutes' walk east along Madero from the cathedral. Wander past the Baroque facade of the **Templo de las Monjas** and the adjacent Palacio Federal to reach tiny **Plaza Villalongin**, a small plaza through the middle of which runs the

José María Morelos y Pavón

A student of Hidalgo, **José María Morelos** took over the leadership of the **Independence movement** after its instigators had been executed in 1811. While the cry of Independence had initially been taken up by the Mexican (Creole) bourgeoisie, smarting under the trading restrictions imposed on them by Spain, it quickly became a mass movement. Unlike the original leaders, Morelos (a *mestizo* priest born into relative poverty) was a populist and genuine reformer. Even more unlike them, he was also a political and military tactician of considerable skill, invoking the spirit of the French Revolution and calling for universal suffrage, racial equality and the break-up of the hacienda system, under which workers were tied to agricultural servitude. He was defeated and executed by Royalist armies under Agustín de Iturbide in 1815 after waging years of guerrilla warfare, a period during which Morelos had come close to taking the capital and controlling the entire country. When Independence was finally gained – by Iturbide, who had changed sides and later briefly served as emperor – it was no longer a force for change, rather a reaction to the fact that by 1820 liberal reforms were sweeping Spain itself. The causes espoused by Morelos were, however, taken up to some extent by Benito Juárez and later, with a vengeance, in the Revolution – almost a hundred years after his death.

Around Michoacán you'll see Morelos's image everywhere – notably the massive **statue** atop Isla de Janitzio – invariably depicted with a kind of bandana over his head. He's also pictured on the **fifty-peso note**, which features the butterfly-net fishers of Pátzcuaro, monarch butterflies and masks for the Danza de los Viejitos.

old **aqueduct**. Built on a winding course between 1785 and 1789, its 253 arches brought water into the city from springs in the nearby hills. Several roads meet here at the **Fuente Las Tarascas**, which features three bare-breasted Tarascan women holding up a vast basket of fruit.

Eastbound roads split three ways here. Madero bears slightly left and, just past the aqueduct, take a peek down the **Callejón de Romance** (Romance Lane), a pretty bougainvillea-draped alley of nineteenth-century homes running down to a couple of fountains. The second of the three roads is **La Calzada Fray Antonio de San Miguel** (named for the bishop who built the aqueduct), a broad and shady pedestrianized walkway that leads down to the wildly overdecorated **Santuario de Guadalupe**, where market stalls, selling above all the sticky local *dulces*, set up at weekends and during fiestas. The last of the three roads, Avenida Acueducto, follows the aqueduct and, 300m along, passes the small **Museo de Arte Contemporáneo** (Tues–Fri 10am–8pm, Sat & Sun 10am–6pm; free), featuring a variety of Latin American work. Behind it is **Bosque Cuauhtémoc**, in which there are some beautifully laid-out flower displays.

Eating and drinking

On a fine day it is hard to resist the temptation of the cafés and restaurants in the *portales* around the Plaza de Armas: fairly expensive for a full meal, but good for snacks or for a breakfast of coffee and *pan dulce*. As ever, the cheapest eating as at the **food market** in Plaza Capuchinas, but Morelia's big Mercado Independencia, just to its south, is on the whole a disappointment, certainly not as large or varied as you'd expect.

Chief of Morelia's specialities are its **dulces**, sweets made of candied fruit or evaporated milk – cloyingly sweet to most non-Mexican tastes, they're very popular here. You can see a wide selection at the **Mercado de Dulces y Artesanías** (see p.368). Morelians also get through a lot of *rompope* (a drink that you'll find to a lesser extent all over Mexico) – again, it's very sweet, an egg concoction based on rum, milk and egg with vanilla, cinnamon or almond flavouring.

Café del Conservatorio Santiago Tapia 363. A peaceful place to enjoy a drink or a snack on the pretty Jardín de las Rosas. They also do good but rather pricey breakfasts (M$70–90).

Café del Teatro in the Teatro Ocampo, on Ocampo and Prieto. Its lush, almost baronial, interior makes this one of the most popular spots in town for good coffee and people-watching. With breakfast for M$40–48 and sandwiches at M$30–50, it's not as expensive as it might be. Try to get a table overlooking the street.

Los Comensales Zaragoza 148. Open till 8pm with a pretty, verdant courtyard setting. The comida corrida is good value at M$65, or pay around the same for elaborate Mexican specialities, including a tasty chicken in rich, dark *mole*.

Copa de Oro Juárez 194-B at Santiago Tapia. An excellent place for fresh *jugos*; also does tortas and breakfasts (but beware – the coffee's instant). Mon–Sat 7.30am–9pm.

Del Olmo Juárez 95. Sophisticated but relaxed café/bar, set around a pretty interior courtyard, with good coffee, and eggs with ham for breakfast.

Dulces Morelianas de la Calle Real Madero 440 Ote. Magnificent old-fashioned candy store with a café serving decadent coffees with drizzles of *cajeta*. The staff even sport colonial dress, and there's a microscopic Museo del Dulces in the back.

Fonda Las Mercedes León Guzmán 47. Upscale Tarascan and Mexican dishes in a swanky setting – all white linen and big wine glasses. Expect the likes of juicy steaks (M$150–190) and salmon *a la plancha* with tarragon (M$175). Daily from 1.30pm.

Gaspachos la Cerrada Hidalgo 67. Nothing like a Spanish *gazpacho*, a Morelian *gaspacho* is a finely chopped fruit salad, topped – if you like – with grated cheese and *chile* powder. Plenty of places around town sell it, but this is the most renowned.

Los Mirasoles Madero 549 Pte ⓣ443/317-5775, ⓦwww.losmirasoles.com. Contemporary Mexican cuisine in a plush conversion of a seventeenth-century mansion – the courtyard is enchanting. There's a full range of Michoacán specialities, including trout tacos and *chamorro* (leg of pork) in *chile* and *pulque* sauce. There's a M$245 tasting menu; otherwise, expect to pay around M$350 for a full meal, and reserve ahead.

San Miguelito Av Camelinas, Fraccionamiento La Loma (at the southern end of Ventura Puente, opposite the Centro de Convenciones, 2km southeast of the centre) ⓣ443/324-2300, ⓦwww.sanmiguelito.com.mx. Superb, unpretentious Mexican dishes such as *sopa tarasca* (M$56) or fish cooked in a banana leaf (M$150).The bar is a recreated bullring. Be sure to sit in the room filled with three hundred effigies of St Anthony and say a prayer for a good spouse.

Shalala Juárez 194. A Christian café, with Christian music Thur, Fri & Sat from 9pm, free wi-fi and good, cheap breakfasts (M$27) and lunches (M$37).

Super Cucina La Rosa Santiago Tapia at Prieto. Filling and tasty *menú del día* for M$55. Breakfast M$35. Mon–Sat 8am–5pm.

El Tragadero Hidalgo 63. At this relaxed café-restaurant you're surrounded by old photos of Morelia. It's a good place for breakfast (M$38.50–46.20) or an inexpensive lunch (menu M$55).

Vegetariano Govinda's Madero 549 Ote. Good, inexpensive, vegetarian fare. Come for breakfast (M$40–47) or the *menú del día* (M$45–56), comprising meat-less versions of Mexican staples.

Listings

Banks and exchange There are plenty of very grand banks with ATMs along Madero Ote, open for exchange on weekday mornings, plus a casa de cambio at Prieto 48 near the Plaza de Armas (but closed Sun).

Entertainment International films are shown at the Museo Regional Michoacáno, the Casa Natal de Morelos and the Casa de la Cultura, several times a week. There are also regular organ recitals in the cathedral, and band concerts in the zócalo (Sun).

Internet access El Jardín, Guillermo Prieto 157 (daily 10am–8pm; M$15/hr); Internet, León Guzmán 231 (Mon–Sat 8am–10pm; M$6–7/hr); On Line, Allende 338 (Mon–Sat 7am–10pm, Sun 9am–10pm; M$8/hr).

Post office Madero 369 Ote (Mon–Fri 9am–6pm).

Pharmacy Farmacia Guadalajara, Morelos Sur 117, on Plaza Ocampo (daily 8am–10pm).

Telephones Telmex, in the post office, has phone and fax offices (Mon–Fri 9am–8pm). There's also a *caseta de larga distancia* at Portal Galeana 103, opposite the front of the cathedral.

The Monarch Butterfly Sanctuary

Each winter more than 150 million monarch **butterflies** (see p.374) migrate from the northeastern US and Canada to the Oyamel fir forests in the lush mountains of Michoacán in order to reproduce. It's an amazing sight any time, but especially in January and February when numbers peak: whole trees are smothered in monarchs, branches sagging under the weight. In the cool of the morning, they dry their wings, turning the entire landscape a rich, velvety orange, while later in the day they take to the air, millions of fluttering butterflies making more noise

Fiestas

Both Jalisco and Michoacán preserve strong native traditions and are particularly rich in fiestas: the list below is by no means exhaustive, and local tourist offices will have further details.

January

New Year's Day (Jan 1). Celebrated in Pátzcuaro (see p.355) and Uruapan (see p.349) with the Danza de los Viejitos (Dance of the Little Old Men; see box, p.351).

Día de los Santos Reyes (Jan 6). Twelfth Night is celebrated with many small ceremonies and dances such as Los Sonajeros (rattles), Las Pastoras (the shepherdesses) and El Baile de la Conquista (conquest). Particularly good at Los Reyes, west of Uruapan, and Cajititlán, 25km south of Guadalajara.

Día de San Sebastian (Jan 20). Traditional dances in Tuxpan (see p.347).

February

Día de Nuestro Señor del Rescate (Feb 1). In Tzintzuntzán (see p.363), the start of a week-long fiesta founded in the sixteenth century by Vasco de Quiroga.

Carnaval (the week before Lent, variable Feb–March). Celebrated everywhere.

March

Festival Internacional de Guitarra (March 17–21) International Guitar Festival in Morelia (see p.365).

April

Palm Sunday (the Sun before Easter Sun). Palm ornament market in Uruapan (see p.349).

Semana Santa (Holy Week). Observed everywhere, but especially in Tzintzuntzán (see p.363).

Expo Feria (variable April–May). Arts and industry show in Morelia (see p.365).

May

Día de la Santa Cruz (May 3). Native dances in Angangueo (see p.375); mariachis and tequila in Tequila (see p.340).

Día del Señor de la Misericordia (last Sun in May). Fiesta and dances in Tuxpan (see p.347).

Corpus Christi (Thurs after Trinity, variable late May–early June). Traditional dances in Paracho (see p.349).

June

Día de San Pedro (June 29). Mariachi and dance festival in Tlaquepaque, Guadalajara (see p.337).

than you'd ever think possible. As the afternoon humidity forces them to the ground, they form a thick carpet of blazing colour.

The best place to see them is in the **Santuario de la Mariposa Monarca** (middle weekend in Nov to last weekend in March daily 9am–4pm; M$55; Ⓦwww.santuario-monarca.com.mx), just outside the village of El Rosario, about 120km east of Morelia. It is best to go early in the morning (and preferably on weekdays, to avoid the crowds), when the butterflies are just waking up and before they fly off into the surrounding woodlands. **Guides**, whose services are included in the entry fee, show you around the sanctuary and give a short explanation of the butterflies'

July

Día de la Preciosa Sangre de Cristo (first Sun in July). Torch-lit religious processions in Quiroga (see p.364).

Día de María Magdalena (July 22). Fiesta in Uruapan (see p.349) featuring a procession of animals.

Día de Santiago Apóstol (July 25). Lively celebrations and fireworks in Tuxpan (see p.347) and Uruapan (see p.349).

August

Fiesta tradicional (Aug 8). Ancient pre-Columbian fiesta in Paracho (see p.349).

Feria Nacional del Cobre (second week in Aug). National Copper Fair in Santa Clara del Cobre (see p.364), near Pátzcuaro.

September

Morelos's birthday (Sept 30). Celebrated in Morelia (see p.365).

October

Fiestas de Octubre (all month). Massive cultural festival in Guadalajara (see p.337).

Día de San Francisco (Oct 4). Saint's day celebrations in Uruapan (see p.349).

Día de la Raza (Oct 12). Uruapan (see p.349) celebrates Columbus's discovery of the Americas.

Día de la Virgen de Zapopan (Oct 12). Massive pilgrimage in Guadalajara (see p.337).

Festival de Coros y Danzas (Oct 24–26). Singing and dancing competitions in Uruapan (see p.349).

November

Día de los Muertos (Day of the Dead; Nov 2). Celebrated everywhere, but especially around Pátzcuaro (see box, p.351). Also picturesque in Zitácuaro.

Arrival of the monarch butterfly (second week of Nov). *Las monarcas* start arriving in Michoacán in big numbers around now.

Festival Internacional de Música (third week of Nov). International Music Festival in Morelia (see p.365).

Feria de Aguacate (variable Nov–Dec). Three-week avocado fair in Uruapan (see p.349).

December

Día de la Inmaculada Concepción (Dec 8). Celebrated in Sayula (see p.346).

La Señora de la Salud (Dec 8). Pilgrimage and dances in Pátzcuaro (see p.355) and Tequila (see p.340).

Día de la Virgen de Guadalupe (Dec 12). Large celebrations in Tapalpa (see p.345).

Pastoral plays (Dec 24). Performed in Tuxpan (see p.347).

lifecycle and breeding habits. For a couple of weeks on either side of the main season, those same guides run the place unofficially, still charging the entry price and offering their services for a tip. There are fewer butterflies but it is still worth the journey anytime from early November to early April. The walk to the best of the monarch-laden trees is about 2km, mostly uphill at an altitude of almost 3000 metres: take it easy if you're not acclimatized.

Practicalities

Visiting the monarchs is possible on **day trips** from Morelia and Mexico City, but it is more satisfying to stay locally (probably in Angangueo) and visit at a more leisurely pace. During the season there are direct buses to El Rosario from Mexico City (Autobuses Zincantepec from Terminal Poniente), but otherwise **getting there** by public transport generally involves changing buses in Zitácuaro (see opposite). From Zitácuaro, buses run to Ocampo (every 15min; 30min) and continue to Angangueo (a further 20min). From Ocampo there is a minibus along a 10km cobbled road to El Rosario (every 15min; 30min). Those with a car can drive direct to El Rosario from Ocampo. If you are staying in Angangueo you could conceivably walk back downhill in a couple of hours.

The closest **accommodation** to the butterfly sanctuary is *Rancho Givali* (ⓣ715/5239-5485 or 01-800/087 6000, ⓦwww.mochilazo.com.mx; ❻), 2km down the hill, which has comfortable rooms, camping and a good restaurant. There are also basic daytime restaurants that line the approach to the sanctuary. All other accommodation and dining options are in Ocampo and Angangueo (see opposite).

The life cycle and habitat of the monarch

The sheer size of the congregation of monarch butterflies in the hills of Michoacán is astonishing, but not as impressive as their 4500-kilometre **migration**. In the fall, when the weather starts to turn cold in the Great Lakes region of the US and Canada, the butterflies head south, taking just four to five weeks to make it to Michoacán. Here, in an area of less than 150 square kilometres, they find the unique microclimate a perfect place to spend the winter. The cool temperatures allow them to conserve energy, the trees provide shelter from wind and precipitation and the fog-laden air prevents them from drying out. Monarchs typically have a **life cycle** of around two to five weeks, but when they fly south they go into a phase known as "reproductive diapause". The same butterflies remain in Michoacán all winter, then breed in spring in time for their caterpillars to dine on the newly emergent milkweed plants – their only food source – before returning to the US and Canada.

Around ten percent of all migrating monarchs get eaten by black-headed grosbeaks and black-backed orioles, but that offers no danger to species survival. The real threat is loss of this crucial mountain **habitat**. This was recognized as far back as 1986, when several key overwintering sites were protected from logging, but the local peasant families need the wood and they were never fully compensated for the loss of this resource. The Mexican government more than tripled the size of the reserves in 2000, but logging continued to a large enough extent that in early 2007 new president Felipe Calderón declared a "zero tolerance" policy against it, and increased policing. To learn more, check out the websites of the Monarch Butterfly Sanctuary Foundation (ⓦwww.mbsf.org), the Michoacán Restoration Fund (ⓦwww.michoacanmonarchs.org) and Monarch Watch (ⓦwww.monarchwatch.org).

Zitácuaro, Ocampo and Angangueo

Most people approaching the butterfly sanctuary change buses at **Zitácuaro**, a small town prettily scattered over low hills at around 1900 metres. Being a little warmer than Angangueo makes it a potential base for visiting El Rosario. There are regular *combis* from the bus station into town, or you can walk (about 1km), turning right as you leave the bus station, then left down Moctezuma till you reach the northern end of Revolución. There are a number of good-value hotels on Revolución around the junction with Hidalgo, of which the cheapest is *Hotel México*, Revolución 22 Sur (Ⓣ715/153-1398; ❶). Nearby restaurants include *La Trucha Alegre* at Revolución 2 Nte, which serves trout in 35 different guises. South of town, the upscale *Hotel Rancho San Cayetano*, at Carretera a Huetamo km 2.3 (Ⓣ715/153-1926, Ⓦwww.ranchosancayetano.com; breakfast included ❼), has a pool and good restaurant set in private woodland.

The nearest substantial village to the El Rosario sanctuary is **Ocampo**, 20km north of Zitácuaro. It is not an especially interesting place, but it has good connections to El Rosario, and you can stay at *Hotel San Carlos*, Zaragoza 8 (no phone; ❷). There are several small, basic **restaurants** around the central square.

Most butterfly visitors stay at **Angangueo**, 9km further on, a former mining town wedged into a valley at almost 2600m: it can be cool in the evenings. The name is Tarascan for "entrance to the cave", presumably an early reference to its mineral extraction potential. The mines have now closed, but with its terracotta-tiled roofs, winding streets and houses stacked up the hillside it is an attractive enough place and offers the best selection of hotels and restaurants around.

Most things happen on Morelos, which becomes Nacional at the point where the minor Matamoros heads off up to the butterfly sanctuary. By far the best **place to stay** is the comfortable and very friendly *Hotel Don Bruno*, Morelos 92, 1km south of the centre (Ⓣ&Ⓕ715/156-0026; ❺), which has its own restaurant and some rooms with fireplace. Right in town, there are simple but clean rooms with bath at *Paso de la Monarca*, Nacional 20 (Ⓣ715/156-0187; ❷); and opposite, *Hotel Juarez*, Nacional 15 (Ⓣ715/156-0023; ❷), with reasonable rooms set around a flower-filled courtyard. **Eating** options are limited, but *Restaurant Los Arcos*, on the main square, serves good breakfasts (M$35) and comidas corridas (M$65 with beer). Angangueo celebrates the **Día de la Santa Cruz** (May 3) with traditional dances.

Travel details

Buses

What follows is a minimum of routes covering the major stops only – it should be assumed that these buses also call at the towns en route. In general the fastest and most efficient operators are Omnibus de Mexico and Tres Estrellas de Oro, though there's little to choose between the first-class companies.

Angangueo to: Ocampo (every 15min; 20min); Zitácuaro (every 15min; 1hr).

Chapala to: Ajijic (every 30min; 20min); Guadalajara (every 30min; 1hr).

Ciudad Guzmán to: Colima (every hour; 1hr); Guadalajara Central Nueva (32 daily; 2hr); Guadalajara Central Vieja (22 daily; 3hr 30min); Manzanillo (3 daily; 3hr); Mexico City (3 overnight; 9hr); Sayula (22 daily; 45min); Tapalpa (4 daily, 2hr).

Guadalajara (Central Nueva) to: Aguascalientes (every 30–60min; 3hr); Colima (approximately every 30min; 3hr); Guanajuato (10 daily; 4hr); Lagos de Moreno (7 daily; 2hr 30min); Manzanillo (every 30min; 5hr); Mazatlán (36 daily; 6hr); Mexico City (every 20–30min, plus numerous overnight; 7hr); Morelia (28 daily; 3–5hr); Pátzcuaro (2 daily; 5hr); Puerto Vallarta (11 daily; 5hr); Querétaro (every

30–60min; 5hr); San Juan de los Lagos (22 daily; 3hr); San Luis Potosí (approximately hourly; 5hr); Tepic (7 daily; 3hr); Tijuana (23 daily; 35hr); Toluca (4 daily; 6hr); Uruapan (25 daily; 5hr).
Guadalajara (Central Vieja) to: Ajijic (every 30min; 1hr 15min); Chapala (every 30min; 1hr); Jocotepec (hourly; 1hr 15min); Tapalpa (9 daily; 3hr); Tequila (every 30min; 1hr 45min).
Morelia to: Aguascalientes (8 daily; 7hr); Guadalajara (40 daily; 3hr 30min); Guanajuato (2 daily; 3hr 30min); León (every 30min; 4hr); Mexico City (Pte) (every 30min; 4hr); Mexico City (Nte) (hourly; 4hr 30min); Pátzcuaro (every 15min; 1hr); Querétaro (hourly; 4hr); Toluca (every 30min; 4hr); Uruapan (every 30min; 2hr); Zitácuaro (every 30min; 3hr).
Ocampo to: Angangueo (every 15min; 20min); El Rosario (every 15min; 30min); Zitácuaro (every 15min; 40min).
Pátzcuaro to: Guadalajara (2 daily; 4–5hr); Mexico City (Pte) (14 daily; 5hr); Mexico City (Nte) (6 daily; 5hr 30min); Morelia (every 15min; 1hr); Quiroga (every 15min; 30min); Uruapan (every 30min; 1hr).
Sayula to: Ciudad Guzmán (22 daily; 1hr); Guadalajara (9 daily; 2hr 30min); Tapalpa 4 daily; 1hr).
Uruapan to: Guadalajara (25 daily; 4hr 30min); Lázaro Cárdenas (28 daily; 3hr 30min); Los Reyes (every 30min; 1hr); Mexico City (Pte) (16 daily; 6hr); Mexico City (Nte) (8 daily; 6hr 30min); Morelia (every 20min; 2hr); Paracho (every 15min; 40min); Pátzcuaro (every 30min; 1hr).
Zitácuaro to: Angangueo (every 15min; 6.15am–9.15pm; 1hr); Mexico City (every 20min; 3hr); Morelia (every 20min; 2hr 40min); Ocampo (every 15min; 30min); Toluca (every 20min; 1hr 30min).

Flights

Guadalajara to: Mexico City (25 daily; 1hr 10min); Ciudad Juárez (2–4 daily; 2hr); Cuidad Obregón (1 daily; 45min); La Paz, Baja California Sur (5–6 daily; 30min); Mérida (2–3 daily; 4hr 10min); Monterrey (8 daily; 1hr 20min); Puerto Vallarta (8–9 daily; 50min); Tijuana (10–12 daily; 3hr); Toluca (6–7 daily; 1hr).
Morelia to: Mexico City (5–7 daily; 50min); Tijuana (2–4 daily; 3hr).

6

Mexico City

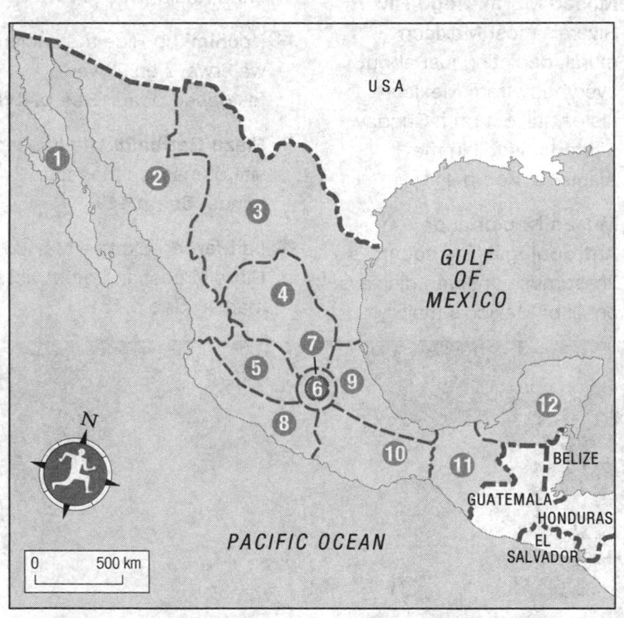

CHAPTER 6 Highlights

✱ **The Zócalo** Mexico City's huge central square, surrounded by the cathedral, Aztec ruins and the Palacio Nacional. See p.395

✱ **Palacio de Bellas Artes** Not only an architectural masterpiece in its own right, with a smashing Art Deco interior, but also home to some of the city's most impressive murals. See p.408

✱ **Museo Mural Diego Rivera** Rivera's most Mexican mural, depicting just about everybody from Mexican history, all out on a Sunday afternoon stroll in the Alameda. See p.411

✱ **Museo Nacional de Antropología** The country's finest museum, with displays on all of Mexico's major pre-Columbian cultures. See p.419

✱ **Coyoacán** Visit the houses where Frida Kahlo and León Trotsky lived, spend an evening checking out the local bars, then come back for the colourful Sunday market. See p.429

✱ **Museo Dolores Olmedo Patiño** A huge collection of works by Diego Rivera and Frida Kahlo. See p.437

✱ **Xochimilco** Ride the ancient waterways on flower-festooned boats. See p.438

✱ **Plaza Garibaldi** The frenetic site of massed mariachi bands. See p.449

✱ **La Merced** Explore Mexico City's largest and most vibrant market. See p.451

▲ Dancers outside the cathedral on the Zócalo

6

Mexico City

Set over 2400m above sea level in a shallow mountain bowl, and crammed with over twenty million people, **Mexico City** is one of the world's most densely populated urban areas. Although it does have a high crime rate, and some terrible pollution (see p.379), the capital is nowhere near as intimidating as you might expect. Nonetheless, you may still prefer to take it in a couple of days at a time, taking days off to visit the places described in the following chapter (see p.461) , all of which are possible as day trips.

The city radiates out from the **Zócalo**, or main square, as much the heart of the modern capital as it was of the Aztec city that once sat here. Immediately to its west, in the streets between the Zócalo and the garden known as the **Alameda**, is the city's main **commercial area**. Beyond that, the glitzy **Zona Rosa**, with trendy **Condesa** to its south, stretches towards **Chapultepec Park** – home to the incredible **Museo Nacional de Antropología** – and the rich enclave of **Polanco**, while Avenida de los Insurgentes leads down to the more laid-back *barrios* of **San Ángel** and **Coyoacán**. Around the outer edges of the city are shantytowns, built piecemeal by migrants from elsewhere in the country. Hidden among these less affluent communities are a number of gems, such as the pyramids of Tenayauca, Santa Cecilia and Cuicuilco, and the canals of **Xochimilco**.

Some history

And when we saw all those cities and villages built in the water, and other great towns on dry land, and that straight and level causeway leading to Mexico, we were astounded. These great towns and cities and buildings rising from the water, all made of stone, seemed like an enchanted vision from the tales of Amadis. Indeed, some of our soldiers asked whether it was not all a dream.

Bernal Díaz, *The Conquest of New Spain*

It's hardly surprising that Cortés and his followers should have been so taken by their first sight of **Tenochtitlán**, capital of the Aztecs. Built in the middle of a lake traversed by great causeways, it was a beautiful, strictly regulated, stone-built city of 300,000 residents. The **Aztec** people (or, as they called themselves, the Mexica) had arrived at the lake in around 1345, after years of wandering and living off what they could scavenge or pillage from settled communities. According to Aztec legend, their patron god Huitzilopochtli had ordered them to build a city where they found an eagle perched on a cactus devouring a snake – this they duly saw on an island in the middle of the lake. It is this legend that is the basis of the nopal, eagle and snake motif that forms the centrepiece of the modern Mexican flag and you'll see the motif everywhere from coins and official seals to woven designs on rugs.

Health and safety in Mexico City

Mexico City comes with an unenviable reputation for overcrowding, grime and crime. To some extent this is deserved, but things are improving, and overall, Mexico's capital is no worse than other cities of the same size and population elsewhere in the developing world. Indeed, the frenzied atmosphere is part of its fascination.

Certainly there is **pollution**. The whole urban area sits in a low mountain bowl that deflects smog-clearing winds away from the city, allowing a thick blanket of haze to build up throughout the day. Conditions are particularly bad in winter, when there is no rain, and pollution levels (reported daily in the English-language newspaper *The News*) tend to peak in the early afternoon. In response, the **Hoy No Circula** ("Don't drive today") law prohibits car use from 5am to 10pm for one day in the working week for vehicles over six years old, the day depending on the car's numberplate. Nonetheless, those prone to **respiratory problems** may have some difficulty on arrival, due to the city's air quality and altitude.

The capital is where the Mexican extremes of **wealth** and **poverty** are most apparent, with shiny, valet-parked SUVs vying for space with pavement vendors and beggars. Such financial disparity fuels **theft**, but just take the same precautions you would in any large city; there is no need to feel particularly paranoid. Keep your valuables – especially credit or debit cards – in the hotel safe (even cheap hotels often have somewhere secure; muggers who catch you with an ATM card may keep hold of you till they have extracted enough cash with it), don't flash large wads of money around and keep an eye on your camera and other valuables in busy market areas. At night, avoid the *barrio* known as **Doctores** (around the Metro station of the same name, so called because the streets are named after doctors), and the area around Lagunilla market, both centres of the street drug trade, and therefore opportunist crime. Note that mugging is not the only danger – abduction for ransom is increasingly common too. **Taxis** have a bad reputation and, though drivers are mostly helpful and courteous, there are reports of people being robbed or abducted (often in stolen taxis). If possible, get your hotel to call you a cab (more expensive), or call one yourself from one of the firms listed on p.390. If you do have to hail a cab in the street, always take one whose registration, on both the numberplate and the side of the vehicle, begins with an L (for "libre" – to be hailed while driving around), and which has the driver's identification prominently displayed within. Better still, find a taxi rank and take a *sitio* taxi that can be traced to that rank (with a number beginning in R, S or T, and again with the driver's ID prominently displayed). Do not take taxis from the airport or bus terminals other than prepaid ones, and avoid taking those waiting outside tourist spots.

The lake proved an ideal site. Well stocked with fish, it was also fertile, once the Aztecs had constructed their *chinampas*, or floating gardens of reeds, and virtually impregnable, too: the causeways, when they were completed, could be flooded and the bridges raised to thwart attacks (or escape, as the Spanish found on the Noche Triste; see p.856).

The island city eventually grew to cover an area of some thirteen square kilometres, much of it reclaimed from the lake, and from this base the Aztecs were able to begin their programme of expansion: first, dominating the valley by a series of strategic alliances, war and treachery, and finally, in a period of less than a hundred years before the Conquest, establishing an empire that demanded tribute from and traded with the most distant parts of the country.

The Conquest

The Aztec empire was firmly established when **Cortés** and his army of only a few hundred men landed on the east coast in 1519 and began their long march on

Tenochtitlán. Several key factors assured their survival: superior weaponry, which included firearms; the shock effect of horses (never having seen such animals, the Aztecs at first believed them to be extensions of their riders); the support of tribes who were either enemies or suppressed subjects of the Aztecs; and the unwillingness of the Aztec emperor to resist openly.

Moctezuma II (Montezuma), who had suffered heavy defeats in campaigns against the Tarascans in the west, was a broodingly religious man who, it is said, believed Cortés to be the pale-skinned, bearded god Quetzalcoatl, returned to fulfil ancient prophecies. Accordingly he admitted him to the city – fearfully, but with a show of ceremonious welcome. By way of repaying this hospitality the Spanish took Moctezuma prisoner, and later attacked the great Aztec temples, killing many priests and placing Christian chapels alongside their altars. Meanwhile, there was growing unrest in the city at the emperor's passivity and at the rapacious behaviour of his guests. Moctezuma was eventually killed – according to the Spanish, stoned to death by his own people while trying to quell a riot – and the Spaniards driven from the city with heavy losses. However, Cortés and a few of his followers were able to escape to the security of Tlaxcala, the most loyal of his native allies, to regroup and plan a new assault. Finally, rearmed and reinforced, their numbers swelled by indigenous allies, and with ships built in secret, the Spaniards laid siege to Tenochtitlán for three months, finally taking the city in the face of suicidal opposition in August 1521.

The city's defeat is still a harsh memory: Cortés himself is hardly revered, but the natives who assisted him, and in particular Moctezuma and Malinche, the woman who acted as Cortés' interpreter, are non-people. You won't find a monument to Moctezuma in the country, though **Cuauhtémoc**, his successor who led the fierce resistance, is commemorated everywhere; Malinche is represented, acidly, in some of Diego Rivera's more outspoken murals. More telling, perhaps, of the bitterness of the struggle, is that so little physical evidence remains: "All that I saw then," wrote Bernal Díaz, "is overthrown and destroyed; nothing is left standing."

Spanish and post-colonial Mexico City

The victorious Spanish systematically smashed every visible aspect of Aztec culture, as often as not using the very stones of the old city to construct the new, and building a new palace for Cortés on the site of the Aztec emperor's palace. Until a few decades ago it was thought that everything had been destroyed; slowly, however, particularly during construction of the Metro and in the remarkable discovery of remains of the **Templo Mayor** beneath the colonial Zócalo, remains of Tenochtitlán have been brought to light.

The **new city** developed slowly in its early years. It spread far wider, however, as the lake was drained, filled and built over – only tiny vestiges remain today – and grew with considerable grace. In many ways it's a singularly unfortunate place to site a modern city. Pestilent from the earliest days, the inadequately drained waters harboured fevers, and the native population was constantly swept by epidemics of European diseases. Many of the buildings, too, simply began to sink into the soft lake bed, a process probably accelerated by regular earthquakes.

By the third quarter of the nineteenth century, the city comprised little more than the area around the Zócalo and Alameda. Chapultepec Castle, Coyoacán, San Ángel and the Basilica of Guadalupe – areas now well within city limits – were then surrounded by fields and the last of the basin's former lakes. Nonetheless, the city was beginning to take its present shape: the Paseo de la Reforma already linked Chapultepec with the city, and the colonial core could no longer accommodate the increasing population. From late 1870 through to 1911 the dictator Porfirio Díaz presided over an unprecedented, and self-aggrandizing, **building**

México, Mexico City and El DF

For clarity, we've referred to Mexico's capital as **Mexico City** throughout this guide, though Mexicans frequently refer to it simply as **México**, in the same way that Americans often refer to New York City as New York. It's a source of infinite confusion to visitors, but the country took its name from the city, so "México" can mean either, and in conversation it most often means the latter. To avoid misunderstandings, the nation may be referred to as La República Mexicana, or occasionally in speeches La Patria, while Mexico City may be referred to as **El DF** ("El Day Effay"), short for "Distrito Federal", the administrative zone that coincides with the city boundaries and contains most of the urban areas. The title **Ciudad de México** is used much less commonly, usually in an official context.

programme that saw the installation of trams, the expansion of public transport and the draining of some of the last sections of the Lago de Texcoco, which had previously hemmed in the city. Jointly these fuelled further growth, and by the outbreak of the Revolution in 1910, Mexico City's residents numbered over 400,000, regaining for the first time in four centuries the population level it had held before the Conquest.

The modern city

As many as two million Mexicans died during the Revolution and many more lost their property, their livelihood or both. In desperation, thousands fled to rapidly industrializing Mexico City in search of jobs and a better life. Between 1910 and the mid-1940s the city's population quadrupled and the cracks in the infrastructure quickly became gaping holes. Houses couldn't be built quickly enough to cope with the seven-percent annual growth, and many people couldn't afford them anyway, so **shantytowns** of scraps of metal and cardboard sprang up. Most neighbourhoods had little or no water supply and sanitation was an afterthought. Gradually, civic leaders tried to address the lot of its citizens by improving the services and housing in shantytowns, but even as they worked a new ring of slums mushroomed just a little further out. As the city expanded, transport became impossible and the city embarked on building the **Metro** system in the late 1960s. The 175th and most recent Metro station was completed in 2000; a twelfth Metro line is expected to open in 2010.

Urban growth continues today: some statisticians estimate that there are a thousand new arrivals each day, mainly from rural areas with high unemployment, and the city now extends beyond the limits of the Distrito Federal and out into the surrounding state of México. Despite the spread, Mexico City remains one of the world's most densely and heavily populated cities, with an unenviable list of major social and physical problems, including an extreme vulnerability to earthquakes – the last big one, in 1985, killed over 9000 people, made 100,000 homeless and left many of the city's buildings decidedly skewed.

Orientation

The traditional centre of the city is the **Zócalo**, or Plaza Mayor, officially called Plaza de la Constitución. The heart of both ancient Tenochtitlán and of Cortés's city, it's surrounded by the oldest streets, largely colonial and unmodernized. To the east, the ancient structures degenerate rapidly, blending into the poorer areas that surround the airport. Westwards, avenidas **Madero** and **Juárez** lead to the

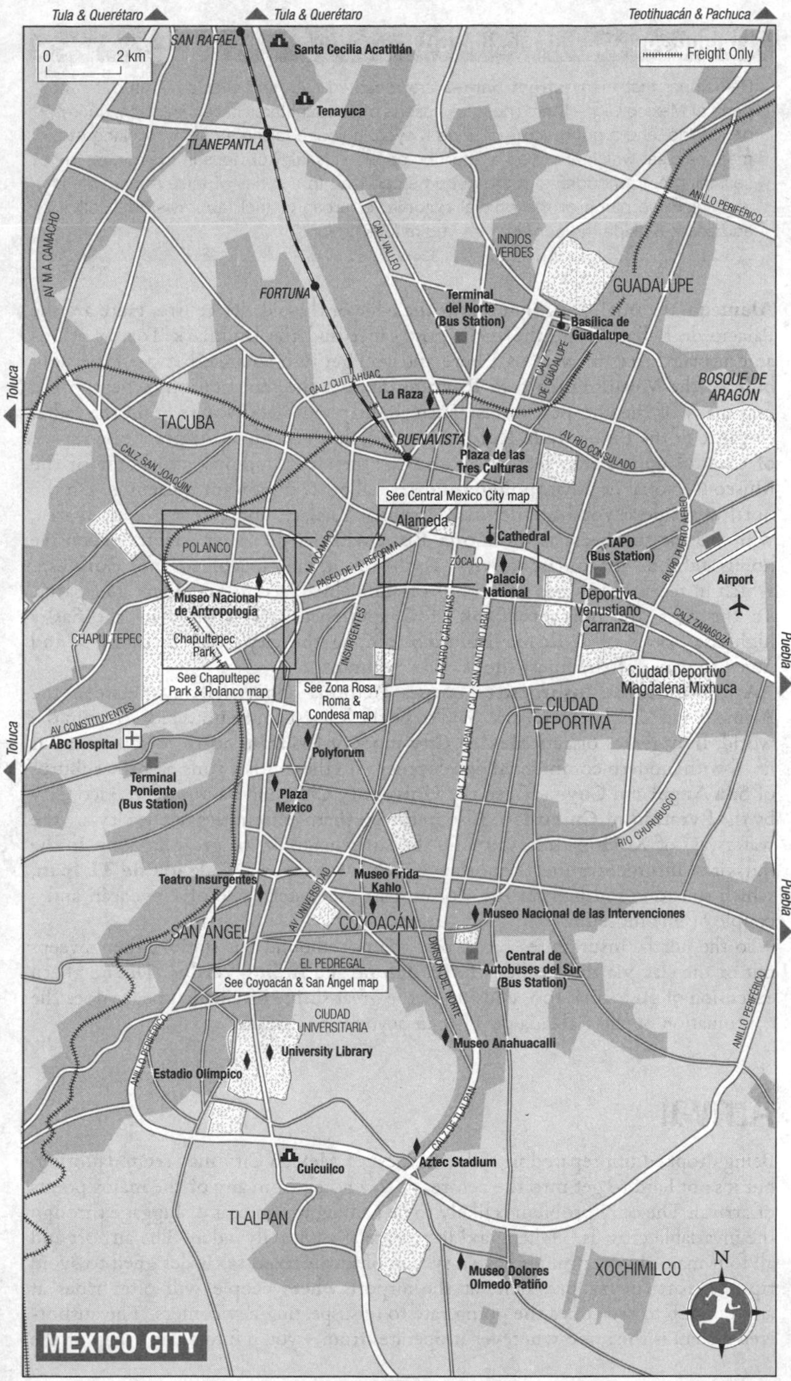

Tula & Querétaro
Tula & Querétaro
Teotihuacán & Pachuca
0 2 km
Freight Only
SAN RAFAEL
Santa Cecilia Acatitlán
Tenayuca
TLANEPANTLA
ANILLO PERIFÉRICO
AV M A CAMACHO
CALZ VALLEO
INDIOS VERDES
GUADALUPE
FORTUNA
Terminal del Norte (Bus Station)
Basílica de Guadalupe
CALZ DE GUADALUPE
BOSQUE DE ARAGÓN
Toluca
CALZ CUITLAHUAC
La Raza
TACUBA
BUENAVISTA
AV RIO CONSULADO
Plaza de las Tres Culturas
CALZ SAN JOAQUÍN
See Central Mexico City map
Alameda
Cathedral
POLANCO
M OCAMPO
ZÓCALO
TAPO (Bus Station)
BLVD PUERTO AEREO
PASEO DE LA REFORMA
Palacio National
Airport
Museo Nacional de Antropología
Deportiva Venustiano Carranza
CHAPULTEPEC
Chapultepec Park
INSURGENTES
LÁZARO CÁRDENAS
CALZ SAN ANTONIO ABAD
CALZ ZARAGOZA
Puebla
See Chapultepec Park & Polanco map
See Zona Rosa, Roma & Condesa map
Ciudad Deportivo Magdalena Mixhuca
CIUDAD DEPORTIVA
AV CONSTITUYENTES
Toluca
ABC Hospital
Polyforum
CALZ DE TLALPAN
Terminal Poniente (Bus Station)
Plaza Mexico
RIO CHURUBUSCO
Teatro Insurgentes
Museo Frida Kahlo
Puebla
AV UNIVERSIDAD
Museo Nacional de las Intervenciones
SAN ÁNGEL
COYOACÁN
DIVISION DEL NORTE
EL PEDREGAL
Central de Autobuses del Sur (Bus Station)
See Coyoacán & San Ángel map
ANILLO PERIFÉRICO
CIUDAD UNIVERSITARIA
ANILLO PERIFÉRICO
Museo Anahuacalli
University Library
Estadio Olímpico
CALZ DE TLALPAN
Aztec Stadium
Cuicuilco
TLALPAN
Museo Dolores Olmedo Patiño
XOCHIMILCO
N
MEXICO CITY
Cuernavaca

Finding your way in Mexico City

Remember that many **street names** are repeated over and over again in different parts of Mexico City – there must be dozens of thoroughfares called Morelos, Juárez or Hidalgo, and a good score of 5 de Mayos. If you're taking a cab, or looking at a map, be clear which area you are talking about – it's fairly obvious in the centre, but searching out an address in the suburbs can lead to a series of false starts unless you know the name of the official **colonia**, or urban district (abbreviated "Col" in addresses outside the centre), that you're looking for.

Alameda, the small park that marks the edge of the old city centre. Here are the Palacio de Bellas Artes, the main post office and the landmark Torre Latinoamericana. Carry on west past here and you get into an area, between the ugly bulk of the **Monumento a la Revolución** and the train station, where you'll find many of the cheaper hotels. Turn slightly south and you're amid the faded elegance of the **Paseo de la Reforma**, which leads down to the great open space of **Chapultepec Park**, recreation area for the city's millions, and home of the Museo Nacional de Antropología and several other important museums. On the northwest side as you head down Reforma is a sedate, upmarket residential area, while to the southeast is the **Zona Rosa** with its shopping streets, expensive hotels and constant tourist activity. To the south, the Zona bleeds into **Condesa**, which in recent years has become *the* fashionable place to eat, drink and party. To the west, the northern flank of Chapultepec Park is lined by the flashy high-rise hotels of **Colonia Polanco**, among the city's chicest districts and home to many of the finest shops and restaurants.

Avenida de los Insurgentes crosses Reforma about halfway between the Alameda and Chapultepec Park. Said to be the longest continuous city street in the world, Insurgentes bisects Mexico City more or less from north to south, and is lined with modern commercial development. In the south it runs past the suburbs of **San Ángel** and **Coyoacán** to the **University City**, and on out of Mexico City by the **Pyramid of Cuicuilco**. Also in the southern extremities of the city are the waterways of **Xochimilco**, virtually the last remains of the great lagoons. In the outskirts, Insurgentes meets another important route, the **Calzada de Tlalpan**, which runs due south from the Zócalo past the eastern side of Coyoacán and a couple of fine museums.

To the north, Insurgentes heads past the northbound bus station, then sweeps out of the city via the basilica of **Guadalupe** and **Indios Verdes**. The northern extension of Reforma, too, ends up at the great shrine of Guadalupe, as does the continuation of the Calzada de Tlalpan beyond the Zócalo.

Arrival

Being dropped unprepared into the vastness of Mexico City may seem daunting, but it's not hard to get into the centre, or to a hotel, from any of the major points of arrival. The only problem is likely to be hauling large items of luggage through the invariable crowds – take a taxi if you are at all heavily laden. The airport and all four major bus terminals have a system of **authorized taxis** designed to avoid rip-offs, particularly prevalent at the airport where people will offer rides at anything up to ten times the going rate to unsuspecting newcomers. The authorized system is the same wherever it operates from – you'll find a large map of the city marked out in zones, with a standard, set fare for each; you pick where you're going, buy a ticket at the booth, then walk outside and present the ticket to one of the waiting cabs. One ticket is good for up to four people to one destination. The driver may drop you a block or two from your hotel rather than take a major detour through the one-way systems (best to accept this unless it's very late at night), and he may demand a large tip, which you're in no way obliged to pay. Most hotels are used to **late arrivals**, so don't be overly concerned if your flight gets in late at night, though it is wise to have somewhere booked in advance for your first night.

By plane

Mexico City's **airport** is surprisingly central, just 6km east of the Zócalo (the views as you come in to land, low over the buildings, are amazing). There are two terminals; most airlines use Terminal 1, which is rather more convenient than the new Terminal 2.

Wherever you come in, you'll find several **ATMs** and numerous **casas de cambio**, open 24 hours and with reasonable rates for US dollars (rates vary, so shop around), though not always such good rates for travellers' cheques or other currencies (they'll usually take Canadian dollars, pounds sterling, euros, Swiss francs and Japanese yen, but nothing else). There are also plenty of pricey restaurants and snack bars, **car rental** agencies (see p.458), a post office, internet offices and 24-hour **left luggage** lockers. There are several airport enquiry desks dotted around, and **tourist information kiosks** in Terminal 1, Sala A (7am–10pm; ⓣ55/5786-9002), and Terminal 2 near exit gate 2 (open 24/7; ⓣ55/2598-3532), which are helpful but have a limited range of information, and only cover Mexico City.

The easiest and safest way to get into town is by pre-paid **authorized taxi**, and there are desks for these in both terminals. Prices vary slightly from firm to firm (Sitio 300 tend to be cheapest, but check the others for comparison); current rates are M$127 to the Zócalo and Alameda, M$162 to the Zona Rosa and M$172 to Polanco. You will probably be accosted by other taxi drivers offering cabs into town, but use only pre-paid authorized cabs, as tourists have been robbed by unauthorized taxi drivers on occasion.

It is also possible to get into town more cheaply by bus or Metro. From Terminal 1 you can use the **Metro** (out of the doors at the end of Sala A, then follow the covered walkway for 200m), but note that large bags are banned (see p.387); otherwise, continue past the Metro station out to Bulevar de Puerto Aéreo and catch a city-bound **bus**. From Terminal 2, the Metro is a very long walk away, but if you head out of the terminal to the main road, you can pick up a bus which will take you to the nearest Metro station (Hangares), or on into town (usually terminating at Metro Garibaldi).

If you don't fancy heading straight into the city so soon after arrival, you can get a **direct transfer to nearby cities**. There are bus stops upstairs from Sala E1 in Terminal 1 and at exit gate 4 in Terminal 2, where you can pick up first-class buses to Cuernavaca, Pachuca, Puebla, Toluca and Querétaro. There are also luxury car and van services, but they're almost ten times the price of the buses. Alternatively, there are hotels nearby (see p.394).

To get from one terminal to the other, there's a monorail service called Aerotrén (upstairs from Sala D in Terminal 1, upstairs in Sala M in Terminal 2), but only passengers with boarding passes are allowed to use this. Otherwise there are red buses (4am–1am; M$10) from exit gate 6 (Sala D) in Terminal 1 and exit gate 4 in Terminal 2.

By bus

Arriving in Mexico City by bus, you will probably find yourself in one of the city's four long-distance **bus stations** (details of which services use which bus station can be found on p.455). All have **Metro stations** pretty much right outside, as well as authorized taxis (see p.389). They also have guarderías (left luggage offices, though TAPO's is very expensive), post and telephone offices and a tourist information kiosk.

From anywhere north of Mexico City, you will probably arrive at the **Terminal del Norte** on Avenida de los Cien Metros. There's a **Metro** station right outside the entrance (Metro Autobuses del Norte; line 5), and trolleybuses just outside, which head down the Eje Central (Lázaro Cárdenas) to Bellas Artes and on to the Central de Autobuses del Sur. Alternatively, if you head four blocks east, you come to Insurgentes, where you can catch the **Metrobús** (see p.389) south, across Reforma and on to the edge of the Zona Rosa. If you want to get a **taxi**, go to the kiosk selling tickets for authorized taxis (about M$85 to the Zócalo and Alameda, M$70 to the Zona Rosa and M$80 to Polanco, all plus M$20 surcharge 10.30pm–6.30am). If you arrive late at night and don't want to search for a hotel in town, there are places nearby (see p.394).

Buses from points east, including a number of places that you may think of as south (such as Chiapas or the Yucatán), will probably drop you at the **Terminal de Autobuses de Pasajeros de Oriente**, known as **TAPO**, which is located on Avenida Ignacio Zaragoza. It has a **Metro** station (Metro San Lazaro; lines 1 and B) just down a connecting tunnel, which also leads you to the stops for city buses and *colectivos* plying Zaragoza towards the Zócalo and the Alameda. In the same tunnel, opposite the Metro entrance, is a sales desk for the authorized **taxis**, which cost M$60 to the Zócalo and Alameda, M$70 to the Zona Rosa and M$80 to Polanco (all plus M$20 10.30pm–6.30am).

Buses from the Pacific coast generally arrive at the **Central de Autobuses del Sur** (Tasqueña or Taxqeña) on Avenida Tasqueña, outside which is a big terminus for local buses and *peseros* (see p.389) to the centre and points south of town, and a **Metro** station (Metro Tasqueña; line 2). To find the Metro, head right as you leave the terminal, and you'll see the sign. Alternatively, to your left, on Avenida Tasqueña, trolleybuses head up the Eje Central (Lázaro Cárdenas) to Bellas Artes, and on to the Terminal del Norte. Authorized **taxis** cost M$95 (M$115 between 9pm and 6am) to the Zócalo, Alameda or Zona Rosa, and M$125 (M$145) to Polanco.

Finally, from some places to the west of Mexico City (mainly for services passing through Toluca), there's the **Terminal Poniente** (Observatorio), at the junction of calles Sur and Tacubaya. To get the **Metro** (Metro Observatorio; line 1), leave from the exit in the middle of the terminal, where it makes a bend (next to the authorized taxi kiosk), and the entrance is straight ahead, hidden behind the market stalls. Authorized **taxis** cost M$70 to Polanco, M$80 to the Zona Rosa and M$98 to the Alameda and Zócalo; from 9pm to 6am you pay M$20 more.

If you are coming into Mexico City on a local service from somewhere nearby, it is also possible that you may be dropped off at the end of one of the Metro lines such as Indios Verdes (line 3) or El Rosario (lines 6 and 7). Obviously, the best way into town from there is by Metro.

City transport

For all its size and frantic pace, once you're used to the city, it is surprisingly easy to get around, with an efficient and very cheap public transport system as well as reasonably priced taxis (see p.389 & p.390).

You'll want to **walk** around the cramped streets of the centre, but remember the altitude – walking gets tiring quickly, especially for the first day or so. If you're heading for Chapultepec or the Zona Rosa, you're better off taking the **bus** or **Metro** – it's an interesting walk all the way down Reforma, but a very long one. As for the outer suburbs, you've got no choice but to rely on public transport. You'll save a lot of hassle if you avoid travelling during **rush hour** (about 7–9am & 6–8pm).

City tours

Tours that take in the city and often include the surrounding area are available from most of the more expensive hotels, and from operators such as American Express (see p.458). The government of the DF runs a one-hour city-centre sightseeing tour on buses in the style of old trams leaving from Juárez by Bellas Artes (daily 10am–6.30pm; M$35), but the commentary is in Spanish only. One of the best city tours is with Turibus (Ⓣ55/5141-1360 ext 2000, Ⓦwww.turibus.com.mx), who run open-top double-deckers on two routes: a northern route taking in the city centre, and a southern route that heads down Insurgentes Sur to Coyoacán and the University. You can get on and off the bus at any stage en route; stops for the northern route include the Zócalo (República de Brasil, on the west side of the cathedral), the Benito Juárez Monument on the south side of the Alameda, and El Ángel on Reforma; at Las Cibeles (Plaza Madrid) in Roma, you can change from the northern to the southern route. Both run every 30–40 minutes, 9am–9pm daily and tickets cost M$125 weekdays, M$145 weekends (M$180/210 for a two-day ticket). Each circuit takes around three hours, and the commentary comes in a choice of languages including English. There's also a night route Thursdays and Fridays 9pm–1am (M$145), run by a single bus doing two circuits only, each taking around two hours.

The Metro and Tren Ligero

Mexico City's superb modern **Metro** system (Ⓣ55/5709-1133 ext 5051 or 5009, Ⓦwww.metro.df.gob.mx) is French-built, fast and quiet. It is crowded (though no more so than its New York or London counterparts) and at peak hours stations designate separate entries for women and children (look for the "Mujeres" signs). **Tickets** (M$2) are sold individually and there is no discount for bulk purchases, though to save time queuing and messing about with tiny quantities of change it makes sense to buy several at a time. In theory you're not allowed **luggage** of any size on the Metro (the official limit is 80cm x 50cm x 30cm), but in practice you can get away with carrying a big bag if you board at a quiet station at a calm time, and these days even a backpack seems to be tolerated at busy times. The first train leaves from each end of the line at 6am Monday to Saturday and 7am on Sunday, with the last train at half-past midnight (and an hour later on Saturday nights).

In general, there are **no maps** of the entire Metro system on platforms, and certainly not on the trains – you'll just find pictographic representations of the line you are on, along with the stations where you can transfer to other lines. The map on p.388 details the system; otherwise you'll need to work out before you set off which way you'll be travelling on each line, and where to change. Direction is indicated by the last station at either end of the line (thus on line 2 you'll want

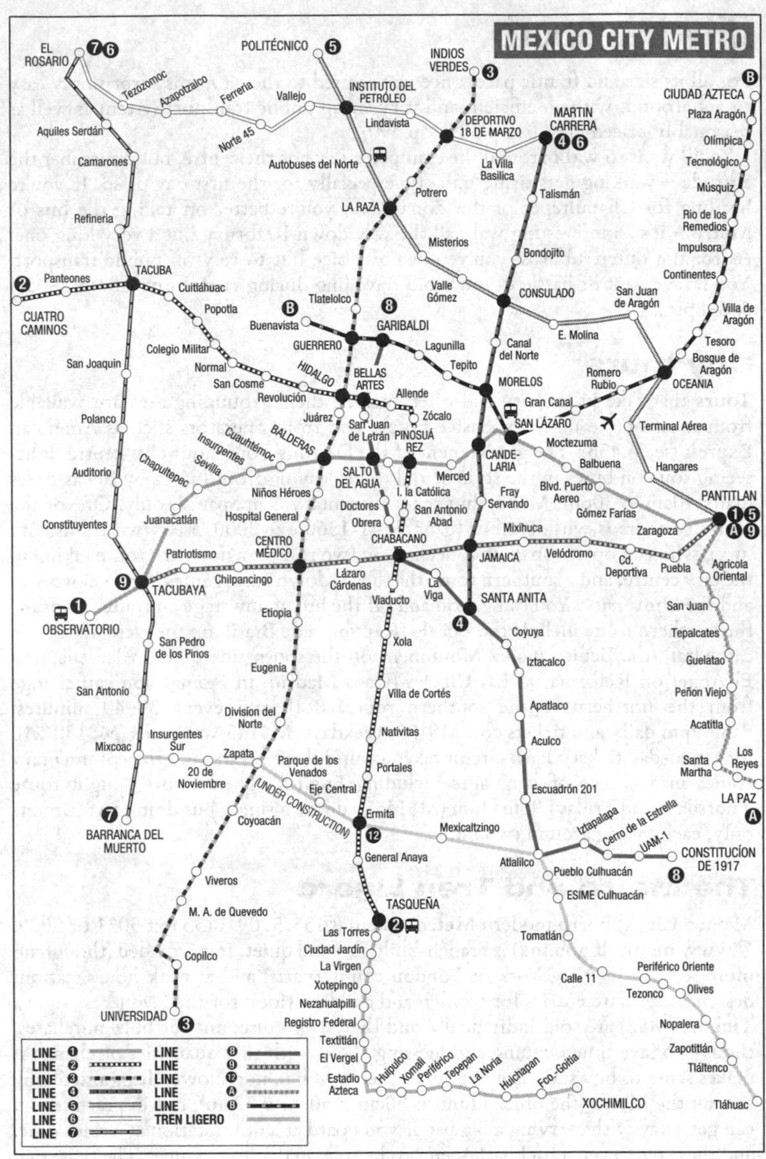

either "Dirección Cuatro Caminos" or "Dirección Tasqueña"); interchanges are indicated by the word "Correspondencia" and the name of the new line.

In addition, there's a **Tren Ligero** (light rail), which runs south from Tasqueña (the southern terminus of line 2) as far as Xochimilco, entirely above ground. It requires a different ticket from the Metro system – when you change at Tasqueña you'll need to buy a Tren Ligero ticket (good for any one-way journey) from the ticket window or the machines on the concourse (M$2).

City buses

Buses in Mexico City are very efficient, if you know where you're going. **Fares** are M$2.50–5, depending on the route and the length of your journey. Buses display their destinations in the front window, which is somewhat more helpful than looking for route numbers, since the latter are not posted up and rarely used, and some buses terminate before the end of the route. One of the most useful routes is along Reforma, and the area just by Chapultepec Metro station at the entrance to the park is also a major bus terminus, from where you can get to almost any part of the city. Note that during **rush hour** it can be almost impossible to get a bus: once they're full, they simply don't stop to let passengers on. On two routes (along Reforma and the Eje Central), the city government in 2008 introduced buses for women only, mostly to tackle the problem of groping on public transport.

There are also **trolleybuses** running in both directions along Lázaro Cárdenas (the "Eje Central", or Central Axis) between Terminal del Norte and Central del Sur (Tasqueña), as well as on some other major routes. Trolleybuses charge a flat fare of M$4.

On Insurgentes, there is a service called **Metrobús** (ⓦwww.metrobus.df.gob.mx), an articulated bus with its own dedicated lane, and fancy bus stops that look more like stations. The Metrobús runs all the way from Indio Verdes in the north to El Caminero in the south, with a less useful east–west line (line 2), with an interchange between the two lines at Nuevo León, south of Chilpancingo. There's a flat fare of M$5, but in order to use the metrobus, you have to buy a card (M$10) from a machine at one of the stations, which you charge up with rides at the same machines. The machines like rejecting coins (keep trying), and there's usually a queue for them, so charge up where you can, but don't add too much as credit has been known to vanish mysteriously from the cards. To buy and charge your card, you must have the exact change. Though it's massively inconvenient if you just want to take the odd journey, there's no other way to pay the fare.

Peseros (colectivos)

Running down the major through routes, especially on Reforma and Insurgentes, you'll find **peseros** (**colectivos**), which are smaller and faster but charge more than the bus (far less than a regular taxi, however) and will let you on and off anywhere along their set route. They're mostly thirty-seater buses or VW vans, usually green with a white roof, and with their destination displayed on the windscreen – drivers of the smaller vehicles may sometimes hold up a number of fingers to indicate how many free seats they have. Like buses, *peseros* have route numbers, but routes often have branches, and a vehicle may start or finish in the middle of a route rather than at the end, so again it's more helpful to check the destination in the window. One of the most **useful routes** runs from Chapultepec Park via Avenida Chapultepec to the Zócalo.

Taxis

Ordinary **taxis** (usually red and gold) come in a variety of forms (some are still VW beetles, though these are gradually disappearing) and have a reputation for robbery at the hands of the drivers (see p.380). You should think twice before taking one, especially if you are on your own, but if you decide to, it's best to take one from a **taxi rank** (*sitio*) rather than hail one in the street. From the airport or bus terminals, always use a **pre-paid authorized taxi**, and never go with a driver who accosts you on arrival with the offer of a cab. Legitimate taxis other than authorized pre-paid ones should have a meter – make sure it's switched on.

Red-and-white radio taxis, which you have to call by phone, charge slightly more, but in general work the same way. Watch out, though, for *turismo* taxis, which lie in wait outside hotels for unsuspecting tourists and charge rates at least triple those of ordinary taxis. In the normal course of events you should avoid them, but they do have a couple of advantages, namely that they're almost always around and that many of the drivers speak some English. They can be worth it if, for example, you need to get to the airport in a hurry (for which they charge no more than an authorized airport cab would) or if you want to go on a tour for a few hours. In the latter case, with some ferocious haggling, you might even get a bargain. If you need to **phone a taxi**, try Servitaxis (ⓣ55/5272-1123) or Taxi-Mex (ⓣ55/5634-9912) or, to the airport, Sitio 300 (ⓣ55/5571-9344), ProTaxi (ⓣ55/2559-0333) or Porto Taxi (ⓣ55/5786-8993). It can be difficult to get a taxi in the rush hour.

Driving

Rental cars (see p.458 for agents' details) are available from the airport and elsewhere, but it is generally better to wait until you are ready to leave the city before renting. There are thousands of agencies throughout the city, and the small local operations are often cheaper than the big chains. Either way, renting a car isn't going to be cheap, and a car can be a liability while you're in the city. Expect to pay M$400–650 a day for the cheapest car with tax, insurance and unlimited mileage, more in July and August; the usual deal for a week is that you pay for six days and get the seventh free. The major operators have offices at the airport and in the Zona Rosa, and some of the smaller companies do too.

If you already have a car, choose a hotel with secure parking and leave it there for the duration of your stay, except possibly to do a tour of the south of the city. Driving in the city is a nightmare, compounded by confusing one-way and through-route systems and by the impossibility of finding anywhere to park. Also note that the "Green Angels" who operate on highways (see p.39) do not operate within Mexico City.

Cycling

If you're brave enough to negotiate Mexico City's streets by **bicycle**, you can borrow one for three hours for free between 10.15am and 6pm Tuesdays to Sundays at one of nine stands across the city centre, of which the most central is just off the Zócalo by the Turibús stop just west of the cathedral (others include El Ángel on Reforma and Las Cibeles in Roma). You must leave your passport as security, and you have to bring the bicycle back to the same stand from which you took it.

A group of local cycling activists called Bicitekas (ⓦwww.bicitekas.org) meets at 9pm on Wednesday evenings at El Ángel on Reforma for a night-time scoot around town.

Information

There are **tourist information** booths run by the government of the DF at the airport (see p.385) and at all four bus terminals. Similar kiosks are dotted around town. None have much printed material to take away, but the staff are usually very helpful and well versed in the ways of the city. The most central is in the **Zócalo** between the cathedral and Monte de Piedad (daily 9am–6pm; ⓣ55/5518-1003;

Metro Zócalo), and there's also one on the other side of the cathedral by the Sagrario. The **SECTUR** (Mexican government) tourist office at Presidente Mazaryk 172, Polanco (Mon–Fri 8am–6pm, Sat 10am–3pm; call 24/7 on ⓣ55/3002-6300 or 078; Metro Polanco), is flush with handouts about Mexico City and the country as a whole – but inconveniently sited a long way from where you are likely to spend your time. The government of the DF also runs a tourist information **website** (ⓦwww.mexicocity.gob.mx), in Spanish and English, with excellent background information, advice, tips and patchy listings, and you can call them toll-free on ⓣ01-800/008-9090.

Useful local **guidebooks**, city **maps** (the best produced by Guia Roji), English-language magazines and pulp paperbacks are sold at Sanborns, street newsstands, the airport and many big hotels.

Accommodation

Accommodation in Mexico City ranges from budget **hostels** to some of the swankiest **hotels** in the country, but the best-value places can fill up quickly, so **booking ahead** is always a good idea.

Most places have 24-hour reception desks and are geared for late arrivals and early departures, and with reasonably cheap taxi fares into the Zócalo or Zona Rosa it seldom makes financial sense to stay near the bus stations or airport. However, if you arrive especially late or are just in transit and need a place to rest up for a while, there are places to stay that are very handy for the **airport** and **Terminal del Norte**.

Unless otherwise noted – and except for the options around the airport and bus station – the establishments below are marked on the "Central Mexico City" map (see pp.396–397).

Hostels

Casa de los Amigos Ignacio Mariscal 132 ⓣ55/5705-0521, ⓦwww.casadelos amigos.org. Metro Revolución. The community-oriented Quaker-run *Casa*, on a quiet street in the house where José Clemente Orozco spent the last decade of his life, pitches itself as a guesthouse, though it still has eight- and four-bed dorms (M$100) as well as a few singles and doubles. Clean and comfortable with a good kitchen (breakfast available), a meditation room/library and occasional film screenings, it is popular with long-stay guests (minimum two-night stay). No alcohol and no smoking. ❸

Hostal Amigo Isabel la Católica 61 ⓣ01-800/746-7835 or 55/5512-3496, ⓦwww.amigohostelgroup.com. Metro Isabel la Católica. Backpackers' hangout with four- to twelve-bed dorms (M$190–220), some without with outside windows, but there are lockers (bring your own padlock), several private rooms, free internet, a luggage deposit, a bar, a kitchen and communal areas. Breakfast included – and dinner too after your first night. ❸

Hostal Moneda Moneda 8 ⓣ01-800/221-7265 or 55/5522-5803, ⓦwww.amigohostelgroup.com. Metro Zócalo. Convivial hostel with eight-bed dorms (M$175), a couple of lounges (one with TV), a decent kitchen and a panoramic rooftop terrace where a buffet breakfast (included) is served. Private rooms are also available, but pricey (M$500). Make a reservation if you are to arrive after 11pm.

Hostel Catedral Guatemala 4 ⓣ55/5518-1726, ⓦwww.hostelcatedral.com. Metro Zócalo. Large, secure and efficiently run modern place behind the cathedral. Open 24hr, it has spotless four- or six-bunk rooms, most with private bathroom (from M$169; HI members and ISIC card-holders M$130; buffet breakfast included) and some private rooms. There's an on-site travel agency, internet access, a café and bar and a rooftop terrace with fabulous views. The only drawbacks are the small kitchen, limited communal areas and noise: bring earplugs and a lock for the lockers. ❸

Hostel Home Tabasco 303, Roma ⓣ55/5511-1683, ⓦwww.hostelhome.com.mx

(see map, p.415). Metro Sevilla. This small twenty-bunk hostel (called "Home" because it was originally a family house) has seen better days and is a little distant from the main sights, but has, as it advertises, a "chilled atmosphere", a kitchen and free internet, and is open 24hr. As well as the six- and eight-bunk dorms (M$170) there's a sunny lounge and a small kitchen.

Mexico City Hostel República de Brasil 8 ⓣ55/5512-7731, ⓔreservaciones@mexicocityhostel.com. Metro Zócalo. Great location and decent enough eight- or twelve-bed dorms (M$140–150), as well as wi-fi and free internet access, but the small, dark private rooms are overpriced, and you may have to go up or down a floor to find a bathroom. ❸

Hotels

Around the Zócalo

Azores Brasil 25 ⓣ55/5521-5220, ⓦwww.hotelazores.com. Metro Allende or Zócalo. Well-situated modern hotel with small but clean and comfy rooms around a central well, each with TV and bath. ❸

Catedral Donceles 95 ⓣ55/5518-5232, ⓦwww.hotelcatedral.com. Metro Zócalo. Very presentable mid-range place. All rooms have TV, FM stereo and telephone, and some have a jacuzzi. Internet access is available, and there's a good restaurant and a terrace overlooking the cathedral. Offers a ten percent discount for cash payment (pesos, dollars or euros). ❹

Gillow Isabel la Católica 17 ⓣ55/5518-1441 to 6, ⓔhgillow@prodigy.net.mx. Metro Allende. Friendly and good-value mid-priced hotel with carpeted rooms, in-house travel agency and leather sofas in the public areas. Cable TV and the expected amenities in rooms (it's worth paying a little extra for a larger room with a small patio or seating area). Ten percent discount for cash payment. ❺

Gran Hotel Ciudad de México 16 de Septiembre 82 ⓣ1-800/088-7700 or 55/1083-7700, ⓦwww.granhotelciudaddemexico.com.mx. Metro Zócalo. Large hotel right on the Zócalo with sumptuous public areas (see p.402), though some of the older rooms don't match the glamorous lobby. The remodelled suites are nice, but cost M$3190. Prices include breakfast. ❽

Isabel Isabel la Católica 63 ⓣ55/5518-1213 to 7, ⓦwww.hotel-isabel.com.mx. Metro Isabel la Católica. Good-value hotel offering services such as taxis and laundry, plus a restaurant and bar. Rooms (with or without bath, the latter on the roof), though a little bit sombre, are quite spacious with TV and safe. Rooms at the back are quieter. It's worth booking a few days ahead. ❷

Juárez Callejón de 5 de Mayo 17 1° ⓣ55/5512-6929, ⓔhoteljuarez@prodigy.net.mx. Metro Allende or Zócalo. Very central, clean and good-value budget tourist hotel, but not recommended for lone women travellers. Avoid room no. 4, which is next to the hotel's main water pump. ❷

Majestic Madero 73 ⓣ01-800/528-1234 or 55/5521-8600, ⓦwww.majestic.com.mx. Metro Zócalo. Luxury Best Western hotel on the Zócalo with bags of character, is considerably cheaper than many of the places in the Zona Rosa and has many of the same facilities. Zócalo views from some rooms. ❾

Montecarlo Uruguay 69 ⓣ55/5518-1418, ⓕ5510-0081. Metro Zócalo. Good-value cheapie with a touch of faded glory, once briefly inhabited by D.H. Lawrence. Quiet and comfortable with a garage and a beautiful inner courtyard that is a little out of keeping with the rather small and dark en-suite rooms. ❷

República Cuba 57 ⓣ55/5512-9517. Old and fairly grotty but also very cheap hotel (especially for two people sharing a double bed) on a quiet street. All rooms have a bathroom; some have TV. ❶

San Antonio Callejón de 5 de Mayo 29 2° ⓣ55/5512-1625 or 6, ⓕ5512-9906. Metro Allende or Zócalo. Quiet, friendly place hidden away in a side street between 5 de Mayo and La Palma. Standards are high considering the price, with light, airy, spotless rooms, good firm beds, decent sheets and free bottled water. It's worth paying the M$20 difference for a room with a private bathroom. ❷

Washington 5 de Mayo 54 ⓣ&ⓕ55/5512-3502. Metro Allende or Zócalo. Good-value hotel very near the Zócalo, with clean, pleasant rooms all with nicely tiled bathroom, cable TV, phone, wi-fi throughout, and free water. ❸

Zamora 5 de Mayo 50 ⓣ55/5512-8245. Metro Allende or Zócalo. One of the more basic downtown hotels. The low prices make the noise, threadbare towels and marginal cleanliness acceptable. Very popular so you may have to book ahead at busy times (though they say, "Pay no attention to cabbies; we always have rooms."). Rooms come with or without bath. ❷

Around the Alameda

Fleming Revillagigedo 35 ⓣ55/5510-4530 or 35, ⓦwww.hotelfleming.com.mx. Metro Juárez. Modern business-style hotel with little imagination to the decor but good facilities – comfortable, carpeted rooms, cable TV, etc – at moderate prices. ❹

Hotel de Cortés Hidalgo 85 ⓣ55/5518-2181, ⓦwww.boutiquehoteldecortes.com. Metro Hidalgo. Very classy boutique hotel in a building dating from 1620, but with rooms that are super-modern and stylish, with wooden deck floors throughout (even in the shower). The hotel also has a spa and fitness centre, a Spanish–Mexican restaurant, two bars and free wi-fi. The price includes breakfast. ❾

Managua Plaza de San Fernando 11 ⓣ55/5512-1312, ⓕ5521-3062. Metro Hidalgo. Good-value, clean and quiet place with a cafeteria that does room service, and rooms with TV, bathroom and free bottled water, all in a restful location facing the Jardín de San Fernando. ❷

Pánuco Ayuntamiento 148 ⓣ55/5521-2916. Metro Juárez. Clean and good-value. Carpeted rooms each have a writing desk and TV – and a lot of fake marble – located in a drab part of town a little distance from the most popular tourist areas, though tolerably close to the Zona Rosa. Parking and a restaurant on site. Tends to be full Fri and Sat. ❷

Around the Revolution Monument

Casa Blanca Lafragua 7 ⓣ55/5096-4500 or 01-800/200-2252, in the US ⓣ1-800/905-2905, ⓦwww.hotel-casablanca.com.mx. Metro Revolución. Attractive but rather impersonal modern high-rise hotel with perfectly decent rooms at prices a good deal lower than a lot of the Zona Rosa places. There's even a rooftop pool, a gym, business facilities and a restaurant. Wheelchair-friendly with an adapted room. Breakfast included. ❽

Mayaland Antonio Caso 23 ⓣ55/5566-6066, ⓔhotelmayaland@hotmail.com. Metro Revolución. Squat and ugly from outside but tastefully decorated within. Good-value rooms all come with cable TV and purified water, though you might want to spend M$90 extra for a more spacious double (with the standard two double beds) or for twin beds and a jacuzzi. ❹

Royalty Jesús Terán 21 ⓣ55/5566-9255. Metro Revolución. Well worn but decent and clean, with very reasonable rates for rooms (some rather dark) with bathrooms, TV and phone. ❶

The Zona Rosa, Roma and Condesa

The hotels listed below are marked on the "Zona Rosa, Roma and Condesa", map (see p.415).

La Casona Durango 280, at Cozumel ⓣ55/5286-3001, ⓦwww.hotellacasona.com.mx. Metro Sevilla. In an early twentieth-century building at the northern end of Condesa, *La Casona* has an understated, if slightly quirky, European-style elegance, with polished wooden floors, antique furniture, a piano in its lounge and quite a collection of art – including masks, original cartoons and paintings. The rooms (which start at M$2293) are all different, with an aesthete's attention to detail. Good on-site restaurant. ❾

Geneve Londres 130 ⓣ55/5080-0800 or 01-800/900-0000, ⓦwww.hotelgeneve.com.mx. Metro Insurgentes. A large, century-old, but thoroughly modern hotel right in the heart of the Zona Rosa with an understated, elegant feel. Rooms are comfortable if unspectacular, with cable TV and mini-bars, but the facilities are excellent, and include the lovely Salon Jardín with its stained-glass and iron roof, a restaurant, gym, spa and on-site *Sanborns* restaurant. ❼

Hotel Del Principado Londres 42 ⓣ55/5207-4606 or 1-800/830-6040, ⓦwww.hoteldelprincipado.com.mx. Metro Insurgentes. The double rooms (with two double beds) are rather more spacious and get rather more light than the ordinary rooms (in which it's worth asking for a king-size bed, as these cost no extra), but they all have a TV and phone, and there's free wi-fi, parking facilities and a laundry service. Rates include a buffet breakfast. ❺

Maria Cristina Rio Lerma 31, Cuauhtémoc ⓣ55/5703-1212, ⓦwww.hotelmariacristina.com.mx. Metro Insurgentes. A lovely colonial-styled little hotel near the Museo Venustiano Carranza. Popular with European visitors, the rooms are bright and quiet, though without the wood panelling and blue tiles of the public areas. ❺

Posada Viena Marsella 28, at Dinamarca ⓣ55/5566-0700 or 01-800/849-8402, in the US ⓣ1-888/698-0690, ⓦwww.posadavienahotel.com.mx. Metro Insurgentes. Lovely fresh and bright rooms decorated in rustic Mexican style, with ceiling fans though no a/c, at this comfortable but unpretentious four-star. The room price is the same for double, king-size or twin beds. ❹

Roosevelt Insurgentes Sur 287 ⓣ55/5208-6813, ⓦwww.hotelroosevelt.com.mx. Metro Insurgentes. The 1938 Art Deco exterior of this mid-range hotel on the edge of Condesa is getting a little shabby, and the corridors are a bit scuffed, but the small rooms are well kept and decorated in a pleasing combination of pink, grey and buff, with pink granite surfaces in the bathrooms. There's a decent restaurant downstairs. ❹

Segovia Regency Chapultepec 328 ⓣ55/5208-8454. Metro Insurgentes. Reliable high-rise hotel with parking facilities. It's often fully booked with business regulars, so reserve ahead, especially during the week. ❺

Polanco

The hotels listed below are marked on the "Chapultepec Park and Polanco", map (see p.416).

Casa Vieja Eugenio Sué 45 ⓣ55/5282-0067, ⓦwww.casavieja.com. Metro Polanco. Very chic and ultra-deluxe small hotel in a suburban house with ten suites (six junior US$351, three master US$491.40, one presidential US$1053), each with supremely comfortable beds, jacuzzi, kitchenette, phone and high-speed internet, fax machine, VCR, stereo, video and music library and stacks of books and magazines. Rich decor with mosaics and quality paintings. There's also a superb restaurant and bar on site. ❾

Nikko Mexico Campos Elisos 204 ⓣ55/5283-8700 or 01-800/908-8800, ⓦwww.hotelnikkomexico.com. Metro Polanco. Not the most expensive high-rise business hotel in the city (rooms start at M$3510) but as luxurious as you could want, with an indoor pool, rooftop tennis courts, gym and acres of glass and marble. ❾

The airport and around

Hilton Mexico City Airport Airport Terminal 1 ⓣ55/5133-0505 or 01-800/003-1400, in the US ⓣ1-800/HILTONS, ⓦwww.hilton.com. Metro Terminal Aérea. An elevator from Sala G (upstairs from Sala E1) takes you up to this swanky hotel which occupies much of the terminal's third floor with its restaurants, bars, gym and very well-appointed, though not especially large, rooms (some with runway views). The multichannel TV even has in-house movies and flight information screens. ❾

Hotel Aeropuerto Blv de Puerto Aéreo 380 ⓣ55/5785-5851, ⓕ5784-1329. Metro Terminal Aérea. The cheapest of the hotels near the airport, with well-maintained rooms (some with runway views); all have TV and phone, plus there's room service from the on-site restaurant. The hotel is three minutes' walk from the terminal: follow signs from Sala A to the Metro, from whose entrance you can see the hotel across the busy road (use the footbridge). ❹

NH Aeropuerto Airport Terminal 2 ⓣ55/5786-5750 or 01-800/903-3300. Metro Hangares. A very sleek, modern hotel, with extremely spacious public areas. Large rooms are equipped with a king-size bed or two double beds. Five-star facilities include a pool, gym and fitness centre. An elevator takes you from the ground floor of the terminal to the sixth floor, where the hotel is located. ❾

Ramada Aeropuerto México Blv de Puerto Aéreo 390 ⓣ55/5133-3232 or 01-800/702-4200, ⓦwww.ramadamexico.com. Metro Terminal Aérea. Attractive business hotel with lower prices than the big airport hotels but still with most of their features and facilities. Located next to the *Hotel Aeropuerto* (see above), so it is barely worth using the hotel's free airport transfer, though it's handy if you suffer from impaired mobility (and the hotel is wheelchair-friendly with an adapted room). ❼

Terminal del Norte and around

Acuario Pte 112 ⓣ55/5586-2677. Metro Autobuses del Norte. Institutional-looking and uninviting, but clean enough if you need a cheap bolt-hole for the night. Leaving the bus station, turn left, then at the major junction (after 100m) turn right across the main road and it's just ahead on the left. ❷

Brasilia Av de los Cien Metros 4823 ⓣ55/5587-8577 or 01-800/503-5212, ⓔhbrasilia@prodigy.net.mx. Metro Autobuses del Norte. Good-value business-style hotel (though sometimes a bit snooty towards backpackers) just 150m southeast of the bus station (turn left as you exit and it's straight ahead of you), where you can get a peaceful sleep in comfortable, carpeted rooms with cable TV and phone. There's a decent if slightly pricey restaurant on site, parking facilities and even room service. ❹

Central Mexico City

The heart of Mexico City is the **Zócalo**, built by the Spanish right over the devastated ceremonial centre of the Aztec city of Tenochtitlán. Extraordinary uncovered ruins – chief of which is the **Templo Mayor** – provide the Zócalo's most compelling attraction, but there's also a wealth of great colonial buildings, among them the huge **cathedral** and the **Palacio Nacional** with its striking **Diego Rivera murals**. You could easily spend a couple of days in the tightly packed blocks hereabouts, investigating their dense concentration of museums and galleries, especially notable for works by Rivera and his "Big Three" companions, David Siqueiros and José Clemente Orozco.

West of the Zócalo the *centro histórico* stretches through the main commercial district past the **Museo Nacional de Arte** to the sky-scraping **Torre Latinoamericana** and the **Palacio de Bellas Artes** with its gorgeous Art Deco interior. Both overlook the formal parkland of the **Alameda**, next to which you'll find a number of museums, principally the **Museo Franz Mayer**, which houses an excellent Alameda-related arts and crafts collection, and the **Museo Mural Rivera**, with the artist's famed *Dream of a Sunday Afternoon in the Alameda*. Further west, the **Revolution Monument** heralds the more upmarket central suburbs, chiefly the **Zona Rosa**, long known as the spot for plush shops and restaurants, though that title has largely been usurped by swanky **Polanco** and hipper **Condesa**.

The Zócalo

The vast paved open space of the **Zócalo** (Metro Zócalo) – properly known as the Plaza de la Constitución – was once the heart of **Aztec Tenochtitlán**, and is today one of the largest city squares in the world after Beijing's Tiananmen Square and Moscow's Red Square. The city's political and religious centre, it takes its name from part of a monument to Independence that was planned in the 1840s for the square by General Santa Anna. Like most of his other plans, this went astray, and only the statue's base (now gone) was ever erected: *el zócalo* literally means "the plinth". By extension, every other town square in Mexico has adopted the same name. It's constantly animated, with pre-Hispanic revivalist groups dancing and pounding drums throughout the day and street stalls and buskers in the evening. Stages are set up here for major national holidays and, of course, this is the place to hold demonstrations. Over 100,000 people massed here in March 2001 to support the Zapatistas after their march from Chiapas in support of indigenous people's rights; in July 2006 the square proved too small to contain the millions of demonstrators who gathered to challenge the result of that year's presidential election, a contest widely believed – especially in the left-leaning DF – to have been fixed. Spreading out from the Zócalo, the crowds reached as far as Reforma.

Though you're not guaranteed to see any protests, among the Zócalo's more certain entertainments is the ceremonial **lowering of the national flag** from its giant pole in the centre of the plaza each evening at sundown (typically 6pm). A troop of presidential guards march out from the palace, strike the enormous flag and perform a complex routine at the end of which the flag is left, neatly folded, in the hands of one of their number. With far less pomp, the flag is quietly raised again around half an hour later. You get a great view of this, and of everything else happening in the Zócalo, from the rooftop *La Terraza* restaurant/bar in the *Hotel Majestic* at the corner of Madero (see p.392).

The Zócalo does, of course, have its less glorious aspects. Mexico City's unemployment rate is tellingly reflected by the people who line up on the west side of the cathedral seeking work, each holding a little sign indicating their trade.

The cathedral

The **Catedral Metropolitana** (daily 7.30am–7.30pm, discretion is required during services; free; Metro Zócalo) holds the distinction of being the largest church in Latin America. Like so many of the city's older, weightier structures, the cathedral has settled over the years into the soft, wet ground beneath – the tilt is quite plain to see, despite extensive work to stabilize the building. The first church on this site was constructed only a couple of years after the Conquest, using stones torn from the Temple of Huitzilopochtli, but the present structure was begun in 1573 to provide Mexico City with a cathedral more suited to its wealth and status as the jewel of the Spanish empire. The towers weren't completed until 1813, though, and the building

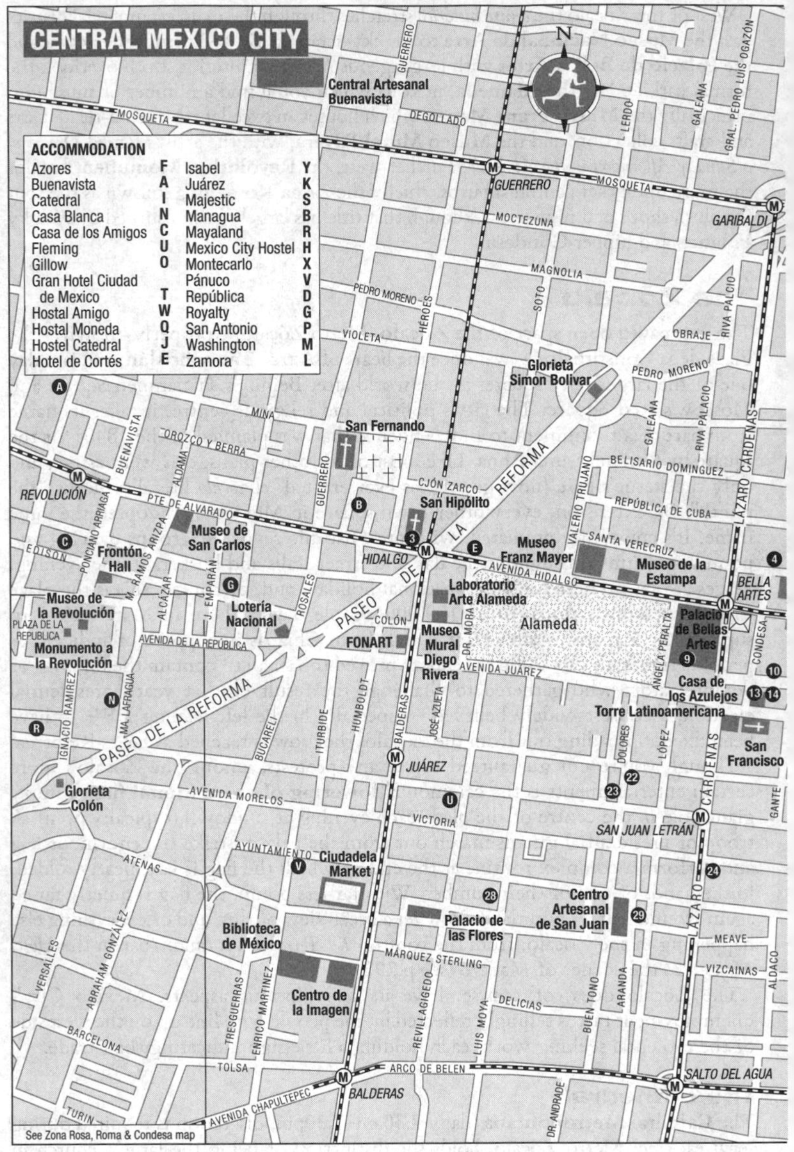

incorporates a plethora of architectural styles. Even the frontage demonstrates this: relatively austere at the bottom where work began soon after the Conquest, it flowers into full Baroque as you look up, and is topped by Neoclassical cornices and a clock tower. If you want to climb the clock tower, join one of the guided tours (M$15) that start roughly hourly from the information desk to the right as you enter.

Inside, although the size of the cathedral is striking, the chief impression is that it's a rather gloomy space, with rows of dimly lit side chapels. It is enlivened

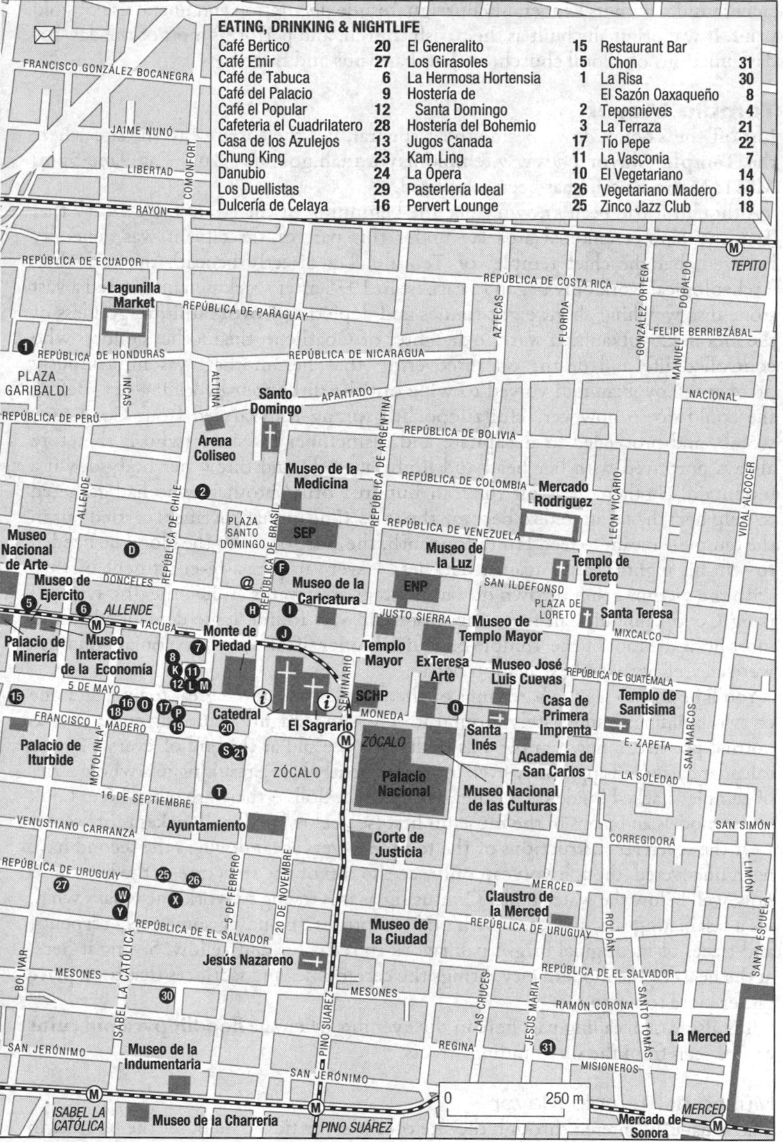

mostly by the **Altar de los Reyes**, a vast gilt *reredos* built of wood between 1718 and 1737 behind the main altar that features effigies of European kings and queens as well as two oil paintings, the *Assumption of the Virgin* and *Adoration of the Kings*. Fans of ornate handiwork will also appreciate the detailed work in gold and wood on the central *coro* (choir).

Next door, the **Sagrario Metropolitano** (daily 7.30am–7.30pm; free), despite its heavy, grey Baroque facade and squat, bell-topped towers, feels both lighter and richer inside, with its exuberant churrigueresque decoration and liberal use of gold paint. It was originally built as the parish church, and performs most of the day-to-day functions of a local church, such as baptisms and marriages.

Templo Mayor

Just off the Zócalo, down beside the cathedral, lies the entrance to the site where the **Templo Mayor** (Ⓦ www.templomayor.inah.gob.mx; Tues–Sat 9am–5pm; M$51; Metro Zócalo) has been excavated.

Although it had been known since the beginning of the twentieth century that Tenochtitlán's ceremonial area lay under this part of the city, it was generally believed that the chief temple, or Teocalli, lay directly beneath the cathedral. Archeological work only began in earnest in 1978 after workmen uncovered a vast stone disc weighing about eight tonnes and depicting **Coyolxauhqui**, goddess of the moon. Coyolxauhqui was the daughter of Coatlicue, the mother goddess who controlled life and death; on discovering that her mother was miraculously pregnant, Coyolxauhqui vowed to wipe out the dishonour by killing her. Before she could do so however, Huitzilopochtli sprang fully armed from Coatlicue's womb, and proceeded to decapitate and dismember his sister (who is therefore always portrayed with her head and limbs cut off) and threw her body down a mountain. He then drove off the four hundred other brothers who had gathered to help her: they scattered to become the stars. The human sacrifices carried out in the temple – meant to feed Huitzilopochtli, the sun god, with the blood he needed to win his nightly battle against darkness – were in part a re-enactment of this, with the victims being thrown down the steps afterwards. When the disc symbolizing Coyolxauhqui's fall from the mountain was found, logic demanded that it must lie at the foot of the Temple of Huitzilopochtli, and so the colonial buildings were cleared away and excavation began.

You'll be able to see the bare ruins of the foundations of the great temple and one or two buildings immediately around it. The site is highly confusing since, as was normal practice, a new temple was built over the old at the end of every 52-year calendar cycle (and apparently even more frequently here), resulting in a whole series of temples stacked inside each other like Russian dolls – there are seven here. Look at the models and maps in the museum first (see below) and it all makes more sense.

Of the seven reconstructions of the temple, layers as far down as the second have been uncovered, though you can only see the top of the structure as the bottom is now well below the water table. Confusing as it is trying to work out what's what, it's a fascinating site, scattered with odd sculptures, including some great serpents, and traces of its original bright paintwork in red, blue and yellow. Seeing it here, at the heart of the modern city, brings the ceremonies and sacrifices that took place rather close to home.

It is also worth calling past here in the evening when the **floodlit pyramid ruins** can be seen from the surrounding streets.

Museo del Templo Mayor

The **museum**, entered through the site on the same ticket, helps set the temples in context, with some welcome reconstructions and models of how Tenochtitlán would have looked at its height. There are some wonderful pieces retrieved from the site, especially the replica **tzompantli** (wall of skulls) as you enter, the eagle in Room 1 with a cavity in its back for the hearts of sacrificial victims, a particularly beautiful *pulque* god statue and, of course, the huge **Coyolxauhqui stone**, displayed so as to be visible from points throughout the museum. The museum's design is meant to simulate the temple, so you climb through it to reach two rooms at the top, one devoted to Huitzilopochtli, the other to Tlaloc.

The best items are towards the top, including some superb stone masks such as the one from Teotihuacán, black with inset eyes and a huge earring, typical of the objects paid in tribute by subject peoples from all over the country. On the highest level are two magnificent, full-size terracotta eagle warriors and numerous large stone pieces from the site. The descent back to the ground level concentrates on everyday life in Aztec times – with some rather mangy stuffed animals to demonstrate the species known to the Aztecs – along with a jumble of later items found while the site was being excavated. There are some good pieces here. Look for the superb turquoise mosaic, little more than a handspan across, but intricately set with tiny pieces forming seven god-like figures; and the two large ceramic sculptures of **Mictlantecihtli**, the god of death, only unearthed in 1994 from tunnels excavated below the nearby Casa de las Águilas.

Palacio Nacional and the Rivera murals

The other dominant structure on the Zócalo is the **Palacio Nacional** (daily 9am–4.30pm; free, but ID required to enter; Metro Zócalo), its more than two-hundred-metres-long facade taking up a full side of the plaza. The so-called New Palace of Moctezuma stood here and Cortés made it his first residence. From 1562 the building was the official residence of the Spanish viceroy, and later of presidents of the republic. The present building, for all its apparent unity, is the result of centuries of agglomeration and rebuilding – the most recent addition was the third storey, in 1927. It still holds the office of the president, who makes his most important pronouncements from the balcony – especially on September 15, when the **Grito de la Independencia** (see p.858) signals the start of the country's Independence celebrations.

The building's chief attraction is the series of **Diego Rivera murals** that decorate the stairwell and middle storey of the main courtyard. Begun in 1929, the murals are classic Rivera, ranking with the best of his work. The great panorama of Mexican history, *México a Través de los Siglos*, around the **main staircase**, combines an unbelievable wealth of detail with savage imagery and a masterly use of space. On the right-hand wall Quetzalcoatl sits in majesty amid the golden age of the

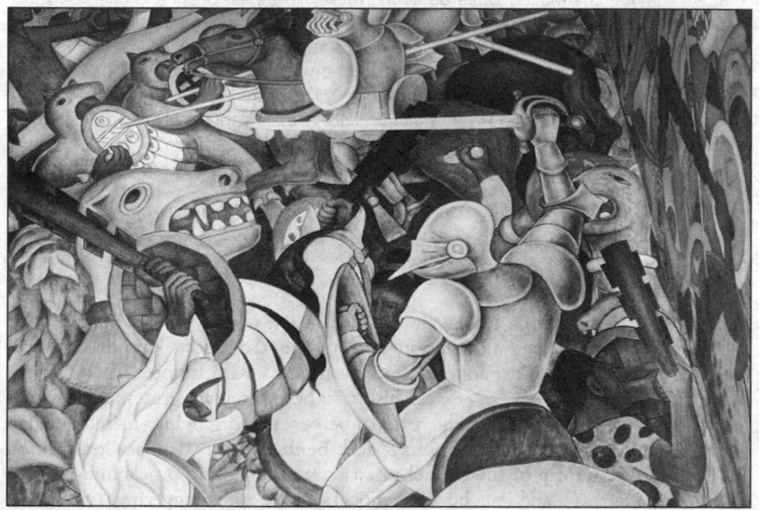

▲ *México a Través de los Siglos* by Diego Rivera, Palacio Nacional

Diego Rivera

Diego Rivera (c.1886–1957), husband of **Frida Kahlo** (see box, pp.432–433), was arguably the greatest of *Los Tres Grandes*, the "Big Three" Mexican artists who interpreted the Revolution and Mexican history through the medium of enormous murals, and put the nation's art onto an international footing in the first half of the twentieth century. His works (along with those of **José Clemente Orozco** and **David Siqueiros**) remain among the country's most striking sights.

Rivera studied from the age of 10 at the **San Carlos Academy** in the capital, immediately showing immense ability. He later moved to Paris, where he flirted with many of the new artistic trends, in particular Cubism. More importantly, though, he and Siqueiros planned, in exile, a popular, native art to express the new society in Mexico. In 1921 Rivera returned from Europe to the aftermath of the Revolution, and right away began work for the Ministry of Education at the behest of the socialist Education Minister, poet and presidential hopeful José Vasconcelos. Informed by his own Communist beliefs, and encouraged by the leftist sympathies of the times, Rivera embarked on the first of his massive, consciousness-raising **murals**, whose themes – Mexican history, the oppression of the natives, post-Revolutionary resurgence – were initially more important than their techniques. Many of his early murals are deceptively simple, naive even, but in fact Rivera's style remained close to major trends and, following the lead of Siqueiros, he took a scientific approach to his work, looking to industrial advances for new techniques, better materials and fresh inspiration. The view of industrial growth as a panacea (particularly in the earlier works of both Rivera and Siqueiros) may have been simplistic, but the artists' use of technology and experimentation with new methods and original approaches often have startling results.

Communism continued to be a major source of motivation and inspiration for Rivera, who was a long-standing member of the Mexican Communist Party. When ideological differences caused a rift in Soviet politics, Rivera supported **Trotsky**'s "revolutionary internationalism", and in 1936, after Trotsky had spent seven years in exile from the Soviet Union on the run from Stalin's henchmen and was running out of countries that would accept him, Rivera used his influence over Mexican President Lázaro Cárdenas to get permission for Trotsky and his wife Natalia to enter the country. They stayed with Diego and Frida rent-free at their Coyoacán house before Trotsky moved down the road to what is now the **Museo Casa de León Trotsky**. The passionate and often violent differences between orthodox Stalinists and Trotskyites spilled over into the art world, creating a great rift between Rivera and ardent Stalinist Siqueiros, who was later jailed for his involvement in an assassination attempt on Trotsky (see box, p.434). Though Rivera later broke with Trotsky and was eventually readmitted to the Communist Party, Trotsky continued to admire Rivera's murals, finding them "not simply a 'painting', an object of passive contemplation, but a living part of the class struggle".

Following the Rivera trail

There is a huge amount of Rivera's work accessible to the public, much of it in Mexico City, but also elsewhere around the country. The following is a rundown of

Valley of México, surrounded by an idealized vision of life in Teotihuacán, Tula and Tenochtitlán. The main section depicts the Conquest, oppression, war, Inquisition, invasion, Independence and eventually Revolution. Almost every major personage and event of Mexican history is here, from the grotesquely twisted features of the conquistadors to the national heroes: balding, white-haired Hidalgo with the banner of Independence; squat, dark Benito Juárez with his Constitution and laws for the reform of the Church; Zapata, with a placard proclaiming his cry of "*Tierra y Libertad*"; and Pancho Villa, moustachioed and swaggering. On the left are post-Revolutionary Mexico and the future (as Rivera envisaged it), with Karl the major Rivera sites organized by region and approximately ordered in accordance with their importance within that area.

Near the Zócalo, the Alameda and Chapultepec

Palacio National (see p.399). Major murals right in the heart of the capital.

SEP (see p.403). There are many of Rivera's early murals around the courtyards of the Ministry of Education.

Palacio de Bellas Artes (see p.408). Rivera's monumental *Man in Control of the Universe* (and others), as well as murals by his contemporaries.

Museo Mural Diega Rivera (see p.411). One of Rivera's most famous murals, *Dream of a Sunday Afternoon in the Alameda*, is on display here.

Museo de Arte Moderno (see p.423). Several quality canvases by Rivera and his contemporaries.

Antiguo Colegio de San Ildefonso (ENP) (see p.403). One relatively minor Rivera mural.

Museo Nacional de Arte (see p.410). A handful of minor canvases.

The southern suburbs

Estadio Olímpico (see p.435). Mosaic relief depicting the relationship between sport and the family.

Museo Dolores Olmedo Patiño (see p.437). A massive collection of Rivera works from almost every artistic period.

Museo Frida Kahlo (see p.431). Just a couple of Diego's works displayed in the house where he and Frida spent some of their married life.

Museo Casa Estudio Diego Rivera y Frida Kahlo (see p.428). Diego's and Frida's pair of houses designed by Juan O'Gorman.

Museo Anahuacalli (see p.436). Large Maya-style house built by Rivera and housing his collection of pre-Columbian sculpture.

Museo de Arte Carrillo-Gil (see p.428). A couple of paintings from Rivera's Cubist period.

Teatro de los Insurgentes (see p.427). Mural depicting the history of Mexican theatre.

Outside the capital

Palacio de Cortés, Cuernavaca (see p.493). Early murals on a grand scale.

Museo Robert Brady, Cuernavaca (see p.494). A few paintings by both Frida and Diego.

Museo Casa Diego Rivera, Guanajuato (see p.275). Relatively minor works and sketches in the house where Diego was born.

Marx pointing the way to adoring workers. Businessmen stand clustered over their tickertape in front of a somewhat ironic depiction of the metropolis with its skyscrapers and grim industrial wastes. Rivera's wife, the artist Frida Kahlo, is depicted, too, behind her sister Cristina (with whom Rivera was having an affair at the time) in a red blouse with an open copy of the Communist Manifesto.

A series of smaller panels was intended to go all the way round the upper (now middle) storey, an over-ambitious and unfinished project. The uncoloured first panel lists the products that the world owes to Mexico, including maize, beans, chocolate, tobacco, cotton, tomatoes, peanuts, prickly pears and chicle (the source of chewing gum). The remainder of the completed paintings reach halfway around and mostly depict the idyll of aspects of life before the Conquest – market day, dyeing cloth, hunting scenes and so on. The last (completed in 1951) shows the arrival of the Spanish, complete with an image of La Malinche (the Indian woman widely perceived to have betrayed native Mexicans) bearing the blue-eyed baby sired by Cortés – the first Mexican *mestizo*.

Also on the middle storey is the chamber used by the Mexican Legislature from 1845 to 1872, when it was presided over by Benito Juárez, who lived in the palace until his death. The room houses the original copy of the 1857 Constitution, which was drawn up there, but is frequently closed for renovations.

Before leaving, take a moment to wander around some of the other **courtyards** (there are fourteen in all), and through the small floral and cactus **gardens**.

Ayuntamiento and Nacional Monte de Piedad

Clockwise round the Zócalo from the Palacio Nacional, the third side is taken up by the city and Federal District administration, the **Ayuntamiento**, while just along from there it is well worth visiting the *Gran Hotel*, 16 de Septiembre 82, to admire the opulent lobby with its intricate ironwork, cage-lifts and wonderful Tiffany stained-glass dome.

Around the corner, on the fourth side of the Zócalo, arcades shelter a series of shops, almost all of which sell hats or jewellery. For an unusual shopping experience, though, you can't beat the **Nacional Monte de Piedad** at the corner of the Zócalo and 5 de Mayo (Mon–Fri 8.30am–6pm, Sat 8.30am–1pm; Metro Zócalo). This huge building, supposedly on the site of the palace in which Cortés and his followers stayed as guests of Moctezuma, is now the National Pawn Shop, an institution founded as far back as 1775. Much of what is pawned here is jewellery, but there's also a wide variety of fine art and sculptures, and just about anything that will command a reasonable price. From time to time they hold major auctions to clear the place out, but it's worth coming here just to take in the atmosphere and watch the milling crowds.

North of the Zócalo

Just a couple of blocks north of the centre the vast openness of the Zócalo gives way to a much more intimate section of small colonial plazas and mostly eighteenth-century buildings. It is still an active commercial area, and is packed with a variety of interesting sights, including ornate churches, small museums and some very fine Rivera and Siqueiros **murals**, all of which can be seen in a few hours.

Santo Domingo and the Museo de la Medicina

Beside the cathedral, Calle Monte de Piedad runs three blocks north (becoming República de Brasil) to the little colonial plaza of **Santo Domingo** (Metro Allende). In the middle of the square, a gently playing fountain honours La Corregidora, here raised on a pedestal for her decisive role in Mexico's Independence struggle. Eighteenth-century mansions line the sides of the plaza along with the fine Baroque church of Santo Domingo, built on the site of the country's first Dominican monastery. Under the arcades you'll find clerks sitting at little desks with ageing electric typewriters, carrying on the ancient tradition of public scribes. You'll see these clerks somewhere in most large Mexican cities – their main function is to translate simple messages into the flowery, sycophantic language essential for any business letter in Spanish, but they'll type anything from student theses to love letters. Alongside them are street printers, who'll churn out business cards or invitations on the spot, on antiquated hand presses.

On the east side of the plaza the **Museo de la Medicina** (daily 9am–6pm; free; Metro Allende) occupies grand rooms around a courtyard that was once the headquarters of the Inquisition in New Spain. It was here that heretics were punished, and although the cruelty of the Inquisition is often exaggerated, it was undoubtedly the site of some gruesome scenes. The extensive museum kicks off with interesting displays on indigenous medicine, religion and herbalism, often with reference to infirmity in sculpture. It is surprising how often skin diseases, humped backs and malformed limbs crop up in pre-Columbian art: note the terracotta sculpture bent double from osteoporosis. The progress of Western medicine from colonial times to the present is also well covered, with an intact nineteenth-century pharmacy, a complete radiology room from 1939 and an obstetrics and gynecology room filled with human embryos in bottles. A "wax room" upstairs shows full-colour casts of various skin ailments, injuries and infections – the diseased genitalia are always a hit with local schoolkids. As you leave, don't forget the "exhibit of the week" room by the entrance.

SEP and Colegio de San Ildefonso

From the Plaza de Santo Domingo, República de Cuba runs a block east to the **Secretaría de Educación Pública (SEP)**, at Brasil 31, with another entrance (the only one in use at weekends) round the corner at Argentina 28 (Mon–Fri 10am–5pm, Sat 10am–4pm, Sun 10am–3pm, upper floors closed on weekends; free; Metro Zócalo. Closed for renovation at the time of writing, but slated to reopen in 2010. This is the Ministry of Education building, where, in 1923 and 1924, Rivera painted his first **murals** on returning from Paris.

The driving force behind the murals was **José Vasconcelos**, a revolutionary Minister of Public Education in the 1920s but better known as a poet and philosopher, who promoted educational art as a means of instilling a sense of history and cultural pride in a widely illiterate population. He is the man most directly responsible for the murals in public buildings throughout the country. Here, three floors of an enormous double patio are entirely covered with frescoes, as are many of the stairwells and almost any other flat surface. Compared with what he later achieved, Rivera's work is very simple, but the style is already recognizable: panels crowded with figures, drawing inspiration mainly from rural Mexico, though also from an idealized view of science and industry. The most famous panel on the ground floor is the relatively apolitical *Día de los Muertos*, which is rather hidden away in a dark corner at the back. Continuing clockwise, there are equally striking images: *Quema de Judas* and *La Asamblea Primero de Mayo*, for example, and the lovely *El Canal de Santa Anita*. On the first floor the work is quite plain, mostly in tones of grey – here you'll find the shields of the states of Mexico and such general educational themes as *Chemistry* or *Physics*, mostly the work of Rivera's assistants. On the second floor are heroic themes from the Revolution. At the back, clockwise from the left-hand side, the triumphant progress of the Revolution is traced, culminating in the happy scenes of a Mexico ruled by its workers and peasants.

More murals, for which Vasconcelos was also responsible, adorn the eighteenth-century **Antiguo Colegio de San Ildefonso** (also called the Escuela Nacional Preparatoria, or **ENP**; Tues 10am–8pm, Wed–Sun 10am–6pm; M$45, free Tues; Metro Zócalo), nearby at Justo Serra 16, with its imposing colonial facade. Many artists are represented, including Rivera and Siqueiros, but the most famous works here are those of **José Clemente Orozco**, which you'll find on the main staircase and around the first floor of the main patio. As everywhere, Orozco, for all his enthusiasm for the Revolution, is less sanguine about its prospects, and modern Mexico is caricatured almost as savagely as the pre-revolutionary nation. *The Trench* depicts three Revolutionary soldiers resigning themselves to death in the battlefield, while *The Destruction of the Old Order* seems to suggest a return to a state of authoritarianism following the Revolution, rather than the ascent of any kind of free or just society.

Museo de la Caricatura and Museo de la Luz

Half a block west of the ENP, Justo Serra becomes Doncelos, home to the **Museo de la Caricatura**, Donceles 99 (Mon–Fri 10am–6pm, Sat & Sun 10am–5pm; M$20; Metro Zócalo), located in a particularly fine example of an eighteenth-century nobleman's dwelling, complete with central courtyard. It exhibits a limited selection of work from Mexico's most famous caricaturists, but without a strong sense of Mexican history and a comprehensive grasp of Spanish much of the impact is lost. It is still worth nipping in to see a small selection of bizarre nineteenth-century prints of skeletal mariachis by José Guadalupe Posada, a great influence on the later **Muralist movement**, and to take a break in the museum coffee shop in the central patio. The most recent cartoons, many of which focus on world affairs, are also extremely sharp, and well worth a look.

A couple of minutes' walk to the northeast stands the ex-Templo de San Pedro y San Pablo, built for the Company of Jesus between 1576 and 1603. Later used as a library, military college and correctional school, it was eventually taken over by the university. The decoration here – plain white, with the arches and pilasters painted in floral designs by Jorge Enciso and Roberto Montenegro – was also influenced by Vasconcelos. The church has since been turned into the **Museo de la Luz** (Mon–Fri 9am–4pm, Sat & Sun 10am–5pm; M$30; Metro Zócalo), a kind of hands-on celebration of all facets of reflection, refraction, iridescence, luminescence and so forth. Good Spanish is essential if you want to learn anything, but it is fun just playing with the optical tricks and effects, and exploring the use of light in art.

Plaza de Loreto and around

Just along from the Museo de la Luz, and three blocks northeast of the Zócalo, the **Plaza de Loreto** (Metro Zócalo) feels a world apart. It is a truly elegant old square, entirely unmodernized and flanked by a couple of churches. On one side is the **Templo de Loreto**, with its huge dome leaning at a crazy angle: inside, you'll find yourself staggering across the tilted floor. **Santa Teresa**, across the plaza, has a bizarre cave-like chapel at the back, entirely artificial. North of the Templo Loreto is a large and not especially exciting covered market, the **Mercado Presidente Abelardo Rodriguez**, inside most entrances of which are a series of large murals dating from the 1930s by an assortment of artists including Antonio Pujol and Pablo O'Higgins.

East of the Zócalo: along Calle Moneda

Calle Moneda, running east from the centre, is one of the oldest streets in the city, and it's fascinating to wander up here and see the rapid change as you leave the immediate environs of the Zócalo. The buildings remain almost wholly colonial, prim and refurbished around the museums, then gradually become shabbier and shabbier. Within four or five blocks you're into a very depressed residential area, with street stalls spreading up from the giant market of La Merced, to the south.

Museo de la SHCP and the Casa de la Primera Imprenta

Just a few steps from the Zócalo, the **Museo de la SHCP**, Moneda 4 (Tues–Sun 10am–5pm; M$8, free Sun), occupies the former archbishop's palace and presents Mexican fine art from the last three centuries in rooms surrounding two lovely open courtyards. The building was constructed over part of Tenochtitlán's ceremonial centre, the Teocalli, and excavations have revealed a few foundation sections for the Templo de Tezcatlipoca pyramid that once stood here. Notice the short flight of stairs, a jaguar carved in high relief and a series of anthropomorphic sculptures. In the galleries, accomplished eighteenth-century canvases by Juan Correa are a nice counterpoint to the small but wonderful collection of Russian icons of the same era. Other highlights include works by Diego Rivera and the stairway mural by José Gordillo, a follower of Siqueiros and Rivera.

On the corner of Licenciado Primo Verdad, the **Casa de la Primera Imprenta** (Mon–Fri 10am–6pm, Sat & Sun 10am–5pm; free) occupies the house where the first printing press in the Americas was set up in 1535, though the only indication of this is the model of the press that sits close to the entrance (away for restoration at last check, but should be back by the time you read this). Archeological finds unearthed during restoration work are displayed in one room; other rooms house temporary exhibits.

Temporary displays are also the stock in trade next door at the **Centro Cultural Ex-Teresa Arte**, Licenciado Primo Verdad 8 (daily 10am–6pm; free), in the former temple of Santa Teresa la Antigua, which has subsided so much that false floors are needed. You can wander around the mainly video and film installations put on by a nonprofit organization funded by the National Institute of Fine Arts.

Museo Nacional de las Culturas and around

Behind the Palacio Nacional, at Moneda 13, is the **Museo Nacional de las Culturas** (Tues–Sun 9.30am–6pm; free. Closed for renovation at the time of writing but slated to reopen in 2010), a collection devoted to the archeology and anthropology of other countries. The museum occupies the sixteenth-century Casa de la Moneda, the official mint until 1848 and later the National Museum, where the best of the Aztec artefacts were displayed until the construction of the Museo Nacional de Antropología (see p.419). Now immaculately restored, with rooms of exhibits set around a quiet patio, it is more interesting than you might guess, though still somewhat overshadowed by so many other high-class museums in the city. One of the more intriguing aspects of the museum is the information on Mexico's historical alignment on the trade routes between Europe and Asia. Every continent is covered, with everything from Korean china to slit gongs from the Marwuasas Islands, and even a reclining nude by Henry Moore.

Just a block beyond the museum is the eye-catching blue and gold **dome** of the church of **Santa Inés**. The dome, though, is the church's only striking feature, and there's little else to admire apart from the delicately carved wooden doors. Painters Miguel Cabrera and José Ibarra are both buried somewhere inside, but neither is commemorated in any way. Around the corner, the church's former convent buildings have been transformed into the **Museo José Luis Cuevas**, Academia 13 (Tues–Sun 10am–5.30pm; M$20, free Sun), an art gallery with changing displays centred on the eight-metre-high bronze *La Giganta* (The Giantess), designed by Cuevas. The only permanent collection is one room full of erotica ranging from pre-Hispanic sculpture to line drawings, some by Cuevas.

A few metres south is the **Academia de San Carlos**, Academia 22 (Mon–Fri 10am–9pm; free), which still operates as an art school, though on a very reduced scale from its nineteenth-century heyday; inside are galleries for temporary exhibitions and, in the patio, copies of classical sculptures. Further up Moneda, which by this time has become Emiliano Zapata, the **Templo de la Santísima Trinidad** boasts one of the city's finest Baroque facades. Again, the church's soft footing has caused it to slump, and plumb lines inside chart its continuing movement.

South of the Zócalo

The area immediately south of the Zócalo warrants a brief foray, particularly if you are en route to the wonderful **La Merced** market. Right on the corner of the Zócalo itself is the colonial-style modern building housing the **Suprema Corte de Justicia** (Mon–Fri 9am–3pm; free, but ID required to enter; Metro Zócalo). Inside are three superb, bitter murals by Orozco named *Proletarian Battles*, *The National Wealth* and *Justice*. The last, depicting Justice slumped asleep on her pedestal while bandits rob the people of their rights, was not surprisingly unpopular with the judges and powers that be, and Orozco never completed his commission here.

Museo de la Ciudad de México and around

A couple of blocks south of the Zócalo, the **Museo de la Ciudad de México**, Pino Suárez 30 (Tues–Sun 10am–5.30pm; M$20; Metro Zócalo), is housed in the colonial palace of the Condes de Santiago de Calimaya. This is a fabulous building, with carved stone cannons thrusting out from the cornice, magnificent heavy wooden doors and, on the far side, a hefty plumed serpent obviously dragged from the ruins of some Aztec temple to be employed as a cornerstone. The rooms are mostly given over to temporary exhibits on all manner of themes, but on the top storey is the preserved studio of the landscape artist **Joaquín Clausell**, its walls plastered with portraits and little sketches that he scribbled between working on his paintings.

Diagonally across the road from the museum a memorial marks the spot where, according to legend, Cortés first met Moctezuma. Here you'll find the church and hospital of **Jesús Nazareno**. The **hospital**, still in use, was founded by Cortés in 1528. As such, it's one of the oldest buildings in the city, and exemplifies the severe, fortress-like construction of the immediate post-Conquest years. The **church**, which contains the remains of Cortés and a bronze plaque to the left of the altar with the simple inscription "H.C. (1485–1547)", has been substantially remodelled over the years, its vaulting decorated with a fresco of the Apocalypse by Orozco.

More or less opposite Jesús Nazareno is a small open space and an entrance to a bookshop-lined subterranean walkway between the Zócalo and **Pino Suárez Metro station**, where an Aztec shrine uncovered during construction has been preserved as an integral part of the concourse. Dating from around the end of the fourteenth century, it was dedicated to Quetzalcoatl in his guise of Ehecatl, god of the wind.

Heading east from here along Salvador or Uruguay takes you to the giant **market** area of La Merced (see p.451). If you walk on Uruguay you'll pass a beautiful cloister, all that remains of the seventeenth-century **Convento de la Merced** (currently closed to the public).

Westwards you can stroll down some old streets heading towards the Zona Rosa, passing several smaller markets. Though still only half a dozen blocks south of the Zócalo, you're well outside the tourist zone down here, and it is instructive to spend a little time watching the city life go by. There's not a great deal to see but you could call in to ask if there any interesting temporary exhibitions at the **Museo de la Indumentaria Mexicana**, José María Izázaga 92 (Mon–Fri 10am–5pm; M$5, ID required to enter; ⓣ55/5130-3300 ext 3415; Metro Isabel la Católica), a former convent. Across the road, a handsome colonial building holds the **Museo de la Charrería**, Isabel la Católica 108 (Mon–Fri 11am–5pm; free; Metro Isabel la Católica), dedicated to all things cowboy, with a collection that includes old photographs, some of them inevitably rather camp, as well as sketches, watercolours, costumes, spurs and brands.

West to the Alameda

The streets that lead down from the Zócalo towards the Alameda – **Tacuba, 5 de Mayo, Madero, 16 de Septiembre** and the lanes that cross them – are the most elegant and least affected by modern development in the city, lined with ancient buildings, traditional cafés and shops and mansions converted into offices, banks or restaurants. When you reach the end of Madero, you've come to the outer edge of the colonial city centre, and should find yourself standing between two of the most striking modern buildings in the capital: the **Torre Latinoamericana** and the **Palacio de Bellas Artes**. Though it seems incredible to compare them, they were completed within barely 25 years of each other.

Along Madero

On **Madero** you'll pass several former aristocratic palaces now given over to a variety of uses. At no. 27 stands a slightly dilapidated mansion built in 1775 by mining magnate José de la Borda (see p.500) for his wife and presided over, on the corner of Bolivar, by a statue of the Virgin of Guadalupe. Still further down Madero, at no. 17, you'll find the **Palacio de Iturbide** (Metro Allende), currently occupied by Banamex and thoroughly restored. Originally the home of the Condes de Valparaiso in the eighteenth century, it was from 1821 to 1823 the residence of the ill-fated "emperor" Agustín de Iturbide. Nowadays it periodically houses free art exhibitions laid on by the bank. In the next block, the last before you emerge at Bellas Artes and the Alameda, the churrigueresque church of **San Francisco** (Metro Bellas Artes) stands on the site of the first Franciscan mission to Mexico.

Opposite San Francisco is the sixteenth-century **Casa de los Azulejos** (Metro Bellas Artes), now a branch of Sanborns, with its exterior swathed entirely in blue and white tiles from Puebla that were added during remodelling in 1737. The building survived a gas explosion in 1994 – though there was quite a bit of structural damage, luckily no one was hurt, and one of the most famous features of the building, the giant Orozco mural on the staircase, suffered few ill effects. Inside you'll find a restaurant in the glassed-over patio, as well as all the usual shopping.

Torre Latinoamericana

The distinctly dated steel and glass skyscraper of the **Torre Latinoamericana**, Lázaro Cárdenas 2 (daily 9am–10pm; M$50; Ⓦ www.torrelatino.com; Metro Bellas Artes), was completed in 1956 and, until a few years ago, was the tallest building in Mexico and, indeed, the whole of Latin America. It has now been outdone by the World Trade Center (formerly the *Hotel de México*, on Insurgentes) and doubtless by others in South America, but it remains the city's outstanding landmark and a point of reference no matter where you are. By world standards it is not especially tall, but on a clear day the views from the 139-metre observation deck are outstanding; if it's smoggy you're better off going up around dusk, catching the city as the sun sets, then watching as the lights delineate the city far more clearly. Having paid the fee, you're whisked up to the 36th floor where, another lift takes you to "El Mirador" on the 42nd floor. Here there is a glassed-in **observation area**, a small **café** on the level above and a series of coin-operated telescopes on the outdoor deck a further level up. Plans in the observation area illustrate how the tower was built, proudly boasting that it is the tallest building in the world to have withstood a major earthquake (which it did in 1985, though others may now rival the claim). The general principle of the construction appears to be similar to that of an angler's float, with enormously heavy foundations bobbing around in the mushy soil under the capital, keeping the whole thing upright.

Palacio de Bellas Artes

Diagonally across the street there's an equally impressive and substantially more beautiful engineering achievement in the form of the **Palacio de Bellas Artes** (Ⓦwww.bellasartes.gob.mx; Metro Bellas Artes). It was designed in 1901, at the height of the Díaz dictatorship, by the Italian architect Adamo Boari and built, in a grandiose Art Nouveau style, of white marble imported from Italy. The construction wasn't actually completed, however, until 1934, with the Revolution and several new planners come and gone. Some find the whole exterior overblown, but whatever your initial impressions, nothing will prepare you for the magnificent interior – an Art Deco extravaganza incorporating spectacular lighting, chevron friezes and stylized masks of the rain god, Chac.

Much of the interior splendour can be seen any time by wandering into the foyer (free) and simply gazing around the lower floor, where there is a good arts bookshop and the *Café del Palacio* restaurant (see p.444). If you want to see more of the building, you might consider visiting the art museum on the middle two floors, the **Museo del Palacio de Bellas Artes** (Tues–Sun 10am–6pm; M$35, free Sun or when there is no special exhibition on; M$30 to take photos, even with a phone). In the galleries here you'll find a series of exhibitions, permanent displays of Mexican art and temporary shows of anything from local art-school graduates' work to that of major international names. Of constant and abiding interest, however, are the great murals surrounding the museum's central space. On the first floor are *Birth of Our Nationality* and *Mexico Today* – dreamy, almost abstract works by **Rufino Tamayo**. Going up a level you're confronted by the unique sight of murals by **Rivera**, **Orozco** and **Siqueiros** gathered in the same place. Rivera's *Man in Control of the Universe (or Man at the Crossroads)*, celebrating the liberating power of technology, was originally painted for Rockefeller Center in New York City, but destroyed for being too leftist – arch-capitalist Nelson Rockefeller objected to Rivera's inclusion of Karl Marx, even though he was well aware of Rivera's views when he commissioned the work. This is Rivera's own copy, painted in 1934, just a year after the original. It's worth studying the explanatory panel, which reveals some of the theory behind this complex work.

▲ Palacio de Bellas Artes, Mexico City

Several smaller panels by Rivera are also displayed; these, too, were intended to be seen elsewhere (in this case on the walls of the *Hotel Reforma*, downtown) but for years were covered up, presumably because of their unflattering depiction of tourists. The works include *Mexican Folklore and Tourism*, *Dictatorship*, the *Dance of the Huichilobos* and, perhaps the best of them, *Agustín Lorenzo*, a portrayal of a guerrilla fighter against the French. None of them was designed to be seen so close up, and you'll find yourself wanting to step back to get the big picture. *Catharsis*, a huge, vicious work by Orozco, occupies almost an entire wall, and there are also some particularly fine examples of Siqueiros's work: three powerful and original panels on the theme of *Democracy* and a bloody depiction of *The Torture of Cuauhtémoc* and his resurrection. The uppermost floor is devoted to the **Museo de la Arquitectura** (same ticket and hours), which has no permanent collection, but frequently has interesting exhibits.

Some of the finest interior decor in the building is generally hidden from view in the main theatre, an important venue for classical music, opera and dance; this is under renovation until at least 2010, but when it reopens, there should be free tours (previously Mon–Fri 1pm & 1.30pm) to see the amazing Tiffany glass curtain depicting the Valley of México and the volcanoes, as well as the detailed proscenium mosaic and the stained-glass ceiling.

Correo Central and Palacio de Minería

Around the back of Bellas Artes, at the corner of Tacuba and Lázaro Cárdenas, you'll find the **Correo Central** (Metro Bellas Artes), the city's main post office. Completed in 1908, this too was designed by Adamo Boari, but in a style much more consistent with the buildings around it. Look closely and you'll find a wealth of intricate detail on the facade, while inside it's full of richly carved wood. On the first floor is the small **Museo Postal** (Tues–Fri 9am–5.30pm, Sat & Sun 9am–2pm; free), housing a rather uninspiring collection of old mailboxes, a few historic documents and objects relating to the postal service and a giant picture made of postage stamps. On the fourth floor, naval buffs will enjoy the **Museum of Naval History** (Tues–Fri 10am–5pm, Sat & Sun 10am–2pm; free; explanations in Spanish only), featuring models of old ships, a reconstruction in miniature of Cortés's waterborne battle against the Aztecs on the Lake of Texcoco, plus photos and artefacts of the 1914 US occupation of Veracruz.

Directly behind the Correo on Tacuba is the **Palacio de Minería** (Ⓦwww.palaciomineria.unam.mx), a Neoclassical building completed right at the end of the eighteenth century and designed by Spanish-born Manuel Tolsá, who is the subject of the devotional **Museo Manuel Tolsá** (Wed–Sun 10am–6pm; M$15; guided tours Sat & Sun 11am & 1pm) within – just a couple of rooms of paintings and architectural drawings, strictly for fans only. The palacio also houses another museum, the more macabre **Torture Museum** (daily 10am–7pm; M$40), which holds instruments of torture and execution from the time of the Inquisition onwards. The exterior of the palacio makes an interesting contrast with the post office and with the Museo Nacional de Arte (formerly the Palacio de Comunicaciones) directly opposite, the work of another Italian architect, Silvio Contri, in the first years of the twentieth century.

The next block to the east has two museums. The Bank of Mexico's **Museo Interactivo de la Economía**, housed in a former seventeenth-century convent at Tacuba 17 (Tues–Sun 9am–6pm; M$50; Ⓦwww.mide.org.mx) has gimmicky exhibits on banking, finance and economics, with buttons you can push to see how money is made or how goods are distributed around Mexico. Around the corner on Filomeno Mata is the small Convento de las Betlemitas, a seventeenth-century convent that now houses the **Museo del Ejército y Fuerza** (Tues–Sat 10am–6pm,

Sun 10am–4pm; free), with a small exhibition of antique arms, and explanations mostly in Spanish.

Museo Nacional de Arte

The **Museo Nacional de Arte**, Tacuba 8 (Tues–Sun 10.30am–5.30pm; M$30, free Sun; Ⓦwww.munal.com.mx), is set back from the street on a tiny plaza in which stands one of the city's most famous sculptures, **El Caballito**, portraying Carlos IV of Spain. This enormous bronze, the work of Manuel Tolsá, was originally erected in the Zócalo in 1803. In the intervening years it has graced a variety of sites and, despite the unpopularity of the Spanish monarchy (and of the effete Carlos IV in particular), is still regarded affectionately. The latest setting is appropriate, since Tolsá also designed the Palacio de Minería (see p.409). The open plaza around the sculpture is now often the scene of intense pre-Columbian drumming and dancing, which usually draws an appreciative crowd.

Though the museum is the foremost showcase of Mexican art from the 1550s to the 1950s, with a collection of over a thousand pieces, its interest is mainly historical. Most of the major Mexican artists are represented, but with essentially mediocre examples spiced only occasionally with a more striking work. It's worth coming here to see something of the dress and landscape of old Mexico, and also some of the curiosities, but don't expect masterpieces.

Temporary displays take up the lower floor (along with a good bookshop and café), leaving the two floors above for the permanent collection. To follow the displays in chronological order, start on the **upper floor**, which covers work up to the end of the eighteenth century. Vast religious canvases take up whole walls, but seldom hold your interest for long, though Miguel Cabrera is particularly well represented with half a dozen works, notably *La Virgen del Apocalipsis*. In the same room there are some fine polychrome sculptures, particularly the diminutive Nativity scene in the glass case. You could hardly miss eighteenth-century painter Francisco Antonio Vallejo's masterwork, the four-canvas *Glorificación de la Inmaculada*, with the heavenly host borne by clouds above the court of Carlos IV.

The museum really comes to life, and modern Mexico begins to express itself, on the **middle floor**, where traditional oils are supplemented by lithographs, sculpture and photography: note the images of nineteenth-century Mexican railways, *pulqueros* tapping the maguey cactus and cattle grazing in the fields of Chapultepec Park. Elsewhere there are a couple of photos by Henri Cartier-Bresson and several by Hungarian-born Katy Horna, who worked in Mexico from 1939 until her death in 2000. The half-dozen Rivera works are mostly minor, though it is instructive to see early works, such as *El Grade de España* from 1914 when he was in Braque mode. Notice too how Rivera's technique influenced many of the other painters of the time, especially Saturnino Herrán and Olga Costa, and look out for the landscapes of the Valley of México by José María Velasco (one of Rivera's teachers).

The Alameda

From behind Bellas Artes, Lázaro Cárdenas runs north towards the **Plaza Garibaldi** (see p.449) through an area crowded with seedy cantinas and eating places, theatres and burlesque shows. West of the Palacio de Bellas Artes lies the **Alameda**, first laid out as a park in 1592, and taking its name from the *alamos* (poplars) then planted. The Alameda had originally been an Aztec market and later became the site where the Inquisition burned its victims at the stake. Most of what you see now – formally laid-out paths and flowerbeds, ornamental statuary and fountains – dates from the nineteenth century, when it was the fashionable place to stroll. It's still popular, always full of people, particularly at weekends, but it's mostly a transient population – office workers taking lunch, shoppers resting their feet, messengers taking a short cut and street vendors selling T-shirts.

Museo de la Estampa and Museo Franz Mayer

On the north side of the Alameda, Avenida Hidalgo traces the line of an ancient thoroughfare, starting from the Teatro Hidalgo, right opposite Bellas Artes. To the west, the church of Santa Vera Cruz marks the **Museo de la Estampa** (Tues–Sun 10am–5.45pm; M$10, free Sun), which concentrates on engraving, an art form that is taken seriously in Mexico, where the legacy of José Guadalupe Posada (see p.264) is still revered. There is no permanent collection, but you may expect anything from engravings and printing plates from pre-Columbian times to the modern age, including works by Posada.

Immediately next door, the **Museo Franz Mayer**, Hidalgo 45 (Tues & Thurs–Sun 10am–5pm, Wed 10am–7pm; M$45, free Tues; ⓦ www.franzmayer.org.mx), is dedicated to the applied arts, and occupies the sixteenth-century hospital attached to the church of San Juan de Dios. It's packed with the personal collection of Mexican arts and crafts of Franz Mayer, a German who settled here in 1913: colonial furniture, textiles and carpets, watches, Spanish silverwork, religious art and artefacts, a valuable collection of sculpture and paintings and some fine colonial pottery from Puebla. There is also much furniture and pottery from Asia, the result of Mexico's position on international trade routes, as well as a library with rare antique editions of Spanish and Mexican authors and a reference section on applied arts. Even if this doesn't sound like your thing, it's well worth seeing. The building is lovely and beautifully furnished, and offers a tranquil escape from the crowds outside. The coffee bar, too, is a delight, facing a courtyard filled with flowers and a fountain – there's a charge of M$5 for those not visiting the museum.

Laboratorio Arte Alameda and Museo Mural Diego Rivera

Almost at the western end of the Alameda, duck down Calle Dr Mora to the **Laboratorio Arte Alameda**, at no. 7 (Tues–Sun 9am–5pm; M$15, free Sun; ⓦ www.artealameda.bellasartes.gob.mx), an art museum built into the glorious seventeenth-century monastery of San Diego. The cool, white interior is filled with temporary exhibitions of challenging contemporary art. They're all superbly displayed around the church, chapel and cloister of the old monastery, a space also occasionally used for evening concerts – mostly chamber music or piano recitals.

One of the buildings worst hit by the 1985 earthquake was the *Hotel del Prado*, which contained the Rivera mural *Dream of a Sunday Afternoon in the Alameda*. The mural survived the quake, and was subsequently picked up in its entirety and transported around the Alameda – it can now be seen in the **Museo Mural Diego Rivera** (Tues–Sun 10am–6pm; M$15, free Sun; ⓦ www.museomuraldiegorivera.bellasartes.gob.mx), at the western end of the Alameda, at the corner of Balderas and Colón. It's an impressive work – showing almost every famous Mexican character out for a stroll in the park – but one suspects that its popularity with tour groups is as much to do with its relatively apolitical nature as with any superiority to Rivera's other works. Originally it included a placard with the words "God does not exist", which caused a huge furore, and Rivera was forced to paint it out before the mural was first displayed to the public.

A leaflet (available at the entrance; M$10) explains every character in the scene: Cortés is depicted with his hands stained red with blood; José Guadalupe Posada stands bowler-hatted next to his trademark skeleton, *La Calavera Catrina*, who holds the hand of Rivera himself, portrayed as a 9-year-old boy; Frida Kahlo stands in motherly fashion, just behind him.

Centro de la Imagen and Biblioteca de México

A short detour south of the Alameda takes you past the excellent **artesanía market** of Ciudadela to a shady open space of the same name. Along the south side of the market are the **Centro de la Imagen** (Tues–Sun 11am–6pm; free; Ⓦcentrodelaimagen.conaculta.gob.mx), with changing photographic exhibits and, next door, the **Biblioteca de México** (daily 8.30am–7.30pm; free), an extensive library also containing rooms where touring art shows are displayed.

Around the Monumento a la Revolución

Beyond the Alameda, avenidas Juárez and Hidalgo lead towards the Paseo de la Reforma. Across Reforma, Hidalgo becomes the **Puente de Alvarado**, following one of the main causeways that led into Tenochtitlán. This was the route by which the Spanish attempted to flee the city on the Noche Triste (Sad Night), July 10, 1520. Following the death of Moctezuma, and with his men virtually under siege in their quarters, Cortés decided to escape the city under cover of darkness. It was a disaster: the Aztecs cut the bridges and, attacking the bogged-down invaders from their canoes, killed all but 440 of the 1300 Spanish soldiers who set out, and more than half their native allies. Greed, as much as anything, cost the Spanish troops their lives, for in trying to take their gold booty with them they were, in the words of Bernal Díaz, "so weighed down by the stuff that they could neither run nor swim". The street takes its name from Pedro de Alvarado, one of the last conquistadors to escape, crossing the broken bridge "in great peril after their horses had been killed, treading on the dead men, horses and boxes". Not long ago a hefty gold bar – exactly like those made by Cortés from melted-down Aztec treasures – was dug up here.

Puente de Alvarado: San Hipólito, San Fernando and the Museo San Carlos

The church of **San Hipólito**, at the corner of Reforma and Puente de Alvarado, was founded by the Spanish soon after their eventual victory, both as a celebration and to commemorate the events of the Noche Triste. The present building dates from 1602, though over the years it has been damaged by earthquakes and rebuilt, and it now lists to one side. West along Puente de Alvarado is the Baroque eighteenth-century church of **San Fernando**, by the plaza of the same name. Once one of the richest churches in the city, San Fernando has been stripped over the years, and is now mostly of interest for its *panteón* (graveyard; Tues–Sun 9am–7pm; free), last resting place of **Benito Juárez** and many of his colleagues in the reform movement, whose names will be familiar from the streets which now bear them: Ignacio Zaragoza, Guillermo Prieto, Miguel Lerdo de Tejada, Melchor Ocampo, Ignacio Comonfort.

At Puente de Alvarado 50 you'll find the **Museo Nacional de San Carlos** (daily except Tues 10am–6pm; free; Ⓦwww.mnsancarlos.com), which houses the country's oldest art collection, begun in 1783 by Carlos III of Spain, and comprising largely European work of the seventeenth and eighteenth centuries with some notable earlier and later additions. Major names are largely absent, but look for the delicate *San Pedro, San Andrés y San Mateo* by fifteenth-century Spanish painter Maestro de Palaquinos, portraits by Reynolds, Rubens and Hals and a luminous canvas of Breton women by the sea (*Mujeres Bretones a la Orilla del Mar*) by another Spaniard, Manuel Benedito y Vives. Travelling exhibitions are also frequently based here.

The building itself is an attractive Neoclassical design by Manuel Tolsá. Its inhabitants have included the French Marshal Bazaine, sent by Napoleon III to advise the Emperor Maximilian – who presented the house to him as a wedding present on his marriage to a Mexican woman – and the hapless Mexican general and sometime dictator Santa Anna. Later it served for a time as a cigarette factory.

Along Juárez to the monument

Leaving the Alameda on Juárez, you can see the massive, ugly bulk of the Monumento a la Revolución ahead of you. The first couple of blocks, though, are dull, commercial streets. The junction with Reforma is a major crossing of the ways, and is surrounded by modern skyscrapers and one older one – the marvellous Art Deco **Lotería Nacional** building. In here, you can watch the winning tickets being drawn each week, although the lottery offices themselves have been moved to an ordinary-looking steel and glass building opposite. Beyond Reforma, Juárez continues in one long block to the **Plaza de la República** and the vast **Monumento a la Revolución**. Originally intended to be a new home for the Cortes (the parliament), its construction was interrupted by the Revolution and never resumed – in the end they buried a few heroes of the Revolution under the mighty columns (including Pancho Villa and presidents Madero, Carranza and Cárdenas) and turned the whole thing into a memorial. More recently the **Museo Nacional de la Revolución** (Tues–Sun 9am–5pm; M$20) was installed beneath the monument (entrance under the north side), with a history of the Revolution told through archive pictures, old newspapers, films and life-size tableaux. Somehow the whole area seems sidelined by the mainstream of city life and is often all but deserted.

Reforma, Zona Rosa, Roma, Condesa and Polanco

West of the Alameda and Revolution monument the tenor of the city changes again, particularly along the grand avenue of **Reforma**, lined by tall buildings, including Mexico's stock exchange. South of here is the tight knot of streets that make up the **Zona Rosa**, one of the city's densest concentrations of hotels, restaurants and shops. The residential districts of **Roma** and **Condesa** warrant attention for their numerous small-time art galleries and, particularly in Condesa, the restaurants. The Paseo de la Reforma runs direct to Chapultepec Park, on the north edge of which lies **Polanco**, home to wealthy socialites and yuppies.

Paseo de la Reforma

Paseo de la Reforma is the most impressive street in Mexico City. Laid out in the 1860s by Emperor Maximilian to provide the city with a boulevard to rival the great European capitals – and doubling as a ceremonial drive from his palace in Chapultepec to the centre – it also provided a new impetus, and direction, for the growing metropolis. The original length of the broad avenue ran simply from the park to the junction of Juárez, and although it has been extended in both directions, this stretch is still what everyone thinks of as Reforma. "**Reforma Norte**", as the extension towards Guadalupe is known, is just as wide (and the traffic just as dense), but is almost a term of disparagement. **Real Reforma**, though, remains imposing – ten lanes of traffic, lines of trees, grand statues at every intersection and perhaps three or four of the original French-style, nineteenth-century houses still surviving. Twenty or thirty years ago it was the dynamic heart of the growing city, with even relatively new buildings being torn down to make way for yet newer, taller, more prestigious towers of steel and glass. The pulse has since moved elsewhere, and the fancy shops have relocated, leaving an avenue now mostly lined with airline offices, car rental agencies and banks, and somewhat diminishing the pleasure of a stroll.

It's a long walk, some 5km from the Zócalo to the gates of Chapultepec, and you'd be well advised to take the bus – they're frequent enough to hop on and off at will. The *glorietas*, roundabouts at the major intersections, each with a distinctive statue, provide easy landmarks along the way. First is the **Glorieta Colón**, with a statue of Christopher Columbus. Around the base of the plinth are carved various friars and monks who assisted Columbus in his enterprise or brought the Catholic faith to the Mexicans. The Plaza de la República is just off to the north. Next comes the crossing of Insurgentes, nodal point of all the city's traffic, with **Cuauhtémoc**, last emperor of the Aztecs and leader of their resistance, poised aloof above it all in a plumed robe, clutching his spear, surrounded by warriors. Bas-relief engravings on the pedestal depict his torture and execution at the hands of the Spanish, desperate to discover where the Aztec treasures lay hidden. **El Ángel**, a golden winged victory atop a forty-metre column, is the third to look out for, and the place to get off the bus for the heart of the Zona Rosa. Officially known as the **Monumento a la Independencia** (daily 10am–5.45pm; free), and finished in 1910, the column stands atop a room containing the skulls of Independence heroes Hidalgo, Aldama, Allende and Jiménez. On weekends (Sat & Sun 11am–1.30pm), you can take an elevator to the top of the monument, but it's a popular ride, so expect queues.

Zona Rosa

To the south of Reforma lies the **Zona Rosa** (Metro Insurgentes), a triangular area bordered by Reforma, Avenida Chapultepec and, to the west, Chapultepec Park. You'll know you're there as the streets are all named after famous cities. Packed into this tiny area are hundreds of bars, restaurants, hotels and shops, all teeming with a vast number of tourists and a cross-section of Mexico City's aspiring middle classes. Until the 1980s this was the city's swankiest commercial neighbourhood, but the classiest shops have moved to Polanco (see p.417) and many of the big international chains have relocated to the out-of-town malls that have sprung up around the Periférico. Though there's no shortage of good shopping, and the selection of restaurants, cafés, clubs and bars in the Zona Rosa is respectable (see p.446 & p.448), it has lost its exclusive feel. You're as likely to spend your time here buying cheap knick-knacks at market stalls and watching street entertainers as admiring the remaining fancy store windows. You might visit during the day to eat well, then return at night for the clubs, and may choose to stay here, but you certainly wouldn't make a special journey for the sights. The zone in general, and particularly the block of Amberes between Estrasburgo and Reforma – has become something of a centre for the city's gay scene, but otherwise, the only real attraction is the **Museo de Cera** (Wax Museum; daily 11am–7pm; M$60; Metro Cuauhtémoc), on the fringes of the Zona, at Londres 6. Thoroughly tacky, with a basement chamber of horrors that includes Aztec human sacrifices, it shares its site with the **Museo de lo Increíble** (same hours and prices; joint ticket for the two museums M$100), a Mexican Ripley's Believe It or Not Museum, which displays such marvels as flea costumes and hair sculpture.

The northern side of Reforma, where the streets are named after rivers (Tiber, Danubio and the like), is a much quieter, posh residential area officially known as **Colonia Cuauhtémoc**, though it's usually just bundled in with the Zona Rosa. Here you'll find some of the older embassies, notably the US embassy, on Reforma, bristling with razor wire and security cameras. Near the much more modest British embassy is the **Museo Venustiano Carranza**, Río Lerma 35 (Tues–Sat 9am–6pm, Sun 9am–5pm; M$37, free Sun; Metro Insurgentes). Carranza was a Revolutionary leader and president of the Republic who was shot in 1920. The building was his home in Mexico City and contains exhibits relating to his life and to the Revolution.

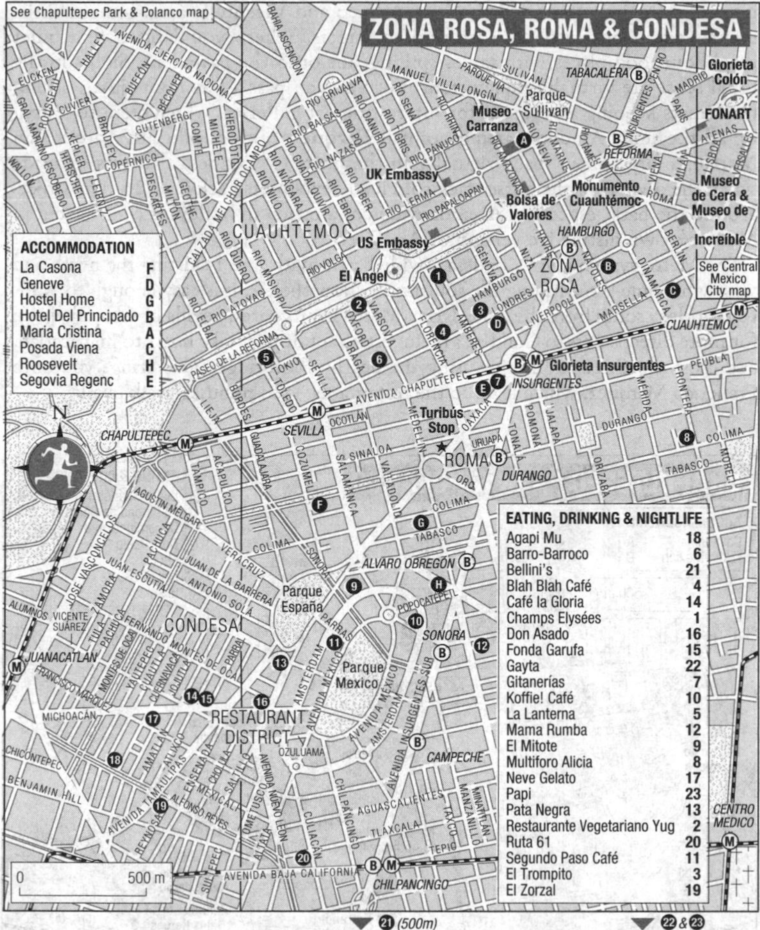

Not far away, just north of the junction of Reforma and Insurgentes, the **Parque Sullivan** hosts free open-air exhibitions and sales of paintings, ceramics and other works of art every Sunday (roughly 10am–4pm); some of them are very good, and a pleasant holiday atmosphere prevails.

Roma and Condesa

South of the Zona Rosa lie the residential districts of **Roma** and **Condesa**, full of quiet leafy streets once you get away from the main avenues that cut through. Both suburbs were developed in the 1930s and 1940s, but as the city expanded they became unfashionable and run-down. That all changed in the 1990s when artists and the bohemian fringe were drawn here by low rents, decent housing and proximity to the centre of the city. Small-time galleries sprang up and the first of the bars and cafés opened. Condesa, in particular, is now one of the best areas for good eating in the city, and definitely the place to come for lounging in pavement cafés or dining in bistro-style **restaurants** (see p.445). The greatest concentration is around the junction of Michoacán, Atlixco and Vicente Suárez, but establishments spread out into the surrounding streets, where you'll often find quiet neighbourhood places with tables spilling out onto the pavement. Sights in the usual sense are virtually nonexistent, but you can pass a few hours just walking the streets keeping an eye out for interesting art galleries, which seem to spring up all the time. A good starting point is **Parque México**, officially Parque San Martín, a large green space virtually in the heart of Condesa that was set aside when the owners of the horse track sold it to developers back in 1924. The streets around the park, especially Avenida México, are rich in buildings constructed in Mexico's own distinctive version of Art Deco.

The Metro system gives Condesa a wide berth, with line 1 skirting the north and west while line 9 runs along the south side. Nonetheless, it is easy enough to **walk to Condesa** south from the Zona Rosa (Metro Insurgentes, Sevilla or Chapultepec); for more direct access to Condesa's main restaurant district take line 1 to Juanacatlán, and cross the Circuito Interior using the nearby footbridge. This brings you onto Francisco Marquez, which leads to the restaurants – ten minutes' walk in all.

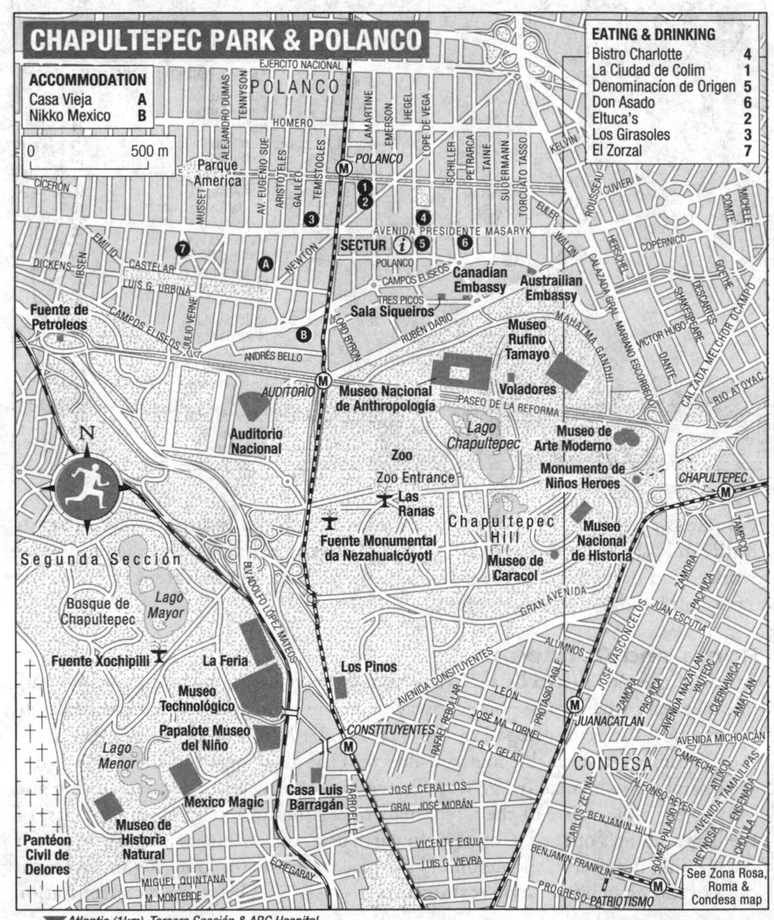

Atlantis (1km), Tercera Sección & ABC Hospital

Polanco

High-priced high-rise hotels line the northern edge of Chapultepec Park, casting their shadow over the smart suburb of **Colonia Polanco**. Unless you've got brand-name shopping in mind or need to visit one of the district's embassies, there's not much reason to come out this way, though it is instructive to stroll along **Presidente Masaryk**, the main drag, watching the beautiful people drive by in their Porsches and Lexus SUVs on their way to the Fendi or Ferragamo stores. Polanco also has great dining and we've recommended a few places on p.446, but bad restaurants don't last long here and you can do just as well strolling along and picking any place you fancy.

The only specific destination is the **Sala de Arte Público David Siqueiros**, Tres Picos 29 (Tues–Sun 10am–6pm; M$10, free Sun; Metro Polanco), a small but interesting collection of the great muralist's later work, including sketches he made for the Polyforum murals (see p.426). They're all displayed in his former residence and studio, donated (along with everything in it) to the people of Mexico just 25 days before his death in 1973. If it is not already playing, ask to see the hour-long **video** (in English) on his life and work made just before his death, and watch it surrounded by his murals, which cover just about every piece of wall space.

Bosque de Chapultepec and the Museo Nacional de Antropología

Chapultepec Park, or the **Bosque de Chapultepec** (Tues–Sun 5am–4.30pm; free), is a vast green area, about a thousand acres in all, dotted with trees, scattered with fine museums – among them the marvellous **Museo Nacional de Antropología** – boating lakes, gardens, playing fields and a zoo. Ultimately, it provides an escape from the pressures of the city for seemingly millions of Mexicans, with the result that the most visited areas get a heavy pounding and some areas are occasionally fenced off to allow the plants to recover. On Sundays, when many of the attractions are free, you can barely move for the throng, but note that on Mondays the entire park and many of the museums are closed.

The park is divided into three sections: the first and easternmost is home to the points of greatest interest, including the Anthropology, Modern Art and Rufino Tamayo museums and the zoo; the Second Section is mostly aimed at kids, with an amusement park, technology museum and natural history museum; and the Third Section contains aquatic and marine parks open at weekends.

The rocky outcrop of **Chapultepec** (Náhuatl for "hill of the locust"), from which the entire area has taken its name, is mentioned in Toltec mythology, but first gained historical significance in the thirteenth century when it was no more than an anonymous island among the lakes and salt marshes of the valley. Here the Aztecs, still a wandering, savage tribe, made their first home, though it proved to be temporary when they were defeated and driven off by neighbouring cities. Once Tenochtitlán's power was established they returned here, channelling water from the springs into the city, and turning Chapultepec into a summer resort for the emperor, with plentiful hunting and fishing around a fortified palace. Several Aztec rulers had their portraits carved into the rock of the hill, though most of these images were destroyed by the Spaniards soon after the Conquest.

Visting the park

Chapultepec is a big place with a lot to do. You could easily spend a couple of days here and still not see everything, but if you are selective you can cover the best of it in one tiring day. Though it can be tempting to visit on Sunday, when a lot of the museums are free and the park is at its vibrant best, the **Museo Nacional de Antropología** and the **zoo** will be packed – if you want to be able to move freely it can be worth coming during the week.

How you approach the park depends on what you want to see first. The easiest access is via the **Chapultepec Metro** station, from where you follow the crowds over a bridge across the Circuito Interior (inner ring road). Straight ahead you'll see the **Niños Héroes monument** and the Castillo containing the **Museo Nacional de Historia.** The entrances to the Museo Nacional de Antropología and its acolytes are grouped together along Paseo de la Reforma, less than a fifteen-minute walk from the Metro station, but if that is where you are headed first it is faster to catch a *pesero* ("Auditorio", "Reforma km 13" and others) anywhere along Reforma. Visitors with kids may want to head straight for the Second Section, either picking up a *pesero* along Constituyentes (routes 2, 24 and others) from Metro Chapultepec, or going direct to Metro Constituyentes and walking from there.

Wherever you go in the park there'll be someone selling **food and drink**, and the Museo Nacional de Antropología has a good (though pricey) **restaurant**. Nonetheless, it is as well to take some snacks (or an entire picnic lunch) and a big bottle of water: museum hopping can be thirsty work.

Chapultepec Hill

As you approach the park from the Chapultepec Metro station you're confronted by **Chapultepec Hill**, crowned by Maximilian's very peaceful-looking "castle". As you climb the hill – and for the less able-bodied, there are land trains that'll take you up and bring you back for M$13 – you pass the modern **Museo de Caracol** (Tues–Sun 9am–4.15pm; M$39, free Sun), devoted to "the Mexican people's struggle for Liberty". Its full name is the Museo Galería de la Lucha del Pueblo Mexicano por su Libertad, but it's colloquially known as the "shell museum" for the snail-like spiralling route through the displays. These trace the history of the constant wars that have beset the country – from Independence, through the American and French interventions to the Revolution.

At the top of the hill, in front of the castle, stands a strange, six-columned monument dedicated to the **Niños Héroes** – it commemorates the cadets who attempted to defend the castle (then a military academy) against American invaders in 1847. According to the story, probably apocryphal, the last six flung themselves off the cliff wrapped in Mexican flags rather than surrender. The **castle** itself was built only in 1785 as a summer retreat for the Spanish viceroy – until then it had been the site of a hermitage established on the departure of the Aztec rulers. Following Independence it served as a military school, but the present design was dictated by Maximilian, who remodelled it in the image of his Italian villa.

Today the castle houses the **Museo Nacional de Historia** (Tues–Sun 9am–5pm; M$51, free Sun; Ⓦ www.mnh.inah.gob.mx). The setting is very much part of the attraction, with many rooms retaining the opulent furnishings left behind by Maximilian and Carlota, or by later inhabitants with equally expensive tastes, notably Porfirio Díaz. Rivalling the decor is a small group of carriages, including the fabulously pompous Cinderella-goes-to-the-ball state coaches favoured by Maximilian. A collection of furniture, glassware and medals leads on to the main attraction of the lower floor, a series of ornate rooms viewed from a black-and-white tiled terrace that affords great views over the park and city. Peer into

Maximilian's office, games room and drawing room, all gilt and dark wood, then move on to Carlota's bedroom and a gorgeous tiled bathroom.

The upper floor is arranged around a formal rooftop garden off which you can visit yet more sumptuous rooms and a magnificent Parisian stained-glass wall imported by Díaz and depicting five goddesses in a Greco-Roman setting. There are several murals here as well, including a number of works by **Orozco** and **Siqueiros**, but the ones by **Juan O'Gorman** most directly attract attention for their single-minded political message.

Museo Nacional de Antropología

The park's outstanding attraction – for many people the main justification for visiting the city at all – is the **Museo Nacional de Antropología** (Tues–Sun 9am–7pm; M$51 Tues–Sat, free Sun; Ⓦwww.mna.inah.gob.mx), one of the world's great museums, not only for its collection, which is vast, rich and diverse, but also for the originality and practicality of its design. Opened in 1964, the exhibition halls surround a patio with a small pond and a vast, square concrete umbrella supported by a single slender pillar around which splashes an artificial cascade. The halls are ringed by gardens, many of which contain outdoor exhibits. If you're rushed, the whole thing can be taken in on one visit, but it is far more satisfactory to spread your visit over two days. The museum can get rather crowded on Sundays when admission is free – it can be worth it to pay the entrance fee and come during the week.

Museum orientation

The museum's rooms, each devoted to a separate period or culture, are arranged chronologically in an anti-clockwise pattern around the central courtyard. As you come into the **entrance hall** there's a small circular space with temporary exhibitions, usually very interesting and devoted to the latest developments in archeology; here too is the small **Sala de Orientación**, which presents an audio-visual overview of the major ancient cultures. Off to the left you'll find the **library** and a **shop** selling postcards, souvenirs, books in several languages on Mexican culture, archeology and history and **guidebooks** (two sizes, in Spanish, English, French or German; M$74 and M$285), which provide photographs and descriptions of most of the important pieces. **The ticket office**, and the **entrance** to the museum proper, is by the huge glass doors to the right, where you can also rent headsets, which effectively take you on a **tour** of the museum's highlights in Spanish, English or French for M$75 (and you have to deposit a piece of ID as security); they're very cursory, but you do get around the whole museum with some form of explanation. Labelling of individual items is mostly in Spanish, though the general introduction to each room is accompanied by an English translation.

A complete tour of the museum starts on the right-hand side with three **introductory rooms** explaining what anthropology is, the nature of and relationship between the chief Mesoamerican cultures and the region's prehistory. It's worth spending time here if only to note the clear acknowledgement of the continuing discrimination against Mexico's native people. These rooms are followed on the right-hand side by halls devoted to the **Pre-Classic**, **Teotihuacán** and **Toltec** cultures. At the far end is the vast **Mexica** (Aztec) room, followed around the left wing by **Oaxaca** (Mixtec and Zapotec), **Gulf of Mexico** (Olmec), **Maya** and the cultures of the **north** and **west**. Every hall has at least one outstanding feature, but if you have limited time, the Aztec and the Maya rooms are the **highlights**; what else you see should depend on what area of the country you plan to head on to. The upper floor is given over to **ethnography collections**, which are devoted to the life and culture of the various indigenous groups today; stairs lead up from each side. Downstairs, behind the hall given over to the cultures of the north and west, is a very welcome **restaurant**.

The entrance from Reforma is marked by a colossal statue of the rain god Tlaloc – the story goes that its move here from its original home in the east of the city was accompanied by furious downpours in the midst of a drought. Just east of the museum is a large open plaza, at one end of which is a small clearing pierced by a twenty-metre pole from which **voladores** "fly". This Totonac ceremony (see box, p.598) is performed several times a day, and loses a lot of its appeal through its commercial nature – an assistant canvasses the crowd for donations as they perform – but it is still an impressive spectacle.

Pre-Classic

The **Pre-Classic** room covers the development of the first cultures in the Valley of México and surrounding highlands – pottery and clay figurines from these early agricultural communities predominate. Notice especially the **small female figures** dated 1700–1300 BC from Tlatilco (a site in the suburbs), which are probably related to some form of fertility or harvest rites. The influence of the growing Olmec culture begins to be seen in later artefacts, including the amazing **acrobat** vase, also from Tlatilco. With the development of more formal religion, recognizable images of gods also appear: several of these, from Cuicuilco in the south of the city, depict **Huehueteotl**, the old god or god of fire, as an old man with flames on his back.

Teotihuacán

The next hall is devoted to **Teotihuacán** (see p.464), the first great city in the Valley of México. A growing sophistication is immediately apparent in the more elaborate nature of the pottery vessels and the use of new materials, shells, stone and jewels. There's a full-scale reproduction of part of the **Temple of Quetzalcoatl** at Teotihuacán, brightly polychromed as it would originally have been. It contains the remains of nine sacrificial victims dressed as warriors, complete with their funerary necklaces: a relatively recent confirmation of human sacrifice and militarism at Teotihuacán. Nearby is a reconstruction of the inside courtyard and central temple of an apartment complex bedecked in vibrant murals representing ritual life in the city, including *The Paradise of Tlaloc*, a depiction of the heaven reserved for warriors and ball-players who died in action.

Toltec

The **Toltec** room begins with vibrant red and blue murals from Cacaxtla near Tlaxcala (see p.480) and then objects from Xochicalco, a city near modern Cuernavaca (see p.499), which flourished between the fall of Teotihuacán and the heyday of Tula. The large stone carvings and pottery show a distinct Maya influence: particularly lovely is the stylized stone **head of a macaw**, similar to ones found on Maya ball-courts in Honduras. Highlights of the section devoted to Tula are the weighty stone carvings, including one of the Atlantean columns from the main temple there, representing a warrior. Also of note are the **Chac-mool**, a reclining figure with a receptacle on his stomach in which sacrificial offerings were placed, and high up, above a large frieze, the **standard bearer**, a small human figure that acted as a flagpole when a standard was inserted into the hole between its clasped hands. Overlooking some human remains, there's an exquisite little mother-of-pearl-encrusted sculpture of a **coyote's head** with teeth made of bone and a bearded man (possibly a warrior in a headdress) emerging from its mouth.

Mexica

Next comes the biggest and richest room of all, the **Mexica Gallery**, characterized by massive yet intricate stone sculpture, but also displaying pottery, small stone objects, even wooden musical instruments. Facing you as you enter is the

▲ Piedra del Sol, Museo Nacional de Antropología, Mexico City

Ocelotl-Cuauhxicalli, a jaguar with a hollow in its back in which the hearts of human sacrifices were placed (it may have been the companion of the eagle in the Templo Mayor museum; the two were found very close to each other, though over eighty years apart). Among the hundreds of other powerful pieces – most of the vast Aztec pantheon is represented – snakes, eagles and human hearts and skulls are prominent. Among the statues is a vast image of **Coatlicue**, goddess of the earth, life and death, and mother of the gods. She is shown with two serpents above her shoulders, representing the flow of blood; her necklace of hands and hearts and pendant of a skull represent life and death respectively; her dress is made of snakes; her feet are eagles' claws. As a counterpoint to the viciousness of most of this, be sure to notice **Xochipilli**, the god of love, flowers, dance and poetry (and incidentally featured on the hundred-peso bill). You'll come across him, wearing a mask and sitting cross-legged on a throne strewn with flowers and butterflies, to the left of the entrance as you come in. Also impressive is a reconstructed version of **Moctezuma's headdress**, resplendent in bright blue quetzal feathers.

The room's undoubted highlight, directly opposite the entrance, is the enormous 24-tonne **Piedra del Sol**, the Stone of the Sun or Aztec Calendar Stone. The latter, popular name is not strictly accurate, for this is much more a vision of the Aztec cosmos, completed under Moctezuma only a few years before the Spanish arrived. The stone was found by early colonists, and deliberately reburied for fear that it would spread unrest among the population. After being dug up again in the Zócalo in 1790 it spent years propped up against the walls of the cathedral. In the centre is the sun god and personification of the fifth sun, Tonatiuh, with a tongue in the form of a sacrificial knife and claws holding human hearts on each side, representing the need for human sacrifice to nourish the sun; around him are symbols for the four previous incarnations of the sun – a jaguar, wind, water and fiery rain; this whole central conglomeration forms the sign for the date on which the fifth world would end (as indeed, with the Spanish Conquest, it fairly accurately did). Encircling all this are hieroglyphs representing the twenty days of the Aztec month and other symbols of cosmic importance, and the whole thing is surrounded by two serpents.

Oaxaca

Moving round to the third side of the museum you reach the halls devoted to cultures based away from the highlands, starting, in the corner of the museum, with the **Zapotec** and **Mixtec** people of **Oaxaca**. Although the two cultures evolved side by side, the Zapotecs flourished earlier (from around 900 BC to 800 AD) as accomplished architects with an advanced scientific knowledge, and also as makers of magnificent pottery with a pronounced Olmec influence. From around 800 AD many of their sites were taken over by the Mixtecs, whose overriding talents were as craftsmen and artists, working in metal, precious stone and clay. The best site in the country for both these cultures is Monte Albán (see p.633).

The Zapotec collection demonstrates a fine sense of movement in the human figures: a reproduction of part of the carved facade of the Temple of the Dancers at Monte Albán; a model of a temple with a parrot sitting in it (in the "Monte Albán II" section); vases and urns in the form of various gods; and a superb jade mask representing the bat god Piquete Ziña. Among the Mixtec objects are many beautifully polychromed clay vessels, including a cup with a hummingbird perched on its rim, and sculptures in jade and quartz crystal. Reproductions of Zapotec and Mixtec tombs show how many of the finer small objects were discovered.

Gulf of Mexico

Next is the **Gulf of Mexico** room, in which are displayed some of the treasures of **Olmec** art as well as objects produced in this region during the Classic period. The Olmec civilization is considered the mother culture of Mexico for its advanced development as early as 1500 BC, which provided much of the basis for the later Teotihuacán and Maya cultures. Olmec figures are delightful, but have many puzzling aspects, in particular their apparently African features, nowhere better displayed than in some of the famed **colossal heads** dating from 1200–200 BC, long before Africa is supposed to have had any connection with the Americas. Many of the smaller pieces show evidence of deliberate deformation of the skull and teeth. The statue known as "the wrestler", with arms akimbo as if at the point of starting a bout, and the many tiny objects in jade and other polished stones are all outstanding. The later cultures are substantially represented, with fine figures and excellent pottery above all. The two most celebrated pieces are a statue of **Huehueteotl**, looking thoroughly grouchy with a brazier perched on his head, and the so-called **Huastec Adolescent**, a young Huastec Indian priest of Quetzalcoatl (perhaps the god himself) with an elaborately decorated naked body and a child on his back.

Maya

The hall devoted to the **Maya** is the most varied, reflecting the longest-lived and widest-spread of the Mesoamerican cultures. In some ways it's a disappointment, since their greatest achievements were in architecture and in the decoration of their temples – many of which, unlike those of the Aztecs, are still standing – so that the objects here seem relatively unimpressive. Nevertheless, there are reproductions of several buildings, or parts of them, friezes and columns taken from them and extensive collections of jewellery, pottery and minor sculpture. Steps lead down into a section devoted to burial practices, including a reproduction of the Royal Tomb at **Palenque** (see p.717) with many of the objects found there – notably the prince's jade death mask. Outside, several small temples from relatively obscure sites are reproduced, the Temple of Paintings from **Bonampak** (see p.723) among them. The three rooms of the temple are entirely covered in frescoes representing the coronation of a new prince, a great battle and the subsequent punishments and celebrations. They are much easier to visit than the originals and in far better condition.

Northern and western societies

As a finale to the archeological collections on the ground floor, there's a large room devoted to the north and the west of the country. **Northern** societies on the whole developed few large centres, remaining isolated nomadic or agricultural communities. The small quantities of pottery, weapons and jewellery that have survived show a close affinity with native tribes of the American Southwest. The **west** was far more developed, but it, too, has left relatively few traces, and many of the best examples of **Tarascan culture** (see box, p.348) remain in Guadalajara. Among the highlights here are some delightful small human and animal figurines in stone and clay, a Tarascan Chac-mool, a jade mask of Malinaltepec inlaid with a turquoise and red-shell mosaic and a two-storey reconstruction of the houses at Paquimé in the Chihuahua desert.

The Ethnography Section

The **Ethnography Section** is on the upper floor. You must cross the courtyard back towards the beginning of the museum before climbing the stairs – otherwise you'll go round in reverse order. The rooms relate as closely as possible to those below them, showing the lifestyle of surviving indigenous groups today through photographs, models, maps and examples of local crafts. Regional dress and reproductions of various types of huts and cabins form a major part of this inevitably rather sanitized look at the poorest (and most oppressed) people in Mexico, and there are also objects relating to their more important cults and ceremonies.

Around the Museo Nacional de Antropología

The enormous success of the Museo de Antropología has led to a spate of other audacious modern **exhibition halls** being set up in the park. Two – the Museo de Arte Moderno and the Museo Rufino Tamayo – are very close by, and together with the adjoining **zoo**, make this one of the finest concentrations of diversions in the otherwise sprawling city.

Museo de Arte Moderno

Some 300m east of the Museo Nacional de Antropología on Paseo de la Reforma lies the **Museo de Arte Moderno** (Tues–Sun 10.30am–5.30pm; M$20, free Sun). This consists of two low circular buildings dedicated to twentieth-century Mexican and Latin American art. The majority of the galleries, along with a separate gallery reached through the **sculpture garden**, are devoted to temporary and touring exhibitions, which are usually well worth inspection. The **permanent collection** is housed on the ground floor of the Sala Xavier Villaurrutia, to the right as you enter, and should not be missed.

All the major Mexican artists of the twentieth century are well represented. Among several works by Siqueiros, the most powerful is *Madre Campesina*, in which a peasant woman carries her child barefoot through an unforgiving desert of cacti. There's a whole corner devoted to Orozco, and oils by Diego Rivera, notably a portrait of his second wife, Lupe Marín, painted in 1938, long after their divorce. Look too for Olga Costa's *Vendedora de Frutas*, whose fruit-seller surrounded by bananas, sugar cane, watermelons, pumpkins, pawpaws, soursops and *mameyes*, all painted in vibrant reds and yellows, is about as Mexican a subject as you could want. The star attraction is Frida Kahlo's *Las Dos Fridas*, which stands out even among the museum's fine representative selection of haunting and disturbing canvases by Kahlo. One of her earliest full-scale paintings, it depicts her on the left in a white traditional dress, her heart torn and wounded, and her hand being held by a stronger Frida on the right, dressed in modern clothes and holding a locket with a picture of her husband Diego Rivera as a boy.

Museo Rufino Tamayo

Hidden among trees across the street from the Museum of Modern Art is the **Museo Rufino Tamayo** (Tues–Sun 10am–6pm; M$15, free Sun; Ⓦwww.museotamayo.org), another fine collection of modern art – this one with an international focus. The modernist structure was built by the artist Rufino Tamayo, whose work in murals and on smaller projects was far more abstract and less political than the Big Three, though he was their approximate contemporary and enjoys a reasonable amount of international fame. There is much of his own work here, and exhibits of his techniques and theories, but also a fairly impressive collection of European and American twentieth-century art – most of it from Tamayo's private collection. Artists represented may include Picasso, Miró, Magritte, Francis Bacon and Henry Moore, though not all of these are on permanent display. First-rate contemporary international exhibits usually find their way here and sometimes take over the space of parts of the permanent collection.

Lago Chapultepec and the Parque Zoológico de Chapultepec

On the south side of Reforma, opposite the Museo de Antropología, lies **Lago Chapultepec**, where you can rent **boats** (M$60–100/hr for 1–5 people, depending on the size of the boat) and while away a leisurely afternoon. At the western side of the lake is the main entrance to the **Parque Zoológico de Chapultepec** (Tues–Sun 9am–4.30pm; free; Ⓦwww.cnf.org.mx), which occupies a large area in the centre of the park and is divided up into climatic zones – desert, tropical, temperate forests, etc – some of which work better than others. Enclosures are mostly open-air and tolerably large, though the animals still look bored and confined, and you wonder about their sanity on a Sunday afternoon when half of Mexico City's children seem to be vying for their attention. Probably the most satisfying sections are the most archetypally Mexican: the desert zone, and the enclosure of **Xoloitzcuintle**, the hairless dogs that represent the last surviving of four pre-Columbian breeds.

All the big beasts make an appearance, too: tigers, bears, lions, bison, camels, giraffes, hippos, elephants and the ever-popular **giant pandas**. The zoo is inordinately proud of these, evidenced by the posters around town that advertise new baby bears when they are born – in fact, this was the first place in the world to breed giant pandas in captivity.

Auditorio Nacional, Los Pinos and Casa Luis Barragán

Continuing west from the zoo, Reforma crosses Calzada Chivatito at Metro Auditorio, beyond which is the **Auditorio Nacional** (Ⓦwww.auditorio.com.mx), a major venue for dance, theatre and music events, with a couple of small theatres and an enormous auditorium. Further out, Reforma leaves the park via the Fuente de Petróleos, a complex of modern skyscrapers surrounding a monument to the nationalization of the oil industry, and heads into Las Lomas, an expensive suburb whose luxury villas are mostly hidden behind high walls and heavy security gates.

Heading south from Metro Auditorio, Calzada Chivatito becomes Molino del Rey, a street named after the major battle here during the Mexican–American War. There are still barracks here, along with **Los Pinos**, the president's official residence, which is strictly off-limits. A couple of footbridges lead from outside the barracks across the *periférico* (Bulevar López Mateos) to the park's Second Section.

Nearby, at Francisco Ramírez 14, the **Casa Luis Barragán** (Ⓦwww.casaluisbarragan.org; visits by appointment only Mon–Fri 10am, 2pm, 4pm & 6pm, Sat 10pm & 1pm; Ⓣ55/5515-4908, Ⓔinformes@casaluisbarragan.org) is a 1948 modernist house designed by Mexican architect Luis Barragán (see p.434), all whitewash and right angles. It's nowadays used for modern art exhibitions.

Nuevo Bosque de Chapultepec: Segunda and Tercera secciónes

Over the years, new sections of parkland have been added to the west of the original Bosque de Chapultepec. These are occasionally still referred to as the **Nuevo Bosque de Chapultepec**, but are more commonly known as the **Segunda Sección**, or Second Section (marked on signs and maps as "2a Sección") and **Tercera Sección**, or Third Section (3a Sección). With very few places to cross the *periférico*, it is difficult to reach the newer parts of the park from the old. It is far better to make a separate visit (see box, p.418) to these sections, especially if you've got kids. There are fewer genuinely compelling reasons to visit either section for adults, though the Second Section is an enjoyable area to stroll about, and a good deal quieter than the main section of the park.

Segunda Sección

Approaching the Second Section from Metro Constituyentes, follow Avenida Constituyentes west for a few metres and then cross it on a footbridge. Follow a short street to the *periférico*, also crossed by a nearby footbridge, to bring you to the **Museo Tecnológico** (daily 9am–5pm; free; Ⓦwww.cfe.gob.mx/mutec), entered on its west side, with its central building surrounded by outdoor exhibits. Despite being sponsored by some of Mexico's biggest companies, these remain unengaging affairs, at odds with the professionalism evident in the displays in most of Mexico City's museums. You can walk around a model of a geothermal power plant and another of a hydro project, as well as assorted bits of machinery and railway rolling stock all too static or inaccessible really to arouse much interest. Inside it is more accomplished, with interactive displays, flight simulators and collections of models. It's a fun place for kids to play, but only educational if their (or your) Spanish is fairly good. There's also a planetarium (free, Spanish only) with shows Mon–Sat 10am, 11am, noon, 1pm, 3pm & 4pm, Sun 10am, 11am, noon, 1.30pm, 3pm & 4pm.

Right next door is **La Feria** (school holidays around Semana Santa; July, Aug & Dec Tues–Sun 10am–8pm; rest of the year Tues–Fri 10am–5pm, Sat 10am–7pm, Sun 10am–8pm; M$50 for entry with no rides included), the city's premier fun park. Here you'll find assorted rides and sideshows, easily the best of which is the old-fashioned wooden roller coaster (*montaña rusa*). A M$100 pass gives you access to most of the rides, but not the very top attractions including the roller coaster (M$20); a M$150 pass gives access to all the rides.

On the other side of the Museo Tecnológico lies **Papalote Museo del Niño**, Constituyentes 268 (Mon–Wed & Fri 9am–6pm, Thurs 9am–11pm, Sat & Sun 10am–7pm; M$99), a kind of cross between an adventure playground and a science experiment, with loads of fascinating hands-on experiments, plus an IMAX cinema (M$90, combination ticket with museum M$125) and a music-and-visuals dome (M$90, combination ticket with museum M$125, combination ticket with museum and IMAX M$160). Adults may feel as if they have entered some sort of psychotic kindergarten, but if you have kids, it will keep them entertained.

Heading west from Papalote you pass the rather tacky **Mexico Magic** fun park (closed for refurbishment at the time of writing) en route to the **Museo de Historia Natural** (Tues–Sun 10am–5pm; M$20, free Tues, M$11.50 to bring in a camera), ten interconnecting domes filled with displays on nature and conservation, biology and geology, including rundowns on Mexico's mineral wealth, flora and fauna. Modern and well presented – and with the obligatory dinosaurs – it is again particularly popular with children.

Tercera Sección

The newest section of the park, the **Tercera Sección**, lies a kilometre further west, beyond the **Panteón Civil de Dolores** cemetery (daily 7am–6pm), where Diego Rivera, José Clemente Orozco and other illustrious Mexicans are buried. To get there catch a *pesero* (route #24 to "Panteón Dolores" or "Atlantis") from Metro Chapultepec or along Avenida Constituyentes.

The main draw in this section – open to the general public only on weekends and public holidays – is **Atlantis** (Sat, Sun & public holidays 10.30am–6pm; M$55), a kind of zoo-cum-circus with marine mammals and assorted birds, some of them trained to take part in various performances, for a number of which there is an additional fee.

South of the centre

Mexico City spreads itself furthest to the south, where a series of old villages that have been swallowed up by the urban sprawl harbour some of the most enticing destinations outside the centre, including the colonial suburbs of **Coyoacán** and **San Ángel**, the archeological site of **Cuicuilco** and the canals of **Xochimilco**.

Insurgentes

Insurgentes, the most direct approach to the suburbs, is interesting in its own right: leaving behind the Glorieta de Insurgentes (the roundabout at Insurgentes Metro station), it runs almost perfectly straight all the way out to the university, lined the whole way with huge department stores and malls, cinemas, restaurants and office buildings. A little under halfway to San Ángel, you pass on the right the enormous **World Trade Center**, crowned by *Bellini's*, an expensive revolving restaurant (see p.445).

Just south of the World Trade Center, and on the right (if heading south) is the garish **Polyforum Siqueiros** (daily 9am–6pm; M$15; ⓣ55/5536-4520 to 24, ⓦwww.polyforumsiqueiros.com.mx; Metrobús Poliforum). Its exterior is plastered in brash paintings by David Siqueiros and some thirty other artists.

Getting to the southern suburbs

It's not at all difficult to get out to any of the sights outside the city centre on **public transport**, but getting from one to the other can be tricky if you're cutting across the main north–south routes. In fact, there is easily enough to see out this way to justify a couple of separate trips, thereby avoiding the slightly complicated matter of traversing the area. And while none of the connections you have to make is impossible, it's worth taking a few short taxi rides between them, from San Ángel to Coyoacán, for example, or from Coyoacán to Rivera's Anahuacalli Museum. If you want to see as much as possible in a day or even an afternoon, you might consider getting a **tourist taxi** (see p.389) to take you round the lot. If you bargain, this may not be as expensive as it sounds; indeed it sometimes seems that you can barely be paying for the petrol used. Alternatively there are **coach tours** run by several of the bigger travel agencies in the Zona Rosa.

For **San Ángel and the University City**, the best approach is along Insurgentes Sur, plied by the Metrobús (see p.389). There are also plenty of *peseros* from the bus stands by Metro Chapultepec or Tasqueña for services along the Calzada de Tlalpan and to the southwest of the city, above all to Xochimilco. If you'd rather stick to the **Metro**, take line 3 to Miguel Ángel de Quevedo, between San Ángel and Coyoacán.

To get to **Coyoacán** from San Ángel, buses head down Altavista by the *San Ángel Inn*; from the centre, buses leave from Metros Chapultepec, Insurgentes or Cuauhtémoc. In each case look for "Coyoacán" or "Colonia del Valle/Coyoacán". There's also a trolleybus that runs down Lázaro Cárdenas against the flow of traffic from a stop close by Bellas Artes. Metro line 3, too, passes close by, though note that Viveros station is considerably closer to the action than Coyoacán station: from Viveros, walk south on Avenida Universidad, then turn left (east) to reach the centre. If you're coming straight from the centre of town down Cuauhtémoc or Lázaro Cárdenas, it makes sense to visit the Kahlo and Trotsky museums (see p.431 & p.433) first, in which case you'll want to get off the bus immediately after passing under Avenida Río Churubusco. The Metro stops are slightly more distant, but a good approach is to take line 2 to General Anaya and walk west from there past the Museo de las Intervenciones and the Trotsky and Frida Kahlo houses.

Inside, it contains what is allegedly the world's largest mural (about 4500 square metres), painted by Siqueiros alone, entitled *The March of Humanity on Earth and Towards the Cosmos*. For the full impact of the changing perspectives and use of sculptural techniques, try to see the **sound-and-light show** (Sat & Sun noon & 2pm; M$30) with taped narration by Siqueiros. Elsewhere, the building houses visiting art exhibitions and a sizeable display of expensive crafts for sale.

Beyond this monster you shortly pass close by the **Plaza México**, the largest bullring in the world, with a capacity of 48,000. You can't actually see it from Insurgentes, but it's only a ten-minute walk along San Antonio, hard by the **Estadio Azul**, a 65,000-seat soccer stadium that is home to Cruz Azul. Finally, just before San Ángel comes the **Teatro de los Insurgentes**, its facade covered in a huge mosaic designed by Diego Rivera depicting the history of Mexican theatre, and assorted historical figures. At the top are Los Insurgentes of Mexico's War of Independence: Hidalgo, Morelos and Benito Juárez on the left, and Zapata on the right.

San Ángel

The upmarket colonial suburb of **San Ángel** lies 12km southwest of central Mexico City, clustered around the point where Insurgentes Sur and Revolución almost meet, linked by the 200-metre-long Avenida La Paz. With its markets, ancient mansions and high-priced shops – Cartier, Italian designer furniture and the like – around flower-draped patios, San Ángel is a very exclusive place to live. It also makes an inviting place to visit, packed with little restaurants and cafés where you can sit outside and watch the crowds go by; it is especially appealing on Saturdays when the delightful **Plaza San Jacinto** is taken over by **Bazar Sábado**, a lively outdoor art market. Initially, the Saturday market was based in one of the mansions on the square, which still opens every weekend selling upmarket crafts and artworks, but nowadays there are stalls in all the surrounding streets, with fairground rides and freak shows. The plaza is surrounded by San Ángel's oldest mansions, notably the eighteenth-century **Casa del Risco**, at no. 15 (Tues–Sun 10am–5pm; free), housing a collection of antique furniture and paintings, with an extraordinary fountain in the patio made from old porcelain plates and cups, broken and unbroken.

Whether you choose to visit on Saturday or one of the quieter days of the week, consider sticking around until evening to blow an appreciable wad of cash on some of the finest dining in the city (see p.446).

Museo del Carmen

San Ángel takes its name from the former Carmelite Convent of San Angelo Mártir, on Revolución just south of its junction with La Paz, which is now run as the **Museo del Carmen** (Tues–Sun 10am–4.45pm; M$41, free Sun). Its three brightly coloured, tiled domes preside over this part of town and add the final touch of grace to what is a lovely example of early seventeenth-century architecture. The church is still used but the rest of the convent has become a museum where just walking through the maze of monks' cells, rooms and courtyards is pleasurable enough, though there's also an extensive collection of colonial religious paintings and furniture. Just about everyone wants to make their way to the crypt to see the dozen **mummies**, found here by troops during the Revolution and thought to be eighteenth-century nuns and monks, now displayed behind glass. Elsewhere, check out the extensive displays on daily life in New Spain and a collection of eighteenth-century oils by Cristóbal de Vallalpando.

Museo de Arte Carrillo-Gil

Heading north along Revolución past a small flower market, you reach the **Museo de Arte Carrillo-Gil**, Revolución 1608 (Ⓦwww.museodeartecarrillogil.com; Tues–Sun 10am–6pm; M$15, free Sun), a surprisingly good museum of modern art that seems a little incongruous in colonial San Ángel. The museum was built in 1974 to house the collection of **Dr Alvaro Carrillo**, a skilled painter and art critic, as well as a friend of Siqueiros and long-time supporter of the avant-garde, who had been amassing works since the 1930s. Three airy and spacious floors feature pieces by Mexicans including Rivera (a couple of Cubist canvases), Siqueiros and most importantly, Orozco, of whose work here *Zapata* and *Christ Destroying His Cross* are the most striking examples. There's also a smattering of international big names, but many are out on loan or stored away to make space for the numerous temporary exhibits and contemporary installations.

Museo Casa Estudio Diego Rivera y Frida Kahlo and the San Ángel Inn

From the Museo de Arte Carrillo-Gil it's just over half a kilometre along Altavista to the **Museo Casa Estudio Diego Rivera y Frida Kahlo**, Diego Rivera 2 (Tues–Sun 10am–6pm; M$10, free Sun), a pair of modernist houses built for Diego Rivera and Frida Kahlo in 1931–32 by the leading contemporary architect, Juan O'Gorman. Tucked behind an organ cactus fence opposite the prestigious *San Ángel Inn* restaurant (see p.446) sits a small compound with a large maroon-coloured house (Diego's)

A walk from San Ángel to Coyoacán

The most enjoyable way to take in San Ángel and Coyoacán on the same day is to put an hour or so aside and **walk** between the two. The most pleasant route, through quiet streets past some of the city's prime real estate (marked on the map on p.430), starts at the main junction in the centre of San Ángel where Revolución passes the Museo del Carmen (see opposite). From here, follow La Paz northeast and cross Insurgentes to reach the **Jardín de la Bombilla**, a small park centred on a blockish concrete monument to General Alvaro Obregón, who was assassinated here in 1928 soon after being re-elected as president. Revolutionary workers (corn cob in one hand, hammer and sickle in the other) flank the monument, and you can duck inside to see the bronze statue of Obregón. On the east side of the park, cross Chimalistac and walk through the tiny Plaza Frederico Gamboa. When you reach the other side, take a left (you're now headed north) and cross Miguel Ángel de Quevedo, passing **Parque Tagle** on your left, then turn right into Arenal. This leads you across Universidad to the **Capilla de San Antonio Panzacola**, a little red chapel sited attractively next to a small stone bridge.

Continue east on the peaceful, cobbled Francisco Sosa, one of the most beautiful streets in the city, and also one of the oldest. Peer over the high walls lining the street to catch a glimpse of some gorgeous residences – the only way to get any closer to these houses is to visit the **Museo Nacional de la Acuarela**, Salvador Nova 88 (daily 10am–6pm; free), a small museum inside one. Devoted to watercolour painting, the collection includes some architectural and graphic art as well. Look for work by early twentieth-century painter Saturnino Herrán, and don't miss the temporary exhibits in a separate gallery reached through a small sculpture garden.

Ten minutes' walk further along Francisco Sosa brings you to the **Plaza Santa Caterina**, a tranquil square overlooked by a mustard-yellow church and with a couple of restaurants. From here it is a short walk to Coyoacán's Plaza Central, reached through a twin-arched gateway.

and a much smaller blue abode (Frida's), connected by a rooftop causeway. From 1933 to 1941 they both stayed here, living and working apart yet still near enough to visit each other and for Frida to deliver Diego's meals. In both buildings the walls are concrete, the floors are wooden and many of the windows go from floor to ceiling – very advanced for the early 1930s and especially for Mexico. Indeed, the whole set-up is in such contrast to the Blue House in Coyoacán (see p.431) that it is hard to imagine that the houses were inhabited by the same people.

Diego's studio contains some of his painting materials, along with personal items, reproductions of some of his work and some large papier-mâché skeletons. Temporary exhibits take up much of Frida's house, though there are a couple of fine portraits of her taken by photographer Nikolas Muray, with whom Frida had an affair in the late 1930s, and some of Frida's own ex-voto paintings of her debilitating accident.

Coyoacán

Around 3km east of San Ángel lies **COYOACÁN**, another colonial township that has been absorbed by the city. Even before the Conquest it was a sizeable place. Originally the capital of a small lakeshore kingdom, it was subjugated by the Aztecs in the mid-fifteenth century. Cortés based himself in Coyoacán during the siege of Tenochtitlán, and continued to live here while the old city was torn down and construction began on the capital of Nueva España. It remains far less touristed than San Ángel, although the plazas are pretty lively, especially at weekends. The focus of the area is the spacious **Plaza Central** (Plaza Hidalgo and the Jardín del Centenario).

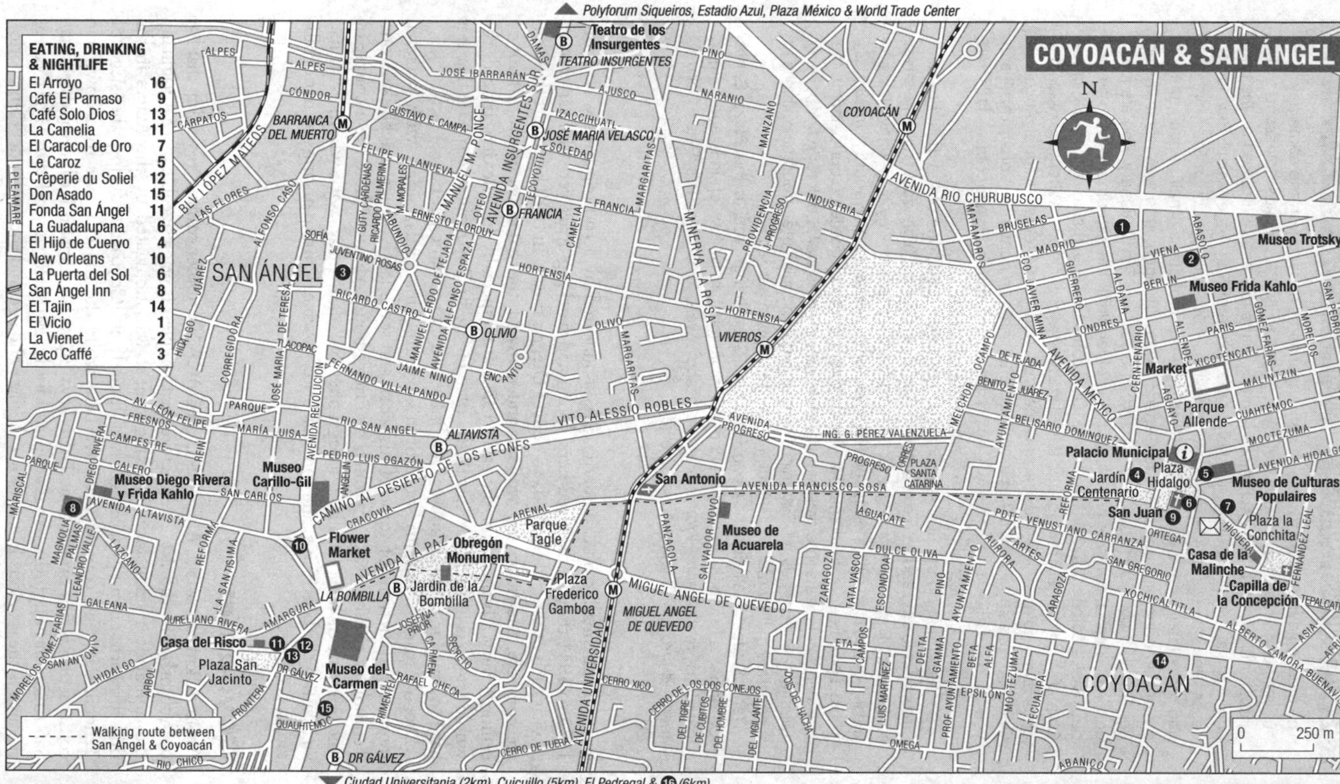
COYOACÁN & SAN ÁNGEL
N
EATING, DRINKING & NIGHTLIFE
El Arroyo 16
Café El Parnaso 9
Café Solo Dios 13
La Camelia 11
El Caracol de Oro 7
Le Caroz 5
Crêperie du Soliel 12
Don Asado 15
Fonda San Ángel 11
La Guadalupana 6
El Hijo de Cuervo 4
New Orleans 10
La Puerta del Sol 6
San Ángel Inn 8
El Tajin 14
El Vicio 1
La Vienet 2
Zeco Caffé 3
Walking route between San Ángel & Coyoacán
0 250 m
Polyforum Siqueiros, Estadio Azul, Plaza México & World Trade Center
Museo Nacional de las Intervenciones
Ciudad Universitania (2km), Cuicuillo (5km), El Pedregal & 16 (6km)
SAN ÁNGEL
COYOACÁN
Teatro de los Insurgentes
TEATRO INSURGENTES
BARRANCA DEL MUERTO
JOSÉ MARIA VELASCO
FRANCIA
OLIVIO
ALTAVISTA
COYOACÁN
VIVEROS
MIGUEL ANGEL DE QUEVEDO
DR GÁLVEZ
LA BOMBILLA
Museo Trotsky
Museo Frida Kahlo
Market
Parque Allende
Palacio Municipal
Plaza Hidalgo
Jardín Centenario
San Juan
Museo de Culturas Populaires
Plaza la Conchita
Casa de la Malinche
Capilla de la Concepción
San Antonio
Museo de la Acuarela
Parque Tagle
Plaza Frederico Gamboa
Obregón Monument
Jardín de la Bombilla
Flower Market
Museo Carillo-Gil
Museo Diego Rivera y Frida Kahlo
Casa del Risco
Plaza San Jacinto
Museo del Carmen
AVENIDA RIO CHURUBUSCO
AVENIDA INSURGENTES SUR
AVENIDA REVOLUCION
AVENIDA UNIVERSIDAD
AVENIDA MÉXICO
AVENIDA FRANCISCO SOSA
MIGUEL ANGEL DE QUEVEDO
MINERVA LA ROSA
VITO ALESSÍO ROBLES
CAMINO AL DESIERTO DE LOS LEONES
AVENIDA LA PAZ
BLV LÓPEZ MATEOS
AVENIDA PROGRESO
AVENIDA ALTAVISTA
MANUEL M. PONCE
PLAZA SANTA CATARINA

Nearby, in the small Plaza la Conchita, the **Capilla de la Concepción** has a wonderful Baroque facade. Overlooking the square, the distinctive red **Casa de la Malinche** (not open to the public) is the house in which Cortés installed his native mistress – and where he allegedly later murdered his wife shortly after her arrival from Spain. No visit to Coyoacán is complete without strolling out to the northern reaches of the suburb to the two main sights, the **Frida Kahlo** and **Leon Trotsky museums**.

Plaza Central

Coyoacán's **Plaza Central** is one of the city's main stomping grounds for artists, artisans and musicians. It is actually made up of two adjoining plazas – **Plaza Hidalgo** and the **Jardín del Centenario**. Bars and cafés ring the plaza. On Sunday, there's a market in the Plaza Central, and the area is taken up by stalls and various rock, folk and reggae bands. It's far and away the most fun place in the city to buy your souvenirs (T-shirts make good buys here, some of them hand-painted), though most of the stuff can be found cheaper elsewhere.

The Plaza Central is also home to the sixteenth-century church of San Juan and the small **Palacio Municipal** (also known as the Casa de Cortés), said to have been built by Cortés himself. Inside the palacio are two **murals** by pupils of Rivera's – one by Aurora Reyes depicting the Conquest, and one by Diego Rosales showing the torture of Cuauhtémoc. The latter is particularly apposite since it was in Coyoacán that the Aztec leader was tortured and finally killed. The murals aren't open to the public, but if you ask at the **tourist office** in the same building (just inside the main entrance, on the right; daily 8am–8pm; Ⓣ55/5658-0221) they might let you take a peek at Reyes's mural, in the Sala de Cabildos, a municipal office. The other mural is in the *capilla* (registry office), which is only open if there's a wedding on – should you stumble upon one you can discreetly put your head round the door for a quick look.

The **Museo de Culturas Populares** (Tues–Thurs 10am–6pm, Fri–Sun 10am–8pm; M$11, free Sun), close to the Plaza Hidalgo at Av Hidalgo 289, has colourful displays on popular cultural forms, mostly dolls, masks and costumes. Avenida Hidalgo also leads to the Museo Nacional de las Intervenciones (see p.436) – to find it, continue down Avenida Hidalgo for about 300m, and bear left down General Anaya, which leads directly to the museum (crossing División del Norte on the way), a fifteen- to twenty-minute walk.

Museo Frida Kahlo

The **Museo Frida Kahlo**, Londres 247, at Allende (Tues–Sun 10am–5.45pm; M$55, ticket also valid for Museo Anahuacalli, see p.436; audio guide M$35; Ⓦwww.museofridakahlo.org; Metro Coyoacán) is just a few minutes' walk from the centre of Coyoacán. The appropriately named Blue House was the Kahlos' family home and this is where Frida was born and spent most of her life, sporadically with husband Diego Rivera, who donated the house to the nation shortly after her death. It was during Frida's and Diego's tenure here in the late 1930s that they played host to the newly arrived **Leon Trotsky** and his wife. Trotsky, ever fearful of assassins, apparently expressed his concern about the ease of access from a neighbouring property, and in a typically expansive gesture Diego simply bought the other house and combined the two. Continually at the centre of the capital's leftist bohemian life, Diego and Frida hosted a coterie of artist and intellectuals at this house – D.H. Lawrence visited frequently, though he had little political or artistic sympathy with Kahlo – or Trotsky.

Several rooms have been set aside as galleries. The first features around twenty relatively minor (and less tortured) examples of Frida's work, from some of her early

Frida Kahlo

Since the 1970s, **Frida Kahlo** (1907–54) has been considered Mexico's most internationally renowned artist, outshining even her husband, Diego Rivera (see p.400), who recognized her as "the first woman in the history of art to treat, with absolute and uncompromising honesty, one might even say with impassive cruelty, those general and specific themes which exclusively affect women". Julie Taymor's 2002 biopic *Frida*, starring Salma Hayek, further consolidated her role as a **feminist icon**. Her work is deeply personal, centred on her insecurities and her relations with her family, her country and her politics. "I paint myself," she said, "because I am so often alone, and because I am the subject I know best." Her relatively short painting career was never prolific and the largest collection of her work is at the **Museo Dolores Olmedo Patiño** (see p.437).

Early life

The daughter of a *mestizo* Mexican mother and Hungarian Jewish father, Frida was born in the Blue House in Coyoacán (now the **Museo Frida Kahlo**, see p.431) in 1907, though she always claimed she was born in 1910, symbolically uniting her birth with the start of the Revolution. When she was 6, she battled a bout of polio that left her right leg withered. She rebounded and, as a precocious 14-year-old at Mexico City's top school, first met **Diego Rivera** (twenty years her senior) who was painting a mural there. She shocked her friends by declaring that she wished to conceive his child "just as soon as I convince him to cooperate", but they didn't meet again for many years.

Marriage to Rivera

At 18, and already breaking free of the roles then ordained for women in Mexico, Frida had begun to pursue a career in medicine when she suffered a gruesome **accident**. The bus she was riding in was struck by a tram, leaving her with multiple fractures and a pelvis skewered by a steel handrail. It was during the months she spent bedridden, recovering, that she first took up a paintbrush. Later in life, she reflected "I had two accidents in my life. One was the bus, the other Diego." After her recovery she fell in with a left-leaning bunch of artists, free-thinkers and Communists where she again met Rivera. Within a year they were married: she a striking, slender woman of 21; he a massively overweight man twice her age with a frog-like face and an unparalleled reputation for womanizing. Diego went about his affairs quite publicly (including briefly

portraits through to her final work, *Viva la Vida*, a still life of sliced watermelons. She painted it in 1954, when the pain and trauma of her recent leg amputation had taken their toll on her painterly control, if not her spirit. Look too for a beautiful charcoal self-portrait from 1932 and the more political *Marxism Gives Health to the Sick* from 1954. A room full of Frida's signature **tehuana dresses** leads to more paintings, including over a dozen by Rivera, such as *Paisaje de la Quebrada*, which shows a rock face at Acapulco into which Diego painted his own face in purple. Alongside are several works by Velasco and Orozco, as well as a Klee and a Tanguy.

Other sections of the house faithfully show the artesanía style that Frida favoured. Witness the blue and yellow kitchen with "Diego" and "Frida" picked out in tiny ceramic mugs on the wall. Its extraordinary decoration continues with bizarre papier-mâché animals and figures, and an impressive collection of *retablos* around the stairway. This leads up to Frida's airy studio where her wheelchair is artfully set next to an easel and, of course, a mirror. Diego's influence in the house is seen more through his interest in Mexico's pre-Hispanic culture. Artefacts are scattered throughout the house and a small collection is displayed in the courtyard on a small two-step pyramid he had constructed there.

with Frida's sister, Cristina). He was furious when Frida took up with other men, but her several affairs with women seemed to delight him. After her death he wrote, "Too late now, I realized that the most wonderful part of my life had been my love for Frida."

Artistic career

Encouraged by Diego, Frida pursued her **painting** career. Over half of her canvases are **self-portraits**: an unsmiling face with dark monobrow above a body often sliced open and mutilated. Increasingly her self-portraits were imbued with sophisticated personal symbolism, with themes of abortion, broken bones and betrayed love explored through the body set in an unlikely juxtaposition of elements.

In 1932 Frida miscarried and was hospitalized in Detroit where she painted *Henry Ford Hospital*. This disturbing depiction of her grief shows her naked body lying on a bed in an industrial wasteland, surrounded by a foetus, pelvic bones and surgical implements all umbilically tied back to her. After returning to Mexico, her circle of friends expanded to include Trotsky (with whom she had a brief affair), Cuban Communist Julio Antonio Mella and muralist David Siqueiros (later implicated in an attempt to kill Trotsky, see p.434). By now Frida and Diego were living in paired houses in San Ángel (see p.428), which allowed them to maintain relatively separate lives. In 1939 they **divorced**, a devastating event Frida recorded in *Self-Portrait with Cropped Hair*, in which her trademark long tresses and indigenous *tehuana* dresses (both much loved by Diego) are replaced by Diego's oversized suit and cropped hair. They **remarried** a year later, with Frida insisting on financial independence and a celibate relationship.

The injuries from her accident dogged her throughout her life, and as her physical condition worsened she found solace in her work (as well as drink and pain-killing drugs), painting *The Broken Column*, in 1944, with her crushed spine depicted as an Ionic column. Despite increasing commercial and critical success, Frida had only one **solo exhibition** of her work during her lifetime, in Mexico City just a year before she died. In her later years she was wheelchair-bound, but continued the **political activism** she had always pursued, and died after defying medical advice and taking part in a demonstration against American intervention in Guatemala while she was convalescing from pneumonia in July 1954. By this stage, she knew she was dying; defiantly, on her last work, she daubed the words "Viva la Vida" – "Long Live Life".

Museo Casa de León Trotsky

Trotsky's House, or the **Museo Casa de León Trotsky**, Río Churabasco 410 (Tues–Sun 10am–5pm; M$35, camera M$15; Metro Coyoacán), where the genius of the Russian Revolution and organizer of the Red Army lived and worked, is about four blocks away and represents virtually the only memorial to Trotsky anywhere in the world. After Lenin's death, Trotsky was forced into exile and condemned to death, and as increasing numbers of countries refused him asylum he sought refuge in Mexico in 1937, aided by Diego Rivera (at the time an ardent Trotskyite), who petitioned President Lázaro Cárdenas on his behalf. Here Stalin's long arm finally caught up with him (see box, p.434), despite the house being reinforced with steel gates and shutters, high walls and watchtowers. Today the fortified building seems at first a little incongruous, surrounded by the bourgeois homes of a prosperous suburb, but inside it's a human place, set up as he left it, if rather dustier: books on the shelves, his glasses smashed on the desk and all the trappings of a fairly comfortable ordinary life – except for the bullet holes.

The assassination of Trotsky

The first attempt on Trotsky's life, in his house at Coyoacán, left more than seventy scars in the plaster of the bedroom walls. At 4am on May 24, 1940, a heavily armed group led by painter David Siqueiros (who had been a commander in the Spanish Civil War and was working under the orders of the Stalinist Mexican Communist Party) overcame the guards and pumped more than two hundred shots into the house. Trotsky, his wife and son survived only by hiding under their beds. After this, the house, already heavily guarded, was further fortified. Unknown to all, though, the eventual assassin had already inveigled his way into the household, posing as a businessman being converted to the cause. Although he was never fully trusted, his arrival at the house on the afternoon of **August 20**, with an article that he wanted Trotsky to look over, seemed innocuous enough. Trotsky invited him into the study and moments later the notorious **ice pick** (the blunt end), which had been concealed under the killer's coat, smashed into Trotsky's skull. He died some 24 hours later, in the hospital after an operation failed to save his life. The killer, who called himself Frank Jackson and claimed to be Belgian, served twenty years in jail, though he never explained his actions or even confessed to his true identity, **Jaime Ramón Mercader del Río**.

Pedregal, the University, Olympic Stadium and Cuicuilco

Around 2km south of San Ángel, Insurgentes enters the great lava field of **El Pedregal**, which gets its name from the vast lava flow that spreads south of San Ángel through the University City and on to the south of Coyoacán. Craggy and dramatic, it was regarded as a completely useless stretch of land, the haunt of bandits and brigands, until the early 1950s, when architect Luis Barragán began to build extraordinarily imaginative houses here, using the uneven lava as a feature. Now it's filled with an amazing collection of luxury homes, though you'll unfortunately be able to see little of what is behind the high walls and security fences even if you drive around. El Pedregal is also home to the **university campus**, the **Olympic Stadium** (Estadio Olímpico) and **Cuicuilco**, the oldest pyramid in central Mexico.

Getting to the area is easy, as it's reached from San Ángel by just about any bus or *pesero* (route #1 or #76, for example) heading south along Insurgentes. All stop outside the Olympic Stadium, right opposite the university library, and many (try those marked "Villa Olímpica", "Cuicuilco" and "Tlalpan") continue on to the pyramid at Cuicuilco, visible on the left just after you pass under the *periférico*. The university can also be reached by Metro (line 3): Copilco is the most convenient station, Universidad much less so as it brings you out at the back of the campus, from where you have to walk all the way through – past the *frontón* courts and medical faculty – to reach the library.

University City

To the east of Insurgentes is the **University City** (Ciudad Universitaria). The campus is dominated by the astonishing, rectangular twelve-storey **library**, each face of which is covered in a mosaic designed by **Juan O'Gorman** – mostly natural stone with a few tiles or glass to supply colours that would otherwise have been unavailable. Representing the artist's vision of the country's progression through history, the focus of the larger north and south faces is on pre-Hispanic and colonial Mexico; on the west wall are the present and the university coat of arms; on the east, the future is ranged around a giant atom. It's remarkable how these have been incorporated as an essential feature of the building – at first it appears that there are no windows at all, but look closely and you'll see that in fact they're an integral part of the design, appearing as eyes, mouths or as windows of the buildings in the mosaic.

More or less opposite the library are the long, low **administration buildings** (*rectoría*), with a giant mural in high relief by Siqueiros (or a "sculptural painting", as he called it), intended to provide a changing perspective as you walk past or drive by on Insurgentes. At the front of the *rectoría* are the university theatre and the **Museo Universitario de Ciencias y Artes** (MUCA; Wed–Sun 10am–5.30pm; free), the latter a wide-ranging general collection, with interactive scientific exhibits, plus displays on contemporary art and culture. Behind them spread out the enormous grounds of the main campus, starting with a large esplanade known as the Plaza Mayor, with sculptural groups dotted around a shallow artificial pond. Towards the back of the *rectoría* are more murals, adorning the **Faculties of Science and Medicine**; continue past these to reach another grassy area with the **Botanical Gardens** and several large walls against which the students play *frontón*.

After over fifty years of use, the campus is beginning to show its age, and while it's no longer the avant-garde sensation it was when it opened, it remains a remarkable architectural achievement. The whole thing was built in just five years (1950–55) during the presidency of Miguel Alemán, and is now one of the largest universities in the world, with some 300,000 students and staff. It's also the oldest on the American continent: granted a charter by Philip II in 1551, the University of Mexico occupied a succession of sites in the city centre (including the Hospital de Jesús Nazareno and what is now the Escuela Nacional Preparatoria), was closed down several times in the nineteenth century and was finally awarded its status as the Universidad Nacional Autónoma de México (UNAM) in 1929.

Estadio Olímpico

Directly across Insurgentes from the university library is the sculptured oval of the 100,000-seat **Estadio Olímpico**, built in 1952. Its main facade is decorated with a mosaic relief by Diego Rivera designed to represent the development of human potential through sport. Most taxi drivers will tell you that the stadium was deliberately designed to look like a giant sombrero, but this, sadly, is not the case; it's undeniably odd, though, half sunk into the ground as if dropped here from a great height and slightly warped in the process.

Cuicuilco

The **Pirámide de Cuicuilco** (daily 9am–5pm; free) is dominated by the circular temple visible to the east of Insurgentes by the *periférico*, around 3km south of the Estadio Olímpico and opposite the former Olympic Village, now a housing complex. This is much the oldest construction of such scale known in central Mexico, reaching its peak around 600–200 BC before being abandoned at the time of the eruption of Xitle (the small volcano that created El Pedregal, which took place around 100–300 AD), just as Teotihuacán was beginning to develop. Not a great deal is known about the site, much of which has been buried by modern housing (completing the work of the lava). The pyramid itself, approached by a ramp and a stairway, is about 25m high by 100m in diameter and is composed of four sloping tiers (of a probable original five), the lowest one made visible only by digging away four metres of lava. A small **museum** displays objects found here and at contemporary settlements.

Calzada de Tlalpan

Along with Insurgentes, the other main approach to the south is the **Calzada de Tlalpan**, which runs south from the Zócalo more or less in parallel with Metro line 2 (initially underground, then running down the middle of the road) and subsequently the Tren Ligero, almost all the way to Xochimilco.

The two train lines provide the easiest access to some fine museums – including Diego Rivera's Anahuacalli and the wonderful Museo Dolores Olmedo Patiño. The Tren Ligero passes the giant **Estadio Azteca** football stadium on its way to the canals of Xochimilco, and Metro line 2 also provides alternative access to the eastern end of Coyoacán.

Museo Nacional de las Intervenciones

Travelling south on Metro line 2, the first station worth stopping at is General Anaya, from where it is a five-minute walk along 20 de Agosto (exit to the west of the Calzada de Tlalpan) to the **Museo Nacional de las Intervenciones**, 20 de Agosto and General Anaya (Tues–Sun 9am–6pm; M$41, free Sun). This occupies the old Franciscan **Convento de Churubusco**, which owes its present incarnation to the 1847 battle in which the invading Americans, led by General Winfield Scott, defeated a Mexican force under General Anaya – another heroic Mexican effort in which the outnumbered defenders fought to their last bullet.

The building itself is a stunner, especially if you arrive at the darkening of day as the lights are coming on in the gardens. The exhibits, all on the upper floor, may not mean a great deal unless you have a reasonable grasp of Mexican history. They're labelled only in Spanish – and not very fully at that – and are dedicated to the history of foreign military adventures in Mexico: skeletons in the cupboards of Britain, Spain, France and the US are all rattled loudly. One section is devoted largely to the Mexican–American wars – with a very different perspective from that of the Alamo. Much of what's on show, however, comprises paintings of generals and flags, and unless you're a history buff you might better spend your time in the pleasant surrounding gardens. Apart from the Metro, the museum is also accessible by *pesero* ("Gral Anaya") from Coyoacán: pick it up by the market at the junction of Allende and Xicoténcatl.

The Trotsky and Frida Kahlo museums and central Coyoacán are about a fifteen-minute walk from the Museo Nacional de las Intervenciones. To reach them, take General Anaya (ahead and over to the right as you come out of the museum), cross División del Norte and go straight ahead for about 500m, by which time General Anaya has merged into Hidalgo. For central Coyoacán and the Frida Kahlo Museum, continue straight on (see map, p.430). For the Trotsky Museum, take a right down Madero (signposted, but not easy to spot) opposite Hidalgo 62.

Museo Anahuacalli

Metro line 2 finishes at Tasqueña, where you can transfer to the Tren Ligero and continue four stops to Xotepingo, a ten-minute walk from the bizarre **Museo Diego Rivera Anahuacalli**, Museo 150 (Tues–Thurs, Sat & Sun 10.30am–5.30pm, Fri 10.30am–4.45pm; M$20, or free with ticket from Museo Frida Kahlo, see p.431; Ⓦwww.anahuacallimuseo.org; Tren Ligero Xotepingo), designed and built by Diego Rivera to house his huge collection of pre-Hispanic artefacts. The museum can only be visited on a guided tour, of which there is one every half-hour until 5pm (except on Friday, when the last one is at 4.15pm). It's an extraordinary blockish structure, started in 1933 and worked on sporadically until Rivera's death, then finished off by Juan O'Gorman and opened in 1963. Inspired by Maya and Aztec architecture, this sombre mass of black volcanic stone is approached through a courtyard reminiscent of a Maya ball-court. The exquisite objects in the collection form part of a thoroughly imaginative exhibit: one small chamber contains nothing but a series of **Huehueteotls**, all squatting grumpily under the weight of their braziers, and the studio has ball-player and animal displays.

The **ground floor** is devoted to objects from the main cultures of the Valley of México – Teotihuacán, Toltec and Aztec – which provided Rivera with an important part of his inspiration. On the **middle floor**, rooms devoted to the west of Mexico (arguably the best such collection in the country) surround the huge airy space that Rivera planned to use as a studio. It's been fitted out with portraits and sketches, including preliminary studies for *Man in Control of the Universe*, his massive mural in the Bellas Artes. On the **top floor** are more Aztec objects, along with pottery and small figures from Oaxaca and the Gulf coast. Up here you can also get out onto the **rooftop terrace**, from where there are magical views of Popocatépetl and Ixtaccíhuatl, both of which seem really close here, their snowy peaks glistening on less smoggy days.

Walking through the dark recesses of the museum, note the ceilings, each with individual mosaic designs, and even the floor of the rooftop terrace, which is inlaid with snake, dog and frog forms, distinct but barely noticeable if you're not looking for them. As you leave the main museum, you'll see a low building diagonally to the left, which houses temporary exhibitions and is worth a visit if only to get a sense of the underlying volcanic rock – part of El Pedregal (see p.434) – which was hewn away to provide building materials for the museum.

To get here from the Xotepingo Tren Ligero station, follow the signs to the Calle Museo exit, double back at the bottom of the steps and take the first left down Museo. After 100m, cross División del Norte, and it's about 500m ahead on your right. On the way, *Antojito Berenice*, Museo 71, is a good little place to stop for a comida corrida (Mon–Fri only).

Museo Dolores Olmedo Patiño

To see the largest private collection of Rivera's work, and to experience one of the city's finest museums, head ten stops further along the Tren Ligero line to the **Museo Dolores Olmedo Patiño** (Ⓦwww.museodoloresolmedo.org.mx; Tues–Sun 10am–6pm; M$41, free Tues; Tren Ligero La Noria). The museum sits amid peaceful and beautifully tended grounds where peacocks strut, oblivious of the busy streets outside. It is built into a seventeenth-century mansion, donated in 1994 by the elderly Dolores Olmedo, a wealthy collector and longtime friend and patron of Rivera's. Over the years she amassed over 130 of his works, all of which are on display here. They span his career, from his Cubist experimentation in the early twentieth century through self-portraits (exhibiting varying degrees of flattery) to 25 sunsets painted in Acapulco from the balcony of his patron's house. The collection is immensely varied, making this perhaps the best place to get a true sense of just how versatile a master he was. Look particularly for three large and striking nudes from the early 1940s, and sketches for his famous paintings of calla lilies.

Rivera's work is reason enough to come here, but the museum also has an outstanding collection of two dozen paintings by **Frida Kahlo**. With the works arranged in approximate chronological order, it is easy to see her development as an artist, from the Riveraesque approach of early works such as 1929's *The Bus*, to her infinitely more powerful self-portraits. Many of her finest works are here, including *Henry Ford Hospital*, *A Few Small Pricks*, *The Broken Column* and *Self-Portrait with Monkey*, the latter featuring a Xoloitzcuintle, a pre-Columbian grey-skinned, hairless dog. To see these creatures in the flesh, wander out into the garden where a few are still kept. There's also a portrait of Kahlo by Rivera elsewhere in the museum in a pastiche of her own style.

Though easily overshadowed by the Rivera and Kahlo pieces, there is also a worthwhile collection of wood-block prints done by **Angelina Beloff**, Diego's first wife, featuring scenes from Mexico and her native Russia.

To get to the museum from La Noria Tren Ligero station, go straight ahead from the exit and take the first left. The museum is a couple of minutes' walk on your left.

▲ *Lanchas* at Xochimilco

Xochimilco

The **floating gardens** adjoining the suburb of **Xochimilco** (Tren Ligero Xochimilco) offer an intense carnival atmosphere every weekend and are likely to be one of your most memorable experiences of the city. Considerable effort has been expended in recent years to clean up the canals and maintain the water levels that had been dropping here, so Xochimilco ("place of the flower fields" in Náhuatl) looks set to remain the most popular Sunday outing for thousands of Mexicans. It's also the one place where you get some feel for the ancient city and its waterborne commerce, thriving markets and dazzling colour – or at least an idealized view of it. Rent any of the colourful boats and you'll be ferried around miles of canals, continually harangued by women selling flowers, fruit and hot food from tiny canoes, or even by larger vessels bearing marimba players and entire mariachi bands who, for a small fee, will grapple alongside you and blast out a couple of numbers. The floating gardens themselves are no more floating than the *Titanic*: following the old Aztec methods of making the lake fertile, these *chinampas* are formed by a raft of mud and reeds, firmly rooted to the bottom by the plants. The scene now appears like a series of canals cut through dry land, but the area is still a very important gardening and flower-producing centre for the city. If you wander the streets of Xochimilco town you'll find garden centres everywhere, with wonderful flowers and fruit in the **market** that enlivens the town centre for much of Saturday (though whether it's healthy to eat food raised on these dirty waters is open to question).

Practicalities

Lanchas (launches) cost from M$110 per hour for up to four people to M$160 for up to twenty. Prices should be posted up at the *embarcadero* (quay), and it's probably best to avoid *embarcaderos* where it isn't. There's a long tradition of milking tourists here, so be certain of what you've agreed on before parting with any money. Remember that there are likely to be sundry **extras**, including the cold beers thoughtfully provided by the boatman, and any flowers, food or music you find yourself accepting on your way. You'll be encouraged to go for two hours, but try to avoid paying upfront or you're likely to get only an hour and a half, which will include a visit to the garden centre of their choice. The boatman won't like it, but you can always take your business elsewhere. Also, be clear which boat you are getting or you are liable to be shuffled to an inferior and less attractive model. You can rent a boat on any weekday for a little less-crowded cruising, but Sunday is by far the most popular and animated day; Saturdays are lively, too, partly because of the produce market. Off the huge central plaza is the lovely sixteenth-century church of **San Bernardino**, full on Sundays with a succession of people paying homage and leaving offerings at one of its many chapels; in the plaza itself there are usually bands playing or mime artists entertaining the crowds.

For the easiest **approach to Xochimilco**, take the Metro to Tasqueña station (line 2) and the Tren Ligero from there to Xochimilco (end of the line); there are also buses and *peseros* from Tasqueña as well as buses direct from the city centre, down Insurgentes and around the *periférico* or straight down the Calzada de Tlalpan. On Sundays many extra services are laid on. To get a boat, go straight ahead from the Tren Ligero station exit and follow the "embarcaderos" signs (about a 10min walk).

North of the centre

Compared to the southern suburbs, the area north of the city centre has less to offer, but two sites of compelling interest – the emotive **Plaza de las Tres Culturas** and the great **Basílica de Guadalupe** – are worth an afternoon of your attention. Further out, and harder to get to, you'll find the pyramids of **Tenayuca** and **Santa Cecilia**, the two most dramatically preserved remains of Aztec architecture in the city.

Plaza de las Tres Culturas

Site of the ancient city of Tlatelolco, the **Plaza de las Tres Culturas** should be your first stop. Today, a lovely **colonial church** rises in the midst of the **excavated ruins**, which are in turn surrounded by a **high-rise housing complex**: all three great cultures of Mexico side by side.

Although there is a Tlatelolco Metro station (line 3), the easiest way **to get to** the Plaza de las Tres Culturas is to take Metro lines 8 or B to Garibaldi and then walk up Lázaro Cárdenas (see p.387). Alternatively, catch one of the buses headed north along Lázaro Cárdenas from near Bellas Artes, or take "La Villa" buses and *peseros* which pass within about three blocks along Reforma on their way to Guadalupe.

The ruins

The ancient ruins of **Tlatelolco** (daily 8am–6pm; free, free guided tours Mon–Fri 9am–2pm, in English by arrangement in advance on ⓣ55/5583-0295; Metro Garibaldi – from the exit, cross Reforma and head north up Lázaro Cárdenas, where you'll find it after 400m on your right) were once the core of a city considerably more ancient than Tenochtitlán, based on a separate but nearby island in the lake. For a long time, its people existed under independent rule in close alliance with the Aztecs of Tenochtitlán, but it was by far the most important commercial and market centre in the valley; even after its annexation to the Aztec empire in 1473 Tlatelolco retained this role. When **Cortés** and his troops arrived, they marvelled at the size and order of the Tlatelolco market. Cortés himself estimated that some 60,000 people – buyers and sellers – came and went each day, and Bernal Díaz wrote:

We were astounded at the great number of people and the quantities of merchandise, and at the orderliness and good arrangements that prevailed...every kind of goods was kept separate and had its fixed place marked for it...Some of the soldiers among us who had been in many parts of the world, in Constantinople, in Rome, and all over Italy, said that they had never seen a market so well laid out, so large, so orderly, and so full of people.

In 1521 the besieged **Aztecs** made their final stand here, and a plaque in the middle of the plaza recalls that struggle: "On the 13th of August 1521", it reads, "defended by the heroic Cuauhtémoc, Tlatelolco fell under the power of Hernan Cortés. It was neither a triumph nor a defeat, but the painful birth of the mixed race that is the Mexico of today." The ruins are a pale reflection of the ancient city – the original temples, whose scale can be inferred from the size of the bases, rivalled those in Tenochtitlán. The chief temple, for example, had reached its eleventh rebuilding by the time of the Conquest – what you see now corresponds to the second stage, and by the time nine more had been superimposed it would certainly have risen much higher than the church that was built from its stones. On top was likely a double sanctuary similar to that on the Templo Mayor of Tenochtitlán. The smaller structures include a square **tzompantli**, or wall of skulls, near which nearly two hundred human skulls were discovered, all with holes through the temples – presumably the result of having been displayed side by side on long poles around the sides of the building.

The church and other buildings around the plaza

The adjacent **Church of Santiago Tlateloco** (still used and not considered part of the ruins) on the site was erected in 1609, replacing an earlier Franciscan monastery. Parts of this survive, arranged about the cloister. In the early years after the Conquest, the friars established a college at which they instructed the sons of the Aztec nobility in European ways, teaching them Spanish, Latin and Christianity. Bernardino de Sahagún was one of the teachers, and it was here that he wrote down many of the customs and traditions of the natives, compiling the most important existing record of daily Aztec life in his famous *Historia General de las Cosas de Nueva España*.

The **modern buildings** that surround the plaza – mostly a rather ugly 1960s housing project but including the Ministry of Foreign Affairs – represent the third culture. The contemporary state of Mexico was rather brutally represented here on October 2, 1968, when troops and tanks were ordered to fire on an almost 250,000-strong **student demonstration**. It was the culmination of several months of student protests over the government's social and educational policies, which the authorities were determined to subdue with only ten days left before the Olympic Games opened in the city. Records of the death toll vary from an official figure at the time of thirty to student estimates of more than five hundred, but it seems clear today that hundreds is more accurate than tens. Mexican philosopher Octavio Paz saw the violence as part of the cycle of history – a ritual slaughter to recall the Aztec sacrifices here – but it's perhaps better seen as an example of at least one thread of continuity between all Mexico's civilizations: the cheapness of life and the harsh brutality of their rulers.

Basílica de Nuestra Señora de Guadalupe

The **Basílica de Nuestra Señora de Guadalupe** (Metro La Villa Basílica, line 6) is in fact a whole series of churches, chapels and shrines set around an enormous stone-flagged plaza and climbing up the rocky hillock where the miracles that led to its foundation occurred. The basilica can be reached by Metro, by **buses** and **peseros** north along Reforma ("Metro La Villa"), or by **trolleybus** along Reforma from Metro Hidalgo ("Indios Verdes").

Origins

The **Virgin of Guadalupe**, Mexico's first indigenous saint, is still the nation's most popular – you'll see her image in churches throughout the country. The Virgin's banner has been fought under by both sides of almost every conflict the nation has ever seen, most famously when Hidalgo seized on it as the flag of Mexican Independence. According to the legend, a Christianized native, **Juan Diego**, was walking over the hill here (formerly dedicated to the Aztec earth goddess Tonantzin) on his way to the monastery at Tlatelolco one morning in December 1531, when he was stopped by a brilliant vision of the Virgin, who ordered him, in Náhuatl, to go to the bishop and tell him to build a church on the hill. Bishop Juan de Zumarraga was unimpressed until, on December 12, the Virgin reappeared, ordering Diego to gather roses from the top of the hill and take them to the bishop. Doing so, he bundled the flowers in his cloak, and when he opened it before the bishop he found the image of the dark-skinned Virgin imprinted into the cloth.

The church and museum

Today Diego's cloak hangs above the altar in the gigantic modern basilica, which takes its name from the celebrated (and equally swarthy) Virgin in the monastery of Guadalupe in Spain. The first church here was built in 1533, but the large Baroque basilica you see now – mostly impressive for its size – was completely reconstructed in the eighteenth century and again remodelled in the nineteenth and twentieth.

Around the back, the **Museo de la Basílica de Guadalupe** (Tues–Sun 10am–5.30pm; M$5) contains a large collection of ex-votos and some of the church's religious art treasures, including a series of slightly insipid early eighteenth-century canvases by José de Ibarra and more powerful oils by Miguel Cabrera and Cristóbal de Villalpando.

To the left of the great plaza is the modern home of the image – a huge **church** built in 1976 with space inside for 10,000 worshippers and for around four times that when the great doors all round are thrown open to the crowds, as they are pretty much every Sunday. You'll find it crowded whenever you visit, and there seems to be a service permanently in progress. The famous cloak, framed in gold and silver, hangs above the main altar. To prevent anyone lingering too long at the spot right underneath you must board a travelling walkway and admire the image as you glide respectfully by.

From the plaza you can walk round to the right and up the hill past a series of little chapels associated with the Virgin's appearance. Loveliest is the **Capilla del Pocito**, in which there is a well said to have sprung forth during one of the apparitions. Built in the eighteenth century, it consists of two linked elliptical chapels, one smaller and one larger, both with colourful tiled domes and magnificently decorated interiors. On the very top of the hill, the **Capilla de las Rosas** marks the spot where the miraculous roses grew.

Around all this, there swirls a stream of humanity – pilgrims, sightseers, priests and salesmen offering candles, souvenirs, pictures of the Virgin, snacks and any number of mementos. On **December 12**, the anniversary of the second apparition, their numbers swell to hundreds of thousands (newspaper reports claim millions). You'll see the pilgrims on the approach roads to the capital for several days beforehand, many covering the last kilometres on their knees in an act of penance or devotion. For others, though, the day is more of a vast fiesta, with dancing, singing and drinking.

Tenayuca and Santa Cecilia Acatitlán

In the extreme north of the city, just outside the boundaries of the Distrito Federal, lie the country's two most wholly preserved examples of **Aztec**-style architecture. They're a little hard to reach by public transport, but thoroughly repay the effort involved if you've an interest in the Aztecs. **Tenayuca** is just off the Avenida de los Cien Metros, some 6km north of the Terminal del Norte. Take the Metro to Deportivo 18 de Marzo (five blocks west of the Basílica de Nuestra Señora de Guadalupe) or La Raza and catch the "Ruta 88" *pesero* northward up Insurgentes to Tenayuca (though be warned that not all "Ruta 88" *peseros* go to Tenayuca, so check first). There are also "Tenayuca" *peseros* plying Lázaro Cárdenas anywhere north of Bellas Artes: ask the driver to drop you at the *pirámide*. *Peseros* take around forty minutes from Deportivo 18 de Marzo.

Route #88 (as well as #79) continues from Tenayuca to **Santa Cecilia Acatitlán**; alternatively, it's a twenty-minute walk, or short taxi ride, from Tenayuca, or a short ride on feeder bus #R10 from San Rafael station on the suburban train line from Buenavista. Some bus tours take both pyramids in on their way to Tula and Tepotzotlán. To return to the city from here, catch a *pesero* to Metro Deportivo 18 de Marzo (lines 3 & 6).

Tenayuca

The twenty-metre-high **Pirámide de Tenayuca** (Tues–Sun 10am–5pm; M$37), plonked right in the main square of the suburb of the same name, is another site that predates Tenochtitlán by a long chalk. Indeed, there are those who claim it was the capital of the tribe that destroyed Tula. In this, its history closely mirrors almost all other valley settlements: a barbarian tribe from the north invades, conquers all before it, settles in a city and becomes civilized, borrowing much of its culture from its predecessors, before being overcome by the next wave of migrants. There's little evidence that Tenayuca ever controlled a large empire, but it was a powerful city and provides one of the most concrete links between the Toltecs and the Aztecs. The pyramid that survives dates from the period of Aztec dominance and is an almost perfect miniature replica of the great temples of Tlatelolco and Tenochtitlán. Here the structure and the monumental double stairway are intact – only the twin sanctuaries at the top and the brightly painted decorations would be needed for it to open for sacrifices again tomorrow. This is the sixth superimposition; five earlier pyramids (the first dating from the early thirteenth century) are contained within it and are revealed in places by excavations which took place in the 1920s. Originally there was a seventh layer built on top, of which some traces remain.

The most unusual and striking feature of Tenayuca's pyramid is the border of interlocking stone **snakes** that must originally have surrounded the entire building – well over a hundred of them survive. Notice also the two coiled snakes (one a little way up the north face, the other at the foot of the south face) known as the "turquoise serpents". Their crests are crowned with stars and aligned with the sun's position at the solstice.

Santa Cecilia Acatitlán

A road leads north from Tenayuca to **Santa Cecilia Acatitlán** (Tues–Sun 10am–5pm; M$37), where there's another pyramid – much smaller and simpler but wholly restored and remarkably beautiful with its clean lines. When first encountered by the Spanish, this was a temple with a double staircase very similar to the others, but the outer structure was stripped away during excavation to reveal an earlier, well-preserved building inside. It's a very plain structure, rising in four steps to a single-roofed shrine approached by a ramped stairway. The studded decorations around the roof represent either skulls or stars. You approach the pyramid through a small museum in a colonial house, whose displays of finds from the site and elsewhere include an Aztec incense burner and a reconstructed nineteenth-century kitchen; in the garden just outside, you are greeted by a large stone skull grinning inanely.

Eating and drinking

Eating out seems to be the main pastime in the capital, with reasonably priced restaurants, cafés, *taquerías* and juice stands on every block.

Costs vary enormously. You can get a decent **comida corrida** pretty much anywhere in town, even in the fancier neighbourhoods (though not in Polanco or Condesa), for M$35–70. Otherwise, there are excellent bargains to be found all over the city in small restaurants and *taquerías*, but as you move up into the mid-range places you can expect to pay something approaching what you would at home. At the top end you can soon find yourself paying big money, especially if you order something decent from the wine list. In upmarket restaurants, a **cover charge** of M$10–50 per head is commonly added to the bill.

The choice of where to eat ranges from traditional coffeehouses to fast-food lunch counters, taking in expensive **international** and rock-bottom **Mexican** cooking along the way. There's a small cluster of **Chinese** restaurants lining Dolores, just south of the Alameda, and food stalls in **markets** throughout the city: Merced is the biggest, but not a terribly pleasant place to eat. At the back of Plaza Garibaldi, however, there's a market hall given over to nothing but food stands, each vociferously competing with its neighbours. Mexico City also abounds in **rosticerías**, roast chicken shops, serving tasty set meals and crispy chicken with beer in a jolly atmosphere. There are quite a few good ones on 5 de Febrero. For lighter, sweeter fare, try a **jugería** (juice bar) or a **pastelería** (cake shop). Both are good bets for flavourful and inexpensive breakfasts.

More so than anywhere else in the country, Mexico City is flooded with **chain restaurants**. American franchise establishments are well represented, along with slightly classier Mexican chains such as *Sanborns* and *VIPS* – on the whole, you're much better off with a comida corrida.

The area **around the Zócalo** and west through to the **Alameda** is packed with places to eat, and there are plenty of tourist traps in the **Zona Rosa**, but for serious dining, especially in the mid-range, head to **Condesa**, about twenty minutes' walk south of the Zona. We've mentioned a few options in this area, but they are really just starting points, and the real pleasure is in simply wandering around and seeing what grabs your fancy. Top-class restaurants are mostly concentrated in **Polanco**. The southern suburbs of **San Ángel** and **Coyoacán** are also good hunting grounds and it is worth sticking around for your evening meal after a day's sightseeing.

Unless otherwise noted, the establishments below are marked on the "Central Mexico City", map (see pp.396–397).

Around the Zócalo

Café Bertico Madero 66. Metro Zócalo. Spacious and friendly café specializing in pasta dishes (M$72), gelati (M$25) and even sushi (M$49–79). Also good for breakfast and great coffee. There's a second, smaller branch at Madero 32, which has internet access.

Café de Tacuba Tacuba 28. Metro Allende. Good coffee and excellent food at a price, though this doesn't deter the folk who've been packing it out since 1912. One of the country's top rock bands is sponsored by the café and thus bears its name.

Café Emir Uruguay 45. Metro Zócalo. Modernized café that's been operating since 1936 and serves good espresso, empanadas, cakes and their own version of baklava (*dulce árabe*).

Café el Popular 5 de Mayo 52. Metro Allende. Cheap place serving simple food 24hr a day. It's almost always crowded, despite the perennially surly service. The turnover is pretty fast, so it's great for breakfast (M$33.50–53.50), coffee and snacks, and also has a lunchime set menu (M$46).

Casa de los Azulejos Madero 4. Metro Bellas Artes. Flagship *Sanborns* restaurant in a wonderful sixteenth-century building (see p.407), with prime seating around a fountain in an enclosed three-storey courtyard. Food is *Sanborns* stock in trade of well-prepared Mexican staples, though a little overpriced. Breakfasts are M$55–90, chicken fajitas M$100 and comidas corridas M$107–128.

Danubio Uruguay 3 ⓣ55/5512-0912, ⓦwww.danubio.com. Metro San Juan de

Letrán. Established restaurant that has specialized in seafood since 1936. As ever, the best deals are the set lunches, in this case a full six courses for M$165, though you can also order from the menu, with most dishes priced at M$145–215.

Dulcería de Celaya 5 de Mayo 39. Metro Allende. A wonderful shop for sweet lovers, with all kinds of sticky delights including *dulce de membrillo* and candied-fruit *comates*.

El Generalito Filomeno Mata 18. Metro Allende. A small but nicely done-out diner, with breakfasts (M$25–37) and comidas corridas (M$45) in pleasant surroundings.

Los Girasoles Plaza Manuel Tolsá, Tacuba 8/10 ⓣ55/5510-3281, ⓦwww.restaurantelosgirasoles.com. Metro Allende. One of the most appealing restaurants in the centre, with Mediterranean decor, a casual atmosphere and great food served at moderate prices. Start with the blue corn quesadillas (M$46) and perhaps follow with turkey in *mole poblano* or *verde* (M$128), then finish with a rose-petal pie (M$58) and espresso. Closes 9pm on Sun & Mon, midnight other days.

Hostería de Santo Domingo Belisario Dominguez 72 ⓣ55/5526-5276. Metro Allende. Full of character, this moderately priced restaurant in part of a former convent looks great, with decorations hanging from the ceiling, artesanía all over the walls and, usually, a pianist and singer in the corner. But the food is not quite as good as they think it is; even their signature *chiles en nogada* (M$195) is better done elsewhere. There's a Sunday buffet 9am–1pm for M$110. A compulsory tip is added to the bill.

Jugos Canada 5 de Mayo 49. Metro Allende. Very good torta and juice bar with decent prices, despite its central location.

Kam Ling Cerrada de 5 de Mayo 14 ⓣ55/5521-5661. Metro Allende. Straightforward Chinese food in seriously large proportions to eat in or take away. There's a buffet for M$55, set menus (M$48–105), or individual dishes (M$50–105) such as squid and green pepper in oyster sauce, and chicken and vegetables, all washed down with huge pots of jasmine tea (M$19).

Pastelería Ideal Uruguay 74. Metro San Juan de Letrán. Bakery with a huge range of cakes, biscuits and moulded gelatine confections.

Restaurant Bar Chon Regina 160. Metro Merced. A veritable eating adventure, with starters such as *mescal* worms, *escamoles* (ant eggs) or *chapulines* (grasshoppers), served with or without guacamole. If you prefer a main course from outside the insect kingdom, there's frogs' legs, armadillo in mango sauce or *chamorro al pilbil* (leg of pork barbecued in a hole in the ground). Main courses M$70–150, though some of the insect dishes are pricier.

El Sazón Oaxaqueño Isabel la Católica 10. Metro Allende. Upstairs family restaurant offering a good-value lunch-time menu (M$40), as well as breakfasts, *antojitos* and chicken dishes.

Teposnieves Donceles 4. Metro Bellas Artes. Local firm selling delicious ices and sorbets in a range of fruit flavours, plus some unlikely ones, such as peanut, rice and tequila.

La Terraza 7th floor of *Hotel Majestic* (see p.392) ⓣ55/5521-8600. Metro Zócalo. Restaurant with a great terrace that's perfect for watching Zócalo life go by over a coffee or a beer (M$25–40). The buffet breakfast (7am–noon; M$130 weekdays, M$150 weekends) and buffet lunch (1–5pm; M$180) are both good and in the evening there's à la carte dining with well-prepared Mexican standards for M$85–150.

La Vasconia Tacuba 73. Metro Allende. One of the best bread and cake shops in the centre, with a huge range of Mexican staples at low prices.

El Vegetariano Filomeno Mata 13. Metro Zócalo. Vegetarian restaurant that's inexplicably decorated with mountain photos. The best deal is usually the healthy four-course *menu del día* (M$63–73), or you can come here for breakfast.

Vegetariano Madero upstairs at Madero 56. This sunny, spacious vegetarian restaurant lurks behind an unprepossessing stairway entrance but offers some of the best-value vegetarian food around, usually with piano accompaniment at lunch time. The four-course M$57 *menu del día* is especially good value, though they also do great breakfasts (from 8am). Metro Zócalo.

Around the Alameda

Café del Palacio inside Bellas Artes. Metro Bellas Artes. An elegant restaurant in Art Deco surroundings. Enjoy limited views of Tamayo's murals as you eat amid business lunchers and pre-theatre diners. Meals are moderately priced, especially if you go for the two-course *menu del Palacio* (available 2–5pm; M$250). The list of what's available isn't huge, but they change it at least monthly. Closes 5.30pm.

Cafetería El Cuadrilatero Luis Moya 73. Metro Balderas. Like Mexico City's other wrestling cafés, *El Cuadrilatero* ("the ring") is owned and run by an ex-wrestler whose old masks are framed on the walls along with photos of his glory days. The food's good, including standard Mexican mains, burgers and tortas (M$50–175) that are big enough for a wrestler or two mere mortals.

Chung King Dolores 27. Metro Bellas Artes. Reasonable chop suey house, one of several in the city's mini-Chinatown, serving the usual standards (chop suey, chow mein, sweet and sour, etc). Set meals M$55–169.

Zona Rosa

The establishments listed below are marked on the "Zona Rosa, Roma & Condesa" map (see p.415).

Barro-Barroco Londres 211. Metro Insurgentes. Small and peaceful café a little away from the main bustle of the Zona, serving coffee, breakfasts and meals at prices that are modest for the area (set menu M$45).

Blah Blah Café Londres 171, at Florencia. Metro Insurgentes. Café, bar and Argentine grill, where an executive steak meal (served 12.30–8pm) will set you back around M$148, or you can have a lighter set meal for M$85.

Champs Elysées Reforma 316 ⓣ55/5514-0450. Metro Insurgentes. Upstairs, one of the capital's finer French restaurants, this place has been reliably feeding the Mexico City elite for almost forty years. Look out on El Ángel as you feast on truly excellent food, complemented by something from the extensive wine list, delicate desserts and a great cheeseboard. Expect to pay M$500 for a full meal. Reservations required. There's now a less formal (and less pricey) bistro downstairs too. Closed Sun.

La Lanterna Reforma 458, at Toledo ⓣ55/5207-9969, ⓦwww.lalanterna.com.mx. Metro Insurgentes. Long-standing and convivial trattoria with an intimate and suitably Italian feel, enhanced by pasta freshly made in-house and combined with some delicious sauces (M$138). The *segundi piatti* (M$170–220) are equally wonderful. Pizzas go for M$135.

Restaurante Vegetariano Yug Varsovia 3 ⓦwww.yug.com.mx. Metro Insurgentes. Worthy contact point for vegetarians and vegans, with set breakfasts, salads and *antojitos* in bright cheery surroundings. There's a particularly good buffet lunch upstairs (1–5pm; Mon–Fri M$75, Sat & Sun M$80) and a great comida corrida (M$65–73). Mon–Fri 7am–9pm, Sat & Sun 8.30am–8pm.

El Trompito Londres 119. Metro Insurgentes. If you're looking for a cheap snack amid the Zona's tourist traps, this modest little *taquería* could be the oasis you need, with tacos, tortas and *alambres* (small kebabs) at low prices in clean surroundings.

Condesa

The establishments listed below are marked on the "Zona Rosa, Roma & Condesa" map (see p.415).

Agapi Mu Alfonso Reyes 96 ⓣ55/5286-1384, ⓦwww.agapimu.com.mx. Metro Juanacatlán or Patriotismo. The best Greek restaurant in the city, but very low-key and affordable as long as you don't go too mad on the *retsina* and Hungarian wines. It's especially fun from Thurs to Sat, when there's live music and Greek dancing. Tue–Sat 1.30–11pm, Sun & Mon 1.30–6pm.

AP Bellini's 45th floor, World Trade Center, Av de las Naciones ⓣ55/9000-8305. Revolving restaurant at the top of the city's third tallest building (see p.426), where business people come to impress their clients, and the romantically inclined enjoy candlelit dinners. Dishes from an international menu are prepared to the highest standards and service is impeccable. Obviously not the cheapest place in town, but not stupidly expensive either: even at the top end of the menu, you can start with smoked salmon, caviar and avocado for M$185, followed by red snapper in lobster and brandy sauce for M$180.

Café la Gloria Vicente Suarez 43. Metro Patriotismo or Juanacatlán. Pleasant little bistro serving pasta dishes, salads or the likes of chicken in tarragon sauce (M$105) or *filet mignon* (M$130). Tasty desserts include profiteroles, chocolate mousse or blueberry cheesecake.

Don Asado Michoacán 77 ⓣ55/5286-0789, ⓦwww.donasado.com.mx. Metro Patriotismo or Juanacatlán. The original branch of a Uruguayan steak house which now has branches in San Ángel and Polanco. Wonderful chargrilled steaks (M$90–140) are the speciality here. It was closed at the time of writing and expected but not certain to reopen; the other two branches remain open in the meantime.

Fonda Garufa Michoacán 93 ⓣ55/5286-8295. Metro Patriotismo or Juanacatlán. Popular Argentine and Italian restaurant with plenty of streetside tables where you can tuck into excellent steaks or something from their extensive range of inventive pasta dishes, all at moderate prices.

Koffie! Café Amsterdam 308, at Celaya. Metro Sevilla. Modern café spilling out onto a quiet leafy street, making it a great spot for a M$55–71 breakfast, especially if you like good strong coffee. Later on, Italian salads, pasta dishes and stuffed baguettes all come in at around M$45–75.

Neve Gelato Michoacán 126. Metro Patriotismo or Juanacatlán. They do crepes and cakes here, but what draws the crowds is the luscious ice cream in flavours fruity (soursop, black cherry, *mamey*) or nutty (toasted almond, amaretto, hazelnut, tiramisú). One scoop for M$29, two scoops for M$45.

Segundo Paso Café Amsterdam 76, at Parras. Metro Juanacatlán. Relaxed, low-lit corner restaurant and café, open on both sides to pavement seating. Salads, pasta dishes and mains such as chicken breast served with *al dente* vegetables are all well prepared. Mains M$65–140.

El Zorzal corner of Alfonso Reyes and Tamaulipas ⓣ55/5273-6023. Metro Patriotismo. Argentine steakhouse serving up juicy slices of steer at M$133–265, and *alfajor* pastries or crepes filled with *dulce de leche* for dessert.

Polanco

The establishments listed below are marked on the "Chapultepec Park & Polanco" map (see p.416).

Bistro Charlotte Lope de Vega 341, at Presidente Masaryk ⓣ55/5105-4194. Metro Polanco. Great little lunch-time bistro where the menu changes every fortnight or so and always offers an interesting and international selection (roast beef and Yorkshire pudding is not unknown). Main courses M$150–225. Only open 1–6pm, and closed Sat.

La Ciudad de Colima Horacio 522, at Lamartine. Metro Polanco. Good but overpriced *jugería* with some unusual *jugos* such as (depending on the season) starfruit (*carambola*), kiwi, sapodilla (*zapote*) and *mamey*.

Denominación de Origen Hegel 406, at Presidente Masaryk ⓣ55/5255-0612, ⓦwww.denominaciondeorigendo.com.mx. Metro Polanco. Classy modern Spanish restaurant with a long bar, lots of whole hams, a whiff of cigars and dishes like *bacalao a la vizcaína* (saltfish Basque-style, in tomato sauce), confit of rabbit with cava or a superb Andalusian gazpacho. Main courses go for M$145–285.

Don Asado Presidente Masaryk 101 (entrance in Petrarca) ⓣ55/2624-2783, ⓦwww.donasado.com. Metro Polanco. Polanco branch of the Condesa Uruguayan steak house (see p.446).

Eltuca's Newton 116, at Lamartine ⓣ55/5545-8388 or 9. Metro Polanco. Forget the rubbish they sell at the international franchise chains: what you get here are proper burgers, made from sirloin steak and grilled over charcoal. You don't get them flipped in an instant, but they're worth the wait. For non-carnivores there are salads, salmon-burgers and veggieburgers. Home delivery available within Polanco.

Los Girasoles Presidente Masaryk 275 ⓣ55/5282-3291, ⓦwww.restaurantelosgirasoles.com. Metro Polanco. Polanco branch of the renowned downtown eatery (see p.444), upstairs in a swish little shopping mall. Main courses around M$150.

El Zorzal corner of Anatole France and Oscar Wilde ⓣ55/5280-0111. Metro Polanco. Polanco branch of the Condesa Argentine steakhouse (see p.446).

San Ángel and south

Establishments in San Ángel are marked on the "Coyoacán & San Ángel" map (see p.430).

El Arroyo Insurgentes Sur 4003, Tlalpan, 6km south of San Ángel ⓣ55/5573-4344. Well off the beaten path, but worth the journey, this unusual restaurant has a small bullring (used by novice bullfighters in bloodless *corridas* from April–Oct) and almost a dozen dining areas that can jointly seat over 2500. There's always a lively atmosphere, helped along by mariachis. The Mexican food is good too – barbecued meats are the speciality – and they usually keep at least four types of flavoured *pulque*. Open until 8pm daily.

Café Solo Dios Plaza San Jacinto 2. Popular hole-in-the-wall café and takeout spot with great espressos, frappés and the usual variations, made from fine Chiapas beans.

Crêperie du Soleil Madero 4-C. Small and peaceful café that's good for an espresso, cakes and, of course, crepes, both sweet (for example three berries, with blackberries, raspberries and strawberries) and savoury (try popeye, with creamed spinach and cheese).

Don Asado Rafael Checa 1 ⓣ55/5616-7240, ⓦwww.donasado.com. San Ángel branch of the Condesa Uruguayan steak house (see p.446). Metro Polanco.

Fonda San Ángel Plaza San Jacinto 3 ⓣ55/5550-1641, ⓦwww.fondasanangel.com.mx. Moderately priced restaurant specializing in contemporary Mexican cuisine. Main courses M$100–240.

San Ángel Inn Diego Rivera 50 at Altavista ⓣ55/5616-2222. Popular with visiting dignitaries and tourists, this late seventeenth-century former Carmelite monastery has been an elegant restaurant with a sumptuous garden setting since 1915. The menu has European overtones, but is mainly Mexican, featuring unusual dishes such as *huitlacoche*, a kind of fungus that grows on corn, served in crepes. Expect to pay at least M$400 per head plus wine (M$50–110 a glass). Reservations required.

Zeco Caffé Revolución 1382 ⓣ55/5663-5434. Metro Barranca del Muerto. Smart modern Italian establishment combining a café and spacious dining area. It is a little inconveniently sited, but worth the journey for excellent risotto and pasta dishes (M$50–135) and a wide range of mains (M$135–225). There's a M$15 per head cover.

Coyoacán

The establishments listed below are marked on the "Coyoacán & San Ángel" map (see p.430).

Café El Parnaso (aka *Café Frida*) Carillo Puerto 2. A sidewalk café with attached bookshop; a good spot for light snacks or just a coffee.

El Caracol de Oro Higuera 22. Laid-back restaurant and juice bar serving salads, pasta dishes, savoury crepes, *chiles* stuffed with various fillings, breakfasts, tea, coffee and excellent juices and energy drinks, and always with plenty of vegetarian options on the menu.

Le Caroz Allende 3, on Plaza Hidalgo. Exellent local bakery with a big range of bread, luscious cakes, jellies and a few savouries.

El Tajín Centro Veracruzano, Miguel Ángel de Quevedo 687 ⓣ55/5659-4447. Veracruz

Pulque and pulquerías

Pulque is the fermented sap of the maguey cactus, a species of agave that grows in the countryside north and east of Mexico City. Traditionally considered a poor man's drink, *pulque* had its heyday in the first half of the twentieth century – as beer and other drinks became more affordable, *pulque*'s stock went down. At one time there were over 1400 **pulquerías** in the capital, but today owners estimate that there are only around a hundred or so left. It's possible, however that Mexico City's *pulquerías* may yet see a revival, as the drink has seen a rise in popularity of late among young Mexicans fascinated with all things pre-Hispanic. Regardless of demand, production continues much as it has done for centuries, with barrels being shipped daily to the capital.

Unless you are looking for them, *pulquerías* are hard to spot; they're concentrated in less salubrious areas of town mostly unvisited by tourists and often have no sign, just a pair of swinging doors guarding a dark interior. Like cantinas, they are traditionally macho territory and women are more likely to receive a respectful welcome when accompanied by male friends.

These places are not set up for anything much more sophisticated than knocking back glasses of the slightly astringent, viscous white beverage, usually ladled out of barrels behind the bar. The emphasis is as much on socializing as drinking, which is a good thing since most *pulque* is only two to four percent alcohol and getting drunk requires considerable commitment. The task is made easier when *pulque* is blended with fresh fruit juices – pineapple, apricot, guava and many others – to form a weaker but more palatable cocktail. The most popular hunting ground is the **Plaza Garibaldi,** where *La Hermosa Hortensia* is always brightly lit and usually has several good flavours served up to a cross-section of men and women, locals and foreigners. During the day you are better off exploring the district south of Bellas Artes, where choices include *La Risa* at Mesones 71, on the corner of Callejón de Mesones (Mon–Sat 11am–8.30pm) and *Los Duellistas* at Aranda 30 (Mon–Sat 9am–9pm), both of which have quite a young clientele.

specialities at medium to high prices; the fish dishes, such as *filete de pescado a la Veracruzana* (in tomato, olive and caper sauce), and *chile poblano* stuffed with seafood, are exquisite. Expect to pay around M$300 per head plus wine.

La Vienet Viena 112, at Abasolo. A good place for refreshments in between visits to the Kahlo and Trotsky houses, this small daytime café serves great coffee and cakes as well as breakfasts and lunchtime menus (M$120–130). Closed at weekends.

Nightlife and entertainment

There's a vast amount going on in Mexico City, which is as much the nation's cultural and social centre as its political capital. **Bars** are dotted all over the city and range from dirt-cheap **pulquerías** and **cantinas** to upscale **lounges** and **hotel bars,** though there are unfortunately few mid-range places.

The **live music** scene has broadened appreciably in recent years, and there are venues for all kinds of bands. Two attractions are particularly worthwhile: the mariachi music in the **Plaza Garibaldi**, a thoroughly Mexican experience, and the **Ballet Folklórico**, which is unashamedly aimed at tourists but has an enduring appeal for Mexicans too.

While Mexican **theatre** tends to be rather turgid (and will of course be in Spanish), there are often excellent **classical music** concerts and **opera** or **ballet** performances by touring companies. Bellas Artes and the Auditorio Nacional are the main venues, but other downtown theatres, as well as the Polyforum and the Teatro de los Insurgentes, may have interesting shows. On most Sundays, there's a free concert in Chapultepec Park near the lake.

Listings for current cinema, theatre and other cultural events can be found in the weekly magazine *Tiempo Libre* (Ⓦwww.tiempolibre.com.mx), which comes out every Thursday and is available at most newsstands.

Bars, clubs and live music venues

As elsewhere in the country, **cantinas** and **pulquerías** are still largely a male preserve. Though there'll often be a few women inside, most unaccompanied female tourists probably won't want to brave the back-slapping macho camaraderie. More civilized **bars**, where you might sit around and chat, are relatively thin on the ground. There are a few, but most concentrate on music, or bill themselves as **antros**, a relatively modern creation somewhere in between a bar and club where you can sit and talk (just about) or dance if the Latin pop hits get you going.

Club-oriented nightlife starts late, with live acts often hitting the stage after 11pm and few places really getting going before midnight. **Entry** can be expensive, ranging up to M$300 for men (women often get in for much less or free), though this is likely to include a drink, or even *bar libre*, where your drinks are free for at least part of the evening. If you stray far from your hotel and stay out after the Metro has closed for the night, be sure to get the bar or club to order a **sitio cab** for you; flagging down a cab late at night is not generally considered safe, especially if you are lost and drunk.

Live music venues are dotted all over town, offering anything from old-fashioned romantic ballads to cutting-edge alternative rock bands. Cuban music is particularly popular, and with Cuba just a short flight away, Mexico City provides a local but international proving ground for the island's talent.

Around the Zócalo and the Alameda

The establishments listed below are marked on the "Central Mexico City" map (see pp.396–397).

La Hostería del Bohemio Hidalgo 107. Metro Hidalgo. An alcohol-free café set around a large open courtyard of the former San Hipolito convent. Smooching couples sit at candlelit tables half-listening to romantic ballads emanating passionately from the live band in the corner.

La Ópera 5 de Mayo 10, near Bellas Artes. Metro Bellas Artes. The best watering hole downtown, in the grand tradition of upmarket cantinas with magnificent *fin-de-siècle* decor – ornate mahogany panelling, a brass-railed bar, gilt-framed mirrors in the booths – and a bullet hole in the ceiling reputedly put there by Pancho Villa. You also can dine here, but most people come for a fairly pricey beer or cocktails in the booths or at the bar. Mon–Sat 1pm–midnight; Sun 1–6pm.

Pervert Lounge Uruguay 70 Ⓣ55/5518-0976. Metro Isabel la Católica. One of the centre's more cutting-edge clubs and nowhere near as sleazy (or as kinky) as it might sound, with DJs from Mexico, the US and beyond, playing a top mix of electronic dance sounds. Thurs–Sat 11pm–4am. Entry M$70–100.

Tio Pepe Independencia 26, at Dolores. Metro Bellas Artes. Convivial cantina with moulded ceilings and wooden bar. Minstrels frequently drop in to bash out a few numbers, and despite the sign on the door, women are free to enter, but will probably feel more comfortable in the saloon next door.

Zinco Jazz Club Motolina 20, at 5 de Mayo Ⓣ55/5518-6369, Ⓦwww.zincojazz.com. Metro Allende. Small but congenial venue, really just a bar/restaurant with entertainment by local jazz bands, tucked away in the vaults beneath the Art Deco splendour of the Banco de México building. Tue–Sat 9pm–2am. Entry M$100 Thurs–Sat, free on Wed.

Zona Rosa, Condesa and Roma

The establishments listed below are marked on the "Zona Rosa, Roma & Condesa" map (see p.415).

Gitanerías Oaxaca 15, Roma Ⓣ55/5514-2027. Metro Insurgentes. Flamenco club with Spanish dancers, complete with frilly skirts and castanets. Wed–Sat 8pm–3am. Entry M$300 guys, M$150 ladies. Reservation particuarly advised Fri & Sat.

Mama Rumba Querétaro 230, at Medellin, Roma Ⓣ55/5564-6920 or 7823. Metro Insurgentes. Reservations are advised for this dance bar. The Hispano-Afro-Caribbean rhythms pumped out by the Cuban house band get the small dancefloor packed, so come prepared to move your feet even if you don't know the steps. Open Wed–Sat 9pm–3.30am, bands come on at 11pm. Wheelchair access.

El Mitote Amsterdam 53, Condesa Ⓣ55/5211-9150, Ⓦwww.elmitote.com. Metro Insurgentes or

Chilpancingo. Tapas bar playing Spanish and international hits to a bright, young clientele. Thurs–Sat 8pm–2.30am. Entry M$30–40. Reservation advisable.

Multiforo Alicia Cuauhtémoc 91, between Colima and Durango, Roma ⓣ55/5511-2100. Metro Cuauhtémoc. "Who hasn't been to Alicia doesn't know rock music", they claim, which may be an exaggeration, but this is definitely the place to catch Mexico's latest rock *ondas*. Most of the action is on Fri & Sat, from 8.30pm, but some shows start as early as 5pm. Expect to pay M$75–100.

Pata Negra Tamaulipas 30, Condesa ⓣ55/5211-5563. Metro Patriotismo or Sevilla. Music bar often featuring live acts, mainly rock. There's no cover charge and it's open Mon–Sat 1.30pm–1.30am.

Ruta 61 Baja California 281, Condesa ⓣ55/5211-7602, ⓦwww.ruta61.com.mx. Metro Chilpancingo. Cosy little blues club with tables (reservation advised). Wed–Sat 8pm–2am; music from 10pm. M$60–100 entry.

San Ángel and Coyoacán

The establishments listed below are marked on the "Coyoacán and San Ángel" map (see p.430).

La Camelia Plaza San Jacinto, San Ángel. Early-evening boozing to recent US and Latin pop hits, either inside or out on the street at this vintage cantina dating from 1931.

La Guadalupana Caballo Calco 7, on Plaza Hidalgo, Coyoacán. Rather a refined and classic cantina (established in 1932), and an excellent place to sink a few beers of an evening. *La Puerta del Sol*, next door, is even more venerable (dating from 1918), but rather smaller, and gets quite crowded.

El Hijo del Cuervo Jardín Centenario 17, Coyoacán ⓣ55/5659-5196. Dark and hip bar with seats overlooking the square and music that ranges from Latin rap to rock. There's no cover charge, and a lively evening atmosphere that runs through to 2.30am Fri night/Sat morning and Sat night/Sun morning.

New Orleans Revolución 1655, San Ángel ⓣ55/5550-1908. Excellent jazz venue-cum-restaurant with very good food at moderate prices. Open Tues–Sun from 6.30pm (band on at 8.30pm), but weekends are much the liveliest unless an international jazz act is playing. Entry M$50–100, depending on what's on.

El Vicio (formerly *El Hábito*) Madrid 13, Coyoacán ⓣ55/5659-1139, ⓦwww.lasreinaschulas.com. Small and quirky fringe theatre and music club, mainly playing jazz. Also on site are *Novo's* restaurant and the Teatro la Capilla.

Plaza Garibaldi

Plaza Garibaldi (Metros Bellas Artes and Garibaldi) is the traditional final call on a long night around the capital's bars, and as the night wears on and the drinking continues, it can get pretty rowdy. The plaza is on Lázaro Cárdenas, five blocks north of Bellas Artes in a thoroughly sleazy area of cheap bars, grimy hotels and several brightly lit theatres offering burlesque and strip shows. Despite a high-profile police presence, **pickpockets** are always a threat and it's best to avoid coming laden down with expensive camera equipment or an obviously bulging wallet.

Hundreds of competing **mariachi** bands gather here in the evenings, all in their tight, silver-spangled *charro* finery and vast sombreros, to play for anyone who'll pay them. A typical group consists of two or four violins, a brass section of three trumpeters standing some way back so as not to drown out the others, three or four men on guitars of varying sizes, and a vocalist, though a truly macho man will rent the band and do the serenading himself. Mariachis take their name, supposedly, from the French *mariage*, it being traditional during the nineteenth-century French intervention to rent a group to play at weddings. You may also come across **norteño** bands from the border areas with their Tex-Mex brand of country music, or the softer sounds of **marimba** musicians from the south. Simply wander round the square and you'll get your fill – should you want to be individually serenaded, pick out a group and negotiate your price.

At the back of the square is a huge market hall in which a whole series of stalls serve simple food and vie furiously for customers. Alternatively, there is at least one prominent *pulquería* on the square (see box, p.447), and a number of fairly pricey restaurant/bars, which try to drown out the mariachi bands with their own canned music, and tempt customers with their no-cover entry. The last Metro leaves at midnight.

Ballet Folklórico

The **Ballet Folklórico** (Ⓣ55/5529-9320 to 22, Ⓦwww.balletamalia.com) is a long-running, internationally famed compilation of traditional dances from all over the country, elaborately choreographed and designed, and interspersed with Mexican music and singing. Despite the billing, it isn't really very traditional – although it does include several of the more famous native dances, they are very jazzed up and incorporated into what is, in effect, a regular musical that wouldn't be out of place on Broadway.

The Ballet Folklórico usually perform in the **Palacio de Bellas Artes** (see p.408), where the theatre is an attraction in itself, but while that is under renovation, they are performing in the Museo Nacional de Antropología (see p.419). Performances are on Sunday at 9.30am and 7.30pm, and Wednesday at 8.30pm. You should try to book at least a couple of days in advance – **tickets** (M$400) are available either from the Bellas Artes box office direct (Mon–Sat 11am–7pm, Sun 8.30am–7pm) or through Ticketmaster (Ⓣ55/5325-9000) – or arrange to go with an organized tour, for which you'll pay a considerable premium.

Cinemas

Mainstream Hollywood movies make it to Mexico just a few weeks after their release in the US and often before they get a British or European release. With the exception of movies for kids, they're almost always in their original language with subtitles, and since you'll usually only pay around M$35–50 (often reduced on Wed), a visit to the flicks can be a cheap and entertaining night out. Movies are **listed** every week in *Tiempo Libre*, as well as in most of the Spanish-language dailies.

There are **cinemas** scattered over most of city, but none near the Zócalo. One of the largest concentrations is along Insurgentes, where half a dozen multiplexes total around fifty screens in all. Handier places can be found in the Zona Rosa (Cinemark Reforma, Reforma 222, at Napoles Ⓣ55/5432-6789; Lumière Reforma, Río Guadalquivir 104, at Reforma Ⓣ55/5514-0000), or in Polanco (Cinemex Casa de Arte, Anatole France 120 Ⓣ55/5280-9156; Cinemark Polanco, Cervantes 397 Ⓣ55/5580-0506).

Markets and shopping

The big advantage of **shopping** in the capital is that you can get goods from all over the country and, if you are flying out of here, you don't have to lug them around Mexico, though they will usually be more expensive than at the source.

One fascinating (and occasionally frustrating) facet of shopping in the capital is the practice of devoting a whole street to one particular trade, which occurs to some extent throughout the city. There are blocks where you can buy nothing but stationery, while other areas are packed exclusively with shoe shops and still others only sell musical instruments. Due to the lack of variety in a given place – and without some luck or good directions – you can spend all day walking through markets without ever finding the items that you seek. This is a hangover from Aztec life, as their well-regulated markets were divided up according to the nature of the goods on sale, and the practice was continued by colonial planners.

Every area of the city has its own **market** selling food and essentials, and many others set up stalls for just one day a week along a suburban street. Less formal **street stalls** spring up all over the city and can take the form of anything from a New Age devotee with a sheet on the pavement selling cheap jewellery, to a relatively sophisticated stand selling pens, watches, computer hard drives and fake designer clothing and bags. The **Centro Histórico** and **Zona Rosa** are good hunting grounds, though the concentration of stalls in these areas is influenced by occasional crackdowns on this illegal but widely accepted trading. At more sensitive times you'll notice vendors alert to the presence of the authorities, and occasionally catch them packing up and sprinting off.

Department stores include El Palacio de Hierro at 20 de Noviembre 3, just south of the Zócalo, and Liverpool, opposite. **Sanborns** at Madero 4, near the main post office, and with branches citywide (see ⓦwww.sanborns.com.mx), sells books, maps and quantities of tacky souvenirs, and also has a sizeable pharmacy.

T-shirts and replica Mexican football shirts can be found in the *tianguis* (street stalls) on San Juan Letrán between Bellas Artes and Salto del Agua, or those in the streets north and east of the Zócalo.

For **crafts**, aside from the markets, there are the craft shops run by **FONART** (ⓦwww.fonart.gob.mx), a government agency that promotes crafts and helps the artisans with marketing and materials. The shops are at Juárez 89, at Balderas (Metro Hidalgo) and Reforma 116, at Milán (Metro Cuauhtémoc). The fixed prices are usually higher than elsewhere, but it is worth visiting to check price and quality before venturing to the markets.

Haggling for a bargain is no longer the thrilling (or daunting) prospect it once was in Mexico City. The nation's increasing prosperity and sophistication means that most things have prices fixed. As a tourist (and especially if your Spanish is poor) you can expect people to try to bump up the price occasionally, but on the whole what you see is what you pay.

Markets

Bazar Sábado Plaza San Jacinto, San Ángel. Very popular open-air art and sculpture market that runs pretty much all day Sat. On Sun it moves to Parque Sullivan, just north of the Zona Rosa (see p.415).

Central Artesanal Buenavista Aldama 187, just east of the former train station. Metro Buenavista. Handicrafts from around the country in what is claimed to be Mexico's largest shop. Rather pricey compared to the Ciudadela and less characterful. Daily 9am–6pm.

Centro Artesanal de San Juan (Mercado de Curiosidades Mexicanas) about five blocks south of the Alameda along Dolores. Metro San Juan de Letrán. Modern tourist-oriented complex that's possibly the least appealing of the major artesanía markets, though there are still deals to be had (particularly in silver) provided you haggle. Mon–Sat 9am–7pm, Sun 9am–4pm.

Ciudadela corner of Balderas and Emilio Donde. Metro Balderas. The best place in the capital to buy regional crafts and souvenirs from every part of the country. If you forgot to pick up a hammock in the Yucatán or some Olinalá lacquerwork in Guerrero, fear not: you can buy them here for not a great deal more. Bargaining has limited rewards. Mon–Sat 11am–7pm, Sun 11am–6pm.

Coyoacán markets Metro Viveros. There are two interesting markets in Coyoacán: the daily markets three blocks up from Plaza Hidalgo are typically given over to food, while on Sun a craft market converges on the plaza itself. There you can buy all manner of *típico* clothing, and lots of trendy variations.

La Lagunilla spreading along Rayon, a couple of blocks north of the Plaza Garibaldi. Comes closest to rivalling La Merced in size and variety, but is best visited on a Sun when the *tianguis* expands into the surrounding streets, with more stalls selling stones, used books, crafts and bric-a-brac. Get there on buses ("La Villa") heading north on Reforma, or walk from Metro Garibaldi.

Mercado de Sonora three blocks south of La Merced on Fray Servando Teresa de Mier. Metro La Merced. This market is famous for its sale of herbal medicines, medicinal and magical plants and the *curanderos* (indigenous herbalists) who go there.

La Merced corner of Izazaga San Pablo and Eje 1 Ote. Metro La Merced. The city's largest market, a collection of huge modern buildings, which still can't contain the vast number of traders who want to set up here. Almost anything you could conceive of finding in a Mexican market (and much more) is sold here, though fruit, vegetables and other foods dominate. Even if you're not buying you could easily spend half a day browsing metre-diameter columns of nopal leaves as high as a man, stacks of dried chiles and all manner of hardware from juice presses to volcanic-stone mortars known as

molcajetes. The Metro takes you right into the heart of things. Daily 6am–6pm.
Palacio de las Flores corner of Luis Moya and Ernesto Pugibet. Metro Salto de Agua or Balderas. A small market selling nothing but flowers – loose, in vast arrangements and wreaths, growing in pots, even paper and plastic. Similar markets can be found in San Ángel and Xochimilco.

English-language books and newspapers

International weeklies are available downtown from **newspaper stands** (especially along 5 de Mayo). Sanborns, dotted all over town, usually have a modest supply of English-language material, much of it business-oriented. Terminal 1 at the **airport** has numerous small shops partly stocked with English-language magazines and airport novels, plus a few foreign newspapers. The best bets are the Cenca store in Sala E2, and Libros y Arte between salas C and D.

American Book Store Bolivar 23, Centro Histórico ⓣ55/5512-0306. Despite the name, their stock of books in English is limited and mostly business- or computer-oriented. OK for a few paperbacks, magazines and newspapers. Mon–Fri 10am–7pm, Sat 10am–5.30pm.
La Torre del Papel Callejón de Betlemitas 6a, beside the Museo del Ejército y Fuerza, near Bellas Artes. Stocks up-to-date newspapers from all over Mexico and Latin America as well as a good showing of US, British, Spanish and Italian newspapers, plus magazines such as *National Geographic*, *The Economist*, *Entertainment Weekly* and *Paris Match*. Mon–Fri 8am–7pm, Sat 9am–2.30pm.

Sport

Sport is probably the city's biggest obsession, and while **football**, **wrestling** and **bullfighting** are the three leading lights, the sporting calendar doesn't stop there. There's **horse racing**, too, throughout the year (afternoons, especially Sat) at the Hipodromo de las Americas on Industria Militar (ⓣ55/5387-0600, ⓦwww.hipodromo.com.mx; Metro Cuatro Caminos); buses and *peseros* heading west on Reforma will take you there – look for "Hipodromo". More exciting horse action is involved in the *charreadas*, or **rodeos**, put on by amateur but highly skilled aficionados most weekends (often free), primarily at the Rancho del Charro, Constituyentes 500 (ⓣ55/5277-8706, ⓦwww.nacionaldecharros.com), close to the Third Section of Chapultepec Park; call or check their website to find out what's going on. **Frontón** (see p.55) used to be played at Frontón México, on Plaza de la República, but it closed when the players went on strike in 1993, and has never reopened.

Football

Fútbol (football, meaning soccer) is undoubtedly Mexico's most popular sport. The big games are held at the 114,000-seat Estadio Azteca, which hosted the World Cup finals in 1970 and 1986, and is home to América (Las Águilas, or The Eagles), the nation's most popular and consistently successful club side. Elsewhere in the city, the university side, UNAM (Las Pumas), have a strong following at the Estadio Olímpico across the road from the university (see p.435); and Cruz Azul (known as Los Cementeros for their long-time sponsorship by a cement company) pack out Estadio Azul right by the city's main bullring (see p.454). Mexico City's other major team, Atlante (Los Potros, "the Colts") shares the Estadio Azteca with América. There are usually at least two **games** every Sunday afternoon from January to June and August to November – check local papers for fixture details – and you can almost always get a **ticket** (M$75–400) at the gate. The exceptions are the big games such as major local derbies, and "El Clásico", when América host Chivas from Guadalajara, the biggest team from the country's second largest city; if you want to be sure of a ticket, they can be bought in advance from Ticketmaster (Ⓣ55/5325-9000, Ⓦwww.ticketmaster.com.mx). Estadio Azteca can be reached by Tren Ligero or Ruta #26 ("Xochimilco") *colectivo*, both from Metro Tasqueña; Estadio Olímpico is reached by "Tlalpan" bus from Metro Chilpancingo; Estadio Azul is reached on foot from Metro San Antonio or from Metrobús station Ciudad de los Desportes on Insurgentes.

Wrestling

Though its popularity has waned in recent years, *lucha libre*, or **wrestling**, remains one of Mexico's most avidly followed spectator sports. Over a dozen venues in the capital alone host fights several nights a week for a fanatical public. Widely available magazines, comics, photonovels and films recount the real and imagined lives of the rings' heroes and villains, though the once nightly telecasts are now a thing of the past.

Mexican wrestling is generally faster, with more complex moves, and more combatants in the ring at any one time than you would normally see in an American or British bout. This can make the action hard to follow for the uninitiated. More important, however, is the maintenance of stage personas, most of whom, heroes or villains, wear masks. The *rudos* tend to use brute force or indulge in sneaky, underhanded tactics to foil the opposition, while the *técnicos* use wit and guile to compensate for lack of brawn. This faux battle, not at all unlike the WWE on-screen antics, requires a massive suspension of disbelief – crucial if you want to join in the fun.

One of the most bizarre features of wrestling was the emergence of wrestlers as political figures – typically still in costume. The most famous of these, **Superbarrio**, arose from the struggle of Mexico City's tenant associations for fair rents and decent housing after the 1985 earthquake to become part of mainstream political opposition, even challenging government officials to step into the ring with him, and acting as a sort of unofficial cheerleader at opposition rallies.

The most famous wrestler of all time, however, was without doubt **El Santo** ("the Saint"). Immortalized in more than twenty movies, with titles such as *El Santo vs the Vampire Women*, he would fight, eat, drink and play the romantic lead without ever removing his mask, and until after his retirement, he never revealed his identity. His reputation as a gentleman in and out of the ring was legendary, and his death in 1984 widely mourned. His funeral was allegedly the second best-attended in Mexican history after that of President Obregón.

Fights can be seen, usually on Tuesdays at the Arena Coliseo, Peru 77 (Metro Allende) and on Fridays at the Arena México, Dr Lucio 197 at Dr Lavista, Colonia Doctores (two blocks south and one east of Metro Balderas, but not a good area to be in at night). Tickets are sold on the door.

Bullfighting

Soccer and wrestling may be more popular, but there is no event more quintessentially Mexican than the **bullfight**. Rooted in Spanish machismo and imbued with multiple layers of symbolism and interpretation, it transcends a mere battle of man against animal. Many visitors arrive in Mexico revolted by the very idea of such one-sided slaughter, but spend an hour watching on TV and you may well find yourself hooked; if nothing else, it is worth attending a *corrida de toros* to see this integral part of the Mexican experience. It is a sport that transcends class barriers; every Sunday afternoon during the winter season men and women from all walks of Mexican society file into the stadium – though some admittedly end up in plush *sombra* (shade) seats while the masses occupy concrete *sol* (sun) terraces.

During the **season** (the longer *temporada grande*, late Oct or early Nov to early April, or the shorter *temporada chica*, July to early Oct) fights take place every Sunday at 4pm at the giant 48,000-seat **Plaza México**, the largest bullring in the world. Each *corrida* lasts around two hours and involves six bulls, all from one ranch, with each of three matadors taking two bulls. Typically there will be two Mexican matadors and one from Spain, which still produces the best performers.

Each **fight** is divided into three *suertes* (acts) or *tercios* (thirds), each announced by a trumpet blast. During the first *tercio*, several *toreros* with large capes tire the bull in preparation for the *picadores* who, from their mounts atop heavily padded and blindfolded horses, attempt to force a lance between the bull's shoulder blades to further weaken him. The *toreros* then return for the second *tercio*, in which one of their number (and sometimes the matador himself) will try to stab six metal-tipped spikes (known as *bandilleras*) into the bull in as clean and elegant a manner as possible.

Exhausted and frustrated, but by no means docile, the bull is now considered ready for the third and final *tercio*, the *suerte de muleta*. The matador continues to tire the bull while pulling off as many graceful and daring moves as possible. By now the crowd will have sensed the bravery and finesse of the matador and the spirit of the bull he is up against, and shouts of "¡Olé!" will reverberate around the stadium with every pass. Eventually the matador will entice the bull to challenge him head-on, standing there with its hooves together. As it charges he will thrust his sword between its shoulder blades and, if it is well executed, the bull will crumple to the sand. However barbaric you might think it is, no one likes to see the bull suffer and even the finest performance will garner the matador little praise without a clean kill. Successful matadors may be awarded one of the bull's ears, rarely two, and perhaps two or three times a season the tail as well. An especially courageous bull may be spared and put out to stud, a cause for much celebration, but this is a rare spectacle.

Elaborate posters around town advertise **upcoming events**, as do most of the major newspapers. Look out too for the weekly coverage of the scene in the press during the season. **Tickets** can be bought at the gate and you can pay as little as M$60 for general admission to sunny concrete benches far from the action. Twenty pesos more and you'll have the luxury of some shade, and from there prices rise rapidly the closer you get to the ring, reaching as much as M$500 for a front-row seat. To get there, take a Metrobús down Insurgentes to Ciudad de los Desportes, or walk ten minutes east from Metro San Antonio.

Moving on from Mexico City

Following privatization, intercity passenger train services ceased to run, and the only service now out of Buenavista station is a suburban train (Ⓦwww.fsuburbanos.com) to Cuautitlán in México state. That leaves a choice for onward travel of either bus or plane. None of the city's four bus stations is very far from the centre of town, and the airport is surprisingly central too. All can be reached easily by Metro.

By plane

The **airport** (Ⓣ55/2482-2424 or 2482-2400, Ⓦwww.aicm.com.mx) is very much within the city limits, only 5km east of the Zócalo. Terminal 1 can be reached by Metro (Metro Terminal Aérea, line 5); Terminal 2 can be reached by bus or *pesero* from Metro Garibaldi (lines B & 8) or Hangares (line 5). To get a cab to either terminal, call the day before to one of the authorized airport taxi firms (Sitio 300 ⓣ55/5571-9344, Nueva Imagen ⓣ55/8421-3701 or Excelencia ⓣ55/2598-3531), or one of the other firms listed on p.390, to arrange a cab from your hotel. For details of airport facilities, see p.385. For the office addresses and phone numbers of the main airlines, see p.31. For domestic flight durations and frequencies, see p.460.

By bus

There are four chief **long-distance bus stations** in Mexico City, one for each point of the compass, though in practice the northbound terminal handles far more than its share, while the westbound one is tiny. All have Metro stations pretty much right outside.

Apart from the major terminals listed below, there are large open-air bus stops at the end of all the Metro lines, with slow services to places up to an hour or so outside the city limits. For destinations in the capital's hinterland it can sometimes be quicker to leave from these.

It's rare not to be able to get onto a bus at short notice, but it can be worth booking in advance for long-distance journeys or for express services to popular destinations at busy times – that way you'll have a choice of seat and be sure of getting the fastest service. Ticket Bus (ⓣ55/5133-2424 within the DF or 01-800/702-8000 toll-free from out of town, ⓦwww.ticketbus.com.mx) – with offices at TAPO bus station, Isabel la Católica 83 in the centre, Hamburgo 254 (at Sevilla) in the Zona Rosa, and Masaryk with Hegel in Polanco, among other places – can book tickets for a small fee with many but not all bus lines.

The box on pp.456–457 indicates which destination is served from which station, but if you're uncertain which bus station you should be leaving from, simply get into a taxi and tell the driver what your ultimate destination is – he'll know where to take you. You'll find places to eat and stalls selling food and drink for the journey in all the terminals, along with ATMs, left luggage offices, post offices and newsstands.

Terminal del Norte

The **Terminal del Norte**, Avenida de los Cien Metros 4907, is the largest of the city's four stations, handling direct routes to and from the US border, and services to every major city north of Mexico City (including the fastest services to Guadalajara and Morelia). To get to it by Metro, take line 5 to Autobuses del Norte. Alternatively, take a trolleybus heading north from Bellas Artes or anywhere along the Eje Central (Division del Norte/Lázaro Cárdenas).

TAPO

Eastbound services use the most modern of the terminals, the Terminal de Autobuses de Pasajeros de Oriente, always referred to as **TAPO**. Buses for Puebla, Veracruz and places that you might think of as south – Oaxaca, Chiapas and the Yucatán, even Guatemala – leave from here. It is also the most central of the bus stations, most easily reached by Metro (Metro San Lazaro; lines 1 and B).

Central de Autobuses del Sur

Buses towards the Pacific coast – Cuernavaca, Taxco and Acapulco in particular – leave from the **Central de Autobuses del Sur**, Tasqueña 1320. You can get there by Metro (Metro Tasqueña; line 2) – take the exit signposted "Autobuses del Sur", and the terminal is over to your left as you leave the station. Alternatively, you can take a trolleybus heading south anywhere along the Eje Central (Lázaro Cárdenas/Division del Norte), for example at Bellas Artes.

Buses to and from Mexico City

Mexico City's **bus stations** are used by hordes of competing companies, and the only way to get a full idea of the **timetable** to and from any given destination is to check each one individually – different companies may take different routes and you can sometimes waste hours by making the wrong choice, though staff are generally very helpful. The following is a list of the main services. You may find that less frequent services use other terminals.

City/town	Bus terminal	
Acapulco	Sur	half-hourly 7.30am–11pm
Aguascalientes	Norte	hourly 9am–midnight
Amecameca	TAPO	every 10min 5.15am–11.20pm
Campeche	TAPO	5 daily
Cancún	TAPO	6 daily
Chalma	Poniente	every 20min 6.30am–9pm
Chetumal	TAPO	3 daily
Chihuahua	Norte	17 daily
Chilpancingo	Sur	hourly 7am–9pm
Ciudad Juárez	Norte	17 daily
Ciudad Obregón	Norte	22 daily
Colima	Norte	5 daily
Córdoba	TAPO	at least hourly 7am–midnight
Cuautla	Sur, TAPO	every 10min 5.45am–11pm from Sur; every 10min 5.20am–11pm from TAPO
Cuernavaca	Sur	every 15min 6am–12.30am
Dolores Hidalgo	Norte	every 40min 5.20am–1am
Durango	Norte	9 daily
Guadalajara	Poniente, Norte	20 daily from Poniente; at least hourly from Norte
Guanajuato	Norte	10 daily
Guaymas	Norte	12 daily
Hermosillo	Norte	22 daily
Ixtapa	Sur	6 daily
Ixtapan de la Sal	Poniente	12 daily
León	Norte	at least hourly 4.45am–midnight
Los Mochis	Norte	22 daily
Malinalco	Poniente	3 daily
Manzanillo	Norte	4 daily
Matamoros	Norte	14 daily
Matehuala	Norte	8 daily
Mazatlán	Norte	1–2 hourly 6am–midnight
Mérida	TAPO	4 daily
Mexicali	Norte	22 daily

Terminal Poniente

For the west, there's the **Terminal Poniente**, at the junction of calles Sur and Tacubaya. The smallest of the terminals, it basically handles traffic to Toluca, but it's also the place to go for the slower, more scenic routes to Morelia, Guadalajara and other destinations in Jalisco and Michoacán, via Toluca. Aside from the Metro (Metro Observatorio; line 1), it can be reached on buses (signed "Metro Observatorio") heading south on Reforma or from the stands by the entrance to Chapultepec Park.

Monterrey	Norte	hourly 6am–11pm
Morelia	Poniente, Norte	half-hourly 5.30am–midnight from Poniente; hourly 6am–11pm from Norte
Nuevo Laredo	Norte	approximately hourly 9am–11pm
Oaxaca	TAPO	18 daily
Orizaba	TAPO	at least hourly 6.30am–12.45pm
Pachuca	Norte	every 10min 5.30am–11.30pm
Palenque	TAPO	2 daily
Pátzcuaro	Poniente, Norte	14 daily from Poniente; 6 daily from Norte
Playa del Carmen	TAPO	4 daily
Puebla	TAPO, Norte, Sur	every 20min 4am–1.30am from TAPO; half-hourly 4am–10pm from Norte; every 50min 6.05am–9.55pm from Sur
Puerto Escondido	Sur, TAPO	5 daily from Sur; 1 daily from TAPO
Puerto Vallarta	Poniente, Norte	6 daily from Poniente; 7 daily from Norte
Querétaro	Norte	every 30min 6am–midnight
Saltillo	Norte	14 daily
San Cristóbal de las Casas	TAPO	5 daily
San Luis Potosí	Norte	at least hourly 6am–11.45pm
San Miguel de Allende	Norte	every 40min 5.20am–1am
Taxco	Sur	hourly 7am–8pm
Tehuacan	TAPO	29 daily
Tehuantepec	TAPO, Sur	2 daily from TAPO, 1 daily from Sur
Teotihuacán	Norte	every 15min 6am–5pm
Tepic	Norte	12 daily
Tepoztlán	Sur	every 20min 7am–10pm
Tijuana	Norte	hourly 6am–11pm
Tlaxcala	TAPO	every 20min 5.40am–9pm (last departure at midnight)
Toluca	Poniente	every 5min 5.30am–10.30pm
Tula	Norte	every 15min 6am–9.30pm
Tuxpan	Norte	hourly 6am–midnight
Tuxtla Gutiérrez	TAPO	12 daily
Uruapan	Poniente, Norte	19 daily from Poniente; 8 daily from Norte
Valle de Bravo	Poniente	every 20min 5am–7.30pm
Veracruz	TAPO	19 daily
Villahermosa	TAPO	24 daily
Xalapa	TAPO	at least hourly 7am–midnight
Zacatecas	Norte	12 daily
Zihuatanejo	Sur	7 daily

Listings

Airlines The main ones are Aerocalifornia, Reforma 322 ☎55/5207-1392 or 01-800/685-5500; Aerocaribe, Xola 535 ☎55/5448-3024; Aerolineas Argentinas, Reforma 195, Cuauhtémoc ☎55/5133-4000 or 01-800/021-4000; Aeromar, airport Terminal 2 ☎55/5133-1111 or 01-800/237-6627; Aeroméxico, Reforma 445 ☎55/5133-4000 or 01-800/0214-7000; Air Canada, Manuel Avila Camacho 1 8° Lomas de Chapultepec ☎55/9138-0280 or 01-800/719-2827; Air France, Poe 90, Polanco ☎55/2122-8282 or 1-800/006-7700; Alaska Airlines, Hamburgo 213 10°, Zona Rosa ☎55/5533-1746; American, Reforma 300, at Amberes ☎55/5209-1400; Avianca, Reforma 195

Ⓣ55/5566-8550; British Airways, Reforma 10–14 Ⓣ55/5628-0500; Continental, Andrés Bello 45 18°, Polanco Ⓣ55/5283-5500; Delta, Horacio 1855, Polanco Ⓣ55/5279-0909 or 01-800/123-4710; Iberia, Ejercito Nacional 436 9°, Polanco Ⓣ55/1101-1550; Interjet, Ejercito Nacional 843-B, Polanco Ⓣ55/1102-5511 or 01-800/322-5050; Japan Air Lines, Reforma 505 36°, Cuauhtémoc Ⓣ55/5242-0150; Lufthansa, Paseo de las Palmas 391, Lomas de Chapultepec Ⓣ55/5230-0000; Mexicana, handiest offices at Juárez 82, at Balderas Ⓣ55/5512-7505, and Reforma 312, at Amberes Ⓣ55/5511-0424; Northwest/KLM, Andrés Bello 45 11°, Polanco Ⓣ55/5279-5390 or 01-800/907-4700; United, Hamburgo 213, Zona Rosa Ⓣ55/5627-0222; US Airways Ⓣ01-800/428-4322.

American Express Central office and clients' mail service at Reforma 350 by El Ángel (Mon–Fri 9am–6pm, Sat 9am–1pm; Ⓣ55/5207-7049). Other offices at the airport and elsewhere in the city.

Banks and exchange ATMs are everywhere, and with the appropriate credit or cash cards you can get money throughout your stay without ever visiting a bank. Besides, many banks will only change money in the morning, and lots are unhelpful for currencies other than US dollars: Banamex is your best bet. Most large hotels and shops will change travellers' cheques and cash dollars, but the quickest and easiest places to change money are casas de cambio, scattered all over town. In the *centro histórico* try Casa de Cambio Puebla, Madero 27, at Bolivar (Mon–Fri 9am–6pm, Sat 10am–4pm) or Cambios Exchange, at Madero 13, near Gante (Mon–Sat 9.30am–7pm, Sun 10am–6pm). You'll find several in the Zona Rosa, especially on Amberes, Londres and Liverpool, and a couple on the south side of Reforma, just south of the Monumento a la Revolución.

Car rental At the airport, as well as local firm Gold Car Rental (Ⓣ55/2599-0090, Ⓔintgold@avantel.net), there are multinational firms including: Avis (Ⓣ55/5762-3688 or 01-800/288-8888, Ⓦwww.avis.com.mx), Budget (Ⓣ01-800/700 1700, Ⓦwww.budget.com.mx), Europcar (Ⓣ55/5786-8265 or 01-800/201-3333, Ⓦwww.europcar.com.mx), Hertz (Ⓣ55/1803-4059, Ⓦwww.hertz.com.mx), National (Ⓣ55/5703-2222 or 01-800/716-6625, Ⓦwww.nationalcar.com.mx) and Thrifty (Ⓣ55/5785-0506 or 01-800/800-2382, Ⓦwww.thrifty.com.mx). Rental cars are exempt from the one day a week driving restriction (see p.38).

Courier services DHL, Madero 70-C, Centro Histórico (Mon–Fri 9am–6pm) and other locations (Ⓣ55/5345-7000 or 01-800/765-6345, Ⓦwww.dhl.com.mx); FedEx, Reforma 308, Zona Rosa (Mon–Fri 9am–7pm, Sat 9am–2pm) and other locations (Ⓣ01-800/900-1100, Ⓦfedex.com/mx_english).

Cultural institutes Several countries maintain cultural institutes and libraries for their nationals within Mexico City, often allowing short-term visitors to use some of their facilities. They can also be useful places for contacts, and if you're looking for work, long-term accommodation or travelling companions their notice boards are good places to start. The US has the Biblioteca Benjamín Franklin, Liverpool 31, at Berlin (Mon–Fri 11am–7pm; Ⓣ55/5080-2185, Ⓦwww.usembassy-mexico.gov/biblioteca; Metro Cuauhtémoc); the UK has the British Council, Lope de Vega 316 (Mon–Fri 8am–8pm; Ⓣ55/5263-1900; Metro Polanco); Canadians can use the Canadian Embassy Library (see below; Mon–Fri 9am–12.30pm).

Embassies and consulates Australia, Rubén Darío 55, Polanco (Mon–Fri 8.30am–5.15pm; Ⓣ55/1101-2200, Ⓦwww.mexico.embassy.gov.au; Metro Auditorio); Belize, Bernardo de Gálves 215, Lomas de Chapultepec (Mon–Fri 9am–1.30pm; Ⓣ55/5520-1274, Ⓔembelize@prodigy.net.mx); Canada, Schiller 529, Polanco (Mon–Fri 9am–1pm & 2–4pm; Ⓣ55/5724-7900, toll-free emergency number for Canadians Ⓣ01-800/706-2900, Ⓦwww.canada.org.mx; Metro Polanco); Ireland, Manuel Avila Camacho 76 3°, Lomas de Chapultepec (Mon–Fri 8.30am–5pm; Ⓣ55/5520-5803, Ⓦwww.irishembassy.com.mx; Metro Polanco or Auditorio); New Zealand, Jaime Balmes 8 4°, Polanco (Mon–Thurs 8.30am–2pm & 3–5.30pm, Fri 8.30am–2pm; Ⓣ55/5283-9460, Ⓦwww.nzembassy.com/mexico; Metro Polanco); South Africa, Andrés Bello 10 9°, Polanco (Mon–Fri 8am–4pm; Ⓣ55/1100-4970, safrica@prodigy.net.mx; Metro Polanco); UK, Río Lerma 71, at Río Sena, Zona Rosa (Mon–Thurs 8am–4pm, Fri 8am–1.30pm; Ⓣ55/5207-2089, Ⓦwww.embajadabritanica.com.mx; Metro Insurgentes); US, Reforma 305 at Danubio, Zona Rosa (Mon–Fri 8.30am–5.30pm; Ⓣ55/5080-2000, Ⓦwww.usembassy-mexico.gov; Metro Insurgentes).

Emergencies All emergency services (police, fire, ambulance) Ⓣ080; police Ⓣ060; fire department Ⓣ068; Red Cross ambulance Ⓣ065; Locatel, which gives information on missing persons and vehicles, medical emergencies, emotional crises and public services Ⓣ55/5658-1111; tourist security Ⓣ01-800/903-9200.

Festivals Celebrations for the Día de los Santos Reyes (Twelfth Night; Jan 6) include a fiesta with dancing at Nativitas, a suburb near Xochimilco. On Jan 17, for the Bendicíon de los Animales, children's pets and peasants' farm animals are taken to the cathedral to be blessed. St Peter's day (June 29) is marked by traditional dancing in San Pedro Actopan, on the southern outskirts of the DF. St Martha's day (July 29) is celebrated in Milpa Alta, near Xochimilco, with Aztec dances and mock fights between Moors and Christians. On Independence Day (Sept 15), the president proclaims the famous Grito at 11pm in the Zócalo, followed by the ringing of the Campana de Dolores and a huge firework display. Santa Cecilia is the patron saint of musicians, and her fiesta on Nov 22 attracts orchestras and mariachi bands from all over to Santa Cecilia Tepetlapa, near Xochimilco. Día de la Señora de Guadalupe (Dec 12) sees a massive pilgrimage to the Basilica of Guadalupe (see p.440), running for several days, with a more secular celebration of music and dancing.

Gay life The Zona Rosa (pink zone) is increasingly becoming a gay zone, and in particular the northernmost block of Amberes between Estrasburgo and Reforma, where you'll find a whole slew of gay and lesbian bars including *Papi, Gayta, Pussy Bar* (for girls) and *Boy Bar* (for boys). The listings magazine *Tiempo Libre* also has a section on gay and lesbian events and locales.

Hospital The American-British Cowdray Hospital (ABC) is at the junction of Observatorio and Sur 136, Col Las Américas (Ⓣ55/5230-8000, Ⓦwww.abchospital.com; Metro Observatorio). Embassies should be able to provide a list of multilingual doctors if necessary (the US embassy maintains a list at Ⓦwww.usembassy-mexico.gov/medical_lists.html).

Internet access Numerous cybercafés all over the city generally charge around M$10–15 per hour. Those in the suburbs (there are several in Xochimilco for example) tend to be slightly cheaper than those in town. In the centre, try: *Hostel Catedral* (see p.391; daily 7am–10pm, but quite pricey, M$20/hr; Metro Zócalo); Lafoel Internet Service, Donceles 80 1°, at República de Brasil (daily 9am–9pm; M$15/hr; Metro Allende). In the Zona Rosa, there are several inside the roundabout at Glorieta Insurgentes.

Laundry Self-service launderettes are surprisingly rare in Mexico City, but most hotels should be able to point one out. Options include: La Maquina, 2nd floor, Plaza Bialos mini-mall, Donceles 87, on the corner of República de Brasil (Mon–Fri 8am–6pm, Sat 9am–2pm); and Lavandería Automática Edison, Edison 91, at Arriaga, near the Plaza de la República (Mon–Fri 9am–7pm, Sat 9am–6pm; Metro Revolución).

Left luggage Most hotels will hold your bags for the rest of the day after you've checked out, and some will allow you to leave excess luggage for several days, sometimes for a small charge. All four main bus terminals and both airport terminals have left luggage facilities (M$40–110 a day depending on the size of your bag).

Opening hours Hours for most businesses in Mexico City are from 10am until 7pm. Very few now close for the traditional 2–4pm siesta.

Pharmacies Sanborns offers a wide range of products at most branches, as well as dispensing some prescription drugs. Other options include El Fénix, Madero 41, at Motolinia, and Isabel la Católica 15, at 5 de Mayo. There are homeopathic pharmacies at Mesones 111-B, at 20 Noviembre, and República Guatemala 16, behind the cathedral.

Photographic supplies Film is available almost everywhere – pharmacies, tourist locales and so on – at reasonable prices, but for specialist needs head to Calle Donceles, between Republica de Argentina and Allende, or Foto Regis at Juárez 56, on the south side of the Alameda (Ⓦwww.fotoregis.com).

Post office The main post office is on Lázaro Cárdenas at Tacuba, across the street from Bellas Artes (Mon–Fri 8am–8pm, Sat 8am–4pm). Branch offices (Mon–Fri 8am–4pm, Sat 8.30am–3.30pm) can be found at Ponciano Arriaga 11, near the Revolution Monument, and Higuera 23 in Coyoacán, among other places.

Spanish courses There are many Spanish courses in the city, though most people prefer to study in such places as Cuernavaca, San Miguel de Allende and Guanajuato. For those who prefer the metropolis, the most prestigious language school in town is the Universidad Autonomo's Centro de Enseñanza para Extranjeros, located at Universidad 3002 in the Ciudad Universitaria (Ⓣ55/5622-2470, Ⓦwww.cepe.unam.mx). Also worth checking out is Ⓦwww.planeta.com/mexico.html, which has good links to Mexican language schools.

Telephones Local, domestic long-distance and international phone calls can be made from any public phone with a phonecard. Cheaper international calls can be made via the internet, though only a few internet locales are offering this service as yet – those which do include a couple inside the roundabout at Glorieta Insurgentes. Otherwise, a number of shops have public phones (for international services look for the blue "Larga Distancia" signs). You can dial direct from most big hotels, but it will cost much more. *Casetas de larga distancia* are closing down in the face of widespread use of cardphones, but you'll find them at all the bus terminals except TAPO.

Tourist cards Should you lose yours, or want an extension, you apply, when your original length of stay is almost finished, to the Instituto de Migración,

Ejército National 862, at the western end of Polanco (Mon–Fri 9am–1pm; ⓣ55/2581-0116; *peseros* from Chapultepec to Toreo run along Ejército Nacional). Extensions are pretty much routine if the period is two weeks or less, and should take around half an hour; go to desk D23 – "Ampliación de Estancia". Longer extensions will require copies, form filling and possibly an onward ticket or proof of sufficient funds.

Travel agencies A particularly good firm for youth and student fares is Mundo Joven (ⓦwww.mundojoven.com), with offices at Guatemala 4 behind the cathedral (ⓣ55/5518-1755), Eugenio Sue 342, at Homero in Polanco (ⓣ55/5250-7191), and Terminal 1, Sala E2 in the airport (ⓣ55/2599-0155).

Travel details

Buses

Mexico City (N = Terminal del Norte; S = Central de Autobuses del Sur/Taxqueña; E = TAPO; W = Terminal Pte/Observatorio) to: Acapulco (S, every 30min; 6hr); Aguascalientes (N, hourly; 6hr); Amecameca (E, every 10min; 1hr 15min); Campeche (E, 5 daily; 17hr); Cancún (E, 6 daily; 24hr); Chalma (W, every 20min, 2hr 30min); Chetumal (E, 3 daily; 18hr); Chihuahua (N, 17 daily; 18hr); Chilpancingo (S, hourly; 3hr 30min); Ciudad Juárez (N, 17 daily; 24hr); Ciudad Obregón (N, 22 daily; 26hr); Colima (N, 5 daily; 11hr); Córdoba (E, hourly; 4hr); Cuautla (S, every 10min; E, every 10min; 1hr 40min); Cuernavaca (S, every 15min; 1hr 30min); Dolores Hidalgo (N, every 40min; 4hr); Durango (N, 9 daily; 12hr); Guadalajara (N, hourly; W, 20 daily; 7hr); Guanajuato (N, 10 daily; 5hr); Guaymas (N, 12 daily; 27hr); Hermosillo (N, 22 daily; 32hr); Ixtapa (S, 6 daily; 10hr); Ixtapan de la Sal (W, 12 daily; 2–3hr); León (N, hourly; 5hr); Los Mochis (N, 22 daily; 21hr); Malinalco (W, 3 daily; 2hr 30min); Manzanillo (N, 4 daily; 12hr); Matamoros (N, 14 daily; 14hr); Matehuala (N, 8 daily; 7hr); Mazatlán (N, every 30–60min; 15hr); Mérida (E, 4 daily; 28hr); Mexicali (N, 22 daily; 30hr); Monterrey (N, hourly; 12hr); Morelia (W, every 30min; N, hourly; 4hr); Nuevo Laredo (N, hourly; 15hr); Oaxaca (E, 18 daily; 6hr); Orizaba (E, hourly; 4hr); Pachuca (N, every 10min; 1hr 15min); Palenque (E, 2 daily; 13hr); Pátzcuaro (W, 14 daily; N, 6 daily; 7hr); Playa del Carmen (E, 4 daily; 22hr); Puebla (E, every 20min; N, every 30min; S, every 50min; 2hr); Puerto Escondido (S, 5 daily; E, 1 daily; 15hr); Puerto Vallarta (N, 7 daily; W, 6 daily; 12hr); Querétaro (N, every 30min; 2hr 40min); Saltillo (N, 14 daily; 10hr); San Cristóbal de las Casas (E, 5 daily; 17hr); San Luis Potosí (N, hourly; 5hr); San Miguel Allende (N, every 40min; 4hr); Taxco (S, hourly; 2hr 30min); Tehuacán (E, 29 daily; 4hr); Tehuantepec (E, 2 daily; S, 1 daily; 10hr); Teotihuácan (N, every 15min; 1hr); Tepic (N, 12 daily; 12hr); Tepoztlán (S, every 20min; 1hr 15min); Tijuana (N, hourly; 42hr); Tlaxcala (E, every 20min; 1hr 40min); Toluca (W, every 5min; 1hr 30min); Tula (N, every 30min; 1hr 15min); Tuxpan (N, hourly; 4hr); Tuxtla Gutiérrez (E, 12 daily; 14hr); Uruapan (W, 19 daily; N, 8 daily; 5hr 30min); Valle de Bravo (W, every 20min; 3hr); Veracruz (E, 19 daily; 7hr); Villahermosa (E, 24 daily; 11hr); Xalapa (E, hourly; 5hr); Zacatecas (N, 12 daily; 8hr); Zihuatanejo (S, 7 daily; 9hr).

Flights

Mexico City to: Acapulco (11–14 daily; 45min); Aguascalientes (7 daily; 1hr); Bajío/León (10 daily; 50min); Campeche (3 daily; 1hr 10min); Cancún (42 daily; 2hr); Chetumal (2 daily; 1hr 50min); Chihuahua (6 daily; 2hr); Ciudad Carmen (4 daily; 1hr 25min); Ciudad Juárez (7 daily; 2hr 20min); Ciudad Obregón (3–4 daily; 2hr 15min); Ciudad Victoria (5–6 daily; 1hr 10min); Colima (3–4 daily; 1hr); Cozumel (1–2 daily; 2hr); Culiacán (5–6 daily; 1hr 45min); Durango (3–4 daily; 2hr); Guadalajara (25 daily; 1hr 10min); Hermosillo (8 daily; 2hr 30min); Huatulco (6 daily; 1hr 10min); Ixtapa/Zihuatanejo (7–9 daily; 50min); La Paz, Baja California Sur (4 daily; 2hr 5min); Lázaro Cárdenas (2 daily; 1hr 10min); Los Cabos (2 daily; 2hr); Los Mochis (2–4 daily; 2hr); Manzanillo (3–4 daily; 1hr 40min); Matamoros (2 daily; 1hr 25min); Mazatlán (6–7 daily; 35min); Mérida (12 daily; 1hr 40min); Mexicali (5 daily; 3hr 15min); Monterrey (30 daily; 1hr 20min); Morelia (5–7 daily; 55min); Nuevo Laredo (2 daily; 1hr 35min); Oaxaca (9–10 daily; 55min); Puerto Escondido (1 daily; 1hr 05min); Puerto Vallarta (9–12 daily; 1hr 20min); Querétaro (2–3; 45min); Reynosa (5–6 daily; 1hr 25min); Saltillo (3 daily; 1hr 25min); San Luis Potosí (9–11; 1hr 15min); Tampico (10–11 daily; 55min); Tapachula (4 daily; 1hr 35min); Tepic (2–3 daily; 1hr 55min); Tijuana (18–21 daily; 3hr 20min); Torreón (8–10 daily; 1hr 25min); Tuxtla Gutiérrez (17 daily; 1hr 20min); Veracruz (15 daily; 50min); Villahermosa (12–14 daily; 1hr 20min); Zacatecas (5–6 daily; 1hr 15min).

7

Around Mexico City

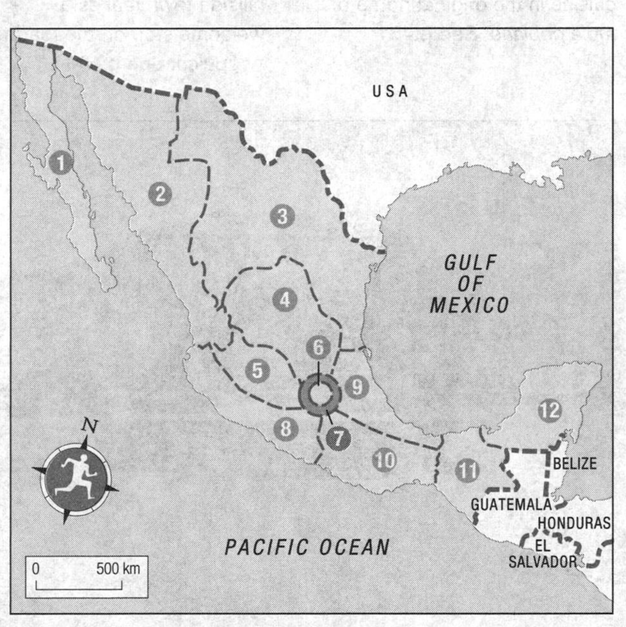

CHAPTER 7
Highlights

* **Teotihuacán** The largest pre-Hispanic site in the country, dominated by the huge Pirámide del Sol. See p.464
* **Real del Monte** A lovely mountain town with fresh air and an unexpected Cornish influence. See p.476
* **Puebla** Marvellous Spanish architecture and wonderful cuisine in the original home of *mole poblano*. See p.481
* **The Great Pyramid of Cholula** What at first glance looks like a hill topped by a pretty church is in fact Mexico's most massive pyramid ruin. See p.487
* **Cuernavaca** Charming colonial city that's a favourite place to study Spanish. See p.490
* **Taxco** This whitewashed hillside town makes a welcome stop on the road to Acapulco. See p.500

▲ Pirámide del Sol, Teotihuacán

7

Around Mexico City

Striking out from Mexico City, there are places worth visiting in every direction. Those covered in this chapter can all be taken in on day trips from the city DF, but many of them – and in particular the wonderful colonial cities of **Puebla**, **Taxco** and **Cuernavaca** – deserve more than just a quick once-over, and really do repay a longer stay.

Much of the region around Mexico City belongs to the **State of México**, whose capital is **Toluca**, to the west, but the state actually reaches all the way round the

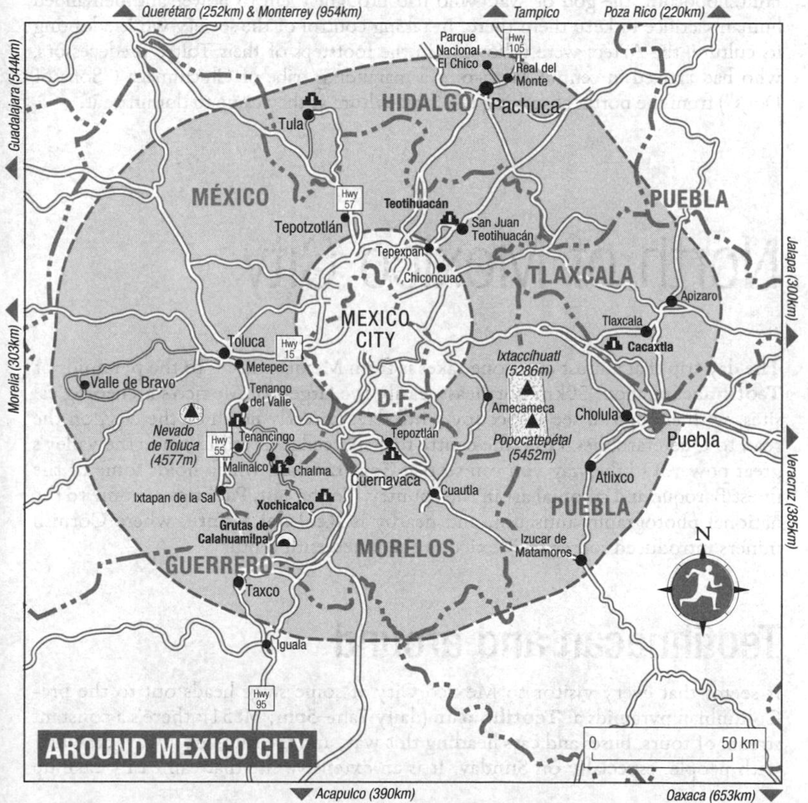

northern edge of Mexico City and covers its eastern side as well. Also encrusted around the capital are the small states of **Hidalgo** (to the north), **Morelos** (to the south) and **Tlaxcala** (to the west). The city of Puebla, though its state sprawls eastward towards Veracruz, is tucked in tidily next to Tlaxcala, just as **Taxco** is next to Morelos, though it actually belongs to Guerrero, the same state as Acapulco.

The heart of this region is the **Valley of México,** a mountain-ringed basin – 100km long, 60km wide and over 2400m high, dotted with great salt- and fresh-water lagoons and dominated by the vast snowcapped peaks of Popocatépetl and Ixtaccíhuatl. Since long before the Mexican nation existed, it has been the country's centre of gravity. Even in the days of the Aztecs, cities such as Texcoco (now in the State of México) and Tlaxcala (now capital of its own little state) vied with Tenochtitlán (Mexico City) for domination.

Also in the region, and particularly to the north of Mexico City, you'll be able to see much older sites such as **Teotihuacán** and **Tula**. Teotihuacán was the predominant culture of the Classic period and the true forebear of the Aztecs. Its style, and its deities – including Quetzalcoatl, the plumed serpent, and Tlaloc, the rain god – were adopted everywhere. The Aztecs, arriving some five hundred years later, didn't acknowledge this debt, but regarded themselves as descendants of the **Toltec kingdom**, whose capital lay at Tula to the north, and whose influence – as successors to Teotihuacán – was almost as pervasive. The Aztecs consciously took over the Toltec military-based society, and adopted many of their gods: above all Quetzalcoatl, who assumed an importance equal to that of their own tribal deity, Huitzilopochtli, the god of war, who had brought them to power and demanded human sacrifice to keep them there. In taking control of the society while adopting its culture, the Aztecs were following in the footsteps of their Toltec predecessors, who had arrived in central Mexico as a marauding tribe of Chichimeca ("Sons of Dogs") from the north, absorbing the local culture as they came to dominate it.

North of Mexico City

The day trip that almost everyone takes is from Mexico City is to the pyramids of **Teotihuacán**, about 50km northeast, easily the largest of Mexico's archeological sites, with enough to see to occupy a full day. Directly north of the city, on the road to Querétaro, lies **Tula**, the centre that succeeded Teotihuacán as the valley's great power. On the way you can stop at **Tepotzotlán**, which holds some of the finest Baroque and colonial art in the country. To the east, **Pachuca** is home to the national photography museum, and nearby is **Real del Monte**, where Cornish miners introduced soccer to Mexico in the nineteenth century.

Teotihuacán and around

It seems that every visitor to Mexico City at some stage heads out to the pre-Columbian pyramids at **Teotihuacán** (daily 7am–5pm; M$51): there's a constant stream of tours, buses and cars heading this way, and the ruins are always crawling with people, especially on Sunday. It is an extensive site that can easily take up

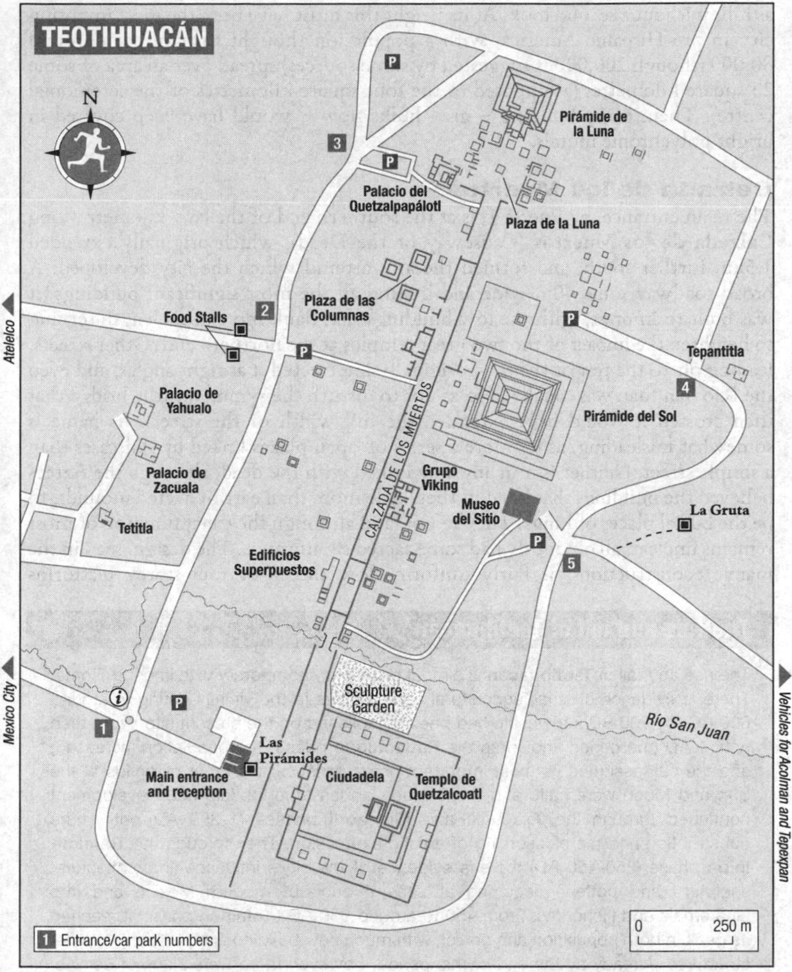

most of a day. It makes sense to plan ahead and it's best to head out here as early as you can manage and do most of your exploration in the cool of the morning before the crowds arrive. From 11am to 3pm it can be very busy, and there is little shade, so you may want to spend that time at a restaurant or in the **museum**, returning refreshed for the photogenic light of the late afternoon. Visitors with limited Spanish will be glad to know that most of the explanatory signs are also in English.

The site

The ruins at **Teotihuacán** are not, on first glance, the most impressive in Mexico – they lack the dramatic hilltop settings or lush jungle vegetation of those in the south – but they reveal a city planned and built on a massive scale, the great pyramids so huge that before their refurbishment one would have passed them by as hills without a second look. At its height this must have been the most imposing city in pre-Hispanic America, with a population thought to have been around 80,000 (though 200,000 is suggested by some sources) spread over an area of some 23 square kilometres (as opposed to the four square kilometres of the ceremonial centre). Then, every building – grey hulks now – would have been covered in bright polychrome murals.

Calzada de los Muertos

The main entrance, by Puerta 1, is at the southern end of the two-kilometre-long **Calzada de los Muertos** (Causeway of the Dead), which originally extended 1.5km further south, and formed the axis around which the city developed. A broad roadway some 40m wide and linking all the most significant buildings, it was built to impress, with the low buildings that flank most of its length serving to heighten the impact of the two great temples at the northern end. Other streets, leading off to the rest of the city, originally intersected it at right angles, and even the Río San Juan was canalized so as not to disturb the symmetry (the bridge that then crossed it would have extended the full width of the street). Its name is somewhat misleading, as it's more a series of open plazas linked by staircases than a simple street. Neither is it in any way linked with the dead, although the Aztecs believed the buildings that lined it, then little more than earth-covered mounds, to be the burial places of kings. They're not, and although the exact function of most remains unclear, all obviously had some sacred significance. The design, seen in the many reconstructions, is fairly uniform: low three- or four-storey platforms

The rise and fall of Teotihuacán

The rise and fall of **Teotihuacán** is almost exactly contemporary with imperial Rome. There is evidence of small agricultural communities in the vicinity dating to around 600 BC; by 200 BC a township had been established on the present site. From then until 1 AD (the period known as the **Patlachique** phase) the population increased, and the city assumed its most important characteristics: the great pyramids of the Sun and Moon were built, and the Calzada de los Muertos laid out. Development continued through the **Tzacualli** and **Miccaotli** phases (1–250 AD) with more construction and the blossoming of artistic expression. Then through the **Tlamimilolpa** phase (250–450 AD) there is evidence of the city's influence (in architecture, sculpture and pottery) occurring at sites throughout modern Mexico and into Guatemala and Honduras. From 450 to around 650 AD (**Xolalpan** phase) it reached its peak in both population and power, with much new building and addition to earlier structures. Already by the end of this period, however, there were signs of decline, and the final phase, the **Metepec**, lasted at most a century before the city was sacked, burnt and virtually abandoned. This is thought to have been the result of attack by northern tribes, probably the **Toltecs**, but the disaster may in the end have been as much ecological as military. Vast forests were cut down to build the city (for use in columns, roof supports and door lintels) and huge quantities of wood burnt to make the lime plaster that coated the buildings. The result was severe soil erosion that left the hillsides as barren as they appear today. In addition, the agricultural effort needed to feed so many people (with no form of artificial fertilizer or knowledge of crop rotation) gradually sapped what land remained of its ability to grow more.

Whatever the precise causes, the city was left, eventually, to a ruination that was advanced even by the time of the Aztecs. To them it represented a holy place from a previous age, and they gave it its present name, which translates as "the place where men became gods". Although Teotihuacán features frequently in Aztec mythology, there are no written records – what we know of the city is derived entirely from archeological and artistic evidence, so that even the original name remains unknown.

consisting of vertical panels (*tableros*) supported by sloping walls. In many cases several are built on top of each other – clearly demonstrated in the **Edificios Superpuestos** (superimposed buildings) on the left-hand side shortly beyond the river. Here, excavated structures underneath the present level may have been the living quarters of Teotihuacán's priests.

La Ciudadela

Directly opposite the entrance at Puerta 1 lies **La Ciudadela**, the Citadel. This enormous sunken square, surrounded by stepped platforms and with a low square altar in the centre, was the city's administrative heart, with the houses of its chief priests and nobles arranged around a vast meeting place. Across the open space stands a tall pyramid construction inside which, during excavations, was found the **Templo de Quetzalcoatl**. With the back of the newer pyramid demolished, the elaborate (Miccaotli phase) temple structure stands revealed. Pyramids aside, this is one of the most impressive sections of the whole site, rising in four steps (of an original six), each sculpted in relief and punctuated at intervals by the stylized heads of Quetzalcoatl, the plumed serpent, and **Tlaloc**, the rain god. Traces of the original paint can be seen in places. This theme – with the goggle-eyed, almost abstract mask of Tlaloc and the fanged snake Quetzalcoatl, its neck ringed with a collar of feathers – recurs in later sites throughout the country.

Pirámide del Sol

The great **Pirámide del Sol** (Pyramid of the Sun) is Teotihuacán's outstanding landmark, a massive structure 70m high and, of Mexico's ancient buildings, second in size only to Cholula (and Cholula is a total ruin). Its base is almost exactly the same size as that of the great Pyramid of Cheops in Egypt, but the lower-angled sides and its stepped nature make it very much lower. There are wonderful views from the top nonetheless, and the bulk is all the more remarkable when you consider the accuracy of its alignment: on two days a year (May 19 and July 25), the sun is directly over the pyramid at noon, and the main west facade faces the point at which the sun sets on these days. This alignment just off the cardinal points determined the line of the Calzada de los Muertos and of the entire city. Equally remarkable is the fact that the 2.5 million tonnes of stone and earth used in its construction were brought here without benefit of the wheel or any beast of burden, and shaped without the use of metal tools. The pyramid you see was reconstructed by **Leopoldo Batres** in 1908, in a thoroughly cavalier fashion. He blasted, with dynamite, a structure that originally abutted the south face, and stripped much of the surface in a search for a more complete building under the present one. In fact, the Pirámide del Sol, almost uniquely, was built in one go at a very early stage of the city's development (about 100 AD), and there is only a very small older temple right at its heart. As a result of Batres's stripping of the stone surface, the temple has eroded considerably more than it might otherwise have done. He also added an extra terrace to the original four.

You approach by a short staircase leading to the right off the Calzada de los Muertos onto a broad esplanade, where stand the ruins of several small temples and priests' dwellings. The main structure consists of five sloping layers of wall divided by terraces – the large flat area at the top would originally have been surmounted by a sanctuary, long disappeared. Evidence of why this massive structure came to be raised here emerged in 1971 when archeologists stumbled on a tunnel (closed to the public) leading to a clover-leaf-shaped **cave** directly under the centre of the pyramid. This, clearly, had been some kind of inner sanctuary, a holy of holies, and may even have been the reason for Teotihuacán's foundation and the basis of its influence. Theories abound as to its exact nature, and many fit remarkably with legends handed down through the Aztecs. It's most likely that the cave was formed by a subterranean spring, and came to be associated with Tlaloc, god of rain but also a bringer of fertility, as a sort of fountain of life.

Alternatively, it could be associated with the legendary "seven grottos", a symbol of creation from which all later Mexican peoples claimed to have emerged, or to have been the site of an oracle, or associated with a cult of sacrifice – in Aztec times the flayed skins of victims of Xipe Totec were stored in a cave under a pyramid.

Pirámide de la Luna

At the end of the Calzada de los Muertos rises the **Pirámide de la Luna** (Pyramid of the Moon), a smaller structure built slightly later (but still during the Tzacualli phase), whose top, thanks to the high ground on which it's built, is virtually on a level with that of the Pirámide del Sol. The structure is very similar, with four sloping levels approached by a monumental stairway, but for some reason this seems a very much more elegant building: perhaps because of the smaller scale, or perhaps as a result of the approach, through the formally laid-out **Plaza de la Luna**. The top of the pyramid offers the best overview of the site's layout, looking straight back down the length of the central thoroughfare. It is perfect for sunset, though as it is then close to closing time the guards will soon chase you down.

Palacio de Quetzalpapálotl and Palacio de los Jaguares

The **Palacio de Quetzalpapálotl** (Palace of the Quetzal-butterfly) lies to the left of the Plaza de la Luna, behind the low temples that surround it. Wholly restored, it's virtually the only example of a pre-Hispanic roofed building in central Mexico and preserves a unique view of how the elite lived at Teotihuacán. The rooms are arranged around a patio whose elaborately carved pillars give the palace its name – their stylized designs represent birds (the brightly coloured quetzals, though some may be owls) and butterflies. In the galleries around the patio several frescoes survive, all very formalized and symbolic, with the themes reduced almost to geometric patterns. **Mural art** was clearly very important in Teotihuacán, and almost every building has some trace of decoration, though much has been removed for restoration. Two earlier buildings, half-buried under the palace, still have substantial remains. In the **Palacio de los Jaguares**, jaguars in feathered headdresses blow conch shells from which emerge curls of music, or perhaps speech or prayers to Tlaloc (who appears along the top of the mural); in the **Templo de los Caracoles Emplumados** (Temple of the Plumed Shells), you see a motif of feathers and seashells along with bright green parrots. Other murals, of which only traces remain, were found in the temples along the Calzada de los Muertos between the two pyramids.

Tepantitla, Tetitla and Atetelco

Mural art was not reserved for the priests' quarters – indeed some of the finest frescoes have been found in outlying apartment buildings. The famous *Paradise of Tlaloc* mural (reproduced in the Museo Nacional de Antropología, see p.419) was discovered at **Tepantitla**, a residential quarter of the old city across the road from the back of the Pirámide del Sol. Only a part of it survives here, but there are others in the complex depicting a procession of priests and a ball-game. All have great vitality and an almost comic-strip quality, with speech bubbles emerging from the figures' mouths, but their themes always have a religious rather than a purely decorative intent. More can be seen at **Tetitla**, to the west of the main site, and **Atetelco**, a little further west, just off the plan on p.465.

Museo del Sitio

Plan to spend at least some of your time in Teotihuacán's excellent **Museo del Sitio** (site hours; entry included in site fee), situated behind the Pirámide del Sol and surrounded by a lovely sculpture and botanical garden. Artefacts from the site are well laid out and effectively lit to highlight the key features of each item in the cool interior. There's just about everything you would expect of a ritual site and living city, from sharp-edged obsidian tools and everyday ceramics to some fine polychrome vessels decorated with animal and plant designs, and a series of five ceremonial braziers or censers ornamented with appliqué flowers, butterflies and shields.

Vast windows framing the Pirámide del Sol take up one entire wall of the next room, where you walk across a glass floor – look down to see a huge relief map of the entire city as it might once have been. This area leads to a second section mostly comprising larger sculptural pieces depicting assorted gods, often bottom-lit to accentuate the gruesome features. There are some superb masks, too, along with a couple of funerary sites modelled on those found under the Templo de Quetzalcoatl.

Practicalities

To get to Teotihuacán you can catch one of the buses that leave every fifteen minutes or so (6am–5pm; 1hr) from Mexico City's Terminal del Norte (see p.455). Go to the second-class (left-hand) side of the bus station and look for the Autobuses Teotihuacán stand in Sala 8 (Ⓣ55/5781-1812); be aware that these buses have from time to time been targeted by bandits, so don't bring a lot of cash or your passport (carry a photocopy instead). A slightly quicker alternative is to catch the Metro to Indios Verdes (line 3) and head to the northern end of Platform J, from where buses leave frequently for "Las Pirámides". A road, the Carretera de Circunvalación, provides access to the main structures through one of six gates (each with parking and lines of souvenir stalls): buses might arrive at any *puerta* (gate), though Puerta 1 and Puerta 2 are the most common. These are also the best places to wait for **buses back to Mexico City** (the last at 6pm), but late in the day most return buses visit all the gates before departing the site.

If you are on a budget it's best to bring all your **food and drink** with you, as anything bought at the site is going to be expensive. The main **restaurant** and bar, *Las Pirámides*, is at the principal entrance at Puerta 1, and has a three-course tourist menu for M$139–169 and some basic à la carte dishes. Prices are high considering the quality of the food, but the view of the site from the top-floor restaurant is great. Cheaper food (including comidas corridas for as little as M$35) is most easily found at the handful of small restaurants beside the ring road at Puerta 2, whose representatives will be on your case as soon as you set foot outside the gate. For something a little special, head for *La Gruta*, 200m west of Puerta 5 (Ⓣ594/956-0104, Ⓦwww.lagruta.com.mx), a fancy restaurant set deep in an open-sided cave, with white-jacketed waiters and a live show on Saturday at 3.30pm, and Sunday at 3.30pm and 5.30pm. At M$150–270 for a main course, the setting is great, but unfortunately the food is rather mediocre.

Around Teotihuacán

On the way to the pyramids you pass a couple of places that, if you're driving, are certainly worth a look, but barely merit the hassle involved in stopping over on the bus, though they can both be accessed easily by *combi* from a junction 500m beyond Puerta 5. At the village of **TEPEXPAN** is a **museum** (Tues–Sun 10am–4.50pm; free) housing the fossil of a mammoth dug up in the surrounding plain (then marshland). There's also a skeleton known as the "Tepexpan Man", once claimed to be the oldest in Mexico but now revealed as less than 2000 years old. This whole area is a rich source of such remains – the Aztecs knew of their existence, which is one of the reasons they believed that the huge structures of Teotihuacán had been built by a race of giants. The museum is a fifteen-minute walk from the village, near the motorway tollbooths, where any second-class bus will drop you; the village itself is attractive, with a good café on Calle de los Reyes, just off the main square. Buses to Metro Indios Verdes and *combis* to Teotihuacán can be picked up at the junction just outside the museum.

A few kilometres towards Teotihuacán (10min by *combi* from Tepexpan, 20min from Teotihuacán) is the beautiful sixteenth-century convent of **San Agustín Acolman** (daily 9am–5.30pm; M$37). Built on a raised, man-made terrace (probably on the site of an earlier, Aztec temple), it's a stern-looking building, lightened by the intricacy of its sculpted facade. In the nave and around the cloister are preserved portions of early murals depicting the monks, while several of the halls off the cloister display colonial religious painting and pre-Hispanic artefacts found here. If you turn right out of the gate, *combis* for Teotihuacán or Tepexpan can be picked up after 100m at the main road. **CHICONCUAC** to the south is rather more of a detour, but on Tuesdays, when there's a large market that specializes in woollen goods, sweaters and blankets, it's included in the itinerary of many of the tours to the pyramids. Again, this is hard to get to on a regular bus, and if you want to visit the market it's easier to do so as an entirely separate trip – buses, again, leave from Mexico City's Terminal del Norte (see p.455).

Tepotzotlán

TEPOTZOTLÁN lies en route from the capital to Tula, and it's possible to visit the two on one long day from the metropolis. Tepotzotlán is also close enough to the city to be a morning's excursion, though once you're there, you may find the town's slow place and colonial charm seduces you into staying longer. On Saturdays, with loads of Mexican visitors, the festive atmosphere is particularly enjoyable, while on Sundays a crafts market draws large crowds. In the week before Christmas, *pastorelas*, or **Nativity plays**, are staged here. Tepotzotlán's *pastorelas* are renowned, and booked up long in advance. At other times of the year, you may catch a concert in the church or cloisters.

Museo Nacional del Virreinato

Atmosphere apart, the reason most people come to Tepotzotlán is to see the magnificent Baroque **Colegio de San Francisco Javier**, now the **Museo Nacional del Virreinato** (Viceroyalty Museum; Tues–Sun 9am–6pm; M$49; Ⓦ www.virreinato.inah.gob.mx). The church was founded by the Jesuits, who arrived in 1580 on a mission to convert the Otomí locals. Most of the huge complex you see today was established during the following century but constantly embellished right up to the expulsion of the Jesuits in 1767. The facade of the church – considered one of the finest examples of churrigueresque architecture in the country – was completed barely five years before this. The wealth and scale of all this gives some idea of the power of the Jesuits prior to their ousting; after they left, it became a seminary for the training of regular priests until the late nineteenth century, when the Jesuits were briefly readmitted. The Revolution led to its final abandonment in 1914.

Iglesia de San Francisco Javier

The main entrance to the Colegio de San Francisco Javier leads into the **Claustro de los Aljibes**, with a well at the centre and pictures of the life of Ignatius Loyola (founder of the Jesuits) around the walls. Off the cloister is the entrance to the church, the **Iglesia de San Francisco Javier**. If the facade is spectacular, it's still barely preparation for the dazzling interior. Dripping with gold, and profusely carved with a bewilderment of saints and cherubim, it strikes you at first as some mystical cave of treasures. The main body of the church and its chapels house five huge gilded cedarwood *retablos*, stretching from ceiling to floor, each more gloriously curlicued than the last, their golden richness intensified by the soft yellow light penetrating through the alabaster that covers the windows. Much of the painting on the main altar (dedicated to the church's patron saint) is attributed to **Miguel Cabrera**, sometimes considered to be Mexico's Michelangelo, whose talents are also on display towards the main church door, which is framed by two large oils, one depicting worshippers bathing in the blood from Jesus' crucifixion wounds.

All this is still only the start, for hidden to one side is arguably the greatest achievement of Mexican Baroque, the octagonal **Camarín de la Virgen**. It's not a large room, but every inch is elaborately decorated and the hand of the native craftsmen is clearly evident in the exuberant carving – fruit and flowers, shells and abstract patterns crammed in between the angels. There's a mirror angled to allow visitors to appreciate the detail of the ceiling without straining their necks. The Camarín is reached through the **Capilla de la Virgen de Loreto**, inside which is a "house" tiled with eighteenth-century *azulejos* – supposedly a replica of Mary's house at Nazareth, in which Jesus grew up. Legend claims the original house was miraculously lifted by angels to save it when Muslims invaded the Holy Land, then deposited in the Italian town of Loreto in 1294.

The rest of the Museo Nacional del Virreinato

Directly off the central cloister are rooms packed with a treasure of beautiful silver reliquaries and crucifixes, censers, custodia, vestments and even a pair of silver sandals; notice too the painted panel depicting the spiritual conquest of New Spain and showing the relative influence of the Franciscans, Augustinians and Dominicans in the sixteenth century, and above it the diagram of churches liberally dotted among the lakes of the Valley of México.

The **upper storey** around the cloister contains more religious painting than anyone could take in on one visit, including portraits of the Society of Jesus and others of beatific eighteenth- and nineteenth-century nuns. Here too is the **Cristo del Árbol**, a crucifix carved towards the end of the seventeenth century from a single piece of wood.

Stairs descend to the **Claustro de los Naranjos**, planted with orange and lemon trees and with a fountain in the middle. Around it are displays of wooden religious statuary – Balthazar and Caspar, two of the three Magi, are particularly fine. Other rooms contain more colonial miscellany – lacquerwork, furniture (notably an inlaid wooden desk) and clothes – and some temporary exhibition space. Outside extends the walled **Huerta**, or garden, some three hectares of lawns, shady trees and floral displays, as well as vegetables and medicinal herbs cultivated as they would have been by the monks. It is not as well tended as it could be, but makes a break from the museum and has a few architectural pieces and large sculptures dotted around, including, at the far end, the original eighteenth-century **Salto del Agua** that stood at the end of the aqueduct carrying water from Chapultepec into Mexico City (a replica of the fountain stands in the capital now, near Metro Salto del Agua).

Returning to the main cloister, you find a mixed bag, with pre-Hispanic statuary leading on to details of Spanish exploration, suits of armour, exquisite marquetry boxes and a sequence of rooms, one filled with ivory statues, another laid out for Spanish nobles to dine, and then the **Botica**, or pharmacy, with bottles, jars, pestles and mortars, and all the other equipment of an eighteenth-century healer.

The **Capilla Doméstica** also opens off the cloister, a whirl of painted and gilded Rococo excess, with a magnificent gilded *retablo* full of mirrors and little figures.

Practicalities

To get to Tepotzotlán from Mexico City, take a bus from Metro Cuatro Caminos or Metro Rosario. The buses are slow, rattling their way round the suburbs for what feels like hours (though the total journey is actually little over an hour) before finally leaving the city. Alternatively, you can take an indirect ("via Refinario") Tula bus or a second-class service to Querétaro, both of which depart from the Terminal del Norte (see p.455), and get off at a road junction about 200m before the first motorway tollbooths, Caseta de Tepotzotlán. From here it's about a fifteen-minute walk west along a minor road to the town of Tepotzotlán, but there's a good chance of being able to hitch, and plenty of local buses. The same road junction by the tollbooths is also the place to pick up buses on to Tula or back to Mexico City.

Tepotzotlán's most central **hotel**, the *Hotel Posada San José*, Plaza Virreynal 13 (Ⓣ55/5876-0520; ❷), has some fairly poky cells at the back and some much more appealing rooms with plaza views (❸). There's a good deal more choice when it comes to **eating and drinking**, with cheap eats around the Mercado Municipal, just west of the plaza, and numerous places around the plaza, most with outdoor seating and many hosting mariachi musicians at weekends. They're all pretty good, so peruse the menus and take your pick: favourites include *Pepe's*, below the hotel, and the slightly more expensive *Restaurant Virreyes*, on the north side of the main square, which serves a wide range of dishes for around M$100–160, special barbecues at weekends (M$149) and a Sunday paella (M$110). Less visible, but still noteworthy, is the fairly pricey *Hostería del Convento*, set beautifully in the seminary's grounds and serving excellent Mexican food for M$94–140 a dish (closed Sun).

Tula

The modern city of **Tula de Allende** lies on the edge of the Valley of México, 50km north of Mexico City. A pleasant enough regional centre with an impressive, if fortress-like, mid-sixteenth-century **Franciscan monastery and church**, it is most notable for the wonderful pre-Hispanic pyramid site of **Tula**, 2km north of the centre.

In legend at least, the mantle of Teotihuacán fell on Tollan, or Tula, as the next great power to dominate Mexico. The Aztecs regarded their city as the successor to Tula and hence embellished its reputation – the streets, they said, had been paved with gold and the buildings constructed from precious metals and stones, while the Toltecs, who founded Tula, were regarded as the inventors of every science and art. In reality, it seems unlikely that Tula was ever as large or as powerful a city as Teotihuacán had been – or as Tenochtitlán was to become – and its period of dominance (about 950–1150 AD) was relatively short. Yet all sorts of puzzles remain about the Toltec era, and in particular their apparent connection with the Yucatán – much of the architecture at Chichén Itzá, for example, appears to have been influenced by the Toltecs. Few people believe that the Toltecs actually had an empire that stretched so far: however warlike (and the artistic evidence is that Tula was a grimly militaristic society, heavily into human sacrifice), they would have lacked the manpower, resources or any logical justification for such expansion.

One possible answer lies in the legends of **Quetzalcoatl**. Adopted from Teotihuacán, the plumed serpent attained far more importance here in Tula, where he is depicted everywhere. At some stage Tula apparently had a ruler identified with Quetzalcoatl who was driven from the city by the machinations of the evil god Texcatlipoca, and the theory goes that this ruler, defeated in factional struggles within Tula, fled with his followers, eventually reaching Maya territory, where they established a new Toltec regime at Chichén Itzá. Though popular for a long time, this hypothesis has now fallen out of fashion following finds at Chichén Itzá that seem to undermine it (see p.790).

The site

Only a small part of **the site** itself (daily 9am–5pm; M$41, free Sun) is of interest: though the city spreads over some considerable area only some of it has been excavated, and the outlying digs are holes in the ground, meaningful only to the archeologists who created them. The ceremonial centre, however, has been partly restored. The centrepiece here is the low, five-stepped pyramid of the **Templo de Tlahuizcalpantecuhtli** (Temple of the Morning Star, or Pyramid B), atop which stand the **Atlantes** – giant, five-metre-tall basalt figures that originally supported the roof of the sanctuary and represent Quetzalcoatl in his guise as the morning star, dressed as a Toltec warrior. They wear elaborately embroidered loincloths, sandals and feathered helmets, and sport ornaments around their necks and legs – for protection, each bears a sun-shaped shield on his back and a chest piece in the form of a stylized butterfly. Each also carries an *atlatl*, or spear-thrower, in his right hand and arrows or javelins in his left.

Other pillars are carved with more warriors and gods. Reliefs such as these are a recurrent theme in Tula: the entire temple was originally faced in sculpted stone, and although it was pillaged long ago you can still see some remnants – prowling jaguars and eagles, symbols of the two great warrior groups, devouring human hearts. In front of the temple is a great L-shaped colonnade, where the partly reconstructed pillars originally supported a huge roof under which, perhaps, the priests and nobles would review their troops or take part in ceremonies in the shade. Part of a long bench survives, with its relief decoration of a procession of warriors and priests. More such benches survive in the **Palacio Quemado** (Burnt Palace – it was destroyed by fire), next to the temple on the western side. Its three rooms, each a square, were once covered, with a small central patio to let light in. The middle one is the best preserved, still with much of its original paint and two Chac-mools.

The main square of the city stood in front (south) of the temple and palace, with a low altar platform in the centre and the now ruinous pyramid of the Templo Mayor on the eastern side. The larger of two **ball-courts** in the central area is on the western side of the square: although also largely ruined, this marks one of the closest links between Tula and Chichén Itzá, as it is of identical shape and orientation to the great ball-court there. To the north of the temple stands the **Coatepantli** (Serpent Wall), elaborately carved in relief with images of human skeletons being eaten by giant snakes; beyond this, across an open space, there's a second ball-court, smaller but in better order.

The whole significance of the site is made much clearer if your Spanish is up to translating all the information presented in the **museum** (daily 9am–5pm; free) located by the entrance, and filled with fragments of Atlantes, Chac-mools and basalt heads, along with assorted bits of sculpture and frieze.

Practicalities

Buses run from Mexico City's Terminal del Norte (see p.455; Autobuses del Valle de Mezquital – the desk furthest to your left when you enter the terminal). Direct buses run every thirty minutes, taking a little less than an hour and a half; slower services via a refinery ("via Refinario") run every fifteen minutes. There are also nine buses a day from Querétaro (2hr 30min). As you approach town, ask to be dropped off beside the train tracks by the *Hotel Sharon*, from where you should be able to walk (1km), pick up a local bus to just outside the site, or get a taxi (around M$30). Buses from Mexico City and Querétaro terminate at the bus station on Xicohténcatl close to the centre of town. From there, the **entrance to the site** is a thirty-minute walk: turn right out of the bus station to the main road (Ocampo), then turn right again, over the river and left before the train tracks (by the *Hotel Sharon*), following signs to "Zona Arqueológica".

To get to the town centre from the bus station, turn right as you leave, take the first left (Rojo del Rio) to the end, where a right turn into Hidalgo brings you to the **cathedral** and main square (Plaza de la Constitución). On the corner of the square with Zaragoza, a small local museum, the **Sala Histórica Quetzalcoatl** (daily except Mon, 9am–5pm; free), has a small display of archeological finds, including a mammoth tusk and some Toltec artefacts. There are several reasonably priced **hotels** nearby – try the *Real Catedral*, next to the museum at Zaragoza 106 (Ⓣ773/732-0813, Ⓦwww.hotelrealcatedral.com; ⑤), with fairly characterful old rooms all with bathroom and 24-hour hot water, but mostly without outside windows. Two other good bets are the *Hotel Cuéllar*, behind the cathedral at 5 de Mayo 23 (Ⓣ773/732-0442, Ⓦwww.hotelcuellar.com; ④), with frumpy rooms, parking and a pool; and the *Casa Blanca*, Pasaje Hidalgo 11, off Calle Hidalgo by no. 129 (Ⓣ773/732-1186 or 01-800/505-2991, Ⓦwww.casablancatula.com; ④), with small but comfortable rooms, off-street parking and bottled water.

Of the **cafés and restaurants** near the main square, the best is the *Casa Blanca* at Hidalgo 114, with a buffet and salad bar for M$129, a set menu for M$79 and breakfasts at M$49–129. In the southwest corner of the square itself, *Cafetería Nevería Campanarioably* is good for burgers, quesadillas and coffee. There are cheaper eating places around the bus station, notably *Azcatmolli* at Rojo del Rio 24, a good place for *antojitos* (M$10 a go), with a slew of cheap *loncherías* between that and the bus station itself.

Pachuca and around

In recent years, **Pachuca**, the capital of Hidalgo state, has burst out of the ring of hills that once hemmed it in, its expansion fuelled by the need to move industry away from Mexico City. By Mexican standards, though, it remains a fairly small city, its centre easily walkable and full of colonial mansions built on the profits of the rich silver-mining country all about. If you have the time, it is worth venturing to nearby towns where the mining heritage is more apparent and the clean mountain air is refreshing.

Arrival and information

The **bus station** is about 5km south of the centre and sees both second-class Flecha Roja and first-class ADO arrivals from Mexico City's Terminal del Norte every ten to fifteen minutes. *Colectivos* outside run frequently to Plaza de la Constitución, one of two main squares in the town centre. The other, the **Plaza de la Independencia**, two blocks away, is Pachuca's zócalo, where most of the action happens. From here, Matamoros runs south past a couple of hotels, becoming Mariano before reaching the Glorieta Revolución. There's a small **tourist office** (daily 8.30am–4pm; Ⓣ771/715-1411) in the base of the **Reloj Monumental** on the zócalo (see opposite).

Accommodation

Of Pachuca's **hotels**, there's nowhere especially classy near the centre, though there are several reasonable places.

América Victoria 203 (a block south of the zócalo) ⓣ771/715-0055. Reasonably cheap, but with rather dingy rooms, some with bath, TV and a king-size bed. ❷

Ciro's Zócalo ⓣ771/715-5351, ⓦwww.hotelciros.com. Offers a slightly higher standard of comfort than typical in Pachuca, but less character. Pleasantly furnished rooms have phone and TV; some also have plaza views. ❹

Emily Zócalo ⓣ771/715-0828 or 01-800/501-6339, ⓦwww.hotelemily.com.mx. Very similar to *Ciro's*, which it faces across the zócalo, but slightly posher, with some suites ❻

Hotel de los Baños Matamoros 205 ⓣ771/713-0700 or 01, ⓕ715-1441. The most characterful place in town, just off the zócalo, with carpeted rooms, each with TV and bathroom around a central, enclosed courtyard. For very little more than the plain rooms, you can opt for type "A" doubles with attractively carved wooden furniture, or type "B" where the craftsmanship is decidedly over the top. ❸

Noriega Matamoros 305 (a block south of the zócalo) ⓣ771/715-0150, ⓕ715-1844. A good-value colonial-styled and plant-filled establishment. You can save MS$50 by opting for a room without TV. ❸

The Town

Nestled below the hills that once provided such bounty, Pachuca's zócalo is dominated by the **Reloj Monumental**, a forty-metre French Neoclassical clock tower funded by the Cornish-born local mining magnate Francis Rule in 1910 to mark a hundred years of Mexican independence. There's a good deal more interest at the late sixteenth-century Ex-Convento de San Francisco, reached by walking three blocks south along Matamoros, then left for 300m along Revolución (which becomes Arista). The ex-convent now operates as the **Centro Cultural Hidalgo**, which contains the **Museo de la Fotografía** (Tues–Sun 10am–6pm; free). Drawing on over a million photographic works stored here as part of the national archive, the museum does a great job of showcasing both Mexican and foreign photographers. Early photographic techniques are illustrated before you move on to the gallery space, where displays change constantly but almost always include images from the Casasola Archive. The pre-eminent Mexican photojournalist of his day, **Agustín Casasola** chronicled both the Revolution and everyday life in its wake, forming an invaluable record of one of Mexico's more turbulent periods. Look too for work by Guillermo Kahlo, father of Frida, and stereoscopic plates of early railway construction, as well as photos by Tina Modotti, an Italian-born American who worked here in the 1930s and was part of the Kahlo/Rivera set.

Pachuca's other museum is the mildly diverting **Museo de Minereía** (Tue–Sun 10am–6pm; M$20), which is one block south and two blocks east of the zócalo at Mina 110 (that's Calle de Javier Mina, not Calle de la Mina), and full of mineral samples and mining equipment.

Eating and drinking

Pachuca is known in Mexico for **pastes**, which originated with the Cornish pasties once made by Cornish miners working in nearby Real del Monte (see p.476). They still come *tradicional* (or *tipo Inglés*), filled with ground meat, onion and potato, as well as with fillings such as chicken *mole* or *refritos*. Though they differ in shape, they're closely related to typical Mexican empanadas, which are usually sold in the same shops stuffed with tuna, pineapple or even rice pudding. You'll find bakeries selling *pastes* all over the region, and even at the bus station.

Alex Steak Glorieta Revolución 102 (about 500m south of the zócalo). Enormous and beautifully prepared steaks cost around M$200.

Mi Antiguo Café Matamoros 115. Good for espressos, croissants and burgers, with set breakfasts (M$55–74) and a lunch-time menu (M$57).

Mirage Guerrero 1210 (a block west of the zócalo and 300m south). Family-style restaurant, where you can try *acos mineros* (chicken tacos with salsa and cheese). Also has a cosy bar.

Reforma Matamoros 111, on the east side of the zócalo. Quite classy restaurant offering a lunch-time menu (M$57) and typical *antojitos* (M$40–50).

Around Pachuca: Real del Monte and Mineral del Chico

Fourteen kilometres north of Pachuca, draped across pine-clad hills, sits **REAL DEL MONTE** (aka Mineral del Monte), a once very wealthy silver-mining town, and, at over 2700m, a nice retreat from Mexico City. There's not a lot to do here, but it is a quietly appealing place where you can wander around the well-tended streets, and carefully explore mining relics in the surrounding hills. The town's architecture is largely Spanish colonial, but is given an odd twist by the almost exclusive use of red corrugated-iron roofing, and the existence of Cornish-style cottages with their double-pitched rooflines. Some 350 **Cornish miners** moved here after 1824 when a British company operated mines that were first opened by the Spanish in the mid-sixteenth century. The British pulled out in 1848, to be replaced by a Mexican successor firm, but many of the miners and their Cornish influence remained, resulting in surprisingly authentic Cornish pasties and the introduction of *fútbol* (soccer), which was played for the first time on Mexican soil here in Real. Indeed, this British community in Mexico went on to found Pachuca football club and the Mexican football league (see box opposite). Many of the miners, who were Methodist rather than Catholic, now rest in the British cemetery (**Panteón Inglés**) on the edge of town (usually locked, but the caretaker should, with luck, be somewhere nearby to open it up).

To get to Real del Monte from Pachuca, walk 200m north of the zócalo along Zaragoza to Calle de Julian Villagran (the northwest corner of Plaza de la Constitución) and pick up one of the very frequent **colectivos**, which drop you close to the centre of Real. Less convenient buses also run hourly from the bus station. Most likely you'll visit on a day trip from Pachuca, but there is tempting **accommodation** in the form of AP *Hotel Real del Monte*, just off the main square on the corner of Iturbide and García (Ⓣ 771/797-1203; ❺), beautifully decorated and furnished, with wooden floors, antique-style furniture and heaters to ward off the chilly nights. The *Restaurant D'Karla* opposite also rents out rooms (Ⓣ771/797-0709; ❹). Several other small **restaurants** are located along Hidalgo, off the central plaza. *La Central* has decent food (most *guisados* M$50–70). *Real de Plateros*, opposite, does the town's best *pastes* (Cornish-style potato, or Mexican-style bean) and empanadas.

Mineral del Chico

The road between Pachuca and Real del Monte passes a road junction, 10km north of Pachuca, from where a side road winds down towards **Parque Nacional El Chico** (Ⓦwww.parqueelchico.gob.mx), which is noted for its impressive rock formations and good hiking. The tiny village of **Mineral del Chico**, 4km from the road junction, is the main base for exploring the park and offers a few restaurants and a couple of luxurious **hotels**: *Posada del Amencer*, right in town at Morelos 3 (full board only Ⓣ771/715-4812, Ⓦwww.hotelesecoturisticos.com.mx; ❼); and *Hotel El Paraíso* (Ⓣ771/715-5654, Ⓦwww.hotelesecoturisticos.com.mx; ❻), about 1km before town. There is no direct public transport from Real del

Football in Mexico

As in much of Latin America, **fútbol** in Mexico is a national addiction, if not an obsession. Turn on the TV and often as not you'll find a match. If you can get to see a live game, it's a different experience entirely.

Football (meaning soccer, of course) was introduced to Mexico in the nineteenth century by a group of Cornish miners in Real del Monte, Hidalgo (see opposite), and it was in that state, by descendants of these Cornishmen, that Mexico's first football club, Pachuca, was founded in 1901. The football **league** was created six years later. The league follows a complicated ladder system: the first division is divided into three tables of six teams each, which are decided by the previous season's placings, with the league champions placed first in table one, second placed top of table two and so on. The top two teams of each table compete in a play-off for the league championship.

There are two **seasons** a year: Apertura (Aug–Nov) and Clausura (Jan–June). At the end of the Clausura season, the two seasons' winners (if they are different) compete to decide that year's champion of champions.

Relegation to a lower division is decided over a two-season (yearly) loss average, so it is, in fact, technically possible to come first in the league and be relegated in the same season. However, relegation need not be the disaster that it might seem. Take, for example, Puebla C.F., who when relegated in 1999 simply bought the team promoted from Primera B (Curtodores), changed their name to Puebla and relocated them, which is perfectly legal under Mexican financial regulations. Similarly, there are no regulations preventing anyone from owning more than one team, which can lead to a clash of interests that are never more than speculated upon; suspicion of corruption is rife but rarely, if ever, investigated.

Matches themselves are always exciting and enjoyed by even the most diehard "anti-futbolistas". Music, dancing and, of course, the ubiquitous **Mexican Wave** make for a carnival atmosphere, enhanced by spectators dressing up and wearing face paint. They're usually very much family affairs, with official salespeople bringing soft drinks, beer and various types of food at fixed prices to your seat. **Stadiums** tend to be mostly concrete, with sitting room only, and can sometimes be dangerously overcrowded, though accidents are thankfully rare. The bigger clubs are those of Mexico City (América, Cruz Azul, Pumas – the national university side – Necaxa and Atlante) and Guadalajara (Chivas, Atlas and Tecos) and the games between any of these can draw crowds of up to 80,000, while smaller clubs like those of Puebla, Irapuato and Celaya may get no more than 10,000 or 15,000 spectators per game. The vast distances between clubs make travelling to away games impossible for many fans, one reason why smaller, more out-of-the-way clubs don't get as much support. Passion for the game means that emotions run high, but this does not usually turn into violence. Opposing fans aren't generally separated, but there's a good relationship between them and an atmosphere of self-policing prevails – part of what makes it an ideal family occasion. The greatest risk is often to the referee, who is frequently escorted from the pitch by armed riot police. The **players**, on the other hand, are accorded a great deal of respect and the more popular ones tend to pick up nicknames, such as "Kikín" (striker Francisco Fonseca – Kicking), "El Pajaro Humano" (goalie Oswaldo Sánchez – the Human Bird), and "Cabrito" (zippy midfielder Jesús Arellano – Little Goat).

For **national games**, of course, the whole country is united, and football has many times been shown to rise above partisan politics. In 1999, despite being outlawed by the government, the EZLN football squad even played an exhibition match against the national side in Mexico City's Estadio Azteca.

For **up-to-date information** on Mexican league teams, fixtures and tables, visit Ⓦwww.futmex.com or www.futbolmexicano.net.

Monte, but *colectivos* from Pachuca can be found on Carranza, 300m north of Plaza de la Constitución.

East of Mexico City

East of Mexico City is the region's second largest city, the thriving and ultra-colonial **Puebla**. This city not only warrants a couple of days of your time in its own right, but makes an excellent base for forays north to more tranquil **Tlaxcala**, and west to **Cholula** with its enormous ruined pyramid. Both were important tributary states of the Aztecs when Cortés marched this way from the coast to pillage and conquer in the name of European civilization. Puebla and Cholula also offer excellent views of central Mexico's twin volcanoes, **Popocatépetl** and **Ixtaccíhuatl**, both currently off-limits due to the continuing threat of eruption, though you can visit the national park which surrounds them.

Tlaxcala and around

Allied to Cortés in his struggle against the Aztecs, as well as with colonial Spain in the War of Independence, **TLAXCALA**, the capital of a tiny state of the same name, has become a byword for treachery. Because of its alliance with Cortés, the town suffered a very different fate from that of nearby Cholula, which aligned itself with the Aztecs (see p.856), and in the long run this has led to an even more total disappearance of its ancient culture. The Spaniards founded a colonial town here – now restored and very beautiful in much of its original colonial glory, but whether because of its traitorous reputation or simply its isolation, development in Tlaxcala has been limited.

The town lies 131km west of Mexico City and 30km north of Puebla in the middle of a fertile, prosperous-looking upland plain surrounded by rather bare mountains. It's an exceptionally pretty and much rehabilitated colonial town, comfortable enough but also fairly dull. Most of the interest lies very close to the zócalo, with its central bandstand, where the terracotta and ochre tones of the buildings lend the city its tag of "Ciudad Roja", the Red City. Its appearance, slow pace and proximity to the nation's capital have drawn a small expat community, though the latter's impact on daily life is minimal.

Arrival and accommodation

Frequent **buses** from Mexico City, Puebla and surrounding towns arrive at the bus station on the edge of the centre. *Colectivos* parked outside run to nearby villages and the zócalo, though it's only a ten-minute walk: exit the bus station and turn right downhill to the next main junction, then take a right down Guerrero for five blocks and left down Juárez. To return to the bus station, take the *colectivo* that stops on the corner by the church just off the zócalo.

Behind the Palacio de Gobierno, on the zócalo, there's a helpful **tourist office** on the corner of Juárez and Lardizábal (Mon–Fri 9am–7pm, Sat & Sun 10am–6pm;

Ⓣ246/465-0968, toll-free from outside the state Ⓣ01-800/509-6557, Ⓦwww.descubretlaxcala.com), where you can pick up useful free maps and book guided tours. Most other facilities – banks, post office and the like – cluster round the zócalo and along Juárez.

Tlaxcala doesn't have any really low-cost **accommodation**. The cheapest and best-value option is *Hotel Alifer*, at Morelos 11, by the junction with Xicohténcatl (Ⓣ246/466-0620 to 22, Ⓦwww.hotelalifer.com.mx; ④), which has comfy, carpeted rooms with TV. For something more high-end, there's *Posada San Francisco*, on the southern side of the zócalo at Plaza de la Constitución 17 (Ⓣ246/462-6022, Ⓦwww.posadasanfrancisco.com; ⑥), occupying a lovely old mansion with colonially furnished rooms, pool and tennis courts.

The Town

The entire north side of the zócalo is taken up by the **Palacio de Gobierno** (daily 8am–6pm; free; enter by easternmost door), whose patterned brick facade is broken by ornate windows and doorways. The building incorporates parts of a much earlier structure, erected soon after the Conquest, and inside boasts a series of brilliantly coloured **murals** by a local, Desiderio Hernandez Xochitiotzin, that took nearly fifty years to complete. The panels depict the history of the Tlaxcalan people from their migration from the north to their alliance with Cortés. The two most spectacular are one on the stairs depicting the Spanish Conquest and another at the bottom showing the Great Market.

To the west of the Palacio de Gobierno, and dominating a small square off the side of the zócalo, stands the tiled facade of the **Parroquia de San José**. It's an attractive building, but except for two fonts beside the door depicting Camaxtli, the Tlaxcalan god of hunting and war, the inside is a disappointment. Note the seventeenth-century painting beside the altar that depicts the baptism of a Tlaxcalan chief, as overseen by Cortés and his mistress, La Malinche.

At the opposite corner of the zócalo, the smaller Plaza Xicohténcatl holds the **Museo de la Memoria** (Tues–Sun 10am–5pm; M$10, free Tues), a modern museum devoted to the cultural history of the region. Its imaginative displays (some interactive) – illustrating pre-Hispanic *tianguis* (markets), Franciscan life under the Spaniards and the ruling hierarchy in Tlaxcala before and after Cortés – make up for the fact that it's light on artefacts.

At the southeastern corner of Plaza Xicohténcatl, a broad, tree-lined path leads up to a triple set of arches. Beyond them, an open area overlooking the city's pretty nineteenth-century bullring is flanked on one side by the Ex-Convento de San Francisco, started in 1537. Wrapped around the convent's cloister, the **Museo Regional de Tlaxcala** (daily 10am–6pm; M$37) covers local life from prehistoric times to the present day – an unexceptional collection but well displayed in a series of whitewashed rooms. The **Catedral de Nuestra Señora de la Asunción** next door is also relatively plain, though it has a beautiful vaulted wooden ceiling decorated in Mudéjar style, the design elements harking back to the Moorish style then common in southern Spain. The Moors were expelled from Spain in 1492, and though their influence continued for some decades, this is only apparent in Mexican churches started immediately after the Conquest. One large chapel, more richly decorated than the rest, contains the font in which Xicohténcatl and other Tlaxcalan leaders were baptized in the presence of Cortés in 1520. Opposite, the lower walls of another chapel bear traces of ancient frescoes.

Tlaxcala's third museum is the **Museo de Artes y Tradiciones Populares**, corner of Mariano Sanchez and 1 de Mayo, three blocks west of the zócalo (Tues–Sun 10am–6pm; M$6). It focuses on traditional crafts and customs, with sections on bell making (including an example cast on the site) and a fascinating room on the manufacture and consumption of *pulque*.

Santuario de Ocotlán

Approaching town you will almost certainly have noticed the twin wedding-cake towers of the **Santuario de Ocotlán**, which overlook Tlaxcala from a hill to the east. The church is about 1km from the zócalo, a fairly steep thirty minutes' walk north along Juárez, then right onto Guridi y Alcocer, which runs past the **Pocito**, a small octagonal shrine. There are great views over the surrounding countryside from up here, but the real interest is the church, its facade a riot of churrigueresque excess that ranks it alongside those at Tepotzotlán and Taxco. Inside, it is no less florid, the huge Baroque *retablo* seeming to spread seamlessly to the dome and along the transept in a frenzy of gilt woodwork. Such exuberance is justified by the miraculous work of the Virgin. According to legend, she appeared to a poor Indian in 1541 with instructions to cure an epidemic with waters from a stream that had miraculously sprung forth. Naturally everyone recovered. Then the Virgin asked the Indian to bring the local Franciscan monks to a forest. Once they were there, fire suddenly burst forth, but though the flames were fierce, they didn't burn the trees. The next day the monks returned, to find that one pine tree (*ocotlán*) contained a wooden image of the Virgin. Now installed on the altar, it is carved and painted very much in the style of the times. The life of Our Lady of Ocotlán is portrayed around the eight walls of the ornate **Camarín de la Virgen** (the Virgin's Dressing Room) behind the altar. In May, the church and surrounding streets host the procession of the Virgin, attended by thousands of pilgrims.

Eating and drinking

For a relatively small city, Tlaxcala seems particularly well stocked with **restaurants** and **bars**, especially around the zócalo and along Juárez. Some of the most inviting are those under the *portales* on the eastern and southern sides of the zócalo, where you can sit outside and watch life go by: try *Los Portales*, Plaza de la Constitución 8, on the east side of the square (Ⓣ246/462-5419), with its broad range of *antojitos*, burgers, salads, pasta dishes and the delicious *sopa tlaxcalteca* (M$45), made from black beans, tortilla chips, cheese, avocado and *chicharrón* (pork crackling). Also on the east side, *Fabrik* at no. 10 has good coffee and crepes, and *Coffee Station* at no. 12, on the south side, has "gourmet" coffee and a range of set breakfasts.

The restaurants all serve alcohol, but for more dedicated drinking go to Plaza Xicohténcatl. On the north side is *Las Ventas*, a convivial saloon bar decorated with paintings of naked women bullfighting, while the southeast corner has the *Cantina de los Amigos* (actually quite a relaxed bar rather than a cantina as such) and the *Pulqueria la Tin Yala*, which claims to have state's the best *pulque*, available in several fruit flavours.

Around Tlaxcala: Cacaxtla and Xochitécatl

Some 17km southwest of Tlaxcala lies the ancient site of **Cacaxtla** (daily 10am–5pm; M$38), where a particularly fine series of murals depicting battle scenes was discovered in 1975. They are clearly Maya in style, which would seem to indicate trade or perhaps even a Maya settlement here.

Two kilometres west of Cacaxtla, the ruins of **Xochitécatl** (same hours and ticket) have three impressive pyramids and monolithic stones. These can be reached by frequent *colectivo* ("San Miguel del Milagro") from Mariano and Lardizábal, or by bus to the nearby village of Nativitas from Tlaxcala or Puebla. Alternatively, every Sunday the tourist office in Tlaxcala organizes **guided tours** to both sites for

M$58; you're picked up in Tlaxcala from outside the post office at the southwest corner of the zócalo at 10am and dropped off at 2.30pm.

The rather less impressive archeological site of **Tizatlán** (Tues–Sun 10am–5pm; M$27), 4km north of town, can be reached by *colectivo* from 1 de Mayo and 20 de Noviembre.

Puebla

East of the capital, the road to **PUEBLA** climbs steeply, with glorious views of the snowy heights of Popocatépetl and Ixtaccíhuatl along the way. Little more than an hour on the bus from Mexico City, Puebla is the republic's fifth largest city (after Mexico City, Guadalajara, Monterrey and Tijuana). The centre has a remarkable concentration of sights – a fabulous **cathedral**, a "hidden" **convent**, museums and colonial **mansions** – while the mountainous surrounding country is in places startlingly beautiful. Nevertheless, Puebla is unlikely to tempt you into staying particularly long and in a couple of leisurely days (or one packed day) you can see the best of the city and nearby **Cholula**.

The city was founded by the Spaniards in 1531, preferring it to the ancient sites of Cholula and Tlaxcala possibly because the memories of indigenous power there remained too strong. It rapidly assumed great importance as a staging point on the journey from the capital to the port at Veracruz and for the shipment of goods from Spain's Far Eastern colonies, which were delivered to Acapulco and transported across Mexico from there. Wealth was brought, too, by the reputation of

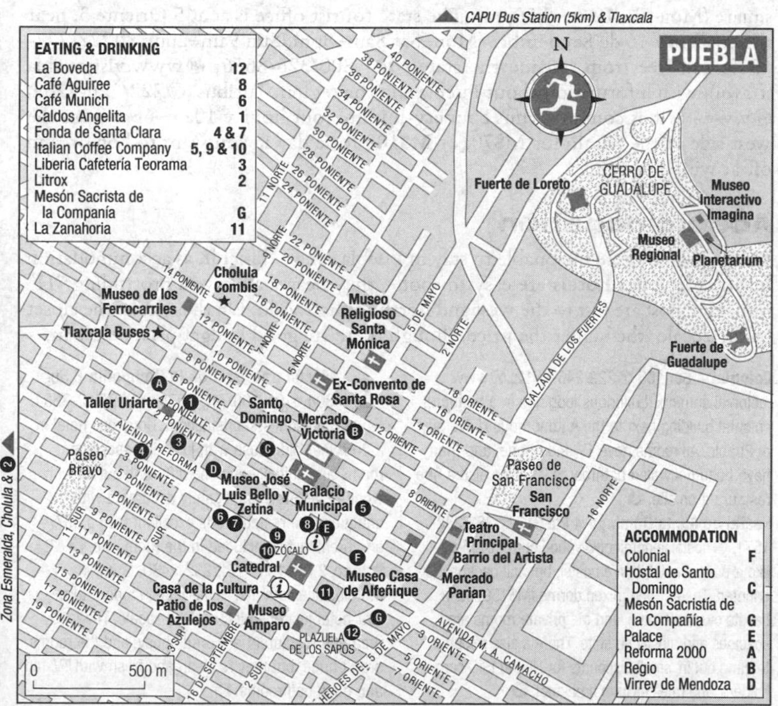

Puebla's ceramics, particularly its tiles. This industry – still very much in evidence – was helped by an abundance of good clays in the region, and by settlers from Talavera in Spain, who brought traditional ceramic skills with them. The city did well out of colonial rule, and, perhaps not surprisingly, it took the wrong side in the War of Independence. As a result, it preserves a reputation for conservatism and traditional values, not dispelled even by the fact that the start of the Revolution is generally dated from the assassination of Aquiles Serdán in his Puebla home.

Military defeat seems to play a larger part in Puebla's history than it does in most of Mexico – the city fell to the Americans in 1847 and to the French in 1863 – but it isn't what's remembered. Rather, it's the greatest victory in the country's history – here, a force of some two thousand Mexicans defeated a French army three times its size in 1862. To this day, Puebla commemorates May 5 (**Cinco de Mayo**) with a massive fiesta, and there's a public holiday throughout the country.

Arrival and information

Puebla's **bus station**, known by the acronym CAPU (Central de Autobuses de Puebla), is 5km northwest of the city centre. There's a guardería, and **authorized taxis** run to the centre of town for M$47; or you can turn right outside and walk about 200m along the main road where you can hop onto one of the frequent local buses and *colectivos* that run to the centre. To get back to CAPU from town, buses can be picked up along 9 Norte or 9 Sur.

For information about the city itself, the municipal **tourist office** at Palafox y Mendoza 14, on the north side of the zócalo (Mon–Sat 9am–8pm, Sun 9am–3pm; ⓣ222/404-5047; ⓦwww.turismopuebla.gob.mx) has free maps and information about the city. It also runs a tourist information kiosk on the south side of the square (Mon–Fri 10am–5.30pm). The state tourist office is at at 5 Oriente 3, near the corner of 16 de Septiembre (Mon–Sat 8am–8pm, Sun 9am–2pm; ⓣ222/777-1519, toll-free from outside the state ⓣ01-800/326-8656; ⓦwww.visitpuebla.travel), with information about Puebla and the region. Túribus (ⓣ222/226-7289, ⓦwww.turibus.com.mx) runs a ninety-minute tour hourly 10am–6pm from the west side of the zócalo for M$70, or M$100 for a day if you want to hop on and off at will.

Accommodation

Finding somewhere reasonable to stay in Puebla can be difficult, as accommodation fills up early, but **hotels** are easy to spot – they nearly all have a protruding "H" sign, and most are just to the west and north of the zócalo. On the whole, the closer to the zócalo, the higher the price, though there are good budget places close in.

Colonial 4 Sur 105 ⓣ222/246-4612, ⓦwww.colonial.com.mx. Luxurious lodgings in a beautiful colonial building next to the Autonomous University of Puebla. All rooms have TV and phone, and many have beautifully tiled bathrooms. There's also a fine restaurant on site. ❺

Hostal de Santa Domingo 4 Pte 312 ⓣ222/232-1671, ⓔhostalstodomingo@yahoo.com.mx. More like a budget hotel than a hostel, but still backpacker-oriented. The ten-bed mixed dorms (M$150) each has its own bathroom, and the private rooms are spacious and mostly en suite. There's also a lounge to hang out in, small discounts for HI and ISIC card-holders, and rates include breakfast. ❸

Mesón Sacristía de la Compañía 6 Sur 304 ⓣ01-800/712-4028 or 222/242-3554, ⓦwww.mesones-sacristia.com. Gorgeous hotel in a 200-year-old house with just nine spacious rooms and suites, each one different, but all with wooden beams and elegantly decorated with antiques. The restaurant is excellent (see p.487) and breakfast is included in the room rate. ❼

Palace 2 Ote 13 ⓣ222/232-2430, ⓦwww.hotelpalace.com.mx. Good-value, modern three-star hotel just one block off the zócalo. The lobby area and restaurant are pretty busy, and the rooms aren't huge, but they're clean and fresh with TV, fan and good bathrooms. ❹

Reforma 2000 4 Pte 916, corner of 11 Nte ⓣ222/242-3363, ⓦwww.hotelreforma2000.com. Comfortable, carpeted, spacious rooms, with TV and phone. Nice bar and restaurant, plus parking facilities. ❸

Regio 5 Mayo 1004 ⓣ222/232-4774. Rock-bottom prices, and basic, yes, but very far from being the worst accommodation in town. It's friendly, decent, housed in a nice old colonial building, and has its own slightly shabby charm. It's worth paying the small amount extra for a room with a private bathroom. ❶

Virrey de Mendoza Reforma 538 ⓣ222/242-3903. Good value and one of the best of the mid-range places, a small hotel with a verdant central courtyard done out in rather violent candy-pink. The big, carpeted rooms, set around it, are rather more tasteful. ❸

The Town

Puebla's **zócalo** is the centre of the numbering system for the ancient grid of streets (lowest numbers are nearest to the centre) and home to the great looming **cathedral** (daily 10.30am–12.30pm & 4–6pm; free), the second largest in the republic. Built between 1562 and the middle of the following century, the exterior is ugly and grey, but the inside improves considerably, with amazing ornamentation in onyx, marble and gilt and a wonderful altar designed by Manuel Tolsá in 1797. The cathedral, and particularly the tower, was partly funded by Bishop Juan de Palafox y Mendoza, an illegitimate son of a Spanish nobleman who grew up with his poor mother but inherited his father's fortune. Behind the cathedral, at 5 Oriente 5, lies the old Archbishop's Palace, which was converted to a library in the seventeenth century (the Biblioteca Palafoxiana, reputed to be the oldest library in the Americas), and houses the original collection of ancient books and manuscripts on the upper floor. Downstairs there's the **Casa de la Cultura** (ⓣ222/246-6922; Mon–Sat 8am–9pm, Sun 8am–6pm; free), which hosts regular exhibitions of local arts and crafts.

Museo Amparo

The undoubted star in Puebla's museum firmament is the modern **Museo Amparo**, 2 Sur 708 at 9 Oriente (daily except Tues 10am–6pm; M$35, free Mon, camera M$50; ⓦwww.museoamparo.com), which concentrates on art from pre-Hispanic Mesoamerica, with additional material from the colonial and more recent eras. Set in a pair of modernized colonial buildings with peaceful courtyards and piped classical music, the collection is the legacy of philanthropist Manuel Espinosa Iglesias, who set up the Amparo Foundation in honour of his wife.

The historical significance of the pieces isn't glossed over, but the focus is firmly on aesthetics, with well-presented cases displaying artefacts to their best advantage. To set the tone, the entrance features an impressive glass replica of a **tzompantli skull-wall** with alternating Olmec and Totonac heads in each of the glass blocks. A room decorated with reproduction **cave paintings** from Altamira in Spain, Arnhemland in Australia, Utah, Norway and Baja California puts Mexico's cultural development into some sort of context before you launch into the main collection. Though far smaller than that in Mexico City's anthropology museum, this is well chosen and a good deal more manageable. It is particularly strong on the Olmecs, a people who greatly influenced life around Puebla and left behind some strikingly beautiful pieces such as the half-metre-wide stone head on display here. Elsewhere notice the exquisite Colima jaguar, the beautiful carved conch shell from the Gulf coast and the sculpture of a kneeling woman from Nayarit with her distinctive face and body painting.

The last section of the museum is devoted to **colonial painting** and rooms of seventeenth- and eighteenth-century furnishings. Everything in the museum is thoroughly documented at strategically located computer consoles, so you probably won't need the rental **headsets** (M$10 plus M$10 deposit; in Spanish,

English, French and Japanese) with their relatively cursory commentary. Free **guided tours** in English and Spanish take place at noon on Sunday.

North of the zócalo

Head north from the zócalo along 5 de Mayo and you'll reach the church of **Santo Domingo** at the corner of 4 Poniente. The chapel here, the **Capilla del Rosario**, is, even in comparison to the cathedral, a quite unbelievably lavish orgy of gold leaf and Baroque excess; a constant hushed, shuffling stream of devotees light candles and pray to the image of the Virgin. Three doors down, the **Museo José Luis Bello y Zetina**, 5 de Mayo 409 (Tues–Sun 10am–4pm; free), displays the paintings and furniture of the wealthy Bello family, who lived here during the nineteenth century – you'll see everything from seventeenth-century Flemish masters to a Napoleonic bedroom suite. It somehow seems too comfortless to be a home yet not formal enough for a museum, though the enthusiasm of your personal guide (whose services are free but not compulsory) may rub off.

Nearby, a passage leads to the glass and iron **Mercado Victoria**, at the corner of 5 de Mayo and 6 Oriente, once Puebla's main market but now a rather sanitized shopping centre. East of the market, candy stores along 6 Oriente sell *camotes*, gooey fingers of sweet potato and sugar flavoured with various fruits – a regional speciality. If you're thinking of buying any to take home, however, note that they only last a couple of weeks. Further along the street, the devotional **Museo Regional de la Revolución Mexicana**, 6 Oriente 206 (Tues–Sun 10am–4.30pm; M$10, free Tues, records the struggles for Liberalism of the Serdán family against the dictatorship of Porfirio Díaz. The assassination of Aquiles Serdán in this house was one of the most important steps in the fall of Díaz: the date of Serdán's death, November 18, 1910, is – in the absence of any firmer indicators – generally recognized as marking the start of the Revolution. The bullet holes in the house have been lovingly preserved, and a huge smashed mirror still hangs on the wall where it appears in contemporary photos of the carnage. Revolution buffs will also enjoy the biographies of key figures in the struggle, photos of the ragtag bands of wide-hatted revolutionaries with their

▲ Dome of the Capilla del Rosario, Iglesia de Santo Domingo

bandoleers and the trap door in the floor under which Serdán spent several fruitless hours trying to avoid his eventual end.

Nine blocks north of the zócalo you'll find the city's remarkable convent, now operating as the **Museo Religioso Santa Mónica**, at 18 Poniente 103 (Tues–Sun 9am–6pm; M$24, free Sun). Here, from the suppression of the church in 1857 until their discovery in 1934, several generations of nuns lived hidden from the public gaze behind a smokescreen of secret doors and concealed passages. Just how secret they were is a matter of some debate – many claim that the authorities simply turned a blind eye – and certainly several lay families were actively supportive, providing supplies and new recruits. But it makes a good story, embellished by the conversion of the building into a museum that preserves the secret entrances along with many religious artworks and a beautiful seventeenth-century cloister. Several simple cells are also in evidence, and from the hidden chapel you can look down through a screen at the still-operating church next door.

In the same general direction, on the corner of 3 Norte, lies the **Ex-Convento de Santa Rosa**, 3 Norte 1203 (Tues–Sun 10am–5pm; M$10, free Tues), whose main claim to fame is that the great *mole poblano* was invented here in its wonderful yellow-tiled kitchens. The kitchens are the highlight of a guided tour that includes rooms full of crafts from around the state of Puebla.

East of the zócalo

The rest of the town's attractions are concentrated mostly to the east and northeast of the zócalo. First stop is the **Museo Casa de Alfeñique**, at the corner of 4 Oriente and 6 Norte (Tues–Sun 10am–5pm; M$15, free Sun), located in an elaborate old mansion covered in Puebla tiles. Within, you can see period furnishings, Puebla ceramics, a small archeological section and an excellent display of colonial art.

At the end of 4 Oriente lies the **Mercado Parian** – mostly given over to rather tawdry tourist souvenirs – and the **Barrio del Artista**, traditionally the artists' quarter, now selling work aimed squarely at the tourist market. The **Teatro Principal**, nearby, is a fine eighteenth-century theatre, said to be the oldest on the continent, which still hosts occasional performances.

West of the zócalo

Follow 4 Poniente west from the zócalo to reach **Taller Uriarte**, 4 Poniente 911 (shop open Mon–Sat 10am–6pm, Sun 11am–5pm; half-hourly tours Mon–Fri 10am–2pm, M$50; ⓣ222/232-1598), about the best known of Puebla's pottery factories. It is a small-scale affair shoehorned into what appears to be just another urban house, but it is well set up for visitors. You can see every stage of the pottery-making process, from forming the plates and bowls to painting the intricate designs in paints whose colours are completely transformed during firing into distinctive blues and yellows.

Press on a few blocks further out to the **Museo Nacional de los Ferrocarriles**, 11 Norte at 12 Poniente (Tues–Sun 9am–5pm; M$10, free Sun), an open-air collection of Mexican railroad cars arranged around Puebla's former train station. Pride of place is given to some menacing-looking steam locomotives, including one 285-tonne monster built in 1946, which was so heavy it could only be run on the most robust lines from Mexico City to the US border.

Cerro de Guadalupe

To the northwest of the centre, crowning the **Cerro de Guadalupe**, the site of numerous nineteenth-century battles and sieges, is the **Centro Cívico 5 de Mayo**, a collection of museums. Neither of the two forts nor any of the museums here is a match for sights downtown, but they are a decent place to spend a couple of hours away from the fumes and the noise of the centre. To get there, take a Ruta #72 *colectivo* (sometimes marked "Centro Cívico") from Héroes del 5 de Mayo, three blocks east of the zócalo.

Your first stop should be the **Fuerte de Loreto** (Tues–Sun 9am–5.30pm; M$37, free Sun), where a moat and high walls protect a large empty parade ground and a small church containing the Museo de la No Intervención. This focuses on the events surrounding the 1862 Battle of Puebla, celebrated on Cinco de Mayo, and records 150 years of the defence of the republic through replicated battle scenes. The views of Popo and Ixta from the battlements are some of the best in Puebla.

The best of the rest of the sights out here is the modern **Museo Regional de Puebla** (Tues–Sun 9am–6pm; M$41, free Sun), largely devoted to the state's archeology and ethnology. There's some exquisite Olmec jade sculpture and sculptural pieces along with a four-metre-high polychrome statue of San Cristóbal from the seventeenth century and sections of wider relevance, such as a detailed explanation of native migration from east Asia through Alaska. Readers with kids will want to traipse across the road to the **Museo Interactivo Imagina** (Mon–Fri 9am–1pm & 2–6pm, Sat & Sun 10am–6pm; M$50, extra for some exhibits), a collection of educational interactive games, or to the adjacent **Planetarium**, with its IMAX screen, which usually has shows twice a day (M$50, joint ticket with Museo Interactivo Imagina M$80; shows Tues–Fri 5pm, Sat 2pm, 3pm & 5pm, Sun 2m, 4pm & 6pm).

The highest point on the hill is occupied by the **Fuerte de Guadalupe** (Tues–Sun 9am–5.30pm; M$37, free Sun), the meagre but well-tended remains of an 1862 fort – really just a few arches and roofless rooms.

Eating and drinking

As with any large Mexican city, there's a huge range of **places to eat** in Puebla, from cheaper places around the Mercado Victoria to good mid-range options around the centre, with better places tucked away in back streets. While in town you should definitely check out the **local specialities**, particularly *mole poblano*, an extraordinary sauce made from chocolate, chiles and any number of herbs and spices. Typically served over chicken, turkey or enchiladas, it is found all over Mexico, but is nowhere better than here, where it was supposedly invented in colonial times for the viceroy's visit to the Convento de Santa Rosa. Should you want to buy some paste to take home (it lasts for ages and doesn't need to be refrigerated), visit Abarrotes Lulu at 16 Poniente 304–A, by Mercado 5 de Mayo.

Another taste sensation is *chiles en nogada*, a dish reputedly concocted in 1821 to celebrate Mexican Independence and made to resemble the colours of the Mexican flag.

Central Puebla is mostly quiet at night and to find any **bars** you'll have to head a few blocks south to the **Plazuela de los Sapos**, near 6 Sur and 5 Poniente, where several lively drinking holes face each other across a small square. The city is pretty quiet until Thursday night, when you might also head around six long blocks west of the zócalo to the Zona Esmeralda, where there's a string of bars and clubs to keep you going. Otherwise, many people head out to **Cholula** to join the lively, student-heavy crowd there, though you'll have to be prepared for a fairly expensive taxi ride back: buses stop running at around 11pm, just when the clubs start warming up.

La Boveda 6 Sur 503. The most happening among a handful of bars and antros on the Plazuela de los Sapos that pump out Latin and US pop hits. Others include *La Farandala* at no. 506, *El Divino* at no. 504, *La Troje* at no. 501, the last of or *La Serenata* at no. 508, which is more of a drinkers' bar.

Café Aguirre 5 de Mayo 4. Predictable and safe restaurant that's a longstanding local favourite and is always popular with business people for its range of breakfast combos, each with juice and coffee (M$45–95), lunch-time menus (M$60), *antojitos* (M$56–86) and tortas.

Café Munich corner 3 Pte and 5 Sur. Basic but reliable restaurant serving a wide range of soups and mains and a great *comida* in a room decorated with photos of Bavarian scenes and drawings of Einstein, Beethoven, Goethe and Wagner. Cheap (M$39) and pricier (M$65) menus are available at lunch time.

Caldos Angelita corner 6 Pte and 9 Nte. A popular no-nonsense diner doling out hearty bowlfuls of wonderful chicken broth (M$23) and excellent *mole poblano* (M$30), but only until 6.30pm.

Fonda de Santa Clara 3 Pte 307, a couple of blocks west of the zócalo ⓣ222/242-2659, ⓦwww.fondadesantaclara.com. The best-known – and most touristy – restaurant in town, serving local food with an upmarket twist in a pretty room decorated with Mexican art, but service is not very good, and the food can be hit or miss. There's a second branch at 3 Pte 920 (ⓣ222/246-1952).

Italian Coffee Company Reforma 121. Teas, infusions, flavoured espresso coffees and cakes in convivial surroundings. Other branches around town include one at 4 Ote 202, and one at 16 Septiembre opposite the cathedral.

Librería Cafetería Teorema 2 Pte 703 ⓣ222/298-0028. Combined bookshop, café and live music venue in an old colonial building with a relaxed bohemian atmosphere, food, beer and coffee, and a smoking area. Gigs usually start around 9.30pm, with acoustic *trova* Sun–Thurs and rock on Fri & Sat. Reservations recommended. Cover M$10–30.

Litrox Juárez 1305. Lively bar west of the town centre in the Zona Esmeralda (Juárez is a continuation of 7 Pte west of the Paseo Bravo) with music nightly from 8pm and no cover charge.

Mesón Sacristía de la Compañía 6 Sur 304 ⓣ222/242-3554. Come here for fine dining in the superb hotel's lovely enclosed courtyard. Try the house *mole* (M$96), preceded by their special soup made with fried tortilla chips, *chicharrón*, cheese and chipotle (M$50). Efficient, friendly service and a good wine list make this one of Puebla's best dining experiences.

La Zanahoria 5 Ote 206 ⓣ222/232-4813. A bustling vegetarian restaurant in Mexican style, with several meat dishes amid the vast array of wholesome herbivorous choices. Burgers and salads are good value, though no match for the M$69 weekend buffet breakfasts and M$49 *menu del día* (replaced by a M$79 buffet on Sun).

Listings

Banks and exchange Banamex, at Reforma 135 (between 3 Nte and 5 de Mayo) is one of several banks that will change money; there's also a casa de cambio in the arcade between the north side of the zócalo and 2 Ote, and others at CAPU.

Buses You'll need to get back to CAPU for all departures except to local destinations such as Cholula, which can be reached by *combi* from 14 Pte at 11 Nte, or Tlaxcala, which (in addition to buses from CAPU) is served by buses from the Flecha Azul terminal on 10 Pte between 11 Nte and 13 Nte, by the railway museum. There are frequent services to Mexico City's Terminal del Norte and TAPO.

Internet access There are a number of places around the zócalo, most charging around M$10 per hour, often with cheap VOIP phone calls too.

Post office The main post office, at 16 de Septiembre and 5 Ote, has an efficient Lista de Correos; there's also a branch office at 2 Ote 411.

Cholula and around

Puebla's expansion in recent years has made **Cholula**, 15km to the west, virtually a suburb. Nonetheless, it retains its small-town charm and has one abiding reason to visit: the **ruins of Cholula**. A rival of Teotihuacán at its height, and the most powerful city in the country between the fall of Teotihuacán and the rise of Tula, Cholula was at the time of the Conquest a vast city of some four hundred temples, famed as a shrine to Quetzalcoatl and for the excellence of its pottery (a trade dominated by immigrant Mixtecs). But it paid dearly for an attempt, inspired by its Aztec allies, to ambush Cortés on his march to Tenochtitlán: the chieftains were slaughtered, their temples destroyed and churches built in their place. The

Spaniards claimed to have constructed 365 churches here, one for each day of the year. Although there are a lot of churches, the true figure certainly doesn't live up to the claim. There may well be 365 chapels within the churches, though, which is already a few hundred more than the village population could reasonably need.

One side of Cholula's large zócalo – the Plaza de la Concordia – is taken up by the ecclesiastical buildings of the **Convento de San Gabriel**, built from 1529 on the site of the temple of Quetzalcoatl. The Gothic main church is of little interest, but behind it is the great mustard-yellow **Capilla Real** (Mon–Sat 9am–1pm & 4.30–6pm), topped by 49 tiled cupolas. Moorish in conception, the interior comes with a forest of columns supporting semicircular arches and immediately recalls the Mezquita in Córdoba, Spain.

The site

Arriving in Cholula you can't miss the **Nuestra Señora de los Remedios** (daily 7am–8pm; free), picturesquely sited atop a hill with Popocatépetl in the background. If you climb up to it, up, you can buy snacks such as *chapulines* (fried grasshoppers) on the way. What's not immediately apparent is that the hill is in fact the remains of the **Great Pyramid of Cholula** – the Pirámide Tepanapa – the largest pyramid ever constructed, though now it's ruined, overgrown and really not much to look at. At 66m, it is lower than the largest of the Egyptian pyramids but with each side measuring 350m it is also squatter and bulkier. As at other sites, the outer shell was built over a series of nested pyramids, constructed between 200 BC and 800 AD, something amply illustrated in the **site museum**. You can find detailed printed guides at the bookshop next to the museum, which can be useful if you have a deep interest in these ancient structures.

Cross the road to reach the **archeological site** (daily 9am–5.30pm; M$41, M$35 to bring in a video camera; ticket includes both museum and site), accessed through a 400-metre-long series of tunnels dug by archeologists, just a fraction of the 8km of exploratory tunnels which honeycomb the pyramid. They're well lit and capacious enough for most people to walk upright, but there's still a palpable sense of adventure as you spur off down side tunnels, which reveal elements of earlier temples and steep ceremonial stairways that appear to go on forever into the gloom. Emerging at the end of one tunnel you'll find an area of open-air excavations, where part of the great pyramid has been exposed alongside various lesser shrines with explanations in English of their importance. Though undoubtedly fascinating, the ruins are a good deal less impressive than some of the more famed sites around the Valley of México. The ring of superimposed structures around the **Patio de los Altares** are certainly worth a look and there are some fine **murals**, but these can be better appreciated in the site museum where replicas are kept.

Practicalities

Buses for Cholula leave the CAPU terminal in Puebla every fifteen minutes or so, and there's a constant stream of *colectivos* from 14 Poniente, between 9 and 11 Norte. In Cholula, the *colectivos* run right by the archeological site, passing en route the Estrella Roja terminal at 12 Poniente 108, from where there are services to TAPO in Mexico City until 7.50pm. Buses to Puebla's CAPU can be picked up across the street at the corner of 3 Sur until around 9pm. From the bus station, head down 5 de Mayo to get to the zócalo; from there, follow Morelos past the train tracks to reach the pyramid.

There are a few **hotels** in Cholula, the most economical being the *Reforma*, Morelos and 4 Sur (Ⓣ222/247-0149; ❷), which has small rooms with tiny bathrooms, but is cosy and decent enough, and also has parking space. For large modern rooms with tiled floors and TV, try the central *Hotel Suites San Juan*, 5 Sur 103 (Ⓣ222/247-0278,

Ⓔinfo@suitessanjuan.com; ④), or the more distant and more upmarket *Villas Arqueológicas*, 2 Poniente 601, south of the pyramid (Ⓣ222/273-7900 or 001-800/001-7333, Ⓦwww.villasarqueologicas.com.mx; ⑥). If you are **camping**, head 2km out along 6 Norte to *Trailer Park Las Américas*, at 30 Oriente (Ⓣ222/261-1793), where you can pitch a tent or park for around M$200 for two people depending on the size of your tent or trailer.

As the home of the Universidad de las Américas campus, Cholula is often packed with students, a good number of whom seem to spend most of their time hanging out at the outdoor cafés and **restaurants** under Portal Guerrero, along one side of the zócalo. This is the place to come to eat. *Café Enamorada*, at no. 1, is eternally popular with coffee lovers, diners and those here to drink while listening to the occasional band. Along the way at no. 7, *Los Jarrones* has a wider menu, a M$60 comida corrida, good food and a more rustic character.

Cholula is generally regarded as the **nightlife** capital of the Puebla region, but while a few bars cluster around 14 Poniente and 5 de Mayo, most of the action has moved about 3km out to Recta a Cholula, the main highway between Cholula and Puebla – thoroughly inconvenient and making taxi rides essential. Establishments also tend to be far apart from each other, making it hard to find the hottest action. The best bet is to ask locally for the current favourite and commit yourself to just one place for the night – not a bad idea when entry can cost M$100 or more.

Around Cholula

If you want to explore some of the churches round about, head for **ACATEPEC**, easily reached by local bus. The spectacular village church here, San Francisco, has a superb Baroque facade entirely covered in glazed bricks and *azulejos* of local manufacture. It's not particularly large but it is beautifully proportioned and quite unexpected in this setting.

Just a kilometre's walk to the northwest, in the village of **TONATZINTLA**, the plain facade of the church of Santa María conceals a remarkably elaborate Baroque treasury. Here local craftsmen covered every available inch in ornament, interspersing bird, plant and native life with the more usual Christian elements. "Chipilo" **buses** from the corner of 3 Norte and 6 Poniente run to both towns.

Popocatépetl and Ixtaccíhuatl

You get excellent views of the snow-clad volcanic peaks of **Popocatépetl** (5452m) and **Ixtaccíhuatl** (5285m) from almost anywhere west of the capital, and viewing from afar is all most people do these days. "Popo" has been rumbling and fuming away since September 1994, and for much of the time since then the region has been on Yellow Alert, with evacuation procedures posted throughout surrounding towns. Activity was renewed in December 2000, culminating in the largest eruption on record. Though there were no devastating lava flows, the crater spat out hot rocks, dust fell on the capital and, on several occasions, Mexico City's airport (over 60km away) was closed for a few hours. Foreign media hyped the eruption excessively and fanned tourist anxiety, but the only real hardship was felt by local villagers, who, evacuated for weeks, were forced to stand idly by while their livestock trampled their fields.

While the area within a two-kilometre radius of Popo still remains closed to the public, the rest of the **Parque Nacional de Volcanes** (daily 7am–10pm; M$22), which surrounds both volcanoes, is open – for details on the latest situation, contact the park office in Amecameca at Plaza de la Constitución 9 (Ⓣ597/978-3830,

Ⓦ www.iztapopo.conanp.gob.mx. In order to enter the park you will need to fill out and submit a formal request, using a form which can be found on the website – the link is on the "Acceso" page). Even a visit to just the Paso de Cortés – the 3800-metre-high pass between the volcanoes – is a memorable experience, with the two giants rising high above you on either side.

"Popo" and "Ixta", as the volcanoes are affectionately known, are the nation's second and third highest peaks (after the 5700m Pico de Orizaba). Their full names come from an Aztec Romeo-and-Juliet-style legend. Popocatépetl (Smoking Mountain) was a warrior, Ixtaccíhuatl (White Lady) his lover, the beautiful daughter of the emperor. Believing Popocatépetl killed in battle, she died from grief, and when he returned alive he laid her body down on the mountain, where he eternally stands sentinel, holding a burning torch. From the west, Ixta does somewhat resemble a reclining female form and the various parts of the mountain are named accordingly – the feet, the knees, the belly, the breast and so on.

Practicalities

If you'd just like to get as close as possible to the mountains, visit **Amecameca** (usually just Ameca), a lovely little town an hour south of Mexico City, reached by "Servicio Volcánes" (AV) buses from TAPO (see p.453; every 20min; 5am–11pm). Dramatic views of the mountain peaks are bizarrely framed by the palms of the zócalo, around which you'll find a couple of good, inexpensive hotels. If Popo quiets down you may again be able to drive or hitch, or get a taxi from Ameca – there are no buses – along the good asphalt road up to the pine-dotted Paso de Cortés. Climbs up Ixta also begin in Ameca; this is a challenging trek for serious mountaineers only, involving a night or two with all your gear at very high altitude, and a technical three-kilometre-long ridge traverse (often requiring ropes) to reach the highest point.

South of Mexico City

Heading south from Mexico City, you climb over the mountains and descend to **Cuernavaca**, which brims with colonial mansions and gardens, and draws visitors on account of its proximity to several important archeological sites, notably the hilltop pyramid sites of **Tepoztlán** and **Xochicalco**. An hour further south the silver town of **Taxco** straggles picturesquely up a hillside, making it one of the most appealing destinations hereabouts.

Cuernavaca and around

CUERNAVACA has always provided a place of escape from the city – the Aztecs called it Cuauhnahuac ("place by the woods"), and it became a favourite resort and hunting ground for their rulers. Cortés seized and destroyed the city during the siege of Tenochtitlán, then ended up building himself a palace here, the Spaniards corrupting the name to Cuernavaca ("cow horn") for no better reason than their

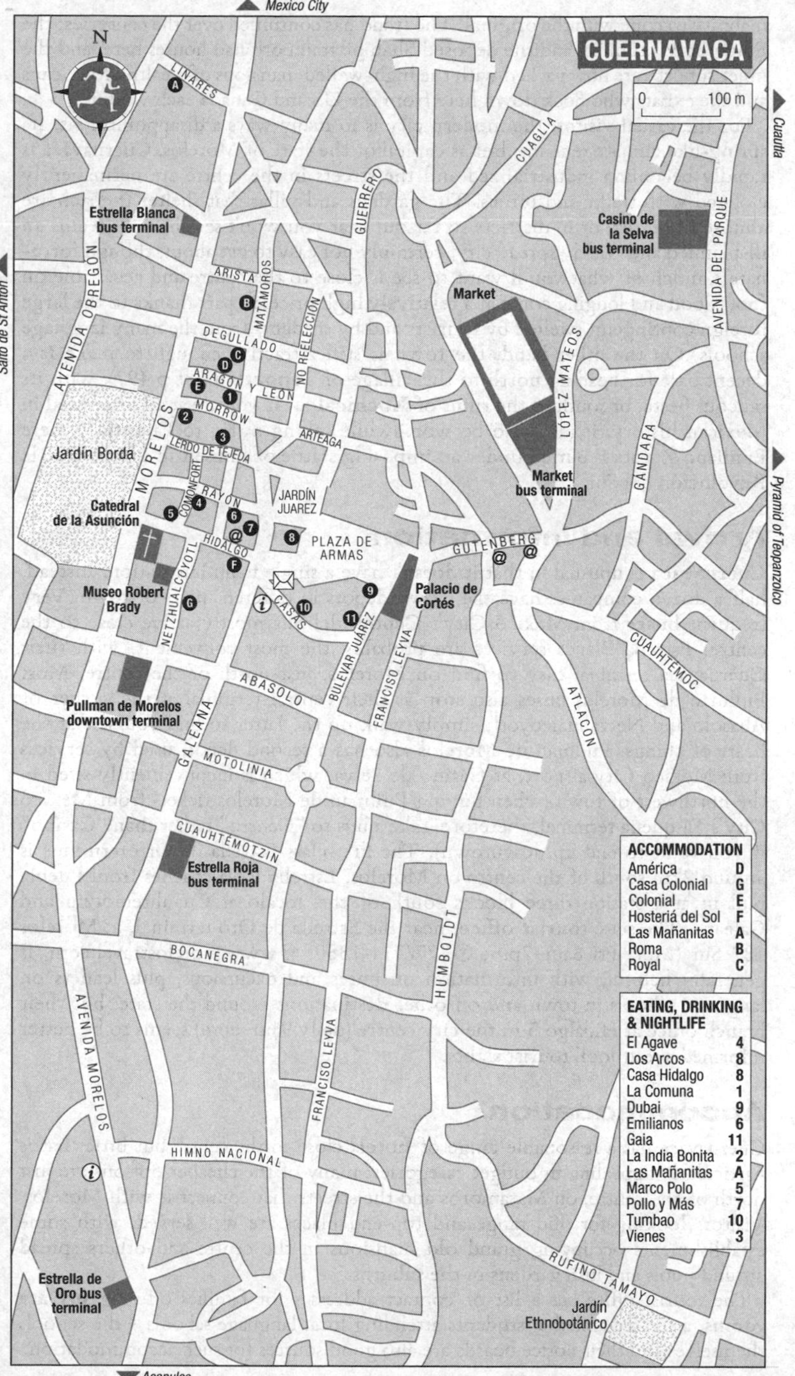
CUERNAVACA
Mexico City
Acapulco
Cuautla
Pyramid of Teopanzolco
Salto de St Antón
0
100 m
Estrella Blanca bus terminal
Casino de la Selva bus terminal
Market
Market bus terminal
Jardín Borda
Catedral de la Asunción
Museo Robert Brady
Palacio de Cortés
JARDÍN JUAREZ
PLAZA DE ARMAS
Pullman de Morelos downtown terminal
Estrella Roja bus terminal
Estrella de Oro bus terminal
Jardín Ethnobotánico
LINARES
CUAGLIA
GUERRERO
ARISTA
MATAMOROS
NO REELECCIÓN
DEGULLADO
ARAGÓN Y LEÓN
MORROW
ARTEAGA
LERDO DE TEJEDA
RAYON
COMONFORT
HIDALGO
MORELOS
AVENIDA OBREGÓN
NETZHUALCOYOTL
CASAS
BULEVAR JUAREZ
FRANCISCO LEYVA
GUTENBERG
LÓPEZ MATEOS
AVENIDA DEL PARQUE
GÁNDARA
CUAUHTEMOC
ATLACON
ABASOLO
GALEANA
MOTOLINIA
CUAUHTÉMOTZIN
BOCANEGRA
HUMBOLDT
AVENIDA MORELOS
HIMNO NACIONAL
RUFINO TAMAYO
ACCOMMODATION
América D
Casa Colonial G
Colonial E
Hosteriá del Sol F
Las Mañanitas A
Roma B
Royal C
EATING, DRINKING & NIGHTLIFE
El Agave 4
Los Arcos 8
Casa Hidalgo 8
La Comuna 1
Dubai 9
Emilianos 6
Gaia 11
La India Bonita 2
Las Mañanitas A
Marco Polo 5
Pollo y Más 7
Tumbao 10
Vienes 3

inability to cope with the original. The trend has continued over the centuries: the Emperor Maximilian and the deposed Shah of Iran both had houses here, and the inner suburbs are now packed with the high-walled mansions of wealthy Mexicans and the expats who flock down here from the US and Canada each winter.

For the casual visitor, the modern city is in many ways a disappointment. Its spring-like climate remains, but as capital of the state of Morelos, Cuernavaca is rapidly becoming industrialized and the streets in the centre are permanently clogged with traffic and fumes. The gardens and villas that shelter the rich are almost all hidden or in districts so far out that you won't see them. It seems an ill-planned and widely spread city, certainly not easy to get about, though fortunately much of what you'll want to see is close to the centre and accessible on foot. Food and lodging come at a relatively high price, in part thanks to the large foreign contingent, swelled by tourists and by students from the many language schools. On the other hand, the town is still attractive enough to make it a decent base for heading north to the village of **Tepoztlán** (see p.497), with its raucous fiesta, or south to the ruins of **Xochicalco**. If you are at all interested in Mexican history, it may also be worthwhile taking a trip to **Cuautla**, where Emiliano Zapata is buried under an imposing statue of himself in Plazuela de la Revolución del Sur.

Arrival and information

Cuernavaca is unusual in that it doesn't have a single main bus station. Instead, half a dozen companies have their own depots in different parts of town. Very frequent **buses** from Mexico City's Central del Sur mostly arrive close to the centre: Estrella Blanca services are probably the most convenient, with their Cuernavaca terminal easy to find on Morelos, just north of the centre. Most Pullman de Morelos buses also stop at their central terminal at the corner of Abasolo and Netzahualcoyotl; simply walk up the latter to find yourself at the heart of things. Pullman de Morelos also has a second depot, used by services from Mexico City airport, at Casino de Selva, which is inconveniently sited in the northwest of town (when buying Pullman de Morelos tickets from Mexico City's Tasqueña terminal, therefore, take a bus to "Centro" rather than "Casino" if you want to end up downtown). The first-class Estrella de Oro terminus is around 2km south of the centre on Morelos. Estrella Roja coaches from Puebla pull in at a station three blocks south of the zócalo at Cuauhtémotzin and Galeana. The state **tourist office**, near the Estrella de Oro terminal, at Morelos 187 Sur (Mon–Fri 8am–7pm; Ⓣ777/314-1880, Ⓦwww.morelostravel.com, is generally helpful, with information on buses and excursions, plus leaflets on language schools in town and on other destinations around the state, but their branch office at Hidalgo 5 in the city centre (daily 9am–6pm) seems to be better informed about local tourist sights.

Accommodation

Cuernavaca has a reasonable range of **hotels** close to the centre but little that is particularly appealing in budget categories: many of the cheaper options are just north of the centre, on Matamoros and the streets that connect it with Morelos. Visitors looking for mid-range and top-end places are well served, with some establishments occupying grand old mansions in the centre and others spread around pools and lush gardens in the suburbs.

The tourist office has a list of contact addresses for families offering **private rooms**, a service aimed at students attending local language schools – the schools themselves and their notice boards are also good sources for such accommodation.

América Aragón y León 14 ☎777/318-6127. Basic but respectable place in a street mostly full of dives; all rooms have bath, but only those at the front have outside windows (the others have windows onto the inner courtyard). ❷

Casa Colonial Netzahualcoyotl 37 ☎777/312-7033, Ⓦwww.casacolonial.com. Gorgeous rooms in a delightful eighteenth-century mansion close to the Museo Robert Brady. With attractive colonial public areas and a pool, this is one of the most appealing places in the centre, and prices include breakfast. TV on request, but no phones. Prices are about fifteen percent higher at weekends. ❼

Colonial Aragón y León 19 ☎777/318-6414. Across the street from the *América* and a bit less basic; the most comfortable hotel on Aragón y León. ❸

Hostería del Sol Callejón de la Bolsa del Diabolo, by Hidalgo 3 ☎777/318 3241. Well-kept little place with some quite charming rooms, nicely decorated with pretty tiles and paintwork, though not all are en suite. ❹

Las Mañanitas Ricardo Linares 107 ☎777/362-0000 or 01-800/221-5299, in the US ☎1-888/413-9199, Ⓦwww.lasmananitas.com.mx. Beautiful luxury hotel, just a 10min walk from the zócalo. The streetfront entrance gives little clue of the oasis within, where peacocks, flamingoes and African cranes strut around a pool and lush gardens. The tiled-floor rooms come with heavy wooden furniture and all the fittings, and there's a superb restaurant on site (see p.496). Prices are about fifteen percent higher at weekends. ❾

Roma Matamoros 17 ☎777/318-8778, Ⓦwww.hotelromacuernavaca.com.mx. Simple but clean budget option with parking space in the central patio and rooms set around it, all with bathroom, overhead fan and TV. ❹

Royal Matamoros 11 ☎777/314-4018, Ⓦwww.hoteles-royal.com. One of a number of similar places along Matamoros; slightly shabby but with comfortable enough rooms with bath, and space for parking. ❸

The Town

At the heart of the city, the **zócalo** comprises the Plaza de Armas and the smaller Jardín Juárez, with its bandstand, to the northwest. Around the twin plazas you'll find a series of cafés where you can sit outdoors under the watchful eye of a huge, black, volcanic-rock **statue of Morelos** that faces the Palacio de Gobierno, across the plaza.

Palacio de Cortés

At the eastern end of the Plaza de Armas, behind the statue of Morelos, is the **Palacio de Cortés**, which houses the **Museo Regional Cuauhnahuac** (Tues–Sun 9am–6pm; M$41). Work on this building began as early as 1522, when, although Tenochtitlán had fallen, much of the country had yet to come under Spanish control – the fortress-like aspect of the palace's older parts reflects this period. Over the centuries, though, it's been added to and modified substantially – first by Cortés himself and later by the state authorities to whom it passed – so that what you see today is every bit a palace. The museum is a good one, spacious and well laid out with a substantial section covering local archeology, including some fine examples of stelae and a lovely seated figure from Xochicalco. In fact, the building is partly constructed over the ruins of a small pyramid, which can be seen in the courtyard and elsewhere. There's also a substantial collection of colonial art, weaponry and everyday artefacts – look for the sixteenth-century clock mechanism from the cathedral and a reproduction of a *cuexcomate*, a kind of thatched granary still found around the state.

The museum's highlight, though, is a series of **murals** around the gallery, painted by Diego Rivera in 1929 and 1930. Depicting Mexican history from the Conquest to the Revolution, they concentrate in particular on the atrocities committed by Cortés, and on the revolutionary Emiliano Zapata, who was born in nearby Cuautla, raised most of his army from the peasants of Morelos and remains something of a folk hero to the locals. From the balcony here, there are wonderful, though sometimes hazy, views to the east with Popocatépetl in the far distance.

▲ Palacio de Cortés, Cuernavaca

The cathedral

From the plaza, Hidalgo runs three blocks west to the **Catedral de la Asunción**, located on the south side of a grassy tree-shaded compound that also contains a couple of other small churches. Founded by Cortés in 1529, the cathedral looks bulky and threatening from the outside (at one stage there were actually cannons mounted along the battlemented roof line), but it has been tastefully refurbished within and stripped almost bare, the modernist approach here an enormous relief if you've grown tired of the churrigueresque and Baroque flamboyance elsewhere. Most of the decor is understated, but traces of murals discovered during the redecoration have been uncovered in places – they have a remarkably East Asian look and are believed to have been painted by a Christian Chinese or Filipino artist in the days when the cathedral was the centre for missions to the Far East. At one time, the main Spanish trade route came through here, with goods brought across the Pacific to Acapulco, overland through central Mexico and on from Veracruz to Spain. If, after viewing the interior of the cathedral you need your fix of golden exuberance, pop into the **Capilla del Santísimo**, where there's a small gilt *retablo* and Stations of the Cross in charcoal on paper.

Until his death in December 2000, Cuernavaca's bishop was **Luis Cervantes**, one of the country's most liberal and outspoken clergymen. Apart from doing up his cathedral, he was renowned for instituting the "Mariachi Mass", something that has been continued by his disciples. Every Sunday, this service is conducted to the accompaniment of traditional Mexican music and usually attracts large crowds.

Museo Robert Brady

South of the cathedral, at the corner of Netzahualcoyotl and 20 de Noviembre, the **Museo Robert Brady** (Tues–Sun 10am–6pm; M$30; Ⓦ www.bradymuseum.org) occupies a former sixteenth-century convent and holds the Iowa-born artist's private collection. Brady moved to Cuernavaca in the 1960s, and lived here until his death in 1986. Filled with art from around the world and decorated in an intensely colourful artesanía style, the museum is a fabulous place, with rooms arranged aesthetically, and without regard to history, geography or classification of artistic styles. As a result, what you see is more like a beautiful home than a typical museum, and is well worth a visit.

The rooms, arranged around a couple of outside patios complete with sculptures and a delightful pool, are filled with works by most of the greats of twentieth-century Mexican art. Even the bathrooms contain works by Diego Rivera and Rufino Tamayo, and there are also pieces by Frida Kahlo, Graham Sutherland, and some particularly good works by Rafael Coronel, including a portrait of Peggy Guggenheim. Everything is labelled in English.

Jardín Borda

Immediately west of the cathedral is the entrance to the **Jardín Borda**, Morelos 103 (Tues–Sun 10am–5.30pm; M$30), a large formal garden adjacent to the mansion of Taxco mining magnate José de la Borda (see p.500). Though it falls short of the grandeur Borda dreamed of when he commissioned the garden in the eighteenth century, both the garden and the mansion are a delightfully tranquil reminder of the haven Cuernavaca once was. Maximilian and Carlota later adopted Borda's mansion as their weekend home, though Maximilian also had another retreat in Cuernavaca that he shared with his native mistress, "La India Bonita".

Out from the centre

About twenty minutes' walk into the suburbs beyond the Jardín Borda is the **Salto de San Antón** (daily 8am–6pm; free), a beautiful 36-metre cascade surrounded by vegetation and natural columns of crystallized basalt. Unfortunately, the site has been overdeveloped and is marred by concrete walkways, litter and a faint stench from the polluted water, but it's still pretty, and the road to the falls passes a number of flower shops and restaurants.

Rather more distant – 2km southeast of the centre, in the Colonia Acapantzingo – is the **Jardín Etnobotánico**, Matamoros 200 (daily 9am–5pm; free), whose grounds and collection of medicinal plants are just about worth taking a taxi (or a long walk) to see. As well as the labelled specimens – coffee, guavas, roses and medicinal herbs – there is a small museum of traditional medicine.

Other sites scattered further out in the fringes of the city include the area's sole significant reminder of the pre-colonial period, the **Pyramid of Teopanzolco** (daily 9am–5pm; M$35). So effectively buried was this site that it took an artillery bombardment during the Revolution to uncover it. Located to the northeast of the centre beyond the train station (which is what the gunners were aiming at), it's a small temple in which two pyramids can be seen, one built over the other. The pyramid can be reached by city bus #6 from Degollado and Reelección.

Eating, drinking and nightlife

You don't need to wander far from the centre to find good **places to eat**: there's a particularly fine group of restaurants around the zócalo, and you can get juices and tortas at any time around the bandstand in the Jardín Juárez. **Evening activity** mostly centres on the Plazuela del Zacate, just a couple of blocks south of the zócalo, where the corner of Galeana and Hidalgo is intersected by Fray Bartolomé de las Casas. Most nights there are large groups hanging around this small triangular area, occasionally popping into one of the fashionable cafés and bars for a beer, or sitting outside listening to someone playing on the makeshift stage. There are also free concerts from the bandstand in the Jardín Juárez every Thursday evening at 6pm.

Restaurants

Los Arcos Jardín de los Héroes 4 ⓣ777/312-1510. Ever-popular restaurant and bar on the south side of the zócalo serving espresso coffee and a wide range of fairly pricey dishes catering to locals and foreign students. In the evening most people are here to drink and listen to the live music, which comes in a variety of styles and abilities.

Casa Hidalgo Jardín de los Héroes 6 ⓣ777/312-2749. Next door to *Los Arcos*, but rather posher, with white table linen, an outside terace, a roof terrace and various balconies with views over the zócalo. Main dishes (M$95–195) include sole with mangoes, or jambalaya.

La Comuna Morrow 6. Small and friendly cooperatively run café, serving, in addition to coffee and beer, comidas corridas for M$35, and excellent breakfasts.

Emiliano's Rayon 5–C. Cheap and cheerful diner offering set breakfasts (M$30), comidas corridas (M$35) and *pozole* (M$55).

Gaia Juárez 102 ⓣ777/310-0031, ⓦwww.gaiarest.com.mx. Stylish restaurant known for its innovative cross-cultural cuisine. Specialities include duck in plum sauce and prawns in tamarind sauce on a bed of couscous and *amaranto* (an indigenous Mexican cereal). Main courses go for around M$135–290.

La India Bonita Morrow 20, just off Morelos ⓣ777/312-5021. Lovely restaurant with a pleasant outdoor patio, excellent but moderately priced food (including set breakfasts at M$60–90) and impeccable service. Expect to pay M$80–160 for delicious mains, or just drop in for a quiet drink at the bar.

Las Mañanitas Ricardo Linares 107 ⓣ777/362-0000 or 01-800/221-5299. People drive hours to visit this well-known restaurant which serves fine international cuisine in the sumptuous grounds of the hotel of the same name. You'll probably part with at least M$600–800 for a full meal but you won't regret it.

Marco Polo Hidalgo 30 ⓦwww.marco-polo.com.mx. Superior Italian restaurant serving up its own home-made pasta (M$75–132), with main courses (if you can fit one in after the pasta) at M$145–185. Alternatively, see if you can get through one of their huge pizzas (M$64–140).

Pollo y Más Galeana 4. Cheap snack bar opposite the zócalo, serving tasty roast chicken, enchiladas and *antojitos*, and M$35 comidas corridas.

Vienes Lerdo de Tejada 302. Austro-Hungarian café, patisserie and restaurant just a block from the zócalo; a great spot for continental-style coffee and pastries.

Bars

El Agave Comonfort 5. Bar/restaurant just north of the zócalo, set around a courtyard with a pretty stone fountain and offering a great range of good rums and tequilas, cheap beers during happy hour (4–6pm) and food in the form of salads and steaks. It's open until there's no one left standing.

Dubai Hidalgo, at southeast corner of Plaza de Armas. Night-time music bar (it doesn't open till 10.30pm) directly opposite the Palacio de Cortés, with an outdoor terrace and an upstairs balcony with views over the zócalo.

Tumbao Casas 11. With fluorescent tropical decor, and DJs mixing everything from salsa to techno, this is the liveliest among a slew of good bars on Casas, which is Cuernavaca's most happening street from dusk until around 2am.

Listings

Banks and exchange Casas de cambio include Gesta on the corner of Galeana and Lerdo de Tejada, plus more at Morrow 9, Matamoros 10 and Hidalgo 7.

Internet access Cyber Gasso, Hidalgo 22–D and Gutenberg 8 (daily 7.30am–9pm; M$7/hr), and Ova-Press, Gutenberg 26–A (daily 7am–11pm; M$5/hr).

Laundry Tintorería Morelos, Matamoros 28, opposite *Hotel Roma* (Mon–Sat 9.30am–8pm).

Pharmacy The handiest pharmacy is the 24hr Farmacia del Ahorro at the corner of Hidalgo and Galeana, just south of the zócalo.

Post office At the southwest corner of the zócalo (Mon–Fri 8am–6pm, Sat 9am–1pm).

Spanish courses The state tourist office has leaflets and brochures issued by several schools offering Spanish language courses in Cuernavaca. One that has been recommended is CETLALIC (ⓣ777/313-2637, ⓦwww.cetlalic.org.mx).

Tepoztlán

An interesting side trip from Cuernavaca is to **TEPOZTLÁN**, just 21km to the northeast and dramatically sited in a narrow valley spectacularly ringed by volcanic mountains. Until recently this was an isolated agrarian community inhabited by Nahuatl-speaking people whose life changed little between the time of the Conquest and the beginning of the twentieth century - it was on Tepoztlán that anthropologist Oscar Lewis based his classic study *Life in a Mexican Village*, in which he traced the effects of the Revolution, as the village was an important stronghold of the original Zapatista movement. In recent years, though, new roads and a couple of luxury hotels have begun to change things – Tepoztlán has become a popular weekend retreat from the capital, with its good selection of restaurants and quality arts and crafts shops, though midweek it is still a peaceful spot. For now, at least, the stunning setting also survives, as does a reputation for joyously boisterous **fiestas** (especially Sept 8, celebrating the conversion of the local ruler to Christianity in 1538).

On Sundays and Wednesdays a **market** is held in the zócalo, on whose eastern side stands the massive **Ex-Convento Dominico de la Natividad**. It was a fortress for a while during the Revolution, but is now in a rather beautiful state of disrepair with some attractive murals still surviving in the cloister. Around the back and accessed off Gonzales, part of the church has been given over to the **Museo de Arte Prehispánico** (Tues–Sun 10am–6pm; M$10), which holds a remarkably good archeological collection.

Several pre-Hispanic temples have been found on the hilltops in the area, and you can see one to the north, perched high up in impossibly steep-looking terrain. This is the **Santuario del Cerro Tepozteco** (daily 9am–5.30pm; M$3, free Sun), reached after an exhausting climb of an hour or so up what is little more than an upgraded dry streambed at times. If you're fit, the hike is worth it for the views from this artificially flattened hilltop, and the chance to inspect the site at close quarters. The small, three-stepped, lime-washed pyramid here was dedicated to Tepoztecatl, a god of *pulque* and of fertility, represented by carvings of rabbits. There were so many *pulque* gods that they were known as the four hundred rabbits: the drink was supposedly discovered by rabbits nibbling at the agave plants from which it is made. This one gained particular kudos when the Spaniards flung the idol off the cliffs only for his adherents to find that it had landed unharmed – the big September fiesta is in his honour. Follow the example of Mexicans and reward your efforts with a picnic lunch (water and soft drinks are available at a price), but do buck the litter-dropping trend and take your empty containers away with you.

Practicalities

Buses between Cuautla (see p.498) and Cuernavaca or Mexico City (Autobuses del Sur) leave you at a caseta on the highway a kilometre west of town at the end of 22 Febrero. Direct second-class buses from Cuernavaca drop you half a kilometre south of town at the end of the main street, 5 de Mayo. One block north of the junction of 22 Febrero and 5 de Mayo is the zócalo, at whose northern end you'll be dropped if you arrive by slower second-class bus from Cuernavaca. For **currency exchange**, there's a Bancomer with an ATM on 5 de Mayo opposite the zócalo.

Many people visit Tepoztlán as a day trip since the **hotels** are fairly expensive. The cheapest is *Posada Ali*, Netzahualcoyotl 2 (Ⓣ739/395-1971; ❹), out towards the ruins and with its lower-cost rooms tucked under the eaves. Larger rooms have sunflower-carved headboards on the beds and wood-beamed ceilings, and everyone has access to the small pool and *frontón* court. If your budget can manage it, *the* place to stay is the elegant but unpretentious *Posada del Tepozteco* at Paraíso 3 (Ⓣ739/395-0010, Ⓦwww.posadadeltepozteco.com; ❾), wonderfully sited above most of the town and with views of the mountains from the manicured gardens and two outdoor pools. The rooms and suites are simple but well equipped, most with their own terrace and jacuzzi. There are plenty of **restaurants** either close to the zócalo or out along the road towards the ruins. For reasonably priced vegetarian dishes, salads, wholemeal bread and good coffee, visit *Govinda Ram* two blocks north of the zócalo on Avenida de Tepozteco (the continuation of 5 de Mayo), or for something slightly more upmarket in colourful surrounds get a table at *Los Colorines*, half a block south along the same street. Two blocks south of the zócalo at 5 de Mayo 21, *Teposnieves* (the original branch of what is now a modest chain) has ice creams and sorbets in more flavours than you can count; fig and mescal is a favourite, but if you want something more unusual, there's chile and cucumber, or carrot sorbet. There are several more branches around town, incuding two on the zócalo at Avenida de la Revolución nos.18 and 24.

Cuautla

Some 42km southeast of Cuernavaca, and an hour and a half by bus, lies **Cuautla**, a pleasant if unexciting little town, where Independence leader and local boy **José Maria Morelos** was besieged by a royalist army in 1812, and where the great revolutionary leader **Emiliano Zapata** is buried, a block south of the zócalo in the Plazuela de la Revolución del Sur. His remains lie under a huge bronze statue depicting him in heroic pose – mustachioed, with a broad-brimmed sombrero on his head and a bandoleer across his shoulder; in one hand he clutches a rifle, and in the other a proclamation demanding "Tierra y Libertad" ("land and freedom").

On the zócalo, the **Casa de Morelos** (Tues–Sun 10am–5pm; M$30), is a beautiful colonial mansion with gardens that was formerly the home of José Maria Morelos (see p.370), and contains archeological finds and items of local historical interest. Three blocks further north along Los Bravo, Cuautla's former train station is now home to the **Museo José Maria Morelos y Pavón** (Tues–Sun 10am–5pm; voluntary donation), which mainly traces the life and times of Morelos, and the Independence movement in this state that bears his name. For train buffs, the 1904 **steam locomotive** and carriages once used by the town's other great local hero, Emiliano Zapata, may be of interest. If you're around on the first or third Saturday of each month, you can take a very short ride on it, with departures every fifteen minutes from 4pm till 8.45pm (M$20; enquiries on Ⓣ735/352-5221).

Cuautla also has something of a reputation for its thermal **spas**, and there are several large complexes a little way out from the centre. The emphasis is more on swimming than luxuriating, but for M$60 you could easily while away an hour or two at Agua Hedionda (Ⓣ735/352-0044, Ⓦwww.aguahedionda.org): take a purple-and-yellow #11 *combi* from Plazuela de la Revolución del Sur (around a 10min trip).

Practicalities

Cuautla has three **bus stations**, all close to each other and a couple of blocks east of the zócalo. There's a small **tourist office** at the old train station, four blocks north of the zócalo on Galeana (daily 8am–8pm; Ⓣ735/352-5221, Ⓦwww.direccionturismocuautla.com). **Hotels** are generally good value. Right on the zócalo, the *Colón* (Ⓣ735/352-2990; ❷) offers simple but clean budget accommodation – it's worth asking for a room with a zócalo view. The *España*, at

2 de Mayo 22 (Ⓣ735/352-2186; ❸), offers a little more comfort, its rooms done out in cool peppermint green and white, and equipped with a TV and fan. There's also the *Defensa del Agua*, Defensa del Agua 34 (Ⓣ735/352-1679; ❸), whose more spacious modern rooms surround a patio with parking space and a small pool. The centre of town has numerous small cheap **restaurants**, but for something a little special make for *Las Golondrinas*, Nicolás Catalán 19–A, a block north of the zócalo (Ⓣ735/354-1350, Ⓦwww.las-golondrinas.com.mx), where fountains splash as you sink back in comfy chairs and tuck into corn and *cuitlacoche* soup (M$39), *ranchera* fish kebabs (M$116) or regional specialities such as barbecued rabbit *molcajete* (M$125); there's also a lunch menu for M$85.

Xochicalco

Some 38km southwest of Cuernavaca lie the impressive hilltop ruins of **Xochicalco** (daily 9am–6pm; M$48). While not much is known of the history of this site or the people who inhabited it, it is regarded by archeologists as one of the most significant in central Mexico because of the connections it shows to both the ancient culture of Teotihuacán and the later Toltec peoples. Xochicalco flourished from around 700 AD to 900 AD – thus overlapping with both Teotihuacán and Tula – and also displays clear parallels with Maya and Zapotec sites of the era.

The setting, high on a bare mountaintop, is reminiscent of Monte Albán (see p.633), the great Zapotec site near Oaxaca. Like Monte Albán and the great Maya sites (but unlike Tula or Teotihuacán), Xochicalco was an exclusively religious and ceremonial centre rather than a true city. The style of many of the carvings, too, recalls Zapotec and Maya art. Their subjects, however, and the architecture of the temples, seem to form a transition between Teotihuacán and Tula. The appearance of **Quetzalcoatl** as a human is especially noteworthy, as he was to turn up in this form at Tula and almost every subsequent site, rather than simply as the feathered serpent of Teotihuacán. The ball-court is almost identical to earlier Maya examples, and similar to those that later appeared in Tula. For all these influences, however, or perhaps because there are so many of them, it's almost impossible to say which culture was dominant: some claim that Xochicalco was a northern outpost of the Maya, others that it was a subject city of Teotihuacán that survived (or perhaps precipitated through revolt) the fall of that empire.

Arriving at the site, first stop in at the **museum**, on a neighbouring hilltop, where you buy your entry **ticket**, and can take a look at some of the more portable pieces unearthed here. A carved stele that once graced one of the lower courtyards (and has now been replaced by a concrete pillar) takes pride of place in the first room, and is followed by numerous slabs of carved stone, a delicate alabaster bowl and some fine jade masks. From here it is a ten-minute walk to the ruins.

The site

Much the most important surviving monument here is the **Pirámide de Quetzalcoatl**, on the highest part of the site. Around its base are carved extremely elaborate plumed serpents, coiling around various seated figures and symbols with astronomical significance – all clearly Maya in inspiration. On top, part of the wall of the sanctuary remains standing, though it now surrounds a large hole. In 1993 the centre of the pyramid was excavated to reveal the remains of an earlier pyramid inside.

The other main point of interest is the **Solar Observatory**, located to the northwest of the main pyramid and down the hill a little, accessed through the northern ball-court. Here you'll find the entrance to some subterranean passages, a couple of natural **caves** augmented by steps and tunnels, one of which features a shaft in the roof that is oriented so as to allow the sun to shine directly in. At astronomical midday (midway between sunrise and sunset) for around five weeks either side of the summer solstice – May 14/15 to July 28/29 – the shaft casts a hexagonal patch of light onto the cave floor. At any time, the custodian should point out the remains of frescoes on the walls.

Practicalities

The quick and comfortable way to the site is by half-hourly first-class **bus** headed to Miacatlán from Cuernavaca's Pullman de Morelos terminal, which will take you to the Crucero de Xochicalco, 4km from the site. There is often a taxi waiting here to run you to the site for about M$20; otherwise you'll have to walk. There's also a very slow and circuitous second-class bus that leaves half-hourly from Cuernavaca's market bus station and takes you right to the site. If you're **driving**, or if you go with a **tour**, you can continue another thirty-odd kilometres down the road beyond Xochicalco to the caves of Cacahuamilpa (see p.504), from where Taxco (see beloe) is only a short distance.

Taxco

Silver has been mined in **TAXCO** since before the Conquest. Supplies of the metal have long been depleted, but it is still the basis of the town's fame, as well as its livelihood, in the form of jewellery, which is made in hundreds of workshops here, and sold in an array of shops (*platerías*) catering mainly to tourists. The city is an attractive place, like some Mexican version of a Tuscan village, with a mass of terracotta-tiled, whitewashed houses lining narrow, cobbled alleys that straggle steeply uphill. At intervals the pattern is broken by a larger mansion, or by a courtyard filled with flowers or by the tower of a church rearing up; the twin spires of **Santa Prisca**, a Baroque wedding cake of a church in the centre of town, stand out above all. Unfortunately, the streets are eternally clogged with VW Beetle taxis and *colectivos* struggling up the steep slopes, and forming an endless *paseo* around the central Plaza Borda. Once you've spent an hour or so in the church and a few museums there's really nothing to do but sit around in the plaza cafés. Still, it is a pleasant enough place to do just that if you don't mind the relatively high prices, and the profusion of other tourists.

Though it might seem a prosperous place now, Taxco's development has not been entirely straightforward – indeed on more than one occasion the town has been all but abandoned. The Spaniards came running at the rumours of mineral wealth here (Cortés himself sent an expedition in 1522), but their success was short-lived, and it wasn't until the eighteenth century that French immigrant **José de la Borda** struck it fabulously rich by discovering the San Ignacio vein. It was during Borda's short lifetime that most of what you see originated – he spent an enormous sum on building the church of Santa Prisca, and more on other buildings and a royal lifestyle here and in Cuernavaca; by his death in 1778 the boom was already over. In 1929, a final revival started with the arrival of American architect and writer **William Spratling**, who set up a jewellery workshop in Taxco, drawing on local traditional skills and pre-Hispanic designs. With the completion of a new road around the same time, a massive influx of tourists was inevitable – the town has handled it all fairly well, becoming rich at the expense of just a little charm.

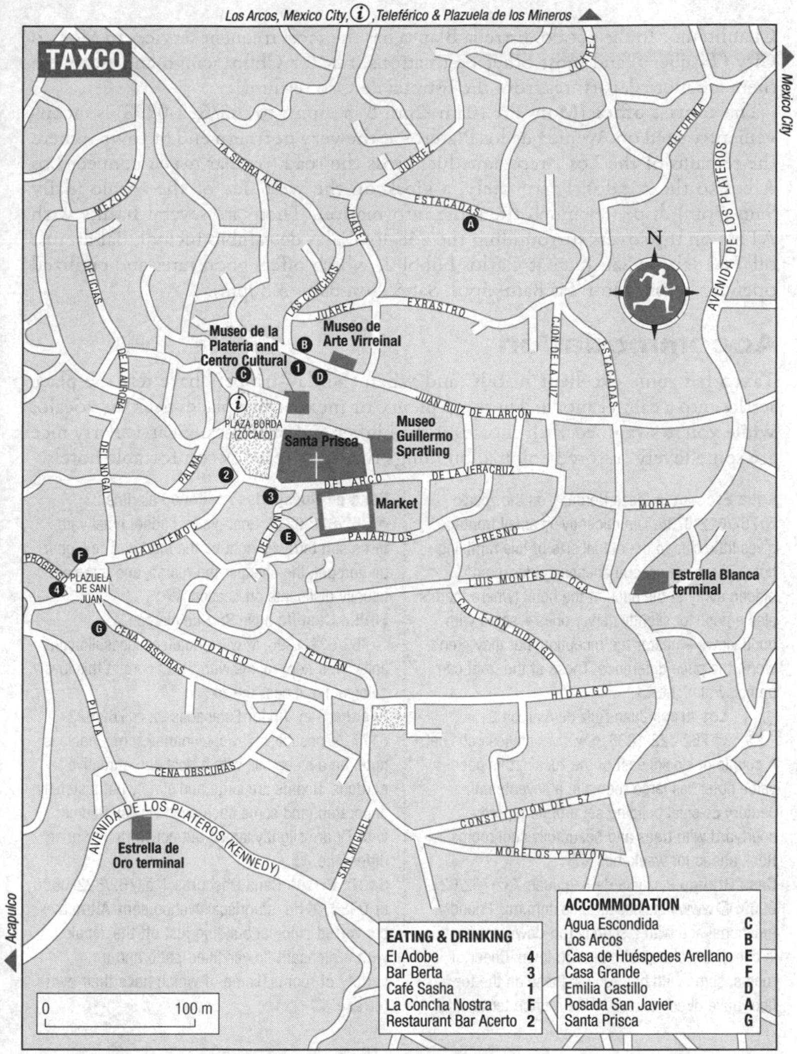

Los Arcos, Mexico City, (i), Teleférico & Plazuela de los Mineros

Mexico City

TAXCO

EATING & DRINKING

El Adobe	4
Bar Berta	3
Café Sasha	1
La Concha Nostra	F
Restaurant Bar Acerto	2

ACCOMMODATION

Agua Escondida	C
Los Arcos	B
Casa de Huéspedes Arellano	E
Casa Grande	F
Emilia Castillo	D
Posada San Javier	A
Santa Prisca	G

Acapulco

Arrival and information

You'll arrive in Taxco on Avenida de los Plateros (formerly Avenida Kennedy), the main road that contours around the side of the valley at the bottom of town. Taxco has two **bus stations**, about 1km apart on Avenida de los Plateros. From either it is a steep fifteen-minute walk or M$30 taxi ride to Plaza Borda, the zócalo. Ignore offers of a free taxi to a "silver mine" – in fact just a small tunnel (not a mine) with a tacky souvenir shop. To get into town from the Estrella Blanca terminal, take a *combi* (M$3.50) or cross the road and turn right up the hill and then left to climb even more steeply past the church of Santa Veracruz to the centre. From Estrella de Oro, head straight up Calle de Pilita, the steep alley directly across from you, until you come to the Plazuela de San Juan, on your right; from there go down

Cuauhtémoc to the zócalo. Estrella Blanca has the most frequent services to Mexico City (Tasqueña) and most other destinations, but for Chilpancingo and Acapulco there are more departures from the Estrella de Oro terminal.

The **tourist office** (Mon–Fri 10am–2pm & 5–6pm; ⓣ762/622-0798) is inconveniently sited on Avenida de los Plateros at the very northern end of town, where the remains of the Los Arcos aqueduct cross the road (regular *combis* connect Los Arcos to the zócalo). Fortunately, a kiosk on the west side of the zócalo (daily 9am–7pm) dispenses much the same information. There are several **banks** with ATMs on the streets surrounding the zócalo. Casas de cambio include Balsas, just off Plazuela de San Juan at Carlos Nibbi 2, which offers good rates and civilized opening hours (Mon–Fri 8am–5pm, Sat & Sun 8am–3.30pm).

Accommodation

Taxco has some excellent **hotels**, and when the day-trippers have left the place settles into a calmer mode. There are plenty of inexpensive places near the zócalo, while you're swamped with choices at the higher end of the scale. Particularly nice are some lovely restored colonial buildings that now serve as comfortable hotels.

Agua Escondida Plaza Borda 4, on the zócalo ⓣ762/622-0736. The deceptively small frontage gives little clue to the actual size of this rambling hotel. There are several cheaper, older rooms hidden away at the back of the hotel (where there's also a pool), or slightly newer ones – some with good views – nearer the reception, but they aren't worth the price difference. Those at the front can be noisy at night. ❹

Los Arcos Juan Ruíz de Alarcón 2 ⓣ762/622-1836, ⓦwww.hotellosarcos.net. A couple of blocks east of the zócalo, this good-value hotel has large rooms in a seventeenth-century colonial building set around a pretty courtyard with trees and beautifully cool rooms. Book ahead for weekends. ❹

Casa Grande Plazuela de San Juan 7 ⓣ762/622-0969, ⓦwww.hotelcasagrande.com.mx. Friendly, functional and with a slightly run-down charm, this is one of the cheapest places in town. Cheerful rooms, some with bathrooms; those on the top floor have direct access to the rooftop terrace. ❸

Casa de Huéspedes Arellano Pajaritos 23 ⓣ762/622-0215. Good-value budget hotel with three sun terraces right by the market. The higher up you get, the cheaper the rooms, and there are usually discounts off-season. ❸

Emilia Castillo Juan Ruíz de Alarcón 7 ⓣ762/622-1396, ⓦwww.hotelemiliacastillo.com. Jolly, well-kept rooms with tiled floors at this lovely colonial hotel near the zócalo. ❹

Posada San Javier Estacadas 32 ⓣ762/622-3177, ⓔposadasanjavier@hotmail.com. Spacious hotel on a steep hill, with a pool and attractive gardens. Rooms are large and simply but tastefully decorated (and some have good views). Rooms with TV are slightly larger, but not worth the price difference. ❹

Santa Prisca Cena Obscuras 1 ⓣ762/622-0080 or 0980, ⓔhtl_staprisca@yahoo.com. Attractive converted colonial building just off the zócalo, with a pleasant flower-filled patio and a variety of rooms, some of which have their own terrace. ❹

The Town

The heart of town is the diminutive **Plaza Borda** (zócalo), ringed by recently restored colonial buildings and dominated by Taxco's one outstanding sight, the church of **Santa Prisca**. Towering over the zócalo, its hyper-elaborate facade was built in a single stint between 1751 and 1759, and displays a rare unity. Inside there's a riot of gilded churrigueresque altarpieces and other treasures, including paintings by Miguel Cabrera, a Zapotec who became one of Mexico's greatest colonial religious artists. His work can be seen in the medallions of the altarpieces; lunettes of the martyrdom of St Prisca and St Sebastian; a series of fifteen scenes from the life of the Virgin in the Episcopal Sacristy behind the altar; and a collection of paintings of prominent townspeople of the age (including Borda), in a side chapel to the left. The *manifestador*, a gilt construction immediately in front of the altar, was designed to display the Holy Sacrament and comes decorated with small statues of Faith, Hope and Charity. It was thought to have been lost until rediscovered in 1988 during renovations.

In the northeast corner of the zócalo, a doorway opens onto a courtyard packed with silver shops, which in turn provides the approach to the **Museo de la Platería**, Plaza Borda 1 (Tues–Sun 10am–6pm; M$10). Turn left and down the stairs to reach this small but worthwhile collection of silver, including beautiful Art Deco cutlery, a coffee jug and a gorgeous teapot from William Spratling's original workshop. The rest of what's on display spans the years since Spratling's time: everything from a walking stick in the form of a snake to modern designs incorporating amethysts found in geodes hereabouts. Almost next door, the **Centro Cultural de Taxco** (Tues–Fri 9am–4pm, Sat & Sun 10am–4pm; free) is really just a showcase for local artists and is worth a quick visit if only for the views over the town from many of the windows.

William Spratling's personal collection of antiquities is contained in the **Museo Guillermo Spratling**, Porfirio Delgado 1 (Tues–Sun 10am–7pm; M$31), right behind Santa Prisca and reached down Calle del Arco at the right-hand side of the church. There are several good pieces, but overall it is disappointing, especially if you've been to the Museo Nacional de Antropología in Mexico City (see p.419). Taxco's most interesting museum, the **Museo de Arte Virreinal**, Juan Ruíz de Alarcón 6 (Tues–Sat 10am–7pm, Sun 10am–4pm; M$20), is housed nearby in the beautiful colonial Casa Humboldt, an old staging inn named after an German explorer-baron who spent just one night here in 1803. Labels in Spanish and English provide detailed and diverting background on the town, its religious art and history, partly focusing on Taxco's importance on the Spanish trade routes between Acapulco and Veracruz. The life and works of José de la Borda and Humboldt both get extensive coverage too, and there's a good collection of ecclesiastical vestments and furniture, including a fine sacristy bench and a kind of waffle iron for making communion wafers.

Beyond these few sights, the way to enjoy Taxco is simply to wander the streets, nosing about in *platerías* and stopping occasionally for a drink. If you're in the market for **silver** you can be fairly sure that the stuff here is the real thing (check for the mark: ".925" or "sterling"), but prices are much the same as they would be anywhere and quality and workmanship can vary enormously: there's everything from mass-produced belt buckles and cheap rings to designer jewellery that will set you back thousands of dollars. The shops off the main streets will be cheaper and more open to bargaining. A section in the **market**, down the steps beside the zócalo, dedicated to silver-hawkers is a good place to start. But the bulk of the market seems to specialize in tacky tourist goods.

There is little of interest in the immediate vicinity, though to while away an afternoon you could follow Benito Juárez to Plazuela el Minero (a small square with a statue of a miner), then head left up Avenida de los Plateros to the northern end of town (around 2km – alternatively take a *combi* from the zócalo to Los Arcos), from where you can catch the **teleférico** (daily 7am–8pm; M$36 return) up to the hilltop *Hotel Monte Taxco* for the pleasant views.

Eating and drinking

Finding somewhere to **eat** in Taxco is no problem: there are several enticing places around the zócalo that are wonderful for watching the world go by. They do tend to be expensive, though, and by sacrificing a little atmosphere you'll do better along some of the streets that lead away from the centre. All except the cheapest of the hotels have their own dining rooms, and for rock-bottom prices, the

market has a section of food stalls, which are better than they look. In the evening everyone gathers around the zócalo to see and be seen, to stroll or to sit outdoors with a coffee or a drink at one of the bars.

El Adobe Plazuela de San Juan 13. Homely restaurant where excellent Mexican food is served for moderate prices either in the cosy interior or on a balcony overlooking the square. There's live music Fri & Sat from 8pm.

Bar Berta Plaza Borda 2. Traditional meeting place almost next to the church, and one of several places in Mexico claiming to be the original home of the margarita. Here it is a tequila and lime mixture known as a "Berta".

Café Sasha Juan Ruíz de Alarcón 1, opposite *Hotel Los Arcos*. Excellent upstairs café with no view to speak of, but an intimate atmosphere with comfy sofas, artesanía decor and even some English-language books for sale. Reliably good and modestly priced food, extending to pizzas, tortas, salads, falafel, garlic bread and daily specials (always including a vegetarian option). Local *músicos* turn up most evenings, making this a relaxed place to drink.

La Concha Nostra upstairs at Plazuela de San Juan 7. Primarily a bar with live rock on Sat, folk on Thurs & Fri (no cover), but also serving breakfasts, meals throughout the day, quesadillas, tacos, pasta and pizza at low prices.

Restaurant Bar Acerto Plaza Borda 4. Directly opposite Santa Prisca and with excellent views, especially if you can get one of the prized window seats. Formerly known as *Bar Paco*, it has been the place to come since 1937 and remains a nice spot for sipping a beer or dining on one of their fairly pricey but well-prepared meals.

West of Mexico City

The terrain west of Mexico City is varied: high and flat due west around the biggest city, **Toluca**, and broken only by the occasional soaring peak, then dropping away on all sides, particularly south of Toluca, where the country becomes ruggedly hilly as you descend. Dotted with small towns of some interest, it also gets progressively warmer and more verdant. The main artery through the region is Hwy-55, which is superseded in places by a modern autopista but still used by most of the buses to the small towns.

Grutas de Cacahuamilpa

Just 20km north of Taxco on the highway to Ixtapan de la Sal and Toluca, you pass close to the vast complex of caves known as the **Grutas de Cacahuamilpa** (open daily with ninety-minute guided tours 10am–5pm; M$60). This network of caverns, hollowed out by two rivers, extends for some 70km. The ninety-minute obligatory tour (in Spanish only) obviously takes in only a fraction of these, passing evocative rock formations, all illuminated to better illustrate their names: "the hunchback", "the bottle of champagne" and others. Among the graffiti you're shown a rather prim note from the wife of Maximilian: "María Carlota reached this point". Alongside, Lerdo de Tejada, who became president in 1872, five years after Maximilian's execution, has scrawled "Sebastian Lerdo de Tejada went further". There's a restaurant and several food stalls by the entrance.

Buses running between Taxco and Ixtapan de la Sal pass within 1km of the entrance: ask to be dropped off at the junction and walk down the hill for fifteen minutes. *Colectivos* to the caves also leave hourly from opposite the Estrella Blanca bus terminal in Taxco.

Festive Mexico

As if Mexico wasn't colourful and noisy enough on any given day, numerous dates throughout the year are dedicated especially to celebration. Everyone puts on their brightest new clothes, cranks up the music and floods the streets to commemorate a saint's day, a great moment in history or even the death of a loved one. Some festivities are regional – a village's annual fiesta, for instance – while others engage the entire nation in a wave of dancing, bright lights and *muchas cervezas*.

Carnaval parade, Morelos ▲

Semana Santa celebrations, El Muerte ▼

Tarahumara dancers, Semana Santa ▼

Religious events

The Catholic calendar provides countless opportunities for celebrating, with many of the biggest events observed with a combination of religious fervour and all-out partying. The **Día de la Virgen de Guadalupe** (Dec 12) is one such occasion. This blue-robed Virgin Mary, often considered a syncretic melding of the Catholic image and the indigenous Mexican goddess Tonantzin, is an icon of Mexico. It was on December 12 in 1531 that Aztec convert Juan Diego tipped open his cloak to reveal a cascade of miraculous winter-blooming roses and the image of the Virgin of Guadalupe imprinted on the fabric. The cloak, with the image still visible, is on display at the Basílica de Nuestra Señora de Guadalupe in Mexico City (see p.440). The most intense festivities take place here; nearly a million visitors attend, some approaching on foot or even on their knees. Similar processions can be seen during **Semana Santa**, or Holy Week (the week before Easter), when pilgrims converge on churches, and people re-enact the Passion of Christ. The most famous staging is in Iztapalapa, outside Mexico City, where the event involves a cast of thousands, buckets of fake blood and more than a million spectators.

Despite its religious affiliation, the week before Lent begins, known as **Carnaval**, is almost purely bacchanalian: expect glittery costumes, elaborate parades, beauty queens and dancing in the streets at these parties in early spring (usually mid- to late February or early March). They're celebrated most vigorously in the coastal cities, including Veracruz and San Miguel on Cozumel. The city of **Mazatlán** claims to have the world's third-largest Mardi Gras party, after New Orleans and Rio de Janeiro.

Cultural festivals

Not all Mexican festivals celebrate the past: the country also hosts some dazzling programmes of contemporary music, art and dance. The largest of these, Guanajuato's **Festival Internacional Cervantino** (see box, p.279), has been happening since the 1970s. Every October, it brings together Mexican marimba legends, French jazz artists, choral music from England and international dance troupes. Smaller but similarly wide-ranging events grace other cities: January's **Ortiz Tirado Music Festival** in Alamos, Sonora, draws leading classical musicians and singers, while every November Monterrey's **Festival Cultural Barrio Antiguo** showcases local rock bands and other eclectic musicians. Several performances are free, and tickets for headlining acts can be very reasonable.

▲ Dance company O Vertigo, Guanajuato festival

▼ Dressed for Independence Day

Independence Day

Party-loving tourists take note: Mexicans celebrate their **Día de la Independencia** on September 16 – not May 5. **Cinco de Mayo** is actually celebrated more enthusiastically in the US, where many *gringos* (who see the date as a chance to have a theme party involving sombreros, nachos and tequila), have come to believe that it's Mexico's equivalent of the US's July 4. In Mexico it's not a big deal. September 16, on the other hand, is a nationwide reason to take to the streets. Festivities begin at 11pm (midnight in the Yucatán) on September 15, when people gather in central plazas for the collective *Grito* – the gutsy cry of "Mexicanos, viva México!", first uttered by the priest Miguel Hidalgo in 1810 as he rallied his congregation to fight the Spanish. Fireworks, dancing and, yes, tequila-drinking carry on into the next day.

▼ Independence Day march, Puebla

Day of the Dead ▲

Dancers at a fiesta, Tabasco ▼

Day of the Dead skeleton ▼

Village fiestas

Even the tiniest village in Mexico has an **annual fiesta**, usually on the name day of the town's patron saint. Fiestas usually last at least a couple of days and often involve some blend of rodeos, bullfights, dancing, fried snacks, carnival rides, fireworks and processions around the church. They offer a great opportunity to see indigenous dances – such as the **Danza de los Viejitos** (Dance of the Little Old Men) in **Michoacán**, or the feather-bedecked **quetzales** in Cuetzalan, **Puebla**.

Día de los Muertos

If visitors know just one Mexican holiday, it's probably the **Day of the Dead**, when families honour and remember those who have died. Actually taking place over two days, November 1 and 2, it's an indigenous tradition unique to Mexico. With a few exceptions (such as the beautiful torch-lighting ceremony and festive dances around Lago de Pátzcuaro), it's usually a private rite. In every home and many businesses people set up *ofrendas* (altars) for the deceased: the centrepiece is always a photograph, lit by candles. In addition to the photo, the person's favourite foods are also placed on the altar, as a way of luring the soul back to this world. For the same reason, strong-scented, bright orange marigolds are often laid in a path leading to the altar, and resinous *copal* incense is lit. On the streets, market stalls brim with eggy, orange-scented *pan de muertos* and colourfully iced sugar skulls. Families usually gather to eat dinner on the night of November 1, then visit gravesites, which are also cleaned and decorated. Far from being a sad time, the Day of the Dead is an occasion for telling funny stories, bonding with family and generally celebrating life.

Ixtapan de la Sal

Continuing north on Hwy-55, the next possible stop is **IXTAPAN DE LA SAL**, not a very attractive town by Mexican standards but a long-established spa whose mineral-rich waters are supposed to cure a plethora of ills. Bathing in Ixtapan's pools is really the only reason to stop, and this can be done either among the slides and fairground-style rides at the **Spa Ixtapan**, at the very top of Juárez (pools Mon–Fri 8am–7pm, Sat & Sun 7am–7pm, M$160; aquatic park daily 9am–6pm, M$160, or M$100 weekdays after 2pm; spa daily 8am–8pm, treatments from M$140 upwards), or more cheaply in the centre of the old town at the **Balneario Municipal**, corner of Allende and 20 de Noviembre (daily 6am–6pm; M$50), which is little more than a geothermally heated swimming pool.

Practicalities

The **bus station** is 3km south of town on Hwy-55, connected to the centre by taxis (M$20), but most buses also stop and pick up at the top of Juárez, which is the town's main drag. The town gets pretty packed out at weekends, when it may be hard to find a room, but there are some very pleasant **hotels** to choose from, among them the friendly *Casa Sarita*, three blocks east and two north of the Balneario Municipal at Obregón 512 (Ⓣ721/143-2745; ④), with nicely decorated, carpeted rooms with TV; discounts are usually negotiable off-season. For more luxury, try the *Avenida*, Juárez 614, towards Spa Ixtapan (Ⓣ721/143-0241, Ⓔisraelalderetemarquez@prodigy.net.mx; ④), a three-star hotel with swimming pool whose rooms and suites all have cable TV, phone and FM radio, and they'll pick you up from the bus terminal for free. Ixtapan's most upmarket address is *Ixtapan Spa Hotel and Golf Resort*, next to the Spa Ixtapan (Ⓣ721/143-2440 or 1-800/498-2726, US & Canada 1-210/495-2477, Ⓦwww.spamexico.com; ⑨). With full-board accommodation only, and the cheapest double room at M$2190, it caters mainly to gringos who've come down to take the waters; facilities include two good restaurants, a piano lounge, a golf course and even a private cinema.

There are numerous **restaurants** along Juárez offering good-value comidas corridas, though if you're just here briefly you may be happy with the juice bar under the central bandstand and the torta shops nearby.

Tenancingo

TENANCINGO is 33km north of Ixtapan de la Sal and is the next village of any size along Hwy-55. The chief reason to be here is its proximity to the Aztec ruins at **Malinalco** (see p.506), which can be reached by regular **buses** (every 15min; 30min), most of which continue on to Chalma, and also on shared taxis. Liqueurs made from the fruits that grow in abundance on the plain surrounding the village and finely woven traditional *rebozos* (shawls) are sold here, many of them produced at the lovely monastery of **El Santo Desierto**. This is also a big flower-growing region and as you pass through you'll see whole fields devoted to one bloom – such as roses and chrysanthemums – and acres of land protected by plastic greenhouses.

Most **buses** stop around the corner of Victoria and Juárez, about five blocks south of the town's tiny zócalo (but Thursdays and Sundays on Madero, five blocks east of Victoria). You can usually change straight onto a bus for Malinalco, or take a shared taxi (from Victoria in front of the market, but Thursdays and Sundays from Iturbide 104 between Guerrero and Madero). If you get stuck there is acceptable

accommodation at *Hotel Lazo*, Victoria 100 (☎714/142-0083; ❷), where rooms are a plain and functional, but always have hot water. Several small cafés nearby serve Mexican staples cheaply.

Malinalco and around

The village of **Malinalco**, 20km east of Tenancingo, is a lovely little place nestled in a fertile, alluvial valley at 1800m and surrounded by rich villas – many of them, complete with swimming pools, the weekend homes of the capital's privileged few. The fact that it is noticeably warmer than most of the towns hereabouts makes it a popular retreat in winter. It centres on the huge Augustinian church of **Santa Mónica** and has a vibrant Wednesday morning **market**, but the real reason to come here is to see the exemplary **Aztec ruins**.

The site

The Aztec **site of Malinalco** (Tues–Sun 9am–5pm; M$41) sits high on a hill to the west of town (follow Guerrero west from the zócalo) and can be reached after a twenty- to thirty-minute walk up a very steep, stepped path. Having only been started in 1501, it was still incomplete at the time of the Conquest but it is undeniably one of the most evocative sites of its kind, carved in part from the raw rock hillside of the Cerro de los Idolos. Looking back over the village and valley, the ruins may be small, but they are undeniably impressive, the main structures and the stairways up to them partly cut out of the rock, partly constructed from great stone blocks. The most remarkable aspect is the circular inner sanctuary of the main temple or **Cuauhcalli** (House of the Eagle), hewn entirely from the face of the mountain. You approach up a broad staircase on either side of which sit stone jaguars – in the centre an all but worn-away human statue would have held a flag. This was the setting for the sacred **initiation ceremonies** in which Aztec youths became members of the warrior elite, and there are images of warriors throughout: to one side of the entrance, a broken eagle warrior sits atop Quetzalcoatl, the feathered serpent; guarding the other side are the remains of a jaguar warrior, representative of the second Aztec warrior class. The doorway of the sanctuary itself, cut through a natural rock wall, represents the giant mouth of a serpent – the entrance was over its tongue, and around it traces of teeth are still visible. Right in the centre of the floor lies the figure of an eagle, and on the raised horseshoe-shaped bench behind are two more eagles and the pelt of an ocelot, all carved in a single piece from the bedrock. Behind the first eagle is a hole in the ground where the hearts of human sacrificial victims would be placed, supposedly to be eaten while still beating as the final part of the initiation into warriorhood.

Other structures at the site include a small circular platform by the entrance, unfinished at the time of the Conquest, and a low pyramid directly in front of the main temple. Beyond this lie two larger temples. The first, Edificio III, again has a circular chamber at the centre, and it is believed that here Aztec warriors killed in battle were cremated, their souls rising to the heavens to become stars. Edificio IV was originally a temple of the sun; much of it was used to construct the church in the village. Below the pyramids, visible from about halfway up the steps to the ruins, you can see another prehistoric building nestling among the mountains. It's still used by local residents as a place of pilgrimage each September 29: formerly a shrine to an Aztec altar-goddess, it is now dedicated to San Miguel.

On the way to the site, you pass the **Museo Universitario Schneider** (Tues–Sun 10am–5.30pm; M$10), a well-laid-out little museum of archeological finds from the area, many donated by local residents who unearthed them while gardening or working on their homes. There's also a suit of conquistador armour, and a reconstruction of the shrine of Cuauhcalli from the site.

Practicalities

The easiest way to reach Malinalco is by **bus** or shared taxi from Tenancingo. Most buses arrive in the central plaza in front of the church of Santa Mónica, but those through to Chalma sometimes hurtle straight down Morelos, which bypasses the centre: ask to be dropped at the end of Hidalgo, which runs 200m to the zócalo. From Mexico City (Terminal Poniente), there are only three direct daily buses to Malinalco (2hr 30min), but departures every twenty minutes for Chalma, from where there are frequent local services. Malinalco has a virtually useless **tourist office** in the town hall at the uphill end of the main plaza (Mon–Sat 9am–5pm; Ⓣ714/147-0111). There are **ATMs** by the town hall and just off the zócalo at Hidalgo 101 (with an internet office next door).

Of the several **places to stay** in town, *Hotel Marmil*, Progreso 67 (Ⓣ714/147-0916, Ⓕ147-0344; ❸), with well-kept country-style rooms, off-street parking, ceiling fans, a pool and cable TV, is ten minutes' walk uphill from the zócalo (if coming by bus from Tenancingo, ask to be dropped near the hotel), and is almost always full at weekends. *Hotel Santa Mónica*, Hidalgo 109 (Ⓣ714/147-0031, Ⓔmali_gro@hotmail.com; ❸), near the plaza on the way to the site, is slightly less well-equipped, though its rooms are pleasantly homely and en suite, around a nice little garden. The best place to stay in town is the super-chic *Casa Limón*, 1km south of the zócalo at Rio Lerma 103 (Ⓣ714/147-0256, Ⓦwww.casalimon.com; ❾), a boutique hotel with elegant stone decor, modern, spacious rooms, a bar, restaurant and pool; very classy, but not worth six times the price of the *Marmil* or *Santa Mónica*, which is what it will cost you.

Come in the middle of the week and you'll find some of the **restaurants** closed, but at weekends there are at least half a dozen places catering to the weekly influx from the capital and Cuernavaca. Everything is close by so you can walk around and take your pick. *Ehecatl*, a block east of the main square on Hidalgo, has good food at low prices. West of the square at Hidalgo 104, by the bridge over the river, *El Puente* has pasta, salads, *antojitos*, plus meat, fish and vegetarian main courses. On the square itself, the best bar-resaurant is *Los Placeres*, which serves excellent food, including vegetarian dishes, lots of salads and delicious breakfasts, and has a great ambience, but it's open only on Fridays, Saturdays and Sundays. One thing that's really good to eat in Malinalco is trout, fresh from a local trout farm, which is widely available in local restaurants.

Around Malinalco: Chalma and Ahuehuete

Nestled among impressive craggy peaks 7km east of Malinalco, **Chalma** is an important place of pilgrimage, although the town itself is a complete dump. Its filthy, muddy streets are lined with stalls offering tacky souvenirs to the pilgrims who converge here every Sunday and at times of special religious significance (especially the first Fri in Lent, Semana Santa and Sept 29), camping out for miles around: so many people come, in fact, that it's impossible to get anywhere near the church. The pilgrims flock here to take part in rituals that are a fascinating blend of Christian and more ancient pagan rites. Originally, the deity Oztocteotl, god of caves, was venerated here in a natural cave. When the first missionaries arrived, he was "miraculously" replaced by a statue of Christ, which was moved in the seventeenth century to a new church, the **Santuario de Chalma**. It is this church that is now the focus of pilgrimage and the site of miraculous appearances by a Christ-like figure. As well as paying their devotions to Christ, the pilgrims bathe in the healing waters that flow from the original cave.

Colectivos leave Malinalco's zócalo every few minutes for Chalma, from where you can continue direct to Mexico City (Terminal Poniente) passing nearby **AHUEHUETE** on the way. There's another heavily visited shrine here, at a spot where a miraculous spring issues from the roots of a huge old tree. Many people stop here before visiting Chalma, and proceed the last few kilometres to that town on foot.

Tenango del Valle and Metepec

Half an hour north of Tenancingo you come to **TENANGO DEL VALLE**, from where you can visit the excavated remains of the large fortified Malatzinca township of **Teotenango** (Tues–Sun 9am–5pm; M$45) nearby. It is a fifteen-minute walk to the entrance, then a steep ten-minute hike up to the site: to get there from the centre of the village, head north along Porfirio Díaz Norte, then take a left up Roman Piña Chan Norte. There's a small museum on site.

Some 25km further north you pass **METEPEC**, famed as a **pottery**-making centre. Brightly coloured wares can be found at craft shops throughout the country; supposedly, the figures that characterize these pots were originally inspired by the saints on the facade of Metepec's sixteenth-century monastery, and in the twentieth century Diego Rivera taught the villagers new techniques of colouring and design. There's a market here on Mondays. From Metepec it is less than 10km on to Toluca (see below).

Toluca and around

The capital of the state of México, **TOLUCA DE LERDO** is today a large and modern industrial centre, sprawling across a wide plain. At an altitude of nearly 2700m, it is the highest city in the country, and comes surrounded by beautiful mountain scenery, dominated by the white-capped **Nevado de Toluca**. It is not a place you'll want to linger, but it is the site of what is allegedly the largest single **market** in the country. Held a couple of kilometres southeast of the centre, just east of the bus station, every Friday (and to a lesser extent throughout the week), the market constitutes the overriding reason to visit. Many visitors stop over on a Thursday night (book accommodation in advance) and then move on, or make an early start from Mexico City on Friday morning.

The market attracts hordes of visitors from the capital, but is so vast that there can be no question of its being overwhelmed by tourists; quite the opposite, many outsiders find themselves overwhelmed by the scale of the place, lost among the thousands of stalls and crowds from the state's outlying villages. Though increasingly dominated by cheap imported goods and clothing, there is still a substantial selection of **local crafts** – woven goods and pottery above all. For an idea of what quality and prices to expect, head first for the Casa de Artesanías, Paseo Tollocan 700 Ote, a few blocks east of the market and very near the bus terminal.

Arrival and orientation

An almost uninterrupted stream of **buses** leaves Mexico City's Terminal Poniente for Toluca throughout the day; the journey takes a little over an hour. Toluca's modern bus station is right by the market and a local bus will take you the last 3km into the centre. *De paso* services from Mexico City to Zitácuaro and Valle de Bravo usually stop on the bypass 500m south of the bus station. To return to the bus station, pick up a *combi* labelled "Terminal" on Sor Juana Inés de la Cruz (a block east of Rayón). The **airport**, further out on Hwy-15, is connected to town by taxi (M$70) and local bus (picked up in town on Santos Degollado).

Unusually for Mexico, the heart of the city is formed not by an open plaza but by a central block surrounded on three sides by the nation's longest series of arcades, built in the 1830s and known as *portales*, lined with shops, restaurants and cafés: **Portal Madero** is to the south along Hidalgo; **Portal 20 de Noviembre** is to the east along Allende; and **Portal Reforma** is to the west along Bravo. The fourth side is taken up by the nineteenth-century **cathedral** and, to its east, the mustard-yellow church of **Santa Cruz**.

Accommodation

In general, Toluca's **hotels** are poor value for your money, with a number of fairly grotty places clustered around the market. But even these fill up by Thursday nights, when **finding a room** can be difficult.

Colonial Hidalgo 103 Ote ⓣ722/215-9700, ⓕ214-7066. One of the better city-centre options, quirky and eccentric with parquet floors and an old-fashioned feel. All rooms have cable TV and 24hr hot water, but you're not allowed to bring in drinks. ❹

Rex Matamoros 101, opposite Portal Madero ⓣ722/215-9300, ⓔhotelrex@prodigy.net.mx. Clean and relatively low-priced, with simple but well-maintained rooms, all with bathroom and TV. ❸

San Carlos Portal Madero 210 ⓣ722/214-4343, ⓦwww.hotelsancarlostoluca.com. Best value in the city centre: very central, with friendly staff and large, comfortable, carpeted rooms. A king-size bed costs no more than an ordinary double bed, so it's worth asking for one. ❹

San Francisco Rayón 104 Sur ⓣ722/213-4415. Business-style hotel with an atrium lobby whose canned music makes it feel rather tacky. The rooms are fine enough, and there's a pool, bar and restaurant. ❻

Terminal Felipe Berriázabal 101 ⓣ722/217-4588. Right by the bus station, with direct access from the terminal, and as functional as you'd expect a bus terminal hotel to be, but it's clean and decent, the rooms are large and have a bathroom, 24hr hot water and TV, and those on the fifth floor upwards are carpeted (with slightly higher rates). ❷

The Town

Most of the central sights are clustered north of the *portales* and the cathedral, close to the massive open **Plaza de los Mártires**, which is dominated on the north side by the Palacio del Gobierno. To the east is the **Plaza Garibay**, rather prettier with shrubbery and fountains stretching down to the **Jardín Botánico Cosmovitral** (Tues–Sun 10am–6pm; M$10), Toluca's botanical gardens. Housed in an enormous, hundred-metre-long Art Nouveau greenhouse the garden structure was built in 1909 and served as the main market until 1975. With predominantly semi-tropical displays, small pools and even a well-tended Japanese corner, it is attractive, but the highlight is undoubtedly the amazing Mexican-muralist-style stained-glass panels by local artist Leopoldo Flores. Come early or late to catch the low sun giving a coloured cast to the plants. The northwestern corner of Plaza Garibay is occupied by the **Museo de Bellas Artes**, on Santos Degollado (Tues–Sat 10am–6pm, Sun 10am–3pm; M$10, free Wed & Sun), which typically shows off some of the best fine arts in the state.

Back on Plaza de los Mártires, the **Museo José Maria Velasco** (Tues–Sat 10am–6pm, Sun 10am–3pm; M$10, free Wed & Sun) occupies two floors of a colonial house and displays a good collection of nineteenth-century paintings, much of it by Velasco, who was born in the state of México in 1840, though he spent much of his life in Mexico City. There's a recreation of his studio, along with busts, portraits and some delightful landscapes, including a delicate rendering of the volcanoes and the Valley of México. Several rooms host temporary exhibits, often featuring work by his contemporaries from the San Carlos academy in the capital.

The state of México makes a point of honouring its artistic sons, and adjoining the Velasco museum (entrance round the corner on Nicolás Bravo) are two more museums dedicated to local painters. The **Museo Felipe Santiago Gutiérrez**, Nicolás Bravo 9 (Tues–Sat 10am–6pm, Sun 10am–3pm; M$10, free Wed & Sun), fills a colonial mansion with sketches, oils and portraits of prominent nineteenth-century Mexicans; but there is more interest next door at the **Museo Taller Nishizawa** (Tues–Sat 10am–6pm, Sun 10am–3pm; M$10, free Wed & Sun), where large abstract landscape canvases by Mexican-Japanese Luis Nishizawa take pride of place alongside pen-and-ink drawings and some of his more recent portraiture.

Centro Cultural Mexiquense

Some 8km west of Toluca, the **Centro Cultural Mexiquense** harbours several museums (all Tues–Sat 10am–6pm, Sun 10am–3pm; M$10, free Wed & Sun) scattered in park-like grounds. Among them are the **Museo Regional**, devoted to the archeology and history of the state, a small **Museo de Arte Moderno** and, perhaps the most interesting, the **Museo de Artes Populares**, a collection of local crafts, ancient and modern, in a restored hacienda. Although local buses run out there (look for "Centro Cultural Las Palomas" along Lerdo), you really need your own transport to explore the place fully.

Calixtlahuaca and Nevada de Toluca

While in Toluca put a couple of hours aside to visit the archeological site of **Calixtlahuaca** (daily 10am–5pm; M$37). This was the township of the Matlazinca people, inhabited from prehistoric times and later subjugated by the Aztecs, who established a garrison here in the fifteenth century. Calixtlahuaca was not a willing subject, and there were constant rebellions; after one, in 1475, the Aztecs allegedly sacrificed over 11,000 Matlazinca prisoners on the **Temple of Quetzalcoatl**. This, several times built over, is the most important structure on the site. Dedicated to the god in his role as Ehecatl, god of wind, its circular design is typical, allowing the breezes to blow freely around the shrine. See also the remains of the pyramid devoted to Tlaloc, and the nearby *tzompantli* (skull wall), both constructed of the local pink and black volcanic stone. Bring something to light your way in the short dark tunnels which reveal evidence of earlier constructions; and don't worry too much about the opening hours since the site is not fenced. A small **museum** is sporadically open.

The site is on a hillside just outside the village of Calixtlahuaca, easily reached by **taxi** (roughly M$50–60) or by a circuitous local **bus** which takes half an hour from the stop on Santos Degollado, one block north of the main square at its junction with Nicolás Bravo.

If you've got your own vehicle – and a sturdy one at that – one trip you should make is to the crater of the extinct **Nevado de Toluca** (Xinantécatl; 4690m), which rises high enough above the surrounding plain for it to rank as Mexico's fourth highest peak. A rough dirt road – impractical during the rainy season or midwinter – leads all the way to the crater rim, from where there are numerous trails leading down to the sandy crater floor and two small lakes, the **Lagos del Sol** and **de la Luna**, right in its heart. From its jagged lip the views are breathtaking: below you the lakes; eastwards a fabulous vista across the valleys of Toluca and

México; and to the west a series of lower, greener hills ranging towards the peaks of the Sierra Madre Occidental. If you do hike down into the crater, remember to take it easy in this thin, high-altitude air.

Eating and drinking

As usual, the markets and outlying areas are the places to go for budget **food**, while around the *portales* there are some good, pricier choices.

Café Hidalgo Hidalgo 233 at Nicolás Bravo, opposite the southwest corner of the *portales*. Coffee or breakfast in pleasantly old-fashioned surroundings.

Hostería de las Ramblas Portal 20 de Noviembre 107, on the east side of the *portales*. Serves an excellent range of *antojitos* at M$45–60, main courses at M$75–135, and breakfasts at M$50–80.

Las Ramblitas Portal Reforma 108, on the west side of the *portales*. Tasty and very reasonable set breakfasts (M$38–57), as well as pozole, enchiladas, *mole poblano* and a M$50 lunch-time menu.

La Vaquita Negra del Portal Portal Reforma 124, at the northeast corner of the *portales*. An excellent deli and *tortería*, selling cheeses and cold cuts by weight or in tortas, which you can eat seated at the counter with big plates of chile pickles to spice them up.

Valle de Bravo

West from Toluca, the road towards Morelia and the state of Michoacán is truly spectacular. Much of this wooded, mountainous area – as far as Zitácuaro – is given over to villas inhabited at weekends by wealthy refugees from the capital, and nowhere more so than the small colonial town of **VALLE DE BRAVO**, reached by turning off to the left about halfway. Set in a deep, pine-clad valley surrounded by low mountains, the town sits on the eastern shore of an artificial lake, **Lago Avandaro**. With terracotta-tiled roofs, iron balconies affixed to many of the older buildings and a mass of whitewashed houses all huddled together, it is an immediately appealing place, something that has drawn a coterie of artistic refugees from the big city. They mostly keep to themselves, leaving the water's edge for weekenders who descend for upmarket relaxation: boat trips, sailing, swimming, water-skiing, riding, paragliding, hiking and golf. If you indulge, it can be an expensive place, but the town itself isn't that pricey and it does make for a very relaxing break provided you come during the week, when fewer people are about and some of the hotels drop their prices.

The zócalo, ringed with restaurants and centred on a twin-towered church, sits on a rise a fifteen-minute walk from the waterfront, where there's a small tourist information kiosk (Mon–Fri 10am–8pm, Sat 10am–9pm, Sun 10am–6pm), and a wharf (*embarcadero*) from which you can take boat rides: either rent one from M$400–500 an hour, or join a *lancha colectiva* for M$40 an hour. The main tourist office is in town at the Auditorio Municipal on Porfirio Díaz (off Juárez between 16 de Septiembre and Independencia).

Practicalities

From Toluca (2hr) and Mexico City's Terminal Poniente (3hr), there are second-class **buses** to Valle del Bravo every twenty minutes. To travel to or from Morelia or Zitácuaro, you'll have to change at a junction called "Monumento", which has buses to Valle once an hour, but don't leave it too late as buses won't stop there after dark. Buses make a long circuit around town before depositing you at the **bus station** on 16 de Septiembre (no guardería). Head downhill and take a right at the end (Juárez) to get to the centre.

Fiestas

January

Día de los Santos Reyes (Twelfth Night; Jan 6). The Magi traditionally leave presents for children on this date: many small ceremonies include a fiesta with dancing at Nativitas, a suburb near Xochimilco, and at Malinalco (see p.506).

Bendicíon de los Animales (Jan 17). Children's pets and peasants' farm animals are taken to church to be blessed – a particularly bizarre sight at the cathedral in México and in Taxco (see p.500), where it coincides with the fiestas of Santa Prisca (Jan 18) and San Sebastián (Jan 20).

February

Día de la Candelaria (Feb 2). Widely celebrated, especially in Cuernavaca (see p.490).

Carnaval (the week before Lent, variable Feb–March). Especially lively in Cuernavaca (see p.490) and nearby Tepoztlán; also in Chiconcuac on the way to Teotihuacán.

March

Palm Sunday (the Sun before Easter Sun). A procession with palms in Taxco (see p.500), where representations of the Passion continue through Holy Week.

Semana Santa (Holy Week). Observed everywhere. There are very famous Passion plays in the suburb of Itzapalapa, culminating on the Friday with a mock Crucifixion on the Cerro de la Estrella, and similar celebrations at Chalma and nearby Malinalco (see p.506). In Cholula (see p.487), with its host of churches, the processions pass over vast carpets of flowers.

April

Feria de la Flor (early April). Cuernavaca's (see p.490) flower festival.

May

May Day (May 1). In Cuautla marked by a fiesta commemorating an Independence battle.

Día de la Santa Cruz (May 3). Celebrated with fiestas and traditional dancing, in Xochimilco (see p.438), Tepotzotlán (see p.470) and Valle de Bravo (see p.511).

Cinco de Mayo (May 5). Public holiday for the Battle of Puebla – celebrated in Puebla (see p.481) itself with a grand procession and re-enactment of the fighting.

Día de San Isidro (May 15). Religious processions and fireworks in Tenancingo (see p.505), and a procession of farm animals through Cuernavaca (see p.490) on their way to be blessed at the church.

Religious festival in Tlaxcala (see p.478; third Mon in May). An image of the Virgin is processed around the town followed by hundreds of pilgrims.

June

Día de San Pedro (June 29). Observed with processions and dances in Tepotzotlán (see p.470) and traditional dancing in San Pedro Actopan, on the southern outskirts of Mexico City.

The best of the more reasonably priced **places to stay** is the AP *Posada Familiar 16 de Septiembre*, 16 de Septiembre 417 (Ⓣ726/262-1222; ❸), which is 100m downhill from the bus station, and has nice, fresh rooms (with TV and bathroom) and a real family atmosphere; slightly upmarket, the *Posada Casa Vieja*, Juárez 101 (Ⓣ726/262-0318, Ⓔposadacasavieja@yahoo.com.mx; ❹), has a variety of rooms, some bigger than others (so it may be worth checking a few), plus ample hot water, and a sunny veranda. Alternatives include *Posada Los Girasoles*, Plaza Independencia 1

July

Día de la Virgen del Carmen (July 16). Dances and a procession with flowers to the convent of Carmen, in San Ángel (see p.427).

Día de Santiago (July 25). Particularly celebrated in Chalco, near Amecameca. The following Sunday sees a market and regional dances at the Plaza de las Tres Culturas (see p.439) and dances, too, in Xochimilco (see p.438).

Día de Santa Marta (July 29). In Milpa Alta, near Xochimilco, celebrated with Aztec dances and mock fights between Moors and Christians.

August

Día de la Asunción (Assumption; Aug 15). Honoured with pilgrimages from Cholula (see p.487) to a nearby village, and ancient dances in Milpa Alta.

September

Independence Day (Sept 15–16). Celebrated everywhere.

Día de San Miguel (Sept 29). Provokes huge pilgrimages to both Taxco (see p.500) and Chalma.

October

Día de San Francisco (Oct 4). A *feria* in Tenancingo (see p.505), with much traditional music-making, and also celebrated in San Francisco Tecoxpa, a village on the southern fringes of the capital.

Fiesta del Santuario de la Defensa (Oct 12). A street party that centres around an ancient church just outside Tlaxcala (see p.478).

November

Día de los Muertos (Day of the Dead; Nov 1–2). Observed everywhere. The shops are full of chocolate skulls and other ghoulish foods. Tradition is particularly strong in San Lucas Xochimanca and Nativitas, both to the south of Mexico City.

Día de Santa Cecilia (Nov 22). St Cecilia is the patron saint of musicians, and her fiesta attracts orchestras and mariachi bands from all over to Santa Cecilia Tepetlapa, not far from Xochimilco.

December

Feria de la Plata (Dec 1). The great silver fair in Taxco (p.500) lasts about ten days from this date.

Día de la Señora de Guadalupe (Dec 12). A massive pilgrimage to the Basilica of Guadalupe (see p.440) runs for several days round about, combined with a constant secular celebration of music and dancing.

Christmas (Dec 25). In the week leading up to Christmas, Nativity plays – also known as *posadas* – can be seen in many places. Among the most famous are those at Taxco (see p.500) and Tepotzotlán (see p.470).

(Ⓣ726/262-2967; ④), right on the main square, clean and cool with firm beds and rooms that are spacious but a bit dark.

Valle de Bravo has a reasonable range of **restaurants**, though not many at the top end of the scale. Some of the cheapest eating is in and around the market, at the end of Juárez on Hidalgo. Another place for good cheap eats is Calle 16 de Septiembre, where the *Cocina Económica* at no. 404 has breafasts and comidas corridas for M$30. The best upmarket choice is *El Portal*, on the zócalo at Plaza

Independencia 101, where you can get salads, pizzas or *antojitos*, followed by steak or chicken, or trout or octopus, at M$63–85 for a main dish. If you like trout (farmed, not from the lake), the tiny *Lonchería Truchas la Estrella* down by the *embarcadero* has trout cooked however you like it (M$70), or their own trout *ceviche* or smoked trout paté.

Travel details

Buses

Cholula to: Mexico City (every 30–60min; 2hr 30min); Puebla (buses every 10–15min; 20min; plus frequent *colectivos*).

Cuautla to: Cuernavaca (Estrella Roja terminal, every 20min; 1hr 20min); Mexico City Autobuses del Sur (Volcanes terminal, every 10min; 2hr); Mexico City TAPO (Volcanes terminal, every 10min; 3hr); Tepoztlán (Volcanes and Estrella Roja terminal, every 10min; 40min).

Cuernavaca to: Acapulco (Estrella de Oro terminal, 11 daily; Estrella Blanca terminal, 5 daily; 5hr); Cuautla (Estrella Roja terminal and market terminal, every 20min; 1hr 20min); Ixtapan de la Sal (Estrella Blanca terminal, hourly; 2hr 3min); Mexico City (Pullman de Morelos terminal, every 15min; 1hr 15min); Mexico City airport (Casino terminal, every 45min; 1hr 30min); Puebla (Estrella Roja terminal, hourly; 3hr 30min); Taxco (Estrella Blanca terminal, 14 daily; 1hr 40min); Tepoztlán (market terminal, every 15min; 45min); Toluca (Estrella Blanca terminal, every 30min; 2hr 30min).

Ixtapan de la Sal to: Cuernavaca (6 daily; 3hr); Mexico City (indirect every 15min; 3hr; direct hourly; 2hr); Taxco (every 40min; 1hr 20min); Tenancingo (every 15min; 45min); Toluca (every 20min; 1hr).

Pachuca to: Mexico City (every 8min; 1hr 15min); Mexico City airport (15 daily; 1hr 40min); Puebla (16 daily; 2hr); Real del Monte (frequent *colectivos*; 20min); Tlaxcala (hourly; 3hr); Tula (every 15min; 1hr 30min).

Puebla to: Cholula (buses every 10–15min; 20min; plus frequent *colectivos*); Cuernavaca (hourly; 3hr 30min); Mexico City TAPO (12–13 hourly; 2hr); Mexico City Terminal del Norte (hourly; 2hr); Mexico City airport (hourly; 2hr 15min); Oaxaca (11 daily; 4hr 30min); Pachuca (16 daily; 2hr); Tlaxcala (every 10min; 40min; plus frequent micros); Veracruz (28 daily; 4hr 30min).

Taxco to: Acapulco (13 daily; 5hr); Chilpancingo (11 daily; 3hr); Cuernavaca (hourly; 1hr 40min); Ixtapan (every 40min; 1hr 20min); Mexico City (hourly; 2hr 15min); Toluca (every 40min; 3hr 30min).

Tenancingo to: Ixtapan de la Sal (every 15min; 45min); Malinalco (every 15min; 30min; plus shared taxis); Toluca (every 10min; 1hr).

Tlaxcala to: Mexico City (every 20min; 1hr 40min); Pachuca (hourly; 3hr); Puebla (every 8min; 40min; plus frequent micros).

Toluca to: Cuernavaca (every 30min; 2hr 30min); Ixtapan (every 20min; 1hr); Mexico City (every 5min; 1hr 30min); Morelia (every 40min; 4hr); Querétaro (hourly; 3hr 30min); Taxco (every 40min; 3hr); Tenancingo (every 10min; 1hr); Tenango del Valle (every 10min; 30min); Valle de Bravo (every 20min; 2hr).

Tula to: Mexico City (every 30–60min; 1hr 30min); Pachuca (every 15min; 1hr 30min); Querétaro (9 daily; 2hr 30min); Tepotzotlán (Caseta de) (every 20min; 1hr).

Flights

Puebla to: Cancún (2 daily; 2hr); Guadalajara (3 daily; 1hr 10min); Hermosillo (1 daily; 2hr 30min); Monterrey (6 daily; 2hr); Tijuana (2 daily; 3hr 30min).

Toluca to: Acapulco (2–3 daily; 50min); Cancún (6 daily; 2hr); Chihuahua (4 daily; 2hr); Culiacán (5–6 daily; 1hr); Guadalajara (6–7 daily; 1hr); Hermosillo (1 daily; 40min); Ixtapa/Zihuatanejo (4 weekly; 50min); Los Cabos (1 daily; 1hr 55min); Mérida (2 daily; 1hr 55min); Monterrey (8 daily; 1hr 25min).

8

Acapulco and the Pacific beaches

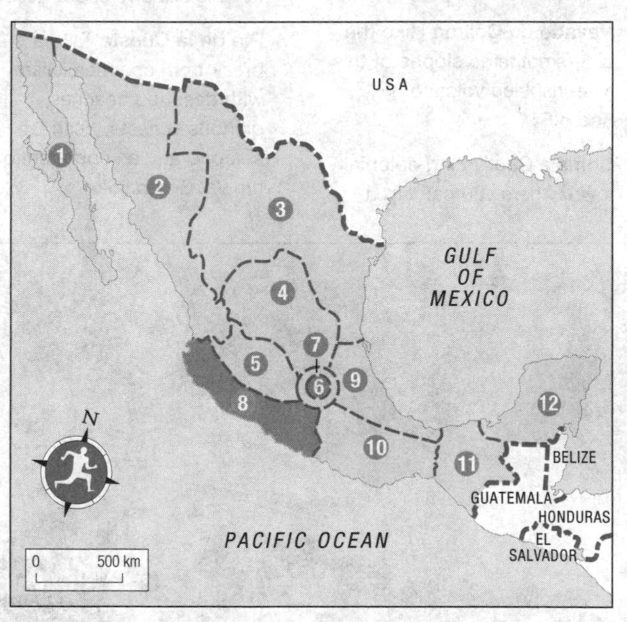

CHAPTER 8 Highlights

* **Puerto Vallarta** Luxury resorts, stylish B&Bs and a languid colonial centre make this an ideal base from which to explore the beaches of the Bahía de Banderas, and to watch humpback whales frolic off-shore from December to April. See p.518

* **Costa Alegre** A tantalizing stretch of coastline punctuated by small, low-key resorts. See p.531

* **Nevado de Colima** Hike the pine-smothered slopes of this awe-inspiring volcano. See p.544

* **Comala** Captivating colonial town, where you can sip a beer and feast on free snacks while mariachis compete for your attention in the plaza. See p.545

* **Barra de Potosí** An untouched beach where you can eat fresh fish and row through a mangrove lagoon. See p.552

* **Acapulco** The king of Mexican resorts is an exhilarating, brash city with romantic dining, serious partying and death-defying cliff divers. See p.553

* **Pie de la Cuesta** Take a break from commercialism with deserted beaches, glorious sunsets, fresh seafood and an unpretentious crowd. See p.562

▲ Acapulco

8

Acapulco and the Pacific beaches

The 800-kilometre stretch of coast between Puerto Vallarta and Punta Maldonado, where the Sierra Madre reaches out to the ocean, is lined with some of Mexico's most popular resorts. Acapulco – the original, the biggest, and for many, the best – is a steep-sided, tightly curving bay that, for all its excesses of high-rise development, remains breathtakingly beautiful, from a distance at least. This is the stomping ground of the wealthy, whose villas, high around the wooded sides of the bay, offer isolation from the packaged enclaves below. It's pricey, but not ridiculously so, and while tourists swarm the congested beaches the city retains a local feel, with the coarse characteristics of a working port.

Puerto Vallarta, second in size and reputation, feels altogether more manageable, with cobbled streets fanning out from a colonial plaza overlooking an oceanfront boulevard. Still, with its party ambience and unbridled commercialism, it is far removed from the tropical village it claims to be: spreading for miles along a series of tiny, rugged beaches, it's certainly a resort. However, if you travel far enough from the downtown beaches you can still find cove after isolated cove backed by forested mountains. For a less commercial experience, **Barra de Navidad**, two hours south of here, is a glorious sweep of sand, surrounded by flatlands and lagoons, with a low-key village at either end. By contrast, **Manzanillo** is first and foremost a port and naval base – despite its lively seaside boardwalk and sail-fishing tournaments its pitch for tourism seems something of an afterthought. **Zihuatanejo** is an attractive, gentle resort where magnificent villas have popped up on the slopes overlooking inviting swathes of sand studded with palms. Its purpose-built neighbour **Ixtapa**, the Pacific coast's answer to Cancún, is far less enchanting, with sterile high-rise developments, shopping malls and an international feel. All along this coast, between the major centres, you'll find **beaches**, some completely undeveloped, others linked to a village with a few rooms to rent and a makeshift bar on the sand.

Most people arrive on the fast – and expensive – **Autopista del Sol** from Mexico City to Acapulco, but the **coast road** is perfectly feasible all the way from the US border to Guatemala. Between Puerto Vallarta and Acapulco, it's a good modern highway, unrelentingly spectacular as it forces its way south, sometimes over the narrow coastal plain, more often clinging precariously to the fringes of the sierra where it falls away into the ocean.

The region is easily traversed by **bus** and all the major resorts have well-connected **airports** with direct flights from Mexico City and the US. Remember that if you've come south from Tepic, San Blas, Mazatlán or points north along the coast, you need to advance your watch an hour: the **time zone** changes at the Jalisco state border, just north of Puerto Vallarta's airport. **Prices** in the resorts, particularly for accommodation, are dictated largely by **season**. High season at the bigger destinations stretches from early or mid-December to after Easter or the end of April, during which time the swankier hotels can charge as much as double the off-season rates and need to be booked in advance; in many resorts a surge in domestic tourism means that prices also rise again in July and August.

Puerto Vallarta and around

Thanks to its mesmerizing sunsets, wide, sandy beaches and a laid-back, colonial centre, **PUERTO VALLARTA** is a small city that depends almost entirely on tourism; it attracts a mixed bag of West Coast Americans, Mexican families (particularly residents of Guadalajara), Spring Breakers, North American retirees and gay visitors taking advantage of its emergence as one of the **gay** centres of Mexico. If you're looking for traditional Mexico you might find this wholly unappealing, but while it's true that PV (as it's known) can be more expensive and certainly more touristy than the average Mexican town, it can also be lots of fun. It is smaller and more relaxed than Cancún and Acapulco, and its location, surrounded by lofty mountains, is spectacular. Behind the beaches there's a vibrant Mexican city, largely undisturbed by the flow of visitors, which means that the choice of tasty, cheap **street food** – especially tacos – is some of the best on the coast, and, contrary to what you might expect, PV is liberally peppered with mid-range hotels, especially during the low season (Aug–Nov).

Puerto Vallarta lies in the middle of the 22-kilometre-wide **Bahía de Banderas**, fringed by endless stretches of sand and backed by the jungle-covered slopes of the Sierra Madre. The town was officially founded in the 1850s (when it was known as Las Peñas – it was renamed in 1918), but there had been a small fishing and smuggling village located where the Río Cuale spills out into the bay for years. Initially developed by the Union en Cuale mining company, it remained a sleepy place until the 1950s, when Mexican airlines started promoting the town as a resort. Their efforts received a shot in the arm in 1963, when John Huston chose Mismaloya, 10km south, as the setting for his film of Tennessee Williams's play *The Night of the Iguana*, starring Richard Burton. The scandal-mongering that surrounded Burton's romance with Elizabeth Taylor – who was not part of the cast but came along – is often deemed responsible for putting Puerto Vallarta firmly in the international spotlight: "a mixed blessing" according to Huston, who stayed on here until his death in 1987, and whose bronze image stands on the Isla Río Cuale in town. Over the last decade, especially, frantic development has mostly overwhelmed the tropical-village atmosphere, though the historic town centre at least retains its charming cobbled streets and white-walled, terracotta-roofed houses.

Orientation

The **Río Cuale**, spanned by two small road bridges and a pedestrianized footbridge, is at the heart of old Puerto Vallarta or just **El Centro**, but the resort zone now covers a vast area for many kilometres north and south of here. The Plaza Principal, official buildings, market and the bulk of the shops and upscale restaurants lie on the north side of the river, Vallarta's busy **Downtown** area, and this eventually morphs into an area of beaches and fancy hotels imaginatively dubbed **Zona Hotelera** by the local authorities. This ends at the upscale **Marina Vallarta** development and the airport. Further north, beyond the Río Ameca, lies **Nuevo Vallarta** and the most expensive resort hotels and condos. The area of El Centro immediately south of the Río Cuale is known as the **old town** and is where you'll find the town beach and the cheaper hotels in what's optimistically labelled the **Zona Romántica** – further south is **Mismaloya**, with a more glamorous appeal.

Arrival and information

The **Central de Autobuses** is around 12km north of the city centre. Equipped with a guardería and long-distance telephones, it is served by local **buses** to and from the centre – buses heading south are usually marked "Olas Altas" or "Centro", while those in the other direction are "Hoteles", "Ixtapa" or "Juntas"; be sure to ask the driver if the bus is going to the city centre, just in case. Fares on all city buses are M$5.50. For **taxis**, buy a ticket at the booth in the terminal – fares to downtown should be pre-fixed M$100. Once in town, you should be able to travel anywhere in the centre of Vallarta for a maximum of M$50 per trip.

Arriving at the **airport** (information on ⓣ322/221-1298), 10km north of the centre on the coastal highway, is a sure reminder that this is gringolandia. Authorized taxis operate on a highly inflated zone system which starts at M$163 (Marina Vallarta) and rises to M$179 for downtown and M$237 for the Zona Romántica

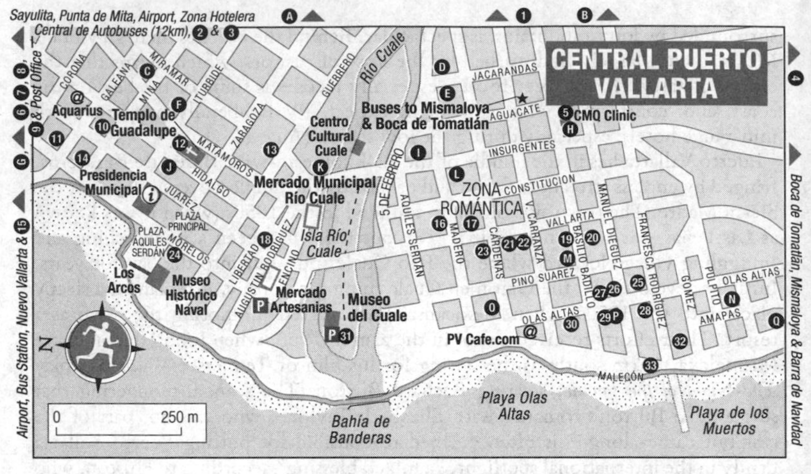

ACCOMMODATION	
Azteca	D
Belmar	I
Blue Chairs Resort	Q
Casa Amorita	F
Casa Kimberley	A
La Casa del Puente	K
Casa Velas Hotel Boutique	G
Los Cuatro Vientos	C
Hacienda Alemana	H
Hortencia	L
Hotel Eloisa	O
Hotel Villa del Mar	E
Oasis Hostel	B
Playa Los Arcos	P
Posada de Roger	M
La Terraza Inn	N
Viva La Vida Hostel	J

EATING & DRINKING	
A Page in the Sun	26
Archie's Wok	32
Café des Artistes	6
Café de Olla	27
El Carbinito	7
Daíquiri Dicks	30
La Dolce Vita	15
Fredy's Tucán	19
Hormiga Feliz	16
Joe Jack's Fish Shack	20
Kaiser Maximilian	29
Langostinos	33
La Michoacana	24
Marisma Fish Tacos	1
Oscar's	31
El Palomar de los Gonzáles	4
Pie in the Sky	23
Planeta Vegetariano	12
Rico's	9
El Torito	21
Las Tres Huastecas	28
Tacos Memo Grill	5
Trio	13

NIGHTLIFE	
Apaches	25
Los Balcones	18
La Bodeguita del Medio	2
Club Roxy	17
Glam	14
Hilo	11
Mandala	8
Memories	10
Paco's Ranch	22
The Zoo	3

or Nuevo Vallarta. *Colectivos* start at M$69 and rise to M$81 and M$93, but only go when full and when enough people are heading in the same direction. In all cases, ignore the hordes of time-share sellers and pay the taxi fare at the ticket booths. If luggage is not a problem, a far cheaper option is to walk out of the terminal onto the main road and catch a **city bus** (marked "Olas Altas" or "Centro") for M$5.50. Regular taxis charge locals around M$80 from here into downtown. All the major **car rental** firms have desks at the airport (see p.528), and you'll find a few ATMs and places to change money.

The **tourist office** (Mon–Sat 8am–8pm, Sun 10am–6pm; ⓣ322/223-2500; ⓦwww.visitpuertovallarta.com) is in the Presidencia Municipal on the Plaza Principal. For up-to-date, if somewhat promotional, information on what's going on in town, pick up the free English-language daily *Vallarta Today* (ⓦwww.vallartatoday.com), available in gringo hangouts. Puerto Vallarta is also well represented on various **websites** such as ⓦwww.puertovallarta.net, ⓦwww.vallarta-info.com (which has the best maps) and ⓦwww.vallartablog.com.

Accommodation

Staying in Puerto Vallarta means opting for one of the many resorts strung out along the coast, or a hotel in Centro, within easy walking distance of Playa de los Muertos and the Plaza Principal. Many **resorts** offer all-inclusive packages, and with a few exceptions, are quite similar; you'll find good deals on the internet, but remember that meals (often you'll have little choice but to eat at the hotel), transport and extra charges can add up. The more affordable options mainly lie south of the Río Cuale in the Zona Romántica, close to the old town – the list below concentrates on the best deals in this area. Free **camping** on any of the more popular beaches around the middle of the bay is prohibited, but if you're reasonably well equipped and protected against mosquitoes, you could try **Punta de Mita** at the northern end of the bay or **Boca de Tomatlán** to the south (where the main road turns inland), each of which from time to time sees small communities established on the sand. At **Yelapa**, a southern beach to which there are boat trips from town (see box, p.524), you might be able to rent a hut or find somewhere to sling a hammock; otherwise there is a good hotel.

Zona Romántica and the old town

Azteca Madero 473, at Jacarandas ⓣ322/222-2750. A longstanding, reliable choice with simple, surgically clean rooms with fans overlooking a peaceful courtyard full of flourishing plants. Street-facing rooms are brighter but noisier. Panoramic views from the rooftop terrace. ❸

Belmar Insurgentes 161 ⓣ322/222-0572, ⓦwww.belmarvallarta.com. Well located and economical, this snug, friendly hotel has clean, pleasant rooms with TV, wi-fi, a/c and closet-size bathrooms – it's M$200 extra for a kitchenette. Request a room with a balcony on the top floor – singles are just M$330. ❹

Blue Chairs Resort Malecón and Almendro 4, at Playa de los Muertos ⓣ322/222-5040, ⓦwww.hotelbluechairs.com. Gay visitors, even if not staying here, will inevitably gravitate to this gay-owned and operated landmark on the town beach. The resort has suites with or without kitchens and ocean views, as well as a rooftop bar and pool. Straight guests are also welcome. ❼

Hacienda Alemana Basilio Badillo 378 ⓣ322/222-2071, ⓦwww.haciendaalemana.com. New hotel with ten crisp, stylish rooms with flat-screen TVs and sauerbraten, bratwurst and German beer in *steins* – they even celebrate Oktoberfest here. Free wi-fi, sauna and gourmet breakfast included, all a short walk from the beach. ❼

Hortencia Madero 336, at Insurgentes ⓣ322/222-2484, ⓦwww.hotelhortencia.com. A variety of whitewashed, clean, spacious quarters with cable TV, free wi-fi and fan in a convenient location. A/c is available for a few extra pesos. ❹

Hotel Eloisa Cárdenas 79 ⓣ322/222-6465, ⓦwww.hoteleloisa.com. The best of the mid-range options, this very friendly, family-run hotel with a Mexican feel has nicely furnished, renovated rooms and studios (with kitchenettes), with cable TV and a/c. There is also a small rooftop pool. ❺

Hotel Villa del Mar Madero 440, at Jacarandas ⓣ322/222-0785. Relaxed, long-time favourite of budget travellers. All motel-style rooms have bathrooms; the larger, more expensive "suites" also have small balconies, a/c, TV and kitchenettes. ❸

Oasis Hostel Libramiento 222 ⓣ322/222-2636, ⓦwww.oasishostel.com. Clean and sociable hostel a 15min walk from the city centre. Dorm beds are available for M$150 per night (M$180 in winter and at Easter), with breakfast and internet access included. Also has two en-suite doubles and a TV room with cable and DVDs. ❸

Playa Los Arcos Olas Altas 380, at Diéguez ⓣ322/226-7102, ⓦwww.playalosarcos.com. The best-equipped and most spacious of the beachfront hotels, with a lively social scene centred around the large pool and adjacent palapa restaurant, where live sports action and beer predominate. Well-appointed rooms with a/c, TV and safe, though they can smell very musty in the rainy season. ❻

Posada de Roger Basilio Badillo 237 ⓣ322/222-0639, ⓦwww.posadaroger.com. Some of the sombre rooms here have seen better days, but they all have a/c, cable TV, safe and fan, and overlook a spacious, shady courtyard where excellent breakfasts are served – the on-site *El Tucan* restaurant is considered the best breakfast spot in town. Only a couple of blocks from the beach, and with a small rooftop pool. ❹

La Terraza Inn Amapas 299 ⓣ322/223-5431, ⓦwww.terrazainn.com. Ten cosy cabañas arranged on beautifully landscaped terraces a short walk from the ocean, all with simple, clean interiors, free wi-fi, cable TV, outdoor patios and tiled floors. Café and pharmacy on site. ❺

Downtown

Casa Amorita Iturbide 309 at Matamoros ⓣ322/222-4926, ⓦwww.casaamorita.com. One of the most enticing downtown hotels, with just five rooms three blocks from the malecón, all with balconies, ornate metalwork beds and cool tiled floors; there's a Venetian tile pool, roof bar and terrace, with spell-binding views of the ocean and cathedral, especially at night. ❾

Casa Kimberley Zaragoza 445 ⓣ322/222-1336, ⓦwww.casakimberley.com. Time-warp shrine-cum-hotel in the house Richard Burton bought for

Liz Taylor in 1964. Except for the Liz memorabilia, the decor is little changed from when she sold it ten years later. Overpriced rooms are scruffy and need upgrading, but Liz fans won't care. The communal living room and bar have unrivalled views over the town, and there is a swimming pool and free breakfast. Prices drop by fifty percent in low season. ❼

La Casa del Puente Libertad at Miramar, just north of the river accessed via *Restaurant La Fuente del Puente* ⓣ322/222-0749, ⓦwww.casadelpuente.com. A real home from home: spacious, bright, elegantly furnished apartments, a wonderful communal area with huge windows overlooking the river and an extremely friendly owner. Only two suites (with fully equipped kitchens) and one double room, so book early (rates drop by fifty percent in summer). ❻

Los Cuatro Vientos Matamoros 520 ⓣ322/222-0161, ⓦwww.cuatrovientos.com. A PV institution, with many return guests. Artistic touches and local handicrafts give the simple, spotless rooms a homely feel. There is a small pool and the terrace has wonderful views. Owner Gloria is a good resource when planning tours or dining out in the area. ❻

Viva La Vida Hostel Juárez 386 ⓣ322/113-0320. Great little hostel, close to the Plaza Principal, offering dorm beds for just M$140, free wi-fi, breakfast and flat-screen TV in the lounge; also has two private rooms (M$300). ❸

Marina Vallarta

Casa Velas Hotel Boutique Pelícanos 311 ⓣ322/226-6688 or 1-866/529-8813, ⓦwww.hotelcasavelas.com. Pick of the elegant new resorts along Vallarta's northern coast, ideal for some serious pampering (and spending). Ultra stylish suites blend Mexican and contemporary decor, and there's plenty of massages, golf, and swimming pools – the private beach club is a 15min walk (or free shuttle ride) away. If you ever decide to venture off the premises, remember it's quite a hike to the old town. ❾

The Town

Apart from the **beaches**, souvenir shops and chi-chi boutiques and galleries that pack the centre of town, there's not a great deal in the way of attractions in Puerto Vallarta. This said, you can still fill a very pleasant hour or two wandering along the **malecón**, the seafront promenade that runs adjacent to Morelos in the downtown area, and on the island in the Río Cuale. The lively **Plaza Principal**, or main square, is north of the river in the heart of town and overlooks the ocean-front boulevard. Here, families gather in the evenings among the balloon sellers and hot-dog stands, while tourists explore the city's restaurants, bars and clubs. The plaza is backed by the **Templo de Guadalupe**, whose tower, topped with a huge crown modelled on one that Emperor Maximilian's wife, Carlota, wore in the 1860s, is a city landmark. Just down from here on the malecón is the **Plaza Aquiles Serdán**, with a strange little amphitheatre and **Los Arcos**, four arches looking out over the sea like a lost fragment of the Roman empire; the original four arches were supposedly taken from a ruined hacienda, while local sculptor Martin Distancia Barragan created these replacements in fine cantera stone. With hawkers, mimes, musicians and food stands, it is one of the best places for people-watching in the city. Here also you'll find the rather stuffy **Museo Histórico Naval** (Tues–Fri 9am–7.30pm, Sat & Sun 10am–2pm & 3–7.30pm; free), which provides a fairly detailed history of the town and region from a nautical perspective, starting with the Spanish Conquest and ending with Mexico's modern navy. Some interesting episodes are covered, but there's not much to see beyond a few dioramas, paintings and photos, and everything is labelled in Spanish.

A short stroll northwards along the malecón brings you past several statues, among them another Puerto Vallarta icon, the *Cabelleo del Mar* created by Rafael Zamarripas, a three-metre-high bronze statue of a seahorse with a naked boy riding on its back. This is a replica of the 1976 original, which ended up floating out to sea after a hurricane struck Puerto Vallarta in 2002. In between the plaza and the statue are many other fantastical sculptures by renowned Mexican and international artists.

South of the plaza, on the **Isla Río Cuale** in the middle of the river, a small park surrounds a clutch of shops and restaurants. On the north side there is the **Centro Cultural Cuale** (ⓣ322/223-0095), which holds all sort of classes and shows local art exhibits, while at the seaward end the **Museo del Cuale** (Tues–Sat 10am–2pm & 3–6pm; free), with half a dozen displays of local pre-Columbian discoveries up to and including the Spanish Conquest, has plenty of English captions. In between the two, restaurants and **galleries** line the middle of the island. Beyond the island further up river, past **John Huston's statue**, there's a park and a patch of river where women come to do the family washing, overlooked from the hillsides by the opulent villas of "Gringo's Gulch".

The beaches

Puerto Vallarta's **beaches** vary in nature as you move round the bay: those to the north, out near Nuevo Vallarta and the airport, are long, flat stretches of creamy white sand – swimming is usually OK here, but the surf gets heavier to the west, with the best breaks around Punta de Mita (see p.529). To the south of Puerto Vallarta are a series of steep-sided coves, sheltering tiny, calm enclaves. The town beach, **Playa de los Muertos** (Beach of the Dead), or "Playa del Sol" as the local tourist office would prefer it known, is south of the river and falls somewhere between the two extremes: not very large, it features coarse, brown sand and reasonably calm surf, despite facing apparently open water. It's also the most crowded of the city's beaches – locals, Mexican holiday-makers and foreign tourists are packed in cheek-by-jowl during the high season. With the omnipresent hawkers selling everything from fresh fruit and tacos to handicrafts and fake jade masks, it can be a far from relaxing experience, but it's always entertaining. Just don't leave anything of value lying about. The **gay** section of this beach is at its southern end, opposite the *Blue Chairs Resort* (see p.521) – look out for the blue chairs.

Some of the best beaches lie to the **south** along Hwy-200; **buses** (M$6) leave regularly from the junction of Carranza and Aguacate south of the Río Cuale, to Mismaloya and Boca de Tomátlan where water taxis continue on to the isolated beaches of Playa las Ánimas (M$20), Quimixto (M$30) and Yelapa (M$60) – see box, p.524. Alternatively, from Playa de los Muertos, **lanchas** (M$100 one way) depart several times daily (usually hourly 9am–6pm) for the same stretches of sand (25–45min). You can also take **taxis** to Mismaloya (M$120) and Boca de Tomátlan (M$140).

Mismaloya

Some 10km south of Puerto Vallarta, the best-known and most accessible beach is **Mismaloya**. Here John Huston filmed *The Night of the Iguana*, building his set at the mouth of what was once a pristine, jungle-choked gorge on the southern side of the gorgeous bay; it's been endowed with a romantic mystique ever since. Plans to turn the set and crew's accommodation into tourist cabins never came to fruition, and now the huge and expensive *Barceló La Jolla de Mismaloya* hotel (ⓣ322/226-0660, ⓦwww.barcelolajollademismaloya.com; ⑨) completely dominates the valley. Crowded with day-trippers and enthusiastic vendors selling everything from coconuts to sarongs, Mismaloya is not without a certain amount of seductive tropical appeal, though it is far from the "Paradise Found" pitched by the tourist office. When you tire of the beach, you can still wander out to the point and the ruins of the film set, where a handful of expensive restaurants sell beer and seafood cocktails. Boats are on hand to take you snorkelling at **Los Arcos**, a federal underwater park around a group of offshore islands, some formed into the eponymous arches. A superb array of brightly coloured fish – parrot, angel, pencil, croaker and scores of others – negotiate the deep rock walls and the boulder-strewn ocean floor. In addition to ninety-minute trips from the beach, boats are rented to groups for unlimited periods. **Diving trips**, including night dives, can also be organized from tour operators in Puerto Vallarta: Chico's Dive Shop, Díaz Ordaz 772 (Ⓣ322/222-1895, Ⓦwww.chicos-diveshop.com), and Vallarta Under Sea, Edificio Marina del Rey, Marina Vallarta (Ⓣ322/209-0025, Ⓦwww.vallartaundersea.com), run trips to Los Arcos (from M$600) and Las Islas Marietas (see p.530) from M$1100, and also rent snorkelling and scuba gear.

Boca de Tomatlán and beyond

If you're after peace and quiet, your best option is to continue along the highway for another 4km past Mismaloya until you reach the once-sleepy village of **Boca de Tomatlán**, which has become a departure point for the *lanchas* that shuttle passengers to and from the southern beaches. Still, it remains picturesque, with a small but beautiful beach in a protected cove dotted with fishing boats and surrounded by densely forested hills. The local speciality, cooked to perfection by the beachside *enramadas* (huts), is *pescado de bara*: a fish impaled on a stick and

Trips from Puerto Vallarta

For the more peaceful and scenic **beaches** further south – **Playa Las Animas**, **Quimixto** and **Yelapa** are the most common destinations – a boat trip is the only means of access. Travel agents all over town tout a variety of excursions, most of which leave from the marina – if you want tranquillity, time your visits to avoid these boats (go in the mornings or late afternoons and avoid Las Animas at lunchtime). Miller Tours, at Paseo de las Garzas 100, between *Hotel Krystle* and *Hotel Crown Paradise* in Nuevo Vallarta (Ⓣ322/224-0585), and Vallarta Adventure, at the marina (Ⓣ322/221-0657, Ⓦwww.vallarta-adventures.com), both have good reputations and charge around M$400 (Las Animas) to M$600 (Yelapa), though compare prices and what's on offer in the way of food and drink – if meals are not included, it's worth taking your own food along. A much cheaper way to travel is via **water taxi** (see p.523).

Unfortunately, the once-remote beauty of many of the southern beaches has been tainted by the invasion of PV tour groups. That said, a number are still quite lovely: **Quimixto**'s crystal waters are home to a colourful profusion of exotic marine life. **Las Animas** is a larger bay and a base for a variety of watersports, including jet skiing, banana boats and parasailing – this is always the busiest beach.

At the old hippie hangout of **Yelapa** there's a small "typical" indigenous village not far from the white-sand beach, and a waterfall a short distance into the jungle. Marketed as an "untouched paradise", it's really more of a luxurious, if rustic, retreat with a contrived alternative vibe; they now have electricity, and long-distance phones, and sushi and massages are all on offer. A short hike through the jungle leads to the Cascada Cola de Caballo, a small waterfall where you can swim. If you've got the time and money, stay for the night, as the beach empties as the sun sets, becoming the perfect spot for total rest and relaxation. Accommodation here is primarily provided by rental apartments; just arriving on the beach and enquiring will usually get you a place (see Ⓦwww.yelapa.info). Alternatively, *Hotel Lagunita* (Ⓣ322/209-5055, Ⓦwww.hotel-lagunita.com; ❼) has beautiful open-air **cabañas**, a pool and beachfront **restaurant** serving Mexican and international food. At **Majahuitas**, between Quiximito and Yelapa, accessed by private boat from Boca de Tomatlán, the eponymous resort is a guaranteed love-it or leave-it experience: eight comfy but simple "casitas ecológicas" have no electricity, phones or internet, and communal meals are served by candlelight. It's not for those who like a fluffy robe and food available at a whim (US Ⓣ1-800/508-7923, Ⓦwww.hoteles.rinconesdemitierra.com/#/majahuitas; ❼). If you want to go **snorkelling** or **scuba diving** at the southern beaches, tours are led by Chico's Dive Shop (see above).

slow-cooked over a barbecue. The Río Horcones, with its thickly forested banks, empties into the sea beside the beach, so there's a choice of fresh or salt water for swimming. Immediately upstream, in the small village of **Las Juntas y Los Veranos**, Puerto Vallarta Canopy Tours offer **exhilarating zipline tours** along cables up to 60m high. The cables link ten treetops and carry you past coffee trees, vanilla vines and agave plants. Tours last from one and a half to two hours and cost around M$1000 (Mon–Sat 8am–8pm, Sun 9am–5pm; ⓣ322/223-6060, ⓦwww.canopytours-vallarta.com).

Eating and drinking

Finding a place **to eat** in Puerto Vallarta is no problem; tourist restaurants offering cocktails by candlelight abound. Inexpensive places to eat are essentially confined to downtown: the **market** – on the north bank of the river by the upper bridge – has a few cheap *comedores* tucked away upstairs, overlooking the river, well away from the souvenir stalls that fill the rest of the building, **taco and hot-dog stands** line the streets (see box, p.526), and vendors on the beach offer freshly caught fish, roasted on sticks. Of the more **expensive places**, most offering some form of music or entertainment, or at least a good view while you eat, you can really take your pick.

Zona Romántica and the old town

Archie's Wok Rodríguez 130 ⓣ322/222-0411. State-of-the-art Asian cooking served in a stylish setting by the wife and daughter of John Huston's former personal chef. Delicious, healthy fare with an emphasis on seafood in Filipino, Thai and Chinese sauces – think Thai garlic shrimps, almond chicken and sizzling fish in banana leaves. A little pricey (mains range M$167–197), but touted by fans as one of the best Asian restaurants in the Americas. Live music at the weekend. Closed Sun and all of Sept.

Café de Olla Basilio Badillo 168, at Olas Altas. Good traditional Mexican food – enchiladas, *carne asado, chile relleno* – served in a lively dining room adorned with local artwork, and delivered by cheerful, attentive waiters. Always popular and brimming with diners who come again and again. Closed Tues.

Daiquiri Dicks Olas Altas 314 ⓣ322/222-0566, ⓦwww.ddpv.com. Informal beachside dining (perfect for sunset drinks) and a varied menu of generous dishes draws a gringo crowd. The signature dish – a whole grilled, seasoned fish served on a stick – is worth the 30min wait. Other crowd pleasers, including lobster tacos and chicken in marsala sauce, are as good as everyone says they are. Daily 9am–11pm.

Fredy's Tucán Basilio Badillo 245, at Vallarta ⓣ322/223-0778. Bright, airy and with tropical decor, this is one of the best venues for Mexican, continental and American breakfasts: omelettes, pancakes, French toast, granola and yogurt and fresh-baked bread are served until 2.30pm in a new dining room, adjacent to the *Posada de Roger* hotel. European football matches are screened in the hotel bar on evenings and weekends.

Joe Jack's Fish Shack Basilio Badillo 212 ⓣ322/222-2099, ⓦwww.joejacks-fishshack.com. Fabulous seafood, but best known for its fish and chips (M$115) and chowders (M$60), the tastiest in town (the M$80 "Tasty" burger is also excellent); sit at the bar downstairs, or enjoy the views from the rooftop dining area. Daily noon–1am.

Kaiser Maximilian Olas Altas 380-B, next to *Playa Los Arcos* hotel ⓣ322/223-0760, ⓦwww.kaisermaximilian.com. Upscale, expensive restaurant (mains M$195–310; early-bird specials before 7pm) with an old-European slant such as traditional Austrian dishes like lamb with rosemary and sautéed squid, as well as more traditional Mexican and international offerings. The restaurant's sidewalk patio is a nice spot for a gourmet coffee and an exceedingly rich pastry. Closed Sun.

Langostinos Playa Los Muertos at Diéguez ⓣ322/222-0894. Phenomenal sunset views and excellent daily special menu (M$55) from the German owners of *Hacienda Alemana*; the German buffets (Wed & Sat; M$225) include draught beer and are well worth making reservations for. Otherwise the menu includes everything from burgers and snacks to fresh fish (M$95) and lobster (M$225). Daily 8am–11pm.

A Page in the Sun Olas Altas 399, at Diéguez ⓣ322/222-3608. A sociable little corner café in a bustling part of town, with outside tables, good coffee, fresh fruit *licuados*, sandwiches (M$45), salads, cakes and a homely ambience, thanks to a stack of games and magazines. It also doubles as a used-book shop. Breakfasts from M$30. Daily 7am–midnight.

El Palomar de los Gonzáles Aguacate 425 ⓣ322/222-0795. Perfect for a romantic candlelit dinner, this elegant mansion carved into the hillside south of the centre has stunning views from its rooftop patio. The seafood dishes are the highlight of the menu (ranging M$175–325), but the Mexican specialities (around M$150) are also well executed. A good wine list and exotic desserts ensure a long, indulgent evening. Evenings only, 6–11pm.

Pie in the Sky Lázaro Cárdenas 247 ⓣ322/223-8183, ⓦwww.pieinthesky.com.mx. Justly praised for fine muffins, cakes, pastries and desserts, they also serve a decent range of rich coffees, teas, cheese and spinach empanadas and chicken pies. Try the addictive *Beso Supreme*, ice cream wedged between two layers of *beso* (chocolate brownie). The main branch is in Bucerias (see p.529). Daily 9am–10pm.

El Torito Vallarta 291, at Carranza ⓣ322/222-3784, ⓦwww.torito.com. Reasonably priced bar and restaurant for sports jocks, with satellite coverage of everything from Serie A to the Super Bowl. They do succulent ribs (M$130) and offer M$25 beers on Thursday nights.

Las Tres Huastecas Olas Altas 444, at Rodríguez. No-frills, cantina-style restaurant a block from Playa de los Muertos that specializes in classic Mexican dishes such as chicken in *mole* sauce and a creative ensemble of fish tacos and enchiladas. One of the cheapest places in this part of town (most dishes under M$70, breakfasts under M$40).

Downtown

Café des Artistes G. Sanchez 740 ⓣ322/222-3228, ⓦwww.cafedesartistes.com. The epitome of Pacific coast gourmet dining. The quality of chef Thierry Blouet's French cuisine matches the sophisticated surroundings – the intriguing menu features shots of foie gras with mango confit (M$280), roasted sea bass ($245) and decadent desserts (from M$90). Eat in the garden or dining room decorated with vivid artwork. Live piano and flute music add to the refined atmosphere. Daily 6–11.30pm.

La Dolce Vita Malecón 674, at Dominguez ⓣ322/222-3852, ⓦwww.dolcevita.com.mx. Pizzas, pasta and other dishes, such as beef carpaccio and chicken cacciatore, at reasonable prices. Live jazz Thurs–Sun.

La Michoacana Plaza Principal. This place has been dishing up heavenly ice cream and fruity ice popsicles since 1957, and remains a firm favourite with the crowds milling around the plaza.

Oscar's Isla Río Cuale (facing the ocean) ⓣ322/223-0789. Come here for magnificent sunsets and a posh, predominantly seafood menu (mains around M$150) served in refined, candlelit surroundings under a giant palapa at the southern end of the island – pelicans usually feed off the beach beyond the bridge. The downside: has been

Taco tour

Numerous **tacos** stalls occupy the streets of Puerto Vallarta at night, offering a tasty introduction to this essential street food. The following tour starts a few blocks east of the malecón in the Zona Romántica and roughly heads north through downtown, though you'd have to be extremely hungry to visit every stall in one night.

Hormiga Feliz ("The Happy Ant") at Madero and Vallarta: This stall has been knocking out delicious *birria*, tacos and quesadillas since the 1970s (from M$4). Usually open Mon–Sat 9am–2pm & 6pm–1am.

Tacos Memo Grill at Badillo and Aguacate: Sumptuous *tacos asada, quesadillas con carne* (M$6), *hamburguesas* and burritos from M$25. Usually open 8pm–2am.

Marisma Fish Tacos on Naranja at Carranza (don't confuse it with the *carne asada* place opposite): The best fish tacos in town (M$10); shrimp tacos from around M$15.

Rico's Mac Tacos Av México 1139. Though this congenial 24hr sit-down place attracts a fair share of tourists, the tacos are excellent and there are lots of bars nearby.

Pepe's Taco Honduras 173, between Peru and México (near *Rico's*): This no-frills stall has been serving mouth-watering *tacos carne asada* (M$8) till the early hours for years.

El Carbonito, across from *Pepe's*: End up at the connoisseurs' favourite – a small (usually unmarked) stall known for serving the finest *tacos el pastor* in the city. The secret; mesquite-infused charcoal and superb, tongue-singeing salsa. Usually open Tues–Sun from 8.30pm. Look out for the top-notch hot-dog stall nearby.

known to allow time-share sellers to approach diners. Politely ignore them.

Planeta Vegetariano Iturbide 270 at Hidalgo ⓣ322/222-3073. Large menu and all-you-can-eat vegetarian buffet (noon–6.30pm; M$75) with a choice of main courses, salads, soup, dessert and a soft drink. The walls are painted with fantastic frescoes, and the food is cheap and deliciously spiced. Mon–Sat 8am–10pm.

Trio Guerrero 264 ⓣ322/222-2196, ⓦwww.triopv.com. An elegant townhouse filled with original art and hanging plants provides the setting for Mediterranean-fusion cuisine prepared by a German and Swedish chef with Michelin credentials. In addition to dishes like rabbit with garlic sauce and braised veal with almond sauce, there are home-made pastas, Lebanese salads, sautéed calamari and an imaginatively prepared selection of seafood dishes. It's a fabulous treat, if you can afford it (mains M$175–220, pastas M$95–175). Daily 6pm–midnight.

Nightlife

The **malecón** (Paseo Díaz Ordez) is the centre of Puerto Vallarta's night-time activity, lined with ornate, hangar-size places that specialize in creating a high-energy party atmosphere – pop, techno and 1980s rock compete for the airwaves with salsa, jazz and the more gentle strumming of marauding mariachis. The greatest concentration of **bars** and **clubs** is downtown along the stretch of the malecón that runs about 400m north of the Plaza Principal. Most of these establishments are at ground level, making it easy to wander along, take your pick of the **happy hours** and compare **cover charges**, which are sometimes nonexistent and sometimes as much as M$200, depending on the night and season. Check ⓦwww.pvscene.com for the latest events and listings. The Zona Romántica also has its share of clubs, which are generally less pretentious and more varied in character. This is where you'll find most of the **gay nightlife** (see ⓦwww.gayguidevallarta.com). In general, Sunday is quiet – some places close – except on the plaza where, from around 6pm, huge crowds gather around the dozens of taco and cake stands and listen to the brass band.

Zona Romántica

Apaches Olas Altas 439 ⓣ322/222-5235. Popular and welcoming gay and lesbian joint where groups gather for martinis and cocktails at happy hour (5–7pm), filling the cosy, indoor bar and sidewalk tables. The closet-sized *Apache* bistro next door serves decent appetizers, steaks and seafood until midnight. Daily 5am–2pm.

Club Roxy Vallarta 217, at Madero ⓣ322/223-2404. A popular bar/club with bands (10pm–2am) playing blues, reggae and rock in an uplifting, if at times raucous, atmosphere that attracts locals and tourists alike. Daily 8pm–4am.

Paco's Ranch Vallarta 278 ⓣ322/222-1889, ⓦwww.pacopaco.com. An unmissable experience, this is the largest and most popular gay club in town. Also drawing a straight contingent, it's a multifaceted venue with DJs playing the latest in techno, hip-hop and pop on the ground floor; Mexican music, a cantina and pool table on the first floor (open from 1pm); a rooftop bar on the second; and strippers in a smaller space connected to the main club by a passageway. There are lively drag shows at 1am & 3am Thurs–Sun.

Downtown

Los Balcones Juárez 182, at Libertad. Puerto Vallarta's oldest gay club (opened in 1986), on three floors with a dancefloor, balconies overlooking the street and, during high season, strippers. Daily 10pm–6am.

La Bodeguita del Medio Paseo Díaz Ordez 858, ⓣ322/223-1585. With graffiti blazoned across the walls, this distinctive restaurant named after the famous Hemingway haunt in Havana is as popular for its *mojitos* (ask for Havana Club 7-year-old rum), *cuba libres* and live salsa bands as it is for its Cuban and Mexican food. Daily noon–2am.

Glam Morelos 460 at Mina ⓣ322/223-5567, ⓦwww.glamclub.com.mx. Booming three-floor dance club, set in a cavernous, slightly camp space adorned with giant Romanesque statues, red sofas, chandeliers and giant video screens. Open daily: bar 8am–11pm, club 9pm–6am.

Hilo Paseo Díaz Ordez 588 ⓣ322/222-5361. Always popular with young, well-heeled locals, this thumping techno club with high ceilings and huge, out-of-place statues of Mexican revolutionary heroes, reverberates with gun-fire beats and attitude. Weekend cover M$75–100. Daily 4pm–4am.

Moving on from Puerto Vallarta

Most long-distance buses depart from the **Central de Autobuses** 12km north of downtown (see p.519). First-class buses serve a long list of destinations including Guadalajara (every 30min; 5hr 30min), Mazatlán (2 daily; 8hr) and Mexico City (9 daily; 13–14hr); there are also frequent buses to Tepic (4hr), where you can change for Mazatlán (M$400). Primera Plus (☎322/290-0715) runs first-class services to Barra de Navidad (4 daily; 3hr 30min) and Manzanillo (3 daily; 5hr). They share their offices at Lázaro Cárdenas 268–9 with ETN (☎322/290-0997), who operates super-deluxe services to Guadalajara and Mexico City (1 daily; 13hr). For second-class buses to Manzanillo (5 daily) and Barra de Navidad (6 daily), try Servicios Coordinados at Cárdenas 268 (☎322/221-0095).

Numerous flights from the airport connect Puerto Vallarta with Mexico City, Guadalajara, Monterrey, Tijuana and Toluca, as well as many destinations in the US and Canada, including Chicago, Dallas, Denver, Houston, Los Angeles, Montréal, New York, Phoenix, San Francisco and Toronto. For further information, see Travel details, p.567.

Mandala Paseo Díaz Ordez 640 ☎322/223-0966. Huge, warehouse-like *discoteca* and video bar, attracting tourists and upscale locals with its Asian-themed interior (think *Buddha Bar*) and Latino pop and dance music. Cover M$100. Daily 6pm–6am.
Memories Mina 207 at Juárez ☎322/205-7906. Sultry bar popular with dating couples who are delighted to be able to hold a conversation (a novelty in a PV bar) in between sips of coffee and speciality cocktails.
The Zoo Paseo Díaz Ordez 630 ☎322/222-4945. Leopard- and zebra-skin chairs and plastic gorillas swinging from the rafters lend a kitsch element to this wildly popular club, where DJs play the latest dance tunes for a hip young clientele. Cover M$100 (free Tues). Daily: bar opens at 10am, club 10pm–4am.

Listings

American Express Centro Comercial Playa de Oro, Paseo de las Garzas 100, Zona Hotelera ☎322/221-3630; holds mail and changes cheques (Mon–Fri 9am–6pm, Sat 9am–1pm).
Banks and exchange Banamex, on the Plaza Principal (Mon–Sat 9am–4pm) has an ATM. There are branches of Banorte downtown, at Díaz Ordaz 690 (Mon–Fri 9am–5pm, Sat 9am–2pm), and in Zona Hotelera, at Francisco Medina Ascensio 500 (same hours). Other ATMs are plentiful. You can change money at the numerous casas de cambio on the streets surrounding the plaza: rates vary, so shop around.
Car rental Alamo, Francisco Medina Ascencio s/n ☎322/221-3030 or the airport ☎322/221-1228; Avis, at the airport ☎322/221-1657 and *Villa del Palmar*, Francisco Medina Ascencio km 3 ☎322/226-1400; and Hertz, also at *Villa del Palmar*, Francisco Medina Ascencio km 3 ☎322/222-0024.
Consulates Canada, Edificio Obelisco, Francisco Medina Ascencio 1951 ☎322/293-0098 (Mon–Fri 9am–3.30pm); US, Paseo de los Cocoteros 85 Sur, Paradise Plaza, Interior Local L-7, Nuevo Vallarta ☎322/222-0069 (Mon–Fri 8.30am–12.30pm, closed every third Wed) – in emergencies call US Consulate General in Guadalajara (☎33/3268-2145).
Emergencies ☎060. Police ☎322/223-2500.
Hospitals English-speaking medics at CMQ Clinic, Basilio Badillo 365, between Insurgentes and Aguacate ☎322/223-1919; and Cruz Roja, Río Balsas and Río Plata ☎322/222-1533.
Internet access Many places (*Pie in the Sky* and *Starbucks*) have wi-fi; the best internet café near the plaza is Aquarius (M$15/hr) at Juárez 532 (24hr), with 15 flat-screen monitors. In the Zona Romántica, try PV Cafe.com at Olas Altas 246 (☎332/223-3308), with seven computers, fax, wi-fi and long distance phones (daily 7am–midnight).
Laundry There are facilities scattered throughout town, all charging around M$45 per load – try Lavandería Blanquita, Madero 407, east of Aguacate (Mon–Sat 8am–8pm).
Pharmacy CMQ, Basilio Badillo 367 ☎322/222-2941, next to CMQ Clinic, is open 24hr; or try Farmacia Guadalajara at Zapata 232 (☎322/222-0101), also 24hr.

Post office The main post office is at Colombia 1014 at Argentina, north of the old town (Mon–Fri 9am–5pm, Sat 9am–1pm).

Travel agents Royale Tours, Francisco Medina Ascencio 2039, ⓣ322/224-8626, ⓦwww.royale-tours.com.

North along the Bahía de Banderas

North of Puerto Vallarta, over the state line in Nayarit, the Bahía de Banderas arcs out to **Punta de Mita**, some 30km away. A summer preserve for Guadalajarans and a winter retreat for motorhome vacationers from the north, these gorgeous beaches offer facilities in just a few spots – **Nuevo Vallarta**, **Bucerías** and **Punta de Mita** – leaving miles of secluded sand for camping and some excellent surf breaks. To get out this direction from Puerto Vallarta, your best bet is to catch any northbound local bus to the Walmart just north of the Marine Terminal in the Zona Hotelera, then flag down an Autotransportes Medina "Punta de Mita" bus (every 10min; Bucerías & Nuevo Vallarta M$12; Destiladeras M$16; Punta de Mita M$20). **Taxis** from downtown are around M$180.

Nuevo Vallarta

NUEVO VALLARTA, 12km north of the airport, is a mega-resort, an ever-expanding cluster of astronomically expensive hotels. Although the beaches here are great, they are backed by ugly buildings and because the hotels tend to be all-inclusive, there's nothing much for the day-tripper to do, save pay a visit to the **dolphins** at Dolphin Adventure (ⓣ322/297-1212 ext 25, ⓦwww.dolphin-adventure.com), an educational centre located at Paseo de la Palmas 39. As well as swimming with dolphins (1hr 30min; US$149), you can also spend a day with a dolphin trainer (US$265).

Bucerías to Playa Destiladeras

For the beach, you're better off pushing on to laid-back **BUCERÍAS**, the last of the bay resorts on Hwy-200, which has wonderful views across the water to Puerto Vallarta from its seafront **restaurants**. *Adriano's* (ⓣ329/298-0088), with bright-orange walls and an extensive range of fresh fish, is superb. For a tea-time treat, visit the locally renowned *Pie in the Sky* **bakery** (ⓣ322/222-8411), opposite the *De Camarón* hotel at Héroe de Nacozari 202, for heavenly chocolate brownies (*beso*), Italian ice cream, bagels and exotic cheesecakes.

Sticking to the coast from here, you leave the main highway, following the signposts for Punta de Mita, passing the beach-free fishing village of **Cruz de Huanacaxtle**, followed by **Manzanillo** and **Piedra Blanca** beaches. The Punta de Mita road continues through increasingly rocky, arid terrain, with small roads dipping down to secluded beaches. The two *enramadas* (**restaurants** under palapas) at **Playa Destiladeras** (8km north of Bucerías) are the only ones in the area, which allows them to charge rather inflated prices for the usual fare – it gets very busy on Sundays. If you've brought a picnic, several places on the beach rent out palapas, tables and chairs for the day for around M$60; **boogie boards** are also available here for around M$35 an hour. **Camping** on the beach is great, but you need to bring everything.

Punta de Mita

PUNTA DE MITA is more developed than Bucerías, with bars, cafés and seafood restaurants strung along the beach area known as **Playa Anclote**. Follow the road parallel to the beach and you'll find the Sociedad Cooperativa de Servicios Turísticos at Anclote 17 (ⓣ329/291-6298, ⓔcooperativapuntamita@prodigy.net.mx), which rents out **snorkelling** and **diving gear** and organizes two-hour *panga* trips

▲ Humpback whale, off the coast of Puerto Vallarta

to a cluster of volcanic islands known as **Las Islas Marietas**, a wildlife sanctuary. The boats hold up to eight people and cost around M$800 – this is probably the cheapest way to get close to the **humpback whales** present in the bay from around December to April, when they come to mate and give birth before returning to the polar waters of the north. Alternatively, you can book an organized whale-watching tour from Puerto Vallarta with an operator such as Open Air Expeditions, Guerrero 339 (Ⓣ322/222-3310, Ⓦwww.vallartawhales.com). **Staying** here usually means splashing out at one of the ultra-luxurious resorts such as *Four Seasons Punta Mita* (Ⓣ329/291-6000, Ⓦwww.fourseasons.com/puntamita; ❾).

Sayulita

On the other side of the Punta de Mita, 22km north of Bucerías on Hwy-200, languorous **SAYULITA** is another popular gringo outpost with an enchanting, jungle-fringed beach, lip-smacking food and some inviting places to stay. The calm was temporarily shattered in 2007 when the town served as backdrop for the cheesy (but commercially successful) Disney movie *Beverly Hills Chihuahua* – many locals were hired as extras. Other than lounging on the sands and making jokes about the movie, the main activity here is **surfing**: the main (right) break in town is in front of *Papa's Palapas*, while you'll find a faster left break north of the river mouth (near the campsite). Lunazul Surf School (Ⓣ329/291-2009, Ⓦwww.lunazulsurfschool.com rents boards (M$200–300/day) and offers lessons (from M$550).

Practicalities

Accommodation is plentiful in Sayulita. Try the exceptionally stylish *Petit Hotel d'Hafa* (Ⓣ329/291-3806; ❺) at Revolución 55 or the cosy *Tia Adriana's B&B* (Ⓣ329/291-302, Ⓦwww.tiaadrianas.com; ❺), which has ten, attractive, clean rooms a short stroll from the beach and wonderfully fresh breakfasts. *Papa's Palapas* (Ⓦwww.papaspalapas.net) rents slightly shabby but cheap bungalows (❸) and suites (❹) right on the beach.

There's also plenty of choice when it comes to **eating**. Of the many institutions in town, everyone tries at least one breakfast at *Rollie's*, Revolución 58, with a vast choice of filling egg, pancake and waffle plates from M$45. Similarly acclaimed, *Sayulita Fish Taco* (Ⓣ329/291-3271, Ⓦwww.sayulitafishtaco.com) at

José Mariscal 13 on the main plaza, knocks out some of the best Baja-style fish tacos (M$20) on the coast, but it also doubles as a tequila bar offering an astounding 250 different brands. For freshly made, filling burritos, seek out Burrito Revolución on the main plaza, with its zesty orange, green and red sauces.

Regular **buses** connect Puerto Vallarta bus station with Sayulita (M$20). **Taxis** cost anything between M$300 and M$700 depending on the group size and your negotiation skills. There are several ATMs in town but no tourist office; check ⓦwww.sayulita.com or www.sayulitalife.com for the latest information.

The Costa Alegre and Bahía de Navidad

The stretch of coast known as the **Costa Alegre** starts about 100km south of Puerto Vallarta. Luxury, taste and style reach a zenith at *Las Alamandas*, km 83 Hwy-200 (ⓣ800/508-7923, ⓦwww.lasalamandas.com; ❾), where beautifully designed villas and suites overlook a breathtaking one-kilometre stretch of private beach. It's beyond La Cumbre (157km south of PV), in the small village of Quemaro, off the main highway.

Further south, the **Bahía de Chamela** comprises a huge, sweeping arc of superb beaches and nine islands, which are popular dive spots. Although large luxury hotels are also cropping up here with alarming frequency, you can still find long sections of untouched beach where you can pitch a tent. To reach **Playa Pérula**, at the northern end of the bay, it's a one-kilometre walk or drive down a dusty track from Hwy-200 (at km 76). There's a small village and you can stay at the average, fourteen-room *Hotel Punta Pérula* (ⓣ315/333-9782; ❹), one block north of the main road at Juárez and Tiburón, or, for slightly more, comfortable, clean rooms with shared kitchen and wheelchair access are available at *Hotel Vagabundo* (ⓣ315/333-9446; ❺), two blocks from the beach at Independencia 100 and Ballena. A little further along Hwy-200 (km72) there's another unpaved road that leads to **Playa Chamela**. Here, the *Paraíso Costa Alegre* (ⓣ315/333-9778, ⓦwww.paraisocostalegre.com.mx; ❺) has attractive oceanfront Polynesian-style cabañas ("Villas Tahitianas") surrounded by palm trees (fan only and no TV). The basic *Bungalows Meyer Chamela* (ⓣ315/285-5252; ❹) has palatable rooms with fan, kitchen and an on-site pool. Otherwise, it's easy to camp on the beach.

At **Playa Careyes**, an upmarket beach resort around 20km further south, expensive villas and luxurious hotels nestle in the hills, including *El Careyes*, km 53.5 Hwy-200 (ⓣ800/508-7923, ⓦwww.elcareyesresort.com; ❽), a chic resort with a spa in idyllic surroundings. Also at Careyes, endangered Olive Ridley **turtles** lay their eggs; biologists have recruited local activists and established a conservation programme – the turtles' eggs are collected before they fall victim to predators and then the babies are released after the eggs hatch in a laboratory.

Playa Tenacatita, a further 40km south along the highway, is another gorgeous beach, with the added attractions of a mangrove lagoon that teems with birdlife and still, clear waters perfect for snorkelling. Lobster- and octopus-fishing is very popular here. The town's name means "red rocks" in Náhuatl; the indigenous people used the russet rocks you'll see to make pottery, ornaments and even to build homes. The **restaurant** on the beach organizes bird-watching boat trips and you can **stay** at the *Hotel Paraíso Tenacatita* (ⓣ314/353-9623; ❸), which has a restaurant and simple rooms built round a courtyard. It's also possible to visit Tenacatita from Barra de Navidad.

Most people choose to press on to the twin towns of **Barra de Navidad** and **San Patricio-Melaque**, 30km further south and among the most enticing destinations on this entire stretch of coastline. They are not undeveloped or totally isolated – indeed, families from Guadalajara come here by the hundreds, especially at weekends – but neither are they heavily commercialized: just small, simple and very Mexican resorts. The entire bay, the **Bahía de Navidad**, is edged by fine sands and, if you're prepared to walk (30min along the beach), you can easily leave the crowds behind.

San Patricio-Melaque

Perched at the northern end of the bay, **SAN PATRICIO-MELAQUE** seems much more typically Mexican than Barra de Navidad (5km further south), with a central plaza, church and largish market. Though it remains popular with Mexican families and budget travellers, Melaque is much scruffier than Barra, more commercial and has a more transitory feel.

The two **bus stations** face each other at the junction of Carranza and Gómez Farías and have frequent connections to Barra de Navidad (every 15min; M$5; 10min), regular buses to Guadalajara (5hr) and Manzanillo (1hr 30min), and four daily first-class buses to Puerto Vallarta (4–5hr). **Taxis** to Barra are around M$50. Opposite the bus station, in the Pasaje Comercial, you'll find the **Casa de Cambio Melaque** (which changes travellers' cheques); one block down Gómez Farías is an **internet** café (daily 9am–2pm & 4–10pm; M$20/hr). Half a block in the other direction there's a Banamex **bank** (Mon–Fri 9am–4pm, Sat 10am–2pm) with a 24-hour ATM; you can also **exchange** travellers' cheques here. The **post office** is on Orozco, around the corner from *Hotel San Patricio*. There's no **tourist office**; the office in Barra de Navidad serves both towns (see p.534).

Accommodation

Accommodation in Melaque is generally very cheap, especially during the low season (Aug–Nov), though little is open at this time. Budget **camping** is an option on the patch of land at the northern end of the beach (from M$30) beyond the restaurants and there's a full-facility campsite right by the beach, *Playa Trailer Park*, Gómez Farías 250, at López Mateos (Ⓣ315/355-5065; M$200), which charges the same for RVs and tents.

Hotel Bahía Legazpi 5 Ⓣ315/355-6894, Ⓦwww.melaquehotelbahia.com. The friendly Moreno family runs this bargain little hotel, a short walk from the beach and one of the best deals in town. Its 23 compact rooms and two kitchenette bungalows enclose a tranquil inner patio and a pool, and come with tiled floors, basic cable TV and fan. ❹, bungalows ❺

Hotel Santa María Abel Salgado Velazco 85 Ⓣ315/355-567. Great budget option, with basic one-bedroom motel-style apartments equipped with kitchenettes, TV and fans, nor far from the beach – the second-floor rooms are generally nicer. The ocean-front pool terrace is a good place to chill. ❸

La Paloma Ocean Front Retreat Av Las Cabañas 13 Ⓣ315/355-5345, Ⓦwww.lapalomamexico.com. Luxurious resort right on the beach, hosted by an amicable bunch of Canadians and featuring spacious studios with kitchen, sun-deck, ocean views and clean, cheerful decor. The on-site Paloma Art Center runs week-long workshops in watercolour painting. ❼

Posada Pablo de Tarso Gómez Farías 408 Ⓣ315/355-5117, Ⓦwww.posadapablodetarso.com. Pleasant, white-painted rooms with TV, fan, terracotta floor tiles around a verdant colonial courtyard and a good pool. ❹

Villas Camino del Mar Francisco Villa 6, corner Abel Salgado Velazco Ⓣ315/355-5207, Ⓦwww.villascaminodelmar.com.mx. Wonderful hideaway on the south side of town offering a range of accommodation in a new building on the road and far better rooms and villas overlooking the beach; some come with kitchenettes, but all have fans only. There's also an inviting pool and patio bar. ❺

Eating and drinking

Some of the best **eating** in Melaque can be had from street stalls around the central plaza, or enjoying the sunset from numerous identical palapa joints along the beachfront – look out especially for *El Pirata Hot Dogs* at the plaza in the evenings, *Juan's Dessert Stand* at Hidalgo and Juárez and *Surf Tacos* on Juárez. During the quieter summer months many restaurants and stalls will be closed.

Flor Morena Juárez 21, on the plaza (no phone). Cosy Mexican diner, knocking out fresh, home-made classics like enchiladas, tamales and tacos, though little seafood apart from their legendary shrimp *pozole*. Dishes for less than M$50 – this is probably Melaque's most popular restaurant, so expect a wait. Wed–Sun 5–11pm.

Hamburguesas Maui Obregón 15 ⓣ315/355-6283. Best takeout option, serving luscious burgers, tortas and fries throughout the day – also some spaces to munch on site. Everything is usually less than M$25. Daily 10am–11pm.

Restaurant Ava Obregón 8 at Gómez Farías ⓣ315/355-7151. Canadian-run place with palapa roof, best known for its ribs (Tues & Fri nights), hamburgers, and dancing and live music in the evenings, though it's usually open at 7am for breakfast. Daily happy hour noon–6pm.

Restaurant Maya Obregón 1 ⓣ315/355-6764. Arguably the best option in Melaque for quality dining, set amongst swaying palms and tiki torches. Fresh fish dishes are prepared with an Asian or Mediterranean twist and the bountiful salads – try the roasted beet, goat cheese and candied walnut – are wholesome and inventive. Brunch (Sun 10.30am–2pm) is also a monumental affair. Mains average M$150.

La Terraza Gordiano Guzmán 4 ⓣ315/355-5313. Serves generous breakfasts of freshly baked bread, granola, fruit and yogurt, as well as traditional Mexican fare in the evening on a cooling, second-floor patio. Daily 7.30am–3pm.

Barra de Navidad

Sitting towards the southern end of the Bahía de Navidad, where the beach runs out and curves back round to form a lagoon behind the town, **BARRA DE NAVIDAD** is easily the most appealing of the communities along the bay. Activities in Barra revolve around the shelved, honey-coloured sands; Sea to Sierra, 21 de Noviembre (ⓣ315/355-8582, ⓦwww.seatosierra.com), runs a variety of land and water tours, including a one-hour boat trip that winds through the mangroves of the Laguna de Navidad (from M$600), horseriding trips (M$250/hr), one-tank dives (M$850) and two- to four-hour mountain-bike tours (from M$500 for 2–4 people). The local *cooperativa* at the jetty also offers fishing trips, lagoon tours (M$200 per boat) and day trips to **Playa Tenacatita** (see p.531; M$2500 per boat).

The opening of the *Grand Bay Hotel* complex across the channel from Barra de Navidad has changed things surprisingly little, not even spoiling the view from the beach or the sedate charm of the town. If you have time, it's worth taking a **boat** over to check out one of the bars or restaurants (casual visitors are not allowed) – you can catch one outside the restaurant *El Manglito* near the jetty; they run across the channel every half-hour from 6am to 6pm (M$10) and, less frequently, to the beaches on the other side. **Colimilla** (M$20 return), across the Laguna de Navidad, is the most popular destination, chiefly for its seafood restaurants such as *Fortino's* (daily 9am–10pm; bring insect repellent if dining after dark), and as a base for the two- or three-kilometre walk over to the rough Pacific beach of Playa de Cocos.

Arrival and information

Buses arrive at the town's main terminals, which are clustered on Veracruz, Barra's main drag. The services you are likely to need – post office, phones and hotels – are all close by; in any case, it only takes twenty minutes to walk around the whole town. **Taxis** line up at Veracruz and Michoacán, with prices to most places fixed: Melaque (M$50), Manzanillo airport (M$300), Manzanillo (M$400), Tenacatita (M$300), Playa Pérula (M$650) and Puerto Vallarta (M$1500). The town now has

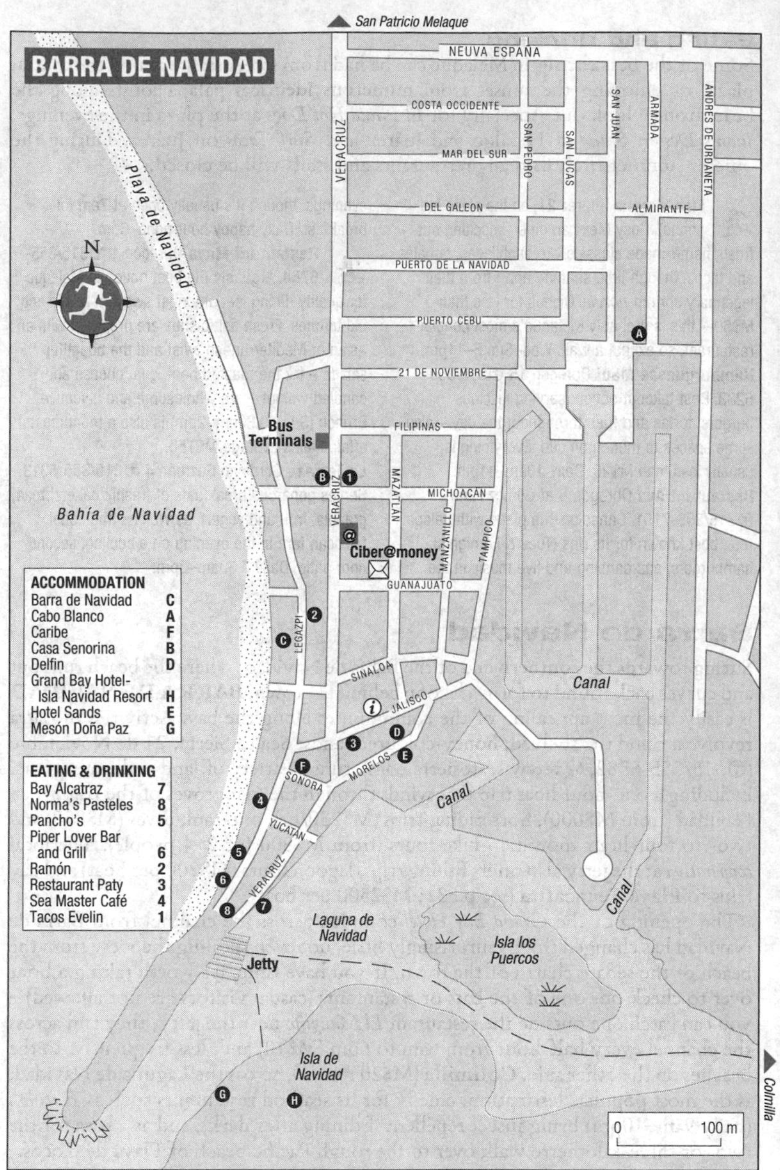

Bancomer and **Banamex** ATM machines on Veracruz but no actual branches; you can **exchange** dollars and travellers' cheques at the Ciber@Money **internet** café at Veracruz 212 (Mon–Sat 9am–2pm & 4–7pm, Sun 9am–2pm). The **post office** is nearby at Mazatlán 17 (Mon–Fri 9am–2pm).

The **tourist office**, Jalisco 67 (Mon–Fri 9am–5pm, Sat & Sun during high season; ⓣ315/355-5100, ⓦwww.barradenavidad.com), serves both Barra de

Navidad and San Patricio-Melaque. The staff can advise on anything happening locally – usually not much.

Accommodation

Although Barra has enough hotels to suit all tastes and budgets, reservations are recommended for the high season (roughly Dec–April). Free **camping** is also a possibility along the beach to the north of town. Should you want to camp, it's easiest to follow the beach, rather than the road, up to a point where you feel comfortable, as beach access is limited.

Barra de Navidad Legazpi 250 ⓣ338/244-4043. For unrivalled beach access, this is a good-value choice – it's right on the sand. Rooms are spartan but comfortable, and with a/c; the best have wonderful sea views. There's also a pool on site. ❻

Cabo Blanco Armada and Puerto de la Navidad (marina) ⓣ315/355-6495 or 01-800/710-5690, ⓦwww.hotelcaboblanco.com. Best for families, this economical resort hotel has more facilities than the price would suggest: palapa bar/restaurant, tennis courts, games room, swimming pool, "Kid's Club" – the list goes on. Rooms come in various sizes and all have a/c, safe, fan and cable TV. Meal plans also run the gamut, from room-only to bed and breakfast to all inclusive. ❺

Caribe Sonora 15 ⓣ315/335-5952. The best of the budget options, with clean, if rather lacklustre, rooms and a pleasant rooftop terrace with rocking chairs. ❷

Casa Senorina Veracruz at Michoacán ⓣ315/ 355-5315, ⓦwww.casasenorina.com. This attractive private home opened as a B&B in 2007, with Moroccan-themed architecture and eight comfy rooms with bath, internet, cable TV and on-site spa. ❻

Delfin Morelos 23 ⓣ315/355-5068, ⓦwww.hoteldelfinmx.com. Bright, arcaded hotel 5min from the beach. Clean, very spacious rooms with fan lead off an attractive balcony with views of the bay. There is a pool with sundeck, a restaurant where breakfast is served and a small gym. ❹

Grand Bay Hotel-Isla Navidad Resort Circuitos de los Marinos, Isla Navidad (across the bay) ⓣ315/331-0500, ⓦwww.wyndham.com/hotels/ZLOGB. Luxurious Wyndham-owned resort with a mountain backdrop, an idyllic location on the bay and a complete range of facilities for golfers and watersports enthusiasts as well as those in need of serious pampering. Rooms are the epitome of taste and style, dripping with marble and exotic woods and with all the expected luxuries. ❽

Hotel Sands Morelos 24 ⓣ315/355-5018. Charming rooms with colonial touches around an inner courtyard and a lush, tropical garden, overlooking the lagoon, where you'll find a swim-up bar and a swimming pool. ❺

Mesón Doña Paz Rinconada del Capitán, Isla Navidad (across the bay) ⓣ01-800/012-9887, ⓦwww.mesondonapaz.com. Beautiful, discreet colonial-style hotel in a stunning setting overlooking the bay. Each room has views of the lagoon and is richly decorated and thoughtfully appointed. An atmosphere of grace and elegance pervades the public areas, which are laden with art and antiques. The large pool has a wet bar and massages; golf and watersports can all be arranged by the superlative staff. ❽

Eating and drinking

Of the many good **restaurants** in Barra, most are on Legazpi, or else at the junction of Veracruz and Jalisco; **seafood** places in particular crowd Legazpi, Morelos and the southern end of Veracruz down towards the point. **Nightlife** is fairly limited but there are a couple of congenial bars where you can play pool, drink, munch on snacks and listen to live music.

Bay Alcatraz Veracruz 12 ⓣ315/355-7041. This tranquil, romantic restaurant occupies a prime spot overlooking the lagoon, with a big menu of soups, salads, meats and fresh fish, but best known for *molcajetes*, delicious combinations of cheese, meats and seafood served in a roughly hewn lava bowl (M$100–150). Daily noon–10.30pm.

Norma's Pasteles Veracruz and Legazpi. This popular stall (manned by the indomitable Norma Torres) sells irresistible slices of home-made cakes and desserts, usually between 3pm and 10.30pm daily. Try the *pastel de tres leches* (sweet milk pudding).

Pancho's Legazpi 53 ⓣ315/355-5176. This earthy restaurant is one of Barra's original palapas, now managed by Pancho's son and serving great fresh seafood: specials include the shrimp "a la diabla" (spicy devilled shrimp) and zesty marlin *ceviche*. Daily 8am–8pm.

Piper Lover Bar and Grill Legazpi 240-C, www.piperlover.com. Facing the beach on Legazpi, this is the best bar in town, with live rock, jazz and especially blues most nights. Daily 10am–2am.

Ramón Legazpi 260, opposite *Hotel Barra de Navidad* ☎315/355-6435. Open all day and with an extensive range of Mexican and international food, including some excellent fish and chips and *chiles rellenos*, especially good with shrimp. Lots of free salsa and chips (crisps) to start. Daily 7am–11pm.

Restaurant Paty Jalisco 52 at Veracruz ☎315/355-5907. The best of a number of similar budget places, serving decent *ceviche*, fresh fish, *carne asada* and fantastic barbecue chicken, as well as all the Mexican staples. Daily 8am–11pm.

Sea Master Café Legazpi 146 at Yucatán ☎315/355-5845. This breezy, laid-back café serves creative meals overlooking the ocean, with popular shrimps in garlic, succulent ribs and the best burgers in town. It's also the perfect place for beers and cocktails in the evening.

Tacos Evelin Veracruz and Michoacán. One of many tiny taco stalls in the centre of town, this one stands out for its juicy *barbacoa* and *carne asada*, all less than M$10. Daily 9am–1pm.

Manzanillo and around

Just ninety minutes south from the Bahía de Navidad, **MANZANILLO** is clearly a working port: tourism – although highly developed – very definitely takes second place to trade. Downtown, criss-crossed by railway tracks, rumbles with heavy traffic and is surrounded by a bewildering array of inner harbours and shallow lagoons that seem to cut the town off from the land. You can easily imagine that a couple of hundred years ago plague and pestilence made sailors fear to land here, and it's not surprising to read in an 1884 guide to Mexico that "the climate of Manzanillo is unhealthy for Europeans, and the tourist is advised not to linger long in the vicinity." While it may still exhibit some of the same coarse characteristics, much of the old town has been spruced up in recent years. This said, few tourists do stay – most head to the hotels and club resorts of the Península de Santiago around the bay to the east – even though Manzanillo is a lot more interesting than the sanitized resort area, and cheaper, too.

Arrival and information

The **Aeropuerto Internacional Playa de Oro** is 30km north of Manzanillo's Zona Hotelera (Hwy-200 km 42). There are no buses here, so you have to take a fixed-price *colectivo* (M$110–130) or **taxi** (M$270–360), with rates set according to a zone system. Alamo (☎314/334-0124), Budget (☎314/334-2270), Hertz (☎314/333-3191) and Thrifty (☎314/334-3282) have **car rental** desks at the airport. The airport **ATM** is temperamental, so make sure you have pesos on arrival.

The **Terminal de Autobuses** is several kilometres northeast of the centre, just off Hwy-200 near Playa Las Brisas. **Buses** (M$5–6) to the main plaza (marked "Jardín" or "Centro") and the beaches (marked "Santiago") leave from the station entrance. **Taxis** should be around M$35 to the centre, but fix the price first. The ETN bus station is much further around the bay, off Hwy-200 at Playa Santiago.

Manzanillo's commercial core, **El Centro**, centres on its main plaza, the **Jardín Alvaro Obregón**, right on the harbour opposite the main outer dock and embellished with rose gardens and exuberant topiary. The 3.5-km boardwalk dotted with palms heading around the bay from here and dominated by the massive 25-metre-tall **sailfish memorial** is best ambled at sunset. All tourist services are a very short walk away. Banamex and Bancomer **banks** (both with ATMs) are next to each other on México, at Bocanegra; and the **post office** is at Galindo 30

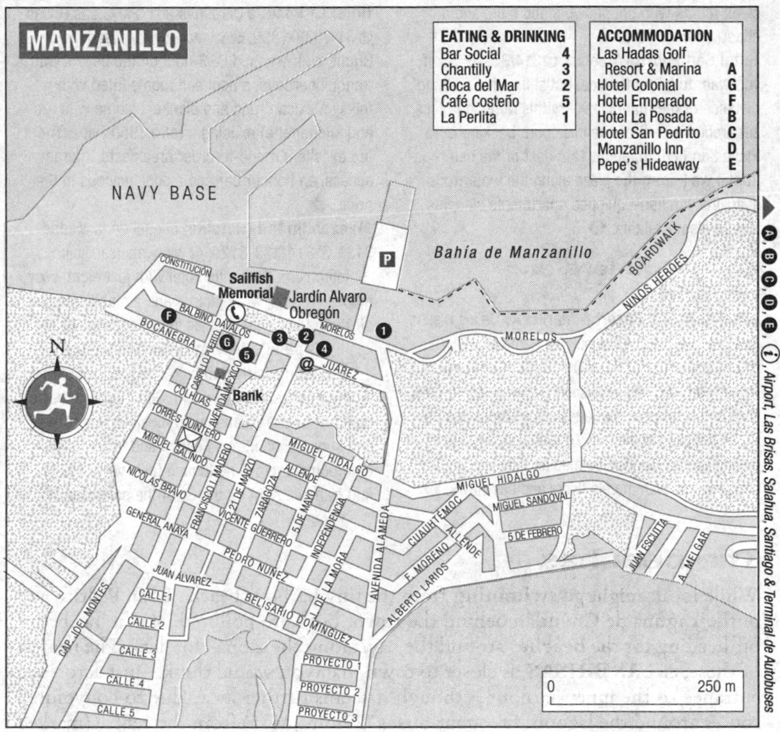

(Mon–Fri 9am–3pm). One of the most central **internet** cafés is Members.com (daily 9am–11.30pm; M$15/hr) at Juárez 116. The helpful **regional tourist office** is north of Playa Azul several kilometres out of town, at Miguel de la Madrid 4960 (Mon–Fri 9am–3pm & 5–7pm, Sat 10am–2pm; ⓣ314/333-2277).

Accommodation

Finding a **place to stay** is no problem in Manzanillo, with most of the budget options close to the plaza in **El Centro**, and a host of mid-range and luxury resorts stretching north around the bay in the **Zona Hotelera**; as the original seaside strip, **Las Brisas** offers a number of dated, monolithic hotels which tend to be cheaper than elsewhere, except when the area is flooded by holiday-makers from Guadalajara, while the rocky **Península de Santiago**, further north, is smothered in luxury resorts. **Prices** at all but the cheapest hotels drop by about 25 percent outside the high season (roughly Dec–May) and Semana Santa. Playa San Pedrito is probably your best bet for **camping**: Manzanillo has no trailer park and all the other beaches are pretty built up.

El Centro

Hotel Colonial Bocanegra 100 ⓣ314/332-1080. This 1940s gem drips with faded colonial grandeur: an Andalucian mosaic-tiled courtyard with a fountain and heavy wooden furnishings add to its allure. The clean, spacious rooms, with a/c and cable TV, are perfectly comfortable. ❹

Hotel Emperador Dávalos 69 ⓣ314/332-2374. Far better value than some of its neighbours, this is one of the best budget deals in town, with small, clean rooms with hot showers and fans, and a cheap *comedor*, too. ❸

Hotel San Pedrito Azueta 3 ⓣ314/332-0535. If you want to be by the sea, but still within walking distance of the main plaza, try this rambling place set around a pool and tennis court, backing onto Playa San Pedrito, about 1km east of the centre (a 20min walk from the plaza along the waterfront); spacious, kitchen-equipped apartments sleeping six are also available. ❺

Zona Hotelera and beyond

Las Hadas Golf Resort & Marina Av De los Riscos and Vista Hermosa, Península de Santiago ⓣ314/331-0101 or 01-800/713-3233, ⓦwww.brisas.com.mx. This amazingly flashy wedding-cake-style hotel complex is where Dudley Moore and Bo Derek frolicked in the film *10*, with a vast range of amenities and Moorish-themed architecture; rooms are all-white, with marble floors and bay views. ❾

Hotel La Posada Cárdenas 201, Playa Las Brisas ⓣ314/333-1899, ⓦwww.hotel-la-posada.info. Bright, pink-washed B&B right on the beach, with tranquil gardens, a pool and rooms fitted with folksy Mexican rugs and blankets (some with a/c and kitchenette) exuding a retro 1950s vibe. There are excellent made-to-order breakfasts, internet access, an honour bar and a pool included in the price. ❺

Manzanillo Inn (Hotelito) Miguel de la Madrid 3181 ⓣ314/333-6120, ⓦwww.manzanilloinn-hotelito.com. Romantic hotel with just eight, cosy, modern rooms, wi-fi, jacuzzi and amiable bar, just off the beach – good deals in low season. ❼

Pepe's Hideaway Camino Don Diego 67, Península de Santiago ⓣ314/333-0616, ⓦwww.pepeshideaway.com. Glittering beachside resort of luxury palapas with mesmerizing views and sunsets, handmade chairs and tables, tiled bathrooms and ceiling fans; it feels very remote and tranquil, right on the tip of the peninsula. ❾

The beaches

While locals might go **swimming** from the tiny harbour beach of San Pedrito and in the Laguna de Cuyutlán behind the town, both are polluted. You're far better off heading for the **beaches** around the bay, along the Zona Hotelera. The nearest of these, at **LAS BRISAS**, is closer to town than you would think – just across the entrance to the inner harbour – though it seems further away due to convoluted routes around the lagoon. Frequent **buses** (20min; M$5) from the centre (marked "Las Brisas") run all the way along the single seafront drive. The six-kilometre beach (which is known as **Playa Azul** at the top end) shelves steeply to the ocean, causing the tide to crash upon the shore; consequently, the beach is not as conducive to swimming as those further around the bay.

Better and more sheltered swimming can be found along the coast further round, where the bay is divided by the rocky Península de Santiago. "Miramar" **buses** run all the way to the far side of the bay, past the settlements of **Salahua** and **SANTIAGO** and a string of beaches. The best of these are around the far edge of the peninsula (get off the bus at Santiago); Playa Santiago, Playa Olas Altas and finally Playa Miramar, the best beach for **surfing** (shops rent boards on the beach).

If you're prepared to walk a little way, you can reach the calm and tranquil waters of the beautiful cove of **La Audiencia**, on the west side of the Santiago peninsula, beneath the *Gran Costa Resort*. From here, if you're feeling reasonably energetic and looking smart enough to get past the guards, you can climb over the hill to the pseudo-private beach of *Las Hadas Golf Resort & Marina* (see above), which is worth seeing even if you can't afford a drink at any of the bars.

Eating and drinking

Rather like the hotels, the cheapest **places to eat** are concentrated around Jardín Alvaro Obregón in Centro, while you'll find modern chains and posher places spread out along the bay on Hwy-200. If you head down México, Centro's main commercial and shopping street, you'll find a whole series of *taquerías*, while there are several very cheap places – grimy and raucous on the whole – in the market area three blocks down México and at the bottom end of Juárez by the railway tracks.

Moving on from Manzanillo

Most long-distance buses depart from the new and hangar-like **Terminal de Autobuses** northeast of town (see p.536). You'll find frequent second-class services to Colima (1hr 30min), Tecomán (1hr), Guadalajara (5–6hr) and **Lázaro Cárdenas** (5 daily; 7hr). First- and executive-class buses also serve **Colima** (every hour; 1hr 30min), Guadalajara (every hour; 6hr), **Barra de Navidad** (11 daily; 1hr 30min) and **Puerto Vallarta** (7hr). Estrella Blanca runs first-class buses to **Acapulco** (3 daily; 12hr), Mexico City (2 daily; 12hr) and Tijuana (2 daily; 38hr). ETN (ⓣ315/344-1050) runs the most comfortable deluxe service from its own terminal at Hwy-200 km 13.5 to Barra de Navidad (3 daily; 1hr 30min), Colima (7 daily; 2hr) and Guadalajara (7 daily; 5hr).

Flights from the airport connect Manzanillo with Mexico City, Los Angeles, Phoenix and Houston – seasonal charters fly direct to Montréal and Calgary.

For further information, see Travel details, p.567.

El Centro

These options are marked on the Manzanillo map, see p.537.

Bar Social Juárez and 21 de Marzo. This classic cantina is a throwback to the 1950s, with crusty old regulars propping up the bar and even older staff. It's all very friendly, though, and perfectly safe for women – an atmospheric place for a couple of beers.

Chantilly Juárez 44 at Madero ⓣ314/332-0194. This bustling restaurant makes a substantial comida corrida, good *antojitos* and the best ice cream in town. Closed Sat.

Roca del Mar Morelos 225, Jardín Alvaro Obregón ⓣ314/332-0302. Diagonally opposite *Chantilly*, this place serves a mind-boggling range of Mexican and international meals, top-value comidas corridas and good espresso and cappuccino – a good choice for sitting outside and watching the action.

Zona Hotelera and beyond

Café Costeño Cárdenas 1613, Playa Las Brisas. Excellent, relaxing place for a coffee – or a frozen cappuccino – inside or on a shady patio. Does tasty oversized American breakfasts or all the classic Mexican dishes from M$40.

Juanito's Miguel de la Madrid km 14, Santiago ⓣ314/333-1388, ⓦwww.juanitos.com. Fun, family restaurant specializing in breakfasts, burgers, chilaquiles, tacos and refreshing drinks (fresh fruit smoothies) since the 1970s. Daily 8am–11pm.

La Perlita Independencia 23, off Miguel de la Madrid, Santiago ⓣ314/120-3753. Venerable seafood restaurant since 1968, now housed in plush modern premises dishing up all sorts of *antojitos*, *ceviche*, shellfish and pastas for around M$100. Daily 6am–midnight.

Le Petit Napoléon Plaza Gaviotas, Paseo de Gaviotas, Playa Azul (off Miguel de la Madrid). For a taste of France make for this small café serving the best crepes on the coast, from apple-smoked sausage to blackberry and chocolate. Crepes M$25–40. Closed Mon & Tues.

La Sonrisa Miguel de la Madrid, Playa Azul. The best tacos on the bay, especially famous for their giant chorizo and *carne asada* quesadillas for M$35. Any taxi driver will know it.

El Vaquero Las Brisas 19 ⓣ314/334-1488. Serves a hearty menu of grilled meats in a suitably cowboy-inspired palapa setting (now has three locations in the area). The fruity sangria is the perfect accompaniment to the mesquite-broiled steaks, sold by the kilo (1kg is enough for four people) or by the gram (350g is considered a regular steak). Closed Sun & Mon.

Cuyutlán and around

If all you need is a heaving ocean and a strip of beach backed by a few *enramadas*, then you're better off skipping Manzanillo altogether in favour of a series of tiny resorts that adorn the shoreline 50–80km beyond. **CUYUTLÁN** is the most appealing, backed by an immense coconut grove that stretches along a narrow peninsula almost to Manzanillo. Popular with Mexican holiday-makers, the old town around the main plaza is sleepy, its inhabitants idling away the day on wooden verandas under terracotta roofs. In spring, the **coast** both here and further south is subject to the **Ola Verde**: vast, dark-green waves up to 10m high that crash down on the fine grey sand. Theories to explain their green hue vary widely – though most experts think it is phosphorescence created by microscopic phytoplankton – but whatever the reason, the Ola Verde has been a part of Cuyutlán lore ever since a huge tidal wave destroyed the town in 1932. At other times of the year the surf is impressive but easier to handle and it's OK to swim (surfers usually head south to Paraíso and Boca de Pascuales (see below).

If you're staying for a couple of days, it's worth taking a trip out to the **Centro Ecológico de Cuyutlán "el Tortugario"**, around 4km on the road to Paraíso (Tues–Sun 10am–5.30pm; M$20) – catch a cab from the plaza (M$50) or stroll south down the beach for about 45 minutes. From July to December, three **turtle** species visit the local beaches to lay their eggs and a team from the centre goes out every night to collect them before they end up as someone's dinner. The newly hatched turtles are then kept in tanks for a couple of days before being released back into the sea. Out of the egg-laying season, there's a resident turtle population and lots of information on hand. The sanctuary has a swimming pool and boats used for the three-hour **tours** (M$75) to Paraíso (see below) and back through the mangrove tunnels of the idyllic, jungly **Laguna Estero Palo Verde**, well known for its birdlife.

There's also the **Museo de Sal** (daily 9am–6pm; donation M$10) in town, two blocks east of the plaza on Juárez, housed in an original, wooden salt *bodega*. Salt was worth more than gold in pre-Columbian times and if you're interested, the retired salt-workers who run the place will talk you through the compound's long history.

Practicalities

To get to Cuyutlán from Manzanillo, you must first catch a bus (every 15min) 50km south to the inland market town of **Armería**, which has a bank, a post office and a long-distance bus stop on the main street (Hwy-200). From Armería, to catch buses to Cuyutlán, 12km west (6am–7.30pm every 30min; M$8.50; 20min), and Paraíso (see below), 6km west of Cuyutlán (every 45min; M$6; 15min), walk two blocks north from the long-distance bus stop, then one block east to the market.

Outside the high season, **hotels** in Cuyutlán are affordable (in low season many places sell three nights for the price of two) and clustered within a block or two of the junction of Hidalgo and Veracruz. The ones to go for are *Morelos*, Hidalgo 185 (Ⓣ313/326-4013; ❷), with clean rooms (the renovated ones are the most comfortable), fans, hot water and the town's best swimming pool; the longstanding *Fénix*, Hidalgo 201 (Ⓣ313/326-4082, Ⓔhotelfenixcuyutlan@yahoo.com; ❸), which has some great old-fashioned rooms opening onto spacious communal verandas; and *San Rafael*, Veracruz 46 (Ⓣ313/326-4015, Ⓦwww.hotelsanrafael.com; ❺), where some lovely rooms lead straight to the beach. All three hotels boast decent **seafood restaurants**.

Paraíso and Boca de Pascuales

With your own vehicle you can reach **PARAÍSO** directly from Cuyutlán, or you could take the Laguna Estero Palo Verde boat tour (see above) and get off at Paraíso. However, if you're travelling by bus you'll have to return to Armería (see above), from where it's another 8km to this minute place – really just a few neglected buildings on either side of the dust-and-cobble street. The beach is peaceful though, with banks of crashing surf and a few uninspired *enramadas* serving essentially the same menu. Only at *Hotel Paraíso*, right on the seafront (☎312/312-1032; ❸), is the feeling of banality and dilapidation dispelled; the older rooms have character, but the new wing is more comfortable, and everyone uses the pool and watches the sunset from the bar. If you **camp** on the beach, they'll let you use a shower, especially if you buy a drink.

Smaller still, **BOCA DE PASCUALES**, 13km from **Tecomán**, is little more than a bunch of palapa restaurants and a beach renowned for huge waves and challenging **surf**; this is a river-mouth beach break with some of the nastiest and fastest tubes in Mexico (breaking right and left) – it's definitely not for the inexperienced. Even swimming can be dangerous, but otherwise it's a fine place to hang out for a few days. Beach **camping** is an attractive proposition here, but there are a couple of surfer-friendly lodges, the best of which is *Paco's Hotel* (☎200/124-7362; ❹), on the way in, offering colourful and cosy rooms, some with air-conditioning (M$50 extra). The best **restaurant**, *Las Hamacas del Mayor* (☎313/103-6903, Ⓦwww.lashamacasdelmayor.com.mx), has been serving top-notch seafood since 1953 and still draws a large crowd, in spite of its remote location. To reach Boca de Pascuales, you'll first need to take a direct bus from Manzanillo to Tecomán, 20km south of Armería. Minibuses run to Boca from Tecomán's bus station (7am–8pm hourly; M$6; 20min). Taxis charge M$80. Buses also run from Tecomán to Colima and Lázaro Cárdenas.

Colima

Inland **COLIMA**, capital of the state of the same name and 100km from Manzanillo, is a distinctly colonial city, and a very beautiful one too, overlooked by the perfectly conical **Volcán de Colima** and, in the distance, the Nevado de Colima. With a handful of sights inside the city limits and interesting excursions nearby, it's a pleasant place to stop over for a night or two. In addition, Colima's Old World ambience, favourable climate – cooler than the coast, but never as cold as in the high mountains – and several good-value hotels and restaurants also make it an appealing destination.

Archeological evidence – much of it explained in the city's museums – points to three millennia of rich cultural heritage around Colima, almost all of it wiped out with the arrival of Cortés's lieutenant Gonzalo de Sandoval, who, in 1522, founded the city on its present site. Acapulco's designation as the chief Pacific port at the end of the sixteenth century deprived Colima of any strategic importance; this, in combination with a series of devastating earthquakes – the most recent in 2003 – means that the city has few grand buildings to show for its former glory. It makes up for this with a chain of shady formal **plazas** called "jardíns" – Colima is known as the "City of Palms" – and a number of attractive **courtyards**, many of which are now used as restaurants and cafés and make wonderfully cool places to catch up on writing postcards.

Arrival and information

Some 2km east of the centre, Colima's **main bus station**, the Terminal Forañea (or Central de Autobuses), handles frequent first- and second-class buses from Guadalajara and Manzanillo. **Taxis** (M$25) and **city buses** #2, #4 and #5 (M$4) run towards the central plaza from the station. Many second-class Manzanillo buses and all local services, including the one to Comala, operate from the **Terminal Rojos**, 7km west of the centre of town. If you arrive here, a #4 or #6 bus will take you to the centre of town; from the centre, take a #2 or buses marked

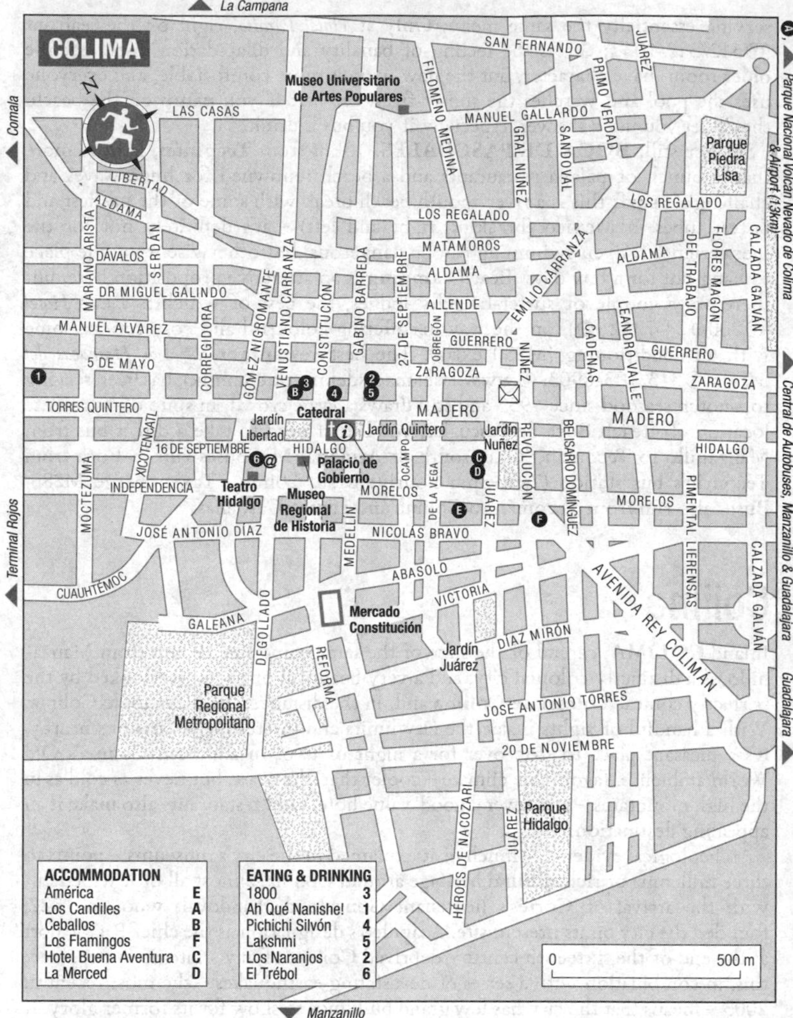

"Rojos" from Madero, at Revolucíon, to get back. The nearest **airport**, Miguel de la Madrid, is 13km northeast of the centre in Cuauhtémoc, with three daily flights from Mexico City on Aeromar (the nearest international airport is Manzanillo). Taxis charge around M$120 into the centre of Colima.

Colima's extremely helpful **tourist office**, inside the Palacio de Gobierno, on Reforma and Hidalgo at the Plaza Principal (Mon–Fri 9am–3pm & 6–9pm, Sat 9am–1pm; ⓣ312/312-4360, ⓦwww.visitacolima.com.mx), has a variety of maps and pamphlets. The **post office** is on Jardín Nuñez, at Madero 247 (Mon–Fri 8.30am–5.30pm). There's a Banamex with an ATM on Hidalgo, a few doors down from the tourist office, and several **casas de cambio** on Juárez, along the western side of Jardín Nuñez. **Internet** access is available at CI@, just off the zócalo at Hildago and Degollado (Mon–Sat 9am–10pm, Sun 10am–4pm; M$15/hr).

Accommodation

Colima has a clutch of reasonable **hotels** within a few blocks of the centre. Sadly, for the most part they don't conform to the regal ambience that pervades the city. **Rates** don't vary much year-round, but places do fill up rapidly during the San Felipe and Todos los Santos fiestas in early to mid-February and late October to early November.

América Morelos 162 ⓣ312/312-0366, ⓦwww.hotelamerica.com.mx. Bland but reliable downtown hotel geared towards Mexican business travellers – it's not as nice as the classic 1920s exterior suggests. Remodelled suites are very comfortable (all with a/c and TV), but the older standard rooms are gloomy. Facilities include a convention centre, chi-chi restaurant, swimming pool and free internet. 5

Los Candiles Camino Real 399 ⓣ312/312-3212, ⓦwww.hotelloscandiles.com. Close to the university (2km from the centre, but on several bus routes), this is a comfortable business hotel. What it lacks in charm it compensates for with its swimming pool, parking, restaurant, and spacious, if rather fusty, rooms with a/c, cable TV, safe and decent bathrooms. Less expensive than its downtown counterparts. 5

Ceballos Portal Medellín 12 ⓣ312/312-4444, ⓦwww.hotelceballos.com. In a prime location, right on the Jardín Libertad, this characterful Best Western-owned colonial hotel exudes Old World grandeur (dating from 1880 it once housed the state governors). Rooms vary enormously; the best are the light and airy, newly refurbished deluxe ones (worth the extra M$100) with hand-painted furniture, French windows and wrought-iron balconies. Standard rooms are more dour with medieval dimensions. 6

Los Flamingos Rey Colimán 18 ⓣ312/312-2525. One of the better budget options. Institutional rooms have private bath, good beds, balconies and TV. 3

Hotel Buena Aventura Juárez 70 ⓣ312/136-1246, ⓦwww.hotelbuenaaventura.com. Fabulous mid-range option, with eleven simple but stylish rooms with tiled floors, a/c, satellite TV and bathroom. You also get free wi-fi, gym, tea and coffee – it's a real bargain. 4

La Merced Juárez 82 ⓣ312/312-6969. Characterful old hotel with passable fan-ventilated rooms with bath around a central patio and some less attractive, newer rooms – the best rooms are at the back. TV and parking. 3

The Town

As in all Mexico's old cities, life in Colima is focused on its central **Plaza Principal** (known as Jardín Libertad) where you'll find the government offices (take a quick look at the distinctly second-rate murals in the Palacio de Gobierno) and the unimpressive Neoclassical cathedral, which dates from 1941. Quite out of character for this part of Mexico, however, the town actually boasts a couple of really good **museums**.

The most central of these, Colima's **Museo Regional de Historia** (Tues–Sun 9am–6pm; M$41, free Sun; ⓣ312/312-9228), stands across the street from the Palacio de Gobierno in a lovely old building that also houses the university art gallery. Move swiftly through the displays on **local crafts** – though the animal and diabolical masks used in traditional dances are interesting – and make for the later rooms, chock-full of **pre-Hispanic ceramics**: gorgeous figurines with superbly expressive faces, fat Izcuintli dogs and people working on mundane, everyday tasks. Though characteristic of western Mexican culture, these examples are specific to Colima, many of them found in *tumbas de tiro* – well-like tombs up to 16m deep, more commonly found in South America and the Pacific Islands. The cultural parallel isn't well understood, but explanatory panels (all in Spanish) show the different styles.

If you've more time to spare, wander eight blocks north of the plaza to the **Museo Universitario de Artes Populares** (Mon–Sat 10am–2pm & 5–8pm, Sun 10am–1pm; M$20; ⓣ312/312-6869), at the corner of Barreda and Gallardo, which has an eclectic but poorly explained collection of folk art, including masks;

Climbing the Nevado de Colima

The **Parque Nacional Volcán Nevado de Colima** comprises two spell-binding volcanoes rising north of Colima. The **Volcán de Colima** (3860m), also known as Volcán de Fuego, is officially still active and smokes from time to time, though there seems little imminent danger. It is far less frequently climbed than its larger and more passive brother, the **Nevado de Colima** (4330m), which, with its pine- and oak-forested slopes, is popular with local mountaineers during the clear, dry winter months. Unless there's a lot of snow – in December and January crampons and an ice axe are essential – and provided you are fit and can get transport high enough, it's a relatively easy **hike** up to the summit. The most popular option is to ascend the Nevado de Colima from the cabin at **La Joya** (3500m); the usual route is via a steep climb to the radio antennae ("Las Antenas"), from where it's another stiff but non-technical walk to the summit. Joining an **organized tour** is the hassle-free alternative and recommended for less experienced hikers: Volcano Tours (Ⓣ312/310-7483, Ⓦwww.colimamagic.com) and Returi (Ⓣ312/308-0487, Ⓦwww.returi.com) offer day trips from Colima and Manzanillo, for around M$800.

Independently, you'll need to set three days aside for the climb, take a sleeping bag and waterproofs, pack enough food and water for the trip and walk from the village of El Fresnito. First, take a bus from Terminal Forañea in Colima to Ciudad Guzmán (about 1hr 30min) and from there catch a bus from stall #21 to **El Fresnito**, where there are very limited supplies. Ask for the road to La Joya – take this and keep right until the route becomes obvious. This rough service road for the radio antennae leads up through cow pastures and goes right past the cabin at La Joya, about six to eight hours' walking (35km). You pay the **entry fee** (M$20) and can tank up from the supply of running water here, but don't expect to stay in the hut, which is often locked, and even if open may be full, as it only sleeps six – bring camping equipment. Plan on a day from La Joya to the summit and back, then another to get back to Colima, though a very fit walker starting before dawn could make the trip back to Colima, or at least Ciudad Guzmán, in a day. Note that **hitching** isn't an option as the logging roads up here are rough, requiring high clearance or 4WD vehicles, and see very little traffic. Check Ⓦwww.nevadodecolima.com for the latest information.

traditional textiles and costumes modelled by enormous papier-mâché figures; shoes; ceramics; images of the Virgin; toy aeroplanes; and a small musical instrument collection – look for the violin made from scrap wood and a Modelo beer can.

The source of some of the museum's treasures is the ruined city at **La Campana** (Tues–Sun 9am–5pm; M$37; Ⓣ312/313-4946), three kilometres northwest of the centre, which dates back to around 1500 BC and is believed to have reached its zenith between 700 and 900 AD. Excavations have revealed some small pyramids, temple remains and one tomb. To get there, head north out of town along Gabino Barreda and take a left onto Tecnológico.

Eating and drinking

For a town of its size, Colima has a great range of places to eat, from restaurants serving **Oaxacan** and local specialities to the region's best **vegetarian** food.

1800 5 de Mayo 15 Ⓣ312/312-9300 (between Carranza and Constitución). Fashionable café and bar attracting mostly local students with tasty *antojitos* (from M$45) comfy couches and billowing drapes. Decent cocktails from around M$30. Tues–Sun 7pm–2am.

Ah Qué Nanishe! 5 de Mayo 267, west of Mariano Arista Ⓣ312/314-2197, Ⓦwww.ahquenanishe.com. The name of this surprisingly inexpensive courtyard restaurant appropriately means "how delicious" in Zapotec. It specializes in dishes from the owner's native Oaxaca: *mole*, *chapulines* (baked grasshoppers) and *tlyaduas* (large flour tortillas). Well worth the walk from the centre. Open 1–11pm, closed Tues.

Lakshmi Madero 265 at Revolución ⓣ312/312-6433. Mainly a wholefood shop and bakery producing great banana and carrot breads and herbal supplements, but with a courtyard restaurant for eat-in veggie burgers, salads, granola, yogurts and nutritious drinks. Mon–Sat 8.30am–9.30pm, Sun 6am–9.30pm.

Los Naranjos Gabino Barreda 34, north of Madero ⓣ312/312-0029. Friendly, smart restaurant where you can get a substantial comida corrida for around M$60 and a good selection of meat dishes, especially beef – try the *arrachera* (thick flank steak). The breakfasts are especially good value; the all-you-can eat buffet (M$70) includes *chilaquiles*, quesadillas, eggs, fruit, tea and coffee. There's a second branch on Constitución. Daily 8am–11.30pm.

Pichichi Silvón Portal Medellín. Hole in the wall, serving crispy *churros rellenos* (M$5) stuffed with chocolate opposite the *Ceballos* hotel.

El Trébol Degollado 59 at 16 de Septiembre ⓣ312/312-2900. Comfortable, cosy and inexpensive place just off the plaza for egg dishes, snacks and light meals. Closed Sat.

Around Colima: Comala

The best time to be in Colima is on a clear winter day when the volcanoes in the **Parque Nacional Nevado de Colima** dominate the scenery to the north. Climbing them, while not that difficult, needs some planning (see box opposite). You can get a closer look, however, by spending an afternoon at **COMALA**, a tidy, quaint town, 10km north of Colima. Here, in the central plaza, you can sip a beer or margarita while enjoying a fantastic view of the mountains and listening to mariachi bands competing for your business. Four **restaurants** huddled together under the plaza's southern portal each try to outdo the other by producing better *botanas* – plates of snacks, dips and tacos – free with drinks from noon until about 6pm. There's little to choose between them – the drinks are uniformly expensive (around M$30 for a beer or soft drink), but you can still get a fairly economical lunch. Friday and Saturday are the liveliest times, when you can mingle with day-tripping, predominantly middle-class Mexicans from Guadalajara; on Sundays and Mondays there are craft markets in the square. A thirty-minute stroll out of town, in the Centro Cultural Nogueras, the **Museo Alejandro Rangel Hidalgo** (Tues–Fri 10am–2pm & 4pm–7pm, Sat & Sun

▲ Nevado de Colima

10am–5pm; M$20; ⓣ312/315-6028) has an engaging display of the eponymous artist's work as well as pre-Hispanic artefacts from Hidalgo's personal collection. Known for his evocative book illustrations, he drew the pictures for the classic Mexican novel *Pedro Páramo,* which was written by his close friend Juan Rulfo and set in Comala (Hidalgo died in 2000 at the age of 73). **Buses** run frequently to Comala from Colima's Terminal Rojos (every 15min; M$7; 20min).

South to Lázaro Cárdenas

Beyond the state of Colima you run into a virtually uninhabited area: there are occasional beaches, but for the most part the mountains drop straight into the ocean – a spectacular sight, but offering little reason to stop. As you move into Michoacán, **CALETA DE CAMPOS**, some 70km short of Lázaro Cárdenas, is the first, and in many ways the best, place to stop. A small village that acts as a service centre for the area, it's friendly and unassuming, with two lovely beaches and impressive ocean views. There is something of a Wild West feel to the place: the streets are unpaved, and horses stand tied to hitching posts alongside the campers of American surfers and the fancy new cars belonging to visitors from the city. Should you decide to stay, there are two **hotels** – *Yuritzi* (ⓣ753/531-5010, ⓦwww.hotelyuritzi.com; ❹, M$150 extra for a/c), Corregidora 10, a modern, well-managed establishment which has its own generator and water supply, and the less expensive, more dilapidated *Los Arcos* (ⓣ753/531-5038; ❸) at Heroica Escuela Naval Militar 5 – as well as a string of bar/restaurants down at the beach and a plethora of taco stands and mini-markets along the main street. For much of the year the place is virtually deserted, but in winter, when Californian beach boys come down in pursuit of sun and surf (the waves are perfect for beginners), and at weekends, when families from Lázaro Cárdenas pile in, it can take on crowds.

Playa Azul

Once a small-time, slow-moving beach surrounded by lagoons, **PLAYA AZUL** has been rather overrun by the growth of Lázaro Cárdenas, 20km away. However, there are still several reasonably priced hotels and a moderate beach, backed by scores of palapa restaurants. But, aside from lying on the sand (the surf and dangerous undercurrents make swimming unsafe) there is really nothing else to hold your attention.

Long-distance **buses** don't pass directly through Playa Azul, so ask to be dropped off at La Mira, the nearest town on Hwy-200 – from here, numerous local buses and *combis* run the remaining 7km down to Playa Azul. Otherwise *colectivos* (M$15; 30min) run back and forth to Lázaro Cárdenas from the centre, and you can also take taxis for around M$150. The road into town crosses four streets, parallel to the beach and running down to the vast plaza at the southern end. As you come in on Carranza you'll pass *Hotel Playa Azul* (ⓣ753/536-0024; ❻), where **rooms** are clustered around a leafy courtyard and have air-conditioning and a pool view. You can also **camp** here (M$150) though the site is little more than a patch of dirt behind the hotel. The pool is a better prospect (M$25 for non-guests), and at weekends their larger pool, complete with water slide, costs no more. For somewhere cheaper, try the comfortable *María Isabela*, on the far side of the plaza (ⓣ753/536-0016; ❹), which has pristine rooms, very friendly staff and a pool of its own. The best accommodation is *Hotel María Teresa*, also on the plaza (ⓣ753/536-0005; ❺), which has attractive rooms, a decent pool and a garden bar/restaurant serving breakfast only (included in the price). **Beachfront restaurants** such as *El Pirata del Caribe* serve mainly seafood lunches and dinners, while the poolside restaurant at *Hotel Playa Azul* has a good range of international food, including pizzas and pasta dishes.

Lázaro Cárdenas

Local buses make the trip from Caleta de Campos to **LÁZARO CÁRDENAS** several times a day. The only reason to come here, however, is if you're trying to get somewhere else – it's strictly industrial, dominated by the huge ArcelorMittal steel-works. If you get stuck for the night, you'll find several small **hotels** in the centre. Close to the bus station, the *Hotel Reyna Pio*, Corregidora 78 (ⓣ753/532-0620; ❸), is a popular inexpensive option with well-maintained, spacious rooms with fan and hot water and friendly, helpful owners. One of the tallest buildings in town, *Hotel de Casablanca*, Nicolás Bravo 475 (ⓣ753/537-3480, ⓦwww.hcasablanca.com.mx; ❺), is a more upscale choice; rooms have phones, wi-fi, TV, air-conditioning and a safe. For a decent meal, make for *El Tejado* (ⓣ753/537-0757) at Ocampo 43 near the cathedral, where great plates of seafood and cold beer is served daily from 8am to midnight.

There are four **bus stations** in town: the ones served by Sur de Jalisco, La Linea, Galeana, Omnibus de México and Parhikuni are opposite one another on either side of Ave Lázaro Cárdenas; to get to the third (at Villa 65), served by Elite, Estrella Blanca and Turistar, walk out the front of the Galeana station, turn right, right again and second right. Estrella de Oro has a terminal at Corregidora 318, one block north. Buses to Caleta de Campos depart from the Galeana station.

Ixtapa

Some 115km south along Hwy-200 from Lázaro Cárdenas, the towns of Ixtapa and Zihuatanejo (see p.548), while only 7km apart, could hardly be more different. **IXTAPA**, a purpose-built, computer-planned "paradise" resort, is, quite simply, one of the most soulless towns imaginable, as well as one of the most expensive. Even now, thirty-plus years down the line, it hasn't yet begun to mellow or wear itself in, and its single coastal drive (Paseo Ixtapa) still runs past a series of concrete boxes of varying heights. These almost completely cordon off Ixtapa's admittedly lovely stretch of **beach** from the road, forcing those who can't afford the hotels' inflated prices to squeeze through a couple of access points or use the hotels' facilities. You might want to visit one of the clubs in the evening, but you will definitely not want to stay.

The beaches

The long 2.5km sweep of **Ixtapa**'s main, hotel-backed **Playa de Palmar** is fine for volleyball or long walks, but often too rough for easy swimming, and plagued by jet skis. Powered watersports are also in evidence at the inappropriately named **Playa Quieta**, some 5km north of Ixtapa, which is dominated by *Club Med* and seemingly perpetual clans of inebriated Spring-Breakers. The water here is wonderfully clear and the surrounding vegetation magnificent, but with the exception of *Restaurant Neptuno*, which predictably specializes in fresh seafood, you won't get anything to eat or drink unless you pay handsomely to enter the confines of the three luxury resorts that dominate the beach.

The next beach along, **Playa Linda** is a huge sweep of greyish sand, with a cluster of *enramadas* at the pier end where the bus (M$7) drops you off. As well as the usual trinket vendors, you can hire horses or rent jet skis and surfboards at the shacks along the beach. To find all the space you need, keep walking away from the crowded pier end: the restaurants are supplanted by coconut groves, which in turn give way to small cliffs and an estuary with birdlife and reptiles.

Boats leave from the pier at Playa Linda for **Isla Ixtapa** (9am–5pm; M$45 return), a small island a couple of kilometres offshore with two fine swimming beaches, a spot reserved for diving and a few restaurants, but nowhere to stay. You can also get there on a daily launch from Zihuatanejo, which leaves at 11am and returns at 5pm (1hr; M$250 round trip).

Practicalities

Some **long-distance buses** now serve Ixtapa directly via the **bus terminal** at Plaza Ixpamar, in the commercial area behind the seafront (Paseo Ixtapa), but otherwise you'll have to change at Zihuatanejo's Central de Autobuses (see p.549); you can catch a local bus (6am–11pm; every 15min; M$7) along the seafront to Ixtapa from the top of Juárez at Morelos. **Taxis** charge according to an exhaustive chart of fixed fares (see p.550); rides between Ixtapa and Zihuatanejo should be around M$60, while Ixtapa to Playa Linda is M$80. Transport from the **Ixtapa-Zihuatanejo International Airport** is the usual over-priced monopoly: *colectivos* charge around M$115 per person, while taxis will be least M$320; in the other direction the fare is just M$150. For information, try the **Oficina de Convenciones y Visitantes** at Paseo de Las Gaviotas 12, near the bus terminal (Mon–Fri 9am–2pm & 4–7pm; ⓣ755/553-1270, ⓦwww.visitixtapazihuatanejo.com). The **hotels** in **Ixtapa** are all expensive: around M$900–1500 in low season, and well over M$1500 in high season – stay in Zihuatanejo instead. One appealing alternative here is *Casa Candiles* (ⓣUS1-717/207-8471, ⓦwww.casacandiles.com; ❼), 65 Paseo de Las Golondrinas (next to the Palma de Real golf course, and not far from the beach), an intimate inn with just three comfy suites, garden and pool.

Ixtapa is the place to come for a raucous night on the town, and though the food choices are generally unexceptional, there are plenty of cheap options on the seafront and a couple of excellent restaurants further out. For superb seafood, seek out local gem *Marisco's el Tiburon de la Costa* (ⓣ755/552-6234) in the village of San José, north of the main resort – if you don't have a car, you'll have to take a taxi but it's worth it. Similarly, *Villa de la Selva* (ⓣ755/553-0362, ⓦwww.villadelaselva.com.mx), south of the resort in a wonderful cliff-side spot at Paseo de la Roca Lote D, serves fabulous contemporary Mediterranean and Mexican dishes from M$150 (dinner only). For something tasty and quick in town, head to *Ruben's Hamburgers* at Centro Comercial Flamboyant for juicy sirloin, cheese and chicken burgers (from M$45).

A typical **night out** starts at *Señor Frog's* (daily 6pm–3am; ⓣ755/553-2282, ⓦwww.senorfrogs.com/ixtapa) in the Centro Comercial La Puerta opposite the *Presidente Inter-Continental* hotel, or *Carlos 'n' Charlie's* (ⓣ755/553-0085, ⓦwww.carlosandcharlies.com) next to the *Posada Real Ixtapa* hotel, two bar/restaurant chains offering food, plenty of alcohol, loud music and dancing, before progressing to the flashy and expensive *Christine* nightclub next to *Hotel Krystal* (daily 10.30pm–6am; cover M$100–200; ⓣ755/553-0456).

Zihuatanejo

ZIHUATANEJO, for all its growth in recent years, has at least retained something of the look and feel of the traditional fishing village it once was. In stark contrast to Ixtapa, what building there has been is small-scale, low-key and low-rise, and the town looks over an attractive bay, ringed by broad, sandy beaches excellent for swimming. This said, it is definitely a **resort**: taxi drivers are forever advertising for

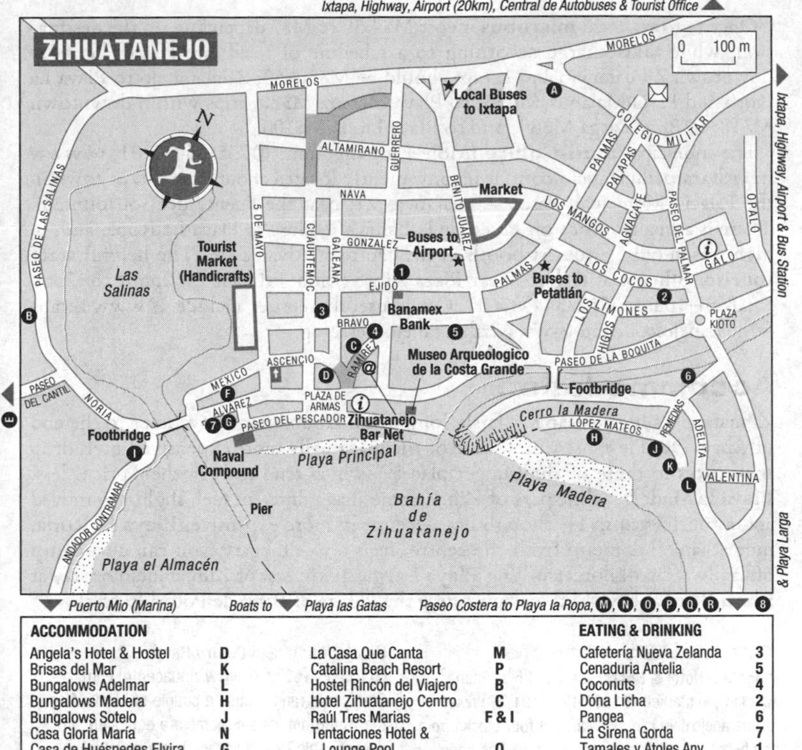

ACCOMMODATION

Angela's Hotel & Hostel	D
Brisas del Mar	K
Bungalows Adelmar	L
Bungalows Madera	H
Bungalows Sotelo	J
Casa Gloria María	N
Casa de Huéspedes Elvira	G
Casa Kau Kan	O
Casa Nancy	E
La Casa Que Canta	M
Catalina Beach Resort	P
Hostel Rincón del Viajero	B
Hotel Zihuatanejo Centro	C
Raúl Tres Marias	F & I
Tentaciones Hotel & Lounge Pool	Q
The Tides	R
Villa Vera Puerto Mio	A

EATING & DRINKING

Cafetería Nueva Zelanda	3
Cenaduria Antelia	5
Coconuts	4
Dóna Licha	2
Pangea	6
La Sirena Gorda	7
Tamales y Atoles Any	1
Zihua Blue	8

customers, trinket and tacky T-shirt shops are abundant and as likely as not there'll be a cruise ship moored out in the bay. Despite the proliferation of luxury hotels, though, there are at least a fair number of small, reasonably priced places to stay as well as some inexpensive restaurants. For some, Zihuatanejo is the ideal compromise – quiet by night, yet with the more commercial excitements of Ixtapa nearby. The one real problem is its popularity – with strictly controlled development, rooms can be hard to find in the centre of Zihuatanejo, a region of barely ten small blocks hemmed in by the main roads into town, the yacht marina and the beach.

Arrival and information

Buses arrive at Zihuatanejo's Central de Autobuses (and the adjacent Estrella de Oro terminal), about 2km and twenty minutes' walk from the centre of town. There are plenty of taxis (M$30) outside the station, and if you walk a couple of hundred metres to the left, you can pick up passing "Zihuatanejo" buses (M$4.50), which will generally drop you off at the top of Juárez.

From the **Ixtapa-Zihuatanejo International Airport**, 20km south of the centre (only 2km off the highway to Acapulco), ignore the crowds of time-share sellers offering lifts and buy transport tickets from the official counters: *colectivos* charge M$115, while taxis will be at least M$280; in the other direction the fare is just M$100.

Once in town, local **microbuses** cost M$4.50 to M$7 depending on the destination, while **taxis** charge according to a schedule of fixed fares; rides between downtown Zihuatanejo and Ixtapa should be M$50–60; Zihuatanejo to Playa La Ropa and Playa Majahua M$35; to Playa Madera M$20; trips within downtown M$18; to Playa Larga M$60; and to Playa Linda M$100.

The municipal **tourist office** (Mon–Fri 8am–4pm; ⓣ755/554-2001, ⓦwww.travelixtapazihuatanejo.com) is inconveniently located about 2km out of town in the Palacio Municipal, Paseo Zihuatanejo 21, near the Fuente del Sol fountain. There is a smaller office on Paseo de la Bahía s/n, close to Playa La Ropa, and, in high season only, a tourist booth in the centre at Álvarez s/n. The helpful **state tourism office** is at Galo 3, near Plaza Kioto (Mon–Fri 8am–3.30pm & 5–7pm, Sat 8am–1pm; ⓣ755/544-8361). Other useful websites include ⓦwww.ixtapa-zihuatanejo.com and ⓦwww.zihuatanejo.net/blog.

Accommodation

Zihuatanejo's **high season** is fairly long, from around mid-November to the end of April. Outside those times some of the marginally more expensive hotels drop their **rates** to those of the budget places – which tend to vary their prices less. **Playa la Madera**, while part of Zihuatanejo, has a different feel, slightly removed and a touch exclusive – though not necessarily more expensive. **Playa la Ropa**, more than a kilometre from the centre, feels a world apart; you can also **camp** officially at two-kilometre-long **Playa Larga**, 10km east of Zihuatanejo or stay at **Playa Blanca**, beyond the airport near the village of Barra de Potosí (p.552).

Central Zihuatanejo

Angela's Hotel & Hostel Mangos 25 at Palmas (behind the market) ⓣ755/112 -2191, ⓦwww.zihuatanejo.com.mx/angelas. Just four blocks from the beach, *Angela's* new modern premises (they moved in 2007) offer pleasant four- and six-bed dorms (M$115 per person) with shared kitchen and bathroom, as well as six private en-suite doubles (M$275). ❸

Casa de Huéspedes Elvira Paseo del Pescador 32 ⓣ755/554-2061. A longstanding favourite budget option with a friendly owner and very good restaurant on site. The six rooms with shared bath are unadorned but perfectly adequate (M$100 extra for a/c). ❸

Casa Nancy Paseo del Cantil 6 ⓣ755/554-2123. Good-value, family-run guesthouse with drab but clean rooms. The hammocks on the roof and peaceful location lend a relaxing vibe, despite being only a 10min walk from the waterfront. ❷

Hostel Rincón del Viajero Paseo de las Salinas 50, La Noria ⓣ755/105-4398, ⓦwww.rinconviajerozihua.4t.com. Tranquil hostel run by laid-back artist Mali (her art graces the walls) and Matias; dorm beds are M$120, with shared kitchen, dining room, hammocks, lush garden, wi-fi (M$10/hr), bike rentals (M$25/hr, M$150/day) and free laundry. There are also private doubles with shared bath (❸) or en-suite (M$50 extra).

Hotel Zihuatanejo Centro Ramírez 2 ⓣ755/554-5330, ⓦwww.zihuacentro.com. Comfy mid-range option a couple of blocks from the waterfront, its a/c rooms are equipped with decent cable TV and access to a small pool, internet café and bar. ❼

Raúl Tres Marias Alvarez 52 ⓣ755/554-6706, ⓔgarroboscrew@prodigy.net.mx. Shiny and spotless, with some sea views from the top floor, a/c and bathrooms with hot water all day. Another, cheaper branch of the same hotel – with unattractive rooms – is at Noria 4, just across the lagoon footbridge (ⓣ755/554-2191). ❹

Villa Vera Puerto Mio Paseo del Morro 5, Playa el Almacen ⓣ755/553-8165, ⓦwww.diamondresorts.com. This luxury boutique hotel sits on the bay just around the corner from downtown within 30 acres of lush gardens, each room coming with a wooden deck and balcony and fabulous views. There is a swimming pool, internet access and bar. ❽

Playa la Madera

Brisas del Mar López Mateos, Playa la Madera ⓣ755/554-2142, ⓦwww.hotelbrisasdelmar.com. Not quite as astronomically priced as many places in these parts, this charming hotel has comfortable, artistically decorated suites with tasteful wooden furnishings. Large private terraces have hammocks from which to enjoy the sea views. Other facilities include a swimming pool, volleyball court, library, fitness centre with sauna, steam room and massages. 7

Bungalows Adelmar Adelita 40, Playa la Madera ☎755/554-9190, ⓔixtsptf@epix.net. Eight immaculately clean, modern apartments, all with well-equipped kitchens – and some with small gardens – an excellent pool and tranquil location close to the beach. Up to four people in a room. 5

Bungalows Madera López Mateos 25, Playa la Madera ☎755/554-3920, ⓦwww.zihua-hotel.com. These hillside bungalows are a great deal, with simple but nicely furnished rooms overlooking the city or the bay, some with kitchens and pools. 5

Bungalows Sotelo López Mateos, Playa la Madera ☎755/554-6307, ⓦwww.bungalowssotelo.com. Comfortable apartments with a/c, satellite TV, balconies, kitchens and great sea views. The most luxurious rooms have jacuzzis on the balcony. 6

Playa la Ropa

Casa Gloria María Playa La Ropa s/n ☎755/554-2055, ⓦwww.zihuatanejo.net/casagloriamaria. A good option for families, these four clean and tidy self-contained bungalows each have two twin beds, a fully equipped kitchen, a spacious bathroom and a dining area. 6

La Casa Que Canta Camino Escéncio, Playa la Ropa ☎755/555-7030 or 01-800/710-9345, ⓦwww.lacasaquecanta.com. *The* place to splurge. Guests rave about this beautifully designed, thatched-roof hotel draped over the hillside. The breezy rooms are luxuriously decorated with traditional Mexican artesanía and the secluded, romantic gardens are composed of labyrinthine pathways that lead to intimate hideaways. There is a stellar restaurant and a spa and fitness centre. 9

Catalina Beach Resort Playa la Ropa s/n ☎755/554-2137, ⓦwww.catalina-beach-resort.com. A good-value beachfront option, *Catalina* is one of the oldest and friendliest hotels in town with great facilities for the price. The rooms do vary – some betray their age more than others, and the new suites are well worth the extra – but the large terraces with hammocks and glorious views are the attraction here. Tropical gardens, a pool and an oceanfront restaurant (complimentary breakfast) are perfect for relaxing. 8

Tentaciones Hotel & Lounge Pool Camino Escéncio, Playa la Ropa ☎755/544-8383. Another gorgeous luxury hideaway, hidden among lush cliffs and ponds above the beach, with just four one-bedroom palapa suites with verandas overlooking the bay, satellite TV, marble-clad bathrooms and all the usual plush amenities. 9

The Tides Playa la Ropa s/n ☎755/555-5500 or 01-866/905-9560, ⓦwww.tideszihuatanejo.com. Lush gardens of hibiscus and bougainvillea hide spacious luxury suites all with terraces and some with small private pools. There's a large infinity pool, too, as well as a private patch of beach, a spa, a fitness centre and other creature comforts. Worth checking out the posh bars and restaurants if you can't afford to stay – it's one of the most expensive hotels on the coast. 9

Playa Larga

Casa Kau Kan Playa Larga s/n ☎755/554-6226, ⓦwww.casakaukan.com. The essence of good taste and discretion, this small, beachside boutique hotel has spacious, artful suites with separate living areas and plush bathrooms. Gourmet food, tranquil pool and gorgeous gardens create an aura of refined pampering in an isolated natural setting with miles of deserted beach (no phones or TVs). 7

Barra de Potosí

Hotel Las Palmas Domicilio Conocido s/n Lote 5, Playa Blanca ☎480/776-0086, ⓦwww.hotellaspalmas.net. This popular luxury retreat is very near the airport, but inconvenient for the town – not that you'll be tempted to leave should you stay here. With just six spacious suites, you'll be pampered like royalty, with a long, bone-white beach on site and fine eating and drinking. 9

Our House Lote 61, Playa Blanca ☎755/113-6114, ⓦwww.ourhouse-zihua.com. One of the best of a handful of B&Bs down here, with three en-suite rooms with access for the disabled, all with beautifully tiled floors, TV and fans (a/c is extra) – breakfast is included. 6

Activities

Zihuatanejo has a few things to distract you from lying on the beach. Quite apart from jet skiing, parasailing and getting dragged around on a huge inflatable banana, you could arrange to go **fishing** for dorado, yellowtail, bonito or big game. Trips, run by Ixtapa Sportfishing Charters (US ☎570/688-9466, ⓦwww.ixtapasportfishing.com) start at around M$2100/day in a small super-*panga*. Zihuatanejo Dive Center, La Noria 1 at Anguila (☎755/544-8554, ⓦwww.zihuatanejodivecenter.com), just across the footbridge close to the pier, organizes **scuba-diving** courses. A one-tank dive for certified divers costs M$650 (two-tanks M$850) while a "discover scuba" course plus one dive for beginners is M$2500. Full PADI certification takes five to six days and costs M$4000.

Just behind the beach you'll find the **Museo Arqueológico de la Costa Grande** (Tues–Sun 10am–6pm; M$10), a small and simple affair not deserving more than twenty minutes, though it does its best to tackle the early history of what has always been a fairly insignificant region. Inside you'll find pre-Columbian archaeological finds such as pottery, tools, simple jewellery and rock engravings, with exhibits beginning with the first settlements in the region and ending with the arrival of the Spaniards.

The beaches

Four main beaches surround the Bahía de Zihuatanejo. **Playa Principal**, in front of Zihuatanejo, is unspectacular, with muddy water, brown sand and persistent hawkers, but is an interesting place to people-watch – the fishermen haul in their catch here early in the morning, selling much of it on the spot. A narrow footpath heads east from the end of the beach across the normally dry outlet of a drainage canal, then winds around a rocky point to the calm waters of **Playa la Madera**, a broad, moderately clean strand of dark sand that shelves softly into the ocean, making it a good option for kids. There's a handful of restaurants and hotels on the hill behind, as well as some expensive condos. Climb the steps between these to get to the road if you want to continue a kilometre or so over the headland, past the *mirador* with great views across the bay, to **Playa la Ropa** (bus M$5) which takes its name – "Clothes Beach" – from silks washed up here when one of the *nao de China* (trading ships from China) was wrecked offshore. This is Zihuatanejo's finest road-accessible beach, palm-fringed for more than a kilometre, with a variety of beachfront restaurants and hotels. You can walk a further fifteen minutes beyond the end of Playa la Ropa to **Playa las Gatas**, named after the nurse sharks that used to populate the waters. Las Gatas is the last of the bay's beaches, its crystalline blue water surrounded by a reef, giving it the enclosed feel of an ocean swimming pool. It's safe for kids, though the sea bottom is mostly rocky and tough on feet. The clear waters are great for **snorkelling** – you can rent gear (M$50/day) from vendors among the rather pricey palapa restaurants. Las Gatas is directly opposite the town and, if the rocky walk doesn't appeal, it is accessible by launches (daily 9am–5pm, last return 5.30pm; 10min; M$35 return) from the Zihuatanejo pier.

For absolute peace and quiet, the best thing you can do is to take a day trip out of Zihuatanejo to **Barra de Potosí**, a tiny community situated at the southern end of the expansive, postcard-perfect, golden sandy beaches of Playa Larga and Playa Blanca, which curve steeply round the bay and keep going as far as the eye can see. To get there, board a Petatlán-bound **bus** from the station on Calle Palmas and ask the driver to drop you off at the village of Los Achotes. From here, pick-up trucks leave when full to run the final bone-rattling twenty minutes to the beach: you'll be dropped off at one end of the bay where a bunch of *enramadas* sell delicious seafood for half the price of the restaurants in town.

Eating and drinking

You can barely move for **restaurants** in Zihuatanejo: the waterfront Paseo del Pescador is the place for fresh fish, expensive drinks and sociable company; the cheapest place, as ever, is the **market**, on Juárez. There isn't much **nightlife** in town, however: for that people head over the hill to Ixtapa (see p.548). Buses (M$7) to Ixtapa run until about 10pm; after that you'll need to get a taxi (M$50–60; M$90 after midnight).

Cafetería Nueva Zelanda Cuauhtémoc 22–30 at Ejido ⓣ755/554-2340. This old-school, diner-style place serves tasty tacos, quesadillas, fajitas and tortas, as well as thick and fruity *licuados*. The American and Mexican breakfasts are bountiful and the cappuccinos the best in town – most dishes are under M$70.

Cenaduría Antelia Nicolás Bravo 14 ⓣ755/554-3091. Open since the 1970s, this snug old-time joint is a great little spot to eat unadulterated Mexican staples for under M$50 – tacos, enchiladas and the like – until midnight. The rich desserts are also worth the havoc they'll wreak on your midriff. The café next door has chairs and tables in a quiet alley off Nicolás Bravo.

Coconuts Pasaje Agustín Ramírez 1 ⓣ755/554-2518, ⓦwww.restaurantcoconuts.com. A charming old house with a stunning patio provides the setting for moonlight dining at *Coconuts*. The food is good, with a varied menu featuring healthy fish, fresh poultry and creative vegetarian dishes. The overall ambience is quite romantic, especially with low-key jazz in the evenings. Open noon–11pm.

Doña Licha Cocos 8 ⓣ755/554-3933. A wide menu of excellent and inexpensive comidas corridas (ribs, tripe and pork chops) served with mountains of rice and beans, has earned this place a loyal following. With a lackadaisical, raw atmosphere, complete with blasting TV and erratic service, the copious platters of food are undoubtedly the main attraction – meals for less than M$75.

Pangea Nuestra Señora de los Remedios s/n, Playa La Madera ⓣ755/102-3270. Specializing in Thai and Indian curries, as well as offering a huge range of Asian veggie dishes and specials. Starters cost between M$30–40, while mains range from M$70–180. Just off Plaza Kioto. Open 6–10pm, closed Wed.

La Sirena Gorda Paseo del Pescador 90 ⓣ755/554-2687. Fairly expensive (M$75–250) but well sited, right where evening strollers can watch you dine on succulent tuna steaks and seafood cocktails, as well as a selection of American dishes, in the balmy night air. Creatively decorated with paintings of the eponymous Rubenesque mermaids. Closed Wed.

Tamales y Atoles Any Guerrero 38, at Ejido. No prizes for what is on the menu at this good-value, bustling, beach joint that packs in locals and tourists looking for its sixteen different kinds of tamales (from M$20), which range from chicken and chile to cheese and squash blossom. The signature dish is *pozole* (pork stew, traditionally eaten on Thurs). Mexican breakfasts served daily.

Zihua Blue Camino Escénico, Playa la Ropa s/n ⓣ755/554-4844, ⓦwww.zihuablue.com. The most stylish place to eat or drink in town, with three levels comprising a terrace, lounge and hookah bar, and excellent restaurant managed by Chef Edmond Benloulou, all with jaw-dropping views of the bay. Expect eclectic contemporary dishes, fusing Mexican, French and Asian styles. Daily 5pm–3am.

Listings

Banks Banamex, on Ejido at Guerrero (Mon–Fri 9am–6pm; 24hr ATM), and Banorte, Ejido 8 at Juárez (Mon–Fri 9am–5pm, Sat 9am–2pm).

Buses The two main bus companies, with services to Mexico City (9hr), Acapulco (4hr) and Morelia (5hr), among other destinations, are Estrella Blanca (ⓣ755/554-3474) and Estrella de Oro (ⓣ755/554-2175).

Emergencies ⓣ066; Cruz Roja (Red Cross) ⓣ065; tourist police ⓣ060 or 755/554-2207.

Internet access There are a numerous cafés in town and especially along Guerrero, most of which charge M$10–20/hr. Try also Zihuatanejo Bar Net at Agustín Ramírez 9, open till 11pm daily.

Pharmacy Farmacia Principal, Ejido 34, at the corner of Cuauhtémoc in Zihuatanejo (Mon–Sat 9am–9pm).

Post office Edificio SCT between Telegrafistas and Palmar (Mon–Fri 8am–6pm, Sat 9am–1pm).

Acapulco

Most people – even if they've not the remotest idea where it is – have heard of **ACAPULCO**, yet few know what to expect upon arrival. Bordered by the rugged Sierra Madre to the east and beautiful Acapulco Bay to the west, the city is considered by many to be the grande dame of the Mexican tourist industry. Acapulco is no tropical paradise – it's a major city – but the truth is, as long as you don't yearn to get away from it all, you'll find almost anything you want here, from magnificent

beaches by day to restaurants, clubs and discos by night. That said, getting from one side of the city to the other can be a very time-consuming and frustrating experience, with perpetual gridlock, grime and choking exhaust fumes. Seething humidity also adds to the oppressive atmosphere, as can the persistent **hawkers**. For lone women in particular, the constant pestering of would-be gigolos can be maddening, while derelict back streets can be dangerous at night for anyone. Drug killings in Acapulco started to make headlines in 2006, and came to the fore in June 2009 when sixteen gangsters and two soldiers were killed in a single shoot-out. Acapulco is much safer than these admittedly horrific incidents suggest; the situation is improving and it's extremely rare for tourists to be affected (see box, p.187).

What Acapulco undoubtedly has going for it, is its stunning **bay**: a sweeping scythe-stroke of yellow sand backed by the white towers of the high-rise hotels and, behind them, the jungly green foothills of the sierra. Even though the town itself has a population of over one and half million and hundreds of thousands of visitors come through each year, it rarely seems overcrowded. There's certainly always space to lie along the beach, partly because of its sheer size, and partly because of the number of rival attractions – everything from hotel pools to parasailing to romantic cruises.

Some history

Acapulco has played an important role in the country's development since being founded by the Spaniards in the 1520s. The **shipping route** between Acapulco and the Spanish colony of the Philippines, on the other side of the Pacific, was once among the most prized and preyed upon in the world. From Acapulco, goods were transported overland to Veracruz and then shipped onwards to Spain. Mexican Independence and the direct route around southern Africa combined to kill off the trade, and in the nineteenth century Acapulco went into a long, slow decline, only reversed with the completion of a road to the capital in 1928. In the 1950s Acapulco became the poster child for exotic glitz and **glamour**, the playground for celebrities like Frank Sinatra and Liz Taylor. Elvis Presley immortalized the resort in the movie *Fun in Acapulco*, and JFK and Jackie spent their honeymoon here. Though American Spring-Breakers still occasionally pile down here in March, it's largely thanks to the toll highway from Mexico City and a burgeoning Mexican middle class that Acapulco has experienced something of a resurgence in recent years – unlike Cancún, Los Cabos and Puerto Vallarta, 75 percent of Acapulco's visitors are Mexican tourists.

Orientation

Acapulco divides fairly simply into two halves: the **old town**, which sits at the western end of the bay, with the promontory of **La Quebrada** rising above it and curving round to protect the sheltered anchorage; and the **resort area**, a string of hotels and tourist services following the curve of the bay east. From Playa Caleta on the southern fringe of the peninsula, a single seafront drive, the **Costera Miguel Alemán** – usually just "Costera" – stretches from the old town around the bay for 10km, linking almost everything of interest. Beyond here on the hills on the eastern side of the bay lie the posh neighbourhoods of Las Brisas and **Acapulco Diamante**, a newly developed area of malls and luxury resorts that encompasses Puerto Marqués, Playa Revolcadero and the beaches all the way south to Barra Vieja.

Arrival and information

Most long-distance **buses** arrive at one of three terminals: many buses (but mainly Estrella Blanca) use the **Central Ejido**, at Ejido 47, 2km north of the

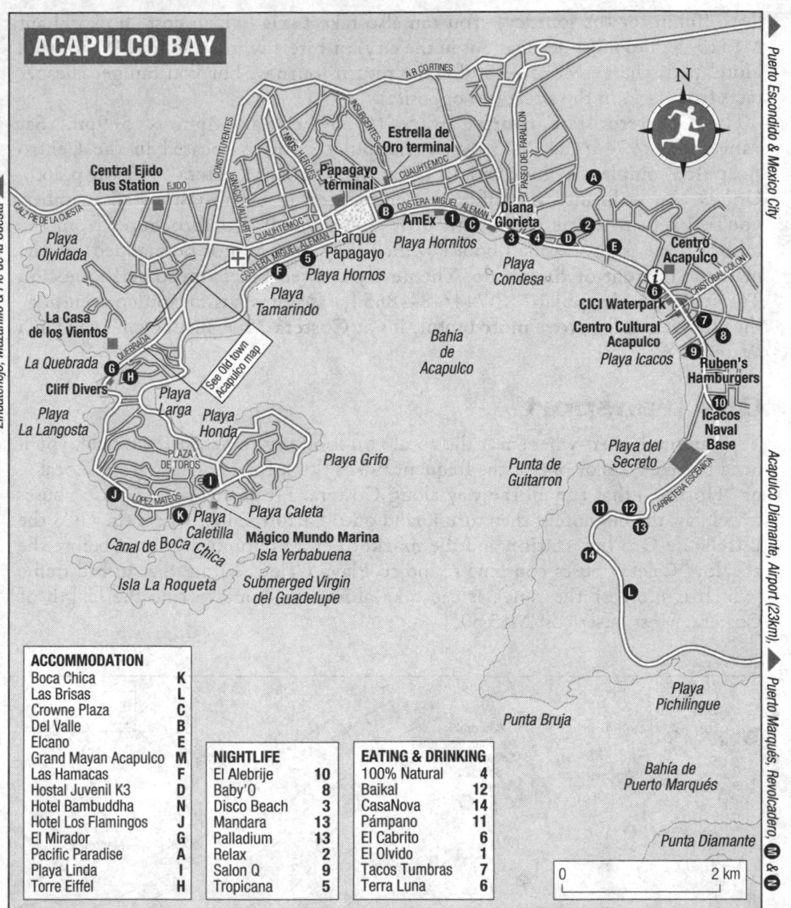

zócalo, from where you can pick up buses (M$5.50) marked "Centro" or "Caleta" to get to the area where the cheaper hotels are located. Most long-distance buses arrive at the Estrella de Oro terminal ("**EDO**"), 3km west of the zócalo at Cuauhtémoc 1490 and Massieu, again connected to the centre by "Caleta" city buses, or to the hotels along Costera by "Río/Base" buses. Some luxury Estrella Blanca and all Turistar Ejecutivo buses (mostly from Cuernavaca and Mexico City) use the **Papagayo** (Central de Lujo) terminal at Cuauhtémoc 1605 behind Parque Papagayo. To get to the zócalo, take a "Zócalo" bus; to get back, take a "CICI" bus to Parque Papagayo and walk across the park. For **taxis**, p.557.

Arriving at the **airport** (information on ⓣ744/435-2060), 23km southeast of the city, you'll find a couple of ATMs, all the major car rental firms (see p.565) and basic information on the city. Transport prices are set according to an expensive zone system: the cheapest option is a shared minibus ride with Móvil Aca (ⓣ744/462-1095, ⓦwww.movilaca.com), which will take you anywhere in the city for M$100 – you need to reserve this service in advance to get back (allow at least 40min for the journey). You can also take **taxis** (which cost an exorbitant M$315–425 to most destinations in the city) or hire a whole van for M$370–460. Hotel taxis charge M$250–300 for the return journey, but you can get cheaper rates from taxis in the street (see opposite).

The Guerrero state **tourist office** (Mon–Fri 9am–3pm & 5–9pm, Sat 9am–2pm; Ⓣ744/484-2423, Ⓦvisiteacapulco.com) is located in the Centro Acapulco complex, a block west of CiCi Waterpark at Costera 4455 (see p.563). Unless you walk into the office and encounter an enthusiastic staff member, you're likely to come away with little but a handful of brochures from the lobby; there is also a small booth (which may or may not be manned) on the malecón in front of the zócalo. The newly created Fideicomiso de Promoción Turística de Acapulco (Ⓣ744/484-8554, Ⓦwww.visitacapulco.com.mx), should eventually prove more useful: it's at Costera 38-A just beyond the CiCi Waterpark.

City transport

You can reach everywhere near the zócalo on foot, but to get further afield, you'll need to take taxis or one of the frequent **buses** (look for "Caleta/Base", "Zócalo" or "Hornos") that run all the way along Costera. From the east, "C Río" buses travel past the big hotels, then turn inland onto Cuauhtémoc, where they pass the Estrella de Oro **bus station** and the **market** before rejoining Costera before the zócalo. "Caleta" buses continue round to Playa Caleta – note that in bad traffic (which is most of the time), it can take almost an hour to ride the length of Costera. Most buses cost M$5.50.

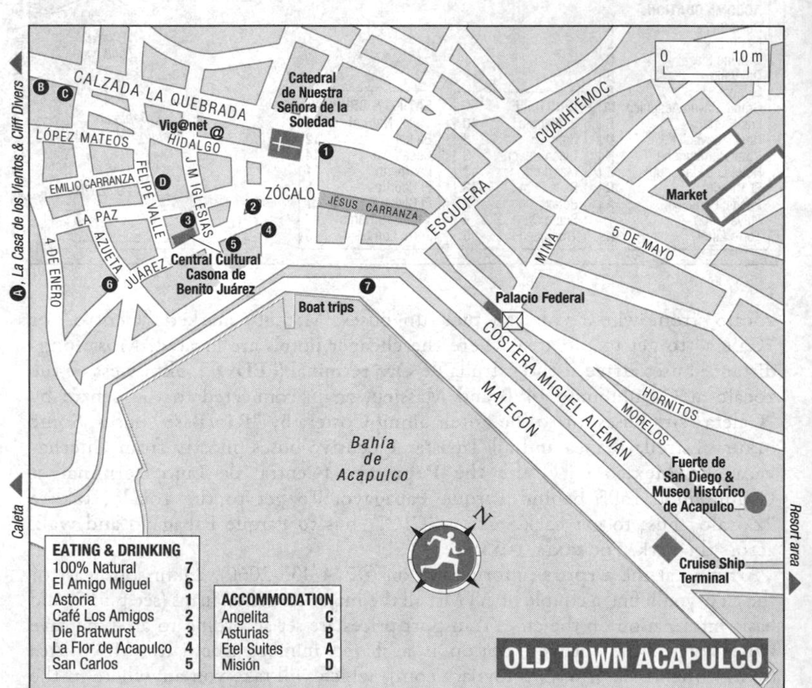

Addresses along Costera

Finding places along Costera can be tricky, as the numbering system is completely meaningless: 50 could be followed by 2010, which is next door to 403. The best **landmarks**, apart from the big hotels, are (moving east from the zócalo): **Parque Papagayo**, the roundabout with the **Diana Glorieta statue** and the **CiCi Waterpark.**

Taxis are plentiful all over the city; at all the bus stations (buy tickets first) and major hotels, they operate on an expensive zone system, which is more or less the same wherever you are (though some hotel taxis charge a little more), with rates usually displayed on boards. Between downtown and the bus stations it's around M$40–50, while locations along Costera range between M$60–100. You'll save money by flagging down the cheaper VW beetle taxis on the street, but even here you'll have to negotiate pretty hard to pay local rates, as these drivers are well aware of the tourist "zone" system; as a rule, these taxis should offer at least M$20–30 less for trips in town, and depending on your negotiating skills, M$200 for trips to the airport.

Accommodation

As with everything in Acapulco, hotel rooms are far less expensive in the **old town**. Head for the streets immediately to the west and slightly inland of the **zócalo**, to calles La Paz and Azueta, and particularly Calzada La Quebrada where it leads up the hill. In contrast to most of Mexico, many hotels in this area charge by the person rather than per room.

You won't find places as cheap out along **Costera**, but if you want to stay by the tourist beaches and the clubs there are a few reasonable options, especially off-season, when even some of the fancier hotels become quite competitively priced. The hotels at the smaller beaches of **Caleta** and **Caletilla**, a ten-minute bus ride from the centre, are rather older than those along Costera, and often booked up in advance. Still further out there's **Pie de la Cuesta**, a quiet alternative 15km north of Acapulco and the only place with official year-round **camping**, at *Acapulco Trailer Park* (Ⓣ744/460-0010, Ⓦwww.acapulcotrailerpark.com; M$220). Most of the newest most luxurious resorts are in the **Diamante** area, a twenty-kilometre drive from the city but much quieter.

Like most of Mexico's top resorts, Acapulco now experiences two **high seasons**: late November or early December through to the end of April (when *norteamericanos* flock south), and July and August, when Mexican families take their summer vacations. If you can, it's best to avoid Christmas and Semana Santa (Easter) altogether, and remember that any US or Mexican public holiday will likely bring the crowds. Thursday to Sunday tends to be busy year-round.

In the centre

These options are marked on the Old Town Acapulco map, see opposite.

Angelita Calzada La Quebrada 37 Ⓣ744/483-5734. One of Acapulco's cheapest options. Spartan but sizeable rooms with private bath and fan lead off a courtyard. Eccentric management keeps life interesting. ❷

Asturias Calzada La Quebrada 45 Ⓣ744/483-6548, Ⓔgerardomancera@aol.com. A welcoming budget option with clean, passable rooms around a courtyard. It is fractionally more expensive than the competition by virtue of its small pool. ❸

Etel Suites La Pinzona 92 Ⓣ744/482-2241, Ⓦwww.acapulcoetelsuites.com. This very hospitable, family-run hotel is extremely clean and well equipped, with 1950s-style three-bed rooms with kitchens, balconies and a/c in lovely gardens overlooking La Quebrada. Good for groups and long-stay guests. ❹

El Mirador Acapulco (Map: Acapulco Bay) Plazoleta La Quebrada 74 ⓣ744/483-1155 or 01-800/021-7557, ⓦwww.miradoracapulco.com. The location of this classic 1930s mid- to-upper-range option – right above La Quebrada – couldn't be better. Lodging is in clean, characterless, Alpine-style rooms with kitchenettes. There are three pools and a bar/restaurant on site, from which you won't have to pay the M$100–250 charge to see the divers plummet. ❺

Misión Felipe Valle 12 ⓣ744/482-3643. The oldest hotel in town has clearly been well used, but still exudes colonial charm and is the best-value option in the centre. Formerly the American consulate and a Wells Fargo office, the house has attractive rooms with mosaic tiles and wooden furnishings spread around a mango-shaded patio. Continental or Mexican breakfasts are included, and there is a book swap. ❹

Torre Eiffel (Map: Acapulco Bay) Inalámbrica 110 ⓣ744/482-1683. This is a great deal for the price, with simple, clean rooms high above La Quebrada and scintillating views across the ocean from the shared balconies – it's a bit of a hike from the zócalo, but once here you can cool off in the small pool. ❸

Caleta and Caletilla

These options are marked on the Acapulco Bay map, see p.555.

Boca Chica on the point at the western end of Caletilla ⓣ744/483-6601, ⓦwww.designhotels.com/bocachica. Beautifully renovated resort carved into the cliff-face at the end of Playa Caletilla and reopened as a stylish Design Hotel – Mexican artist Claudia Fernández has decorated the 1950s interior, with a luxurious spa, gym, massage cabañas, pool terrace, and special sushi takeout menu adding to the allure. ❼

Hotel Los Flamingos López Mateos ⓣ744/482-0690, ⓦwww.hotellosflamingos.com. An Acapulco retro classic, this landmark 1930s hotel was once owned by a Hollywood gang that included Tarzan (Johnny Weissmuller), Cary Grant and John Wayne. The "coco loco" cocktail was apparently invented here, and the lush gardens and sublime sunset views from Acapulco's highest cliffs are a perfect accompaniment. The rooms have seen better days but are still spacious, characterful and comfortable. ❺

Playa Linda Costera Gorieta de Caleta 1, just as you reach Caleta ⓣ744/482-0814, ⓦwww.playalindaacapulco.com. Modern hotel with nicely decorated rooms, some with sea-view balconies, a short walk from the beaches. All rooms (sleeping up to four) have a/c, TV and fully equipped kitchenettes. ❹

Along Costera and Las Brisas

These options are marked on the Acapulco Bay map, see p.555.

Las Brisas Carretera Escénica 5255 ⓣ744/469-6900, ⓦwww.brisas.com.mx. Overlooking the eastern end of the bay, high above the ocean amidst blossom-smothered gardens, this luxury resort is probably the most exclusive in the city. Its individual villas offer private swimming pools, breakfasts and pink jeeps to every occupant. You access the water via the beach club below, and every room has a sea-view terrace. ❾

Crowne Plaza Costera 123 ⓣ744/440-5555, ⓦwww.ichotelsgroup.com. Certainly the most memorable building on the beach (it's like a curved pyramid), with clean, bright modern rooms with cable TV and an attractive pool right on the beach. Internet is M$150/day. ❻

Del Valle Manuel Gómez 150, opposite the eastern entrance to Parque Papagayo ⓣ744/485-8336. *Del Valle* has a convenient location, spacious, well-maintained rooms (some with a/c), a pool and private kitchens (outside the rooms) that can be rented for M$100 a day. ❹

Elcano Costera 75 ⓣ744/435-1500. This renovated 1950s monolith with an all-pervasive nautical theme feels fresh: spic-and-span blue and white rooms have tiled floors, cable TV, comfortable beds and well-proportioned bathrooms, though the a/c can be weak. The best rooms have terraces overlooking the ocean, but all rooms have ocean views. There's a beachside pool, jacuzzi, gym and two bars. ❼

Las Hamacas Costera 239, 1km east of the zócalo ⓣ744/483-7709, ⓦwww.hamacas.com.mx. Ageing better than its peers, *Las Hamacas* is the closest Costera gets to international standard close to the old town – though the beach here is dirty and very crowded. Bright, clean rooms are comfortable, with cable TV, a/c and spacious bathrooms. There is a swimming pool, a beachside restaurant and a gym. ❺

Hostal Juvenil K3 Costera 116, opposite the *Fiesta Americana* hotel ⓣ744/481-3111, ⓦwww.k3acapulco.com. This well-positioned hostel is a clean, friendly place with small, a/c four-bed dorms (M$180/person; M$160 HI members), lockers, a kitchen and snack bar. Rates include breakfast and internet use. Private rooms ❹

Pacific Paradise Punta Bruja 1, near Playa Condesa ⓣ744/481-1413, ⓦwww.pacificparadise.com.mx. Mediterranean-style budget resort with spotless, attractive rooms on three floors. Situated a few blocks back from Costera, so nights are quieter and it's better value than many of the beachside establishments. ❹

Diamante

These options are marked on the Acapulco Bay map, see p.555.

Grand Mayan Acapulco Av de las Palmas 1121, Playa Diamante ⓣ744/469-6000, ⓦwww.mayanresorts.com. Currently the gold standard in Acapulco luxury, though if you stay here you may not leave; it's a self-contained, all-inclusive resort. The beach is tranquil, and the facilities first class (including a huge pool, an interior lake and an aqua park with waterfalls and slides), but travelling into the city can be time-consuming and expensive from here – most guests hire drivers. Minimum three-night stay. ❾

Hotel Bambuddha Carretera Barra Vieja km 37 ⓣ744/444-6406, ⓦwww.hoteles.rinconesdemitierra.com/bambuddha. This gorgeous Asian-themed boutique hotel, with bamboo palapas right on the beach, is a wonderfully languid retreat, specializing in yoga, meditation and detox programmes. ❼

Pie de la Cuesta

Baxar Hotel Fuerza Aerea 356 ⓣ744/460-2502, ⓦwww.baxarhotelacapulco.com. Rustic chic epitomised, this intimate beachside enclave has colourful, breezy rooms with tiled private bath and mosquito nets (some have a/c). The restaurant serves great fresh fish and there's a pool and guaranteed relaxation. ❻

Bungalows María Cristina Fuerza Aerea 351 ⓣ744/460-0262. Good-value budget suites with fully equipped kitchens and balconies for up to five people; the rooms are fine, too. ❹

Hacienda Vayma Fuerza Aerea 378 ⓣ744/460-2882, ⓦwww.vayma.com.mx. A low-key, arty place to hang out with hip Mexicans from the capital and *laissez-faire* Europeans. Modern bungalows with spatially challenged bathrooms (cold water) are functional, but the main attractions here are the setting, relaxed vibe and fantastic restaurant. The suites have more creature comforts: a/c, terrace and hot water. ❻

Villa Nirvana Fuerza Aerea 302 ⓣ744/460-1631, ⓦwww.lavillanirvana.com. Delightful retreat with immaculate, spacious rooms with tiled floors, painted in soothing pastels and nicely furnished with local crafts, set around an attractive garden and great pool. Rooms with kitchen facilities and a little beach cottage also available. ❹

The Town

No one comes to Acapulco for the sights. By day, if people aren't at the beach, drinking cocktails with umbrellas or asleep, they're mostly scouring the expensive shops. If you only do one thing in Acapulco, though, make sure you see its most celebrated spectacle, the leap of the daredevil **high divers** (see p.562).

In the **old town** the zócalo is a shady, languid place, but other than cheap places to eat and drink, lacks character – even the **Catedral de Nuestra Señora de la Soledad** is a modern construction from 1950, with a slightly bizarre blue dome that resembles a Russian Orthodox church. About the only place in Acapulco that gives even the slightest sense of the historic role the city played in Mexico's past is the **Museo Histórico de Acapulco** (Tues–Sun 9am–6pm; M$41, free Sun) a short walk away inside the **Fuerte de San Diego**. This impressive, if heavily restored, star-shaped fort was established in 1616 to protect the Manila galleons from foreign corsairs but was severely damaged by an earthquake in the eighteenth century – what you see today dates from the 1776 reconstruction. The building's limited success in defending the city against pirate attacks is charted inside the museum, where displays also extend to the spread of Christianity by proselytizing religious orders, Mexico's struggle for independence and a small anthropological collection. Air-conditioned rooms make this a good place to ride out the midday heat, and you can pop up on the roof for superb views over Acapulco.

The only other cultural diversion in the centre is **La Casa de los Vientos** ("Exekatlkalli"), on Cerro de la Pinzona, near La Quebrada, where Diego Rivera spent the last two years of his life with his former model and partner, Dolores Olmedo Patiño, who bought the vacation home in 1951. Rivera spent eighteen months working on five grand **murals** here between 1955 and 1957, several preserved in his studio on the grounds; sadly the house has remained in private hands since Olmedo's death in 2002 and off-limits. At the time of writing, the government was trying to buy the property – the tourist office should know the latest. In the meantime, fans traipse up here to see the twenty-metre mural that covers the entire outside wall of the house, made of seashells and coloured tiles, depicting Tlaloc, the Aztec god of rain, fertility, and lightning and various other figures from Aztec mythology.

Acapulco also has two mildly entertaining cultural centres, both of which host temporary art exhibitions and various cultural events with a regional bias. The more absorbing is housed in a lovely old property near the zócalo at Juárez and

▲ Acapulco

Felipe Valle, the **Central Cultura Casona de Benito Juárez** (daily 8am–6pm; free; ⓣ744/483-5104). At the other end of the bay, the **Centro Cultural Acapulco** (daily 8am–9pm; free; ⓣ744/484-3814) at Costera 4834 (next to the CiCi Waterpark) is a small complex of galleries and a crafts store set around a garden just off the main road.

The beaches

To get to the best of the sands **around Acapulco Bay** from the centre of town, you have to get on a bus or take a taxi.

Caleta, Caletilla and La Roqueta

Playas Caleta and **Caletilla** (any "Caleta" bus from Costera) have a quite different atmosphere from those in the main part of the bay. Very small – the two are divided only by a rocky outcrop and breakwater – they tend to be crowded, but the water is almost always calm and the beach is reasonably clean. You can sit at shaded tables on the sand, surrounded by Mexican matrons whose kids are paddling in the shallows, and be brought drinks from the cafés behind. There are showers here, too, and, on the rock, the **Mágico Mundo Marino** (daily 9am–6pm; M$60, kids M$30), a waterpark with a predictable aquarium and sea lion show, decent water slides and a choice of the pool or the bay to swim in.

From outside the waterpark, small boats ply the channel to the islet of **La Roqueta**, where there are more and yet cleaner beaches (you can rent a picnic table for M$50) and beer-drinking burros, one of the town's less compelling attractions. Catch one of the frequent glass-bottomed boats to the island (daily 8am–5pm) and keep your ticket for the return journey; it'll cost M$40 for a direct launch or M$60 for one that detours past the **submerged bronze statue of the Virgin of Guadalupe**.

From all three beaches you can rent snorkelling gear for around M$70 (though you'll see the most fish and coral off Roqueta), kayaks and small boats (motor, sail and pedal) by the hour.

Along Costera and on to Revolcadero

The main beaches, despite their various names – Tamarindo, Hornos, Hornitos, El Morro, Condesa and Icacos – are in effect a single sweep of sand. It's best to go some considerable distance round to **Playa Condesa** or **Playa Icacos**, in front of hotels (which make good points of reference) such as the monolithic *Grand Hotel*, where the beach is far less crowded and considerably cleaner. It's easy enough to slip in to use the hotel showers, swimming pools and bars – there's no way they're going to spot an imposter in these thousand-bed monsters. The beaches around here are also the place to come if you want to indulge in such frolics as being towed around the bay on the end of a parachute, water-skiing or sailing. Outfits offering all of these are dotted at regular intervals along the beach; charges are standard, though the quality of the equipment and the length of the trips varies.

Beyond the end of the bay, across the hills to the south, are two other popular beaches: **Puerto Marqués** and **Playa Revolcadero**. On the way you'll pass some of the fanciest hotels and villas in Acapulco, as well as some mesmerizing views of the city. Puerto Marqués (buses marked "Puerto Marqués") is the first of the beaches, a sheltered, deeply indented cove with restaurants and beach chairs right down to the water's edge, overlooked by two more deluxe hotels. You can continue by road to Revolcadero (though only an occasional bus comes this far) or get there by boat down a narrow inland channel. The beach, a long exposed stretch of sand, is beautiful but frequently lashed by heavy surf that makes swimming impossible. This whole area is being developed as another major resort zone

Acapulco's divers

Acapulco's famed **clavadistas** (cliff divers) having been plunging some 35m from the heights of La Quebrada into a rocky channel since the early 1920s (organized officially since 1934), timing their leap to coincide with an incoming wave. Mistimed, there's not enough water to stop them hitting the bottom, though the chief danger these experts seem to face is getting back out of the water without being dashed against the rocks. It could easily be corny, but it's undeniably impressive, especially when floodlit at night. The **dive times** – 12.45pm, 7.30pm, 8.30pm, 9.30pm and 10.30pm – are rigidly adhered to. A typical display involves four exponents, three taking the lower (25m) platform with two diving simultaneously, the fourth diving from the upper level after first asking for the Virgin's intervention at the clifftop shrine. The final diver carries a pair of flaming torches. From the road you can see the spectacle for nothing, but you'll get a much better view if you go down the steps from the Plazuela de Quebrada to a **viewing platform** (M$35 adults, M$10 kids) more or less opposite the divers. Get here early for a good position. Alternatively, you can sit in the lobby bar at *El Mirador Acapulco* hotel (M$100 cover includes two drinks) or watch from their expensive *La Perla* restaurant (minimum M$250 charge per person). To get there, simply climb the Calzada La Quebrada from the town centre, about fifteen minutes' walk from the zócalo. Heading back, hotel taxis will charge M$40 into the centre, M$70 to the bus terminals and M$90–110 along Costera.

known as **Acapulco Diamante**, with deluxe hotels lining the coast all the way to the airport and the former village of Barra Vieja.

Pie de la Cuesta

Pie de la Cuesta, around 15km north of Acapulco, is far more serene than the city and a good place to watch the sun sink into the Pacific or to ride horseback along the shore, though most of the horses here are a little worse for wear – their owners on the beach will try to charge rates in US$s, but you should be able negotiate hourly rates of M$150–200, especially mid-week. The sand extends for miles up the coast, but at the Acapulco end, where the bus drops you, there are several rickety bars and some tranquil **places to stay** (see p.559).

Behind the beach, and only separated from the ocean by the hundred-metre-wide sandbar on which Pie de la Cuesta is built, lies the **Laguna de Coyuca**, a vast freshwater lake said to be three times the size of Acapulco Bay, which only connects with the sea after heavy rains. Fringed with palms, and rich in bird and animal life, the lagoon is big enough to accommodate both the ubiquitous noisy jet skiers and the more sedate **boat trips** that visit the three lagoon islands. Various outfits along the hotel strip offer tours – prices hover around M$85 per person – but it's worth checking what's on offer and how long the cruise is, as times tend to differ. Most boats stop on one island for lunch (not included in the price) and swimming. The bus from Acapulco ("Pie de la Cuesta") runs every ten minutes or so from Costera south of the zócalo (M$5.50). The last bus back leaves around 8pm.

Activities

Acapulco Bay has a multitude of watersports activities and tours on offer. Touristy **cruises** depart from the docks along the malecón in front of the zócalo, with boats such as the **Aca Rey** (Ⓣ744/484-7080) catamaran charging around M$320 for three hours around the bay. For more of a thrill, Shotover Jet runs high-speed trips (50min) up the Papagayo River for M$500 per person (hourly 9.30am–4.30pm; M$650 with transport; Ⓣ1-800/509-5992, Ⓦwww.shotoverjet.com.mx).

Heading east along the bay from Playa Hornitos to Playa Icacos, kiosks offer everything from banana boats to jet skis, snorkelling to parasailing. The more professional outfit Fish-R-Us, Costera 100 (ⓣ744/482-8282, ⓦwww.fish-r-us.com) runs **sea-fishing** (from M$2800 per boat) and **scuba-diving** (from M$850) tours as well as cruises around the bay. Night-time excursions (typical catch are sailfish, dorado and red snapper) are particularly appealing, illuminated by the lights of the town shining out from all around the coast. Going east along Costera, at Playa Icacos, the **CiCi Waterpark** (daily 10am–6pm; M$120; ⓣ744/484-1970, ⓦwww.cici.com.mx) where you can splash around in swimming pools and on water slides and watch or swim with performing dolphins, makes for a welcome break from the beach. The other amusement park along Costera, the fifty-acre **Parque Papagayo**, at Playa Hornos (daily 8am–8pm; free), attracts picnicking families and joggers with its green spaces, aviary, rollerskating rink, boating lake and fairground rides.

Eating and drinking

Though it may not seem possible, there are even more **restaurants** than hotels in Acapulco. To eat cheaply, though, you're confined to the area around the **zócalo** where no-frills joints serve unmemorable but filling comidas corridas. Eating by the **beach** – where there's some kind of restaurant at every turn – is of course very much more expensive, and increasingly so as you head east, although the food is decent enough. Throughout the tourist zone, especially along Costera, you'll find the usual US and Mexican chains such as *Señor Frog's* and *Hard Rock Café*.

Heading towards the hills of **Acapulco Diamante**, Costera has world-class restaurants where delectable food, flawless service and goose-bump-inducing views are likely to be the highlight of your stay. Prices are, of course, on a par with upscale New York and London, but well worth the splurge.

In the centre

These options are marked on the Old Town Acapulco map, see p.556.

El Amigo Miguel Juárez 31 ⓣ744/483-6981. Two locations at the junction of Juárez and Azueta, both serving good soups, *antojitos* and seafood – sea bass, garlic shrimp and broiled Pacific lobster – at reasonable prices in clean, if institutional, surroundings with a pleasant second-floor dining room.

Astoria Inland end of the zócalo next to the cathedral ⓣ744/483-2944. Tucked just off the plaza under the shade of a huge tree, this is a cheap, quiet café with tables that spill out onto the pavement. The (mostly fried) dishes are predictable but satisfying – it's a good bet for a quick coffee and a giant torta.

Café Los Amigos La Paz 10 ⓣ744/482-2390. Popular shady spot just off the zócalo. Excellent breakfasts and tortas served all day (from M$25), plus daily specials of spaghetti, pork chops and the like (main dishes M$50–70). Hawkers are actively discouraged, so it's relatively peaceful.

Die Bratwurst José Azueta 10 ⓣ744/127-1523. Clean, modern German-owned place that knocks out tasty comidas corridas for M$45,and decent breakfasts M$38–45, though it's mostly the usual Mexican classics (with one or two German dishes), with a focus on chicken and fish.

La Flor de Acapulco on the zócalo ⓣ744/421-7649. With a balcony overlooking the square, this is not the cheapest option, but is a pleasant spot to linger over hearty staples including *arroz con mariscos* (M$70), *mojarra frita* (M$70), chicken *mole*, fish *pastor*, *pozole* (on a Thurs) or pork tacos. It's a popular meeting place for solo travellers, with occasional live music.

San Carlos Juárez 5, one block from the zócalo ⓣ744/482-6459. Another no-frills budget restaurant in the centre, with the added allure of a breezy patio, serving good *pozole* and comidas corridas all day for M$40; soups, pastas, fried fish and steaks all less than M$50.

Along Costera and beyond

These options are marked on the Acapulco Bay map, see p.555.

100% Natural Costera 126 ⓣ744/484-8440; Costera 200 ⓣ744/485-3982; Costera 112 ⓣ744/484-6447; Costera in the old town ⓣ744/480-1450; ⓦwww.100natural.com.mx. A chain of 24hr "healthy" eating places, serves good salads, fruit shakes and burgers (pastries start at M$30).

Baikal Carretera Escénica 16 & 22 ⓣ744/446-6867. The best restaurant in the city, with seductive views of the bay from floor-to-ceiling windows in the classically stylish dining room. The small menu is a fusion of everything from traditional Mexican to French and Asian. Escargots sit atop jumbo seared scallops, and lobster tail is bathed in a creamy white-wine sauce and surrounded by fluffy peaks of mashed potato. Average mains are around M$250. Reservations essential (request window seating).

CasaNova Carretera Escénica 5256, just south of *Las Brisas* hotel ⓣ744/446-6237. This is one of Acapulco's most highly regarded restaurants, as much for its spectacular location nestled in a hillside overlooking the bay as for its fine northern Italian cuisine. The menu features succulent veal chops, spaghetti with seafood and a selection of Mediterranean-style fish dishes.

El Olvido Costera inside Plaza Marbella ⓣ744/481-0203, ⓦwww.elolvido.com.mx. Upscale nouvelle cuisine, combining traditional Mexican flavours with French and Italian dishes. Good *crema quemada* (Mexican-style *crème brûlée*) and dreamy views of the bay from the dual-level, open-air dining room.

Pámpano Carretera Escénica 33 ⓣ744/446-5636, ⓦwww.modernmexican.com. An Acapulco institution and part of the Richard Sandoval stable (Placido Domingo is also an owner), with a variety of exquisite contemporary Mexican dishes, featuring plenty of seafood and fish dishes (mains M$200–300). The views from the understated, but elegant, dining room are wonderful. Closed Tues.

Tacos Tumbras Costera, 62 opposite Oceanic 2000 ⓣ744/484-1100. Cheap local chain with a couple of outdoor restaurants on Costera, with plastic furniture and meat roasted at the counter. The clubbers' and taxi drivers' late-night favourite for its very succulent tacos *carne asada*. Daily 7pm–5am.

Terra Luna Costera 54, west of CiCi Waterpark, opposite the *Hard Rock Café* ⓣ744/484-2464, ⓦwww.terralunaacapulco.com. Excellent crepes as well as Italian pastas, seafood and imaginative salads.

Nightlife and entertainment

You could spend several weeks in Acapulco simply trawling its scores of **night-clubs** and **bars**, discos and dinner-dances – there are people who claim never to have seen the town during daylight hours. Anywhere with music or dancing will demand a hefty **cover charge** – usually not less than M$300 in high season for men and M$250 for women – before they even consider letting you in, though this usually includes a **free bar**. Most clubs open at 11pm and close at 6am, the majority strung out along **Costera**, beyond CiCi Waterpark. If you're not easily intimidated, you could also try some of the old town **bars and cantinas**, but these aren't recommended for women on their own.

More refined entertainment can be found at Centro Acapulco, which features a year-round programme of events, including classical concerts by the Orquesta Filarmónica de Acapulco (ⓦwww.filarmonicadeacapulco.org.mx).

El Alebrije Costera 3308 ⓣ744/484-5902. Opposite the *Grand Hotel*, this cavernous, rather tacky, dance hall with light shows is popular with a youngish local crowd post-1am and couples earlier in the evening. The music runs the gamut of mainstream pop and rock and Latin tropicana. Cover at the weekend is around M$360 for men, M$260 for women, and includes all drinks (usually watered down).

Baby'O Costera 22, east of CiCi Waterpark ⓣ744/484-7474, ⓦwww.babyo.com.mx. Set in an imitation cave, this is one of the more consistently popular clubs and as well as one of the most expensive (cover M$300–600) – drinks are not included. The well-dressed, well-heeled crowd is usually high on attitude if they have managed to get in – *Baby'O* tries to maintain a spurious exclusivity by turning people away at the door. All in all a mainstream affair, with cheesy 1980s music mixed with house and Latin.

Disco Beach Costera, Playa Condesa ⓣ744/484-8230. A notorious hook-up beach party with all the requisite gimmicks and contests. The more casual dress code – shorts and flip-flops – draws a young, fun crowd. Wed is "ladies night". Cover around M$300.

Mandara Carretera Escénica, north of *Las Brisas* hotel ⓣ744/446-5711, ⓦwww.acapulcomandara.com. Elegant club complete with terraced levels designed to see and be seen ("Philippe Starck-style"), as well as large windows overlooking the bay. Exclusive and luxurious, cover around M$400.

Palladium Carretera Escénica Las Brisas, Playa Guitarrón ⓣ744/446-5490, ⓦwww.palladium.com.mx. It's all about the glorious bay view at this justifiably hyped club with the best music selection – techno, house and hip-hop – in the city. A slightly older and dressier, but less pretentious, crowd adds to the friendly, gregarious atmosphere. Considered the best disco in the city, and long queues testify to its kudos. Cover around M$400.
Relax Lomas del Mar 4, opposite *El Presidente* hotel ⓣ744/484-0421. While not as gay-friendly as Puerto Vallarta (see p.518), Acapulco does have some gay bars and discos: this is one of the more reliable – small and a little claustrophobic, but featuring strippers and other live shows.
Salon Q Costera 23, east of CiCi Waterpark ⓣ744/481-0114. Live Latin music that draws hard-core salsa and merengue aficionados, who come to dance all night. The reasonable cover charge (M$200; no free bar) and a slightly older clientele give it an accessible vibe.
Tropicana Costera, Playa Hornos. One of a series of similar bar/restaurants that tend to play *cumbia*, merengue and salsa as much as American rock. Diners take to the dancefloor later in the evening (cover around M$50).

Listings

Banks and exchange Banks (particularly Banamex) and casas de cambio (slightly poorer rates) are numerous along Costera.
Buses The first-class Estrella de Oro terminal at the corner of Cuauhtémoc and Wilfrido Massieu (city buses marked "C Río" from opposite the zócalo) handles hourly buses to Mexico City (5hr). The much larger Central Ejido (aka Estrella Blanca; ⓣ744/469-2028; city buses marked "Ejido" or "Mocimba") handles the unified services of several companies, while luxury Estrella Blanca and all Turistar Ejecutivo buses (mostly from Cuernavaca and Mexico City) use the Papagayo (Central de Lujo) terminal at Cuauhtémoc 1605 behind Parque Papagayo. You can also get to Chilpancingo, Puerto Escondido and Taxco, while first- and second-class buses run to Zihuatanejo; many continue to Lázaro Cárdenas.
Car rental Alamo ⓣ744/484-3305; Avis ⓣ744/462-0075; Budget ⓣ744/481-2433; Hertz ⓣ744/485-8947.
Consulates Canada, Centro Comercial Marbella, Prolongación Farallón at Costera ⓣ744/484-1305; UK, Plaza Arrecife, Suite 105, Costera 2408 ⓣ744/484-3331; US, *Hotel Continental Emporio*, Costera 121, Office 14 ⓣ744/481-0100.
Emergencies ⓣ066; Cruz Roja ⓣ065 or 744/445-5912; Emergency IMSS Hospital, Cuauhtémoc 95, ⓣ744/445-5353; police ⓣ744/486-8220; tourist complaints ⓣ744/484-4416.
Internet access Try Vig@net at Hidalgo 8, just west of the zócalo (daily 8am–midnight; M$10/hr).
Laundry Lavandería Coral, Juárez, at Felipe Valle (Mon–Fri 9am–2pm & 4–7pm, Sat 9am–5pm; M$13/kg).
Pharmacy Plenty of 24hr places in the hotel zone along Costera, and Botica Acapulco near the zócalo at Carranza 3 (also 24hr).
Post office At Costera 215, three blocks east of the zócalo (Mon–Fri 8am–5.30pm, Sat 9am–1pm).
Telephones Long-distance and collect calls can be made from Caseta Alameda (Mon–Sat 9am–8pm), west of the zócalo, on La Paz, next to *Café Los Amigos*.
Travel agents One of the best is Acuario Tours (ⓣ744/485-6100, ⓦwww.acuariotours.com), at Costera 186, but there are numerous agents interspersed between the hotels along Costera.

Chilpancingo

Nestled in a bowl in the Sierra Madre Occidental, 130km north of Acapulco, restful **CHILPANCINGO**, Guerrero's modest state capital since 1870, makes a cool stop-off – it's higher than 1000m – on the trip inland to Mexico City. Well off the tourist circuit and lent a youthful tenor by the large student population, it has a traffic-free zócalo, which is a good place to get a sense of the town's dynamic atmosphere.

The modern **Ayuntamiento** and **Palacio de Gobierno** combine a harmonious blend of Neoclassical and colonial influences. The latter is adorned with a huge bronze sculpture, *El Hombre Hacia el Futuro*; there's more monumental metalwork, along with busts of famous Guerrerans, in the Alameda, three blocks east along Juárez.

Fiestas

February

Día de la Candelaria (Feb 2). Celebrated in Colima with dances, processions and fireworks.

Fiesta Brava (Feb 5). A day of bullfights and horse races in Colima.

Carnaval (the week before Lent; variable Feb–March). Acapulco and Manzanillo are both famous for the exuberance of their celebrations; rooms can be hard to find.

March

Fiesta de San Patricio (March 10). Exuberant celebrations in San Patricio-Melaque continue for a week.

Semana Santa (Holy Week). Widely observed: the Palm Sunday celebrations in Petatlán, just south of Zihuatanejo, are particularly fervent.

May

Cinco de Mayo (May 5). Celebrations in commemoration of the victorious battle of Cinco de Mayo, especially in Acapulco.

Festival de las Lluvias (May 8). Celebrated in Mochitlán, near Chilpancingo, the festival has pre-Christian roots: pilgrims, peasants and local dance groups climb a nearby volcano at night, arriving at the summit at dawn to pray for rain. Manzanillo celebrates its **Founder's Day**.

Día de San Isidro (May 15). A week-long festival in Acapulco.

Founder's Day (May 31). In Puerto Vallarta.

June

Día de la Marina (Navy Day; June 1). Celebrated in the ports, particularly Puerto Vallarta, Manzanillo and Acapulco.

September

Día de Santiago (Sept 28). Celebrated in several villages immediately around Acapulco.

November

Feria (first week of Nov). Colima's major festival runs from the last days of October until November 8.

Día de los Muertos (Day of the Dead; Nov 2). Widely observed, with picturesque traditions in Atoyac de Alvarez, just off the Acapulco–Zihuatanejo road.

December

Día de la Virgen de Guadalupe (Dec 12). In honour of the patroness of Mexico. Acapulco has fervent celebrations, while in Manzanillo the celebrations start at the beginning of the month. In Puerto Vallarta they continue until the end of it.

Directly opposite its replacement, the former Palacio de Gobierno houses frequently changing exhibitions in the **Instituto Guerrerense de Cultura** and the excellent little **Museo Regional de Guerrero** (both Tues–Sun 9am–6pm; free). Well-laid-out displays – some labelled in English – record the history of the state's native peoples from their migration from Asia across the Bering land bridge thirty thousand years ago to the Maya and Teotihuacán influences on their pottery and stelae and the coming of the Spaniards. But the city's most dramatic chapter – vividly depicted on murals around the internal courtyard – came with the Independence struggle. After Hidalgo's defeat in the central highlands it was left to the southern populist movement, fuelled by the spread of land-grabbing haciendas and led by the skilled tactician **José María Morelos**, to continue the campaign. With almost the whole country behind them, they forced the Spaniards – who still held Mexico City – to attend the Congress of Chilpancingo in 1813, where the Declaration of Independence was issued and the principles of the constitution – chiefly the abolition of slavery and the equality of the races – were worked out. Ultimately the congress failed, and within two years the Spaniards had retaken Guerrero and executed Morelos.

Practicalities

Buses from Mexico City (3hr 30min) and Acapulco (1hr 30min) arrive at either the Estrella Blanca or Estrella de Oro terminals, opposite each other, 2km east of the zócalo on 21 de Marzo – turn right and then right again along Juárez. Minibuses run into town along Juárez and back out along the parallel Guerrero. Madero crosses these two streets just before the zócalo, and it's around here that you'll find all the essential services.

If you want to **stay** overnight, you'll be perfectly comfortable at the *Del Parque*, at Colón 5 (☎747/472-1285; ④), which has well-equipped, spacious, brightly decorated rooms and bathrooms, and a very good café/restaurant. You can **eat** light snacks or cake with an espresso at *El Portal*, beside the cathedral on Madero, or find more substantial meals at *Taco Rock* inside *Del Parque*, which turns into a popular bar at night.

Travel details

Buses

Bus services all along the coast are frequent and fast, with the possible exception of the stretch between Manzanillo and Lázaro Cárdenas, and there are almost constant departures on the major routes heading inland. The following list covers first-class services – second-class services are usually just as frequent.

Acapulco to: Chilpancingo (every 30min; 2hr); Cuernavaca (10 daily; 4–5hr); Guadalajara (5 daily; 17hr); Lázaro Cárdenas (5 daily; 6–7hr); Manzanillo (1 daily; 12hr); Mexico City (frequently; 6hr); Puerto Escondido (5 daily; 7hr); Puerto Vallarta (5 daily; 18hr); Taxco (5 daily; 5hr); Tijuana (2 daily; 49hr); Zihuatanejo (at least hourly; 4–5hr).

Barra de Navidad to: Guadalajara (every 30min; 6–7hr); Manzanillo (every 30min; 1hr 30min); Puerto Vallarta (18 daily; 5hr).

Chilpancingo to: Acapulco (every 30min; 2hr); Mexico City (hourly; 3hr 30min).

Colima to: Comala (every 10–15min; 20min); Guadalajara (at least hourly; 3hr); Lázaro Cárdenas (4 daily; 6–7hr); Manzanillo (frequently; 1hr 30min); Mexico City (8 daily; 11hr); Puerto Vallarta (3 daily; 6hr); Tecomán (every 15min; 45min); Tijuana (2 daily; 38hr).

Manzanillo to: Acapulco (3 daily; 12hr); Barra de Navidad (frequently; 1hr 30min); Colima (frequently; 1hr 30min); Guadalajara (frequently; 5–6hr); Lázaro Cárdenas (7 daily; 6hr); Mexico City (4 daily; 12hr); Puerto Vallarta (at least hourly; 5–7hr); Tijuana (2 daily; 38hr).

Puerto Vallarta to: Acapulco (2 daily; 18hr); Barra de Navidad (9 daily; 3hr 30min); Colima (2 daily; 6hr); Guadalajara (at least every 30min; 6hr); Lázaro Cárdenas (3 daily; 12hr); Manzanillo (6 daily; 5–7hr); Mazatlán (7 daily; 8hr); Mexico City (8 daily; 14hr); Tepic (frequently; 2hr 30min).

Zihuatanejo to: Acapulco (hourly; 4hr); Ixtapa (continuously; 15min); Lázaro Cárdenas (hourly; 2hr); Manzanillo (3 daily; 7–8hr); Mexico City (frequently; 9hr); Morelia (6 daily; 8hr); Puerto Vallarta (2 daily; 12–13hr); Salina Cruz (2 daily; 17–18hr); Tijuana (2 daily; 40hr).

Flights

This section of Mexico's coast is well served by flights, with international services to Acapulco, Puerto Vallarta and Zihuatanejo and domestic flights to various points in between. Guadalajara and Mexico City are accessible from Manzanillo and Ixtapa/Zihuatanejo; Ixtapa/Zihuatanejo also has seasonal flights to numerous locations in the US and Canada.

Acapulco is connected to North America by numerous seasonal flights (typically Nov–April) to Chicago, Dallas, Los Angeles, Montréal, Newark and Toronto. Scheduled flights to: Guadalajara (1 daily); Houston (1daily); Mexico City (frequent); Monterrey (3 weekly); Phoenix (1 weekly); Tijuana (1 daily); Toluca (1 daily).

Puerto Vallarta is one of the busiest air hubs in Mexico, with flights to: Atlanta (1 daily); Calgary (1 weekly); Chicago (5 weekly); Dallas (daily); Denver (4 weekly); Detroit (1 daily); Guadalajara (5–7 daily); Houston (1–3 daily); Los Angeles (2–4 daily); Mexico City (frequent); Minneapolis (1 daily), Monterrey (frequent); Montréal (2 weekly); Newark (1 weekly); New York JFK (1 daily); Phoenix (2–3 daily); Portland (7 weekly); San Francisco (5 daily); Salt Lake City (1 daily); Seattle (3 daily); Tijuana (4 weekly); Toluca (1 daily); Toronto (2 weekly); Vancouver (1 weekly).

Veracruz

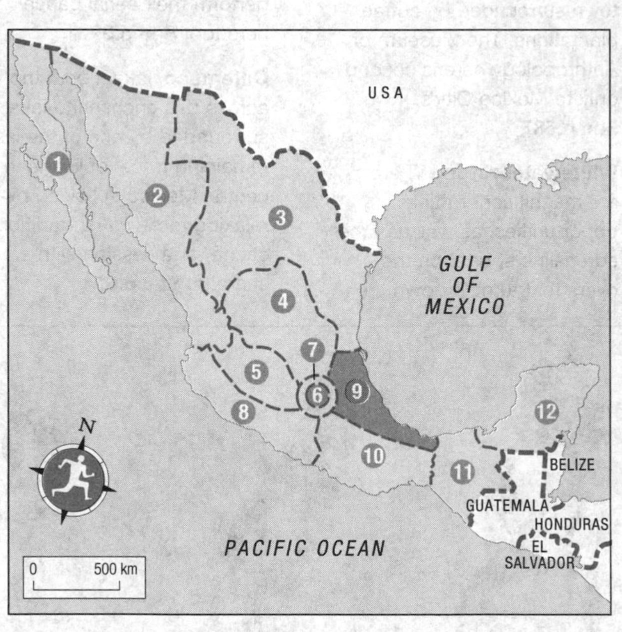
USA
1
2
3
4
5
6
7
8
9
10
11
12
GULF OF MEXICO
BELIZE
GUATEMALA
HONDURAS
EL SALVADOR
PACIFIC OCEAN
N
0
500 km

CHAPTER 9 Highlights

✱ **Veracruz** Show your fiery side and salsa with divas wearing outrageous costumes at the city's exuberant Carnaval. Afterwards, relax with an ice-cold mint julep and soak up the sounds of marimba in the zócalo, one of Mexico's most vibrant plazas. See p.577

✱ **Xalapa** Enjoy the café culture in this university town surrounded by coffee plantations. The Museum of Anthropology here is second only to Mexico City's. See p.587

✱ **Whitewater rafting** There are magnificent rafting opportunities, as well as other adrenaline sports, on the rivers that tumble down the tropical valleys of the Sierra Madre Oriental. Take a tour from one of the cities, or head directly to the riverside towns of Jalcomulco or Tlapacoyan. See p.593

✱ **El Tajín** Explore the unique pyramids and ruins at this magnificent remnant of Classic Veracruz civilization; the awesome *voladores* perform their aerial dance here too. See p.597

✱ **Catemaco** Take a boat trip across this enchanting lake, surrounded by one of the last remaining tracts of jungle in central Mexico, followed by a relaxing *temazcal*, a traditional sauna, or a session with a shaman. See p.604

▲ Carnaval, Veracruz

Veracruz

The central Gulf coast is among the least-visited yet most distinct areas of Mexico. From Mexico City, you descend through the southern fringes of the Sierra Madre Oriental, past the country's highest peaks, to a broad, hot and wet coastal plain. In this fertile tropical zone the earliest Mexican civilizations developed: **Olmec** culture dominated the southern half of the state from 1200 BC, while the civilization known as **Classic Veracruz** flourished between 250 and 900 AD at centres such as El Tajín. Today, **Huastec** and **Totonac** culture remains strong in the north. Cortés began his march on the Aztec capital from Veracruz, and the city remains, as it was throughout colonial history, one of the busiest ports in the country. Rich in agriculture – coffee, vanilla, tropical fruits and flowers grow everywhere – the **Gulf coast** is also endowed with large deposits of oil and natural gas.

The few non-Mexican tourists who find their way here are usually just passing through. In part, at least, this is because the area makes no particular effort to attract them; the **weather** can also be blamed – it rains more often and more heavily here than just about anywhere else. Yet even in the rainy season the torrential downpours are short-lived, and within a couple of hours of the rain starting, you can be back on the streets in bright sunshine. Though there are long, windswept **beaches** all down the Atlantic coast, they are less beautiful than their Pacific or Caribbean counterparts, while the larger coastal towns are primarily commercial centres, of little interest to the visitor.

That said, domestic tourism to the area is increasing rapidly, both to the beaches and, increasingly, for **adventure tourism** – climbing, whitewater-rafting, kayaking, canyoning and more – around the eastern slopes of the **Sierra Madre** and the rivers that flow off it. **Veracruz** itself is one of the most welcoming of all Mexico's cities; it's too busy with its own affairs to create a separate life for visitors so you're drawn instead into the steamy tropical port's day-to-day workings, and its obsession with music. Less than an hour north lie **La Antigua** and **Villa Rica**, where Cortés established the first Spanish government on the American mainland, and **Cempoala**, ruined site of the first civilization he encountered. **El Tajín**, near the coast in the north of the state, is one of the most important archeological sites in the country, and **Filo Bobos**, only recently excavated, is also well worth a visit. The colonial cities in the mountains are also delightful: **Xalapa**, seat of the Veracruz state government, is the finest, with its balmy climate, beautiful highland setting and superb anthropology museum. This area, and the high mountains around **Córdoba** and **Orizaba**, are the playground of the adrenaline tourist too. To the south, **Catemaco** is a spell-binding lake set in an extinct volcanic crater, where you can see the last remaining tract of Gulf coast **rainforest**. The area is renowned as a meeting place for native *brujos* and *curanderos*, witches and healers.

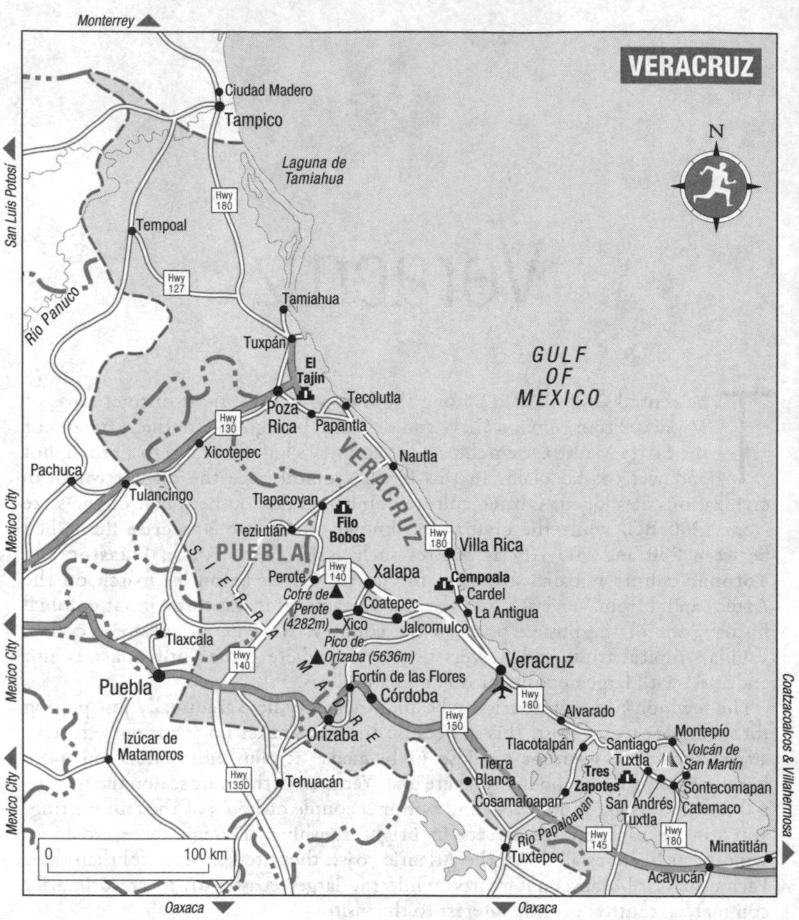

The state also has some great **food** – not only local coffee, fruit and vanilla but also seafood. *Huachinango a la Veracruzana* (red snapper Veracruz-style) is served across the country, and is of course on every menu here. But there are many more exotic possibilities, from langoustines and prawns to *jaiba*, large local crab; look out for anything made with *chile chipotle*, a hot, dark-brown chile with a very distinctive (and delicious) flavour – *chilpachole de jaiba* is a sort of crab chowder that combines the two. Sweet tamales, too, are a speciality, and to wash it all down, the brewery at Orizaba produces some of the best beers in the country.

The route from Mexico City

If you take the direct route – the excellent Hwy-150 – from Mexico City to Veracruz, you'll bypass every major town en route; if you're driving yourself, note that the tolls along this stretch of road are extremely high (about M$450). For those pressed for time, the fast highway is a blessing – Veracruz and the coast are very much the outstanding attractions – but the cities in the mountains merit a stop if you have the time. Regardless of how fast you go or what form of transport you take, the journey is one of the most beautiful in Mexico: as Ixtaccíhuatl gradually disappears behind you, the snow on the **Pico de Orizaba** comes into view, and the plains of corn and maguey in the west are supplanted on the eastern slopes by woods of pine and cypress, and by green fields dotted with contented cows out to pasture.

It's worth noting, however, that this is the rainiest area of the country, and while the damp brings bounties in terms of great coffee and a luxuriance of flowers, downpours can become a problem. Particularly irritating – especially in October and November – is what the locals call *chipichipi*, a persistent fine drizzle caused by warm airstreams from the Gulf hitting cooler air as they reach the eastern face of the sierra. Drivers should also watch out for the fog that frequently cloaks the higher sections of this road.

Orizaba

The first major town en route, midway between Puebla and Veracruz, **ORIZABA** is an industrial city and a major brewing centre: giant Cervecería Cuauhtémoc Moctezuma produces some of the best **beer** in the republic, including globally famous brands Sol and Dos Equis – ask at the tourist office (see below) for details of tours. Despite the industry, the historic centre remains compact and attractive; because the old city was built up against a hill, development has spread in one direction only, so the *centro historico* is right on the edge of town, with more modern development sprawling to the east and south. There's not a great deal to see, but it makes an enjoyable short break or overnight stop.

Arrival and information

The ADO **bus station** is on Oriente 6 near Sur 11; most second-class services also stop here or very nearby. Oriente 6 is Orizaba's main commercial street, and you'll find big business **hotels** and numerous restaurants here: head five blocks west and three north for the Parque Castillo at the heart of the old town, where the helpful **tourist office** (Mon–Fri 8am–3pm & 4–8pm, Sat noon–8pm, Sun noon–4pm; ⓣ272/728-9136) is on the ground floor of the Palacio de Hierro. There's an **ATM** in the bus station, and plenty more in the shopping area between here and the centre; the **market** is just off Parque Castillo.

Accommodation

Casa Real Ote 6 464 just up from the ADO on the opposite side of the street ⓣ272/724-0077, ⓦwww.casarealorizaba.com. Pleasant, low-rise, business-style hotel with rooms around a tiled courtyard and good facilities including a small pool and wi-fi. Smart and comfortable. ❺

Mediterraneo Corner of Ote 6 and Sur 11 ⓣ272/724-4000, ⓦwww.hotel-mediterraneo.com.mx. Probably the best value in this area, right next to the ADO but with well-soundproofed modern rooms, mostly air-conditioned, with wi-fi. ❸

Plaza Palacio Pte 2 #2 ⓣ272/725-9933, ⓔhotelplazapalacio_ori@hotmail.com. Facing the Palacio de Hierro and cathedral across a pedestrianized street, this could hardly have a better location. Rooms are simple, with fan and cable TV, but comfy and quiet. ❸

Posada del Viajero Madero Nte 242 ⓣ272/726-3320. Decent budget choice just half a block from the Palacio de Hierro facing the market. ❶

The Town

The **Parque Castillo**, at Colón and Madero, marks the centre of the old town. Here you'll find the Catedral de San Miguel and the **Palacio de Hierro**, which houses not only the helpful **tourist office** (Mon–Fri 8am–3pm & 4–8pm, Sat noon–8pm, Sun noon–4pm; ⓣ272/728-9136), but also a tiny one-room Museo de

Cerveza and, upstairs, a small Museo Arqueologico. Between them these won't detain you for more than twenty minutes, but the building itself is well worth a look, an extraordinary nineteenth-century iron structure, prefabricated in Belgium. West of the plaza, Colón continues towards the looming **Cerro del Borrego**, atop which a vast Mexican flag flies and from where, if you brave the stiff climb, there are fabulous views of the city. Along the way, Colón crosses the **Río Orizaba**, where an attractive riverside walk winds beneath the city's many bridges. Colón continues past the **Palacio Municipal** before ending at the **Alameda**, a shady park beneath the Cerro. There's just one other significant sight in the city, the **Museo de Arte** (Tues–Sun 9am–6pm; M$10), whose 36 works by Diego Rivera constitute one of Mexico's finest collections of this iconic artist. Housed alongside other Mexican art from colonial to contemporary in a fine colonial building, they make this the most worthwhile visit in the city. Unfortunately it's a long way out – over a dozen blocks east of the centre on Av Oriente 4 at Calle 25 Sur.

Eating and drinking

There are plenty of taco stands in the historic centre, but surprisingly few places to sit down and eat: the bulk of those are out on Oriente 6.

La Braza Ote 6 by the ADO. Fast-food style grill that's always busy, day and night.

Cafeteria Dauzon corner of Colón Ote and Nte 4. A great café and cake shop that also serves a very good-value lunchtime *comida* (M$45).

Gran Cafe de Orizaba Parque Castillo, in the Palacio de Hierro. Wonderful, old-fashioned café with a terrace facing the cathedral. Great coffee, but little in the way of food.

Restaurante Jardin Pte 2, inside the Plaza San Juan, just beyond the Palacio Municipal on the opposite side of the road. Probably the top choice in the historic centre, serving tasty meals in a lovely, tiled colonial courtyard; cool and peaceful.

Quick Lunch Pte 2, opposite the *Hotel Plaza Palacio*. Basic lunch stop with excellent rotisserie chicken.

Pico de Orizaba

Orizaba is situated close to the foot of the loftiest peak in Mexico, the **Pico de Orizaba** (Citlaltépetl), a perfectly formed, snow-capped volcano. There is a fair amount of disagreement over its exact height – 5636m seems the most widely accepted, though locals often claim more – but there's no disputing that it's a beautiful sight and a seriously challenging climb, for experienced mountaineers only. Numerous local companies offer guides and facilities, mostly based in the village of **Tlachichuca**, which at 2600m is where the main trails begin. To get there take a second-class bus to the small town of Serdán (2hr), where you change for Tlachichuca itself (1hr); there are also occasional buses direct from Puebla. Details of the climb (Oct–May only) can be found in R.J. Secor's *Mexican Volcanoes*. Reliable operators include long-established Servimont (ⓦwww.servimont.com.mx) and Summit Orizaba (ⓣ245/451-5082, ⓦwww.summitorizaba.com), both with their own accommodation in Tlachichuca, and Pico de Orizaba Xtreme (ⓣ271/713-2926, ⓦwww.picodeorizabaxtreme.com), who also offer a variety of other eco- and adventure-tourism options around Orizaba.

Fortín de las Flores

FORTÍN DE LAS FLORES, "Fortress of the Flowers", lies 15km northeast of Orizaba at a point where a beautiful minor route cuts across country to Xalapa (see p.587), nearly 150km north. Its name is singularly appropriate: you'll see flowers, including wild orchids and cultivated gardenias, all over the place – in the plaza, at the hotels, on the hillsides. Rain, which is frequent from May to December, and the region's constant muggy warmth ensure their growth. Flowers are also big business

▲ Climbing the Pico de Orizaba

here, with a series of huge nurseries and garden centres lining the road towards Córdoba, and a giant flower festival in late April or early May. There's not a lot to do other than enjoy the torpid atmosphere, but it's a far quieter place to take a break than Orizaba or Córdoba. You can fully appreciate the luxuriance of the vegetation a couple of kilometres west of town at the **Barranca del Metlac**, the spectacular ravine you'll have crossed on the way from Orizaba. Coffee and fruit trees flourish at the top, while the banks of the gorge itself are thick with a stunning variety of wild plants, which attract hummingbirds and insects of all kinds.

Practicalities

The town is laid out on a grid, at the heart of which is the large Parque Principal, bordered by avenidas 1 and 5 and calles 1 and 3. Local **buses** from Córdoba will drop you off here, most others at the tiny ADO bus station on Avenida 2 at Calle 6, a short walk away. Six blocks along Avenida 2 at no.210, between calles 5 and 7, is the *Hotel Fortín de las Flores* (Ⓣ271/713-0108, Ⓦwww.hotelfortindelasflores.com.mx; ❹). Built in 1935, this was the hotel that helped establish Fortín as a resort in the 1950s and it's still the most comfortable **place to stay** in town, with air-conditioned rooms with cable TV, a restaurant, pool and internet connections. The *Hotel Fortín* takes up most of the block; in the remaining corner, cheaper accommodation is available at the motel-like *Hotel Bugambilia* (Ⓣ272/713-1350; ❸), Avenida 1 305 at Calle 7, also with internet in the lobby and a small café. The *Hotel Posada Loma*, on the eastern edge of town opposite the market on the main road to Córdoba (Ⓣ271/713-0658, Ⓦwww.posadaloma.com; ❺), has comfortable, air-conditioned rooms and bungalows around a pretty garden with pool; an excellent breakfast (also open to non-guests) is included.

A tiny **tourist office** is on Avenida 1 at the corner of Calle 5, the main road junction in town, and there's a Banamex **bank** with ATM on Calle 1 on the zócalo. **Internet** cafés include Infinitum, Avenida 3 between calles 1 and 2, and Konekta, upstairs in the corner of the zócalo at Avenida 5 and Calle 1. The

Cafeteria Kiosco, in the centre of the lower half of the zócalo between the Palacio Municipal and the Catedral, is a great spot for breakfasts and simple meals. For more substantial **food**, the *Central de Mariscos*, Calle 1 just off Avenida 1 on the zócalo, is a fishmonger and fish restaurant serving a great *coctel de camarón*. *Lolo*, at Calle 1 #6 between avenidas 2 and 4, is a slightly more formal place.

Córdoba

It's a short local bus ride from Fortín to **CÓRDOBA**, and indeed these days the two places are barely separate – linked along the road by a continuous string of superstores and factories. At the centre of the area's coffee trade, Córdoba is a busy modern city built around an attractive colonial centre. Founded in 1618 by thirty Spanish families – and so also known as the "City of the Thirty Knights" – its main claim to fame is that in 1821 the last Spanish viceroy, Juan O'Donoju, signed the **Treaty of Córdoba** with General Iturbide here, formally giving Mexico independence. The signing took place in the Palacio de los Condes de Zevallos, now known as the **Portal de Zevallos**, on the northern edge of the central Plaza 21 de Mayo.

Arrival and information

Central Córdoba is easy to navigate: Avenida 1 and Calle 1 intersect at the Palacio Municipal on the Plaza 21 de Mayo: avenidas run east–west, with even numbers north of the zócalo and odd numbers south. Calles run north–south, with even numbers west of the zócalo and odd numbers east. The **bus terminal** (for first- and second-class services) is 3km south of the centre at Privada 4 between calles 39 and 41, a short taxi ride to the zócalo (buy a ticket first), or hop on a local bus marked "Centro". For Fortín de las Flores and Orizaba, you'll find local buses on Avenida 2. The **tourist office** (Mon–Fri 9am–7pm, Sat 9am–1pm) is in the Palacio Municipal; local tours are organized by Turismo Recreativo (ⓣ271/713-0216, ⓦwww.turismorecreativo.com.mx). For **internet** access try *Infinitum*, Calle 1 219 between avenidas 2 and 4, or *Cafe Internet*, upstairs at the corner of Calle 3 and Avenida 2.

Accommodation

Most of the big modern **hotels**, along with fast food and fancier restaurants, are some way north of the centre on the old highway.

Bello Avenida 2 at Calle 5 ⓣ271/712-8122, ⓦwww.hotelbello.com/cordoba. A mid-market business-style hotel, with wi-fi in the rooms. ❺

Iberia Avenida 2 919 ⓣ271/712-1301. One of numerous budget options on this street, a pleasant place with a/c rooms as well as slightly cheaper ones with fan. ❷

AP Mansur Avenida 1, corner of Calle 3 ⓣ271/712-6000, ⓦwww.hotelmansur.com.mx. Great central hotel with fantastic balconied rooms overlooking the cathedral in a characterful old building. ❹

Virreynal Avenida 1 at Calle 5 ⓣ271/712-2377, ⓦwww.hotelvirreynal.com. Next door to the *Mansur* and very similar in style. ❹

The City

There's not a great deal specifically to seek out in Córdoba: the animated zócalo is the main focus, surrounded by arcaded *portales*, many of which, including the famous Porta de Zevallos, are given over to handicraft shops and cafés, where you can sit and sample Córdoban coffee or julep, a rum and mint cocktail. The twin-towered **Catedral de la Inmaculada Concepción**, facing the Palacio Municpal across the plaza, is one of the most richly adorned religious buildings in the state – started in 1621, it contains a revered image of the Virgin Mary to the right of the altar. Nearby, on Calle 3 half a block off the zócalo between avenidas 3 and 5, is the **Museo de la Ciudad** (Tues–Sun 9am–2pm & 4–7pm; free). Housed in a beautiful colonial building with gorgeous mountain views from its upper storey, the museum's exhibits (labelled in Spanish only) encompass some thirty centuries of local history, from Olmec and Totonac ceramics and sculpture, through Independence, to mementos of the Mexico '68 Olympics.

Eating and drinking

La Colonial Calle 5, opposite *Hotel Bello*. A huge bakery with great *pan dulce*; takeaway only.

Las Delicias Avenida 2 307 between calles 3 and 5 ⓣ271/712-9494. A good bet for tasty inexpensive *comidas* in the centre of town.

Los 30's Avenida 9 2004 between calles 20 and 22 ⓣ271/712-3379. Excellent crepes at this option in the restaurant zone near the highway.

Mi Kasa Avenida 5 between calles 2 and 4 212-A ⓣ271/712-7613. For a break from Mexican food, try the sushi and other Japanese specialities at this comfortable restaurant.

Monkah Café Bar Below the museum on Calle 3. More of a bar than a café, with frequent club nights and live music events.

La Parroquia Portal de Zevallos ⓣ271/712-1853. A lovely, if pricey, traditional café on the zócalo.

El Patio de la Abuela Calle 1 208, between avenidas 2 and 4 ⓣ271/712-0606. *El Patio* serves good-value breakfasts and *comidas*.

El Tabachin Portal de Zevallos ⓣ271/712-1853. Alongside the *Cafe La Parroquia*. The best location in town, for an upmarket restaurant serving steaks and more traditional Mexican fare.

Veracruz

VILLA RICA DE LA VERACRUZ was the first town founded by the Spanish in Mexico, a few days after Cortés's arrival on Good Friday, 1519. Though today's city occupies the area of coast where he first came ashore, made camp and encountered Aztec emissaries, the earliest development – little more than a wooden stockade – was in fact established some way to the north (see p.595) before being moved to La Antigua (see p.585) and finally arriving at its present site in 1589. The modern city is very much the heir of the original; still the largest port on the Gulf coast, its history reflects every major event from the Conquest onwards. "Veracruz", states author Paul Theroux, "is known as the 'heroic city'. It is a poignant description: in Mexico a hero is nearly always a corpse."

Your first, and lasting, impression of Veracruz, however, will not be of its historical significance but of its present-day vitality. Its dynamic zócalo, pleasant waterfront location and relative absence of tourists make the city one of the most enjoyable places in the Republic in which simply to sit back and observe – or join – the daily round. This is especially true in the evenings, when the tables under the *portales* of the plaza fill up and the drinking and the marimba music begin, to go on most of the night. **Marimba** – a distinctively Latin-Caribbean sound based around a giant wooden xylophone – is *the* local sound, but at peak times there are also mariachi and *norteño* bands and individual crooners all striving to be heard over each other. When the municipal band strikes up from the middle of the square, confusion is total. Veracruz's riotous nine-day **Carnaval** celebrations rival the best in the hemisphere, while the **Festival Internacional Afrocaribeño**, usually held in July or August, showcases dance and music performances from all over the Caribbean and Africa, film showings and art exhibitions.

Some history

Though tranquil enough today, the port's past has been a series of "invasions, punitive missions and local military defeats…humiliation as history". The problems started even before the Conquest was complete, when **Pánfilo Narváez** landed here on his ill-fated mission to bring Cortés back under the control of the governor of Cuba, and continued intermittently for the next four hundred years.

Throughout the sixteenth and seventeenth centuries, Veracruz and the Spanish galleons that used the port were preyed on constantly by the English, Dutch and French. In the **War of Independence** the Spanish made their final stand here, holding the fortress of San Juan Ulúa for four years after the country had been lost. In **1838** the French occupied the city, in what was later dubbed "The Pastry War", demanding compensation for French property and citizens who had suffered in the years following Independence; in **1847** US troops took Veracruz, and from here marched on to capture the capital. In January **1862** the French, supported by Spanish and English forces that soon withdrew, invaded on the pretext of forcing Mexico to pay her foreign debt, but ended up staying five years and setting up the unfortunate Maximilian as emperor. Finally, in **1914**, US marines were back, occupying the city to protect American interests during the Revolution. These are the "Cuatro Veces Heroica" of the city's official title, and form the bulk of the history displayed in the museums here.

Arrival and information

The ADO first-class **bus station** is about 3km from the centre at Díaz Mirón 1698, with the AU second-class terminal right behind it facing Lafragua. To reach the centre, buy a ticket for a **taxi** (M$25) from the booth on the south side of the first-class terminal (left as you exit). To take a bus (M$6), walk to the stop on Díaz Mirón to the right as you exit, and take any – most will have "Díaz Mirón" or

"Centro" on the windscreen. They mostly end up on Independencia as it runs past the zócalo. The **airport** is about 10km south of the city. Taxis between here and the centre cost M$165; buy a ticket from the taxi desk in the terminal.

Although Veracruz is a large and rambling city, the **centro histórico** (its old downtown area) is relatively small and easy to navigate – anywhere further afield can be reached by **local bus** from somewhere very near the zócalo. All trips within the city (and as far as Boca del Río) are M$6, or M$7.50 for the newer 'express' buses, often (but not always) painted yellow. Taxis charge according to a zone system and are pretty honest – trips in the centre will cost you about M$25, to the bus station M$30. If your hotel calls for one it will be more expensive (M$50 and up), though this is generally a safer option at night.

The **tourist office**, on the ground floor of the Palacio Municipal right on the zócalo (Mon–Fri 8am–8pm, Sat & Sun 10am–6pm; ⓣ229/989 8817, ⓦwww.veratur.gob.mx), has basic information and helpful staff on hand, though not always English speakers.

Accommodation

There's a **hotel** right next to the first-class bus station, and several very cheap and rather grim places around the back of the second-class terminal, but unless you've arrived late at night or face a very early departure, there's no point staying this far out. The other inexpensive places are mostly within a couple of blocks of the zócalo; they're nothing to write home about, and often noisy, but at least you should find a clean room with a fan. The best deals in the city are in the **mid-range**, and there are some decent hotels along the malecón within walking distance of the zócalo. If you want more luxury, head to the **beach**, where resort-style hotels front the *playas* of Villa del Mar, Mocambo and Boca del Río in an ever-expanding hotel zone

City Centre

Amparo Serdán 482 ⓣ229/932-2738, ⓦwww.hotelamparo.com.mx. One of a cluster of cheap places close to the zócalo. Rooms are basic but clean, with fan and TV. ❷

Casa Blanca Trigueros 49 ⓣ229/200-4625, ⓦcasablanca.hotel.sitiosprodigy.com.mx. The pick of the budget places near the centre, with tiny but comfortable rooms around a pretty tiled courtyard. Very clean and quiet; some with a/c. ❸

Central Díaz Mirón 1612 ⓣ229/937-2222, ⓦwww.hotel-central.com.mx. If you have to stay out by the bus station, you may as well make it here: right next to the ADO, modern, comfortable, efficient and reasonably well-soundproofed rooms, most with a/c and wi-fi. ❸

Colonial Miguel Lerdo 117 ⓣ229/932-0193, ⓦwww.hcolonial.com.mx. Ageing option on the zócalo, with a swimming pool, garage (extra) and a/c. Some rooms have been refurbished, including the priciest, which have great views over the square; others are in desperate need of a make-over. ❺

Gran Hotel Diligencias Independencia 1115 ⓣ229/923-0280, ⓦwww.granhoteldiligencias.com. The most modern, and best, of the hotels on the zócalo, elegantly refurbished with cable TV and wi-fi in the rooms, plus most other facilities and a small terrace pool. ❼

Holiday Inn Centro Histórico Morelos 225 ⓣ229/932-4550, ⓦwww.holidayinn.com. Charming hotel built out of the renovated half of the nineteenth-century Faro Benito Juárez, with all the modern conveniences and a pretty pool enclosed by a courtyard embellished with elegant tiling. Look out for bargain deals at the Holiday Inn website. ❻

Imperial Miguel Lerdo 153 ⓣ229/932-1204, ⓦwww.hotelimperialveracruz.com. If faded glory is your thing, you'll love the *Imperial*, an eighteenth-century building whose once magnificent public areas boast marble floors, a striking stained-glass ceiling and the first lift installed in Mexico (still going strong). The standard rooms, though they have a/c and comfy beds, are basic and faded and represent poor value, however, so only really worth it if you go for one of the large suites (❻–❽), decorated with colonial-style furniture, some of which look right onto the zócalo. ❺

Mar y Tierra Ávila Camacho at Figueroa ⓣ229/931-3866, ⓦwww.hotelmarytierra.com. Mid-priced seafront option, a 15–20min walk from the zócalo. A/c rooms in the old section are much smaller, so it's worth the extra for a newer room: both sections have many rooms with sea views at no extra cost. ❺

Royalty Ávila Camacho 503 ⓣ229/932-2844. Exceptionally ugly seafront hotel whose marble-walled corridors plainly saw their heyday twenty years ago; but it's exceptional value, with wonderful views from the a/c rooms at the front, and cheaper ones in the old part at the back with fan, TV and small balcony. ❸–❹

Ruíz Milán Paseo del Malecón ⓣ229/931-2121, ⓦwww.ruizmilan.com. Not quite as fancy as the facade and public areas might lead you to believe, this is nonetheless a comfortable, business-style hotel in a great location. Three grades of room – the best are at the front – all with a/c and cable TV, plus a small indoor pool and hot tub, and a good restaurant. ❹–❺

Trianon Héroes de Nacozari 76 ⓣ229/932-2844, ⓦwww.hoteltrianon.com.mx. Very friendly, central budget hotel whose a/c rooms with internet and cable TV are popular with local business folk. Big discounts often available. ❹

Acuario to Boca del Río

Bello Ruíz Cortines 258 ⓣ229/922-4828, ⓦwww.hotelbello.com. About 5km south of the centre, the *Bello* is among the cheaper modern options in one of the busiest restaurant and nightlife sections en route to Boca del Río, hence often fully booked. There's a courtyard pool, and rooms are business-like and comfortable: those on the upper floors at the back have views to the sea, a couple of blocks away. ❻

City Express Ávila Camacho 2375 ⓣ229/923-0900, ⓦwww.cityexpress.com.mx. In the seafront hotel zone beyond the *Lois*, this is a brand-new budget chain hotel, rather out-of-place here, but great value, with a pool and free wi-fi and buffet breakfast included. ❻

Fiesta Americana Ávila Camacho ⓣ229/989-8989, ⓦwww.fiestaamericana.com. Dominating the Playa de Oro, this massive resort has a giant pool and spacious rooms and balconies, all with sea views. One of the longest-established in the hotel zone, but still among the best, with a great beachfront position. ❽

Lois Ruíz Cortines 10 ⓣ229/937-8290, ⓦwww.hotellois.com.mx. On the very busy seafront junction of Ruíz Cortines and Ávila Camacho, close to the *Bello* and surrounded by restaurants and nightlife. The designer lobby and public areas are deceptively attractive: rooms are large and comfortable, but pretty bland. Outdoor pool, and good sea views from many rooms (better on the upper floors). ❼

Mocambo Ruíz Cortines 4000 at Playa Mocambo ⓣ229/922-0200, ⓦwww.hotelmocambo.com.mx. Grand old beachside hotel complex built in 1932 with lots of dark wood and a nautical theme. Though rather faded, it's wonderfully atmospheric – you half expect Frank Sinatra to be wandering through the lobby – facilities include large indoor and outdoor pools, a children's play area and several restaurants, among which is the well-regarded, formal *La Fragata*. ❼

Playa Paraiso Ruíz Cortines 3500 at Playa Mocambo ⓣ229/923-0700, ⓦwww.playaparaiso.com.mx. Villa and hotel complex with direct access to Mocambo beach, and across the road from Plaza las Americas and the World Trade Center. Comfortable, modern rooms in the main building, plus pricier villas and bungalows closer to the beach and pools. ❼

The city centre

The attractive **zócalo** is the heart of life in Veracruz in every sense – the place where everyone gathers, for morning coffee, lunch, afternoon strolls and at night. After dark, especially, it has an extraordinary energy, with tables set out under the *portales*, non-stop music and strolling crowds. The imposing **Catedral de Nuestra Señora de Asunción**, consecrated in 1721, dominates the square. Its most striking feature is its tiled dome, though the whole place is in a sad state of disrepair, with decay seeming to advance more quickly than the permanent, slow renovation. On the plaza too is the elegant **Palacio Municipal**, one of the oldest in Mexico, originally built between 1609 and 1627, though it assumed its current form in the eighteenth century. The **Fototeca de Veracruz** (Tues–Sun 10am–7pm; free), alongside, hosts beautifully presented photography exhibitions.

The malecón and the harbour

It's just a couple of blocks from the zócalo, past a stupendously tacky Mercado de Artesanías, down to the harbourfront promenade, the **malecón**. This is a worthwhile stroll at any time of day or night – evenings are particularly animated as street vendors and entertainers compete for your attention, illuminated by the twinkling lights of the ships in the port and the spotlit 'dancing' fountains outside the PEMEX building. *Tranvía* city tours start from here, and *lanchas* depart for harbour jaunts or across to the fortress (see box, p.582).

The latter, the **Castillo de San Juan de Ulúa** (Tues–Sun 10am–4.30pm; M$41, free Sun), is a tremendous fortification, clearly visible across the harbour it so singularly failed to protect. Today the fortress, originally an island, now connected to the mainland by a causeway, is mostly an empty ruin of endless battlements and stairways. Apart from a small **museum**, the main attraction is the **prison** – many political prisoners died during the rule of Díaz in three dark, unpleasant cells known as El Purgatorio, La Gloria and El Infierno (Purgatory, Heaven and Hell). At weekends and in high season, *lanchas* regularly cross the harbour to the castle (around M$30); otherwise the easiest way to get here is to take a taxi, which should be no more than M$35 if you hail one on the street – ask it to wait if you want to guarantee a ride back.

Towards the end of the malecón, the old **Faro** (lighthouse) stands alongside the **PEMEX tower**, a fine example of early modern Mexican architecture (or concrete brutalism), built in 1952. Outside are various memorials to the city's heroes, including a giant statue of Venustiano Carranza in front of the *faro*, looking exactly as John Reed describes him in *Insurgent Mexico*: "A towering, khaki-clad figure, seven feet tall it seemed…arms hanging loosely by his side, his fine old head thrown back." Carranza is further immortalized in the nearby **Museo Histórico Naval** (Tues–Sun 10am–5pm; free; labelling in Spanish only), where one room looks in detail at the events of 1914, when US troops occupied Veracruz and Carranza subsequently established his Constitutionalist government here. There's plenty more on the various heroic defenders of the city, but also fascinating exhibits on earlier history and seafaring in general.

Not far from the museum, the blackened and threatening walls of the **Baluarte de Santiago** (Tues–Sun 10am–4.30pm; M$41 for museum, fortifications free) make a bizarre sight, stranded as they are three blocks from the sea, with the cannon threatening only the passing traffic. The sole survivor of what were originally nine forts along a 2650-metre-long wall, the Baluarte was built in 1635 to help fend off constant attacks by pirates and buccaneers; at the time, it stood at the water's edge. The small museum inside has a few pieces of exquisite pre-Columbian gold jewellery discovered in 1976 by a local octopus fisherman. By the time the authorities got wind of his find, most of it had been melted down and sold, but what little remains is lovely.

Museums and cultural centres

About five blocks south of the zócalo on Zaragoza, the **Museo de la Ciudad** (Tues–Sat 10am–6pm, Sun 10am–3pm; free) occupies a former nineteenth-century orphanage. The exhibits cover local history and folklore from the city's earliest inhabitants to the 1950s. Inevitably, given the scope of material covered, it's rather a potted version, and many of the exhibits go completely unexplained (the few labels are in Spanish only), but there's some beautiful Olmec and Totonac sculpture, including one giant Olmec head; thought-provoking information on Mexico's African population, much of which was concentrated in this area after the slave trade; and enlightening sections on the social movements of the early twentieth century and the celebrated music and dance culture of the city.

Nearby are several cultural centres. The headquarters of the **Instituto Veracruzano de Cultura** occupy an old convent on Francisco Canal (Tues–Sun 9am–8pm; free). As well as regularly changing art exhibitions in its galleries, other rooms off the courtyard house classes and events, and you can also pick up information about cultural happenings across the city. Just a block away, **Las**

Atarazanas were colonial warehouses that once backed onto the harbour; inside are more temporary exhibition spaces, while the main facade is at the back. More prestigious art shows are generally held at the **Casa Principal** (daily 10am–8pm; free), a fine, converted eighteenth-century residence at Mario Molina 315.

Acuario to Boca del Río: the beaches

You wouldn't make a special trip to Veracruz for its **beaches**, but for an afternoon's escape to the sea, they can be very enjoyable. Strips of sand hug the coast for some 12km southeast of the centre, linked together by Bulevar María Ávila Camacho, which runs all the way to Boca del Río. For the most part this is not attractive, with concrete strip development all the way, and a six-lane highway right behind the beach, but it is where much of the city's modern life is concentrated. About halfway to Boca, Avenida Ruíz Cortines cuts inland, taking a short-cut away from the beach: here is some of the city's most recent development, including vast shopping malls like the Plaza las Americas, and many of the biggest, newest hotels. **Buses** (marked "Boca del Río", "Playas" or "Mocambo") head out from Zaragoza just next to the zócalo in Veracruz. Most take the quick route via Ruíz Cortines; for the scenic route along the coastal road take buses marked "Penacho" or join the open-air **tour buses** from the malecón (see box below). Direct services also run from the second-class bus station.

Swimmable beaches start a couple of kilometres from the centre, just beyond the Plaza Acuario shopping centre, home of the **Acuario de Veracruz** (Mon–Thurs

Tours, boat trips and watersports

City tours mostly depart from the malecón, where you'll find the traditional *tranvías* – buses done up to look like old trolley-cars – along with various rival tour buses. They leave every half-hour or so for a 45–60 minute tour of the old town (M$50, children M$30); the price includes a drink (a powerful *torito* for adults) and it's especially fun at night, when the *tranvías* are lit up. There are also bus tours down to Boca del Río (same price) and **boat trips** around the harbour (M$80). All of these are more frequent at weekends and in high season, and busier in the late afternoon and evening.

There are plenty of other opportunities to take to the water in Veracruz. Asdic (ⓣ229/935-9417, ⓦwww.asdic.com.mx), which runs the harbour tours, also offers evening sailings in its disco catamaran; and from a base on the beach by Plaza Acuario it sails around the Isla de los Sacrificios (now a nature reserve) to **Cancuncito**, a semi-submerged sandbar in the bay where you can disembark and swim. Banana boats and jet-skis are also available here.

There's remarkably good **diving** at pretty good rates on a large number of little-visited reefs and beaches within the **Parque Nacional Sistema Arrecifal Veracruzano**. To see marine life in the Gulf of Mexico at close quarters, head for one of the city's dive shops: Mundo Submarino (ⓣ229/980-6374, ⓦwww.mundosubmarino.com.mx), Ávila Camacho 3549, a couple of blocks north of Ruíz Cortines; Tridente (ⓣ229/260-5272, tridente_ver@hotmail.com), Ávila Camacho 353, a block or so north of the *Royalty* hotel; or Scubaver (ⓣ229/932-3994, ⓦwww.scubaver.net), Hernandez y Hernandez 563, near the *Mar y Tierra* hotel. Veracruz Adventures, Ávila Camacho 681-A by the *Hotel Novomar* (ⓣ229/931-5358, ⓦwww.veracruzadventures.com) also offers diving, as well as **snorkel trips** and **kayaks** for rent.

For more adventurous tours further afield, above all **whitewater-rafting** (mostly at Jalcomulco, see p.593), but also canyoning, rappelling and the like: operators include Amphibian (Lerdo 117, in the *Hotel Colonial*, ⓣ229/931-0997, ⓦwww.amphibianveracruz.com); Mexico Verde (Ruíz Cortines 4300, in the *Crowne Plaza* hotel, ⓣ01-800/362-8800, ⓦwww.mexicoverde.com); and Aventura Extrema (Sanchez Tagle 973, ⓣ229/202-6557, ⓦwww.aventuraextrema.com.mx).

10am–7pm, Fri–Sun 10am–7.30pm; M$70, children M$35), a modern aquarium with some large ocean fish. This first section is the **Playa Villa del Mar**. The water here is not the cleanest, but it's popular with locals who frequent the many beachside palapa restaurants (for outrageously overpriced seafood) and there are boat trips to Cancuncito and the **Isla de Sacrificios**, more or less directly offshore (see box opposite). More attractive sands are further south, though: in particular in the area where Ávila Camacho and Ruíz Cortines join up again. Here **Playa Mocambo** is one of the best strips of sand, helped by the fact that the main road is for once not right alongside: there are plenty of beach bars, and a small water park with slides. It's also easy to get to, as all the buses come past – get out at the *Hotel Mocambo* or Plaza las Americas. The **Playa de Oro**, immediately north, is also attractive.

Boca del Río lends its name to the whole southern half of this coast, but it's actually a small town in its own right, ten minutes or so further by bus, located, as the name suggests, at the mouth of the Río Jamapa. There are more long, grey-sand beaches here, but the main attraction is the river. A string of small restaurants lines the riverfront in town, all offering seafood at prices which the fierce competition ensures are reasonable. You can also take trips upstream: a *lancha* costs about M$350 an hour, or at busy times you should be able to join a tour for around M$50.

Eating and drinking

"**A la Veracruzana**" is a tag you'll find on menus all over the country, denoting a delicious sauce of onions, garlic, tomatoes, olives, chiles and spices, served with meat or fish. Try *pescado a la Veracruzana*, *pulpos a la marinera* (baby octopus), *arroz a la tumbada* (Veracruz-style rice, packed with seafood) or *empanadas de camaron* (shrimp turnovers). Local liquors include the mind-wiping *toritos* (made with fruits and blended with condensed milk and a tot of brandy) and *el popo* (a beverage made of cacao and rice).

Despite all the local specialities, it's surprisingly hard to get a decent meal in the centre, especially in the evening. The zócalo is ringed by **bars** and **cafés**, but these are really places to drink and though most do serve food, it's generally an overpriced afterthought. There are a number of great places serving local **coffee** too. Proper restaurants, though, are relatively scarce: the old market building on Landero y Coss between Serdán and Mariano Arista has a whole series of small and cheap **fish restaurants** and cooked-food stalls, many of them lunchtime-only, but most of the places that are busy in the evening are down in the hotel zone, well south of the centre.

Bola de Oro Mario Molina 240-A. A tiny, traditional coffee shop where they grind and roast their own local coffee and serve it as *café lechero*. One of several similar places on this block.

El Cacharrito Ruíz Cortines 15, next to *Hotel Lois* ⓣ229/935-9246. Argentine restaurant in the hotel zone, serving fabulous steaks (M$200 up) and Argentine wines. Somewhat formal and pricey, but worth it.

El Cochinito de Oro Zaragoza at Serdán ⓣ229/932-3677. This friendly, no-frills eatery has been around for fifty years, offering a reasonable selection of seafood dishes for no more than M$75. The menu is translated into English and there are good value *comidas*, but it's closed in the evening.

La Gaviota Trigueros 21 ⓣ229/932-3950. A useful address for nocturnal revellers, *La Gaviota* is open 24hr and offers fortifying, meaty dishes and snacks along with a well-stocked bar should you wish to keep the party going; three-course lunchtime *comida* for M$55.

Gran Café de la Parroquia Gómez Farías 34 on the malecón ⓣ229/937-2584, and Ruíz Cortines 1815 ⓣ229/130-0200. A Veracruz institution that claims to have been going for two hundred years. The original malecón branch comprises two vast white dining rooms occupying nearly a whole block. *Café lechero* is the speciality – effectively a latte; you are brought a glass with black coffee, chink the glass with a spoon and another waiter arrives bearing a kettle of milk, which he adds from a great height. They serve full meals too (M$50–100 for a main). The new hotel-zone branch is equally large, and if anything even busier.

Gran Café del Portal Independencia 1187 at Zamora, opposite the cathedral ☎229/931-2759. The coffee (roasted on the premises) is undeniably good, and you can order pricey food from a varied menu from breakfast until midnight. Don't expect a tranquil meal – you'll be serenaded by the house marimba band at any time of day, and will probably draw the attention of plenty of street vendors.

Neveria Morales Zamora 15 at Landero y Coss. Fabulous, refreshing ice creams in tropical fruit and nut flavours; easily the match of fine Italian *gelati*, and only distantly related to the creamy US variety.

Parrilla Suiza Ruíz Cortines 444, near *Hotel Bello*. A big, lively Mexican restaurant in the hotel zone serving tacos and grills in a semi-outdoor setting.

Las Piragüas Riverfront boulevard, corner of Revolución, Boca del Río ☎229/986-2889. One of many seafood restaurants on the Boca del Río waterfront – excellent fish *comidas* for around M$90.

Café Punta del Cielo Mariano Arista at Independencia. A spacious modern café with cappucinos, lattes, muffins and wi-fi.

Samborcito 16 de Septiembre 727 ☎229/931-4388. Large, no-nonsense local favourite with fans twirling under a palapa roof. A bit of a walk from the centre in an area that feels like a Caribbean shanty-town, but worth it for the *picadas* (thick tortillas with cheese), tamales and other delicious Veracruz dishes.

Sanborn's Independencia 1069, at Miguel Lerdo ☎229/931-0219. The Veracruz branch of the national department store and restaurant chain. Food ranges from Mexican snacks to filet mignon, served in an a/c dining room or the cosier adjoining café. Hearty breakfasts from M$60–70. Daily 7am–1am.

Nightlife and entertainment

An evening spent at an outdoor table under the *portales* on the **zócalo** is entertainment in itself, as mariachi, marimba and *norteño* bands compete for your attention with street vendors, fortune-tellers and uniformed nurses offering to take your blood pressure. Most Thursday and Saturday evenings the municipal band or a folkloric dance troupe strikes up from the bandstand, and local couples dance *danzón* across the square, adding to the general madness. The municipality often organizes **outdoor musical performances** elsewhere in the centre of Veracruz, too, on the otherwise quiet Plazuela La Lagunilla for example.

Bars and most of the best places for **dancing**, however, are generally out of the centre, on the coast road or in the commercial strip along Ruíz Cortines. As ever, clubs change pretty rapidly, but many of the bigger ones are close to the *Hotel Lois* around the junction of Ruíz Cortines and Ávila Camacho, including places such as *Cerebro* and *Sky*, directly opposite the *Lois* on Ruíz Cortines.

La Casona de la Condesa Ávila Camacho 1520 in the hotel zone Ⓦwww.casonadelacondesa.com. Club attracting a more mature crowd to its warehouse space for rock and party nights. Wed to Sun from 10pm.

Kachimba Ávila Camacho at Médico Militar in the hotel zone. Salsa and hot Latin sounds, with a Cuban orchestra playing Thursday to Saturday from 8pm (M$100 cover).

Noize Ávila Camacho at Calle 7 Ⓦwww.thenoizeveracruz.blogspot.com. Beachfront club for *reggaetón* and themed club nights. Thursday to Saturday from late.

Regis Miguel Lerdo on the zócalo. Along with its neighbours, *Bar Palacio* and *La Tasca*, this is the place to take in the zócalo action over a beer or traditional mint julep (or *jullep*) – prepared with dark rum, dry sherry, vermouth, sugar and mint.

El Rincón de la Trova Plazuela La Lagunilla. Friendly bar-restaurant with excellent Afro-Cuban sounds (Thurs–Sat 8pm–3am), and food during the day, every day.

Listings

Airlines AeroMéxico ☎01-800/021-4000 or 229/937-1765, Ⓦwww.aeromexico.com; Mexicana, Ruíz Cortines 1516 ☎229/921-7391, Ⓦwww.mexicana.com; Continental, Ruíz Cortines 1600 ☎01-800/900-5000 or 229/922-5801, Ⓦwww.continental.com; InterJet, Ávila Camacho 3549 ☎01-800/011-2345 or 229/935-3453, Ⓦwww.interjet.com.mx; Vivaaerobus Ⓦwww.vivaaerobus.com.

Banks Branches of all the main banks, where you can change travellers' cheques and find ATM machines, are around the junction of Independencia and Benito Juárez.

Bus tickets Most tickets can be bought downtown at the Ticket Bus booth, inside the Farmacia del Ahorro on Independencia at Mario Molina.

Car rental Most of the big international companies have offices at the airport, and a few are also represented at the larger hotels in the hotel zone.

Hospital The big hospitals are mainly south of the centre towards the bus station, including Hospital General, 20 de Noviembre 1074 ⓣ229/932-2705. Call ⓣ060 for an ambulance.

Internet access There are a few internet cafés near the zócalo (see map, p.578), including one on Miguel Lerdo just west of 5 de Mayo, one on Morelos and two on Mariano Arista between Independencia and Clarijero. All charge around M$14/hr.

Laundry Lavandería Mar y Sol, Madero 16 (Mon–Sat 8am–6.30pm; M$30/kg), or a much cheaper, nameless place on 16 de Septiembre, beyond Manuel Doblado (M$10/kg).

Left luggage In the second-class bus station (M$28 per day, per piece).

Pharmacies They're everywhere. Handiest is the Farmacia del Ahorro just off the zócalo by the *Gran Café del Portal* on Independencia at Mario Molina: there's a Ticket Bus booth and ATM inside. This is a chain that also offers home (or hotel) delivery service ⓣ229/937-3525. Farmacia Issste is in the Super Issste supermarket, on 16 de Septiembre between Mariano Arista and Morales.

Police ⓣ229/938-0664 or emergency ⓣ066.

Post office On the Plaza de la República (Mon–Fri 8am–4pm, Sat 9am–1pm).

Shopping Coffee, vanilla and cigars are the souvenirs most Mexicans take home from Veracruz, and you'll find all of these (along with fake designer watches and bags) all around the zócalo. Fabulously kitsch souvenirs, shells and cheap T-shirts are on offer at the stalls of the Mercado de Artesanías at the top of the malecón, corner of Landero y Coss. Upstairs opposite this, at Mario Molina 23 and Landero y Coss, is the state-run Popularte shop, with high-quality (and high-priced) furniture, clothing, ceramics and jewellery. There's high-class artesanía at Libros y Arte too, a classy book and craft shop under the Fototeca, just off the zócalo.

Taxis Taxi del Golfo ⓣ229/938-9050; Servi Taxi ⓣ229/934-6299 or 934-0620.

Telephones There are Ladatel phones throughout the city, and several fax and copy centres where you can make international calls – including at the internet place on Madero, near the zócalo.

La Antigua, Cempoala and Cardel

Heading north from Veracruz, there's a short stretch of toll highway as far as Cardel, at the junction of the coastal highway and the road up to Xalapa. **LA ANTIGUA**, site of the second Spanish settlement in Mexico (it's often incorrectly described as the first – Villa Rica is further north, see p.595), lies 2km off this road, 20km north of Veracruz. Although it does see an occasional bus, you'll find it much easier and quicker to take one heading for Cardel (about every 30min from the second-class terminal in Veracruz) and get off at the toll booths. From here it's about twenty minutes' walk up a signed road.

For all its antiquity, there's not a great deal to see in La Antigua; however, it is a beautiful, cobble-streeted tropical village on the banks of the **Río La Antigua** (or Río Huitzilapan). At weekends it makes a popular excursion for Veracruzanos, who picnic by the river and swim or take boat rides. In the semi-ruined centre of the village stand some of the oldest surviving Spanish buildings in the country: on the plaza are the **Edificio del Cabildo**, built in 1523, which housed the first *ayuntamiento* (local government) established in Mexico, and the **Casa de Cortés**, a fairly crude stone construction, which, despite the name, was probably never lived in by Cortés and is now a ruin. Nearby is the tranquil **Ermita del Rosario**, the first Christian church built in New Spain, which also dates from the early sixteenth century, though it's been altered and restored since. On the riverbank stands a grand old tree – the **Ceiba de la Noche Feliz** – to which it is claimed that Cortés moored his ships. A pedestrian suspension bridge crosses the river near the tree, and on this stretch of the bank are *lanchas* offering river trips and a little row of restaurants with waterside terraces. There's good food at *Las Maravillas*, in the middle of the row, distinguished by its bright pink paint and tablecloths.

Cempoala

The ruins of **CEMPOALA** (or Zempoala, daily 9am–5pm; M$37, free Sun), 12km north of Cardel and 4km west of Hwy-180, though not as dramatic as El Tajín further north, make for an absorbing detour – most weekdays you'll have them to yourself. The first native city visited by the conquistadors, Cempoala quickly became their ally against the Aztecs. When Cortés arrived, the city, under the leadership of Chicomacatl (dubbed the "Fat Chief" by conquistador Bernal Díaz del Castillo), had been under Aztec control for little over fifty years. Its people, who numbered some 25,000 to 30,000, had already rebelled more than once and were only too happy to stop paying their tribute once they believed that the Spaniards could protect them. This they did, although the inhabitants must have begun to have second thoughts when Cortés ordered the idols of their deities to be smashed and replaced with crosses and Christian altars.

Cortés left Cempoala in August 1519 for the march on Tenochtitlán, but the following May he was forced to return in a hurry by the news that Pánfilo Narváez, on a mission to bring the conquistadors back under the control of the governor of Cuba, had come after him with a large force. Cortés mounted a surprise attack on the newly arrived Spaniards, who were camped in the centre of Cempoala, and won a resounding victory: Narváez was wounded (but survived), many of his generals were captured and most of the men switched sides, joining the later assaults on the Aztec capital.

The **ruins** date mostly from the Aztec period, and although the buildings have lost their decorative facings and thatched sanctuaries, it's one of the most complete surviving examples of an Aztec ceremonial centre – albeit in an atypical tropical setting. The double-stairway pyramids, grouped around a central plaza, must have resembled those of Tenochtitlán, though on a considerably smaller scale. Apart from the main, cleared site, consisting of the **Templo Mayor** (the largest and most impressive structure, where Narváez made his stand), the Gran Pirámide and the Templo de las Chimeneas, there are lesser ruins scattered throughout, and around, the modern village. Most important of these are the **Templo de las Caritas**, a small temple on which a few carvings and murals can still be seen, in open country just beyond the main site, and the circular **Templo de Ehecatl** (Temple of the Wind God) on the opposite side of the main road through the village.

The site takes a couple of hours to explore; if you're coming by **bus** there are a few direct second-class services from Veracruz, but it's generally quicker to go to **Cardel** and change there: Cardel has very frequent first-class services from both Veracruz and Xalapa, and even more second-class. Coming from **La Antigua**, you can go back to the main road, get a second-class bus to Cardel and go on from there. From Cardel there are plenty of green-and-white **taxis** (M$60) to the site, but the local buses marked "Zempoala" that leave from the bus station are cheaper (M$10).

Cardel and Chachalacas

CARDEL is a busy little town which can make a convenient stopover; there's nothing to see but plenty of facilities, including hotels, restaurants, banks and shops, mostly very close to the plaza. The second-class **bus terminal** is right on the main plaza; ADO is a couple of blocks beyond on Zapata. Top choice for **accommodation** is the smart *Bienvenido Hotel* (Ⓣ296/962-0777, Ⓦwww.hotelbienvenido.com.mx; ❸), just off the plaza between the two bus stations at

Sur 1, which has comfortable air-conditioned rooms, wi-fi and a decent coffee-shop-style restaurant. The *Hotel Cardel* (Ⓣ296/962-0014; ❸), on Zapata between the plaza and ADO, is also air-conditioned and comfortable, but its smaller, simpler rooms cost only marginally less.

From Cardel you can head 10km northeast to the mouth of the Río Actopan and a long beach at **Chachalacas** (another short bus journey), a small fishing village that has transformed itself into a low-key resort popular with domestic tourists. At weekends and holiday periods it can be packed; the rest of the time almost entirely deserted. The seafront is lined with inexpensive seafood **restaurants** – try *La Huella*, in the middle of the village, for great seafood cocktails, rich in cilantro and chile – and there are plenty of cheap rooms and modest **hotels**, stretched out for some kilometres to the north. Of these, the *Hotel San Juan* (Ⓣ296/962-5524; ❹), about 800m out of town, is a simple place with a small pool and air-conditioned rooms with TV; the *Hotel Chachalacas* (Ⓣ296/962-5242, Ⓦwww.hotelchachalacas.com; ❻) is a much fancier place at the entrance to town near the river mouth, with bungalows and children's play areas around the pool.

Xalapa

The capital of the state of Veracruz, **XALAPA** is a big city, but remarkably attractive despite its relative modernity and traffic-laden streets. It is set in countryside of sometimes breathtaking beauty, sprawling across a hillside below the volcanic peak of the **Cofre de Perote** (4282m) and with views to the snow-capped Pico de Orizaba, with a warm, damp climate that encourages rich, jungly vegetation. In addition to these natural advantages, Xalapa has been promoted by its civic leaders as a **cultural centre**, with an international jazz festival in August and a classical and traditional music festival in June, as well as many lesser events year-round. Home, too, of the **University of Veracruz** and the exceptional **Museo de Antropología**, it's a lively place, enjoyable even if you simply hang out in one of the many wonderful cafés in the centre of town, sip the locally grown coffee and watch life pass by. For adrenaline junkies and lovers of nature there's much more, though, as Xalapa is also close to numerous rivers: as they crash down from the high sierra to the coast these create numerous spectacular **waterfalls** and some of Mexico's finest opportunities for **whitewater-rafting** and kayaking.

Arrival, information and tours

Xalapa's modern **bus station**, with separate sections for first- and second-class services, is a couple of kilometres east of the centre on 20 de Noviembre. You can get to the centre by regulated taxi, booked from a booth underneath the station (follow the signs). To catch a bus or *combi*, walk down through the shopping mall to 20 de Noviembre and look for those marked "Centro"; note that going back to the bus station, they're marked "CAXA" (Central de Autobuses de Xalapa). Xalapa's **tourist office** occupies a kiosk under the arches at the Palacio Municipal, opposite Parque Juárez (Mon–Sat 8am–2pm & 2.30am–8.30pm; Ⓣ228/842-1214, Ⓦwww.xalapa.net or www.xalapa.gob.mx); the same kiosk houses a Ticket Bus operation, so you can get your tickets in advance (another branch, with longer hours, is at Enriquez 13 east of the zócalo).

A number of companies offer trekking adventures, jungle tours and especially rafting trips in the region; see also Jalcomulco (p.593) and Tlapacoyan (p.593). Those with local offices include Amigos del Río, Chilpancingo 205 (Ⓣ228/815-8817, Ⓦwww.amigosdelrio.com.mx) and Veraventuras, Santos Degollado 81

CENTRAL XALAPA

NIGHTLIFE

Cubanias	7
Santa Anna	6
Ibiza Club	8
Rio Latino	1

EATING & DRINKING

Café Chiquito	12
La Casona del Beaterio	10
La Fonda	2
Italian Coffee Company	11
Café Lindo	4
La Parroquia	9
Il Postodoro	5
T-Grill	3

ACCOMMODATION

Cantón Juárez	B
Casa Regia	H
Clara Luna	D
Hostal de la Niebla	E
Limón	C
María Victoria	F
Mesón del Alférez	G
Posada del Caféto	I
Posada La Mariquinta	A
Principal	H

(ⓣ228/818-9579, ⓦwww.veraventuras.com). A rafting day trip costs around M$750–800 per person.

Accommodation

There are some truly elegant hotels in Xalapa, many housed in charming, historic eighteenth-century haciendas, as well as some good budget choices.

Cantón Juárez Juárez 65 ⓣ228/818-4021. Big, high-ceilinged rooms in a simple old courtyard hotel that's recently been done up, with new bathrooms, marble-tile floors and TV. Can be noisy at the front. ❸

Casa Regia Hidalgo 12 at Canovas ⓣ228/812-0591. This brightly decorated and friendly place has peaceful, cosy rooms with TV, constant hot water and a breakfast area near the lobby. ❸

Clara Luna Ávila Camacho 42 ⓣ228/167-8000, ⓦwww.claralunahotel.com.mx. Comfortable four-star, international-style hotel close to the centre; rooms have internet and there's wi-fi in communal areas. ❼

Hostal de la Niebla Zamora 24 ⓣ228/817-2174, ⓦwww.delaniebla.com. Clean and friendly hostel, affiliated with YH International. There's internet, simple breakfasts of bread and coffee (included), cable TV in the common room, hot water and large lockers. A place in a six-bed dorm costs M$120 (YHI members), M$130 (ISIC card holders) or M$145 (everyone else). Private rooms also available. ❸

Limón Revolución 8 ⓣ228/817-2204, ⓔhotellimon@prodigy.net.mx. One of the best budget options, close to the centre, with small, very clean rooms around a narrow, leafy courtyard embellished with ornate tiling. Rooms have TV and 24hr hot water, and there's a laundry. ❷

María Victoria Zaragoza 6 ⓣ228/818-6011, ⓦwww.hotelmariavictoriaxalapa.com. High-rise hotel that looks like an office block, on a busy road. Worn furnishings and a rather institutional feel, but it's clean and comfortable, with a/c, TV and wi-fi: rooms at the back are quiet and have stunning views. ❹

Mesón del Alférez Sebastian Camacho 2 at Zaragoza ⓣ228/818-0113, ⓦwww.pradodelrio.com. Beautiful converted colonial house, once belonging to Alférez Real de Xalapa, the last Spanish viceroy of Veracruz. Each room is unique, luxurious and charmingly decorated, and there's an excellent restaurant (*Hostería de la Candela*) with some vegetarian options. Breakfast is M$55. 6

Posada del Caféto Canovas 8 ⓣ228/817-0023, ⓦwww.pradodelrio.com. Under the same management as the Mesón del Alférez: rooms are set around a pretty courtyard garden; some have balconies, all have TV and bath. The on-site café serves breakfast (included) and has books to read. 4

Posada La Mariquinta Alfaro 12 ⓣ228/818-1158, ⓦwww.lamariquinta.xalapa.net. Meticulously restored colonial hacienda with attractive, comfortable rooms with cable TV and phone. There is a tranquil inner garden, a common room with a vast collection of books and an English- and French-speaking owner. More expensive extended-stay apartments are available in an adjoining, concrete and wood extension, a fine example of modern Mexican architecture. Discounts offered if you stay longer than three nights. 5

The City

Xalapa's appealing colonial downtown is centred on the **Parque Juárez** (the zócalo), its trees filled with extraordinarily raucous birds at dusk. There are stunning mountain views towards the Cofre de Perote from the south side of the plaza, where the land drops away steeply. Xalapa's contemporary arts crowd meets up at the **Agorá de la Ciudad** (Tues–Sun 10am–10pm; free; ⓦwww.agora.xalapa.net), a cultural centre built under this edge of the plaza, where there are often interesting temporary exhibitions. Also beneath the plaza, at Herrera 5, the **Pinacoteca Diego Rivera** (Tues–Sun 10am–7pm; free) showcases a few works by Rivera and other Mexican artists, along with more temporary exhibition space. Next door at Herrera 7 the **Museo Casa de Xalapa** (MUXA; Tues–Sun 10am–7pm; free) is a lovely seventeenth-century colonial home in whose rooms a small, modern museum of local history (lots of interactivity, but mainly in Spanish) has been installed.

The **Palacio de Gobierno**, on the east side of the plaza, has interesting murals by Chilean artist José Chaves Morado. Beside it, on the adjoining Parque Lerdo, is the eighteenth-century **Catedral**. Inside there's a richly decorated nave, a striking Calvary at the altar and a chapel dedicated to Rafael Guízar y Valencia (1878–1938), who was canonized as **St Rafael Guízar** in 2006 – the first bishop born in the Americas to receive the honour. He is most admired for resisting the state's persecution of the church in the 1920s and 1930s, forming a "guerrilla ministry" and later becoming the bishop of Veracruz; behind the cathedral, at the corner of Juárez and Revolución, there's an entire **museum** dedicated to him (Mon–Sat 9am–2pm & 4–8pm, Sun 9am–2pm; free). Finally in the centre, there's yet more temporary art exhibition space at the **Galería de Arte Contemporáneo** (daily 10am–7pm; free), Xalapeños Ilustres 135.

Museo de Antropología and Museo Interactivo

Beyond question the city's outstanding sight is the **Museo de Antropología** (Tues–Sun 9am–5pm; M$40; ⓦwww.uv.mx/max), a brilliant museum with arguably the best archeological collection in the country after that in Mexico City. The collection is excellent in both scope and quality, and makes for a wonderful introduction to the various pre-Hispanic cultures of the Gulf coast. The building itself is also lovely, flowing down the hillside in a series of marble steps. Start your visit at the top of the hill, where the first halls deal with the **Olmecs**. There are several of the celebrated colossal stone heads, a vast array of other statuary and some beautiful masks. Later cultures are represented mainly through their pottery – lifelike human and animal figurines especially – and there are also displays on the architecture of the major sites: El Tajín, Cempoala and so on. Finally, with the **Huastec** culture come more giant stone statues. Some larger, less valuable pieces are displayed in landscaped gardens outside. Labels are in Spanish only, though there are a few English information sheets. There's a **café** on the first floor, and also

Parklife in Xalapa

Xalapa is renowned for its **parks** and their wonderful tropical flora. A couple of fine potential picnic spots are within walking distance of the centre. The **Parque Los Tecajetes** (Tues–Sun 6am–6pm), ten minutes' walk west of the zócalo along María Ávila Camacho, is a pristine public park with lush vegetation and plenty of shaded seating areas. South of the zócalo, Herrera leads steeply down towards the **Paseo de los Lagos**, where walkways lead around a series of small, artificial lakes edged by parkland; popular with runners in the morning and strolling families later on. In the north of the city, the entrance to the woody **Parque Ecológico Macuiltépec** is close to the Archeological Museum. At 1590m, the easily climbable Macuiltépec is the highest of the hills on which the town is built, and from its *mirador* you might catch a glimpse of the Gulf. There are panoramic views of the city even if you don't make it to the peak, and it also has a small **Museo de la Fauna** (Tues–Sun 10am–6pm; M$10) with a reptile house and aviary. Finally, on the edge of the city on the old road to Coatepec, about 3.5km from the centre, the **Jardín Botánico Francisco Clavijero** (daily 9am–5pm; M$5) boasts an impressive collection of plants native to the state.

a shop selling fantastic, though expensive, masks. The museum lies 3km from the zócalo on the outskirts of town – to get there take a bus marked "Museo" from Camacho, on the northwest corner of the Parque Juárez, or a taxi.

Another worthwhile museum on the edge of town, especially if you have kids, is the **Museo Interactivo** (Mon–Fri 9am–6pm, Sat & Sun 10am–7pm; M$25, M$45 with IMAX; Ⓦwww.mix.org.mx), southeast of the centre on Murillo Vidal. Along with a permanent exhibit of Mexican cars and planes and a massive IMAX cinema, the museum features a planetarium and rooms dedicated to different sciences, such as space exploration, with interactive displays and impressive models. Take a taxi or a bus marked "Murillo Vidal".

Eating and drinking

Good **food** is abundant in Xalapa. The city is home to the **jalapeño pepper**, and there's also great local **coffee** (mostly grown in nearby Coatepec; see opposite), consumed in great quantities in the city's numerous **traditional cafés**. Many of these can be found along Nicolás Bravo or its continuation Primo Verdad, and there are plenty of appetizing **restaurants** and some enticing *jugo* and torta places in the couple of blocks between here and the zócalo.

Café Chiquito Nicolás Bravo 3 Ⓣ228/812-1122. One of the largest and most distinctive cafés, with plenty of wooden tables around a colonial courtyard. There's a reasonable menu, mostly of snacks and sandwiches (M$30–40), plus excellent breakfasts, along with the usual range of caffeinated beverages.

Café Lindo Primo Verdad 21. Traditional café with good sandwiches in addition to Mexican-style snack foods. Lively, primarily young clientele in the large, dimly-lit dining and drinking area.

La Casona del Beaterio Zaragoza 20 Ⓣ228/818-2119. Hundreds of old photographs adorn the walls at one of the city's best restaurants, which serves up fine, reasonably priced Mexican food and breakfasts. Tables are arranged around a small courtyard with running water. Live traditional music Thurs–Sun.

La Fonda Callejón del Diamante 1 Ⓣ228/818-7282. Justifiably popular lunch-time spot (plenty of room upstairs if the street-level dining room is full) on a bustling 'alternative' alley. Copious and very cheap comidas corridas or an à la carte choice of chicken, meat and some seafood dishes for M$50 and up.

Italian Coffee Company Down steps off the south side of Parque Juárez. Café with a fabulous setting and a terrace enjoying the views south from the zócalo. A very popular and busy meeting place.

La Parroquia Zaragoza 18 Ⓣ228/817-4436. Venerable fifty-year-old establishment best known for its breakfast menus starting at around M$40, but whose unpretentious and busy dining room is also open for lunch and dinner. Another, smarter branch at María Ávila Camacho 72 (mains M$50 and above).

Il Postodoro Primo Verdad 11 ⓣ228/841-2000. Homemade pasta, delicious pizzas (from M$45) and a variety of flavours of ice cream at this welcoming Italian restaurant. Excellent wine list.

T-Grill Xalapeños Ilustres 1 ⓣ228/124-1504. Mexican-style fast food, with excellent tacos, tortas, quesadillas and steaks, and tortillas made fresh in front of you. Try the *tacos de arrachera*.

Nightlife and entertainment

Xalapa is a city of great creative energy. A number of **bars** offer live music and occasional poetry readings or theatre; downtown there are several lively places on the Callejón del Diamanate, and especially down Callejón de la Perla. Louder **clubs** and bars tend to be further out, though there's a small group on Ávila Camacho around its junction with Victoria, close to the Parque los Tecajates. If you're in the mood for something more relaxed, the **Teatro del Estado,** Ávila Camacho at Ignacio de la Llave (box office ⓣ228/817-3210), hosts regular **concerts** by the Orquesta Sinfónica de Xalapa, in addition to dance and theatre (in Spanish only), while the **Agorá de la Ciudad** in Parque Juárez has arts events and a small cinema and theatre as well as its galleries. The giant Plaza las Américas mall on the edge of town has a good multiplex **cinema**.

Cubanias Callejón González Aparicio 1 (Callejón de la Perla). Cuban-themed restaurant and bar. A great late-night spot for Cuban music, mojitos and Cuba libres.

Ibiza Club Camacho 101 ⓦwww.ibizaclub.com.mx. The biggest of the downtown clubs, with spectacular light shows, visiting DJs and music that's mainly house and techno. Thurs–Sun from 10pm.

Rio Latino Av Principal 26, Las Trancas, on the edge of the city, near the Plaza las Américas (ⓦwww.riolatino.com). Big, two-storey club with two separate bar areas, a big screen, regular live music and themed party nights. Wed–Sat from 10pm.

Santa Anna Callejón González Aparicio (Callejón de la Perla). Lively bar-restaurant in this busy alley – a good place for an early evening beer.

Listings

Banks and exchange There are plenty of banks and ATMs around the centre, including HSBC on Parque Juárez and Bancomer on Parque Lerdo.

Flights Aeromar (ⓣ01-800/237-6627, ⓦwww.aeromar.com.mx) operates two daily flights to Mexico City from the airstrip at Lencero, just outside the city.

Internet access Try El Sarcofago, on Allende immediately below the Agorá, Ciber 10 on Mata, or Ciberbazar, tucked away in the Bazaar Enríquez indoor market, just east of the Parque Juárez.

Laundry Lavandería Diamante, Rojano 21-A (daily 9am–8pm; M$20/kg), a block north of the post office.

Post office The main post office (Mon–Fri 8am–7.30pm, Sat 9am–5pm, Sun 9am–noon) is on Zamora, at Diego Leño, and is also where you'll find a Western Union office.

Around Xalapa

A number of appealing excursions can be made into the jungly country around Xalapa; Coatepec, Xico and the Hacienda El Lencero are all very close by.

Coatepec

COATEPEC, less than 15km south, is an enjoyable little town with a beautiful setting and fine colonial architecture, and a very popular weekend outing for folk from the city. Much of the coffee consumed in Xalapa is grown around Coatepec – the aroma is unmistakeable as you drive in – and this, along with fresh trout (*trucha*) from the river, is the speciality at many local cafés and restaurants. In May, the **Feria del Café** celebrates the local crop, and there's a big celebration in September to honour the local patron saint, San Jeronimo.

Thanks to all the local visitors there are a number of very comfortable hotels and excellent places to eat here. Locals like the riverside **restaurants** alongside the old road from Xalapa, on the edge of town; in the centre *Finca Andrade*, Lerdo 5 on the zócalo (ⓣ228/816-4887, ⓦwww.fincaandrade.com; main courses M$80–100), is an excellent, elegant restaurant which also serves good *cafe lechero* and *pan dulce*; the *Arcos de Belem* (ⓣ228/816-5265), almost next door at no. 9, is a simpler place; *El Tío Yeyo* (ⓣ228/816-3645), a block over at Santos Degollado 4, specializes in fresh fish, particularly trout served in a variety of delicious sauces. There are a number of high-class **artesanía** outlets around the zócalo, especially in the Plazuela El Zaguán, next to Finca Andrade. More modest, but still lovely, alternatives to the better-known but overpriced *Posada Coatepec* (ⓣ228/816-0544, ⓦwww.posadacoatepec.com.mx; ❽) are the *Posada San Jeronimo* (ⓣ228/816-5486, ⓦwww.posadasanjeronimo.com; ❺), 16 de Septiembre 26, and *Mesón del Alférez* (ⓣ228/816-6744, ⓦwww.pradodelrio.com; ❺), Jiménez del Campillo 47. At the opposite end of the price scale is the *Hostal Cafe-tal apan* (ⓣ228/816-6185, ⓦwww.elcafe-tal.com), Aldama 51, a friendly place with dorm beds, and use of the kitchen, for M$150. You can get information here (or on the website) about tours of their **coffee plantation**, about 5km out of town, where they have set up a small coffee museum and a sanctuary for local wildlife.

Buses run regularly from Xalapa to Coatepec; most frequent are the local services from the Terminal Excelsiór (also known as Los Sauces, after the market next to it), 2km southwest of the zócalo, though there are also second-class buses from the main terminal.

Xico

XICO lies 8km beyond Coatepec. It's another small colonial town, but the big attraction here is the **Cascada de Texolo**, to which you'll see signs on the edge of town as you enter. The falls lie 2km along a rough, cobbled road (just about driveable, or forty minutes' hot walk); beside the road along the way, coffee is grown in the shade of banana palms. If you're scared of heights, this may not be for you, as you emerge right at the top of the main 80m cascade, with only some hopelessly inadequate-looking railing to prevent you plunging over. It's a beautiful spot, though, with lots of wildlife and a couple of restaurants: the *Mirador* on the far side has the best view, but it's a stiff climb up. Five minutes' walk upstream is the **Cascada la Monja**, a far smaller fall, but one where you can get very close to the bottom, and enjoy the cooling spray. Locals swim here, but it's not recommended.

Like Coatepec, Xico is a popular outing from Xalapa, and has a number of surprisingly fancy **restaurants**. These are mostly clustered in the lower half of town towards the falls, half a dozen blocks downhill from the main plaza; two of the best are right next to each other at Zaragoza and Matamoros, near the tiny Capilla del Llanito – *Casa Xiqueña* and *El Campanario*. Nearby there's an exceptionally helpful municipal **tourist office** (little English spoken) on the small Plaza los Portales, on Hidalgo, with plenty of information on the local area and places to stay in the surrounding countryside. Local **buses** run frequently from Coatepec to Xico, as well as from the Xalapa bus terminals.

Hacienda El Lencero

Off the highway to Veracruz, 10km outside Xalapa, the **Museo Exhacienda El Lencero** (Tues–Sun 10am–5pm; M$45) is a colonial hacienda that was once the property of controversial general and president Antonio López de Santa Anna. It is preserved in its full nineteenth-century splendour, and both the grounds, with plenty of gentle walks, and the surrounding countryside are stunning. A good, formal restaurant occupies part of the main building; if you don't have transport of your own, it's best approached by taxi (15–20min; M$40–50).

Jalcomulco

JALCOMULCO is the prime spot in Veracruz for **whitewater-rafting** and other adventure sports including kayaking, canyoning, rappelling and mountain-biking. The village is about 25km southeast of Coatepec, on the banks of the Río Antigua (also known as the Río de los Pescados). The journey descends from the highlands into a steamy and impressive valley where the river runs through a series of rapids of varying intensity. Local **buses** run at least hourly throughout the day between Coatepec and Jalcomulco, and there are half a dozen or so direct connections with Cardel and Xalapa.

A dozen or more **operators** have bases here, the majority of them on the river-bank some way out of town where they offer all-inclusive packages including accommodation, meals and activities, so there's a lot to be said for booking in advance. Among the best are Mexico Verde (Ⓣ01-800/362-8800, Ⓦwww.mexicoverde.com; inclusive day trip M$850; three days, two nights from M$2820), one of the longest established, whose "eco-resort" has accommodation in safari-style luxury tents; Aldea Ecoturismo (Ⓣ01-800/563-0530, Ⓦwww.aldeajalcomulco.com.mx), where accommodation is in rather more luxurious villas sleeping four to six (two nights for four people from M$7200); and Ecco Sports (Ⓣ279/832-3559, Ⓦwww.eccosports.com; two nights from M$2200), with more solid hotel-style accommodation with wi-fi, in town. All of these have pools and *temazcales* (traditional sweat lodges) and offer a wide variety of activities. Locally, Viajes Aventura on the main square (Ⓣ279/832-3580, Ⓦwww.raftingsinlimite.com) can arrange everything from backpacker accommodation to zipwires to inclusive rafting packages. Nearby, *Nachita* is the best of several **restaurants** with terraces overlooking the river; it's right by the pedestrian *puente colgante* (suspension bridge). On the far bank *Los Cachanes* serves up great fish and seafood. There are **internet** connections at Ali-internet and Ciber Jalisco, both close to *Nachita*.

Tlapacoyan

Another centre for rafting and river adventures is **TLAPACOYAN**, bounded to the south by the Río Bobos and to the north by the Río María de la Torre, some 70km north of Xalapa en route to the coast at Nautla. An unspoilt, friendly place and a centre of citrus-fruit production, Tlapacoyan is surrounded by forested hills and pre-Columbian ruins, most important of which are the massive, little-known sites of **Filo Bobos**.

Buses to Tlapacoyan run from Veracruz, Cardel, Xalapa, Papantla, Puebla and Mexico City. First and second-class terminals are opposite each other, and pretty central, at Zaragoza and Ferrer: walk uphill on Ferrer then right at 5 de Mayo for the zócalo. Here you'll find a couple of good, modest **hotels** and **places to eat**. Best of them is the *Posada Oliver* (Ⓣ225/315-4212, Ⓦwww.hotelposadaoliver.com; ❸), Cuauhtemoc 400, a very pleasant place with a colonial courtyard, closely followed by it sister hotel, just half a block away at Cuauhtemoc 300, the marginally cheaper *Plaza* (Ⓣ225/315-0520, Ⓦwww.hotelplazatlapacoyan.com; ❸). Budget rooms are available at the *San Agustín* (Ⓣ225/315-0023; ❷), across the square. The *San Agustín* also has a restaurant, or try *Las Ranas*, near *Posada Oliver*, for good *licuados* and tacos.

To arrange a **rafting** trip, contact the very helpful guys at Rios y Rapidos (mobile Ⓣ225/104-2180, Ⓔriosyrapidos@hotmail.com; rafting from M$450, packages including accommodation from M$1950), Cuauhtemoc 407 just off the plaza. Most of the rafting actually takes place near **El Encanto**, about 5km from the centre of town off the Nautla road. There's a waterfall here, and spectacular river views enjoyed by a couple of rafting camps. At *Filobobos Camp* (Ⓣ225/315-1784, Ⓦwww.filoboboscamp.com.mx; full day of activities M$600, three-day

▲ Kayaking near Tlapacoyan

package M$2000) you can try a variety of activities in addition to rafting, including a zipwire, and there's camping along with some basic cabins; *Titanic* (Ⓣ225/321-5966; ⑤), next door, offers 4WD trips to the waterfall (M$100) as well as rafting, and has more camping space, plus a couple of lovely rooms with elegant bathrooms, air-conditioning and cable TV.

Filo Bobos

Work is ongoing at the **Filo Bobos** archeological project (daily 8am–5pm), some 15km from Tlapacoyan, where you can explore two of the several pre-Hispanic sites identified along the Río Bobos valley, **El Cuajilote** and **Vega de la Peña**. Both are well worth visiting as much for the beauty of their locations, the birdlife and the serenity, as for the ruins themselves. No one yet knows for certain who occupied the Filo Bobos sites. Signs of a fertility cult suggest a **Huastec** influence, yet the other sculptures found are more Totonac in style, and the earliest buildings at El Cuajilote, which may as far back as 1000 BC, are decidedly Olmec. Archeologists speculate that Filo Bobos was the centre of an as yet unknown Mesoamerican civilization, which provided an important trade link between the Gulf coast, its environs and the central valleys.

Check locally about access, as new roads and facilities are being built, but expect to walk at least part of the way; you should be able to arrange a tour from El Encanto (see p.593), but contact one of the camps there in advance if you want to be sure. **El Cuajilote** is the more impressive site, with platforms and pyramids arranged around a rectangular central plaza measuring 31,500 square metres. The surrounding buildings appear to be a series of temples dedicated to a fertility cult: a monolithic, phallic stele more than two metres tall and oriented to the stars stands in the middle of the plaza, and at Shrine A4 more than 1500 other phallic figurines were found, though none remains at the site today. You can also make out a ball-court and some sculptures, including one of a giant frog – it's speculated that this may also be a fertility symbol.

Vega de la Peña covers some eight thousand square metres. There's little doubt that structures buried beneath the lush greenery here extend beyond that;

some archeologists believe they may have stretched as far as Nautla. If true, this would radically alter the accepted conception of Mexican and Mesoamerican pre-Columbian history, placing this coast in a far more prominent position than previously thought. What you see here today are small buildings, with more palatial dwellings than at El Cuajilote, and a small ball-court.

The north

Beyond Cardel, where the express highway ends, there's very little to stop for in the long coastal stretch (about 4hr on the bus) to Papantla. Around 15km north of Cardel is the sleepy village of **Villa Rica**, the first Spanish settlement in New Spain. Established by Cortés in 1519, it was abandoned in 1524 for La Antigua, and only foundations remain today, close to the normally deserted beach. Some 3km inland are the similarly sparse ruins of the nearest Totonac town, **Quiahuitzlán** (daily 8.30am–5pm, but unreliable; M$27), with the great basalt outcrop known as the Peñon de Bernal looming above. What you can see today is primarily a cemetery, with over seventy small stone tombs, but it's utterly tranquil and has incredible views over the coast. This exceptionally scenic area of steep, green hills makes Mexico's only **nuclear plant**, on the coast at Laguna Verde, just beyond, even more of a shock.

At **Nautla**, 153km from Veracruz, you pass the largest town en route to Papantla, surrounded by coconut groves. Beyond is the so-called **"Costa Esmeralda"**. There are hotels, some of them pretty fancy, trailer parks and campsites all the way up here, but they are just metres from the highway, which runs close to the shore. The grey sand is mostly desolate and windswept, and it's not really a place you'd want to stay.

Tecolutla

Only in the very final stretch of the Costa Esmeralda, where the highway turns inland, bypassing **TECOLUTLA**, does the beach offer much temptation. A growing resort, Tecolutla is pretty much the closest beach to Mexico City – easily accessed via the toll highway to Tuxpán – and can be very busy on Mexican holidays, especially Semana Santa. The rest of the time it's an enjoyably laid-back beach town with bargain accommodation, and a possible alternative base for Papantla and El Tajín. With the coast on one side and the broad Río Tecolutla on the other, the town occupies a point at the river mouth, with a lighthouse at its furthest point – the older and more attractive development is at this end of town. Seek out the **Campamento Tortuga** (ⓣ766/846-0467, ⓦwww.vidamilenaria.org.mx), right in the middle of the beach, where they have been rescuing and releasing sea turtles for 35 years; you can see hatchlings and injured turtles, and from June to November you can join them each morning (7.30–9am) as they release baby turtles to find their way to the sea.

Good seafood **restaurants** line both the beach and the riverfront (where many also offer boat trips), while every other building in town seems to offer **rooms**, with a concentration of budget places around the bus station. *Dora Emilia* (ⓣ766/846-0185; ❸), on the main street at Hidalgo 45, has a small pool and air-conditioned rooms ranged around a courtyard. Beachfront properties are slightly more expensive, though out of season bargains are on offer – try the friendly, bright-yellow *Hotel Playa* (ⓣ766/846-0020, ⓦwww.hotelplayaentecolutla.com; ❹), Obregón 45, for air-conditioned rooms with cable TV around a pool; or the *Hotel Tecolutla* (ⓣ766/846-0011, ⓦwww.hoteltecolutla.com.mx; ❺), the original hotel here, right at the point by the *faro*, with slightly old-fashioned rooms (not all a/c) but a fabulous position and good facilities including a large pool. There are first-class **buses** from Tecolutla to Mexico City (7hr) and Papantla (1hr) and very frequent second-class services to Papantla via Gutiérrez Zamora, the closest point on the highway. Change at Gutiérrez Zamora for first-class services to Vercaruz (3hr 30min), Tuxpán (2hr 30min) and elsewhere.

Papantla

PAPANTLA, 227km from Veracruz, is the most attractive town on the route north, straggling over an outcrop of low, jungly hills. Even so, if it weren't for the proximity of El Tajín, few people would consider staying here. In addition to being one of the most important centres of the Mexican **vanilla** industry – the sweet, sticky odour frequently hangs over the place, and vanilla products are on sale everywhere – Papantla is also one of the last surviving strongholds of **Totonac** culture. On the edge of the zócalo, the huge **Mural Cultural Totonaca** depicts the clash between modern and traditional life, with sculpted images of Totonac gods, myths and the pyramids of El Tajín alongside oil rigs and farm machinery (the tourist office has a leaflet describing this in detail). You'll also see Totonacs wandering around barefooted in loose white robes, especially in the Hidalgo market, and can regularly witness the amazing dance-spectacle of the **Voladores de Papantla** in front of the cathedral and at El Tajín (see box, p.598). On the terrace above the murals and zócalo stands the solid **Catedral de la Asunción**, above which you can climb to the **Volador monument**, a giant statue affording tremendous views of the town.

Arrival and information

First-class **buses** use the ADO terminal on Juárez, just off the main road through town; walk uphill and you'll soon be able to see the cathedral above you, about ten minutes' walk (if you have heavy luggage you might consider a taxi, for about M$20). **Moving on**, there are ten daily first-class buses to Veracruz (4hr) and Tuxpán (1hr 30min) and half a dozen daily to Xalapa (4hr), Mexico City (6hr) and Tecolutla (1hr); most are *de paso* though, so book ahead. The second-class terminal is much closer to the centre on 20 de Noviembre – walk steeply uphill past the Mercado Hidalgo to reach the zócalo.

There's a small **tourist office** (Mon–Fri 9am–5pm) in the Ayuntamiento building on the zócalo. You'll find plenty of information here, and usually an English speaker. All of the major **banks**, where you can change travellers' cheques and find ATM

El Baile de los Negritos

Popular at festivals across the state of Veracruz, the frenetic **Baile de los Negritos** is a Totonac dance dating back to colonial times, when African slaves were imported to work on local plantations, often living and labouring alongside *indígenas*. Stories abound as to the origin of the dance: the most popular version has it that a female slave and her child escaped from a plantation near Papantla and lived in the dense jungle with local indigenous groups. After her child was poisoned by a snake bite, the mother, using African folk medicine, danced herself into a trance. The Totonacs around her found the spectacle highly amusing and, it is said, began to copy her in a spirit of mockery.

The costumes of the dance are influenced by colonial dress, and the dancers wear a snake motif around the waist. The dance is directed by a "Mayordomo", the title given to plantation overseers in the colonial era. Good opportunities to see the dance are **Corpus Christi** (late May–June) in Papantla, or in Tlapacoyan (p.593) at the **Feast of Santiago** (July 25), dedicated to the town's patron saint, or the **Day of the Assumption** (Aug 15); at other times it's held on a smaller scale in other village festivals in the area.

machines, are on Enríquez, just off the opposite side of the zócalo. You'll find a couple of **internet** cafés on 20 de Noviembre near the Mercado Hidalgo. The latter is one of two **markets** right by the zócalo; the other, the Mercado Juárez, lies on the opposite (uphill) side of the Ayuntamiento; they're basically working markets, but you can stock up here on small bottles of locally produced vanilla, and both have food stalls.

Accommodation

Hotel Provincia Express Enríquez 103 on the zócalo ⓣ784/842-1645. One of a small local chain of business hotels. Slightly worn modern rooms with a/c, cable TV and phones; internet in the lobby. ❹

Hotel Pulido Enríquez 205, downhill from the zócalo ⓣ784/842-0035. Basic courtyard hotel with a choice of rooms with fan or a/c. The former are some of the cheapest in town and also some of the quietest, thanks to a position away from the main traffic routes and around an internal courtyard. ❷

Hotel Tajín Domínguez 104 beside the cathedral ⓣ784/842-0121, ⓦwww.hoteltajin.com.mx. The town's top hotel, which isn't saying a great deal. Some rooms have good views across the city; others face only the corridor. There's a small pool which clients of the café can also use, and wi-fi in communal areas. ❹

Hotel Totonacapán Olivio at 20 de Noviembre, just below the second-class bus terminal ⓣ784/842-1220. Friendly, modern place whose rooms have a/c and cable TV. There's wi-fi downstairs. ❹

Eating and drinking

Papantla has an enticing spread of **local specialities** to sample, chief of which is *sacahuil* or *zacahuilt*, a giant tamale of chicken and beans, which you'll find in the markets. These are also the place to head for cheap eats: on the whole, the restaurants aren't great.

Café Catedral Below the cathedral at Domínguez and Curato, by *Hotel Tajín*. Ultra-traditional café serving little other than coffee and *pan dulce* (also to take away) at old-fashioned wooden tables.

La Hacienda Reforma alongside the Ayuntiamento ⓣ784/842-0633. Upstairs, with a balcony in a corner of the zócalo. Decent value *comidas*, but generally few customers and little atmosphere.

Plaza Pardo Enríquez on the zócalo ⓣ784/842-0059. Open from breakfast till late, the *Plaza Pardo* has an unbeatable position with a first-floor terrace overlooking the zócalo. Unfortunately the food can be disappointing – probably best for breakfast or an evening beer.

Sorrento Enríquez on the zócalo ⓣ784/842-0067. Next door to the *Plaza Pardo* at street level, and also open all day, the view and ambience at the *Sorrento* are far less attractive, the food considerably tastier.

Totonaco In the *Hotel Tajín* ⓣ784/842-0121. Despite being a hotel restaurant, with all the atmsophere that implies, this is rightly one of the most popular (and expensive) in town.

El Tajín

EL TAJÍN is by far the most important archeological site on the Gulf coast. The principal architecture here dates from the Classic period (300–900 AD); the city declined in the early Post-Classic (900–1100 AD) and by the time of the Conquest it had been forgotten. Our knowledge of it comes entirely from archeological enquiries made since the accidental discovery of the site in 1785 – El Tajín remains one of the most enigmatic of all of Mexico's ancient cities. No one even knows who built it: some claim it was the Huastecs, others the Totonacs. Although "Tajín" means thunderbolt in Totonaca, experts consider it unlikely to have been built by their ancestors. Most archeologists prefer not to speculate too wildly, instead calling the civilization "**Classic Veracruz**". You'll notice many of its hallmarks at El Tajín, including niches in temple walls and complex ornamental motifs known as "scrolls", which are most prevalent on items and bas-reliefs associated with the ball-game (look at some of the stone "yokes" in the site museum). Classic Veracruz influence was widespread, and is strongly felt at Teotihuacán (see p.464), to the extent that some believe that city may have been built by Veracruzanos.

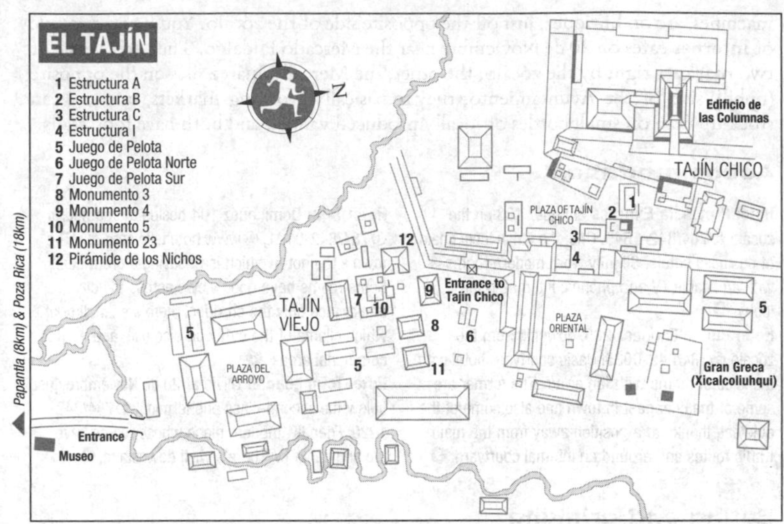

Despite many years of effort, only a small part of the huge site has been cleared, and even this limited area is constantly in danger of being once more engulfed by the jungle: green mounds sprout from the trees in every direction, each concealing more ruins. The site (daily 9am–5pm; M$51) divides broadly into two areas: **Tajín Viejo**, which centres on the amazing Pirámide de los Nichos, and **Tajín Chico**, a group of official residential buildings belonging to the city's ruling class built on an artificial terrace. The site **museum**, by the entrance, has a model of the site worth examining before you venture in, along with a collection of the more delicate stonework

The Voladores de Papantla

Although the full significance of the dance of the **voladores** has been lost over time, it has survived much as the earliest chroniclers reported it, largely because the Spanish thought of it as a sport rather than a pagan rite. It involves five men: a leader who provides music on flute and drum, and four performers. They represent the five earthly directions – the four cardinal points and straight up, from earth to heaven. After a few preliminaries, the five climb to a small platform atop a pole, where the leader resumes playing and directs prayers for the fertility of the land in every direction. Meanwhile, the dancers tie ropes, coiled tightly around the top of the pole, to their waists and at a signal fling themselves head-first into space. As they spiral down in increasing circles the leader continues to play, and to spin, on his platform, until the four hit the ground (hopefully landing on their feet, having righted themselves at the last minute). In all, they make thirteen revolutions each, symbolizing the 52-year cycle of the **Aztec calendar**.

In **Papantla** (performances in front of the cathedral Fri, Sat & Sun 11am–6pm, 4 times a day) and **El Tajín** (regular performances outside the entrance to the ruins starting at 11am) it has become, at least partly, a tourist spectacle, as the permanent metal poles attest. In local villages there is still more ceremony attached, particularly in the selection of a sufficiently tall tree to act as the pole, and its temporary erection in the place where the dance is to be performed. Note that performances are nominally free, though if you catch one of the regular shows in Papantla or El Tajín you'll be expected to make a "donation" of at least M$10 per person – one of the dancers will walk round with a hat.

salvaged from the ruins, notably murals and columns, bits of pottery and statues – displays are primarily labelled in Spanish, but there are a few English explanations.

Tajín Viejo

From the site entrance, a track leads through a small group of buildings to the **Plaza del Arroyo**, the city marketplace, and into the heart of Tajín Viejo. Around the plaza are several **ball-courts**, the most prominent of which is the South Court, or **Juego de Pelota Sur**; it looks like a wide avenue between two small pyramids. Seventeen such courts are known here, and more possibly lie unexcavated; it's thought that the game took on a greater importance here than at any other known site (see p.876). The superb bas-relief sculptures that cover the walls of the South Court include portrayals of a decapitated player, and another about to be stabbed with a ritual knife by fellow players, with Death waiting to his left. (Such bas-reliefs are a constant feature of the site, adorning many of the ball-courts and buildings, with more stacked in the museum).

The unique **Pirámide de los Nichos** is the most famous building at El Tajín, and indeed one of the most remarkable of all Mexican ruins. It rises to a height of about 20m in six receding tiers, each face punctuated with regularly spaced niches; up the front a steep stairway climbs to a platform on which the temple originally stood. If you tally up the niches, including those hidden by the stairs and those, partly destroyed, around the base of the temple, there are 365 in all. Their exact purpose is unknown, but clearly they were more than mere decoration: theories include each one holding some offering or sacrifice, one for each day of the year, or that they symbolized caves – the dwellings of the earth god. Originally they were painted black, with the pyramid in red, to enhance the impression of depth. Niches are also present on other buildings at the site, some bearing the attributes of **Quetzalcoatl**, the plumed serpent, El Tajín's most depicted god.

Around the plaza in front of the pyramid stand all the other important buildings of Tajín Viejo. Opposite is **Monumento 3**, a similar pyramid without niches, and behind it **Monumento 23**, a strange steep-sided bulk, one of the last structures to be built here. To the right of the Pirámide de los Nichos, Monumento 2, a low temple, squats at the base of **Monumento 5**, a beautiful truncated pyramid with a high decorative pediment broken by a broad staircase; on the left, Monumento 4 is one of the oldest in El Tajín, and only partly restored.

Tajín Chico

From the back of Monumento 4 the path continues past the **Juego de Pelota Norte**, with its worn relief sculptures, onto the levelled terrace of **Tajín Chico**, home of the city's elites. Originally this raised area was supported by a retaining wall, part of which has been restored, and reached by a staircase (which is no longer there) opposite the ball-court. Only parts of the buildings themselves now survive, making a rather confusing whole. **Estructura C** and the adjoining **Estructura B** are the most impressive remains here: Estructura C has stone friezes running around its three storeys, giving the illusion of niches. In this case, they were purely decorative, an effect that would have been heightened by a brightly coloured stucco finish. It also has the remains of a concrete roof – originally a huge single slab of poured cement, unique in ancient Mexico. **Estructura A** had a covered interior, and you can still see the entrance covered by a false arch of the type common in Maya buildings. To the left of Estructura C, **Estructura I** features internal and external murals, and was probably the residence of some major political or religious figure. On the hill above Tajín Chico stood the **Edificio de las Columnas**, which must have dominated the entire city. El Tajín's most famous ruler, 13 Rabbit, lived here – bas-reliefs on columns recorded his exploits, and some of these are now on show in the museum. The building is partly restored, and bits of broken, pre-Columbian pottery litter the area, but this part of the site is closed.

From the terrace of Tajín Chico you can walk down the stone path to the **Gran Greca** complex, also known as Xicalcoliuhqui, with its spiral walls containing two ball-courts and more pyramids. It has been only partially cleared of jungle, but you can stroll along the walled edges to get a sense of its vast size. Built towards the end of the city's life, it is regarded as a sign of growing crisis, Tajín's rulers becoming increasingly obsessed with monumental projects in order to maintain control over a disenchanted populace.

Transport

The easiest way to **get to El Tajín** is from Papantla, 8km away. Local buses (M$8) take around fifteen minutes and can be picked up at the PEMEX gas station on Madero, the main road a few blocks downhill from the zócalo (take 20 de Noviembre) – coming from the plaza, buses should be heading to your left (west). Note that any bus to Poza Rica will pass the ruins, though you'll have to walk 500m from the main highway. **Taxis** to Tajín from Papantla cost around M$50. Both buses and taxis drop you off at the collection of touristy stalls and cheap restaurants that surround the entrance.

Moving on, the local buses continue to **Poza Rica** (30min), where you can connect with services to Mexico City as well as up or down the coast. Poza Rica, 21km from Papantla, is not a place of any delights – a dull, oil-boom city – so if you want to stay somewhere overnight you're much better off continuing north towards Tuxpán, about an hour up the coast. **Poza Rica airport** operates flights to Mexico City, Reynosa and Villahermosa.

Tuxpán

TUXPÁN (or Tuxpam, pronounced "Toosh-pam") offers a far preferable overnight stay to its uglier southern neighbour, Poza Rica, on the journey up the coast to Tampico (see p.213). The town is built on the north bank of the broad Río Tuxpán, where giant tugs and half-built oil-rigs lend an industrial air, and where in the evening half the town comes to stroll as the traffic rushes past them. There's only one real sight, the **Museo de la Amistad México–Cuba** (Mon–Sat 9am–7pm, Sun 9am–2pm; free), on the far bank. Occupying the house where Fidel Castro spent a year planning his revolutionary return to Cuba, the museum, comprising one small room of unlabelled photos, and another where a video is shown, focuses on Castro, Che Guevara and Spanish imperialism in the Americas; there's usually a guide around who can give you a rundown on the displays. The revolutionaries sailed from Tuxpán in December 1956 aboard the *Granma* yacht, almost sinking on the way, and arrived in Cuba to find Batista's forces waiting. A replica of the *Granma* stands on the riverbank. To get there, take one of the small boats (M$3) that shuttle across the river from in front of the Palacio Municipal. On the other side walk inland a couple of blocks and then turn right on Obregón: the museum is right at the end of the street where it hits the river.

The only other reason to stick around Tuxpán is some long, if mediocre, beaches at **Barra de Tuxpán**, by the river mouth some 12km east of town. **Buses** (marked "Playa") run all day along riverside Bulevar Reyes Heroles, past fishing boats and tankers, and arrive twenty minutes later at a vast stretch of grey sand. There are restaurants and changing rooms here and some palapas where you can sling a hammock.

Arrival and information

The first-class ADO **bus** terminal lies on Rodríguez near the junction with Juárez, half a block from the river and some 300m east of the Palacio Municipal. Ómnibus de México (with both first- and second-class services) is further east along riverfront Reyes Heroles, beyond the huge bridge across the river. There are regular departures for Tampico, Veracruz and Mexico City (direct and via Poza Rica), as well as numerous daily services to Papantla. To get to the centre from either bus station, head west along the river to the Palacio Municipal and cathedral: behind these runs Juárez, and in the four blocks from here to the **Parque Reforma**, Tuxpán's liveliest plaza, you'll find **banks**, shops and most other things you might need, including the bulk of the hotels and restaurants. Several **internet** cafés are on Garizurieta, which heads off Juárez between the hotels *Reforma* and *Florida*, and there's another opposite the *Posada San Ignacio*, close to Parque Reforma. The helpful, well-stocked **tourist office** (Mon–Fri 9am–7pm, Sat 10am–6pm; ⓣ783/834-6407) is in the Palacio Municipal, at Juárez 20.

Accommodation

Hotel Reforma Juárez 25 opposite the cathedral ⓣ783/834-0210, ⓔhotelreforma@prodigy.net.mx. The town's best hotel: traditional but classily refurbished. A/c rooms with flat-screen cable TVs and fridges. ❺

Hotel Riviera Tuxpan Reyes Heroles 17-A ⓣ783/834-8123, ⓦwww.rivieratuxpan.com. One of the few hotels in the centre with a river view, though by no means from all rooms. It's a Best Western, so comfortable and efficient (with wi-fi), if a little dull. ❺

Posada San Ignacio Ocampo 29, one block north of Parque Reforma ⓣ783/834-2905. The best budget choice; a brightly painted courtyard hotel hidden away down an alley; quiet rooms with fan and TV. ❷

Hotel Sara Garizurieta 44 ⓣ783/834-0010, ⓦwww.hotelsara.com.mx. Slightly worn business hotel, but good value (discounts for cash); there's a rooftop pool and it's just a couple of blocks from the ADO (head inland, then left). ❹

Eating and drinking

A kiosk in the centre of the Parque Reforma houses a series of little snack bars and *licuado* places, serving to plastic tables set out on the square. There are plenty of food stalls in and around the **market** too – it's on the riverfront between Rodriguez and Pípila, opposite the ADO. Younger locals hang out along the river downstream of the centre, where there are numerous fast-food places.

Antonios Juárez 25 in the *Hotel Reforma* ⓣ783/834-1146. With linen tablecloths, good steaks and live music on Fridays and Saturdays, this is the chicest restaurant in town (M$60–110 for mains).

El Atracadero Reyes Heroles ⓣ783/835-5166. Floating restaurant and bar; pricey steaks, excellent paella, and great atmosphere.

El Mejicano Morelos 49 on Parque Reforma. Enjoyable, straightforward Mexican restaurant, with good guacamole and a M$50 buffet.

Nuevo 303 Pípila, between Juárez and the river. One of numerous simple choices beside the market, this place is open 24 hours, and busy with locals for almost all of them.

South of Veracruz

Leaving Veracruz to the south, Hwy-180 traverses a long expanse of plain, a country of broad river deltas and salty lagoons, for nearly 150km, until it hits the hills of the volcanic **Sierra Tuxtla**, known as "La Suiza Veracruzana" (the Switzerland of Veracruz), home to the townships of **Santiago Tuxtla** and **San Andrés Tuxtla**. Although plainly named by someone who'd never been to Switzerland, this beautiful country of rolling green hills makes a welcome change from the flat plains, and the cooler climate is an infinite relief. The idyllic **Lago de**

Catemaco around which the last expanse of Gulf coast **rainforest** is preserved, makes a rewarding place to break the journey south, with plenty of opportunities to explore the nearby mountains and coast. Beyond the Tuxtla mountains, low, flat, dull country leads all the way to Villahermosa (see p.729).

Historically, the region's great claim to fame is that it was the birthplace of Mexico's first civilization, the **Olmecs**. Here lies the **Volcán de San Martín**, where the Olmecs believed the earth to have been created; they built a replica "creation mountain" at their city, La Venta, on the border with Tabasco (see p.738). Their second major city, at **Tres Zapotes**, near Santiago Tuxtla, is now little more than a mound in a maize field. For most modern Mexicans, however, this part of southern Veracruz, especially around Lago de Catemaco, is best known as the "**Tierra de los Brujos**" (land of the witches/wizards).

Tlacotalpan

TLACOTALPAN is a beautiful, languid town on the north bank of the broad Río Papaloapan. An important port and railhead in the eighteenth and nineteenth centuries, it now has just six hundred permanent inhabitants, but its elegant colonial architecture has led to its being declared a Unesco World Heritage Site. At the weekend it can be packed with locals, who come here to eat at the riverside restaurants, fish, swim or take boat rides on the river, browse the artesanía shops and hang out in the bars and cafés on the plaza. Come on a weekday afternoon and you'll find the place all but deserted.

Among Mexicans, Tlacotalpan is best known as the place where musician and composer **Agustín Lara** (1900–70), whose works have been interpreted by the likes of Pavarotti, Carreras and Domingo, spent his early childhood. Two museums and a cultural centre honour the man, but unless you're a huge fan they're not worth the admission – the true pleasure here is simply to wander the streets, admiring the architecture (many of the buildings are labelled with their history) and soaking up the steamy, tropical atmosphere. On the zócalo, the Plaza Zaragoza, are two magnificent churches and a florid, wrought-iron bandstand; Enriquez and Miguel Chazaro, parallel streets heading west from here, are lined with magnificent colonnaded houses. The most enjoyable of the town's few sights is the **Museo Salvador Ferrando** (Tues–Sun 10.30am–5pm; M$15), on Alegre on the Plaza Hidalgo. Named after one of the town's most respected painters, it's a fine old house containing an Old Curiosity Shop of paintings, antique furniture, historical artefacts and junk, around which you're given a lightning conducted tour in Spanish.

Practicalities

Tlacotalpan lies some 70km south of Veracruz, 10km inland on the winding road that heads towards Tuxtepec (and eventually Oaxaca). There are frequent **buses**, and there's a lot to be said for coming second class, because these will drop you right in the heart of town: the ADO terminal is west of the centre on the road out towards Tuxtepec. There's a small **tourist office** (Mon–Fri 9am–3pm) in the Palacio Municipal, just off the Plaza Hidalgo at Alegre 6; at busy times a tourist information kiosk also operates on the waterfront Plaza Colon. The **market** occupies a wonderful nineteenth-century building on the waterfront, just east of the centre; there's a **bank** with ATM by the *Hotel Doña Lala*. At the beginning of February, the **Fiesta de la Virgen de la Candelaria** is celebrated with bull runs, special food stalls and folk-music concerts – the main "procession" takes place on the river, where the image of the Virgin is floated downstream amongst a mass of assorted riverboats.

If you're looking for somewhere to **stay**, the upmarket *Hotel Posada Doña Lala* (Ⓣ288/884-2580, Ⓦwww.hoteldonalala.com; ⑤), close to river and zócalo at Carranza 11, is the fanciest place in town, comfortable if a bit stuffy, with a smart restaurant serving great seafood. Cheaper alternatives include the *Reforma* (Ⓣ288/884-2022), Carranza 2 just off the zócalo, where there's a choice of basic rooms with fan (❸) or air-conditioning (❹) – a couple of the latter have lovely balconies over a smaller plaza at the back – and the bright blue-and-yellow *Posada Don Diego* (Ⓣ288/884-3221; ❸), Gutierrez Zamora off Carranza near the market, where internal air-conditioned rooms are quiet, modern, clean and comfortable. The riverside **restaurants** in Tlacotalpan are famed for their delicious, cheap seafood; try for example *Las Riberas del Papaloapan*, close to the market. There are also a couple of surprisingly rowdy **bars** on the zócalo.

Santiago Tuxtla

SANTIAGO TUXTLA is much the smaller of the two Tuxtlas, a quiet country town which can make for a peaceful overnight break. Buses stop on the main road a short walk downhill from the zócalo, where a giant **Olmec head**, 3.4m high, is proudly displayed – this is the largest ever found, and unusual also for its closed eyes, scowling mouth and simplified features. The small **Museo Tuxteco** (Tues–Fri 9am–6pm, Sat & Sun 9am–5pm; M$37), on the south side of the plaza, has another giant head which by contrast is the smallest known, yet far more expressive and finely worked than that outside. Its other star exhibit is a figure, probably an altar, known as "El Negro" – visiting celebrities and locals come here to rub their thumbs over his forehead, which reputedly provides positive energy and miraculous cures.

There are a couple of excellent **hotels** in town, the best of them the *Mesón de Santiago* (Ⓣ294/947-0167, Ⓦwww.mesonsantiago.com.mx; ❹), 5 de Mayo in the corner of the zócalo, a lovingly converted colonial building with elegant rooms around a courtyard with a small pool. Just a few doors down 5 de Mayo on the zócalo, the marginally cheaper *Gran Santiago Plaza* (Ⓣ294/947-0300, Ⓦwww.hotelgransantiagoplaza.com; ❹), could hardly be more of a contrast – a thoroughly incongruous, seven-storey, circular concrete construction. The rooms are comfortable and efficient, though, and it also has Santiago's most formal **restaurant**. Simpler places include *Super La Joya*, on the zócalo, where you can eat standard Mexican fare at tables outside (around M$40 for breakfast or comida corrida); inside it's a supermarket and **internet** café. Bar-restaurant *La Yegua Panda*, on Juárez just off the zócalo, has more good food and is also the centre of what local nightlife there is, while *Antojitos Gaby*, on the small Plaza Cervantina to the side of the *Mesón de Santiago*, serves excellent local specialities – try the *memelas*, like giant quesadillas filled with meat and cheese. There are two **ATMs** at the Palacio Municipal on the zócalo, and another on the main road opposite the bus station: from here frequent buses continue towards San Andrés (20min) and Catemaco (45min).

Tres Zapotes

Around 23km from Santiago, the Olmec site of **Tres Zapotes** was one of the longest-lasting of all Olmec cities, occupied from 1200 BC to around 1000 AD. It's a slow journey out here, and frankly barely worth it unless you are an obsessive collector of Olmec heads: another is on display in the renovated **museum** (daily 9am–6pm; M$27). Other than this the museum contains little that is not duplicated elsewhere – its main interest lies in a series of stelae inscribed with Olmec glyphs – while of the site itself, nearby, virtually nothing can be seen apart from green mounds. To get there take Hwy 179 (towards Isla) for about 8km, and then turn right. Local **buses** (M$20) take around an hour, departing from close to the junction of the highways, by the river below the zócalo; you can also find **taxis** (around M$100, or *colectivos* for not much more than the bus) on this riverside road.

San Andrés Tuxtla

SAN ANDRÉS TUXTLA is the administrative centre of the region, and a far larger place with every facility you might need. Surrounded by tobacco fields, it's also home to several **cigar factories** where you can watch *puros* being hand-rolled. The **Santa Clara** factory (Ⓦwww.santaclarapuros.com), established in 1830, on the highway one block from the ADO bus station (Catemaco direction), welcomes visitors – it's fascinating, informal and there's very little pressure to buy.

One popular outing from San Andrés is to the **Salto de Eyipantla** (M$6), a powerful waterfall 50m wide and 40m high, about 9km away. Frequent local buses signed "El Salto" (M$5.50; 30min) run from a stop opposite the *Hotel del Parque*.

Practicalities

Local **buses** from Catemaco or Santiago will take you right into town, but the majority drop you at the top of the hill where the highway passes by; from here, Juárez leads straight down to the zócalo, a fifteen-minute walk or M$15 taxi ride. There's a helpful **tourist office** here in the Palacio Municipal (office hours, but a booth is open outside on busy weekends) and most **accommodation** and other facilities are nearby. The *Hotel Figueroa* (Ⓣ294/942-0257; ❷), Pino Suárez 10 at Belisario Domínguez, a couple of blocks northeast of the plaza, is the pick of the budget options, with basic but comfortable rooms along with a friendly welcome and lots of information and brochures on what is happening in the region. The *Hotel del Parque* (Ⓣ294/942-0198, Ⓦwww.hoteldelparque.com; ❺), Madero 5 on the zócalo, has the best position in town, and recently refurbished air-conditioned rooms with cable TV and wi-fi. The *Hotel Posada San Martin* (Ⓣ294/942-1036, Ⓦwww.hotelposada-sanmartin.com; ❹), halfway to the bus station at Juárez 304, has air-conditioned motel-style units arranged around a peaceful garden and a small pool.

There are plenty of **restaurants and cafés** around the centre: sip a coffee while people-watching at the *Italian Coffee Company* on the zócalo, or at popular *Winni's* (also food: M$42 *menú del día*) almost next door. Several more good places to eat are on Madero southwest of the zócalo: the *Refugio la Casona* at no. 18 (Ⓣ294/942-1496) is a pretty restaurant in a colonial building, with courtyard dining at the back and occasional live music. *Montepio* (Ⓣ294/942-0735), at the end of the alley off Madero opposite the *San Andrés* hotel, has excellent steaks (M$140–150), a good wine list and a bar that welcomes women. In the other direction, the *Palapa la Hueva Jarocha*, on Juárez a block and a half from the zócalo, is a big, popular place for *mariscos*, grilled meat and tacos. Cheaper eats can be found around the excellent **market**, on 5 de Mayo west of the zócalo.

Banks with ATMs are mostly in the shopping streets north of the zócalo: HSBC and Santander are at the junction of 16 de Septiembre and Carranza, just off Juárez. Try *Pl@y.net*, on the street off the zócalo past the cathedral, for **internet**, or a place in the Plaza Jardín, on Juárez by the *Palapa la Hueva Jarocha*.

For **moving on**, Catemaco is around 11km east, and Santiago is 13km to the west: both are easily accessible via frequent buses that depart in front of the giant Fenix supermarket at Pino Suárez and Constitución, two blocks east of the zócalo. There are also frequent buses to Veracruz from the main terminal, but note that buses to Villahermosa tend to leave in the evening, getting you there in the early hours.

Catemaco

Squatting on the western shore of the enchanting Lago de Catemaco, and by tradition a centre of native witchcraft, **CATEMACO** is a much more picturesque spot to break the journey before the long leg south. With an impressive backdrop of volcanic mountains, the lake and nearby marshland and lagoons are a haven for wildlife, supporting large colonies of **water birds**, including herons, cormorants, wintering ospreys and dozens of other resident and migratory species.

Arrival and information

The **ADO** first-class terminal, surely the most scenic in the country, faces the lake on the eastern edge of town, about a five-minute walk from the centre. Some second-class buses also terminate at the ADO station, but most stop at the AU terminal on the main highway on the edge of town. Buses from San Andrés Tuxtla will drop you at Lerdo and Revolución, directly inland from the ADO. In the other direction, buses make the thirty-minute trip to San Andrés from the same place, which is also the starting point for *piratas* (*colectivo* pick-ups) heading to Sontecomapan and the beaches (see p.607). **Share-taxis** to San Andrés leave from halfway up Carranza towards the main highway, near the mound known as El Cerrito.

On the zócalo, two blocks from the waterfront, there's a **tourist office** in the Palacio Municipal (Mon–Fri 9am–3pm & 6–9pm; also a booth on the highway at the entrance to town at busy periods), a bank and a couple of **ATMs**. There are **internet** cafés on Carranza, including *Open Cybercafe*, about four blocks from the zócalo.

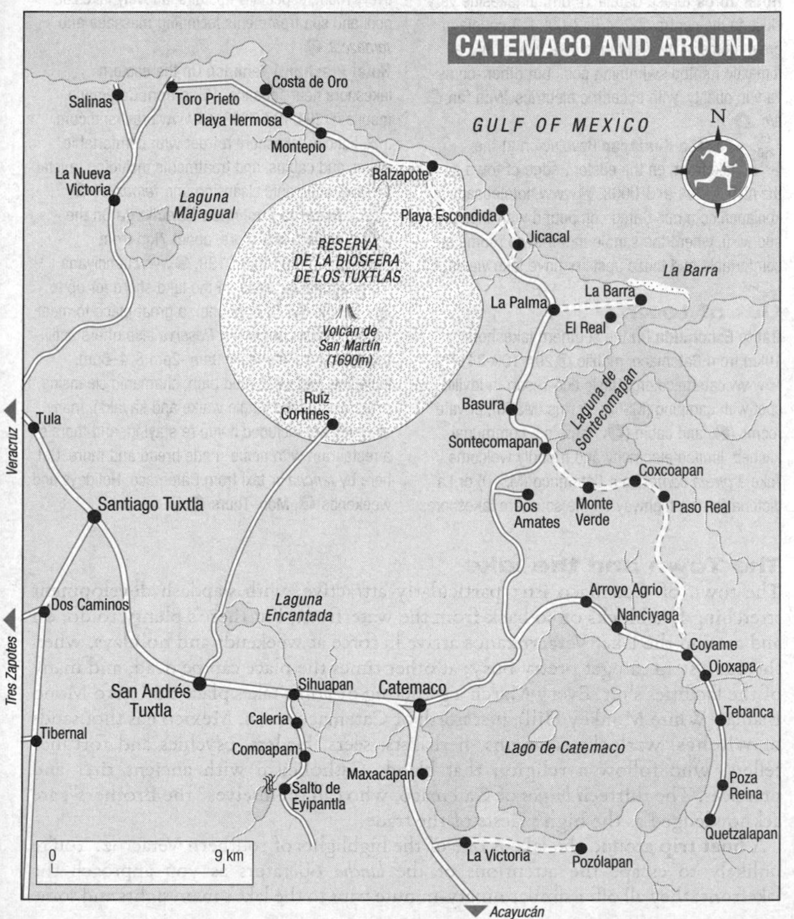

Accommodation

Hotel standards are not very high here, though there are some great, back-to-nature eco-resorts around the lake.

In town

Hotel Los Arcos Madero 7, between the zócalo and the lake ⓣ294/943-0003, ⓦwww.arcoshotel.com.mx. Pleasant, a/c rooms with TV around an attractive pool. Some of the higher rooms have lake views. ④

Catemaco Hotel Carranza 8 on the zócalo ⓣ294/943-0203, ⓦwww.hotelcatemaco.net. Great position, a good café and comfy rooms. Excellent-value singles but otherwise overpriced. ⑤

Hotel Julita Teresa García 10 on the lakeside very close to the centre ⓣ294/943-0008. Good-value budget option, with simple, clean and bright rooms with fans. ②

Hotel Juros Teresa García 14 on the lakeside very close to the centre ⓣ294/943-0084. A couple of great rooms at the front with lake views, and a fantastic rooftop swimming pool, but other rooms vary in quality, with eccentric electrics. With fan ③, a/c ④

Posada Koniapan Revolución at the lakefront, on the eastern edge of town by the ADO ⓣ294/943-0063, ⓦwww.hotelposadakoniapan.com.mx. Gated compound with a pool and wi-fi, where the simple motel-style rooms are comfortable and those upstairs have lake views. ④

Out of town

Bahia Escondida On the southern lakeshore, 10km from Catemaco, mobile ⓣ294/109-3417, ⓦwww.catemaco.org. Basic eco-resort in idyllic spot with camping (M$50), dorms (M$70), private rooms (③) and cabin (④); there's a communal kitchen, limited electricity and friendly welcome. Take a *pirata combi* from Catemaco (M$10) or La Victoria (on the highway on the southern lakeshore; M$5) to Pozólapan, followed by a ten-minute walk, or a *lancha* from Catemaco. ⑥

Ecobiosfera Dos Amates, 10km from Catemaco on the road to Sontecomapan, mobile ⓣ294/114-5849, ⓦwww.ecobiosfera.com. Fairly basic cabañas, close to nature in a stunning hillside position overlooking the lake; also camping from M$50. They run all sorts of excellent nature and cultural tours from here, in particular into the Reserva de la Biosfera and to various waterfalls. ④

La Finca Hwy 180km147, on the west bank of the lake about 2km from town ⓣ294/947-9700, ⓦwww.lafinca.com.mx. The best hotel on the lake, with stunning views from almost every room, especially upstairs, a lovely lakeside pool and spa treatments including massage and *temazcal*. ⑦

Hotel Prashanti Tebanca On the eastern lakeshore near Tebanca, 15km from Catemaco, mobile ⓣ294/107-7998, ⓦwww.prashanti.com.mx. Fancier lakeshore retreat with comfortable rooms and cabins, and treatments including crystal therapy, shamanic cleansing and *temazcal*. ⑥

Reserva Ecológica Nanciyaga On the eastern lakeshore, about 7km from Catemaco ⓣ294/943-0199, ⓦwww.nanciyaga.com. Simple cabañas on the lake shore for up to four people (no TV or phone); a great place to meet young Veracruzanos. The *Reserva* also offers activities to non-guests (daily 9am–2pm & 4–6pm; including *temazcal*, mud bath, shamanic cleansing, massage, guided jungle walks and kayaks), many of which are included if you're staying, and there's a restaurant with home-made bread and more. Get here by *lancha* or taxi from Catemaco. Holidays and weekends ⑥, Mon–Thurs ④

The Town and the lake

The town of Catemaco isn't particularly attractive, with slapdash development stretching five blocks or so back from the waterfront, but there's plenty to do, on and around the lake. Veracruzanos arrive in force at weekends and holidays, when the main strip can get pretty busy; at other times the place can be dead, and many of the facilities shut. Every March a gathering of *brujos* takes place on Cerro Mono Blanco (White Monkey Hill), just north of Catemaco town. Mexico has thousands of **witches**, warlocks, shamans, herbalists, seers, healers, psychics and fortune-tellers, who follow a religion that blends Catholicism with ancient rites and practices. The thirteen *brujos* of Catemaco, who call themselves "the Brothers", are acknowledged as the high priests of the trade.

A **boat trip** around the lake is one of the highlights of southern Veracruz. You're unlikely to escape the attentions of the *lancha* operators as you approach the lakefront: they all offer similar ninety-minute trips to the lake's main sights and some of its beaches (M$450 for a boatload, though bargain at quiet times; M$80 *colectivo*, in busy periods only). On the tiny **Isla de los Changos** there are stump-tailed macaques (monkeys native to Thailand), introduced here by Veracruz University in 1974 – they look bored stiff in their restricted habitat. In 1988, endangered Mexican howler monkeys were introduced to the much larger Agaltepec Island; these are far more active and aggressive. You are almost guaranteed to see a huge variety of **birds** too – herons, egrets, cormorants and shags, as well as more exotic kingfishers and ospreys. **Morelet's crocodiles**, a relatively small species (up to 3m long), live in the lake too, nesting on the far bank. They're well fed and, apparently, never attack. Certainly plenty of people swim in the lake: stick to the main **beaches** and close to others if you feel uneasy. Playa Espagoya is just a short walk beyond the eastern edge of town, with Playa Hermosa and Playa Azul not much further beyond. **Other activities** include kayaking, mountain-biking, jungle tours, shamanic spiritual cleansing, *temazcales* and more; many of them can be organized by Catemaco Tours (mobile ⓣ294/941-5849, ⓦwww.catemacoturs.com), on the lakefront just east of the centre, or through the various lodges around the lake, especially *Nanciyaga* and *Ecobiosfera* (see "Accommodation", opposite).

Catemaco is an important place of pilgrimage for Catholics as well as followers of shamanism. The focus for pilgrims (and the festival held here on July 15–16) is the **Iglesia de Nuestra Señora del Carmen** on the zócalo, one of the prettiest churches in Veracruz, with beautifully painted walls and ceilings, stained glass and a striking dome. They come to venerate its miraculous statue of the Virgin of Carmen, who is said to have appeared to a fisherman in 1714 in a narrow grotto known as **El Tegal**, roughly twenty minutes' walk around the lakeshore towards Playa Azul.

Eating, drinking and entertainment

Seafood **restaurants** abound along the lakefront, most offering the local speciality, *mojarra* (small perch from the lake), best sampled when cooked *a'la tachagovi* – with a delicious hot sauce. A few more modern places, serving shocking innovations like cappuccino and pizza, are also starting to appear. At the other end of the scale the **market**, half a block from the zócalo on Madero, has plenty of cooked-food stalls.

Bossa Nova Lakefront just east of the centre. Jazz café playing some cool sounds on a lovely upstairs terrace with lake views.

Cafe Catemaco *Catemaco Hotel*. Café overlooking the zócalo, with the best breakfast in town, and wi-fi.

La Casita Matamoros between Bravo and Melchor Ocampo, a few blocks north of the plaza (hard to find, so ask). Well-priced Mexican dishes and seafood, perennially popular with locals.

La Casona Aldama 4 ⓣ294/943-0813. Enchanting old building on the zócalo which has plenty for seafood- and meat-lovers, served in an attractive dining room looking out onto a verdant garden or on a balcony over the zócalo. Try the *arroz a la tumbada*, lemon-scented rice with seafood (mains M$60–70).

Il Fiorentino Lakefront by *Bossa Nova*. Italian restaurant serving decent pizza, calzone and pasta dishes; evenings only during the week, from lunchtime at weekends.

Fractal Naturaleza Lakefront in the centre of town. Café and shop serving smoothies, coffee and muffins and selling quality souvenirs and handicrafts, plus traditional medicines.

La Panga Lakefront west of the centre. Quite a few lakefront restaurants in this direction have terraces; *La Panga* goes one better, with a couple of palapas right out in the lake, accessed by a jetty. Primarily a bar – a great place for a sundowner.

Los Sauces Lakefront towards the ADO ⓣ294/943-0548. Some of the most consistently good seafood on the lakeshore, in a quiet spot with great views from the upper floor.

Sontecomapan and the coast

From Catemaco a paved road heads 18km to the coast and the small fishing village of **Sontecomapan**. Here you can take a variety of *lancha* trips through the

Fiestas

February

Día de la Candelaria (Feb 2). The final day of a week-long fiesta, complete with dances, boat races and bulls let loose in the streets, in Tlacotalpan (see p.602). Colourful fiesta in Jaltipán, near Acayucán, which includes the dance of La Malinche (Cortés's Indian interpreter and mistress, who is said to have been born here).

Carnaval (the week before Lent; variable Feb–March) is celebrated all over the region, most riotously in Veracruz (see p.577).

March

Congreso de Brujos (first Fri in March). Shamans, witches, wizards and healers from across Mexico attend purification rituals and celebrations in and around Catemaco (p.604), amid a festival that attracts plenty of visitors.

Fiestas de San José (March 18–19). In Naranjos, between Tuxpán and Tampico, a fiesta with many traditional dances. In Espinal, a Totonac village on the Río Tecolutla, not far from El Tajín and Papantla, you can witness the spectacular voladores.

Semana Santa (Holy Week). Re-creations of the Passion are widespread in this area. You can witness them in Papantla (see p.596), where you'll also see the voladores; in Coatzintla, a Totonac village nearby; in Cotaxtla, between Veracruz and Córdoba; and in Otatitlán. Naolinco, a beautiful village near Xalapa, stages a mock Crucifixion on Good Friday. Also celebrations in Catemaco (see p.604) and in the port of Alvarado – a ribald Fish Fiesta following the spirit of the Veracruz Carnaval.

April

Feria de las Flores (late April or early May). Flower festival in Fortín de las Flores (see p.574).

May

Feria del Cafe (first two weeks of May). Coatepec (p.591) celebrates the local crop.

Corpus Christi (variable; the Thurs after Trinity Sun). The start of a major four-day festival in Papantla (see p.596) with regular performances by the voladores.

June

Día de San Juan (June 24). Celebrated with dancing in Santiago Tuxtla (see p.603), and in Martinez de la Torre, near Tlapacoyan, where the voladores perform.

mangroves on the freshwater **Laguna de Sontecomapan**, which offers good **bird watching** possibilities. The most common trip is all the way to the mouth of the Laguna at **La Barra**, about 4km away (also accessible via a very rough road), where there's a lovely stretch of sand, usually deserted. The journey costs M$450 for the entire boat, including an hour or so at the beach; at busy periods you can get a *colectivo* ride for M$80. At La Barra, *La Sirenita* serves up tasty fresh seafood, while *Los Amigos* (Ⓣ294/943-0101, Ⓦwww.losamigos.com.mx; ❸) offers a variety of simple **cabañas** on a jungly hillside, as well as single beds in dorm-like "Ecoalbergues" with shared bathroom for M$170 (M$50 for breakfast). There's a simple restaurant here, as well as hiking trails and kayaks and a *temazcal*.

Beyond Sontecomapan a good road heads northwest along the coast for some 40km, before turning inland to rejoin the main highway beyond Santiago Tuxtla; the route is regularly traversed by *piratas*. Only one short section has been deliberately left unpaved, where it passes through the **Reserva de la Biosfera los Tuxtlas**, a nature reserve most easily visited on a tour with *Ecobiosfera* (see p.606). Some of Veracruz's most alluring and least-visited **beaches** lie off this road,

July

Día de la Virgen del Carmen (July 15–16). A massive pilgrimage to Catemaco (see p.604), accompanied by a fiesta which spills over into the following day. At the same time, Xico (p.592) has a week-long celebration of Mary Magdalene.

Día de Santiago (July 25). Celebrated with fiestas in Santiago Tuxtla (see p.603) and Coatzintla; each lasts several days. In Tlapacoyan (see p.593) you can see the bizarre Baile de los Negritos (see box, p.596).

August

Day of Assumption (Aug 15). Widely celebrated, particularly in Tlapacoyan (see p.593), where you can see El Baile de los Negritos, and with a week-long festival in Tuxpán (see p.600) that includes dancing and the voladores.

September

Independence Day (Sept 15–16). Celebrated everywhere.

San Jeronimo (last week of Sept). Big celebrations in Coatepec (see p.591).

October

Fiesta de la Virgen del Rosario (Oct 7). In La Antigua (see p.585) the patroness of fishermen is honoured with processions of canoes on the river, while Alvarado, outside Veracruz, enjoys a fiesta filling the first two weeks of the month.

November

Día de los Muertos (Day of the Dead; Nov 2). Observed everywhere.

December

Dia del Niño Perdido (Dec 7). Huge candle-lit processions in Tuxpán (p.600).

Día de la Virgen de Guadalupe (Dec 12). Widely observed, especially in Huatusco, Cotaxtla, and Amatlán de los Reyes, near Córdoba.

Christmas (Dec 25). Celebrated everywhere. There's a very famous festival in Santiago Tuxtla (see p.603) that lasts until Twelfth Night (Jan 6).

although in the early stages most of them are at least a couple of kilometres away, down very poor dirt tracks. At **Playa Escondida**, a beautiful stretch of sand some 30km from Catemaco and 3km off the main road, the *Hotel Icacos* (Ⓣ294/942-0556, Ⓦwww.paradorecoturisticoicacos.com; ❸) is a simple place for a Robinson Crusoe existence. At **Montepio**, 39km from Catemaco, the road finally runs right by the coast. This is almost a resort, with a couple of posadas, the better of which, the *San José* (book through *Posada San José* in San Andrés Tuxtla Ⓣ294/942-1010; ❸), has a small pool and simple rooms with fan and sea views. The beach here offers warm, shallow swimming – people also swim in the nearby river – and is lined with palapa restaurants serving seafood and *cocos fríos*. At holiday times there are *lanchas* and banana-boat rides; out of season there are barely half a dozen people on the entire beach. Beyond Montepio, the coast is being promoted as the **Costa de Oro**, though as yet there's no real development, and only the odd isolated place to stay; there are excellent beaches at Playa Hermosa and Costa de Oro, though, and a popular dive spot at Roca Partida – the split rock.

Acayucán and Coatzacoalcos

Travelling along the **northern shore** of the Isthmus of Tehuantepec – the narrowest part of Mexico – you'll almost inevitably pass through **ACAYUCÁN**, where the coastal highway and the trans-isthmus highway meet, though the toll expressway wisely gives a wide berth to all the towns in this region. An enormous bus station and equally giant market cater to passing travellers; there's little otherwise but mud, dust and noise, though the **market** stalls can be a good place to stop off for provisions such as nuts, cheese, fresh pineapple and corn bread. Make your visit a short one and, if you have any choice at all, press straight on through to Villahermosa (see p.729). If you have to **stay**, go for the *Hotel Plaza* (Ⓣ924/245-0088; ❸) at Victoria 37 or the more comfortable *Kinaku* (Ⓣ924/245-0410, Ⓦwww.hotelkinaku.com; ❺), nearby at Ocampo Sur 7, whose air-conditioned rooms have cable TV and wi-fi.

The coast from here to the Tabasco border is less attractive still, with a huge industrial zone stretching from the dirty concrete town of Minatitlán to **COATZACOALCOS** (formerly Puerto México, the Atlantic railway terminus), dominated by a giant oil refinery. If you have to stop in this area, Coatzacoalcos is definitely the better choice: big enough to have a real centre and with plenty of hotels and restaurants around the camionera. Coatzacoalcos also boasts a spectacular modern bridge – known as Coatzacoalcos II – by which the main highway bypasses the town. If you're on a bus heading downtown you'll cross the Río Coatzacoalcos by an older, lesser suspension bridge. In legend, Coatzacoalcos is the place from which Quetzalcoatl and his followers sailed east, vowing to return.

Travel details

Buses

First-class buses are mostly operated by Autobuses de Oriente (ADO; Ⓦwww.ado.com.mx) – remarkably slick and efficient. Second-class is dominated (at least on long hauls) by Autobuses Unidos (AU), more of a mixed bag. This is a brief rundown of the routes, mainly taking into account the ADO services, and should be regarded as a minimum.

Papantla to: Mexico City (6 daily; 6hr); Poza Rica (frequently; 30min); Tlapacoyan (4 daily; 3hr); Tuxpán (10 daily; 1hr 30min); Veracruz (10 daily; 4hr); Xalapa (7 daily; 4hr).

Poza Rica to: Mexico City (8 daily; 5hr); Tuxpán (frequently; 1hr); Veracruz (frequently; 4hr 30min).

San Andrés Tuxtla to: Catemaco (frequently; 30min); Coatzacoalcos (9 daily; 2hr 30min); Veracruz (frequently; 3hr).

Tuxpán to: Mexico City (9 daily; 6hr); Poza Rica (frequently; 1hr); Tampico (10 daily; 3hr); Veracruz (6 daily; 5hr 30min); Xalapa (7 daily; 6hr).

Veracruz to: Cancún (4 daily; 20hr); Cardel (frequently; 30min); Catemaco (9 daily; 3hr 30min); Coatzacoalcos (10 daily; 5hr 30min); Córdoba (frequently; 1hr 45min); Mexico City (24 daily; 5hr 30min); Oaxaca (1 daily; 7hr); Orizaba (frequently; 2hr 30min); Papantla (6 daily; 4hr); Poza Rica (frequently; 4hr 30min); Puebla (frequently; 3hr 30min); San Andrés Tuxtla (12 daily; 3hr); Tuxpán (15 daily; 5hr 30min); Villahermosa (6 daily; 7hr); Xalapa (frequently; 2hr).

Xalapa to: Fortín de las Flores (7 daily; 3hr); Mexico City (15 daily; 5hr); Papantla (7 daily; 4hr); Veracruz (frequently; 2hr).

Flights

Poza Rica to: Mexico City (3 daily; 50min); Reynosa (1 daily; 1hr 40min); Villahermosa (1 daily; 1hr 40min)

Veracruz to: Cancún (1 daily; 1hr 35min); Ciudad del Carmen (1 daily; 1hr); Guadalajara (1 daily; 1hr 25min); Houston, Texas (1 daily; 2hr 10min); Mérida (2 daily; 1hr 15min); Mexico City (7 daily; 50min); Monterrey (3 daily; 1hr 30min); Tampico (2 weekly; 1hr); Villahermosa (2 daily; 50min).

Xalapa to: Mexico City (2 daily; 55min).

10

Oaxaca

USA
GULF OF MEXICO
PACIFIC OCEAN
BELIZE
GUATEMALA
HONDURAS
EL SALVADOR
N
0 500 km
1
2
3
4
5
6
7
8
9
10
11
12

CHAPTER 10 Highlights

* **Oaxaca** Indigenous traditions fuse with colonial grandeur in one of Mexico's most hypnotic cities. See p.616
* **Oaxacan food** The rich *moles*, potent mescals and aromatic dishes of this exquisite regional cuisine are best experienced in Oaxaca city. See p.629
* **Monte Albán** A potent symbol of Zapotec power, these ruins were once an astounding ancient city with a population of over twenty thousand. See p.633
* **Teotitlán del Valle** Experience the rich artisan traditions of Oaxaca's Valles Centrales while shopping for iconic *tapetes* (rugs). See p.638
* **Mitla** The ancient Zapotec ceremonial centre with sublime greca stonework is considered to be without peer in Mexico. See p.640
* **Benito Juárez** Stay in a Tourist Yú'ù cabin in this quaint village named after Oaxaca's most famous son, where you can hike in gorgeous mountain surroundings. See p.642
* **Puerto Escondido** Ride the Mexican pipeline – or just watch – at this world-famous surfing spot. See p.648
* **Mazunte** See the queens of the sea, female Golfina turtles, in this tranquil oceanside town, or take a trip to the local crocodile lagoon. See p.663

▲ Surfing in Puerto Escondido

10

Oaxaca

The state of **Oaxaca** is one of the most enticing destinations in Mexico. **Indigenous traditions** remain powerful in this area and nowhere else in the country are the markets so infused with colour or the fiestas so exuberant. The old languages are still widely spoken, and there are traditions in the villages that long pre-date the Spanish Conquest. Here too the landscapes make a fundamental break with the barren deserts of the north, replaced by thickly forested hillsides, or in low-lying areas by swamp and jungle.

The striking differences of the region are compounded by the relative lack of development. Industry is virtually nonexistent, and while the city of Oaxaca and several coastal hot spots such as Puerto Escondido have thrived on tourism, the rest of the state is woefully underdeveloped – the "Mexican economic miracle" has yet to reach the south. Indeed, the region has witnessed considerable **political disturbance** in recent years. In autumn 2006 the political situation reached its nadir when striking teachers clashed with riot police in a dispute that had begun over wages and mushroomed into protests over the alleged corruption of state governor Ulises Ruíz Ortíz.

The city of **Oaxaca** is the region's prime destination, close enough to Mexico City to attract large numbers of tourists to its fine crafts stores, markets, seemingly constant fiestas, cobbled, gallery-lined walkways and sophisticated restaurants. Here you can see one of the region's – and the whole of Latin America's – most magnificent **Baroque churches**, notably Santo Domingo, which fuses Spanish and native influences to spectacular effect. Nearby, the Zapotec and Mixtec ancient sites at **Monte Albán**, **Yagul** and **Mitla** are less well known than their contemporaries in central and eastern Mexico, but every bit as important and impressive.

The Pacific resorts of **Puerto Escondido**, **Puerto Ángel** and **Huatulco** are now firmly on the map and are easily reached from the city, though their reputation for being unspoiled beach paradises is no longer justified – Escondido in particular is a resort of some size, and Huatulco, conceived as an environmentally conscious international development, is a characterless resort with an artificial Mexican flavour. Yet along this coast you'll discover some of the emptiest and best **Pacific beaches** in Mexico, including tranquil **Mazunte**, accessible from the main centres. The resorts are all around 250km from Oaxaca city, reached via spectacular mountain roads that take a minimum of six hours to traverse. The highway robberies that once plagued this part of Mexico are largely a thing of the past – increased security makes bus travel safe – but it's still advisable to avoid driving at night. Many people prefer to **fly** down, either from Oaxaca to Escondido – an experience in itself – or direct from Mexico City to Escondido or Huatulco.

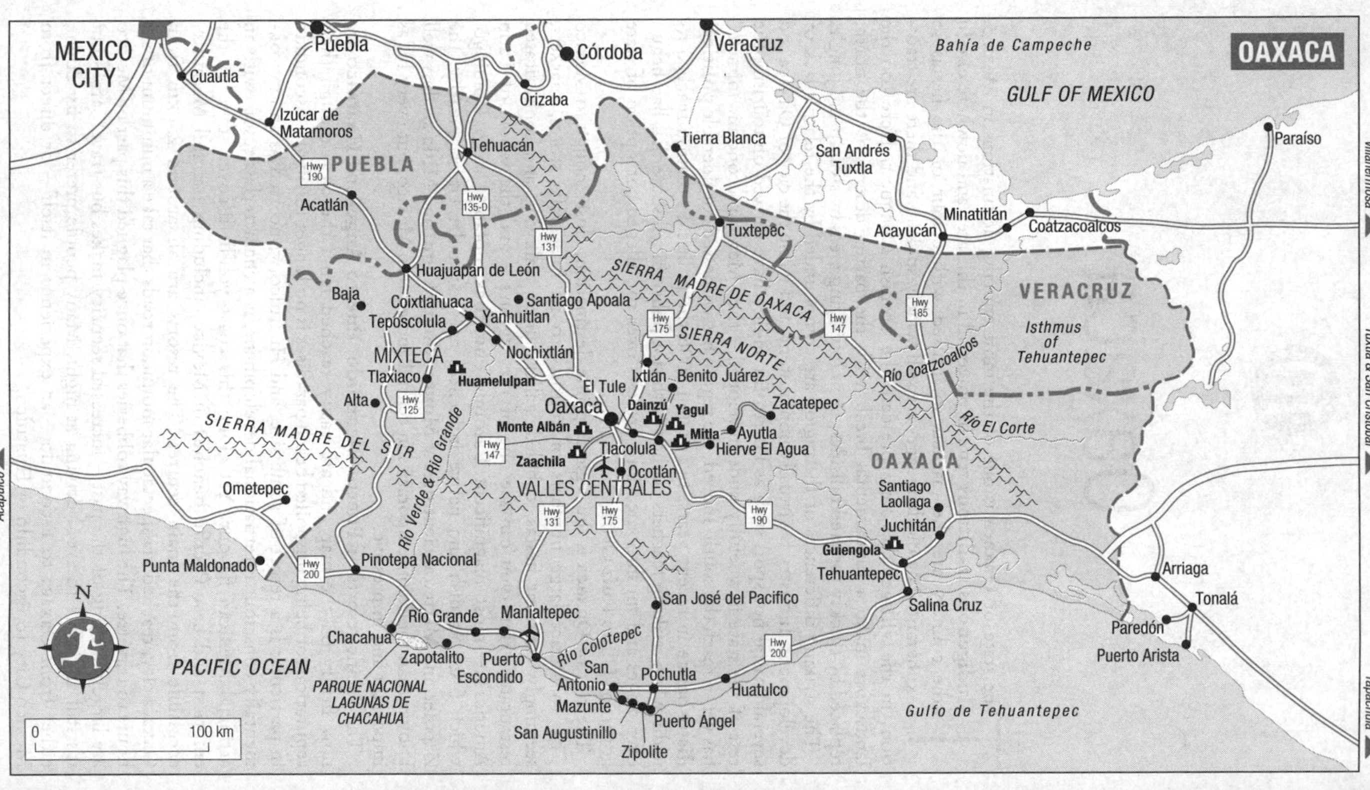
OAXACA
MEXICO CITY
Cuautla
Puebla
Izúcar de Matamoros
Acatlán
PUEBLA
Tehuacán
Orizaba
Córdoba
Veracruz
Tierra Blanca
San Andrés Tuxtla
Bahía de Campeche
GULF OF MEXICO
Paraíso
Villahermosa
Minatitlán
Coatzacoalcos
Acayucán
Tuxtepec
VERACRUZ
Isthmus of Tehuantepec
Tuxtla & San Cristóbal
Río Coatzcoalcos
Río El Corte
Huajuapan de León
Baja
Coixtlahuaca
Santiago Apoala
Teposcolula
Yanhuitlan
Nochixtlán
MIXTECA
Tlaxiaco
Huamelulpan
Alta
SIERRA MADRE DE OAXACA
SIERRA NORTE
Ixtlán
Benito Juárez
El Tule
Oaxaca
Dainzú
Yagul
Zacatepec
Monte Albán
Mitla
Ayutla
Hierve El Agua
Tlacolula
Zaachila
Ocotlán
VALLES CENTRALES
SIERRA MADRE DEL SUR
Río Verde & Río Grande
OAXACA
Santiago Laollaga
Juchitán
Guiengola
Tehuantepec
Salina Cruz
Arriaga
Tonalá
Paredón
Puerto Arista
Tapachula
Acapulco
Ometepec
Punta Maldonado
Pinotepa Nacional
Río Grande
Manialtepec
Chacahua
Zapotalito
Puerto Escondido
Río Colotepec
San José del Pacifico
San Antonio
Pochutla
Huatulco
Mazunte
San Augustinillo
Zipolite
Puerto Ángel
PACIFIC OCEAN
PARQUE NACIONAL LAGUNAS DE CHACAHUA
Gulfo de Tehuantepec
Hwy 190
Hwy 135-D
Hwy 131
Hwy 175
Hwy 147
Hwy 185
Hwy 125
Hwy 200
N
0
100 km

The fastest route to Oaxaca **from Mexico City** is the 465-kilometre toll-road **Hwy-135**, which links to the Mexico City–Puebla–Córdoba autopista and takes only five hours. On the way you can stop at the spa town of **Tehuacán** or explore the **Mixteca**, one of the state's most intriguing regions and home to some of the finest colonial buildings in the country.

To reach Oaxaca **from Acapulco**, it's probably quickest to go through Mexico City, though there are frequent buses down the Pacific coast to **Puerto Escondido** or Pochutla, the service town for **Puerto Ángel**. However, if you are travelling along the Pacific coast, it seems a pity to miss out on the region's excellent beaches just to get to Oaxaca quickly.

Tehuacán

If you decide to travel via the autopista from Mexico City to Oaxaca, the only place that merits a stop as you speed along is **TEHUACÁN**, the source of a good percentage of the bottled mineral water (Peñafiel, now owned by Dr. Pepper Snapple Group) consumed throughout Mexico. It's the second largest town in the state of Puebla, but despite some rapid development precipitated by the manufacture of stone-washed denim here in the 1990s, it still feels like an old-fashioned spa town: relaxed, easy-paced, temperate in every sense of the word and with a centre full of buildings from the early twentieth century. The tiled, arcade-fronted house on the main plaza, with its Moorish flourishes, was obviously designed with Vichy or Evian in mind and bears a plaque to Señor Don Joaquim Pita, who first put the water here in bottles. Take a look at the underside of the colonnade for highly graphic murals depicting the five regions that make up Tehuacán district. A more pedestrian introduction to the region fills the halls of the **Museo del Valle de Tehuacán** (Tues–Sun 10am–5pm; M$37; ⓣ238/382-4045), in the elegant Ex-Convento de Carmen at Reforma Norte 200, which features a bright tiled dome that dominates the skyline in this part of town. A tiny collection of prehistoric relics shores up the thinly illustrated story of maize in Mesoamerica and particularly in the Tehuacán valley, which was the first place where the crop was truly cultivated (rather than simply harvested) some six or seven thousand years ago – ample evidence that this was one of the earliest settled areas in Mexico.

All this can be seen in a couple of hours, but if you decide to stay in town you can fill the time by heading out to the **springs** on the outskirts to sample the clean-tasting water. You might also take a dip at Balneario San Lorenzo (Tues–Sun 6.30am–6pm; M$35; ⓣ238/371-3227), a large complex of sun-warmed pools (including one Olympic-sized affair) that draws from local springs and is known for its relaxation-inducing high lithium content. Catch a bus from the Autobuses Unidos terminal to San Lorenzo Teotipílco, a suburb 5km west of the centre (the spa is at Av 5 de Febrero no. 301). Alternatively, you can pamper yourself with a *temazcal* (a pre-Hispanic steam bath), sauna and massage at the pleasant *Hotel Aldea del Bazar* (ⓣ427/272-1535, ⓦwww.aldeadelbazar.com; ④), a five-minute taxi ride from the centre of town at Calzada Adolfo López Mateos 3351.

Practicalities

Most long-distance **buses** arrive at the ADO station on Independencia, two blocks west of the plaza. Second-class buses from Mexico City, Oaxaca and elsewhere arrive at the Autobuses Unidos station near the junction of 5 Oriente and 5 Sur, on the opposite side of the centre.

The most comfortable **place to stay** in the centre of Tehuacán is the *Hotel México*, Independencia at Reforma Norte, one block west of the plaza (Ⓣ238/382-2419; ④), which has a pool, parking and clean, modern, well-appointed rooms. Budget hotels can be found near the plaza. **Banks** (with ATMs) and other services are mostly on Reforma.

Oaxaca

The city of **OAXACA** sprawls across a grand expanse of deep-set valley, 1600m above sea level. Its colour, folklore, numerous fiestas, indigenous markets and magnificent colonial centre make it one of the country's most rewarding destinations. The city has recovered from an outbreak of violence in 2006, when teacher protests escalated into bloody conflict, and it remains a safe destination, though tensions do persist (see p.868).

Once central to the **Mixtec** and **Zapotec** civilizations, the city had a limited role during the early years of the Spanish Conquest. **Cortés**, attracted by the area's natural beauty, created the title of Marqués del Valle de Oaxaca, and until the Revolution his descendants held vast estates hereabouts. For practical purposes, though, Oaxaca was of little interest to the Spaniards, with no mineral wealth and, due to the rugged mountain terrain, no real agricultural value (though coffee was grown). This meant that the **indigenous** population was largely left to get on with life and did not have to deal with much outside influence beyond the interference of a proselytizing Church. Nevertheless, by 1796 it had become the third largest city in Nueva España, thanks to the export of cochineal and, later, textile manufacturing. An earthquake destroyed much of the city in 1854; another quake in 1931 hampered the slow rebuilding process.

Today Oaxaca is well on its way to becoming an industrial city – the population is over 250,000, the streets are choked and noisy and a thin veil of smog often enshrouds the valley – yet it remains easy to navigate. In the **colonial centre**, thanks to strict building regulations, the city's provincial charm is hardly affected and just about everything can be reached on foot. Oaxaca is widely seen as the artistic centre of Mexico, with several state-run and private galleries, craft and jewellery masterclasses and regular exhibitions. You'll also see the state's most famous son, **Benito Juárez**, commemorated everywhere in Oaxaca, a privilege not shared by **Porfirio Díaz**, the second most famous Oaxaqueño, whose dictatorship most people have chosen to forget.

Surrounding Oaxaca is some extraordinary topography, making an impressive backdrop to the city skyline at sunset. The Sierra Madre del Sur enters Oaxaca state from the west, while the Sierra Madre de Oaxaca runs down from Mexico's central volcanic belt. The two ranges meet in the centre of the state and between them, converging in Oaxaca city, lie the three **Valles Centrales**.

Arrival

Oaxaca has two main **bus stations**; both are around 2km from the centre, upwards of twenty minutes' walk. The first-class terminal (with 24-hour guardería) is on Calzada Niños Héroes de Chapultepec, northeast of the centre; from here your best bet is to find a taxi (around M$35). If you prefer to walk, turn left along the main road for about three blocks to Juárez, then left again for ten blocks to Independencia and right three blocks to the central Plaza de la Constitución. Once you reach Juárez you can also pick up **city buses** (M$4.50). The second-class terminal (guardería 6am–9.30pm; M$7) is west of the centre by the Mercado de

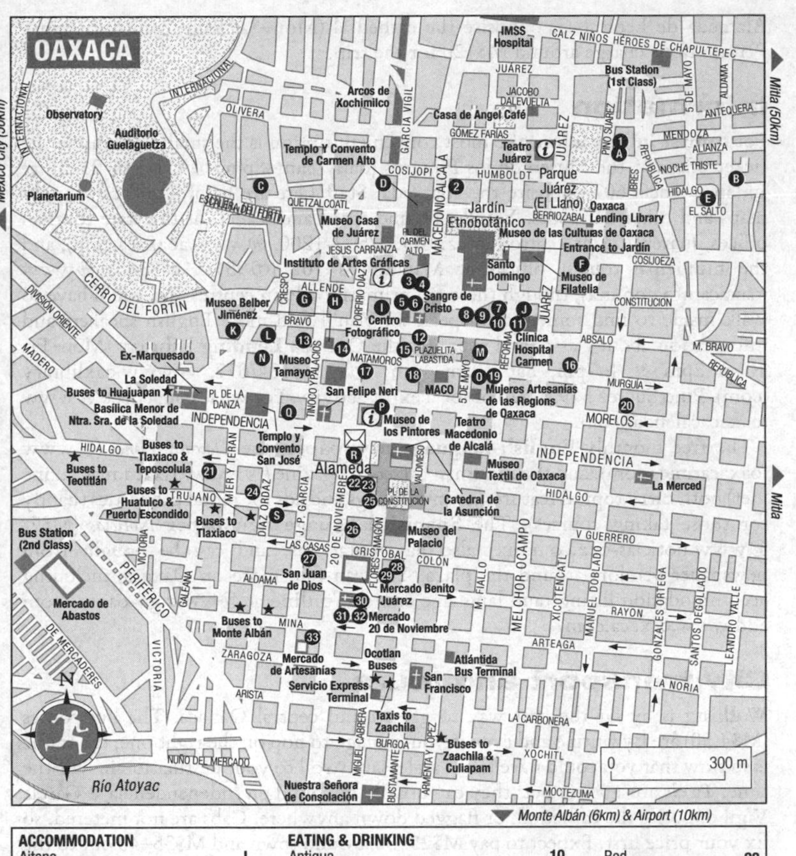

ACCOMMODATION

Aitana	L
Camino Real Oaxaca	M
Casa Arnel	B
Casa de las Bugambilias	J
Casa Cid de León	P
La Casa de los Milagros	N
Casa Oaxaca	I
Las Golondrinas	G
Hostal Casa del Sótano	H
Hostal Pochón	C
Hostel Don Nino	A
Hotel Azucenas	K
Hotel Cazomalli	E
Las Mariposas	F
Monte Albán	R
Paulina Youth Hostel	S
Posada del Centro	Q
Posada Don Mario	D
Principal	O

EATING & DRINKING

Antigua	10
Bar del Jardín	25
Biznaga	3
Café Alex	24
Café Gecko	9
La Casa de la Abuela	23
Casa Oaxaca	1
Cenadería Libres Tlayudas Doña Martha	20
Como Agua Pa' Chocolate	22
La Crêpe	12
Los Danzantes	6
El Manantial Vegetariano	13
Maria Bonita	2
Marco Polo	1
Mayordomo	31
La Olla	11
Cafe de Oaxaca Orgánica	7
Pizza Nostrana	4
El Teatro Culinario	5
Red	28
Le Soledad	32

NIGHTLIFE

La Barcina	21
El Borgo Jazz	19
Candela	16
Casa del Mezcal	29
La Cucaracha	14
La Divina	8
La Farola	26
El Famoso	27
Freebar	18
Mesoal Don Ageve	30
Musical Tobala	33
La Nueva Babel	17
La Tentación	15

Abastos. Smaller minibus services tend to have their own terminals south of Calle Mina, a short walk from the plaza.

From the **airport** (Aeropuerto Internacional Xoxocotlán), around 10km south of the city, a *colectivo* service, Transportación Terrestre Aeropuerto (ⓣ951/514-4350), will drop you right by the plaza for about M$44. On leaving, you should buy tickets in advance wherever possible – they're sold at the company's office at

Alameda de León 1-G, opposite the cathedral (Mon–Sat 9am–2pm & 5–8pm). Private **taxis** charge around M$120 for the trip.

Information

For **tourist information**, the most convenient option is the small desk inside the ticket office of the Museo de los Pinteros (daily 8am–8pm; Ⓣ951/516-0123), at Independencia 607 opposite the Alameda. Staff here are helpful and can supply maps and other handouts. You'll also find maps and leaflets at the state tourism offices, Juárez 703 (at Teatro Juárez; Ⓣ951/502-1200, Ⓦwww.aoaxaca.com), and the municipal tourist offices at Matamoros 102 (Ⓣ951/516-8365, Ⓦwww.oaxacainfo.gob.mx), though these are primarily admin centres and you'll have to walk inside to find someone to speak to. You'll find more English speakers and information about classes and events at the **Oaxaca Lending Library** (Mon–Fri 10am–2pm & 4–7pm, Sat 10am–1pm; Ⓣ951/518-7077, Ⓦwww.oaxlibrary.com), Pino Suárez 519, a hub of local expat activity. For what's on, check Ⓦwww.oaxacacalendar.com.

The free monthly **English-language newspaper**, the *Oaxaca Times* (Ⓦwww.oaxacatimes.com), and the monthly *Oaxaca* magazine (Ⓦwww.oaxaca.magazzine.net) both carry topical features, events listings and ads for rental properties (handy for those taking courses). The **Spanish-language newspaper** *Noticias* (M$7; Ⓦwww.noticias-oax.com.mx) also has rental ads, and can be bought from newspaper vendors around the plaza. You can find more on Oaxaca, including accommodation listings and language courses, **online** at Ⓦwww.go-oaxaca.com and www.oaxaca.com.

City transport and tours

Walking is by far the best way to get around central Oaxaca. The bus routes (M$4.50) are Byzantine and even if you manage to hop on the right one, the traffic is so slow that you could have taken a pleasant stroll to your destination in half the time. **Taxis** are a better bet; they can usually be found on Independencia at García Vígil opposite the cathedral, or flagged down anywhere. Cabs are not metered, so fix your price first. Expect to pay M$25–30 around town and M$35–40 out to the first-class bus terminal.

Alternatively, several tour operators **rent bicycles** and run bike tours: try Bicicletas Pedro Martínez (Ⓣ951/514-5935, Ⓦwww.bicicletaspedromartinez.com) at Aldama 418 inside Mesón la Brisa, or Bicicletas Bravo, García Vigil 406 (Ⓣ951/516-0953, Ⓦwww.bikeoaxaca.com). Rentals start at around M$30/hr, while one-day tours start at M$1100.

The Oaxaca Lending Library (see above) organizes excellent English-speaking guided **walking tours** of Oaxaca's churches (Tues & Sat 10am; M$95). Day trips to Monte Albán and nearby villages (such as El Tule) cost around M$180; operators include Cantera Tours, Constitución 100-7 (Ⓣ951/516-0512) and Turismo El Convento de Oaxaca (Ⓣ951/516-1806, Ⓦwww.oaxacaexperts.com) at the *Camino Real*. Rancho Buenavista, San Pedro Ixtlahuaca (Ⓣ901/228-2951, Ⓦwww.ranchobuenavista.com.mx), organizes more adventurous hiking, mountain-biking (from M$400) and rock-climbing (from M$600) expeditions. Expediciones Sierra Norte, M. Bravo 210-I (Ⓣ951/514-8271, Ⓦwww.sierranorte.org.mx), and Tierraventura, Abasolo 217 (Ⓣ951/501-1363, Ⓦwww.tierraventura.com), lead treks to the Sierra Norte mountains outside Oaxaca City.

Accommodation

The cheapest **hotels** tend to be **south of Independencia**, especially between the old market and Calle Trujano, although they are dwindling in number as more upscale hotel offerings pop up in the touristy zone near the **plaza** and **north of Independencia**. In this area, both prices and quality tend to be higher, though there are some surprisingly good-value establishments. In general, **rates** tend to drop by ten to thirty percent outside the Christmas, Semana Santa, July and August high seasons. It's often worth asking for a *descuenta* (discount) – the worst they can say is no.

Around the Plaza de la Constitución

Monte Albán Alameda de León 1 ⓣ951/516-2777. Beautiful, if cavernous, colonial-style hotel opposite the cathedral. Excellent value, given the location, with some lovely external rooms and gloomier internal ones. Nightly *folklórico* dancing takes place in the main hall. ❺

Posada del Centro Independencia 403 ⓣ951/516-1874. Pleasant rooms around a tiled courtyard, most with shared bath and some with private bath; a good deal, although front rooms face a heavily trafficked street. ❹

North of Independencia

Aitana Crespo 313 ⓣ951/514-3788, ⓦwww.hotelaitanaoaxaca.com.mx. With more attention to detail than most hotels in this range, the well-managed *Aitana* has fine rooms with cable TV, safe, free wi-fi, coffee-makers, fan and spacious bathrooms with shower, bathtub and hairdryer, all grouped around a leafy courtyard. There are panoramic views from the rooftop terrace, which has sun loungers and tables. It's five blocks west of Santo Domingo. ❻

Camino Real Oaxaca 5 de Mayo 300 ⓣ951/516-0611, ⓦwww.camino-real-oaxaca.com. Oaxaca's priciest hotel (from M$3000 a night), in the beautifully converted sixteenth-century Ex-Convento de Santa Catalina. Candles light the way through arcaded, flower-filled courtyards to characterful, if medievally dimensioned, rooms and idyllic gardens. If a night's stay is beyond your budget, a lingering coffee or cocktail in the courtyard is a worthy substitute. Take a tour of the hotel Wed–Fri 5pm (40min; free). ❾

Casa Arnel Aldama 404 ⓣ951/515-2856, ⓦwww.casaarnel.com.mx. Between the plaza and first-class bus station (within walking distance of both), *Casa Arnel* is a popular family-run place. Reasonably priced rooms (with or without bath – some smaller than others) sit around a leafy courtyard. There's a rooftop bar, where breakfast (additional cost) is served, internet, laundry and a library; they also offer tours in Oaxaca and outlying areas. Newer rooms and apartments (around M$4000 a month) lie across the street. ❹

Casa de las Bugambilias Reforma 402 ⓣ951/516-1165, ⓦwww.lasbugambilias.com. Peaceful and central colonial B&B beside *La Olla* café, just south of Santo Domingo. Eight comfortable, airy rooms (individually decorated with work by local artists) with private bath. Rates include breakfast. ❻

Casa Cid de León Morelos 602 ⓣ951/514-1893, ⓦwww.casaciddeleon.com. With just four suites, all beautifully and idiosyncratically restored by owner, poet and artist-in-residence Leticia Rodríguez, this is one of Mexico's most memorable hotels. Each spacious room is crammed with antiques, books and trinkets – a regal, timeless aura pervades every artfully conceived nook and cranny. There is a lovely terrace where breakfast is served, and the staff are charming and efficient. ❾

La Casa de los Milagros Matamoros 500 ⓣ951/501-2262, ⓦwww.casadelosmilagros.com. Justifiably a mid-range favourite, this small, family-run, colonial hotel has just three immaculate, individually styled rooms in a dream home setting. There's a beautiful communal kitchen, a dining room and a patio – the "Ángeles" room even has its own waterfall. ❼

Casa Oaxaca García Vigil 407 ⓣ951/514-4173, ⓦwww.casa-oaxaca.com. If you are going to splurge, *Casa Oaxaca*, the personal favourite of Gabriel García Marquéz, is the place. Seven tastefully serene, spacious rooms are set around a pristine white courtyard with a tiled pool and sumptuous restaurant. With an emphasis on intimacy and tranquillity, the service is faultless and Oaxacan artistry is woven through every immaculate detail. Delicious breakfast included. ❾

Las Golondrinas Tinoco y Palacios 411 ⓣ951/514-3298, ⓦwww.hotellasgolondrinas.com.mx. Tidy, pristine rooms in an old colonial house, each with separate reception area and bathroom. The main draw is the gorgeous, flower-filled courtyard where breakfast is served. Very tranquil with a distinctly local flavour. ❹

Hostal Casa del Sótano Tinoco y Palacios 414 ⓣ951/516-2494, ⓦwww.hoteldelsotano.net. Just two blocks from Santo Domingo, this smart, modern hotel retains a traditional feel with folk-art flourishes and comfy rooms, all with a/c. Earth tones and dark wood evoke fancy monks' quarters – some are very small, so ask to see a few first. There's an inviting terrace café and a lovely art gallery on the premises, both run by the same friendly character. Basic breakfast is included. ❺

Hostal Pochón Callejón del Carmen 102, between Tinoco y Palacios and Crespo ⓣ951/516-1322, ⓦwww.hostalpochon.com. Close to Santo Domingo, this is the best hostel in town. Dorms (for 2 and 4 people; M$120), double rooms and shared bathrooms are all surgically clean, and the colourful patio and common areas have an inviting traveller hangout vibe. There is cable TV, free internet, cheap international calls, a substantial breakfast and efficient, welcoming staff. Discounts for group and online bookings. ❸

Hostel Don Nino Pino Suárez 804 ⓣ951/515-8985, ⓦwww.hosteldonnino.com. Stylish hostel well worth the slight walk out of the centre, with dorm beds for M$150 plus breakfast, hot showers, cable TV room and free internet. Also offers comfortable doubles. ❺

Hotel Azucenas M. Aranda 203 at Matamoros ⓣ951/514-7918, ⓦwww.hotelazucenas.com. Another gorgeous colonial mansion with ten luxurious rooms and a spread of welcoming extras; morning coffee in your room, buffet breakfast, self-serve rooftop bar and wi-fi. ❹

Hotel Cazomalli Salto 104, near Aldama ⓣ951/513-3513, ⓦwww.hotelcazomalli.com. Quaint little posada with comfy rooms in a colonial house with a gorgeous rooftop breakfast area. ❹

Las Mariposas Pino Suárez 517 ⓣ951/515-5854, ⓦwww.lasmariposas.com.mx. Delightful colonial-style hotel with spacious, thoughtful rooms, some with kitchenettes and all with private bathrooms, clustered around a vibrant courtyard complete with flowers and fish-filled fountains. The staff are very helpful and happy to provide a wealth of information on tours. Very popular with long-stay Spanish students. Breakfast and internet access are included. ❹

Posada Don Mario Cosijopí 219 ⓣ951/514-2012, ⓦwww.posadadonmario.com. The house where Rufino Tamayo, Oaxaca's most famous contemporary painter, was born is now a sociable hostel popular with language students, with bright, cheerful public areas and clean, if rather gloomy, double rooms for around M$300 per night, or M$350 with private bath (singles M$220–270). Dorm beds are M$120 and breakfast is included. Internet access and tour information available. ❸

Principal 5 de Mayo 208 ⓣ951/516-2535. Colonial-style choice with a central courtyard and friendly owner. Simple, functional rooms with private bathrooms grouped around a lovely garden suggest a pricier place. Rooms to the rear are quieter. Good value considering the colonial flourishes and location. ❹

South of Independencia

Paulina Youth Hostel Trujano 321 ⓣ951/516-2005, ⓦwww.paulinahostel.com. Revamped hostel, ultra-clean and white with bargain dorms from M$150. There are separate dorm rooms for men and women, clean bathrooms and some private rooms (❸). There's also a small garden with fountains, beer for sale in the lobby and a rooftop lounge.

The City

Simply being in Oaxaca, wandering through its streets and absorbing its life, is an experience, especially if you happen to catch the city during a **fiesta** (they happen all the time – the most important are listed on p.671). Nonetheless, you should definitely take time out to visit the **Museo de las Culturas** and the **Museo Tamayo**, the **markets** (craft shopping in Oaxaca is among the best in the entire country), the churches of **Santo Domingo** and **La Soledad**, and to get out to **Monte Albán** and **Mitla**. While you could certainly cover the city's highlights in a leisurely two days, it's easy to stay for much longer.

Around Plaza de la Constitución

Plaza de la Constitución, closed to traffic and surrounded by *portales* (arcades) sheltering languid cafés, sees a steady stream of beggars, hawkers, business people, tourists and locals. It continues to be Oaxaca's kaleidoscopic central reference point, and features some of the best free entertainment in the city – especially displays of music, song and dance. On Sundays and many weekday evenings you'll find a band playing in the centre, or else a performance or exhibition opposite the cathedral. On the south side of the square, the Neoclassical former Palacio de Gobioern has been transformed into the fancy **Museo del Palacio** (Tues–Sat 9.30am–7pm, Sun 9.30am–5pm; free), an ambitious project that symbolizes the earnest post-2006 efforts to rebuild the city. This is essentially an ethnographical museum, albeit presented in a very modern and interactive manner, with hands-on exhibits and all sorts of displays. Starting with the evolution of life on Earth, the museum covers the development of human society across the planet (with reference to Oaxaca), but everything is labelled in Spanish only. It's worth wandering in to view the murals by Arturo García Bustos in any case; painted between 1985 and 1987 they smother the main staircases of the courtyard. The first mural depicts the country's history: at the top are the revolutionary Ricardo Flores Magón (left), Benito Juárez and his wife Margarita Maza (centre) and José María Morelos (right). Porfirio Díaz appears below Juárez, with a sword. At the bottom right, Vincente Guerrero's execution at Cuilapam is shown. The left wall shows ancient Mitla and is supposed to evoke the native roots of the country.

You can reach the **Catedral de la Asunción** at the northwest corner of the square by crossing to the Alameda de León, a more diminutive version of the plaza. Begun in 1553, the cathedral wasn't completed until the eighteenth century, thanks to several earthquakes. Since then it's been repeatedly pillaged and restored; as a result, despite a fine Baroque facade, it's not the most enchanting Oaxaca church. It is impressively large, though, with a heavy *coro* (choir) blocking the aisle in the heart of the church and a ring of chapels dedicated to various saints surrounding the nave. These days, most of the services are held in the Capilla del Señor del Rayo, centred on a calvary embellished with gold votives, at the far end of the nave near the altar. Just across from the cathedral, the **Museo de los Pintores Oaxaqueños** (Tues–Sun 10am–8pm; M$20; Ⓣ951/516-5645) at Independencia 107 shows mainly temporary exhibits of modern Oaxacan painters, and the quality is usually very high.

Along Independencia

Walk east along Independencia for a couple of blocks from the cathedral to arrive at the **Teatro Macedonio de Alcalá**, built in 1909 in the French style fashionable during the dictatorship of Porfirio Díaz. Still operating as a theatre and concert hall, it's typical of the grandiose public buildings that sprang up across Mexico in the early twentieth century – behind the *belle époque* exterior, the interior (if you can see it – try going to a show, or sneaking in before one), is a magnificent swath of white marble and red plush.

Just around the corner, the **Museo Textil de Oaxaca** (Wed–Mon 10am–8pm; free, donations requested; Ⓣ951/501-1617, Ⓦwww.museotextildeoaxaca.org) at Hildalgo 917 is a showcase for the state's high-quality textile traditions, though it also has temporary exhibitions of textiles from all over the world. Opened in 2008, largely via funds supplied by Alfredo Harp Helú, the ex-Banamex owner turned philanthropist, the museum occupies an artfully renovated eighteenth-century mansion.

North of the Plaza de la Constitución

Heading north from the Plaza de la Constitución, Valdivieso crosses Independencia to become **Macedonio Alcalá**, the city's pedestrianized shopping street, home to the best, and most expensive, Mexican and Oaxacan crafts. This is the place to come for exquisitely intricate silver designs and finely executed, imaginative textiles: check the quality of the goods here before venturing out to the villages where many of the crafts are made, and where the selection tends to include pieces of varying quality and lower prices. Strolling north from the plaza along Alcalá you'll come to **MACO**, the **Museo de Arte Contemporáneo** (daily except Tues 10.30am–8pm; M$30; ⓣ915/514-1055, ⓦwww.museomaco.com), housed in a seventeenth-century building widely regarded as Cortés's house although actually built after his death. Founded in 1992, the museum hosts temporary exhibits of national and regional contemporary art that can include anything from collections of Zapotec folk art and political caricatures to video installations focusing on the impact of Mexican immigration to the US. It should reopen at the end of 2010, after a comprehensive renovation (until then only a couple of galleries are open). One block west of Alcalá at Bravo 116 you'll find more art at the **Centro Fotográfico Alvarez Bravo** (daily except Tues 10am–8pm; free; ⓣ951/516-9800, ⓦwww.cfmab.blogspot.com), established by painter Francisco Toledo, which has three exhibition rooms displaying historical and contemporary photographs, plus an excellent reference library.

Santo Domingo de Guzmán

Two blocks further up Alcalá from MACO stands one of the real highlights of Oaxaca, the church of **Santo Domingo de Guzmán** (daily 7am–1pm & 4–8pm; no sightseeing during Mass; free), consecrated in 1611. One of the finest examples of Mexican Baroque, this extravaganza is elaborately carved and decorated both inside and out, the external walls (10m thick in some places) are solid and earthquake-proof, the interior extraordinarily rich. Parts were damaged during the Reform Wars and the Revolution – especially the chapels, pressed into service as stables – but most of the interior was restored during the 1950s. Notice especially the great gilded main altarpiece, and, on the underside of the raised choir above you as you enter, the family tree of Felix de Guzmán, father of St Dominic (the founder of the Dominican Order), in the form of a vine with leafy branches and tendrils, busts of leading Dominicans and a figure of the Virgin right at the top.

▲ Santo Domingo de Guzmán, Oaxaca

Most striking of all, the church drips with white and gold leaf throughout, beautifully set off in the afternoon by the light that floods in through the window. Looking back from the altar you can appreciate the relief scenes high on the walls, the biblical events depicted in the barrel roof and the ceiling of the choir, a vision of the heavenly hierarchy with gilded angels swirling in rings around God. The adjoining **Capilla de la Virgen del Rosario** (completed in 1720) is also richly painted and carved: the Virgin takes pride of place in another stunning altarpiece, all the more startlingly intense in such a relatively small space.

Museo de las Culturas de Oaxaca and around

Next to the church, the old Convento de Santo Domingo has been restored to house the absorbing **Museo de las Culturas de Oaxaca** (Tues–Sun 10am–7pm, last entry 6.15pm; M$51, plus M$30 camera). If you don't read Spanish, it's worth renting the M$50 audio-guide at the entrance to make the most of your visit.

Construction of the *convento* began in 1572, and the church held its first Mass in 1608; from then until 1812 it was occupied by Dominican friars. During the Revolution, the building served as barracks for the Mexican army. The damage inflicted during this period wasn't restored until the 1990s, when the exhibits were installed. The museum traces the history of Oaxaca in an expansive and elaborately executed labyrinth of galleries that hold displays detailing the pre-Hispanic period through to the present day. The archeological finds defy hyperbole, especially the true highlight here: sala 3, dedicated to the magnificent **Mixtec jewellery** discovered in Tomb 7 at Monte Albán (see p.635), including a couple of superb gold masks and breastplates. This lavish treasure trove constitutes a substantial proportion of all known pre-Hispanic gold, since anything the conquistadors found they melted down. The museum also owns smaller gold pieces, as well as objects in a wide variety of precious materials – mother-of-pearl, obsidian, turquoise, amber and jet among them. The final galleries, in typically idealistic style, are dedicated to the pluralism of modern Mexico; an enlightening video shows members of each of the state's fifteen indigenous peoples speaking their own language.

Through the museum windows you'll catch tantalizing views of the mountains, as well as another hidden artistic masterpiece – the cactus garden, or **Jardín Etnobotánico** (visits by signing up in advance for a guided tour only; English tours Tues, Thurs & Sat 11am–1pm, M$100; Spanish tours Mon–Sat 10am, noon & 5pm, M$50). Beyond the garden's sensual appeal – specifically an ornate collection of orchids and plumeria – the tours are also extremely illuminating. The grounds preserve species native to Oaxaca and provide information on plants and insects, such as the *cochinilla* that dwells inside certain varieties of cactus and secretes a substance that is used to produce natural dyes for textiles. The entrance is at Reforma and Constitución. Oaxaca is also the proud mother of Mexico's only stamp museum, the **Museo de Filatelia**, housed in a sober mansion near the garden entrance at Reforma 504 (Tues–Sun 10am–8pm; free). It has a respectable permanent exhibition of Mexican stamps, letters, philatelic instruments and seals.

Across the road from the Museo de las Culturas at Alcalá 507, the **Instituto de Artes Gráficas** (daily except Sat–Fri 9.30am–8pm; donation) is another one of many cultural centres in the state sponsored by painter Francisco Toledo. Established in 1988, it displays changing exhibits of works by nationally renowned artists including José Guadalupe Posada, Rodolfo Nieto, Vicente Rojo and Toledo himself. It's worth popping in just to amble around the rooms of what was once a rather grand colonial house and to spend an hour in the excellent art library and idyllic reading room. There are also evening music recitals.

North along García Vigil

The **Museo Casa de Juárez** (Tues–Sat 10am–7pm; M$37, use of video camera M$35 extra), a block to the west of the Museo de las Culturas at García Vigil 609 (and opposite the fortress-like Temple y Convento de Carmen Alto, now mostly government offices), is where Oaxaca's most famous son, **Benito Juárez** (see box below), lived between 1818 and 1828. The house belonged to bookbinder Antonio Salanueva, who virtually adopted the young Benito after hiring him, providing him with a crucial leg-up in Mexican society. The renovated house contains a small collection of the young Zapotec's possessions along with seminal historical documents. Wander through the kitchen, bedroom and dining area exhibits to get an idea of what life must have been like

Benito Juárez

Despite the poor judgement he exhibited in his later years, **Benito Juárez** ranks among Mexico's greatest national heroes. He was the towering figure of nineteenth-century Mexican politics, and his maxim – "*El respeto al derecho ajeno es la paz*" ("Respect for the rights of others is peace") – has long been a rallying cry for liberals. A **Zapotec**, he strove against nineteenth-century social prejudices and, through four terms as president, successfully reformed many of the worst remnants of Spanish colonialism, earning a reputation for honesty and fair dealing.

Juárez was born in **San Pablo Guelatao** in 1806. His parents died when he was 3, and he grew up speaking only Zapotec; at the age of 12 he was adopted by priests and moved to **Oaxaca**, where he began to study for the priesthood, which included learning Spanish. Turning his talents to law, he provided his legal services to impoverished villagers free of charge, and by 1831 had earned a seat on Oaxaca's municipal council, lending his voice to a disenfranchised people. Juárez rose through the ranks of the city council to become **state governor** from 1847 to 1852, on a liberal ticket geared towards improving education and releasing the country from the economic and social stranglehold of the Church and the aristocracy. In 1853, the election of a conservative government under Santa Anna forced him into eighteen months of exile in the US.

Liberal victory in 1855 enabled Juárez to return to Mexico as minister of justice and give his name to a law abolishing special courts for the military and clergy. His support was instrumental in passing the **Ley Lerdo**, which effectively nationalized the Church's huge holdings, and bills legalizing civil marriage and guaranteeing religious freedom. In 1858, President Ignacio Comonfort was ousted by conservatives enraged by these reforms, and Juárez, as **the head of the Supreme Court**, had a legal claim to the presidency. However, he lacked the military might to hold Mexico City and retired to Veracruz, returning three years later, victorious in the War of Reform, as constitutionally elected **president** on the basis of his attempts to reduce the power of the Church. Stymied by an intractable Congress and empty coffers, Juárez suspended all national debt repayments for two years from July 1861. To protect their investments, the British, Spanish and French sent their armies in, but when it became apparent that Napoleon III had designs on the control of Mexico, the others pulled out, leaving France to install Hapsburg **Archduke Maximilian** as puppet emperor. Juárez fled again, this time to Ciudad Juárez (originally called Paso del Norte) on the US border, but by 1867 Napoleon III had buckled under Mexican resistance and US pressure, and Juárez was able to return to the capital and his army to round up and execute the hapless Maximilian.

Juárez was returned as president in the 1867 elections but alienated much of his support through attempts to use Congress to amend the constitution. Nevertheless, he secured another term in the 1870 elections, spending two more years trying unsuccessfully to maintain peace before dying of a heart attack in 1872.

for the middle class in early nineteenth-century Oaxaca (though nothing is original to the house).

Four blocks north, shadowing García Vigil beyond Cosijopí, the **Arcos de Xochimilco** are remnants of the eighteenth-century aqueduct of San Felipe. The surrounding streets are a pleasant place to stroll with multi-coloured, low-slung, colonial-style houses surrounded by crumbling walls draped in bougainvillea, hole-in-the-wall taco joints, snoozing dogs, street lanterns and giant cacti. On Fridays and Saturdays, check out the small **organic market** (9.30am–4pm) at Santo Tomas Xochimilco church, north of Niños Héroes or beneath the arches in the Parque el Pochote at García Vigil 817/819 (check with the tourist desk for the latest location).

Northwest of the Plaza de la Constitución

Northwest of the plaza at Morelos 503 (three blocks west of Alcalá), lies the **Museo Rufino Tamayo** (Mon & Wed–Sat 10am–2pm & 4–7pm, Sun 10am–3pm; M$35), a private collection of pre-Hispanic artefacts gathered by the Oaxaqueño abstract artist Rufino Tamayo (1899–1991), set in an attractive house that dates from 1902. Rather than try to explain the archeological significance of its contents, the collection is deliberately laid out as an art museum, with the focus on aesthetic form, and includes some truly beautiful items from all over Mexico, with pottery and carvings from pre-Classic civilizations. Aztec, Maya and western indigenous cultures all feature strongly, though there's surprisingly little that is Mixtec or Zapotec.

One block north, at Matamoros 307, the **Museo Belber Jiménez** (Mon–Fri 10am–2pm & 4–6pm, Sat 10am–2pm; M$20; ⓣ951/514-5095, ⓦwww.museobelberjimenez.org) is Oaxaca's newest museum and a worthy introduction to the region's artistic heritage. Set around a small courtyard, the galleries here display the private collection of renowned jeweller Francisco Jiménez and wife Ellen Belber, a treasure trove that includes some magnificent gold Mixtec jewellery, colonial chains and necklaces and a fine collection of twentieth-century silver work by some of Mexico's great masters, including American expats Frederick Davis and William Spratling. There's also a selection of Oaxacan folk art, from rugs and traditional clothing to pottery and lacquer chests. Pride of place goes to the necklace given to Frida Kahlo by Diego Rivera in 1937, engraved with the words "Amor", and a woollen Mexican flag, presented to President Díaz on a visit to Oaxaca.

Around the corner at J.P. García and Independencia, the church of **San Felipe Neri** is mostly Baroque, with a richly decorated proliferation of statues on the plateresque facade. It's the interior decor, though, that really makes it interesting. The church was completed in 1773 and later used as barracks during the Revolution. By the 1920s it badly needed to be repainted, which it was – in an incongruous Art Nouveau style. The building's other claim to fame is that it's the church in which Benito Juárez and Margarita Maza were married in 1843.

Basílica Menor de Nuestra Señora de la Soledad

Not far to the west of San Felipe Neri along Independencia, the **Basílica Menor de Nuestra Señora de la Soledad**, built between 1682 and 1690, is one of Mexico's most important religious sites. It contains a statue of the Virgen de la Soledad, Oaxaca's patron saint since 1909, one of the most revered images of Mary in the country.

The story goes that in the early colonial period (dates vary), a statue of the Virgin was mysteriously found in the backpack of a mule en route to Guatemala; some versions claim that the Virgin herself miraculously appeared. The basilica was consequently constructed in her honour (the rock where this miracle is supposed to have happened is now surrounded by an iron cage on your right as you enter the church). The diamond-encrusted crown that adorns the statue of the Virgin inside the basilica is a replica of the original, which was stolen during the 1980s. The sumptuously decorated church, built in the late seventeenth century but with a more recent facade, is set on a small plaza surrounded by other buildings associated with the Virgin's cult. It's a peaceful spot to watch Oaxaqueño life unfold over an ice cream or sorbet, both of which are sold in a beguiling variety of flavours at a cluster of stands – try *tuna* (cactus) and mescal in combination. The adjoining Plaza de la Danza is the setting of outdoor concerts, *folklórico* performances and specialist craft markets. Ramshackle stalls behind the ice-cream vendors sell brightly coloured religious icons. Just at the back of the church courtyard there's the small **Museo Religioso de la Soledad** (daily except Wed 10am–2pm & 4–6pm, Wed 10am–2pm only; donation only) devoted to the cult. It's a bizarre jumble of junk and treasure – native costumes displayed on permed blonde 1950s mannequins; ex-voto paintings giving thanks for miracles and cures – among which the junk is generally far more interesting.

South of the Plaza de la Constitución

The **markets** are the main reason most travellers venture south of the plaza. Traditionally, **Saturday** is market day, and although nowadays the markets operate daily, it's still the day to come if you want to see the old-style *tianguis* (markets) at their best. *Indígenas* flood in from the villages in a bewildering variety of costumes, and Mixtec and Zapotec dialects replace Spanish as the *lingua franca*. The majority of the activity, as well as the serious business of buying and selling everyday goods, happens at the sprawling **Mercado de Abastos**, by the second-class bus station. This is the place to go for fruit, vegetables, meat, herbs, spices and all manner of household goods, from traditional cooking pots to wooden utensils and furniture – you could spend a couple of hours lost in here.

Just one block south of the plaza, the **Mercado Benito Juárez Maza** makes for an easier target, where raw meat, fruit, clothes and bag stalls blend with some of the best budget eateries in town (see p.629). There are also plenty of stalls more obviously focused on tourists: mescal, local cheese and *mole* are the products of choice. South of the market, on 20 de Noviembre at Aldama, the 1890 church of **San Juan de Dios** (replacing a far earlier church) attracts villagers and market traders who've come to town for the day and want to pay their respects, but the real highlight sits just behind it. The **Mercado 20 de Noviembre** is essentially a giant food court, a cacophony of sights, smells and tastes. Indigenous women wander labyrinthine corridors amidst plumes of incense, inviting you to try curious Oaxacan dishes such as *chapulines* (crunchy baked grasshoppers) and *chicharrones* (crispy pork fat). An excellent place to eat, the market is lined with *comedores* serving inexpensive food, such as *chiles rellenos* and tamales (see p.629 for full review). You'll also find the best **mescal** and **chocolate** stores around here (see box opposite).

Finally, the **Mercado Artesanías**, two blocks southwest on 20 de Noviembre between Mina and Zaragoza, is the site for village handicrafts such as *rebozas* (shawls), rag dolls and green china; plenty of fresh produce and flowers; and the infamous *chapulines* (fried grasshoppers). While many of the goods here can be much cheaper than in the smaller markets, be warned that it's very touristy – you're harassed far more by the vendors and you may have to bargain fiercely to get your price. Always check the quality of the goods before you buy; *sarapes*, in particular, are often machine-made from chemically dyed artificial fibres. You can tell real wool by plucking out a thread – artificial fibres are long, thin and shiny, woollen threads short, rough and curly. There are numerous **shops** around the plaza and on Alcalá that will give you a good idea of the potential quality of items you can buy in the market, or try the **Mujeres Artesanias de los Regionales de Oaxaca** at 5 de Mayo 204 (daily 9am–8pm).

Eating and drinking

The food in Oaxaca is sensational. The cheapest places to eat are in the **markets**, either in the section of the Mercado de 20 de Noviembre around 20 de Noviembre and Aldama, or in the market by the second-class bus station, where you'll find excellent tamales. You'll also find a medley of stalls dotted around the **plaza** and along its peripheral streets that serve filling staples such as *elote* (corn on the cob) and *flautas* (deep-fried, rolled tortillas filled with mozzarella-like string cheese or meat). Other happy hunting grounds include the stalls on García Vigil near the Carmen Alto, and the organic market near the aqueduct (see p.625).

In addition to stalls, the plaza is ringed by **cafés** and restaurants where you can sit outside – irresistible as ever and not as expensive as their position might lead you to expect – and there are plenty of simple places for everyday meals in the

Mescal and cacao

The markets are the best place to indulge in two of Oaxaca's favourite treats. **Mescal**, the Oaxaqueño drink of choice, is sold everywhere in bottles that usually have a dead *gusano* worm in the bottom. Legend has it that the creature lives on the cactus-like maguey plant (it's actually a type of caterpillar) and is there to prove that the ingredients are genuine (this is debatable; these days most of the worms are farm-raised and inserted as a marketing ploy). You don't have to eat the worm, though few people are in any state to notice what they're ingesting by the time they reach the bottom of the bottle. Mescal and tequila are similar drinks – tequila is simply a speciality type of the more varied mescal. True tequila is made only from the prized blue agave species, while mescal may be a combination of a number of types of maguey. Both alcohols are made from the sugary heart of the plant, which is baked, pulverized and then distilled. These liquors were developed around the same time, when the Spaniards introduced distillation after the Conquest. Surrounding the Mercado 20 de Noviembre are clusters of **mescal stores** where you can, rather dangerously, taste before you commit to buying; good brands include Monte Albán, Rey Zapoteco, Beneva and Oro de Oaxaca. Some of the best shops are *El Famoso* at J.P. García 405, *Mescal Don Agave* at Aldama 209 and *Mescal Tobala* at 20 de Noviembre 606–608. Most shops are open daily 9am–9pm, and sell small bottles from M$70.

Several towns produce mescal, but the original is **Santiago Matatlán**, 45km from Oaxaca City. You'll see **mescal tours** advertised everywhere, but one of the best guides is Canadian expat Alvin Starkman, owner of the *Casa Machaya* B&B (ⓣ951/132-8203, ⓦwww.oaxacadream.com).

On the south side of the market, your nose will lead you to Calle Mina, which is lined with **spice** vendors selling plump bags of the chile-and-chocolate powder that makes up most Oaxacan *moles*. Cinnamon-flavoured chocolate powder is also available, for cooking or making into drinking **chocolate**. One of the best places in this area to try a mug of hot chocolate laced with almond, cinnamon, sugar or chile is *Mayordomo*, the Willy Wonka of Oaxaca. The main branch is at the corner of Mina and 20 de Noviembre; luscious hot chocolate served with bread is M$15, malts are M$10, and you can buy pure cacao served by the kilo (M$60) and all sorts of boxes of chocolates (M$50 for a large one). Nearby *La Soledad* at Mina 212 has a row of old bean-crushing machines and is drenched in the overpowering aroma of sweet cacao – choc addicts beware.

streets round about. On the pricier end, there are some colonial-style and contemporary upscale restaurants that offer nouvelle Mexican dishes that use local herbs and produce to create imaginative, and usually healthier dishes – most street food tends to be fried, often in lard. Oaxaca also provides welcome relief for **vegetarians**, especially those who have been restricted to endless *huevos* and quesadillas in other parts of the country.

Around the plaza

Bar del Jardín Portal de Flores 10, on the plaza. One of the best cafés on the plaza for a coffee or cocktail and some people-watching. Don't go for the food, but if hunger overwhelms you there is a passable, if uninspired, menu of soups, sandwiches, enchiladas and breakfasts. (Not to be confused with the *Café del Jardín*, next to *Casa de la Abuela*.)

La Casa de la Abuela Hidalgo 616. Touristy and with erratic service, but the great views over the plaza from the second floor compensate and most dishes are not that expensive (M$38–50). Serves locally inspired takes on classic dishes, tailored to an American palette.

Como Agua Pa' Chocolate Hidalgo 612 Altos, just off the plaza ⓣ951/516-2917. Romantic restaurant with cuisine inspired by *Like Water for Chocolate*, essentially a fusion of Mediterranean and Mexican styles (think quails in rose-petal sauce or prawns in orange sauce). Known particularly for its table-side flambéed dishes, exquisite *mole* sauces and the second-floor views across the Alameda. Mains M$150–180.

North of Independencia

Antigua Reforma 401. Close to Santo Domingo, this café is a popular breakfast choice, with a range of American, continental and Mexican combinations. There's also a selection of pastries and sandwiches for a quick lunch, and a lively post-dinner scene with wine, mescal and gourmet liqueur coffees.

Biznaga García Vigil 512 ⓣ951/516-8000. Inside a lemon-walled courtyard festooned with artwork, a chalk-board outlines the daily menu, which usually ranges from wholesome salads and soups to *pastor*-style (tomato, oil, cilantro) fish and chicken *milanesa* filled with cheese. Some of the more elaborate dishes can fall short of their adjective-heavy descriptions, but when it's good it's delicious. They admit service can be slow – sip an excellent margarita or Belgian beer while you wait. Main dishes average M$100.

Café Gecko 5 de Mayo 412. Come here for inexpensive omelettes, yogurt and granola, coffee and snacks (mains from M$50), which you can eat indoors or within a leafy courtyard (inside Plaza Fray Gonzalo Lucero, opposite San Domingo). Open until 8pm weekdays, 11pm at weekends.

Casa Oaxaca García Vigil 407 ⓣ951/514-4173. Contemporary Mexican cuisine with an international twist from chef Alejandro Olmedo. Dishes such as chiles stuffed with *ceviche*, red snapper coated with *guajillo* sauce and a decadent chicken *mole* are served in the candlelit courtyard of the hotel of the same name. Service is formal and charming. Most entrées are upwards of M$150. Reservations required.

Cenadería Libres Tlayudas Doña Martha Libres 212. Incredibly popular late-night snack stop, cooking up tasty flame-grilled *tlayudas* (plate-sized tortillas char-grilled and stuffed with meat, cheese, and beans for M$35) to lines of hungry clubbers and taxi-drivers. Take a number and expect to wait up to 40min. Daily 9pm–4am.

La Crêpe Alcalá 307. There may not be much Oaxacan flavour to the food, but it's popular with locals, and the smart, lively setting, conveniently location overlooking Alcalá, make this a great international choice. Vast range of sweet and savoury crepes (M$44–60) from squash and cheese to nutella and banana, as well as fruit salads, ice creams and a range of excellent salads (from M$42). Good dessert stop-off when the music draws the pre-party crowd.

Los Danzantes Alcalá 403 ⓣ951/501-1184, ⓦwww.losdanzantes.com. One of the best choices in town with a slick, nouveau-design setting, good cocktails – try the mescal margarita – and imaginative dishes like mango- and mint-infused octopus, shrimp *ceviche*, barbecue chicken strips tossed with fried cactus and Oaxacan chocolate soufflé. The friendly staff are efficient and graciously opinionated. Prices start from around M$120, with lunch menu from M$75.

El Manantial Vegetariano Tinoco y Palacios 303. Vegetarian Mexican breakfasts, affordable veggie burgers and fruit shakes are the order of the day at this small but excellent wholefood restaurant. The Sunday buffet (M$75) is a bargain.

Marco Polo Pino Suárez 806 ⓣ951/501-1184. Daily fresh seafood specials in a snug, rustic setting right by the Parque Juárez (aka El Llano). There's a lovely outdoor patio and a brick oven; very good fish dishes – refreshingly not all fried – and wonderful *ceviche* are the menu highlights. Not the best value for money in town, but certainly a very pleasant way to spend an evening. Also popular for breakfasts (M$39–52).

Maria Bonita Alcalá 706 ⓣ951/516-7233. Family-run restaurant one block north of Santo Domingo, serving reasonably priced Oaxacan specialities: *tasajo* (beef strips), fried squash blossoms, *mole* tamales, *quesillo* (string cheese) and *tlayudas* topped with lard. Mains cost M$50 to M$120. Breakfasts are good, too (from M$40) – try the *enfrijoladas*, baked tortillas filled with beans and Oaxacan string cheese.

La Olla Reforma 402 ⓣ951/516-6668, ⓦwww.laolla.com.mx. Quaint, relaxed café/gallery with a reliable breakfast menu featuring Oaxacan specialities, enchiladas and *chilaquiles* as well as more wholesome choices – the most popular restaurant in town for tourists looking for an easy introduction to Oaxacan cuisine.

Pizza Nostrana Allende 150. While Oaxaca's Italian culinary reputation is nonexistent, this is the best option in town for well-executed and varied pasta dishes with a vegetarian slant. The intimate, old-fashioned atmosphere and its location close to Santo Domingo lend a romantic, relaxed vibe.

El Teatro Culinario Allende 107, inside *Casa Crespo*, west of Alcalá ⓣ951/516-0918, ⓦwww.elteatroculinario.com. Best restaurant in Oaxaca, with chef José Luis Díaz creating fabulous, artful interpretations of traditional Oaxacan food like *xicamatl* (turnip) spaghetti, cactus salad and *huevos chorizo* (done with whole eggs on sausage). M$600 for dinner for two. Daily 1– 2.30pm & 7–10pm.

South of Independencia

Café Alex Díaz Ordaz 218 at Trujano ⓣ951/514-0715. Popular with locals and travellers alike, this boisterous Mexican-style diner offers extensive breakfast menus ranging from omelettes, yogurt and hot cakes to refried beans, *huevos rancheros* and fresh fruit *licuados* – it also opens early by Oaxaca standards. Free wi-fi. Mon–Sat 7am–9.30pm, Sun 7am–1pm.

Mercado 20 de Noviembre 20 de Noviembre at Aldama. This food market can be overwhelming, but each section has a speciality – if in doubt follow the biggest crowds. Entering from the north side, you'll encounter *caldos menudos* (aromatic tripe stew) specialists; *Angelita* (stall 179) is a good bet here. Beyond, the *comedores* take over, where tamales and regular Mexican dishes rule: try *Comedor Bety* (M$20 plates). On the east side, in a separate row, the roast meat stalls serve *carne asada* on tables with plenty of salsa.

Mercado Benito Juárez Las Casas and 20 de Noviembre. Make for the *Hawai* stall in the centre of the market, which sells fresh *jugos* and tortas, or *Chagüita*, a venerable local institution, to grab a beer, mescal or exotic ice-cold *sabores* (35 flavours) including *beso de ángel*, piña colada and tamarindo. Visit *El Arte Oaxaqueños* for sweet pastries.

Land of the seven moles – Oaxacan cuisine

Oaxaca is a wonderful city for gourmands, while the state is known as the "land of the seven *moles*" after its most famous sauces: *negro* or *mole Oaxaqueño* (the most popular, made with chocolate giving a distinct roasted flavour), *amarillo*, *coloradito*, *mancha manteles*, *chichilo*, *rojo* and *verde*. *Moles* are typically served with chicken or enchiladas, but you don't have to go to one of the smart restaurants serving contemporary Oaxacan cuisine to sample them: *mole negro* is often better from street or market vendors. Other specialties include **tamales**, worth trying in any form, and **chapulines**, crunchy seasoned grasshoppers. **Tlayudas**, giant crisp tortillas dressed with beans and a mild Oaxacan string cheese called **quesillo**, are staples of cafés and street stands after dark.

The place to go for exceptional home-made **ice cream** is the plaza in front of the church of La Soledad, full of rival vendors and tables where you can sit and gorge yourself while watching the world go by. Flavours are innumerable and often bizarre, including *elote* (corn), *queso*, *leche quemada* (burnt milk; even worse than it sounds), *sorbete* (cinnamon-flavoured sherbet) and exotic fruits like *mamey*, *guanabana* and *tuna* (prickly pear; a virulent purple that tastes wonderful). There are also more ordinary varieties like chocolate, peanut and coconut. You can buy local organic **coffee** at *Café de Oaxaca Orgánica* (Mon–Thurs 9am–10pm, Fri & Sat 9am–11pm) opposite *Casa de las Bugambilias* at Reforma 401, and drink it next door at *Café La Antigua*. For **mescal** and **chocolate** see box, p.627.

Red Las Casas 101 ☎951/514-6853. A bustling, no-frills joint that looks a bit like a fast-food place, serving generous portions of whole fish dishes, mixed seafood soups, prawn cocktails, *ceviche* and octopus for M$80 – spotlessly clean, though.

Nightlife

If you're not content sitting around the plaza over a coffee or a beer or whiling away a balmy night to the accompaniment of mariachi or brass bands, Oaxaca has a handful of decent bars and clubs to sample. Most open daily 7pm to 3am, though clubs won't get busy till after midnight and usually close Sunday to Wednesday (exceptions are noted below). The *guelaguetza* **folk dances** at the *Casa de Cantera, Federico Ortiz Armengol 104* (daily 8.30pm; M$140; ☎951/515-3768, Ⓦwww.casadecantera.com), *Camino Real Oaxaca* (Fri 7pm; M$315; 3hr; see p.619) and *Monte Albán* at Alameda de León 1 (daily 8.30pm; M$70; 90min; ☎951/516-2777) are aimed squarely at tourists, but will at least give you a taster of the famous festival if you can't attend the real thing.

La Barcina Hidalgo 218, between Galeana and Mier y Tieran. Check out the best of Oaxaca's burgeoning rock scene at this lively bar – the bands are pretty good, everything from ska and reggae, to punk and garage. Doors open at 7pm most nights. Cover M$25.

El Borgo Jazz Murguía 202. This popular bar reopened in 2009 opposite the *Camino Real*, and though it remains the home of ebullient Oaxaqueños rubbing shoulders with language students and tourists, it's now dedicated to serving live jazz at weekends.

Candela Murguía 413 ☎951/514-2010. Set in a charming colonial house, *Candela* is a restaurant by day, but the place really comes alive after 11pm when the dancefloor is packed with locals and tourists coming to practise their salsa, rumba and merengue, accompanied by a live band. Try to arrive before 10pm at the weekend in order to secure a table. M$50 cover.

Casa del Mezcal Flores Magón 209. Longstanding, classic Mexican cantina in the market district, open since 1935, with cheap shots of mescal and a fairly liberal attitude to female patrons (though it's generally frequented by men).

La Cucaracha Porfirio Díaz 301-A. It's hard to miss this roomy colonial-style bar with a roadhouse feel. If you want to expand your repertoire of tequila or mescal with a M$100 selection of different shots in a loud and often frenzied environment, this is the place. Live entertainment and dancing at the weekend.

La Divina Gurrion 104. Arguably the best bar in town, this friendly, funky space in front of Santo Domingo is decorated with masks and model animals; dripping candles on chunky wooden tables add a gothic feel. There is a good variety of beer, spirits and tequila, and unlike many other local bars, the music won't blow your ears off.

La Farola 20 de Noviembre 3 at Las Casas. Classic cantina since 1916, with wooden tables, friendly bar staff and two floors. Come here to drink fine mescal: Rey Zapoteco, Beneva and Oro de Oaxaca are the favoured brands.

Freebar Matamoros 100-C. Dark and dingy space that becomes a packed madhouse on weekends, with locals and some foreigners dancing to alternative music and spilling into the street.

La Nueva Babel Porfirio Díaz 224. Loungey wine bar also serving coffee and snacks, and sometimes featuring live folk music, salsa (*son Cubano*) and poetry readings, usually from 9.30pm (free). Opens as a café during the day. Closed Sun.

La Tentación Matamoros 101 ☎951/514-9521, Ⓦwww.latentacion.com.mx. With just a few tables and two-for-one drink deals most nights (Tues for cocktails), this is a good place for a drink and boogie. Depending on the season, there is live Latin music (Thurs–Sat) and ska/reggae on Tuesdays – it's often packed with sweaty, gyrating gringos and Mexicans. Tues–Sun 10pm–3am, cover M$10–20.

Listings

Airlines Aeroméxico, Hidalgo 513 ☎9/516-1066; Aerotucán ☎951/502-0840; Aviacsa, Pino Suárez 604 ☎951/516-4577; Mexicana, Fiallo 102 ☎951/516-5797; Aerovega, Alameda de León ☎951/516-4982.

American Express Viajes Jalietza, Murguía 500-A at Pino Suárez ☎951/501-5656 (Mon–Fri 8am–9.30pm, Sat 8am–8pm, Sun 9am–4pm).

Banks and exchange Scotiabank, Independencia 801 and Alcalá, has an ATM and good rates

Moving on from Oaxaca

For the Valles Centrales and Mixteca, see the relevant sections. Further information available in Travel details, p.672.

To the Oaxaca coast

For buses to the **Oaxaca coast**, you have two principal choices: long-distance coach lines or faster, more cramped minibuses. OCC (first class) and ADO GL (executive class) from the first-class station (see p.616), take a huge detour along Hwy-190 (via Salina Cruz) to **Huatulco** (M$258), with OCC going on to **Pochutla** (M$266) and **Puerto Escondido** (M$272), a 10–11hr marathon. It's much faster to take one of the many minibus operators to Pochutla (for Puerto Ángel) or direct to Puerto Escondido (around six hours), though you'll need a constitution of iron to take the curves and bumps (be warned: many travellers throw up and need a day to recover). The long-distance coaches are much more comfortable, though even Hwy-190 has plenty of stomach-churning bends. Of the faster minibuses, Oaxaca Pacifico runs to Pochutla (M$100), Puerto Escondido (M$115) and Huatulco (M$120) from its terminal at Armenta y López 121, south of La Noria; Autotransportes Turisticos Huatulco at Trujano 600, between Galeana and Victoria, has minibuses to Huatulco for M$160, five times a day (4am–8pm), and to Puerto Escondido (M$150); Autoexprés Atlántida (☎951/514-7077) at Noria 110 and Armenta y López is a smart outfit with daily minivans to Pochutla (M$120) every two hours from 7am to 7pm (plus an overnight 11.30pm service); Servicio Express at Arista 116 and Cabrera runs to Puerto Ángel and Puerto Escondido for about the same rates. Estrella de Valle runs from the second-class terminal to Pochutla at night (M$100), Escondido (M$115) and Puerto Ángel (M$100).

Long-distance buses

For long-distance **buses**, always try to buy tickets at least one day in advance, especially for popular destinations like San Cristóbal de las Casas. Ticketbus offices, one on Valdivieso by the cathedral (☎951/516-3820) and another at Díaz 102A at Independencia (Mon–Sat 8am–10pm, Sun 9am–4pm; ☎951/514-6655, Ⓦwww.ticketbus.com.mx), sell tickets for first-class lines. OCC, ADO GL and UNO (deluxe class) run frequent services from the first-class bus station (see p.616) to Mexico City (6hr) and Puebla (4–5hr), and just three or four buses to San Cristóbal (11hr), Tuxtla Gutiérrez (10hr), Veracruz (6–7hr) and Villahermosa (12hr). Slower, cheaper, more frequent and less comfortable services leave from the second-class bus station, for Mexico City (mostly overnight), Pinotepa Nacional, Tuxtla Gutiérrez and other destinations; buses to the Chiapas coast are particularly cheap (Tapachula just M$310, Arriaga M$180).

Flights

Oaxaca airport operates principally to serve as a connection to **Mexico City**; for other destinations you'll need to change there. Prices increase dramatically during Mexican holiday times, but expect to pay around M$1100 to Mexico City and M$2200 to Mérida.

Aerovega (☎951/516-4982, Ⓦwww.oaxaca-mio.com/aerovega.htm) flies tiny Cessna aircraft (daily 8.30am) to Puerto Escondido for around M$1200; buy tickets at Alameda 1, opposite the cathedral. It's around ten times more expensive than a minibus, but takes just 30 minutes – very tempting if you're short of time. Aerotucán (☎951/502-0840, Ⓦwww.aerotucan.com.mx) flies to Huatulco and Escondido for similar rates. Their office is at Carranza 303 and Eucaliptos. The airport is about 10km south of the city on the road to San Bartolo Coyotepec and Ocotlán; contact Transportación Terrestre Aeropuerto (see p.617) for a relatively cheap pick-up (M$44 per person).

(Mon–Fri 9am–5pm, Sat 10am–3pm); Banamex, Hidalgo 821, has an ATM and Western Union service (Mon–Fri 9am–4pm, Sat 10am–2pm); Banorte is at García Vigil 103, between Morelos and Independencia (Mon–Fri 9am–5pm, Sat 9am–2pm). Casas de cambio litter the town centre.

Books and maps There are a number of bookshops selling Spanish and English titles, as well as museum shops and reference libraries. Amate, Alcalá 307, has an excellent selection of new and second-hand English-language books (including literature, travel, archeology and cooking) and magazines. You can get new and second-hand English books about Oaxaca, Mexico and Latin America from Librería Universitaria, Guerrero 108, just off the plaza (Mon–Sat 10am–3pm & 4.30–8.30pm). The expat-run Oaxaca Lending Library (see p.618) has over 30,000 books in English and Spanish – there is a small membership fee to take out books and use the free wi-fi (M$130/1 month; M$200/2 months; M$265/3 months).

Car rental Alamo, 5 de Mayo 203 (ⓣ951/514-8534); Hertz, Alcalá 100 (ⓣ951/516-2434). Both firms have desks at the airport, and you can also try locally based Only Rent A Car (ⓣ951/501-0816, ⓦwww.onlyrentacar.com) at 5 de Mayo 215 and Alcalá 401.

Cinema You can see international and Mexican films for free at the Cine Pochote, García Vigil 817 (for listings see ⓦelpochote.blogspot.com or the *Oaxaca Times*).

Consulates Canada, Pino Suárez 700 (ⓣ951/513-3777); US, Alcalá 407, Office 20 (ⓣ951/514-3054). Other consulates in Oaxaca move regularly – check at the tourist office for the latest information.

Emergencies Dial ⓣ066; the tourist police are located at Independencia 607 (ⓣ951/516-0123, 514-2155 or 01-800/903-9200).

Hospitals Clínica Hospital Carmen at Abasolo 215 (ⓣ951/513-3777) usually has English speakers on hand. The vast IMSS Hospital is at Porfirio Díaz 141, north of the centre (ⓣ951/515-6021).

Internet access Internet cafés are abundant; most have copy and printing services, and some have long-distance call booths. Open latest is Café Internet, upstairs at Valdivieso and Independencia – it closes most nights at 11pm; also Inter@ctive at Alcalá 503, (across from Santo Domingo (rates around M$6/hr).

Laundry Lava-Max, Bravo y Tinoco y Palacios (Mon–Sat 8.30am–9pm; M$13/kg); Lavandería Antequera, Murguía 408 (Mon–Sat 8am–2pm & 4–8pm).

Massages and saunas Traditional *temazcal* sauna (M$250) and massage (M$250) are offered in a peaceful garden on the outskirts of town through *Casa de las Bugambilias,* Reforma 402 (ⓣ951/295-1165; reserve at least a day in advance), a short taxi or cheap bus ride from the centre of town.

Post office Antonio de Leòn 2 at Independencia, on the Alameda (Mon–Fri 8am–7pm, Sat 9am–1pm). It has fax services and Ladatel phones for collect calls.

Spanish courses Some of the most popular language classes are offered by Amigos del Sol, Calzada San Felipe del Agua 322, meeting at Pino Suárez 802 at Llano park (ⓣ951/133-6052, ⓦwww.oaxacanews.com/amigosdelsol.htm; from M$120/week, 15hr); the teachers are very friendly and student ability is properly assessed by tests on arrival. Similar services are offered at the small-scale Becari Language School, Plaza San Cristóbal, M. Bravo 210 (ⓣ951/514-6076, ⓦwww.becari.com.mx; M$120/week, 15hr). The Instituto Cultural Oaxaca, Juárez 909 (ⓣ951/515-3404, ⓦwww.icomexico.com; from M$115/week, 15hr) is renowned for its high standards and immersion courses, while Academia Vinigúlaza, Abasolo 503 (ⓣ951/513-2763, ⓦwww.vinigulaza.com; from M$105/week, 15hr) specializes in small groups and only hires native-speaking teachers. If you're interested in Oaxacan cuisine, you can learn to cook while practising Spanish at the Seasons of My Heart cooking school, Rancho Aurora, AP#42, Admon 3 (ⓣ951/508-0469, ⓦwww.seasonsofmyheart.com; half-days from M$500).

Volunteering The Oaxaca Street Children Grass-roots project (Centro de Esperanza Infantil) aims to bring a brighter future to Oaxaca's neediest children. You can contribute to their food and medical programme, or volunteer with them in Oaxaca by visiting or contacting the centre at Crespo 308 (ⓣ951/501-1069, ⓔstreetchildren@spersaoaxaca.com.mx).

Yoga and meditation Classes offered several times a week at *La Casa del Ángel*, a New-Age café at Jacobo Dalevuelta 200, between Reforma and Juárez (ⓣ951/545-3203). Listings for other alternative health practitioners can be found in the *Oaxaca Times.* Calipso Gym, Allende 211 (ⓣ951/516-8000, ⓦwww.calipso.com.mx), offers day passes (from M$120) for aerobic and yoga classes and their weight rooms.

Monte Albán

The extraordinary Mesoamerican city of **MONTE ALBÁN** is one of the world's great archeological treasures, legacy of the advanced Zapotec culture that dominated this part of Mexico well over one thousand years ago. Founded around 500 BC, most of the city was abandoned by 950 AD, though the Mixtecs later used it as a magnificent burial site, and the main structures were cleared and restored in the 1930s. Today it's the great flattened mountain-top (750m by 250m), the scale of the monuments and the views over the valley that impress more than any individual aspect of the site. Late afternoon, as the sun sinks into the valley, is the best time to see it.

Some history

It seems almost madness to have tried to build a city here, so far from the obvious livelihood of the valleys and without any natural water supply (in the dry season water was carried up and stored in vast urns). Yet that may have been the Zapotecs' point – to demonstrate their mastery of nature. By waging war on potential rivals, the new city soon came to dominate an area that extended well beyond the main valley – the peculiar *danzante* figures carved in stone that you can see at the ruins today are widely considered to be depictions of prisoners captured in battle. By 200 AD, the population had expanded to such a degree that the Zapotecs endeavoured to level the Monte Albán spur completely to create more space, essentially forming a massive plateau. The resulting engineering project boggles the mind: without the aid of the wheel or beasts of burden, millions of tons of earth were shifted to build a vast, flat terrace on which the Zapotecs constructed colossal pyramids, astronomical observatories and palaces. What you see today is just the very centre of the city – the religious and political heart – the dominating apex of the region between 300 and 700 AD. On the terraced hillsides below lived a bustling population of between 25,000 and 30,000 craftsmen, priests, administrators and warriors, all of whom, presumably, were supported by tribute from the valleys. It's small wonder that so top-heavy a society was easily destabilized. This said, there is still much speculation as to why, just like Teotihuacán, the site was ultimately abandoned.

Getting there

Monte Albán (daily 9am–5pm; M$51) is just 9km southwest of Oaxaca, up a steeply switchbacking road. There are two principal competitors for the Monte Alban run, both based on Calle Mina and both offering similar minibus services; compare prices first as these sometimes differ. At the time of writing Autobuses Turisticos (☎951/516-5327) at Mina 505 (tickets at no. 501) was offering return tickets for M$51, while Transportadora Turistica (☎951/117-9601), which stops at the *Hotel Rivera del Ángel* at no. 518 and no. 504-B further along, was selling return tickets for just M$38.

Departures usually run every thirty minutes from 8.30am to 3.30pm, while official returns start at noon and finish at 5pm – you'll normally be allocated a fixed return time, giving three hours at the site (8.30am–noon, 9.30am–1pm and so on), but it's OK to come back before noon if you finish early, or take a different bus in the afternoon if you stay longer (if there's space). Both companies also run tours of the whole region, and have English-speaking staff.

Heading back it's sometimes possible to hitch a ride or find a taxi (M$100), and walking is also a realistic option: more than two hours, but downhill almost all the way – get a guard or one of the kids selling "genuine antiquities" to show you the path. The route is an eye-opening experience, veering through slum dwellings that are a far cry from the comforts of much of the city below. There's a car park, restaurant and souvenir shop by the entrance, and a small **museum** in the same complex: the collection is tiny, but there are some important finds on display, including the carvings of the "dancers" (see opposite), some intricate sculptures, ceramics and some gruesome mutilated skulls, presumably victims of the Zapotecs.

The site

You enter the site at its northeast corner. Sombre, grey and formal as it all appears now, in its heyday, with its roofs and sanctuaries intact, the whole place would have been brilliantly polychromed. The **Plataforma Norte**, straight ahead as you enter, may have been the most important of all the temples at Monte Albán, although now the ceremonial buildings that line its sides are largely ruined. What survives is a broad stairway leading up from the Gran Plaza to a platform enclosing a square patio with an altar at its heart. This ceremonial centre was constructed between 400 and 750 AD, when Monte Albán was at its zenith. At the top of the stairs are the remains of a double row of six broad columns, which would originally have supported a roof to form a colonnade, dividing this plaza from the main one.

The Gran Plaza

The main path takes you south along the eastern side of the Plataforma Norte to the **Gran Plaza**, the vast, ceremonial focus of the city surrounded by all the major buildings of Monte Albán. As you enter you'll pass the **Juego de Pelota** (ball-court), a simple I-shaped space with no apparent goals or target rings, obviously an early example. The ball-game was used as a means to solve conflict – it is believed that the losing team was sacrificed to the gods (see p.876). Otherwise, the platforms on the east side of the plaza are relatively late constructions, dating from around 500 AD onwards. Facing them from the middle of the plaza is a long tripartite building (**Edificios G, H** and **I**) that must have played an important role in any rites celebrated here. The central section has broad staircases by which it can be approached from east or west – the lower end temples have smaller stairways facing north and south. From here a complex of tunnels runs under the site to several of the other temples, presumably to allow the priests to emerge suddenly and miraculously in any one of them. You can see the remains of several of these tunnels among the buildings on the east side.

South of this central block, **Monticulo J**, known as the observatory, stands alone in the centre of the plaza – at 45 degrees to everything else – and its arrow-shaped design marks it out from its surroundings. Although the orientation is almost certainly for astronomical reasons, there's no evidence that this was actually an observatory; more likely it was built (around 250 AD, but on the site of an earlier structure) to celebrate an earlier victory. The carvings and hieroglyphics on the back of the building apparently represent a list of towns captured by the Zapotecs: much of the imagery at Monte Albán points to a highly militaristic society. In the vaulted passage that runs through the heart of the building, several more panels carved in relief show *danzante* figures (dancers) – these, often upside down or on their sides and in no particular order, may have been reused from an earlier building.

The southern end of the Gran Plaza is dominated by its tallest structure, the unrestored **Plataforma Sur**, a vast square pyramid offering the best overview of the site, as well as fine panoramas of the surrounding countryside. Heading from here back up the western side of the plaza, you'll pass **Monticulo M** and **Sistema IV**, probably the best-preserved buildings on the site. Both consist of a rectangular platform reached by a stairway from the plaza. Between Monticulo M and Sistema IV, the gallery and building of **Los Danzantes** (the Dancers), are the most interesting features of Monte Albán. A low wall extending from Monticulo M to the base of the Danzantes building forms the **gallery**, originally faced all along with blocks carved in relief of "dancers". Among the oldest (dating from around 500 BC) and most puzzling features of the site, only a few of these *danzantes* remain – the originals are now all preserved in the museum and what you see here are replicas. The significance of the nude male figures is disputed: many of them seem to have been cut open and may represent sacrificial victims or prisoners; another suggestion is that the entire wall was a sort of medical textbook, or that the figures really are dancers, ball-players or acrobats. Whatever the truth, they show clear **Olmec** influence, and many of them have been pressed into use in later buildings throughout the site.

The outer buildings

Several lesser buildings surround the main plaza, and although they're not particularly interesting, many contain tombs in which rich treasures were discovered (as indeed did some of the main structures themselves). **Tumba 104**, reached by a small path behind the Plataforma Norte or from the main entrance, is the best preserved of these, with polychrome frescoes vividly revealing the mystical symbolism of the Zapotec gods. One of several in the immediate vicinity, this vaulted burial chamber still preserves excellent remains of murals. **Tumba 7**, where the important collection of Mixtec jewellery now in the Oaxaca Museum was found, lies a few hundred metres down the main road from the site entrance. Built underneath a small temple, it was originally constructed by the Zapotecs towards the end of Monte Albán's heyday, but was later emptied by the Mixtecs, who buried one of their own chiefs here along with his magnificent burial trove.

The Zapotec and Mixtec heartland

The region around Oaxaca can be divided into two parts: the **Valles Centrales** (or Valle de Oaxaca), which radiate from the state capital to the south and east, towards Mitla, Ocotlán and Zaachila; and the **Mixteca**, which extends northwest towards Puebla and arcs down to the Pacific coast via Tlaxiaco and Pinotepa

Staying in local communities around Oaxaca

Indigenous communities in the mountains and valleys of Oaxaca have been developing their ecotourism potential since the 1990s, when the **Tourist Yú'ù** (pronounced YOU) – Zapotec for "house" – programme was established. These small, self-contained *cabañas ecoturísticas* were designed to bring income to the local villages while minimizing the disruptive effects of mass tourism. These days many villages organize **tours** (from hiking and fishing to adventure sports and horseriding) and some sort of "community lodging", from **homestays** to simple but comfy **cabins** usually arranged through a Comité local de Ecoturismo. Either type of accommodation makes a convenient and economical base for exploring the villages and archeological sites of Oaxaca state. Many communities have particular **handicraft traditions**, such as carpet-weaving, wickerwork or pottery; others have museums devoted to local archeological finds and the life of the villagers.

The best place for information and reservations – ideally made a few days in advance, especially for the more accessible sites – is Oaxaca's tourist offices at Independencia 607 or Juárez 703 (see p.618). For the Sierra Norte and the Pueblos Mancomunados contact Expediciones Sierra Norte (see p.618), which coordinates all the local community programmes in that area. For Ixtlán contact Ecoturixtlán (p.643) directly. Note that the Tourist Yú'ù in Teotitlán del Valle and Tlacolula are now closed.

Cabins usually cost M$140–450, depending on how many people are sharing, with a bedroom, a fully equipped kitchen and outside shower and toilets (which can also be used by people camping in the grounds). Campers pay around M$45.

Nacional. The Valles Centrales include the state's most famous and frequented archeological centres, craft villages and colourful markets, while the Mixteca, rich in ruined Dominican convents and ancient towns and villages, is less visited but well worth exploring.

This area saw the development of some of the most highly advanced civilizations in pre-Hispanic Mexico, most notably the Zapotecs and Mixtecs. Their craft skills – particularly Mixtec weaving, pottery and metalworking – were unrivalled, and the architecture and planning of their cities stand out among ancient Mexico's greatest achievements. Traditional ways of life and indigenous languages are still vigorously preserved by Mixtec and Zapotec descendants in villages today.

Car rental is as pricey here as anywhere in the country, but if you are planning extensive exploration of the valleys it may prove worthwhile, allowing you to trade a week of long **bus rides** for a couple of days of independence; see p.632 for agents. Note that poor signposting in this area can be frustrating, and that getting in and out of Oaxaca is a nightmare, unless you travel at dawn. Note also that many of the towns outside Oaxaca don't observe daylight-saving time, so your watch might be an hour off local time.

Some history

The Valles Centrales are the cradle of some of the earliest civilizations in Mexico. The story begins with the **Zapotecs**, who founded their first city – now called San José Mogoté and little more than a collection of mounds a few kilometres north of the state capital – some time before 1000 BC. As the city grew in wealth, trading with Pacific coastal communities, its inhabitants turned their eyes to the stars, and by 500 BC they had invented the first Mexican calendar and were using hieroglyphic writing. At this time, San José, together with smaller villages in the area, established a new administrative capital at Monte Albán, a vantage point on a mountain spur overlooking the principal Oaxaca valley (see p.633). Just like Teotihuacán, Monte Albán mysteriously began to implode from about 700 AD, and the Zapotec influence across the Valles Centrales waned. Only Yagul and Mitla, two smaller cities in the principal valley, expanded after this date, though they never reached the imperial glory of Monte Albán. As the Zapotecs disappeared, the gap they left behind was slowly filled by the **Mixtecs**, pre-Hispanic Mexico's finest craftsmen, who expanded into the southern valleys from the north to occupy the Zapotecs' magnificent cities. Influenced by the Zapotec sculptors' abstract motifs on the walls at Mitla, the Mixtecs concentrated their artistic skills on metalwork and pottery, examples of which can be seen in the state capital's museums. By the fifteenth century, the Mixtecs had become the favoured artisans to Mexico's greatest empire, their conquerors, the **Aztecs**; Bernal Díaz recounts that Moctezuma only ate from plates fashioned by Mixtec craftsmen.

The road to Mitla: Valle de Tlacolula

Hwy-190 provides access to some of the most alluring villages of the **Valle de Tlacolula**, slicing some 45km east of Oaxaca towards **Mitla** (see p.640), before cutting south to Tehuantepec and the coast. The route is well served by *colectivos* and buses from the second-class terminal (every thirty minutes or so), making day trips possible, even without a car. Check with the tourist office, or see the box on p.638, for which village has a market on the day you're going. If you want to explore the valley further, it's a good idea to stay in one of the villages, some of which have self-catering facilities (see box opposite), which are as comfortable as many of Oaxaca's budget hotels.

Santa María del Tule

At **Santa María del Tule** (or just El Tule), 13km east on Hwy-190 as you head out of Oaxaca, you pass the famous **Árbol del Tule** in a churchyard by the road. This mighty tree, said to be at least 1500 years old (some say 3000), is a good 36m round (the signboard claims a girth of 58m, but this is disputed by most experts), slightly fatter than it is tall (around 30m), and weighs in around 500 tons. A notice board gives all the vital statistics, though some of these are rather dubious: suffice to say that it must be one of the oldest living (and flourishing) objects on earth, and it's a species of cypress (*Taxodium mucronatum*) that has been virtually extinct since the colonial era. Known as a Montezuma Cypress or *Ahuehuete* in Mexico (from the Náhuatl), it became the national tree in 1910. Sadly, the Tule tree has recently come under threat from industry and housing projects sapping its water supply. Local environmentalists are pushing for Unesco status in order that an integrated programme of ecological protection, including reforestation of the surrounding area, could be applied – the site was added to Unesco's World Heritage Tentative List in 2001, but has yet to be nominated.

A tacky souvenir market takes advantage of the passing trade, and there are various food and drink stalls. If you want to avoid the tourist hype, sit on the left-hand side of the bus (heading to Mitla) and you may get a glimpse of the tree as you pass. A close-up look, for M$3 (daily 9am–5pm), provides a better view; the tree is mightily impressive. **Buses** for El Tule (M$4.50) depart from the second-class bus station every thirty minutes but can take an hour to get there: to save time catch the same bus one block east of Oaxaca's baseball stadium on Niños Héroes and Blv Eduardo Vasconcelos (they say "Tule" on the top); you can also take the buses to Mitla (see p.640), but you'll have to walk from the highway.

Dainzú

Barely unearthed, the main allure of the ancient Zapotec site of **DAINZÚ** (daily 8am–6pm; M$31) resides in its raw appeal, with few tourists or imposing facilities

Market days in the villages around Oaxaca

Despite Oaxaca's many craft stores, if it's quality you're after, or if you intend to buy in quantity, visiting the villages from which the goods originate is usually a far better, cheaper bet. Each has a different speciality (rugs in Teotitlán del Valle, or black pottery in San Bartolo Coyotepec, for example; see below & p.643), and many have their own market each week. At these you will be able to see the craftspeople in action and you may be able to have your own design made up; quite apart from all that, a village market is an experience in itself.

Monday Miahuatlan: mescal, bread, leather. Ixtlan de Juárez: flowers, produce.

Tuesday Santa Ana del Valle: rugs. Santa Maria Atzompa: pottery.

Wednesday Etla: cheese, flowers.

Thursday Zaachila: meat, nuts. Ejutla: mescal, embroidered blouses.

Friday Ocotlán: flowers, meat, pottery, textiles.

Saturday Oaxaca: everything. Tlaxiaco: leather goods, blankets, *aguardiente* (the local firewater), baskets.

Sunday Tlacolula: mescal, ceramics, rugs, crafts.

to detract from soulful contemplation. Just over 20km from Oaxaca on Hwy-190 and some 7km on from Tule, Dainzú stands partially excavated in a harsh landscape of cactus-covered hills around 1km south of the main road. It was established around 700–600 BC, and carvings here are reminiscent in style, rather than scale, of *Los Danzantes* at Monte Albán, most notably at **Edificio A**, a tomb adorned with a magnificently carved jaguar head. It's the first structure you come across on entering the site, a large, rambling construction set around a courtyard and with elements from several epochs. Nearby is the **ball-court**, only one side of which has been reconstructed. Higher up the hill, **Edificio B** is the best-preserved part of the site; along the far side of its base a series of dancer figures can be made out, similar to the Monte Albán dancers except that these clearly represent ball-players.

Teotitlán del Valle

A short drive beyond Dainzú a road branches off Hwy-190 to **TEOTITLÁN DEL VALLE**, 4km north and the most famous weaving town in Oaxaca. All over the village you see bold-patterned and brightly coloured **rugs** and **sarapes**, some following traditional designs from Mitla, others imitating twentieth-century designs, among them those of Dutch graphic artist M. C. Escher. Century-old recipes are still used in the production of dyes, namely indigo, pomegranate and cochineal. The cochineal beetle secretes a substance that, when dried, creates an inimitable blood-red colour. Rugs are mainly the product of cottage industry: even if you're not buying, poke your head into the compounds with rugs hanging outside. Most weavers will be more than happy to provide a demonstration of pre-Hispanic weaving techniques. When dropped off the bus, you'll probably be pointed along a street to the left, which leads to the **Mercado de Artesanías**. You'll see the widest range here – ask to rummage in the back and you'll find some especially nice deals – and prices are generally cheaper than in Oaxaca. Be sure to check the quality, as some rugs are wool blends and machine-woven.

On the main plaza stands the absorbing **Museo Comunitario Balaa Xtee Guech Gulal** (Tues–Sun 10am–2pm & 4–6pm; M$10) with displays on pre-Hispanic artefacts and information about carpet-weaving and life in the area. Inside the local **church**, the **Templo de la Virgen de la Natividad**, whose walls are studded with bits of Zapotec temple, worship is a syncretic fusion of Catholic and indigenous ritual.

Practicalities

Teotitlán has a few worthy **restaurants**. A favourite with locals as well as tour groups, *Tlamanalli*, Juárez 39 (Tues–Sun 2–5pm), serves delicious local classics such as squash-blossom soup and stewed chicken; the menu changes daily (mains M$80–200). The less expensive *La Cúpula*, on the road into town, offers authentic Zapotec food, including hearty *pozole* soup, adjacent to a fine weaving shop. A wonderful place to **stay**, where you can immerse yourself in the indigenous traditions of the region for a couple of days, is *Casa Sagrada* (Ⓣ951/516-4275, Ⓦwww.casasagrada.com; ❾), a nature retreat that offers cosy rooms adorned with artesanía in a glorious setting and delicious food – breakfast and dinner are included. They can also arrange horseback tours (M$590/2hr, or longer excursions; Ⓦwww.horsebackmexico.com), and taxi pick-up from Oaxaca for M$180. A cheaper but comfy alternative is *Las Granadas* at 2 de Abril no. 9 (Ⓣ951/524-4232, Ⓦwww.lasgranadasoaxaca.com; ❸). There are direct **buses** (M$15) and *colectivos* (M$20) out here every hour or so from the second-class bus station in Oaxaca.

Tlacolula and Santa Ana del Valle

Just six kilometres beyond the turning to Teotitlán del Valle, **TLACOLULA** is a rather scruffy village, but worth a stop to see its sixteenth-century church, the **Parroquia de la Virgen de la Asunción**, about 1km to the south of Hwy-190. The interior is as ornate as Oaxaca's Santo Domingo, though less skilfully crafted. In the adjoining Capilla del Señor de Tlacolula, some gory carvings of martyrs include a decapitated St Paul. The best day to go is Sunday, when there's one of the most important **markets** in the valley (see box opposite). **Buses** leave frequently for Tlacolula from Oaxaca's second-class bus station (M$10; 1hr).

From Tlacolula a road leads 4km north to **SANTA ANA DEL VALLE**, smaller than Teotitlán but with a fine selection of locally produced **rugs**. Lucio Aquino Cruz and his younger brother Primo, at Madero 14, make some of the most exquisite floor coverings in Mexico – it's worth visiting their house just to see them, even if they are beyond your price range. Alternatively, place orders with Lucio for your own designs and you can see the production from beginning to end.

One side of the small central square is devoted to the **Museo Shan-Dany** (Mon–Sat 10am–2pm & 3–6pm; M$10). Its name is Zapotec for "foot of the hill", and it marks the exact spot where a couple of **tombs** were discovered in the 1950s, though excavated more recently. Probably contemporary with Dainzú and Monte Albán, the Zapotec site here boasts some fine glyphs. Excavations have also been carried out beneath what are now basketball courts outside, enough pots and stones being recovered to fill the small but impressive cooperatively run museum. The local weaving industry is also covered and, though panels are all in Spanish, the gist is clear enough. There's a tranquil and well-managed **Tourist Yú'ù** (see box, p.636) in Santa Ana if you want to stay, the local **baker** makes delicious bread, and there's a shop where you can buy basic **provisions**. To **get here**, take a bus to Tlacolula and get off on the outskirts of town on Hwy-190 by the Pemex station. From here you can take taxi or local bus (usually every 10min), or even hike the 6.5km into Santa Ana.

Yagul

One of the least-visited archaeological sites in the region, **YAGUL** (daily 8am–6pm; M$37) lies just to the north of the highway at about the 35-kilometre mark – just a couple of kilometres uphill from where the bus from Oaxaca stops. Its location, atop a large, cactus-dotted plateau overlooking the entire Tlacolula valley, is its major draw. The large site spreads expansively across a superb defensive position, and although occupied by the Zapotecs from a fairly early date, its main features are from later on (around 900–1200 AD, after the fall of Monte Albán) and demonstrate **Mixtec** influence. On the lowest level is the **Patio de la Triple Tumba**, where the remains of four temples surround an altar and the entry to the **Triple Tomb**, whose three funereal chambers show characteristically Mixtec decoration. Immediately above the patio, you'll see a large and elegantly simple ball-court, and a level above this, the maze-like **Palacio de los Seis Patios**. Probably a residential complex, this features six small courtyards surrounded by rooms and narrow passages. Climbing still higher towards the crest of the hill and the fortress, you pass several lesser remains and tombs, while from the fortress itself there are stunning views, and a frightening rock bridge to a natural watchtower.

Mitla

The town of **MITLA** ("Place of the Dead"), where the bus from Oaxaca finally drops you, is some 4km off Hwy-190 and just ten minutes' walk from the site of the famous ruins. It's a dusty little place where you'll be harassed by would-be guides and handicraft vendors (there's also a distinctly second-rate crafts market by the ruins). Good **accommodation** can be found at the *Hotel Don Cenobio* (Ⓣ951/568-0330, Ⓦwww.hoteldoncenobio.com; ⑤), Juárez 3 at Morelos, or the budget *La Zapoteca* (Ⓣ951/568-0026; ③), at 5 de Febrero 12, on the way to the ruins. *Restaurant Don Cenobio*, located in the hotel, is the most stylish place to try local Oaxacan specialities at reasonable prices.

Mitla reached its apogee during the post-Classic period, when Monte Albán was in decline. Construction at the site continued up until the late fifteenth century, at which point it was finally conquered by the Aztecs. The abstract designs on the buildings seem to echo patterns on surviving **Mixtec** manuscripts, and have long been viewed as purely Mixtec in style. But more recent opinion is that the buildings were built by **Zapotecs** and that the city was a ceremonial centre occupied by the most important Zapotec high priest. This Uija-Tao, or "great seer", was described by Alonso Canesco, a fifteenth-century Spaniard, as being "rather like our Pope", and his presence here would have made Mitla a kind of Vatican City.

A few minutes south by local bus from Mitla you'll find the small town of **Santiago Matatlán**, mostly dedicated to mescal production (see p.627), where

▲ The ruins at Mitla

you can visit the ateliers in which the drink is made, enjoy free samples from the town stores, and eat the maguey plant itself. Be warned that a few samples of home-made mescal can wreak havoc with your senses.

The site

While the **site** itself (daily 8am–5pm; M$37, free Sun) may not have the grandiose scale and setting of Monte Albán, Mitla impresses with its superlative bas-reliefs and geometric designs, You'll see it at its best if you arrive towards closing time, when the low sun throws the patterns into sharp, shadowed relief, and the bulk of the visitors have left.

There are five main complexes here, each magnificently decorated with elaborate stone mosaics that are considered peerless throughout Mexico. The **Grupo de las Columnas** is the best preserved and most impressive of these, and the obvious place to head for from the entrance. The first large courtyard in the Grupo de las Columnas is flanked by constructions on three sides – its central **Templo de las Columnas** is magnificent, precision-engineered and quite overpowering in effect. Climbing the broad stairway and through one of three entrances in its great facade, you come to the **Salón de las Columnas**, named after the six monolithic, tapered columns of volcanic stone that supported its roof. A low, narrow passageway leads from here into the small inner patio (**Patio de las Grecas**), lined with some of the most intricately assembled of the geometric mosaics; each of the fourteen different designs here are considered representative of the universe and the gods. Four dark rooms that open off the patio continue the mosaic theme. It is in these rooms that the Uija-Tao would have lived. If the latest theory is correct, the Zapotec architects converted the inner room of the traditional Mesoamerican temple, in which priests usually lived, into a kind of exquisitely decorated "papal flat" arranged around a private courtyard. The second courtyard of the Columns group, adjoining the southwestern corner of the first, is similar in design though less impressive in execution. Known as the **Patio de las Tumbas**, it does contain two cross-shaped tombs, long since plundered by grave-robbers. In one, the roof is supported by the **Columna de la Muerte**; legend has it that if you embrace this, the gap left between your hands tells you how long you have left to live, hand-widths being translated into years remaining (mercifully you can no longer hug the column to test this myth).

The **Grupo de la Iglesia**, a short distance north, is so called because the Spaniards built a church over, and from, much of it in 1590 (Templo de San Pablo Apóstol). Two of its three original courtyards survive, however, and in the smaller one the mosaic decoration bears traces of the original paint, indicating that the patterns were once picked out in white from a dark-red background.

Three other groups of buildings, which have weathered the years less well, complete the site. All of them are now right in the modern town, fenced off from the surrounding houses: the **Grupo de los Adobes** can be found where you see a chapel atop a pyramid; the **Grupo del Arroyo** is near Los Adobes; and the **Grupo del Sur** lies right beside the road to the main site.

Hierve el Agua

Before the environmental degradation worsens, you should visit **HIERVE EL AGUA** (daily 9am–6pm; M$15), the site of a spectacular calcified formation that resembles a bubbling **waterfall**. The site is some 25km east of Mitla, down a side road that leads to **San Lorenzo Albarradas** (Hierve el Agua lies just beyond the village). The mineral concentration causes the water to bubble out of the ground and become petrified over the vertiginous cliff-tops, forming a stunning stalactite; it is a beautiful sight and the panoramas from above the pools, where there several

stalls serving tacos and other snacks, are jaw-dropping. Sadly, tourism here threatens to be more destructive than in the rest of the valley: San Lorenzo can barely support the volume of visitors it receives and disputes between local villagers over how to split the proceeds often closes the site – check with the state tourism office to see if it's open. It is advisable to hire a car to get here; the only public transport is provided by *camioneta* (pick-up truck) from Mitla (M$25 per person), which leave when full. There are a few basic **cabañas ecoturísticas** (M$70) here (though check in advance to see if they are operating), as well as a few simple *comedores*, which close after sunset. Alternatively, tour groups from Oaxaca often take in Hierve El Agua as part of day trip that includes Mitla and Teotitlán del Valle.

The Sierra Norte and the Pueblos Mancomunados

North of the Oaxaca valleys lies the **Pueblos Mancomunados** (literally "joint villages") of the Sierra Norte, a pristine world of pine forests, mist-cloaked mountains and rustic Zapotec villages. The hills are laced with more than a hundred kilometres of signposted rural **footpaths and country roads**, suitable for hikers and mountain-bikers of all abilities, and almost every community offers simple accommodation, local guides and a roster of activities. The paths have been used for centuries by local people accustomed to sharing resources with surrounding communities and the villages are an impressive example of social organization, with eight small towns perched on common land. The landscape is spectacular – some sections of the pine forest have been classified by the World Wildlife Foundation as being the richest and most varied on earth. The **biodiversity** is also phenomenal, with birdlife, butterflies and mammals, including ocelot, puma and jaguar. It's a rewarding place to spend a few days, enjoying nature and getting firsthand experience of rural Oaxacan life.

Don't expect one afternoon to be enough time to really see this area; a visit requires forward planning and at least a couple of days to be worthwhile. The most efficient way to go is through one of the **tour operators** in Oaxaca (see p.618). Tierraventura and Expediciones Sierra Norte organize trips with guides, transport, accommodation and meals for around M$1500 for two days.

Benito Juárez

Perched on a ridge overlooking the Oaxaca valleys (18km north of Teotitlán) and surrounded by pine trees, the little village of **BENITO JUÁREZ** is known for its spectacular sunsets – in clear weather you can see all the way to Mexico's highest mountain, Pico de Orizaba (5636m), from the *mirador* (see p.574). The village makes a good base for exploration of the **Pueblos Mancomunados**, and there's a river where you can **fish** for trout. One of the most enchanting hikes is along the 15km high-altitude footpath between the isolated villages of Latuvi and San Miguel Amatlán, which passes though mystical cloud forest and is believed to be part of a larger pre-Columbian route that connected the Zapotec cities in the Valles Centrales with the Gulf of Mexico – you can still see the remains of an old road along the trail (tours usually take two days to hike this route).

If you prefer to travel independently, the small but extremely helpful **tourist information** office (Mon–Sat 9am–5pm; ☎951/545-9994) in Benito Juárez, next to the town square, has excellent maps which show the varying demands of each trek, and rents out reliable mountain bikes (M$100/3hr), but only with a Spanish-speaking guide (M$120/day, plus M$50 access fee). Next door, the simple and friendly **restaurant** serves cheap breakfasts, *comidas* and hot drinks, and sells sandwiches and water.

Basic accommodation is limited to the Tourist Yú'ù Benito Juárez (Ⓣ951/545-9994; ❸), managed by Expediciones Sierra Norte and the local ecotourism cooperative, which has one dorm with bunk beds (for ten people) and nine cabins with kitchens (make sure the caretaker switches on the hot water before he disappears for the night). **Camping** is also an option, but contact Expediciones Sierra Norte in advance (from M$45). This area has extremes of altitude and temperature – it's advisable to let your body acclimatize before engaging in any strenuous physical activity, to drink plenty of water and wear sunscreen. Temperatures drop dramatically at night, so take warm clothing and a sleeping bag (the Tourist Yú'ù can provide wool blankets).

Ixtlán

IXTLÁN, a pretty Zapotec village near San Pablo Guelatao (the birthplace of Benito Juárez) and 61km north of Oaxaca, is in an area of great natural beauty, and its cloud forests and pine and oak woodlands are claimed to be home to five hundred bird varieties and six thousand species of plants. Before you visit, get in touch with the locally run **Ecoturixtlán** (Ⓣ951/553-6075, Ⓦwww.ecoturixtlan.com.mx) at 16 de Septiembre at the corner of Revolución. They organize tours (from M$300) of all the local beauty spots (Mirador del Cerro Cuachirindo, the Grutas del Arco, the Cascada del Mesofilo and the gentle woodlands of the Bosque Mesofilo), as well as the eighteenth-century village church, the Templo Santo Tomàs Apòstol. The also rent thirteen basic but comfy **cabañas** ($550 for two) in the forest bordering the village, run the best local *comedor*, and arrange a host of bird-watching tours, rent bikes (M$30/hr), and arrange ziplining (from M$15), horseriding (M$100/hr) and rapelling (M$50).

Ixtlán is accessible either by direct **bus** from Oaxaca's second-class station (2 daily; M$30), Cuenca first-class bus (M$40) or by *colectivo* (all around 2hr).

Valle de Zimatlán-Ocotlán

The **Valle de Zimatlán-Ocotlán** that runs almost due south of Oaxaca doesn't have the same concentration of interesting villages and sites as the Valle de Tlacolula, but poking through the communities or admiring the beauty of the area by bike could easily occupy a day or so, especially on **market days**. Again, you can travel around the area by **public transport**, but **cycling** on rented bikes from Oaxaca isn't as arduous as it might sound, especially if you are careful about the midday heat. Oaxaca Pacifico runs buses to Ocotlán via Hwy-175 for M$15 from its terminal at Armenta y López 121, south of La Noria in Oaxaca.

San Bartolo Coyotepec

Thirteen kilometres south of Oaxaca on Hwy-175 lies **SAN BARTOLO COYOTEPEC**, an otherwise dreary town famed for its shiny black pottery, **barro negro**, which can be found in crafts shops all around Oaxaca state, but is only made here. From the bus stop, a road lined with vendors leads to the workshop where, in 1934, one **Doña Rosa** developed a technique for adding the unique lustre to the previously ordinary pottery made in San Bartolo. The pottery may now be too weak to carry mescal to market on the back of a mule, as it did for centuries, but Doña Rosa's invention has yielded a new, purely ornamental vocation that now draws thousands of tourists every year. Although Doña Rosa died in the 1980s, her family still runs the biggest *alfarería* or workshop at Juárez 24 (daily 9am–7pm; Ⓣ951/551-0011), an unashamedly touristy showroom with pieces ranging from beautifully simple amphorae to ghastly clocks. Prices are supposed to be fixed, and at the factory they probably are, but places down the road will haggle; just remember your piece has to get home and the stuff is fragile.

The other main attraction here is the **Museo Estatal de Arte Popular Oaxaca** (Tues–Sun 10am–6pm; M$20; ⓣ951/551-0036) at Independencia on the south side of the plaza, featuring Oaxacan folk art (usefully divided by town), including the black pottery, and two halls of temporary handicraft exhibits.

The best way to **get here** is via *colectivo* from the Mercado de Abastos in Oaxaca, or on one of the many Automorsa minibuses from Miguel Cabrera and Zaragoza – you could also take the minibuses for Ocotlán and the coast (just ask to be dropped off in San Bartolo).

San Martín Tilcajete and Santo Tomás Jalieza

Ocotlán buses continue south, passing **SAN MARTÍN TILCAJETE**, a sleepy town (29km from Oaxaca) whose main street is lined with workshops carving, painting and polishing bright copal-wood figurines known as *alejibres*, which come in all manner of designs – from Day of the Dead skeletons to whimsical creatures. Although not as famous as those in Arrazola (see below), there are still some attractive examples. It's easy to wander through the shops and observe the process. *Colectivo* taxis in Oaxaca run from Arista between Cabrera and Bustamente to San Martín Tilcajete.

To the east of the highway is **SANTO TOMÁS JALIEZA**, where women specialize in weaving cotton on backstrap looms. An all-women's cooperative market in the centre of town sells thick cotton tablecloths and placemats, backpacks, clothing and belts at fixed (though generally reasonable) prices.

Ocotlán

Forty minutes from Oaxaca lies **OCOTLÁN**, chiefly noted for the red **clay** figures crafted here by the Aguilar sisters. On the approach into town, look out on the right for the adjacent workshops of Josefina, Guillermina, Irene and Concepción, each of whom produces slightly different items, in the distinctive Aguilar style originated by their mother. Again, you can find examples in Oaxaca, but a trip out here allows you to see the full range, including figures of animals, men and buxom women at work and play, and even Nativity scenes (apparently no subject matter is off-limits), all often gaudily decorated in polka dots or geometric patterns. Prices here also tend to be much cheaper. Try to make it on a Friday when the weekly **market** takes place not far from the **Parroquia de Santo Domingo de Guzmán**, with its elegantly restored facade and multiple domes richly painted with saints.

Ocotlán is also the birthplace of famous Oaxacan artist **Rodolfo Morales** (1925–2001), who set up the Fundación Cultural Rodolfo Morales here, in his old home at Morelos 108 (Mon–Fri 10am–2pm & 4pm–7pm; ⓣ951/571-0952). The foundation has provided the town with its first ambulance and computer centre, as well as establishing conservation and land-restoration projects. The former convent (next to the church), for example, has been turned into an **art museum** (daily 9am–6pm; M$15) featuring Morales's work in addition to sombre sacred art from the Santo Domingo church, and a restaurant.

Arrazola, Cuilapam and Zaachila

The other major region of interest in this area is along, or beside, Hwy-147 that runs southwest from Oaxaca past the foot of Monte Albán to Zaachila and eventually back to Hwy-175 at San Bartolo Coyotepec. Taxis de Zaachila on Bustamante at Zaragoza run to Zaachila for M$9; Autotransportes Añasa at Bustamante 606 (near Xochitl) has buses to Cuilapam and Zaachila for M$5.

SAN ANTONIO ARRAZOLA, an easy five-kilometre cycle ride off to the right from Hwy-147 (10km southeast of Oaxaca), is the home of the local woodcarvers and painters who produce many of the delightful boldly patterned *alejibres*, animals made from copal wood, that you'll see for sale in Oaxaca and all over Mexico, most of them reasonably priced. The man responsible for transforming this local craft into an art form was Manuel Jiménez (1919–2005), still very much revered in Oaxaca. Following on the heels of his success, entrepreneurial townspeople have turned their skills to carving, creating a thriving cottage industry that produces a fantastical profusion of spiky figures and polka-dot, hooped or expressionist styles. Carvers from other villages are catching on to the popularity but few, if any, are better than in Arrazola.

The village of **CUILAPAM**, 14km southeast from Oaxaca, seems insignificant beneath the immense sixteenth-century hulk of the Dominican **Ex-Convento de Santiago Apóstol**, which, though badly damaged, is still an impressive place to wander around, with a Renaissance twin-aisled nave and largely intact vaulting. The church was never finished, but the original roof still remains on one section, and Mass is said here amid the clangs and echoes of ongoing restoration work. The real interest, however, lies around the back in the **cloister** (daily 9am–6pm; M$31), which features a few faded frescoes on the wall. Look out for the sign pointing to the back wall, where **Vicente Guerrero** was executed by firing squad in 1831 after spending his captivity here.

Buses from Oaxaca continue 5km from Cuilapam to **ZAACHILA**, which has a Thursday **livestock market** that makes for a very entertaining spectacle. Come here then and you've got the best chance of being able to get into the **zona arqueológica** (nominally daily 9am–5pm; M$31), up behind the multi-domed church on the main plaza. The Zapotec town is thought to have flourished from 1100 to 1521, though it was taken over by the Mixtecs towards the end of this period and much of the site remains unexcavated. There's not a great deal to see, but you can step down into the two opened tombs dating from the early sixteenth century – out of what is probably a much larger site – and, when your eyes become accustomed to the gloom, pick out detailed bas-relief geometric figures on the lintel and owls guarding the entrance. Two marvellous glyphs show who was interred here: Señor 9-Flower, probably a Mixtec priest, depicted carrying a bag of copal for producing incense. The revered gentleman was found buried with lavish jewels that are now displayed in the archeological museum in Mexico City, comparable to those discovered in Tomb 7 at Monte Albán.

The Mixteca

The two areas of Oaxaca's Mixteca region – the barren hills of the **Mixteca Baja** and the mountainous, pine-clad **Mixteca Alta** – are not obvious tourist destinations: the pre-Hispanic sites here are far less spectacular than those in the Valles Centrales and there are no artisan centres to compare with Teotitlán or Arrazola. However, the colonial buildings are widely regarded as some of the country's most important, and the low number of visitors means that you are likely to have vast crumbling monasteries and Mixtec ruins to yourself; the main appeal is their aching, faded glory and the spine-tingling sense that you're witnessing a scene that has remained relatively unchanged since before Cortés.

Public transport through the region is fairly easy; from Oaxaca, Autotransportes de Tlaxiaco (5am–5pm) runs every thirty minutes to Tlaxiaco (M$65; 3hr) and Teposcolula (M$50; 3hr) from Díaz Ordaz between Trujano and Las Casas. OCC also runs comfy first-class buses to Tlaxiaco (M$136; 3hr). Hwy-135D, one of the country's best roads, cuts through the Baja's deforested hillsides, eventually reaching Mexico City. Hwy-125 leads off Hwy-135 to the south, traversing the steeper slopes of the Mixteca Alta, eventually arriving at Puerto Escondido via a long and circuitous route.

The Baja: Yanhuitlán, Teposcolula and Coixtlahuaca

Among the **Mixteca Baja**'s highlights are three **Dominican monasteries** – Yanhuitlán, Teposcolula and Coixtlahuaca – imposing relics of Mexico's imperial past. Once centres of mass conversion but virtually abandoned by the 1970s, all three of them have been expertly restored and can easily be visited as a day trip from Oaxaca if you have your own transport; it's less easy if you're relying on public transport, though still possible (see below). If you want to stay, there are plenty of basic hotels on the route from Oaxaca.

Head northwest out of Oaxaca on Hwy-190 for about 120km to reach the first monastery, the **Templo y Ex-Convento de Yanhuitlán** (Mon–Sat 8am–4pm; M$31), the permanent seat of the diocese of the Mixteca during the sixteenth century (the word *convento* was used to describe both monasteries and convents at the time). The church is massive, built on an enormous pre-Hispanic platform overlooking the village, no doubt intended to remind the Mixtecs of the supremacy of the new religion. The vaulted ceiling is a soaring 27m tall. Inside are many original paintings and sculptures – the main altarpiece, dating to 1570, is the work of the Spanish artist Andrés de la Concha. The **Ex-Convento de San Pedro y San Pablo** in **Teposcolula** (Mon–Sat 8am–4pm; M$31), 30km south of here on Hwy-125, has one of the finest *capillas abiertas* in the Americas, completed in the 1560s. These graceful open-air chapels were used for mass preaching and conversion, and are only found in the New World; looking a bit like a cathedral chopped in half, the Teposcolula *convento*'s elegant Romanesque columns, arches and cloisters lie open on one side.

Further north, the **Ex-Convento de San Juan Bautista**, at **Coixtlahuaca** (2km east of the Hwy-135D Coixtlahuaca exit), dates from 1576 and is one of the best preserved of the region's colonial structures; a comprehensive five-year restoration should be complete by 2010 (when entry should be the same as the other two monasteries). If you do get inside, look out for unusual sculptures on the facade depicting grand rosettes, symbols of the Passion and John the Baptist, flanked by sts Peter and James. Red slivers of paint hint at the polychrome finish that would have once glorified the sombre building. There's an impressive churrigueresque altarpiece within the church.

Buses take about an hour and a half to reach Yanhuitlán. You can catch the next bus, or a taxi, to Teposcolula, less than 25km away. From Teposcolula, take a cab or catch a second-class bus to **El Crucero**, at the junction of Hwy-125, Hwy-190 and Hwy-135D, about 10km from the town. Frequent first- and second-class buses heading to Mexico City or Oaxaca stop here. Catch one going towards Mexico City and get off after about 20km at the turn-off to Coixtlahuaca. The monastery is about 2km up a side road.

Santiago Apoala

About 98km north from Oaxaca, reached by following Hwy-190 to the town of **Nochixtlán**, and then heading 40km north on an unpaved road, is the rural village of **SANTIAGO APOALA**, tucked into a captivating high valley. Here you'll find the **Picturas Repuestas**, five-thousand-year-old glyphs considered to be the oldest example of Mixtec drawing. It's a wild place, ideally located for hiking, biking and various other outdoor activities involving the nearby rivers, lagoons and falls; one rewarding hike is to follow the trail alongside the Apoala River to the sixty-metre **Cola de Serpiente** waterfall – you can swim in the pool at the bottom. Many of the trails are badly marked and it is advisable to take a guide with you. The village ecotourism cooperative, **Comité de Turismo de Santiago Apoala** (Ⓣ551/151-9154), can arrange meals, accommodation, organize expeditions and guides (M$120/day) and provide general information;

it offers basic *cabañas* (from around M$200) and campsites for M$35. They also rent bikes for around M$100/day.

The best way to reach Apoala is to take a second-class bus or *colectivo* from Oaxaca to Nochixtlán, where a taxi or microbus (Wed & Sat 1pm, Sun noon) can make the remaining climb into the mountains and into the village's lush, spring-fed valley.

The Alta: Tlaxiaco and around

Hwy-125 climbs into the **Mixteca Alta** after Teposcolula, entering majestic pine forest as it gets closer to Tlaxiaco. On the way, about 50km after Teposcolula, lies **San Martín Huamelulpan**, 2km up a side road. This tiny mountain village has an extensive and mostly unexplored Mixtec archeological site, with two large plazas cut out of a hill, a ball-court and some temple complexes. Some of the sculptures found here have been embedded in the walls of the eighteenth-century colonial church. Other artefacts from the ruins are displayed in the small **Museo Comunitario Hitalulu** (Mon–Fri 9am–5pm; M$10), which also has information about indigenous medicines – these are still used by traditional healers in the local community. The surrounding countryside is picturesque, with deer and coyotes in the woodland, and a variety of unusual plants.

TLAXIACO, a fifteen-minute bus ride beyond Huamelulpan, is famed for its *pulque* (best savoured at the Saturday market stalls), the lightly fermented drink made from cactus. The city once served as the economic heart of the Mixteca, and consequently its important **Saturday market** attracts indigenous people from across the region – many still wear traditional dress. An attractive town square and nearby good-value hotels could serve as a base for exploring the countryside and the Mixtec and Triqui villages nearby. The *Hotel del Portal* (ⓣ953/552-0154; ❸), in a converted colonial house on the main plaza, is a wonderful **place to stay**, especially if you make sure you get a room in the old building. The rather grandiose **restaurant** within serves fresh juices and special dishes such as *molcajete*, a stone bowl of hot stewed meat and vegetables. Slightly better rooms can be found on the edge of town at the *Hotel Del Llano* (ⓣ953/552-0848; ❸), Carretera Putla km 56.5.

Moving on from Tlaxiaco, Autobuses Fletes y Pasajes buses leave for **Pinotepa Nacional** (5–6 daily; 5hr), where you can change for Puerto Escondido and the Pacific coast.

San José del Pacífico

The 250-kilometre journey south from Oaxaca to the coast is dramatic, passing through mountainous forests and descending into tropical lowlands. On route via Hwy-175, perched on the side of a pine-smothered mountain and enveloped in plumes of mist, you'll find **SAN JOSÉ DEL PACÍFICO**, renowned for its hallucinogenic mushrooms. Around three hours' drive south from Oaxaca, it's the best place to break the journey, or to stay for a day or two if you want to enjoy the forest trails and cool mountain air before descending to the tropical lowlands of the coast. Many people also make the short trip from nearby Zipolite, just two hours away (see p.661) for a relaxing overnight stay. The *Cabañas/Hotel La Puesta,* on the main road (ⓣ951/100-8678, ⓦwww.sanjosedelpacifico.com) has a good **restaurant** serving *comidas*, *dulces* and mescal, plus you can stay here in wooden **cabañas** (❸) with incredible views over the valley (try to get one of the cabañas furthest from the restaurant so that you get a clear view). Round the corner, in the centre of the village, there is a pleasant café, *Rayito del Sol*, and small grocery store where you can stop and buy coffee, cakes and excellent *tortas de quesillo*. It gets chilly at night here in winter (although it heats up during the day), so bring warm clothing and a sleeping bag and indulge in some mescal.

Puerto Escondido and around

Though no longer the tranquil hangout it was thirty years ago, **PUERTO ESCONDIDO** ("Hidden Port") remains an irresistible location for most travellers to Oaxaca. With direct flights from the capital, kilometres of sandy beaches and an international surf reputation as home of the "**Mexican Pipeline**", Escondido has firmly established itself as a destination: you'll find the standard strings of souvenir shops, crowded bars, internet cafés and no-frills restaurants along the Adoquín (the main pedestrian strip), as well as constantly spiralling prices that for the most part do not correspond to quality. This said, the town has retained a somewhat languid air; small-scale, casual and uninhibited, there is still the hint of the village it once was, and it's a world away from resorts such as Cancún. This is most evident in the early morning, when fishermen return to Playa Principal, their boats laden with marlin and red snapper, and while there are a tremendous number of **hotels** to choose from, the majority tend to be small and basic, catering to long-stay travellers. Most of the visitors are young, with **surfing** high on their agendas.

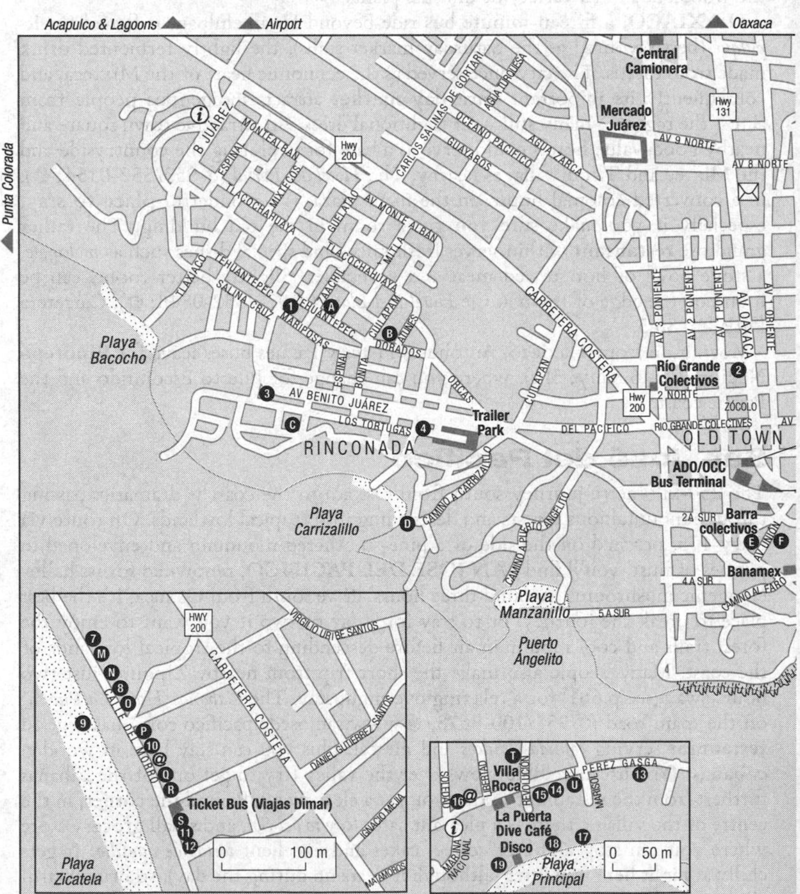

Indeed, it is along the surf beach, **Zicatela**, less than a kilometre away from the centre and divided from the main beach of Playa Principal by a rocky outcrop known as Rocas del Morro, that most of the recent changes have taken place. Where once stood just a few weather-beaten huts, there's now a thriving community with a clutch of hotels – most with pools, since the sea is almost always too rough for swimming – and open-air rustic restaurants serving everything from burgers to fresh fish and Mexican staples. Non-surfers and surfer groupies have also latched onto the relaxed pace, and Zicatela is now as much a destination as Escondido town itself, especially between August and January when the weather is ideal. During the rainy season the town has a much more vacant, lacklustre air – the oppressive humidity creates a marshy, mosquito-ridden beachfront. At either end of the dry season, Escondido is packed for **surf tournaments**.

Despite Zicatela's laid-back atmosphere, **muggings** have occurred in the past, and bright new lighting has been installed in many areas – it's inadvisable to walk in any dimly lit areas at night, but if you use the normal precautions, there shouldn't be any problems.

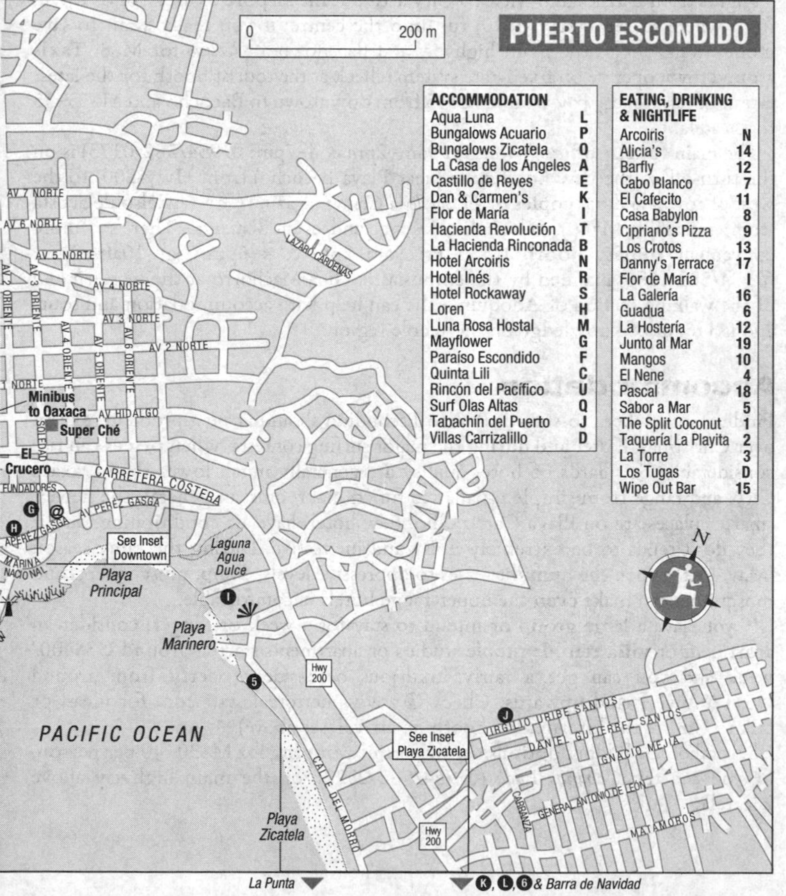

Orientation, arrival and information

Puerto Escondido can be loosely divided into two zones. The **old town** sprawls across the hill behind the bay, separated by Hwy-200 from the newer **tourist zone** along the coast. This starts at **Playa Principal** and **Avenida Pérez Gasga** behind it, the town's main thoroughfare. Half of the latter street is pedestrianized and known as **El Adoquín** – Spanish for "paving stone". **Playa Marinero** separates Playa Principal from **Playa Zicatela** (hidden behind rocks at the east end of the bay), which runs east and then south from here.

Puerto Escondido has two main **bus stations**; the smart, modern OCC/ADO terminal sits on the hill near **El Crucero**, the junction where the main road between the old town and the tourist zone crosses the Carretera Costera (Hwy-200). From El Crucero it's a ten-minute walk to the centre and about twenty to Zicatela; taxis to the latter should cost M$25–35. Turistar and Estrella Blanca (and Sur second-class buses) operate out of the new **Central Turistica de Autobuses** (aka Central Camionera), another 2km north on Avenida Oaxaca. Taxis from here charge M$25 downtown and M$40 to Zicatela. **Minibuses** from Oaxaca city drop you in the centre of the old town, close to the OCC station (see box, p.656).

Flights from Oaxaca and Mexico City arrive at the **airport** 3km north of town, from where shared taxis (M$40) run into the centre; if you really want to save money walk out to the main highway and flag down a *colectivo* for M$8. **Taxis** around town operate on fixed-rate system (check at the tourist booth for the latest rates). Locals usually pay around M$35 from downtown to Bacocho and M$25–35 to Zicatela.

The main **tourist office** (Mon–Fri 9am–2pm & 4–7pm; ⓣ954/582-0175) is on the turn-off to the new hotel zone (near Playa Bacocho) from Hwy-200, to the west of town, and has copies of *El Sol de la Costa* magazine (ⓦwww.elsoldelacosta.com; normally M$10), which has festival and event **listings**. There's a more convenient **tourist booth** (Mon–Fri 9am–2pm & 4–6pm, Sat 10am–2pm; ⓣ954/582-1186) manned by the enthusiastic Gina Machorro at the western end of the walking section of Adoquín – she can help with accommodation and tours and is a fount of knowledge on the whole region.

Accommodation

Finding somewhere to stay in Puerto Escondido shouldn't be a problem, except over Christmas, Easter and during the major surfing contests, when **prices** can rise considerably. Standards of hotel quality are generally much lower than Oaxaca City, and range from simple cabañas to functional rooms; in general, the newer, smarter places are on Playa Carrizalillo. Few hotels have air-conditioning, and if they do it tends to be extremely noisy and ineffective. During the rainy season (May–Oct), when the humidity rises to oppressive levels, damp, musty sheets and mosquitoes can make even the upper-range hotels uncomfortable.

If you have a large group or intend to stay for a week or longer, consider an apartment or **villa rental**; simple studios or apartments start at around US$400/week and you can get a fairly luxurious beachside property from around US$1700/week and upwards. Check ⓦwww.puertorealestate.com for ideas, or talk to Gina at the information booth on arrival (see above).

Several of the budget options below permit **camping** for M$30–40 per person, or you can try *Cabañas Edda* (ⓣ954/582-2322), on the main highway above Zicatela.

The old town, Playa Principal and Playa Marinero

Castillo de Reyes Pérez Gasga 210 ⓣ954/582-0442. Centrally located, this roomy, castle-themed hotel with large, clean, fan-cooled rooms is a few blocks uphill from the Adoquín on a noisy street. A few artisan embellishments add to the warmth of the place. ❸

Flor de María 1a Entrada, Playa Marinero ⓣ954/582-0536, ⓦwww.mexonline.com/flordemaria.htm. With a perfect location on Playa Marinero, within easy reach of Zicatela and the Adoquín, and offering great-value, laid-back comfort, this is a traveller favourite. Some of the fan-cooled rooms have balconies and all have fresh, tiled bathrooms and a safe. There's a rooftop pool with an excellent restaurant (breakfast included during low season) and great views. ❹

Hacienda Revolución Revolución 21 ⓣ954/582-1818, ⓦwww.haciendarevolucion.com.mx. Attractive hotel in a colonial mansion a short walk up the hill from the Adoquín, with a tranquil courtyard, and simple but clean rooms – the revolution theme is maintained with displays of Pancho Villa-like memorabilia. ❹

Loren Pérez Gasga 507 ⓣ954/582-0057. High-standard, brightly painted hotel away from the ocean but with a good pool and impressively low off-season prices, which can be slashed by up to fifty percent – no a/c in rooms though. ❸

Mayflower Andador Libertad s/n ⓣ954/582-0367. Travellers love or hate this well-managed place overlooking the Adoquín. Double rooms and dormitories (M$90), a bar, a communal kitchen and ample common areas foster a long-term, sociable traveller vibe – but this is definitely what the locals call "gringolandia". Some upper rooms have little balconies where you can glimpse the Pacific. ❸

Paraíso Escondido Unión 10 ⓣ954/582-0444, ⓦwww.hotelpe.com. One of the best-maintained hotels in the area, located on the hill before the Adoquín, with stellar views and lush gardens. Tidy rooms all have balconies and are artistically decorated with kitsch mirrors, tiles and sculptures (some have dipping pools). There is also a central, pretty pool, bar and restaurant area. It's a real bargain in low season (M$675). ❺

Rincón del Pacífico Pérez Gasga 900 ⓣ954/582-0056, ⓦwww.rincondelpacifico.com.mx. Can be cheap in low season; slightly motel-like, but clean, decent-sized rooms with a/c and cable TV overlooking the beach and its own stone courtyard – look for the entrance at *Danny's Terrace*. ❹

Zicatela

The hotels below are listed in order of distance from Playa Principal.

Tabachín del Puerto Calle del Moro s/n ⓣ954/582-1179, ⓦwww.tabachin.com.mx. Just one block from the beach, this eclectic cluster of six studios, some with large, breezy balconies, is crammed with books, knick-knacks and vases that add to its quirky, comforting appeal. The owner is keen to help with any tours, and substantial vegetarian breakfasts are included. Fans, a/c and cable TV in each room. ❺

Luna Rosa Hostal Calle del Morro s/n ⓣ954/118-7398, ⓦwww.zicatela.org/lunarosa. Novel, women-only hostel, with spacious dorms (M$100) and private rooms right on the beachfront (above Cinemar Zicatela) – very popular with solo female travellers and surfers. Lockers, hot water and kitchen included. ❸

Hotel Arcoiris Calle del Morro s/n ⓣ954/582-1494, ⓦwww.hotel-arcoiris.com.mx. This is one of the better-value options if you want to be at the heart of the Zicatela surfing action. Functional rooms with private baths and fans – some have kitchenettes – are set back from the shore in a modern three-storey block, but do need upgrading. The main draws here are the relaxing and friendly vibe, the luxuriant gardens with secluded pool, and the restaurant with great views and a decent fish and meat dishes. ❺

Bungalows Zicatela Calle del Morro s/n ⓣ954/582-0798, ⓦwww.bungalowszicatela.com.mx. A modest jumble of large rooms, most with a kitchen. The action is centred around the pool and adjacent restaurant with bar. ❹

Bungalows Acuario Calle del Morro s/n ⓣ954/582-1027, ⓦwww.oaxaca-mio.com/bunacuario.htm. A laissez-faire hotel with simple lodgings to suit low- and mid-range budgets. With an attractive pool and bar, a gym (M$15/day for non-guests), an a/c internet café and a communal vibe, there would be no need to leave if you weren't right in the centre of Playa Zicatela. There are a lot of mosquitoes, though, and some furnishings are faded and musty – ask to see a few rooms. Cabins ❹, a/c rooms ❺

Surf Olas Altas Calle del Morro 310 ⓣ954/582-2315, ⓦwww.surfolasaltas.com.mx. For the more chi-chi surfer, this large, spotless, but rather banal, hotel has more creature comforts – safe, a/c, TV – modernity and order to it than the other hotels but lacks some of their organic charm. ❼

Hotel Inés Calle del Morro s/n ⓣ954/582-0792, ⓦwww.hotelines.com. With an artistic feel, a sauna and spa, the German-managed *Inés* has plentiful facilities for this price range. With rooms for various budgets; sharing a cabaña with a group is especially economical. There's a hotel pool and a pleasant restaurant. ❹

Hotel Rockaway Calle del Morro s/n ⓣ954/582-0668, ⓦwww.hotelrockaway.com. A dedicated surfer resort. Pleasant palapa cabins with private showers flank one side of a large swimming pool while facing a newly constructed, comfortable but sterile, hotel with a/c, queen-size beds and cable TV. The lively on-site bar draws the older Jimmy Buffet-style contingent in town, and there's a surf shop and a volleyball court. Very good value, especially in the low season when hotel doubles drop to M$400, singles M$300. Cabins ❷, rooms ❺

Dan & Carmen's Jacaranda 14 ⓣ954/582-2760, ⓦwww.casadanycarmen.com. Very cool place with lots of character, a short walk behind the beach. A variety of rooms are available, each with a kitchen, terrace, great views and artfully decorated bathrooms. Larger rooms are very spacious and cost-effective for groups or families. Reservations advised in the high season. ❹

Aqua Luna Vista Hermosa s/n ⓣ954/582-1505, ⓦwww.hotelaqualuna.com. Smart, minimalist hotel with neat, well-equipped rooms – as close to a boutique hotel as you'll get in Zicatela. Hospitably run by a Canadian–Mexican couple who are knowledgeable about the area, it makes a very pleasant base. There's also the added allure of a swimming pool, palapa bar, wide-screen TV, pool table and laundry service. ❸

Rinconada, Playa Carrizalillo and Playa Bacocho

La Casa de los Ángeles Zaachila 9 ⓣ954/582-0889, ⓦwww.casadelosangelesboutique.com. Tranquil, luxurious boutique hotel away from the action for non-surfing Escondido visitors; there are six one-bedroom suites, with kitchen, living room and terrace, and access to a health club and rooftop palapa. ❼

La Hacienda Rinconada Atunes 15 ⓣ954/582-0279, ⓦwww.suiteslahacienda.com. Thanks to their gracious French owner, the six very comfortable, spacious bedrooms with kitchenettes and a/c ooze home-spun style. Outside, a colonial theme prevails, with flower-filled patios and a swimming pool surrounded by tropical foliage. A 5min walk from Playa Carrizalillo, it's not cheap, but one of the better places if you are inclined to splurge. ❼

Quinta Lili Cangrejos 104 ⓣ555/406-4759, ⓦwww.quintalili.com. Fabulous deal, just off the beach, with neat, spacious rooms, LCD TVs, iPod docks, fans and balconies with sea views, all set in a whimsical beach house, half-palapa, half-Moorish palace. Excellent breakfasts and helpful hosts. ❺

Villas Carrizalillo Carrizalillo 125 ⓣ954/582-1735, ⓦwww.villascarrizalillo.com. In a peaceful spot above its beautiful namesake beach, these discreet, spacious, individually designed villas with kitchens and stunning views are perfect for young couples and families who want a few home comforts away from the party scene. There is free internet, lap-tops and aquatic equipment for rent and a welcoming atmosphere – but the area is developing rapidly. ❽

The beaches

Apart from **shopping** for international surf designs, beachwear and crafts (some tacky, some classy), Escondido offers little beyond the standard **beach activities**: swimming, surfing, lazing on the sand, eating, drinking and watching beautiful sunsets, though if you have time there are a growing number of places offering everything from salsa to cooking lessons, in addition to the usual Spanish – ask at the information booth.

The choice of **beaches**, even within a couple of kilometres of town, is impressive. Note that wherever you are, the surf should be treated with respect – the waters along Zicatela, especially, have a lethal **undertow**.

It's possible to take a **boat** (M$50) to all the beaches below, and some further afield, from the beach in front of the *Hotel Rincón del Pacífico* on Playa Principal. It should then return to pick you up at an agreed time. The same boats charge M$400 for a full tour of the coast, beaches and local turtles (45min), while specialized turtle tours are M$1500.

Playa Principal and Playa Marinero

Puerto Escondido has several beach areas, beginning with the town beach (**Playa Principal**), which stretches round to the east and south from the old town centre, frequented primarily by Mexican families. The sand here is perhaps a little overused, and shared, too, with the local fishermen and the activities of the port. A little to the east, beyond where the **Laguna Agua Dulce** occasionally reaches the sea, **Playa Marinero** is quieter and sometimes graced with gentle waves – it's a good place to learn to surf.

Playa Zicatela

The real big stuff is past Playa Marinero, beyond the little headland, where **Playa Zicatela** stretches for 2km, cluttered with palapa bars the whole way; this is the preferred hangout of most foreign travellers. One of the world's top surf beaches, Zicatela ("place of big thorns") regularly receives beach breaks of around four metres and can maintain the surf swell for days on end. This spot is referred to as the "**Mexican pipeline**", because the breaking waves curl into perfect cylinders – permitting expert surfers to momentarily ride inside the tubes. Surfboards and boogie boards can be rented from a number of places along Zicatela beach. When the waves are really nasty, consider your strength and fitness (you can check the wave reports online at one of the internet cafés, or ask in one of the surf shops) before venturing into the water: occasionally even experienced surfers drown, although there are *salvavidas* (lifeguards) patrolling the beach. If the pipeline is too much for you to handle, continue east for a little over a kilometre down the beach to **La Punta** ("the point"). La Punta is a much easier break, though it can also be exceptional when the swell is up. It usually provides good, slower waves that are excellent for longboarding and is recommended as a spot to learn to surf when the waves are smaller.

Puerto Ángelito to Punta Colorada

Everything is much calmer in the coves to the west of the town. **Puerto Ángelito** is the closest, divided in two by a rocky outcrop, with a second beach, slightly further inland from Ángelito, called **Manzanillo**. They're about twenty minutes' walk from town, either by a track that leads to the left off Peréz Gasga, or direct from the highway on a signed road leading down opposite *El Padrino* restaurant (the two paths meet above the beach). An alternative is the concrete footpath that sets out from the western end of the town beach, dipping and turning over the coastal rocks and eventually climbing up to a road. Follow this inland, then turn left along the road signposted "Playa Manzanillo", which turns into steps going down to the beach. You can also drive or get a taxi to drop you off at the top of the steps to the beach. Both little inlets have small beaches and excellent snorkelling among the rocks (if you can avoid the boats), but you'll have to bring your own gear or rent some at great expense (M$100/half-day) from the makeshift restaurants lining the beach.

The next bay, **Playa Carrizalillo**, is a spell-binding cove reached by continuing west along the same track. At the end you have to scramble down over 160 steps to reach the sand, guaranteeing that there won't be too many other people around – it's the best beach in the area and well worth the effort. **Playa Bacocho** is further, following the highway out towards the airport and then cutting through the new hotel zone. There aren't a great number of hotels here yet, so the sand is still somewhat secluded, though swimming isn't considered safe – the beach is pounded by heavy surf and has a **strong undertow**. **Punta Colorada**, a little-visited, clean beach around the point at the far end of Bacocho is perfect for body-boarding and boogie-boarders; you'll get tubes, and left and right breaks up to two metres high – it tends to be shallow however.

Activities

Activities and ecotourism adventures are big business in Puerto Escondido, with everything from lagoon trips to cycling, camping, rock climbing, bird watching and tours of hot springs and coffee plantations on offer. Viajes Dimar (Ⓦwww.viajesdimar.com) can arrange almost anything and has offices in town at Pérez Gasga 905-B (at *Hotel Casa Blanca*; Ⓣ954/582-1551) and Zicatela (at the *Bungalows Puerta del Sol*; Ⓣ954/582-2305).

Surfing lessons are offered at several places: the most reliable are Central Surf (Ⓣ954/582-2285, Ⓦwww.centralsurfshop.com) on Zicatela, and Oasis Surf Academy (Ⓣ954/104-2330, Ⓦwww.oasissurffactory.com) at Juárez 1 (in front of *Cafecito*) over in Rinconada. Rates tend to be around M$300/hr, with **board rentals** from M$150/day.

Several outfits offer **scuba diving**, including the Puerto Dive Center (Ⓣ954/102-7767, Ⓦwww.puertodivecenter.com), which runs four-day courses from US$320 and two-tank dives from US$65; Aventura Submarina (Ⓣ954/582-2353) is also worth checking out. Both have offices on the Adoquín. **Fishing** trips can be arranged by Omar Sportfishing (Ⓣ954/559-4406, Ⓦwww.tomzap.com/omar.html); Captain Omar Ramírez also does dolphin and whale-watching tours from his base on Playa Puerto Ángelito. Rates are around; M$500/hr.

For something a little less energetic, Temazcalli, 10min out of town on Hwy-200 past Zicatela beach and over the bridge, at Infraganti and Temazcalli (Ⓣ954/582-1023, Ⓦwww.temazcalli.com), has a range of spa treatments, from **massages** (M$350) to **temazcal** (traditional sauna; M$300).

Escondido is also a popular place to study **Spanish**. Among the most highly recommended are the Oasis Language School (Ⓣ954/109-1319, Ⓦwww.oasislanguageschool.info) at Juárez 2 in Rinconada, offering private lessons (90min) for US$75/week (one class per day), or two-hour group lessons for the same price per week. They can also arrange homestays or apartment rentals for around US$125/week. The Instituto de Lenguajes (Ⓣ954/582-2055, Ⓦwww.puertoschool.com), on the main road behind Zicatela, also offers popular private lessons for US$12/hr, group lessons for US$8/hr and various packages for food and lodging.

Eating, drinking and nightlife

It doesn't cost much to eat well in Escondido. Many of the restaurants and cafés are laid-back, low-key affairs open to cool breezes and with plenty of natural light. The **seafood** is always fresh, and you can vary your diet with **vegetarian** food, excellent bread and cakes and **Italian** food from the inordinately large number of Italian restaurants. For cheap snacks, it's worth strolling into the old town to the **Mercado Juárez** and the taco stalls along Oaxaca, and you can buy self-catering provisions at the *Super Che* supermarket near El Crucero. You should also check out the up and coming **Rinconada** area, with another enticing assortment of restaurants and bars. **Nightlife** is concentrated here and along the bars of Pérez Gasga near Playa Principal, though plenty of restaurants double as watering holes along Zicatela as the sun goes down.

There are arthouse **films** on show at Cinemar Zicatela, at the east end of Zicatela, usually in English or with subtitles (fifteen people only). The schedule is on view outside – there are two showings nightly (7 & 9pm; M$45).

Old town, Playa Principal and Playa Marinero

Alicia's Pérez Gasga (near *Danny's Terrace*). No-frills, inexpensive cafeteria with a broad menu including seafood, Italian and authentic Mexican dishes. For lunch, the comida corrida is great value (M$45).

Los Crotos Pérez Gasga Ⓣ954/582-0025. At the edge of the Playa Principal, an unassuming joint that sparkles at night and serves an unpretentious menu of extremely fresh whole grilled fish.

Danny's Terrace Pérez Gasga 900 ⓣ954/582-0257. Seafood specialist, known for its high-quality dishes such as prawn curry (M$110) and prawn tacos (M$80). Daily 7am–11pm (happy hour 5–7pm).

Flor de María Playa Marinero. Attached to the hotel of the same name, *Flor de María* is an inviting place for a quiet meal. The menu features dishes like stuffed peppers, roast meats and pastas.

La Galería Pérez Gasga ⓣ954/582-2039. One of the best Italian joints in town, with platters of home-made tortellini, spaghetti, ravioli and gnocchi as well as delicious salads and an array of pizzas, all served in a polished setting with art displayed on the walls and exposed brick. Mains average M$90–100.

Junto al Mar Pérez Gasga. At the western end of the Adoquín, opening onto the sea, this rustic, open-air restaurant sticks to unadulterated grilled seafood dishes that are tasty and well proportioned. With views over Playa Marinero, there is plenty of beach action to entertain at sunset.

Pascal Andador Gloria, Playa Principal ⓣ954/103-0668. Fabulous restaurant and bar right on the beach, this French-owned place serves up all sorts of fresh seafood, pastas and occasionally live music – most main dishes range M$75–150. Open from 6pm daily.

Sabor a Mar Playa Marinero ⓣ954/102-7090. Easy to miss, the relaxed open-air place serves some of the best seafood in town – just ask for the freshest fish of the day.

Taquería La Playita 3 Nte (just west of Oaxaca). Escape "gringolandia" with a stroll into town for the best *tacos pastor* on the coast. Open from 7pm only.

Wipe Out Bar Pérez Gasga. This multilevel bar and club is the favourite spot on the Adoquín for surfers and travellers, so don't come here looking for a quiet drink – it gets packed and rowdy, with hip-hop and electronica blaring most nights. Wed–Sat 7.30pm–2am.

Playa Barocho, Rinconada and Playa Carrizalillo

El Nene Juárez 14, Rinconada. Great Mexican restaurant with a few sidewalk tables, tasty tacos (M$36), *hamburguesas* (M$35), natural juices, and the special, *chili con carne*. It also has the best margaritas in town. Open 2–10pm.

The Split Coconut Guelatao at Tlacochahuaya, Barocho ⓣ954/582-0736, ⓦwww.jardin-real.com. Favourite expat bar serving mouth-watering barbecue and burgers, with live music on Sundays, good wi-fi, satellite TV and daily happy hour 3–5pm. The July 4 celebrations are big here. Closed Mon & Tues.

La Torre Juárez 427, Rinconada ⓣ954/582-1119. This smart and locally popular restaurant is noted for its delectable steaks (from M$115), fresh fish (M$105), sandwiches (M$55) and Chinese (Thurs) and BBQ ribs (Fri) nights. The outdoor garden seating is great in the summertime. Tues–Sun 5–11pm.

Los Tugas *Villas Carrizalillo*, Carrizalillo 125 ⓣ954/582-0995. Fine dining in a posh palapa restaurant, with mesmerizing views of the bay – try and get a table on the edge of the terrace. Expect an international menu featuring pastas, curries, grilled meats and seafood – also does US-style and Mexican breakfasts. Mon–Sat 8am–1pm, 5–10pm, usually closed Sun.

Zicatela

The restaurants and bars below are all on the seafront and listed in order of distance from Playa Principal.

Cabo Blanco ⓣ954/582-0337. Hit-or-miss seafood on the beach at reasonable prices. Fish and shrimp are dressed with a more imaginative choice of sauces than at other similar restaurants: try the Thai curry or lime, wine and cream. Live music most nights draws a boisterous crowd. Mains start at M$60.

Cipriano's Pizza Thin, crispy, cheesy pizzas, served at romantic tables wedged into the sand.

Arcoiris The main draw here is the elevated beachfront location, but the traditional Mexican dishes are generally very good value and tasty. An uninspired selection of international dishes include pastas and mercilessly fried fish. There are also vegetarian comidas corridas – bland, but meat-free; strict vegetarians should request that their meal not be fried in animal fat.

Casa Babylon Arty, friendly, late-night bar next door to the *Hotel Arcoiris*. Board games, mellow music and a useful reference library with travel books and *National Geographic* magazines. Opens 10.30am–2pm and 8pm till late.

Mangos Always crowded, with hearty breakfasts for just M$19–35, and an eclectic menu that includes chow mein, BBQ ribs and grilled chicken. Daily 7am–midnight (happy hour 6–11pm).

La Hostería ⓣ954/582-0005. Wood-oven pizzas (M$75–130) and imaginative Italian and nouvelle Mexican dishes are served with flair and a decent wine selection. It's also one of the best places for creative vegetarian dishes. Substantial breakfasts are available.

Barfly (upstairs from *Hostería*), ⓦwww.barfly.com.mx. The hub of Escondido's bar scene, this eclectic

Moving on from Puerto Escondido

First-class buses depart from the ADO/OCC terminal near El Crucero, or the Central Turistica de Autobuses (aka Central Camionera), another 2km north on Avenida Oaxaca; OCC is best for **Oaxaca** (M$270; 10–12hr) and destinations in **Chiapas**, while Turistar and Estrella Blanca (at Central) are faster for **Mexico City** (M$680; 12hr) and **Acapulco** (M$350; 8hr); departures are not frequent, so check in advance. OCC is also best for frequent buses to **Huatulco** (M$80; 2hr 30min) and **Pochutla** (for Puerto Ángel; M$50; 1hr 30min). Second-class buses from the OCC terminal charge around M$30 for Pochutla and M$40 for Huatulco. **Ticketbus** has convenient agent offices on Pérez Gasga and Zicatela. To avoid the twelve-hour trip to **Oaxaca**, take one of the faster (but often vomit-inducing) minibuses from the centre of town: Express Bus (6am–10pm) at the *Hotel de Ángel* at 1 Norte and Oaxaca, and Villa del Mar (5am–6.30pm; both M$150 & 6hr), one block down on Hidalgo just west of Oaxaca.

You can get daily thirty-minute **flights** to Oaxaca with Aerotucán (☎954/582-1725) and Aerovega (☎954/582-0151); the approximate cost one way is M$1200–1400. There are also daily Mexicana (see p.35) flights to Mexico City, with the best prices available in advance online (from around M$1400).

For further information, see Travel details, p.672.

lounge with a balcony overlooking the beach plays good international music and has comfy cushions for you to lie on while you sip a frosty cocktail.

El Cafecito ☎954/582-0516. Justifiably longstanding favourite, this local chain has another branch in Rinconada. Wonderful, wholesome breakfasts (under M$50) and *jugos* (M$21) compete with the aromas of freshly baked pastries (M$13) and Oaxacan coffee from sister *Panaderia Carmen's*, served in an open-air palapa. The lunchtime menu has an international flavour, with burgers, whole-grain sandwiches and burritos. Tasty, simple seafood dishes and other filling Mexican staples feature in the evening (M$70–100).

Guadua On the beach at Tamaulipas, near La Punta ☎954/107-9524, Ⓦwww.guadua.com.mx. Breezy palapa on the sand, serving the high-quality fusion cuisine of chef Ricardo Morales, who combines fresh, local ingredients with Asian and European cooking styles; think seared tuna with teriyaki sauce or fish *ceviche* with mango and mint. Fabulous cocktails. Tues–Sun 5–11pm.

Listings

Banks and exchange There's a casa de cambio on the Adoquín (Mon–Sat 9am–9pm, Sun 9am–5pm), although better rates are available just up the hill at the busy Banamex on Pérez Gasga near the *Paraíso Escondido* (Mon–Fri 9am–5pm, Sat 10am–2pm), which also has an ATM. There is also an HSBC ATM halfway along the Adoquín and in Zicatela along Morro. Also in Zicatela, there's a cambio in front of *Bungalows Acuario* (see p.651).

Internet access There are several slightly pricey internet cafés in Zicatela and on Pérez Gasga charging around M$15/hr. Venturing outside the tourist zone around the Adoquín leads to cheaper, M$10/hr internet access – head north of the Carretera Costera on any major street.

Laundry Lava Max, towards the east end of the Adoquín, offers self-service machines or a drop-off laundry service for M$15/kg.

Police ☎954/582-0498; help line ☎954/540-3816; tourist police ☎954/582-3439.

Post office In the old town at Oaxaca and 7A Nte (Mon–Fri 9am–3pm & 6–8pm, Sat 9am–1pm), though you can get stamps from postcard vendors (at a half-peso premium) and chance your luck with the mail boxes along Pérez Gasga.

Telephones There are several Telmex card phones on the Adoquín, and in Zicatela.

Around Puerto Escondido: the lagoons

Unless you're a hardcore surfer or ardent sun-worshipper, a few days relaxing on the beach is usually sufficient before you feel the need to explore. In addition to a range of activities on offer (see p.654), there are also a few boat excursions around Puerto Escondido that make for enjoyable, accessible day trips.

Laguna Manialtepec

Laguna Manialtepec, about 15km west of the city (km 124 on Hwy-200 to Acapulco), is cut off from the sea most of the year, forming a freshwater lake extraordinarily rich in **birdlife**. You can easily spot fifty-odd species (there are said to be 270 in total), including parrots, hawks, falcons, ospreys, kingfishers and ibises. The most convenient way to visit is to take an organized **tour** through one of the travel agencies in Puerto Escondido. Hidden Voyages Ecotours (ⓦwww.peleewings.ca) runs trips led by Canadian ornithologist Michael Malone (Dec 15–March 25 daily, except Thurs and Sun; 7am–noon; M$600, by kayak M$750). Contact Viajes Dimar (p.654) for additional information. Alternatively, Lalo Ecotours (ⓣ954/588-9164, ⓦwww.lalo-ecotours.com) is open throughout the year in the village of **LAS NEGRAS** on the shores of the lagoon; they rent kayaks and boats and run a variety of tours by boat (M$400; 3hr) or kayak (M$400/day), guided hikes (M$400/half-day) and evening tours to see the phosphorescence in the water (M$250/2hr). They also tour Chacahua (see below; M$600/day) and offer horseback tours to the Atotonilco hot springs (M$400/half-day).

If you can get enough people together it is worthwhile organizing a boat trip independently; take a taxi for around M$100, or a Río Grande-bound *colectivo* from 2A Norte and 3A Poniente for M$10 (ask to get off at *El Gallo*). At restaurant *Isla del Gallo* (on the main highway), you can hire a **boat** for four passengers and captain (2hr 30min; M$700) or rent kayaks for around M$50/hr. *La Puesta del Sol* (ⓣ954/588-3867), further along the lake, is a palapa restaurant right on the water serving tasty food and offering a similar roster of services.

Parque Nacional Lagunas de Chacahua

The **Parque Nacional Lagunas de Chacahua**, some 75km west of Puerto Escondido (another 60km along Hwy-200 from Manialtepec), makes for a more diverse venture – in order to visit independently you will need a couple of days at least. This 150,000-hectare park is a refuge of mangroves, sand dunes and forests that teem with birdlife, turtles and crocodiles. On the shores of the lagoon the village of **CHACAHUA** is interesting in itself, with a small Afro-Mexican population and a huge beach where you can rent basic **cabañas** (❶) by the water. The lagoon is calm enough in parts but also has some good surf, though the currents are strong, so check where it's safe to swim. There's also space to **camp** and a row of outdoor seafood restaurants where you could hang a hammock. To **get here** from Escondido catch the *colectivo* (see above; every 20min; M$20/person) to **Río Grande**, 50km west of Puerto Escondido on Hwy-200, then change to one of the frequent minibuses (M$10) to the port of **Zapotalito**. From here you can take a *lancha* to the village and the wonderful sands at **Playa Chacahua**; boats all the way cost around M$400, but it's just M$250 if you travel half-way via *camioneta*. If you're prepared to wait, *colectivo* boats charge around M$50 and M$25 per person respectively. A two-hour boat tour will cost around M$1000 per boat (six people). You should be able to negotiate a **taxi** all the way to Zapotalito from Escondido for M$400–500. For more information check ⓦwww.lagunasdechacahua.com.

Barra de Navidad

An ecotourism project has been established in **BARRA DE NAVIDAD**, ten minutes east of Puerto Escondido on Hwy-200 (the turning, on the right, comes just after the bridge that crosses the lagoon). For M$80, locals will take you on a 45-minute walking tour around the **Laguna Las Naranjas**, a local **crocodile** lagoon, and nearby deserted beach – a haven for **birdlife**. You can also take a short tour of Galo's **Iguanario** when you arrive (donation requested only); get off at the last stop (the first right after crossing the Río Colotepec) and walk 50m to the Iguanario on the left, where you can see a motley collection of iguanas, crocodiles and turtles. **Colectivos** marked "Barra" run here from the highway near El Crucero in Escondido (M$4 per person) – you can get more information at the tourist booth on the Adoquín (see p.650).

Once here you can **eat** at *La Huerta de Don Juan y Doña Lola* (☎954/588-3269) on the main avenue; enjoy home-cooked fish and shellfish under a huge palapa with plastic tables and chairs in the midst of lush palms.

Puerto Ángel and around

Some 65km from Puerto Escondido, at the junction of Hwy-175 from Oaxaca and coastal Hwy-200, the oppressive, shabby town of **Pochutla** is the service hub for a string of beach towns and resorts that unfurl east towards the Isthmus of Tehuantepec. **Puerto Ángel**, now firmly on the tourist radar, is a dusty, rough-hewn village that draws budget travellers with its unpretentious, low-key vibe and picturesque setting with crescents of golden sand backed by craggy, jungle-covered hills. Four miles west, the beautiful beach of **Zipolite** has gained a reputation for its liberal-minded, 1960s European hippy vibe, while north over the headland, attractive **San Agustinillo** has a more restrained feel. Further west, **Mazunte** is the main nesting site for Golfina turtles and, as yet, remains an unspoiled enclave where you can escape civilization on pristine beaches.

Pochutla

Anyone visiting Puerto Ángel and the other beach communities along the coast comes through **POCHUTLA**, a scruffy town on Hwy-175, 2km north of Hwy-200. Apart from catching a bus or changing money – there are no banks at the beaches beyond Puerto Ángel – there's no reason to stop here.

The **bus stations** – the second-class Estrella Blanca (☎958/584-0380), Oaxaca Pacífico (☎958/584-0349) and the first-class OCC (☎958/584-0274) – are close to each other on Lázaro Cárdenas, which runs from Hwy-200 into the centre of town. Daily first-class services cover Huatulco, Mexico City, Oaxaca, Puerto Escondido and San Cristóbal de las Casas; daily second-class buses leave for the same destinations and local villages.

Further along Cárdenas, HSBC (Mon–Fri 8am–7pm, Sat 8am–3pm), with ATM, will change travellers' cheques and dollars as well as issue cash advances. Scotiabank (Mon–Fri 9am–5pm) or Bancomer (Mon–Fri 8.30am–4pm), both with ATM, will change **money**. If for some reason you get stuck here, the best **hotel** in the centre is the clean, well-run *Costa del Sol*, Cárdenas 47 (☎958/584-0049; ❸). The usual **food** options ring the plaza, but the best place to eat is out of town, just north of Puerto Ángel on Hwy-175, where the *Finca de Vaqueros* outdoor barbecue restaurant is famous with locals for grilled meats of every kind. Two cowboy brothers keep the place open every day of the year, but it's a hassle to get to without a car.

"Pasajeras" (covered pick-up trucks) head down frequently to Puerto Ángel, Zipolite and Mazunte from Cárdenas, along with **colectivos** or *especial* **taxis**; one of these taxis may cost well over five times as much, so go *colectivo* – you shouldn't have to wait long for fellow passengers and fares rarely top M$15 per person. In Puerto Ángel, the taxis drop off at the rank by the dock. If you want to go further, over to Playa del Panteón for example, make this clear as you set out or you'll be charged an outrageous amount for the last part of the journey (you probably will be anyway, but at least you'll be prepared).

Puerto Ángel

Though it's well established as a tourist destination, **PUERTO ÁNGEL** still goes about its business as a small, down-at-heel fishing port with minimum fuss. Everything remains resolutely low-key – you may very well find pigs and chickens mingling with the visitors on the streets – and locals fish off the huge concrete dock, catching yellowtail tuna and other gamefish with a simple rod and line. Though it has a gorgeous setting – around a sheltered bay and ringed by mountains – the beaches are less than pristine. Small hotels, rooms and simple places to sling a hammock, however, are abundant, with some of the most promising on the road between the main village and the Playa del Panteón. If you're on a tight budget Puerto Ángel can be a fun place to spend a few days, meandering and sampling the superb local **seafood**, while the fabulous *Casa Bichu* will appeal to those willing to splurge.

Arrival and information

Buses from Oaxaca City and *colectivos* from Pochutla drop off at the junction of Vasconcelos and Uribe (there's also a taxi stand here), the de facto centre of town and a short stroll from the **tourist information booth** at the pier entrance on Uribe (Mon–Fri 10am–noon & 4–8pm, Sat–Sun 10am–noon); actual hours tend to be erratic. The town's only **bank** is Banco Azteca on Uribe (daily 9am–9pm), but Bancomer (near *Hotel Soraya*) and HSBC (at the Agencia Municipal) now have ATMs. The **post office** is on Avenida Principal, the main road into the centre, while you can access the **internet** (M$15/hr) at Gel@Net, Vasconcelos 3 (just off Uribe).

Accommodation

Puerto Ángel's **hotels** are a bit scattered, but the village is small enough that you should be able to find someone to mind your bags while you look around. The places listed below represent only a fraction of the total, but you'll find little better.

Bahía de la Luna Playa la Boquilla ⓣ958/589-5020, ⓦwww.bahiadelaluna.com. An escape for couples happy to do without creature comforts, this jungle retreat close to beautiful La Boquilla beach (wonderful snorkelling) is hard to beat. Bungalows for two to five people cling to the hillside, and a restaurant/café on the beach serves fresh fish. It also offers holistic therapy treatments, personal development workshops and yoga, and sea kayaks and scuba gear are available to rent. Taxis are around M$100 from town. ❻

Buena Vista La Buena Compañia s/n ⓣ958/584-3104, ⓦwww.labuenavista.com. A short walk along the footpath north from Uribe, next to the Arroye River. After the fork to the left, you will find one of the best hotels in Puerto Ángel set back from the main road. Accommodation is arranged over three floors, with an ocean view from the top-floor restaurant terrace and a rooftop swimming pool. The quiet rooms may not be well equipped – not even hot water – but the Robinson Crusoe ambience is part of the appeal. ❺

La Cabaña Playa del Panteón ⓣ958/584-3105, ⓦwww.lacabanapuertoangel.com. Chilled-out beachside hotel, with spotlessly clean rooms with bathrooms, small fridge, cable TV and fans (some with a/c); free coffee and tea in the mornings, and the rooftop terrace has spectacular views. ❹

Casa Arnel José Azueta 666 ⓣ958/584-3051, ⓦwww.casaarnel.com.mx. This sister hotel of the *Casa Arnel* in Oaxaca (see p.619) has clean rooms with fans and bathrooms and a hammock area, all in a homely environment. ❸

Casa Bichu Bahía de Estacahuite ⓣ958/584-3489, ⓦwww.casabichu.com. This sumptuous ecofriendly boutique hotel and spa opened in 2009 and is the first truly luxurious option in the area (it's in a secluded bay a short drive south of town). Rooms are decked out in rattan and wickerwork (the hotel is built from 90 percent natural materials), in palapa cabins nestled within the palms on a steep hillside – all with stunning views. Excellent restaurant on site, and everything here is recycled. ❾

Casa de Huéspedes Gundí y Tomas Uribe 2 ⓣ958/584-3068, ⓦwww.puertoangel-hotel.com. One of the best budget options in the village, this jungle-clad, German-run guesthouse has simple, if rather worn, rooms with fans, mosquito nets and random folksy flourishes. The atmosphere is very friendly – travellers exchange tales in the open-fronted lounge area. The restaurant serves very good food, especially the bountiful breakfasts. Private bath ④, shared bath ③, bungalow ⑤

Hotel Soraya Vasconceles s/n ⓣ958/584-3009. A bland but efficient choice, right in the centre of town overlooking the pier. There is little character to this modern hotel – rooms are basic with frilly bedspreads, fan (some with a/c and terrace) and private bath – but it is clean and spacious and the staff are very helpful. ④

Puesta del Sol Uribe s/n ⓣ958/584-3315, ⓦwww.puertoangel.net/puesta_del_sol.html. The pick of the cheaper hotels. Not much in the way of a view but spotless, spacious rooms (hot water for a few dollars more) around a garden with hammocks, laundry, internet access, library, satellite TV and communal space lined with photos. ④

The beaches

Puerto Ángel has two, rather scruffy, beaches: **Playa Principal** is right in front of the town, and **Playa del Panteón** is opposite, beyond a rocky promontory and the mouth of a small stream. Panteón is the cleaner of the two, reached by road or a path around the base of the cliffs to the west. Here there is some interesting snorkelling around the rocks, though the stretch of sand is not without a profusion of tenacious hawkers. By the afternoon, though, it's in shade, so most people wander round to the town beach. With just a little more effort you can visit one of the far better beaches either side of Puerto Ángel. To the west is the more primitive **Zipolite** (see opposite), while to the east, about fifteen minutes' walk up the Pochutla road and then down a heavily rutted track to the right, is tranquil **Estacahuite**. Here you'll find three tiny, sandy coves divided by outcrops of rock and the swish *Casa Bichu*. The rocks are close in, so you can't swim far, but there's wonderful **snorkelling** (beware of sharp coral and undercurrents) and rarely more than a handful of other people around. You can rent snorkelling gear here (M$150/day), or hire it from cafés on the Playa del Panteón and bring it with you.

There are other lovely beaches near Estacahuite, including idyllic **Playa del Boquilla**, where you'll find the *Hotel Bahía de la Luna* and a **restaurant**, accessible by boat from Puerto Ángel. Boquilla is signposted from the main road to Pochutla, but it's inadvisable to drive down here, as the seven-kilometre road is in a terrible state. A better idea is to arrange a boat trip in advance to both beaches, turtle-spotting along the way.

Eating and drinking

Beto's Uribe s/n, on the outskirts of town on the way to Zipolite. High-quality seafood at very good prices served in an unassuming, low-key setting. It becomes a lively spot for drinks later on in the evening.

Buena Vista La Buena Compañia s/n ⓣ958/584-3104, ⓦwww.labuenavista.com. People come from all over the area to this romantic hotel restaurant serving a reliable menu of Mexican and Italian classics in a lovely floral setting overlooking the bay. Reservations recommended in high season.

El Rincón del Mar No phone. Precariously balanced on a cliff between playas Principal and Panteón. Boasting windy views of the ocean, this locally renowned restaurant serves the best fish and seafood in the area. The thick, seared loins of tuna are mouth-watering, and the nightly specials menu features imaginative renditions of the daily catch – bonita, lobster, shrimp, snapper – all invariably delicious.

Susy's Playa del Panteón, right on the beach. The most reliable place for fish, shrimp, pasta, cold beers and soft drinks if you're having a day at the beach, although better seafood platters can be found elsewhere.

Villa Serena Florencia Uribe s/n. At its namesake hotel, this is a popular place with European and American travellers, serving hearty Italian staples such as antipasto, pasta *bolognese*, *arrabiata* and marinara, as well as large, leafy salads, pizzas and traditional Mexican fare.

Zipolite

Though some people rave about Puerto Ángel for its laid-back lifestyle, others are ecstatic about **ZIPOLITE**, 3km along the road north. Everything here revolves around the beach. Hippies started coming here in the 1970s (allegedly looking for a spot to witness an eclipse) and even today the travellers' grapevine is alive with tales of the widely available hallucinogens, low living costs and liberal approach to **nudity** – rumours that are largely well founded, much to the chagrin of the locals. Certainly, nude bathing – predominantly at the western end of the beach – is sanctioned by the local military; keep cover handy for trips to the restaurants. As for drugs, grass, mushrooms and acid are just as illegal as – though more prevalent than – anywhere else in Mexico; unscrupulous dealers are not above setting people up. **Theft**, particularly along the beachfront at night, can be a problem, but seems in no way to detract from the lure of a few days of complete abandon.

The origin of the name "Zipolite" is uncertain – one theory is that it comes from the Náhuatl word meaning "beach of the dead", hence the constant references to it as the "playa de los muertos". The **beach** itself is magnificent, long and gently curving, pounded by heavy surf with a **riptide** that requires some caution – drownings are depressingly common (although there are lifeguards, as well as flags denoting danger levels up and down the beach). It is divided into three segments: Roca Blanca towards the western end, Centro in the middle and Playa del Amor at the eastern end nearest Puerto Ángel. Palapa huts line all three, catering to visitors' basic accommodation and dining needs, as do a handful of restaurants offering seafood and pasta. **Hammocks** (M$50) are strung from every rafter, and many places rent basic **rooms**; it can be worth getting a room just to have a safe place to store your gear.

Zipolite is a good base for **trips** to nearby places such as Mazunte or Puerto Escondido, as accommodation is abundant and inexpensive. Taxis run up and down the road behind the beach, but a better and cheaper way of getting around is by *colectivos*, which run along the same route. All of the palapas along the beachfront advertise **boat trips** out to sea for about M$165, where you can snorkel and sometimes spot turtles, dolphins and, if you're really lucky, whales on their way up to Baja California. Scuba **diving** is also offered, but the reef isn't particularly impressive here.

Arrival and information

The main road coming into Zipolite from Puerto Ángel runs east to west; a turn to the left takes you onto the road immediately behind the beach, which has a **laundry** and a few small shops with **internet** access, beach gear and other bare necessities, but for anything other than the simplest needs you'll have to catch the *colectivos* that run to Puerto Ángel and on to Pochutla (every 20min until around 8pm). Follow the road to the end onto a dirt track to get to the more peaceful, western end of the beach.

Accommodation

Most **accommodation** options feature shared bathrooms (cold water) and are fitted with mosquito nets; a few have fans.

El Alquimista ⓣ958/587 8961, ⓦwww.el-alquimista.com. Features fourteen cosy palapas right on the beach (west end) and one of the best restaurants in town (see p.662), as well as a bonfire parties at night. The artfully designed cabañas have private bathroom, hammocks, terrace and fan. ❻

Brisa Marina Av Roca Blanca ⓣ958/584-3193. This more substantially constructed, three-storey American-run place offers a range of simple rooms, some with private baths and balconies. ❷

Las Casitas ⓣ958/585-7263, ⓦwww.las-casitas.net. Set back from the western end of the beach, this pleasant collection of five partially open-air (mosquito nets provided) cabañas, some with kitchens, come with private bathrooms and hammocks. ❸

Castillo Oasis Calle del Amor 97 ⓣ958/1061-763, ⓦwww.costachica.net/castillooasis. At the far eastern end of Zipolite beach (near Playa del Amor), with five clean, beautifully designed rooms in a leafy green oasis; all come with hammocks, and a couple have bathrooms. ❸

Lo Cósmico ⓦwww.locosmico.com. One of Zipolite's best options, this idyllic hotel lies at the western end of the beach. It has beautiful cabañas, some sleeping up to six people, with views of the coast, a restaurant (Tues–Sun 8am–4pm) serving delicious crepes and a secluded beach out front. Hammocks are also available in the winter for M$50 per night, on a special "hammock terrace". ❷

La Loma Linda ⓦwww.lalomalinda.com. Six colourful, thoughtfully designed cabañas on the hillside overlooking the middle of the beach, all with hammocks, fans, fridges, stellar views and tiled bathrooms. Hosts the popular Solstice Yoga Center (ⓦwww.solstice-mexico.com), which runs five-day yoga programmes (includes meals and accommodation) from US$750. ❺

Lyoban Hostal ⓣ958/584-3177, ⓦwww.lyoban.com.mx. Located in the centre of the village next to the church, this friendly hotel has space to lock luggage as well as pool and ping-pong in the lounge. Choice of hammocks (M$80), "rustic" rooms with shared bath (M$250) or en-suite rooms with fan. ❸

Posada México Av Roca Blanca ⓣ958/584-3194, ⓦwww.posadamexico.com. Currently the most popular place to stay in Zipolite: the ten cosy rooms (some in cute two-storey palapas) equipped with double beds, hammocks, safes and mosquito nets are a real bargain, and there's excellent Italian food and cocktails, all right on the beach. ❶

Posada San Cristóbal ⓣ958/584-3191, ⓔposadasancristobal@hotmail.com. Plain but adequate rooms with private bath, fans and safe, in a two-storey building on the beach – rooms face the gardens and get a cooling breeze in the morning. ❷

Shambhala ⓦwww.shambhalavision.tripod.com. Next door to *Lo Cósmico*, this long-established and slightly eccentric meditation retreat is tucked away up the side of a hill by a rocky outcrop. It boasts beautiful vistas and shares the *Cósmico*'s beach area, with some shabby and some nicer, new cabañas, shared bathrooms and a terrace for hammocks. The area at the top of the hill behind the cabins is a meditation spot and a great place to watch the sun rise (or set) over the bay. No alcohol or drugs permitted. ❶

Eating, drinking and nightlife

Zipolite is a great place for cheap and fresh food, with most of the popular **restaurants** located along the western beachfront: *El Alquimista* (ⓣ958/587-8961) gets packed in the evenings with diners looking for seafood, chicken, steak and pizza accompanied by chilled-out music (mains M$60–140), while *Posada San Cristóbal* (see above) covers backpacker staples such as eggs, pancakes and salads (from M$40). *El 3 Diciembre* (Wed–Sun 7pm–2am; ⓣ958/584-3157) is best known for its tasty pizzas (from M$60), but also serves vegetarian Mexican dishes, *pozole* and home-made cheesecake, at the start of the road behind the beach. *Pachamama* (on the beach, no phone), has a happy hour and keeps going until late, and the popular but cheesy open-air **disco** *La Puesta* kicks off around midnight (Tues–Sat), and winds down 2–4am.

San Agustinillo

Rounding the headland north of Zipolite you come to **SAN AGUSTINILLO**, another fine beach graced with good surfing waves (though you can also swim here). It has a more restrained vibe than Zipolite, with some charming and upmarket places to stay and eat. The sand is backed by restaurants, which offer space for a hammock or small rooms for rent in addition to reasonably priced, fresh seafood. Few **hotels** have phones: *Un Sueno* (ⓦwww.unsueno.com; ❺) has twelve stylish, breezy cabañas with private bath at the east end of the beach. *Posada La Termita* (ⓣ958/107-8135, ⓦwww.posadalatermita.com; ❺) offers four rooms on the seafront, all en suite with fan and mosquito nets; the bonus here is the restaurant, with specialities from Argentina and Italy, and mouth-watering pizza. The four luxurious beach-side cabins at *Cabañas Punta Placer* (ⓦwww.puntaplacer.com; ❻) contain eight circular rooms, gorgeous all-white spaces with drape beds, bathrooms and tranquil terraces. Catch any Mazunte-bound *camioneta* from Zipolite to get here.

Mazunte

Further west is the tiny village of **MAZUNTE**. Though it has grown in recent years, it remains a languid, laid-back place with a dazzling beach. It's more peaceful than Zipolite, and lacking the hippie-party vibe. In addition, the surf is less powerful here, and at the western end of the beach, beyond the rocky outcrop, there's a smaller bay where the waves are even gentler and it's safer to swim. The village's name is derived from the Náhuatl word "maxonteita", which means "please come and spawn", a reference to the **Golfina turtles** that come here to breed, although it was once the site of an abattoir that, at its most gruesome, supposedly slaughtered three thousand of the creatures a day. In 1990, the Mexican government bowed to international pressure and effectively banned the industry overnight, removing in one fell swoop the livelihood of the villagers, who then turned to slash-and-burn agriculture. Since then, Mazunte has been declared a reserve, and more sustainable, long-term ecotourism programmes have been encouraged, including the cooperative *Cosméticos Naturales* (Mon–Sat 9am–4pm, Sun 9am–2pm; Ⓣ958/583-9656), which you see as soon as you enter the village, set up with help from companies such as The Body Shop and selling beauty products made from local ingredients and organic produce. The government-funded **Centro Mexicano de la Tortuga** (Wed–Sat 10am–4.30pm, Sun 10am–2.30pm; M$22; guided tours in Spanish every 15min; Ⓣ958/584-3376, Ⓦwww.centromexicanodelatortuga.org), at the east end of the village, features an aquarium with some particularly large turtles and a turtle research centre. It's well worth the visit, especially as proceeds go towards the conservation of this majestic species.

Don't leave Mazunte without following the trail next to the *Balamjuyuc* (see p.664), which runs past the remains of some unmarked **ruins** to **Punto Cometa** (a 30min walk) – an entrancing park on top of the rocky headland next to Mazunte beach and the southernmost point in Oaxaca, where you get mesmerizing views at sunset. The "jacuzzi", a rocky pool that fills with foamy surf as the waves rush in, can be accessed by scrambling down the rocks at the south end of the headland – it makes a good photo but it's not safe to go in. Another nearby treat is the crocodile lagoon at **Playa Ventanilla**, about 2km to the west, where you can test your heart rate by going out on the water in a shallow boat to navigate among the scaly inhabitants. There are around four hundred in the lagoon, as well as a rich profusion of birdlife. It can be reached by *colectivo*, or by taxi (about M$40); the boat trips (M$50/person; *lanchas* accommodate 10) are arranged by the village cooperative, *Servicios Ecoturísticas* (Ⓣ958/589-9277) which can also organize horseriding tours in the area (around M$250).

Arrival and information

You can save time and money **getting to Mazunte** from Puerto Escondido by getting dropped off at **San Antonio**, a cluster of just a few houses and a restaurant, from where you can hitch or take a taxi (M$30) for the 5km to Mazunte. Otherwise, the bus drags you through Pochutla and Puerto Ángel before arrival. *Colectivos* from Mazunte go to Zipolite, Puerto Ángel and Pochutla (every 30–40min), but if you can time it correctly, it makes sense also to return through San Antonio.

In the village, Café Internet Dafne is open until 10pm (M$10/hr), but there are no banking facilities in Mazunte, so make sure you withdraw enough money in Pochutla or Escondido (where there are ATMs) before coming here.

▲ Golfina turtle, Mazunte

Accommodation

All of the palapas on the beach have **cabañas** and hammock space, along with **restaurants** serving basic breakfasts, seafood and pasta. If you are equipped and feel so inclined, you can pitch your tent right along the beach (free).

Alta Mira ⓣ958/584-3104, ⓦwww.labuenavista.com. Set discreetly up the hill, this is one of the most enchanting options in town, with smart bungalows with tiled bathrooms and jaw-dropping views from the terrace restaurant. Some rooms do not have electricity (solar power is being introduced), but that adds to the alluring atmosphere in the evening, when the bungalows are lit with candles. 5

Cabañas Balamjuyuc ⓣ958/101-1808, ⓦwww.balamjuyuc.com.mx. This friendly place has impressive views of the ocean and five comfy, brightly coloured shared-bath cabañas. Also has a restaurant and a basic palapa for M$80. Massages are offered, as are turtle-viewing trips and surfing lessons. 3

Cabañas Ziga ⓣ958/583-9295. At the east end of the beach (near the turtle centre), this congenial option has a range of rooms with fan and mosquito net (the more comfortable rooms have private bathrooms; ③), flower-filled gardens and glorious sea views from the patio restaurant, which serves decent Mexican and international fare. ②

Casa Pan de Miel ⓣ958/100-4719, ⓦwww.casapandemiel.com. Five luxurious modern a/c suites overlooking the beach (adults only), with satellite TV, bathroom, kitchenette and wi-fi. Small pool and yet more stellar views included. ⑦

El Copal Calle de Panteón s/n ⓦwww.elcopal.com.mx. Gorgeous cluster of four palapas surrounded by palms and terraces above Playa Mermejita (near Punta Cometa), blending modern amenities (free wi-fi) with an ecofriendly ethos (candles at night, cold water, dry toilets and recycling). Closed Oct. ⑤

Posada Arigalan ⓣ958/111-5801, ⓦwww.arigalan.com. Between San Agustinillo and Mazunte, this is one of the best places in the area, with stunning views from its six modern but charming rooms; all have private baths (some with hot water) and fan; three "suites" have a/c and king-size beds. ⑤

Posada del Arquitecto ⓔinfo@posadadelarquitecto.com. Solid choice at the western end of the sandy stretch, past the rocks at the second small bay with the area's best swimming. Has hammocks (M$50) and eco-conscious cabañas with private bath. ④

Eating and drinking

There are some appealing **food** options in Mazunte, including the excellent Italian-run restaurant *La Dolce Vita*, on the main road (daily 4–11pm), which has brick-oven pizza, pastas with seafood for under M$100 and occasional movies in the evenings. *La Empanada*, also on the main road, offers cheap Asian fusion – sushi and stir-fry – as well as fillers like hearty sandwiches on home-made bread and blended juices (try the delicious cucumber and lemon); the gregarious *Tania*, further along, has good-value Mexican and vegetarian fare. At the western end, on the sandy path that leads down to the beach, *El Agujón* is another great snack joint with delicious fresh bread, quesadillas, tortas and pizzas.

Huatulco and around

At **HUATULCO**, some 35km from Puerto Ángel, the latest of Mexico's purpose-built resorts is well under way. The government began developing the coastline in the 1980s, with the intention of constructing an environmentally conscious international destination, though so far, only 20 percent of visitors hail from overseas (mostly Canada). The area is what it aims to be: a safe, sanitized, manicured resort with a beautiful setting. You could be anywhere – it just happens that you're in Mexico. The long-term effects of the tourism influx are still hard to predict and will largely depend on whether the infrastructure (especially the sewage treatment plants) can keep pace with the demand. With an overriding emphasis on coiffured hotels, Huatulco is certainly not the place for budget or independent travellers keen to experience the real Mexico, but if lying on the beach, snorkelling and tripping off to coffee plantations and attractive coves are your priorities, you could do much worse.

Arrival, information and activities

Huatulco is the umbrella name for a resort area encompassing nine bays and over thirty beaches, with **La Crucecita** the main inland settlement and the village of **Santa Cruz Huatulco** the primary focus on the coast.

If you're travelling by **bus** you'll end up at one of the terminals on the northern edge of La Crucecita: OCC, ADO GL and Sur (second-class) services arrive at the terminal on Bulevar Chahué at Rescadillo, while Estrella Blanca buses and Turistar have a station further up the road at Avenida Carpinteros. Moving on to the beaches you have to take a taxi; rates are fixed at around M$20 to Santa Cruz and Chahué, and M$30 to Tangolunda (the rates are usually listed on the dashboard).

From Huatulco's **airport**, some 17km west of La Crucecita, *colectivos* offer fixed rates of around M$90 to Santa Cruz, La Crucecita and Chahué, and around M$100 to Tangolunda (buy a ticket at the booth in the terminal). **Taxis** from the airport are extortionate (M$700 to Puerto Ángel, M$300 to La Crucecita), though you'll pay much less if you walk 500m out of the terminal towards the highway and the waiting cars of Sitio Agua JE El Zapote (ⓣ958/107-2772, ⓦwww.taxihuatulco.com): Santa Cruz/La Crucecita (M$120), Tangolunda (M$160), Puerto Ángel (M$350) and San Agustín (M$180).

You'll find a **tourist information** kiosk (Mon–Fri 9am–2pm & 4–7pm, Sat 9am–1pm) at the Parque Central in La Crucecita, and a **post office** a few blocks east at Blv Chahué 100, close to a number of **banks** (with ATMs). Hurricane Divers (ⓣ958/587-1107, ⓦwww.hurricanedivers.com), on Santa Cruz beach, offers **dive trips** (from M$950) in the area, along with PADI and NAUI certification (from M$3500 for four days). They also speak English. Copalita River Tours run **rafting and kayaking trips** from their office (from M$650/day) in the *Posada Michelle* (see below); Explora Mexico also runs class-3 rafting day trips (M$700), as well as less challenging excursions, out of Huatulco (ⓣ958/587-2058, ⓦwww.explorahuatulco.com).

Accommodation

With hotel development mushrooming, finding a budget **place to stay** in **La Crucecita** is easier than it used to be, and outside the high season (Dec, Semana Santa, July & Aug) prices can drop by up to fifty percent. The best resorts and hotels can be found at **Tangolunda** and at **Playa Conejos**, a five-minute drive east of Tangolunda.

La Crucecita and Playa Chahué

Hotel Flamboyant Gardenia at Tamarindo ⓣ958/587-0113, ⓦwww.hotelesfarrera.com/flamboyant. This charming three-storey house on the northwest side of the plaza features pleasantly decorated a/c rooms with cable TV grouped around a courtyard and an enticing swimming pool. ❻

Misión de los Arcos Gardenia 902 ⓣ958/587-0165, ⓦwww.misiondelosarcos.com. The most polished option in town, with white stucco suites with cable TV and a/c. There is a decent restaurant, free internet, a gym and access to a nearby pool. ❹

Plaza Conejo Guamúchil 208 ⓣ958/587-0054, ⓦwww.plazaconejomexico.com. Among the best of the cheaper options, this spotless colonial-style hotel offers ten simple rooms, all with a/c, cable TV, private bath and internet. ❹

Posada Eden Costa Zapoteco 27 at Chahué, Sector R ⓣ958/587-2480, ⓦwww.edencosta.com. Popular mid-range option just one block from Playa Chahué, with eight rooms and three suites, all with terraces leading out to the pool and free wi-fi. Excellent on-site restaurant (see p.668). ❻

Posada Michelle Gardenia 1301 at Palo Verde ⓣ958/587-0535. Friendly hotel with a range of very cheap singles and doubles, some are showing their age so check rooms first. A good place to arrange tours. ❸

Villa Blanca Juárez and Zapoteco ⓣ958/587-0606, ⓦwww.hotelesvillablanca.com. Solid mid-range option near Playa Chahué at the southern end of town, with spacious, modern a/c rooms and terracotta floors overlooking the gardens and pool; the breakfast buffet is one of the best in the area. ❻

Tangolunda

Dreams Huatalco Resort & Spa Juárez 4 ⓣ958/583-0400, ⓦwww.dreamsresorts.com/drehu. Best value of all the major resorts, with excellent deals online, great service and a huge roster of amenities. Modern, stylish rooms overlook the bay and come with LCD satellite TV, DVD players and balconies. ❻

Quinta Real Juárez 2 ⓣ958/581-0428, ⓦwww.quintareal.com. Unabashed luxury in an exotic whitewashed property embellished with Moorish domes and curves, just off the beach. With lavish suites, a private beach club, posh restaurants and a colony of torpid iguanas in the nearby palms, you are unlikely to venture much further. 9

Playa Conejos

Agua Azul La Villa Juárez s/n ⓣ958/581-0265, ⓦwww.bbaguaazul.com. For a slice of tranquillity close to the beach the best option is this Canadian-run B&B overlooking the bay. The ambience is welcoming and sociable, the hosts are knowledgeable, and excellent breakfasts are served in a communal palapa dining room/lounge area. Adults only. 8

Villa Sol y Mar ⓦwww.villasolymar.com. An intelligent choice for groups, a gorgeous apartment complex close to the beach with continental breakfast included; you rent one of five suites or the whole property, with fabulous views of the sunset and coast. No kids from Thanksgiving to Easter. 6

La Crucecita

The purpose-built town of **LA CRUCECITA** is the main service centre for the resort area. Though designed to house the ten thousand locals needed to support and staff the bayside hotels, it is now becoming a tourist centre in its own right, probably helped along by the lack of cheap hotels elsewhere. You won't find much to see beyond the **Parque Central** (main plaza) and the modern **Parroquia de Nuestra Señora de Guadalupe** (which houses a twenty-metre mural of the Virgin of Guadalupe, said to be the world's largest), along with pizza joints, costly tourist shops and internet cafés. Nevertheless, in its fifteen years of existence, it has matured well to become a friendly, functional place. You'll find the best of the budget accommodation here, and plenty of cheap places to eat.

Santa Cruz Huatulco and the beaches

Just 2km from La Crucecita, **SANTA CRUZ HUATULCO** was conceived as the token "Mexican village", something it patently fails to be. In fact, it feels more like the Mexican section at Epcot Centre, just dressed up with a marina, handicraft stalls, a few relatively inexpensive seafood restaurants and a handful of condos. Santa Cruz's **harbour**, though, is the local transport hub. From here, fishing and diving trips can be organized, or you can just catch one of the boats (on demand) that ply the coast to the more remote bays. **Playa Santa Cruz** is small and overcrowded and you're better off taking a *lancha* (M$200 per boat) to the next beach along the bay (2.5km by road), the attractive but busy **Playa La Entrega**, where Mexican families congregate and palapas serving fresh seafood flank the gentle surf.

Just over 1km west from La Entrega is **Bahía Maguey**, best accessed on one of the horseback rides or *lanchas* (M$500) that leave from the *embarcadero* in Santa Cruz. Its tranquil, blue waters curve around jungly headlands. Just beyond Maguey are the pristine sand dunes of **Bahía Cacaluta**, where much of the movie *Y Tu Mamá También* was filmed. It is reached by walking through the jungle from the coastal road, or for a more exhilarating route you can take one of the excellent ATV tours from Santa Cruz; contact Xpert & Professional Travel at Plaza Coyula 11, behind Banamex (ⓣ958/587-1290, ⓦwww.huatulcobays.com). **Bahía San Agustín** has the furthest western beach from Santa Cruz (over 30km by road; *lanchas* will be around M$1200), and is popular with Mexican holiday-makers. It has very good snorkelling, offshore reefs for diving and plenty of amenities.

Around 2km to the east of Santa Cruz and just south of La Crucecita is the largest beach, at **Bahía Chahué**, with a marina and upscale hotels. Over the headland, **Bahía Tangolunda** is by far the most developed resort area, with luxury hotels, chi-chi homes and an eighteen-hole golf course. The only public access is by the road near the *Quinta Real*, a further 3km northeast from Chahué. Unless you are a guest, there is very little to do and in the restaurants you will pay upscale New York or London prices.

Eating and drinking

The best-value **restaurants** surround the Parque Central in La Crucecita, but there are some exceptional places in the posh resorts along the coast if you fancy a splurge. For something cheaper, hit *Los Portales* at Bugambilia 603 on the plaza in La Crucecita for addictive nachos and cold beer.

Ay Caray Palma Real 310, La Crucecita ⓣ958/587-2655; also at Playa Maguey. Everyone loves this laid-back place overseen by the indomitable Alfredo, especially good for fresh fish and fish tacos – fishermen can also take their catch to be cooked on site. The Maguey beach branch is perfect for lazing away the afternoon over a cold beer.

Café Dublin Carrizal 502, La Crucecita. Welcoming Irish-themed pub serving giant, juicy hamburgers and chilled beer (but Guinness in cans only). It has darts and screens major sports events. Open from 6pm.

La Crema Gardenia 311, La Crucecita. Eclectic nightlife venue with a diverse clientele, lively rock music and tasty pizza (try the Crema Special) and baked potatoes – the bar is upstairs. Open from 7pm but go after 9pm if you want to avoid a long wait for food (it closes around 2am).

L'Echalote *Posada Eden Costa* (see p.666), ⓣ958/587-2480. Exceptional restaurant featuring an eclectic menu that blends Asian, Mexican and European traditions, everything from Vietnamese dishes to Spanish classics and fabulous fondue (the owners hail from Switzerland and Laos). Dinner only, most mains range M$100–150.

Kristal Rose Cocotillo 218, La Crucecita ⓣ958/106-0912. Popular with locals and tourists alike and managed by the affable English-speaking Juan Ferra, this cosy restaurant offers decent seafood and service; try the tortilla soup or anything with shrimp (the steaks are pretty average).

Ve El Mar Manzana 20, Lote 10, Sector A, Playa Santa Cruz ⓣ958/587-0364. It's hard to beat this seafood restaurant for waterside dining, fresh fish and zippy cocktails; try the pineapple scooped out and filled with dorado, or the reasonably priced sweet Pacific lobster.

The Isthmus of Tehuantepec

The **Isthmus of Tehuantepec**, where the Pacific and the Atlantic are just 210km apart and the land never rises to more than 250m above sea level, is the narrowest strip of land in Mexico. It's a hot and steamy region, with a fascinating and unique cultural identity. The people are descendants of various indigenous groups, principally Zapotec. Historically, the Zapotec *indígenas*, especially those in the south, have been a **matriarchal** society. Though you'll still find women dominating trade in the markets (they are renowned for their tenacious, even aggressive, sales skills) while the men work in the fields, this is a tradition that is dying faster than most others in macho Mexico. Nevertheless, some elements remain: the women exude pride, dressed in ornate handwoven dresses and draped with gold jewellery; it's still the mother who gives away her child at a wedding (and occasionally still the eldest daughter who inherits land); and on feast days the women prove their dominance by climbing to the rooftops and throwing fruit down on the men in the Tirada de Frutas.

The best reason to stop in this region is if there's a **fiesta** going on, as they're among the most exciting in the country. Otherwise, you can go straight across – from Oaxaca to **Tuxtla Gutiérrez** or **San Cristóbal** in Chiapas – in a single, very long, day. Most first-class buses now bypass the grimy port town of Salina Cruz, dominated by a giant oil refinery, and the best place to stop is Tehuantepec itself, around 250km from Oaxaca City, or nearby Juchitán.

Tehuantepec

The modest town of **TEHUANTEPEC** visibly preserves many of the Isthmus's local traditions, has some of the **best fiestas** in the region and is generally an extremely pleasant place to stop, with a fine plaza and several inexpensive hotels. In the evening, the plaza really comes alive, with singing birds and people strolling and eating food from the stalls set up by the townswomen, who proudly wear the traditional flower-embroidered *huipil* and floor-length velvet skirt of the Zapotec. Tehuantepec is a tiny place where a walk of ten blocks in any direction will take you out into the countryside. Perhaps because the town is so concentrated, it's extraordinarily noisy considering its size and remote location. The din of passing buses is made worse by the flatbed motor tricycles (*motos*) that locals use as taxis. If you do stop for a bit, pop into the **Casa de la Cultura**, housed in the remains of the Dominican Ex-Convento Rey Cosijopí, on Callejón Cosijopí (Mon–Fri 9am–2pm & 5–8pm, Sat 9am–2pm; free). It features a random collection of archeological pieces and exhibits of local costumes and art. Construction of the *convento* was begun in 1544 at the behest of Cortés and it was named after the incumbent Zapotec king. Just west of the plaza there is an indoor **market**, which sells fruit, herbs, bread, flowers and other local produce.

The ruins of Guiengola

The hilltop fortress of **GUIENGOLA** (daily 8am–5pm; free) 15km north of Tehuantepec, was the Zapotec stronghold on the isthmus, and in 1496 its defenders successfully fought off an Aztec attempt to gain control of the area, which was never fully incorporated into their empire. It continued to be a centre of resistance during the early years of the Conquest and was a focus of Indian revolt against Spanish rule throughout the sixteenth and seventeenth centuries.

At the site you'll see remains of pyramids and a ball-court, but the most striking feature is the massive **defensive wall**. By definition, Guiengola's superb location makes it somewhat inaccessible and it's probably best to take a **taxi**, though **buses** to Oaxaca do pass the turn-off to the site, 8km from Tehuantepec on the main road (look out for the "Ruinas Guiengola" sign). From here it's a hot, seven-kilometre walk uphill. The site is open daily, and if the caretaker is around you may be asked to pay a small fee, though you'll almost certainly have the place to yourself.

Tehuantepec practicalities

Buses stop at the OCC terminal at the northern edge of town on Hwy-185, a short *moto* ride (M$15) or walk from the centre. There's a **post office** and bank on the north side of the plaza; on 5 de Mayo itself you'll find a **Bancomer** with good rates and an ATM, as well as a Banorte. **Hotels** aren't far away: *Donaji* (Ⓣ971/715-0064; ❸), at Juárez 10, two blocks south of the plaza, is one of the best, with clean rooms with TV, air-conditioning (worth the extra few pesos) or fan overlooking the Parque Juárez. There is also a gym and pool. Just outside the centre on the road to Oaxaca (15min walk), the *Guiexhoba* (Ⓣ971/715-1710; ❺) has the largest, most comfortable, motel-style rooms with air-conditioning and fridge, convenient parking, a sizeable pool and a restaurant that serves good local and international dishes. *Hotel Oasis*, Ocampo 8 (Ⓣ971/715-0008; ❸), is one block south of the plaza and has clean rooms with air-conditioning or fan.

For cheap **places to eat** try the Mercado de Jesús on the west side of the plaza, or the steaming taco carts lining the east side of the square. Be sure to try some of the **corn bread** that local women hawk to everyone arriving on the bus. For something more colourful, try *Scarú* at Leona Vicario 4 (north of the square next to the *Donaji*), which has murals depicting Tehuantepec life and offers seafood, pasta and cocktails until 11pm.

While Tehuantepec is a major stopping point en route to Oaxaca or the Chiapas coast, few **buses** originate here, so moving on, you may find it easier to take one of the constant stream of buses to **Juchitán**, 26km away (see p.670), and continue

Fiestas

January

New Year's Day (Jan 1). Celebrated everywhere, but particularly good in Oaxaca and Mitla.

Día de San Sebastián (Jan 20). Big in Tehuantepec.

February

Día de la Candelaria (Feb 2). Colourful Indian celebrations in Santa María del Tule.

Carnaval (the week before Lent; variable Feb–March). At its most frenzied in the big cities – especially Oaxaca – but also celebrated in hundreds of villages in the area.

May

Día de San Isidro (May 15). Peasant celebrations everywhere – famous and picturesque fiestas in Juchitán.

June

Día de San Juan (June 24). Falls in the midst of festivities (June 22–26) in Tehuantepec.

July

Fiesta de la Preciosa Sangre de Cristo (first Wed in July). Teotitlán del Valle, near Oaxaca, holds a festival with traditional dances and religious processions.

Guelaguetza (last two Mon in July). In Oaxaca, a mixture of traditional dancing and rites on the Cerro del Fortín. Highly popular; tickets for the good seats are sold at the tourist office.

August

Fiestas (Aug 13–16). Spectacular festivities in Juchitán (Vela de Agosto) and Tehuantepec (Fiesta del Barrio de Santa María Relatoca).

from there. The main long-distance routes, operated by first-class OCC and ADO, serve Oaxaca, Mexico City, Tuxtla Gutiérrez, Huatulco and Villahermosa, and there are also buses to San Cristóbal and Puerto Escondido; you can buy **tickets** in advance. Several second-class companies also operate between the main towns on the isthmus.

Juchitán

JUCHITÁN, just 26km east of Tehuantepec, is a dusty commercial centre clogged with traffic and somewhat lacking in tourist infrastructure. Despite this, the city has a rich cultural life, offering glimpses into the matriarchal society the region is known for, with widely observed native traditions and near-constant **fiestas**, also known as **velas**. Although they take place throughout the year, in May there seem to be daily parties, where women dress in colourful *traje* and men in formal wear for all-night marathons of music and dancing. The residents are also known for strong political views, socialist leanings and a relatively tolerant attitude towards homosexuality; it's one of the few places in Mexico where gay men live openly, sometimes even attending *velas* in drag.

The **Casa de la Cultura** (Mon–Fri 9am–2pm & 5–7pm, Sat 9am–1pm; free) on Belisario Domínguez beside the church, was started by Francisco Toledo (who was born in Juchitán), and offers a tiny archeological display with pre-Hispanic stone carvings and pottery shards, an art library and occasional exhibitions of local artists.

Fiesta de San Bartolomé (Aug 24). In San Bartolo Coyotepec, near Oaxaca.

Blessing of the Animals (Aug 31). In Oaxaca locals bring their beasts to the church of La Merced to be blessed.

September

Fiesta del Señor de la Natividad (Sept 8). In Teotitlán del Valle.

Independence Day (Sept 16). Celebrated everywhere.

October

Feria del Árbol (second Mon in Oct). Based around the famous tree in Santa María del Tule.

November

Día de los Muertos (Day of the Dead; Nov 2). Observed everywhere, with particularly strong traditions in Xoxocotlán and in Atzompa.

December

Día de la Inmaculada Concepción (Dec 8). Observed widely. There are traditional dances in Juquilla, not far from Puerto Escondido, and Zacatepec, on the road inland from Pinotepa Nacional.

Fiesta de la Virgen de la Soledad (Dec 18). Celebrations in Oaxaca in honour of the patroness of the state – expect fireworks, processions and music.

Fiesta de los Rabanos (Radish Festival; Dec 23). There's an exhibition of statues and scenes sculpted from radishes in Oaxaca.

Christmas Eve (Dec 24). In Oaxaca there's music, fireworks and processions before midnight Mass. *Buñuelos* – crisp pancakes that you eat before smashing the plate on which they are served – are dished up at street stalls.

A cooling day trip from Juchitán is to the natural clear-water **spring** (M$10) in **Santiago Laollaga**, about 36km northwest of town. The concrete swimming pools by the car park can be overrun by kids, but a short walk upstream leads to natural pools by the spring's source, perfect for a refreshing dip followed by a beer in one of the streamside restaurants – although the occasional duelling stereos can mar the peaceful atmosphere. There is nowhere to stay in town, unless you want to camp. You can get to Santiago Laollaga quickly by car, north through **Ixtepec**, or by buses on the same route in about an hour. The spring is at the northern edge of town.

Practicalities

The main **bus** station is on Prolongación 16 de Septiembre near the main highway, and you won't have long to wait, whichever direction you're heading – taxis into the centre cost around M$15. Unfortunately, Juchitán doesn't offer much in the way of good-value **accommodation**, and therefore Tehuantepec makes a better base. The best place to stay is the spartan but clean and comfortable *Hotel Lopez Lena Palace* (Ⓣ971/711-1388; ❺) at 16 de Septiembre 70, which has institutional rooms with cable TV. You'll also find the **post office**, a **Banamex** and some good **places to eat** on the main plaza (Jardín Juárez), notably the *Casagrande* at Juárez 12 (Ⓣ971/711-3460), which serves delicious local dishes with an emphasis on fish and seafood in an elegant cool atrium.

Travel details

Buses

The following frequencies and times are for first-class services. Scores of second-class buses usually cover the same routes, taking ten to twenty percent longer.

Huatulco to: Acapulco (7 daily; 10hr); Oaxaca (4 daily; 7hr); Pochutla (6 daily; 1hr); Puerto Escondido (hourly; 2hr 30min); Salina Cruz (almost hourly; 3hr); San Cristóbal (2 daily; 10hr); Tehuantepec (10 daily; 3hr 30min); Juchitlán (1 daily; 4hr).

Oaxaca to: Mexico City (at least two every 30min; 6hr); Pochutla (5 daily; 6hr); Puebla (hourly; 4hr 30min); Puerto Escondido (4 daily; 9hr 30min); San Cristóbal de las Casas (3 daily; 12hr); Tehuacán (3 daily; 3hr); Tehuantepec (at least hourly; 5hr); Veracruz (4 daily; 7hr); Villahermosa (5 daily; 12hr).

Pochutla to: Huatulco (hourly; 1hr); Oaxaca (14 daily; 7–8hr); Puerto Escondido (hourly; 1hr 30min); San Cristóbal (1 daily; 11hr).

Puerto Escondido to: Acapulco (3 daily; 8hr); Huatulco (hourly; 2hr 30min); Mexico City (2 daily; 18hr); Oaxaca (6 daily; 8–9hr); Pochutla (7 daily; 1hr 30min); Salina Cruz (1 daily; 5hr); San Cristóbal de las Casas (2 night buses; 14hr); Tehuantepec (1 daily; 6hr).

Tehuacán to: Córdoba (2 daily; 2hr 30min); Mexico City (hourly; 4hr); Oaxaca (6 daily; 4hr); Veracruz (3 daily; 3hr 30min).

Tehuantepec to: Mexico City (at least 12 daily; 11hr); Oaxaca (hourly; 4hr 30min); Puerto Escondido (5 daily; 7hr); Tuxtla Gutiérrez (6 daily; 5hr); Veracruz (2 daily; 7hr 30min); Villahermosa (7 daily; 7hr).

Flights

Huatulco to: Oaxaca (daily); Mexico City (5 weekly); Toluca (4 weekly); Houston, Texas (1 weekly); numerous charter services to Canada.

Oaxaca to: Guadalajara (2 daily); Huatulco (daily); Los Angeles (3 weekly); Mexico City (10 daily); Monterrey (2 weekly); Puerto Escondido (2 daily); Tijuana (4 weekly); Tuxtla Gutiérrez (2 daily).

Puerto Escondido to: Mexico City (daily); Oaxaca (2 daily).

Chiapas and Tabasco

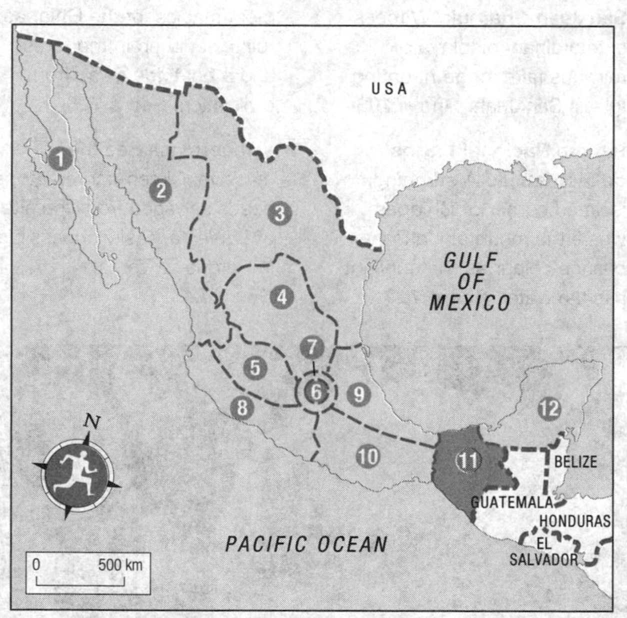

CHAPTER 11

Highlights

* **Cañón del Sumidero** Enjoy a boat ride through this spectacular gorge, with jungle-covered cliffs soaring a thousand metres above the Río Grijalva. See p.693
* **San Cristóbal de las Casas** The most enchanting colonial city in Chiapas, surrounded by villages rich in indigenous culture. See p.694
* **San Juan Chamula** Witness extraordinary displays of religious faith in the haunting Iglesia San Juan. See p.703
* **Parque Nacional Lagos de Montebello** A stunning, isolated corner of Chiapas where the mountain lakes change colour as the sunlight hits the water. See p.709
* **Palenque** Visit the evocative ruins of one of the greatest Maya cities, then bathe in the refreshing cascades outside the town. See p.714
* **Bonampak** Over one thousand years old, the vivid murals here provide a startling insight into ancient Maya culture. See p.723
* **Yaxchilán** For many, the most magical of the Chiapas ruins, set deep in the forest and a boat ride away from civilization. See p.725
* **Villahermosa** See the massive, Olmec-carved stone heads salvaged from the site of La Venta, easily accessible in Parque La Venta. See p.729

▲ Olmec head, Parque La Venta, Villahermosa

11

Chiapas and Tabasco

Endowed with a stunning variety of cultures, landscapes and wildlife, **Chiapas**, Mexico's southernmost state, has much to tempt visitors. Deserted Pacific beaches, rugged mountains and ruined cities buried in steamy jungle offer a bewildering choice of settings, and many **indigenous traditions** survive intact. Administered by the Spanish as part of Guatemala until 1824, when it seceded to join newly independent Mexico, the state is now second only to Oaxaca in Indian population: about 25 percent of its four million people are thought to be *indígenas*, most of Maya origin, but totalling some fourteen ethnic groups in the state. Their numbers were bolstered in the 1980s, when refugees fled the conflicts in Guatemala.

Travellers usually head straight for the colonial town of **San Cristóbal de las Casas**, tucked among the mountains in the geographic centre of the state and surrounded by strongholds of **Tzotzil** and **Tzeltal** Maya culture, the largest indigenous groups. Ancient customs and religious practices carry on in these mountain villages, melded with the trappings of modern Mexico. As picturesque as life here may sometimes seem, villagers often live at the barest subsistence level, with their lands and livelihoods in precarious balance. These tensions helped fuel the 1994 **Zapatista rebellion** (see p.678), and although that conflict is now barely palpable, many of the core issues have yet to be fully resolved.

One continuing legacy of the rebellion is a heavy **military** presence, keeping an eye on the eastern half of the state, primarily in the **Lancandón forest region** along the **Carretera Fronteriza** (Frontier Highway). Many villages here are at least nominally occupied by the Zapatistas. But as the military has fanned out across the country to combat drug cartels and illegal immigration, Chiapas now feels no more militarized than anywhere else. Though you'll see plenty of signs announcing Zapatista loyalty, visitors are treated with full respect, and you'll never get an inkling of problems at the state's main attractions, such the **Parque Nacional Lagos de Montebello** or the ruins of **Yaxchilán** or **Bonampak**.

Steamy and low-lying, the state of **Tabasco** is less aesthetically attractive than its neighbour state, with a major oil industry to mar the landscape. But the region is the heartland of the **Olmecs**, Mexico's earliest developed civilization, and there are rural pockets of the state that see virtually no tourists, only birds and wild animals. **Villahermosa**, the vibrant, modern capital, has a wealth of parks and museums, the best of which is **Parque La Venta**, where the original massive Olmec heads are on display. In the extreme southwest, bordered by Veracruz and Chiapas, a section of Tabasco reaches into the Sierra de Chiapas up to 1000m high. Here, in a region almost never visited by outsiders, you can splash in pristine rivers in **Tapijulapa** and explore the astonishing ruins of **Malpasito**, a city of the mysterious **Zoque** culture.

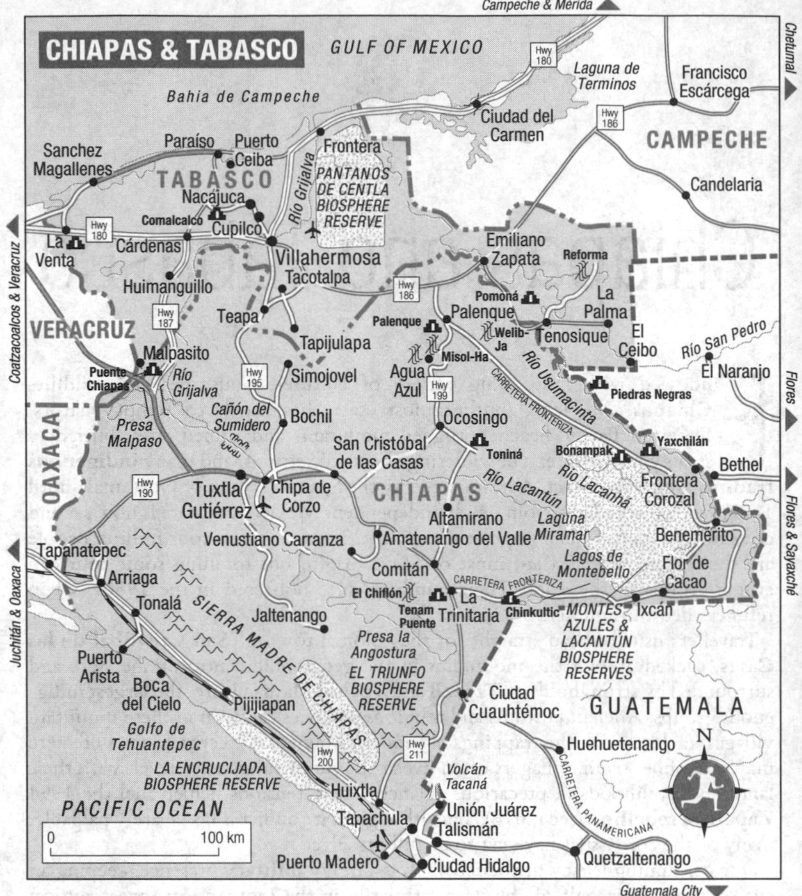

Chiapas

The state of **Chiapas** rises from the Pacific coastal plain, backed by the peaks of the Sierra Madre de Chiapas, through the mainly agricultural Central Depression, irrigated by the Río Grijalva, up to the highlands, **Los Altos de Chiapas**. Beyond the highlands, to the north the mountains drop down to the Gulf coast of Tabasco, while to the east a series of great rivers, separated by the jungle-covered ridges of the **Lacandón forest**, flow into the Río Usumacinta, which forms the border with Guatemala. The **climate**, like the land, varies enormously. You could spend the morning basking on the beach at **Puerto Arista**, and then a chilly night in the old colonial capital of **San Cristóbal de las Casas**. As a rule, the lowlands are hot and humid, with heavy afternoon rainfall in summer, and while days in the highlands can also be hot, by evening you will often need a sweater.

Though it's a relatively small part of Mexico, Chiapas has the greatest **biological diversity** in North America. Its forests are home to howler monkeys, red macaws and jaguars, though casual visitors are guaranteed to see these animals only at the **zoo** in the state capital of **Tuxtla Gutiérrez**, which houses animals native to the state. In the huge **Montes Azules Biosphere Reserve**, reached from Palenque, a section of the largest remaining rainforest in North America has been preserved. From Ocosingo you can make forays into its heart, **Laguna Miramar**, a truly isolated, pristine wilderness destination. There's **cloud forest** in the south, protected in **El Triunfo Biosphere Reserve** and, far easier to visit, the beautiful lakes and hills of the **Parque Nacional Lagos de Montebello**.

The Classic-period Maya site of **Palenque**, on the northern edge of the highlands, is one of Mexico's finest ancient sites. The limestone hills in this area are pierced by crystal-clear rivers, creating exquisite waterfalls – most spectacularly at **Agua Azul**. Palenque is the best starting point for a trip down the **Usumacinta valley**, to visit the remote ruins of **Bonampak** and **Yaxchilán**. The Frontier Highway pushes south beyond these sites through the town of Benemérito, where you can get a boat to **Guatemala**. Buses serve the full length of the highway, enabling you to travel on to the **Lagos de Montebello** and around to San Cristóbal. This remote eastern half of the state is also the home of the **Lacandón Maya**, who retreated into the forest when the Spaniards arrived, and shunned all outside contact until fifty years ago.

Travelling around Chiapas is not difficult: the main cities are connected by a network of good, all-weather roads, and the **Panamerican Highway** passes from west to east through some of the state's most spectacular scenery. In the south the coastal highway offers a speedy route from **Tonalá**, near the Oaxaca border, to **Tapachula**, almost on the frontier with Guatemala. In very out-of-the-way places, particularly in the jungle, travel is by dirt roads, which, though generally well maintained, can cause problems in the rainy season. These more remote places are also fairly well served by public transport, though it's more likely to be *combis* and trucks taking people and produce to and from markets than the comfortable buses of the main roads.

The Chiapas coast

Running parallel to the coast about 20km inland, Hwy-200 provides a fast route from the Oaxaca border to Tapachula: if you're heading straight for **Guatemala**, this is the road to take. It traverses the steamy coastal plain of the **Soconusco**, once a separate province within Guatemala, but forced into union with Mexico by Santa Anna in 1842 and promptly absorbed by Chiapas. From the highway, the 2400-metre peaks of the **Sierra Madre de Chiapas**, little-visited mountains penetrated by roads only at their eastern and western extremities, are always in view. Not far from the Oaxaca border, the first point of interest is **Puerto Arista**, the only place on the Chiapas coast that even remotely resembles a resort town. The plain itself is a fertile agricultural area, mainly given over to coffee and bananas, though there are also many *ranchos*, where cattle grow fat on the lush grass. **Tapachula**, the "capital" of the Soconusco plain, is cut off from the rest of Chiapas by the mountains, but has frequent connections to the southern border crossings into Guatemala; on the way there you can easily visit the ancient Olmec and Maya site of **Izapa**. From Tapachula you can also take a relaxing trip up through coffee plantations to the delightful little town of **Unión Juárez**, the base for expeditions to **Volcán Tacaná**, the highest peak in Chiapas.

Visiting Chiapas: the legacy of the Zapatista rebellion

On **January 1, 1994**, the day that the North American Free Trade Agreement (**NAFTA**) came into effect, several thousand lightly armed rebels calling themselves **Zapatistas** (after early twentieth-century revolutionary Emiliano Zapata) occupied San Cristóbal de las Casas, the former state capital and Chiapas's major tourist destination. The Zapatistas declared themselves staunchly against globalization, as well as local efforts by paramilitary groups to force indigenous people off the land. When the Mexican army recovered from its shock, it launched a violent counter-attack, but international solidarity with the rebels soon forced the Mexican government to call a halt. A ceasefire was agreed in 1995, and negotiations have continued over the years, as yet to conclude in a peace treaty. But the issue of indigenous rights has now spread beyond the borders of Chiapas. During the 2006 presidential elections, **Subcomandante Marcos**, the "chief spokesman" of the Zapatistas, embarked on a non-aligned campaign across Mexico to spread awareness of indigenous power. That same year, large-scale disturbances in Oaxaca also made Chiapas seem relatively peaceful.

In the years since the rebellion, **tourists** have always visited Chiapas with no problems other than delays due to army checkpoints. But the government is hostile to foreign Zapatista sympathizers, as their presence is considered undue (and, in fact, illegal) influence on Mexican politics, so showing obvious Zapatista support in Chiapas can potentially lead to deportation. For more information on the conflict's issues, visit the website of **SIPAZ**, the International Service for Peace, Ⓦwww.sipaz.org, as well as the official Zapatista websites, Ⓦwww.enlacezapatista.ezln.org.mx and www.zeztainternazional.ezln.org.mx (in Spanish).

Tonalá

The gateway to the main beach resorts of Chiapas, the market town of **TONALÁ** is 39km from the Oaxaca state border and just off Hwy-200. With a population of 67,000, it has all the basic services but not much to see. Tonalá means, quite aptly, "hot place" in Náhuatl, and you're better off pressing on to the coast, where the beachside accommodation can be more appealing. All the **bus** companies terminate along Avenida Hidalgo, the town's main street: the main first-class companies (OCC and ADO) pull in about 500m west of the plaza; second-class, to the east. A taxi to the centre costs about M$15.

Everything you need in Tonalá is either on the *parque central* (plaza) or within a couple of blocks of it. The main feature of the park is the **Estela de Tlaloc**, a large, standing stone carved by the Olmecs, depicting the rain god Tlaloc and showing the influence of Teotihuacán. The **Templo de San Francisco de Asís**, built in 1794 and a couple of blocks northeast of the plaza, merits a quick peek for its pretty pink facade, ceiling murals and impressive gold *retablo*.

Practicalities

The most convenient **place to stay** in Tonalá, handy for catching first-class buses in the early hours, is the *Grajandra* (Ⓣ966/663-0144; ④) at Hidalgo 204. A couple of doors east from the bus station, it offers good value for money, with large, clean, comfortable en-suite rooms with cable TV, air-conditioning, a pool and wi-fi. *Galilea* (Ⓣ966/663-0239; ④) is well located in an attractive old building on the east side of the plaza, and has clean, basic rooms with air-conditioning and TV, as well as private parking. It also has a good **restaurant** overlooking the plaza. A few other restaurants ring the plaza; one of the best is *El Tizoncíto*, on Hidalgo, just off the western side of the plaza. For breakfast, don't miss the sidewalk vendors of chilled *pozole* on the north side of the plaza. Cheaper snacks can be found at the **Mercado La Libertad**, south of the plaza at Matamoros. There are plenty of

internet cafés around the plaza, including Caseta Cristy on 16 de Septiembre on the north side of the plaza (daily 9am–11pm; M$10/hr), and several others along Hidalgo towards the first-class bus station.

Leaving Tonalá, OCC has first-class departures to Tuxtla Gutiérrez (11 daily 2.10am–8.25pm; 3hr 15min), Tapachula (nearly hourly; 3hr 45min), Oaxaca (one daily at 10.40pm; 9hr) and Mexico City (4 daily 4.10–9.40pm; 14hr), and there are a few ADO GL services as well, plus plenty more second-class Rapidos del Sur buses. In the bustling market area, orange shared taxis (on Matamoros between 5 de Mayo and 20 de Marzo) leave when full for **Puerto Arista** (22km south) and **Boca del Cielo** (37km; both M$15/person), while *combis* for Puerto Arista depart one block away on Juárez between 5 de Mayo and 20 de Marzo. The green-striped **city taxis** charge considerably more for the journey to Puerto Arista (M$80 per car).

Puerto Arista

Although this sleepy village may not be everyone's idea of a perfect beach resort, **PUERTO ARISTA**, with its miles of grey sand, flocks of frigatebirds and crashing waves, does offer a chance to escape the unrelenting heat of the inland towns. It's a bit run down, but it's a handy place to stop if you've been doing some hard travelling. While the waves are refreshing, be aware of the potentially dangerous **riptides** that sweep along the coast – never get out of your depth.

You can easily get transport from Puerto Arista 15km down the coast to **Boca del Cielo** ("Mouth of Heaven"), a cluster of houses and fishing boats on the landward side of Laguna la Joya, where you can board a *lancha* and speed across to a beautiful beach. It's best at high tide, when the water comes right up to the restaurants, and at sunset. That said, without your own transport you'll need to head back well before 7pm, as it's almost impossible to find a taxi after dark. Some of the palapa restaurants will let you sling a hammock for a small fee, though if you plan to sleep outdoors be prepared for mosquitoes. The beaches along this stretch of coast are used by **turtles** for nesting: in October, the turtles emerge during the early hours of the morning to deposit their eggs beneath the sand; the next year, in June and July, the hatchlings struggle out to reach the sea.

Practicalities

The road from Tonalá joins Puerto Arista's only street, Avenida Matamoros, at the lighthouse in the centre of town. Ahead lies the busiest section of beach, with hotels and restaurants packed closely together; walk a couple of kilometres left or right and you'll be on a deserted shoreline. Unless you arrive at Christmas or Semana Santa, the place has a slight ghost-town feel, with at least as many buildings abandoned or boarded up as occupied.

There are many **hotels** in Puerto Arista but generally few customers: you could try to bargain with a couple of the places listed here – and you can always **camp** on the beach for free. Turn right at the lighthouse (facing the beach) and the most convenient place to stay is *Lizeth*, with its cramped but clean rooms (ⓣ994/600-9038; ❹). Further up the road are a couple of more upmarket, but rather overpriced alternatives: *Hotel Safari* (ⓣ994/600-9036; ❼), which offers poolside suites for up to eight people, and *Arista Bugambilias* (ⓣ994/600-9044; ❺), a smart option around 500m from the lighthouse, with rooms and suites around a small pool and private garden right on the beach. Take a left at the lighthouse and accommodation is rather thinner on the ground – you'll walk a long way before you find the first decent option. It's around 1km to *Lucero* (ⓣ994/600-9042, ⓦwww.hotel-lucero.com; ❹), just back from the beach, with a pool and suites with air-conditioning and wi-fi. If you take the left turn before *Lucero* you'll soon come across signs for *José's Camping and Cabañas* (ⓣ994/600-9048; ❶, or ❷ with bath), the friendliest place in Puerto Arista and great for budget travellers. Accommodation is in sturdy thatched bungalows with electric lighting; some are en suite, but the shared bathrooms are very clean and have a dependable water supply. There's a flower-filled patio with hammocks and a pool, and camping is also possible if you have your own tent.

For food, a couple of dozen beachfront palapa **restaurants** near the lighthouse serve seafood, but only five or six are ever open at once, and there's little that distinguishes them in terms of cost (M$70–100 for most dishes), menu (*mojarra*, crab and shrimp feature heavily) or quality. At night, stalls sell tacos along the main street, and there are a couple of basic restaurants for *antojitos* on the main road near the lighthouse.

From Tonalá to Tapachula

It's 223km between Tonalá and Tapachula. If you have your own vehicle you can explore some of the side roads leading from Hwy-200, either up into the mountains, where heavy rains give rise to dozens of rivers and waterfalls, or down to near-deserted beaches. (Note that the highway is two lanes each direction, often out of sight of each other. Be sure you don't pull back onto the road going the wrong way; you must use the signed U-turn points.) Around **PIJIJIAPAN**, 75km from Tonalá, a series of dirt roads lead to unspoiled beaches and lagoons with opportunities for fishing, swimming or merely relaxing in the sun. The best of these is **Playa Palo Blanco**, 20km due south of Pijijiapan and accessible by *combi* (M$15). Most of the coastal villages, including Palo Blanco, are actually on the landward side of narrow lagoons, separated from the ocean by sand bars. These sand bars block many rivers' access to the sea, causing marshes to form and providing a superb wetland habitat, protected as the **La Encrucijada Biosphere Reserve**, 45km of coastline and an important wintering point for North American migrant birds, as well as home to such rarities as the azure-rumped tanager. One jumping-off point for visits is Embarcardero de las Garzas; look for it signed off the highway around Escuintla. Travelling **by bus**, it's much more difficult (though still possible) to take in destinations off the main road, and you need to be prepared to hitch and camp. At **HUIXTLA**, 42km before Tapachula, Hwy-211 breaks off from Hwy-200 to snake over the mountains to join the Panamerican Highway near Ciudad Cuauhtémoc and the Guatemalan border at La Mesilla. The road offers stupendous mountain views and is traversed by buses running between Tapachula and Comitán and San Cristóbal de las Casas.

Tapachula

Set in the imposing shadow of the four-thousand-metre Volcán Tacaná, the busy commercial city of **TAPACHULA** is just 16km from Guatemala and a major transit point between Mexico and Central America. As a border city as well as the capital of the Soconusco, it has a lively cultural mix, including immigrants from Central America, as well as small German and Chinese communities. The Germans were invited to settle here by the Mexican government in the 1880s as part of a scheme to boost the economy. They eventually established the state's coffee industry and left a legacy of fine haciendas around the city. The Chinese initially came to work on the railway, in part because the rebellious locals refused to do so; the most visible sign of their community today is the high proportion of Chinese restaurants in the city centre.

While the surrounding countryside offers some worthwhile diversions, there's not much to see in the city itself. As always, the centre of activity is the **plaza**, a pleasant place to while away an evening listening to the marimba bands. Look out

for vendors selling *jocotes*, so-called hog plums – they look like giant olives and are pickled in rum.

The main attraction here is the **Museo Arqueológico del Soconusco**, in the former Palacio Municipal, a gold-trimmed colonial gem on the west side of the plaza. It was closed for renovation at the time of writing, but has displays of prehistoric and Olmec finds and a decent collection of artefacts from Izapa and other local sites (explanations in Spanish only).

Arrival, orientation and information

All the main **bus stations** are north of the centre; the various second-class companies have their terminals within walking distance of the plaza, while first-class OCC (also the terminal for Tica and Linea Dorada buses from Guatemala) is further out, at 17a Calle Ote between avenidas 1a and 3a Nte. A taxi to the centre costs about M$25, and walking takes about twenty minutes. From Tapachula's **airport** (Ⓣ962/626-4079), 18km south on the road to Puerto Madero on the coast, a *colectivo* into town costs M$80 per person. Buy a ticket at the Transportes Terrestre booth just outside the arrivals hall. If you are in a group, it works out cheaper to take a taxi for around M$120.

The town's **layout** is a little confusing, for while the streets are laid out in the regular numbered grid common in Chiapas, the main plaza, **Parque Hidalgo**, is actually three blocks west and one block north of where Calle Central meets Avenida Central.

The **city tourist office** is on the plaza in the former Palacio Municipal (daily 9am–4pm; Ⓣ962/628-7725, Ⓦwww.turismotapachula.gob.mx). The **regional tourist office** (Mon–Fri 8am–8pm, Sat 8am–2pm; Ⓣ962/625-5409) is inconveniently located 2km west of the centre in Plaza Kamico on the main road to the border. The main **banks** are one block east of the plaza, with HSBC at 1a Calle Pte and 2a Avenida Nte, but for **changing cash** and travellers' cheques you'll get much quicker service from Cambio de Divisas, 2a Av Nte 9, between Calle Central and 1a Calle Pte (Mon–Fri 9am–5pm, Sat 9am–2pm); you can also get

Guatemalan quetzales here. The **post office** (Mon–Fri 9am–3pm, Sat 9am–1pm) is a long way southeast of the plaza at 1a Calle Ote, between avenidas 7a and 9a Nte. The Guatemalan **consulate** is at Calle Central Ote 42, at the junction with 5a Avenida Nte (Mon–Fri 10am–3pm & 4–6pm; ⓣ962/626-1525). **Visas** are currently not required for citizens of Europe, North America, South Africa, Australia, New Zealand and many other nations – the office is worth a visit, however, to stock up on free maps and information if you're headed over the border. There are plenty of **internet** cafés around the centre of town: *Angelito's* (Mon–Fri 8am–8pm, Sat 8am–3pm, Sun 9am–2pm: M$10/hr) is on the way to the bus station on Avenida Central Nte, beyond 7a Calle Pte.

Accommodation

Tapachula has no shortage of places to stay, with options for almost every budget. There is at least one **hotel** near any of the bus stations. Your best bet is the area immediately east of the plaza, where there are several good-value hotels along avenidas 4a Nte and 1a, 3a and 5a Pte. The cheapest places are west of the plaza, where the market straggles down the hill, and though most are rather desperate-looking there are one or two good budget options.

La Amistad 7a C Pte 34 between avenidas 10 and 12 Nte ⓣ962/626-2293. The best budget hotel in the city, clean, with fan-only rooms around a flower-filled courtyard. Free drinking water, but M$30 extra for TV. If you're driving, however, *Villa del Sol* is better value because it has parking. ❷

Casa Mexicana 8a Av Sur 19 ⓣ962/626-6605, ⓦwww.casamexicanachiapas.com. Historic and beautifully decorated hotel arranged around a flower-laden courtyard, tastefully adorned with art and antiques. There's wi-fi, a pool and a good restaurant. ❺

Fénix 4a Av Nte 19 ⓣ962/628-9600, ⓦwww.fenix.com.mx. Best-value hotel in the centre, with large rooms with either fan (❸) or a/c (❹), and decent bathrooms. There's a cooling fountain in the courtyard plus leafy gardens complete with parrots. Rooms are surprisingly tranquil given the central location; the remodelled a/c rooms, for about M$100 more, are substantially nicer.

Hostal del Ángel 8a Av Nte 16 ⓣ962/625-0142. Smart hotel just south of the plaza. The seventeen rooms are equipped with cable TV and a/c and arranged around a courtyard. ❹

Hotel Santa Julia 17a C Ote 5, at 1a Av Nte ⓣ962/626-3140. A tidy, slightly old-fashioned hotel just down the street from the OCC bus station (turn left). All rooms have a/c and TV. ❸

Villa del Sol 3a C Pte 45 ⓣ962/626-6193. This clean and friendly option offers large, bright rooms with cable TV, phone and wi-fi, as well as free parking. Rooms without a/c are cheaper (❷). The small downside is its location on a grungy block down from the market. ❸

Eating and drinking

Stalls around the plaza sell cheap local food, while 1a Calle Poniente is lined with inexpensive **restaurants**, most with breakfast options and a comida corrida. As usual, there are budget places to eat and some fine *panaderías* around the market, beginning with the row of **juice bars** on 10a Avenida Poniente, just west of the plaza. Los Portales, a row of restaurants on the south side of the plaza, is a good place for drinks, while the city's liveliest **clubs** are clustered in the Zonas Discotecas, 2km east on Calle Central Oriente.

Bambú 7a C Pte 23. The most appealing of several economical Chinese restaurants along this street; also has a takeaway option should the traffic fumes put you off eating in the open-fronted restaurant – a lunchbox with three dishes plus rice is M$35. *El Carboncito* next door serves great *tacos al pastor* (M$5).

Los Comales Plaza (southwest corner). The busiest place on the plaza, the fluorescent-lit *Los Comales* is open 24hr, serving seafood and a range of Mexican favourites, including a spicy *caldo de pata* (trotter soup, M$60). Other main dishes are about M$80. There's live marimba on weekend evenings.

Los Jarrones 1a C Pte 18. Clean and a/c restaurant in the *Hotel Don Miguel* with a varied, if slightly pricey, menu. Try the *tacos de camarón* (M$80) or pastas (M$40–50).

Moving on from Tapachula

First-class **buses** (and some of the better second-class services) leave from the OCC terminal; taxis to the terminal from anywhere in the centre should be no more than M$25. Luxury ADO GL/Platino services are available to **Tuxtla Gutiérrez** (11 daily), Oaxaca (1 daily), Mexico City (3 daily) and Veracruz (2 daily). OCC has services to all the above, including eleven daily departures to Tuxtla Gutiérrez (6am–midnight). All buses to **Comitán** (6 daily) and **San Cristóbal** (7 daily) are *via altos* and head over the mountains, starting at 7.30am (last one at 11.30pm). All first-class and most second-class buses to Tuxtla are *via costa*, and head up the coast through Tonalá. For **Guatemala City,** three first-class companies offer daily direct services: Trans Galgos (6am, 10.30am, 11.45pm; ⓣ962/625-4588), Linea Dorada (3pm) and Tica Bus (daily 6am; ⓣ962/626-2880); the latter two are a bit cheaper, though the buses aren't as nice. All run from the OCC terminal; buy tickets from a kiosk in the arrivals hall. At the border crossing at Talismán, you'll have to get off the bus for Mexican immigration, walk across the bridge, pass through Guatemalan immigration and then reboard.

The main **second-class bus** operators are TRF, at the corner of 16a Avenida Norte and 3a Calle Poniente, and AEXA, opposite. The main **combi** terminals lie along 5a Calle Poniente beyond the market, between avenidas 12a and 14a Norte. Unión y Progreso runs frequent services to Cacahoatán (30min) for Unión Juárez, as well as to the Talismán Bridge (30min) for Izapa and the Guatemalan border every three to five minutes. Next door, Omnibus de Tapachula runs frequent buses to Ciudad Hidalgo (45min), while Costeños de Chiapas, opposite, provides a virtually identical service. If you're staying on the other side of the plaza, Gen. Paulino Navarro also offers regular *combis* to Hidalgo (every 8min 4.30am–9.45pm) from its terminal on 7a Calle Ote and Avenida Central Nte. **Shared taxis** to Hidalgo leave from 7a Calle Pte, between 2a Avenida and 4a Avenida Nte.

Tapachula's **airport** (ⓣ962/626-4189), 18km from town, is served by three daily flights to Mexico City, operated by Aeroméxico (C Central Ote 4; Mon–Fri 9am–7pm, Sat 9am–6pm; ⓣ962/626-7757). You can buy tickets from airline offices in town, or from helpful agent Aeropromociones y Viajes at 4a Av Nte 18-B (ⓣ962/625-0017).

For further information, see Travel details, p.746.

Jordán 2a Av Nte 6. Tranquil Christian bookshop with small restaurant at the front, with a big menu of Mexican staples (M$40–50), many of them vegetarian. There's free wi-fi too. Open 7am–9pm.

La Parrilla 8a Av Nte 20, just south of the plaza. South-American-style *parillas* (grills, from M$85) as well as a delicious *taquiza mixta*, with five mouth-watering types of supertacos (M$60), all served in a fast-food-style diner.

Pronto's 1a C Pte 11. One of several good-value budget options along this street, this open-front cafeteria has the added advantage of being open 24hr. Try the *menudo sinaloense*, a typical Mexican *caldo* (broth) for M$40, or the large fried chicken (M$50).

Tortas German 8a Av Nte at C Central Pte. Enjoy big stuffed sandwiches on an airy raised terrace just above street level.

Ruta del Café

The **Ruta del Café** refers to a number of charming old haciendas built north of Tapachula by German coffee barons in the early twentieth century. As it's a long, winding drive through *pequeña Alemania*, the area is best for extended stays, rather than a day trip, and you'll need your own transport or a taxi (M$300–400) to get up here. Three of the haciendas provide accommodation and/or tours: **Finca Irlanda** (ⓣ962/625-9203, ⓦwww.grupopeters.com), which became the world's first certified organic producer in 1967; the **Argovia Finca Resort** (ⓣ962/626-2966, ⓦwww.argovia.com.mx), which has an upscale restaurant and offers walking tours; and **Finca Hamburgo** (ⓣ962/625-1812, ⓦwww.fincahamburgo.com), established in 1888 and still run by the same German-Mexican family. All three require advance reservations and offer only all-inclusive lodging packages, at similar rates. *Finca Hamburgo* (which is the most absorbing) has two-night all-inclusive ecotourism packages starting at US$224 per person in high season. It has an office in Tapachula at 9a C Ote 54-A, near 11a Avenida Norte.

Santo Domingo and Unión Juárez

If you're travelling by bus, the small towns of **Santo Domingo** and **Unión Juárez** offer a similar taste of the area's coffee culture as the Ruta del Café, but make for much easier destinations, and are more manageable as day outings. This said, there are still no direct buses from Tapachula, and you have to change at the town of **Cacahoatán**, approximately halfway and thirty minutes from the city (see box, p.683). The route follows the road to Talismán and the border for much of the way; it's best to bring your passport in case of security checks. Once in Cacahoatán, frequent **buses** leave from the station across the street from the Unión y Progreso terminal. Shared **taxis**, which are slightly faster, also wait here. Domingo usually takes around thirty minutes, with Juárez an additional ten to fifteen minutes up the mountain. As the road climbs up the lush green valley of the Río Suchiate, which forms the border with Guatemala, the bananas and cacao give way to coffee and you begin to enjoy good views of two majestic **volcanoes**: Tacaná, at 4092m, the highest peak in Chiapas; and the 4220-metre peak of Tajumulco, the highest mountain in Guatemala.

Santo Domingo

Around 35km from Tapachula, **SANTO DOMINGO** is a sleepy village with a wonderfully restored 1920s coffee-plantation house, Casa Braun, or just "**Casa Grande**" (daily 8am–8pm; free).The three-storey wooden house, set in beautiful gardens, and with balconies all around, was the home of Enrique Braun Hansen, whose German origins are reflected in the building's architectural style – early North American meets Alpine hotel, with predominately Art Nouveau interiors. Now part of a community-based tourism project, the house includes a good restaurant on the ground floor, a swimming pool out back for guests and the **Museo de Café** (free), with displays and photos charting the area's history and the coffee-making process. Opposite the main entrance, around 100m along the street and just off the main road, *Hotel Santo Domingo* (Ⓣ962/627-0055, Ⓦwww.centroecoturisticosantodomingo.com; ❷) is a good-value **place to stay**, where rooms with spacious, private baths and comfortable beds are set around a patio garden. Get off the bus at the lower end of the village, near the plaza, and you should be able to follow the signs for the "Centro Turístico" – the house is around 200m from the main road. Moving on, you can pick up buses to Juárez on the main road.

Unión Juárez

The small town of **UNIÓN JUÁREZ**, 51km from Tapachula, is one of the last remaining areas for the Mam people in Mexico (most of this Maya group lives in Guatemala). Perched at 1100m on the flank of the **Volcán Tacaná**, the community is the starting point for some of the finest hiking in southern Chiapas, passing scores of waterfalls. With a guide, you can reach the summit of the volcano, where a monument symbolizes the kinship between Mexico and Guatemala. Fernando Valera Fuentes (Ⓔfernandao772@hotmail.com), an excellent Spanish-speaking guide, leads three-day trips up Tacaná for about M$1000; the price includes government approvals and equipment. The best time to climb is between November and March, particularly December and January.

Unión Juárez has two **hotels**: the budget but comfortable *Posada Aljoad*, half a block off the west side of the plaza (Ⓣ962/647-2025; ❷), which has simple but neat rooms with private bathrooms (with hot water) around a courtyard, and a decent, inexpensive restaurant; and the good-value *Hotel Colonial Campestre*, which you pass as you enter the town (Ⓣ962/647-2015; ❸). Rooms and suites here are comfortable and spacious, with en-suite bathrooms and TV. The *Campestre* has a pleasant **restaurant**, and on the north side of the plaza, the *Carmelita* serves an inexpensive menu of meat, chicken and tacos. *La Montaña*, nearby, is slightly better, with comfortable wooden tables and chairs and tasty tamales stuffed with egg, plums, chicken and olives. You can sit outside and enjoy views of Pico de Loro, a steep, rocky outcrop that actually looks like its namesake – a parrot's beak. All the coffee served in the village is organic, and can be purchased freshly roasted. Buses pull in on the west side of the plaza and depart for Cacahoatán from the east side (every 15min until 8pm; last bus to Tapachula 9pm from Cacahoatán).

The ruins of Izapa

About 14km east of Tapachula, the road to the border passes right through the archeological site of **Izapa** (Wed–Sun 8am–5pm; free), an important, if little-visited, group of ruins. Besides being easy to get to, the site is large – with more than eighty temple mounds – and significant for its evidence of both the Olmec and Maya cultures. Izapa culture is seen as a transitional stage between the Olmecs and the Classic Maya period. Many of the best carved monuments have been removed to museums, but you can still see early versions of the rain god Chac and other gods, many in rather sad-looking huts surrounded by barbed wire. From its founding before 1250 BC, Izapa flourished up to and throughout the Maya pre-Classic period, until around 300 AD; most of what remains is from the later part of this period, perhaps around 200 AD.

Entry is officially free, but in practice the gatekeepers at each section appreciate small donations. The **northern side** of the site (left of the road as you head to the border) is the most interesting. There's a ball-court and several stelae, which, though not Olmec in origin, are carved in a recognizable Olmec style. The **southern side** (Grupo A and B), is down a track about 1km back along the main road towards Tapachula. These sections are more overgrown, but you can spot altars with animal carvings – frogs, snakes and jaguars – and several unexcavated mounds. To **get to Izapa**, take any bus or *combi* to the Talismán border and ask the driver to drop you at the site, which is signposted from the road.

The Guatemalan border: Talismán Bridge and Ciudad Hidalgo

Both of these southern crossing points are easy places to enter Guatemala (see box, p.686) – which one you head for depends largely on your ultimate destination. But neither is a place to linger. **Talismán Bridge** is closer to Tapachula (16km) and better for onward connections if travelling by bus, especially to Quetzaltenango and the Western Highlands. Apart from a few grubby hotels and unappealing *comedores* there is nothing in Talismán; El Carmen, on the Guatemalan side, isn't much better. **Leaving Mexico**, you shouldn't have to pay departure tax of any kind: though each Mexican state seems to follow slightly different rules, the only official fee payable is the **non-immigrant fee** of around US$20 (the exact amount in pesos changes from year to year), which should have been paid on entry to the country. Most airlines include the fee in the price of a ticket, but if you entered Mexico by land and didn't pay upon leaving the border zone, you'll have to go to a bank in Tapachula before you leave. Make sure they stamp your tourist card after

Crossing into Guatemala

There are two major **crossings** (Talismán Bridge and Ciudad Hidalgo, open 24hr) and several minor points of entry (Frontera Corozal, see p.724; Ciudad Cuauhtémoc, see p.710; Benemérito, see p.727; and El Carmen Xhan) from Chiapas into Guatemala, as well as one from Tabasco (El Ceibo; see p.743). Crossings are relatively trouble-free at the larger points these days, though procedures at Frontera Corozal, Ciudad Cuauhtémoc and El Ceibo are rather more unpredictable. These are notorious entry points for illegal immigrants and the *aduanas* consist of little more than armed soldiers manning riverside tables – the soliciting of **illegal fees** sometimes still occurs at these crossings. Requesting a receipt is often a sufficient response to get them to waive the fee, but it may well be less hassle to pay. The only genuine tax is the **non-immigrant fee** (usually around US$20), which should have been paid on your arrival (and included in the cost of most flights). If for some reason this fee was not paid, and you do not intend to return before your tourist card expires, you can make payment at any city bank before departure. If you will be returning to Mexico you will be allowed to proceed in possession of your current tourist card free of charge.

Citizens of the US, Canada, South Africa, the EU, Australia and New Zealand **do not require visas** to enter Guatemala. Citizens of other countries should check with the Guatemalan consulate in Tapachula (see p.682). Note that Mexico observes daylight-saving time, making it one hour later here during the summer than in Guatemala.

you've paid – you'll need this to exit the country. **Changing money** is also best done in Tapachula, where rates are more favourable and you can check the official exchange rate beforehand.

Guatemala City is five to six hours away. Buses are usually waiting, but these typically travel along the Carretera al Pacifica via Tecún Umán (closer to Ciudad Hidalgo). The faster option is one of the international bus services from Tapachula direct to Guatemala City (see box, p.683). For **Quetzaltenango** and other destinations in the Western Highlands, take a shared taxi to **Malacatán** and continue from there. Travelling **into Mexico** you'll be given a tourist card at immigration; *combis* head to Tapachula, and first-class buses go from Tapachula onwards. You may have your passport checked along Hwy-200, so be prepared.

South of Talismán Bridge, and 37km from Tapachula, the border town of **CIUDAD HIDALGO** is a very busy road crossing, but useful only if you're aiming for the beaches along the Carretera al Pacifica (Pacific Highway) or the ruins at Abaj Takalik near Retalhuleu (connected to Hidalgo's Guatemalan neighbour **Tecún Umán** with regular buses). The OCC terminal is one block from immigration, where you can pick up shuttles to Tapachula every fifteen minutes. If you get stuck (try not to), the *Mazari* (Ⓣ962/698-0098; ❸), at 3a Avenida Norte and 5 Calle Oriente, is one of the better choices, with clean, comfortable rooms. Plenty of willing locals offer to pedal you across the Puente Rodolfo Robles to Umán in Guatemala, but it's an easy walk. You have to pay M$5 to cross the bridge.

The Chiapas highlands

There is nowhere in Mexico so rich in scenery as **highland Chiapas**. Forested mountains and jungle valleys – flush with vivid orchids, brilliantly coloured birds and monkeys – are studded with rivers and lakes, waterfalls and dramatic gorges, including the enormous **Cañón del Sumidero**. In addition, the area's relative isolation has allowed the **indigenous population** to carry on with their lives little affected by Catholicism and modern commercialism, especially evident in the villages of **San Juan Chamula** and **San Lorenzo de Zinacantán**, near the large market town of **San Cristóbal de las Casas**. Older generations in particular preserve traditional dress and folk practice, and this includes an aversion to **photography**. Be sensitive of taking pictures, especially of anything that might have religious significance; donning **native clothing**, the patterns on which convey subtle social and geographic meaning, can also cause offence.

Strong and colourful as these cultures are, the economic and social lot of the *indígena* population in this region lags far behind the rest of Mexico. This is in part due to the long duration of the *encomienda* system of forced labour, which remained in place here long after the end of Spanish colonialism. Many small villages still operate at the barest subsistence level. It's worth noting that many indigenous communities and some local transport operators refuse to observe the **time change** in summer, preferring *la hora vieja* – the old time, or, as some savvy marketers have dubbed it, 'Zapatista time'. For the ascent by car into the hills from Tonalá and the coast highway, a short toll highway (M$23) outside Arriaga bypasses about twenty kilometres of almost comically winding road.

Tuxtla Gutiérrez

Though not actually in the highlands, **TUXTLA GUTIÉRREZ** is the main gateway from central Mexico and a major transport hub. As the capital of Chiapas,

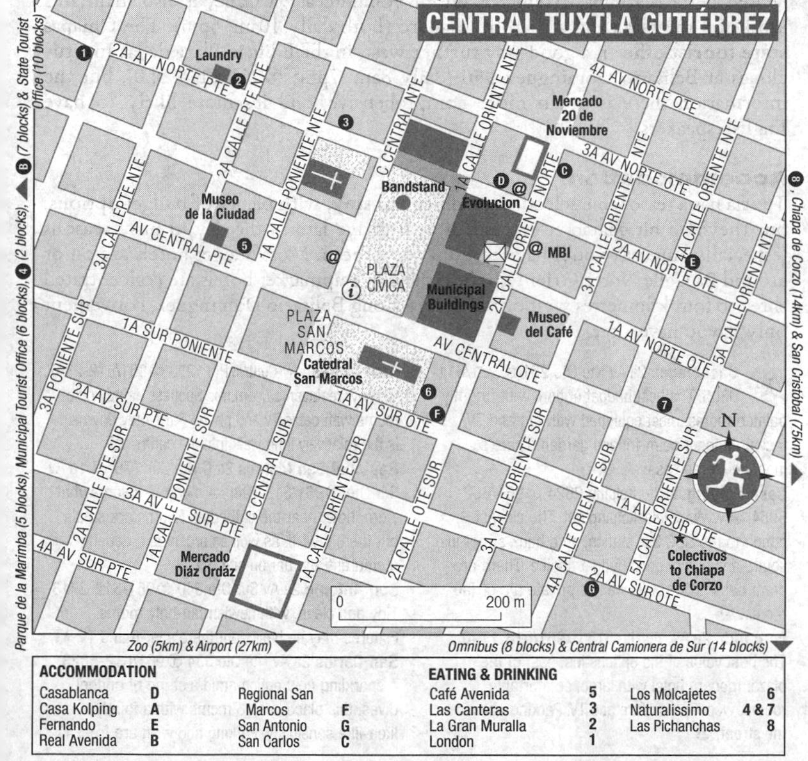

it does its best to deny most of the state's attraction and tradition – it's a fast-growing, modern, crowded city of about 500,000. (If you prefer a more rural setting, press on to Chiapa de Corzo; see p.691.) A couple of **museums** can fill your time if you stay here, and the city is the best base from which to approach the cliff-tops and *miradores* of the **Cañón del Sumidero** (see p.693), the real highlight of the area. Other day trips to surrounding attractions are better organized in San Cristóbal, a little over an hour's drive east (see p.694).

Arrival and information

Tuxtla's airport, **Aeropuerto Ángel Albino Corzo**, is inconveniently located 27km south of the city. All the major car rental companies and top hotels have desks in the arrivals hall, but as yet there is nowhere to change money. There is a small Bancomer ATM tucked away in the departures hall upstairs, but this is often out of order. To get anywhere, you have to take a **taxi**; buy tickets at the desk in the arrivals hall. It's about M$200 to Tuxtla or Chiapa de Corzo (both take 35–45min).

First-class **buses** pull into the large ADO/OCC station on 5a Avenida Norte Poniente, in the Plaza del Sol mall on the northwest side of town. Taxis to the centre cost M$30. The main second-class terminal, the Central Camionera de Sur, is on Avenida 10a Sur Oriente at 15a Calle Oriente Sur. Scores of smaller companies and *colectivos* pull in here; taxis to the centre cost M$25. A confusing number of **colectivos** shoot around town, but you can walk to most sights.

The **municipal tourist office** (Mon–Fri 8am–8pm, Sat 8am–2pm) is at the Museo de la Marimba, Avenida Central Poniente at 9a Calle; it also maintains kiosks on the plaza and at Parque Madero (both daily 10am–6pm). The Chiapas **state tourist office** is a good way further west, in the Edificio Plaza de las Instituciones at Belisario Domínguez 950 (daily 8am–7pm; ⓣ961/617-0550), but the information there is much more comprehensive, and it's more likely to have English speakers.

Accommodation

Tuxtla has a reasonable selection of **places to stay**, with plenty of budget options, but they're a bit characterless, and if you arrive late in the day in busy seasons (especially August), you'll have to hunt for a room. Most budget hotels are on or around 2a Calle Norte Oriente, while the city's upmarket hotels are concentrated three to four kilometres west of the centre along Belisario Domínguez, convenient only if you have a car.

Casablanca 2a Av Nte Ote 251 ⓣ961/611-0305. The best budget option, with brightly painted rooms, most equipped with a/c and TV, facing an inner palm-fringed garden. There's luggage storage as well. ❷

Casa Kolping Adolfo Kolping 2624 ⓣ961/602-6954, ⓦwww.hoteleskolping.net. The closest option to the OCC bus station, on a back street just south, and a very good budget choice. There are dorm beds (M$110) as well as private a/c or fan rooms. ❸

Fernando 2a Av Nte Ote 515 ⓣ961/613-1740. The best value of the options just east of the plaza: modern hotel with large, comfortable rooms, wooden furniture and TV. Parking across the street. ❸

Real Avenida Av Central Pte 1230 ⓣ961/612-2347, ⓦwww.realavenida.com.mx. Spotless, faintly chic rooms with cable TV and phone – the only downside is the relatively long walk into the centre. ❹

Regional San Marcos 2a C Ote Sur 176, at 1a Av Sur Ote ⓣ961/613-1940. A modern, if somewhat worn, hotel near the cathedral. Rooms are small, but there's wi-fi, as well as a/c, plus a decent restaurant and bar on site. ❹

San Antonio 2a Av Sur Ote 540 ⓣ961/612-2713. Tidy and clean, with newish fan-only rooms. Fixtures may be basic, but there's wi-fi and TV. ❷

San Carlos 2a Av Nte Ote 334 ⓣ961/612-5323. A sparkling new option amid a string of budget dives, this place has 16 rooms with a faintly Ikea-like sensibility. Parking and wi-fi are free. ❸

The City

The **plaza**, known as the Plaza Cívica, is an expanse of ostentatious marble, fountains and a statue of General Joaquín Miguel Gutiérrez Canales (1796–1838), former governor of Chiapas and campaigner for *indígena* rights. Just opposite, across Avenida Central, the whitewashed **Catedral de San Marcos** (daily 6am–2pm & 4–9pm) was established in the sixteenth century. Its bell tower is one of the leading local entertainments: every hour a mechanical procession of the twelve apostles goes through a complicated routine accompanied by a carillon of 48 bells.

Unlike in many Mexican cities, the central plaza is not the true social centre. Head west along Avenida Central Poniente, at 2a Calle Poniente Sur, past the **Museo de la Ciudad** (daily 9am–6pm; free), with its small but absorbing collection of photos and memorabilia, to the **Parque de la Marimba**, between calles 8 and 9. This is where evening crowds gather, often for live music, as well as to lounge in the various modern cafés around the perimeter. Real fans can visit the **Museo de la Marimba** (Tues–Sun 10am–8pm; M$50) on the corner, which highlights the history of the musical genre (displays in Spanish only).

About 1km northeast of the centre, **Parque Madero** is another place where locals go to stroll in late afternoon and evening. A promenade leads off 5a Avenida Norte Oriente, first passing the pleasant **Jardin Botánico** and the less interesting **Museo Botánico** (Tues–Fri 9am–3pm, Sat 9am–1pm; free) opposite, and on to the **Museo Regional de Chiapas** (Tues–Sun 9am–5pm; M$33, free Sun), which details the history of pre-Hispanic Chiapas and the results of the Conquest. The highlights are the intricately carved human fencers from the ruins of Chiapa de Corzo (see p.692). At the end of the promenade is the city theatre and next to it the **Museo de Paleontología** (Tues–Fri 10am–5pm, Sat & Sun 11am–5pm; M$10), which displays local fossils, amber and the skeleton of a sabre-tooth tiger.

At research time, the **Museo del Café** was just about to open, on 2a Calle Oriente Norte, just north of Avenida Central, in an old colonial house. Exhibits detail the history and use of coffee in Mexico.

The zoo

If you're interested in local wildlife, it's worth heading out to the Zoológico Miguel Álvarez del Toro, or **ZOOMAT** (Tues–Sun 9am–5pm; M$20), 5km south of the city centre. It claims to have every species native to Chiapas, and as far as zoos go, it's not bad, with good-sized cages, natural vegetation and freshwater streams. A number of animals, including *guaqueques negros* (agoutis) – rodents about the size of a domestic cat – and large birds such as currasows and chachalacas, are free to roam the zoo grounds. The *vivario* contains a vast collection of snakes, insects and spiders.

The **bus** is very roundabout and can take up to 45 minutes, so you might prefer a **taxi**. The bus, #60, marked "Cerro Hueco" or "Zoológico", leaves from 1a Calle Oriente Sur between avenidas 6a and 7a Sur Ote, a bit of a walk from the centre.

Eating and drinking

The centre of Tuxtla has dozens of reasonably appetizing **restaurants**, and you need never wander more than a block or so on either side of Avenida Central to find something in every price range, including juice bars and bakeries. The very **cheapest** places are in the Mercado Díaz Ordáz, Calle Central Sur, between avenidas 3a and 4a Sur Oriente; there's also a string of pleasant, inexpensive lunch operations on 1a Avenida Norte, just west of Calle Central, with set menus for M$35 or so. Most popular for socializing and people-watching are the terrace restaurants under the arches on **Plaza San Marcos** behind the cathedral, and, for a younger scene, the cafés and bars around **Parque de la Marimba**.

Moving on from Tuxtla Gutiérrez

ADO and OCC first-class **buses** depart from the station on the northwest side of the city, near the *libramiento norte* ring road. OCC has very frequent departures for **Tonalá**, **Tapachula, Comitán** and **San Cristóbal**, and seven buses daily to **Palenque** via **Ocosingo**. Other destinations include Mexico City, **Villahermosa**, Cancún and Oaxaca. ADO GL and Platino go to Cancún (2.30pm, 6pm & 11.30pm), Comitán (5.25am & 10.15am), Oaxaca (9.30pm), Palenque (2.30pm), Villahermosa (6pm & 11.30pm), and more frequently to Mexico City, Tapachula and San Cristóbal. Note that first-class buses to Villahermosa travel via the Puente Chiapas, which looks less direct but is much faster than going over the mountains. The second-class terminal, at 10a Avenida Sur Oriente and 15a Calle Oriente Sur, is used by Autotransportes Tuxtla Gutiérrez (ATG), and serves San Cristóbal, Oaxaca, Villahermosa, Mérida, Palenque and Cancún. **Colectivos** for Bochil and San Cristóbal depart from the 9a Avenida side. The most frequent service to San Cristóbal is with Omnibus, from a dedicated terminal on 4a Avenida Sur Oriente at 15a Calle Oriente Sur.

For **Chiapa de Corzo** (30min), hop on one of the *colectivos* that leave from the southeast corner of 1a Avenida Sur Oriente at 5a Calle Oriente Sur.

Tuxtla's **airport** has frequent flights to Mexico City (Click Mexicana and InterJet); taxis should take you to the airport for about M$200.

For further information, see Travel details, p.746.

Café Avenida Av Central Pte 230. An authentic Mexican coffee shop (they grind their own beans), where old men sip black coffee to a background of mariachi music and slow service.

Las Canteras 2a Av Nte Ote at 1a C Pte. An open, airy restaurant serving traditional *chiapaneco* cookery, often accompanied by live marimba – the atmosphere is somewhat more refined, but don't expect a quiet meal. Mains from M$100–120, and a good-value set lunch.

La Gran Muralla 2a Av Nte Pte 334. Passable Cantonese restaurant, with a wide range of Chinese dishes for anyone needing a break from Mexican food. Daily noon–11pm.

AP London 2a Av Nte Pte at 4a C Pte Nte. A casual restaurant-bar, decorated outside with caricatures of Elvis and Marilyn Monroe and inside with lots of plants and twinkly lights – great atmosphere and inexpensive, wide-ranging menu.

Los Molcajetes Plaza San Marcos. One of a string of restaurants behind the cathedral, this sit-down taco and grill operation offers bargain combo meals. Especially satisfying are the *tacos machos*, grilled steak and poblano peppers on flaky flour tortillas.

Naturalissimo 6a C Pte Nte 124, just off Av Central Pte. Bright vegetarian chain restaurant; it's inexpensive (no more than M$40 for most dishes), clean and modern, and offers a solid daily set lunch. Mon–Sat 7am–10.30pm, Sun 8am–10.30pm. There's a second branch on Av Central Ote, five blocks east of the plaza.

Las Pichanchas Av Central Ote 837, east of the plaza between calles 7 and 8 Ote. A bit touristy, but a great place for dinner, with marimba all evening, folk dancing 9–10pm and excellent *chiapaneco* food all dished up in a two-storey house with a courtyard. Try the *platón de botana regional* (a selection of local snacks: cheese, sausage, tortas). Most dishes are M$60–70. Daily noon–midnight.

Listings

Airlines InterJet, Belisario Domínguez 1748 ☎800/011-2345 (Mon–Sat 9am–7pm); Mexicana, Plaza Veranda 7, 8 y 9 Col Arboledes ☎961/602-5769.

Banks There are plenty of banks along Avenida Central, with a branch of HSBC right on the plaza (C Central Nte 137).

Car rental Hertz, Belisario Domínguez 1195 (☎961/617-7777), and at airport; Alamo, Europcar and others have airport locations.

Internet access Widely available, particularly along 2a Av Nte Ote. MBI, 2a C Ote Nte 220, just off 2a Av Nte Ote, is open daily 9am–9pm.

Laundry Lavandería Zaac, 2a Av Pte Ote 440 (Mon–Fri 8am–2pm & 4.30–8pm, Sat 9am–4pm; M$30/kg, minimum 3kg).

Post office The main post office is at 1a Av Nte Ote, behind the Palacio de Gobierno (Mon–Fri 8.30am–4pm, Sat 8.30am–1pm).

Travel agent Viajes Miramar, Av Central Pte 1468 ⓣ961/613-3983, ⓦwww.viajesmiramar.com.mx.

Chiapa de Corzo and around

An elegant town of about 70,000, **CHIAPA DE CORZO** overlooks the **Río Grijalva**. As it's barely twenty minutes east from Tuxtla, it makes a scenic alternative to the big city, though it's best known as the starting point for boat rides through the **Cañón del Sumidero** (see p.693), and is quite a tourist scene during Mexican holiday times. The first Spanish city in Chiapas, it was officially founded in 1528, though it had already been an important centre in pre-Classic times. A stele found here bears the oldest **Long Count date**, corresponding to December 7, 36 BC, yet discovered. The ruins that remain are on private land behind the Nestlé plant, at the far end of 21 de Octubre on the edge of town (see p.692).

The most striking feature of Chiapa de Corzo is the elaborate sixteenth-century **Fuente Colonial**, which dominates the central Plaza Ángel Albino Corzo. Built of brick in the Mudéjar style, in the shape of the Spanish crown, the fountain is one of the most impressive surviving early colonial monuments in Mexico. It has become a state symbol – you may recognize it from Chiapas licence plates. Just behind the fountain, the huge tree bursting from its confines is **La Pochota**, a national monument to the suffering of the *indígenas* under Spanish rule, said to have been standing here when the town was founded.

On the northwest side of the plaza, the **Casa Museo Ángel Albino Corzo** (daily 10am–2pm & 6–9pm; free) is the former residence of the national reformer for whom the town was named. Housing an interesting jumble of period furniture

▲ Fuente Colonial during a fiesta, Chiapa de Corzo

and historical artefacts, it features two cannon used in the so-called Pastry War against France in 1838 (explanations in Spanish only). On the southern side of the plaza, *portales* house a series of reasonably priced handicraft stores, which continue south along 5 de Febrero towards the river and *embarcadero*. Behind the *portales* is the lovely **Templo de Santo Domingo de Guzmán** and ex-convent, with a tall nave and timbered ceiling. Forming part of the complex, behind the main entrance to the church, is the **Centro Cultural** (Tues–Sun 10am–5pm; free), an ambitious new project that is gradually converting the old convent into a series of tasteful galleries and art studios. Upstairs on the first floor, the **Museo de Laca** recounts the history of lacquer-making in Mexico, from pre-Hispanic times to the present, featuring various lacquered objects from gourds to pots and chests.

Practicalities

Buses from Tuxtla travel along Avenida Cuauhtémoc, north of the plaza, terminating near the Nestlé plant – get off at Calle Mexicanidad, or where the driver says "parque", and turn right for the plaza. Heading back, buses cut across the top of the plaza (Avenida 21 de Octubre) and are easy to pick up. Moving on, though, you typically have to backtrack to Tuxtla, as the main highway bypasses the town about 4km to the north. One alternative is to take a taxi from the plaza all the way to San Cristóbal (about M$350). Heading to the airport, however, there's little point going to Tuxtla as taxis cost the same (M$200).

There are two good **hotels** in town: the central *Los Angeles* (Ⓣ961/616-0048; ❸), on the southeast corner of the plaza, which has small but comfortable en-suite rooms in a renovated building around a courtyard; and the more upmarket *Hotel La Ceiba*, Domingo Ruíz 300 (Ⓣ961/616-0389; ❺), three blocks west from the plaza, which encloses a tranquil palm-filled garden with a small pool and caged parrots, and offers simple but very comfortable rooms with air-conditioning and cable TV. For **food**, don't miss the vendors near the **market** (southeast of the plaza), who specialize in *cochito horneado*, chile-roasted pork in a rich broth. Several **restaurants** specialize in *chiapaneco* cuisine, though they tend to be a little overpriced: *El Campanario*, behind the municipal building on Coronel Urbina 5 (just east off the plaza) is the best, with an inviting garden and courtyard, though it closes at 7pm. *Los Corredores*, at the southwest corner of the plaza at Madero 35, offers Mexican favourites. The *embarcadero* along the river is a pretty spot for a drink, though nothing differentiates the somewhat pricey seafood restaurants here, and most start to wind down early.

The ruins of Chiapa de Corzo

On an ancient trade route high above the Río Grijalva, the ruins of **Chiapa de Corzo** comprise some two hundred structures scattered over a wide area of private property, shared among several owners and sliced in two by the Panamerican Highway (Hwy-190). This is the longest continually occupied site in Chiapas, begun as a farming settlement in the early pre-Classic period (1400–850 BC). By the late pre-Classic period (450 BC–250 AD), it was the largest centre of population in the region. What you see today are mainly low pyramids, walls and courtyards.

There's a small example of the ruins in the middle of the road, just beyond the terminal for buses to Tuxtla on the edge of town, but to **get to the main site** from the plaza, take any microbus heading east, get off at the junction with Hidalgo and follow the signs. After about fifteen minutes, you'll come to an unmarked gate in a fence on the right; go to the house (officially closed Mon) and pay the M$10 **fee** to the family who farm among the ruins. **Walking**, it's about 3km northeast from the plaza in Chiapa de Corzo, passing the beautiful sixteenth-century church ruin of **San Sebastián** on 21 de Octubre along the way.

Cañon del Sumidero

On the highway east from Chiapa de Corzo towards San Cristóbal, you catch occasional glimpses of the lower reaches of the **Cañón del Sumidero**. Through this spectacular cleft the Río Grijalva runs beneath cliffs that reach 1000m in height in places, the rock walls sprinkled with patches of bright green vegetation. The typical tour is on a mesmerizing **boat ride** down the river from Chiapa de Corzo, or you can drive along the rim from Tuxtla.

From Tuxtla, Autobús Panorámico (Sat & Sun 9am & 1pm; 3hr 30min; M$80) runs a bus from the plaza along the road that borders the rim of the canyon, passing all the main *miradores* – the best views are from **La Coyota**. The buses go only when five or six people turn up. There's no public transport to the area.

In Chiapa de Corzo, several companies offer regular boat trips down the canyon, all for the same price (8am–5pm; M$150/person). The first office you reach is Turística de Grijalva (Ⓣ961/600-6402), on the west side of the plaza. Or you can head straight south down the street to the *embarcadero*, where other companies operate. During Mexican vacation times, boats fill with the requisite ten people almost immediately, and it doesn't matter where you buy your ticket; in slower times, it's best to show up early and go from company to company to see which boat is closest to full. Tours last a couple of hours, snaking through the whole gorge to the Chicoasén Dam, which forms a lake at the northern end. Along the way you pass several waterfalls, including the remarkable **El Árbol de Navidad**, where calcareous formations covered with algae resemble a Christmas tree from a distance. Crocodiles and spider monkeys can often be spotted, as well as vast numbers of pelicans, egrets and cormorants.

Bochil and Simojovel

Just beyond Chiapa de Corzo, Hwy-195 cuts off to the north. It's an inconvenient route, as there's no continuous bus service, but for those with time and inclination, it's a part of mountainous Chiapas that's well off the tourist track. Second-class buses run from Tuxtla only as far as Pichucalco, and from there you can catch another to Teapa in southern Tabasco (see p.736). The road climbs through mountains wreathed in cloud to **BOCHIL**, some 60km from Tuxtla and a centre for the **Tzotzil Maya**. There are a couple of simple **places to stay**, including the *Posada San Pedro* (no phone; ❷), whose basic rooms are set out around a courtyard on 1 Calle Poniente Norte, a block from the plaza; head for Banamex at the top of the plaza and turn right. *Combis* run regularly up to **SIMOJOVEL**, 40km away at the head of a spectacular valley. The pretty town is the source of most of the amber you'll find sold in local markets, and plenty of shops sell it, often for a bit less than elsewhere in the state.

El Triunfo Biosphere Reserve

Cradled within the slopes of the Sierra Madre de Chiapas, on the northern edge of the Soconusco (see p.677), the dense cloud forest of the **El Triunfo Biosphere Reserve** is a refuge for hundreds of species of birds (including the rare quetzal). The jumping-off point for the reserve is the town of **JALTENANGO**, also known as **Ángel Albino Corzo**, ringed with coffee plantations. But it's best to contact the reserve several weeks in advance if you intend to visit. Based in Tuxtla, the Fondo de Conservación El Triunfo (Ⓣ961/125-1122, Ⓦwww.fondoeltriunfo.org), at C San Cristóbal 8, is responsible for tourism. It runs four-day packages that include transport from Tuxtla, lodging at the simple *Campamento El Triunfo* in the mountains, a guide at the coffee *fincas* and in the wilderness and porters, for about M$5100 per person. **Buses** to Jaltenango leave Tuxtla several times a day from the Cuxtepeques y Anexas station at Calle 10 Oriente Norte and Avenida 3 Norte Oriente.

San Cristóbal de las Casas and around

Just 75km from Tuxtla Gutiérrez, **SAN CRISTÓBAL DE LAS CASAS** – or Jovel, as many locals call it – is almost 1700m higher, at 2100m. Even in August, the evenings are chilly, and the tile-roofed houses huddle together in the bowl of a small valley. San Cristóbal's distinctive colonial charm, fascinating **indigenous villages** nearby and, of course, Zapatista cachet have made it a major stop on the travel circuit. But the city of 200,000 has held up to tourism well, with pedestrianized central streets and a low-key social scene in a cosmopolitan mélange of small bars and restaurants. It's also a great base for studying at one of the numerous Spanish-language schools.

San Cristóbal was designed as a Spanish stronghold against an often-hostile indigenous population – the attack here by **Zapatista rebels** in January 1994 was only

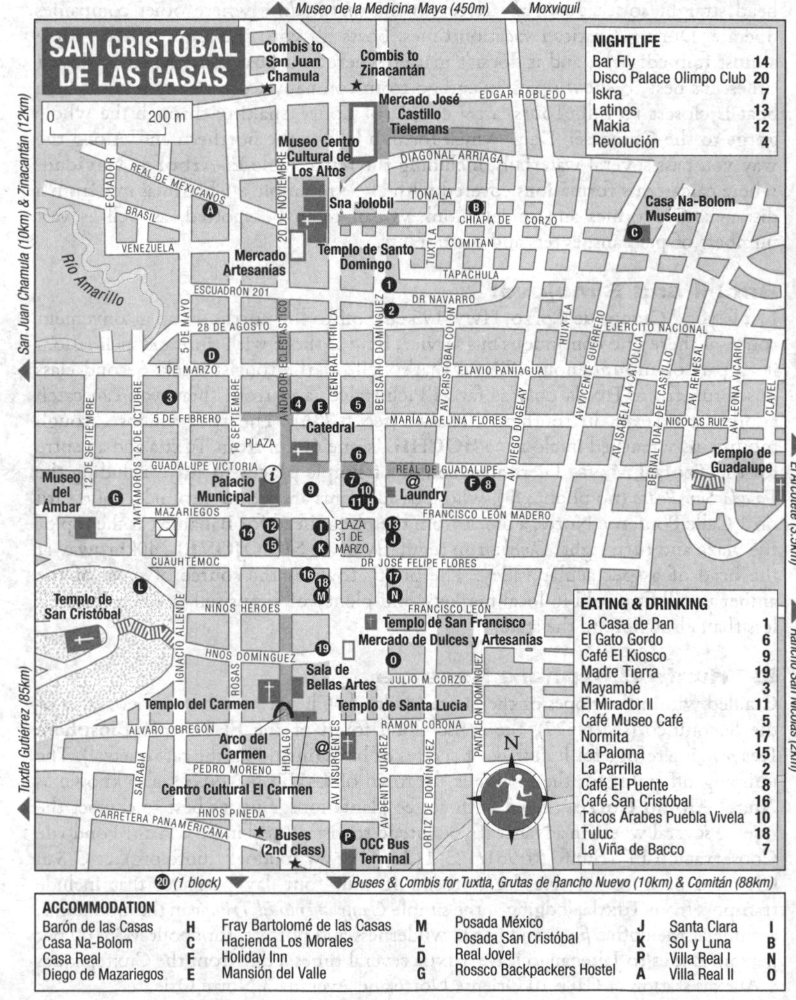

the latest in a long series of uprisings. It took the Spaniards, led by conquistador Diego de Mazariegos, four years to pacify the area enough to establish a town here in 1528. The so-called Villareal de Chiapa de los Españoles was more widely known as Villaviciosa (Evil City) for the oppressive exploitation exercised by its colonists. In 1544, Bartolomé de las Casas was appointed bishop, and he promptly took an energetic stance in defence of the native population, playing a similar role to that of Bishop Vasco de Quiroga in Pátzcuaro (see box, p.348). His name – added to that of the patron saint of the town – is still held in something close to reverence by the local population. Throughout the colonial era, San Cristóbal was the capital of Chiapas (at that time part of Guatemala), but lost this status in 1892 as a result of its continued reluctance to accept the union with Mexico. This spirit of rebellion was revived by the Zapatistas in 1994. Although it was the main focus of their attack, the town was only occupied for thirty hours, and no tourists were harmed.

Arrival and information

The toll highway from Tuxtla Gutiérrez to San Cristóbal (M$38) rises quickly from the plains, breaking through the clouds into pine forests. As the modern parts of the city sprawl unattractively along the highway, first impressions of San Cristóbal itself are not the best, but the centre has none of this unchecked development. Whether you arrive by first- or second-class **bus**, you'll almost certainly be just off the Carretera Panamericana (Hwy-190), which becomes Bulevar Juan Sabines Gutiérrez at the southern edge of town, though if you've arrived from Bochil, you'll be just north of the market area. For the centre, turn right out of the OCC **first-class terminal**, and it's seven blocks north on Insurgentes to the plaza. Most **second-class** services stop along the highway to either side of the OCC terminal. **Taxis** within the centre should cost no more than M$20.

The helpful **state tourist office**, in the Palacio Municipal (Mon–Fri 8am–8pm, Sat 9am–8pm, Sun 9am–2pm; ⓣ967/678-1467), has free city maps, up-to-date lists of hotels, bus times and event information, as well as English-speaking staff. The **municipal tourist office** (daily 8am–8pm; ⓣ967/678-0665) is just next door; it also staffs kiosks on both plazas.

Accommodation

Vast numbers of visitors and competition for business mean that San Cristóbal has some very good-value **hotels**. There are a few reliable places around the OCC terminal, but walking up Insurgentes to the plaza, you'll pass more establishments in all price ranges. Most of the best **budget options** are found in the streets east of the plaza, particularly along Real de Guadalupe and in its vicinity. An ever-larger proportion of hotels here call themselves "**posadas**", and most live up to the convivial ambience this is presumably meant to convey, but it's always worth seeing your room before you pay. Even the most basic places now have hot water, though not necessarily all of the time. Nights can be pleasantly cool in summer, but cold in winter, so make sure there are enough blankets.

For **longer stays**, check out the many notice boards in the bus stations, language schools and popular cafés, where you'll find rooms and even whole houses for rent. The closest official **campsite** is at *Rancho San Nicolás*, 2km east of the centre along the extension of Francisco León (ⓣ967/678-0057; M$60).

Barón de las Casas Belisario Domínguez 2 ⓣ967/678-0881, ⓔhotelbaron@hotmail.com. Well-run budget hotel with a bit of colonial charm, one block east of the plaza. Rooms are simple, with tiled floors and spotless bathrooms with plenty of hot water. TV is M$20 extra. The owners speak English. ❸

Casa Na-Bolom Vicente Guerrero 33 ⓣ967/678-1418, ⓦwww.nabolom.org. Very comfortable rooms with fireplaces and private bathrooms around courtyards, and lovely private cottages in the tranquil gardens. All are decorated with textiles, artefacts and photos taken by Gertrude Blom (see p.698). Rates include breakfast (with organic produce from the garden) and entry to the museum. ❺

Casa Real Real de Guadalupe 51 ⓣ967/678-1303, ⓔhotelcasareal2009@gmail.com. Large rooms with double beds have only shared baths, but there is hot water, and a *pila* for washing clothes on the sunny, flower-filled rooftop terrace. It's M$85 per person, so very good value for singles. ❷

Diego de Mazariegos 5 de Febrero 1 ⓣ967/678-0833, ⓦwww.diegodemazariegos.com.mx. San Cristóbal's most polished colonial hotel, set in two buildings on either side of General Utrilla. Spacious rooms – all featuring a fireplace, antique furniture and beautifully tiled bathrooms – are arranged around attractive courtyards. Book ahead, as it's often busy with tour groups. ❺

Fray Bartolomé de las Casas Niños Héroes 2, at Insurgentes ⓣ967/678-0932, ⓔhotelfraybartolome@prodigy.net.mx. Split into two sections, this hotel has an older part with more charm, as it's arranged around a pretty courtyard with a central fountain. The newer section is far less appealing. ❸

Hacienda Los Morales Ignacio Allende 17 ⓣ967/678-1472, ⓦwww.hotelhaciendalosmorales.com. Past an antiques-crammed lobby and restaurant, stone cabins sprawl up the hillside garden four blocks west of the plaza. Each rustic-feeling room has a fireplace and a porch or terrace for enjoying the views across town. Breakfast included. ❹

Holiday Inn 1 de Marzo 15 ⓣ967/678-0045, ⓦwww.hotelesfarrera.com. Never mind the less-than-chic chain association – this is the most luxurious place to stay in the centre, in an old hacienda with a pink-walled courtyard and beautifully decorated rooms. Significant discounts often available online. ❻

Mansión del Valle Diego de Mazariegos 39 ⓣ967/678-2582, ⓦwww.mansiondelvalle.com. Stylish white rooms decorated with local embroidery make this mid-range hotel feel a bit special. There's a big roof terrace, wi-fi and a decent restaurant. The smaller *Mansión de Los Angeles*, Francisco Madero 17, is another good option, under the same ownership. ❻

Posada México Josefa Domínguez 12, at Francisco Madero ⓣ967/678-0014, ⓦwww.hostellingmexico.com. The HI-affiliated hostel is a colonial-style place with a big courtyard. There's a whole roster of activities, wi-fi in the dorms (M$100) and plenty of space to relax. Private rooms have shared bath. ❶

Posada San Cristóbal Insurgentes 3 ⓣ967/678-6881. Spacious, wood-panelled rooms with *azulejo*-tiled bathrooms and TV, an excellent restaurant and a leafy covered courtyard with fountain; the best value of the options around the plaza. ❹

Real Jovel Insurgentes 66 ⓣ967/678-1668, ⓔhotel_real-jovel@hotmail.com. Adjacent to the OCC bus terminal and open into the early hours for late arrivals. Bright, airy rooms with tiled en-suite bathrooms. Good value – it's M$80 extra for TV. ❸

Rossco Backpackers Hostel Real de Mexicanos 16 ⓣ967/ 674-0525, ⓦwww.backpackershostel.com.mx. One of the best hostels in Chiapas, with enthusiastic English-speaking owners, clean, renovated dorms (M$50; there's a separate dorm for women) and rooms. There's also free internet, breakfast, lockers, cable TV in the common room, daily use of gym, Spanish lessons and a cosy campfire in the garden every evening. ❶

Santa Clara Insurgentes 1, at the corner of the plaza ⓣ967/678-1140, ⓔhotelstaclara@hotmail.com. The spacious, plant-filled patio and lobby of this colonial mansion are adorned with period artefacts, though the rooms are a bit worn. Its heated pool makes it good value, though, and big discounts are often available if you pay in cash. ❺

Sol y Luna Tonalá 27 ⓣ967/678-5727, ⓦwww.solylunainn.com. For a very private-feeling space, book one of the two large rooms at this beautifully decorated guesthouse, each with a double bed and wood-burning stove. ❹

Villa Real I and II two locations on Benito Juárez, 8 and 24-A I ⓣ967/678-2930 & II ⓣ967/678-4485. Comfortable, well-furnished, carpeted rooms all with private bathrooms, cable TV and access to parking facilities. *Villa Real I* is the older but cheaper of the two. I ❷, II ❸

The City

Plaza 31 de Marzo, usually referred to simply as *el parque*, is at the heart of the city, encircled by a cluster of attractive colonial mansions and the sixteenth-century **cathedral**, which boasts an ornate, pale orange facade, impressive *artesanado* ceiling and grand *retablo*. The finest of the mansions is **La Casa de las Sirenas**, now the *Hotel Santa Clara*, which is said to have been built by the conquistador Andrés de la Tovilla in the mid-sixteenth century and has a very elaborate doorway around the corner on Insurgentes. In the middle of the plaza there's a bandstand and a café.

Cutting through the centre is the **Andador Eclesiástico**, a pedestrianized thoroughfare that connects the Templo del Carmen, 300m south of the plaza (on Hidalgo), to Santo Domingo, 400m to the north (on 20 de Noviembre). It's lined with touristy shops, slick restaurants and ice-cream parlours. The **Templo del Carmen** stands opposite the Arco del Carmen, which spans the road, and once served as the gateway to the city. Built in 1677, it shows a slight Mudéjar (Moorish) influence. The church is not particularly inspiring architecturally, but on the other side of the arch, the **Centro Cultural El Carmen** (daily 9am–5pm; free) contains a couple of galleries of contemporary painting and craftwork around gardens filled with traditional Maya plants. Considering the amount of artistic activity in and around San Cristóbal, these sights are pretty disappointing, though partly explained by a serious fire in 1993 that destroyed much of the city's artwork, including several eighteenth-century religious paintings.

Local crafts

A major draw for visitors to San Cristóbal is the indigenous crafts tradition, with every village in the area specializing in a distinctive style of weaving, embroidery and more. Many of the salespeople in San Cristóbal are from nearby villages – in fact, many are so-called *expulsados*, evangelical Protestants who have been expelled from their communities for converting. To eke out an existence they have turned to craft-making, with tourists as their main source of income. As a result, the city is a textile collector's dream, with vibrant **woven blankets** and intricately **embroidered clothing**. If you see something you like (here or in any village), you should buy it, as there's no guarantee you'll see it again in the next town.

The plaza in front of Santo Domingo church, filled with **craft stalls**, is often the best place to buy souvenirs. Part of the former *convento* next door has been converted into a craft cooperative (**Sna Jolobil**) that sells textiles and other village products (Mon–Sat 9am–2pm & 4–6pm). The quality here is generally good, but the prices higher than elsewhere. The **Mercado de Artesanías y Dulces** on Insurgentes is another worthwhile place to look for local crafts, although traders here are less willing to barter.

Other **craft shops** include the Tienda de los Artesanos de Chiapas, at the corner of Hidalgo and Niños Héroes (Tues–Sun 9am–2pm & 5–8pm), a state-sponsored venture where the weaving and embroidery are as high-quality as you'll find in any museum. Artesandia, 28 de Agosto 6, sells women's clothing with traditional embroidery but tailored in modern styles – pieces are expensive but beautifully done.

Taller Leñateros, Flavio Paniagua 54, is one of the more fascinating. Here you can see the process of making **paper** by hand from such diverse items as banana leaves, cornstalks and bamboo, coloured with natural dyes. The finished sheets become beautiful cards and notebooks. Delicate, decorative **wrought iron** is on display at Metalistería Hermosillo, Jardinera 12.

Amber is another special product of this region, sold mostly in the form of jewellery. If you're serious about buying, first visit the **Museo del Ámbar**, in the **Convento de la Merced** off Belisario Domínguez (Tues–Sun 10am–2pm & 4–7.30pm; M$20). The English-speaking staff can explain the various types, as well as sell you some exquisite pieces. Real amber is exceptionally light, gives a resin-like odour when rubbed and is rarely sold with insects trapped inside it – if someone tries selling you a scorpion in amber, it's definitely a con: there are only five real pieces in existence. Tierra de Ámbar, Real de Guadalupe 16, is another trustworthy store, though you should be okay in most shops – just don't buy from street sellers. In the same vein, if you're interested in **jade**, visit the small **Museo del Jade**, 16 de Septiembre 16 (Mon–Sat noon–8pm, Sun noon–6pm; M$30; ⓦwww.eljade.com), for beautiful displays of ancient jewellery and new pieces for purchase.

Templo de Santo Domingo Guzmán

Five blocks north of the plaza, the **Templo de Santo Domingo Guzmán** is the most intrinsically interesting of San Cristóbal's churches. Constructed between 1547 and 1551, the church's lovely pinkish Baroque stucco facade combines Oaxacan and Guatemalan styles. Inside, it's gilded everywhere, with a wonderfully ornate pulpit – if you see it in the evening, by the light of candles, you might well believe it's solid gold. To the left of the main entrance (beyond Sna Jolobil), the **Museo Centro Cultural de los Altos** (Tues–Sun 10am–2pm & 4–6pm; M$25, free Sun), tells the story of the city, with vivid portrayals of how the Indians fared under colonial rule.

The market

San Cristóbal's daily market, the **Mercado José Castillo Tielemans**, lies beyond Santo Domingo along General Utrilla. It's an absorbing place, largely because its chaos and the crowds in its souk-like lanes contrasts with the rather manicured centre of town, where the indigenous people in traditional dress can seem a bit like part of the scenic background. Here, commerce is the important thing, and every villager in town for the day participates fully – arguing over prices of herbs and fried ants, selecting the best live chickens, picking through piles of dried fish. The market is far bigger than it first appears, with sections for housewares, clothing and more in a network of narrow covered alleys alongside the back of the main structure.

Casa Na-Bolom

Behind Santo Domingo, Chiapa de Corzo leads east towards the **Casa Na-Bolom** (daily 10am–5pm; tours in English at 4.30pm; M$35, M$45 with tour) at Vicente Guerrero 33, also housing one of the best hotels in San Cristóbal (see p.696) and a **library** of local anthropology (daily 10am–4pm; free). This was the home of Danish explorer and anthropologist Frans Blom, who died in 1963, and his Swiss wife, Gertrude, an anthropologist and photographer who died in 1993. Today it's renowned as a centre for the study of the region's indigenous cultures, particularly of the isolated Lacandón Maya. Buy tickets across the road from the main complex, in the gift shop in the **Jardín de Jaguar**, which also contains a few exhibits and information boards about the various ethnic groups in Chiapas. In one corner is a replica of a traditional highlands house, made with wooden walls covered with mud and a roof thatched with grass.

Back across the street, the main museum occupies rooms set around a series of beautiful courtyards – it's not particularly large, and a guided tour can be illuminating, if you're able to time your visit for one. The museum exhibits discoveries from the site of **Moxviquil** (see p.702) and explains the history and culture of the Chiapas highlands and the Lacandón forest. There's also a collection of items belonging to Frans Blom, including the detailed maps for which he is known. After the tour, you can watch a film (mainly in English) about the life of the Bloms and specific ecological, cultural and political aspects of life in Chiapas.

The whole centre is overseen by the Asociación Cultural Na-Bolom, which arranges some small-scale volunteer cultural and agricultural projects, though you'll need to speak Spanish to participate; write or email for details (see the hotel review on p.696 for contact info).

Museo de la Medicina Maya

About 500m north from the centre on General Utrilla, the **Museo de la Medicina Maya** (Mon–Fri 10am–6pm, Sat & Sun 10am–5pm; M$20) provides an absorbing journey through the world of Maya medicine, complete with medicinal plants growing in the gardens and a herbal pharmacy on site to dispense remedies. You'll learn more than you ever thought to ask about Maya midwifery, and it's a great place to visit before heading out to the church at San Juan Chamula, as it explains a lot of the rituals you might see performed there.

Guadalupe and San Cristóbal

On either side of town, two churches perch on hilltop sites: **Templo de Guadalupe** to the east and **Templo de San Cristóbal** to the west. Neither offers a great deal architecturally, but the climbs are worth it for the views – San Cristóbal, especially, is at the top of a dauntingly long and steep flight of steps. Best not to climb up to either of these relatively isolated spots after dark; we have received reports of women being subjected to harassment at San Cristóbal.

Eating and drinking

San Cristóbal has no lack of places to eat, with a huge variety of economical **restaurants** in the streets immediately east of the plaza, especially on Madero. Where the city really scores, however, is in lively places that cater to a disparate, somewhat bohemian crowd. Enticing menus feature plenty of **vegetarian** options. A battery of sweets-sellers regularly set up under the *portales* on the west side of the plaza, and a much smaller, more locally used plaza north on Belisario Domínguez often has snack carts and stands selling clove-spiked *ponche*, a warm pineapple drink that's great on a chilly night.

Cafés

Café El Kiosco in the plaza. In a great location under the bandstand, where you can enjoy a coffee at the outdoor tables and watch the world go by.

Café El Puente Real de Guadalupe 55. Popular café serving inexpensive salads, soups, sandwiches, cakes and an inviting organic buffet (2–5pm; M$60); also acts as a cultural centre, with internet access, live music, lectures and films. Closed Sun.

Café Museo Café María Adelina Flores 10. Delicious coffee and some of the best *chocolate con leche* in town, served in the café of a small museum, where beautiful illustrations depict the history of the coffee trade in Mexico. The café also sells organic beans from a cooperative of local coffee producers (one of which you can visit – ask at the museum for information). Open Mon–Sat 9am–9pm.

Café San Cristóbal Cuauhtémoc 2, near Insurgentes. This tiny, no-frills coffeehouse is a popular spot for locals to play chess and read the newspaper.

Restaurants

La Casa de Pan Dr. Navarro 10. A superb range of reasonably priced vegetarian food and baked goods, made with local, organic ingredients. Open from morning till night, the place serves as a meeting place for expat development workers, and there's usually live music at night. Closed Mon.

El Gato Gordo Real de Guadalupe 20. Inexpensive and deservedly popular backpacker place serving Mexican and international dishes with great-value specials and set lunches from M$35. You can also read the newspapers, watch TV and listen to music. Closed Tues.

Madre Tierra Insurgentes 19, opposite the Mercado de Artesanías. European-style restaurant in a colonial house serving great, healthy food including home-made soups, salads and pastas. The upstairs terrace bar has good views of ancient walls and red-tiled roofs, and the bakery and deli next door sell whole-wheat bread and carrot cake until 8pm Mon–Sat.

Mayambé 5 de Mayo 10. A vegetarian-friendly place with Indian, Thai and Lebanese food; there's a M$40 *menú*. The owners speak excellent English and there are books and internet access. Mon–Sat 9am–11pm.

El Mirador II Madero 16. The best cheap Mexican restaurant on Madero, with good meat-and-bean-filled tortas and comidas corridas.

Normita Juárez at José Flores. A great little restaurant serving Jaliscan specialities and inexpensive breakfasts from M$25. Daily 7am–11pm.

La Paloma Hidalgo 3, just south of the plaza ☎967/678-1547. A sixteenth-century mansion houses a refined restaurant and hip upstairs coffee-house. The menu is broad, and ingredients are fresh, though some items border on bland – think of this more as an opportunity to relax in comfort for about M$150 for dinner. Open till 11.30pm.

La Parrilla Belisario Domínguez near Dr. Navarro. A relaxed, reasonably priced restaurant in a courtyard, specializing in grilled meats, including *alambres*, which are similar to kebabs. Closed Mon.

Tacos Árabes Puebla Vivela Belisario Domínguez 8. Taco meat is grilled on a vertical skewer with a real wood fire, then sliced up for elementally good tacos on a flour tortilla that's halfway to Lebanese flatbread. *Mamelas*, chewy blue corn patties, are topped with fresh herbs and cheese. Dinner only.

Tuluc Insurgentes 5. Justifiably popular Mexican diner, with a good comida corrida and dinner specials from M$50, mains from M$40. This is the first place in town to open in the morning (6.30am), ideal if you have to catch an early bus.

La Viña de Bacco Real de Guadalupe 7. A snug little tapas bar that looks straight out of Spain – but there's a big selection of Mexican wines by the glass, as well as a platter of locally made cheeses, sausages and ham (M$80). You get a free bite-size *botana* with each glass, and snacks start at just M$5.

Nightlife

The major bar strips are on Real de Guadalupe and the pedestrianized street north of the plaza, but there are many smaller bar/cafés on quieter blocks throughout the centre, many with a mellow candlelit atmosphere. On a practical note, this is a rare town in Mexico where there's good wine to drink, as well as beer. Many of the city's cafés and bars host **live music** in the evenings, usually salsa or Latin, and only rarely impose a cover charge. *Madre Tierra* (see p.699) also has a bar and live music upstairs.

Bar Fly Rosas 4. Bar and club with lively theme nights featuring reggae, funky jazz and trance. Wed–Sat from 10pm.

Disco Palace Olimpo Club Crescendo Rosas 59. The only real club in town is eight long blocks south of the plaza, with a relatively young crowd enjoying a raucous blend of Latino dance and hypnotic techno. Thurs–Sat from 9pm.

Iskra Real de Guadalupe 53. House-brewed beer, with Communist trimmings. There's also live music and a generally young party atmosphere.

Latinos Madero 14. Boisterous bar and *discoteca* playing a variety of live and recorded music, from salsa and reggae to jazz and rock. Mon–Sat 8pm–3.30am.

Makia Hidalgo at Mazariegos. Fashionable, dimly lit bar and club, with a good mix of locals and travellers. Thurs–Sat from 9pm.

Revolución 20 de Noviembre and Flavio Paniagua. Zapatista chic is the style at this bar on the pedestrian street. It serves light snacks and drinks. Cocktails from M$36, and two-for-one drinks daily noon–7pm.

Listings

Airlines InterJet, Real de Guadalupe 14, at *Hotel Real del Valle* ⓣ800/011-2345 (Mon–Sat 9am-6pm); Mexicana, Francisco Madero 8 ⓣ967/678-9309 (Mon–Sat 9am–8pm, Sun 10am–3pm).

Banks and exchange Several bank branches (with ATMs) surround the plaza; most will exchange dollars and give cash advances (mornings only). HSBC is at Mazariegos 6. You'll get much quicker exchange, however, at good rates from the casa de cambio at Real de Guadalupe 12-A (Mon–Sat 9am–2pm & 4–8pm, Sun 9am–1pm); it changes most major currencies and usually has Guatemalan quetzales.

Bike rental An enjoyable way to get out to the surrounding villages. Los Pingüinos, Ecuador 4-B (ⓣ967/678-0202, ⓦwww.bikemexico.com/pinguinos), has well-maintained bikes for M$150/day, and leads day outings and multiday tours. German and English spoken. Ruta Nahual, Real de Guadalupe 123 (ⓣ967/124-2110, ⓔrutanahual@hotmail.com) does numerous biking day trips.

Books Librería Chilam Balam, at General Utrilla 33 near Dr. Navarro (daily 9am–8pm), has the best selection, including academic and educational books; also guides and topographic maps of Chiapas. Librería La Pared, Hidalgo 2 (Tues–Sat 3–7.30pm, Sun 3–7pm), has new guidebooks (including *Rough Guides*) and the largest selection of new and secondhand books in English and other languages in southern Mexico; you can rent, trade or buy. Other useful stores are Librería Soluna, Real de Guadalupe 13-B (daily 9am–8pm), with a fair choice of books, including guides; and Casa Na-Bolom, Vicente Guerrero 33, which has an excellent library (daily 10am–2pm; free) and sells some books and maps of the Lacandón forest.

Immigration office ⓣ967/678-7910. The office itself (Mon–Fri 9am–3pm) is a couple of kilometres west of the centre, at the junction of the Carretera Panamericana and Diagonal Centenario.

Internet access It's scarcely possible to walk a block in the centre without coming across a place. Most open 7–9am and close around 10pm – the price is usually M$10/hr. Try Fast Net, Real de Guadalupe 15-D, or Caféteria del Centro, at no. 7.

Laundry Lavandería Las Estrellas, Real de Guadalupe 75; Lavandería Sol, Real de Guadalupe 45; lavandería at Belisario Domínguez 5–B; lavandería at Hermanos Domínguez 12. All are closed Sun and cost M$15/kg.

Post office Ignacio Allende between Diego Mazariegos and Cuauhtémoc (Mon–Fri 8.30am–7pm, Sat 9am–1pm); in addition, most hotels have Mexipost boxes, and many of the larger ones sell stamps.

Spanish courses El Puente, Real de Guadalupe 55 (ⓣ967/678-3723, ⓦwww.elpuenteweb.com), is the longest-established language school in San Cristóbal; they also have courses in Maya. Instituto de Lenguas Jovel, Francisco Madero 45 (ⓣ967/678-4069, ⓦwww.institutojovel.com), is also recommended. Both can arrange accommodation with local families.

Telephones Librería La Pared, Hidalgo 2 (Tues–Sat 3–7.30pm, Sun 3–7pm), has the cheapest long-distance and international rates, at M$15/min to North America and M$20 to Europe. There are Ladatel phones on the plaza, under the arches of the Palacio Municipal, and in the OCC terminal, but you need a phonecard to operate them.

Travel agencies and tours San Cristóbal has dozens of tour agencies, most doing the same four standard tours to local villages, the Cañón del Sumidero, Lagos de Montebello and Palenque and Agua Azul. You can also arrange tours further afield to Bonampak and Yaxchilán. Sombrero Tours, Belisario Domínguez 8-A (ⓣ967/631-6936), is one such agency, and also rents scooters (from M$80/hr). Horse-riding tours can be arranged at Casa Utrilla, General Utrilla 33, leaving at 9am and 1pm (ⓣ967/100-9611; M$150 to Chamula). One of the best local tour agencies is OTISA, Real de Guadalupe 3-C (ⓣ967/678-1933, ⓦwww.otisatravel.com). For local and national adventure tours, try Viajes Pakal, Cuauhtémoc 6 (ⓣ967/678-2818, ⓦwww.pakal.com.mx). City tours are provided by El Coleto, a bus which leaves 10am–1pm & 4–7pm from outside the Mercado de Artesanías on Insurgentes (minimum five people).

Moving on from San Cristóbal

First-class buses for destinations in the state and throughout the Yucatán leave from the OCC terminal at the south end of Insurgentes, near the ring road, with **second-class** buses departing either side. AEXA (across the highway), runs first- and second-class buses to similar destinations. You can also buy first-class tickets from the Ticket bus office (Mon–Sat 7am–11pm, Sun 9am–5pm; ⓣ967/678-0921) closer to the centre at Real de Guadalupe 5. **Tuxtla Gutiérrez** is served frequently by first-class buses, and *combis* also tout for customers outside the bus stations on the main highway – for **Chiapa de Corzo** they'll drop you on the main highway, where you have to catch a local bus into town. **Villahermosa** is not so well served, though there are two first-class services daily with OCC (11.20am & 11pm); it's easier to get any bus to Tuxtla and change there. For **Palenque**, there are eleven daily first-class departures. All buses going to Palenque call at **Ocosingo**, and in addition there's ample passenger-van traffic: just go to the highway and someone will call out to you. OCC has the most comfortable service to **Ciudad Cuauhtémoc** via Comitán (6 daily) on the Guatemalan border. To Comitán only, you'll find any number of *combis* along the highway, with hourly departures. There are nine daily services to **Tapachula** and three overnight services for Oaxaca; for more choice to the latter, head to Tuxtla. The first-class companies all have overnight services to Mexico City (7 daily). For Campeche and Mérida, there's a first-class service at 6.20pm. Buses for the Yucatán coast (4 daily) go via Chetumal, where you can catch connections to Belize, and make all major stops to Cancún. Bochil buses (1hr 30min) depart from north of the market area.

Heading to Tuxtla's **airport** (the nearest in operation), you can take a direct bus organized by tour agencies: see Astur Viajes (ⓣ967/678-3917) in the *portales* on the east side of the plaza. Travel agency Chincutik, Real de Guadalupe 34 (ⓣ967/678-7021), runs a daily shuttle bus to **Guatemala**.

For further information, see Travel details, p.746.

Around San Cristóbal: Grutas de Rancho Nuevo, El Arcotete and Moxviquil

Some organized outings go to the popular **Grutas de Rancho Nuevo** (daily 9am–5.30pm; M$10), an enormous cavern extending deep into a mountain about 10km to the southeast of San Cristóbal. It's easy enough to visit it by bus or bike, though, since the area is well signed, just off the main road to Comitán. By **bike**, it's about a fifty-minute ride, uphill most of the way from San Cristóbal. There's an average restaurant here for refreshment, and you can hire horses for about M$50 per hour. Although the cave system is quite extensive, only 400m of pathway are open to the public.

Another favourite trip is to **El Arcotete**, a natural limestone arch that forms a bridge over a river. To get there, follow Real de Guadalupe out of town, past the Guadalupe church, where it becomes the road to Tenejapa; El Arcotete is down a signed track to the right about 3.5km past the church.

Moxviquil, a completely deserted and ruined Maya ceremonial site, is a pleasant excursion of a few hours on foot from San Cristóbal; it's best, however, to study the plans at the Casa Na-Bolom first (see p.698), as all you can see when you get there are piles of rough limestone – in fact, the tourist office will tell you there's nothing to see at all. To reach the site, find Avenida Yajalon, a few blocks east of Santo Domingo, and follow it north to the end (about 30min) at the foot of tree-covered hills, in a little settlement called Ojo de Agua. Head for the highest buildings you can see, that is, two timber shacks with red roofs. The tracks are at times indistinct as you clamber over the rocks, but after about 300m a lovely side valley suitable for camping opens up on your left. The main path veers gradually to the right, becoming quite wide and leading up through a high basin ringed by pine forest. After 3km you reach the village of Pozeula; the ruins are ahead of you across a valley, built on top of and into the sides of a hill.

Chamula and Zinacantán

Almost everyone who stays in San Cristóbal visits the Tzotzil Maya villages of **SAN JUAN CHAMULA** and **SAN LORENZO DE ZINACANTÁN**. Both

Useful words in Tzotzil and Tzeltal

	Tzotzil	Tzeltal
To ask permission	Chíkhelav	Ya shka shan
Hello	Kúshee	Bish chee
Goodbye	Batkun	Bónish
Please	Avokoluk	Há wokolook
Thank you	Kalaval	Wókolawal
Sorry/Excuse me	Tsik bunjoomul	Pasbón
Yes	Chabal	Heech
No	Moo yuk	Ho'o

villages have retained much of their unique cultural identity, particularly in religion, which is a blend of traditional animist belief and Catholicism. The church at Chamula, in particular, is one of the most moving sights in Mexico. But it's also one of the most intensely sacred spots in the country, and photography is banned (it's also generally not appreciated by most villagers).

It's hard not to feel a sense of intrusion in these settings, where you may be a spectator at some intense religious ritual. For many visitors, an organized tour (very easy to arrange in San Cristóbal) at least contains the sense of imposition, and helps explain some of the rituals. If you come on your own, you'll feel a bit less conspicuous in busy tourist times (August, primarily), when there's a bit of crowd cover and a festive atmosphere. It may help to learn a few words of the native language. Villages to the west of San Cristóbal are generally **Tzotzil**-speaking, and those to the east speak **Tzeltal**, but each village has developed its own identity in terms of costume, crafts and linguistics. Some simple words are given in the box above.

Transport and tours

Inexpensive *combis* leave frequently for Chamula, Zinacantán and other villages from Edgar Robledo, just north of the market in San Cristóbal. Though an **organized tour** (about M$140/person) can feel a little rushed and contrived, it's usually more informative, not to mention easier, as there are no direct *combis* between Chamula and Zinacantán. Tours depart at 9.30am, go to both villages and return to San Cristóbal around 2pm (see "Listings", p.701, for recommendations, though there is little difference between companies).

San Juan Chamula

SAN JUAN CHAMULA (usually referred to as just Chamula) is the closest indigenous village to San Cristóbal (10km), as well as the most frequently visited. Though thousands of residents have been cast out in recent decades for converting to Protestant faiths, Chamula still has a population of 15,000, with more than 90,000 in the surrounding municipality. Over the years it's been far more against change than Zinacantán, putting up fierce resistance to the Spaniards from 1524 to 1528, then acting as the centre of a rebellion described as the second "Caste War" from 1867 to 1870, inspired by the uprising in the Yucatán.

Traditional practices are maintained here, especially in religion – a visit to the 200-year-old **Iglesia de San Juan Bautista** can be a humbling and moving experience. Before you enter, buy a ticket (M$20) from the "tourist office" in the Palacio Municipal, on the right-hand side of the plaza as you face the church. The inside is glorious, the floor covered with pine needles and the light of a thousand candles casting an eerie glow. Lining the walls are statues of the saints adorned with offerings of clothes, food and mirrors (thought to aid communication with the laity), while above the altar, San Juan, patron saint of the village, takes pride of place. The customs practised inside the church incorporate aspects of Christian and Maya beliefs – each villager prays by clearing an area of pine needles and arranging a "message" in candles, and rituals frequently involve tearful chanting and singing. There are no priests, Masses or marriages here, only baptisms, and the church is open 24 hours, reflecting its important role as a place of healing for the sick – Tuesdays and Fridays are particularly special days for prayer.

During the annual Kinta Jimultik, the **carnival** (five days in Feb/March), representatives of all the villages in the area attend in traditional dress, marching in circles around the church and up to strategically placed crosses on the hillsides for the first four days. On the final day, which coincides with the last of the five ill-fated days of the Maya calendar, purification rites and fire-walking ceremonies take place in the plaza.

Admission to the church also grants entry to the **Museo Etnográfico** (daily 8am–7pm), behind the Palacio Municipal. Rooms display artefacts of village life, musical instruments and costumes from Chamula and other villages. Remember that taking **photographs** in the church is expressly forbidden, and no foreign visitors are admitted after 7pm.

San Lorenzo de Zinacantán

An easy seven-kilometre walk from Chamula and surrounded by steep, pine-forested hills, **ZINACANTÁN**, 12km from Cristóbal, is more open than its neighbour. The locals here have embraced flowers as an export crop, and the hillsides are dotted with greenhouses. Traditional practices have not completely disappeared, and are on impressive display during fiestas. Some older men still wear the rose-pink and blue-green ponchos with silver threads (called *pok 'ul*), decorated with tassels and embroidered flowers, and the same colours and designs feature in the women's costumes. Tours include a visit to a typical house, where you'll see the family altar, women weaving beautiful table mats decorated with large embroidered flowers and the house fire where tortillas are prepared. You might also be invited to taste *posh*, the local spirit, made from sugar cane and sometimes flavoured with fruit or cinnamon. Zinacantán also has a museum, the **Museo Ik'al Ojov** ("Our Great Lord"), which has displays of costumes from different hierarchical groups and a tableau of a house interior (daily 8.30am–5pm; donation requested). The museum is a short walk downhill from the main plaza (follow the signs) and the **Iglesia de San Lorenzo**. Independent visitors must pay M$15 at the kiosk at the entrance to the village; this includes entrance to the church, and you will almost certainly pick up a few small children who want to lead you to craft shops. It's worth going because some, such as Artesanías Maria Isabel, also serve delicious handmade tortillas to hungry shoppers. Note that photography isn't permitted in the church, nor even in the churchyard.

San Cristóbal to Guatemala: Comitán and Montebello

Beyond San Cristóbal, the Panamerican Highway continues to the border with Guatemala through some of the most scintillating scenery in Chiapas. Thirty-seven kilometres from San Cristóbal it passes **Amatenango del Valle**, a Tzeltal-speaking village that's a favourite stop for tours, due to its reputation for beautiful unglazed pottery, produced with the traditional pre-Hispanic method of building the fire around the piece, rather than placing it in an oven. **Comitán de Domínguez** (or just Comitán) is the only place of any size in this area – a jumping-off point not only for the **Guatemalan border** and for the **Parque Nacional Lagos de Montebello**, but for the Classic-period Maya site of **Tenam Puente**.

Comitán

An attractive colonial city, **COMITÁN** is 88km from San Cristóbal and strategically poised on a rocky hillside, surrounded by rolling farms and wild countryside in which orchids bloom. The final place of any note before the border with Guatemala, Comitán is also a supply centre for the surrounding agricultural area. The city has an elegant historic core and a small but absorbing market, and it makes a good place to rest up before heading into the Lacandón forest or Guatemala.

Once a major Maya population centre (the ruins of Bonampak and Yaxchilán, even Palenque, are not far, as the parrot flies), Comitán was originally known as Balún Canán ("Nine Stars", or "Guardians"), but was renamed Comitán ("Place of Potters" in Náhuatl) when it came under Aztec control. At 1560m, it's not as high as San Cristóbal but can still be milder than the sweltering lowlands.

Arrival and information

Buses stop along the Panamerican Highway (known as Bulevar Dr. Belisario Domínguez), the wide commercial strip through town; only OCC has a terminal, between 7a and 8a Avenidas Sur, while all others just pull in at the roadside. From the terminal, it's a long six or seven blocks' east to the centre. To walk, turn left out of the terminal, cross the road, then after about three blocks, go right on 1a Calle Sur Poniente. The main plaza is a further seven blocks east. A booth in the terminal will call a **taxi** if required, though they are easy to find. Any journey within the city boundary costs about M$20.

The helpful **state tourist office** (Mon–Fri 8am–6pm, Sat & Sun 9am–2pm; ⓣ963/632-4047) is on 1a Avenida Oriente Norte (Avenida Castellanos), on the second floor of the Plaza Margarita shopping centre. For anyone moving on to Guatemala and needing a visa, the **Guatemalan consulate** is inside the complex at 1a Calle Poniente Sur 35, three blocks west of the plaza (Mon–Fri 9am–5pm;

Ⓣ&Ⓕ963/632-2669). Note that many shops and offices in Comitán observe the afternoon siesta between 2 and 5pm.

Accommodation

Comitán has plenty of good-value **hotels** in all price ranges. The cheapest places are just west of the plaza, but standards vary; we've noted the best of them. Nights here are much cooler than days, even in the height of summer, so you'll need at least one blanket, and air-conditioning is generally irrelevant.

Delfín Av Central Sur 21-A, right on the plaza Ⓣ963/632-0013. Pleasant, colourful and spacious, with large en-suite rooms and cable TV – so long as you get one of the back rooms, around the quiet courtyard. Front rooms are noisy from cars parking and plaza hubbub. ❸

Hospedaje San Francisco 1a Av Ote Nte 13 Ⓣ963/632-0194, Ⓔsamuel22f@prodigy.net.mx. Best of the budget options, with en-suite bathrooms and some rooms with TV. Rooms on the front courtyard are bigger and brighter. ❷

Hotel del Virrey Av Central Nte 13 Ⓣ963/632-1811. This attractive colonial hotel has a historic atmosphere set by a pretty, flower-filled courtyard and a welcoming feel set by the friendly staff. The rooms are bright and clean, with en-suite bathrooms, laundry and cable TV. ❹

Internacional Av Central Sur 16 Ⓣ963/632-0110. Smart, modern hotel with a stylish edge. It's calm and cool past the wrought-iron doors. Cable TV, car park and a good restaurant, *Girasoles*. ❹

Plaza Tenam Av Central Nte, opposite *Hotel del Virrey* Ⓣ963/632-0436. One of the newer hotels in the area, with clean, modern rooms but a bit less character than the older places – not bad value though, for cable TV and telephone. ❸

Posada Casa Lupita 3a C Sur Ote 22 Ⓣ963/632-3362, Ⓔposadacasalupita@hotmail.com. A converted home run by a friendly family, the *Lupita* has just five rooms, in various configurations, all with new beds. Bathrooms are wedged in odd corners but clean. There's a nice front patio covered in bougainvillea. ❸

Posada El Castellano 3a C Nte Pte 12 Ⓣ963/632-3347, Ⓦwww.posadaelcastellano.com.mx. A good alternative if *Hotel del Virrey* is full, this place has old-fashioned style, including an attractive courtyard with a fountain, as well as all the modern amenities, such as wi-fi, parking and laundry. Rooms have telephone and cable TV, and there's a charming restaurant. ❹

The City

Comitán's spacious, manicured **plaza** is arranged on several levels around a central bandstand. The whitewashed **Palacio Municipal** dominates the north side, while the seventeenth-century **Templo de Santo Domingo**, with its partially exposed Neoclassical stone facade, is to the east. Inside is a spacious nave, timbered ceiling and marble-covered altar. On the plaza's southeast corner, the **Centro Cultural Rosario Castellanos** (Mon–Fri 8am–5pm; free), named after the respected poet and author who grew up nearby, has a pretty courtyard featuring a mural depicting the city's history. On the same block, just off the plaza, the splendid little **Museo de Arqueología** (Tues–Sun 9am–6pm; free) offers a chronology of local Maya sites through displays of jewellery and pottery, as well as some unsettling tooth necklaces and children's skulls deliberately deformed for ceremonial purposes.

One block south of the plaza along Avenida Central Sur, the most evocative of the city's museums is the **Casa Museo Belisario Domínguez** (Mon–Sat 10am–6.45pm, Sun 9am–12.45pm; M$5), once the home of the local doctor and politician who was assassinated in 1913 for his outspoken opposition to Huerta's usurpation of the presidency. Though it's packed with memorabilia (including a solemn display of the famous anti-Huerta speech that precipitated his murder), it's hard to appreciate unless you understand Spanish. Most interesting is the pharmacy, its shelves lined with diverse lotions and potions, where Domínguez would administer free treatment to the poor. A block further south, the **Museo de Arte Hermíla Domínguez de Castellanos** (Tues–Sat 10am–6pm, Sun 9am–12.45pm; M$5) is named after his wife, and houses a vibrant collection of largely modern artworks by Mexican artists; several canvases by Oaxacan painter Rufino Tamayo are displayed in one room.

Just around the corner, the twin-towered **Templo de San José**, skirted with white and gold and featuring a blend of Gothic and Baroque architecture, is the most unusual of the city's churches. Its interior is particularly attractive, with tiled floors and stained-glass windows. Also worth seeking out is the Neoclassical **Iglesia de San Caralampio**, constructed in 1852 with an elaborately painted stucco facade, two blocks east of the plaza along 1a Calle Norte Poniente. It is dedicated to a martyr who became an object of devotion after cholera and smallpox epidemics decimated the town in the nineteenth century. A fiesta in his name is celebrated in mid-February. Alongside the plaza out front, Comitán's cold, potable mountain-spring water gushes from a row of fountainheads.

Eating and drinking

Apart from in the hotels, most of the best **places to eat** in Comitán are on the plaza. For good-value Mexican food served in clean surroundings, try *Restaurante Acuario*, which has tables under the arches on the west side of the plaza. *Café Quiptic*, on the east side next to Santo Domingo, is the smartest place to eat, serving hearty breakfasts under the stone arches from 8am, with very good coffee. Try the *desayuno chiapaneco*, a breakfast of spicy local tamales. For evening snacks, *Los Portales del León*, overlooking the plaza opposite San Caralampio, is an upmarket cantina and grill; it opens at 8pm most nights. The **market**, one block east of the plaza, is filled with fruit stands and is ringed with some very good *comedores* – it's also a beautiful sight, with golden light casting a sepia-tone glow over the stacks of herbs and chiles in its narrow aisles.

If you're in the mood for a drink you should try **comiteco**, a rich local spirit made from agave (as tequila is) and flavoured with fruits, and available virtually nowhere else. It's smoother than tequila, and a good deal cheaper. Most places will serve it (even if it's not on the menu) for around M$30 for a large glass. You can

Moving on from Comitán

First-class buses depart the OCC terminal regularly for **Tuxtla** and **San Cristóbal**, and there are also two ADO GL buses to Tuxtla at 3pm and 3.30pm; the 3pm one continues to Mexico City. There are seven buses daily to **Tapachula**, and a couple to **Palenque** (1.45pm & 9.15pm). Buses to **Ciudad Cuauhtémoc** on the border leave five times daily, but it's cheaper and more convenient to take the Alfa y Omega *combi* from Bulevar Dr. Belisario Domínguez, opposite 1a Calle Sur Poniente. Transportes Cuxtepeques runs *combis* to Tuxtla via Amatenango del Valle (1hr) and San Cristóbal from Bulevar Domínguez at 2a Calle Norte Poniente, from 5am to 9pm. Transportes Francisco Sarabia, at 3a Av Pte Sur 10 (between Calle Central Poniente and 1a Calle Sur Poniente) runs an hourly *combi* service from its ramshackle terminal to **Tenam Puente** (on the half-hour; 20min).

For the **Lagos de Montebello** and the Frontier Highway, take one of the frequent *combis* run by Transportes Lagos de Montebello from their terminal at 2a Av Pte Sur 23, between calles 2 and 3 Sur Poniente. Buses all the way to Palenque via **Benemérito** and **San Javier** (for Bonampak) start at 4am, leaving once every hour until 9.30am, and take around ten hours. Buses to the lakes are more frequent, with services to Laguna Bosque Azul (1hr), Tziscao, Maravillas and Ixcán leaving around every thirty minutes throughout the day from 3am. Transportes Tzoyol runs buses to **Amititlán** (3hr; for boats to Laguna Miramar) from its small terminal 3km from the centre along 4a Avenida Poniente Sur, near 13a Calle Sur Poniente, from 4am to 2pm.

For further information, see Travel details, p.746.

buy excellent-quality bottles (from M$65) at Comiteco Nueve Estrellas (daily 9.30am–3pm, 5–9pm) on 1a Avenida Poniente Sur near 2a Calle Sur Poniente.

Nightlife

Comitán has a number of lively, fairly polished bars dotted around town. Among the more popular spots is *La Jima*, a block south of the plaza on Avenida Central Sur, which opens at 9pm Thursday to Saturday and hosts boisterous theme nights for hip-hop, cumbia and more. *Jarro Café*, two blocks northwest of the plaza along 1a Avenida Poniente Norte, transforms from a quiet coffee bar by day to a rock hangout at night, while *Matisse*, opposite at no. 16, is a fitting location for evening cocktails. *La Casa de Abajo*, C Central Pte 31, is a smart bar in rustic surroundings. **Free** entertainment is supplied in the form of live marimba, played in the plaza most Thursdays and Sundays from 7pm.

Listings

Banks and exchange Bancomer (Mon–Fri 8.30am–4pm), on the plaza, is useful for currency exchange and dollar cash advances, and also has an ATM. HSBC is at 2a C Sur Pte 7, just down from the plaza.
Internet access Widely available. Ciber@dictos (daily 9am–9pm; M$10/hr), at the end of Pasaje Morales on the north side of the plaza, has a fast connection, but there are plenty of other options on and around the plaza.
Post office One and a half blocks south of the plaza on Av Central Sur (Mon–Fri 8am–6pm, Sat 9am–5pm, Sun 9am–1pm).
Tours The Tranvía Turistico El Cositía is an open-sided tourist bus that takes in all the sights, leaving from the plaza outside Santo Domingo at 9am and 4pm (M$50), but only if there's a minimum of five people.
Travel agents Viajes Tenam, Pasaje Morales 11 (Ⓣ963/632-1654), can arrange domestic and international flights, as well as organize day trips to local attractions such as El Chiflón.

El Chiflón

A waterfall some 120m high is the attraction at Centro Ecoturístico Cascadas El Chiflón (daily 7am–6pm; M$15; Ⓦwww.chiflon.com.mx), not far from the village of Tzimol and about 40km southwest of Comitán. It's a popular day outing from Comitán, as well as from San Cristóbal de las Casas. Trails run along the river, past smaller cascades with pale blue mineral-rich waters, and there are twelve private-bath rooms (❹), should you want to stay overnight. From Comitán, take a *combi* with Rápidos de la Angostura, on Bulevar Domínguez at 1a Calle Sur Poniente; they run every half-hour or so 5am to 6pm. (Tour operators sometimes also call the place Cascadas Velo de Novia, or Bridal Veil Falls – this is the official name of the park entrance and ecotourism centre, with similar facilities, on the west side of the river, when you come from San Cristóbal.)

Tenam Puente

The Maya ruins of **Tenam Puente** (daily 9am–4pm; M$31), 14km south of Comitán and 5km off the main road, cover a large area, and are easily reached by bus (see box, p.707). A path leads up past the guard's hut and into a meadow with a huge stone terrace. The site, uncovered by Frans Blom in 1925, marks a settlement which was at its peak from 600 to 900 AD and finally abandoned around 1200 AD. The most important group of ruins, the acropolis, has three ballcourts and a twenty-metre-high pyramid that affords magnificent views of the Comitán valley. To get to it, keep climbing the stone terraces until you reach the highest point.

Parque Nacional Lagos de Montebello

The **Parque Nacional Lagos de Montebello** lies 50km southeast of Comitán, along the border with Guatemala. The park encompasses beautiful wooded country in which there are more than fifty lakes, sixteen of them very large, and many of them with small restaurants providing local food and basic cabañas. The combination of forest and water is reminiscent of Scotland or Maine, with miles of hiking potential; for the less energetic, roadside viewpoints provide glimpses of many lakes, lent different tints by natural mineral deposits and the angle of the sun. The lakes themselves are actually a series of cenotes (sinkholes) formed by the erosion of limestone over millions of years. You could see quite a bit of the park in a long day trip – buses cover the route all day from 3am, with the last bus leaving the park entrance around 7.30pm – but to really enjoy it, and to visit the small but spectacular **ruins of Chinkultic**, you're better off staying in or near the park.

The main route through the park is the **Carretera Fronteriza**, the Frontier Highway (Hwy-307). It splits from the Panamerican Highway 16km outside Comitán, at the village of La Trinitaria. From there, the park entrance is a further 36km. Past the park, the road roughly follows the line of the Guatemalan border and is paved all the way to Palenque. In the recent past, there were frequent **army checkpoints** along this road – you may still be asked for your passport at any time. The soldiers are invariably polite, but make sure your tourist card is valid.

The road to the park

The most comfortable of the several **places to stay** along the road to the park is the *Museo Parador y Hotel Santa María* (Ⓣ963/632-5116, Ⓦwww.paradorsantamaria.com.mx; ⑨), 22km from the La Trinitaria junction, then 1.3km along a dirt track on the right. A former hacienda, it's a lovely place, furnished with antiques and oil paintings and steeped in colonial history. There's hot water and electricity but rooms are also lit with oil lamps. A small **museum** (daily 9am–6pm; M$20) in the grounds is filled with religious paintings and other ecclesiastical art from the seventeenth century.

At km 31 on the Frontier Highway, a two-kilometre track leads off to the left to the Classic-period Maya ruins of **Chinkultic** (daily 9am–5pm; M$37). Only a relatively small portion of the site has been cleared and restored, but it's well worth a visit if only for the dramatic setting. Climb the first large mound as you enter the site, and you're rewarded with a view of a small lake, with fields of maize beyond and forested mountain ridges in the background. Birds, butterflies and dragonflies abound, and small lizards dart at every step. A ball-court and several stelae have been uncovered, but the highlight is undoubtedly the view from the top of the tallest structure, **El Mirador**. Set on top of a steep hill, with rugged cliffs dropping straight down to a cenote, the temple occupies a commanding position; peaceful now, this was clearly an important hub in ancient times.

Back on the Frontier Highway, you'll find a cluster of **budget accommodation** on the left side at km 32 – buses and *combis* stop right outside. First, just a kilometre or so past the turning for Chinkultic, there's the *Hospedaje and Restaurant La Orquídea* (①), better known as *Doña María's*. Here, half a dozen simple cabins with electricity and shared cold showers sit among the pines. Next door, and a step above in comfort, *El Pino Feliz* (Ⓣ963/102-1089; ①) has eight rooms in wooden cabins with shared, hot-water showers, and serves home-cooked meals (M$30).

Park practicalities

The park entrance is at km 36, and most *combis* continue to one of the prettiest lakes, **Laguna Bosque Azul**, 3km straight ahead, via a spur from the main highway. This route passes a park ticket booth (M$10), then dead-ends at the lake parking lot.

From here, you can take the dirt track a few hundred metres further to a fork. The left-hand path, signposted "Gruta San Rafael del Arco", heads into the jungle through an exquisitely forested gorge and eventually to a massive limestone arch over a river and, at the end, a cave in the cliff-face. On the northwest side of Bosque Azul you can rent basic **cabañas** at *Doña Josefa* (Ⓣ963/632-5971; ❶) or hire scrawny horses at the car park from local children for M$50 per person.

Buses headed for destinations further along the Frontier Highway bear right at the park entrance and pass turnings for several other lakes. One is **Laguna Tziscao**, 9km on, where there is another ticket booth (M$10) and you can swim and take a tour on a wood *balsa* (**raft**), for M$70 for half an hour or M$100 for one hour. The last buses back to Comitán from here leave at around 5pm. Just further east, a road leads south 2km to a tiny settlement on the lake's edge; you can rent simple wood cabañas here (Ⓣ963/633-5244; ❶).

The Frontier Highway east

The main road continues beyond the lakes and through mountains with spectacular views, rushing rivers and precipitous ridgelines on its way around the border to Palenque. The largest settlement – which is not saying much – along the road is **Las Maravillas de Tenejapa**, a pretty village about two hours from Lake Tziscao. About 20km east of Flor de Café, you pass the turn to *Las Guacamayas* (Ⓣ664/134-1138; ❺) a remote yet polished ecotourism operation run by the tiny village of Reforma Agraria. There are **cabins**, a restaurant and space to camp (M$50); guides can lead you down the Río Lacantún and through the forest, which teems with wildlife, including endangered red macaws.

If you drive straight through on the Frontier Highway, plan to carry on at least to Benemérito (see p.727), the closest place on the highway with lodging, and at least three hours from the Lagos de Montebello. It's possible to reach Palenque in the same day, but you would have no time to stop at Bonampak (see p.723) and Yaxchilán. In late 2009, a Pemex station was being installed in Benemérito, making it less likely that you'll need one of the scores of roadside petrol vendors. Due to its proximity to the border, as well as the strong Zapatista loyalties here, this route has several army checkpoints – keep your passport at hand. It also still has a reputation for being a risky place to drive after dark.

Ciudad Cuauhtémoc and the Guatemalan border

A visit to the Lagos de Montebello is a good introduction to the landscapes of Guatemala, but if you want to see the real thing up close, it's only another 60km or so from the junction at La Trinitaria juncion (served by plenty of passing buses) to the **Mexican border post** at **CIUDAD CUAUHTÉMOC**. It's not a city at all – just a few houses, the immigration post, a restaurant and the OCC bus station; the two hotels are not recommended.

The **Guatemalan border post** is at **La Mesilla**, a three-kilometre taxi ride away. As always, it's best to cross in daylight – you may not be able to get your passport stamped after 8pm. Officials at La Mesilla were once notorious for exacting illegal charges from tourists, though things are much improved. **Buses** onwards to Huehuetenango (2hr; US$1.50) and Quetzaltenango (3hr 30min; US$4) wait just over the border, leaving at least every hour between 6am and 5pm. The **money-changers** will give you reasonable rates for travellers' cheques or dollars, but not as good for pesos. **Getting into Mexico** is easy: the Mexican tourist card will be issued free, and vans or buses will be waiting to take you to **Comitán** (1hr 30min; about M$38).

San Cristóbal to Palenque

If you're heading from San Cristóbal to the Yucatán, the best route takes you 203km to **Palenque** (5hr), via **Ocosingo** (88km), along Hwy-186 and then Hwy-199. It's an unrelenting winding road, but an impressive and beautiful journey, through spectacular valleys, lush with greenery, and tiny villages, where women's colourful clothing is different in each one. It's worth making a pit-stop at Ocosingo, the starting point for excursions to the **Toniná ruins** or light-aircraft trips to mesmerizing **Laguna Miramar**, deep in the pristine forests of the **Montes Azules Biosphere Reserve**. Beyond Ocosingo the road passes the pretty waterfalls at **Agua Azul**, though in practice it's easier to visit these from Palenque. If you're travelling by bus you won't have any problems, but in lieu of *topes* (speed bumps), local vendors often try to stop cars with a rope held across the road. It's best to keep off the road at night.

Ocosingo

Its streets lined with single-storey, red-tiled houses and its air thick with the scent of wood smoke, **OCOSINGO** makes a good place to escape the tourist crowds of San Cristóbal or Palenque. The town has stayed close to its country roots, with farmers in cowboy hats in from their ranches and local women selling *maíz* from great bubbling vats. Central to town life is the **plaza**, surrounded by *portales*, a big old country church on the east side and the modern *ayuntamiento* opposite.

Buses stop on the main road or at the small OCC terminal nearby. To get to the plaza turn right out of the terminal and walk back uphill a few blocks until you reach Avenida Central. Turn left and walk down to the plaza, where you'll find pretty much everything you need within a block or two. Local **taxis** charge M$15 for trips anywhere in town.

Practicalities

Accommodation options are plentiful. The *Hotel Central* (☎919/673-0024; ❷) is hard to miss on the north side of the plaza, but though all rooms have fans, hot water and cable TV, none has air-conditioning. *Hotel San José*, just off the northeast corner of the plaza along Calle 1 Oriente Norte (☎919/673-0039; ❷), is a great budget option, with clean, comfortable rooms, some with cable TV and air-conditioning. Colourful *Hospedaje Esmeralda* (☎919/673-0014), a block north of the plaza on Calle Central Norte, has both en-suite (❸) and shared-bath rooms (❷). It's a popular travellers' meeting place, as the friendly staff can help you book flights over the ruins (see p.712) from the airfield outside town as well as flights to **Laguna Miramar** (about M$2500 for four people); a day trip to **Bonampak** and **Yaxchilán** by air is around M$6500 (for four people).

The *Esmeralda* also has a good restaurant, and several other budget **places to eat** are on the square. *El Campanario*, on the north side, is one of the best, with an English menu, hearty plates of Mexican classics (breakfasts M$30–40, tortas M$15) and beers. *El Desván*, on the opposite side of the plaza is recommended for its upstairs terrace, and also serves pizza. In the **food market**, or *tianguis*, traditionally dressed indigenous women sell fruit and vegetables and locally produced cheeses, including the round waxy *queso de bola* and the delicious creamy *queso botanero*. To get there turn right at the church for one block, then left along Calle 2 Sur Oriente for another four.

There are a couple of **ATMs**, one at Banamex on the plaza, and another at Banco Santander opposite *Hospedaje Esmeralda* on Calle Central Norte. **Internet** cafés include Compu Centro, near the plaza on Calle Central Norte (daily 9am–2pm &

4–9pm; M$8/hr), and Xanav (9am–2pm & 4–10pm; M$8/hr), which doubles as a travel agent, at no. 40-C.

Leaving Ocosingo by road is easy enough until mid-evening, with buses, frequent *combis* and shared taxis to San Cristóbal, and buses and regular *combis* to Palenque. The last second-class buses in either direction officially leave at 7.30pm – though they're *de paso* and so are likely to be later. First-class OCC services continue after midnight, with buses to San Cristóbal at 1.40am and 6am and Palenque at 3.25am. **Taxis** to Palenque are far more expensive (around M$650), though you might be able to negotiate.

Toniná

Some 14km east of Ocosingo, the Classic-period Maya site of **TONINÁ** (museum daily 8am–5pm, site daily 9am–3.30pm; M$41 including museum) is large and impressive, yet it sees few visitors. At its height, Toniná was a great regional power: the city defeated Palenque and captured its ruler in 699 AD, and from then until after 900 AD, when it became the last of the great Maya centres to fall victim to whatever disaster led to them all being abandoned, it was probably the greatest power in the Usumacinta basin. It's also the place where the **latest Long Count date**, corresponding to 909 AD, was recorded, and like all the major Maya centres, it was abandoned not long after.

At the site entrance is a good **museum**, with a helpful model of the site, as well as drawings of some of the relief carvings still in place in the buildings. It also displays some of the more fragile sculptures from the site, many of which are images of bound prisoners and of decapitation – a bit unnerving when packed together in the gallery space.

The **ruins** themselves, a five-minute walk from the entrance, are virtually all one enormous building, the **Acrópolis**, a series of seven artificial terraces built into the hillside and incorporating dozens of temples and other buildings. This is the "house of stone" that gave the site its Tzeltal name. A flashlight is useful to explore the labyrinthine interiors and internal staircases. Of the remaining stucco reliefs, the finest is the enormous (16m x 4m) **Mural de las Cuatro Eras**, on the sixth platform. This amazingly well-preserved stucco codex tells the story of Maya cosmology by following the eras of the world as they were created and destroyed. The worlds are depicted as decapitated heads surrounded by flowers. A grinning, skeletal Lord of Death presents a particularly graphic image as he grasps a skinned human head. At the summit is the **Templo del Espejo Humeante** (Temple of the Smoking Mirror), built around 840 AD, and a great vantage point across the valley.

To reach Toniná **from Ocosingo**, take one of the frequent *combis* (M$10) that leave from the market area – look for those marked "Predio/Ruinas". A taxi will cost around M$70 one way. Near the ruins, a small **café** sells packaged snacks, locally grown macadamia nuts and espresso, from local coffee. For a spectacular **flight** over the ruins (M$1000 for four people, plus guide) contact *Hospedaje Esmeralda* (see p.711).

Laguna Miramar

A much more remote excursion from Ocosingo is a visit to **Laguna Miramar**, in the heart of the Lacandón forest. Miramar, at 40km long the largest lake in southeast Mexico, is now part of the enchanting **Montes Azules Biosphere Reserve**, the largest surviving area of rainforest in North America. The high-canopy forest is home to abundant wildlife, including howler and spider monkeys, tapirs and jaguars, and there are rivers and caves to explore. An island in the lake has traces of a fortress, which was a Maya stronghold until it was finally conquered in 1559. It's best to avoid the rainy season (June–Oct).

You can visit Miramar on your own or on an organized tour. To **travel independently** takes some time and effort. The jumping-off point is the *ejido* and major army base of San Quintín, where most transport drops you. From there, you need to catch a lift or walk the 2km to the *ejido* of **Emiliano Zapata**. When you arrive, if not directed to the relevant person, ask for the *comisario* or *presidente*, either of whom will be able to organize the practicalities, charged per day: M$100 for a guide, M$50 for a porter, M$100 for the use of canoe (highly recommended) and around M$30 per person to camp or sleep in hammocks in lakeside palapas. Then it's a further nine-kilometre hike to the lake from here. There are a few shops and simple cafeterías in San Quintín, but supplies in Emiliano Zapata are very basic, so it's best to bring your own food.

Getting to Laguna Miramar

By far the easiest method of transport is to **fly** to **San Quintín** in a light aircraft from Servicios Aéreos de San Cristóbal (Ⓣ963/632-4662, Ⓦwww.serviciosaereos sancristobal.com), arranged by the *Hospedaje Esmeralda* in Ocosingo (see p.711). If you can't fill a plane (the hotel-arranged tours are US$500 for four people), you can also contact the airline directly – if they have space they might let you fly one way for M$350.

Of the **overland** options, the most established route is the bone-shaking six- to seven-hour, 130-kilometre ride in a pick-up truck **from Ocosingo** to San Quintín (M$75). Trucks known as *tres toneladas* leave between 9am and noon, depending on demand, from the depot behind Ocosingo market on 3a Calle Sur Oriente. In theory, the journey is faster **from Comitán**, where you first take a frequent *combi* to the small town of Las Margaritas, 16km northwest (M$25), then pick up another *tres toneladas* to San Quintín, about three to four hours away. But this route passes through **La Realidad**, a celebrated Zapatista stronghold, and may lead to extra hassle at military checkpoints in the area – check with the Comitán tourist office, or *Hospedaje Esmeralda*, before trying this.

A more expensive but far more exciting alternative is to take a Transportes Tzoyol *combi* from Comitán to Amatitlán, in Guatemala, then arrange a **boat** (M$1000; 3hr) to take you up the Río Jatatè to Emiliano Zapata.

North to Palenque: Agua Azul and Misol-Há

A series of magnificent **waterfalls** is the chief attraction along the winding mountain road between Ocosingo and Palenque. The dazzling cascades on the Río Shumulhá at **Agua Azul** and the exquisite falls at **Misol-Há** are more easily visited on a day trip from Palenque (see p.714), though it is possible to visit them independently and stay nearby.

Agua Azul

The impressive waterfalls of **Agua Azul**, in the Parque Nacional Agua Azul, 58km north of Ocosingo and 4km off the main road, are now a major tour-bus destination. The main cascades lie near the car park at the end of the access road, with several smaller but equally appealing rapids stretching for 1km up the river. The whole area is certainly picturesque, though the river near the lower falls is lined with rows of souvenir stalls and snack vendors. Adjust your expectations accordingly, and it still makes for a pleasant trip.

If you come **by bus** (not on a tour), you'll be dropped at the turn-off to the falls on the main highway, where you'll probably have to walk 45 minutes downhill to the waterfall (and at least an hour's sweaty hike back up, or an M$10 taxi ride). Villagers have set up two tolls along the road; at each (if manned), you'll be charged M$10. If you need to stay near the falls, simple **cabañas** (❷) are for rent

– ask at the Modulo de Información near the car park – but they're not as nice as the ones at Misol-Há (see below).

If it's safe to walk upstream (it may not be in the rainy season), you'll come across a perilous-looking bridge over the river and eventually reach an impressive gorge where the **Río Shumulhá** explodes out of the jungle-covered mountain. At the right time of year, the river is alive with butterflies. Higher up, the swimming is a little safer, too – but don't go in at all if you're not a strong swimmer. People drown here every year, and though a few signs warn of **dangerous currents**, they don't begin to mark all the perilous spots. Although you may want to get as far from the tourist scrum as possible, keep in mind that violent attacks have occurred here in the past. A heavy federal police guard has proved a major deterrent, but you're always safer with other people nearby.

Back on the highway heading north, it's another 64km to Palenque – some tours call at **Agua Clara**, another waterfall 10km from Azul, which is good for swimming but otherwise not as attractive.

Misol-Há

Only 18km from Palenque, **Misol-Há** (M$15) is a much easier day trip than Agua Azul if travelling by public transport, and in many ways far more pleasant, with none of the slapdash development present at its celebrated neighbour. A 25-metre waterfall provides a stunning backdrop to a pool that's safe for swimming, and a fern-lined trail leads along a ledge behind the cascade – refreshing from the spray and mist even if you don't swim. It's an easy 1.5km walk downhill from the road (though not so much fun in the other direction); there's an additional M$10 charge if you arrive by car. The San Miguel *ejido* manages the area, offering a decent **restaurant** catering to tour groups, as well as inexpensive **accommodation** in some beautiful wooden cabañas (Ⓣ55/5329-0995 or 916/345-03456, Ⓦwww.misol-ha.com; ❸); each cabin has a private bathroom and electricity, and some also have kitchens. The organization recommends advance reservations, especially during Mexican holiday times.

Palenque

Set in thick jungle buzzing with insects, the ancient Maya **ruins of Palenque** are for many the finest of Mexico's Maya sites: less crowded than Chichén Itzá, larger than Uxmal, and with the most spectacular setting. It is a relatively small site – you can see everything in a morning – but a fascinating one, strongly linked to the lost cities of Guatemala while displaying a distinctive style.

Nine kilometres east of the ruins, the rather helter-skelter **town of Palenque** has 65,000 inhabitants and every facility a visitor might need. An excellent base for exploring the ruins and the waterfalls in the nearby hills, it is lively enough, with music in the turquoise-painted plaza most evenings, but – save for a small **museum** on the plaza, devoted to the textiles of Chiapas – it has no real intrinsic appeal. As there are a number of excellent camping sites, cabañas and hotels near the ruins, you may prefer not to stay in town at all.

Arrival and information

Arriving on any long-distance bus (except for Lagos de Montebello vehicles), you'll be at one of two nearly adjacent **bus terminals** on Juárez, just off the main highway through town. If you know when you're leaving it's worth buying your onward ticket as soon as you arrive – or at any rate as soon as possible – as buses

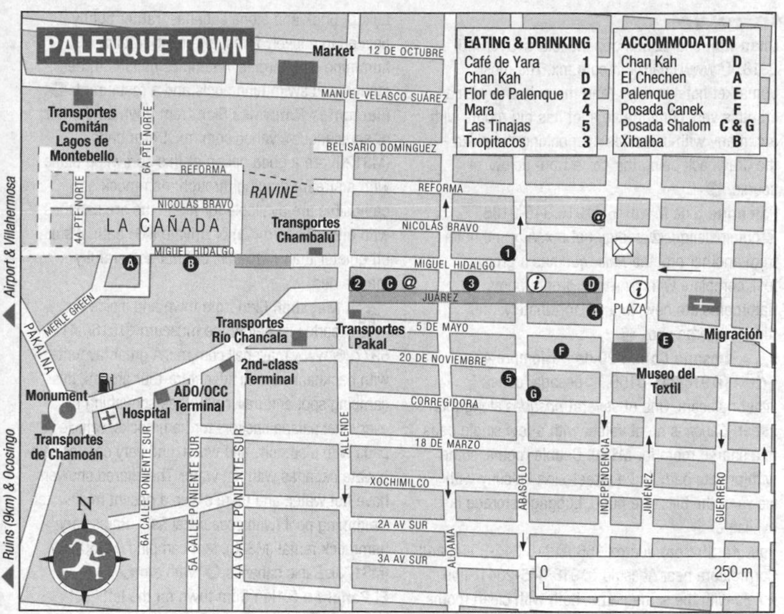

out of Palenque can be very crowded, particularly the more popular first-class services towards Mérida or San Cristóbal de las Casas. Palenque's three main streets, avenidas Juárez, 5 de Mayo and Hidalgo, all run parallel and lead straight up to the **plaza**, the Parque Central.

The **tourist office** (Mon–Sat 9am–9pm, Sun 9am–3pm; ⓣ916/345-0356) is in the Plaza de Artesanías on Juárez at the corner of Abasolo, a block below the plaza; the staff will very sweetly give you wrong information, and a street map if you're lucky. There's another booth on the east side of the plaza, with sometimes sharper staff. You'll generally get better **information** from local tour operators (see "Listings") or at your hotel.

Accommodation

Palenque has seen a massive boom in **hotel** construction in recent years. There are plenty of places on the rather noisy streets leading from the bus stations to the plaza, especially Hidalgo and 20 de Noviembre. A quieter option is the area called **La Cañada**, named for the ravine that divides it from the town centre. With brick-paved streets and soft lighting, it feels a little like a chic subdivision. It's set in a swath of trees (birds and monkeys are audible in the morning) and only a short walk from the action. Most hotels here are more upmarket, but there's one very good budget option. (Hotels in the centre and in La Cañada are marked on the Palenque Town map above.) For more isolation, opt for places lining the **road to the ruins**, in every category from luxury hotel to campsite – though the latter options are becoming fewer. A taxi from the OCC bus station to these places should cost about M$50, but during daylight hours, it's just as easy to flag down one of the many *combis* headed for ruins. Note that high season here is Mexican vacation times – July, August, Christmas and Semana Santa; outside that time, rates can drop significantly.

In town

Chan Kah Juárez at Independecia ⓣ916/345-0318, ⓦwww.chan-kah.com.mx. The most upmarket hotel in town (and the only one with a lift), this very comfortable spot has big rooms with a/c, many with balconies overlooking the plaza – the drawback being the noise from below, of course. ❹

Palenque 5 de Mayo 15 ⓣ916/345-0188, ⓔhotelpalenque@prodigy.net.mx. A grand hotel from another era, the *Palenque* has a groovy Sixties feel, complete with two-tone green rooms. Bathrooms are new, though, fortunately, and there's a large pool. ❺

Posada Canek 20 de Noviembre 43 ⓣ916/345-0150, ⓔposada_canek@hotmail.com. One of several *posadas* along this street, *Canek* is great value, with a few single beds in a shared room for M$60. Double rooms, some with private bath and a street-side balcony with views of the hills, are huge. Luggage storage is available. ❷

Posada Shalom Juárez 156 ⓣ916/345-0944, and Corregidora near Abasolo ⓣ916/345-2641. Two hotels with the same name, both with clean rooms, cable TV and tiled private bathrooms. Luggage storage, parking and laundry service available. ❷

La Cañada

El Chechen Merle Green at Hidalgo ⓣ916/345-1008. Just sixteen rooms, run by a conscientious family, all with private bath (the brown tiles look sketchy, but they're actually new and clean). Parking. ❸

Xibalba Merle Green at Hidalgo ⓣ916/345-0411, ⓔxibalba02@prodigy.net.mx. Pretty white rooms are accented with green and brown, giving a vaguely natural feel, even if rooms are not very large. Staff are friendly, and there's a good restaurant and a helpful travel agency. ❺

On the road to the ruins

Chan Kah Resort Village 4km from town on the left ⓣ916/345-1134, ⓦwww.chan-kah.com.mx. Luxury brick and stone cabañas, rather tightly packed in a lovely forest and river setting, humming with birdlife. Amenities include three stone-lined swimming pools and a restaurant. ❼

Elementos Naturales 6km from town on the left ⓔenpalenque@yahoo.com.mx. Dorm beds (M$120) are a good option at this sprawling place with a stream running through; hammock or campsites are available for M$50, as are cabañas with either shared (❷) or private (❸) bath. It's a bit quieter than *Mayabell*, but not so carefully maintained.

Mayabell 6km from town and inside the park, just before the museum ⓣ916/341-6977, ⓦwww.mayabell.com.mx. A great favourite with backpackers and adventure-tour groups, this camping spot and trailer park has something for everyone: palapa shelters for hammocks, vehicle pads with electricity and water, and very comfortable private cabañas with hot water. The shared showers have hot water, and there's also a decent freshwater swimming pool (with occasional fish). Rates vary: hammock rental (M$20), tent camping (M$50), RV (M$170). Basic cabañas ❶, with a/c ❺.

El Panchán 5.1km from town on the left, just before the park entrance ⓦwww.elpanchan.com. A large complex incorporating several privately run cabaña operations, separated by screens of trees and sharing a couple of restaurants, an internet cafe and laundry. The vibe may be a little too nouveau-hippie for some, but most places here are excellent value, and it's easy to take a *combi* here, then walk around comparing rates. One drawback is that there's no swimming pool. *Margarita and Ed's* (ⓣ916/341-0063, ⓔedcabanas@yahoo.com; ❷) is the cleanest and best-value option, with thatched cabins or conventional double rooms with a/c. *Jungle Palace* (ⓣ915-348-0520; ❶) has a stream running between its shared-bath thatch cabañas, and a "no drums" policy. *Don Mucho's* should be avoided if you want an early night – the cabañas are right by the restaurant of the same name, where there's live music, fire-spinning, etc every night.

Eating and drinking

Food in Palenque town is fairly basic, and most restaurants serve up similar dishes, often just pasta and pizza, to customers who've really only come for the ruins. There are also several places along the road to the site – some of which cater mainly to tour groups – including a couple in El Panchán (see "Accommodation" above). The bigger hotels in La Cañada have a restaurant attached and, though standards are generally fine, prices are higher than in the centre. Bargains can be found among the set menus posted on boards outside most restaurants. **Avenida Juárez** also has several budget options between the bus stations and the plaza, while **Avenida Hidalgo** has more Mexican-style food, with several taco places and even a couple of seafood restaurants. There's a good Mexican **bakery**, *Flor de Palenque*, on Allende just off Juárez.

Café de Yara Hidalgo at Abasolo. Good café, both in terms of coffee and the casual atmosphere. Try the cappuccino (from a proper espresso machine) and breakfasts especially. Dinner, with European as well as Mexican dishes, is also decent, and it's a reliable spot to get a green salad.

Chan Kah Juárez at Independencia, on the plaza. The hotel has a first-floor terrace bar/restaurant with great views over the action on the plaza. Prices reflect the location (and aren't worth it for the standard Mexican food), but this is a good place for an early evening drink.

Mara Juárez at Independencia, on the plaza. A pleasant little café from which to watch the plaza scene. Tacos are good here, but you can get big platters as well – or just a cold beer.

Las Tinajas 20 de Noviembre at Abasolo. Pleasant, family-run restaurant, open morning till night and popular for its vast menu of hearty meats, fish, chicken and pasta in addition to the usual Mexican fare. No comida corrida, but most dishes are around M$85, and all are big enough to share.

Tropitacos Juárez between Allende and Abasolo. The biggest skewer of *pastor* pork in town, served hot and fast to the constant drone of blenders whipping up fruit drinks. Go for the *torta de bisteck*, garnished with griddle-fried cheese, if you want something more substantial.

Listings

Banks and exchange Several banks along Juárez will change travellers' cheques and have ATMs.

Internet access There are a few places along Juárez: try Red M@aya (daily 9am–10pm; M$15/hr) at no. 133 between Allende and Aldama. In La Cañada area, the hotels run something of a cartel, ripping off isolated customers with a charge of M$25/hr. *El Panchán* also has internet access (10am–11pm; M$15/hr).

Laundry Several in town, including Azul Lavanderia, 2a Avenida Sur Ote, just east of the plaza (Mon–Fri 9am–2pm & 5–8pm, Sat 9am–2pm).

Post office On Independencia, a block from the plaza (Mon–Fri 9am–6pm, Sat & Sun 9am–1pm).

Tours Walk the streets of Palenque and you'll be accosted by touts offering a huge variety of tours to local attractions, above all the waterfalls at Agua Azul and Misol-Há (see p.713) and the ruins of Bonampak and Yaxchilán (see p.723 & p.725). There are also trips to Tikal in Guatemala or to Toniná, and adventure tours, including kayaking and horseriding. Prices vary according to season (and even time of day if there's one seat left to fill) but start from around M$100 for the waterfalls, M$600 for a day trip to Bonampak and Yaxchilán. Be sure to check what's included – entrance fees, meals and English-speaking guides most importantly. Two of the more reliable agents are Na Chan Kan (Ⓣ916/345-0263, Ⓔnachan@tnet.net.mx), with a small office on Juárez, just up from the bus station, and a main office on Hidalgo at Jiménez, and Viajes Shivalva, based at the *Hotel Xibalba* in La Cañada (Ⓣ916/345-0411).

The ruins of Palenque

The **ruins of Palenque** occupy the top of an escarpment marking the north-western limit of the Chiapas highlands. Superficially, the site bears a closer resemblance to the Maya sites of Guatemala than to those of the Yucatán, but ultimately the style here is unique – the **towered palace** and **pyramid tomb** are like nothing else, as is the abundance of reliefs and inscriptions. The setting, too, is remarkable. Surrounded by jungle-covered hills, Palenque is right at the edge of the great Yucatán plain – climb to the top of any of the structures and you look out over an endless stretch of low, pale-green flatland. If you arrive early enough in the day, the mist still clings to the treetops and the howler monkeys are roaring off in the greenery.

Founded around 100 BC as a farming village, it was four hundred years before Palenque began to flourish, during the Classic period (300–900 AD). Towards the end of this time the city ruled over a large part of modern-day Chiapas and Tabasco, but its peak, when the population is thought to have numbered some

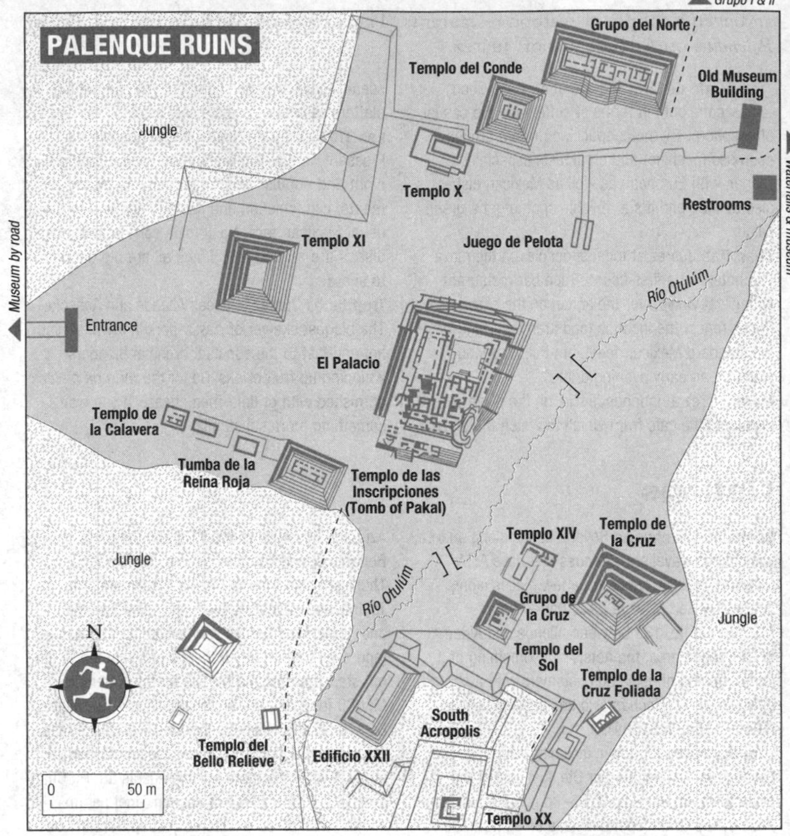

100,000, came during a relatively short period in the seventh century, under two rulers: **Hanab Pakal (Jaguar Shield)** and **Chan Bahlum (Jaguar Serpent)**. Almost everything you can see (and that's only a tiny, central part of the original city) dates from this era.

El Palacio and around

As you enter the site, **El Palacio**, with its extraordinary watchtower, stands ahead of you. The path, however, leads to the right, past a row of smaller structures – one of them, the so-called **Tumba de la Reina Roja** ("Tomb of the Red Queen"), is open inside, and you can climb in to see a sarcophagus still in place. This is nothing, though, compared with the structure's neighbour, the enormous **Templo de las Inscripciones**, an eight-step pyramid, 26m high, built up against a thickly overgrown hillside. You are not permitted to climb the pyramid, so you just have to imagine the sanctuary on top, filled with a series of stone panels carved with hieroglyphic inscriptions relating to Palenque's dynastic history. Deep inside the pyramid is the **tomb of Hanab Pakal**, or Pakal the Great (615–683 AD). Discovered in 1952, this was the first such pyramid burial found in the Americas, and is still the most important and impressive. Some of the smaller objects found inside – the skeleton and the jade death mask – are on display at the Museo Nacional de Antropología in Mexico City (see p.419), but the massive, intricately carved stone **sarcophagus** is still inside; a reproduction is in the site museum (see p.720).

The centrepiece of the site, **El Palacio**, is in fact a complex of buildings constructed at different times to form a rambling administrative and residential block. Its square **tower** is unique, and no one knows exactly what its purpose was – perhaps a lookout post or an astronomical observatory. Throughout you'll find delicately executed **relief carvings**, the most remarkable of which are the giant human figures on stone panels in the grassy courtyard, depicting rulers of defeated cities in poses of humiliation. An arcade overlooking the courtyard held a portrait gallery of Palenque's rulers, though many of these have been removed.

South of El Palacio and adjacent to the Templo de las Inscripciones, a small path leads to the **Templo del Bello Relieve (Templo del Jaguar)**. More temples are being wrested from the jungle beyond, but the paths are closed, and though the path leads eventually to the *ejido* of Naranjo, you won't be permitted to pass much further into the forest without a guide. Even so, clambering around here, it's easy to believe you're walking over unexcavated buildings, as the ground is very rocky and some of the stones don't look naturally formed.

The Grupo de la Cruz and around

The main path then leads across the Río Otulúm, one of several streams that cascade through the site. The Otulúm was once completely lined with stone and used as an aqueduct; the reinforcement also kept the stream from overflowing its banks and undermining the foundations of the surrounding buildings.

The path leads uphill to end in the plaza of what's called the **Grupo de la Cruz**, oddly oriented away from Palenque's more central buildings. The **Templo del Sol**, the **Templo de la Cruz** and the **Templo de la Cruz Foliada** are all tall,

▲ The ruins at Palenque

narrow pyramids surmounted by a small temple with an elaborate stone roofcomb. All contain carved panels representing sacred rites – the cross found here is as important an image in Maya iconography as it is in Christian, representing the meeting of the heavens and the underworld with the land of the living. On the right-hand side of the Templo de la Cruz, God L, one of the gods of the underworld, is depicted smoking tobacco – so far the oldest known image of someone smoking. A small path next to the Templo de la Cruz Foliada leads to the only open portion of the South Acropolis, a building with a replica relief carving, covered with elaborate glyphs and a triumphant king.

The Grupo del Norte and around

Following the Río Otulúm to the northern edge of the cleared site, you reach the lesser buildings of the **Grupo del Norte** and the **Juego de Pelota** (ball-court), on lower ground across a grassy area from El Palacio. Beyond them, two **paths** lead downhill towards the museum. One goes down some perilous stairs behind Grupo del Norte, leading to **Grupo I** and **Grupo II**, intricate complexes of interconnected rooms. The other path follows the stream as it cascades through the forest and flows over beautiful limestone curtains and terraces into a series of gorgeous pools (no swimming allowed, though). The paths join again just after a suspension bridge crossing the river; eventually the route emerges on the main road opposite the museum. If you don't want to exit here, and want to make a loop, it's best to go down via Grupo I and II – the steeper route – then make your way back up by the other, somewhat easier trail.

The museum

Palenque's excellent **museum** (Tues–Sun 9am–4.30pm, included in site entry), on the road 1.5km from the site entrance, will give you a good idea of the scale of Palenque, and a look at some of its treasures. Many of the glyphs and carved relief panels found at the site are on display, as are examples of the giant ceramic

Ruin practicalities

Getting to the ruins of Palenque, nine kilometres from town, is straightforward. Two **combi** services, Chambalú and Pakal, run at least every fifteen minutes (6am–6pm; M$10 one way) from their terminals near Juárez, and will stop anywhere along the road to the ruins – useful if you're staying at one of the hotels or campsites near the ruins. After 6pm, you'll have to either walk or take a **taxi** (M$60). There are also plenty of organized **tours** from town (see p.717).

The **ruins** (daily 8am–5pm, last entry 4.30pm; M$48 including museum) are in the **Parque Nacional de Palenque**, which takes an additional M$22 at the park gate, just after *El Panchán*. (If you're staying inside the park, at *Mayabell*, say, you only have to pay once.) The main road first passes a nice *artesanías* shop, a café and the site **museum** – it's possible to buy a site ticket here, after 9am (but not on Mondays, when the museum is shut), then enter at the gate across the road, hiking up to the main part of the site via the waterfalls trail. But most people will press on to the main site entrance, at the top of the hill another 2km up a winding road. In this area, there's a small **café** and numerous souvenir stalls selling drinks, as well as toilets and some expensive lockers. Guides officially cost M$350 for groups of up to seven people, but that's open to negotiation.

Even if you have your own **car**, you may still prefer to take a *combi*, as this enables you to exit on the downhill side of the site by the museum, and spare yourself having to hike back up to your vehicle. There's also very limited parking space at the main entrance at the top of the hill.

Moving on from Palenque

Leaving Palenque by **bus**, there are **first-class** departures from the ADO/OCC terminal to Mérida (4 daily) via Campeche. There are also first-class departures for Oaxaca (1 daily at 5.30pm); Cancún (5 daily), via Chetumal; and overnight buses to Mexico City (2 daily). Buses for **Tuxtla Gutiérrez** (10 daily) all call at **Ocosingo** (2hr 30min) and **San Cristóbal** (5hr). The main regional transport hub is **Villahermosa** (10 daily), and you may find it easier to get there and change for your onward journey. You can also get a *de paso* first-class bus to Emiliano Zapata in Tabasco (9 daily), for **Tenosique** and Guatemala. Luxury ADO GL services run to Cancún via Chetumal at 9pm; and to Tuxtla via San Cristóbal at 7.05am. **Second-class** buses – Auto Cardeso, Expreso Azul and others – run to Cancún, **Tuxtla**, and Villahermosa from a terminal just down the street.

Transportes Comitán Lagos de Montebello, on Velasco Suárez, just past the market, and Transportes Río Chancalá, on 5 de Mayo, have numerous departures to destinations along the Frontier Highway, beginning at 3.40am. All go to the turn-off (*crucero*) for **Frontera Corozal** (for Yaxchilán), and Montebello's early-morning departures continue all the way to Comitán via Benemérito and the Lagos de Montebello. Transportes de Chamoán, on the west side of the traffic circle by the statue of the Maya head, runs regular **minivans** to Frontera itself; these cost a bit more (M$70, rather than M$60), but you don't have to pay for a taxi into town. You can find **taxis** on the northeast corner of the plaza to: **Agua Azul** (return, with 2hr waiting time), **Bonampak** (return, with 2hr waiting time), Frontera, Ocosingo, Palenque ruins and around town.

For further information, see Travel details, p.746.

incense-burners in the form of gods or mythological creatures. An intricate model of El Palacio reveals how it would have appeared in the Classic period – with the tops of the buildings adorned with roofcombs.

The back wing is devoted to a replica of Pakal's sarcophagus lid from the Templo de las Inscripciones – entrance is restricted to small groups, every 30 minutes or so. One of the most renowned iconographic monuments in the Maya world, the engraved sarcophagus lid depicts Pakal at the moment of his death, falling into Xibalba, the underworld, symbolized by a monster's jaws. Above the dead king rises the **Wakah Kan** – the World Tree and the centre of the universe – with **Itzam-Yé**, the Celestial Bird, perched on top representing the heavens. So that the deified king buried here should not be cut off from the world of the living, a psychoduct – a hollow tube in the form of a snake – runs up the side of the staircase, from the tomb to the temple.

The Usumacinta valley and the Frontier Highway south

The Carretera Fronteriza (**Frontier Highway**) provides access to the Lacandón forest and the valley along the Río Usumacinta, and the great Maya sites located here: **Bonampak**, famous for its murals, and **Yaxchilán**, a vast ruined city on the riverbank. The remote highway, which roughly follows the line of the Guatemalan border, has a reputation as a dangerous place – as recently as 2003, Mexican federal police escorted tourists in convoys. A steady military presence has made the area relatively safe, however, and though it's not advisable to drive the road after dark, it is no problem to travel this way in your own car without an escort. Army checkpoints are frequent, so be sure to carry your passport.

Tourism infrastructure has grown, making the trips described below significantly easier – though visiting this area is still one of the better adventures in this part of Mexico. It used to be that the only way to visit Bonampak and Yaxchilán was with a **tour** from Palenque (see p.717). That's still the easiest option, whether you go on a day trip or an overnight, with accommodation at the Lacandón Maya community of **Lacanjá Chansayab**, where the Lacandón Maya have lived for millennia.

But it's no longer difficult to make the trip on your own, giving you the option of arriving at the remote sites relatively alone. Independent travel can also be substantially cheaper, although the final cost will depend on finding people to share the boat from the settlement of **Frontera Corozal** to Yaxchilán. The starting point for **DIY trips** is the Transportes de Chamoán *combi* office in Palenque (see box, p.721). And if you have a chance, pick up an information sheet on the Lacandón community from **Casa Na-Bolom** in San Cristóbal (see p.698) before you set off.

If you intend to push on into **Guatemala**, you can get a boat a short distance upstream from Frontera Corozal to **Bethél** across the border, and from the fast-expanding town of Benemérito you can occasionally take a longer trip on a trading boat upstream to **Sayaxché** (also in Guatemala), on the Río de la Pasión. See p.727 for the description of the road past Benemérito.

Welib-Ja

About 30km southeast of Palenque, the beautiful waterfalls of **WELIB-JA** (9am–5pm; M$10) see fewer visitors than Agua Azul or Misol-Há. And because they're only 500m from the road, they're also easier to reach by public transport (take the Chamoán *combi* and ask to be let off at the *cascadas*). A forest path leads alongside the river and down to the base of a towering split cascade, close enough for the mist to spray over you. There are a few palapas for picnicking in the shade, as well as a protected kids' swimming area, upstream from the falls. A few breeze-block **rooms** (❷) are available for overnight stays. Getting back to Palenque shouldn't be hard, as long as you start looking for a ride by 4.30pm or so – flag down standard *combi* vans as well as the pick-up trucks that serve the smaller *ejidos*.

Lacanjá Chansayab and Bonampak

For the settlement of Lacanjá and the ruins of Bonampak, you need to get off the bus at **San Javier** (about 3hr and 132km from Palenque), where there's a large palapa on the right side of the road. Taxis usually wait here to take passengers either to the village, or to a parking area 3km down the road, where *combi* vans cover the final stretch to the ruins.

If you want to spend the night in the area, the easiest option is right at the *combi* parking area, a simple place called *Camping Margarito* (from M$70/person), which also runs a **restaurant**. But there are more – and nicer – **camping spots and cabañas** in and on the way to the village, reached in 2.5km by the other road leading out of the parking area. It's easiest if you have a particular spot in mind – the village is too spread out to walk around comparing options. Prices at all places run about M$25 for camping, M$80 for dorm beds where available, M$200 for shared-bath rooms and M$300–400 for private-bath options – the differences come in the upkeep of the facilities. None of the ten or so operations currently has a phone, but there's little chance you'll wind up with nowhere to sleep.

The first place you pass en route to the village is *Campamento Servicios Turísticos Lacandones*, where the tent sites are set by a rushing river; a few concrete cabañas

The Lacandón

You may already have encountered the impressively wild-looking **Lacandón Maya**, dressed in simple white robes and selling exquisite (and apparently effective) bows and arrows at Palenque. Until recently, they were the most isolated of all the Mexican Indian groups. The ancestors of today's Lacandón are believed to have migrated to Chiapas from the Petén region of Guatemala during the eighteenth century. Prior to that the Spanish had enslaved, killed or relocated the original inhabitants of the forest. The Lacandón refer to themselves as "Hach Winik" (true people). Appearances notwithstanding, some Lacandón families are (or have been) quite wealthy, having sold timber rights in the jungle, though most of the timber money has now gone. This change has led to a division in their society, and most live in one of two main communities: **Lacanjá Chansayab**, near Bonampak, a village predominantly made up of evangelical Protestants, some of whom are keenly developing low-impact tourist facilities (see opposite); and **Nahá**, where a small group still attempt to live a traditional life, and where it is possible to arrange stays in local homes. The best source of information on the Lacandón in Chiapas is Casa Na-Bolom in San Cristóbal de las Casas (see p.698), where you can find a manuscript of *Last Lords of Palenque*, by Victor Perera and Robert Bruce (Little Brown & Co, 1982). *Hach Winik*, by Didier Boremanse (University of Albany, 1998), is an excellent recent study of Lacandón life and history.

have private bathrooms. *Ya'aj Ché*, further along on the right, is much preferable, a very tidy spot next to a small stream – a few lovely shared-bath wood cabins have good mosquito nets and porches overlooking the water, or you can go for the large concrete rooms with en-suite facilities. *Río Lacanjá*, to the left at the main village junction, is popular with tour groups – it doesn't get too excited about walk-up business, though it does have a nice set of cabins. Other recommended spots are run by old hands Vicente Kin Bor and Enrique Paniagua – look for signs at the village junction.

From the village, hiking trails lead to **Cascada Ya Toch Kusam** (M$35), a magical waterfall, in about an hour and a half, and on to Bonampak (better done with a guide, for about M$200) in another hour and a half. The hikes are wonderful in the dry season (Jan to late April) – be prepared for mud at other times.

Bonampak: the site

Relatively small compared with other ruined Maya cities, what makes **BONAMPAK** (daily 8am–5pm; M$41) unique is its fascinating **murals**, evocative memorials to a lost civilization. The outside world first heard of Bonampak, meaning "painted walls", in 1946, when Charles Frey, an American who'd skipped to the Mexican forest during WWII, was shown the site (but apparently not the murals) by Lacandón who still worshipped at the ancient temples. The first non-Maya ever to see these murals – astonishing examples of Classic Maya art – was the American photographer Giles Healey, who arrived shortly after Frey's visit, sparking a long and bitter dispute over exactly who was responsible for their discovery. Bonampak's actual buildings, most from the eighth century, are small and not the most spectacular, but the murals definitely make it worth the visit – there is very little like them elsewhere in the Maya world, and even in their decayed state, the colours are vivid and the imagery memorable.

Bonampak lies in a small national park controlled by and for the Lacandón on the fringe of the much larger Montes Azules Biosphere Reserve. However you get here, you can enter the forest only in Lacandón transport – no other vehicles are allowed in. When you get off a *combi* at the highway, **taxis** are usually waiting by a big palapa to take you about 3km to a parking area at the turn for the village of Lacanjá Chansayab (M$50). There, you'll get on a rattling old *combi* to the ruins (M$70 round trip, with 1hr waiting time). You can also **rent a bike** (M$75) to ride up to the ruins, but the business is set up another 250m past the parking area for the *combis*, and the *combi* drivers may tell you that the bikes don't exist. Once you've seen the ruins, head back to the San Javier junction, where you can catch a **bus** or *combi* to Palenque.

At the **site entrance** there are toilets and a couple of huts selling snacks and souvenirs. After crossing an airstrip, you are at the northwest corner of **La Gran Plaza**, which is 110m long and bounded by low walls – the remains of some palace-style buildings. In the centre of the plaza **Stele 1** shows a larger-than-life **Chaan Muan II**, the last king of Bonampak, dressed for battle – at 6m, it is one of the tallest stele in the Maya world. You'll encounter other images of him throughout the site. Ahead, atop several steep flights of steps, lies the **Acrópolis**. On the lower steps, more well-preserved stelae show Chaan Muan with his wife, Lady Rabbit, preparing himself for blood-letting and apparently about to sacrifice a prisoner. From the highest point of the acropolis there's an impressive sense that you're surrounded by primeval forest – the Selva Lacandona – with just a small cleared space in front of you.

The murals

Splendid though these carvings are, the highlight of the site is the modest-looking **Edificio de las Pinturas**, halfway up the steps. Inside, in three separate chambers and on the temple walls and roof, the renowned **Bonampak murals** depict vivid scenes of haughty Maya lords, splendidly attired in jaguar-skin robes and quetzal-plume headdresses, their equally well-dressed ladies; and bound prisoners, one with his fingernails ripped out, spurting blood. Dating to around 790 AD, these paintings show the Bonampak elite at the height of their power: unknown to them, the collapse of the Classic Maya civilization was imminent. Some details were never finished, and Bonampak was abandoned shortly after the scenes in the temple were painted. Though you can't enter the rooms fully, the vantage point inside the doorway is more than adequate to absorb what's inside, and though no more than three people are permitted to enter at any one time and queues are possible, you shouldn't have to wait long. Having said that, time and early cleaning attempts have clearly taken their toll on the murals, and apart from a few beautifully restored sections, it takes some concentration and imagination to work out what you're looking at.

In **Room 1**, an infant wrapped in white cloth (the heir apparent?) is presented to assembled nobility under the supervision of the lord of Yaxchilán, while musicians play drums, pipes and trumpets in the background. **Room 2** contains a vivid, even gruesome, exhibition of power over Bonampak's enemies: tortured prisoners lie on temple steps, while above them lords in jaguar robes are indifferent to their agony. A severed head rolls down the stairs and Chaan Muan II grasps a prisoner (who appears to be pleading for mercy) by the hair – clearly about to deal him the same fate. **Room 3** shows the price paid for victory: Chaan Muan's wife, **Lady Rabbit**, prepares to prick her tongue to let blood fall onto a paper in a pot in front of her. The smoke from burning the blood-soaked paper will carry messages to ancestor-gods. Other gorgeously dressed figures, their senses probably heightened by hallucinogenic drugs, dance on the temple steps.

Frontera Corozal and Yaxchilán

Fifteen kilometres beyond San Javier is the turn for **FRONTERA COROZAL**, the gateway to **Yaxchilán**, one of the most enigmatic Maya ruins in Mexico. The ancient city can only be approached by boat along the Río Usumacinta, and though Frontera is the point of embarkation there's not much in the village itself.

The turn-off to Frontera (*combi* drivers call this the *crucero de Corozal*) is marked by a *comedor* and shop selling basic supplies. If your *combi* doesn't go further, you can pick up a taxi for M$20 for the ride 15km down the road to town. On the edge of town, a kiosk collects a "conservation fee" of M$15 per person. Visitors' first destination is the *embarcadero* on the banks of the Usumacinta, where you catch the boats to Yaxchilán. There's a Mexican **immigration post** (see box, p.686, for border procedures) 200m back along the main road coming in, and the community **museum** (7am–7pm; free) is across the road. It showcases the history of the settlement, founded only in 1976, and the relationships between the Chol, Lacandón and Tzeltal people, local archeology (there are a few large stelae) and flora and fauna. Its **restaurant** also has one of the only **telephones** in the village. The true centre of the village – a couple of scrappy **plazas** and a market – is about 400m south from the main paved road and 300m back from the river; *combis* usually pass this way.

Should you want **to stay**, there are a few options. *Escudo Jaguar* (Ⓣ00502/5353-5637, in Guatemala, Ⓦwww.escudojaguarhotel.com; ❸ shared bath, ❹ private) is the longest-established place, and though its rooms are clean, spacious and comfortable, they're also the top choice for every tour group and can fill up early. Their bright-pink, concrete aesthetic may also not chime with your vision of ecotourism. The alternative is *Nueva Alianza* (Ⓣ00502/5353-1395, in Guatemala, Ⓦwww.ecoturlacandona.com; ❷ shared bath, ❸ private), behind the museum. It has big group rooms in wood cabañas (M$110/person), camping space (M$50 per tent) and private cabañas, many in an area kept dark at night, so you feel a bit more in the wilderness. Both hotels have decent **restaurants**, and there's one other very bare-bones operation selling fried chicken about 500m back along the main road.

Yaxchilán: the site

A larger and more dramatic site than Bonampak, **Yaxchilán** (daily 8am–4.30pm; M$49) was an important Classic-period centre. From around 680 to 760 AD, the city's most famous kings, Escudo Jaguar (Shield Jaguar) and his son Pájaro Jaguar IV (Bird Jaguar), led a campaign of conquest that extended Yaxchilán's sphere of influence over the other Usumacinta centres and made possible alliances with Tikal and Palenque. The buildings occupy a natural terrace above the river, with others climbing steep hills behind - a superb natural setting. Not so many people make the trip to this evocative site, and you'll often be alone in the forest with nothing but moaning howler monkeys around you. Giant trees keep the site shady, but nonetheless the jungle heat can be palpable – bring plenty of water, as there are no services at the ruins.

From the entrance, the main path leads straight ahead to the Gran Plaza, but if you have the energy for climbing, it's more rewarding to explore the wilder parts of the site first. Follow the branching path to the right that leads up the hillside to the **Pequeña Acrópolis**, a set of thirteen buildings. A lintel on the most prominent ruin, known as **Edificio 42**, depicts Escudo Jaguar with one of his warriors. Walk behind here to find another narrow trail down through the jungle, over several unrestored mounds, until you reach a fork: to the right, the path climbs steeply once again until it reaches, in about 10 minutes, Edificios 39–41, also called the **Templos del Sur**, 90m above the river level – buildings that probably had some kind of astronomical significance. High above the main forest, this is also a good spot to look for canopy-dwelling birds like parrots, though the trees also obscure any view.

Getting to Yaxchilán

To reach Yaxchilán, you need a *lancha* – a narrow riverboat with benches along the side and a tin roof for shade. A number of companies compete for business, but prices are all similar. If you're looking to share a boat to bring down the cost, your best bet is to head to the *embarcadero* at the riverfront. As with all the operations, fares here vary with group size, with one or two people paying M$680 between them, three paying M$780, four M$800 and so on up to the maximum of ten passengers. You could also check at *Escudo Jaguar*, as this is listed in many guidebooks as the main boat operator.

You also need to buy your **site entrance ticket** at the INAH office by the museum (or your boat company will send someone to buy it for you), as cash is not kept at the isolated ruins. You can also hire a **guide** here (M$280 for between one and three people), though only a few speak English; during high season (July, August, Christmas and Semana Santa), the guides wait at the site itself. The company, Siyaj Chan (Ⓣ00502/5047-5908, in Guatemala; Ⓦwww.siyajchan.blogspot.com), also leads six-hour **hiking trips** for M$1000 to Gruta Tzolkin, a cave deep in the forest.

The **river trip** is fabulous in itself, down a broad, fast-flowing river with Mexico on one bank, Guatemala on the other; depending on the state of the river the journey downstream to Yaxchilán takes around half an hour; the return can be twice as long. To allow enough time at the site, the latest you should get on a *lancha* is 2pm. If you're headed **back to Palenque** or Lacanjá Chansayab the same day, you'll have to go much earlier, as the last buses and *combis* leave from in front of the *embarcadero* at 4pm. The earliest you can leave for the site in the morning is 8am, when the INAH office opens.

Retrace your steps back to the main path, and continue on until it emerges at the back of **Edificio 33**, the most famous building at the site, also know as **El Palacio**. It overlooks the main plaza from a high terrace. The lintels here are superbly preserved, and inside one of the portals is a headless statue of Pájaro Jaguar IV. In ancient times the building was a political court; more recently, it served as a religious site for the Lacandón Maya.

Descending 40m down the stairs in front brings you to the long **Gran Plaza**. Turn back to look up at the Palacio: with the sun shining through the building's roofcomb and tree roots cascading down the stairs, this is what you imagine a pyramid lost in the jungle should look like, especially if you've been brought up on Tintin. To your left, just above the level of the plaza, **Edificio 23** has a few patches of coloured stucco around its doorframes – just one patch of many well-preserved paintings and relief carvings on the lintels of buildings surrounding the long green lawn. Some of the very best works were removed in the nineteenth century and are now in the British Museum in London, but the number and quality of the remaining panels are unequalled at any other Maya site in Mexico. Many of these depict rulers performing rituals. This can also be seen on **Stele 1**, right in the middle of the plaza, near the base of the staircase. It depicts Pájaro Jaguar IV in a particularly eye-watering bloodletting ceremony, ritually perforating his penis. **Stele 3,** originally sited at Edificio 41, has survived several attempts to remove it from the site and now lies at the west side of the plaza, where it shows the transfer of power from Escudo Jaguar to Pájaro Jaguar IV.

Heading back to the entrance, be sure to pass through **El Laberinto** (The Labyrinth) at the plaza's northeast corner, the most complex building on the site, where you can walk down through dim passages out onto the main path.

On from Frontera Corozal and Yaxchilán

Entering Guatemala is relatively easy, with plenty of *lanchas* between Frontera Corozal and **Bethél**, a thirty-minute boat ride upstream, plus any time spent waiting for the boat to fill up. Trips across to Bethél have a set fare of M$300 for one to two people and M$450 for four. There's a Guatemalan **immigration post** (see box, p.686, for border procedures) in Bethél, from where buses normally depart at noon and 5pm for **Flores** (for Tikal; US$5), a five-hour ride, mostly along dirt roads. Alternatively, you can **stay** in the simple but comfortable *Posada Maya* cabañas (❶), on the riverbank amid the small Maya **ruins of Bethél**.

Escudo Jaguar in Corozal can arrange trips **downstream from Yaxchilán** to the impressive ruins of **Piedras Negras** on the Guatemalan bank. If you go in a single, long day, it's M$3800 for one to five people; an overnight trip costs M$4400. There are rapids above the site, meaning you may well have to get out and walk along the bank at times. It's a beautiful journey, though, and well worth making if you have the time. Below the site the river speeds through two massive canyons.

The southern Usumacinta

Following the Frontier Highway south a further 35km from Frontera Corozal brings you past the tiny settlement of **BOCA LACANTÚN**, where a bridge carries the road over the enormous Río Lacantún. You can expect any bus along this road to be stopped by immigration or army officials, so keep your passport handy. At the confluence of the Lacantún and Usumacinta rivers is an unusual Maya monument, the **Planchon de Figuras**, a great limestone slab of unknown origin carved with glyphs, birds, animals and temples. If you're travelling by river, the beautiful **Chorro cascades** are just downstream.

Benemérito and onwards

The sprawling frontier town of **BENEMÉRITO**, 2km beyond Boca Lacantún, is the largest settlement in the Chiapas section of the Usumacinta valley, and an important centre for both river and road traffic. If you're **arriving by boat** from Guatemala you'll be met by Mexican soldiers who'll probably check your passport, though the nearest **immigration office** is at Frontera Corozal (see p.725). Along the highway, which is about 2km from the river, there's a hospital, market, shops, *comedores*, a petrol station and a few desperately basic **hotels**. Buses from Transportes Comitán Lagos de Montebello pull in on the highway at the southern end of town; they head north every couple of hours throughout the day, but the last one heading south along the Frontier Highway to Lagos de Montebello and Comitán passes through around 3pm. For information on the rest of the Frontier Highway, including the *Las Guacamayas* eco-lodge, see p.710.

By river to Sayaxché

If you hope to get by boat **from Benemérito to Sayaxché** in Guatemala you'll need patience, a good deal of money or both. **Trading boats** (taking at least 12hr) are the cheapest method of transport, but as there's no proper schedule you just have to hope there's one going when you want to. To reach Sayaxché in one day you'll need to leave early. Fast boats are now making the trip in less than three hours, stopping at the various sites en route, but you'll have to charter them at a cost of US$200–250 per boat. **Entering Guatemala**, you'll get your passport stamped at the army post at **Pipiles**, at the confluence with the Río de la Pasión. There's no Mexican immigration here; make sure you get an exit stamp in Frontera Corozal (see p.725).

Tabasco

Despite the best efforts of the state tourism board, few visitors view the state of **Tabasco** as more than a transit corridor for Palenque, as most people have to change buses in the capital city, **Villahermosa**. Crossed by numerous slow-moving tropical rivers on their way to the Gulf, the low-lying, humid region is the homeland of the ancient **Olmec**, **Maya** and **Zoque** cultures. There are numerous **archeological sites** here, such as **Comalcalco**, a Maya site north of Villahermosa, and the most important Olmec site, **La Venta**, west of the capital.

Villahermosa ("Beautiful Town"), the state capital, is often maligned for not living up to its name, but it has some attractive patches, notably the **Parque Museo La Venta**, a beautifully done outdoor archeological exhibition of the legendary Olmec stone heads, and the pedestrian-friendly historic downtown.

Tabasco's **coast**, alternating between estuaries and sand bars, salt marshes and lagoons, is off the beaten track for most visitors. Hwy-180 runs very close to the shore, however, enabling you to reach the beaches with relative ease. Though the sands are a bit buggy, and the views often marred by the offshore oil industry, they do have the virtue of being frequented only by locals, if at all. All have somewhat limited facilities – even the main coastal town, **Paraíso**, is a tiny place. Much of inland Tabasco is very flat, consisting of the flood plains of a dozen or so major rivers, which proved a hazard when floodwaters washed over the state in 2007 and 2008 – but, impressively, little evidence of these disasters remains. In fact, the state's borders are largely marked by rivers, and **boat trips** along the Grijalva and the Usumacinta are the best way to glimpse remote ruins and the region's abundant birdlife. You can also travel by river into the Petén in **Guatemala**, leaving from La Palma, near **Tenosique**, in the far eastern corner of the state and near the Classic Maya site of **Pomoná**.

In the far south of the state, around **Teapa**, the foothills of the **Sierra Puana** offer a retreat from the heat and humidity of the lowlands. Waterfalls spill down from the mountains, and a few small spas (*balnearios*) have developed. Village tracks provide some great **hiking trails** and, despite the proximity to Villahermosa, you can enjoy a respite from the well-travelled tourist circuit.

Tabasco **cuisine** relies heavily on tropical fruits and seafood, as well as the *pejelagarto*, or freshwater gar, a green-fleshed, pike-like fish that's usually barbecued and served with chile, lime and a salsa of deadly, caper-size chillies. But **Tabasco Sauce** isn't actually a speciality: although Tabasco peppers are named after the state, they don't grow here, and the celebrated condiment is an American product made from peppers grown in Louisiana.

Some history

Little is known about the **Olmec culture**, referred to by many archeologists as the mother culture of Mesoamerica. Its legacy, which included the Long Count calendar, glyphic writing, a rain deity and probably also the concept of zero and the ball-game, influenced all subsequent civilizations in ancient Mexico. The fact that it developed and flourished in the unpromising environment of the Gulf coast swamps 3200 years ago only adds to its mystery. Olmec civilization began to decline around 400 BC, and over the next thousand years the plains were gradually absorbed by the great Maya cities to the east, an influence most notable at **Comalcalco** (see p.739). After the collapse of Classic Maya civilization, Tabasco became something of a crossroads, its great rivers important trade routes to the interior, though its remaining Maya communities were relatively unorganized.

When **Hernán Cortés** landed at the mouth of the Río Grijalva in 1519, he easily defeated the local Chontal Maya. However, the town he founded, Santa María de la Victoria, was beset first by indigenous attacks and then by pirates, eventually forcing a move to the present site and a change of name to "Villahermosa de San Juan Bautista" in 1596. For most of the colonial period, Tabasco remained a relative backwater, since the Spanish found the humid, insect-ridden swamps distinctly inhospitable. **Independence** did little to improve matters, as local leaders fought among themselves, and it took the **French invasion** of 1862, and Napoleon III's imposition of the unfortunate Maximilian as emperor of Mexico, to bring some form of unity, though Tabasco offered fierce resistance to this foreign intrusion.

The industrialization of the country during the dictatorship of Porfirio Díaz passed agricultural Tabasco by, and even after the **Revolution** it was still a poor state, dependent on cacao and bananas. Though **Tomás Garrido Canabal**, Tabasco's socialist governor in the 1920s and 1930s, is still respected as a reformer whose laws regarding workers' rights and women's suffrage were decades ahead of the rest of the country, his period in office was also marked by intense **anticlericalism**. Priests were killed or driven out (a process vividly brought to life in Graham Greene's *The Power and the Glory*), all the churches were closed, and many of them, including the cathedral in Villahermosa, torn down. The region's **oil**, discovered in the 1930s but not fully exploited until the 1970s, provided the impetus to bring Tabasco into the modern world, enabling capital to be invested in the agricultural sector and Villahermosa to be transformed into the cultural centre it is today.

Villahermosa

VILLAHERMOSA, the state capital, is a virtually unavoidable road junction: sooner or later you're almost bound to pass through here on the way from central Mexico to the Yucatán or back, especially if you hope to see Palenque (see p.717). It's a large and prosperous city, and at first glance it can seem to be subject to as bad a case of urban blight as any in Mexico. The longer you stay, though, the more compensations you discover. Quite apart from the **Parque La Venta** and sudden vistas of the broad sweep of the **Río Grijalva**, there are attractive plazas, quiet old streets, impressive ultramodern buildings and several art galleries and museums. In the evening, as the traffic disperses and the city cools, its appeal is heightened, and strolling the pedestrianized streets around the **Zona Luz**, as the historic downtown core is known, or the lively malecón, where everything stays open late, becomes a genuine pleasure. Villahermosa's modern commercial centre, **Tabasco 2000**, 2km northwest of the Zona Luz, is a smart area of government buildings, a conference centre and high-end hotels, where oil-industry business travellers hang out.

Arrival, transport and information

Villahermosa's busy regional **airport**, the Aeropuerto Carlos A. Rovirosa, lies about 13km east of the centre on the main road towards Escárcega and Palenque. No buses run to the centre from here; a taxi will set you back around M$200. The **bus stations** are pretty close to each other northwest of the Zona Luz: the **first-class station** (known as El ADO – pronounced *ah-day-oh*) is a modern building on Javier Mina just off Ruíz Cortines. There's luggage storage and an information booth, usually unstaffed. *Combis* ply the road outside, but to **get to the Zona Luz** requires changing buses at the market – it's less hassle (and less confusing) to take a

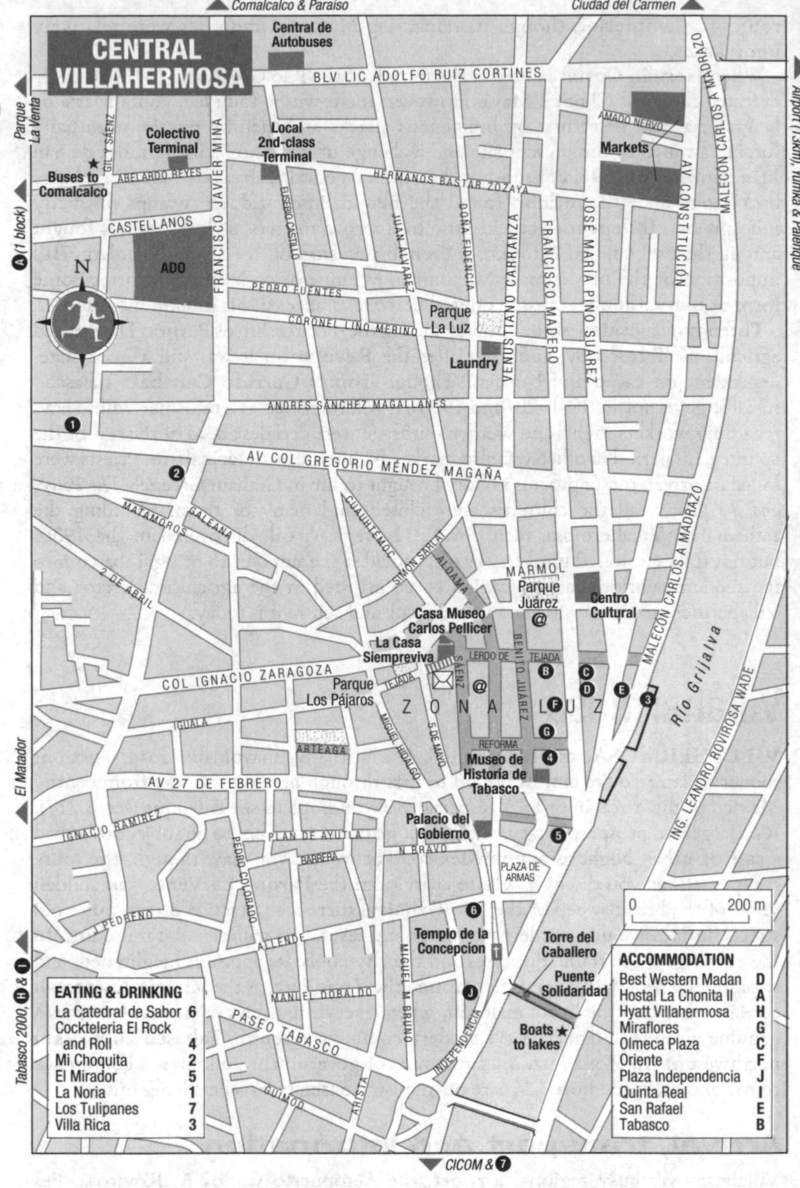

taxi (M$20). Walking takes around twenty minutes: head east on Merino or Fuentes, opposite the station, for six or seven long blocks, and then turn right (south) at Madero, which will eventually get you to the pedestrianized streets north of the Plaza de Armas.

Villahermosa's main **second-class** terminal, the Central de Autobuses, is on Ruíz Cortines. To walk into the centre, turn left on Ruíz Cortines, then follow the highway to its junction with Madero and turn right. Villahermosa's humidity might make you consider taking **taxis** more frequently – rates are M$20 within most of the city. The **local bus** system comprises a confusing jumble of *combi* minivans, with the **Mercado Pino Suárez** acting as the main hub. Fares are a standard M$5.

Despite the growth in visitor numbers in recent years, there's no handy **tourist office** in Villahermosa. Booths at the airport, history museum, Parque La Venta and ADO bus station can offer only leaflets, and the main state and federal office (Mon–Fri 8am–6pm, Sat 8am–1pm; ⓣ993/310-9700 ext 5238, ⓦwww.visitetabasco.com), on Avenida de los Ríos south of Paseo Tabasco in Tabasco 2000, is too far away from the centre to be of much use. To get to Tabasco 2000 from Parque Juárez, walk north along Madero and catch a *combi* marked "Fracc Carrizal".

Accommodation

Hotels in Villahermosa are no bargain on the low end, though you can find some reasonable-value places. Most of the **budget** options are on Madero or Lerdo de Tejada, close to the heart of things – though none is particularly praiseworthy. A few of the more **upmarket** hotels, on the other hand, are actually well priced when compared with more touristy cities, but a steady stream of PEMEX employees can keep the rooms full. With a couple of exceptions, these pricier places are located in the Tabasco 2000 district, about 2.5km west of the centre along Paseo Tabasco – this area isn't far from La Venta, but away from the centre.

Best Western Madan Madero 408 ⓣ993/314-0518, ⓦwww.bestwestern.com. Excellent-value mid-range option, with quiet a/c in the well-kept modern rooms and exceptionally nice staff. The café downstairs is a busy meeting place. If you need a place near the bus stations, try the equally good *Best Western Maya Tabasco* on Ruíz Cortines, midway between the two. ❺

Hostal La Chonita II Abelardo Reyes 217 ⓣ993/312-2053, ⓦwww.hostelachonita.com. Not a bargain hostel (M$150/person), but clean and lovely compared with the city's budget hotels, with bikes, wi-fi and a/c. Handy location near the bus stations.

Hyatt Villahermosa Juárez 106 ⓣ800/233-1234, ⓦwww.villahermosa.regency.hyatt.com. Best luxury hotel in town, close to the Laguna de Ilusiones and on the edge of Tabasco 2000, just off Paseo Tabasco. Comfortable, well-furnished a/c rooms and suites with beautiful tiled bathrooms, and big discounts at the weekends. Also has two of the best restaurants in town. ❼

Miraflores Reforma 304 ⓣ993/312-0022, ⓦwww.miraflores.com.mx. A bit cheaper than the *Best Western*, this independent hotel has all the same amenities (parking, a lobby bar and café, lobby wi-fi), though they're not all quite as slick and new. Rooms have nice balconies, and the staff are friendly. ❺

Olmeca Plaza Madero 418 ⓣ993/358-0102, ⓦwww.hotelolmecaplaza.com. Slick modern rooms, great locations and a swimming pool. Rack rates can seem a little steep, but desk clerks are often able to conjure up "promotions" if you look like you might head to rival *Best Western Madan*. ❺

Oriente Madero 425 ⓣ993/312-0121. The best of the budget options, though a bit pricier than its neighbours – you're paying for a big tile-floor room that's actually clean, with a very firm bed and a decent bathroom. The mint-green paint job and pink staircase are a bonus. ❸

Plaza Independencia Independencia 123 ⓣ993/312-1299, ⓦwww.hotelesplaza.com.mx. Comfortable, well-furnished rooms and suites in a quiet area just off the Plaza de Armas. Front rooms have balconies with views over the river. Room maintenance can be a little spotty, but there's a lift, a pool, a good restaurant, a bar with live music and secure parking. ❺

Quinta Real Paseo de la Choca 1402 ⓣ993/310-1300, ⓦwww.quintareal.com. The best of the city's luxury hotels, in grand mansion style, with vast rooms and two pools. It's 5km west from the centre, but right by the city's outer ring road, making it easily accessible for drivers, yet not too far from Parque La Venta. ❼

San Rafael Constitución 240 ⓣ993/312-0166. A bit ratty, but notable for its cheap fan-only rooms, and, perhaps more importantly, its splendid old tiled floors, soaring ceilings and brilliantly painted walls. A few rooms have a/c and TV, but for that, you're better off elsewhere. ❶

Tabasco Lerdo de Tejada 317 ⓣ993/312-0077. Of two adjacent budget hotels (the other is called *San Miguel*), this is the marginally better one: rooms (all with private bath) are small and spartan, but functional, and there are some quiet ones in the back of the building. ❷

The City

Most visitors to Villahermosa head straight out to **Parque La Venta**, the obvious highlight of the city, but the **Zona Luz** in the old centre also warrants some exploration. The narrow streets contain several absorbing museums and galleries, particularly the **Museo de Historia de Tabasco**, housed in one of the state's most ornate buildings. If you have more time, it's worth heading out to **Yumká**, an enjoyable safari park and ecological research centre.

Zona Luz

The oldest part of Villahermosa can be found **downtown**, in the **Zona Luz**, where vestiges of the nineteenth-century city (the original colonial buildings were built mostly of wood and have perished) survive on streets busy with shoppers and commerce. Many of the main shopping blocks are now pedestrianized, and the buildings along them are gradually being cleaned up and restored. At the northern end of the Zona, Parque Juárez, at the junction of Madero and Zaragoza, is bustling in the evenings, as crowds swirl around watching the street entertainers. Facing the plaza on the east side, the futuristic glass **Centro Cultural de Villahermosa** (Tues–Sun 10am–8pm; free) presents changing exhibitions of art, photography, and costume, as well as film screenings and concerts – stroll by and check out the schedule.

West of the park, on the corner of Sáenz and Lerdo de Tejada, the distinctive pink and purple paint on **La Casa Siempreviva** immediately catches the eye. One of the few fully restored houses from the early twentieth century, it has beautiful tiled floors and arched stained-glass windows. It's usually open as a gallery with a small café, and is the anchor for a bit of an arts scene in the surrounding blocks. Just a couple of doors down at Sáenz 203 is another old mansion turned into a museum – the **Casa Museo Carlos Pellicer** (Tues–Sat 10am–7pm, Sun 10am–4pm; free), filled with exhibits related to the life of Carlos Pellicer, a poet and anthropologist born in Villahermosa and the driving force behind the rescue of the stone carvings of La Venta. In the side streets round about are a number of other small **art galleries** – look for signs of current exhibitions. The steps at the far end of Lerdo lead up to the small, tree-shaded **Parque Los Pájaros**, where budgerigars sing in a large, globe-shaped cage.

Heading on south, Villahermosa's **Museo de Historia de Tabasco**, at the corner of 27 de Febrero and Juárez (Tues–Sun 9am–7pm; M$15), provides a quirky, detailed account of the state's development. The main attraction, however, is the 1915 building itself, tiled inside and out with colourful patterns from all over Europe and the Middle East – each room is different and dazzling.

A couple of blocks further south, the grand **Palacio del Gobierno** looks onto the **Plaza de Armas**, a patch of green adjacent to a sprawling expanse of concrete. You can poke your head inside the government building to see what temporary exhibition is on, but the building is attractive on its own, with classical columns, turreted corners and a clock tower. Across the park lies the pretty white **Templo de la Concepción** – commonly called "La Conchita". The church was first built here in 1799, but this and its successor were each demolished twice over – the present building dates only from 1945. Facing this traditional civic layout and overlooking the Río Grijalva is a more modern public space, usually busy in the cool of the evening, when there's often live music. Steps lead up to the **Puente Solidaridad** footbridge over the river, overshadowed by a rather bleak square tower, its observation deck unreliably open to the public. Cross the water to reach jetties with boats offering tours up and down the river, or walk back up to the cluster of riverside bars and restaurants adjacent to the Zona, where the *Capitán Beuló II* offers cruises (Tues–Sun 3.30pm & 6.30pm; M$90) – check at the *Olmeca Plaza* (see p.731).

If you're tempted, incidentally, by glimpsing the impressive-looking spires of Villahermosa's **Catedral del Señor de Tabasco**, know that it's a longer walk than it looks, about twenty minutes up Paseo Tabasco. Once you get there, you'll find that the spires are just about all that exists – the rest of the Gothic building, begun in 1973, is only very slowly being constructed.

The CICOM complex

A fifteen-minute walk south from the Zona Luz, or a short *combi* ride, brings you to Villahermosa's cultural centre, **CICOM** – the Centro de Investigaciones de las Culturas Olmeca y Maya. The complex includes a museum, concert hall, a beautiful theatre, a research library and a fine restaurant (see p.735), along with the centrepiece, the **Museo Regional de Antropología Carlos Pellicer Cámara**. Unfortunately, it is shut for a massive overhaul; the vast collection of Olmec and Maya artefacts is expected to reopen in late 2010 or early 2011; ask at the history museum before you make the trek. There are other small museums in the complex (devoted to music and contemporary art), but they don't merit a trip on their own.

Parque La Venta and the Museo de Historia Natural

A visit to Villahermosa's **Parque La Venta** (daily 8am–4pm; M$40) could easily fill half a day. The most important artefacts from the Olmec site of La Venta, some 120km west of Villahermosa, were transferred here in the late 1950s, when they were

▲ Great blue heron, Parque La Venta

threatened by Pemex oil explorations. Little is known about the **Olmec culture**, referred to by many archeologists as the mother culture of Mesoamerica (see p.873).

Just inside the entrance, a display familiarizes you with what little is known about the Olmecs, as well as the history of the discovery of La Venta. The most significant and famous items in the park are the four gigantic **basalt heads**, notable for their African-looking features. Additionally, there's a whole series of other Olmec stone sculptures. To conjure a jungle setting, monkeys, agoutis (large rodents) and coatis (members of the racoon family) wander around freely, while crocodiles, jaguars and other animals from the region are displayed in sizeable enclosures. At night, there's a rather good **sound-and-light show** (Tues–Sun at 8, 9 & 10pm; M$100) that involves strolling from monument to monument, dramatically illuminated amidst the shadowy trees – buy tickets and enter at a second gate, about 250m southwest along Paseo Tabasco.

Parque La Venta is set inside the much larger **Parque Tomás Garrido Canabal**, which stretches along the shore of an extensive lake, the **Laguna de Ilusiones**. There are walking trails here and boats for hire, or you can climb the Mirador de los Águilas, a tower in the middle of the lake. Also in the park, opposite the La Venta entrance, the small **Museo de Historia Natural** (Tues–Sun 9am–5pm; M$15) features displays on the geography, geology, animals and plants of Tabasco, focusing on the interaction between humans and the environment.

To get to La Venta, take a taxi or hop on one of the *combis* that run along Madero in the city centre ("Tabasco 2000", "Circuito 1", "Parque Linda Vista", "Fracc Carrizal", among others); they also run along the highway from the second-class bus terminal. A taxi from the centre costs M$40.

Beyond La Venta, many of the *combis* continue down Paseo Tabasco to the **Tabasco 2000** area. This extension of the city is an impressive, if soulless, example of modern Mexican architecture, with concrete shopping malls, government buildings and a planetarium, as well as a number of large hotels.

Yumká

Villahermosa's major ecological attraction, **Yumká** (daily 9am–5pm, last entry 4pm; Ⓦwww.yumka.org; M$50, children M$25), named for the Chontal Maya dwarf-god who looks after forests, is an enjoyable combination of a safari park and an environmental studies centre. The park covers more than six square kilometres, so after a guided walking tour of the Tabasco jungle, complete with monkeys, you board a train for a tour round paddocks representing the savannas of Africa and Asia. Elephants, rhinos, giraffes and antelopes are rarely displayed in Mexico and almost never in such spacious surroundings. After a stop at the **restaurant**, you can take a boat tour of the lagoon (M$20), where, in addition to hippos, there are good bird watching opportunities.

Yumká is 14km from the centre of Villahermosa, just past the airport. **Combis** leave regularly from along Amado Nervo behind the market at the top end of Avenida Constitución, and a park-operated **shuttle bus** (M$15) departs from Ruíz Cortines, west of Parque La Venta, on weekends at 9am, 10.30am, noon and 1.30pm. A taxi costs M$170.

Eating and drinking

The Zona Luz boasts mostly **fast food** – with a couple of exceptions noted below. Head for Calle Aldama, north of its junction with Lerdo de Tejada: right on this junction there's a *Flor de Michoacan* ice-cream place, and heading up Aldama you'll find half a dozen taco joints. As ever, the **market** – here, a vast, tidy two-storey complex trimmed with white wrought-iron trellises – is good for fruit, bread, and cheap tacos: it's several blocks north of the Zona Luz on Constitución. For **nightlife**, check out the various nightclubs on the malecón around 27 de Febrero, some facing the river and others on structures jutting into the river – they're all far smarter than you might expect.

La Catedral de Sabor Independencia, adjacent to the Templo de la Concepción. Cool down with a refreshing *horchata de coco* – a Tabasco speciality – at this little sidewalk stand. You can also sit down inside, in a more formal café.

Cockteleria El Rock and Roll Reforma 307. A bustling place with excellent seafood cocktails (M$80), *ceviche* and prawns, accompanied by, yes, blaring rock-and-roll from the jukebox. There's slightly quieter seating upstairs.

Mi Choquita Javier Mina 304-A. No-frills local place with plastic tables and chairs offering good breakfasts from M$25 and regional dishes in a typical Tabascan style as well as Spanish/Castilian classics like roast lamb – there's a decent *menu del día* for M$43.

El Mirador Madero 105. Seafood restaurant with river views and a slightly time-warp classiness. Prices are not unreasonable – a full dinner runs about M$300 per person. Mon–Sat noon–8pm.

La Noria Gregorio Méndez 1008. Very cheap Lebanese and Middle Eastern restaurant with food you are unlikely to find elsewhere in the state.

Los Tulipanes In the CICOM complex. A lovely riverfront restaurant, a bit formal and unstinting on the a/c. Come here to sample delicious renditions of Tabasco cuisine: shrimp with coconut and passionfruit salsa, fresh corn tortillas stuffed with seafood, crab soup. Very well priced, considering the massive portions. Open till 6pm.

Villa Rica Corredor Turístico Malecón (end of Zaragoza) ⓣ993/312-1801. One of the best options on the waterfront, with excellent seafood, prawns and shellfish and a smart riverside setting (mains from M$100). Handy for a post-dinner bar crawl along the malecón.

Listings

Airlines Aeromar, Av de los Ríos 1110, Plaza Usumacinta, Tabasco 2000 ⓣ993/316-8510; Aeroméxico, Carlos Pellicer Cámara 511 ⓣ993/314-9262; Mexicana, Vía 3, no. 120 Local 5 y 6 Plaza D'Atocha Mall, in Tabasco 2000 ⓣ993/316-3132.

Banks and exchange There are branches of all major banks at the airport and in the centre, on Madero or Juárez, and you can easily change cash and travellers' cheques. Most banks have ATMs.

Internet access Try Ciberware at Aldama 521 (M$5/hr) or G&C on Zaragoza (daily 9am–1am; M$10/hr). Opposite the ADO station, Blue Network Internet is open similar hours (M$5/hr).

Laundry Lavandería La Paz, on Coronel Lino Merino 403, near Madero (8am–8pm Mon–Sat, 8am–2pm Sun; M$18/kg).

Post office The main post office is in the Zona Luz at Sáenz 131 on the corner of Lerdo (Mon–Fri 9am–3pm, Sat 9am–1pm).

Travel agents and tours There's no shortage of travel agencies in the Zona Luz, and all the big hotels have a tour desk to arrange domestic flights and trips to Palenque. Creatur, Paseo Tabasco 1404, on the right just beyond Ruíz Cortines (ⓣ993/310-9900, ⓦwww.creaturviajes.com), is the best in the region, with multilingual staff.

South of Villahermosa

South of Villahermosa is an area of exceptionally beautiful highland. The foothills of the Sierra de Chiapas are heavy with banana plantations, but higher up, thick forest remains, and the roadside pools and wetlands are as wild as ever. The highlights of this region include numerous **caves and grottoes**, as well as several accessible spas, created by tectonic activity, in the main town of **Teapa**. From here, you can catch a series of second-class buses over the mountains, a good slow route into the mountains of Chiapas.

Moving on from Villahermosa

Villahermosa is a regional transport hub, with excellent air and bus connections to every corner of the country and state.

To get to the **ADO bus station** from the centre, catch a *combi* from the malecón heading for "Chedraui". From here, ADO, OCC and TRT operate dozens of services to all major destinations. The front of the station deals with services originating here; tickets for *de paso* services are sold in a separate complex behind. Services include Campeche (19 daily), Cancún (19 daily), **Emiliano Zapata** (4 daily), **Frontera** (26 daily), Mérida (19 daily), Mexico City (21 daily), Oaxaca (3 daily, in the evening), Palenque (12 daily), **Tenosique** (13 daily), **Tuxtla Gutiérrez** (19 daily, most via Puente Chiapas) and Veracruz (23 daily). There are five buses to San Andrés Tuxtla, most in the morning. Most buses into Chiapas travel via Puente Chiapas, which seems circuitous but knocks several hours off the journey. For **San Cristóbal**, there are just three direct services; it's often easier to change at either Tuxtla or **Palenque**.

The **Central de Autobuses** (the main second-class terminal) has buses to virtually everywhere in the state and all the main cities beyond, including **Tenosique** ten times a day (5am–5.30pm), **Teapa** every half-hour (5am–9pm; 1hr), and **Tacotalpa** and **Coatzacoalcos** (the latter for La Venta; 2hr 30min), on the same schedule. There's another, more dilapidated second-class terminal near the ADO, off Eusebio Castillo near Zozaya, with frequent buses to Emiliano Zapata, Frontera and Paraíso, as well as Palenque and Escárcega. Several companies run buses to **Comalcalco** (1hr), the best of which is Comalli Bus, on Gil y Sáenz above Abelardo Reyes, not far from the ADO (4.45am–10pm). Just south of here on Gil y Sáenz, *combis* run to Nacajuca (for Cupilco; 30min), and pale yellow *colectivos* go from Castellanos, just east of Gil y Sáenz. Just to the north, off Ruíz Cortines, La Sultana runs a comfortable service to Teapa (5am–10.30pm, every 30min). **Shared taxis** are usually faster and not that much more expensive: the terminal is just north of the ADO on Abelardo Reyes. Taxis leave when full for Palenque, Paraíso, Frontera and Tacotalpa, taking four or five people, but you won't have to wait long, at least in the morning.

From the **airport** (☎993/356-0157), flights depart for Mérida, Mexico City, Poza Rica and Veracruz. Continental flies to Houston, Texas, once a day.

For further information, see Travel details, p.746.

Teapa and the southern hills

Fifty-nine kilometres to the south of Villahermosa, the small, friendly town of **TEAPA** is a lovely base for the spas and caves nearby. Most second-class buses pull in at the **market** near the edge of town: to get to the centre, walk a couple of blocks down the hill and turn left at the green clock onto Méndez, which takes you to the plaza. Teapa's **hotels** are good value: try the *Quintero* (☎932/322-0045; ❸) at Eduardo Rosario Bastar 108, which has comfortable modern rooms.

There's swimming in the Río Teapa in town, but it's better on the **Río Puyacatengo** (open daily; free, vehicles M$5), 3km east (walk or take the bus for Tacotalpa; taxis charge M$15). Follow signs for *balnearios* just off the road to the right of the bridge, where big natural pools form in the river, and several restaurants serve food. Two-bed cabañas here cost M$200. Eight kilometres west of Teapa, on the old mountain highway to Tuxtla Gutiérrez, the **Hacienda Los Azufrés spa** has a classy hotel (☎932/327-5806; ❹) with a huge pool, spa baths and a restaurant serving local specialities, including *pejelagarto*. You can also organize guided walks, rent bikes and camp here (M$65), and fishing rods are also available to rent; if you're not staying overnight, the spa pools cost M$30. Catch a second-class bus towards Pichucalco.

Green-and-white *colectivos* run from Bastar, next to the plaza in Teapa, to the spectacular **Grutas del Coconá** (daily 9am–5pm; M$30), 4km northeast. Eight chambers are open to tourists. A stroll through the caves, which also contain a small museum displaying pre-Hispanic artefacts found inside, takes about 45 minutes. They're surprisingly humid, lined with oddly shaped stalactites and stalagmites. You could also walk to the caves from Teapa (45min): from Méndez, head for the Pemex station and turn right, following the sign. When you get near the forested hills, the road divides; bear left and cross over the rail track.

Tapijulapa

To escape the humidity of the lowlands, head up the valley of the Río Oxolotán to the Sierra Puana, Tabasco's "hill country". This is an extraordinarily picturesque area, with quiet colonial towns set in beautiful wooded valleys, and a turquoise river laden with sulphur. The main destination is **TAPIJULAPA**, a beautiful whitewashed village with narrow cobbled streets that could, at first glance, be mistaken for a mountain town in Spain. It's celebrated for its wicker craftsmen, who have workshops all over town, and as the starting point for a beautiful natural park. If you're just going for the day, you'll need to make a fairly early start. To get to the village from Teapa, take a bus to Tacotalpa from the OCC terminal on Méndez (every 30min; 20min), then on to Tapijulapa (hourly departures; 45min). The last bus back to Teapa (with connections to Villahermosa) leaves at 7pm, but there are also a couple of simple and relaxing **places to stay**. *Posada Don Julian* (Ⓣ932/322-4007; ❶) is on the main plaza, with a restaurant at street level and a row of four basic (cold water, fan only) but tidy en-suite rooms just below, opening onto the river. *Hotel Comunitario* (no tel; ❶), with three rooms, is further along the main street on the left, under the arcades. From the edge of the village, the main street, Avenida López Portillo, leads downhill to a pretty little **plaza**; on weekends, local women serve exceptionally delicious tamales and other inexpensive **food** in the large civic building.

But you probably won't make it this far before you're accosted by kids offering to take you to **boats** for the **Parque Natural Villa Luz** (daily 8am–5pm; free), with its spa pools, cascades and caves. Two companies charge the same price (M$30 round trip, with two hours' waiting time) for the short ride upstream; the better established operation is past the plaza: follow López Portillo till it dead-ends, then turn right to the river. The natural park's outstanding feature – not least for its powerful aroma – is the stream running through it, which owes its cloudy blue-white colour to dissolved minerals, especially sulphur. Where it meets the Río Oxolotán, it breaks into dozens of cascades and semicircular pools. Thousands of butterflies settle on the riverbanks, taking nourishment from dissolved minerals, and jungle trees and creepers grow wherever they find a foothold – a truly primeval sight. From the boat dock, well-signed trails (no need for a guide) lead 1.5km to the waterfalls, passing the **Casa Museo Tomás Garrido Canabal** (daily 8am–5pm; free), the country retreat of Canabal, the controversial former governor of Tabasco, which contains a few of his personal effects as well as Zoque artefacts and handicrafts from the area. Another path leads to the **Cuevas de las Sardinas Ciegas** – the caves of "blind sardines", sightless fish with translucent scales that have adapted to the cave's sulphur-rich waters. The gases in the cave are so powerful that it's impossible to breath inside, but you can peer into their precipitous entrances. In Maya cosmology the openings are believed to lead to the underworld (Xibalba). During Semana Santa, the local people catch the fish and dedicate them to the rain god, Chac. Beyond the caves are a couple of *albercas*, stream-fed **swimming pools** said to have therapeutic properties.

You can also take an easy three-kilometre **walk** to the park: cross the tributary river on the suspension bridge (to the right before you reach the plaza), head left on the concrete path, across the football field, then follow the track over the hill, keeping close to the main river – about 35 minutes in all. And for those travelling by **car**, the main entrance to the park is on the main highway toward Oxolotán, a few kilometres past the turn for Tapijulapa.

West of Villahermosa

West of Villahermosa the main attractions are a series of isolated ruins, the most famous being the Olmec site at **La Venta**, although the best pieces now reside in Villahermosa. The little-known ancient Zoque people also flourished in this area, and the ruins at **Malpasito** reflect that unique culture.

La Venta

The small town of **LA VENTA**, on the border between Tabasco and Veracruz, 128km from Villahermosa, would be of little interest were it not for the nearby **archeological ruins** (daily 10am–5pm; M$37). The town is served by a steady stream of **buses** from Villahermosa and Coatzalcoalcos (see box, p.736), so there's no need or real reason to stay. The ancient city, the name of which remains unknown, was occupied by the Olmecs between 1200 and 400 BC and is regarded as their most important centre. Most of the finest pieces found here, including the famous **basalt heads** – extraordinary because the material from which they were hewn does not occur locally in the region and must have been imported from what is now Veracruz, Oaxaca or Guatemala – were transferred to Villahermosa's Parque La Venta in 1957 and 1958. The **museum** at the entrance to the site (800m north of the bus station) has a model of the grounds, as well as glass cases with rather confusing displays of unlabelled pottery. The site itself retains some replicas of the sculptures and heads now displayed in Villahermosa, and few weathered stelae and monuments, but the highlight is the huge grass-covered mound, about 30m high, clearly a pyramid, with fluted sides believed to represent the ravines on the flanks of a sacred volcano. The climb up is worth the effort for the views and the breeze. Paths below take you through the jungle – fascinating for its plants and butterflies, but haunted by ferocious mosquitoes.

Malpasito

Some 100km southwest of Villahermosa, between the borders of Veracruz and Chiapas, a narrow triangle of Tabasco thrusts into mountains known as the **Sierra Huimanguillo.** These rugged peaks are not that high, only up to 1000m, but in order to fully appreciate them, you'll need to do some hiking: not only to canyons and waterfalls, but also to the ruins of **MALPASITO** (daily 9am–4pm; M$31), with their astonishing **petroglyphs**. A car, however, is necessary. Although you can get to the ruins by bus, it arrives too late to visit the ruins, and there is no reliable overnight accommodation in the village (a small guest cabin was under repair in 2009; in a pinch, ask in the village for Guillermo Pérez, who rents rooms).

The site and waterfalls

The post-Classic **Zoque** ruins are overshadowed by jagged, jungle-covered mountains, the highest point in Tabasco. Though the ruins bear a certain resemblance to Palenque (see p.718), the Zoque were not a Maya group – one of the few things known about them. On the way into the site you pass terraces and grass-covered mounds, eventually arriving at the unique **ball-court** (see p.876). At the top of the stone terraces forming the south side of the court, a flight of steps leads down to a narrow room, with stone benches lining either side. Beyond this, and separate from the chamber, is a square pit more than two metres deep and 1.5m wide. This room may have been used by the ball-players to make a spectacular entrance as they emerged onto the top of the ball-court.

But the most amazing features of this site are its **petroglyphs**. More than three hundred have been discovered so far: animals, birds, houses and more, etched into the rock. One large boulder is covered in enigmatic flat-topped triangles surmounted by a square or rectangle, and shown above what look like ladders or steps – stylized houses or launching platforms for the chariots of the gods, depending on your viewpoint.

While in the area, you can cool off at the nearby **Cascadas Las Pavas** (9am–5pm; M$50), a beautiful set of waterfalls, set in a tranquil spot down a path through dense flowering trees, and often surrounded by butterflies. To get here, backtrack along the road to town, and bear left at the fork.

Comalcalco and the north coast

The journey from Villahermosa along **the coast**, either west to Veracruz or east to Campeche, is extraordinarily beautiful. The road hugs the shore, and it's never hard to find deserted beaches and lagoons. Attractive as the coastal route is, it's undeniably slow and almost no tourists travel it, preferring the inland route to the Yucatán in order to stop by Palenque on the way. Even if this is your intention, you'll be well rewarded by spending a day north of Villahermosa, at the ruins of **Comalcalco**.

Cupilco

On the road north from Villahermosa to Comalcalco, you wind through the heart of Tabasco's **cacao-growing region**, with a few minor diversions along the way. Thirty kilometres out of Villahermosa, the main road passes through **CUPILCO**, notable for its roadside church, the **Templo de la Virgen de la Asunción**. Decorated in gold and blue with floral patterns, it's a beautiful example of the distinctive *tabasqueño* approach to sacred spaces. In the area around Comalcalco several **cacao haciendas** have opened their doors to visitors. The first you pass, 2km before Comalcalco, is Hacienda de la Luz (Ⓣ933/334-1126), which runs a **chocolate museum** (M$30), while Hacienda Cholula (Ⓣ933/334-3815) is a further 3km beyond the ruins. Either makes a pretty diversion if you're in your own car; bus travellers will find Hacienda Cholula a little easier to reach, as it's just off the main highway.

Comalcalco

The Classic-period site of **COMALCALCO** (daily 8am–5pm; M$41 including museum), 58km north of Villahermosa, is an easy, very worthwhile trip from the city. The westernmost Maya site, Comalcalco was occupied around the same time as Palenque (250–900 AD), with which it shares some features, and it may have been ruled by some of the same kings. The area's lack of building stone forced the Chontal Maya to adopt a distinctive form of construction: kiln-fired brick. As if the bricks themselves were not sufficient to mark this site as different, the builders added mystery to technology: each brick was stamped or moulded with a geometric or representational design before firing, with the design deliberately placed facing inwards, so that it could not be seen in the finished building.

Most **buses from Villahermosa** (see box, p.736) take an hour and a quarter; you'll likely be dropped off at or near the ADO terminal on the main highway (Comalcalco is west of the road). Green *combis* (M$5), found outside the ADO terminal, ply the route to the ruins, and any second-class bus heading north will pass by, but you'll have to walk about 1km to the site entrance. Ask the driver for "ruinas", or get off after about five minutes, when you see the sign. The ruins are on the right along a long straight paved road; some *combis* go all the way there, but otherwise it's a fifteen-minute walk. Taxis charge M$20. There's a small **restaurant** and toilets at the site, and plenty of buses back to Villahermosa (look for TRT buses, which take the fast route via Cárdenas, every 45 minutes, or Allegro and Comalli buses, which go via Cupilco) or on to Paraíso (20min), running along the highway.

The museum

You can see the astonishing designs on the bricks in Comalcalco's marvellous **museum**, though the labels are in Spanish only. Animals depicted include crocodiles, turtles, frogs, lizards, dogs and mice, while those portraying the sculpted faces of rulers display an advanced level of artistic development. One of the most amazing figures is of a skeleton that appears to be leaping out at you from the surface of the brick. The abundant clay that provided such a versatile medium for architects and artists here also formed the basis for many more mundane artefacts. Comalcalco means "place of the *comales*" – fired clay griddles for cooking tortillas – and these and other clay vessels have been excavated in great numbers. Some of the largest jars were used as **funerary urns** and several are on display here, including one with an intact skeleton.

The site

Though there are dozens of buildings at Comalcalco, only around ten or so of the larger ones have been restored. Because the brickwork is so fragile, you're not allowed to enter or climb on many of them, but you can follow a path up to Structure 3 and around the Palacio. Entering the site, you first come to **Temple I**, the main structure of the **North Plaza Cluster**, a tiered pyramid with a massive central stairway. Originally, the whole building (like all of the structures here) would have been covered with stucco made from oyster shells, sculpted into masks and reliefs of rulers and deities, and brightly painted. Only a few of these features remain – the exposed ones protected from further erosion by shelters, while others have been deliberately left buried. Facing Temple I at the opposite end of the site is the **Gran Acrópolis**, a complex of buildings, some still being excavated, raised above the plaza. Here you can climb up to **El Palacio** for some excellent close-up views of the brickwork, including a series of massive brick piers and arches that once formed an enormous double corbelled vault, 80m long and over 8m wide – one of the largest enclosed spaces the Maya ever built. There's a fine stucco mask of Kinich Ahau, the Maya sun god, on **Templo VI**, and at the side of **Temple V** a small, corbel-arched room contains stucco reliefs of nine, richly dressed, half-life-size figures apparently in conversation or even argument – they may represent the **Lords of Xibalba**, the Maya underworld.

The north coast

Skirting the coast and passing through areas of wetland teeming with wildlife, the little-travelled **north coast** road is a treat. Mangroves and lagoons are covered with flocks of feeding water birds, and if you look hard enough you may spot the odd crocodile. However, if it's beaches that you've come for, you are likely to be disappointed – the sand is grey-brown and, though generally clean, you've always got the oil refinery in sight to the east. There are few hotels along this stretch, but plenty of spaces for **camping** – if you can stand the swarms of mosquitoes and sandflies.

Paraíso

If you want to travel on the coastal route, catch one of the frequent buses passing the Comalcalco turn-off to **PARAÍSO**, 17km away on the banks of the Río Seco. A weekend escape for Villahermosa residents, it's a sleepy place, with some beaches nearby – pleasant enough if you need to wind down, and a better place to spend the night than Frontera (see below). Paraíso's ADO **bus station** is 1km south of the centre along Benito Juárez, the main road. Turn right out of the station and keep walking: eventually you'll see the town's most distinctive monument – the twin-towered colonial church – across the river up ahead. The main second-class station, with departures for points along the coast, is north of the centre and well served by *combis*; to make the fifteen-minute walk, turn south (left) and aim for the church towers. One quality **hotel** is *Sabina*, on the east side of the plaza (Ⓣ933/333-0016; ④), with freshly painted, clean air-conditioned rooms with TV, private bathrooms and drinking water. There are plenty of juice bars around the plaza and a couple of decent, moderately priced **restaurants**: *Real de la Costa* on the east side is good, with a wide selection of Mexican food, meats, pastas and seafood dishes. The nearest beach, **Playa Limón**, where locals go for picnics on weekends, is a twenty-minute *combi* ride north of Paraíso. **Taxis** to the beaches cost M$30, and there are a couple of daily first-class buses to Frontera.

Puerto Ceiba and the coast road east

Ten kilometres east of Paraíso, the road passes through **PUERTO CEIBA** on the shores of the **Laguna de Mecoacán**. There's a *parador turístico* here offering boat trips (M$280 for up to fourteen people) and a restaurant serving regional dishes and fish straight out of the lake. The road then crosses **Laguna Santa** to the east, and there are turn-offs for several decent beaches before it meets Hwy-180, 50km or so north of Villahermosa. The first is **Playa Azúl**, where you can rent boats and jet skis; **Playa Pico de Oro**, 6km or so further on, is more tranquil. If you're travelling light you could easily camp at any of these and get back to the main road in the morning.

Frontera and the Pantanos de Centla Biosphere Reserve

About 50km beyond Paraíso the bus will drop you in **FRONTERA**, a pleasant, if uninspiring, working town and port – once the main port for southern Mexico, as river steamers provided the only access to the roadless interior. Graham Greene visited in 1938 and wrote about it (in less than flattering terms) in *The Lawless Roads*, but the town has changed little since then, and now the sole reason most people stay is to visit the 17,200-square-kilometre **Pantanos de Centla Biosphere Reserve**. Among the more exotic species protected here (few of which you are actually likely to encounter) are jaguar and tapir, osprey and tiger heron, and, in the water, manatee and crocodile; the mangrove forests are also full of rare orchids and bromeliads. To get into the reserve, you will almost certainly need your own transport, unless you're lucky enough to catch one of the few *combis* to Jonuta – head through Frontera and continue west on the highway a few kilometres, then take the Jonuta road, just before the huge bridge over the river. Ten kilometres south, on the riverbank, the Desarrollo Ecoturístico Punta Manglar (ⓣ913/398-1688; open daily, but most activities available only at weekends) offers guided walks, canoe and ferry trips, and other educational **activities** in the reserve, plus it has a small **restaurant** for refreshment. A few kilometres further down, the Centro de Interpretación Uyotot-Já (Tues–Sun 9am–5pm; M$20 admission includes a guided tour; ⓣ913/131-3274) is a larger tourist centre with an observation tower, restaurant, boat trips (from about M$500 for up to ten people) and walkways over the marshy riverbanks. There are also a few cabañas here for **spending the night**, plus a restaurant.

If you **arrive in Frontera** by second-class bus, turn left out of the bus station and walk two blocks along Madero to get to the plaza or, from the first-class bus station, left along Zaragoza, then right, and walk three blocks down Madero from the other direction. **Buses** for Villahermosa or Ciudad del Carmen leave every one or two hours during daylight hours, and four buses daily go to Veracruz. Everything you'll need is around the tastefully modern plaza, including a couple of nondescript **hotels**; the renovated *Marmor Plaza* (ⓣ913/332-0001; ④) at Juárez 202, just left of the delicate Gothic-style church, is the best option, with reasonable-value rooms equipped with air-conditioning. For tasty shrimp or a hearty comida corrida, try *El Conquistador*, in an old colonial building, at Juárez 8.

East to the Usumacinta and Guatemala

Heading east from Villahermosa, Hwy-186 cuts across northern Chiapas before swinging north into Campeche to Francisco Escárcega, then east again as the only road across the base of the Yucatán Peninsula to Chetumal. At Catazajá, in Chiapas, 110km from Villahermosa, is the junction for **Palenque**. If you've already been there and want to see Tikal in Guatemala's Petén, you can go via **Tenosique** and **La Palma**, although it's quicker and cheaper to go from Frontera Corozal (see p.727); however, if you go this way, through this odd, seldom-visited side of Tabasco, you could stop at the nearby ruins of **Pomoná**. You'll pass through the town of **Emiliano Zapata** on the way, though there's little reason to stop unless you're coming from Palenque, in which case you'll probably need to change buses here.

Tenosique

Road and railway cross the Río Usumacinta at Boca del Cerro, 8km southwest of **TENOSIQUE**, where the now placid river leaves some pretty impressive hills. **Buses** arrive at a small terminal close to the highway, 2.5km out of town. Inexpensive *colectivos* and shared taxis (M$20) run frequently to the centre; get off when you see a large white church with red trim on the right. Streets are numbered according to the Yucatán system, with even numbers running north–south, and odd numbers running east–west. Between the main street, Calle 26 (also called Pino Suárez), which leads up to the plaza, and Calle 28, you'll find pretty much everything you needs.

There's not a lot to do in Tenosique. Its main claim to fame is as the birthplace of Mexican national hero Pino Suárez (September 8, 1869). His former house is on Calle 26, across the road from the church towards the plaza; it's now painted blue and white, as it's the offices of Telcel. If you have **to stay**, *Hacienda Tabasqueña*, C 26 no. 512 (☎934/342-2731; ❷), is the best option, with comfortable, spacious en-suite rooms, some with air-conditioning (❸). Most of the **restaurants** in the centre are unimpressive and cheap, and have similar menus. A row of inexpensive *comedores* lines the front of the market, just off the northwest corner of the plaza, while *Los Tulipanes*, on the corner of calles 27 and 22, has a somewhat better menu of Tabasco specialities, including *pejelagarto*. It's under a large palapa and features live marimba in the afternoons, though it tends to close in the early evening. Several places with **internet** access are along Calle 28, charging around M$10 an hour.

If you are going **to Guatemala** you'd be wise to stock up on provisions here: there's a good **bakery** opposite the *Hotel Roma*. The **banks** in Tenosique aren't interested in changing money, but Bancomer on the plaza has an ATM; for Guatemalan quetzales ask around in the shops on Calle 28, where you should find someone who will give better rates than the boatmen. For **moving on**, there are at least thirteen daily bus services to Villahermosa. For the Yucatán, there are four buses to Escárcega and points east in the evening up to 8pm, but otherwise it's best to get one of the frequent buses to **Emiliano Zapata** and change there.

The ruins of Pomoná

On the road from Emiliano Zapata, about 30km west of Tenosique, the ruins of **Pomoná** (daily 10am–5pm; M$34) are reached 4km down a signed track. Although the site, located in rolling countryside with views of forested hills to the south, makes a pleasant diversion, a visit is really only for the dedicated. The restored structures date from the Late Classic period; the site's largest building is a stepped pyramid with six levels. Pomoná was a subject of the much larger city of Piedras Negras in Guatemala, further up the valley of the Usumacinta. The small **museum** (daily 10am–4pm) houses some interesting carved panels and stelae, made even more mysterious by the omission of any explanations as to what you're seeing.

Reforma and the Reserva Ecológica Cascadas de Reforma

North of Tenosique a road heads about 70km through the **Reserva Ecológica Cascadas de Reforma** (daily 8am–6pm; M$22), where the Río San Pedro forms four pretty waterfalls. There's a swimming area in the natural pools here, along with restaurants and toilets. Major excavations at the site of **Moral-Reforma** in mid-2009 uncovered an amazing collection of stucco decoration, stelae and masks; expect the site to reopen to the public, with these new finds, in late 2010.

El Ceibo and the Río San Pedro to Guatemala

It's more convenient to enter Guatemala at the heavily policed border crossing of **EL CEIBO**, 60km southeast of Tenosique, rather than the town of La Palma, cutting travel time to Flores to around six hours in total. **Buses** leave Tenosique every hour from 6am to 5pm behind the market on the corner of calles 45 and 16, and take an hour to reach the border. From there, you can pick up a minibus (about M$30) to cross the new bridge to El Naranjo in Guatemala – but be sure to get your passport stamped by both Mexican and Guatemalan

Fiestas

The states of Chiapas and Tabasco are extremely rich in festivals. Local tourist offices should have more information on what's happening.

January

New Year's Day (Jan 1). San Andrés Chamula and San Juan Chamula (see p.703), both near San Cristóbal, have civil ceremonies to install a new government for the year.

Día de San Sebastián (Jan 20). In Chiapa de Corzo (see p.693), a large fiesta with traditional dances (including the masked *parachicos*) lasts several days, with a re-enactment on Jan 21 of a naval battle on the Río Grijalva. The event is big, too, in Chamula and Zinacantán (see p.704), near San Cristóbal.

February

Día de la Candelaria (Feb 2). Colourful celebrations at Ocosingo (see p.711).

Fiesta de San Caralampio (Feb 11–20). In Comitán (see p.705), celebrated with a parade to San Caralampio church, where elaborate offerings are made and dances held in the plaza outside.

Carnaval (the week before Lent; variable Feb–March). Celebrated in hundreds of villages throughout the area, but at its most frenzied in the big cities, especially Villahermosa (see p.729). San Juan Chamula (see p.703) also has a big fiesta.

March

Anniversary of the foundation of Chiapa de Corzo (March 1). Town fair with kiddie rides, live music and more.

Semana Santa (Holy Week). Widely observed. There are particularly big ceremonies in San Cristóbal de las Casas (see p.694). Ciudad Hidalgo (see p.686), at the border near Tapachula, has a major week-long market.

April

Feria de San Cristóbal de las Casas (April 1–7). Festival in San Cristóbal de las Casas (see p.694) celebrating the town's foundation. A Spring Fair is generally held here later in the month.

Feria de Villahermosa (second half of April). Villahermosa (see p.729) hosts its annual festival, with agricultural and industrial exhibits and the election of the queen of the flowers.

Día de San Pedro (April 29). Celebrated in several villages around San Cristóbal, including Amatenango del Valle (see p.704) and Zinacantán (see p.704).

May

Día de la Santa Cruz (May 3). Celebrated in San Juan Chamula (see p.703) and in Teapa (see p.736), between Villahermosa and San Cristóbal.

Día de San Isidro (May 15). Peasant celebrations everywhere – famous and picturesque fiestas in Huistán, near San Cristóbal. Also, there's a four-day nautical marathon (variable dates) from Tenosique to Villahermosa, when watercraft from all over the country race down 600km of the Río Usumacinta.

immigration before you leave, as there is no office on the Guatemala side. *Lanchas* up the Río San Pedro – previously the only way to cross – are less frequent now, but still an option, up until sunset; they're about M$40 for the thirty-minute trip.

June

Día de San Antonio (June 13). Celebrated in Simojovel (see p.693), near San Cristóbal, and Cárdenas (Tabasco), west of Villahermosa.

Día de San Juan (June 24). The culmination of several days' celebration in San Juan Chamula (see p.703).

July

Día de San Cristóbal (July 17). Celebrated enthusiastically in San Cristóbal de las Casas (see p.694) and in nearby villages such as Tenejapa and Amatenango del Valle (see p.704). This is just one highlight in over a week of festivities.

Día de Santiago (July 25). Provokes widespread celebrations, especially in San Cristóbal de las Casas (see p.694).

Fiesta de Santo Domingo de Guzmán (last week of July, first week of August). Comitán's fair, with concerts, rodeos and more.

August

Fiesta de San Lorenzo (Sunday nearest Aug 10). Celebrated in Zinacantán (see p.704), with much music and dancing.

Día de Santa Rosa (Aug 30). Celebrated in San Juan Chamula (see p.703), when the locals don traditional garb and play Tzotzil harps and instruments outside the church.

September

Independence Day (Sept 14–16). In Chiapas, independence celebrations are preceded by those in honour of the state's annexation to Mexico.

October

Día de la Virgen del Rosario (first Sun in Oct). Celebrated in San Juan Chamula and Zinacantán (see p.703 & p.704) with Tzotzil folk music and dances. There's also a special craft market.

Día de los Muertos (Day of the Dead; Nov 1–2) The most captivating celebration of the Day of the Dead in Chiapas takes place in Comitán (see p.705), where the cemeteries overflow with flowers and ornate altars. Families make offerings and hold dances, to the accompaniment of traditional music.

December

Día de la Virgen de Guadalupe (Dec 12). An important day throughout Mexico. There are particularly good fiestas in Tuxtla Gutiérrez (see p.687) and San Cristóbal de las Casas (see p.694), and the following day another in nearby Amatenango del Valle (see p.704).

Feria and cheese expo (Dec 17–22). Held in Pijijiapan (see p.680), on the coast highway to Tapachula.

Opposite the dock at **EL NARANJO** are some large, overgrown **ruins**, where the bigger pyramids are surmounted by posts bristling with machine guns. At least eight daily **buses** leave El Naranjo for **Flores** (3hr); most will pass by the dock but if you get stuck here it's only a ten-minute walk to the main road and a number of rather desperate hotels and *comedores*.

Travel details

Buses

Departures given are for direct first-class services; there are likely to be at least as many second-class buses (and often *combis* as well) to the same destinations. See also the "Moving on from..." sections of larger city accounts.

Comitán to: Ciudad Cuauhtémoc (5 daily 8.50am–7.20pm; 1hr 30min); Mexico City (6 daily 2.10pm–8.40pm; 15hr 30min); Palenque (7hr) via Ocosingo (1.45pm & 9.15pm; 4hr); Tapachula (7 daily 9.35am–1.55am; 6hr); Tuxtla Gutiérrez (3hr) via San Cristóbal (19 daily; 2hr).

Palenque to: Campeche (4 daily; 5hr); Cancún (5 daily; 13hr); Emiliano Zapata (9 daily; 1hr); Mérida (4 daily; 8hr); Mexico City (2 daily at 9pm and 9.30pm; 13hr); Oaxaca (1 daily at 5.30pm; 15hr); San Cristóbal (10 daily; 5hr); Tuxtla Gutiérrez (10 daily; 6hr); Villahermosa (10 daily 7am–9.35pm; 2hr 30min). Second-class buses run along the Frontier Highway for the junctions to Bonampak (3hr) and Yaxchilán (3hr 30min).

San Cristóbal to: Cancún (18hr) via Chetumal (4 daily 12.05–4.45pm; 12hr); Ciudad Cuauhtémoc, for Guatemala (6 daily; 3hr 30min) via Comitán (6 daily; 2hr), for Lagos de Montebello; Mérida (13hr) via Campeche (1 daily at 6.20pm; 10hr); Mexico City (7 daily; 14hr); Oaxaca (6.05pm, 8pm & 10.45pm; 12hr); Palenque (5hr) via Ocosingo (11 daily; 2hr 15min); Tapachula (9 daily 7.45am–1.05am; 8hr); Tuxtla Gutiérrez (frequently; 1hr); Villahermosa (2 daily at 11.20am & 11pm; 7hr).

Tapachula to: Comitán (6 daily; 6hr); Guatemala City (5 daily; 5–6hr); Mexico City (8 daily 12.30–8pm; 17–19hr); Oaxaca (2 daily; 11–12hr); San Cristóbal (7 daily 7.30am–11.30pm; 8hr 30min); Tonalá (hourly; 4hr); Tuxtla Gutiérrez (16 daily 6am–midnight; 5hr 30min–7hr 30min); Veracruz (2 daily at 2pm & 8.30pm; 13–14hr); Villahermosa (3 daily; 11–12hr).

Tuxtla Gutiérrez to: Cancún (5 daily 10.55am–11.30pm; 17–19hr); Ciudad Cuauhtémoc, for Guatemala (3 daily; 4hr 30min); Comitán, for Lagos de Montebello or the Guatemalan border (19 daily; 3hr); Mérida (4 daily; 12hr 30min–14hr); Mexico City (12 daily; 12hr); Oaxaca (4 daily 11.30am–23.55pm; 10hr); Palenque (6hr) via Ocosingo (7 daily 6am–midnight; 3hr 30min); San Cristóbal (hourly; 1hr); Tapachula (20 daily; 5hr 30min–7hr); Tonalá (15 daily 6am–11.20pm; 3hr 30min); Villahermosa (15 daily 5am–11.45pm; 5hr).

Villahermosa to: Campeche (19 daily; 6hr); Cancún (19 daily; 12–14hr); Chetumal (6 daily; 8hr 30min); Emiliano Zapata (4 daily; 2hr 45min); Mérida (19 daily; 8–10hr); Mexico City (21 daily; 11hr); Oaxaca (3 daily, 6–9.25pm; 13–14hr); Palenque (12 daily; 2hr 15min); San Andrés Tuxtla (5 daily; 5hr–6hr 30min); San Cristóbal (3 daily, 7am–noon; 6–7hr 30min); Tapachula (2 daily at 3.35am & 5.30pm; 11hr 30min); Tenosique (13 daily, 4am–7pm; 3hr 45min); Tuxtla Gutiérrez (16 daily via Puente Chiapas, 4–5hr; 3 daily via Bochil, 8hr); Veracruz (23 daily; 6–9hr).

Ferries

Frontera Corozal (Yaxchilán) to: Bethél, Guatemala (several daily, no schedule; 30min).

El Ceibo (near Tenosique) to: El Naranjo, Guatemala (frequent; 30min).

Flights

Villahermosa is the main regional airport, with international services to the US (Houston, Texas) as well as direct flights all over Mexico. In Chiapas, only Tapachula and Tuxtla Gutiérrez receive commercial flights, though Servicios Aéreos San Cristóbal, based in Ocosingo (T 963/632-4662, W www.serviciosaereossancristobal.com), operates light aircraft to Bonampak and San Quintín (for Laguna Miramar).

Tapachula to: Mexico City (3 daily).

Tuxtla Gutiérrez to: Mexico City (11 daily).

Villahermosa to: Houston (1 daily); Mérida (3 daily); Mexico City (17 daily); Poza Rica (4 daily); Veracruz (3 daily).

12

The Yucatán

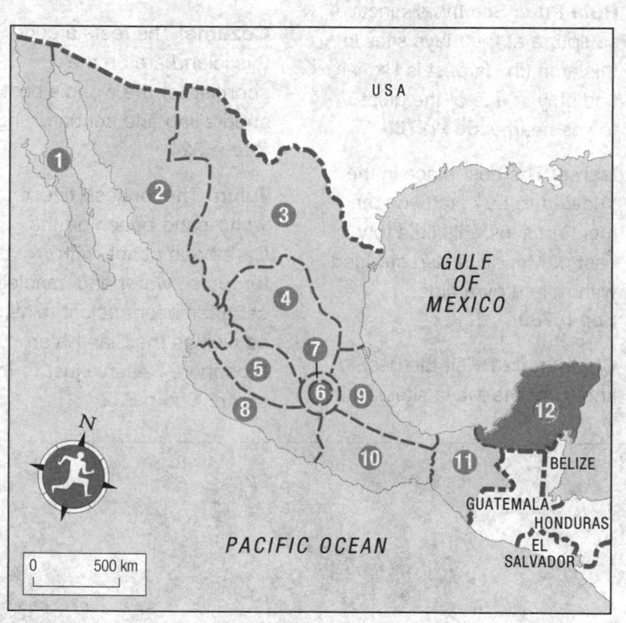

CHAPTER 12 Highlights

* **Campeche** This lovely walled city with narrow streets and pastel-coloured houses is kept immaculate by its proud citizens. See p.753

* **Mérida** Although the "White City" is the largest on the peninsula – alive with music and Sunday markets – it retains a tranquil charm. See p.764

* **Ruta Puuc** See the distinctive sculpture at the Maya sites in this area (the largest is Uxmal), and stay in one of the quiet towns nearby. See p.780

* **Izamal** The best place in the Yucatán to buy craftwork and meet artisans, this little town east of Mérida is also studded with ruined pyramids. See p.789

* **Chichén Itzá** Visit the best-known of the Maya sites, with its vertiginous temple, Chac-mool figures and dramatic, snail-shaped observatory. See p.790

* **Cenotes** On a peninsula with no rivers and few lakes, these water holes and caverns played an essential role in ancient Maya survival and spirituality. Today, they're a refreshing spot to swim. See p.799

* **Cozumel** The reefs around this island are on the shortlist for the world's best snorkelling and scuba diving. See p.824

* **Tulum** The longest, finest white-sand beach on the Caribbean coast, with turquoise water and candlelit cabañas near ancient ruins, as well as the Sian Ka'an Biosphere Reserve just to the south. See p.832

▲ Tulum

12

The Yucatán

The three states that comprise the Yucatán Peninsula – Campeche, Yucatán and Quintana Roo – are among the hottest and most tropical parts of Mexico, though they lie further north than you might imagine: the capital of Yucatán state, **Mérida**, is actually at a higher latitude than Mexico City. Until the 1960s, when proper road and rail links were finally completed, the Yucatán lived out of step with the rest of the country and had almost as much contact with Europe, Cuba and the US as with central Mexico, resulting in a very distinct culture. Tourism has since made major inroads, especially in the north around the great **Maya sites**, such as Chichén Itzá, and on the **Quintana Roo coast**, where development has centred on the "super-resort" of **Cancún** and the islands of **Mujeres** and **Cozumel**, but is now shifting to the so-called Riviera Maya, the stretch of beachfront that includes **Playa del Carmen** and **Tulum**. But away from the big centres, especially in the south, where towns are sparsely scattered in thick jungle, there's still a distinct pioneering feel.

In northern Yucatán state, the landscape is relatively spare: shallow, rocky earth gives rise to stunted trees, and underground springs known as cenotes are the only source of water. Campeche state, by contrast, boasts a huge area of **tropical forest**, the Calakmul Biosphere Reserve – though the trees are being thinned in places for cattle ranching and timber. The entire peninsular coastline is great for spotting **wildlife** – notably turtles at the Sian Ka'an Biosphere Reserve in Quintana Roo and flocks of flamingoes at Celestún and Río Lagartos in Yucatán – but the most spectacular, white-sand **beaches** line the Caribbean coast, where magnificent offshore **coral reefs** form part of the second largest barrier reef system in the world.

Some history

The peninsula's modern boom is, in fact, a reawakening, for this has been the longest continuously settled part of the country, with evidence of Maya inhabitants as early as 2500 BC. The **Maya** are not a specifically Mexican culture – their greatest cities were in the lowlands of modern Guatemala, Belize and Honduras. They did, however, produce a unique style in the Yucatán and continued to flourish here long after the collapse of the earlier, grander civilizations to the south. This was done in spite of natural handicaps – thin soil, heat and lack of water – and invasions from central Mexico. Indeed, the Maya still live in the Yucatán, both in the cities and in rural villages, in many cases remarkably true to their old traditions and lifestyle, despite the hardships of the intervening years: ravaged by European diseases, forced to work on vast colonial *encomiendas* or, later, subjected to the semi-slavery of debt peonage.

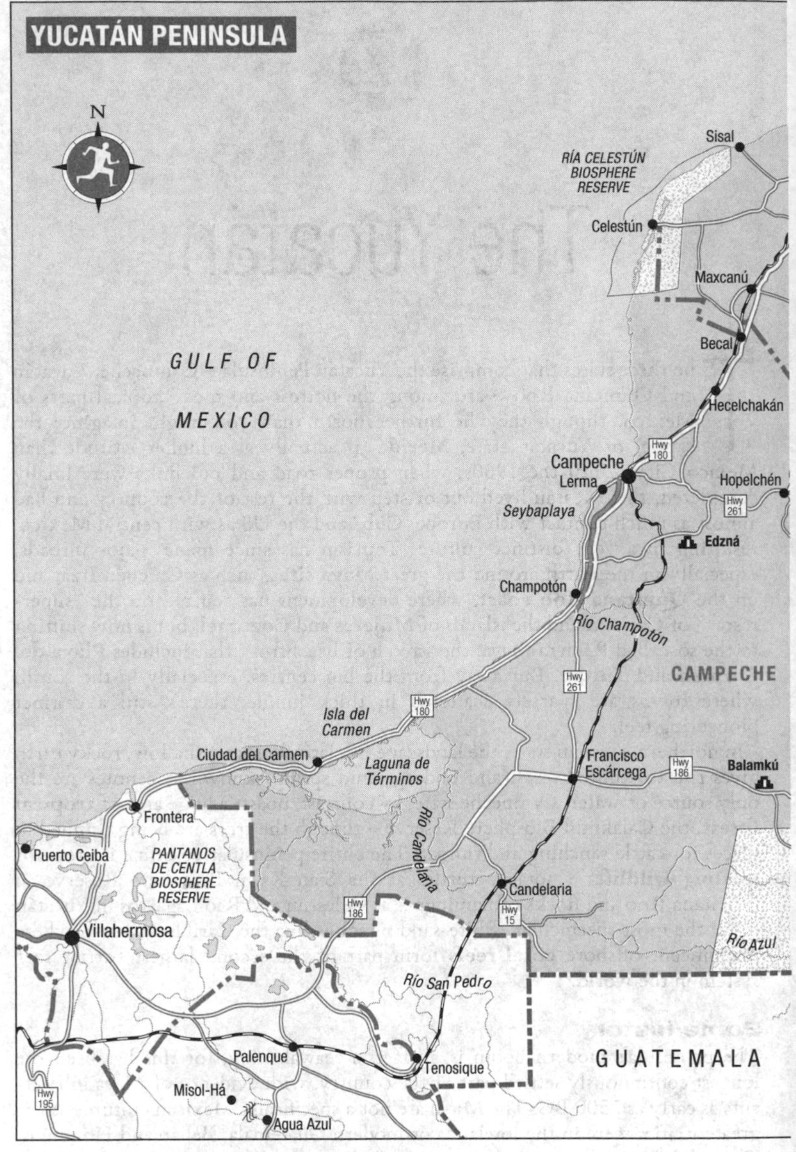

The florescence of Maya culture, throughout its extensive domain, came in the **Classic period**, from around 300 to 900 AD, an age in which the cities (most over the border to the south) grew up and Maya science and art reached their height. The Maya calendar, a complex interaction of solar, lunar, astral and religious dates, was far more complex and accurate than the Gregorian one. Five hundred years before the European Renaissance, the Maya had already developed

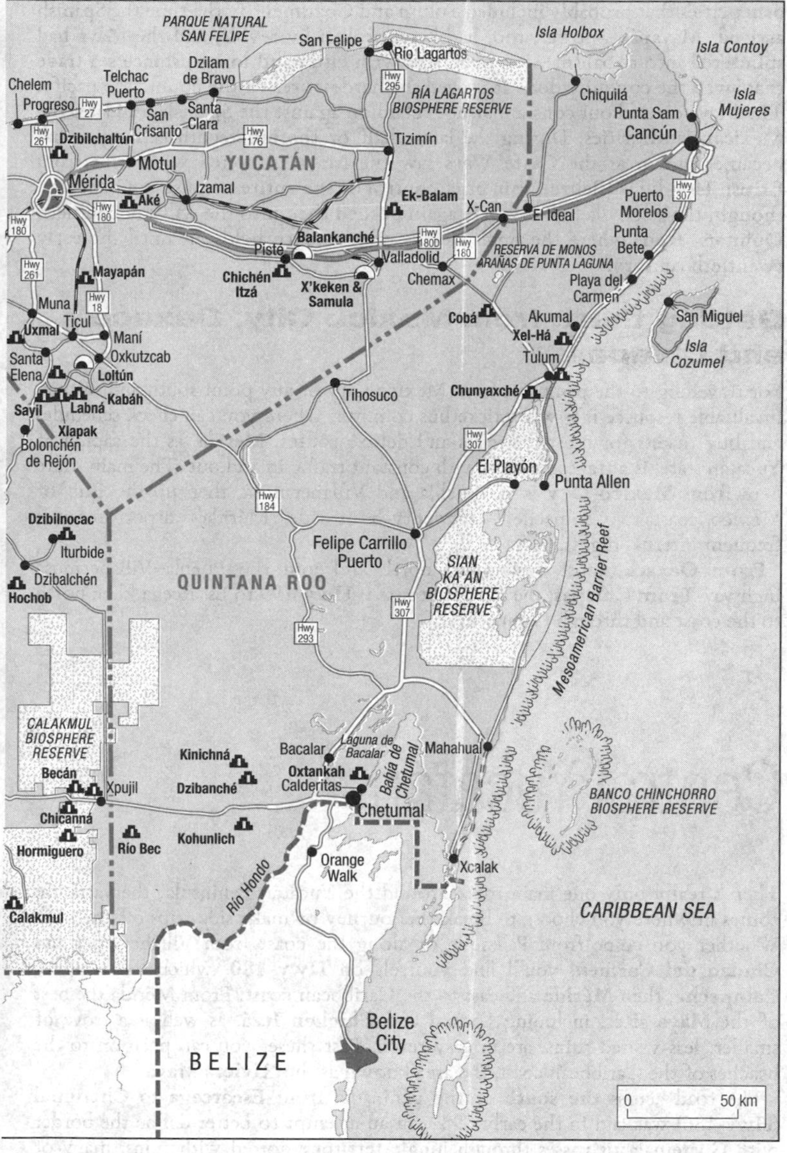

a sophisticated perspective in art and an elaborate mathematical and hieroglyphic system. In the early ninth century AD, growing military tension and a prolonged drought saw the abandonment of many of the southern lowland cities (Tikal and Calakmul among them), while the cities of the north – such as Chichén Itzá, Uxmal and the Puuc sites – began to flourish. These in turn collapsed around 1200 AD, to be succeeded by Mayapán and a confederacy of other cities that probably included Tulum and Cozumel. By the time the Spanish arrived, Mayapán's power, too, had been broken by revolt, and the Maya had splintered into tribalism – although still with cities and long-distance sea trade that awed the conquistadors. It proved the hardest area of the country to pacify. The Maya carried out constant armed rebellion against the Spanish, and later the Mexican, authorities. During the latter half of the nineteenth century, what became known as the **Caste Wars** saw the Maya, supplied with arms from British Honduras (Belize), gain brief control of the entire peninsula. Gradually, though, the guerrilla fighters were again pushed back into the wilds of southern Quintana Roo, where the final pockets of resistance held out until the early twentieth century.

Getting there from Mexico City, Oaxaca and Chiapas

For travelling to the peninsula from Mexico City or any point south and east, an invaluable resource is Ⓦwww.ticketbus.com.mx, where you can check schedules and buy tickets for most first-class and deluxe routes. Mérida, as the capital of Yucatán state, is a transport hub, with constant traffic in and out. The main route here **from Mexico City** is via Puebla and Villahermosa, then up the Gulf of Mexico coast to Campeche – a twenty-hour ride. Mérida's airport receives frequent internal flights.

From Oaxaca, most buses head north and join the Puebla–Villahermosa highway. **From Chiapas**, the standard route is Hwy-199 to Escárcega, then north to the coast and through Campeche.

Central Yucatán

There's really only one main route around the Yucatán Peninsula; the variation comes in where you choose to break the journey or make side trips off the trail. Whether you come from Palenque or along the coast from Villahermosa and **Ciudad del Carmen**, you'll find yourself on **Hwy-180**, which heads up to **Campeche**, then **Mérida** and east to the Caribbean coast. From Mérida the best of the **Maya sites**, including **Uxmal** and **Chichén Itzá**, as well as a trove of smaller, less-visited ruins, are in easy reach. Past these, you can push on to the beaches of the Caribbean coast, the area known as the **Riviera Maya**.

The road across **the south** of the peninsula from **Escárcega** to **Chetumal** (Hwy-186) was laid in the early 1980s in an attempt to better define the border with Guatemala; it passes through jungle territory dotted with ruins, many of them still being excavated. The star is the enormous site of **Calakmul**, located deep in a reserve near the border with Guatemala; from the top of its main pyramid, the tallest in the Maya world, the tropical forest stretches to the horizon like a green sea. You can get accommodation and arrange tours to all of the ruins at **Xpujil**, on the border between Campeche and Quintana Roo states.

Campeche

Capital of the state that bears its name, beautiful **CAMPECHE** is one of Mexico's finest colonial gems. At its heart, relatively intact, lies a historic port town still surrounded by hefty defensive **walls and fortresses**; within them, interspersed with the occasional grand Baroque church, are elegant eighteenth- and nineteenth-century houses painted in pastel shades, hundreds of which have been restored to their former glory. Nonetheless, the place doesn't feel like an outdoor museum, with appliance stores and internet cafés occupying many of the historic shopfronts. Around the old **centre** are the trappings of a modern city that is once again becoming wealthy, while the **seafront**, built on reclaimed land, provides a thoroughly modern vista. Though the city is less lively, its immaculately preserved and tranquil streets compare favourably with Mérida's, and *campechanos* live up to their reputation as some of the most gracious people in Mexico.

Some history

In 1517, a crew of Spanish explorers under Francisco Hernández landed outside the Maya town of Ah Kin Pech, only to beat a hasty retreat on seeing the forces lined up to greet them. Not until 1540 did second-generation conquistador **Francisco de Montejo the Younger** found the modern town. Until the

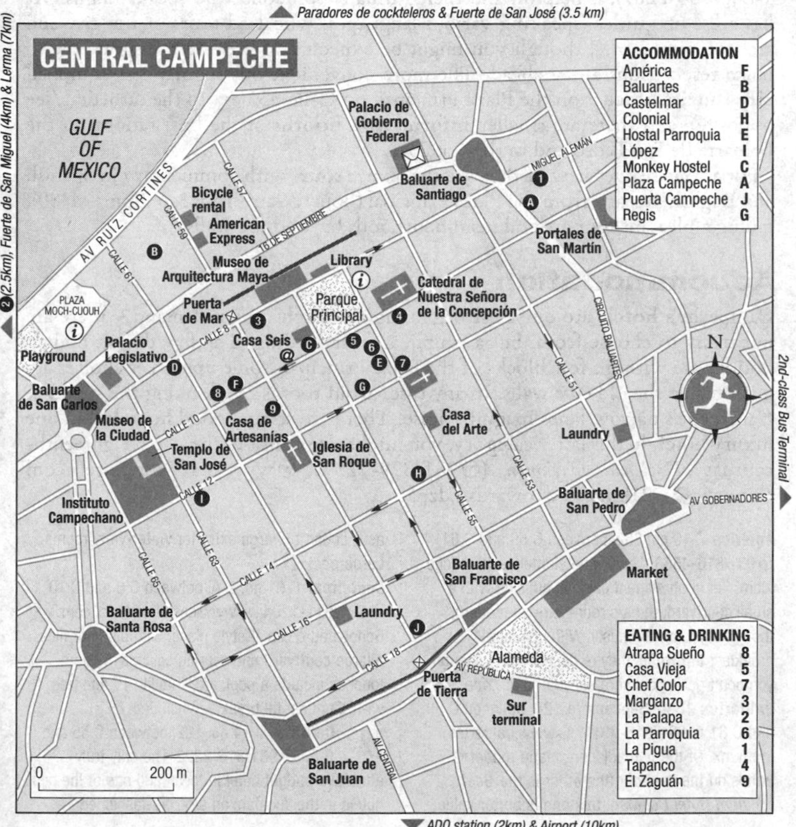

nineteenth century, Campeche was the peninsula's chief port, exporting mainly **logwood** (source of a red dye known as hematein) from local forests. It was an irresistible target for **pirates** until locals prevailed upon the Spanish authorities to fortify the city: construction of the walls, with eight massive *baluartes* (bulwarks), began in 1686 after a particularly brutal massacre. Although large sections of the walls have been replaced by a ring road, two major sections survive, along with seven of the eight *baluartes*.

Arrival and information

Campeche has two **bus stations**, one each for first- and second-class services, as well as a separate terminus for local and rural buses. The **first-class ADO** station is about 2km from the centre on Avenida Central; taxis line up outside (M$40 to the centre), as do buses and *colectivos* (M$5; look for "Mercado" or "Centro"). The **second-class** terminal is 600m northeast of the centre on Gobernadores; to get downtown, either walk or cross the street in front of the station and take a city bus, also marked "Centro" or "Mercado". All of these buses will head to the market, just outside the city wall on the landward side. To get from the **airport**, about 10km southeast of town, you'll have to take a **taxi** (M$80).

Campeche's **state tourist office**, in the Plaza Moch Couoh on 16 de Septiembre opposite the Palacio de Gobierno (daily 8am–4pm & 6–9pm; ⓣ981/811-9229 or 1-800/900-2267), is helpful, and there's usually someone who speaks English. It has a list of **guides** (speaking various languages) who lead tours of the city and archeological zones, though you might be expected to provide transport; try to make reservations a day ahead. The more convenient but slightly less equipped **city tourist office** is on the Plaza Principal, on Calle 55 next to the cathedral (see opposite), and there are smaller **information booths** at the bus stations, in the Baluarte de San Pedro and in the Casa Seis.

For a concise overview of the city, the *tranvía* **tour**, with commentary in Spanish and English, departs from the Plaza Principal (hourly 9am–1pm & 5–9pm; M$80), taking a pleasant tour around neighbourhoods beyond the walls.

Accommodation

Campeche's **hotels** are only just beginning to match tourist demand – there are not many to choose from, but a couple are outstanding. The few decent budget options are within a few blocks of the Plaza Principal; some upmarket choices are just outside the old city walls. In any case, avoid rooms overlooking the street, as Campeche's narrow lanes magnify noise. There are several good **hostels** and one luxury hotel; in this latter category, you might also consider the lavish eighteenth-century *Hacienda Uayamón* (ⓣ981/829-7257, ⓦwww.starwoodhotels.com/luxury; ❾), 21km away towards Edzná.

América C 10 no. 252, between C 59 and C 61 ⓣ981/816-4588, ⓦwww.hotelamericacampeche.com. Set in an elegant colonial building with a small courtyard, the a/c rooms are all modern, though occasionally musty. With continental breakfast thrown in, they're decent value, though you don't get a pool here, as you do at *López*. ❹

Baluartes 16 de Septiembre 128, between C 59 and C 61 ⓣ981/816-3911, ⓦwww.baluartes.com.mx. Of the two adjacent bland modern hotels on the seafront (the other is the *Best Western Hotel Del Mar*), this one is better value, as it doesn't charge extra for water-view rooms. Large pool. ❻

Castelmar C 61 no. 2-A, between C 8 and C 10 ⓣ981/811-1204, ⓦwww.castelmarhotel.com. Renovated colonial-style place, with old floor tiles, a large courtyard and soaring ceilings. Modern touches include a pool, a/c, satellite TV and free wi-fi. Continental breakfast included. ❼

Colonial C 14 no. 122, between C 55 and C 57 ⓣ981/816-2222. The only truly attractive budget hotel in town, and one of the best hotels in the Yucatán: an airy, old-fashioned courtyard building with immaculately kept rooms in Easter-egg hues. Book ahead. ❷

Hostal Parroquia C 55, between C 10 and C 12 ⓣ981/816-2530, ⓦwww.hostalparroquia.com. Next door to the restaurant of the same name, this converted colonial home has a good mix of attractive dorms (M$100 per bed) and private rooms with high ceilings (❷) around a very pleasant courtyard. Somewhat limited kitchen, but laundry services available; rates include continental breakfast.

López C 12 no. 189, between C 61 and C 63 ⓣ981/816-3344, ⓦwww.hotelllopezcampeche.com. A nicely renovated hotel catering to Mexican business travellers (complete with free wi-fi and a newspaper in the morning); modern a/c rooms are in a pretty Deco-era building with open halls, though bathrooms can be musty. There's even a small pool. ❹

Monkey Hostel C 57 at corner of C 10 ⓣ01-800/CAMPECHE, ⓦwww.hostalcampeche.com. In a prime location on the west side of the plaza, this long-established backpacker haven has helpful staff, clean rooms and a host of services, from laundry to local tours. Breakfast is included. Single-sex dorm beds are M$85; basic double rooms are also available. ❷

Plaza Campeche C 10 at Circuito Baluartes ⓣ981/811-9900, ⓦwww.hotelplazacampeche.com. Outside the old wall on the north side, the *Plaza Campeche* is a colonial-look high-end place with friendly service. Large rooms have marble baths and dark-wood furniture and there's a small pool, a bar and wi-fi. The same management's *Plaza Colonial* (C 12, just inside the walls) has smaller, slightly cheaper rooms. ❼

Puerta Campeche C 59 no. 61, between C 16 and C 18 ⓣ981/816-7508, ⓦwww.starwoodhotels.com/luxury. Located just inside the Puerta de Tierra, Campeche's finest hotel occupies the shell of a colonial home and warehouse. The pool winds through crumbling walls, overlooked by a breezy terrace (great for an evening drink). ❾

Regis C 12 no. 148, between C 55 and C 57 ⓣ981/816-3175. Seven very large rooms, all with a/c, arranged around a small patio – a reasonable alternative to the *Colonial* or the *López*, and about halfway between the two in price. ❸

The City

One of the greatest pleasures to be had in Campeche comes from simply wandering the streets or the **malecón** (Avenida Ruíz Cortines) – especially in the early evening, when the heat lessens and locals also come out to stroll, and on Sundays, when the plaza is closed to cars for a mellow, all-evening party. Churches, mansions and fortresses punctuate each block, though only the **archeological museum** in the Fuerte de San Miguel can be described as a "must-see".

As you explore, remember that even-numbered **streets** run parallel to the sea, starting with Calle 8, just inside the ramparts; odd-numbered streets run inland. The central **Plaza de la Independencia**, or *parque principal*, is bordered by calles 8, 10, 55 and 57. Outside the old city wall, the grid system is less strict; the **market**, just outside the wall by the Puerta de Tierra, is as far as you're likely to need to venture into the modern city.

Starting on the plaza, the most central landmark is **La Catedral de Nuestra Señora de la Concepción** (daily 6.45am–8pm). Founded in 1540, it's one of the oldest churches on the peninsula. The bulk of the construction, though, took place much later, and what you see now is a wedding-cake Baroque structure; look in the adjacent museum (11am–5pm; donation) for a seventeenth-century statue of Christ, interred in a dark wood and silver catafalque, among other relics. Across the plaza is the **Centro Cultural Casa Seis** (daily 9am–9pm; free), which has an elegant permanent display of Baroque interiors. It also hosts art shows and performances, including musical *serenatas* most Thursdays. On the seaward side of the plaza, the Baluarte de la Soledad, just south of the public library, houses the **Museo de Arquitectura Maya** (Tues–Sun 9.30am–5.30pm; M$31), a collection of columns, stelae and other stone details arranged by regional style – Chenes, Puuc, etc. Its presentation of a sketch outline of the decoration next to most of the carved stone helps train your eye to see the details. From here, you can head southwest along the line of the wall to the **Baluarte de San Carlos**, which has cannons on the battlemented roof and, underneath, the beginnings of a network of ancient tunnels that runs under much of the town. Sealed off now, the tunnels provided refuge for the populace during pirate raids, and before that were probably used by the Maya. The *baluarte* houses Campeche's **Museo de la Ciudad** (Tues–Sun 9.30am–5.30pm; M$29), a tiny but rather lovely collection of local memorabilia that includes models of ships, with Spanish commentary.

The other remaining chunk of wall is on the landward side of the old city – hence the name **Puerta de Tierra** (daily 9am–4pm; M$10 for access to the wall and a small museum). It hosts a perfunctory pirate museum (M$30), but you can also pay just to climb the ramparts (M$10) and walk along the top of the walls in either direction, to the Baluarte de San Juan or the Baluarte de San Francisco. The views are intriguing: from the **Baluarte de San Francisco** to the north, you can see the busiest parts of the new town and the **Alameda Francisco de Paula Toro**, the Havana-inspired promenade next to the market; heading south towards the **Baluarte de San Juan**, you can gaze down over the neatly restored colonial facades in the centre and see how much still lies derelict behind them. An optional audio-guide (M$40) identifies some of the other visible landmarks. Every Tuesday, Friday and Saturday, there's an enjoyable **sound-and-light show** (8pm; M$50, or M$80 with translation) starting from the Puerta de Tierra and walking along the wall in the company of the "soldiers" guarding it.

Beyond the city wall

On a steep hill on the southwest side of town, about 4km from the centre, the **Fuerte de San Miguel** houses Campeche's impressive **Museo Arqueológico** (Tues–Sun 9.30am–5.30pm; M$37). Plaques are in Spanish only, but the beautiful relics from all over the peninsula speak for themselves. Maya artefacts from Edzná and Jaina make up much of the collection; highlights include delicate Jaina figurines, fine sculpture and pre-Hispanic gold. But the best part is the treasure from the tombs at Calakmul, including the first mummified body to be found in Mesoamerica, unearthed in 1995. The jade death masks are mesmerizing. Enjoy the view over the ramparts, too, which is wonderful at sunset. To get here, you can take a city bus along the coast road (look for "Lerma" or "Playa Bonita"), but that will leave you with a stiff climb up the hill to the fort.

On the north side of the city, about 3.5km from the centre and directly uphill from the *paradores de cockteleros* (see opposite), the **Fuerte de San José** (Tues–Sun 9.30am–5.30pm; M$31) faces down a giant statue of Benito Juárez on the neighbouring hill. It is home to a museum of armaments and a collection of items from the colonial era. It's at the top of an even steeper hill than the southern fort and takes in a dramatic view; buses to look for are marked "Morelos" or "Bellavista", starting from in front of Alameda. A taxi to either museum from the centre costs about M$30.

If you're desperate for **beaches**, take one of the buses along the waterfront marked "Playa Bonita" or "Lerma", two seaside destinations just south of Campeche; Playa Bonita is the better of the two, with palapas for shade, but it can still be rather dreary and empty on weekdays.

Eating and drinking

Restaurants abound in the centre, especially along calles 8 and 10. **Seafood**, available almost everywhere, is a good bet; try the *pan de cazón* (tortillas layered with shredded shark meat) or shrimp (*camarones*) in spicy sauce. For breakfast, the cafés along Calle 8 near the government offices offer everything from tacos to fresh juices and pastries. Later in the day, the café in the centre of the plaza serves excellent coffee and home-made ice cream. The blocks around the Instituto

Campechano (C 10 at C 63) hold numerous snack joints catering to students, and Campeche's **market**, just east of the walled city, is surrounded by *comedores* offering cheap and tasty lunches. Another local favourite is the stretch of *paradores de cockteleros* on the malecón – these seafood-vending kiosks are open until around 4pm (a taxi costs about M$30). At **night**, people head to Portales de San Martín (see p. 000) for snacks. Bars aren't open late, but stop by the rooftop bar at the hotel *Puerta Campeche* (Fri & Sat only) for the gorgeous view.

Atrapa Sueño C 10 between C 59 and C 61. Vegetarian snacks from M$40, alongside handicrafts.

Casa Vieja C 10 no. 319, on Plaza Principal. Cuban-owned restaurant with well-appointed balcony overlooking the main square that serves tasty international cuisine. Prices match the classy setting, but if your budget doesn't stretch to a full meal, just stop in for a rum cocktail.

Chef Color C 55 at C 12. Cafeteria-style service and plastic folding chairs give this little lunch spot the feel of a church basement, but the home-made food – hearty dishes like pork with beans – is delicious, fast and cheap. Lunch only.

Marganzo C 8 no. 267 between C 57 and C 59. Somewhat touristy but still pleasant and not as expensive as it looks. The varied menu includes tasty crab quesadillas and generous *botanas* (bite-size snacks).

La Palapa Resurgimento, 2.5km south along the malecón from the city centre. A good destination for a malecón stroll, this large bar is right on the water, and delicious *botanas* are served with every drink.

La Parroquia C 55 no. 8 between C 10 and C 12. Traditional, family-run café with high ceilings, echoing with the clink of dishes and buzz of conversation. The excellent-value *pan de cazón* and other local dishes are popular with locals, but breakfasts, with house-made yogurt, are best. Open 24hr.

La Pigua Alemán 179-A ☎981/811-3365. Follow C 8 north to find one of the city's most legendary restaurants, a pretty, somewhat elegant spot with exceptionally delicious seafood such as creamy shrimp soup, fresh filets with garlic and herbs. Open for lunch and dinner; for the latter, make reservations if possible.

Tapanco C 10 between C 53 and C 55. Hip bi-level café and convenience store across from the cathedral, with beers, coffee and sandwiches.

El Zaguán C 59 between C 10 and C 12. Small, friendly restaurant/bar, with wooden booths, serving inexpensive but good local and Mexican specialities, including *pan de cazón* and *mole poblano*. Closed Sun.

Listings

Airlines Aeroméxico ☎981/816-3109 or 01-800/021-4010; InterJet ☎01-800-011-2345, at airport only.

American Express In the VIPS travel agency, C 59 between Ruíz Cortines and 16 de Septiembre behind the *Best Western Hotel Del Mar* (Mon–Fri 9am–8pm, Sat 9am–1pm; ☎981/811-1100).

Banks and exchange HSBC, C 10 at C 55, is just off the main square and has an ATM; Banorte is on the plaza.

Baseball The major-league Campeche Piratas play at the Estadio Nelson Barrera Romilón, on the malecón north of the centre, inland from the *paradores de cockteleros*. Good seats cost about M$100.

Bike rental Aventura (☎981-811-9191 ext 405), on C 59 in the *Best Western Hotel Del Mar* parking lot, rents cruisers with baskets (M$25/hr) and leads tours around town.

Car rental Europcar, at the airport (☎55/5207-5572, www.europcar.com); Localiza (☎981/811-3187), in the *Hotel Baluartes*; Maya Car Rental (☎981/816-0670), in the *Best Western Hotel Del Mar*.

Internet access There are internet cafés on every street in the centre of Campeche, most charging approx M$10/hr. You can send a fax from Ah-Kim-Tel caseta, C 10 between C 57 and C 59.

Laundry Klar, C 16 no. 305 at C 61; Lave Klin, Circuito Baluartes Nte between C 14 and C 16. Both charge about M$10/kg (Klar has a 3kg minimum).

Post office In the Palacio de Gobierno Federal, 16 de Septiembre at C 53 (Mon–Fri 8.30am–3.30pm, Sat 9am–1pm).

Shopping Casa de Artesanías Tukulná, C 10 no. 333 between C 59 and C 61, is a particularly well-stocked craft shop; look for Panama hats and Campeche-style *lotería* sets. Casa Seis, on the plaza, has a smaller but also quite fine selection.

Taxis Within the city, they are inexpensive, but sometimes not plentiful. Look for them at taxi stands around the centre or call ☎981/816-2363, 816-2359 or 816-2355.

Moving on from Campeche

To get back to the **bus stations**, look for "Av Central or "ADO" (first-class) or "Gobernadores", "Universidad" or "Terminal Sur" (second-class). The first-class station has ADO, OCC and some ATS service. Buses leave relatively frequently for Ciudad del Carmen, Escárcega, Villahermosa, Mérida and Cancún. A direct **bus** goes to the Mérida airport at least three times a day. You can also get as far as Chetumal, San Cristóbal de las Casas (via Palenque) and Veracruz. The Edzná Tours travel agency on Circuito Colonias at Calle 8 doubles as a TicketBus office, to spare you a trek out to the station.

You'll need Sur or ATS service at the second-class terminal for stopping buses on Hwy-180 (Hecelchakán, etc.); for Escárcega, Hopelchén, Bolonchén de Rejón and Iturbide (for Dzibilnocac); or for Uxmal and Santa Elena. *Colectivos* for most of the same destinations depart from Gobernadores as well – you'll pass the marked stops on the walk to the bus station. For Champotón, Seybaplaya or Sabancuy, go to the auxiliary Sur terminal on República just inland from the Puerta de Tierra. For Edzná there are departures from in front of this same terminal (though they're not Sur buses) hourly from around 7am to early afternoon. There are daily **flights** from the airport (ⓣ981/816-6656) to Mexico City.

For further information, see Travel details, p.850.

Tours Servicios Turísticos Xtampak, C 57 no. 14 between C 10 and C 12 (Mon–Sat 8am–3pm & 5–9pm; ⓣ981/811-6473), runs trips to Edzná (M$200 half-day, transport only; or M$850 with guide, lunch and other stops), as well as Calakmul and the Chenes sites. *Monkey Hostel* (see "Accommodation", p.755) also runs day trips. Nómadas, Ruíz Cortines 61 (ⓣ981/816-2935, ⓦwww.nomadastravel.com.mx, is a good all-purpose, student-friendly agency.

Around Campeche: Edzná and the Chenes sites

Some 50km east of Campeche lie the impressive ruins of **EDZNÁ** (daily 8am–5pm; M$41), one of the few sites in the area accessible by bus. Though this is where the so-called **Chenes** style of architecture (*chen* means "well" and is a fairly common suffix to place names hereabouts) dominated, Edzná is far from a pure example of it, also featuring elements of Río Bec, Classic Maya and Puuc design. At the height of its power, between 250 BC and 150 AD, it was a large city, on the main route between the Maya communities of the highlands and the coast. The ruins show evidence of a complex drainage and irrigation system that probably supported a large agricultural project and more than a thousand people.

The most important structure here is the great **Templo de los Cinco Pisos** (Temple of the Five Storeys), a stepped palace-pyramid more than thirty metres high. Unusually, each of the five storeys contains chambered "palace" rooms: while both solid temple pyramids and multistorey "apartment" complexes are relatively common, it is rare to see the two combined in one building. At the front, a steep monumental staircase leads to a three-room temple, topped by a roofcomb. It's a hot climb, but the view takes in the dense greenery and the hills that mark this side of the peninsula. As you look out over two plazas, the further of which must have been capable of holding tens of thousands of people, it is easy to imagine the power that the high priest or king commanded. Beyond lie the unexcavated remains of other large pyramids, and behind them, the vast flat expanse of the Yucatán plain. Inside the west-facing temple, a stele of the god of maize was illuminated by the sun twice a year, on the dates for the planting and harvesting of the crop.

Lesser buildings surround the ceremonial precinct. The **Nohochná** (Casa Grande, or Big House), a palace on the northwest side, is some 55m long and contains a room used as a *temazcal* (traditional sauna), with stone benches and hearths over which water could be boiled. Over in the **Pequeña Acrópolis**, the **Templo de los Mascarones** contains two eerie masks representing the sun god, rising on the east (left-hand) side and setting on the west.

Buses leave from Campeche in front of the Sur terminal on República south of the market (see opposite) in the mornings; the last ride back to Campeche is at 3.45pm, but check with the driver on the way there. A **sound-and-light show** on Friday and Saturday (8pm; M$112) involves walking among the illuminated buildings. Alternatively, you could join an **organized trip** from Campeche (see opposite).

Other Chenes sites

Most of the ruins that exhibit undiluted Chenes style (marked by colonnaded facades and monster-mouth doorways, evolved from the Río Bec further south) are accessible only with a car or exceptional determination. One site, **Dzibilnocac** (daily 8am–5pm; free), is relatively accessible by **bus**, as it's 1km east of the village of Iturbide (or Vicente Guerrero, according to many road signs), which gets regular second-class service from Hopelchén and Campeche; to be on the safe side, arrive early and check return times. The buildings here show the ultradecorative facades typical of the Chenes style – its restored western temple pyramid is quite pretty.

About 15km southwest of the village of Dzibalchén (follow signs to Chencoh), **Hochob** (daily 8am–5pm; M$31) has an amazing three-room temple (low and fairly small, as are most Chenes buildings), with a facade richly carved with stylized snakes and masks. The central chamber is surmounted by a crumbling roofcomb, and its decoration, with fangs, eyes and ears, creates the effect of a huge face, with the doorway as a gaping mouth.

If you're driving, you can continue south to Xpujil – it's a good back route that avoids a lot of the truck traffic that plagues Hwy-186. **HOPELCHÉN**, about 90km east of Campeche, is the biggest town in the area, and home to a Mennonite community since the 1980s. To **stay** the night, the only option is the basic but clean *Los Arcos* (Ⓣ982/822-0123; ❸), Calle 23 on the corner of the plaza, near where the buses stop.

South of Campeche: the coast

Continuing south from Campeche, Hwy-180 splits into free (*libre*) and toll (*cuota*) roads. The slower *libre* route winds between hills, with striking vistas of the green Gulf waters, while the toll highway (M$55) is straight and fast to **Champotón**, a scrappy port town renowned for its delicious and cheap shrimp cocktails. It's also where many buses turn inland, following Hwy-261 southeast towards Escárcega for the Río Bec area and Chetumal (via Hwy-186) or Palenque. Hwy-180 continues along the coast to Villahermosa via **Ciudad del Carmen**. Although this city isn't really a compelling destination (nor worth pausing at during a longer bus trip), the ride down the coast is fast and pretty, with the road just a few feet from the water most of the way. At **Isla Aguada**, the Puente de la Unidad (M$52 toll) crosses the eastern entrance to the **Laguna de Terminos**, linking **Isla del Carmen** to the mainland. Be careful not to exceed the 50-kph speed limit; traffic cops posted at either end of the bridge are notorious for demanding heavy fines on the spot.

Ciudad del Carmen

The only town of any size on 35-kilometre-long Isla del Carmen, midway between Campeche and the state border with Tabasco, **CIUDAD DEL CARMEN** doesn't merit a special trip except perhaps during Carnaval, which it celebrates with gusto, or its lively **fiesta** in the second half of July (see p.849). If you do wind up here, you'll find a crowded old centre surrounded by modern sprawl, and exceptionally bad traffic. The conquistadors landed here in 1518, but the first real settlers, in 1633, were pirates who used the island as a base of operations. Nowadays the money's in shrimp (an enormous bronze prawn presides over one central traffic circle) and oil, with many rigs just offshore in the Gulf. That industry has forced prices up, so you won't find many bargains.

Practicalities

Ciudad del Carmen is a very big place, but once you find your way downtown, you won't need to stray more than a few blocks. ADO (first-class) and Sur (second-class) **buses** use the same station on Avenida Periférica Oriente, a very long way out. To get to the centre, take a taxi or *colectivo* (5am–11pm; about 20min and M$60). There's a downtown ADO ticket office on Calle 24, next to the *Hotel Zacarias*. You can pick up a map from the **tourist office** – just a desk in the modern building jutting toward the water from the malecón in front of the central Parque General Ignacio Zaragoza (Mon–Fri 8am–3pm). The **post office** (Mon–Fri 9am–3pm) is on the corner of calles 22 and 27, while Banamex, on the corner of Calle 24 at the edge of the park, and Bancomer, Calle 24 at the corner with Calle 29B, both have **ATMs**. A handy **internet** café is in the Plaza Delfin, on Calle 20 across from the Plaza de Artesanías y Gastronomía, on the malecón.

Most of the budget **accommodation** in town is around the plaza near the waterfront. The big, basic *Hotel Zacarias* (Ⓣ938/382-3506; ④), on the plaza at the corner of Calle 24 and Calle 31, has rooms with a choice of air-conditioning or fan; more luxurious is the *Hotel del Parque*, on Calle 33 between the plaza and the waterfront (Ⓣ938/382-3046; ④), where all rooms have air-conditioning, TV and a phone. **Food** in Ciudad del Carmen is a mixture of specialities from the Yucatán Peninsula and spicier flavours from Tabasco, with a stress on shellfish. One of the nicer places is *La Fuente,* Calle 20 and Calle 29, on the waterfront, a traditional Mexican café serving simple food round the clock. Other good, low-priced **restaurants** are grouped together in a couple of complexes on the malecón just north of the park.

Escárcega to Xpujil

Heading south from Champotón on the inland route, Hwy-261 meets the east–west Hwy-186 at **Escárcega** (officially Francisco Escárcega, though the full name is seldom used). The town is the gateway for a number of **Maya sites** that opened to tourists only in the 1990s, known as the **Río Bec sites**; a much smaller village, **Xpujil**, lies further east and is the usual stop for visitors to the ruins. The largest ancient Maya complex, the city of Calakmul, is surrounded by the **Calakmul Biosphere Reserve**, a vast area of tropical forest once heavily populated by lowland Maya, which stretches all the way into the Petén region of Guatemala (where the ruins of Tikal are situated). Several of the sites are every bit as exciting as more northern ones such as Chichén Itzá.

Escárcega

A dusty town straggling along the road and old train tracks, **ESCÁRCEGA** is not an ideal stopover, but you may need to change buses here (and there's bearable lodging if you do get stuck overnight). The ADO **first-class bus station** is at the west end of town, at the junction of Hwy-261 and Hwy-186; from there, it's 1.5km east to the east end and the Sur **second-class bus station** (you can buy tickets for all services at ADO). You'll find an **ATM** in the next block south of the Sur station. The **food** options are basic, but a little better closer to the ADO station; try the 24-hour *La Teja*, southwest across the traffic circle. If you need to **stay**, the gaily painted *Hotel Escárcega*, on the town's main drag (Ⓣ982/824-0186, Ⓔhotelescarcega@hotmail.com; ❷), has tidy enough rooms with air-conditioning or fan, but if you definitely want air-conditioning, *Gran Hotel Colonial del Sureste*, a bit further east (Ⓣ982/824-1908; ❸), is better value. **Getting out of town** is relatively easy: there are nine first-class buses daily to Mérida (4hr 30min) and more to Campeche (2hr); six run to Palenque (though all depart in the middle of the night or early morning; 3hr 30min), and four to San Cristóbal de las Casas (8hr). Services to Xpujil (2hr 30min) go four times daily – you're better off with Sur (second-class) for this destination; express service to Chetumal (4hr) goes five times during the day, with many more services in the middle of the night.

Xpujil

The ramshackle village of **XPUJIL**, 150km east of Escárcega (and 120km east of Chetumal), on the border with Quintana Roo, is the main base for exploring the region. Basically a one-street town straddling Hwy-186, it offers nothing more remarkable than the ancient Maya site it's named for, though it does have an unofficial **tourist information** office (Ⓣ983/871-6064; Tues–Sun 9am–1pm & 4–7.30pm) at the east end. Of the two main **places to stay**, *Hotel Calakmul*, about 500m west of the bus station (Ⓣ983/871-6029), is marginally preferable, with tidy air-conditioned rooms (❹) or a few very rustic wood cabins with shared bath (❸). *Mirador Maya*, 500m further (Ⓣ983/871-6005, Ⓔmirador_maya@hotmail.com; ❸), has marginally cheaper cabins with porches and private baths. Both have decent, if slightly overpriced, **restaurants**; others in town close relatively early. There's an **internet** café by the bus station, two **laundries**, several Ladatel **phones** and a small **post office**. A **petrol station** is just east of town.

A far better accommodation option is 10km north of Xpujil in the tranquil village of **Zoh-Laguna**. *Cabañas and Restaurant Mercedes* (Ⓣ983/114-9769; ❷) offers spotless cabins with private baths, and the kindly owners can fix tasty meals on request. You might fall asleep to your neighbour's satellite TV, but you'll wake up to the sound of turkeys, pigs and other roaming village livestock. If you don't have your own car, you can get a taxi from Xpujil for M$40.

Leaving Xpujil, there are four **buses** a day to Chetumal, and seven to Escárcega, though you may not always be able to secure a seat, as first-class buses can be packed with through travellers. The schedule in the station does not include several second-class Caribe buses – enquire about these if you're stuck. Second-class buses run north out of town through the Calakmul Biosphere Reserve, past the Chenes sites and eventually to Mérida via Dzibalchén, Hopelchén and the Ruta Puuc – also a handy back route for anyone **driving from Campeche**.

The Río Bec sites

The Río Bec style, characterized by long, low buildings with narrow roofcombs and matching towers (really, dramatically elongated pyramids) at each end, can be seen at a number of sites in this region. The intricate carvings and dense jungle setting make these sites some of the most striking in the Yucatán.

A typical express visit to the area involves spending the night in Xpujil, taking a taxi the next morning to visit Calakmul and Balamkú, returning to Xpujil to see the ruins there and then leaving on a late bus to Chetumal or Campeche. Two days gives you more flexibility, as does **renting a car** in Chetumal or Campeche. But taking taxis can cost about the same, and leave you with the option with continuing straight on. **Taxis** can be arranged at either of the tourist hotels in Xpujil – though you may in some cases get a slightly better rate directly from the drivers gathered at the crossroads in town. Prearranged taxis (round trip, with waiting time) charge by the number of people in the car: to Calakmul and Balamkú or to Kohunlich and Dzibanché costs between US$60 for one person and US$100 for four. To Chicanná and Becán (see below) is half that; this latter option always includes Xpuhil, even though you can walk there. Alternatively, you could take an organized **tour** to Calakmul from Campeche (see "Listings", p.758, for details) or, if your Spanish is up to it, with the experienced team at Servidores Turísticos de Calakmul (Ⓣ983/871-6064), which runs the unofficial tourist office in Xpujil. Tours may costs more, but a good guide can really make the area come alive, as many of the sites have little or no signage.

Xpuhil

The most accessible of the Río Bec sites, though also the smallest, is **XPUHIL** (the site is spelt according to the traditional Maya name), less than 300m west along the highway from the bus station (daily 8am–5pm; M$37) in the town of Xpujil. Dating from between 500 and 750 AD, it is in excellent shape, and it has three striking ersatz pyramids, with almost vertical and purely decorative stairways.

Becán

Becán (daily 8am–5pm; M$41), 6km west of Xpujil and then 500m north on a signed track, is unique among Maya sites in being entirely surrounded by a dry moat, sixteen metres wide and four metres deep. This moat and the wall on its edge form one of the oldest known defensive systems in Mexico, and have led some to believe that this, rather than present-day Flores in Guatemala, was the site of Tayasal, an early capital of the Itzá, who later ruled at Chichén Itzá. First occupied in 600 BC, Becán reached its peak between 600 and 1000 AD. Unlike the sites in the northern Yucatán, many of the buildings here seem to have been residential rather than ceremonial; in fact, the tightly packed structures – with rooms stacked up and linked by internal staircases – create a strong sense of urbanism, akin to modern apartment blocks.

Chicanná and Balamkú

The buildings at **Chicanná** (daily 8am–5pm; M$37), 2km west from Becán and just south of the highway, are the precursors of the Chenes style, with their elaborate decoration and repetitive masks of Chac; the gaping, square-carved doorway at the impressive Structure II gives the site its name ("House of the Serpent Mouth"). The rest of the building is covered in smaller masks of hook-nosed Chac, made up of intricately carved mosaic pieces of limestone, many still painted with red stucco.

After visiting the site, stop across the highway for a drink and a dip in the pool at *Chicanná Ecovillage Resort* (Ⓣ981/811-9192, Ⓦwww.chicannaecovillageresort.com; ❼), which also offers the most comfortable rooms around (though the "eco" label isn't really accurate). A bit further west on the highway, *Rio Bec Dreams* (Ⓦwww.riobecdreams.com; ❹) is a smaller **lodging** option (with cosy cabins), as well as a great travellers' resource: the owners are archeology buffs who can advise on the latest site openings and arrange good tours. Non-guests can stop in at the **restaurant**, with its varied (non-Mexican) menu.

The main draw at **Balamkú** (daily 8am–5pm; M$31), 50km beyond Chicanná and 5km west of the turn-off to Calakmul, is the elaborate, beautifully preserved seventeen-metre-long stucco frieze. It's inside the central palace; ask the caretaker to let you in. The embellished wall, crawling with toads, crocodiles and jaguars, seems to undulate in the dim light, and the rolling eyes of the red-painted monster masks, though smaller than those at Kohunlich (see p.847), are perhaps more alarming here.

Hormiguero and Río Bec

Hormiguero and **Río Bec** (the latter gives its name to the region's dominant architectural style) are accessible only by dirt road – and Río Bec is rarely even reachable by that. At Hormiguero (daily 8am–5pm; M$34), 22km south from the main crossroads in Xpujil, excellently preserved carved monster mouths from the Late Classic era adorn the two excavated buildings, which are topped with impossibly steep towers. It's a small site, but the decoration and the wild jungle setting make it a particularly transporting one. Keep your eyes on the forest floor here as you explore – Hormiguero has its name ("anthill") for good reason. There are no buses; taxis charge about M$150 round trip with waiting time.

The scattered buildings of the city of Río Bec, 10km east of Xpujil and south of the *ejido* of 20 de Noviembre, are usually closed to visitors, though some years it opens for a few months in the spring. If you do visit, you will see the most extreme example of the Río Bec false-pyramid style: as at Xpujil, the "steps" on the twin towers were never meant to be climbed – the risers actually angle outward. Ask at the tourist office in Xpujil about arranging an expedition on horseback.

Calakmul

The ruined Maya city of **Calakmul** (daily 8am–5pm; M$41, plus M$40 per car and M$40 per person for the biosphere reserve) is one of the best places for quiet contemplation of the culture's architectural legacy. Though the complex is only partially restored and a long drive south of Hwy-186 (down a signposted road midway between Escárcega and Xpujil), its location in the heart of the jungle and its sheer size make it irresistible. Probably the biggest archeological area in Mesoamerica, it has nearly seven thousand buildings in the central area alone and more stelae and pyramids than any other site; the great pyramid here is the largest Maya construction in existence, with a base covering almost five acres. The view of the rainforest from the top is stunning, and on a clear day you can even glimpse the tip of the Danta pyramid at El Mirador in Guatemala. Arrive early (the gate to the biosphere on Hwy-186 opens at 7am) to look for **wildlife** such as wild turkeys, peccaries, toucans and jaguars. Even if you don't spot anything, you'll likely hear booming howler monkeys and raucous frogs.

During the Classic period, the city had a population of about 200,000 and was the regional capital. A *sacbé* (Maya road) running between Calakmul and El Mirador (another leads on to Tikal) confirms that these cities were in regular communication. Calakmul reached its zenith between 500 and 850 AD but, along with most other cities in the area, it was abandoned by about 900 AD. Excavations begun in the 1980s have so far uncovered only a fraction of the buildings, the rest being earthen mounds.

Some of Calakmul's treasures are on display in the archeological museum at Campeche (see p.756), including two hauntingly beautiful jade masks. Another mask was found in a tomb in the main pyramid as recently as January 1998. At the site, ask about a huge interior stucco **frieze**, substantially larger and more ornate than the one at Balamkú (see above).

A few kilometres inside the reserve, Servidores Turísticos Calakmul, an excellent ecotourism organization, maintains *Yaxche* (ⓣ983/871-6064), a **campsite** with basic cabins (❷) and space for tents (M$50). It also rents gear, and will point you to **nature trails** within the reserve. You can try stopping in for a **meal**, but as the kitchen uses all local products, it may not have provisions on hand in slow seasons. In that case, you could try the **lodge** *Puerta Calakmul*, down a dirt road just after the entrance gate to the reserve; it rents pretty private cabins and has a pool too (ⓣ998/892-2624, ⓦwww.puertacalakmul.com.mx; ❼). As of late 2009, new regulations regarding **driving** into Calakmul were set to be enacted – you may have to take dedicated transport from the gate, as is the situation at Bonampak (see p.723).

From Campeche to Mérida

Two routes run from Campeche north to Mérida. First-class buses take **Hwy-180**, once the colonial Camino Real. The highway bypasses most of the towns along the way, but signposts direct you to two worthwhile detours: **Hecelchakán**, about 80km from Campeche, which has a small **archeology museum** on the main square (Mon & Tues 8am–4pm, Wed–Sun 8am–7pm; M$31) with figures from Jaina and objects from other nearby sites; and **Becal** (35km further), one of the biggest centres for the manufacture of baskets and the ubiquitous Yucatecan **jipis**, or "Panama" hats (the original Panama hats came from Ecuador). Shops throughout town sell them, and it's interesting to see a village so consumed with a single cottage industry – a fountain made of concrete hats even graces the town square. This area has two special **accommodation** possibilities: *Hacienda Blanca Flor* (ⓣ999/925-8042, ⓦwww.blancaflor.com.mx; ❼), near the village of Poc-Boc, is a great opportunity to stay in a rambling, antiques-crammed old house; it has somewhat dated decor in the rooms, but a wonderful feeling of overgrown decay. Just over the border of Yucatán state near the town of **Granada** (turn off Hwy-180 at Maxcanu) is the small but markedly more luxurious *Hacienda Santa Rosa* (ⓣ999/910-0174, ⓦwww.starwood.com/luxury; ❾); you can also **eat** here, but it's a good idea to call ahead and tell the staff you're coming.

The longer route to Mérida goes via Hopelchén and Muna, passing the great sites of **Sayil**, **Kabáh** and **Uxmal** (see p.781). With a car you could easily visit all three, perhaps stopping also at **Bolonchén de Rejon**, a pretty village of stone houses and rolling hills, and still get to Mérida within the day. Near Bolonchén, you'll see signs for the nearby **Grutas de X'tacumbilxuna'an** (daily 9am–5pm; M$50, or M$80 with translation), 3km south, but though deep and rather dramatically lit, the area you actually visit is limited, and it feels a bit overpriced. By bus, this route is slightly harder, but with a little planning – and if you set out early – you should be able to get to at least one site. Kabáh is the easiest because its ruins lie right on the main road.

Mérida

Even if practically every road didn't lead to **MÉRIDA**, it would still be an inevitable stop. Nicknamed "La Ciudad Blanca" after its white limestone buildings (now covered in peeling layers of gem-coloured paint), the capital of Yucatán state is in every sense the leading city of the peninsula, with a population of some 1.6 million. But within its historic core, there's a sense of small-town graciousness coupled with an extremely lively and sometimes avant-garde cultural scene. It draws thousands of visitors, both Mexican and foreign, and has seen a rash of expat investment in the last decade. But even as the buzz increases, the city retains its grace and manners: every street in the centre boasts a well-maintained colonial church or museum, and locals still ride in little horse-drawn taxis, which gather by the plaza in the evenings. Not only can you live well here, but you can also find good beaches nearby, and it's a great base for excursions to the Maya sites of Uxmal and Chichén Itzá (see p.781 & p.790).

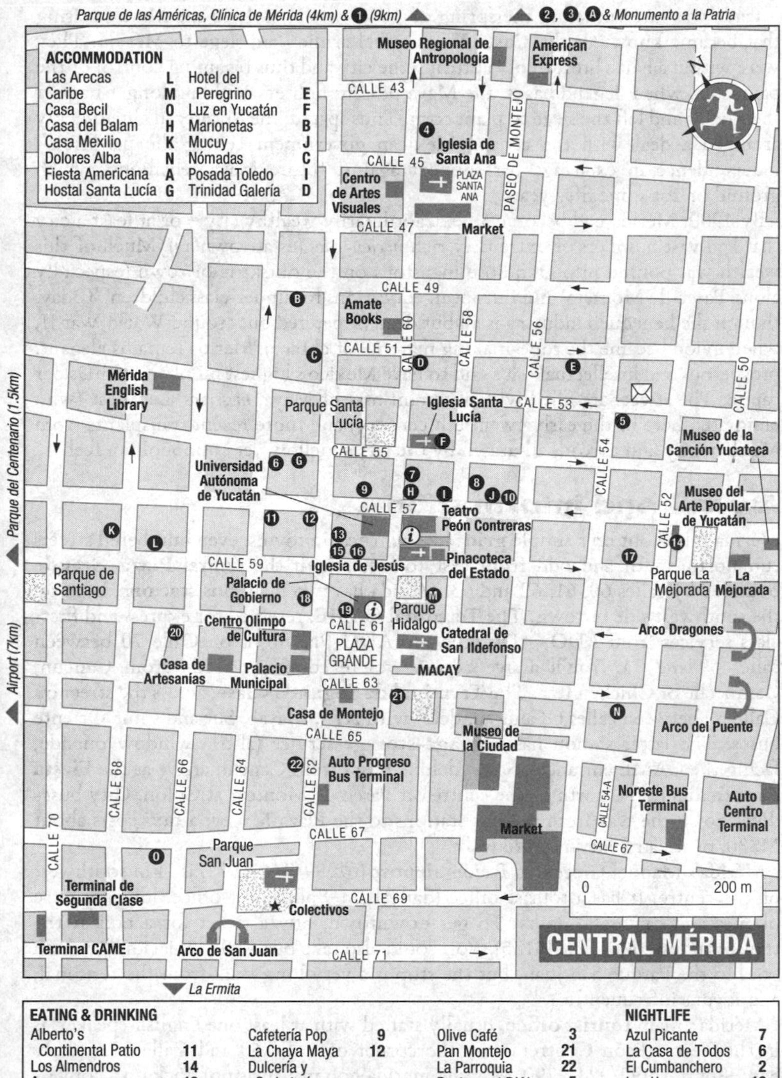

EATING & DRINKING

Alberto's Continental Patio	11	Cafetería Pop	9	Olive Café	3
Los Almendros	14	La Chaya Maya	12	Pan Montejo	21
Amaro	16	Dulcería y Sorbetería El Colón	19	La Parroquia	22
Café Alameda	8	Jugos California	21	Restaurant D'Al	5
Casa de Frida	20	El Marlin Azul	13	Savia	17
Café La Habana	15			El Trapiche	18

NIGHTLIFE

Azul Picante	7
La Casa de Todos	6
El Cumbanchero	2
Los Henequenes	10
Mambo Café	1
Pancho's	15
La Quilla	4

Some history

Founded in 1542 by conquistador Francisco de Montejo the Younger, Mérida is built over, and partly from, the ruins of a Maya city known as **Tihó** or Ichcansihó. Like the rest of the peninsula, it had little effective contact with central Mexico until the 1960s and looked to Europe for influence. This is especially evident in the architecture of the older houses, built with French bricks and tiles that were brought over as ballast in ships that exported **henequen**, the rope fibre that was Yucatán's "green gold" from early in its colonization to World War I.

Trade was interrupted in the spring of 1849, when, early in the Maya uprising that became known as the **Caste Wars**, rebel armies laid siege to Mérida. They were within a hair's breadth of capturing the city and thus regaining control of the peninsula, when, legend has it, the Maya peasant fighters could no longer neglect their fields and left the siege to plant corn. Thus spared, the Yucatecan elite quickly arranged a deal with the central Mexican government ceding the peninsula's independence in exchange for support against future Maya rebellions, which ground on for some fifty years.

By 1900, Mérida had become an extraordinarily wealthy city – or at least a city that had vast numbers of extremely rich *haciendados* (estate owners). Much of this wealth was poured into grandiose mansions on the outskirts of town (especially along Paseo de Montejo) and European educations for upper-class children. Today, though the henequen industry is all but dead (it petered out around World War II, when nylon became the rope-making material of choice), Mérida remains elegant, prosperous and intellectual – it's said to have Mexico's highest number of PhDs per capita. The streets are filled with a vibrant mix of Maya, *mestizos*, Lebanese (who emigrated here in the early twentieth century) and more recent transplants from Mexico City and abroad, all drawn by the city's mellow yet cosmopolitan feel.

Arrival and information

Mérida is laid out on a simple **grid**: like all Yucatán towns, even numbered streets run north–south and odd from east to west, with the central **Plaza Grande** bounded by calles 60, 61, 62 and 63. Mérida has two main **bus stations**, both on the southwest side of town. The **Terminal CAME**, reserved for express and first-class services from ADO, ADO GL and ADO Platino, is on Calle 70 between calles 69 and 71. You'll arrive here if you're coming directly from Cancún, Campeche or Chichén Itzá. The **Terminal de Segunda Clase**, across the street on Calle 69 between calles 68 and 70, deals with ATS, Mayab, Sur and some Oriente buses. The latter station has **luggage-storage** service (also a window outside, facing the CAME entrance). Some deluxe buses from Cancún arrive at the **Fiesta Americana** hotel, north of the centre off Paseo de Montejo at Colón. City buses don't go all the way from the bus stations to the Plaza Mayor; a **taxi** costs about M$30, or it's a twenty-minute walk.

Mérida's Manuel Crecencio Rejón **airport** (Ⓣ999/946-1372) is 7km southwest of the centre. It has a tourist office (daily 8am–8pm), post office, long-distance phones and car-rental desks. To get downtown, buy a ticket for a taxi at the transport desk outside (M$135). You could also take bus #79 ("Aviación"), which goes to the Parque San Juan, but the stop is a very long walk from the terminal, and it runs infrequently.

Mérida's main **tourist office**, usually staffed with at least one English-speaker, is in the Teatro Peón Contreras, on the corner of Calle 60 and Calle 57A (daily 8am–8pm; Ⓣ999/924-9290, Ⓦwww.merida.gob.mx/turismo). Pick up a copy of the excellent *Yucatán Today* (Ⓦwww.yucatantoday.com), in English and Spanish. Other **tourist information booths** are in the Palacio de Gobierno on the Plaza

Mayor and on Paseo de Montejo at Colón, just south of the *Fiesta Americana* hotel. The website Yucatan Living (Ⓦwww.yucatanliving.com) is another excellent resource, posting a weekly events calendar and commenting on local bars, restaurants and news.

Mérida's tourism bureau gives a free **walking tour** Mon–Sat at 9.30am; reserve at the office in the Palacio de Gobierno. Horse-drawn carriages (*calesas*) are M$200 for a one-hour trip around the centre and up Paseo de Montejo. Two bus tours go further afield than you'd walk: avoid the eyesore red double-deckers in favour of the festive open-sided one that departs from Parque de Santa Lucía (Sun 10am & 1pm, Mon–Sat 10am, 1pm, 4pm & 7pm; M$75; Ⓣ999/927-6119).

Accommodation

Although Mérida can get crowded at peak times, you should always be able to find a good, reasonably priced **hotel** room. Unless you have a very early bus to catch, there's not much point in staying in the grimier area near the **main bus stations**, nor in the generic upmarket hotels along **Paseo de Montejo**; the far more desirable options are all within a few blocks of the central plaza – which is still just a long walk or a short cab ride from the furthest transport and sights. In addition to the usual hotels, Mérida has excellent **B&Bs**, smaller inns and even **hostels**, all housed in converted old homes complete with vintage tile floors and lofty ceilings.

A glamorous alternative is to stay in a **rental house** from Urbano Rentals (Ⓦwww.urbanorentals.com); they can be quite reasonable if you're travelling with a group or family. Or you could stay outside town in a **hacienda**. One of the best is *Xcanatun*, 12km north of the city on the way to Progreso (Ⓣ999/930-2140, Ⓦwww.xcanatun.com; ⑨), but if you're happy to go further afield, check the state tourism website (Ⓦwww.yuctan.travel) for a full list.

Hotels

Caribe C 59 no. 500, Parque Hidalgo Ⓣ999/924-9022, Ⓦwww.hotelcaribe.com.mx. One block from the plaza, on a pretty, small square of its own. Rooms don't have any particular flair, but the views of the cathedral and plaza from the rooftop pool are lovely. There's also a travel agency and parking on site. ⑤

Casa Becil C 67 between C 66 and C 68 Ⓣ999/924-6764, Ⓔhotelcasabecil@yahoo.com.mx. Small hotel with very friendly and helpful staff, close to the main bus stations. A few rooms have a/c, and there's a shared kitchen. But if you don't need this proximity you can find better value closer to the plaza. ③

Casa del Balam C 60 no. 488 at C 57 Ⓣ999/924-2150, Ⓦwww.hotelcasadelbalam.com. Good combo of colonial-house style – tiled floors, dark-wood furniture – with the amenities of a large hotel. Rooms have fridges and bathtubs, and there's a shady pool and cosy, wood-panelled bar. Breakfast included. ⑦

Dolores Alba C 63 no. 464 between C 52 and C 54 Ⓣ999/928-5650, Ⓦwww.doloresalba.com. Popular mid-range place situated around two courtyards (one colonial-style, and one sporting a dazzling array of mirror glass) and a large swimming pool. Rooms in both sections have TV, phone and a/c. With parking, laundry facilities and more, you get a lot for your money, but it is a bit out of the way. ④

Fiesta Americana C 56 at Colón Ⓣ999/942-1111, Ⓦwww.fiestaamericana.com. Just off Paseo de Montejo, Mérida's top business-class hotel is often booked with tour groups, but it's a bit of a hike from the centre. It's mentioned here primarily as a landmark: the lobby houses a number of travel and car agencies, as well as a terminal for express buses. ⑦

Mucuy C 57 no. 481 between C 56 and C 58 Ⓣ999/928-5193, Ⓦwww.mucuy.com. Quiet and well run, with clean, good-value rooms (a/c is M$50 extra), a small pool and a truly hospitable owner. English-speaking staff and a laundry on the premises. ③

Posada Toledo C 58 no. 487, at C 57 Ⓣ999/923-1690, Ⓔhptoledo@finred.com.mx. Grand, well-kept colonial building with beautiful tiled floors and heaps of antique furniture. Single rooms can be a little small, but the "honeymoon suite" is an amazing confection of French antiques and gold trim. ③

Trinidad Galería C 60 no. 456 at C 51 Ⓣ999/923-2463, Ⓦwww.hotelestrinidad.com. Wonderfully eccentric hotel crammed full of bizarre artefacts, sculptures and paintings. Rooms upstairs are lighter and more spacious, but all are individually decorated (some have a/c). Also has a pool, a small breakfast café and two art galleries. The *Trinidad* (C 62 at C 55), under the same ownership, has several cheaper rooms with shared bath, and guests can use the pool at the *Galería*. ❸

B&Bs and inns

Las Arecas C 59 no. 541 between C 66 and C 68 ⓣ999/928-3626, ⓦwww.lasarecas.com. Small, colonial-style guesthouse (one of the few run by a *meridano*) that's a fantastic bargain. Rooms around the small garden courtyard are simply furnished, but four of the five have a/c, and there's wi-fi throughout the house. ❸

Casa Mexilio C 68 no. 495 between C 59 and C 57 ⓣ999/928-2505, ⓦwww.casamexilio.com. One of Mérida's real treasures, this very attractive B&B, in a restored colonial townhouse, is a fascinating labyrinth of individually decorated rooms, tranquil gardens, sun terraces and a pool. The full breakfast (included) is delicious. ❺

Del Peregrino C 51 no. 488 between C 54 and C 56 ⓣ999/924-5491, ⓦwww.hoteldelperegrino.com. A quiet, beautifully remodelled house, with an especially nice outdoor kitchen, *Del Peregrino* has tidy, simply furnished tile-floor rooms. ❹

Luz en Yucatán C 55 no. 499 between C 58 and C 60 ⓣ999/924-0035, ⓦwww.luzenyucatan.com. Delightful studio rooms and apartments in a rambling house, decorated in rich colours, plus a pool and plenty of comfortable public space. The owners can arrange massages, Spanish lessons and more. Rates are negotiable for longer stays. ❺

Marionetas C 49 no. 516 between C 62 and 64 ⓣ999/928-3377, ⓦwww.hotelmarionetas.com. No antique clutter in this fully renovated colonial home – rooms are sunny, sparely furnished and spacious. The owner designed many of the traditional-style floor tiles herself, and the breakfasts (included) are generous. Pool and free parking. ❼

Hostels

Hostal Santa Lucía C 55 no. 512 between C 62 and C 64 ⓣ999/928-9070, ⓦwww.hostalstalucia.com. A decent back-up if *Nómadas* is full, with beds for M$95. Nice location near Parque Santa Lucía.

Nómadas C 62 no. 433 at C 51 ⓣ999/924-5223, ⓦwww.nomadastravel.com. The longest-established hostel is a smooth operation, with co-ed and single-sex dorms (M$109), space for hammocks (M$75) and fan-only private rooms. There's even a pool. ❸

The City

Any exploration of Mérida begins naturally in the **Plaza de la Independencia**, also called the Plaza Grande or Plaza Mayor. It's the hub of city life, particularly in the evenings, when couples meet on park benches and trios of *trovadores* wait to

▲ Sunday street party in Mérida

be hired for serenades. The plaza is ringed by some of Mérida's oldest buildings, including the simple **Catedral de San Ildefonso** (daily 6am–noon & 5–8pm), built in the second half of the sixteenth century. Most of the church's valuables were looted during the Mexican Revolution. One object that was destroyed, the **Cristo de las Ampollas**, has been recreated and is the focal point of a **fiesta** from mid-September through to mid-October. According to legend, this "Christ of the Blisters", which is in a chapel to the left of the main altar, was carved from a tree in the village of Ichmul, which had burned for a whole night without showing the least sign of damage; later, in 1645, the church at Ichmul burned down, and the crucifix survived, though blackened and blistered.

Beside the cathedral, the former bishop's palace has been converted into shops, offices and the **MACAY** (Museo de Arte Contemporáneo Ateneo de Yucatán; 10am–6pm daily, closed Tues; M$20), which has the best modern art collection in the region, with permanent displays featuring the work of internationally acclaimed Yucatecan painters Fernando Castro Pacheco, Gabriel Ramírez Aznar and Fernando García Ponce.

On the south side of the plaza stands the **Casa de Montejo**, a palace built in 1549 by Francisco de Montejo, the first conquistador to attempt to bring the peninsula under the control of Spain. His initial effort, in 1527, failed, as did several later forays; however, his son, Francisco de Montejo the Younger, did what the father could not, and secured the northern part of the peninsula in the 1540s. The building now belongs to Banamex, and most of it is used as office space. During weekday business hours, visitors can see the lavishly restored wood-panelled dining room, off the back right corner of the Moorish-feeling courtyard. Above a staid doorway of Classical columns, the facade is decorated in the manically ornate plateresque style (probably the first instance of it in the New World), with conquistadors depicted trampling savages underfoot.

Across the plaza from the cathedral, the **Palacio Municipal** is another impressive piece of sixteenth-century design, with a fine clock tower. Next door, the modern **Centro Olimpo de Cultura** contains an auditorium, a planetarium and an art gallery showing local works and travelling exhibits.

Completing the square, the nineteenth-century **Palacio de Gobierno** (daily 8am–10pm; free) is a must-see; enormous, aggressively modernist murals by Fernando Castro Pacheco cover the walls on the ground floor and in the large front room on the second floor. They powerfully depict the violent history of the Yucatán and the trials of its indigenous people.

North and east of the Plaza de la Independencia

Most of the remaining monuments in Mérida lie north of the plaza, bordering Calle 60 and Paseo de Montejo. Calle 60 is one of the city's main commercial streets, lined with fancy hotels and restaurants. It also boasts a series of colonial buildings, starting one block north of the plaza with the seventeenth-century Jesuit **Iglesia de Jesús**, on the corner with Calle 59. It was built using stones from the original Maya city of Tihó, and a few pieces of decorative carving are visible in the wall on Calle 59. In the same block of Calle 59, the **Pinacoteca del Estado Juan Gamboa Guzmán** (Tues–Sat 8am–8pm, Sun 8am–2pm; M$31) houses a collection of nineteenth-century portraits of prominent Yucatecans and Mexican leaders – Emperor Maximilian, who was executed less than three years into his reign, looks particularly hapless among the crowd of presidents. Back on Calle 60, continuing north, you reach **Teatro Peón Contreras**, a grandiose Neoclassical edifice built by Italian architects in the heady days of Porfirio Díaz. Across the street stands the **Universidad Autónoma de Yucatán**, a highly respected institution that has existed, under various names, since 1624.

Detour east on Calle 57 to Calle 50 for the **Museo del Arte Popular de Yucatán** (Tues–Sat 9.30am–7pm, Sun 9am–2pm; M$20), a small but flawless collection of Mexican craftwork. Behind the former monastery of La Mejorada, on Calle 57 between calles 50 and 48, the **Museo de la Canción Yucateca** (daily 9am–5pm; M$15, free Sun) details the diverse musical influences on the local *trovadores*, from pre-Columbian traditions to Afro-Cuban styles.

Returning to Calle 60, one block north of the Teatro Peón Contreras the sixteenth-century **Iglesia Santa Lucía** stands on the elegant plaza of the same name – a small square that was once the city's stagecoach terminus. Three blocks further, **Plaza Santa Ana** is bordered by a cluster of market stalls. The surrounding neighbourhood is developing an art scene – see what's on at the **Centro de Artes Visuales** (Mon–Fri 9am–10pm, Sat & Sun 9am–7pm; free), the university's exhibition space. Up and down the block are several private galleries. Head east from here a couple of blocks to reach the south end of Paseo de Montejo.

Paseo de Montejo and beyond

Paseo de Montejo is a broad boulevard lined with trees and modern sculptures. It's also lined with the magnificent mansions of the henequen-rich grandees who strove to outdo one another around the end of the nineteenth century. One of the most striking, the Palacio Cantón, at Calle 43, houses Mérida's **Museo Regional de Antropología** (Tues–Sat 8am–8pm, Sun 8am–2pm; M$41). The Beaux Arts palace, grandly trimmed in wrought iron and marble, was built at the beginning of the twentieth century by Francisco Cantón Rosado, the railway tycoon, state governor and general who was a key supporter of dictator Porfirio Díaz. The walk **to the museum** from the plaza takes about thirty minutes; you can also get there on a "Paseo de Montejo" bus running up Calle 56, or in a horse-drawn **calesa** taxi (about M$100 from the centre to the museum).

The collection is short on actual relics, but it's a useful introduction to the sites and Maya culture nonetheless, with displays covering everything from prehistoric stone tools to modern religious practice and an informative emphasis on ancient Maya daily life and belief. Upstairs, temporary exhibits examine Mérida's history and specific archeological sites. Most displays are in both Spanish and English. The **bookshop** offers leaflets and guidebooks in English for dozens of ruins in the Yucatán and the rest of Mexico.

Another fifteen minutes' walk north on Paseo de Montejo, past scores of mansions, brings you to the **Monumento a la Patria**, covered in neo-Maya sculptures relating to Mexican history. You could also visit **Parque de las Américas**, west on Colón, which is planted with a tree from every country on the American continent. Travellers with children – or anyone who wants to see modern Mérida at leisure – can head for the green space of **Parque del Centenario**, west of the plaza (head straight out along Calle 59 to Avenida Itzáes). It contains a **zoo** (free admission), with a miniature train running through it.

South of the Plaza de la Independencia

The streets get more crowded and the shops more jumbled as you head towards Mérida's main **market**, a huge place between calles 67, 69, 54 and 56. In two vast joined halls plus a clutch of stalls around the periphery, more than two thousand vendors ply their trades. It's a wild scrum of consumer goods, from freshly hacked-up beef to hand-tooled leather belts to numerous varieties of bananas. Arrive before noon to see the most bountiful foodstuffs; **craft shops** (many in a separate wing on Calle 56-A at Calle 65) are open all day.

On Calle 65 at Calle 56, the grand **Museo de la Ciudad** (Mon–Fri 9am–8pm, Sat & Sun 9am–2pm; free) occupies the beautiful old central post office. The exhibits trace city history from ancient Maya times through the henequen boom (text in Spanish and English). There's also a gallery of local contemporary art in the building.

Shopping

For **crafts**, prices in the market are no great shakes, unless you're an unusually skilled and determined haggler. Before buying anything, head for the **Casa de Artesanías** (Tues–Sat 9am–8pm, Sun 9am–1.30pm), in the Casa de la Cultura on Calle 63 two blocks west of the plaza. Run by a government-sponsored organization, the shop sells consistently high-quality crafts, including delicate silver filigree jewellery; the clothing options are somewhat limited, though.

One of the most popular souvenirs of Mexico is a **hammock** – and Mérida is probably the best place in the country to buy one. If you want something you can realistically sleep in, exercise a degree of care and never buy from street vendors or even a market stall – their products are invariably of poor quality. Comfort is measured by the tightness of the weave and the breadth: because you're supposed to lie in a hammock diagonally to be relatively flat, the distance it stretches sideways is as crucial as the length (although obviously the woven portion of the hammock, excluding the strings at each end, should be at least as long as you are tall). Cotton threads (*hilos de algodón*) are more comfortable and better hold their shape, but nylon is easier to wash. (Sisal hammocks are generally scratchy and very poor quality – avoid them.) As a guideline, a decent-size cotton hammock (*doble* at least) will set you back about M$250. For a **specialist dealer**, head to Tejidos y

Yucatecan cuisine

Though it varies across the peninsula, food in the Yucatán has a few unifying elements, most based on **traditional Maya combinations** and accented with many earthy **spices**. The most popular dishes are:

Puchero A mutable stew that often includes chicken, beef, pork, squash, cabbage and sweet potato in a broth seasoned with cinnamon and allspice, all garnished with radish, coriander and Seville orange

Poc-chuc A combination of pork with tomatoes, onions and spices, widely considered the region's signature dish

Sopa de lima Chicken broth with a fragrant local citrus and tortilla chips, and the most popular appetizer or evening snack

Pollo or cochinita pibil Chicken or suckling pig wrapped in banana leaves and cooked in a *pib*, a pit in the ground, the shredded meat then utilized in many other snacks

Papadzules Tacos filled with hard-boiled eggs and covered in a very rich red and green pumpkin-seed sauce

Pavo en relleno negro Turkey in a black, burnt-chile sauce

Salbutes Crisp corn tortillas topped with shredded turkey, pickled onions, avocado and radish, ubiquitous at dinner time

Panuchos The same as *salbutes*, with an added dab of beans

Chaya A spinach-like green that's reputed to cure everything that ails you, often blended into a drink with pineapple

Huevos motuleños A sweet-savoury mix of fried eggs and beans on a crisp tortilla, topped with mild salsa, ham, cheese, peas and fried banana slices.

Little of this is hot, but go easy with the *salsa de chile habañero* that most restaurants have on the table. It's also called *xnipek*, Maya for 'dog's nose', because the fiery chile induces a clammy sweat.

Cordeles Nacionales, very near the market at Calle 56 no. 516-B, just north of Calle 65. More a warehouse than a shop, it has hundreds of hammocks stacked against every wall, sold by weight; a high-quality, dense-weave *doble* weighs about a kilo and a half and costs M$250. Similar stores include El Campesino and El Aguacate, both on Calle 58, and La Poblana, Calle 65 no. 492, near Calle 60.

Other good buys include **clothing**, in particular men's *guayabera* shirts, which both Cubans and *meridanos* claim to have invented; Panama hats, known here as *jipis*; and *huipiles*, which vary wildly in quality, from factory-made, machine-stitched junk to hand-embroidered, homespun cloth. Mérida's distinctive *trova* **music** is available in many gift shops on CD; it's especially cheap at the weekly serenade on Parque Santa Lucía, where vendors sell remastered classics or newer songs in the same vein. You can also try the gift shop at the Museo de la Canción Yucateca (see p.770).

Eating and drinking

Good **restaurants** are plentiful in the centre of Mérida, though the best (and some of the least expensive) are open only for lunch. At dinner, many restaurants are a bit overpriced and cater largely to foreigners; locals tend to frequent the **snack stalls** on Plaza Santa Ana (Calle 60 at Calle 47) and Parque de Santiago (Calle 59 between calles 70 and 72) for *panuchos*, *salbutes* and *sopa de lima*. There are also sidewalk cafés on the **Parque Hidalgo**, along Calle 60 between calles 61 and 59. **Juice bars** – notably *Jugos California*, on the southwest corner of the plaza – serve all the regular juices, as well as home-made root beer, and *La Parroquia* (Calle 62 between calles 65 and 67) is a **lechería**, serving cinnamon-laced chocolate milk, fruit plates and yogurt. The **bakery** *Pan Montejo*, at the corner of calles 62 and 63, also makes a good breakfast.

Cafés

Café Alameda C 58 between C 55 and C 57. This old-fashioned lunch café, a popular Lebanese hangout, serves *garbanzos* (hummus) and other Middle Eastern standards.

Café La Habana C 62 at C 59. A good place to spy on Mérida's older bohemian crowd, who smoke and debate, while black-and-white-clad waiters dish out Mexican-style diner fare. There's free wi-fi, and decent coffee. Open 24hr.

Cafetería Pop C 57 between C 60 and C 62. A good breakfast joint with vintage 1960s decor that also serves hamburgers, spaghetti and Mexican snacks. Close to the university, it's favoured by students and professors. Daily 7am–midnight.

Mérida's free entertainment

The historic centre hosts a party nearly every night of the week, all free and attended largely by locals. Many films and concerts happen at the **Centro Olimpo de Cultura**, on the northwest corner of the plaza. In addition, these are the recurring events:

Monday *Jarana* folk dances, in or in front of the *ayuntamiento* (city hall) on the west side of the main plaza. 9pm.

Tuesday Big band music, heavy on the mambo, Parque de Santiago (C 72 at C 59); *trova* at the Centro Olimpo. 8.30pm.

Wednesday Concert at the Centro Olimpo. 9pm.

Thursday Serenata Yucateca, traditional *trova* music, Parque Santa Lucía; classical music at the Centro Olimpo. 9pm.

Saturday Noche Mexicana, music from all over Mexico, at the start of Paseo Montejo, Calle 56-A; jazz, salsa and more on the Plaza de la Independencia. 8pm.

Sunday Car-free centre: in the morning (8am–noon), bicycles take over the streets for the Bici-Ruta; in the afternoon and evening, the plaza is filled with music, dancing, food stalls and more. There's also a flea market in the Parque Santa Lucía.

Dulcería y Sorbetería El Colón C 61, on the north side of the plaza. Popular spot for exotic fruit sorbets. There's another branch on Paseo de Montejo between C 39 and C 41, a good place to stop after the archeology museum.

Olive Café Paseo de Montejo between C 37 and C 39. In case you need your modern espresso fix, along with some gelato. Good cultural calendar too. Closed Sun.

La Quilla C 60 between C 43 and C 45. Near a strip of galleries, this funky café-bar (see p.774) is adorned with art and sagging sofas.

Restaurants

Alberto's Continental Patio C 64 no. 482 at C 57 ⓣ999/928-5367. Old-world Mérida, with a beautiful courtyard and formal service. The food, which blends Mexican and Middle Eastern flavours, is erratic in quality and ungodly expensive. It's best for snacks, a drink, and a chat with the charming Lebanese owner.

Los Almendros C 50 between C 57 and C 59, in the Plaza Mejorada. One of Mérida's most venerable Yucatecan restaurants is marred by inconsistency, but when it's on, it serves delicious, moderately priced food. The dressier wing, *Gran Almendros*, with a separate entrance around the corner, has slightly higher prices, but can be fun on a busy Sunday afternoon.

Amaro C 59 no. 507 between C 60 and C 62. *Amaro* is set in a lovely tree-shaded courtyard with a fountain and a romantic guitarist Wed–Sat. The food is a little overpriced, but there are lots of veggie options, such as *crepas de chaya* – though many are heavy on cheese.

Casa de Frida C 61 no. 526 at C 66 ⓣ999/928-2311. Specializing in *chiles en nogada*, this eclectic little restaurant is painted in candy colours and has a cosy back patio.

La Chaya Maya C 62 at C 57. A simple, sparkling-clean restaurant with a thorough menu of Yucatecan specialities, heavy on the *chaya* (a nutritious wild green), pumpkin seeds and other earthy flavours.

El Marlin Azul C 62 between C 57 and C 59. Longtime local favourite for seafood, including great fish tacos and perfect fresh *ceviche*. It closes at 4.30pm, however, and there's no sign on the blue awning.

Restaurant D'Al C 54 at C 53. A typical *cocina económica* serving hearty, stick-to-your-ribs daily specials (about M$30), but open into the evenings. Also, beer is served – a rarity at this type of hole-in-the-wall restaurant.

Savia C 59 between C 52 and C 54. A vegetarian's delight, with big salads and sandwiches.

El Trapiche C 62 between C 59 and C 61. Basic, budget-friendly Yucatecan restaurant, open for every meal, from fresh juices for breakfast to *poc-chuc* for dinner.

Entertainment and nightlife

In addition to all the free entertainment (see opposite), there are **mariachi nights** in hotel bars and **salsa dancing** in nightclubs. On Fridays, the **Ballet Folklórico de la Universidad de Yucatán**, presents a colourful performance of traditional Mexican and Maya ceremonies at the Centro Cultural Universitario, Calle 60 at Calle 57 (9pm; M$30). Also check the schedule at **Teatro Peón Contreras**, which hosts some excellent musicians, and tickets are usually very affordable; the symphony orchestra plays alternating Fridays and Sundays October–April.

Apart from hard-drinking cantinas (and there are plenty of these in the city, including a couple on Calle 62, just south of the plaza), many of Mérida's **bars** double as restaurants, with relatively early closing times to match.

Azul Picante C 60 between C 55 and C 57. This small salsa club caters more to tourists than some of the others listed here, but it offers free lessons early in the evenings, as well as Mexican- and Caribbean-themed nights. A couple of other decent bars are in adjacent buildings.

La Casa de Todos C 64 at C 55. Very small student bar – more of a clubhouse, really – with a strong leftist bent. Most nights there's a rousing folksinger or two on the tiny stage; other nights, young punk bands. Wed–Sun after 9pm.

El Cumbanchero Paseo de Montejo at C 39. More convenient than *Mambo Café*, this small salsa bar is owned by the son of the late Rubén González, of Buena Vista Social Club. Dancing starts around dinner time, with an older crowd at first, who then give way to younger dancers around 10pm. Also open for brunch on Sun.

Los Henequenes C 56 at C 57. A modern reinvention of a traditional bar serving *botanas* (snacks) and beers, set in an old house and generally busy in the late afternoon. It's perhaps a little *too* modern, but it does have a local clientele, two-for-one beer specials and live music.

Mambo Café In the Plaza Las Américas mall. Worth the cab ride (about M$50) if you're looking to mingle with salsa-mad locals. Touring Dominican and Cuban bands often play here. Cover is usually M$50. Wed–Sat 10am–3am.

Pancho's C 59 between C 60 and C 62. A steak restaurant with a pricey haute Mexican menu, this sprawling space is nonetheless better as a bar, with tasty mojitos and margaritas. Try to hit the happy hour, 6–8pm Mon–Fri.

La Quilla C 60 between C 43 and C 45 ⓦwww.laquilla.blogspot.com. This artist-friendly café really takes off in the evenings – it often hosts hip-hop shows, DJs, films and other cool events (cover M$20 or M$30), starting at 9pm or so. Even on quiet nights, it's a nice place to drink a beer.

Listings

Airlines Mexicana, Prolongación de Montejo 91, at C 17 ⓣ999/944-9105.

American Express Paseo de Montejo 492, between C 41 and C 43 ⓣ999/942-8200, ⓕ942-8210 (Mon–Fri 9am–5pm, Sat 9am–noon).

Banks Most are around C 65 between C 60 and C 64, have ATMs and are open 9am–4pm. The most centrally located is Banamex, in the Casa de Montejo on the south side of the plaza; it also has an ATM.

Moving on from Mérida

As the biggest travel hub in the Yucatán, Mérida has a profusion of **bus stations**, each theoretically dedicated to certain bus companies and regions; in practice, routes and services overlap a bit – see the chart, opposite, for frequencies from each station. The fastest long-distance services—ADO, semi-deluxe ADO GL or deluxe Platino—go from the **Terminal CAME** and, mostly for Cancún, the **Fiesta Americana** terminal off Paseo de Montejo. You might be able to find a comparably fast and cheaper trip at the **Terminal de Segunda Clase,** across the street from the CAME; also come here if you want a bus to any town between Mérida and Campeche, or a town on the Ruta Puuc.

Buses at the **Noreste** terminal, on Calle 67 at Calle 50, serve coastal towns east and west of Progreso (such as Chelem, Dzilam de Bravo and San Felipe) and some points on the Ruta de Conventos southeast of Mérida (such as Mayapán). For Dzibilchaltún and Progreso, go to the **AutoProgreso** station on Calle 62 between calles 65 and 67. AutoCentro, Calle 65 at Calle 48, specializes in Izamal, and provides the only service to the ruins of Aké.

Additionally, **colectivos** often provide more frequent service to destinations an hour or two outside the city, and to smaller villages. These, as well as small buses to Dzibilchaltún, Oxkutzcab and Ticul, congregate on **Parque San Juan** (Calle 62 at Calle 69). For Progreso, colectivos leave from the east side of Calle 60 between calles 65 and 67. Principal destinations and the corresponding bus stations and services can be found in Travel details, p.850.

Flights depart from Lic. Manuel Crecencio Rejón airport (ⓣ999/946-1530, ⓦwww.asur.com.mx) for Mexico City, Cancún and Villahermosa, as well as Houston; to get to the airport, catch bus #79 ("Aviación") from Parque San Juan. A taxi from the centre costs about M$100.

The Ruta Puuc bus

Infrequent buses make the ruins on the **Ruta Puuc** (see p.780) difficult to visit without a car, but Autotransportes del Sur (ATS) offers a day-trip service for tourists that's budget-friendly (M$146), if a bit rushed. The bus leaves at 8am every day from the Terminal de Segunda Clase, visiting Uxmal, Sayil, Kabáh and Xlapak. To go to Uxmal only, it's M$41. You get just long enough at each site to form a general impression, and there's no guide or lunch included in the price.

Buses from Mérida

For bus station locations, see opposite.

City/town	Bus terminal	Frequency
Campeche	CAME	at least hourly, round-the-clock
	Fiesta Americana	1 daily at midnight
	Segunda Clase	every 30min 4.15am–7.15pm
	Noreste	hourly 5.20am–8.20pm
Cancún	CAME	at least hourly, round-the-clock
	Fiesta Americana	9 daily 6am–8.30pm
	Segunda Clase	every 30min 6am–midnight
	Noreste	hourly 5am–10.20pm
Celestún	Noreste	hourly 5.15am–10.30pm
Chetumal	CAME	4 daily
	Segunda Clase	7 daily 7am–midnight
Chichén Itzá	CAME	4 daily
	Segunda Clase	hourly 6am–midnight
	Noreste	hourly 5.20am–10.20pm
Chiquilá/Holbox	Segunda Clase	1 daily at 11.30pm
Ciudad del Carmen	Noreste	hourly 4am–1.35am
	Segunda Clase	5 daily
Dzibilchaltún	AutoProgreso	hourly 5am–midnight
Dzilam de Bravo	Noreste	7 daily 5am–8pm
Escárcega	CAME	6 daily 8.30am–midnight
	Segunda Clase	3 daily
Felipe Carrillo Puerto	Segunda Clase	10 daily 4am–11.55pm
Izamal	Noreste	every 45min 4.45am–9pm
Mahahual	Segunda Clase	Thu–Sat 11.30pm in summer
Maní, via Mayapán	Noreste	hourly 5.30am–8pm
Mexico City	CAME	5 daily
Oxkutzcab	Segunda Clase	hourly 6am–6pm
	Noreste	hourly 5.30am–8pm
Palenque	CAME	5 daily
Playa del Carmen	CAME	14 daily 6.30am–3.45am
	Segunda Clase	8 daily, with 2 via Cobá
Progreso	AutoProgreso	every 30min
Río Lagartos	Noreste	3 daily
San Felipe	Noreste	1 daily at 5.30pm
San Crisanto	Noreste	3 daily
Santa Elena	Segunda Clase	5 daily
Ticul	Segunda Clase	hourly 6am–6pm
	Noreste	3 daily
Tizimín	Noreste	hourly 5.30am–5.30pm
Tulum	CAME	5 daily
	Segunda Clase	8 daily 5am–11.55pm, with 2 via Cobá (5am & 9.55pm)
Valladolid	CAME	13 daily 6am–7.30pm
	Segunda Clase	hourly 6am–midnight
	Noreste	hourly 5am–10.20pm
Villahermosa	CAME	hourly 7.15am–1.35am
	Segunda Clase	3 daily

Bike rental On Sun mornings for the Bici-Ruta (see p.772), bicycles are for rent on the plaza; the rest of the week, contact Exiquio Cetina, ⓣ999/982-0940, ⓔexiquiocetina@yahoo.com.

Bookstores Amate Books, C 60 between C 49 and C 51 (closed Mon), has an excellent selection of English-language titles on Mexican culture, plus Latin American literature and even magazines and guidebooks. For maps, head to Librería Burrel, C 59 between C 60 and C 62, or Sanborn's, in the *Fiesta Americana*. Librería Dante, on the west side of the plaza and on C 59 opposite Burrel, also sells some guidebooks as well as field guides. The Conaculta bookstore adjacent to Teatro Daniel Ayala, C 60 just north of the plaza, carries art books, guides and music, mostly in Spanish. Alternatively, borrow books from the extensive Mérida English Library, C 53 between C 66 and C 68.

Car rental Family-run Mexico Rent a Car, with offices at C 57-A between C 58 and C 60, and at C 62 no. 483-A, has very good rates with insurance (ⓣ999/927-4916, ⓔmexicorentacar@hotmail.com). International agencies have offices in a strip on C 60 between C 55 and C 57 and in the *Fiesta Americana*.

City buses The city-bus system is very convoluted, but in general, northbound buses run up Calle 56. For Paseo de Montejo, look for #17 on Calle 59 between calles 56 and 58, or #18 on Calle 56 at Calle 59. You can flag buses down at any corner; fares (usually M$5) are posted on the doors.

Consulates Opening hours are limited, so phone ahead. Belize, C 53 no. 498 at C 58 ⓣ999/928-6152, ⓔconsbelize@dutton.com.mx; Cuba, C 1-D no. 320 between C 42 and C 44, Col. Campestre ⓣ999/944-4216, ⓔconscubaamer1@prodigy.net.mx; Netherlands, C 64 no. 418 between C 47 and C 49 ⓣ999/924-3122, ⓔpixan2003@prodigy.net.mx; US, C 60 no. 338-K between C 29 and C 31, Col. Alcala Martín ⓣ999/942-5700, ⓔmeridacons@state.gov.

Hospitals Mérida is the Yucatán's centre for medical care – there is no shortage of doctors. Clinica de Mérida hospital, Itzáes 242 at Colón (ⓣ999/942-1800, ⓦwww.clinicademerida.com.mx), is accustomed to dealing with foreigners.

Internet and telephone Casetas are not numerous; you're better off with VOIP at the internet cafés (about M$20/hr), which dot every street in central Mérida, and especially C 61 west of the plaza. There's free wi-fi in most of the city's parks.

Laundry Lavandería La Fe, C 64 between C 55 and C 57 (closed Sun).

Post office C 53 between C 52 and C 54 (Mon–Fri 8am–4.30pm, Sat 9am–1pm).

Taxis Taxis can be hailed all around town and from ranks at Parque Hidalgo, the post office and Parque San Juan. The ones at ranks charge according to a zone system – usually M$30 around the centre, and up to M$70 to the outskirts. Cars roving the streets (signed "Radio Taxi") use meters, and are often cheaper.

Tourist police This special squad roams the plaza giving directions and otherwise helping visitors (ⓣ999/925-2555 ext 260).

Travel agents and tours Ecoturísmo Yucatán (ⓣ999/926-7756, ⓦwww.ecoyuc.com.mx) runs a day trip to the cenotes at Cuzamá. Red de Ecoturismo de Yucatán, C 56-A no. 437, near the Monumento a la Patria (Mon–Fri 10am–2pm, Sat 4–6pm; ⓣ999/926-7756, ⓦwww.redecoturismo.com), is a network of small community eco-adventure projects, offering activities like bike trips and camping excursions. Student travel agency Nómadas (ⓣ999/948-1187, ⓦwww.nomadastravel.com.mx) has good-value excursions to Uxmal and Chichén Itzá, plus excellent plane fares to Mexico City; Yucatan Trails, C 62 no. 482 between C 57 and C 59 (ⓣ999/928-2582, ⓔyucatantrails@hotmail.com), runs Cuba trips and a handy one-way Mérida–Chichén Itzá–Cancún package; they also offer luggage storage for a small fee.

North of Mérida: the coast

A wide, fast road (Hwy-261) connects Mérida with the coast to the north, first passing the ancient Maya complex of **Dzibilchaltún**, then arriving after 36km in the port of **Progreso**, on which *meridanos* descend en masse in summer.

It's easy enough to visit both Dzibilchaltún and Progreso from Mérida: **combis for Chablecal**, which leave from Parque San Juan (calles 62 and 69) about every thirty minutes, stop near the ruins; leaving, you can walk or hitch a ride back to the main highway, where you can flag down a Progreso- or Mérida-bound bus or *combi*. *Combis* return to Mérida from the corner of calles 80 and 31 near the post office, on the north side of Progreso's Parque Central (leaving on summer Sunday evenings, with the rest of the weekend crowds, you'll have a very long wait). To go straight to the coast from Mérida, **buses** leave from the AutoProgreso terminal on Calle 62 between calles 65 and 67.

Due west of the city, the little village of **Celestún** offers a very different coastal experience, as it's surrounded by a large nature reserve. In fact, most people hit the beach only after taking a boat tour around a long inlet that's home to a massive flamingo colony.

Dzibilchaltún

The archeological importance of the ruins of the ancient city of **Dzibilchaltún** (daily 8am–5pm; M$79) is hardly reflected in what you actually see. What it lacks in grandiosity, though, it makes up for in the excellent small **Museo del Pueblo Maya** (Tues–Sun 8am–4pm), which examines the persistence of Maya culture until modern times. There's also a very pretty **cenote**, in which you can swim, and the area is part of an **eco-archeological park**, where birders can catch the rough-winged swallow and the Yucatán woodpecker. Allow about two hours to see everything.

The place was settled from 1000 BC right through to the Conquest, the longest continuous occupation of any known site. More than eight thousand structures have been mapped, but unfortunately, little has survived, in particular because the ready-dressed stones were a handy building material, used in local towns and in the Mérida–Progreso road. There is very little signage at the site, so it's worth hiring a **guide** (M$200 for up to six people) at the main entrance.

From the museum at the entrance, a meandering nature trail leads to the **Templo de las Siete Muñecas** (Temple of the Seven Dolls). The temple was originally a simple square pyramid, subsequently built over with a more complex structure. Later still, a passageway was cut through to the original building and seven deformed clay figurines (dolls) were buried, with a tube through which their spirits were meant to commune with the priests. The structure is remarkable for being the only known Maya temple to have windows, and for having a tower in place of the usual roofcomb. On the **equinoxes**, the sun shines straight through the tower doors, in a display of ancient astronomical savvy that draws a crowd of tourists.

One of the ancient causeways that linked the city's major points runs straight from the temple to another cluster of ruins. The centre of the grassy field is dominated by the shell of a Franciscan chapel. A little further west, **Cenote Xlacah**, in addition to providing the ancient city with water, was of ritual importance to the Maya: more than six thousand offerings – including human remains – have been discovered in its deeper end. It's also home to several types of fish, including the Yucatán tetra, a type of sardine found only in the peninsula.

Progreso and around

First impressions of **PROGRESO** – a working port with a six-kilometre-long concrete pier – can be uninspiring, especially at the end of a summer weekend when crowds of day-trippers have pulled out, leaving beer bottles and food wrappers in their wake. But the beach, really the only reason to visit, is long and broad, with fine sand, and it makes for a pleasant day out from Mérida. If you're here in the winter, the beach will be empty, except perhaps for a few intrepid tourists from one of the cruise ships that dock here occasionally.

Progreso is a small place, and it's not difficult to find your way around. The **bus station** is on Calle 29 (running east–west, four blocks south of the water) at the corner of Calle 82. Calle 80, one block east, is the main street, running north–south and dead-ending at the beach. The **tourist office** (Mon–Fri 8am–2pm, Sat

8am–1pm; ⓣ969/935-0114) is here, in the Casa de la Cultura at Calle 27, but it has only a free map and a couple of flyers. On cruise-ship days, the courtyard at the front hosts a crafts market. Also on Calle 80 is the lively city **market** (the fruit and veg vendors are usually shut by 2pm), along with a few **banks** with ATMs, and a couple of **internet** cafés.

Hotels in town range from very seedy to somewhat overpriced, but Progreso is a popular family destination, so many have large rooms ideal for groups. The high season is July, August and Semana Santa; outside of that, prices drop considerably. Best bets include the *Hotel Progreso*, Calle 29 no. 142 at Calle 78 (ⓣ969/935-0039; ❷), and *San Miguel*, just across the street (ⓣ969/935-1357; ❸) – they're both several blocks back from the beach with clean, air-conditioned rooms. A couple of other, more upscale hotels cluster on the east side, just off the end of the main beach: *Casa Isidora*, on Calle 21 between calles 58 and 60 (ⓣ969/935-4595, ⓦwww.casaisidora.com; ❺) and *Yakunah*, further east between calles 48 and 50 (ⓣ969/935-5600, ⓦwww.hotelyakunah.com.mx; ❺), are both set in old houses, with pretty tiled floors and a pool.

For **eating**, try the lively *Eladio's*, on the malecón at Calle 80, where you can make a meal of the tasty *botanas* that come free with beers. Equally popular is *Sol y Mar*, across the street, for seafood snacks, and *Le Saint Bonnet*, a family restaurant on calles 19 and 78 that serves more elaborate seafood and has a pool. All of these places also set out tables on the beach. For cheap comidas corridas, the town's small market has several good stalls; also try the area around the **plaza** at Calle 80 and Calle 31 – *El Cordobés*, on Calle 80, is a good place for coffee and snacks.

Beaches east of Progreso

Heading **east from Progreso**, the shorefront behind the beach is built up all the way to the village of **Chicxulub Puerto** some 5km away, where the excellent *Restaurante Moctezuma* (aka "Los Barriles", for the giant wood barrels that form its front entrance), just east of the plaza, is a favourite destination for a late seafood **lunch**. After this, bus and car traffic is shunted away from the beach and onto Hwy-27, which runs a bit further inland. At km 15 on the highway, a **viewing platform** (free; follow signs for the *mirador turístico*) over the Uaymitún inlet is a great place to see flocks of **flamingoes.** Go at sunset, but before the 6pm closing time (7pm in summer), for your best chance of spotting them; the caretakers rent binoculars for M$10.

The road continues to **Telchac Puerto**, a laid-back seaside village popular in the summer with escapees from Mérida, then another 9km to **San Crisanto**, where a village organization leads **mangrove tours** (M$40; 1hr 30min) in small rowboats with four or five people – great for bird watching, and you end at a cenote for a swim. The same group also rents large **cabañas** (❺), for up to six people (ⓣ991/105-3710 or 991/910-4310, ⓦwww.sancrisanto.org). The office is just south of the crossroads, towards the baseball field.

With more time, it's possible to get even further east along an ever-narrowing road to where the coast reverts to a wild state. In the village of **Santa Clara** (really just a few buildings between the sea and the salt flats), the beach is tranquil and the seafood fresh. At the end of the road, **Dzilam de Bravo** has a sea-defence wall rather than a beach. The real draw here is **Bocas de Dzilam**, a state nature reserve in the Parque Natural San Felipe. Set in 620 square kilometres of coastal forests, marshes and dunes, the *bocas* are freshwater springs on the seabed. The water's minerals encourage turtles, tortoises, crocodiles and dozens of bird species. To arrange a tour, walk east from the plaza to the fishing port, where a few boat captains are equipped to take you out; expect to pay about M$400 for three or four hours. A more direct way to the town is a second-class **bus** in Mérida from the Autobuses del Noreste terminal (see p.774).

Beaches west of Progreso

Venturing **west from Progreso** is not as promising, though in the 19km of coast road you will find a few more beach villages: **Yucalpetén**, **Chelem** and **Chuburná**, respectively fifteen, twenty and thirty minutes from Progreso and easy day trips from Mérida, have clean, wide beaches and some **accommodation** and restaurants. *Hotel Sian Ka'an* (ⓣ969/935-4017; ❺), in Yucalpetén, is one good option, offering oceanfront rooms ideal for groups or families, with balconies and kitchenettes. *Costa Azul*, just down the road in Chelem, is a highly recommended fish **restaurant**.

Beyond Chuburná, the coast road, which was damaged by Hurricane Isidore in 2002, is not passable, and you'll have to turn inland again. It's not worth making a detour back to the coast at **Sisal**; it's hard to believe this was Mérida's chief port in colonial times (and gave its name to the henequen fibre exported from here), as now it's practically deserted.

Celestún

Were it not for its amazing flamingo-filled lagoon, **CELESTÚN** – 93km west of Mérida, at the end of a sandbar on the peninsula's northwest coast – would be little more than a one-boat fishing village. To see the birds – most numerous from November to May, when blue-winged teal and shovellers also migrate – in the warm waters of the 146,000-acre **Ría Celestún Biosphere Reserve**, hire a boat at the official *parador turístico*, just past the bridge on the main road into town. Ask the bus driver to drop you here, as it's a twenty-minute walk back from the main square.

The standard tour (M$780 for up to six; approx 1hr) stops at the flamingo feeding grounds and a freshwater spring amid mangroves; the longer trip (M$1380 for up to six; approx 2hr) also visits a "petrified forest" (really, a spooky swath of salt-choked trees). Guides (M$300/1hr, M$400/2hr) are definitely recommended – all speak English and can identify most of the birds you'll see. If you'd like to join a larger group, show up around 10am, as that's when most people arrive, usually on the 8am bus from Mérida.

You may be approached by unlicensed captains outside the *parador*; they will offer a competitive price, but their deep-keel boats are not designed for the inlet, and some passengers have found themselves pushing their craft out of the mud.

For extended **bird-watching** tours, look for Alberto Rodriguez Pisté, a fluent English-speaker and longtime birder; he's one of the expert guides at the *parador turístico*, and if he's not there, he can usually be found at *Restaurant Celestún*, on the waterfront.

Practicalities

Buses for Celestún depart sixteen times daily from Mérida's Noreste terminal (see p.774) beginning at 5.15am; the trip takes about two hours. The village has half a dozen **places to stay**: beachfront *María del Carmen*, Calle 12 no. 111 at Calle 15 (ⓣ988/916-2170, ⓔmcrodriguez@hotmail.com; ❹) is the best bet on the beach, with balconies overlooking the water; air-conditioning is an option. *Posada Marina Luciely*, on the plaza (ⓣ988/916-2144; ❸), has the cheapest rooms, basic but tidy, with fans. If you really want to escape, the remote and lovely *Eco Paraíso Xixim* (ⓣ988/916-2100, ⓦwww.ecoparaiso.com; ❾) is 10km north of town. Operating primarily on wind and solar power, it has fifteen rustic-looking but very comfortable cabañas (all renovated in 2009), excellent showers and a deserted beach; rates include breakfast.

Of the several **seafood restaurants** along the beach, *La Palapa* is the biggest and priciest, but unfortunately one of the only reliable ones. For home cooking, visit the *loncherías* by the market (just off the inland side of the plaza). There's also a bakery, an internet café, a bank and a petrol station.

If you're travelling by car, you might be tempted by the small road south to Chunchucmil, rather than the straight highway back to Mérida. Don't be – it's colossally potholed and very slow going for most vehicles.

South of Mérida: Uxmal, the Ruta Puuc and the Ruta de Conventos

About 80km south of Mérida in the Puuc hills lies a group of important archeological sites, well restored and many of them uncrowded with visitors. The chief attraction on the so-called **Ruta Puuc** is **Uxmal**, second only to Chichén Itzá (see p.790) in tourist appeal as well as size and historical significance, though greater in the beauty and harmony of its unique architectural style. Hwy-261 carries on from Uxmal to the lesser site of **Kabáh**; shortly after that, bearing east on a smaller side road, you pass **Sayil** and **Labná**. From Labná you can continue to the farming town of **Oxkutzcab**, on the road between Muna and Felipe Carrillo Puerto, and head back to Mérida via **Ticul** and Muna. Or you can follow another scenic route, the **Ruta de Conventos,** north to Maní and its Franciscan monastery then past other fortified churches and the Maya ruins of **Mayapán**.

The distinctive Puuc sites clearly evolved from themes in the Río Bec and Chenes regions: you'll see the same gaping monster mouths and facades decorated in mosaic-like Xs and checkerboards. In both cases, though, the techniques reflect a new strategy of mass production – the mask-covered front of the Codz Poop at Kabáh, for instance, is dotted with hundreds of consistently round carved eyes that form both a regular decorative pattern and individual images of the rain god Chac. A new core-and-veneer style of construction, rather than stone blocks stacked with mortar, yielded sounder buildings with a smoother appearance, which is highlighted by the tendency to leave the lower registers of buildings unadorned. However, though related architecturally, each site is actually quite distinct from the others.

Hacienda hopping

Along the Ruta Puuc are numerous ruined henequen plantations, in various states of repair. The closest one to Mérida, **Hacienda Yaxcopoil** (Mon–Sat 8am–6pm, Sun 9am–1pm; M$50, kids free), on the edge of the village of the same name, is also one of the most dramatic. At its height, it employed four hundred people, but now the main house stands in a state of picturesque disrepair – peeling walls, sagging ceilings, rooms full of mildewed tablecloths and faded pictures. It also has a wonderful **room to rent**, a huge, tiled, high-ceilinged space with two double beds. You can cook over a fire or they'll bring meals in for you (ⓣ999/927-2606, ⓦwww.yaxcopoil.com; ❺).

Just west of Hwy-261, about 30km north of Uxmal, the attractively refurbished **Hacienda Ochil** (11am–7pm; ⓣ999/910-6035, ⓦwww.haciendaochil.com) operates as a good Yucatecan restaurant (mains M$85), a small **museum** and some excellent handicraft workshops. Some of the old train tracks along which carts of henequen were transported have been restored. The entry fee of M$20 is waived if you're eating at the restaurant. About 8km off Hwy-261 to the east, **Hacienda Temozón** (ⓣ999/923-8089, ⓦwww.luxurycollection.com; ❾) is one of the peninsula's best hotels, with a rather lavish international restaurant. Breakfast, however, is not too expensive.

If you're travelling by bus, *Yaxcopoil* and *Ochil* lie right beside the road, so it's easy enough to be dropped here and flag down another to continue your journey.

Getting to the sites

Because the sites are far apart, and on a road poorly served by buses, it's best to **rent a car**: in two days you can explore all of the key sites, spending the night in Santa Elena or Ticul. For details of car rental agencies, see p.776. If your budget doesn't allow for a car, opt for the **Ruta Puuc day-trip bus** (M$146) from Mérida (see p.774). It's a bit rushed, leaving you only a short time at each set of ruins, but Uxmal is the last stop, so it's possible to stay later here and pay for a different bus back. Scores of Mérida travel agencies offer pricier Puuc-route trips that include meals and a guide.

Uxmal

Meaning "thrice-built", the UNESCO world heritage site of **UXMAL** (pronounced OOSH-mal; daily 8am–5pm; M$111) represents the finest achievement of the Puuc-region Maya culture before it fell into its ultimate decline near 1000 AD. Its spectacular buildings are encrusted all over with elaborate, and sometimes grisly, decoration. It's potentially more rewarding than a visit to Chichén Itzá, as the crowds are (somewhat) smaller, the decorative detail is fascinating, and you can still climb one of the pyramids. Try to arrive close to opening time (the drive from Mérida takes about an hour); you can see the major buildings in a couple of hours and leave before the buses start arriving.

As in all Maya sites in the Yucatán, the face of **Chac**, the rain god, is everywhere. Chac must have been more crucial in this region than almost anywhere, for Uxmal and the other Puuc sites have no cenotes or other natural sources of water, relying instead on *chultunob*, jug-shaped underground cisterns, to collect and store rainwater (most have been filled in, to prevent mosquitoes breeding, but Kabáh has an extant one).

Little is known of the city's history, but the chief monuments, which marked its peaks of power and population, were erected around 900 AD. Sometime after that, the city began to decline, and by 1200 Uxmal and the other Puuc sites, together with Chichén Itzá, were all but abandoned. The reasons are unknown, although political infighting, ecological problems and loss of trade with Tula, near Mexico City, may have played a part. Later, the **Xiu dynasty** settled at Uxmal, making it one of the central pillars of the League of Mayapán (see p.787), but a rebellion in 1441 overthrew that alliance and put an end to centralized Maya authority over the Yucatán.

The site

The main restored buildings are set out on a roughly north-south axis in a large cleared site; the alignment of individual buildings often has astrological significance, usually connected with Venus or the sun. Little is known of the history, but what is clear is that the chief monuments and the city's peaks of power and population, fall into the Terminal Classic period, 800–1000 AD. Though there are indications of settlement long before this, most of the buildings that you see date from this time.

The Pirámide del Adivino

Entering the site, you first see the most remarkable of all Mexican pyramids, the **Pirámide del Adivino** (Pyramid of the Magician), soaring at a startling angle from its uniquely oval base. The legend of the pyramid's creation tells that an old sorceress who lived in a hut where the pyramid now stands hatched a dwarf son from an egg and encouraged him to challenge the king to a series of tests – all of which the dwarf won, thanks to a little magic. Finally the king challenged him to build a pyramid overnight: the dwarf succeeded, and became ruler of Uxmal.

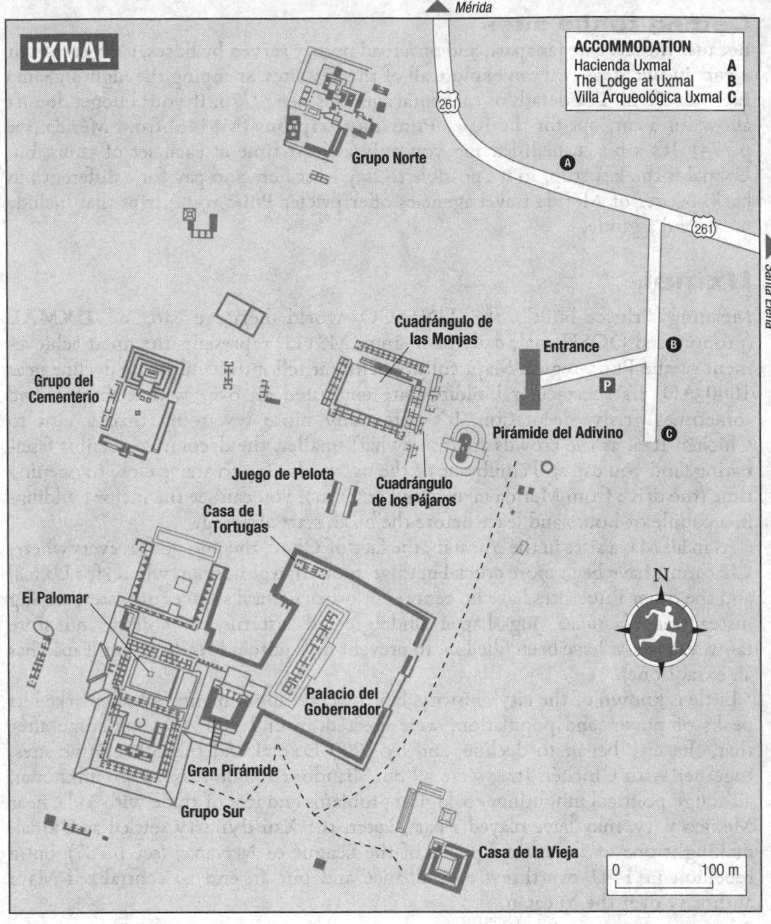

Archeological evidence, however, shows at least five stages of construction – six if you count the modern restoration, which may not correspond to any of its earlier incarnations. At the base of the rear (east) stairway, a tunnel reveals **Templo III**, one of the earlier levels. Walk around to the west face of the pyramid into the **Cuadrángulo de los Pájaros** (named for the macaws that stud the roofline of the building on the west side) to admire the even steeper stairway that runs down either side of a second, earlier sanctuary in a different style. Known as the **Edificio Chenes** (or Templo IV), as it reflects the architecture of the Chenes region (see p.758), the building's entire front forms a giant mask of Chac. At the bottom of the west face, divided by the stairway, is the very first stage of construction.

The Cuadrángulo de las Monjas and the Casa de las Tortugas

Behind the pyramid, the **Cuadrángulo de las Monjas** (Nunnery Quadrangle) is a beautiful complex of four buildings enclosing a plaza. Despite the Spanish name, it wasn't a convent; theories range from a military academy to a sort of earthly paradise, where intended sacrificial victims would spend their final months in debauchery. The four buildings, probably constructed between 895 and 906 AD, are each set on a slightly different level, possibly representing the four main levels of the Maya universe. The facade of each is decorated with complex reliefs, and the quadrangle itself is a slightly irregular shape, apparently to align with Venus.

Maya architectural skills are at their finest here, as the false vaults of the interiors are taken about as wide as they can go without collapsing (wooden crossbeams provided further support), and the frontages are slightly bowed in order to maintain a proper horizontal perspective. The **north building**, probably also the oldest, has a strip of plain stone facade (from which doors lead into vaulted chambers) surmounted by a slightly raised panel of mosaics, featuring geometric patterns and human and animal figures, with representations of Maya huts above the doorways. The **west building**, which has been heavily reconstructed, boasts even more varied themes, and the whole of its ornamentation is surrounded by a coiling, feathered rattlesnake with the face of a warrior emerging from its jaws. The **east building** mirrors the west one in its proportions; its snake decorations, however, run in long horizontal bars.

An arched passageway through the middle of the **south building**, the lowest of the four, is directly aligned with the **ball-court** (ham-handedly rebuilt with cement) outside. Today a path leads through here, between the ruined side walls of the court and up onto the levelled terrace on which stand the Palacio del Gobernador (see below) and the **Casa de las Tortugas** (House of the Turtles). This very simple, elegant building, named after the stone turtles carved around the cornice, demonstrates another constant theme of Puuc architecture: stone facades carved to resemble rows of narrow columns. These, marked with bands of masonry, probably represent the Maya huts still in use today, with walls of bamboo or saplings lashed together.

The Palacio del Gobernador and the Grupo Sur

The **Palacio del Gobernador** (Governor's Palace) marks the finest achievement at Uxmal. Arriving at the then virtually unknown site in June 1840, explorer and writer John L. Stephens did not doubt its significance. "If it stood this day on its grand artificial terrace in Hyde Park or the Garden of the Tuileries," he later wrote, "it would form a new order…not unworthy to stand side by side with the remains of the Egyptian, Grecian and Roman art." The palace faces east, away from the buildings around it, probably for astronomical reasons – its central doorway aligns with the column of the altar outside and the point where Venus rises. The use of light and shade on the long, low facade lends a remarkable harmony, as do the strong diagonals that run through its broad band of mosaic decorations. Close up, the mosaic features masks of Chac alternating with grid-and-key patterns and highly stylized snakes. Moreover, the patterns vary in depth, lending a fascinating texture to the facade.

Behind the palace stand the ruinous buildings of the **Grupo Sur** (South Group), with the partly restored Gran Pirámide (Great Pyramid) and El Palomar (Dovecote, or Quadrangle of the Doves). You can climb the rebuilt staircase of the **Gran Pirámide** to see the temple on top, decorated with macaws and more masks of Chac – some of these have even smaller carved faces set inside their mouths. **El Palomar** was originally part of a quadrangle like that of the Nunnery, but the only building to retain any form is this, topped with the great latticed roofcomb that gives it its name: it looks somewhat like a dovecote.

The outlying structures are rather anticlimactic, but the scrub forest is the perfect place to spot some of the Yucatán's more distinctive birds, such as the turquoise-browed motmot, with its pendulum-like tail, particularly along the path that runs off the south side of the Palacio del Gobernador. The trail leads to an odd display of small **stone phalluses**, protected by a thatch roof – collected from all over the site, they're evidence of a fertility cult centred on Uxmal. (They're also worked into the back of the building on the west side of the Nunnery Quadrangle.)

Visiting Uxmal

Several **buses** a day run direct from Mérida to Uxmal in about an hour, and any bus heading down the main road towards Hopelchén will drop you a short walk from the entrance. There's a pay car park at the entrance to the site, where the **visitor centre** includes a small museum, bookshop with guides to the site, crafts store, snack bar and ATM. **Guides** cost about M$550 for a small group. A **sound-and-light show** (M$40, or included in price of day entrance ticket) starts at 7pm in winter and 8pm in summer. The commentary is in Spanish (translation equipment M$25) and of dubious historical accuracy, but the lighting effects highlight the relief decorations beautifully. No buses run back to Mérida after the hour-long show.

Several **hotels** are close to the site, none in the budget category. All are subject to sudden arrivals of huge tour groups, which can make quality of service and food erratic, but are likely to offer good deals when not full. Two are right at the site's entrance: *Villa Arqueológica Uxmal* (ⓣ997/974-6020, ⓦwww.villasarqueologicas.com.mx; ⑤) is the best value here, with a pool and tennis courts, though the rooms are relatively small; *The Lodge at Uxmal* (ⓣ998/877-2495, ⓦwww.mayaland.com; ⑧) is more spacious, if a bit overpriced, and its breezy **restaurant** and bar, *La Palapa*, is a convenient spot for a cool drink. Across the main highway from the site entrance, the colonial-style *Hacienda Uxmal* (ⓣ998/887-2495, ⓦwww.mayaland.com; ⑧) is a sister hotel to *The Lodge*, with similar rates. Other accommodation nearby but not within walking distance includes budget options in Santa Elena (see below) or the ultra-luxury of *Hacienda Temozón* (see box, p.780).

Santa Elena

The village of **SANTA ELENA**, sixteen kilometres south of Uxmal, and just seven from Kabáh, is worth visiting mainly for the magnificent view from its large **church,** which dominates the skyline for miles around from a position atop a small hill. Beside the church is a morbidly interesting small **museum** (daily 8am–6pm; free) with displays on local funerary practices, including the 200-year-old mummified remains of four children discovered under the church floor in 1980.

Two exceptionally pleasant (and popular, so book ahead) **places to stay** are both on Hwy-261 as it bypasses the village centre. The *Flycatcher Inn* (no phone, ⓦwww.flycatcherinn.com; ⑤) is the first you reach, a B&B with seven rooms and a separate guest cottage, all decorated with local craftwork and furnished with lovely beds; air-conditioning is optional. It's about a five-minute walk south from the main square, or buses from Mérida will drop you on the highway very nearby. A little further south is *Sacbe Bungalows* (ⓣ985/858-1281, ⓦwww.sacbebungalows.com.mx; ③), where a hospitable Mexican–French couple offer basic but spotless bungalow rooms, all with porches, dotted about spacious grounds; there's a cottage with a kitchen as well. Breakfast and supper are available. In between the two hotels are two small **restaurants**: *El Chac Mool* does decent, inexpensive local food (closes at 8pm), while *The Pickled Onion* (Mon–Sat 1–9pm, Sun 5–9pm), which has a pool for guests, has a more international menu but also does excellent versions of local dishes; vegetarians will appreciate the fresh salads and the *chaya* soufflé.

Ticul

Located 80km south of Mérida on Hwy-184, **TICUL** is another good base for exploring the Puuc region, though not especially scenic. Historically an important centre of Maya shamanism, it's also a shoe-producing town, full of shops stocked with wildly impractical sparkly sandals. It's well served by **buses** to and from Mérida and with services to Cancún and the east coast.

The centre of town is around the junction of calles 25 and 26, with a large plaza to either side, plus a massive church and several **hotels**. Simplest of these is the friendly *Sierra Sosa*, Calle 26 no. 199-A between calles 23 and 21 (Ⓣ&Ⓕ997/972-0008; ❷), where basic rooms have a shower and fan (upstairs is better), though air-conditioning and TV are available. A smarter alternative is the *Plaza,* Calle 23 no. 202 between calles 26 and 26-A (Ⓣ997/972-0484, Ⓦwww.hotelplazayucatan.com; ❸), with TV, telephone and air-conditioning in all rooms. For a little greenery, head to *Posada Jardín* at Calle 27 no. 216 between calles 28 and 30 (Ⓣ997/972-0401, Ⓦwww.posadajardin.com; ❸), which has four excellent-value cabins with separate sleeping and sitting areas, air-conditioning, TV and fridge, set in a bright garden with a small pool.

Ticul's best-known **restaurant**, *Los Almendros*, is the original location of what is now a small chain and claims to have invented *poc-chuc* and other Yucatecan dishes – unfortunately that's no guarantee you'll get a great meal, but it's worth a try. It's on Calle Principal heading out of town towards Oxkutzcab, in a big building complete with a pool, and packed with families at weekends. Back in the centre, for an inexpensive *comida*, try *Restaurante & Cocktelería La Carmelita*, at the corner of calles 23 and 26. At night, don't miss the tortas at the front of the market on Calle 23 between calles 28 and 30.

Buses from Mérida and elsewhere use a station directly behind the church at the corner of calles 24 and 25-A. **Colectivos and trucks** for Mérida as well as Santa Elena, Oxkutzcab and surrounding villages set off when they're full from various points in the immediate vicinity of the bus station: for Mérida around the corner of calles 24 and 25, other destinations mainly from Calle 25-A alongside the church. Other practicalities are also central – the Banamex **bank** facing the plaza on Calle 26 just off Calle 25 has an ATM; directly opposite is a good **internet café**.

Kabáh

The extensive site of **KABÁH** (daily 9am–5pm; M$37), meaning "Mighty Hand", stretches across the highway some 25km from Uxmal. Much of it remains unexplored, but the one great building, the **Codz Poop**, or Palace of Masks, lies not far off the highway to the east, near the main entrance. The facade of this amazing structure is covered all over, in ludicrous profusion, with goggle-eyed, trunk-nosed masks of Chac – to get into the doorways, you need to tread over the mask's noses. Even in its present state – with most of the long, curved noses broken off – this remains one of the strangest and most striking of all Maya buildings, decorated so obsessively, intricately and repetitively that it seems the product of an insane mind. A couple of lesser buildings are grouped around the Codz Poop, in front of which stands a rare working *chultun* (cistern), with a concave stone floor gathering water into the underground chamber.

On the other side of the road is an unusual circular **pyramid** – now simply a green conical mound that, once you spot it, is so large you can't believe you missed it. It is believed that the building, erected on a natural elevation, functioned as a place where priests offered sacrifices or interpreted divine messages. Just beyond, a sort of triumphal arch marks the point where an ancient thirty-kilometre causeway, or *sacbé*, from Uxmal entered the city.

Sayil

A sober, restrained contrast to the excesses of Kabáh, the site of **Sayil** (daily 8am–5pm; M$37) lies some 5km along a smaller road heading east off the highway from a junction 5km beyond Kabáh. Once one of the most densely populated areas in the Puuc region, Sayil was home to an estimated 17,000 people from 700 AD to 1000 AD. It is dominated by one major structure, the eighty-metre-long **Gran Palacio** (Great Palace), built with three storeys, each smaller than the one below. Although several large masks of Chac adorn a frieze around the top of the middle level, the decoration mostly takes the form of bamboo-effect stone pillaring – seen more extensively here than at any other Puuc site. The interiors of the middle level, too, are lighter and airier than usual, thanks to the use of broad openings, their lintels supported on fat columns.

Few other structures have been cleared, and those that have been are widely scattered in the forest – a walk to these remote spots is a long, hot one, but it gives you a better sense of the scale of the old city, as well as a chance to view wildlife like hummingbirds. From the Gran Palacio a path leads through the forest to the small temple of **El Mirador**, and in the other direction to a stele, carved with a phallic figure and now protected under a thatched roof. The path (in fact, a former ceremonial *sacbé*) carries on to the **Palacio Sur**, a large, little-restored structure with another characteristic bamboo facade.

Xlapak and Labná

The minor road continues from Sayil past tiny **XLAPAK** (daily 8am–5pm; free), the smallest and least-visited of the Puuc sites. If you have the time, stop to see the one restored building, a small, elegant palace with huge Chac masks above its doorways and geometric patterns on the facades. Three kilometres after Xlapak, the ancient city of **LABNÁ** (daily 9am–5pm; M$37), historically far smaller and less important than Sayil, is in many ways a more impressive site. There has been more excavation here, so the main buildings can all be seen as part of a harmonious whole. The **Palacio**, near the entrance, bears traces of sculptures including the inevitable Chac, and a crocodile-snake figure with a human face emerging from its mouth – thought to symbolize a god emerging from the jaws of the underworld. Remnants of a *sacbé* lead from here to the **Arco de Labná**. Originally part of a complex linking two great squares, like the Nunnery at Uxmal, it now stands alone, richly decorated on both sides: on the east with geometric patterns, on the west (the back) with these and niches in the form of Maya huts or temples. Nearby is **El Mirador**, a barely restored temple mound topped by the well-preserved remains of a tall roofcomb. An inner passageway at one time led to the site's principal temple.

Grutas de Loltún

Just before you reach Oxkutzcab on the road from Labná, the **Grutas de Loltún** (daily by guided tour only at 9.30am, 11am, 12.30pm, 2pm, 3pm & 4pm; M$66), are the most impressive caves in the Yucatán, at least among those that are developed for visitors. The hour-long tour (for which you can request an English-speaking guide) concentrates on strange rock formations and patterns in giant stalactites and stalagmites. The caves were revered by the Maya as a source of water. At the entrance, a huge bas-relief warrior guards the opening to the underworld, and throughout are traces of ancient paintings and carvings on the walls. The surrounding jungle is visible through the collapsed floor of the last gallery, and ten-metre-long tree roots find an anchor on the cavern floor.

Across the road is a decent **restaurant**, *Lol-tún*, with tasty *panuchos* and other standards. From Oxkutzcab, you can take a **colectivo** or truck; they leave from Calle 51 next to the market, and if you get there by 8.30am you may be able to catch the truck taking the cave employees to work. **Getting back** is less easy, as the trucks are full of workers and produce, but if you wait something will turn up. The short taxi ride from the town will cost you approximately M$50.

Oxkutzcab

From Labná, you can head back to Mérida on the fast Hwy-18 (look for signs just north of the Grutas de Loltún), or you can stop off in the village of **OXKUTZCAB**, 25km northeast from Labná. It's a decent rest stop after completing the Ruta Puuc, with a huge **fruit market**. Calles 51 and 50 edge the main park and the mercado, with a Franciscan church between them.

Buses to Mérida via Ticul (2hr) leave about every hour from the **bus station** at the corner of Calle 56 and Calle 51; *colectivos* come and go from beside the mercado on Calle 51. One clean, basic **hotel**, *Hospedaje Duran* (Ⓣ997/975-1748; ❷), is centrally located on Calle 51 opposite the fruit market, but the *Hotel Puuc*, on Calle 55 at Calle 44 on the way out of town towards Labná (Ⓣ997/975-0103, Ⓦwww.oxkutzcab-hotelpuuc.com; ❸), is much preferable and costs only marginally more for bright, clean rooms with air-conditoning and TV, and has a good restaurant next door. The Banamex **bank** on Calle 50, opposite the park, has an ATM, and there's an **internet** café at the corner of calles 51 and 52. **Restaurants** and cafeterias skirt the market.

Ruta de Conventos

The "Convent Route" – Hwy-18 from Oxcutzcab to Mérida – may have no more impressive churches than anywhere else in the Yucatán, but it is a pretty drive. Every town along the route has an immense fortress church, but the historic highlights are **Maní** and the late Maya site of **Mayapán**.

The **churches** date mainly from the seventeenth century or even earlier, as the Spanish were trying to establish their control. They were built so huge partly to impress, as a sign of the domination of Christianity over traditional gods (often on the site of Maya temples, using the stone from the older buildings), and partly as fortresses and places of refuge in times of trouble.

Maní

Twelve kilometres north of Oxkutzcab is the small town of **MANÍ**. Founded by the Xiu after they abandoned Uxmal, at the time of the Conquest it was the largest city encountered by the Spanish in the Yucatán, though almost no trace now survives. Avoiding a major confrontation, Maní's ruler, Ah Kukum Xiu, converted to Christianity and became an ally of the Spanish. In 1548 one of the earliest and largest **Franciscan monasteries** in the Yucatán was founded here. This still stands, surrounded now by Maya huts, and just about the only evidence of Maní's past glories are the ancient stones used in its construction and in walls around the town. In front of the church, in 1562, Bishop Diego de Landa held his infamous auto-da-fé, in which he burned the city's records (because they "contained nothing in which there was not to be seen the superstitions and lies of the devil"), destroying virtually all surviving original Maya literature. Méridans often come down here on day trips to dine at ✱ *El Príncipe Tutul-Xiu*, Calle 26 between calles 25 and 27 (Tues–Sun 11am–7pm), a festive palapa-roof **restaurant** that has been serving Yucatecan standards for more than thirty years – it can be an absolute zoo on Sundays, but the food is always delicious.

Mayapán

Roughly halfway between Maní and Mérida, the ruins of **MAYAPÁN** (daily 8am–5pm; M$31), the most powerful city in the Yucatán from the thirteenth to the fifteenth century, sit right beside the road. According to Maya chronicles, it was one of the three cities (the others being Chichén Itzá and Uxmal) that made up the **League of Mayapán**, which exercised control over the entire peninsula from around 987 to 1185. The league broke up when the **Cocom** dynasty of Mayapán attacked and overwhelmed the rulers of an already declining Chichén Itzá, establishing themselves as sole controllers of the peninsula. However, archeological evidence suggests that Mayapán was not a significant settlement until the thirteenth century. The rival theory has Mayapán founded around 1263, after the fall of Chichén Itzá.

Whatever its history, Mayapán was a huge city by the standards of the day, with a population of some 15,000 on a site covering five square kilometres, in which traces of more than four thousand buildings have been found. Rulers of subject cities were forced to live here, perhaps even as hostages, where they could be kept under control. This hegemony was maintained until 1441, when Ah Xupan, a Xiu leader from Uxmal, finally led a rebellion that succeeded in overthrowing the Cocom and destroying their city – thus paving the way for the tribalism that the Spanish found on their arrival and facilitating considerably the Conquest. What can be seen today is in some ways a disappointment – the buildings were crude and small by Maya standards, at best poor copies of what had gone before, and only a few have been restored (a visit doesn't take long). This less-than-grand architecture has led to the society being dismissed as decadent and failing, but a case can be made for the fact that it was merely a changing one. As the priests no longer dominated here (hence the lack of great ceremonial centres), what grew instead was a more genuinely urban society: highly militaristic, no doubt, but also far more centralized and more reliant on trade than previous Maya culture.

East of Mérida: Aké and Izamal

The land east of Mérida and north of Hwy-180 is particularly dense with Maya towns and villages. All laid out according to the same orderly Spanish plan, around a central plaza and church, they are uniformly pretty, but the excellent regional crafts centre of **Izamal** in particular merits a detour. It's easy enough to come from Mérida on a day trip, but don't leave before sunset, when the place takes on a perfect golden glow, thanks to the striking ochre-yellow that covers all of the buildings. You may even consider staying a night or two and making this a base for day trips, if you want a break from cities. On the scenic, slow route to Izamal (via the hammock-weaving towns of Tixkokob and Cacalchén), you also pass **Aké**, an intriguing Maya ruin now inextricable from a neighbouring henequen factory. Public transport runs frequently to Izamal, but Aké requires a car, or at least a taxi south from Hwy-180, where the closest second-class bus runs about every 45min.

Aké

Midway between Izamal and Mérida on the back road via Cacalchén, the **Aké ruins** (9am–5pm; M$27) are partially integrated into an inhabited village and working henequen plantation. Aké was probably in alliance with the old city of Izamal, as it is linked to it by one of the peninsula's largest *sacbeob* (Maya roads). The most impressive building here is the **Edificio de las Pilastras**, a large platform topped with more than twenty stone pillars. The henequen **hacienda**, San Lorenzo de Aké, a fine example of neo-French architecture from the end of the nineteenth century, intermingles with the Maya rubble, and you're welcome to wander through the antique-looking machinery to see the fibre-making process. An Auto Centro bus makes the 45-minute trip from Mérida to the ruins six times daily, roughly every three hours; the last bus back is at 8pm.

Izamal

The exceptionally scenic town of **IZAMAL**, 72km east of Mérida, is a beautiful, tranquil place to spend a night or two, or longer, as a more rural alternative to the big city. It was formerly an important religious centre for the Maya, where they worshipped **Itzamná**, mythical founder of the ancient city and one of the gods of creation, at a series of huge pyramid-temples. Most of these are now no more than low mounds in the surrounding country, but several survive in the town itself, and are fascinating to see right in the middle of the residential grid. The largest, **Kinich Kakmó** (daily 8am–8pm; free), dedicated to the sun god, has been partly restored. It's just a couple of blocks north of the two adjacent central plazas – ask for directions from the roving brown-clad tourist police.

In 1552 Fray Diego de Landa (later responsible for a vicious Inquisition and auto-da-fé in Maní) lopped the top off a neighbouring pyramid and began building the grand **Convento de San Antonio de Padua** (daily 8am–9.30pm; donation), which now anchors the main squares. The porticoed atrium is particularly beautiful in the late afternoon. Inside the complex is a statue of Nuestra Señora de Izamal (usually in a small chapel behind the main altar, reached through a side hall and stairs), the patroness of the Yucatán. The statue inspires pilgrims from all over the peninsula, especially during the fiesta dedicated to her in August and again in December, when penitents climb the convent's broad stairway on their knees. A few evenings a week, a **sound-and-light show** (Tues, Thurs, Fri & Sat 8.30pm; M$50) is projected on the facade of the main church.

Izamal is also renowned as a refined **crafts centre**. A free **map**, available from most hotels and businesses, identifies workshops of wood-carvers, papier-mâché artists and other artisans; be sure to visit Don Esteban, on Calle 26 at Calle 45, whose jewellery made from henequen spines is striking and modern, and whose effusive character is memorable. To get around, you can rent a bicycle (M$40 for 2hr) from the **Centro Cultural y Artesanal** (Mon–Wed & Fri 10am–8pm, Thurs & Sat 10am–10pm, Sun 10am–5pm; M$20) on the plaza. Its museum showcases choice pieces of craftwork from all over Mexico; there's also a small café and a quiet back room where you can get a foot massage. On the south side of the convent plaza, Hecho a Mano, a particularly good craft and **folk-art shop**, is stocked with everything from Mexican wrestling masks to Huichol yarn paintings from Nayarit, as well as excellent photography by one of the owners; note that the hours (Mon–Sat 10am–2pm & 4–7pm) can be erratic.

Practicalities

Of the few **hotels** in town, *Posada Flory*, on Calle 30 at Calle 27 just off the plaza (Ⓣ988/954-0562; ❷), is a bargain, with nine homely rooms with optional air-conditioning, operated by a chatty, hospitable woman. For a bit more, *Macan Ché B&B*, Calle 22 between calles 33 and 35 (Ⓣ988/954-0287, Ⓦwww.macanche.com; ❺), is an assortment of comfortable cottages tucked among rambling gardens east of the plaza; rates include breakfast, and other meals are available as well. A few kilometres south, near the town of Sudzal, is the rambling, artfully decorated *Hacienda San Antonio Chalanté* (Ⓣ988/954-0287, Ⓦwww.haciendachalante.com; ❺), well worth the drive if you have your own transport; it's bookable through *Macan Ché*, but be sure to specify the hacienda, to avoid confusion.

For **food** in town, the palapa-roof *Kinich*, on Calle 27 between calles 28 and 30, is a popular spot for **lunch**, while *El Toro*, on Calle 33 just south of the convent, is open for **dinner**, with a hearty Yucatecan menu of dishes like *chaya* tamales and *queso relleno*. *Los Arcos*, under the portales on the east side of the north plaza, makes enormous tortas and delicious fresh fruit drinks. You can enjoy coffee or ice cream at *Los Mestizos*, a small courtyard **café** in the arcade next to Hecho a Mano.

Buses arrive at a small station one block west of the main plaza. Services run back to Mérida about twelve times daily (the last one goes at 7pm) and hourly to Valladolid and Cancún till 1am (though faster Oriente buses go only three times daily, via Tizimín). In the north plaza you'll find a Banorte **bank** with ATM, while on the main plaza is a **post office** (Mon–Fri 8am–2.30pm) and the very friendly **tourist office** (daily 9am–6pm; ⓣ988/954-0009). An **internet café** is on Calle 32, just south of the bus station. A **laundry** is on Calle 30 two blocks north of the north plaza. **Horse-drawn carriages** lined up around the plaza will take you for a pleasant *paseo* around the town (20min; M$80). If you're **driving** here, know that most streets are one-way, but very haphazardly signed.

Chichén Itzá

The most famous, the most extensively restored and by far the most visited of all Maya sites, **Chichén Itzá** lies conveniently along the main highway from Mérida to Cancún, a little more than 200km from the Caribbean coast. A fast and very regular bus service runs all along this road, making it perfectly feasible to visit as a day's excursion from Mérida, or en route from Mérida to the coast, or even as a day out from Cancún, as many tour buses do. But both to do the ruins justice and to see them when they're not entirely thronged with tourists, an overnight stop is well worth considering – either at the site itself or, less extravagantly, in the nearby village of **Pisté** or in Valladolid, which is both convenient and inexpensive (see p.796).

Arrival and practicalities

Arriving at Chichén Itzá, Hwy-180 *libre* curves around the site to the north, making an arc that merges with the site access road (the original highway straight through) at both ends. All first-class buses drive right up to the site entrance. All buses stop in Pisté as well, at one of two stations, on the west end of town (eastbound buses) or the east end (westbound buses).

The main **entry to the site** (daily winter 8am–5pm; summer 8am–6pm, last entry an hour earlier; M$111) is on the west side. A huge **visitor centre** (open until 10pm) houses a museum, restaurant, **ATM** and shops selling souvenirs, film, maps and guides. **Guided tours** of the ruins can be arranged here: private tours in one of four languages (Spanish, English, German or Italian) cost approximately M$480 and last ninety minutes; group tours cost a little less. You can also buy tickets and get in at the **smaller eastern gate** by the *Hotel Mayaland*, where there are fewer facilities. You can book two-hour **horseback trips** around the wilder, southern part of the site, Chichén Viejo, at the hotel reception area (M$500 with guide). A **sound-and-light-show** in Spanish runs nightly (7pm in winter, 8pm in summer; included in price of day entrance ticket); it's a bit of a yawn, but it does recreate the shadow-serpent effect (see p.793) on the stairs of El Castillo, and it's the only thing to do in the evening.

About 3km west of Chichén Itzá, **Pisté** is an unattractive village straddling the road. Its main function is providing visitors with accommodation (see p.792), so they can get up early enough to beat the buses that arrive at the ruins around 10.30am. There's an **internet** café here, opposite the **bus station**, at the east end of town.

Accommodation

Visitors to Chichén Itzá have a choice of staying in a handful of more expensive **hotels** immediately **east of the ruins** (all but one are on the short access road

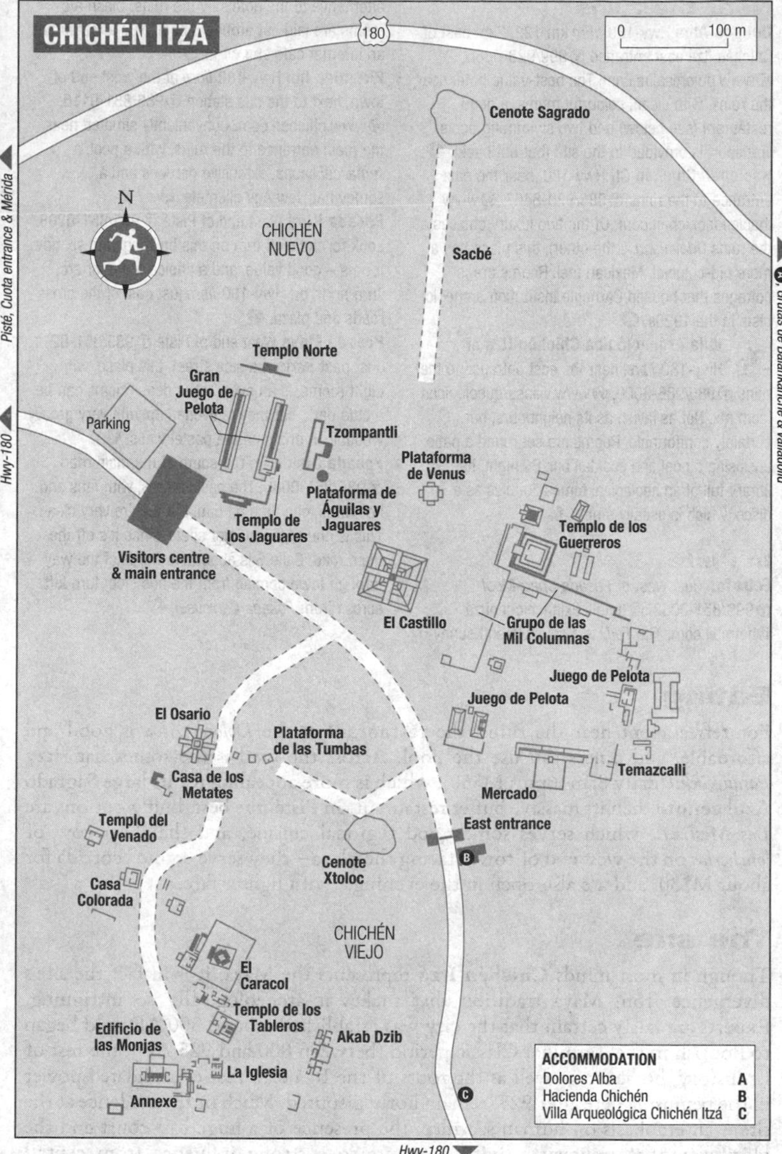

off Hwy-180, signposted "Zona Hotelera"), or along the main street in the town of **Pisté**, to the west of the site. In Pisté, most hotels are on the main road, between the village and the ruins, so it's easy to shop around for the best deal – though quality can be low and occupancy high; the reliable *posadas* have only a few rooms apiece. You can **camp** or sling up a hammock at the *Pirámide Inn* (M$55).

Near the ruins

Dolores Alba Hwy-180 *libre* km 122, 2km east of Chichén Itzá east entrance ⓣ999/928-5650, ⓦwww.doloresalba.com. The best-value hotel near the ruins, with clean, colourful rooms, a good restaurant (see below) and two swimming pools. Transport is provided to the site (but not back). ④

Hacienda Chichén Off Hwy-180, near the east entrance to the ruins ⓣ985/920-8407, ⓦwww.haciendachichen.com. Of the two luxury choices at the ruins (*Mayaland* is the other), this place has a more old-colonial, Mexican feel. Rooms are in cottages that housed Carnegie Institution archeologists in the 1920s. ⑧

Villa Arqueológica Chichén Itzá off Hwy-180 *libre*, near the east entrance to the ruins ⓣ985/986-6000, ⓦwww.villasarqueologicas.com.mx. Not as lavish as its neighbours, but certainly comfortable. Rooms are set round a patio enclosing a pool and cocktail bar. By night, its library full of archeological tomes doubles as a disco, which is usually empty. ⑤

In Pisté

Felix Inn Just west of *Posada Chac-Mool* ⓣ999/851-0033, ⓔhotelfelixinnchichenitza@hotmail.com. The *Felix* is a sensible and sunny alternative to the hotels by the ruins. Clean a/c rooms are laid out around a pool, plus a restaurant, an internet café and wi-fi. ⑥

Pirámide Inn Hwy-180 *libre* at the west end of town, next to the bus station ⓣ985/851-0115, ⓦwww.chichen.com. Conveniently situated near the main entrance to the ruins, with a pool, a *temazcal* sauna, extensive gardens and a somewhat New Age clientele. ③

Posada Kary West end of Pisté ⓣ985/851-0208. Look for the pink trim on this building with six tidy rooms – good value, and a choice of fan or a/c. Turn north off Hwy-180 *libre* just east of the crossroads and plaza. ③

Posada Maya West end of Pisté ⓣ985/851-0211. Just past *Kary* on a side street, this place, with eight rooms, is an even better deal. Rooms can be a little dark, but they're livened up with very groovy woodblock prints on the pastel walls. ②

Posada Olalde On C 6 south of the main road ⓣ985/851-0086. The basic rooms, with fans and hot water, can be a bit dim, but they're very clean. This is one of the quieter spots, since it's off the main road. Calle 6 is about two-thirds of the way through town coming from the bus stop; turn left across from *Posada Carrousel*. ③

Eating

For refreshment near the ruins, the **restaurant** at the *Dolores Alba* is good and affordable, and diners can use the pool. Across the road is the somewhat ritzy *Parque Ikkil* (daily 8am–6pm; M$60), which is more appealing for its large Sagrado Azul **cenote** than its massive buffet restaurant. In Pisté, the best dining options are *Las Mestizas*, which serves some good regional cuisine, and the short row of *loncherías* on the west end of town, facing the plaza – they serve comida corrida for about M$30, and are also open in the evenings, with lighter fare.

The site

Though in most minds **Chichén Itzá** represents the Maya, it is in fact the site's divergence from Maya tradition that makes it archeologically so intriguing. Experts are fairly certain that the city was established around 300 AD, and began to flourish in the Terminal Classic period (between 800 and 925 AD); the rest of its history, however, as well as the roots of the Itzá clan that consolidated power in the peninsula here after 925, remain hotly disputed. Much of the evidence at the site – an emphasis on human sacrifice, the presence of a huge ball-court and the glorification of military activity – points to a strong influence from central Mexico. For decades researchers guessed this was the result of the city's defeat by the Toltecs, a theory reinforced by the resemblance of the Templo de los Guerreros to the colonnade at Tula, near Mexico City (see p.473), along with Toltec-style pottery remains and numerous depictions of the Toltec god-king, the feathered serpent Quetzalcoatl (Kukulcán to the Maya).

Work since the 1980s, however, supports a theory that the Itzá people were not Toltec invaders, but fellow Maya who had migrated from the south (an explanation for their subjects referring to them as "foreigners" in texts). The Toltec artefacts, this view holds, arrived in central Yucatán via the Itzás' chief trading partners, the **Chontal Maya**, who maintained allegiances with Toltecs of central Mexico and Oaxaca.

Chichén Nuevo

The old highway that used to pass through the site is now a path dividing the ruins in two: the Itzá-era **Chichén Nuevo** (New or "Toltec" Chichén) to the north and Terminal Classic **Chichén Viejo** (Old Chichén) to the south. If it's still reasonably early, head first to the north and **El Castillo** (also called the Pyramid of Kukulcán), the structure that sits alone in the centre of a great grassy plaza. It is a simple, relatively unadorned square building, with a monumental stairway ascending each face (though only two are restored), rising in nine receding terraces to a temple at the top. The simplicity is deceptive, however, as the building is in fact the **Maya calendar** rendered in stone: each staircase has 91 steps, which, added to the single step at the main entrance to the temple, amounts to 365; other numbers relevant to the calendar recur throughout the construction. Most remarkably, near sunset on the spring and autumn equinoxes, the great serpents' heads at the foot of the main staircase are joined to their tails (at the top of the building) by an undulating body of shadow – an event that lasts just a few hours and draws spectators, and awed worshippers, by the thousands.

Inside El Castillo an **earlier pyramid** survives almost intact, and in the temple's inner sanctuary, archeologists discovered one of the greatest treasures at the site: an **altar**, or perhaps a throne, in the form of a jaguar, painted bright red and inset with jade "spots" and eyes.

The "Toltec" plaza

El Castillo marks one edge of a **plaza** that formed the focus of Chichén Nuevo, and in addition to a *sacbé* leading to **Cenote Sagrado**, all its most important buildings are here, many displaying a strong Toltec influence in their structure and decoration. The **Templo de los Guerreros** (Temple of the Warriors), lined on two sides

▲ Grupo de las Mil Columnas, Chichén Itzá

by the **Grupo de las Mil Columnas** (Group of the Thousand Columns), forms the eastern edge of the plaza. These are the structures that most recall the great Toltec site of Tula, both in design and in detail – in particular the colonnaded courtyard (which would have been roofed with some form of thatch) and the use of Atlantean columns representing battle-dressed warriors, their arms raised above their heads. The temple is richly decorated on its north and south sides with carvings and sculptures of jaguars and eagles devouring human hearts, feathered serpents, warriors and, the one undeniably Maya feature, masks of the rain god Chac, with his curling snout. On top (now visible only at a distance, as you can no longer climb the structure) are two superb examples of figures called **Chac-mools**, once thought to be introduced by the Toltecs: offerings were placed on the stomachs of these reclining figures, which are thought to represent either the messengers who would take the sacrifice to the gods or perhaps the divinities themselves. The "thousand" columns alongside originally formed a square, on the far side of which is the building known as the **Mercado**, although there's no evidence that this actually was a marketplace. Near here, too, is a small, dilapidated ball-court.

Walking west across the plaza from El Castillo, you pass the **Plataforma de Venus**, a raised block with a stairway up each side guarded by feathered serpents. Here, rites associated with Quetzalcoatl when he took the form of Venus, the morning star, would have been carried out. Slightly smaller, but otherwise identical in design, the adjacent **Plataforma de Águilas y Jaguares** features reliefs of eagles and jaguars holding human hearts. Human sacrifices may have been carried out here, judging by the proximity of a third platform, the **Tzompantli**, where victims' heads likely hung on display. This is carved on every side with grotesque grinning stone skulls.

Gran Juego de Pelota and the Templo de los Jaguares

Chichén Itzá's **Gran Juego de Pelota** (ball-court), on the west side of the plaza, is the largest known in existence, with walls some 90m long. Its design is a capital "I" surrounded by temples, with the goals, or target rings, halfway along each side. Along the bottom of each side runs a sloping **panel** decorated with scenes of the game. Although the rules and full significance of the game remain a mystery, it was clearly not a Saturday afternoon kick-about in the park; for more on the game's significance, see p.876. On the panel, the players are shown proceeding from either side towards a central circle, the symbol of death. One player, just right of the centre (whether it's the winning or losing captain is up for debate) has been decapitated, while another holds his head and a ritual knife. Along the top runs the stone body of a snake, whose heads stick out at either end. The court is subject to a whispering-gallery effect, which enables you to be heard clearly at the far end of the court, and to hear what's going on there.

The **Templo de los Jaguares** overlooks the playing area from the east side. At the bottom – effectively the outer wall of the ball-court – is a little portico supported by two pillars, between which a stone jaguar stands sentinel. The outer wall panels, the left and the right of the interior space, are carved with the images of Pawahtuns, the gods who supported the sky and who are thought to be the patrons of the Itzá people. Inside are some worn but elaborate relief carvings of the Itzá ancestors inserted in the Maya creation myth – a powerful demonstration of their entitlement to rule.

Cenote Sagrado

The **Cenote Sagrado** lies at the end of the *sacbé* that leads about 300m off the north side of the plaza. It's an almost perfectly round hole in the limestone bedrock, some 60m in diameter and more than 30m deep, the bottom third full of water. It was thanks to this natural well (and perhaps another in the southern half of the site) that the city could survive at all, and it gives Chichén Itzá its name (literally "at the edge of the well of the Itzá"). The well was regarded as a portal to the underworld, called Xibalba, and the Maya threw in offerings such as statues, jade and engraved metal disks (a few of them gold), as well as human sacrifices – all of them boys, recent research has shown. People who were thrown in and survived were believed to have prophetic powers, having spoken with the gods.

Chichén Viejo

The **southern half of the site** is the most sacred part for contemporary Maya, though the buildings here are not in such good condition. They were built for the most part prior to 925 AD, in the architectural styles used in the Puuc and Chenes regions. A path leads from the south side of El Castillo to the major structures, passing first the pyramid **El Osario** (the Ossuary; also called the High Priest's Grave), the only building in this section that shows Toltec-style detail. Externally it is very similar to El Castillo, but inside a series of **tombs** was discovered. A shaft, first explored at the end of the nineteenth century, drops down from the top through five crypts, in each of which was found a skeleton and a trap door leading to the next. The fifth is at ground level, but here too was a trap door, and steps cut through the rock to a sixth chamber that opens onto a huge underground cavern: the burial place of the high priest.

Follow the main path and you arrive at **El Caracol** (the Snail, for its shape; also called the Observatory), a circular, domed tower standing on two rectangular platforms and looking remarkably like a modern-day observatory. The roof has slits aligned with various points of astronomical significance. Four doors at the cardinal points lead into the tower and a circular chamber. A spiral staircase leads to the upper level, where observations were made.

Immediately to the south, the so-called **Monjas** (Nunnery) palace complex shows several stages of construction. Part of the facade was blasted away in the nineteenth century, but it is nonetheless a building of grand proportions. Its **annexe**, on the east end, has an elaborate facade in the Chenes style, covered in small heads of Chac that combine to make one giant mask, with the door as a mouth. By contrast, **La Iglesia**, a small building standing beside the convent, is a clear demonstration of Puuc design, its low band of unadorned masonry around the bottom surmounted by an elaborate mosaic frieze and roofcomb. Masks of Chac again predominate, but above the doorway are also figures of the four mythological creatures that held up the sky – a snail, a turtle, an armadillo and a crab.

South of Las Monjas, a path leads, after about ten minutes, to a further group of ruins that are among the oldest on the site, although they are unrestored; this is a good area for bird watching, with few people around to disturb the wildlife. Just east of Las Monjas, is the **Akab Dzib**, a relatively plain block of palace rooms that takes its name ("Obscure Writings") from undeciphered hieroglyphs found inside. Red palm prints – frequently found in Maya buildings – adorn the walls of some of the chambers. Backtrack along the main path to the building opposite El Osario, the **Plataforma de las Tumbas**, a funerary structure topped with small columns; behind it is a jungle path that heads back to the main east–west road via the site's other water source, Cenote Xtoloc.

Around Chichén Itzá: Grutas de Balankanché

Just 1.6km east of the *Dolores Alba* hotel (see p.792), the **Grutas de Balankanché** are a refreshingly cool way to pass an hour. These damp caverns were reopened in 1959, when a sealed passageway was discovered, revealing a path to an underground

Moving on from Chichén Itzá

In Pisté, there are two bus stations: if you're heading east, go to the station at the east end of town, near the *Pirámide* hotel; westbound buses go from a small station just east of the crossroads at the west end. Many second-class Oriente buses (nearly hourly departures) and first-class ADO buses (just a few) depart from both Pisté and the ruins themselves to **Mérida** (1hr 45min), **Valladolid** (45min) and **Cancún** (3–4hr) (last one at 9.30pm, in either direction).You can bypass Cancún by taking a second-class bus to **Tulum** (4 daily; 2hr 30min); the 7.30am bus stops at **Cobá** (2hr).

altar to Chac. Tours with taped commentary (in English daily 11am, 1pm & 3pm; M$50) lead past an underground pool, stalagmites and stalactites to a huge rock formation that resembles a ceiba, the Maya tree of life. Around its base lie many of the original Maya offerings, such as clay pots in the shapes of gods' faces.

Valladolid and around

The second city of Yucatán state, **VALLADOLID** is around 40km east of Chichén Itzá, still close enough to beat the crowds to the site on an early bus, and of interest in its own right. Although it took a severe bashing in the nineteenth-century Caste Wars, it has retained a strong colonial feel and exudes the unpretentious attitude of a rural capital, catering to the farmers and ranchers who live nearby, while village women gather in the plaza to sell hand-embroidered *huipiles* and other crafts.

Arrival and information

Valladolid's **bus station** is on Calle 39 at Calle 46, a block and a half west of the plaza. The plaza is bounded by calles 39, 40, 41 and 42. The **tourist office**, on the southeast corner of the plaza (Mon–Sat 9am–8.30pm, Sun 9am–1pm), has plenty of information, including free maps of Valladolid and details of in-house **tour operator** Viajes Valladolid (Ⓣ985/856-1857), though it's a pretty casual set-up, and the office is often unattended; however, most hotels and souvenir shops on the plaza also have **maps**.

With its small scale and light traffic, Valladolid is a good place to get around by **bike**; you can also reach nearby cenotes via bike paths. Bikes can be hired from MexiGO Tours (see p.798), which also runs guided trips, as well as a shop on Calle 40 just north of the plaza and the Rey de Béisbol sports shop, Calle 44 no. 195 between calles 39 and 41. The latter owned by Antonio "Negro" Aguilar, a one-time pro baseball player and all-around entertaining man. Rates start at M$15 per hour.

Accommodation

Valladolid's budget hotels are good, and higher-end places are excellent value. Also note that *Genesis Retreat* (see p.800) is only about twenty minutes outside town.

Casa Hamaca C 49 at C 40 on the southwest corner of Parque San Juan Ⓣ985/856-5287, Ⓦwww.casahamaca.com. Set in a garden packed with fruit trees, this bed-and-breakfast is a quiet retreat. Expansive rooms in the big two-storey building are decorated with elaborate murals and glossy red tile floors. There's also a pool, and massage and other healing treatments available. ❽

Casa Quetzal C 51 no. 218 Ⓣ985/856-4796, Ⓦwww.casa-quetzal.com. A pleasant alternative to the plaza hotels, *Casa Quetzal* is a very comfortable guesthouse with a big pool. ❺

Lili C 44 no. 192 between C 37 and C 39 Ⓣ985/856-2163. One block off the plaza, this small, homely hotel rents 21 basic rooms (those upstairs get a little more light) at reasonable rates. ❷

María de la Luz C 42 between C 39 and C 41 ⓣ985/856-1181, ⓦwww.mariadelaluzhotel.com. The best value on the plaza, *María de la Luz* offers clean, comfortable rooms with (somewhat noisy) a/c, all arranged around a small pool. ④

María Guadalupe C 44 no. 198 between C 39 and C 41 ⓣ985/856-2068. The best of Valladolid's cheapies, with well-kept rooms featuring private baths and optional a/c in a small two-storey 1960s building. *Colectivos* for Cenote Dzitnup leave from outside. ②

El Mesón del Marqués C 39 no. 203 on the plaza ⓣ985/856-2073, ⓦwww.mesondelmarques.com. Lovely hotel in a former colonial mansion, overlooking a courtyard with fountains and lush plants. There's a wonderful palm-fringed pool, and one of the best restaurants in town (see p.798). Rates include full breakfast. ⑤

Zací C 44 no. 191 between C 37 and C 39 ⓣ985/856-2167. Pleasant, modern, three-storey hotel with a quiet courtyard and pool that make it exceptionally good value. The big rooms have a fan, or, for a few dollars more, a/c and TV. ③

The City

The most famous of Valladolid's churches to have survived the Caste Wars is the sixteenth-century **Iglesia de San Bernardino de Siena**, 1km southwest of the plaza (Wed–Mon 9am–noon & 5–8pm; Mass daily 6pm). Franciscan missionaries began work on it shortly after the Spanish established Valladolid as an outpost in 1545. In 1848 Maya rebels sacked the church; despite this, a fine Baroque altarpiece from the eighteenth century remains, as do some striking seventeenth-century paintings on the side walls.

Closer to the plaza, on Calle 41 between calles 38 and 40, the **Museo de San Roque** (Mon–Sat 9am–8pm; free) displays objects from the site of Ek-Balam (see p.799), embroidery and other craftwork. If you need to cool down after a morning spent wandering, **Cenote Zací**, on the block formed by calles 34, 36, 37 and 39 (daily 8am–6pm; M$20) has broad stairs leading down into a huge cavern, with an open-air restaurant at the top. Unlike at many cenotes, swimming is not permitted.

As the *huipil*-clad statue in the plaza's fountain suggests, Valladolid is a good place to purchase craftwork; in addition to the women selling their embroidery, you can also visit the Bazar de Artesanías, the **craft market** on Calle 44 at Calle 39, or Yalat, a very nice shop on the northwest corner of the plaza that stocks clothing, chocolate and soaps. The central city market, the **Mercado Municipal**, is on Calle 32 between calles 35 and 37.

Eating, drinking and nightlife

Whatever your budget, to eat well in Valladolid you don't have to stray from the plaza, where you can get inexpensive **snacks and coffee** (at *Mayan Coffee*, on the west side) or treat yourself at a refined **restaurant**. As for **nightlife**, there are a couple of bars, but not much beyond people-watching on the plaza, where there's usually some live music on Sundays.

El Bazar northeast corner of the plaza. Houses a dizzying selection of inexpensive, busy *loncherías* and pizzerias. It's also about the only place in town, except *Hostería El Marqués*, where you can have a big meal after 9pm.

La Casa del Café Kaffè C 44, on Parque la Candelaria. This place serves organic coffee, juices and little snacks to members of the local arts scene. 9am–1pm and 6.30pm–midnight.

Doña Hermelinda C 44 between C 37 and C 39. Succulent stewed pork with white beans is the core ingredient here – you can have it as a taco, a *torta* or (the best) a *pibihua*, a hollowed-out round of chewy fried corn. Open till 8pm.

Hostería El Marqués C 39 no. 203, in *El Mesón del Marqués*. Valladolid's best (and quite reasonably priced) restaurant is set in an interior courtyard on the plaza. Don't be put off if you see it packed with a tour group – the excellent menu features Yucatecan classics such as *sopa de lima* and *poc-chuc*, along with city specialities like *escabeche de Valladolid* (chicken in a spicy vinegar broth). Open till 10.30pm daily.

María de la Luz C 42, on the plaza. This popular terrace restaurant has a basic Mexican and Yucatecan menu. Good-value (M$60) breakfast buffet with American and Mexican dishes offered daily. Open daily till 9pm.

Restaurante San Bernardino de Siena C 49 no. 227. Locally known as *Don Juanito's*, this family-run restaurant with decent prices is a great place for a lazy lunch or dinner, two blocks behind Iglesia de San Bernardino. Grilled fish and meat are the specialities. Open till 8pm.

Squimoz C 39 between C 44 and C 46. A small cafe with a pretty back garden; ice cream, coffee and light snacks are on the menu. Open 7am–9.30pm Mon–Sat, till 3pm Sun.

Yepez II C 41 between C 38 and C 40. Friendly open-air bar and restaurant opposite the Museo de San Roque with live music after 9.30pm, as well as very cheap Mexican snacks (*queso fundido* for M$20). Families come for dinner, but the crowd becomes predominantly male (not too rowdy, though) once the music starts. Open daily till 2am.

Listings

Banks Bancomer, next door to the post office on the plaza, changes travellers' cheques and has an ATM.

Colectivos Those travelling to Chichén Itzá (M$20) depart from Calle 46 between calles 37 and 39; most others go from points along Calle 44.

Internet There are a couple of cafés on C 41 west of the plaza (daily 7am–10pm).

Laundry C 40 at C 33.

Post office On the plaza, C 40 near the corner of C 39 (Mon–Fri 9am–3pm).

Tours MexiGO Tours (C 43 no. 204-B between C 40 and C 42 ⓣ985/856-0777) runs trips to Río Lagartos, Chichén Itzá and Cobá, as well as bike trips to local houses and cenotes.

Around Valladolid

From Valladolid, the vast majority of traffic heads straight to Cancún and the Caribbean beaches. A few places merit taking time out to explore, however – whether the beautiful sculpture at the ruins of **Ek-Balam**, the cenotes of **X'keken** and **Samula** or, further afield, the flamingo colony at **Río Lagartos** or the beach at **San Felipe**. If you want to go all the way to the coast as a day trip, you'll need to make an early start – the last bus from Río Lagartos for Tizimín leaves at 5pm. You'll have to return at least to Tizimín to continue on to Mérida or Cancún.

Cenotes X'keken and Samula

Perhaps the most photogenic swimming hole in the Yucatán, the remarkable **Cenote X'keken**, also called Dzitnup like the nearby village (daily 7am–6pm; M$25), is 7km west of Valladolid on Hwy-180 *libre*. Visitors descend through a cramped tunnel into a huge vaulted cave, where a nearly circular pool of crystal-clear turquoise water glows under a shaft of light from an opening in the ceiling. A swim in the ice-cold water is a fantastic experience. Across the road, at the even more impressive (thanks to spooky natural lighting) **Cenote Samula** (daily 8am–5pm; M$25), the roots of a huge tree stretch down into the pool.

Colectivos run to the village of Dzitnup from outside the *María Guadalupe* hotel in Valladolid (M$15; see p.797). Any westbound second-class **bus** will drop you at the turn-off, 5km from Valladolid; then it's a walk of 2km down a signed track. You could also take a taxi or, best of all, **cycle** from Valladolid on the paved bike path; the most scenic route is down Calle 41-A to San Bernardino, then along Calle 49, which eventually connects to Avenida de los Frailes, then the old highway and the *ciclopista*.

Ek-Balam

Notable for the high quality and unique details of its fantastically preserved stucco sculpture, **Ek-Balam** (daily 8am–5pm; M$31) is nonetheless rarely crowded. The compact site, enclosed by a series of defensive walls, is really only the ceremonial centre; the entire city, which was occupied from the pre-Classic period through to the Spanish Conquest, spreads out over a very wide area, punctuated by *sacbeob* leading out in all directions.

The entrance is along one of these ancient roads, leading through a freestanding four-sided arch. Beyond are two identical temples, called **Las Gemelas** (the Twins), and a long **ball-court**. The principal building, on the far side of the plaza, is the massive **Acrópolis**, the stones along its two-hundred-metre-long base adorned with bas-reliefs. Thatched awnings at the top protect the site's finest treasure, an elaborate stucco frieze fully uncovered only recently; 85 percent of what you see is original plaster from the ninth century that didn't even require retouching once the dirt was brushed away.

A staircase leads up the centre of the building. On the first level, two doorways flanking the steps display near-matching designs of twisted serpents and tongues; in the right-hand carving, the snake's tongue is emblazoned with a glyph thought to represent the city. Just below the summit, a **Chenes-style doorway** in the form of a giant gaping mouth is studded with protruding teeth. This is the **entrance to the tomb** of Ukit-Kan-Lek-Tok, Ek-Balam's king in the mid-ninth century. The lower jaw forms the floor, while skulls, lilies, fish and other symbols of the underworld carved below reinforce its function as a tomb gateway. Back on the ground, in the plaza, an exceptionally well-preserved **stele** depicts a king receiving the objects of power from Ukit-Kan-Lek-Tok, the smaller seated figure at the top of the stele. Given the rich detail at the site, it's worth hiring a **guide** for about M$250 for a small group.

Juan Canul, who has worked on many excavations, is recommended; ask for him at the ticket desk.

In the parking area at the site, you'll find someone selling tickets to **Cenote Xcanché** (daily 9am–5pm; M$30), a seemingly bottomless pool that's a two-kilometre walk from the ruins.

In the nearby village of Ek-Balam, *Genesis Retreat* (no phone; www.genesisretreat.com; 4) is a beautiful **ecolodge** with a big garden and a bio-filtered pool; guests can take tours around the village and in the nearby forest. The vegetarian **café** (daily 1–3pm) makes a great stop after the ruins, with organic, local produce and lots of raw foods. If you take a taxi, be aware that some drivers may attempt to take you to another, less savoury lodge around the corner – *Genesis* has a doghouse labelled "Concierge" out front.

The village and ruins are easily reached by from Valladolid in a **colectivo** (M$50), departing from Calle 44 just west of the plaza.

Tizimín

Travelling by bus from Valladolid north to Río Lagartos, you have to transfer in **TIZIMÍN**, the unofficial capital of Yucatán's cattle country, 51km from Valladolid. It's a pleasant enough city, but of little interest to travellers except during Epiphany in early January, when the Feria de los Tres Reyes draws both Catholic pilgrims and cowboys. If you're coming through around lunchtime, though, it's worth making time in your bus schedule for a meal at *Tres Reyes*, a great **restaurant** with hand-patted, chewy tortillas, black-as-ink beans and succulent meats – the soul of Yucatecan cooking. It's on the plaza, which is bounded by calles 50, 51, 52 and 53 – a ten-minute walk from the two bus stations, around the corner from each other at Calle 46 and Calle 47. Should you wind up staying, the best of the modest **hotels** in the centre is *Hotel San Carlos*, on Calle 54 between calles 51 and 53 (986/863-2094; 4), while *Posada Maria Antonia*, on C 50 between C 53 and C 51, just off the plaza (986/863-2384; 2) is a good cheap choice. Tizimín also has direct **bus** services to and from Mérida and Cancún.

Río Lagartos

The village of **RÍO LAGARTOS**, 100km north of Valladolid, is protected from the Gulf of Mexico by a long barrier island; it's on a small spit surrounded on three sides by water and inhabited much of the year by tens of thousands of **pink flamingoes** (Nov–May most migrate to Celestún, on the west coast). The flamingoes alone make a visit worthwhile, as the town itself is somewhat dreary.

A day-trip from Valladolid is manageable, but if you want to **stay the night**, *Cabañas Escondidas* (986/862-0121; 3) has a few simple cabins, all with private bath, facing the waterfront on Calle 14 just south of Calle 19; next door, *Posada Isla Contoy* (986/862-0000; 4) has slightly fancier solid rooms; and the surprisingly flashy *Tabasco Río* is at Calle 12 no. 91 (986/862-0116; 4). There is **no bank or ATM** in town, so plan accordingly.

As soon as you arrive at the **bus station** (on Calle 19 just east of the main north–south street through town) or get out of your car, you'll be approached about boat tours to see the flamingoes. Several experienced guides operate in town: ask for Ismael Navarro and Elmer Canul of Río Lagartos Expeditions (986/862-0452, www.riolagartosexpeditions.com) at the *Restaurante Isla Contoy*, on the waterfront on the west side, or Diego Nuñez at *Las Palapas de la Toreja* restaurant, on the north malecón, near Calle 14. Both operations run **boats** to visit the many feeding sites; a two-hour tour usually costs about M$700 for a maximum of seven people; a three-hour trip includes a "spa treatment" at some mud flats. As well as flamingoes, you're likely to see fishing eagles, spoonbills and, if you're lucky, one of the very few remaining crocodiles after which Río Lagartos was (mis)named.

San Felipe

If it's beaches you're after, head to the tidy town of **SAN FELIPE**, where an offshore spit is lined with white sand. The town, which is also a popular destination for sport-fishing, is 12km west of Río Lagartos; many of the buses from Tizimín to Río Lagartos come out here as well. There's one good **hotel**, *San Felipe de Jesús,* Calle 9 between calles 14 and 16 (Ⓣ986/862-2027, Ⓔhotelsf@hotmail.com; ⑤), which also has a decent restaurant. To get to the beach, take a boat (M$15/person) from the east end of the malecón, where you can also get basic **tourist information** and buy tickets for various bird watching and nature tours (from M$250 for up to five people). At Mexican holiday times – July, August and Semana Santa – the beach is crowded; the rest of the year, though, it's quite deserted, and you can set up **camp** here. If you do, be sure to bring protection against mosquitoes.

Quintana Roo and the Caribbean coast

Mexico's furthest east coast was a backwater for most of modern Mexican history, its tropical forests exploited for their mahogany and chicle (from which chewing gum is made), but otherwise unsettled, a haven for outlaws, pirates and Maya living beyond the reach of central government. In the 1970s, however, the stunning palm-fringed white-sand **beaches** on the Caribbean and the magnificent offshore **coral reefs** began to be developed for **tourism**: the first highways were built and new towns settled, and **Quintana Roo** finally became a full state (as opposed to an externally administered federal territory) in 1974.

Along the north coast, facing the Gulf of Mexico, remote spots like **Isla Holbox** feel relatively untouched by time. But the stretch of **coast** between **Cancún** and **Tulum**, known as the Riviera Maya, is one of the most heavily touristed areas of Mexico. Cancún and **Playa del Carmen**, along with the islands of **Mujeres** and **Cozumel**, have become desirable package-tour destinations, and are overdeveloped as a result. Images of the Maya appear everywhere, but the foreign-owned, all-inclusive resort companies make sure little of their profit ever goes to Mexico, much less to the indigenous villages that dot the jungle.

Further south, the scene is a bit calmer: sea turtles nest on the beaches within the **Sian Ka'an Biosphere Reserve**, while the inlets shelter manatees and the mangrove swamps clamour with birdlife. The coast south of the biosphere – dubbed the Costa Maya – is on its own development trajectory, but it's still your best bet for hammock camping. The vast, beautiful **Laguna de Bacalar** is a crystal-clear lake that's rich in wildlife and an affordable alternative to the beaches.

Prices on the Caribbean coast

Because Cancún, Cozumel and the big towns in the Riviera Maya cater largely to tourists, local businesses often quote **prices** in US dollars, and accept payment in that currency. Moreover, prices for major attractions, tours and the like are often pegged to the exchange rate, so a US$70 hotel room could be M$700 one week and M$770 the next. Occasionally in this section, we give prices in US dollars because it is more accurate.

Chetumal, the state capital and a duty-free border town, is chiefly important as a gateway to and from Belize.

Inland Quintana Roo is barely populated, let alone visited. There are some **Maya sites**, though they are not as accessible or as restored as the pristine open-air museums of Yucatán state. **Cobá**, a lakeside ruin between Tulum and Valladolid, has some of the Maya world's tallest temples, but is only partially excavated, hidden in jungle swarming with mosquitoes. The early Classic site of **Kohunlich**, famous for its giant sculpted faces of the Maya sun god, lies in the heart of the Petén jungle that stretches into Guatemala and Belize.

The Gulf Coast: Isla Holbox

Although most traffic between Mérida and the coast heads directly east to Cancún, it is possible to turn north at Valladolid (on the bus) or at the small town of El Ideal (if you're driving) to reach **Chiquilá**, on the Gulf coast, where you can board the ferry for **ISLA HOLBOX** ("ol-BOSH"), a small island that offers a very rustic beach hideaway. The lone village has sand streets and a genuinely warm feel. So far, a good part of the island is remains wild, and all manner of **birds**, including flamingoes, thrive here. But the main attraction is the rare **whale sharks** that congregate just off the cape between mid-May and mid-September. Tours to see and swim with the gentle animals take the better part of a day (about M$900/ person, including lunch and snorkel gear), and can be arranged through your hotel and any number of guides in town. A dive shop at *Posada Mawimbi* (see opposite) does **snorkelling** excursions. The whale shark season unfortunately overlaps with the absolutely fearsome mosquitoes that arrive at the end of the summer and stay until the rains stop – be prepared.

Arrival and information

The direct **bus for Chiquilá** leaves Mérida (6hr) and Valladolid (3hr) in the middle of the night and arrives in time for the 6am ferry. Transferring in Tizimín (3hr) is a little easier, with a choice of three day-time buses. Coming from the east, the easiest route to Chiquilá is from Cancún (3hr), on an early-morning Mayab bus or the 1.45pm Noreste bus. If you're **driving**, don't take the toll highway, as there's no nearby exit; turn north off Hwy-180 *libre* at the tiny town of El Ideal.

The **Chiquilá ferry** for Holbox leaves nine times daily, roughly every two hours between 6am and the 7pm (30min; M$60). Secure parking is available near the pier (set the price before you leave – usually about M$30 for any portion of a day). If you're with a group or arrive between ferries, you might want to hire a private boat (about M$500). But don't miss the last ferry: Chiquilá is not a place to get stranded. There's a restaurant, basic hotel, store and petrol station, but little else.

Although a couple of restaurants on Holbox take credit cards, there's **no ATM** there, nor in Chiquilá – plan accordingly.

When you arrive on the island, you'll be greeted by *triciclo* taxis, which can spare you the ten-minute trek to the plaza, straight ahead from the ferry dock; the maximum charge is M$60, to the very furthest hotels. On the main square, which locals call the *parque*, is an **internet** café and a **money-exchange**. Very few people have cars; locals use the *triciclos* and electric **golf carts**. The latter are available to rent from several outlets near the *parque*.

Accommodation

Low-key hotel development stretches east of Holbox town for a couple of kilometres; only one property lies far to the west. Out of season (early summer and before Christmas), rates for some of the high-end rooms can fall by almost half; August, however, can be priced as high as Christmas and Easter weeks. All of the hotels on the **beachfront** are mid-range to luxury, but there are a few decent cheaper options away from the water, as well as the excellent *Ida y Vuelta* **campground and hostel**, with screened shelters for tents or hammocks (M$110) and a few beds (M$150), plus clean bathrooms and a shared kitchen (Ⓣ984/875-2358, Ⓦwww.camping-mexico.com). It's on the eastern edge of town, just 200m from the beach, behind *Xaloc*.

Casa las Tortugas On the beach two blocks east of the plaza Ⓣ984/875-2129, Ⓦwww.holboxcasalastortugas.com. A great little collection of round, two-storey cabañas, decorated with polka-dots and tucked among dense greenery. A/c is optional; breakfast is included. ❻

Faro Viejo Benito Juárez, at the beach Ⓣ984/875-2217, Ⓦwww.faroviejoholbox.com.mx. Modern, a/c rooms directly on the beach (the only stretch in town that's free of fishing boats), all with porches. A few suites are ideal for groups, with kitchenettes. ❼

Posada Los Arcos West side of the plaza Ⓣ984/875-2043. Clean, basic rooms, some with kitchenettes, around a small courtyard. Choice of a/c or fan. ❸

Posada Mawimbi On the beach next to *Casa las Tortugas* Ⓣ984/875-2003, Ⓦwww.mawimbi.net. Similar to *Casa las Tortugas* in layout, but with a few less expensive rooms. Opt for an upstairs room if you prefer fresh breezes. ❺

Villas Chimay On the beach 1km west of town Ⓣ984/875-2220, Ⓦwww.holbox.info. A wonderful hideaway, and the only lodging on the western beach. Self-sufficient with wind and solar power, and plenty of space between the well-designed bungalows. ❺

Villas Los Mapaches On the beach two blocks west of the plaza Ⓣ984/875-2090, Ⓦwww.losmapaches.com. Comfortable bungalows with kitchenettes. ❻

Xaloc On the beach at the east edge of town Ⓣ984/875-2160, Ⓦwww.holbox-xalocresort.com. Eighteen cabañas with rough-hewn wooden canopy beds and well-appointed bathrooms. The property is smartly divided into areas for families and adults only, with a pool in each section. Free kayaks and snorkel gear. ❻

Eating and drinking

The village has very little choice in terms of **restaurants**, but a few are quite good. On the east side of the plaza, *La Cueva del Pirata* is a tasty Italian restaurant, complete with hand-made fresh pasta. Just west of the plaza, off the beach-facing side, *Viva Zapata* serves great fresh fish in banana leaves, as well as chipotle shrimp, pasta and more; the first-floor palapa is a good place to watch the sun go down. On the beach, family-owned *Leo's* serves inexpensive fish and Mexican dishes, and there are also a couple of small *loncherías*. Don't expect any **nightlife** – the closest thing to a full bar is *Carioca's*, on the beach just north of the plaza. Locals generally lounge around on the plaza, where there might be a traditional Mexican *lotería*, or some vendors or musicians.

Cancún

If nothing else, **CANCÚN** is proof of Mexico's remarkable ability to get things done in a hurry – so long as the political will exists. In the late 1960s, the Mexican government decided to develop a new resort area to diversify the economy. Computers crunched weather data, and surveyors scouted the country's natural attractions to identify a 25-kilometre-long barrier island just off the northern Caribbean coast as the ideal combination of beautiful beaches, sparse population and accessible position. Construction of the resort paradise began in 1970, and when the first hotel opened in 1974, it relied on a generator for electricity and trucked-in water. In the twenty-first century, Cancún has struggled to shed its reputation for tacky fun (Spring Break happens only a month a year, after all), and it has also successfully courted Mexican tourists. But it is facing a mild crisis as seasonal storms in recent years have significantly eroded parts of the beach, the city's literal raison d'être.

Independent travellers often find the glitz of the hotel strip off-putting and the beachfront pleasures expensive, and, for anyone who has been out in the rest of the Yucatán or is eager to get there, all the concrete can be a downer. But a night spent here on the way in or out doesn't have to be wasted, so long as you appreciate the city as an energetic, successful frontier experiment, rather than lament its lack of history. A closer look reveals lively salsa clubs, bare-bones beach bars and inexpensive taco stands, all frequented by *cancunenses* who are friendly and proud of their city's prosperity.

Cancún has two parts: the *zona comercial* on the mainland (also called the **centro** or downtown), which has developed a bit of soul in its short lifetime, and the *zona hotelera*, a narrow, 25-kilometre-long barrier island lined with hotels and tourist amenities. It encloses a huge lagoon, so there's water on both sides. **Paseo Kukulcán** runs the length of the hotel zone, from the airport up to **Punta Cancún** (where the road splits around the convention centre and a warren of nightclubs and bars) and back onto the mainland. From Punta Cancún it's a half-hour bus ride to **Avenida Tulum**, the main avenue in the downtown area that runs north–south and eventually turns into Hwy-307, the highway that follows the length of the Caribbean coast.

Arrival, information and city transport

Charter flights from Europe and South America, along with direct scheduled flights from dozens of cities in Mexico and North and Central America, land at **Cancún International Airport** (Ⓦ www.cancun-airport.com), 20km south of the centre. Most international flights arrive at terminal 3, while domestic flights and some charter flights come into terminal 2 (terminal 1 is currently not in use). In both of the main terminals, you'll find **currency exchange** desks just past customs. In terminal 3, there's an **ATM** too, but at terminal 2, you have to walk outside and turn right and head for the one in the departures hall, which also has luggage **lockers**. An **airport bus** (M$40) runs nearly every thirty minutes to downtown (7.45am–12.30am), while **shared vans** take you to any part of the hotel zone for a fixed price (US$15); buy tickets at the respective desks outside customs. **Taxis** cost at least US$50.

Arriving by bus, you'll pull in at the city's main **bus station**, in the heart of downtown; it has **luggage storage**. You can walk to most downtown hotels.

Avenida Tulum, downtown Cancún's main north–south street, is lined with shops, banks, restaurants and travel agencies. The **tourist office** is a few minutes' walk south of the bus station, inside the city hall at Tulum 26 (daily 9am–8pm;

☎998/884-8073). The friendly bilingual staff will help with even the smallest enquiries. They also dish out free maps and leaflets, but nothing you can't get at any travel agency or hotel reception. Other "tourist information" **kiosks** are usually pitching time-shares or tickets to the big nature parks down the coast.

To get to and around the *zona hotelera*, **city buses** marked "Tulum–Hoteles, Ruta 1" run along Tulum every few minutes; the fare is M$6 in downtown and

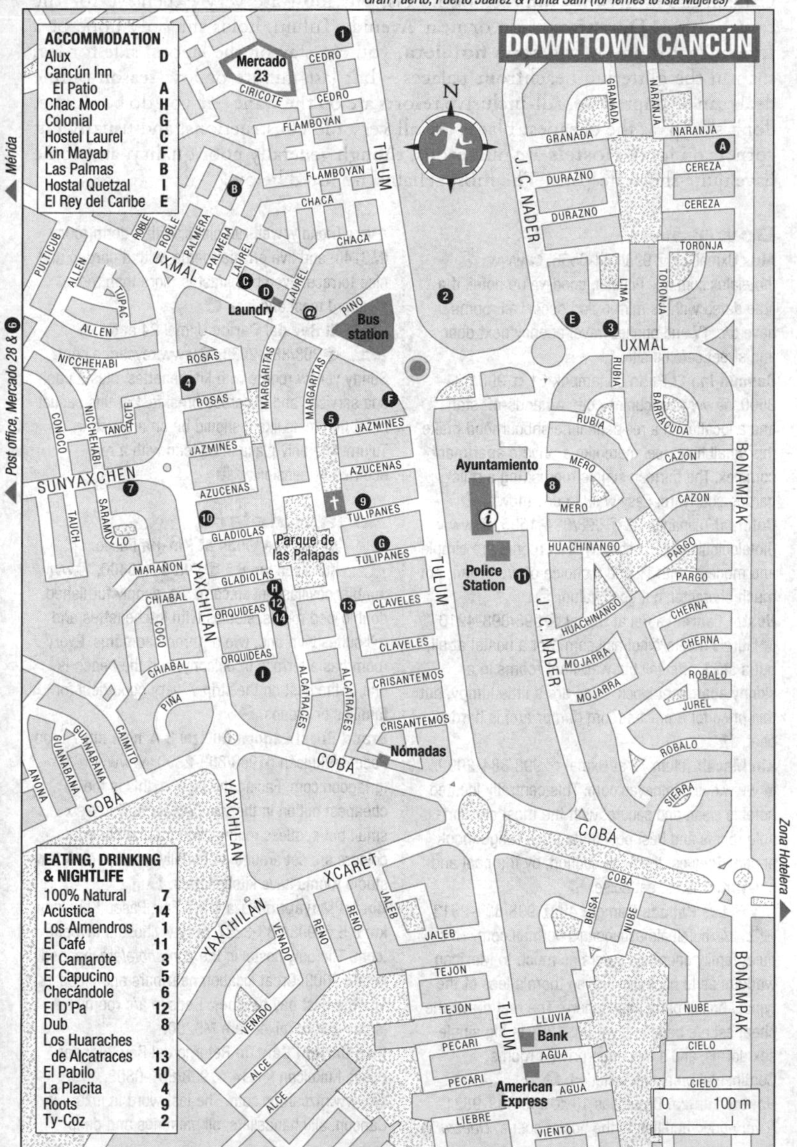

M$8.50 within and to anywhere in the hotel zone. **Taxis** are plentiful and can be hailed almost anywhere – the trip between downtown and Punta Cancún in the *zona hotelera* costs around M$110, based on a complex zone system (they're just M$15 within the downtown area). A **car** isn't necessary within the city, but it's not a liability either, as parking is not too difficult.

Accommodation

Cancún has a dizzying number of hotels, but most are very expensive for the casual visitor. **Downtown**, on or near Avenida Tulum, holds the only hope of a true budget room; in the **zona hotelera**, you can stay on the lagoon side for less than in the glittering beachfront palaces – but last-minute or low-season online deals can be impressive. All-inclusive resorts are on the wane – if you do book one, don't skimp, as the cheapest places are all very old constructions, and usually cut corners on food. **Hostels** are numerous, though generally poor quality, and some have quite short lifespans. The most reliable are listed below.

Downtown

Alux Uxmal 21 ⓣ998/884-0556, ⓦwww.hotelalux.com.mx. Popular, good-value hotel, if a little dated with its mirror-clad decor; all rooms have a/c, TV and phone. Travel agency next door and street café on site. ❺

Cancún Inn El Patio Bonampak 51 ⓣ998/884-3500, ⓦwww.cancuninn.com. A hands-off staff and a location in a residential neighbourhood make this small hotel feel more like a private apartment complex. The thirteen simple rooms ring a quiet garden courtyard. Easy walk to downtown. ❺

Colonial Tulipanes 22 ⓣ998/884-1535, ⓦwww.hotelcolonialcancun.com. Well-lit rooms are simple and modern, with TV and a choice of a/c or fan; not much character, but good value. ❺

Hostel Laurel Laurel at Uxmal ⓣ998/898-4210, ⓔlaurel41hostel@hotmail.com. Not a hostel at all, but a stack of small but well-kept rooms in a skinny apartment block. Beds are a little lumpy, but this price for a private room (fan or a/c) is hard to beat. ❸

Kin Mayab Tulum 75 at Uxmal ⓣ998/884-2999, ⓦwww.hotelkinmayab.com. This centrally located hotel is clean and secure, with the most comfortable rooms and best pool in its price range (book ahead). Request the back section, by the pool and away from the street noise. ❺

Las Palmas Palmera 43 ⓣ998/884-2513, ⓔhotelpalmascancun@hotmail.com. This quiet family operation caters as much to Mexican workers as to backpackers, so there's less of the typical hostel party atmosphere. The real draw: the cheapest a/c beds in town (M$120), in big single-sex dorms, and a few huge private rooms. Continental breakfast included. ❸

Hostal Quetzal Orquideas 10 ⓣ998/883-9821. A very good addition to the hostel scene, *Quetzal* is a very friendly, well-run place, with a dorm room (M$140) and five private rooms, with a garden and nice terrace. Even breakfast is more than the standard toast and jam. ❸

El Rey del Caribe Uxmal 24 at Nader ⓣ998/884-2028, ⓦwww.reycaribe.com. Sunny yellow rooms with kitchenettes, plus a pool, spa services and generous breakfast at this casual hotel that feels like it should be on a beach in Tulum. The only place in Cancún with a real ecofriendly sensibility. ❺

Zona hotelera

Ambiance Villas at Kin-Ha Paseo Kukulcán km 8.5 ⓣ998/891-5400, ⓦwww.ambiancevillascancun.com. Big, simply furnished double-bed rooms, studios with kitchenettes and full suites with one, two or three bedrooms. Every room has a terrace or balcony, and the beach is one of the best on the strip. A very good deal for families or groups. ❼

Grand Royal Lagoon Quetzal 8-A, near km 7.5 on Paseo Kukulcán ⓣ998/883-2890, ⓦwww.grlagoon.com. Facing the lagoon, this is the cheapest option in the *zona hotelera*. Thirty-six small but spotless rooms decorated in cheerful colours are set around an equally small pool. A few studio rooms have kitchenettes. ❹

Hostal Mayapan Plaza Maya Fair, Paseo Kukulcán km 8.5 ⓣ998/883-3227, ⓦwww.hostalmayapan.com. The only hostel in the *zona hotelera*, opened in late 2009. Great location near bars and clubs and the best bay beaches. Beds in a/c rooms (same-sex or mixed) are M$200.

Ritz-Carlton Cancún Retorno del Rey 36, near Paseo Kukulcán km 14 ⓣ998/881-0808, ⓦwww.ritzcarlton.com. The last word in luxury in Cancún: all chandeliers, oil paintings and deep

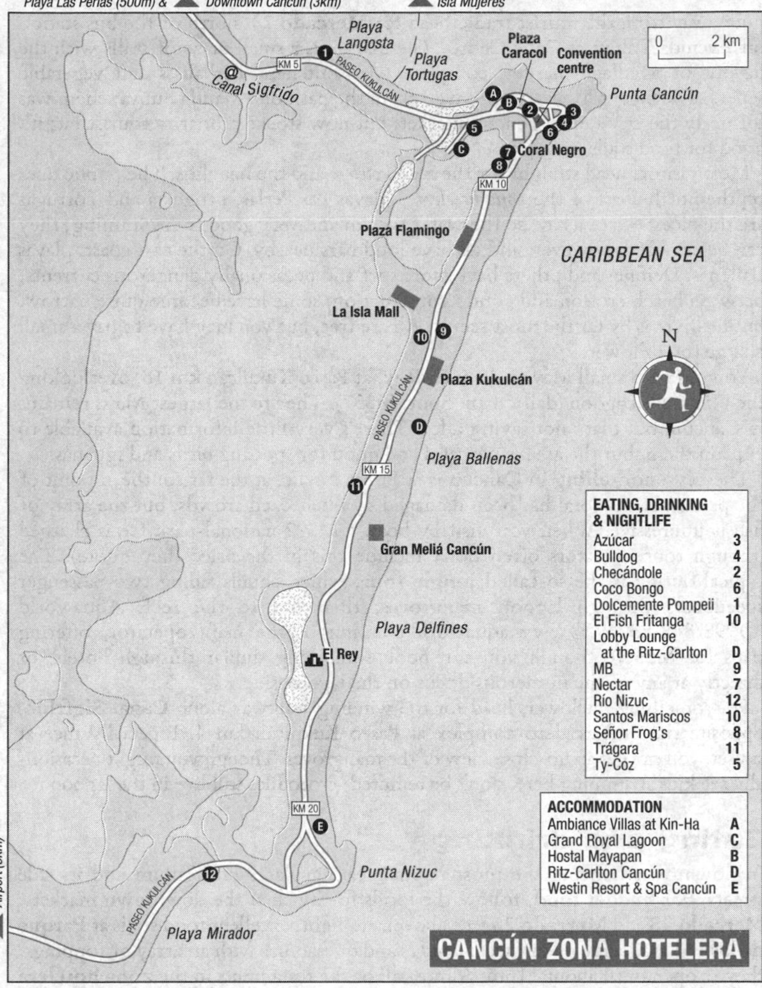

carpeting. Even if it doesn't seem particularly Mexican, it's still an impeccably run hotel. Prices can drop by half in the low season. ⑨

Westin Resort & Spa Cancún Paseo Kukulcán km 20 ⓣ998/848-7400, ⓦwww.westin.com. Striking, minimalist accommodation with pillow-top beds, deluxe showers and impressive views. An additional west-facing beach and pool on the lagoon get afternoon sun. Isolated (and quiet), but a free shuttle runs up to sister hotel the *Sheraton*, closer to the action. ⑧

The city and beaches

There's little in the way of sights in **downtown Cancún**, though it is a pleasant place to stroll in the evenings, particularly around the central **Parque de las Palapas,** which is ringed with food stalls and often serves as a venue for live music; smaller parks in the neighbourhood host craft or art shows. For a sense of the city's hum away from the tourist trade, head for **Mercado 23**, north of the bus station off Avenida Tulum at Calle Cedro. The market is a small maze of stalls with the flavour of a village market, complete with butchers, herbalists and vegetable sellers. The bigger **Mercado 28**, west from the park on Avenida Sunyaxchén, was formerly the city's main general market, but now stocks primarily tourist tat; it's good for food stalls, though.

Most visitors head straight for the *zona hotelera* and the **beaches**. The public ones on the north coast of the *zona hotelera* – playas Las Perlas, Langosta and Tortugas are the nicest – face a bay, so the water is calm and very good for swimming; they can be crowded, however, and all have loud bars nearby. On the east coast, playas Ballenas, Delfines and others have more surf and occasionally dangerous currents; between beach erosion and condo construction, some have become quite narrow, but Delfines is by far the most scenic. All are free, but you may have to pay a small charge for a shower.

You can see a small Maya ruin at **El Rey**, at Paseo Kukulcán km 18, overlooking the Nichupté Lagoon (daily 8am–5pm; M$37). They're the largest Maya remains in Cancún, but that's not saying a lot. There's very little information available to explain them, but the area is peaceful and good for spotting birds and iguanas.

The best **snorkelling** in Cancún is at Punta Nizuc, at the far southern point of the peninsula. Its coral has been damaged by unchecked crowds, but the array of fish is impressive. When you visit by boat, a M$22 national-park fee is charged (though tour operators often don't include this in the price they quote). The typical outing is the so-called **jungle tour**, which entails riding two-passenger speedboats through lagoon mangroves, then out to the reef. Aquaworld (Ⓣ998/848-8326, Ⓦwww.aquaworld.com.mx) is the main operator, offering trips for M$600, though you can book something similar through hotels, or directly at any of the numerous docks on the lagoon side.

For something mellower, head for the winding walkway along **Canal Sigfrido**, opposite the Embarcadero complex at Paseo Kukulcán km 4. Especially nice at sunset, you can get an up-close view of the mangroves. Though you might occasionally see kids swimming here, don't be tempted: crocodiles still live in the lagoon.

Eating and drinking

In downtown Cancún, the most popular eating-places line Tulum and its side streets. For **budget food**, follow the locals for lunch at the downtown markets: **Mercado 28** and **Mercado 23** (see above). At night, excellent food stalls at **Parque de las Palapas** serve open-face *huaraches* and quesadillas with an array of toppings; they're open until about 11pm. Almost all of the restaurants in the **zona hotelera** are geared towards one thing only: parting tourists from their money. But the few recommended here are solidly delicious. If you're staying on the beach, you're often better off taking a cab or bus downtown, where you'll find more satisfying food at reasonable prices, plus a congenial mix of people.

Downtown

These options are marked on the Downtown Cancún map, see p.805.

100% Natural Sunyaxchén 26 at Yaxchilán. As the name implies, the menu at this largely vegetarian restaurant is decidedly wholesome, with fruit salads, veggie burgers and fresh Mexican dishes. Breakfasts are delicious and inventive; try poached eggs over nopal leaves with spinach and an almond cream sauce.

Los Almendros Tulum 66. The original restaurant in the town of Ticul (see p.784) is credited with inventing the emblematic Yucatecan pork dish *poc-chuc*. This branch is somewhat stiff, with bright lights and white tablecloths, but the food is well prepared and reasonably priced. Nightly specials on Mon, Wed, Thurs and Sun.

El Café Nader 5, behind the city hall. A buzzing terrace frequented by Cancún's journalists. Good coffee and *pan dulce* for breakfast, plus a simple, reasonably priced lunch and dinner menu with basics like steak and fries and *enchiladas de mole*.

Checándole Xpuhil 6. A buzzing, popular restaurant that has been around since the earliest days, with a breezy terrace and a selection of satisfying and fresh-tasting Mexican classics. Mains such as enchiladas start at M$70; set lunch is M$45. Closed Sun.

El D'Pa Alcatraces, at the southwest corner of Parque de las Palapas. Typical French sweet and savoury crepes and decent wine by the glass. Sidewalk tables or sit inside among plush furniture. Closed Mon.

Dub Nader at Mero. Chilled-out hip café, often with a DJ providing a live soundtrack. It opens at 8am for a cappuccino fix, then segues into ice cream and sandwiches, then wine and light snacks (*jamón serrano*, olives, salads) at night – when a couple of other stylish places on the same street open up.

Los Huaraches de Alcatraces Alcatraces 31 (or enter on Claveles). This sparkling cafeteria-style restaurant serves up hearty breakfasts and hot lunches as well as lighter snacks like *huaraches* and quesadillas. It's all very fresh, and the staff are happy to explain the various dishes. Closed Mon.

El Pabilo Yaxchilán 31, in the *Xbalamqué* hotel. Mellow literary coffee shop (a '*cafébrería*') with very good cappuccino, espresso and snacks. Live guitar music or readings at night. A bulletin board has notices of art openings, concerts and the like.

La Placita Yaxchilán at Rosas. Open-air grill restaurant that's open at lunch but very lively at night, when this street gets packed with bar-hoppers.

Ty-Coz Tulum behind *Comercial Mexicana*. A sandwich shop where French and Mexican tastes mix: the warm ham-and-cheese *baguette económico* is slathered with garlic-herb mayo and studded with pickled jalapenos. Coffee and croissants for breakfast. Open till 10pm.

Zona hotelera

These options are marked on the Cancún Zona Hotelera map, see p.807.

Checándole Plaza El Parián, Paseo Kukulcán km 8.7. A branch of the downtown standby (see above). Daily 2–8pm.

Dolcemente Pompeii Pez Volador 7 near Paseo Kukulcán km 5 ⓣ998/849-4006. A rare casual restaurant catering to Mexican families and hotel-zone residents with mammoth portions of hearty Italian food, from hand-made pastas (M$110 and up) to gelato. Hard to find because it's not affiliated to a mall or hotel: turn north in front of the giant Mexican flag. Closed Mon.

El Fish Fritanga Paseo Kukulcán km 12.5. Hidden behind a *Domino's*, this lagoon-side seafood specialist is inexpensive, laid-back and frequented by residents – there's even a bit of beach, so you can stick your feet in the sand while you eat.

MB Paseo Kukulcán km 12, in *Aqua*. Miami chef Michelle Bernstein created the gutsy Italian and Spanish flavours at this unpretentious modern restaurant; don't miss the salt-caramel-and-chocolate cake. Mains from M$200.

Río Nizuc off Paseo Kukulcán near km 22. *Ceviche* and *tikin-xic* fish grilled in banana leaves are popular with locals at this casual place among the mangroves near the opening to the lagoon. Daily 11am–5pm.

Santos Mariscos Paseo Kukulcán km 12.5. Hip little seafood joint, with a really wide-ranging and well-priced menu, in the strip mall immediately south of *El Fish Fritanga*. Open till 11pm, midnight on weekends.

Ty-Coz Paseo Kukulcán km 7.5. A branch of the French-Mexican sandwich shop (see above).

Entertainment and nightlife

As Cancún's goal is to encourage some two million visitors a year to have fun, the **zona hotelera**'s array of huge dance clubs, theme bars and top-volume everything (most clustered around Punta Cancún and rolling from about 10pm till the wee hours) is lavish – or remorseless, depending on your mood. **Downtown**, people often dance on weekend evenings at the Parque de las Palapas to traditional Mexican music, and the stretch of Avenida Yaxchilán north of Sunyaxchén is a popular local hangout, with terrace restaurant-bars and karaoke open till 3am or 4am, all punctuated by roving *trovadores*.

Downtown

These options are marked on the Downtown Cancún map, see p.805.

Acústica Alcatraces, south of Parque de las Palapas. Live *trova* music most nights, in a warm, mellow atmosphere. The crowd is usually a bit younger than at *El Rincón del Vino*, just across the park, which has similar live music.

El Camarote In the *Plaza Kokai* hotel, Uxmal 26 ⓣ998/884-3218. Older

gentlemen play backgammon and cards at this nautical-themed terrace bar. In the back, a small stage hosts crooners of sad ballads (M$30 cover).

El Capucino Margaritas near Azucenas. Local reggae and jam bands play for a mixed clientele of students and bohemians. Cover is M$25 on weekends.

Roots Tulipanes 26. Funky little live jazz and blues club that also serves dinner.

Zona hotelera

These options are marked on the Cancún Zona Hotelera map, see p.807.

Azúcar At *Dreams Cancun*, Punta Cancún. Very popular, classy salsa club with a ten-piece house band. Cover is usually about M$80; music starts around 10pm. Closed Sun.

Bulldog South end of *Krystal* hotel, Paseo Kukulcán km 9.5. Outside of high Spring-Break season, this is frequented more by local kids, with hip-hop and *rock en español* on the speakers, and the occasional touring band.

Coco Bongo In the Forum by the Sea shopping centre, Paseo Kukulcán km 9.5. Vast state-of-the-art rock and pop disco popular with US college kids. Open till 5am; cover charge at weekends only.

Lobby Lounge at the Ritz-Carlton Retorno del Rey 36 near Paseo Kukulcán km 14. Soak up the ersatz Continental feel while sitting in overstuffed chairs and listening to the tinkling piano. The giveaway you're in Cancún: the sea view, exhaustive tequila menu and *ceviche* bar.

Nectar Paseo Kukulcán km 9.5. Hip indoor-outdoor lounge with DJs with a taste for techno. There's a little patch of sand for dancing, and a view over the lagoon.

Señor Frog's Paseo Kukulcán km 9.5. Practically synonymous with the name Cancún, the *Frog* is the first stop off the plane for the Spring-Break hordes. Go for live reggae or karaoke night, or just as an anthropological experience.

Trágara Paseo Kukulcán km 15.6. Velvet couches, numerous aquariums and mosaic trim on every surface set a super-cool mood in this breezy lagoon-front lounge – the perfect spot for a sunset drink and a snack from the Asian-fusion finger-food menu.

Listings

Airlines InterJet, Plaza Hollywood ⓣ800-011-2345; Mexicana ⓣ998/881-9045.

American Express Tulum 208 at Agua ⓣ998/884-4000 (Mon–Fri 9am–5pm).

Moving on from Cancún

First- and second-class **buses** go from the terminal at the corner of Tulum and Uxmal. If you're going any distance, you'll have a good selection of ADO GL (semi-deluxe) and Platino (deluxe) services, in addition to usual ADO and various second-class lines. Well-served destinations include **Campeche**, **Chetumal**, **Tulum**, **Mérida** and **Valladolid**. ADO runs one bus daily to **Mahahual** (at 7.30am; service increases in August). There's a second-class service to **Izamal** and to **Chiquilá**, for Isla Holbox, on Noreste (1.45pm) or Mayab (7.50am & 12.40pm). You could even conceivably head all the way to San Cristóbal de las Casa (18hr) or Mexico City (24hr). For **Playa del Carmen**, buses depart every ten minutes, stopping at Puerto Morelos; you could also take a **colectivo**, which is marginally cheaper – one service leaves from the parking area across Avenida Tulum from the bus station. And there's also a bus to Playa direct **from the airport** (hourly, 9.30am–11.30pm).

If you're heading west **by car** to Valladolid, Chichén Itzá and Mérida, you can choose between the free road (*libre*) or the toll highway (*cuota*). From the bus station, drive north on Tulum about 1km, then turn onto Avenida López Portillo. After a few kilometres you have the choice of which road to join; just south of the Cancún airport, there's an entrance to the *cuota* only. The drive to Mérida costs M$338; to Chichén Itzá, M$267.

From Cancún airport, frequent **flights** go to Mérida, Veracruz and Mexico City, as well as numerous international destinations, including Belize City on Maya Island Air. From downtown and the *zona hotelera* a taxi to the airport costs about M$200, and the bus from downtown costs M$40.

For further information, see Travel details, p.850.

Banks Most banks (usually Mon–Fri 9.30am–3pm, Sat 9.30am–1pm) are along Tulum between Uxmal and Cobá and in the biggest shopping malls – Kukulcán, Plaza Caracol – in the *zona hotelera*. The HSBC, Tulum 192, stays open until 7pm on weekdays.

Car rental At the airport, at most hotels and various locations downtown. Buster Rent a Car, C 35 between López Portillo and Bonampak (☎998/883-0510, ⓦwww.busterrentacar.com), is one reputable local firm.

Consulates Canada, Plaza Caracol, Paseo Kukulcán km 8.5 ☎998/883-3360; Germany, Punta Conoco 36, SM 24 downtown ☎998/887-2127; UK, *Royal Sands*, Paseo Kukulcán km 13.5 ☎998/848-8229; US, Plaza Caracol, Paseo Kukulcán km 8.5 ☎998/883-0272.

Hospital The largest hospital close to the *zona hotelera* is AmeriMed, Tulum Sur 260, behind Plaza las Américas ☎998/881-3400 or 881-3434 for emergencies, ⓦwww.amerimed-hospitals.com.

Internet access Immediately across from the bus station and northwest on Uxmal are several internet cafés; some are casetas as well. In the *zona hotelera*, web access is significantly more expensive; there's one café at Paseo Kukulcán km 4, opposite the Embarcadero.

Laundry Lavandería Las Palmas, on Uxmal just west of the bus station (daily 6am–9pm; M$13/kg). In the *zona hotelera*, at Paseo Kukulcán km 7.5, near *Ty-Coz* (see p.809).

Post office Sunyaxchén at Xel-Ha (Mon–Fri 8am–6pm, Sat 9am–1pm).

Travel agencies and tours Most hotels in the *zona hotelera* have in-house agencies that can arrange day trips to the chief Maya sites or other attractions along the coast. Otherwise, the student-friendly agency Nómadas is at Cobá 5, just west of Tulum (☎998/892-2320, ⓦwww.nomadastravel.com.mx) and leads affordable tours to Chichén Itzá and other nearby attractions.

Isla Mujeres

Just a few kilometres off the easternmost tip of Mexico, **ISLA MUJERES** is substantially mellower than Cancún, drawing people for long stays despite the lack of tourist attractions and wild nightlife. A hippie hangout in the 1970s, the tiny island still retains an air of bohemian languor, with wild-haired baby-boomers passing on travel wisdom to a new generation of young backpackers.

Physically, however, Mujeres is hardly the desert island it was thirty years ago, and its natural attractions have been developed considerably. Thousands of day-trippers visit from Cancún, and the **Garrafón coral reef** off the southern tip is now almost completely dead (though fish still flourish here). Prices, too, have risen. But the island can still seem a respite to those who've slogged across Mexico, or to anyone overwhelmed by Cancún – the low wooden buildings and narrow streets have a genuine Caribbean feel.

The attractions here are simple: first there's the beach, then there's the sea. And when you've tired of those, you can cruise around the island to more sea, more beaches and the tiny Maya temple full of female figures that the conquistadors chanced upon, which gave the place its name. But you'll want to be back under the palms on **Playa Norte**, the big west-facing beach, by late afternoon: Isla Mujeres is one of the few places along Mexico's eastern shoreline where you can enjoy a glowing sunset over the water.

Arrival, information and tours

Passenger **ferries** (see box, p.812) arrive at Isla Mujeres town at two adjacent piers; the car ferry comes in further south on Avenida Medina, just past the edge of town. From the piers, it's about a twenty-minute walk to the opposite side of the island and the most distant hotels. The **tourist office** (Mon–Fri 9am–6pm, Sat & Sun 9am–4pm; ☎998/877-0307) is on Medina just northwest of the passenger ferry piers. Here you can pick up leaflets and maps.

The ferry to Isla Mujeres

Passenger **ferries** (15min; M$70) for Isla Mujeres leave from Gran Puerto in Cancún on the mainland and, about 250m further north, Puerto Juárez, every thirty minutes (6.30am–10.30pm). To get to the ferry terminals, catch a bus ("R-13" or "R-1 – Pto Juárez") heading north from the stop on Tulum opposite the bus station (15min), or take a taxi from Avenida Tulum (around M$50). There's also a less frequent ferry service from Playa Tortugas in the *zona hotelera* (30min; M$140).

There's also a **car ferry** (M$185 per car with one driver, M$14 per extra person), but you don't need a vehicle, as the island is quite small and has plenty of bicycles and mopeds for rent. The boat leaves from Punta Sam, a few kilometres north of Puerto Juárez.

The best way of getting around the small island is by **moped** (M$120/hr) or bicycle (M$120/day). Virtually every other storefront rents out both forms of transport for approximately the same rates. David II, Guerrero at Matamoros, has well-maintained cruiser bikes

There are several **dive shops** on the island – recommended is Enrique's Unique Dives, Medina 1, by the PEMEX station (Ⓣ998/145-3594, Ⓦwww.divingisla mujeres.com), which offers a range of trips, including some to the "Cave of the Sleeping Sharks", where tiger, bull, grey reef, lemon and nurse sharks are regularly encountered. You can also take **snorkelling** trips with a couple of *lancheros* cooperatives, which are set up on the piers (M$240; 2hr). The main day outing, to which scores of touts devote their efforts, is a boat trip to the bird sanctuary of **Isla Contoy**. You can see colonies of pelicans and cormorants and occasionally more exotic sea birds, as well as a sunken Spanish galleon. The experienced captains at La Isleña Tours, on Morelos one block back from Medina, run a relaxed *faux*-castaway trip that takes about seven hours, with lunch caught straight from the sea, for US$55.

In recent years, the *lancheros* have begun offering tours (about M$1250) to see the **whale sharks** that gather off the coast in August and September – a trip more commonly taken from Isla Holbox (see p.802). While every shop touts the trip, only a small number of boats have the permit. Boats usually leave at 8am, and the trip to the sharks takes a couple of hours; there's lunch and reef snorkelling on the way back.

Accommodation

Isla Mujeres is short on good **budget places to stay**. Though rates are lower than in Cancún, so is the quality. Most of the reasonably priced options are on the north-western edge of the island; some of the less expensive waterfront views are on the northeastern side, where the sea is generally too rough for swimming. There is no official **campsite** on Isla Mujeres, but you can pitch your tent or hang a hammock (M$85) on the grounds of the *Poc-Na* **hostel**, Matamoros at Carlos Lazo (Ⓣ998/877-0090, Ⓦwww.pocna.com), which opens directly onto a beach. The hostel has other sleeping options, from dorm beds (M$120) to private rooms with air-conditioning (❹), though it can be less than spotless and has no public kitchen.

Casa Sirena Hidalgo, between Bravo and Allende, no phone Ⓦwww.sirena.com.mx. Very nicely redone home that has kept some old details, such as tiled floors, and added modern bathrooms and a breezy roof terrace. Three-night minimum; advance reservations required. ❼

Chi Chi's & Charlie's Northwest corner of the island, end of Av Rueda Medina Ⓣ998/877-0491. The bar on the prime beach spot for sunset-watching also rents twelve rooms – simple, but new construction, so they're in good shape, and certainly the best beachfront deal. ❺

Francis Arlene Guerrero 7 at Abasolo ⓣ998/877-0310, ⓦwww.francisarlene.com. Pretty, small hotel with well-tended courtyards and clean (if rather brightly painted) rooms with plenty of comforts – good value, especially as there's a choice of a/c or fan. ⑤

El Marcianito Abasolo 10 ⓣ998/877-0111. Though lacking the view that *Vistalmar* has, this is otherwise a comparable budget option, with clean rooms, all with one double bed. ③

María Leticia Juárez 28 between Mateos and Matamoros ⓣ998/877-0832, ⓕ877-0394. Big, airy rooms with or without kitchens and sitting rooms – great for long stays, but you must book ahead. ③

Las Palmas Guerrero 20 ⓣ998/274-0062, ⓦwww.laspalmasonisla.com. Friendly Canadian-owned operation, in an old courtyard building revamped with very comfortable beds, a plunge pool, wi-fi and a great roof terrace. ⑤

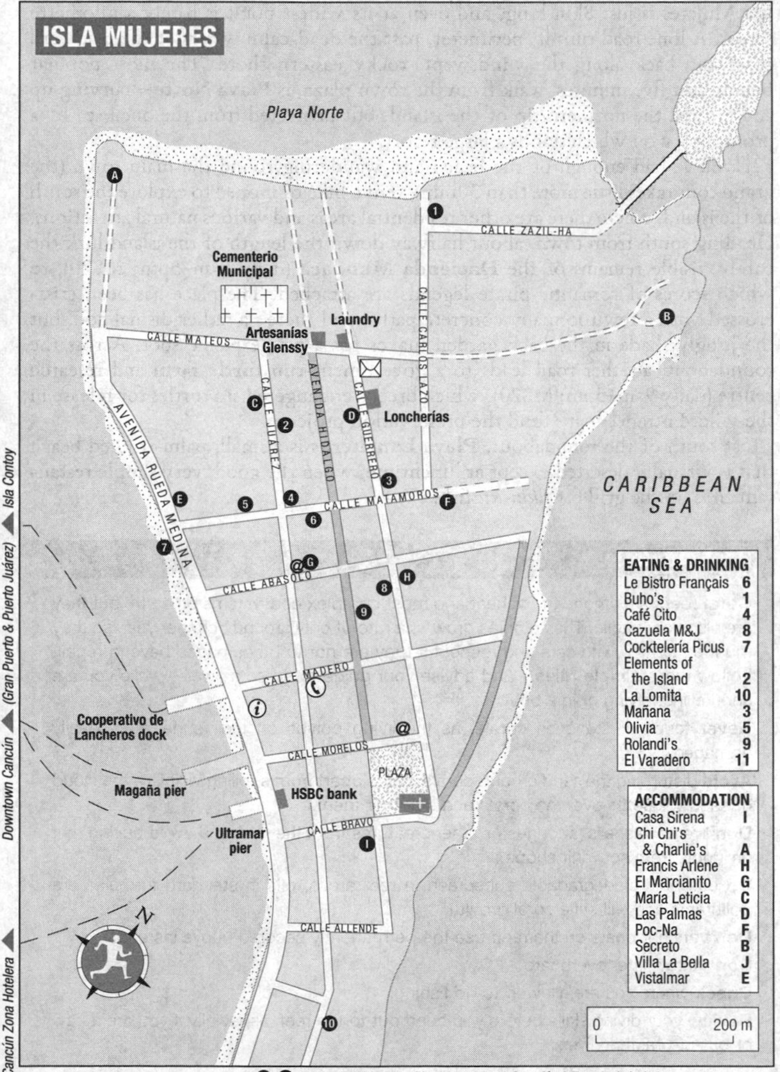

Secreto on the northeastern shore of the island ☎998/877-1039, ⓦwww.hotelsecreto.com. Whitewashed modern hotel with fluffy beds and outdoor lounge by the pool and a partially sheltered cove. Very good service. Continental breakfast included. ❾

Villa La Bella 2.5km southeast from the ferry, on the northeastern shore ☎998/888-0342, ⓦwww.villalasbrisas.com. A beautifully designed guesthouse outside the main town, perched above crashing surf (swim in the pool instead). The five rooms all have king-size beds. Full breakfast included. ❽

Vistalmar Medina at Matamoros ☎998/877-0209. Brightly painted, old-fashioned hotel (the colours change every year or two) just north of the ferry pier and central downtown. Good value, with choice of a/c or fan and big shared terraces with sea views. ❸

The island

Isla Mujeres is just 8km long, and even at its widest point is barely a kilometre across. A lone road runs its perimeter, past the dead-calm waters of the landward coast and back along the windswept, rocky eastern shore. The most popular **beach**, just five minutes' walk from the town plaza, is **Playa Norte** – curving up and around the northern tip of the island, but protected from the open sea by a promontory on which stands a large resort.

If you've had enough of the beach and wandering round the main town (the grand tour takes little more than 30min), rent a bike or moped to explore the south of the island, where there are other residential areas and various natural attractions. Heading south from town, about halfway down the length of the island lurk the barely visible remains of the **Hacienda Mundaca** (daily 9am–5pm; M$20), to which scores of romantic pirate legends are attached. The place has been criss-crossed with a few too many concrete paths, and there's a rather dismal zoo, but the jungly shade in the back garden makes for a prime picnic spot. Across the roundabout, another road leads to a government-run **turtle farm** and research centre (daily 9am–5pm; M$20), which breeds endangered sea turtles for release in the wild. Entrance helps fund the preservation project.

Just south of the roundabout, **Playa Lancheros** is a small, palm-fringed beach that is virtually deserted except at lunchtime, when the good, very simple restaurant fires up the grill for *tikin-xic* fish.

Reef etiquette

Coral reefs are among the richest and most complex ecosystems on earth, but they are also very fragile. The colonies grow at a rate of only around 5cm per year, so they must be treated with care and respect if they are not to be damaged beyond repair. Follow these **simple rules** – and advise your guide to do so as well – while you are snorkelling, diving or in a boat.

Never touch or stand on corals, as the living polyps on their surface are easily damaged.

Avoid disturbing the sand around corals. Quite apart from spoiling visibility, the cloud of sand will settle over the corals and smother them.

Don't remove shells, sponges or other creatures from the reef, and avoid buying reef products from souvenir shops.

Do use only biodegradable sunscreen in reef areas; oils in standard formulas are pollutants and will stifle coral growth.

Don't anchor boats on the reef: use the permanently secured buoys instead.

Don't throw litter overboard.

Check where you are allowed to go fishing.

Review your diving skills before you head out to the reef, especially if you are a new or out-of-practice diver.

▲ *Buho's* beach bar, Isla Mujeres

At the southern end of the island, the **Garrafón** reef is enclosed in a nature park (daily 9am–6.30pm; Ⓦwww.garrafon.com) with a zipline and "snuba" (swim underwater with an oxygen line). It's pricey, and can be crowded with Cancún day-trippers. For snorkelling, you're better off going on a trip with the *lancheros* (see p.812). The entrance to the park is almost at the southern tip of the island – beyond, the road continues to the old lighthouse, surrounded by *faux*-Caribbean houses containing shops and a restaurant. From there you can visit a somewhat gratuitous sculpture park and the **Templo de Ixchel**, at the southeastern tip (M$30; free with Garrafón ticket). It's not much of a ruin (the fertility figures the Spaniards spotted here have been removed), but it is very dramatically situated on low rocky cliffs.

Eating and drinking

The area along and around Hidalgo between Morelos and Abasolo is lined with **restaurants** and **bars**. For inexpensive, basic Mexican food and great fruit salads, head for the **loncherías** on Guerrero between Mateos and Matamoros. At night, food vendors set up on the main plaza.

Le Bistro Français Matamoros 29, at Hidalgo. Vaguely French café with a varied, inventive and delicious menu (fish with fennel and capers, for instance) at reasonable prices. Good breakfasts too.

Buho's Playa Nte at Carlos Lazo, in front of *Cabañas María del Mar*. In high season, this beach bar is the liveliest in town, with loud rock music, swinging hammock chairs and a well-attended happy hour.

Café Cito Juárez at Matamoros. Visit this colourful, cheery restaurant for healthy yogurt-granola breakfasts or more decadent crepes and waffles, along with very good coffee.

Cazuela M&J Guerrero across from *Francis Arlene*. This casual café serves inexpensive (mostly Mexican) breakfasts. Its speciality is egg dishes baked in small casseroles (*cazuelas*). Daily 7am–2pm.

Cocktelería Picus Medina just north of the ferry piers. Small beachfront hut serving fresh and inexpensive *ceviche* and shrimp cocktails. Lunch-only in the low season.

Elements of the Island Juárez 64. This tasty café below a yoga studio serves organic eggs and excellent coffee. Thurs–Tues 7.30am–1pm.

La Lomita Juárez 25-B, two blocks southeast of the plaza. Home cooking that's worth the hike up the hill, and the wait: locals line up for a helping of the daily lunch special.

Mañana Matamoros at Guerrero. Brightly painted breakfast and lunch café serving everything from falafel to *churrascos* (Argentine-style steak sandwiches). A secondhand book shop occupies one corner.

Olivia Matamoros between Juárez and Medina ☎998/877-1765. A wide-ranging Mediterranean menu, from Moroccan to Israeli flavours, is served in a pretty garden. Mains from M$70. Very popular, so reserve in high season. Tues–Sat 5–9.30pm.

Rolandi's Hidalgo, between Madero and Abasolo. Part of a small family-run chain serving great wood-oven pizza, lobster, fresh fish and other northern Italian dishes with salads.

El Varadero West coast, adjacent to Puerto Isla Mujeres. This super-casual Cuban restaurant is nestled among palm trees a little way out of town. Garlicky pork and refreshing mojitos are the specialities.

Listings

Banks HSBC, with an ATM, is directly across the street from the Ultramar ferry pier.

Books *Mañana* café (see p.815) sells second-hand books in several languages, including guidebooks.

Bus tickets Check schedules and purchase tickets for ADO and affiliate buses at a kiosk at the Ultramar ferry pier.

Internet One next to El Marcianito, on Abasolo between Hidalgo and Juárez, can also download photos from cameras; one on the northwest side of the plaza has cheap international calling too.

Laundry Lavandería Mis Dos Angelitos, Guerrero at Mateos (Mon–Sat 8am–11pm; M$10/kg).

Post office Guerrero at Mateos (Mon–Thurs 9am–4pm).

The east coast: Cancún to Playa del Carmen

The white-sand beach between Cancún and Tulum, known as the Riviera Maya, has become nearly as large a tourist draw as Cancún itself. The quietest town, **Puerto Morelos**, is actually the closest to Cancún, just 15 minutes' drive; the **Mesoamerican Barrier Reef** begins offshore here and extends all the way to Honduras. Further south, the phenomenal growth of **Playa del Carmen**, once known only as the departure point for boats to Cozumel, has transformed a fishing village into a major holiday destination renowned for its chic nightlife. **Tulum**, where the beach is finest, is a yogacentric, *faux*-rustic resort spot.

Finding a relatively deserted stretch of beach is increasingly difficult, though not impossible, and many visitors based in Cancún rent a car to explore the coast. Bus and *colectivo* service along Hwy-307 is cheap and efficient, but be prepared for at least a half-kilometre walk, or a longer taxi ride, towards the water.

Puerto Morelos and around

Leaving Cancún behind, the first town south along the coast is **PUERTO MORELOS**, 20km away. Still a working fishing town, it's unpretentious and calm, which tends to draw visitors for long stays – but even the cheapest hotels might be over budget for some travellers. The reef offshore is also very healthy, making for good **diving and snorkelling**. Inland, on the dirt road to Central Vallarta, are some beautiful cenotes. With a direct bus service from the Cancún airport (see p.804), it's easy for visitors to bypass Cancún altogether, making Puerto Morelos their first stop along the Riviera Maya.

Arrival and information

Buses going down the coast leave Cancún's bus station every ten minutes and drop you thirty minutes later at the highway junction, where taxis wait to take you the 2km into town (about M$25). On the plaza, you'll find several **long-distance telephones**, an **internet** café, a supermarket, a couple of **exchanges** and an **ATM**, though no actual bank. Marand Travel (Ⓦ www.puertomorelos.com.mx), on the southwest corner of the plaza, is the unofficial tourist info spot, dispensing maps and advising on hotels. There's a **laundry** just south of the plaza, across from *Posada Amor*.

Accommodation

Beachfront hotels in Puerto Morelos are significantly cheaper than in Playa del Carmen or Cancún, so this might be a place to treat yourself if your budget allows. But there are no set **campsites** or **hostels**.

Amar Inn on the seafront 500m north of the main plaza Ⓣ 998/871-0026, Ⓔ amar_inn@hotmail.com. Bohemian, family-run hotel with eight large, well-furnished rooms and cabañas, some with kitchenettes. Delicious Mexican breakfast included in rates. ⑤

Maya Echo C 2 in the *zona urbana* Ⓣ 998/208-9148, Ⓦ www.mayaecho.com. With two spacious guestrooms in the forest on the inland side of the highway, the "peanut house" is a great chance to experience the jungle and the non-touristy side of Puerto Morelos in relative comfort. It's also a handy place for solo travellers to get settled, under the wing of hostess Sandra, a longtime Mexico resident. ⑤

Ojo de Agua on the seafront 400m north of the plaza Ⓣ 987/871-0027, Ⓦ www.ojo-de-agua.com. Bright, sunny rooms (some have a/c) with colourful decor, most overlooking a giant pool; beyond lies a clean beach. The restaurant/bar occasionally hosts a live band. Ocean-view rooms don't cost more. ⑤

Posada Amor Av Rojo Gómez just south of the plaza Ⓣ 998/871-0033, Ⓔ pos_amor@hotmail.com. Not on the beach, but friendly, and one of the longest-running hotels in town. Some of the quirky, individually decorated rooms are the least expensive around, while some other, larger ones with private baths are worth the extra money; ask to see a few. ⑤

Posada El Moro Rojo Gómez 17, just north of the plaza Ⓣ 987/871-0159, Ⓦ www.posadaelmoro.com. Ten clean, relatively new rooms, some with kitchens, in a pretty little garden; rooms at the back are preferable, as the bar across the street can be noisy at night. Amenities are excellent for the price: there's a small pool, and continental breakfast is included. ⑤

The Town

The road from Hwy-307 ends at the small, modern **plaza** in the centre of Puerto Morelos. The only proper streets lead north and south for a few blocks, parallel to the beach. The plaza has a small church, a baseball court and a taxi rank, and hosts a produce market on Wednesdays. It's also home to the wonderful Alma Libre (Oct–April Tues–Sat 9am–noon & 6–9pm), probably Mexico's most extensive secondhand English-language **bookshop** (you can also get your digital photos transferred to CD here). Ahead lies the **beach**, a wooden **dock** and a **lighthouse**, knocked off-kilter years ago by a hurricane, but kept as a local icon. Reasonably priced **craftwork** can be found at Hunab-Ku Artesanía, two blocks south of the plaza on Rojo Gómez. Here you can often see the artisans at work. If you're in town on a Sunday, don't miss the "**jungle market**", where members of a women's cooperative sell their wares (winter only, Sun 10.30am), which include great food as well as handicrafts. It's on the inland side of the highway – tell the cab driver "zona urbana, Calle Dos".

With a healthy stretch of reef only 600m offshore, Puerto Morelos is a great place to learn to **dive**. Long-established Almost Heaven Adventures, on Rojo Gómez one block north of the plaza (Ⓣ 987/871-0230, Ⓦ www.almostheavenadventures.com), offers certification courses and one- and two-tank dives (US$55–75) and snorkelling trips (M$350 per person; 2hr), as well as sport-fishing charters. It also leads tours to some inland **cenotes**, accessible via a turn-off from the main highway, marked by a modern concrete Maya arch. Most have been developed as big-budget package-tour destinations, but a couple, such as Siete Bocas and Tres Bocas, are good for diving.

On the east side of the highway, opposite the turn for the cenote route, the **Jardín Botánico Dr Alfredo Barrera Marín** (also signposted as Yaax Ché; Nov–April daily 8am–4pm, May–Oct Mon–Sat 9am–5pm; M$70) provides a good overview of the Yucatán's flora. A three-kilometre path leads through medicinal plants, ferns, palms, some tumbledown Maya ruins and a mock-up *chiclero* camp, where you can see how the sap of the *zapote* (sapodilla) tree is tapped before being used in the production of gum.

Eating and drinking

For a town of its size, Puerto Morelos has a disproportionately high number of great **places to eat**, offering a mix of local cuisine and flavours brought in by various expats (expect higher prices at the latter, of course). Most places are on the plaza, where everyone seems to convene at night. The bar at *Hacienda Morelos* occasionally hosts **live music**, as do a few restaurants. The tastiest snacks can be found at *El Tío*, just north of the plaza on Avenida Melgar, which does shrimp tacos in the morning and tortas and *panuchos* at lunch; also look out for a few informal eateries run out of people's front yards.

Bara Bara Rojo Gómez south of the plaza, next to *Posada Amor*. PM's hippest venue, a small bar with DJs spinning reggae and house music, and bartenders mixing actual cocktails. Closed Mon.

Don Pepe Olé Rojo Gómez north of the plaza. A sometimes rowdy local bar scene, which starts in the afternoon. Karaoke is the entertainment of choice once the sun goes down.

Hola Asia South side of the plaza. Get your fix of General Tso's chicken, or sample other Asian delicacies such as Thai fish with tamarind or Indonesian-style coconut shrimp. The rooftop tiki bar is nice at sunset – and the main expat hangout in town. Closed Tues.

John Gray's Kitchen Niños Héroes north of the plaza ⓣ998/871-0665. Visitors from Cancún often make the short drive down for dinner at this small, casually elegant restaurant with combos like pan-roasted duck breast with chipotle, tequila and honey, or mac-and-cheese with shrimp and truffle oil. Closed Sun.

Lonchería Mimi Niños Héroes north of the plaza. Look for the pale-green façade on this tidy *cocina económica*, where a team of women cook up daily specials in a spotless open kitchen. Go early, as food tends to run out – and the four tables fill up fast.

Mama's Rojo Gómez, one block north of the plaza. Homely American-owned breakfast and lunch joint, offering breakfast burritos with veggie chorizo, oatmeal, fruit smoothies and a wide range of baked goods. Closed Mon.

La Petita Melgar half a block north of the plaza. This small wooden house is a fishermen's hangout and a local favourite for enjoying the catch of the day, sold by the kilo and available fried, grilled or in *ceviche*.

La Suegra de John Gray Melgar opposite *La Petita*. John Gray's mother-in-law cooks up chile-laced shrimp tacos, hearty soups and other tasty food that's ideal for the beachfront setting. Open Tues–Sun noon–8pm.

Punta Bete and Playa Maroma

Jutting out north of Playa del Carmen, the sedate beach called **PUNTA BETE** has a mix of high- and low-end hotels facing the slightly rocky water—and the area is small enough that the hotels are the only draw. The mellow mini-resort *Petit Lafitte* (US ⓣ01-800/538-6802, ⓦwww.petitlafitte.com; ➒) is a relative bargain, a low-key place with loyal regulars; rates include breakfast and dinner. *The Tides Riviera Maya* (ⓣ984/877-3000, ⓦwww.tidesrivieramaya.com; ➒), on the other end of the price scale, is an extremely lovely hideaway. In this same category, *Maroma*, 10km north of Punta Bete on Playa Maroma (ⓣ998/872-8200, ⓦwww.orient-expresshotels.com; ➒), is elegant yet informal, and with a strong Mexican style. The whitewashed hotel has a wonderful spa and an exceptionally personal feel.

Playa del Carmen

Once a soporific fishing village where travellers camped out en route to Cozumel, **PLAYA DEL CARMEN** (often called simply Playa) has mushroomed in recent years to become a trendy place touted as the next Miami Beach – and, from a local's perspective, a goldmine of employment in construction. Not only do Mexico City's elite pop in, but so do day-trippers from Cancún and passengers from cruise ships. As a result, the town's main centre of activity, Avenida 5 (also called **La Quinta**), a long, pedestrianized strip one block back from the sea, is often packed to capacity with tourists rapidly emptying their wallets in pavement cafés, souvenir outlets and designer-clothes shops. Nonetheless, the low-rise development and numerous European-owned businesses make it, compared with Cancún, seem positively cosmopolitan and calm. The **nightlife** in particular has a hip edge, and you'll also find sophisticated cuisine, hotels for most budgets and diverse shops. Everywhere visitors will want to go is compact and pedestrian-friendly – even a walk to the **Playa Norte**, the better **beach** on the north side of town, is an easy one.

For anyone interested in **scuba diving**, Tank-Ha, on Calle 10 between avenidas 5 and 10 (Ⓣ984/873-0302, Ⓦwww.tankha.com), is a good place to start. The shop offers PADI certification courses, one- and two-tank dives (US$45–75) and twice-daily snorkelling tours (9am & 1.30pm; US$40; 3hr). **Kiteboarding** specialists Ikarus give basic instruction on the beach in Playa, then take you up or down the coast for in-water lessons; visit the shop on Avenida 5 at Calle 20 (Ⓣ984/803-3490, Ⓦwww.kiteboardmexico.com) for details.

Arrival, information and city transport

Playa del Carmen has two **bus stations**. One is on Avenida 5 at Avenida Juárez, the main street running east–west from the highway to the beach, for short-haul buses between Cancún and Tulum; it has short- and long-term luggage storage. The other station, on Avenida 20 between calles 12 and 14, handles long-distance buses. From both, a **taxi** to the hotels furthest north should be no more than M$17. From the international **airport** in Cancún, buses run hourly to Playa (9.30am–11.30pm; M$90). Coming by **ferry** from Cozumel, you arrive at a pier at the end of Calle 1, the southern edge of Playa's public beachfront – the town extends north and inland from here.

Tourist info kiosks, on Juárez near Avenida 15 and on the main plaza (daily 9am–9pm; Ⓣ984/873-2804, Ⓔturismo@solidaridad.gob.mx), have bilingual staff who do their best to answer any enquiries. They stock the useful *Playa del Carmen*, with hotel and restaurant listings. Online, you can prep for your trip or get news on upcoming events at Ⓦwww.playa.info.

Accommodation

Hotels are being built all the time in Playa, so you'll have no difficulty finding a room. Competition keeps prices relatively low, but it's still virtually impossible to get a room for less than M$400 in high season – which here includes the European vacation months of July and August, as well as mid-December to April. In general, the further from the water, the cheaper the accommodation; the central beach is somewhat eroded, so seafront hotels are generally not good value. Hotels on Avenida 5 can be noisy due to the bars.

The town has one place for **camping**, beachfront *Cabañas La Ruina* (M$150; see p.821), and one recommended **hostel**, the big, groovy *Youth Hostel Playa*, Avenida 25 at Calle 8 (Ⓣ984/803-3277, Ⓦwww.hostelplaya.com), which is further from the beach but more comfortable, with dorm rooms (M$120) and a variety of private options.

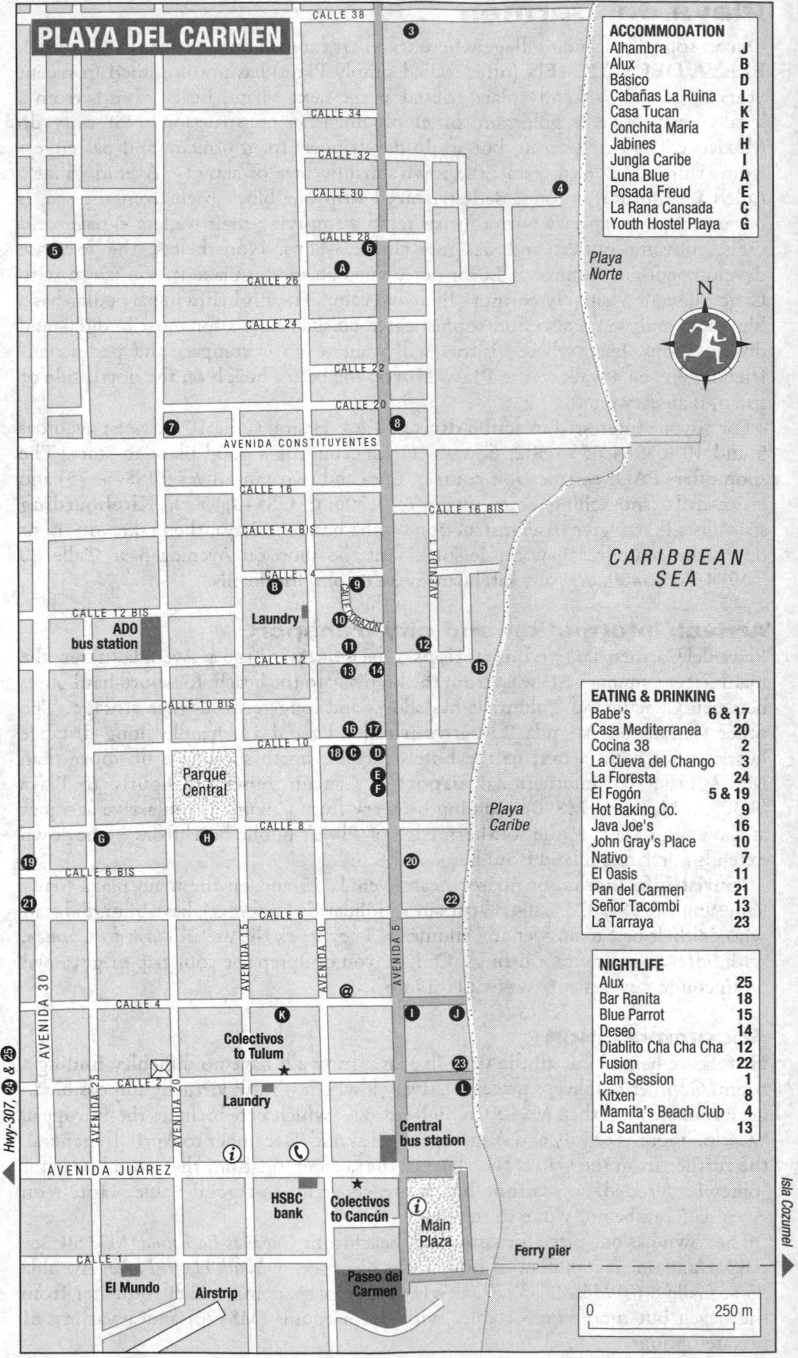
PLAYA DEL CARMEN
ACCOMMODATION
Alhambra J
Alux B
Básico D
Cabañas La Ruina L
Casa Tucan K
Conchita María F
Jabines H
Jungla Caribe I
Luna Blue A
Posada Freud E
La Rana Cansada C
Youth Hostel Playa G
EATING & DRINKING
Babe's 6 & 17
Casa Mediterranea 20
Cocina 38 2
La Cueva del Chango 3
La Floresta 24
El Fogón 5 & 19
Hot Baking Co. 9
Java Joe's 16
John Gray's Place 10
Nativo 7
El Oasis 11
Pan del Carmen 21
Señor Tacombi 13
La Tarraya 23
NIGHTLIFE
Alux 25
Bar Ranita 18
Blue Parrot 15
Deseo 14
Diablito Cha Cha Cha 12
Fusion 22
Jam Session 1
Kitxen 8
Mamita's Beach Club 4
La Santanera 13
CALLE 38
CALLE 34
CALLE 32
CALLE 30
CALLE 28
CALLE 26
CALLE 24
CALLE 22
CALLE 20
AVENIDA CONSTITUYENTES
CALLE 16
CALLE 16 BIS
CALLE 14 BIS
CALLE 14
CALLE 12 BIS
CALLE 12
CALLE 10 BIS
CALLE 10
CALLE 8
CALLE 6 BIS
CALLE 6
CALLE 4
CALLE 2
CALLE 1
AVENIDA JUÁREZ
AVENIDA 30
AVENIDA 25
AVENIDA 20
AVENIDA 15
AVENIDA 10
AVENIDA 5
AVENIDA 1
CALLE CORAZÓN
Playa Norte
CARIBBEAN SEA
Playa Caribe
ADO bus station
Laundry
Parque Central
Colectivos to Tulum
Central bus station
HSBC bank
Colectivos to Cancún
Main Plaza
Ferry pier
El Mundo
Airstrip
Paseo del Carmen
Hwy-307, 24 & 25
Isla Cozumel
Playacar
1 & 2
N
0
250 m

Alhambra On the beach at C 8 ⓣ984/873-0735, ⓦwww.alhambra-hotel.net. With gleaming white a/c rooms and a small pool, this is the strongest beachfront option. Daily yoga classes and treatments offered by the resident massage therapist. ❽

Alux C 14 between Av 10 and Av 15 ⓣ984/803-2482, ⓦwww.hotelalux.com. Like its downtown Cancún counterpart, this *Alux* is a little frumpy, but a good deal. A/c is optional, and some rooms have kitchenettes. ❹

Básico Av 5 at C 10 ⓣ984/879-4448, ⓦwww.hotelbasico.com. Cool industrial design meets an equally cool clientele – the rooftop pools (converted water tanks) are a hot spot. Also look for the same owners' *Deseo* hotel, at C 12: equally sharp style, and marginally quieter. ❾

Cabañas La Ruina C 2 on the seafront ⓣ984/873-0405. Long-established bargain slice of the good life on the beach despite large hotels all around. The cheapest cabañas have shared bath. ❸

Casa Tucan C 4 between Av 10 and Av 15 ⓣ984/873-0283, ⓦwww.casatucan.de. A Playa institution and still one of its best bargains. Offers basic rooms (some with palapa roofs and shared bath) and excellent-value studios, a big swimming pool, a friendly restaurant and a generally mellow vibe. Book in advance. ❺

Conchita María Av 5 between C 8 and C 10 ⓣ984/873-2336, ⓔhotelconchitamaria@hotmail.com. Surprising budget operation on a prime block – fifteen fan-only rooms, a couple with small kitchenette and terrace. Top-floor rooms are best, though reached by a dodgy staircase. ❸

Jabines C 8 between Av 15 and Av 20 ⓣ984/873-0861. A reliable budget hotel filled with greenery, facing a modern plaza. Rooms are a little dark, but quieter than most. ❸

Jungla Caribe Av 5 at C 8 ⓣ984/873-0650, ⓦwww.jungla-caribe.com. On a prime corner on La Quinta, this hotel is nonetheless serene inside, thanks to a shady courtyard (so overgrown, in fact, you can hardly see the pool). Stairs trimmed in black-and-white tiles ascend like an Escher etching to large, cool rooms. It's clean, a little quirky and an especially good bargain in the off season. ❻

Luna Blue C 26 between Av 5 and Av 10 ⓣ984/873-0990, ⓦwww.lunabluehotel.com. Relatively far from the noisy fray, yet still close to the beach, *Luna Blue* is built around a central garden with tall palms and other shady trees. Rooms have curvy, palapa-covered terraces, white-washed walls and lots of windows. ❺

Posada Freud Av 5 between C 8 and C 10 ⓣ984/873-0601, ⓦwww.posadafreud.com. Pretty rooms with colourful details smack in the middle of the action at reasonable (and often negotiable) rates. Ground-floor rooms can be a little loud – it may be worth asking for a back, upstairs room. ❺

La Rana Cansada C 10 no. 132 between Av 5 and Av 10 ⓣ984/873-0389, ⓦwww.ranacansada.com. One of the oldest hotels in Playa, "The Tired Frog" is friendly, sparkling clean and laid-back. It has communal kitchen facilities and various room options, including a smart two-level suite with beer delivery by bucket from the bar downstairs. Optional a/c. ❹

Eating and drinking

Playa del Carmen is heaving with **restaurants** of every kind, and even the traditional Mexican places stay open late. The pedestrianized section of **Avenida 5** is lined with tables at which you can eat all sorts of cuisine – but if you're on a **budget** you'll need to search out where locals go: try the taco carts on Juárez close to the beach (breakfast and lunch only), food stalls on Avenida 10 at Calle 6 (open at night) and various restaurants on Avenida 30. There's a **supermarket** on Avenida 30 at Calle 20, and the smaller *DAC store*, half a block north, has great produce. One warning: the turnover in restaurants in Playa is so high as to make a guidebook writer despair – half these places may have closed by the time you go looking for them; the good news is that new places will have opened.

Cafés

Hot Baking Co. C 14 at C Corazón. Bakery-café for fresh muffins, bagels, brownies and giant cinnamon rolls. Heartier eaters can choose from omelettes and grilled sandwiches.

Java Joe's C 10 between Av 5 and Av 10. Caffeine junkies stumble to this open-sided coffee bar in the late morning or early afternoon – the regulars are party-happy expats, and the brew is super-strong.

Pan del Carmen Av 30 at C 6. Pick up inexpensive bread, sweet and savoury *hojaldres* (filled puff pastry) and *pan dulce* at this fragrant Mexican bakery.

Nativo Av 30 between Constituyentes and C 20. Delicious fresh-fruit smoothies and other healthy Mexican food, next to the *DAC* market.

Señor Tacombi C 12 between Av 5 and Av 10. Clubbers flock to this 24hr taco vendor built in a groovy VW bus – you'll pay more, but the variety is good, and its breakfast combos are tasty too.

Restaurants

Babe's C 10 between Av 5 and Av 10. This Swedish-owned Thai noodle house – which also serves a fine Cuban mojito – typifies Playa's international hodgepodge. Dishes like *pad thai* start at M$90 for a huge portion. An outpost at Avenida 5 and Calle 28 has a longer menu.

Casa Mediterranea Av 5 between C 6 and C 8. Tucked inside the Jardín del Marieta, amid art galleries, this modest little trattoria (there are only about six seats) serves delectable fresh pasta, such as fettucine with shrimp and squash, for M$120 and up. Unpretentious and delicious.

Cocina 38 Av 5 at C 38. Minimalist and upscale, this chic little foodie haven does creative, confident seafood as well as heartier items like pork belly. The short menu changes often, and even the smallest details, like the chocolates with the coffee and the Mexican house wine, are well chosen. Mains start at M$180.

La Cueva del Chango C 38 between Av 5 and the beach. This garden restaurant serves till 11pm, but it's a local favourite especially for long, late breakfasts. The menu includes tasty empanadas and crepes (about M$65) and house-roasted coffee. Closes at 2pm Sun.

La Floresta West side of Hwy-307, just north of Av Juárez. This big palapa next to the highway is a road-tripper's delight, serving overstuffed *tacos de camarón*, the perfect marriage of batter-fried shrimp, mayo and chunky tomato salsa. Seafood cocktails and *ceviches* are available too. Closes at 4.30pm.

El Fogón Av 30 at C 6 bis. A basic, brightly lit taco joint that's generally mobbed with locals; anything off the grill is recommended. No booze is served, but you can wash down all the meat with a big selection of *aguas frescas*. There's another branch on Av 30 near C 28.

John Gray's Place Corazón, north of Av 5, between C 12 and C 14 ⓣ984/803-3689. An outpost of an excellent restaurant in Puerto Morelos (see p.818), with the same varied, tasty menu and a great Mexican wine list – or try the signature "smoky margarita" made with mescal. Closed Sun.

El Oasis C 12 between Av 5 and Av 10. There's a full menu of seafood dishes, but the star attraction is the batter-fried shrimp tacos, served with *pico de gallo* and a smear of mayonnaise – cheap for this part of town, and tasty. Closed Sun.

La Tarraya on the seafront at C 2. This local institution has been open for more than thirty years, well before Playa was a gleam in a developer's eye. It still serves standard beach fare like *ceviche* and *pescado frito* (M$90/kg) with plenty of cold beer.

Nightlife and entertainment

At night, La Quinta becomes one long street party, and you can find any sort of music in the array of **bars**, though by 10pm or so, most people will wind up around the intersection with Calle 12, which has the highest concentration of cool **clubs** and **lounges**, and the area can stay lively till 3am or 4am. If you're looking for a mellower atmosphere, head north of Constituyentes, even as far up as Calle 40. Drinks aren't cheap, but don't let that stop you from going out, as it's easy to meet people, and happy-hour specials can ease you into the night without depleting funds too rapidly.

Bars

Bar Ranita C 10 between Av 5 and Av 10. A crew of regulars – mostly expats – hang out at the horseshoe-shaped bar in this snug and mellow wood-panelled spot. A welcome break from Playa's generally top-volume scene.

Deseo Av 5 at C 12. The poolside bar at the stylish hotel draws its inspiration from Miami Beach, with beds to lounge on, over-the-top cocktails and bartenders as attractive and ostentatious as the crowd.

Diablito Cha Cha Cha C 12 at Av 1. Mexico-goes-rockabilly is the loose theme at this retro-cool lounge – you can fuel up on Asian snacks, or just go straight to vanilla martinis and the like.

Fusion C 6 at the beach. This mellow beach bar, lit with kerosene lamps and tables in the sand is a great slice of old-fashioned, pre-club-scene Playa.

Kitxen Av 5 between Av Constituyentes and C 20. This cool bar-restaurant is owned by a member of legendary Mexican rock group Los Jaguares, so live bands often accompany good bar-snack food.

El Tigre Av 10 between C 2 and C 4. Good local spot for beers, *ceviche* and ridiculously generous *botanas*. Women will probably feel more comfortable accompanied by a man; the billiards area upstairs is men-only. Closes by 5pm.

Moving on from Playa del Carmen

Typically, long-haul **buses** go from the station on Avenida 20 between calles 12 and 14, and short-haul services leave from the central station, Juárez at Avenida 5. You can buy tickets for all routes at either station. The most frequent service is Cancún, every 10 minutes; Cancún airport service goes every hour 7am–9pm. Departures for Tulum and Chetumal are at least hourly, as are Mérida and Valladolid buses (ten of these go to Cobá, after two hours; four stop in Chichén Itza, after four hours). You can also get to San Cristóbal de las Casas (four of the five buses stop in Palenque) and Villahermosa (15 daily).

The best way to reach smaller towns or beaches just north and south of Playa is by **colectivo**; the Cancún service departs frequently from Juárez in front of the main bus station, and vans heading south to Tulum leave from Calle 2 between avenidas 10 and 15. **Taxis** can also take you anywhere you need to go along the coast – they're more expensive than *colectivos*, but far cheaper than any tour company, even when you pay for waiting time.

For further information, see Travel details, p.850.

Clubs

Alux Juárez, 400m west of Hwy-307 ⓣ984/803-2936, ⓦwww.aluxlounge.net. It's expensive and a trek from the main drag (tell the cab driver "ah-LOOSH"), but how often do you get to party in a Technicolor-lit cave? French-tropical dinner menu starts at 8pm; a DJ or a floor show of belly dancers and jazz musicians begins around 10pm. Usually no cover; drinks are M$80 and up.

Blue Parrot on the beach at C 12. As the rest of Playa goes upscale, this longtime beach haunt, also known as the *Dragon Bar*, stays true to its casual, anything-goes vibe, with tables in the sand, a young crowd and two-for-one drinks 7–10pm.

Jam Session Av 5 at C 40. Wed–Sat 9am–2pm, Sun 6pm–2am. A mellow alternative to Calle 12: a house band plays blues, jazz and whatever else strikes their fancy, sometimes joined by visiting musicians.

Mamita's Beach Club on the beach at C 30. The coolest place to be during the day, with a hip but not overbearing party atmosphere and a live DJ. Chairs and umbrellas are for rent, but you can spread a towel at the water's edge and still get waiter service. Occasionally hosts blow-out nighttime dance parties.

La Santanera C 14 between Av 5 and Av 10. Super-stylish club with a comfortable, breezy lounge area, diverse music and good strong drinks. The scantily clad party crowd – equal parts visitors and residents – usually staggers out around 5am. No cover.

Listings

Banks HSBC, Juárez between Av 10 and Av 15 (Mon–Fri 9am–7pm); Bancomer, Juárez between Av 25 and Av 30 (Mon–Fri 9am–4pm). Both have ATMs.

Books El Mundo, C 1 Sur between Av 20 and Av 25, has English and Spanish titles. Closed Sun.

Car rental All the large car-rental companies have outlets in Playa – most are situated on the main coastal highway at the turn-off into town or in Plaza Marina near the Cozumel ferry pier at C 1 Sur. Try Localiza, Juárez between Av 5 and Av 10 (ⓣ984/873-0580).

Internet access and telephones The streets off Av 5 hold numerous internet cafés; one on C 4 between Av 5 and Av 10 doubles as a caseta. There's also a Telmex caseta on Juárez between Av 10 and Av 15.

Laundry Lavandería Lamat, Av 10 between C 12 and C 14; Lavandería Lua, C 2 between Av 10 and Av 15.

Post office Av 20 at C 2 (Mon–Fri 8am–2pm); geared to dealing with tourists.

Shopping La Sirena, Av 5 at C 26, has great folk art and candy-colour paintings of Mexican wrestlers; Caracol, Av 5 between C 6 and C 8, has very high-quality textiles; Paseo del Carmen, at the south end of Av 5, is a pretty outdoor mall.

Isla Cozumel

A forty-kilometre-long island directly off the coast from Playa del Carmen, **ISLA COZUMEL** caters primarily to the mainstream tastes of the cruise-ship passengers that put ashore here – during the high season, up to twenty liners a week dock at the piers south of the main town of **San Miguel** (often called just Cozumel). But you can escape to the wild, windy eastern shore – or underwater, as the island offers the best **diving** in Mexico, with spectacular drop-offs, walls and swim-throughs, some beautiful **coral gardens** and a number of little-visited remote reefs where you can see larger pelagic fish and dolphins. The island is also good for **bird watching**, as it's a stopover on migration routes and has several species or variants endemic to Cozumel.

Over the years, island culture has developed distinct from that of the mainland, with *cozumeleños* relishing their lifestyle, which is somehow even more easy-going than on the rest of the coast; San Miguel hosts a particularly colourful celebration of **Carnaval**, the decadent week prior to Lent.

Some history

Before the Spaniards arrived, the island appears to have been a major Maya centre, carrying on sea trade around the coasts of Mexico and as far south as Honduras and perhaps Panama. This ancient community – one of several around the Yucatán coast that survived the collapse of Classic Maya civilization – shows evidence of large-scale trade, specialization between centres and even a degree of mass production. A US air base, built during World War II, has erased the ancient city, however, and the lesser ruins scattered across the roadless interior are mostly unrestored. (The airfield did bring a degree of prosperity; converted to civilian use, it remains the means by which many visitors arrive.)

After about 1600 Cozumel was virtually deserted. In the mid-nineteenth century, though, as the Caste Wars made life on the peninsula unstable, the island became a place of refuge, and by the 1880s, the town of San Miguel was established as a home for the growing population.

Arrival and information

The **passenger ferry dock** is right in the centre of San Miguel, with the plaza directly across the street. From the **airport**, where there's an **ATM**, a *combi* van service makes the short trip into town (about M$50).

A branch of the **tourist office** (Mon–Sat 8.30am–5pm; ⓣ987/872-7585, ⓦwww.islacozumel.com.mx) is in the complex on the east side of the plaza, upstairs. There are dozens of **dive shops** in town – Deep Blue, Salas at Avenida 10

The ferry to Cozumel

Two competing **passenger ferry** services, Mexico Waterjets and Ultramar (both M$140), depart from the pier at Calle 1 Sur in Playa del Carmen for San Miguel in Cozumel nearly every hour between 6am and 11pm, though sometimes service is cut in slow seasons. Transbordadores del Caribe (ⓣ987/872-7688, ⓦwww.transcaribe.com.mx) operates a **car ferry** to Cozumel from Puerto Calica (also called Punta Venado), 7km south of Playa del Carmen. It runs four times Mon–Sat (4am, 8am, 1.30pm & 6pm) and twice on Sunday (6am & 6pm), with a crossing time of about 1hr 15min; at M$550 per car (with one driver) and M$60 per passenger, it's worthwhile only if you'll be staying on the island more than a few days. Departures from Cozumel back to Calica are between 6am and 8.30pm (8am & 8pm on Sun).

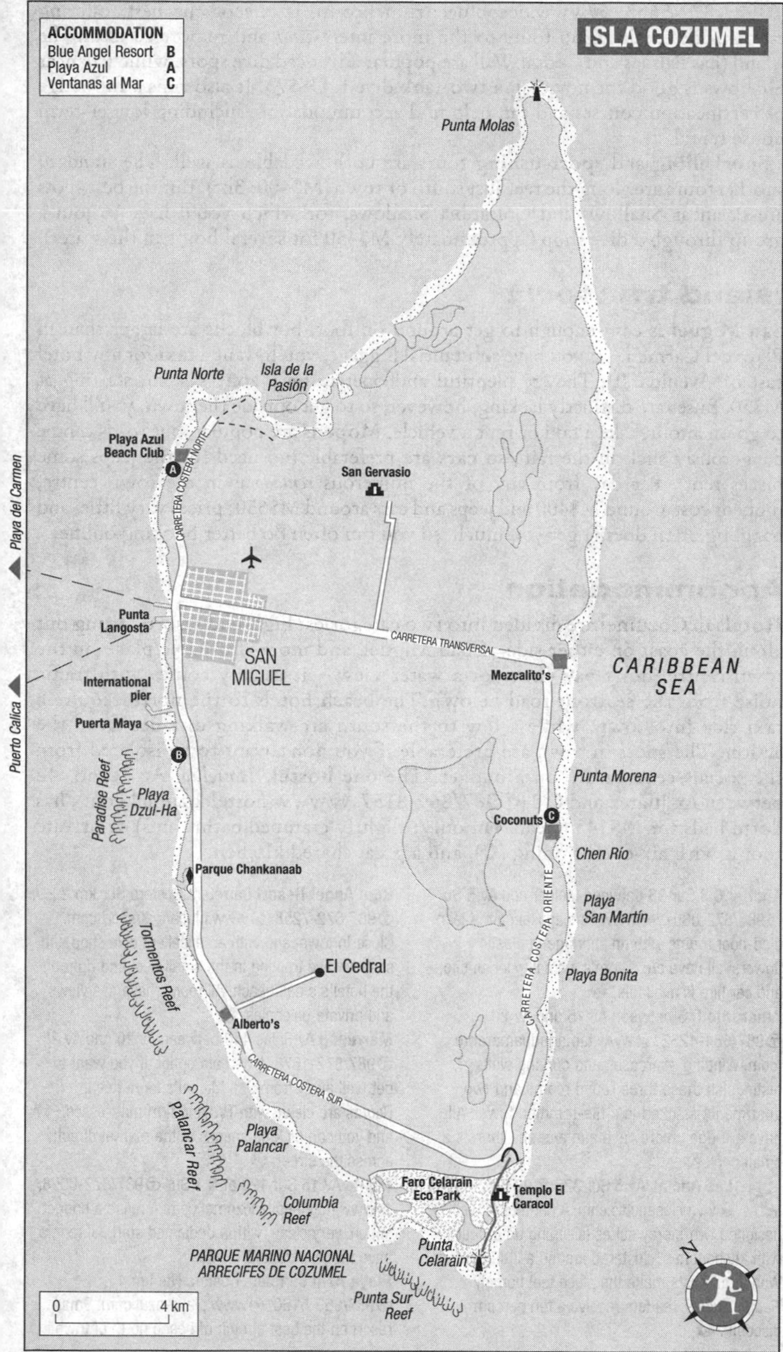
ISLA COZUMEL
ACCOMMODATION
Blue Angel Resort B
Playa Azul A
Ventanas al Mar C
Punta Molas
Punta Norte
Isla de la Pasión
Playa Azul Beach Club
CARRETERA COSTERA NORTE
San Gervasio
Playa del Carmen
Punta Langosta
SAN MIGUEL
CARRETERA TRANSVERSAL
Mezcalito's
CARIBBEAN SEA
International pier
Puerta Maya
Puerto Calica
Paradise Reef
Playa Dzul-Ha
Punta Morena
Coconuts
Chen Río
Parque Chankanaab
Playa San Martín
CARRETERA COSTERA ORIENTE
Tormentos Reef
El Cedral
Playa Bonita
Alberto's
CARRETERA COSTERA SUR
Palancar Reef
Playa Palancar
Faro Celarain Eco Park
Templo El Caracol
Columbia Reef
Punta Celarain
PARQUE MARINO NACIONAL ARRECIFES DE COZUMEL
Punta Sur Reef
0
4 km
N

(Ⓣ987/872-5653, Ⓦwww.deepbluecozumel.com), is one of the best, offering tailor-made small-group tours to the more interesting and remote reefs off the island (Las Palmas and Cedral Wall are popular advanced dive spots, while Palancar Shallows is good for novices); a two-tank dive is US$73. It also runs a full range of certification courses and can help find accommodation, including longer-term house rental.

Snorkelling and **sport-fishing** tours are both available as well. The standard snorkel tours are along the reef just south of town (M$400; 3hr). But the best spots are Palancar Shallows and Colombia Shallows, for which you'll have to join a group through a dive shop (approximately M$450 for several hours in the water).

Island transport

San Miguel is easy enough to get around on foot, but blocks are larger than in Playa del Carmen – if you have substantial luggage, you'll want a **taxi** for any hotel east of Avenida 10. They're plentiful and operate on a zone system, starting at M$30. Buses are distinctly lacking, however, so to get outside the town, you'll have to go on a tour, take a taxi or rent a vehicle. **Mopeds** are popular, but roads can be dangerously slick in the rain, so **cars** are preferable (no need for the jeeps some places rent). Per day from any of the numerous *rentadoras* in the town centre, mopeds cost around M$400 and jeeps and cars around M$650; prices vary little, and haggling often doesn't get you much, so you can often do better booking online.

Accommodation

Hotels in Cozumel are divided into two categories: high-end resorts strung out along the coast on either side of San Miguel, and more affordable places in the town centre (don't pay extra for a water view – it usually comes with traffic noise from the seafront road below). The beach hotels to the north require a taxi ride into town, while a few to the south are walking distance from the action. The spots in town are preferable if you don't want to be isolated from the social scene or are on a budget. The one **hostel**, *Hostelito*, Av 10 no. 42 between Av Juárez and C 2 (Ⓣ987/869-8157, Ⓦwww.hostelcozumel.com), has dorm beds for M$145 (clean, fan only; slightly cramped bathrooms) or private rooms with air-conditioning (❹), and a great shared kitchen.

Aguilar C 3 Sur 98 between Melgar and Av 5 Sur Ⓣ987/872-0307, Ⓦwww.hotelaguilar.com. Clean, tiled-floor rooms with no shortage of plastic flowers; all have a/c. There's a small pool on site, and car hire is available. ❹

Amaranto C 5 between Av 15 and Av 20 Ⓣ987/564-4262, Ⓦwww.tamarindoamaranto.com. Winding staircases and curving walls distinguish these three round rooms and two apartments stacked in a tile-trimmed tower. All have a fridge, microwave and a/c, and there's a small pool. ❹

Las Anclas Av 5 Sur 325 Ⓣ987/872-5476, Ⓦwww.lasanclas.com. A handful of well-designed two-storey suites (sleeping up to four) with kitchenettes, clustered around a little garden. Wonderful hosts make the place feel homely. *Rough Guides*' readers receive a ten percent discount. ❻

Blue Angel Resort Carretera Costera Sur km 2.2 Ⓣ987/872-7258, Ⓦwww.blueangelresort.com. Close to town, and with an excellent dive shop and shallow dive training in the small pool and right off the hotel's small beach. All rooms have sea views and private balconies. ❻

Marruang Av Salas 440 between Av 20 and Av 25 Ⓣ987/872-1678. A bargain option if you want to get well away from San Miguel's tourist centre. Rooms are clean, with TVs and firm mattresses, and you can pick up snacks at the market directly across the street. ❸

Pepita Av 15 Sur 120 at C 1 Sur Ⓣ987/872-0098, Ⓦwww.hotelpepitacozumel.com. A reliable budget option, very clean, with a dedicated staff. All rooms have fridges, a/c and TV. ❹

Playa Azul Carretera Costera Nte km 4 Ⓣ987/869-5160, Ⓦwww.playa-azul.com. Small resort on the best stretch of beach north of town, with fifty elegant ocean-view rooms; the pool is a bit small, however. Rates include breakfast and greens fees at the nearby golf club. ⑨

Saolima Salas 260 between Av 10 and Av 15 ⓣ987/872-0886. Basic and old-fashioned, but clean rooms. Overall, it's pretty unremarkable, but really the only decent option in this price range. ③

Tamarindo B&B C 4 no. 421 between Av 20 and Av 25 ⓣ987/872-6190, ⓦwww.tamarindocozumel.com. At this French-owned B&B, rooms have cosy nooks and whimsically placed windows; two full suites have kitchenettes, and come at bargain rates. Two of the five rooms share a kitchen, while two others have private kitchens. A/c is an option in some rooms. ④

Ventanas al Mar On the east coast, 5km south of *Mezcalito's* beach bar and the intersection with the Carretera Transversal ⓦwww.ventanasalmar.biz. The empty east coast's only hotel has gigantic rooms with terraces overlooking the crashing surf. Breakfast is included and for other meals you get a discount at the neighbouring beach bar, or stock up on groceries for the kitchenette in your room. ⑥

The Island

The town of **San Miguel** – the only inhabited spot on the island – is short on sights, but thick with hotels and other services. Day trips to the small ruins of **San Gervasio**, as well as the beaches and parks around the coast, require a bit of planning. Most visitors to the island stick with the placid west coast, which is additionally protected by a string of reefs, but the east coast is a truly rustic escape.

San Miguel

Along the malecón (Avenida Rafael Melgar), **downtown San Miguel** is devoted to tourism: restaurants, souvenir shops, tour agencies and jewellery stores lure in the huge cruise-ship clientele. As a result, it's all too often uncomfortably crowded and you may be hassled by aggressive salespeople. The weekends, though, are blissfully free of cruise ships – none generally stop on Cozumel on Sunday, and only a couple arrive on Saturday and Monday (to check the ships' schedules, visit ⓦwww.cruisecal.com). If you shop, try not to do it on a cruise-ship day (prices may rise), and don't buy **black coral**, an endangered, beautiful type of sea life which is unfortunately sold everywhere.

The attractive **Museo de la Isla de Cozumel**, on the malecón between avenidas 4 and 6 (Mon–Sat 9am–5pm, Sun 9am–4pm; M$36), has small displays of the flora, fauna and marine life of the island, as well as a good collection of Maya artefacts and old photos. It occasionally hosts live music and theatre events – check with the tourist office.

The western shore

The easiest **beaches** to get to are north of the town. It's far more fun, though, to rent a car and head to the more isolated places in the other direction. Heading **south of San Miguel**, there's accessible **snorkelling** just off the coast, starting at several hotels and beach clubs. Most rent snorkel gear for about M$150; if you think you might visit a few spots, it's worth buying your own. The best place for wade-in snorkelling is **Playa Dzul-Ha**, where you'll find the open-air *Money Bar* and a dive shop. The current here usually runs north to south, so you can swim north and drift back, or drift down to the *Fiesta Americana* and walk back along the road. The bar here will probably ask you to pay M$50 for a bracelet – this is a legitimate charge for maintaining the reef as a national park. Dzul-Ha is reached only by the smaller coastal access road – bear right (west) at *El Presidente Inter-Continental* hotel.

Tourists are usually steered right to the **Parque Chankanaab**, or "Little Sea" (daily 7am–5pm; M$170; ⓦwww.cozumelparks.com), due south of San Miguel. It's a lovely lagoon, but overdeveloped, and you'll probably want to skip it unless you have kids, as there's a protected children's beach. A large arch on the inland

side of the road at km 17.5 marks the turn for the village of **El Cedral**, founded in 1847. There's little to see, but in late April and early May, the village hosts the ten-day-long Fiesta de la Santa Cruz, a huge fair with bullfights, prize-winning livestock and dancing.

Immediately opposite the turn for El Cedral is **Alberto's** beach club, the most rustic option on the west coast, with a great beach and snorkelling. There's nothing but a small restaurant, boasting fish fresh-caught with its own boats. Just a couple of kilometres south, at km 19, the last western beach is **Playa Palancar** (daily 9am–6pm). A restaurant serves good *tikin-xic*, and there's a dive shop (closed Sun) where you can arrange a boat ride out to Palancar Gardens just offshore.

Faro Celarain Eco Park

The southernmost point of the island is a protected reserve for diverse wildlife, the **Faro Celarain Eco Park** (also called Parque Punta Sur; daily 9am–3pm; M$120; ⓦwww.cozumelparks.com). The site contains several lovely beaches, the Punta Celarain **lighthouse** and the **Templo El Caracol**, which may have been built by the Maya as a lighthouse, and is worth visiting to hear the sounds produced when the wind whistles through the shells encrusted in its walls. You can climb to the top of the lighthouse for amazing views over the coast, or visit the adjacent **museum of navigation** (daily 10am–4pm; same ticket) in the former lightkeeper's house. A bus transports visitors between various sites (or you can rent bicycles), including viewing towers over a network of lagoons and a beach restaurant serving good fried fish. This is also a prime spot for **bird watching**, as the mangroves host both migratory and endemic species, including the extremely rare Cozumel vireo.

The eastern shore and San Gervasio

As for the **rest of the island**, Cozumel's rugged, windy eastern shore remains undeveloped because, as on Isla Mujeres, it faces the open sea and is usually too rough for **swimming**. From Parque Punta Sur, you can complete a circuit of the southern half of the island by following the road up the windswept eastern shoreline. There are a couple of good, if basic (no running water or electricity), restaurants at **Chen Río** and **Punta Morena** – the latter is popular with kitesurfers. The beaches here are often deserted, but swim only where you see others, as currents can be dangerous. The main road cuts back across the middle of the island to town.

Midway along this road, called the Carretera Transversal, then 6km north, **San Gervasio** (daily 7am–5pm; M$77) is the only excavated Maya site on the island. Built to honour Ixchel, the goddess of fertility and weaving, and apparently modelled on Chichén Itzá, with several small temples connected by *sacbeob*, or long white roads, San Gervasio was, between 1200 AD and 1650 AD, one of the most important centres of pilgrimage in Mesoamerica – though it's not particularly impressive now. As part of a larger nature reserve, however, the site is worth a visit for the numerous birds and butterflies you can spot early in the morning or late in the day.

Eating and drinking

A good number of San Miguel's **restaurants** are tourist traps catering to a dull palate, but beyond the plasticky chains and dull steakhouses, you can find some bargain meals, and a couple of places worthy of serious pesos. In general, you're better off sticking to casual cafés, rather than the more formal restaurants – though don't rule out a seemingly empty restaurant, as many have back gardens where the real action is. The cheapest snacks of all can be found at the main market, the Mercado Municipal, on Salas between avenidas 20 and 25. *Panadería Cozumeleña*, Calle 3 at Avenida 10, is a good **bakery** with an adjacent coffee shop. The laziest lunches can be had at the palapa bars dotted every few kilometres along the southwestern and eastern coasts. Evening entertainment centres on the Plaza del Sol, which is ringed with **bars** blasting classic rock. On Sunday evenings the crowd is a little more mellow and mixed, as local families come out to chat and listen to strolling musicians.

Cafes

Coffeelia C 5 Sur 85 between Melgar and Av 5. The proud local owner presides over her homely kitchen in this sweet café with outdoor space. The menu mixes fresh Mexican dishes, smoothies and huge Dutch-style pancakes.

Del Museo Melgar between C 4 and C 6, at the Museo de la Isla de Cozumel. Enjoy a quiet breakfast or early lunch on the upstairs balcony of the museum with a view of the sea. The food – from *huevos rancheros* to club sandwiches – is fresh and filling. Closed Sun.

Zermatt C 4 Nte at Av 5. Bakery serving delectably light sugar doughnuts, among other sweet treats.

Restaurants

La Candela Av 5 at C 6 Nte. Really friendly home-cooked breakfast and lunch place, with a selection of hot dishes – just point at what looks good. Fresh fish specials and breezy terrace seating.

Casa Denis C 1 between Av 5 and Av 10. A little wooden-frame house, this is the best bet for eating near the plaza. Bigger meals can be bland, so best to stick with a beer and some *panuchos* and watch the action from your sidewalk table.

El Chef Av 5 at C 5 Sur. Charming, personal place where the chef-owner devises new specials every day, such as various pizzas, grilled fish and, for lunch, fresh sandwiches. The same owner runs *Le Bistrot*, down the street at Calle 7, good for poached-egg dishes at breakfast.

La Cocay C 8 between Av 10 and Av 15 ☎987/872-5533. Formal service and inventive dishes such as pork in currant sauce – plus very rich desserts. The menu (mains about M$160) changes seasonally. Closed Sun.

Conchita del Caribe Av 65 between C 13 and C 15. This locally famous informal seafood spot is worth the cab ride deep into town. The generous portions of *ceviche* are particularly good. Closes at 6pm.

Especias C 3 Sur at Av 5 ☎987/876-1558. Inexpensive Argentine, Mexican and even occasionally Thai meals, served by an exceptionally friendly husband and wife team. The breezy rooftop is a good place for a sunset beer. Closed Sun.

Kelley's Av 10 between Salas and C 1 Sur. Big open-air bar with a pool table and live music on weekends – you might see your divemaster or tour guide there off-hours. Tasty American food during the day.

Guido's Melgar 23 between C 6 and C 8 ☎987/872-0946. Guido's is probably best known for its delectable lasagne, a dense stack of garlicky tomato sauce, meat, cheese and house-made pasta. Also serves crisp-crust pizza (from M$160) from its wood oven; seafood mains are about M$220. There's also a lovely garden at the back. Lunch and dinner; closed Sun.

Pancho's Melgar 27 at C 8 Nte ☎987/872-2141. By no means "authentic" Mexican – especially at lunch, when it's a favourite with cruise-ship passengers – but the best service on the island. Very good margaritas, tortilla chips hot out of the fryer and fresh-tasting, slightly dressed-up Mexican dishes; strong veggie selection too. Closed for lunch Sat & Sun.

Rock'n Java Melgar 602 between C 7 and Av Quintana Roo (C 11) ☎987/872-4405. Healthy sandwiches, salads and veggie chile (all between M$60 and M$120) are balanced out by fantastically rich and delicious desserts, such as German chocolate cake, at this seafront diner. Sat 7am–2pm, closed Sun.

Sabores Av 5 between C 3 Sur and C 5 Sur. Real home cooking – in an actual house – at this lunch-only *cocina económica* – walk through the living room and kitchen and out to the huge shady garden. Unfortunately, there have been reports of a waiter trying to overcharge – know that the set price (M$45) includes a choice of mains, soup and an all-you-can-drink jug of *agua de jamaica*.

Listings

Banks HSBC (Mon–Fri 9am–7pm) is on Av 5 at C 1 Sur.

Consulate US, Plaza Villamar, Juárez at C 5 ☎987/872-4574.

Internet access Internet cafés are scarce in the centre of town; there is one place on Melgar near *Rock'n'Java*.

Laundry Two adjacent laundries on C 11 (Av Quintana Roo) just east of Melgar (M$12/kg).

Post office Melgar at C 7 Sur (Mon–Fri 9am–4pm, Sat 9am–1pm).

Moving on from Cozumel

Returning to Playa del Carmen, **passenger ferries** leave Cozumel nearly hourly 5am–10pm, although this can fluctuate according to the season. From the airport, there are **flights** to Cancún, Atlanta and Houston. You can buy **bus tickets** for mainland travel at the ADO office on Avenida 10 at Calle 2.

From Playa del Carmen south to Tulum

Like the beaches to the north, much of the seafront **south of Playa del Carmen** has been developed into resorts or condominium villages, and their access gates line the east side of Hwy-307, leaving little or no access to the sea for non-guests. There are just a couple of good beach spots, but inland you'll find some good **cenotes**.

First you have to get past the massive tourist attraction that is **Xcaret** (daily 8.30am–9pm in winter; 8.30am–10pm in summer; US$69; ⓦwww.xcaret.com), 6km south of Playa del Carmen. With a museum, tropical aquarium, "Maya village", beach, some small authentic ruins, pools and more than a kilometre of subterranean rivers down which you can swim, snorkel or float, it's like having all of the Yucatán's attractions in one handy place – and it's remarkably untacky for what it is. Anyone on a longer trip can happily skip the place, though.

Twenty-five kilometres further south, **Xpu-ha** is an especially lovely stretch of beach, curving around in a gentle arc. An all-inclusive resort, *Catalonia Royal Tulum*, breaks up the view, but serves as a landmark for access roads. You can **camp** (M$70) or stay in basic cabañas at *Bonanza Xpu-ha* (no phone; ❺); for just a day visit, you're charged a small parking fee. Turn onto the second narrow dirt road south of the *Catalonia* – *not* the road to Playa Xpu-Ha Beach Club, though this place has a good **restaurant**. At the other end of the price spectrum, and just north of *Catalonia*, is *Esencia* (US ⓣ984/873-4835, ⓦwww.hotelesencia.com; ❾), neck and neck with *Maroma* and *The Tides Riviera Maya* (see p.818) for best small luxury hotel in the area; rare for this type of beach property, kids are welcome.

Another 10km south (turn at "Akumal Playa"), **Akumal** is primarily a condo community, but its bay offers beautiful snorkelling, and the chummy *Turtle Bay* **restaurant** has delicious whole-grain bread and fresh fish. You can rent bikes and snorkel gear at the *Hotel Club Akumal*. South of central Akumal, on Aventuras beach (reached by the next turn off the highway), Aquatech Divers (ⓣ984/875-9020, ⓦwww.cenotes.com) is one of the most respected **cave-diving** operations in the Yucatán.

Exploring the cenotes

The area north and west of Tulum has one of the largest concentrations of **cenotes** on the peninsula, including **Ox Bel Ha**, which at almost 170km, is the longest water-filled cave system in the world. Many of these freshwater sinkholes are accessible from Hwy-307 or off the road to Cobá. Some, like Hidden Worlds (see p.832), have been developed as adventure centres, and the guides and marked trails at these places can help put first-time visitors at ease in dark water and tight spaces. But it's also worth visiting one of the less developed alternatives, such as **Grand Cenote**, 4km up the road to Cobá from Tulum (8am–6pm; M$100), where the only service is snorkel-gear rental, so you can float above stalagmites and other rock formations – all the fun of cave exploration, with none of the scrabbling around. Zacil-Há, 4km further (M$30), is a local hangout and a great beginner pool, as you can see the sandy bottom.

Divers must have open-water certification for **cavern diving** (in which you explore within the reach of daylight), but **cave diving** (in which you venture into closed passageways and halls) requires rigorous training.

Local development may threaten cenotes in the long run, but clumsy visitors can do more damage in the short term: wear only **biodegradable sunscreen**; **do not touch** the surprisingly delicate stalactites; never break off anything as a souvenir; **mind your flippers**, as it's easy to kick up silt or knock into the rocks; and be very careful climbing in and out of the water – use the paths and ladders provided.

A few kilometres south of Akumal and immediately south of Chemuyil, **Xcacel** is a sea-turtle research station and pristine beach where visitors are welcome between 8am and 6pm; there are no services. It's only 500m from the highway – handy if you're coming by bus or combi. The next big landmark is **Parque Xel-ha** (daily 8.30am–5.30pm in winter, till 6pm in summer; US$68 including all food and drink; Ⓦwww.xelha.com.mx), a natural water park built around a system of lagoons, inlets and caves. It's a beautiful place and great for children, but like Xcaret, it's nothing you won't see elsewhere. Across the highway, the small and only partly excavated **ruins of Xel Há** (daily 8am–5pm; M$37) are notable for the stucco paintings in the Grupo Pájaros and miniature, chest-high temples that resemble ones found at Tulum.

Just south of the ruins, **Hidden Worlds** (tours daily 9am–3pm; Ⓣ984/877-8535, Ⓦwww.hiddenworlds.com.mx) is a park area encompassing some exceptionally beautiful cenotes and caverns. Guided group snorkelling (US$30) and diving (US$60 for one tank) trips run several times a day, with options for ziplines and the like. You can also visit glimmering **Dos Ojos** cenote on your own, for M$50 paid at a separate entrance just to the north on Hwy-307.

Tulum

To visitors, **TULUM** can mean several things. First, it's one of the most picturesque of all the ancient Maya sites, poised on fifteen-metre-high cliffs above the impossibly turquoise Caribbean. Tulum also refers to a stretch of broad, white beach that's the finest in the Riviera Maya, dotted with lodging options that range from bare-bones to ultra-swank; many of them, as well as many ultra-casual beach bars, still show their backpacker-friendly roots in style, if no longer in price. Finally, it's a booming town (often called **Tulum Pueblo** to distinguish it from the beach) that has evolved from roadside waystation to real population centre, where visitors can arrange tours into the Sian Ka'an Biosphere Reserve (see p.839), among other things.

Arrival and information

Coming into the Tulum area on Hwy-307 from the north (it's 130km from Cancún), you arrive first at the well-marked pedestrian and bus entrances to the **ruins** – the site itself is on the water, 1km east. There's a dedicated long-haul bus stop here, so you don't have to double back from town.

Another kilometre or so south along the highway is a traffic light marking the main intersection, what locals call *el crucero*. Turn left here to follow the road 3km to the **beach**, where most of the local accommodation is strung along a narrow but paved road running north–south along the water. To the north (left) are a few hotels, the better publicly accessible **beaches** and, after 2km, a back entrance to the ruins. To the south (right), hotels dot 7km of road; after that, you're at the border of the Sian Ka'an Biosphere Reserve and the road turns to dirt.

Back on Hwy-307 (here called Avenida Tulum), the centre of **town** is just a little further south. The **bus** station, open 24 hours, is near the southern end; **colectivos** stop almost next door. To get to the beach hotels, you'll need a **taxi** (starting at M$40); rates are posted in the median where taxis gather, just north of the station. Tulum's taxi drivers have a reputation for denying the existence of hotels that don't pay them commission; if you have planned on a particular hotel, insist on being taken there.

There's a **tourist info kiosk** with erratic hours on Avenida Tulum at Calle Osiris, just north of the HSBC bank, or you can pick up good free maps at the *Weary Traveler* hostel, just south of the bus station, and elsewhere around town.

Accommodation

Although Tulum's beach is an obvious draw, you may want to stay in **town** if you arrive late in the day, have a limited amount of time (and money) or prefer hot water round-the-clock. Hotels in the *zona hotelera* along the **beach road** do not connect to the electric grid, relying instead on varying combinations of solar panels, windmills and diesel generators; most have power for only about six hours in the evening. Depending on your point of view, the candle-lit ambience is rustic charm or expensive primitivism, and the thatched palapa roofs on most places can be a liability in the rain.

Basic sand- or cement-floor **cabañas** made this area famous with hippie backpackers, but they're in short supply now (and are plagued with reports of theft), as ritzier places, with prices to match, have sprung up. There are now very few mid-range beds on the beach, and, as in Playa del Carmen, most hotels also charge high-season rates in the European holiday period of July and August.

For **hostel** accommodation, *The Weary Traveler* (Ⓣ984/871-2390; M$120), just south of the bus station, is a longstanding destination for budget travellers, though *Casa del Sol*, about 300m south of bus station and one block west (Ⓣ984/129-6424, Ⓔcasadelsoltulum@yahoo.com; M$120), has brighter dorms and rooftop cabañas. *El Crucero* (see below) also offers some dorm beds (M$100). You can **camp** at *Camping La Caireta*, 4km south on the beach road (Ⓣ984/135-9323; M$100; M$300 for tipis).

In town

El Crucero East side of Hwy-307, by the pedestrian entrance to the ruins Ⓣ984/871-2610, Ⓦwww.el-crucero.com. Fun, friendly hotel convenient for visiting the archeological site. Choose dorm beds, standard rooms or deluxe rooms with a/c and distinctive murals painted by a local artist. The bar/restaurant is extremely hospitable. ❸

Don Diego de la Selva West side of Hwy-307, south of town Ⓣ984/114-9744, Ⓦwww.dtulum.com. Quiet French-owned hideaway set back from the highway, with a pool and big, white rooms with terraces; two have fans, while the other six have a/c. Guests have access to *Don Diego de la Playa* (see below). ❻

Kukulcán Av Tulum between Beta and Orión Ⓣ984/871-2423. Opened in 2009, this basic budget hotel has clean tiled-floor rooms that open onto small garden spaces at the back – a nice patch of green in town. All rooms have ceiling fans, and some have a/c. Wi-fi too. ❸

Posada Luna del Sur Luna Sur 5 Ⓣ984/871-2984, Ⓦwww.posadalunadelsur.com. Exceptionally comfy, tranquil rooms sent around a small garden, with welcoming and helpful staff to create an intimate B&B atmosphere. No children. ❺

Teetotum On the road to the beach, 200m from Hwy-307 Ⓣ984/745-8827, Ⓦwww.teetotumhotel.com. Four sharply designed rooms with iPod docks, quiet a/c and mod furniture. Other perks include rooftop yoga classes, a small pool and a great café (see p.836). Its location on the road to the beach hits a sweet spot: quiet, but walking distance to town and an easy bike ride (on free bicycles) to the water. ❼

On the beach road

Cabañas Copal 700m south of the junction with the highway access road Ⓣ01-800/123-3278, Ⓦwww.cabanascopal.com. The round, cement-floor cabañas are quite crowded in, but they're relatively well priced; if you're looking to go cheap, try to nab one of two shared-bath cabins (US$35). There's electricity only in public areas but plenty of hot water, and a clothing-optional beach. Good spa on site. ❻

Cabañas Zazil-Kin 2.4km north of the junction; no phone, Ⓦwww.hotelstulum.com/zazilkin. Cement-floor cabañas with shared or private bath (cold water only). Perennially popular, with a lively bar scene. A five-day minimum is required for most reservations; otherwise, just arrive early – rooms go fast. ❹

Don Diego de la Playa 4km south of the junction Ⓣ984/114-9744, Ⓦwww.dtulum.com. From the owners of *Don Diego de la Selva*, attractive tribal-look tents and one cabaña right on the beach, with shared bath. ⑤

Dos Ceibas 5.5km south of the junction ⓣ984/877-6024, ⓦwww.dosceibas.com. Small, attractive hotel in front of a turtle-hatching beach. Yoga and meditation classes offered. The cheapest cabaña (US$60) has a bathroom outside; all are spacious and colourful. ⑤

Nueva Vida de Ramiro 4.5km south of the junction ⓣ984/877-8512, ⓦwww.tulumnv.com. Peaceful, quirky eco-hotel which relies entirely on wind turbines. Attractive wood cabins on stilts and newer cement cabins with big tiled bathrooms, are built over and around untamed greenery. The beach is great and the restaurant serves tasty seafood. With several suites and whole houses, it's a good choice for families. ⑦

Las Ranitas 5.4km south of the junction ⓣ984/877-8554, ⓦwww.lasranitas.com. This understated but comfortable French-owned hotel has well-designed breezy rooms and two suites for families, plus tennis courts, a pool and an excellent library. The biggest perk: 24hr electricity. ⑧

Xbalamqué 7km south of the junction no phone. This "ecohostel" on the inland side of the road has very simple but clean back-to-nature cabañas with shared bath and sporadic power. Out back there's access to a cenote. ③

Zamas 1.2km south of the junction ⓣin the US 1-415/387-9806, ⓦwww.zamas.com. Enormous, comfortable rooms, some right on one of the prettiest stretches of beach in Tulum. Hot water and electricity are plentiful, but the style remains bohemian. Good restaurant on site (see p.837). ⑦

The town and the beaches

Tulum **town** offers all the basic tourist services and an increasing number of good dinner restaurants and bars, but it's devoid of typical attractions. The place is generally empty of visitors by day because they've all decamped to the **beach**, the longest, most impeccable stretch of sand outside Cancún. The most popular spot is **El Paraiso Beach Club**, about 2km north from the junction with the road to town, with a fully stocked bar and friendly vibe; there's also a **kiteboarding** school here, Extreme Control (ⓣ984/745-4555, ⓦwww.extremecontrol.net). For solitude, head immediately north along the sand to Playa Maya, a public beach that's generally empty. It's followed by **El Mariachi Beach Club**, which is more of a locals' hangout where you can get super-fresh *ceviche*. You can also pop into the sea anywhere else, as long as you don't use the lounge chairs maintained by hotels.

The ruins

On a sunny day, with the turquoise sea glittering behind the weather-beaten grey stones, your first glimpse of the **Tulum ruins** (daily: May–Oct 8am–7pm; Nov–April 7am–6pm; M$51) can be quite breathtaking, despite the small scale of its buildings, all clustered in a compact mass. When the Spaniards first set eyes on the place in 1518, they considered it as large and beautiful as Seville. They were, perhaps, misled by their dreams of El Dorado and the brightly painted facades of the buildings, for architecturally Tulum is no match for the great Maya cities. Most built after 1200, the structures seem a bit haphazard because walls flare outward and doorways taper in – not the effect of time, but an intentional design, and one echoed in other post-Classic sites along the coast like El Rey in Cancún and San Gervasio on Cozumel.

Tickets are sold at the site **entrance**, about 1km from the main highway and parking area, where there's also a warren of souvenir shops; a shuttle (M$20) runs between the parking area and the ruins. You can also approach from the south, parking at the dead-end of the beach road and walking in. The site itself takes only an hour or so to see, though you may want to allow time to **swim** at the tiny, perfect beach that punctuates the cliffs. Arrive in the early morning or late afternoon to avoid the worst crowds.

You walk in through a breach in the wall that surrounded the city on three sides; the fourth faced the sea. Passing through the wall on the north side, you are in front of the **Casa del Noroeste**, one of the many small-scale buildings which typify the site, with their slanty walls and narrow windows. Closer to the sea sits the **Casa del Cenote**, a square structure straddling what was once a water-filled cave, the source of life for the settlement. On the bluff above and to the right are the **Templos Miniaturas**, several small-scale temples, complete with tiny lintels and mouldings, which were probably used as shrines. Skirt the small beach to reach the **Templo del Díos Descendente**. The small, upside-down winged figure depicted above the temple's narrow entrance appears all over the city, but in only a handful of places elsewhere in the Maya world. It may represent the setting sun, or the bee god, as honey was one of the Maya's most important exports. Immediately adjacent, the **Castillo**, on the highest part of the site, commands fine views in every direction – but to protect the worn stones, visitors may now only look up at the building from the base of the hill. The pyramid may have served not just as a temple, but also as a lighthouse. Even without a light, it would have been an important landmark for mariners.

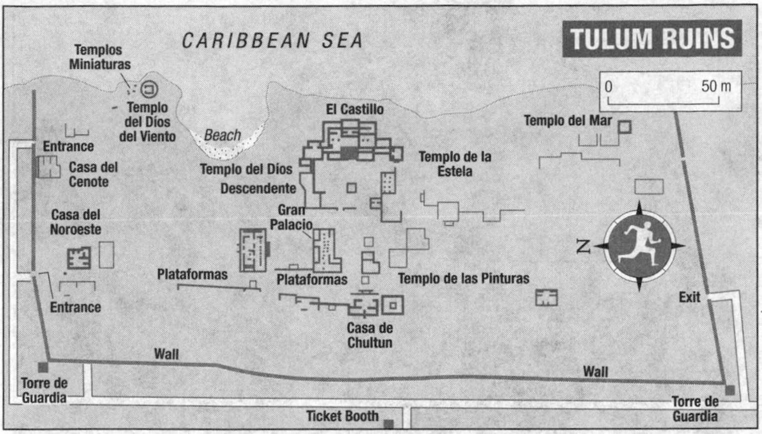

Away from the sea, a cluster of buildings is arranged on a city-like grid, with the chief structures set on stone platforms along parallel streets. Of these, the **Templo de las Pinturas** (Temple of the Paintings) is intriguing: the intricate carvings on its exterior slowly reveal themselves as you look closely. The corners form glowering masks trimmed with feather headdresses, and the "descending god" can be spotted in one niche. Unfortunately, you can no longer view the interior murals (actually on the *exterior* of an older, smaller temple, which has been preserved by the surrounding gallery), but one remarkable scene, created at a later date than the others, shows the rain god Chac seated on a four-legged animal – likely inspired by the conquistadors on horseback.

The best view is from the cliff edges to the south of the Castillo. A small trail leads along the edge, delivering a great perspective on the sea and the ruins, then loops down through the greenery.

Eating and drinking

Because the accommodation in Tulum is spread over 10km and the town is so far from the beach, almost every hotel has its own restaurant – ranging from cheap to very chic. Guests tend to stick to the restaurants in their own hotels, but a few **places to eat** along the beach road merit a special trip. In town, a number of

▲ Tulum ruins

inexpensive **cafés** serve comida corrida and rotisserie chicken, and there's an increasing number of cheerful, mid-range places run by European expats. As for nightlife, *Mezzanine* hosts a beach party every Friday, while *El Paraiso Beach Club* often has some kind of event around the full moon; otherwise, some hotel **bars** expand into a dancing scene.

In town

La Casa del Buen Pan Sagitario Pte at Alfa. Savour the a/c along with organic coffee and a flaky croissant at this bakery that does both Mexico and European treats. Nice shaded garden area, too.

Cetli Tulum town, C Polar at C Orión ⓣ984/108-0681. Chef-owner Claudia trained in Mexico City's premier culinary academy; at her casual restaurant, try refined versions of Mexican classics (about M$180), such as a delicate green-almond mole. Breakfast, with fresh juices and *chilaquiles*, also served.

La Nave East side of Av Tulum between Orion and Beta. A busy hangout with fresh-fruit breakfasts, inexpensive pizza from a wood-fired oven (M$55 and up) and Italian staples like fresh gnocchi.

El Tacoqueto Tulum town, east side of Av Tulum at C Acuario. A dependable *lonchería* with gut-busting daily specials (feel free to poke your head in the kitchen to see what looks good) for about M$50, or delicious hot-off-the-grill tacos for even less.

Teetotum On the road to the beach, 200m from Hwy-307. For breakfast, go big with french toast (with farmer's cheese and caramelized bananas), or smaller, with a basket of baked goods and house-made jam. The eclectic lunch menu includes both a BLT sandwich and a Vietnamese summer roll.

Urge Taquito West side of Hwy-307, one block north of the traffic light (*el crucero*). Roadside taco place specializing in shrimp tacos, which you can dress up with fixings from the salsa bar or the epic condiments rack. Mon–Sat noon–5pm.

On the beach

Ak'iin Beach Club 4km south of the junction, on the beach road. Two-for-one drinks from noon till 7pm and big swinging lounge beds make this a nice place to spend the day. At night there's usually a DJ at work – Saturdays are the best.

Hechizo 7.5km south of the junction, on the beach road ⓔhechizo_tulum@yahoo.com. This gem of a restaurant is owned by a former *Ritz-Carlton* chef and features a short, sophisticated international menu that changes frequently. Email to reserve one of the eight tables. Closed Mon and parts of the low season.

Mezzanine 800m north of the junction, on the beach road ⓦwww.mezzanine.com.mx. Channelling Ibiza chic, this super-cool bar-lounge does excellent cocktails and Thai snacks; it's the only place on the beach where you can regularly find a dance scene in high season, every Friday. Helpfully, its morning menu includes, next to the smoothies, a special of coffee, cigarettes and a shot of tequila.

Posada Margherita 2.5km south of the junction, on the beach road, at *Posada Margherita* hotel ⓣ984/100-3780. Fantastic Italian restaurant with great seafood; the antipasto platter, served on a slice of a tree trunk, is a bounty of piquant cheeses, cured meats and olives. Prices are higher than the sand-floor setting might suggest (around M$140 for mains), but the food is worth it.

Qué Fresco 1.2km south of the junction, on the beach road, at *Zamas*. Very popular mid-range restaurant with fresh salads, pastas and some of the healthier Mexican dishes. Its beachside setting makes it a great way to start the day, too.

La Vita è Bella 1.6km north of the junction, on the beach road. Reasonably priced sandwiches and wood-oven pizzas are served until 11pm; a cocktail bar opens at 9.30pm, and a European party crowd often gets dancing later under the big palapa.

La Zebra 4.6km south of the junction, on the beach road. Live music Thursday through the weekend, but the Sunday salsa party is the biggest draw, for both tourists and residents – hone your skills early with free classes at 6pm (coinciding with happy hour). There's a huge selection of tequilas, and the restaurant's Mexican food is good as well.

Listings

Banks HSBC, with an ATM, is in the middle of town, about 300m north of the bus station on the east side of Av Tulum.

Bike rental The excellent Iguana Bike Shop, on Satélite at Andrómeda (ⓣ984/871-2357, ⓦwww.iguanabike.com), has the best-maintained rental bikes. It also runs tours to nearby cenotes and Playa Xcacel.

Car rental National chains Hertz and Europcar are here, on Av Tulum, as is Buster (ⓣ984/133-9111, ⓦwww.busterrentacar.com), on Av Tulum at Jupiter, opposite the bus station and a little south.

Colectivos Passenger vans run very frequently to Playa del Carmen and every hour or so to Felipe Carrillo Puerto, stopping anywhere in between on request. They gather near the bus station.

Diving There are dozens of dive shops in town and on the beach. Reliable operators include Cenote Dive Center, west side of Av Tulum at Osiris (ⓣ984/871-2232, ⓦwww.cenotedive.com) and Acuatic Tulum, on the beach at *Cabañas Zazil-Kin* (ⓦwww.acuatictulum.com.mx).

Laundry Lavandería Los Gemelos, Av Tulum between Osiris and Beta. Lavandería Burbujas, two blocks east of Av Tulum on Jupiter.

Post office West side of Av Tulum, between Satélite and Osiris (Mon–Sat noon–3pm).

Transfers West side of Av Tulum, between Satélite and Osiris (Mon–Sat noon–3pm).

Tours On the north edge of town, near the entrance to the ruins and *El Crucero* hotel, Sian Ka'an Info Tours (ⓣ984/871-2499, ⓦwww.siankaan.org) is one of the most reputable companies leading nature tours into the reserve. Savana Travel, on Av Tulum next to *La Nave*, is a full travel agency and also offers local tours.

Cobá

Set in muggy rainforest 50km northwest of Tulum, the crumbling ancient city of **COBÁ** (daily 7am–6pm; M$51) is a fascinating and increasingly popular site. The clusters of buildings are spread out over several kilometres, so the area can absorb lots of visitors without feeling crowded, and you can ramble through the forest in peace, looking out for toucans, egrets, coatis and myriad tropical butterflies, including the giant iridescent blue morpho. A visit here requires at least a couple of hours; renting a **bicycle** just inside the site entrance (M$30) is highly recommended. Although the ruins aren't as well restored as those at Tulum, their scale is much more impressive, and the dense greenery and wildlife make a good counterpoint to the coast.

Ceramic studies indicate that the city was occupied from about 100 AD up until the advent of the Spaniards – the site is even mentioned in the *Chilam Balam* of Chumayel, a book of Maya prophecy and lore written down in the eighteenth century, well after the city had been abandoned. The city's zenith was in the Late

Classic period, around 800 AD, when most of the larger pyramids were built and its wealth grew from links with the cities of Petén, in lowland Mexico and Guatemala. These cities influenced Cobá's architecture and use of stelae, typically seen only in the southern Maya regions. Cobá also prospered later through its connections with coastal cities like Tulum, and several structures reflect the style found at those sites.

The centrepiece of the site is the giant pyramid **Nohoch Mul**, taller than El Castillo at Chichén Itzá and, in its narrow and precipitous stairway, resembling the pyramid at Tikal in Guatemala; at the top, a small temple, similar to structures at Tulum, dates from around 1200. The view takes in nearby lakes, as well as the jungle stretching uninterrupted to the horizon.

If you're feeling intrepid, head 1km down a shady *sacbé* to **Grupo Macanxoc**, a cluster of some twenty stelae, most carved during the seventh century AD. Stele 1 shows part of the Maya creation myth and the oldest date recorded in the Maya Long Count calendar system, which tracks the days since the moment of creation. Other stelae depict a high number of women, suggesting that Cobá may have had female rulers. Clambering between the carvings, you're crossing not natural hills, but unreconstructed buildings; in a way, these offer a more palpable sense of the civilization that thrived here than some of the more immaculately rebuilt structures.

Practicalities

Eleven **buses** a day run to Cobá from Tulum. The first one leaves Tulum at 7.15am (arriving at 8.15am), and the next one, which continues to Chichén Itzá after stopping in Valladolid, arrives in Cobá at 10.10am – you could therefore theoretically cover both sites via public transport from Tulum, though you would be very rushed. Two first-class buses run back to Tulum from Cobá, at 1.30pm and 3.30pm. A taxi from Tulum to Cobá costs about M$340 each way.

The **village** of Cobá, where the bus stops, is little more than a cluster of houses and cabañas a few hundred metres from the site entrance, which fronts a small lake filled with crocodiles. **Hotels** are few, but two are quite comfortable: *Villa Arqueológica Cobá* (Ⓣ984/206-7001, Ⓦwww.villasarqueologicas.com.mx; ❺), overlooking the lake, offers a modest bit of luxury, complete with a swimming pool and an archeological library; the *Hotelito Sac-bé* (Ⓣ984/206-7140; ❸), on the south side of the main street through the village, is leagues better than the other budget option in town, with five clean rooms offering various amenities (some have a/c). There's a decent **restaurant** in front of the lake, *La Pirámide*, which serves Yucatecan specialities.

Around Cobá

After visiting the ruins, you can make a trip to a group of **cenotes** north of town (M$45); buy tickets and arrange a taxi (M$200 round trip) at the entrance to the site parking area. Outside Cobá, back at the traffic circle on the main highway, if you follow signs for Nuevo X-Can, after 18km kilometres you reach the **Reserva de Monos Arañas de Punta Laguna**, which protects one of the northernmost populations of spider monkeys. From the reserve's entrance kiosk, you're required to hike with a guide (M$40/person, plus M$200 for a guide for a group of up to ten people) to where the monkeys usually congregate – there's no guarantee you'll see them, but they're at their liveliest in the early morning (guides are around from 6am or so) and after about 3.30am. You can also rent canoes at the lake here.

The Sian Ka'an Biosphere Reserve

Sian Ka'an means "the place where the sky is born" in Maya, which seems appropriate when you experience the sunrise in this beautiful part of the peninsula. Created by presidential decree in 1986 and made a World Heritage Site in 1987, the **Sian Ka'an Biosphere Reserve** is a huge, sparsely populated region sprawling along the coast south of Tulum. One of the largest protected areas in Mexico, it covers 1.3 million acres. Only about a thousand permanent inhabitants are found here, mainly fishermen and subsistence farmers gathered in the village of **Punta Allen**.

It contains all three of the principal ecosystems found in the Yucatán Peninsula and the Caribbean: the area is approximately one-third **tropical forest**, one-third fresh- and saltwater **marshes** and **mangroves** and one-third marine environment, including a section of the Mesoamerican Barrier Reef. All five species of Mexican **wild cat** – jaguar, puma, ocelot, margay and jaguarundi – live in the forest, along with spider and howler monkeys, tapir and deer. More than three hundred species of **birds** have been recorded (including fifteen types of heron and the endangered wood stork, the largest wading bird to breed in North America) and the coastal forests and wetlands are important feeding and wintering areas for North American migratory birds. The Caribbean beaches provide nesting grounds for four endangered **marine turtle** species, while extremely rare West Indian manatees have been seen in the inlets. Morelets and mangrove **crocodiles** lurk in the lagoons.

Although you can enter the park unaccompanied (M$24), on the road south from Tulum's beach hotels, you will benefit more from an organized tour, which is easily arranged in Tulum. One of the best operators is Sian Ka'an Info Tours, part of a non-profit group called Centro Ecológico de Sian Ka'an (CESIAK), which funds its research and educational programmes with several **tours**: one by day through the ancient Maya canals that criss-cross the marshy areas here, and a late-afternoon excursion that takes in sunset inside the reserve (US$70 each); half-day kayaking trips are also an option (US$45), as is unguided kayak rental (US$20/3hr). These are great trips around the fringes of the reserve's vast open spaces, with excellent opportunities for bird watching. You can reserve a spot at the office in Tulum (see "Listings", p.837).

CESIAK also offers **accommodation** at the rigorously ecofriendly *Boca Paila Camps* (Ⓣ984/871-2499, Ⓦwww.siankaan.org; ❺), hidden among the trees in a prime location near the beach; guests share bathrooms (with composting toilets), but there is hot water, thanks to solar and wind power. The staff are very well informed about the reserve, and the inexpensive **restaurant** is great at sunset, for its view across the jungle. Note that although there are many enticing stretches of sand along the road from Tulum, biosphere regulations **prohibit camping** on the beach to control erosion – which is not to say it's not done, unfortunately.

Punta Allen

Right at the tip of a narrow spit of land, with a lighthouse guarding the northern entrance to the **Bahía de la Ascensión**, the remote fishing village of **PUNTA ALLEN** is not the kind of place you stumble across by accident. With a population of just five hundred, it's the largest village inside the reserve. Bonefish and tarpon in the bay are a draw for active travellers; layabouts come for the feeling of being entirely cut off from the world. The beach is more for hammock-lounging than swimming, though, as there's lots of sea grass, and, depending on the currents, a bit of rubbish.

The road south from Tulum has helped maintain Punta Allen's special quality: it's famously rutted and flooded in the rainy season, and can still be very slow going during the dry months, typically requiring at least three hours for the fifty-kilometre drive. A **colectivo** (daily at 2pm; M$220) runs from next to the taxi syndicate in Tulum (call ⓣ984/879-8040 in the morning to reserve a seat). Another goes from Felipe Carrillo Puerto (see opposite) via an even more bone-rattling route to Vigia Chico (also called El Playón), where launches (M$50 for 2–3 people) cross the bay to the village. In any case, take plenty of cash (there's **no bank**), and plan to spend at least a couple of nights, as the Tulum colectivo **leaves** at 5am, and the launch for the Carrillo Puerto service goes at 7am (reserve your seat beforehand at Tienda Caamal).

Practicalities

Entering Punta Allen from the north, past the naval station on the right and beached boats on the left, the first and cheapest of the **accommodation** options is the bohemian *Posada Sirena* (ⓣ984/877-8521, ⓦwww.casasirena.com; ❺), with four different rooms. *Cuzan Guesthouse* (ⓣ983/834-0358, ⓦwww.flyfishmx.com; ❺), a bit further south, specializes in **bonefish tours** and rents cabañas and tipis, some with hot water. Its **restaurant** is good, though you need to book meals if you're not staying here. Next door, *Serenidad Shardon* (ⓣ984/876-1827, ⓦwww.shardon.com; ❼) has the most comfortable beach houses, as well as dorm beds (US$15) and **camping** space (M$150).

A **mobile shop** in a truck travels the peninsula on Wednesdays and Saturdays, selling fresh items you can't get in the few village *tiendas*, reaching Punta Allen sometime in the afternoon or evening, depending on road conditions. Hotels have **watersports equipment** for rent and can arrange boat tours – for instance, a three-hour snorkelling tour, during which you might see some of the local loggerhead turtle population, costs about M$1200 for a boat.

Chunyaxché

The little-visited ruins of **CHUNYAXCHÉ** (daily 8am–5pm; M$31), also known as **Muyil**, for the nearby village, lie on the north border of the biosphere, about 20km south of Tulum. Catch any second-class **bus** from Tulum to Chetumal and ask to be dropped at the gate on the east side of the highway. Despite the size of the site – probably the largest on the Quintana Roo coast – and its proximity to Hwy-307, you're likely to have the place to yourself, as few visitors to the Yucatán travel further south than Tulum.

Muyil was continuously occupied from the pre-Classic period until after the arrival of the Spaniards in the sixteenth century. There is no record of the inhabitants coming into direct contact with the conquistadors, but they were probably victims of depopulation caused by European-introduced diseases. Most of the buildings you see today date from the post-Classic period, between 1200 and 1500 AD. The tops of the tallest structures, just visible from the road, rise 17m from the forest floor. There are more than one hundred mounds and temples, none of them completely clear of vegetation, and it's easy to wander around and find buildings buried in the jungle, but climbing them is forbidden.

The centre of the site is connected by a *sacbé* to the small **Muyil lagoon** 500m away. This is joined to the large Chunyaxché lagoon and ultimately to the sea at **Boca Paila** by an amazing **canalized river** – the route used by ancient Maya traders. A boardwalk (M$40) leads through the mangroves to the lagoon and rickety wooden viewing towers. You can potentially enter the biosphere this way, if a representative from the local fishing cooperative happens to be there to offer a **boat tour** (M$300/person; 2hr) to even less explored sites, some of which appear to be connected to the lagoon or river by **underwater caves**.

Ancient Mexico

When the Spanish arrived in what is now Mexico in 1519, they were astonished to find a thriving, previously unknown civilization. In fact, the Aztecs, still expanding their sphere of influence from their base at Tenochtitlán, were just the latest in a string of Mesoamerican cultures to make their mark on the region over a rich, two-thousand-year history. Centuries later, our understanding of these cultures continues to develop, even as physical remains further decay. New theories constantly emerge, and the worlds of the ancient Olmecs, Toltecs, Maya, Zapotecs and Aztecs remain as fascinating to us as they were to the conquistadors.

Olmec head, La Venta ▲

Toltec ruins at Tula ▼

The Olmecs

The earliest-known Mesomerican civilization, the **Olmecs** flourished in the jungles of southern Veracruz and Tabasco as early as 1150 BC. Their culture died out around the fourth century BC and though very little has survived, what has is enormous: seventeen colossal **basalt heads**, the largest around three metres tall. Unearthed in the 1930s at **San Lorenzo Tenochtitlán** and **La Venta**, these boulders are carved with strikingly realistic features and handy dates. Archeologists, who previously credited the Maya with being the first culture in these regions, had to readjust their timeline of Mesoamerican development. The details of Olmec society remain unclear, but its artistic and religious influences can be seen in its pottery and in its worship of the feathered serpent and a god of rain; figures that evolved into the Aztec Quetzalcoatl and Tlaloc, and the Maya Kukulcán and Chac.

Teotihuacán and the Toltecs

The first of the powerful cultures in Mexico's central plain, the rulers of **Teotihuacán** (see p.464) built the largest city in ancient Mesoamerica. At the height of its dominance, between 150 and 450 AD, it was home to nearly 100,000 people. Yet these rulers and their subjects have never been clearly identified. The **Toltecs**, who held sway over the same region from their capital of **Tula** (see p.474) during the Classic period (900–1200 AD), are nearly as inscrutable. The Aztecs regarded both as their spiritual ancestors, and adopted many of their gods and customs from them, including a grisly fixation on decoration with skulls and sacrificial hearts.

The Maya

While Teotihuacán ruled over central Mexico, an even more impressive society dominated much of what is now southeastern Mexico, Guatemala and Belize. At its height, the **Maya** population is thought to have been roughly two million, spread around at least forty substantial cities, including **Chichén Itzá**, **Calakmul** and **Uxmal** (see p.790, p.763 & p.781). More than any other Mesoamerican culture, the Maya have been subject to the fantasies of explorers, who have credited them with everything from creating a pacifist utopia (a theory that unravelled when the bloody murals at Bonampak were brought to light) to being enlightened extraterrestrials. After 1200 AD, the Maya empire splintered into a loose confederation of city-states, but despite the best efforts of the Conquest, the culture was never completely obliterated, and even helped fuel a rebellion in the nineteenth century.

▲The ruins at Tulum

▲ Murals at Bonampak

▼ Jaina figurine of woman writing

The Jaina figurines

Little of ancient Mexico survives that is not made of stone. Perhaps the most famous other Mesoamerican artworks are the **Jaina figurines**, a collection of clay people and animals that accompanied the dead at the Maya burial ground of Isla Jaina, off the coast of the Yucatán Peninsula. The statuettes depict a broad range of individuals – from queens to weavers, from ball players to the sick and elderly – and are one of our clearest records of the everyday life of the era. They show a great deal about how people lived, what they wore and what they looked like, while their expressive features give a clear impression of the Maya as people, rather than just pyramid-builders.

Monte Albán ▲

Mural depicting the Aztec city of Tenochtitlán ▼

Painting of the Piedra del Sol Aztec calendar ▼

The Zapotecs

Often overshadowed by larger empires to the north and east, the **Zapotecs**, who ruled from **Monte Albán** (see p.633) in Oaxaca, are believed to have developed the first full writing and calendar systems in Mesoamerica.The Zapotecs reached the height of their power in the Classic period, resisted being overtaken by the Aztecs and were subdued only by the Spanish

The Aztecs

Ruling from **Tenochtitlán** (see p.855), the **Aztecs** were the last and most successful Central Mexican empire – more than a million people still speak the Aztec language of Náhuatl and the very name México, derives from the Aztecs' name for themselves, Mexica. The Aztec empire existed for less than a hundred years, but dominated an area equal to that of any of its predecessors.

Archeological adventures

▸▸ **Bask on the beach at Tulum** Built on sea trade, this late Maya settlement commands breathtaking views of the water and its private beach. See p.832.

▸▸ **Spot wildlife at Calakmul** In the heart of a huge biosphere reserve, this is the country's most remote site, and rewarding for nature lovers. See p.763.

▸▸ **Kayak and hike at Filo Bobos** Several barely known sites line the Río Bobos valley in Veracruz; it's a spectacular hike to reach them, while the river is home to some of Mexico's best whitewater rafting and kayaking. See p.594.

▸▸ **Stay with the Maya at Lacanjá** To really appreciate the ruins here – as well as nearby Bonampak and Yaxchilán – spend the night in this traditional Lacandón village. See p.722.

Leaving the site, particularly if you're making your way up to Tulum, should be easy enough, provided you don't leave it too late; continuing south could prove a little more difficult, as buses to Chetumal run only every two hours and *colectivos* are often full when they pass.

From Tulum to Chetumal

The road from Tulum to Chetumal skirts the Sian Ka'an Biosphere Reserve and heads inland amid ever-denser forest, past **Felipe Carrillo Puerto**, a crossroads on the routes to Valladolid and Mérida; through Limones, where a road heads east to the region known as the **Costa Maya** (the coastal towns of Mahahual and Xcalak); along the beautiful **Laguna Bacalar**, as scenic as any Caribbean beach; and on to **Chetumal**, the gateway to Belize and a good point from which to explore **Kohunlich** and other Maya sites.

Felipe Carrillo Puerto

A slow-paced agricultural town with a population of about 15,000, **FELIPE CARRILLO PUERTO** doesn't look like much on the surface; however, following its role as capital of the independent "Zona Maya" during the nineteenth-century Caste Wars (when it was called Chan Santa Cruz), it is still an important cultural and spiritual centre for the modern Maya. In the 1850s rebels from the north gathered forces here and took guidance and inspiration from a miraculous talking cross that told them to fight on against their oppressors – you can still visit the **Santuario de la Cruz Parlante**, built on the site of the talking cross (its remnants have been moved to a smaller town nearby). Turn west off the main street (Calle 70 or Avenida Juárez) at the PEMEX, Calle 69; the complex is at Calle 62. Back on the plaza, the Franciscan-style **church** was in fact built by the rebel Maya as a temple – using the slave labour of captured white fighters, no less; it was consecrated as a Catholic church in 1948. The small **tourist office**, on Calle 70 at Calle 59 (Mon–Fri 9am–4pm; Ⓣ983/267-1452), has information on surrounding Maya villages, or stop in at Xiimbal Tours, in the Balam-Nah **internet café** on the plaza. The **colectivo to Punta Allen** (2 daily at 9am & 3pm; 3hr) leaves from the first block east out of the main traffic circle. There are several reasonable **hotels** around the plaza (where the **bus station** is also located) – *Hotel Esquivel*, on Calle 63 between calles 66 and 68 (Ⓣ983/834-0344, Ⓔesquivelhotel@yahoo.com; ④), is the most reliable. The best **place to eat** in the evenings is taco specialist *La Placita Maya*, two blocks south of the bus station.

The Costa Maya

South of Carrillo Puerto, a dead-straight road turns east to the beaches that line the 250km of coast between the southern edge of the Sian Ka'an reserve and the Belize border. The **Costa Maya**, as the area is known, still has a very end-of-the-world feel, despite heavy development pressure. The two towns in the area, **Mahahual** and the smaller **Xcalak**, had only enjoyed regular electricity for a few years before Hurricane Dean hit hard in 2007. Now largely rebuilt, Mahahual is once again welcoming passengers from Puerto Costa Maya, a slick cruise-ship port. Divers also come here, for **Banco Chinchorro**, a coral atoll littered with shipwrecks and designated a biosphere reserve in 2003, and the reefs closer to Xcalak.

So far, infrequent transport to this area has helped keep the tourist droves at bay, though this may change with the inauguration of a **water-taxi service** connecting

Xcalak, Chetumal and San Pedro in Belize, set to begin in late 2009, followed later by a road across the border. Meanwhile, one direct **bus** to Mahahual leaves Cancún daily at 7.30am (often rising to two or three in August), or you can take a bus to Limones and transfer to a bus coming from Chetumal. This latter service departs from Chetumal at 6am, 4pm and 7.30pm daily from the main bus terminal (though only the first two, by Caribe, also go past the hotels south of Mahahual and on to Xcalak). To connect, you should be in Limones by 7.30am, 5.30pm or 9pm, respectively. **Leaving** Mahahual, Caribe (second-class) buses start in Xcalak, then cut over to the coast road at *Xahuayxol* (see below), passing the coast-road hotels en route to Mahahual. ADO buses serve only Mahahual.

Mahahual

Puerto Costa Maya is out of sight north of **MAHAHUAL** (60km east of Hwy-307), but its influence is felt on cruise-ship days (check Ⓦwww.cruisecal.com for the ship schedules), when the village springs to life with souvenir stands and jet-ski rentals along the slick seafront promenade – a surreal juxtaposition with the rest of the ramshackle town. There's **no bank**, and the **ATM seldom works**. To avoid any crowds, plan your visit for cruiseship-free days, or just head down the bumpy dirt beach road south of town. The main **dive shop**, Dreamtime Diving (Ⓣ983/700-5824, Ⓦwww.dreamtimediving.com), runs trips to Banco Chinchorro.

For **accommodation**, seek out the wonderfully secluded and very comfortable *Mayan Beach Garden*, in Placer, 20km north of Mahahual (Ⓦwww.mayanbeachgarden.com; ❻). The best budget option is *Las Cabañas del Doctor*, on the south edge of town (Ⓣ983/832-2102, Ⓦwww.lascabanasdeldoctor.com; ❸), where you can choose palapa-roof cabins or cement rooms, all with private bath. It's another 5.5km down the coast road to the white stucco cottages at *Balamku* (Ⓣ983/839-5332, Ⓦwww.balamku.com; ❻), built to stringent ecofriendly guidelines. Much further south, at km 29, wind-powered *Xahuayxol* (Ⓣ983/837-4564, Ⓦwww.xahuayxol.com; ❺) is on a beautiful section of beach, with wood cabins and a good restaurant. For food, make the trek to *Travel In'*, just south of *Balamku*, for fresh-baked bread and healthy treats. In town, a **grocery store** is on the main street (Calle Huachinango), across from the *100% Agave* **bar**.

Xcalak

XCALAK, less than 20km south of Mahahual, can only be reached by a paved road that runs a bit inland. Once the largest town in Quintana Roo, today it's a desolate village that still hasn't recovered from being flattened by a hurricane in 1955. As it has no real beaches, the main reason to visit is its superb **snorkelling**, **diving** and **fishing**. For more information on Xcalak, check out the good website, Ⓦwww.xcalak.info, maintained by relocated American and Canadian residents. The best place to **stay** here is *Tierra Maya* (Ⓣ983/831-0404, Ⓦwww.tierramaya.net; ❻), a welcoming guesthouse a short drive north of town; it also has a bit of a sandy beach. Back in town, the **dive shop** XTC (Ⓦwww.xtcdivecenter.com) runs snorkelling trips (M$300; 2hr), offers open-water certification courses (M$3750) and has a licence to dive at Banco Chinchorro. For **eating**, plan to be in town on the weekend, when the extremely casual yet supremely delicious *Leaky Palapa*, on the northern edge of the village, is open to serve fresh-caught fish (closed in the low season); reservations are recommended (by email Ⓔleakypalapa@yahoo.com).

Laguna Bacalar

Back on Hwy-307, some 35km north of Chetumal, the gorgeous **Laguna Bacalar** stretches along the east side of the road. It resembles the Caribbean Sea, sparkling clear and ranging in colour from palest aqua to deep indigo. About 45km and 1km wide, it's the second largest lake in Mexico (after Laguna de Chapala, south of Guadalajara), but still attracts only a small number of Mexican tourists and a small expat community with a bent for ecology and yoga.

The small town on the edge of the lake, **Bacalar**, was once a key point on the pre-Columbian trade route, and unexcavated **Maya remains** surround the lake. The *Chilam Balam* of Chumayel, one of the Maya's sacred books, mentions it as the first settlement of the Itzá, the tribe that occupied Chichén Itzá. All this is detailed in the interesting **Museo de San Felipe Bacalar** (Tues–Thurs & Sun 9am–7pm, Fri & Sat 9am–8pm; M$52), set in a restored fort built by the Spanish for protection against pirates from Belize (then British Honduras), and later used as a Maya stronghold in the Caste Wars. The fort is just off the plaza – about 1.2km from the highway, where the bus stops. In town, you can go **swimming** at the *balneario municipal*, down the hill from the fort and left (north) along the lakeshore drive (10am–6pm; M$5). Or head south a few kilometres along this road to the inky-blue "bottomless" **Cenote Azul** (daily 8am–8pm; free), which is busy with swimmers, dive-bombing teens and live musicians at weekends. Several **restaurants** capitalize on the lake view, but more reliable is the basic yet satisfying *Orizaba*, one block off the northwest corner of the town's plaza, or the veggie-friendly *Gaia*, just south of the plaza.

To **spend the night**, check out *Casita Carolina*, a bit south of the fort on the lakeshore drive (Ⓣ983/834-2334, Ⓦwww.casitacarolina.com; ❸), a guesthouse with seven rooms and a spacious back garden. At the south end of the road along the water (about M$35 in a taxi from the plaza), the wonderfully kitsch and comfortable *Hotel Laguna Bacalar* (Ⓣ983/834-2206, Ⓦwww.hotellagunabacalar.com; ❺) is decorated with seashell-encrusted countertops and plaster pillars galore; there's a pool that's also open to anyone dining at the restaurant.

The lake harbours a wide variety of **birdlife**, and a couple of places outside the town are good nature havens: *Villas Ecotucan*, 5km north (Ⓣ983/834-2516, Ⓦwww.villasecotucan.info; ❺), has large cabañas on attractively landscaped grounds between the lake and acres of uncleared forest. Just south of here, *Juumyaxche* (Ⓣ983/102-0523) has space for **camping** (M$60), as well as kayaks for guests' use. *Colectivos* and second-class buses can drop you on the highway near the entrances to both places.

Chetumal and around

If you're heading south to Belize or Guatemala, you can't avoid the capital of Quintana Roo, **CHETUMAL**, 15km from Belize – the neighbouring country's influence is reflected in everything from the language (many people speak English) to the clapboard houses. Obliterated by Hurricane Janet in 1955, the city is a hodgepodge of modern concrete buildings (some even exuding a bit of 1960s flair) and a few old wooden houses with porches that remain from the settlement's earliest days. As the state capital and a border town, Chetumal is bustling but largely oblivious to tourists – which can be refreshing after the hedonism of the Riviera Maya. Although it can't really be praised as a destination for its own sake, it does make a decent one- or two-day stop for resting and restocking, as everything's relatively cheap. You could also take day or overnight trips to the Río Bec archeological sites west from here, though car rental is the one thing in Chetumal that's not a great deal.

Arrival and information

Chetumal's main **bus station** is on the north side of town, a short taxi ride from the centre (about M$20). A **bus ticket office** in town, on Belice between Gandhi and Colón, handles long-haul services. The central part of Chetumal is strung along **Avenida de Niños Héroes**, the town's main street, which runs south to the waterfront. The city **tourist office**, on 5 de Mayo at Carmen Ochoa (Mon–Fri 8.30am–4pm; ⓣ983/835-0500), is happy to provide information on buses, hotels and tours; they can also advise on nearby attractions in Belize.

Accommodation

Most of Chetumal's **hotels** are on or near Niños Héroes in the few blocks back from the malecón – the options on the high and low ends are both good, but there's little in the mid-range. There is only one **hostel** – *Chetumal Hostel* (Sicilia 262 at Av San Salvador, ⓣ983/832-8317), with dorm beds for M$95 – but you might wind up paying more in taxi fares, as it's quite far from the centre.

Caribe Princess Obregón 168 ⓣ983/832-0520, ⓦwww.caribeprincesschetumal.com. A couple of steps up from the real budget places, popular with Mexican business travelers. Rooms all have a/c and were remodelled in 2008 – though they look like they were designed in 1988. Free parking. ④

Los Cocos Niños Héroes 134 ⓣ983/832-0544, ⓦwww.hotelloscocos.com.mx. A better deal than the *Holiday Inn*, with large, comfortable rooms (the recently redone "premier" category is worth the upgrade), a pool and a sprawling terrace bar and restaurant. ⑤

Guadalupe del Carmen Zaragoza 226 ⓣ983/832-8649. Exceptionally clean and tidy two-storey hotel, and a little roomier than budget competitor *María Dolores*; some rooms have a/c. ③

Holiday Inn Niños Héroes 171 ⓣ983/835-0400, ⓦwww.holidayinn.com. All the usual comforts of a chain hotel, plus an on-site travel agency. Compared with the giant suites at *Los Cocos*, though, you're paying for the name (though discounts are often available online). ⑥

Juliet Efraín Aguilar 171 ⓣ983/129-1871, ⓦwww.hoteljulietchetumal.com. On a pedestrian walkway just off Niños Héroes, this place has clean all-white rooms with TV and fan (a/c is optional). Unlike other budget hotels, there's wi-fi. ③

María Dolores Obregón 206 ⓣ983/832-0508. Basic budget offering, popular with backpackers, with slightly cramped rooms, but an excellent restaurant downstairs. ②

Ucum Gandhi 167 ⓣ983/832-0711, ⓦwww.hotelucumchetumal.com. One of the better deals in town, though it looks unpromising from the motel-like front section. Rooms in the back building, by the huge pool, are brighter and have a choice of a/c or fan. ②

The Town

The main attraction, on Avenida de Niños Héroes at the northern edge of the centre, is the **Museo de la Cultura Maya** (Tues–Thurs & Sun 9am–7pm, Fri & Sat 9am–8pm; M$50). It has nifty exhibits on the Maya calendar and counting system, and a re-creation of one of fresco rooms at Bonampak. The *Alegoría del Mestizaje* **sculpture** out front is one of the most striking depictions of the popular theme of the intermingling of Spanish and indigenous cultures, showing the Mexican born of a conquistador and a Maya woman.

Immediately south is a little warren of shops and *loncherías* – what's called the "old" **market** (the newer, larger one, where most of the fresh produce is sold and buses for Belize gather, is 1km northwest along Niños Héroes). A couple of blocks further south, the **Centro Cultural de las Bellas Artes**, in a striking 1936 neo-Maya-style school, now houses the romantic memorabilia of the **Museo de la Ciudad** (Tues–Sun 9am–7pm; M$10) as well as the state schools for the performing arts – there's usually live music here on weekend evenings. From here, Niños Héroes continues down to the bay and the **malecón**, popular for evening strolls and

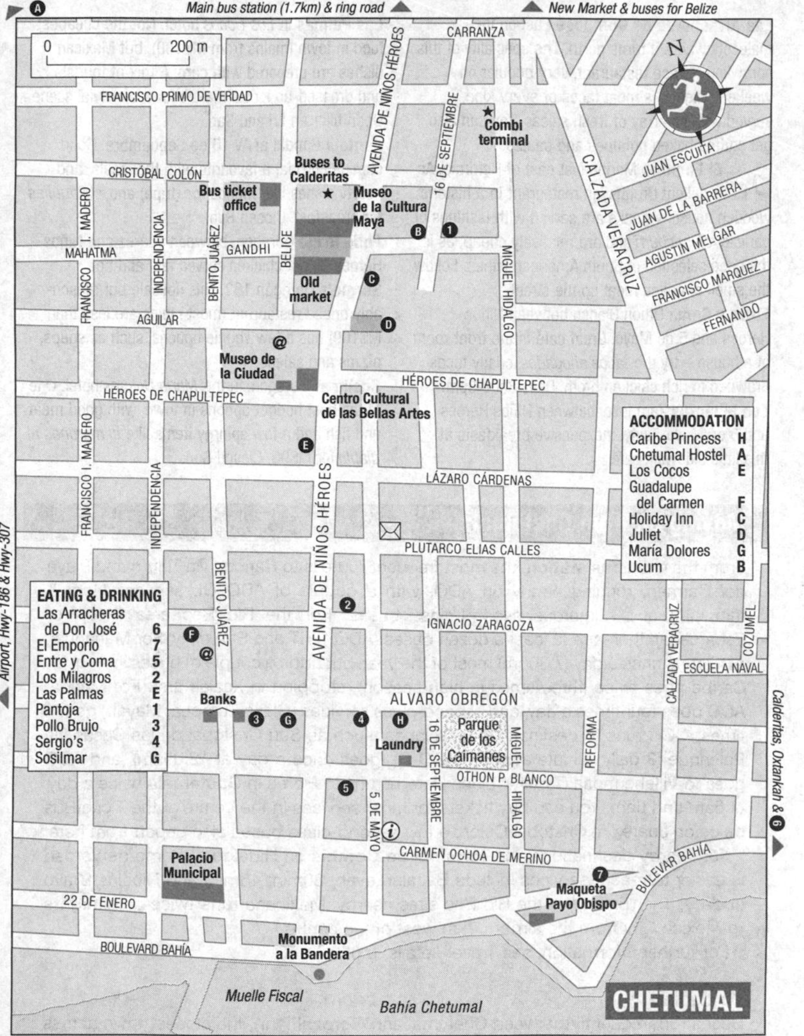

fishing. A few blocks east, behind the modern Palacio Legislativo, a small Caribbean house contains the fascinating **Maqueta Payo Obispo** (Tues–Sun 9am–1pm & 5–9pm; free), a hand-carved scale model of Chetumal as it looked in the 1920s.

Eating and drinking

The intersection of Niños Héroes and Obregón has the highest concentration of restaurants, while the **market stalls** south of the Museo de la Cultura Maya have good, inexpensive fare at lunch. **Nightlife** isn't particularly vibrant, but on weekend evenings the plaza has food stalls, and residents flock to the bar/restaurants strung along the seafront east of the plaza.

Las Arracheras de Don José East on the malecón, where it turns north. The speciality of this sprawling terrace restaurant, very popular on weekend nights, is meat tacos of every kind, served with an array of fresh salsas. You can also get stuffed baked potatoes and pastas.

El Emporio Merino just east of Reforma. An excellent Uruguayan restaurant in a historic wooden house – steaks are served with lashings of garlicky *chimichurri* and are relatively cheap, as is the good selection of South American wines. Follow the smell of grilled meat up the street.

Entre y Coma Othon Blanco between Niños Héroes and 5 de Mayo. Great café in the front room of a house – try the *tacos ahogados*, crispy tacos drowned in rich chicken broth. Daily 8am–3pm.

Los Milagros Zaragoza, between Niños Héroes and 5 de Mayo. Tasty, inexpensive breakfasts at this little sidewalk café.

Las Palmas in *Los Cocos* hotel. Not the cheapest food in town (mains from M$100), but Mexican dishes are prepared with care. A mix of tourists and dressed-up locals makes for a convivial scene. Open till 1am Fri and Sat.

Pantoja Gandhi at Av 16 de Septiembre. Good comida corrida, a favourite with the locals, and hearty dishes like *mondongo* (tripe) and *chilaquiles* for breakfast. Closed Sun.

Pollo Brujo Obregón, between Juárez and Niños Héroes. Roast chicken served fast and hot.

Sergio's Obregón 182. This upscale but reasonably priced restaurant (most mains are less than M$100) has a few veggie options, such as soups, pizzas and salads.

Sosilmar Obregón, in the *María Dolores* hotel. One of the best budget options in town, with good meat and fish and a few splurgy items like *camarones al diablo* for M$90. Closed Sun.

Moving on from Chetumal

From the main **bus station**, the most frequent route is to Cancún via Tulum and Playa del Carmen, running hourly on ADO, with a couple of ADO GL services (4am & midnight) and numerous second-class buses. For the Río Bec area (Xpujil or Escárcega), there are at least a dozen buses (ADO, TRT and Sur) daily. For Mahahual, ADO runs once a day (7.30pm) most of the year, but adds a couple of buses in August; Caribe goes twice (three times in high season), stopping in Xcalak first. For Mérida, ADO goes four times a day, and second-class services (Clase Europea, Mayab) go ten times. OCC runs to destinations in Chiapas, such as San Cristóbal de las Casas via Palenque (3 daily, all late at night; ADO GL goes once a day at 12.05am), and ADO goes to Villahermosa (7 daily). Linea Dorada runs to Flores in **Guatemala** twice a day, at 5am and 6am. You can buy tickets for most services in the centre at the TicketBus office on Juárez at Cristóbal Colón; a few second-class buses also depart from here.

For nearby destinations, the **Terminal de Combis** on Hidalgo at Primo de Verdad is easier to reach; services include Bacalar (every 30min; 45min) and Nicolás Bravo (4 daily; 1hr 15min), for the Río Bec sites nearby. Mexicana runs twice-daily **flights** to Mexico City from the airport, 2km west of the centre.

For further information, see Travel details, p.850.

To Belize

Buses run frequently between Chetumal and **Corozal** (1hr), the closest town across the border, though you must get off the bus and walk over the bridge at Subteniente López, 8km west of Chetumal. Citizens of the UK, US, Canada, Australia and New Zealand do not need a visa to enter Belize; if you are planning to return to Mexico, make sure to keep your tourist card, or you will have to purchase another.

The cheapest, very rattle-trap buses leave from the *mercado nuevo* on the north side of town on Calzada Veracruz, between 4am and noon; you can get over the border for about M$20 – a few of these buses continue on to **Orange Walk** (2hr 30min) and **Belize City** (5hr). First-class service on Linea Dorada, San Juan and Premier Lines departs from the main bus station (5 daily; 3hr to Belize City). Note that cars rented in Mexico cannot typically be driven into Belize. There's no air travel straight from Chetumal, but there is a water-taxi service (Fri–Mon at 3pm) from the main pier in Chetumal to San Pedro on Ambergris Caye, operated by San Pedro Water Taxi (Ⓣ501-2/26-2194 in Belize, Ⓦwww.sanpedrowatertaxi.com).

Listings

Car rental Europcar, Niños Héroes 129, opposite *Los Cocos* hotel, and at the airport ⓣ55/5207-5572; Aventura Maya in *Hotel Los Cocos* ⓔaventuramaya@hotelloscocos.com.mx.
Internet access Plenty of options; Web Center, on Aguilar, just south of the old market, is cheap and has fast connections.
Laundry Lavandería Centro, Othon Blanco between 16 de Septiembre and 5 de Mayo (daily 8am–8pm; M$13/kg).
Post office Plutarco Elias Calles at 5 de Mayo (Mon–Fri 8am–6pm, Sat & Sun 9am–12.30pm).
Tour operators Operators are not plentiful in Chetumal, and often need several days' advance notice to arrange something for you. On the plus side, because there are not yet many fixed routes, you can often tailor a trip precisely to your tastes. Villa Manatí, Blvd Bahía 301 (ⓣ983/129-3204, ⓦwww.villamanati.com.mx) runs day trips to the Río Bec sites (M$650; M$500 for guide).

Around Chetumal

Near Chetumal are several refreshing escapes. At weekends, the town descends en masse on **CALDERITAS**, a small seaside resort just 6km north around the bay; the best **place to stay**, the *Yax-Há* RV park (ⓣ983/834-4127, ⓔyax_ha1@yahoo.com; ⑤) has nice rooms and a large picturesque garden with swimming pool right on the seafront. You can hire a **boat** at the adjacent *El Rincón de las Tortugas* bar (ⓣ983/834-4220) for various day outings: to the beaches on the nearby empty island of Tamalcab (M$400 for 6–8 people); a tour around the bay to look for manatees (M$1500; 3hr); or to several other nature spots. **Buses** to Calderitas leave frequently from Cristóbal Colón west of Héroes, behind the museum.

Seven kilometres north of Calderitas, **OXTANKAH** (daily 8am–5pm; M$37, free Sun) is a small Maya site with the remains of a maritime city occupied principally in the Classic period (200–600 AD) and developed to exploit ocean resources – specifically salt. Allegedly, it was also the site of the first *mestizaje*, where shipwrecked Gonzalo Guerrero married into a Maya family and fathered mixed-blood children. What remain are the ruins of several buildings around two squares, with an architectural style similar to that of the Petén region, and a chapel built by the Spanish conquerors. It's a peaceful wooded place with trees – *ceiba, yaxche* – and other flora neatly labelled. You'll need your own transport to get there (follow the shoreline north through Calderitas) or a taxi (M$200 round trip with waiting time).

Kohunlich and other Maya sites in the south

The only way from Chetumal back towards central Mexico is across the bottom of the peninsula along Hwy-186. The main reason to stop anywhere along here is for the seldom-visited Maya ruins. Together with the archeological sites in Xpuhil and further east (see p.762), these sites represent a fascinating period of architectural decoration, enhanced by the dense jungle that surrounds some of them. If you stop for only one, make it the Classic Maya city of **KOHUNLICH**, set some 60km from Chetumal, then another 9km off the road from the village of Francisco Villa (daily 8am–5pm; M$49).

The ruins, seldom visited by anyone other than enormous butterflies and wild parrots, are beautifully situated, peering out above the treetops. The buildings date from the late pre-Classic to the Classic periods (100–900 AD) and the majority are in the Río Bec architectural style. Foliage has reclaimed most of them, except for the **Templo de los Mascarones**, which is named after the five two-metre-high stucco masks that decorate its facade. Disturbing enough now, these wide-eyed, open-mouthed images of the sun god, Kinich Ahau, once stared out from a background of smooth, bright-red-painted stucco. Also look for an

Fiestas

January

New Year's Day (Jan 1). Beginning of the Feria de los Tres Reyes in the cow town of Tizimín (see p.800), an important religious and secular gathering during which lots of steak is consumed.

Fiesta de Polk Keken (Jan 6). Celebrated in Lerma, near Campeche, with many traditional dances.

Día de la Virgen de Santa Inés (Jan 16–21). An ancient festival with roots in Maya tradition celebrated in Dzitas, north of Chichén Itzá.

February

Día de la Candelaria (Feb 2). Candlemas: colourful celebrations and candlelight processions at Tecoh and Kantunil. The whole week before (beginning Jan 25) is a fiesta in Valladolid (see p.796).

Carnaval (the week before Lent; variable Feb–March). At its most riotous in the big cities – especially Mérida (see p.764) – but is also celebrated in Tixkokob, Campeche and Chetumal (see p.753 & p.843), as well as on Isla Mujeres and Cozumel (see p.811 & p.824) with particularly Caribbean flair. The village of Hocaba adds a sombre note, with re-enactments of the Inquisition of the Maya in the sixteenth century.

March

Feria de las Hamacas (March 20). In Tecoh, a hammock-producing village near Mérida.

Equinox (March 21). Huge gathering to see the serpent shadow at Chichén Itzá (see p.000).

April

Semana Santa (Holy Week). Celebrated with particularly colourful Passion plays in Mérida (see p.764) and Maní (see p.787).

Festival of honey and corn (April 13–17). Traditional celebrations in Hopelchén (see p.759).

Fiesta de San Telmo (April 14–22). Progreso (see p.777) celebrates the patron saint of fishermen.

May

Día de la Santa Cruz (May 3). The excuse for another fiesta in Hopelchén (see p.759); also celebrated in, among other towns, Celestún (see p.779) and Felipe Carrillo Puerto (see p.841).

Feria del Jipi (May 20). In Becal (see p.764), celebration of the Panama hat, which is the major industry in the town.

Sport-fishing tournament (last weekend in May). Occasion for a town-wide party in Puerto Morelos (see p.816).

June

Fiesta de San Pedro y San Pablo (June 26–30). Celebrated on Cozumel (see p.824) and in Panaba, north of Tizimín.

elite residential area called the **27 Escalones**, worth the detour to see the great views over the jungle canopy from the cliff edge on which it is built (prime real estate was just as valuable 1400 years ago, it seems).

A few kilometres east along Hwy-186 is the turn to **Dzibanché** and **Kinichná** (8am–5pm; M$41); set in a drier area with sparse trees, these two neighbouring ruins are an interesting contrast to Kohunlich. Kinichná's hulking pyramid, built in metre-high stones, layer upon layer by successive leaders, barely clears the trees,

July

Fiesta de Nuestra Señora del Carmen (July 15–30). Festival for the patron saint of Ciudad del Carmen (see p.760). Motul also celebrates, with lots of dancing.

Feria de Holbox (July 31). Celebrations on Isla Holbox (see p.802).

Maya ceremony (dates variable). Held in Edzná (see p.758) for the god Chac, to encourage, or celebrate, the arrival of the rains.

August

Día de la Asunción (August 15). Assumption Day, celebrated in Oxcutzcab for a week prior, and in Izamal the week following (see p.789).

September

Día de San Roman (Sept 14). In Dzan, near Ticul, the end of a four-day festival with fireworks, bullfights, dances and processions. In Campeche (see p.753), the **Feria de San Roman** lasts until the end of the month. Also marks the beginning of the season of "Los Gremios", the workers' processions to honour the Cristo de las Ampollas at the cathedral in Mérida; daily pilgrimages begin on Sept 27 and continue until Oct 17.

Equinox (Sept 21). Another serpent spectacle at Chichén Itzá (see p.790).

Día de San Miguel (Sept 29). Celebrated with a major festival in Maxcanú, as well as on Cozumel.

October

Pilgrimage (Oct 18). Centred on Izamal (see p.789), in honour of the miraculous Black Christ of Sitilpech, it starts ten days of celebration, culminating in dances on the night of Oct 28.

November

Feria del Estado de Yucatán (first two weeks of Nov). Typical thrill rides, agricultural exhibits and fried foods at the fairgrounds south of Mérida (see p.764).

Día de los Muertos (Day of the Dead; Nov 1–2). Celebrated everywhere as Hanal Pixan, the Maya equivalent, though usually as a private event. Mérida is the exception, with altars on display in the centre.

December

Día de la Inmaculada Concepción (Dec 8). Widely celebrated, but especially in Kantunilkin, Izamal (see p.789) and Champotón, each of which has a fiesta starting several days earlier. Izamal's and Kantunilkin's fiestas include bullfights.

Día de la Virgen de Guadalupe (Dec 12). Celebrated everywhere, but look for runners on the roads around Mérida (see p.764) in the days prior; church groups organize days-long relays as penance. On Isla Mujeres (see p.811), the week prior celebrates the church's statue of the Virgin.

Día de Nuestra Señora de la Estrella (Dec 27). Peto celebrates until Jan 2 with a trade fair, bullfights and dancing.

but you can look over the surrounding terrain (and spot a glimse of Dzibanché), now broken into farmland.

There is no public transport from Chetumal to these sites, and they are too far off the highway to walk in. The easiest way to visit this area is to take a taxi tour from **Xpujil** (see p.761). It's also possible to start off from Chetumal by taking a *combi* to the town of Nicolás Bravo, then hiring a taxi from there (about M$500), ending by flagging down a second-class bus back to Chetumal or onward to Xpuhil.

Travel details

Buses

The most useful bus services are those between Mérida and Cancún and those provided by Mayab and Riviera, which run at least every thirty minutes between Cancún and Playa del Carmen. Second-class buses and *combis* or *colectivos* will get you around locally and to the nearest major hub. The following frequencies and times are primarily for first-class services, most on ADO, but second-class times are given where there is no first-class available. Check Ⓦwww.ticketbus.com.mx for up-to-date schedules on major routes in the peninsula with ADO, plus some Sur, ATS, OCC and Mayab services.

Campeche to: Cancún (8 daily, 3.20am–11.30pm; 7hr); Chetumal (1 daily at noon; 6hr 30min) via Xpujil (4hr 30min); Ciudad del Carmen (hourly; 3hr); Escárcega (12 daily; 2hr 15min); Mérida (every 30min; 2hr 30min); Mérida airport (up to 5 daily, 5.45am–3pm; 2hr 30min); Playa del Carmen (2 daily at 11.30pm & 3.20am; 8hr); San Cristóbal de las Casas (2 daily at 9.45pm & 12.55am; 10–12hr); Uxmal (5 daily, 6am–5pm; 2hr); Veracruz (1 daily at 10.15pm; 11hr 30min); Villahermosa (hourly; 6–7hr).

Cancún to: Campeche (12 daily; 7hr); Chetumal (hourly, 4am–12.30am; 6–7hr); Chiquilá (3 daily; 3hr); Mahahual (1 daily at 7.30am; 5hr 30min); Mérida (hourly; 4hr 30min); Mexico City (5 daily; 23–26hr); Playa del Carmen (every 10min; 1hr 15min) via Puerto Morelos (30min); Tizimín (at least 7 daily; 4hr); Tulum (hourly; 2hr 15min); Valladolid (8 daily; 3hr); Villahermosa (hourly; 12–15hr).

Chetumal to: Bacalar (every 30min: 1hr); Belize City via Orange Walk (5 daily; 3hr); Campeche (1 daily; at 6.15pm; 6hr 15min); Cancún via Tulum and Playa del Carmen (hourly; 5hr 30min–7hr); Escárcega (14 daily; 4.15am–midnight; 4hr); Flores, Guatemala, via Belize City (2 daily; 12hr); Mahahual (3 daily; 2hr 30min); Mérida (4 daily 7.30am–11.30pm; 5hr 30min–6hr 30min); Mexico City (1 daily at 4.30pm; 20hr); San Cristóbal de las Casas (4 daily; 12hr) via Palenque (7hr); Villahermosa (7 daily; 8–9hr); Xcalak (2 daily; 4hr 30min); Xpujil (14 daily, 4.15am–midnight; 2hr).

Mérida See box, p.775.

Playa del Carmen to: Cancún (every 10min; 1hr 15min); Cancún airport (hourly 7am–9pm; 1hr); Chetumal (hourly 5.30am–1.45am; 4–5hr) via Tulum (1hr); Chichén Itzá (5 daily, 6.10–11.50am; 4hr); Cobá (10 daily; 2hr); Mérida (hourly 6.30am–12.30am; 4–5hr); Palenque (4 daily; 11hr 30min); San Cristóbal de las Casas (5 daily; 17–20hr); Valladolid (14 daily; 3hr); Villahermosa (15 daily, 12.30pm–10.30pm; 12–15hr).

Tulum to: Cancún (frequently; 2–3hr); Chetumal via Felipe Carrillo Puerto and Bacalar (hourly 6.40am–12.40am; 3hr 15min–4hr); Chichén Itzá (5 daily; 3hr); Cobá (11 daily; 1hr); Mahahual (1 daily at 9.55am; 3hr 15min); Mérida (5 daily 5am–1.40am; 4hr); Playa del Carmen (frequently; 1hr); San Cristóbal de las Casas (2 daily, 6.25pm & 8.30pm; 16hr) via Palenque (11hr); Valladolid (14 daily; 2hr).

Ferries

Ferry services run frequently to **Isla Mujeres, Cozumel** and **Isla Holbox**. Although there are car ferries to all three islands, it's not worth taking a vehicle to Holbox and Mujeres; for Cozumel, the trip might make sense if you'll be spending more than a few days there.

Passenger ferries

Chetumal to: San Pedro, Ambergris Caye, Belize (Fri–Mon at 3pm; 1hr 45min).

Chiquilá to: Isla Holbox (9 daily; 30min).

Playa del Carmen to: Cozumel (hourly 6am–11pm; 30min).

Puerto Juárez and **Gran Puerto**, Cancún to: Isla Mujeres (every 30min 6.30am–10.30pm; 15min).

Car ferries

Chiquilá to: Isla Holbox (2 daily; 1hr).

Puerto Calica, Playa del Carmen to: Cozumel (7 daily; 1hr 15min).

Punta Sam to: Isla Mujeres (5 daily; 1hr).

Flights

Campeche to: Mexico City (3 daily; 1hr 50min).

Cancún to: Atlanta (5 daily; 3hr); Belize City (1 daily; 1hr 15min); Charlotte (3 daily; 3hr); Chicago (5 daily; 4hr); Dallas (4 daily; 3hr); Houston (6 daily; 2hr 30min); Los Angeles (2 daily; 5hr 40min); Mérida (1 daily; 1hr); Mexico City (17 daily; 2hr 30min); Miami (6 daily; 1hr 40min); New York (8 daily; 4hr); Philadelphia (3 daily; 3hr 40min); Toronto (3 daily; 4hr); Veracruz (2 daily; 2hr).

Chetumal to: Mexico City (2 daily; 2hr 10min).

Ciudad del Carmen to: Houston (1 daily; 2hr 40min); Mexico City (7 daily; 1hr 40min).

Cozumel to: Atlanta (1 daily; 3hr); Cancún (6 daily; 30min); Houston (1 daily; 2hr 30min).

Mérida to: Cancún (1 daily; 50min); Houston (1 daily; 2hr 15min); Mexico City (18 daily; 2hr); Villahermosa (3 daily; 1hr).

Contexts

Contexts

History

The nation of Mexico, with its current borders, has existed for little over 150 years. The story of the political entity known as Mexico can be traced to the Spanish Conquest. Our knowledge of anything pre-dating that is largely taken from histories recorded long after the events or from archeological conjecture, as the Spanish did their best to erase all traces of the cultures that preceded them.

These earlier cultures were not confined to present-day Mexico, but spread throughout the area referred to as **Mesoamerica**, which extends from central Mexico well into Central America. The north of this region was occupied by native peoples who never abandoned their nomadic, hunter-gatherer existences; the south was ruled by a succession of powerful empires, including the Aztecs and the Maya, who at one time spread all the way from southeastern Mexico into what is now Honduras. Some of the world's most extraordinary societies flourished in this region, creating – without the use of metal tools, draught animals or the wheel – vast cities, intricate statuary and a mathematical and calendar system more advanced than those known in the "civilized" world.

The **framework** set out below is based on archeological theories that are generally, but by no means universally, accepted. There are still major gaps in modern knowledge – especially concerning the extent and nature of the contact between the societies and their influence on each other – which, should they ever be filled, may overturn many existing notions.

The earliest peoples

The exact date when human beings first crossed the Bering land bridge into the Americas is debatable (as is the very theory of the migration from North Asia), but the earliest widely accepted date is around 13,000 years ago. Successive waves of nomadic Stone Age hunters continued to arrive until around 6000 BC, pushing their predecessors gradually further south.

The first signs of settled habitation in Mexico – the cultivation of corn, followed by the emergence of crude pottery, stone tools and even some trade – seem to come from the **Archaic** period, around 8000 to 2000 BC. The first established civilization did not appear until the **pre-Classic** or **Formative** era (2500 BC to 250 AD) with the rise of the Olmecs.

Still the least understood of all the ancient societies, the **Olmecs** thrived in the low-lying coastal jungles of Tabasco and Veracruz. Many of their political, cultural, artistic and architectural innovations can be observed in later Mesoamerican cultures. What you see of them in the museums today is a magnificent artistic style, exemplified in their sculpture and famous colossal basalt heads. These, with their puzzling "baby-faced" features, were carved from monolithic blocks and somehow transported over 90km from the quarries to their final settings – proof in itself of a hierarchical society commanding a sizeable workforce.

Classic civilizations

By the end of the **pre-Classic** period, the Olmec civilization was already in decline – La Venta, the most important cultural centre, seems to have been abandoned around 400 BC, and the other towns followed over the next few hundred years. As the Olmec weakened, new civilizations grew in strength and numbers, establishing cities throughout central Mexico. These sites, such as Monte Albán, near Oaxaca were obviously influenced by the earlier Olmec. To the north, in the Valley of México (where Mexico City now stands, an area then known as Anahuac), many small cities expanded. Tlatilco, one of the towns in this region, hoarded Olmec objects, suggesting significant contact with Monte Albán to the south – at least through trade. Meanwhile, there were hints of bigger things to come: Cuicuilco (now in the capital's suburbs) was an important city until it was buried by a volcanic eruption around the beginning of the first century AD; at the same time, the first major buildings of the city of Teotihuacán were being constructed.

Teotihuacán, the first truly urban society, dominated central Mexico at the beginning of the **Classic Period** (250–900 AD). Its architectural and religious influences reached as far south as the Maya heartland of Guatemala. Even today, the ruins of the city, with the great Pyramids of the Sun and Moon, are an impressive testimony to the civilization's strength. Very little is known about Teotihuacán (even the name was coined later by the Aztecs – it means "the place where men became gods"), but what is certain is that the city's period of dominance ended between 500 and 600 AD, and that within a century it had been abandoned altogether. Mysteriously, several societies throughout Mesoamerica, particularly the Maya, seem to have been disrupted at around the same time.

The great **Maya** centres, above all their cities in the lowlands of Guatemala and Honduras, also reached the peak of their artistic, scientific and architectural achievements in the Classic period. These survived longer than Teotihuacán, but by around 800 AD had also been abandoned. In the Yucatán the Maya fared rather better, their cities revived from about 900 by an injection of ideas from central Mexico and, archeologists now propose, new leaders from the south. The famous structures at Chichén Itzá mostly date from this later phase, around 900 to 1100 AD.

In general, the Classic era saw development everywhere – other important centres grew up on the Gulf coast at El Tajín and in the Zapotec areas around Monte Albán – but was followed by rapid decline. There are numerous theories to account for this, but none is entirely convincing, although the fall of Teotihuacán must have affected its trading partners throughout Mexico. In all likelihood, once started, the disasters – probably provoked by some sort of agricultural failure or ecological disaster – led to a loss of faith in rulers and perhaps even rebellion, and had a knock-on effect.

Toltecs and Aztecs

The start of the **post-Classic** era (900–1520 AD) saw the beginning of a series of invasions from the north which must have exacerbated any existing problems. Wandering tribes would arrive in the fertile Valley of México, like what they saw, build a city adopting many of the styles and religions of their predecessors in the area, enjoy a brief period of dominance and be subdued in turn by a new wave of invaders, or **Chichimeca**. All such marauding tribes were known as Chichimec, which implies barbarian (even if many of them were at least semi-civilized before they arrived), and all claimed to have set out on their journeys from the legendary seven caves of Chicomoztoc. Of the many people who founded cities in the valley in this bellicose era, two names stand out – the Toltecs and the Aztecs.

The **Toltec** people, who dominated the central valleys around 950–1150 AD, were among the first to arrive – indeed, some say that it was a direct attack by them that destroyed Teotihuacán. Later, they assumed a mythical significance for the Aztecs, who regarded them as the founders of every art and science and claimed direct descent from Toltec blood. In fact, it appears that the Toltecs borrowed most of their ideas from Teotihuacán.

Nevertheless, there were developments under the Toltecs. In particular, the cult of **Quetzalcoatl** assumed new importance: at Tula, the Toltec capital, the god is depicted everywhere, perhaps embodied as a king or dynasty of kings, and it was from here that he was driven out by the evil god Texcatlipoca. (The prediction of his return was later to have fatal consequences for the Aztecs.) The structure of Toltec society was at least as militaristic as it was religious, and human sacrifice was practised on a far larger scale than had been previously recorded.

When the **Aztecs** (or Mexica) arrived in central Mexico around the end of the twelfth century they found numerous small city-states, with none in a position of dominance. They spent some years scavenging and raiding until about 1325 – when legend has it that they saw the prophesied sign (an eagle perched on a cactus devouring a snake) telling them to build their own city.

The new city, **Tenochtitlán**, was to become the heart of the most formidable of all Mexican empires, but its birth was not easy. The chosen setting, an island in a lake (now Mexico City), was hardly promising, and the city was at first a subject of its neighbours. The Aztecs overcame the lack of arable land by growing crops on floating reed islands that they fashioned in the lake. This agricultural success led to self-sufficiency and a burgeoning population. They became the most powerful civilization in the valley, and around 1428 formed the so-called Triple Alliance with neighbouring Texcoco and Tlacopán, establishing the **Aztec empire**. The empire's achievements were remarkable – in less than a hundred years the Aztecs came to control, and demand labour tribute and taxes from, the whole of central and southern Mexico. Tenochtitlán grew huge – the invading Spanish could not believe its size and grandeur – but even as it expanded, the gods continued to demand more war: to suppress rebellious subjects, and to capture fresh victims for the constant rituals of human sacrifice.

Meanwhile, other societies had continued much as they had before the Aztec rise. In present-day Oaxaca, the Zapotecs were subjected to invasions by **Mixtecs** from the mountains. By war and alliance the Mixtecs came eventually to dominate this region – developing the trades of the potter and goldsmith as never before – and fell to the Aztecs only in the last years before the Spanish Conquest. In the Yucatán, the **Maya** were never conquered, but their civilization was in decline and any form of central authority had broken down into city-states. Nevertheless, they carried on trade all around the coasts, and Christopher Columbus himself (though he never got to Mexico) encountered a heavily laden boat of Maya traders, plying the sea between Honduras and the Yucatán. On the Gulf coast Aztec supremacy was total by the time the Spanish arrived, but they were still struggling to subdue the west.

The Spanish Conquest

Hernán Cortés landed on the coast near modern Veracruz in the spring of 1519. With him were just 550 men, a few horses, dogs and a cannon; yet less than three years later the Spaniards had defeated the Aztecs and effectively established control over most of Mexico. Several factors enabled them to do so. First was Cortés himself, as ruthless a leader as any in history: he burned the expedition's boats within days of their arrival, so that there was literally no turning back. In addition, his men had little to lose and much to gain, and their metal weapons and armour were greatly superior to anything the Aztecs had (although many Spaniards adopted Aztec-style padded cotton, which was warmer, lighter and almost as protective). Their gunpowder and cannon could also wreak havoc on opposing armies, both physically and psychologically. The horses and attack dogs, too, terrified the Aztecs. None of these, though, in the end counted a fraction as much as Cortés's ability to form alliances with tribes who were fretting under Aztec subjugation and whose numbers eventually swelled his armies tenfold.

Moctezuma, the Aztec leader, could certainly have destroyed the Spanish before they left their first camp, since his spies had brought news of their arrival almost immediately. Instead he sent a delegation bearing gifts of gold and jewels which he hoped would persuade them to leave in peace. This served only to inflame the greed of the Spanish. By all accounts Moctezuma was a morose, moody and indecisive man, but his failure to act against Cortés had deeper roots: he was heavily influenced by religious omens, and the arrival of Cortés coincided with the predicted date for the return of **Quetzalcoatl**. The invaders were fair-skinned and bearded, as was Quetzalcoatl, and they had come from the east, where the deity had vanished. Moreover, it seemed they bore a peaceful message like that of the god, for one of their first acts when they conquered a city was to ban human sacrifice. So although he put obstacles in their way, even persuading his allies to fight them, when the Spanish finally reached Tenochtitlán in November 1519, Moctezuma welcomed them as his guests. They promptly repaid his hospitality by taking him prisoner within his own palace.

This first phase of the Conquest, during which Spanish troops skirmished with a number of other Indian tribes and made allies of many – most significantly the **Tlaxcalans** (or Tlaxcalteca) – lasted for about a year. In April 1520 news came of a second Spanish expedition, led by Pánfilo de Narváez, who was under orders from the governor of Cuba, to capture Cortés and take him back to Cuba (Cortés's mission had always been unofficial, and many others hoped to seize the wealth of Mexico for themselves). Again, though, Cortés proved the more decisive commander – he marched back east, surprised Narváez by night, killed him and persuaded most of his troops to switch allegiance.

Meanwhile, the Spaniards left behind in Tenochtitlán had finally provoked their hosts beyond endurance by killing a group of priests during a religious ceremony, and were under siege in their quarters. Cortés, with his reinforcements, fought his way back into the city on June 24, only to find himself trapped as well. On June 27, Moctezuma (still a prisoner) was killed – stoned to death by his own people while attempting to appeal for peace according to the Spanish, though rumour has it that he was garrotted by Cortés himself. Finally Cortés decided to break out on the night of June 30 – still commemorated as **Noche Triste** – when the Spanish lost over half their number on the causeways across the lake. Most of them were so weighed down with gold and booty that they were barely able to move, let alone swim in the places where the bridges had been destroyed.

Once more, though, the Aztecs failed to follow up their advantage, and the Spanish survivors managed to reach their allies in Tlaxcala, where they regrouped. The final assault on Tenochtitlán began in January 1521, with more supplies and fresh troops, tens of thousands of whom were Tlaxcalteca and other Indians. The city, besieged, was also ravaged by an epidemic of smallpox, among whose victims was Moctezuma's successor, Cuitláhuac. The Aztecs held out for several more months under **Cuauhtémoc** – in Mexican eyes the only hero of this long episode – but on August 13, 1521, Tenochtitlán finally fell to the Spanish.

Although much of the country remained to be pacified, the defeat of the Aztec capital made it inevitable that it would be.

Colonial rule

By dint of his success, Cortés was appointed governor of this new territory, although in practice he was watched over by minders from Spain and never had much real freedom of action. In 1535 **Nueva España** (New Spain) was formally established. There followed nearly three centuries of direct Spanish rule, under a succession of 61 viceroys responsible to the Spanish king. By the end of the sixteenth century the entire country had been effectively subjugated, its boundaries stretched by exploration from Panama to the western states of the US (although the area from Guatemala south, including the Mexican state of Chiapas, was soon under separate rule).

When the Spaniards arrived, the **native population** of central Mexico was at least 25 million; by the beginning of the nineteenth century the total population of Nueva España was just six million, and at most half of these were pure-blooded natives. Some had been killed in battle, a few as a result of ill-treatment or simply from being left without homes or land to live on, but the vast majority died as a result of successive epidemics of European diseases to which the New World had no natural immunity. The few survivors found the burden of labour placed on them ever-increasing as their numbers dwindled – for certainly no European came to Mexico to do manual work – and became more and more like slaves.

The first tasks, in the Spanish mind, were reconstruction, pacification and conversion. Tenochtitlán, destroyed in the war, had been subsequently pillaged and burnt, its population dispersed. In a deliberate policy of destroying all reminders of Aztec power, the remaining stones were used to construct the new city, **México** (Mexico City). At first there was quite remarkable progress: hundreds of towns were laid out according to a plan drawn up in Spain, with a plaza surrounded by a grid of streets. Thousands of churches were built (by 1800, the count reached 12,000), often in areas that had been sacred to the Indians, or on top of their pyramids; mass conversions were the order of the day. In a sense the indigenous peoples were used to all this – the Aztecs and their predecessors had behaved in a similar manner – but they had never experienced a slavery like that which was to follow.

The Church, which at first championed indigenous rights and attempted to record native legends and histories and educate the children, grew more and more concerned with money. Any attempt to treat the Indians as human was, in any case, violently opposed by Spanish landowners, to whom they were rather less than machines (in fact, cheaper than machinery, and therefore more expendable). By the end of the colonial era, the Church owned more than half of all the land and wealth in the country, yet most native villages would be lucky to see a priest once a year.

In a sense Mexico was a wealthy nation – certainly the richest of the Spanish colonies – but its riches were confined to the local elite and the imperialists in Spain. The governing philosophy was "what's good for Spain is good for Mexico", and it was towards this end that all **trade**, industry and profit were exclusively aimed. No local trade or agriculture that would compete with Spain was allowed, so the cultivation of vines or the production of silk was banned; heavy taxes on other products – coffee, sugar, tobacco, cochineal, silver and other metals – went directly to Spain or to still poorer colonies. Since the "Spanish Galleon" (actually more of a convoy) sailed from Veracruz just once a year and was even then subject to the vagaries of piracy, this was a considerable handicap.

All this didn't prevent the growth of a small class of extraordinarily wealthy **hacendados** (owners of massive estates) and **mine-owners**, whose growing confidence is shown in the architectural development of the colonial towns, from fortress-like huddles at the beginning of the colonial era to the full flowering of Baroque extravagance by its end. However, it did stop the development of any kind of realistic economic infrastructure, even of decent roads linking the towns: just about the only proper road in 1800 was the one that connected Acapulco with Mexico City and Veracruz, by which goods from Spain's colonies in the Far East would be transported cross-country before being shipped on to Spain.

Even among the wealthy Spanish-descended landowners there was growing **resentment**, fuelled by the status of those among them born in Mexico: only **gachupines**, Spaniards born in Spain, could hold high office in the government or Church. Of the six million people in Mexico in 1800, only 40,000 were *gachupines* – the rest were **criollos** (creoles, born in Mexico of Spanish blood) who were generally educated, wealthy and aristocratic, and **mestizos** (of mixed race) who dominated the lower ranks of the Church, army and civil service, or lived as anything from shopkeepers and small ranchers to bandits and beggars.

Independence

By the beginning of the nineteenth century Spain's status as a world power was in severe decline. In 1796 British sea power had forced the Spanish to open their colonial ports to free trade. At the same time, new political ideas were transforming the world, and memories of the French Revolution and the American War of Independence were still fresh. Although the works of such political philosophers as Rousseau, Voltaire and Paine were banned in Mexico, the opening of the ports made it inevitable that their ideas would spread – especially since it was traders from the new US who most took advantage of the opportunities. Literary societies set up to discuss these books quickly became centres of **political dissent**.

The spark, though, came when the French invaded Spain in 1808, and Napoleon placed his brother Joseph on the throne. Colonies throughout Latin America refused to recognize the Bonaparte regime (and the campaigns of Bolívar and others in South America began). In Mexico, the *gachupine* rulers proclaimed their loyalty to Ferdinand VII (the deposed king) and hoped to carry on much as before, but creole discontent was not so easily assuaged. The literary societies continued to meet, and from one, in Querétaro, emerged the first leaders of the Independence movement: **Father Miguel Hidalgo y Costilla**, a creole priest, and **Ignacio Allende**, a disaffected junior army officer.

When their plans for a coup were discovered, the conspirators were forced into premature action, with Hidalgo issuing the famous *Grito de Dolores* (culminating in the rallying cry, *Méxicanos, viva México!*) from his parish church in Dolores on September 16, 1810. The mob of Indians and *mestizos* who gathered behind the banner swiftly took the towns of San Miguel, Guanajuato and others to the north of the capital, but their behaviour – seizing land and property, slaughtering the Spaniards – horrified the wealthy creoles who had initially supported them. In spring 1811, Hidalgo's army, huge but undisciplined, moved on the capital, but at the crucial moment Hidalgo threw away a clear chance to overpower the royalist army. Instead he chose to retreat, and his forces broke up as quickly as they had assembled. Within months, Hidalgo, Allende and the other ringleaders had been captured and executed.

By this time most creoles had rejoined the ranks of the royalists. However, many *mestizos* and much of the indigenous population remained in a state of revolt, with a new leader in the *mestizo* priest **José María Morelos**. Morelos was not only a far better tactician than Hidalgo – instituting a highly successful series of guerrilla campaigns – he was also a genuine radical. By 1813 he controlled virtually the entire country, with the exception of the capital and the route from there to Veracruz, and at the **Congress of Chilpancingo** he declared the abolition of slavery and the equality of the races. The royalists, however, fought back with a series of crushing victories. Morelos was executed in 1815, and his forces, led by **Vicente Guerrero**, were reduced to carrying out the occasional minor raid.

Ironically, it was the introduction of liberal reforms in Spain, of just the type feared by the Mexican ruling classes, which finally brought about **Mexican**

Independence. Worried that such reforms might spread across the Atlantic, many creoles pre-empted a true revolution by assuming a "revolutionary" guise themselves. In 1820, **Agustín de Iturbide**, a royalist general but himself a *mestizo*, threw in his lot with Guerrero; in 1821, he proposed the **Iguala Plan** to the Spanish authorities, who were hardly in a position to fight, and Mexico was granted independence. With self-determination, though, came none of the changes which had been fought over for so long – the Church retained its power, and one set of rulers had simply been changed for another, local set.

Foreign intervention

In 1822, Iturbide proclaimed himself emperor; a year later, deserted by many of his former allies, he was forced to abdicate and go into exile, and a year after that, attempting to return to the country, he was arrested and executed by firing squad. It was the first of many such events in a century which must rank among the most confused – and disastrous – in any nation's history. Not only had Independence brought no real social change, it had left the new nation with virtually no chance of successful government: the power of the Church and of the army was far greater than that of the supposed rulers; there was no basis on which to create a viable economy; and if the state hadn't already been bankrupted by the Independence struggle, it was to be cleaned out time and again by the demands of war and internal disruption. There were no fewer than 56 governments in the next forty years. In what approaches farce, the name of **General Antonio López de Santa Anna** stands out as the most bizarre figure of all – the man became president or dictator on eleven separate occasions and masterminded the loss of more than half of Mexico's territory.

Santa Anna's first spell in office immediately followed Iturbide – he declared Mexico a **republic** (although he himself always expected to be treated as a king, and addressed as His Most Serene Majesty) and called a constitutional convention. Under the auspices of the new constitution, the republic was confirmed, the country divided into thirteen states, and **Guadalupe Victoria**, a former guerrilla general, elected its first president. He lasted three years, something of a record. In 1829, the Spanish attempted a rather half-hearted **invasion**, easily defeated, after which they accepted the fact of Mexican independence. In 1833, Santa Anna was elected president (officially) for the first time, the fifth man to hold the post thus far.

In 1836, a rather more serious chain of events was set in motion when Texas (Mexican territory but largely inhabited by migrants from the US) declared its independence. Santa Anna commanded a punitive expedition that besieged **the Alamo** in the famous incident in which Jim Bowie and Davy Crockett, along with 150 other defenders, lost their lives. Santa Anna himself, though, was promptly defeated and captured at the battle of San Jacinto, and rather than face execution he signed a paper accepting **Texan independence**. Although the authorities in Mexico refused to accept the legality of its claim, Texas was, de facto, independent. Meanwhile, in 1838, the French chose to invade **Veracruz**, demanding compensation for alleged damages to French property and citizens; the "Pastry War" (so called on account of one of the French claimants, who owned a *patisserie* in Mexico City) lasted about four months, during which Santa Anna lost a leg.

In 1845, the US annexed Texas, and although the Mexicans at first hoped to negotiate a settlement, the redefinition of Texas to include most of Arizona, New Mexico and California made yet another war almost inevitable. In 1846, clashes between Mexican troops and US cavalry in these western zones led to the declaration of the **Mexican-American War**. Following defeats for the Mexicans at Palo Alto and Resaca, three small US armies invaded from the north. At the same time

General Winfield Scott took Veracruz after a long bombardment, and commenced his march on the capital. Santa Anna was roundly defeated several times, and in September 1847, after legendary resistance by the Niños Héroes (cadets at the military academy), Mexico City itself was captured. In 1848, by the **Treaty of Guadalupe Hidalgo**, the US paid $15 million for most of Texas, New Mexico, Arizona and California, along with parts of Colorado and Utah; in 1854, the present borders were established when Santa Anna sold a further strip down to the Río Grande for $10 million under the **Gadsden Purchase**.

Reform

Mexico finally saw the back of Santa Anna when, in 1855, he left for exile in Venezuela, but the country's troubles were by no means at an end. A new generation had grown up, knowing only an independent Mexico in permanent turmoil and espousing once more the liberal ideals of Morelos. Above all, this generation saw its enemy as **the Church**: immense, self-serving and far wealthier than any legitimate government, it had further sullied its reputation by refusing to provide funds for the American war. Its position enshrined in the constitution, it was an extraordinarily reactionary institution, bleeding the peasantry for the most basic of sacraments (few could afford official marriage, or burial) and failing to provide the few services with which it was charged. All education was in Church schools, which for 95 percent of the population meant no education at all.

Benito Juárez, a Zapotec Indian who had been adopted and educated by a priest and trained as a lawyer, led this liberal movement through several years of civil war. When the **liberals** first came to power following Santa Anna's exile they began relatively mild attempts at **reform**: permitting secular education, liberating the press, attempting to distance the Church from government and instituting a new democratic constitution. The Church responded by threatening to excommunicate anyone co-operating with the government. In 1858, there was a conservative coup, and, for the next three years, **internal strife** on an unprecedented scale. With each new battle the liberals proclaimed more drastic reforms, churches were sacked and priests shot, while the conservatives responded by executing anyone suspected of liberal tendencies. In 1861, Juárez emerged triumphant, at least temporarily. Church property was confiscated, monasteries closed, weddings and burials became civil affairs and set fees were established for the services of a priest.

It wasn't until 1867 that most of these **Reform Laws** were fully enacted, though, for the conservatives had one more card to play. At the end of the civil war, with the government bankrupt, Juárez had suspended payment of all foreign debts, and in 1861 a joint British, Spanish and French expedition occupied Veracruz to demand compensation. It rapidly became clear, however, that the French were after more than mere financial recompense. Britain and Spain withdrew their forces, and Napoleon III ordered his troops to advance on Mexico City. Supported by Mexican conservatives, the aim was to place **Maximilian**, a Habsburg archduke, on the throne as emperor.

Despite a major defeat at **Puebla** on May 5, 1862 (now a national holiday), the French sent for reinforcements and occupied Mexico City in 1863. The new emperor arrived the following year. In many ways, Maximilian was a pathetic figure. He came to Mexico with almost no knowledge of its internal feuds (having gleaned most of his information from a book on court etiquette), and expecting a victorious welcome. A liberal at heart – he refused to repeal any of Juárez's reforms – he promptly lost the support of even the small group of conservatives that had initially welcomed him. While his good intentions seem undeniable, few believe that he would have been capable of putting them into practice even in the best of circumstances. And these were hardly ideal times. With Union victory in the **US Civil War**, the authorities there threw their weight behind Juárez, providing him with arms and threatening to invade unless the French withdrew (on the basis of the Monroe doctrine: America for the Americans). Napoleon, already worried by the growing power of Bismarck's Prussia back home, had little choice but to comply. After 1866 Maximilian's position was hopeless.

His wife, the Empress Carlota, sailed to Europe to win fresh support, but Napoleon had made his decision, and the Vatican refused to contemplate helping a man who had continued to attack the Church. The constant disappointments eventually drove Carlota mad; she died, insane, in Belgium in 1927. Maximilian, meanwhile, stayed at the head of his hopelessly outnumbered troops to the end – May 15, 1867 – when he was defeated and captured at **Querétaro**. A month later, he faced the firing squad.

Juárez reassumed power, managing this time to ride through the worst of the inevitable bankruptcy. The first steps towards **economic reconstruction** were taken, with the completion of a railway from Veracruz to the capital, encouragement of industry and the development of a public education programme. Juárez died in office in 1872, having been re-elected in 1871, and was succeeded by his vice-president, **Sebastián Lerdo de Tejada**, who continued on the same road, though with few new ideas.

Dictatorship

Tejada was neither particularly popular nor spectacularly successful, but he did see out his term of office. However, there were several Indian **revolts** during his rule and a number of plots against him, the most serious of them led by a new radical liberal, **Porfirio Díaz**. Díaz had been a notably able military officer under Juárez, and in 1876, despite the re-election of Tejada, he proclaimed his own candidate president. The following year he assumed the presidency himself, then consolidated power to effectively become dictator for the next 34 years. At first his platform was a radical one – including full implementation of the Reform Laws and a decree of no re-election to any political office – but this was soon dropped in favour of a brutal policy of **modernization**. Díaz did actually stand down at the end of his first term in 1880, but he continued to rule through a puppet president, Manuel González, and in 1884 resumed the presidency for an unbroken stretch until 1911.

In many ways the **achievements** of his dictatorship were remarkable: some 16,000km of railway were built, industry boomed, telephones and telegraph were installed and major towns, reached at last by reasonable roads, entered the modern era. In the countryside, Díaz established a police force – the notorious *rurales* – which stamped out much of the banditry that had plagued the nation. Almost every city in Mexico seems to have a grandiose theatre and elegant public buildings from this era. But the costs were high: rapid development was achieved basically by handing over the country to **foreign investors**, who owned the majority of the oil, mining rights, railways and other natural resources. At the same time, there was a policy of massive land expropriation, in which formerly communal village holdings were handed over to foreigners or simply grabbed by corrupt officials.

Agriculture, meanwhile, was ignored entirely. The owners of vast haciendas could make more than enough money by relying on the forced labour of a landless peasantry, and had no interest in efficiency or production for domestic consumption. By 1900 the whole of Mexico was owned by some three to four percent of its population. Without land of their own, peasants had no choice but to work on haciendas or in forests, where their serfdom was ensured by wages so low that they were permanently in debt to their employers. The rich became very rich indeed, while the poor had lower incomes and fewer prospects than they had a century earlier.

Once the *rurales* had done their job by making the roads safe to travel, they became a burden – charging for the right to travel along roads they controlled and acting as a private police force for employers. In short, slavery was reintroduced in all but name, and up to a quarter of the nation's resources came to be spent on internal security. The press was censored, education strictly controlled and **corruption** rife.

Revolution

By the onset of the **twentieth century**, Díaz was old and beginning to lose his grip on reality. While he had every intention of continuing in power until his death, a real middle-class opposition began to develop, concerned above all by the racist policies of their government (which favoured foreign investors above native ones) and by the lack of opportunity for themselves – the young educated classes. Their movement popularized the slogan of "no reelección", and in 1910 **Francisco Madero** stood against Díaz in the presidential election. The dictator responded by imprisoning his opponent and declaring himself victor. Madero, however, escaped to Texas, where he proclaimed himself president, and called on the nation to support him.

This was an entirely opportunist move, for at the time there were no revolutionary forces, but several small bands immediately took up arms. Most important were those in the northern state of Chihuahua, where **Pancho Villa** and **Pascual Orozco** won several minor battles, and in the southwest, where **Emiliano Zapata** began to arm Indian guerrilla forces. In May 1911, Orozco captured the major border town of Ciudad Juárez, and his success was rapidly followed by a string of Revolutionary victories. By the end of the month, hoping to preserve the system, if not his own role in it, Porfirio Díaz had fled into exile. On October 2, 1911, Madero was elected president. Like the originators of the independence movement before him, Madero had no conception of the forces he had unleashed. He freed the press, encouraged the formation of unions and introduced genuine **democracy**, but failed to do anything about the condition of the peasantry or the redistribution of land. Zapata prepared to act again.

Emiliano Zapata was perhaps the one true revolutionary in the whole long conflict to follow. His battle cry of "**¡Tierra y libertad!**" ("Land and liberty!") and his insistence that "it is better to die on your feet than live on your knees" still make him a revered figure among the peasants – and revolutionaries of the namesake EZLN – of the present day. By contrast, the rest were mostly out for personal gain: Pancho Villa, a cattle rustler and bandit in the time of Díaz, was by far the most successful of the more orthodox generals, brilliantly inventive, and ruthless in victory. But his motivation seems to have been personal glory. He appeared to love fighting, and at one stage, when a Hollywood film crew was travelling with his armies, allegedly arranged his battles so as to ensure the best lighting conditions and most impressive fight scenes. (The result was the silent film *Life of Villa*, released in 1912.)

In any case, Madero was faced by a more immediately dangerous enemy than his own erstwhile supporters: US business interests. **Henry Lane Wilson**, US ambassador, began openly plotting with **Victoriano Huerta**, a government general, and **Felix Díaz**, a nephew of the dictator, who was held in prison. Fighting broke out between supporters of Díaz and those of Madero, while

Huerta refused to commit his troops to either side. When he did, in 1913, it was to proclaim himself president. Madero was shot in suspicious circumstances (few doubt an assassination sanctioned by Huerta), and opponents on the right, including Díaz, either imprisoned or exiled. The new government was promptly recognized by the US and most other foreign powers, but not by Madero's former supporters within the country.

Constitution versus Convention

Villa and Zapata immediately took up arms against Huerta, and in the north Villa was joined by **Alvaro Obregón**, governor of Sonora, and **Venustiano Carranza**, governor of Coahuila. Carranza was appointed head of the **Constitutionalist** forces, though he was always to be deeply suspicious of Villa, despite Villa's constant protestations of loyalty. At first the Revolutionaries made little headway – Carranza couldn't even control his own state – although Obregón and Villa did enjoy some success raiding south from Chihuahua and Sonora. But almost immediately the new US president, **Woodrow Wilson**, withdrew his support from Huerta and, infuriated by his refusal to resign, began supplying arms to the Revolution.

In 1914, the Constitutionalists began to move south, and in April of that year US troops occupied Veracruz in their support (though neither side was exactly happy about the foreign presence). Huerta, now cut off from almost every source of money or supplies, fled the country in July, and in August Obregón occupied the capital, proclaiming Carranza president.

Renewed fighting broke out straight away, this time between Carranza and Obregón, the Constitutionalists, on one side, and the rest of the Revolutionary leaders on the other, the so-called **Conventionalists** whose sole point of agreement was that Carranza should not lead them. The three years of fighting that followed were the most bitter and chaotic yet, with petty chiefs in every part of the country proclaiming provisional governments, joining each other in factions and then splitting again, and the entire country in a state of anarchy. Each army issued its own money, and each forced any able-bodied men it came across to join it. It was reckoned that about 900,000 people were killed between 1910 and 1921, out of a total population of 15 million.

Gradually, however, Obregón and Carranza gained ground – Obregón defeated Villa several times in 1915, and Villa withdrew to carry out raids into the US, in the hopes of provoking an invasion (which he nearly did: US troops led by General "Black Jack" Pershing pursued him across the border but were never able to catch up, and withdrew following defeat in a skirmish with Carranza's troops). Zapata, meanwhile, had some conspicuous successes – and occupied Mexico City for much of 1915 – but his troops tended to disappear back to their villages after each victory. In 1919, he was tricked into a meeting with one of Carranza's generals and assassinated. Villa retired to a hacienda in his home state and was murdered in 1923.

The end of the Revolution

Meanwhile, Carranza continued to claim the presidency, and in 1917 he set up a constitutional **congress** to ratify his position. The document it produced – the present constitution – included most of the Revolutionary demands, among them workers' rights, a mandatory eight-hour working day, national ownership of all mineral rights and the distribution of large landholdings and formerly communal properties to the peasantry. Carranza was formally elected in May 1917 and proceeded to make no attempt to carry out any of its stipulations, certainly not with regard to land rights. In 1920, Carranza was forced to step down by Obregón, and was shot while attempting to escape the country with most of the contents of the treasury.

Obregón, at least, was well intentioned – but his efforts at land reform were again stymied by fear of US reaction: in return for American support, he agreed not to expropriate land. In 1924, **Plutarco Elias Calles** succeeded him and initiated some real progress towards the ideals of the Revolutionary constitution. Work on large public-works schemes began – roads, irrigation systems, village schools – and about eight million acres of land were given back to the villages as communal holdings. At the same time, Calles instituted a policy of virulent **anticlericalism**, closing churches and monasteries and forcing priests to flee the country or go underground.

These moves provoked the last throes of a backlash, as the **Catholic Cristero** movement took up arms in defence of the Church. From 1927 until about 1935 isolated incidents of vicious banditry and occasional full-scale warfare continued, eventually burning themselves out as the stability of the new regime became obvious, and religious controls were relaxed. In 1928, Obregón was re-elected, but was assassinated three weeks later in protest at the breach of the "no reelección" clause of the constitution. He was followed by **Portes Gil**, **Ortíz Rubio** and then **Abelardo Rodríguez**, who were all controlled behind the scenes by Calles and his political allies, who steered national politics to the right in the bleak years of the 1930s Depression.

The road to modern Mexico

By 1934 Mexico enjoyed a limited degree of peace. A new culture had emerged – most boldly reflected in the great murals of **Diego Rivera** and **José Clemente Orozco** that began to adorn public buildings throughout the country – in which native heroes like Hidalgo, Morelos, Juárez and Madero replaced European ideals. Everyone in the Republic claimed Indian blood – even if the indigenous peoples themselves remained the lowest stratum of society – and the invasion of Cortés was seen as the usurpation of the nation's march to its destiny, a march which resumed with Independence and the Revolution. At the same time, there was a fear in these early days that Calles was attempting to promote a dynasty of his own.

With the election of **Lázaro Cárdenas** in 1934, such doubts were finally laid to rest. As the spokesman of a younger generation, Cárdenas expelled Calles and his supporters from the country, simultaneously renaming the broad-based party that Calles had set up the **PRI** (Party of the Institutional Revolution); it was to stay in power for the rest of the century. Cárdenas set about an unprecedented programme of reform, redistributing land on a huge scale (170,000 square kilometres during his six-year term), creating peasant and worker organizations to represent their interests at national level and incorporating them into the governing party. He also relaxed controls on the Church to appease internal and international opposition.

In 1938, Cárdenas nationalized the **oil companies**, an act which has proved one of the most significant in shaping modern Mexico and bringing about its industrialization. For a time it seemed as if yet more foreign intervention might follow, but a boycott of Mexican oil by the major consumers crumbled with the onset of **World War II**, and was followed by a massive influx of money and a huge boost for Mexican industry as a result of the war. By the time he stood down in 1940, Cárdenas could claim to be the first president in modern Mexican history to have served his full six-year term in peace, and to have handed over to his successor without trouble.

Through the war, industrial growth continued apace under **Manual Ávila Camacho**, and Mexico officially joined the Allies in 1942. **Miguel Alemán** (1946–52) presided over still faster development, and further extensive public works and land reform – major prestige projects, like the University City in the capital, were planned by his regime. Over the next thirty years or so, massive oil income continued to stimulate industry, and the PRI maintained a masterly control of all aspects of public life. Though it was an accepted fact that governments would line their own pockets first – a practice which allegedly reached its height under **José López Portillo** (1976–82) – the unrelenting populism of the PRI, its massive powers of patronage and, above all, its highly visible and undoubted progress maintained it in power with amazingly little dissent.

This is not to say there were no problems. **1959** saw the repression of a national railway strike during which ten thousand workers lost their jobs and their leaders were jailed. In **1968**, hundreds of students were massacred in Tlatelolco Square in Mexico City in the government's heavy-handed attempt to stem the pro-democracy student movement that threatened Mexico's image as the Olympic Games neared (Mexico's were the first Olympics to be held in the "Third World" and were seen as an opportunity to promote the regime). The PRI was unable to buy off the students due to their rotating leadership, and unwilling to negotiate for fear of losing face. Although the massacre did put an end to student unrest, or at least any public manifestation of it, after Tlatelolco the opposition gradually saw fewer reasons for working within the system; guerrilla movements sprang up in Guerrero state, for example. The PRI was still very much in control, though, and snuffed out these movements by the mid-1970s.

Economic crisis

By the 1980s, however, the PRI was losing its populist touch. The years between 1970 and 1982, later dubbed the "**Docena Trágica**" (tragic dozen), saw rapid growth based on booming oil prices. But this growth was accompanied by inflation and devaluation of the peso; vast sums were misappropriated, corruption flourished as never before, and by 1982 Mexico had run up a foreign debt of almost $100 billion, borrowed against future oil earnings. When the 1980s bubble burst and the price of oil collapsed, the government of **Miguel de la Madrid** (1982–88) found itself faced with unprecedented economic crisis on a national and international scale. A US-educated financier, he adopted **austerity measures** imposed by the World Bank. Such policies won acclaim from international bankers, but at home they produced massive unemployment and drastically reduced standards of living (the average wage-earner lost fifty percent of his or her purchasing power), and inflation was barely held down to one hundred percent a year. An exploding population only added to the country's problems, and the huge level of illegal **emigration** to the US had little impact. Some of the wide panoply of interests covered by the PRI – from the all-powerful unions to the top businessmen – began to split off.

This movement against the PRI was accelerated in 1985, when a huge **earthquake** hit the capital. The quake revealed widespread corruption – many of the buildings that collapsed were government-owned and turned out to have been constructed using inferior materials – exacerbated by inadequate official rescue efforts. The country became increasingly polarized: in the relatively wealthy, US-influenced north, the right-wing **PAN** (National Action Party) won a string of minor elections, while in the south opposition was far more radical and left-wing: a socialist/peasant alliance held power for a while in Juchitán (Oaxaca) before being ousted by strong-arm tactics.

In this climate, the **1988 election** was tainted by allegations of fraud. Predictably, the PRI candidate, **Carlos Salinas de Gortari**, was declared the comfortable winner. It is widely believed, however, that **Cuauhtémoc Cárdenas**, son of the much loved Lázaro, actually gained the majority of the votes, having split from the PRI and succeeded in uniting the Mexican left for the first time since the Revolution.

Salinas continued on the path of economic and political reform, attempting at least to attack corruption and liberalize the economy. His policies, however, while popular overseas and with the elite at home, were disastrous domestically. By 1993, nearly forty million Mexicans were living below the official **poverty** line (about half the population), while 24 were listed in the Forbes list of the 500 wealthiest men in the world, most grown rich on privatized utilities. To boost foreign investment, Salinas expanded the "**maquiladora**" programme, which allowed foreign companies to set up assembly plants along the US-Mexican border while enjoying substantial tax concessions. He also pushed through the North American Free Trade Agreement (**NAFTA**; **TLC** in Spanish), which created a free market between Canada, the US and Mexico. None of this was popular, especially among those on the left, but perhaps the most important change from a domestic point of view was the amendment of Article 27 of the constitution. This article had been written to protect communal village landholdings, known as **ejidos**; under Salinas, their status shifted from state property to private property, allowing them to be sold.

The Chiapas uprising

On New Year's Day 1994, NAFTA took effect and at the same time an armed guerrilla movement known as the **Zapatista Army of National Liberation** (EZLN) took control of San Cristóbal de las Casas and four other municipalities in the state of Chiapas. The guerrillas were mainly indigenous villagers, and their action took the country almost entirely by surprise; they demanded an end to the feudal system of land tenure in Chiapas, free elections, the repeal of NAFTA and the restoration of Article 27 of the constitution. The government reacted with a predictable use of force, committing numerous human-rights abuses along the way, including the bombing of civilians and the torture and murder of prisoners, particularly in the town of Ocosingo. Long hidden from the world, the repressive side of the Mexican state – together with the plight of the country's indigenous peoples – was front-page news throughout the world. To Salinas's credit, he prepared the ground for peace negotiations by ordering a ceasefire within twelve days.

At the beginning, **negotiations** progressed with remarkable speed as the government made concessions to the guerrillas. The star of the talks was **Subcomandante Marcos**, the main spokesman for the Zapatistas. The balaclava-clad, pipe-smoking guerrilla became a cult hero, his speeches and communiqués full of literary allusions and passionate rhetoric (he was later exposed as, allegedly, Rafael Guillén, a philosophy professor from Mexico City, though this did little to dent his popularity). Negotiations ended in March, when an accord was drawn together. The EZLN then sent the accord back to its community bases for them to vote on it, a process complicated by the inaccessibility of many villages and the different languages and dialects spoken. While the accord was being considered, the army and the guerrillas maintained an uneasy truce, and Mexicans were given ample time to dwell on events in Chiapas.

In the meantime, with elections due, Mexico was hit by a wave of **political assassinations**, in particular of leading PRI figures. Many believe that these were linked to internal party disputes, as the so-called party "dinosaurs" felt threatened by moves to democratize the political system and to attack corruption. Senior members of the PRI were also implicated in money laundering, presumably linked to the drug trade.

In June the EZLN rejected the accord with the government, and in July a leftist candidate for the governorship of Chiapas, Amado Avendaño Figueroa, met with a suspicious "accident" when a truck with no numberplates collided with his car, killing three passengers; Avendaño lost an eye. In national elections in August the PRI triumphed, helped by an electorate that had been shaken by the uprising. **Ernesto Zedillo** was declared president in what appeared a relatively clean election, the party also sweeping up most senate and governorship posts that were on offer

In **Chiapas**, however, where the PRI also claimed to have won the governorship, Avendaño declared himself "rebel governor" after denouncing the elections as fraudulent; as many as half the municipalities in the state refused to pay taxes. Both the **PRD** (the left-wing alliance formed by Cuauhtémoc Cárdenas) and the EZLN supported his move. The EZLN warned that if the PRI candidate, Eduardo Robledo, was sworn in, the truce with the government would be at an end. By this point Chiapas was essentially in a state of **civil war**. Ranchers and landowners organized paramilitary **death squads** to counter a mobilized peasantry. Land seizures and roadblocks were met with assassinations and intimidation, and a build-up of federal troops in the state only made things worse. On January 8, 1995, Zedillo attended the swearing-in of the PRI governor of Chiapas. Ten days later, the EZLN deployed its forces, breaking the army cordon surrounding its positions and moving into 38 municipalities (it had previously been confined to four). That this was accomplished, as was their later retreat, virtually undetected, right under the noses of government troops, showed their familiarity with the terrain, their discipline and the folly of the "surgical strike" tactic that many in the military had been contemplating.

In the meantime the Mexican economy was once again under immense pressure, with foreign investors deserting the country in the face of the uncertainty. The government briefly launched an offensive against the EZLN, resulting in thousands of peasants, terrified by the army and by right-wing landowners' paramilitary groups, becoming internal refugees. The EZLN, though, enjoyed considerable public sympathy, especially in view of its largely non-violent methods, and the government was forced to call off the army and set up **new negotiations**.

These proved to be even more protracted than the 1994 talks, but eventually resulted in the **San Andrés Accords on Rights and Indigenous Cultures** (named after the village near San Cristóbal where the talks took place), signed in February 1996. The accords guaranteed indigenous representation in national and state legislatures, but to this day they have not been fully implemented. For a while relations between the Zapatistas and the government hit a new low, while the remorseless increase of the military presence on the Zapatistas' perimeter appeared to give the paramilitary groups even greater freedom to operate. This culminated in the December 1997 **Acteal Massacre**: 45 displaced Tzotzil Indians, 36 of them women and children, were murdered at a prayer meeting by forces linked to PRI officials. The killings brought worldwide condemnation, and at last some action from the government, with a purge of the local government and military.

In the twenty-first century, an uneasy peace continues to reign in Chiapas. Recent governments have made some progress at least in implementing the San Andres accords, but there's still a heavy military presence in the state, where the EZLN continues to wield a huge amount of influence. They have attempted to expand their non-violent campaigning methods across the country and to a broader spectrum of the population, allying with unions and urban groups on the left.

The new millennium

Despite the crisis in Chiapas, Mexico's **political reforms** continued, with limits on campaign spending and the establishment of a federal electoral body in 1996. The following year, the PRI lost its majority in the Chamber of Deputies (the lower house of Congress) as well as control of Mexico City, where a PRD mayor was elected. But the biggest change of all came on July 2, 2000, when **Vicente Fox Quesada**, the PAN candidate, was voted in as president. It was a landmark event: not only was he the first opposition candidate ever to have been democratically placed in power, it was also the first peaceful transition between opposing governments since Independence. Most remarkably, though, it was the end of seven decades of PRI rule – the world's longest-lasting one-party dynasty, surpassing even the Soviet Communist party.

A former Coca-Cola executive and governor of Guanajuato, the media-savvy, fiscally conservative Fox had wooed the business sector and wowed the general public with his campaign promise of *cambio* ("change"), encouraging hopes that he would shake up the system of political patronage and corruption. However, little of the much-vaunted *cambio* was realized: Fox's ambitions for constitutional and structural reforms were hampered by the fractured nature of PAN and by the PRI, which still controlled Congress, more than half the state governorships and most of the bureaucracy. In spite of his political shortcomings, however, the president for the most part retained his popularity, and set the stage well for the July 2006 election – which, in many ways, was even more crucial than the previous one, as it would either prove the PAN victory a fluke or help consolidate the party's power.

Unfortunately, it is still not clear whether PAN passed its test. Fox's would-be successor was **Felipe Calderón**. His campaign started easily enough, with polls showing him well ahead of his main opponent, the PRD's **Andrés Manuel López Obrador**, the popular leftist former mayor of Mexico City, with the PRI nowhere. But allegations about Calderón's financial dealings, a ruthless assault on a teachers' sit-in in **Oaxaca** and the EZLN-led **Otra Campaña** ("other campaign", with Subcomandante Marcos himself as "Candidate Zero"), which endorsed no candidate but drummed up fervour for workers' rights and other populist issues, helped boost Obrador's standing. The official election **results** took four days to deliver, and showed Calderón winning by a margin of just 0.58 percent, or 243,934 votes. The numbers told the story of a divided Mexico – every state north of the capital (for the most part, the wealthier part of the country) supported Calderón, while Obrador took all of the poor, southern states with large indigenous populations. The only exception in the south was Yucatán state, not coincidentally home to a substantial upper class.

With the decision so close, the battle immediately went to the courts. Obrador alleged irregularities and demanded a complete recount. Millions of his supporters took to the streets, occupying the Zócalo in Mexico City and scores of other cities. After the electoral court confirmed Calderón's victory in late August, Obrador declared himself head of an **alternative government**, and urged his followers to continue their resistance. Meanwhile, the confrontation in Oaxaca had grown more violent – another uncomfortable reminder that Mexico had not completely shed its "Third World" image. After several deaths, heavily armed *federales* were sent in, facing down rock-throwing protesters amid the rubble that once was a gem of a colonial plaza.

Many Mexicans were simply relieved when Calderón was sworn in to the presidency peacefully on December 1, 2006. Legitimate or not, his government has been widely accepted as the initial outrage faded away; ironically it has perhaps helped that PAN does not control a majority of either the Congress or the Senate. Despite relative stability and continuing economic growth (Mexico has the eleventh largest economy in the world), the nation continues to face huge **challenges**. The outbreak of **swine flu** in 2009 did nothing to help tourism or the country's international image, while Mexico's relationship with the US, if better than it sometimes has been, remains problematic – the 370-mile **border fence** proposed by President Bush in 2006 was a rather brutal symbol of how intractable the debate over **illegal immigration** has become. Internally, one of the main effects of the splintering of PRI dominance and the lack of a majority for the president in the legislature, has been increasing decentralization, and the **devolution of power to the states**. Since the PRI and the PRD control many state governorships, their representatives are keen to see more power at state level, and commonly trade this off for support for government initiatives; whether this is a sensible policy at the national level, and whether they will regret it should they gain the presidency, remains to be seen.

Drugs, however, dominate the agenda and the headlines. Calderón has determined to face the problem head-on, and committed 45,000 army personnel, as well as 5000 *federales*, to what can only be described as a war against the cartels that control the transportation of drugs through Mexico, and across the border to the US (as well as feeding a growing internal drug culture). Casualties in this war are high, and the government is hampered by the vast wealth of the drug barons and the corruption this entails; few local police forces are untainted (hence the deployment of the army and federal police), and senior politicians continue to be implicated. At least 10,000 people are thought to have been killed in drug-related violence in the first three years of Calderón's regime (some put the figure much higher) – the majority in fighting between the cartels, or in revenge attacks by them. This, even more than ongoing divisions in the south, seems the greatest threat to Mexico's stability.

Chronology

11,000 BC ▶ First waves of Stone Age migrants from the north. Earliest evidence of humans in the central valleys.

8000–2000 BC ▶ Archaic period. First evidence of settlement – cultivation, pottery and tools in the Valley of México.

2000 BC–250 AD ▶ Pre-Classic period. The first simple pyramids and magnificent statuary at the Gulf coast sites – San Lorenzo, La Venta and Tres Zapotes. Rise and dominance of the Olmecs, whose influence is seen everywhere, especially Monte Albán. Early evidence of new cultures in the Valley of México – Cuicuilco and Teotihuacán.

250–900 AD ▶ Classic period. Teotihuacán dominates central Mexico, with evidence of its influence as far south as Kaminaljuyu in Guatemala. Massive pyramids at Teotihuacán, decorated with stucco reliefs and murals. Monte Albán continues to thrive, while El Tajín on the Gulf coast shows a new style in its Pyramid of the Niches. Maya cities flourish in the highlands of Guatemala and Honduras, as well as the Mexican Yucatán: all the great sites – Uxmal, Palenque, Chichén Itzá, Edzná, Kabáh – are at their peak.

900–1520 AD ▶ Post-Classic period. In central Mexico, a series of invasions by warlike tribes from the north. Toltecs make their capital at Tula (c.900–1150); new use of columns and roofed space – Chac-mools and Atlantean columns in decoration. At Chichén Itzá, a revived city demonstrates new styles, possibly the result of contact with Tula.

C10 ▶ Mixtecs gain control of Oaxaca area. Mixtec tombs at Monte Albán, but seen above all at Mitla.

C11 ▶ League of Mayapán, a confederation of city-states in the Yucatán. Maya architecture in decline, as Mayapán itself clearly demonstrates.

C13 ▶ Arrival of the Mexica in central Mexico. Many rival cities in the Valley of México, including Tenayuca, Texcoco and Culhuacán.

1345 ▶ Foundation of Tenochtitlán – rapid expansion of the Aztec empire and growth of all the great Aztec cities, especially Tenochtitlán itself. In the east, cities such as Cholula and Zempoala fall under Aztec influence, and in the south the Mixtecs are conquered. To the west, Purépecha (or Tarascan) culture is developing, with their capital at Tzintzuntzan. Maya culture now concentrated in coastal cities such as Tulum.

1519 ▶ Cortés lands in present-day Veracruz.

1521 ▶ Tenochtitlán falls to the Spanish, who destroy many ancient cities. Early colonial architecture is defensive and fortress-like; churches and mansions constructed in Mexico City and elsewhere; monasteries with huge atriums for mass conversions. Gradually replaced by more elaborate Renaissance and Plateresque styles.

1524 ▶ First Franciscan monks arrive.

1598 ▶ Conquest officially complete.

C17–C18 ▶ Colonial rulers grow in wealth and confidence. Baroque style dominates new religious architecture – great cathedrals at Mexico City and

Puebla, lesser ones at Zacatecas, for example. Towards the end the still more extravagant churrigueresque style appears: magnificent churches around Puebla and at Taxco and Tepotzotlán.

1810 ▸ Hidalgo proclaims Independence. Development of the Neoclassical style through the influence of the new San Carlos art academy.

1821 ▸ Independence achieved.

1836 ▸ Texas declares independence – battles of the Alamo and San Jacinto.

1838 ▸ Brief French invasion.

1845 ▸ Texas allies with the US in the Mexican-American War.

1847 ▸ US troops occupy Mexico City.

1848 ▸ Half of Mexican territory ceded to US by the Treaty of Guadalupe Hidalgo.

1858-61 ▸ Reform Wars between liberals under Benito Juárez and Church-backed conservatives. Many churches damaged or despoiled.

1861 ▸ Juárez triumphant; suspends payment of foreign debt. France, Spain and Britain send naval expeditions.

1862 ▸ Spain and Britain withdraw. Invading French army defeated on May 5.

1863 ▸ French take Mexico City. Maximilian becomes emperor.

1866 ▸ French troops withdraw.

1867 ▸ Juárez defeats Maximilian.

1876 ▸ Porfirio Díaz accedes to power. Porfiriato period sees an outbreak of Neoclassical and grandiose public building: Palacio de las Bellas Artes and Post Office in Mexico City, theatres and public buildings throughout the country.

1910 ▸ Francisco Madero stands for election, sparking the Revolution. Another period of destruction.

1911 ▸ Díaz flees into exile.

1911–17 ▸ Vicious revolutionary infighting continues.

1920 on ▸ Modern Mexico. Modern architecture in Mexico is among the world's most original and adventurous, combining traditional decorative colours and vast murals with streamlined forms and technology. The Museo Nacional de Antropología and University City in the capital are architectural highlights.

1929 ▸ PRI founded (initially known as the PRD or Party of the Democratic Revolution).

1938 ▸ Oil companies nationalized.

1994 ▸ NAFTA comes into force. Zapatista uprising.

2000 ▸ PAN candidate Vicente Fox Quesada elected president; end of PRI hegemony.

2006–present ▸ Felipe Calderón, controversially elected in 2006, institutes a fierce campaign against the drug cartels, provoking an ongoing murderous war.

The pre-Columbian belief system

The Spanish Conquest and subjugation of Mesoamerica saw the destruction of more than just the physical culture of some of the most advanced societies in the world at the time. More important for the Spanish were the suppression of "alien" cultures and the propagation of Catholicism. All traces of traditional religion and culture were to be rooted out. In their attempts to do these things, hundreds of thousands of books were burnt, priests executed and temples overturned. Such is the tenacity of traditional beliefs, though, that even five hundred years of effort have not been enough to eradicate them entirely, as anyone who has entered a rural Mexican church or witnessed the rituals of the Day of the Dead can attest.

Much of our knowledge of **ancient Mesoamerican beliefs** is derived from the surviving traditions of contemporary indigenous groups, which have been handed down through the generations. Further fragments are gleaned from various Spanish accounts, from hieroglyphs and images carved into ruined buildings, from sculpture and pottery, from jewellery retrieved from tombs and from the few surviving written records.

Shamanism: the root of Mesoamerican culture

By all appearances, the great **Mesoamerican civilizations** comprised some of the purest **theocracies** the world has known. Every aspect of life was a part of a cosmic interplay between the material world and the dreamlike spirit world. This spirit world was home to a pantheon of gods and the souls of dead ancestors. The priests and kings who governed Mesoamerica had privileged access to this realm, communicating with its denizens while in a state of trance, predicting the effect of the spiritual on the material from the motion of the stars, and maintaining the balance between the two worlds, thus avoiding misfortune or disaster. Every part of life was sacred, as were the days of the week and the cardinal points with their associated deities and spiritual properties. Every event, from the planting of crops to the waging of war, had to occur at the correct spiritual time.

This elaborate belief system had its roots in **shamanism**, whose origins pre-date agriculture and settled village life. This is still the religion of the nomadic communities of Siberia, whose ancestors were the first to populate the Americas. In the shamanic universe everything is alive, not only in the material world but, more truly, in the spiritual. A rock has a soul every bit as much as a jaguar or a human being, and this soul can be separated from the physical form, a feat achieved by spiritually adept individuals known as shamans. The shaman's soul is able to travel through the **spirit world**, communing with gods, demons or ancestors or even appearing in the material world in another form, such as an animal. But the spirit world is an ambivalent place, containing both paradise, populated by the good, and its opposite, inhabited by gods and demons and the souls of the evil.

These malevolent and benevolent forces make the relationship between the **material and spiritual worlds** a delicate one. Disease, for instance, is not merely a physical condition; it is also a spiritual one which may result from the imprisoning of a soul by an evil spirit, or some other imbalance. The shaman, in a state of trance, can correct imbalances – journeying to free the soul, and thus making the material person well again. But in the shamanic universe, you rarely get something for nothing, and if a powerful spirit or a god is involved, sacrifice may be required to recompense that spirit.

The legacy of the shaman can still be found in Mexican religion. The **Day of the Dead** celebrations have their roots in a shamanic conception of the universe, as do the rituals of modern Mexican witchcraft. The best contemporary examples, though, are the belief systems of the tribes of northern Mexico, such as the **Yaqui** (whose shamanic traditions have been immortalized by Carlos Castaneda) or the **Huichol**.

Huichol shamanism

In the province of Nayarit in the desert of northern Mexico, the **Huichol** have survived the dominance of the Aztecs, the Spanish Conquest of western Mexico, subsequent exploitation, the Revolution and the technological leaps of the twentieth century. More than any other people in Mexico, they have remained faithful to the spiritual beliefs of their ancestors, and their way of life has changed little in thousands of years.

Like all shamanic communities, the Huichol see the material and spirit worlds as two poles of one universe. The border between the two is blurred: the communities are in regular communication with their dead ancestors, most of whom live in the underworld, and who often sneak back into the world of the living to steal their maize beer. The spirit world is used as a constant reference for occurrences in the material, with shamans, known as **maracames**, providing the readings that inform the community. However, two facets of Huichol cosmology – the orientation of their sacred buildings to the four cardinal points and a belief in a "first place" where their ancestors had been gods – stand out as distinctly Mesoamerican.

The most important Huichol structures, **xirikis**, are precisely aligned with north, south, east and west, each of which has a particular spiritual connotation. Each *xiriki* is home to a disembodied ancestral shaman whose soul inhabits a quartz crystal attached to a ceremonial arrow lodged in the roof. Contemporary shamans use the spiritual strength of these crystals to travel to the Huichol spirit world.

The centre of this spirit world is called **Wirikuta**. In the everyday, physical world, this is a dull stretch of desert in northwest Mexico, some 500km from Nayarit. In the spiritual world it is the Huichol womb of creation – the ground from which the sky and the stars emerged at the beginning of time, and the paradise where humans were created by the gods, and where for a while they lived with them as equals. The Huichol frequently visit Wirikuta in pilgrimages that involve taking peyote to induce trance-like states. A shaman guide orchestrates key rituals throughout the journey to protect the pilgrims from deceitful spirits, and interprets the landscape along the way: a waterhole becomes a spiritual gateway; shreds of cactus, the bones of ancestors. Plants, animals, rivers and mountains all have associated spirits and an individual, symbolic, sacred meaning.

Every aspect of Huichol life is filled with symbolism. Their bright weavings and intricate beaded masks reflect the spiritual reality behind the material, often depicting the three most sacred symbols of all: **corn**, the substance of creation; **deer**, hunted for food but also revered; and **peyote**, the trance-inducing cactus. Gourds covered in brightly coloured beads, spelling out the wishes of their maker, are offered to the gods as sacrifices.

The Olmecs: the roots of Mesoamerican shamanism

Archeological research at **Olmec** sites tells us that many of the Huichol's beliefs were common to the first great Mesoamerican civilization, whose cities and pre-occupations formed a template traced by subsequent cultures. The Olmecs, who flourished on Mexico's Gulf coast around 1400–400 BC, were the first Mesoamerican civilization literally to set their cosmology in stone, making a record of their rulers, and the gods and spirits with whom they communed. Like the Huichol, they had a place of creation: the mighty volcano of **San Martín** in the south of modern Veracruz state. They built a replica – a sacred artificial mountain, complete with fluted sides – in their city at **La Venta**. This was the original Mesoamerican **pyramid**, a feature that recurred in virtually every society that followed: the Classic Maya conceived of their cities as a living landscape of artificial mountains and trees, while the Aztec Templo Mayor was a dual pyramid representing the two sacred mountains of Coatepec and Tonacatepetl.

Into the base of their volcano pyramid the Olmecs embedded huge stone **stelae**, one portraying ruling dignitaries communicating with gods and spirits – shamans, who, because of their crucial role in maintaining the balance between the material and spiritual, had come to govern Olmec society. Such stelae (which perhaps shrank to become the Huichol rooftop arrowheads), seem to have been regarded as embodiments of the gods or kings they represented – spiritual telephones to the dead and the divine, whose users operated them in a trance state. These were the first stelae in Mesoamerica, and later versions fill the plazas of ruined cities all over Mexico and Central America.

One stele at La Venta depicts a **World Tree**, a symbol of the "axis mundi" at the centre of the Mesoamerican universe: its roots in the earth, its branches in the heavens, linking the underworld with the earth and sky. Though this was perhaps the first such representation, World Trees have been found in cities all over Mesoamerica and are portrayed in Teotihuacán mythology and in the **Codex Borgia**, one of the most beautiful of the few surviving Aztec books. At the Maya site of Palenque there are several, including one on the lid of a ruler's sarcophagus: symbols and events of Maya mythology are written in the patterns and motion of the stars, and the ruler is shown falling through a World Tree inscribed in the night sky – the Milky Way.

Opposite Mexico's first pyramid, the Olmecs built a **gateway** to the shamanic spirit world in the form of a sunken, court-shaped plaza with an enormous pavement of blocks made of the mineral serpentine. They added two large platforms on either side of the entrance into the court and deposited huge quantities of sacred serpentine inside. These two platforms were topped with mosaics and patterns depicting aquatic plants, symbols of a gateway to the spirit world. Such symbols appeared all over Mesoamerica in the ensuing centuries, often decorating ball-courts or ceramics.

Other surviving artefacts speak of stranger shamanic aspects to Olmec religion. **Statuettes** of half-jaguar, half-human babies probably depict the awakening of latent shamanic powers and associations with spirit animals – in the Mesoamerican pantheon each soul has its companion spirit animal. **Mirrors** found at Olmec cities – made of highly polished minerals such as hematite – were symbols of portals to the spirit world, an idea developed by the Aztecs, whose god, Tezcatlipoca ("Smoking Mirror") governs shamans and sorcerers in the Toltec and Aztec pantheon. In the Aztec creation myth, Tezcatlipoca assisted Quetzalcoatl in the creation of the world.

The Olmec shaman-rulers also recompensed the gods and spirits through whom they kept the crucial balance between the material and the spiritual world. They probably developed human **sacrifice** and ritual blood-letting for this purpose. And though there were different emphases, the basic structure of Olmec society – a theocracy ruled over by a priestly and regal elite who communicated with and propitiated the spirit world through sacrifice – would change little throughout Mesoamerica until the advent of Cortés. But there were some important developments. An increasing preoccupation with divining and balancing the material and the spiritual led to the invention of the calendar and writing, and the ball-game and sacrifice became ever more crucial, particularly in central Mexico, where the appetites of the malevolent and bloodthirsty Mesoamerican gods increased with each new civilization.

The calendar

The Mesoamericans believed that the relationship between the spirit and material worlds was recorded in the stars, and that certain astronomical configurations were ominous. For both the Maya and Aztecs, the stars were embodiments of gods and the constellations re-enactments of cosmic events. This preoccupation led to the invention of the **calendar**, probably by the Zapotecs of Monte Albán around 600 BC. Subsequent depictions of calendars can be seen across the spectrum of Mesoamerican art, notably on the Aztec Piedra del Sol (Sun Stone), now in the Museo Nacional de Antropología in Mexico City, and in the paintings in Maya codices.

By the time of the Classic Maya (250–900 AD), a 260-day calendar had become the fundamental map of the relationship between the spirit and material worlds, and the highest tool of prediction and divination outside the trance state itself. Every number and day had its own significance; each of the twenty day names was connected with a specific god and a particular direction, passing in a continuous anticlockwise path from one day to the next until a cycle of time was completed. This calendar was used alongside a 365-day calendar, roughly matching the solar year, but lacking the leap days necessary to give it real accuracy. This was divided into eighteen groups of twenty days plus an unlucky additional five days. Each twenty-day grouping and each solar year also had a supernatural patron. When the two calendars were set in motion and were running concurrently, it took exactly 52 years for the cycle to repeat. In addition to these two calendars, the pre-Classic Maya developed what is known as the **Long Count**, recording the total number of days elapsed since a mythological date when the first great cycle began (August 11, 3114 BC, to be exact). For Mesoamerican civilizations, the ending of one cycle and the beginning of another heralded apocalypse and, afterwards, a new age and a reassertion of the ordered world from the disordered and demonic; one symbol of this new age was the construction of new temples over the old every 52 years. The Maya Long Count will end on **December 23, 2012**, and there are many who believe that this date will herald the end of the world.

Sacrifice

At the beginning of the 365-day cycle, the Aztecs extinguished all fires and smashed all ceramics throughout their empire. At midnight, when the fire star was seen overhead, priests ripped out the heart of a warrior and started a new fire in his chest – for the Aztecs, **sacrifice** was crucial in maintaining harmony and the continuance of cosmic events. If the forces of the spirit world were not kept in balance, chaos and death would reign.

The ruling shaman-priests were vital to the continued existence of the world, and sacrifice was one of their main tools: Mesoamericans believed that they were not so much living on borrowed time, but on time won by trickery from the gods of death. Maya vases, buried with the dead, often depict scenes from the *Popul Vuh*, the creation epic of the Quiché Maya, in which the Hero Twins defeat the **Lords of the Underworld** through a series of shamanic tricks and their skill at the ball-game. Central Mexican mythology went still further: life is not won from death, it is quite literally stolen. In one story, Quetzalcoatl and Xolotl descend to the underworld, where they trick the god of death, Mictlantecuhtli, into giving them sacred bones left over from a previous creation. These bones are taken to the paradise of **Tamoanchán** – the central Mexican equivalent of the Huichol Wirikuta, or the Olmec San Martín – where they are ground into meal. The gods then let their blood into the ground meal, and humans are born. After the creation of people, the gods convene in darkness at Teotihuacán, where they decide to create a new sun. This, too, depends on sacrifice, and the two gods hurl themselves into a fiery furnace to become the sun and the moon.

The bloody creation mythology of central Mexico is filled with the presence of the Lords of the Underworld trying to regain the life that was stolen from them; none was more preoccupied with this than the Aztecs. The Aztec empire was enslaved to the Lords of the Underworld's seemingly insatiable appetite for **human hearts** – the price of continuing life and order. The conquistador Bernal Díaz recounts the sacrifice of fattened children, women and captured warriors with horror, and concludes that the Aztec priests were slaves of the powers of darkness, an idea suggested even in their own mythology. The great Toltec prince **Topiltzin Quetzalcoatl**, renowned for his wisdom and holiness and founder of the great city of Tula, decided to make an end to human sacrifice and attempted to convince the inhabitants of Tula to give it up. He was unsuccessful, however, as the shamanic god, Tezcatlipoca, tricked the Toltecs and forced Topiltzin Quetzalcoatl into exile. Topiltzin Quetzalcoatl built a raft and left "for the east" from the Gulf coast, promising to return one day to banish false rulers and reinstate a higher order, where human sacrifice would play no part. It is a well-known irony that Cortés landed on the Gulf coast, whence Topiltzin Quetzalcoatl was said to have left, at the time predicted for his return.

The ball-game

The Mesoamerican **ball-game**, once played all over pre-Hispanic Mexico and Central America, and still played in some villages in Oaxaca and the northwest, seems to have been imbued with shamanic symbolism and the Mesoamerican mythology of death.

Like so much of Mesoamerican religious tradition, the game was developed by the Olmecs, probably from an earlier prototype. A carving dating back to 900 BC, found at the Olmec city of **San Lorenzo**, depicts a ball-player kneeling to receive a ball; ball-players were depicted at Dainzú, outside Oaxaca, sometime after 150 BC, and ball-courts appear in the pre-Classic Maya city of Izapa in Chiapas. The game was usually played in a ball-court shaped like the letter I. The players, in teams of two or three, would score points by hitting the ball with their upper arms or thighs, through hoops or at markers embedded in the court walls. Heavy bets were placed by supporters, and the penalty for losing the most important games was death (though there have been suggestions that the winners were sacrificed in some cities).

The Classic Veracruz civilization was obsessed with the ball-game – there are more than seventeen courts in their most important city, **El Tajín**. Most are covered with superb bas-reliefs showing all aspects of the game, including sacrifice: one depicts a player having his chest cut open while a grinning skeleton rises from a pot. This figure appears in many of the carvings at Tajín, and is almost certainly an underworld lord – a personification of death. In Maya mythology, the ball-game is played against the Lords of the Underworld, most famously by the Hero Twins of the *Popul Vuh*. The largest court at **Chichén Itzá** is covered in bas-reliefs of aquatic plants, which are traditionally associated with an opening to the underworld. Still more depict the death rituals that were associated with the game. One shows a player holding the severed head of a captive. The stump of his neck spouts serpents – symbols of the spiritual life force contained in blood – which transform into water lilies, showing how the sacrifice opens the way to the spirit world.

Environment and wildlife

Mexico is one of the world's most biologically diverse countries, with the second highest number of mammal species for its size (about 500), more than a thousand species of birds, at least 30,000 species of higher plants (including half of the world's pines) and more reptile species (700) than anywhere else on the globe. Many of these are endemic, and this diversity, combined with the country's vast size (1,960,000 square kilometres) and tremendous range of natural environments, make Mexico an ideal location for the visiting naturalist, irrespective of expertise.

Unfortunately, much of Mexico's natural beauty is under threat either from direct hunting or from the indirect effects of **deforestation** and **commercialization**. It is vital that visitors show a responsible attitude to the natural environment, and endeavour to support the educational programmes that are seeking to preserve these remnants. Not only is it extremely irresponsible to buy, even as souvenirs, items that involve wild animals in their production, but it is also generally **illegal** to bring them back to the UK or the US. This applies specifically to: tortoiseshell; black coral; various species of butterfly, mussels and snails; stuffed baby crocodiles; cat skins; and turtle shells. Trade in living animals, including tortoises, iguanas and parrots (often sold as nestlings) is also illegal, as is the uprooting of cacti.

Geography and climate

The distinct geographical pattern seen in Mexico, in conjunction with the climatic variation from north to south, creates a series of isolated **biomes**, each with its individual flora and fauna. The **Tropic of Cancer** divides the country laterally, technically placing half the country inside and half outside the tropics.

The predominant geographical features tend to be southward continuations of formations in the US: the **Sierra Madre Oriental** in the east is an extension of the Rocky Mountain range, while the **Sierra Madre Occidental**, to the west, is an extension of the **Sierra Nevada** range. The highlands and the intermontane basins between form the lofty **Northern Plateau**, which extends from Mexico City to the western tablelands of the US. Further south (between latitudes 18 and 20 degrees north), the range of volcanoes known as the **Sierra Volcánica Transversal** cuts across the country, from the Pacific coast almost as far as the Gulf of Mexico. The lands south of this range are primarily coastal plains and plateaus with intermittent higher ranges, such as the **Oaxaca** and **Chiapas uplands**.

Most of the landmass is subject to the prevailing **trade winds** that blow from the northeast across the Gulf of Mexico. Cool currents keep the Pacific coastal waters colder and the air drier than the Atlantic coast, while the sharp escarpments of the Sierra Madre Oriental, creating a vast rain shadow, contribute to the aridity of the Northern Plateau. Rainfall is variable, scant in the arid deserts of the north Pacific and interior sierras but extremely heavy in the tropical cloud forests and rainforests of the southeastern slopes of the **Sierra Madre del Sur** and sections of the Gulf coast (the **rainy season** extends from late May to October or November).

Vegetation

The influence of long-term **deforestation** for charcoal or slash-and-burn agriculture has substantially denuded large areas of Mexico. Today the northern mountains contain tracts of conifer, cedar and oak, especially around Durango, where the largest **pine forest** reserves are found. At lower altitudes, grass-covered **savannas** are interrupted by the occasional palm or palmetto tree, and the riverbanks are graced with poplar and willow. **Tropical rainforests**, which border the Gulf of Mexico, form a band that extends southwards from Tampico across the base of the Yucatán Peninsula and northern Oaxaca. They contain mahogany, cedar, rosewood, ebony and logwood. **Seasonal tropical forest** and **dry scrub** cover the remaining areas of the Gulf coast and the lowlands of the Pacific coast. One particularly notable tree is a single **ahuehuete** (Montezuma cypress) in the state of Oaxaca, which measures 36m around; it's alleged to be at least 1200 years old.

Extensive **mangrove forests** once lined much of the Gulf coast and the Caribbean, and grew along sheltered reaches of the Pacific shore, but tourism along the coasts has eaten away at the swamps – a short-sighted move, as runoff from the trees' root systems nourishes the coral reefs that draw tourists.

The flatter lands of the north, the north Pacific and portions of central Mexico are characterized by dry scrub and grassland – better known as the **Sonoran** and **Chihuahuan Deserts**, though they are hardly the empty sands that the term "desert" conjures. The most conspicuous vegetation here is the **cactus**. Various species adorn these flatlands: the **saguaro** is a giant, tree-like growth which can exceed 15m in height, whereas the columns of the **cereus** cactus stand in lines, not dissimilar to fence posts, and can reach 8m. Another notable variety is the **prickly pear** (*nopal*) which produces a fruit (*tuna*) that can be eaten raw or used in the production of sweets. Other harvested varieties include the pulpy-leaved **maguey cactus** (a member of the agave family), whose fermented juice forms the basis of tequila, mescal and *pulque*, and **henequen** (another agave), which was once grown extensively on the Yucatán Peninsula and used in the production of rope. The temperate grasslands are composed primarily of clumped bunch grass and wiry, unpalatable **curly mesquite**. Low-lying shrubs found amongst these grassy expanses include spindly ocotillo, **creosote** bush and palm-like **yucca**, with **mesquite** and **acacia bushes** in the more sheltered, damper areas.

Flowers are commonplace throughout Mexico and form an integral part of day-to-day life. Once, **frangipani** and **magnolia** were considered to be of such value that they were reserved for the Aztec nobility. Today the blue blossoms of **jacaranda** trees and purple and red **bougainvillea** still adorn the walls of cities and towns during the spring and summer. Even the harsh arid deserts of the north are carpeted with wild flowers during the brief spring that follows the occasional rains; the cacti blooms are particularly vivid. Many of these floral species are indigenous to Mexico, including **cosmos**, **snapdragons**, **marigolds** and **dahlias**. In the wetter areas, several species of **wild orchid** are endemic, while more than eight hundred other species have been classified from the forests of Chiapas alone.

The tropical forests provide supplies of both **chocolate** (from the cacao trees of Chiapas) and **vanilla**. Also harvested are **chicle**, from the latex of the **sapodilla** tree, used in the preparation of chewing gum, and **wild rubber** and **sarsaparilla**. The pharmaceutical industry makes use of **digitalis** from wild **foxgloves** and various **barks** used in the preparation of purges and disinfectants. One medicinal plant unique to Mexico is **Discorea composita**, which is harvested in Veracruz, Oaxaca, Tabasco and Chiapas, and is used in the preparation of a vegetable hormone that forms an essential ingredient of the contraceptive pill.

Insects

Insect life is abundant throughout Mexico, but numbers and diversity reach their peak in the tropical rainforests. For the most part, insect life makes itself known through the variety of bites and sores incurred whilst wandering through these areas: **mosquitoes** are a particular pest, with malaria still a risk in some areas. Openings in the tree canopy also attract a variety of colourful **butterflies**, **gnats** and **locusts**. The **garrapata** is a particularly tenacious tick found everywhere livestock exists, and readily attaches itself to human hosts. A range of **scorpions**, whose sting can vary from extremely painful to definitively lethal, is found throughout the country.

In the forests, long columns of **leafcutter ants** crisscross the floor in their search for tasty bits of fungus on tree bark, and surrounding tree trunks provide ideal shelter for large nests of **termites**. Carnivorous **army ants** also sweep through in waves, devouring grasshoppers and other pests but leaving greenery untouched. One species of ant, local to Tlaxcala, provides for seasonal labour twice each year: first, during the egg stage, when it is harvested for a highly prized form of caviar, and secondly during the grub stage, when it is an equally loved food source. The most spectacular insect migration can be seen in winter in eastern Michoacán, where thousands of **monarch butterflies** hatch from their larval forms en masse, providing a blaze of colour and movement (see p.374).

Fish, reptiles and amphibians

The diversity of Mexican inland and coastal habitats has enabled large numbers of both marine and freshwater species to survive. Among the freshwater species, **rainbow** and **brook trout**, **silversides** and **catfish** are particularly abundant (as are European **carp** in certain areas, where it has been introduced). The most highly regarded is a species of **whitefish** found in Laguna de Chapala and Lago de Pátzcuaro, where it forms the basis of a thriving local fishing industry.

Offshore, Mexican waters contain over one hundred marine species of significance, including varieties of tropical and temperate climates, coastal and deep waters, surface and ground feeders and sedentary and migratory lifestyles. Among the most prevalent are **goliath grouper** (which can grow up to 5m), **swordfish**, **snapper**, **king mackerel**, **snook**, **tuna**, **mullet** and **anchovy**. **Shrimp**, **crayfish** and **spiny lobster** are also important commercial species. The marine fishing grounds on the Pacific coast are at their best off the coast of Baja California, where the warmer southern waters merge with subarctic currents from the north. Similarly, deep ocean beds and coastal irregularities provide rewarding fishing in the waters of the Campeche bank in the Gulf of Mexico.

Reptiles are widely represented throughout Mexico. The lower river courses that flow through the southern forests are frequented by **iguanas**, **crocodiles** and their close relative, the **caiman**. **Lizards** range from tiny nocturnal lizards along the Gulf coast to **tropical iguanas**, which can reach up to 2m in length. **Marine turtles**, including the loggerhead, green, hawksbill and leatherback, are still found in many places on both the Atlantic and Pacific coasts, though several species are endangered. Hunting of both adults and eggs is now illegal, and a number of official and unofficial turtle sanctuaries have been established, with positive results on the population. Several kinds of **rattlesnake** are common in the deserts of northern Mexico, and further south the rainforests hold a substantial variety of other snakes, including the **boa constrictor**, **fer-de-lance**, **bushmaster** and the small **coral snake**. Amphibian life includes salamanders, several types of **frog** and one marine toad that measures up to 20cm in length.

Birds

More than five hundred species of tropical birds live in the rainforests and cloud forests of southern Mexico alone. Among these are resplendent **macaws**, **parrots** and **parakeets**, which make a colourful display as they fly amongst the dense tree canopy. The cereal-eating habits of the parrot family have not endeared them to local farmers, and for this reason (and their continuing capture for sale as pets) their numbers have been seriously depleted in recent times. Big-billed **toucans** perch on lower branches and a few larger game birds, such as **curassow**, **crested guan**, **chachalaca** and **ocellated turkey** can be seen on the ground, amid the dense vegetation.

Particularly rare are the brilliantly coloured **trogons**, including the dazzling **quetzal**, which inhabits the cloud forests of the Sierra Madre de Chiapas (in El Triunfo Reserve). The ancient Maya coveted its long, emerald-green tail feathers, which were used in priestly headdresses; its current status is severely endangered. The drier tropical deciduous forests of northern Yucatán to the east, the Pacific coastal lowlands and the interior lowlands provide an ideal habitat for several predatory birds including **owls** and **hawks**. The most familiar large birds of Mexico, however, are the carrion-eating **black** and **turkey vultures** – locally *zopilote* – often seen soaring in large groups. The Yucatán is also one of the last remaining strongholds of the small **Mexican eagle**, which features in the country's national symbol.

Large numbers of coastal lagoons provide both feeding and breeding grounds for a wide variety of aquatic birds – some of them winter visitors from the north – including **ducks**, **herons** and **grebes**. Foremost amongst these are the substantial flocks of graceful **flamingoes** which can be seen at selected sites along the western and northern coasts of the Yucatán Peninsula. In the north of Mexico, where the harsher and drier environment is less attractive, outlying towns and villages form a sanctuary for a variety of **doves** and **pigeons**, and the areas with denser cover have small numbers of **quail** and **pheasant**. Any water feature in these drier zones, as well as wetland areas further south, provides attractive migration stopover sites for North American species, including **warblers**, **wildfowl** and **waders**.

Mammals

Zoologists divide the animals of the Americas into two categories: the **Nearctic** region of the mid-latitudes, in which the native animals are of North American affinity, and the **Neotropical** region of the lower latitudes, in which the fauna is linked to that of South America. The Isthmus of Tehuantepec marks the border between these two regions, serving as a barrier to many larger mammalian species.

The Nearctic region is predominantly composed of open steppe and desert areas and higher-altitude oak and pine forests. Relatively few large mammals inhabit the highland forests, although one widespread species is the **white-tailed deer**, which is still hunted as a source of food. The northern parts of the Sierra Madre Occidental mark the southernmost extent of several typically North American mammals, such as **mountain sheep** and **black** and **brown bears**, though the latter are near extinction. Bears live in the Cumbres de Monterrey National Park, and wild horned **sheep** can be seen at the San Pedro Mártir National Park in Baja California. Other mammals include **deer**, **puma**, **lynx**, **marten**, **grey fox**, **mule sheep**, **porcupine**, **skunk**, **badger**, **rabbit** and **squirrel**. A large array of smaller **rodents**, and their natural predators, the **coyote** and the **kit fox**, are also widespread throughout the forests. Nowadays the extensive grassland plains are frequented only by sporadic herds of white-tailed deer; the days of the pronghorn and even the bison have long passed under the burden of overhunting. Within the desert scrub, the **peccary** is still widely hunted, and rodents, as ever, are in abundance, forming an ample food supply for the resident **bobcats**, **ocelots** and even the occasional **jaguar** – more commonly associated with the country's jungle regions, but also at home in the drier areas and known to roam across the US–Mexico border.

Baja California forms an outstanding wildlife sanctuary for marine mammals, harbouring nearly 40 percent of the world's species. Isla Guadalupe is one of the few remaining breeding sites of the endangered **elephant seal**, and the only known mating and nursery sites of the **grey whale** are around Guerrero Negro.

Although some southern species (notably the opossum and armadillo) have succeeded in breaching the Tehuantepec line, and now thrive in northern Mexico and the southern US, on the whole the **Neotropical** region holds a very different collection of mammals. The relationship between these species and the lush vegetation of the tropical rainforest and the highland cloud forests is particularly apparent. Many species are arboreal, living in the tree canopies: these include **spider** and **howler monkeys**, **opossums**, **tropical squirrels**, the racoon-like **coati** and the gentle **kinkajou**.

Because of the paucity of grass on the shaded forest floors, ground-dwelling mammals are relatively scarce. The largest is the **tapir**, a distant relative of the horse, with a prehensile snout, usually found near water. Two species of **peccary**, a type of wild pig, wander the forest floors seeking their preferred foods (roots, palm nuts and even snakes), and there's also the smaller **brocket deer**. The **agouti** and the spotted **cavy** are large rodents living along the streams and riverbanks. These are hunted by large cats, including the **jaguar**, **puma** and **ocelot**.

The drier tropical and subtropical forests of northern Yucatán, the Pacific coastal lowlands and the interior basins produce a more varied ground cover of shrubs and grasses, which supply food for the **white-tailed deer** and abundant small rodents, including the spiny tree **rat** and the **paca**, which in turn provide food for a variety of predators such as the **coyote**, **margay** and **jaguarundi**. Other large mammals which can still be found in small numbers are **anteaters**, **opossums** and **armadillos**. The reefs and lagoons which run along the Quintana Roo coast have small colonies of the **manatee**, or sea cow, a docile creature which feeds on sea grass.

Wildlife sites

It would be almost impossible to compile a comprehensive list of sites of wildlife interest in Mexico, particularly as so much can be seen all over the country. The following is a selection of some of the outstanding areas, particularly ones that are easily accessible or close to major tourist centres. The few zoos that exist in Mexico are generally depressing places, but there is one outstanding exception – the conservation-oriented **Zoológico Miguel Álvarez del Toro** in Tuxtla Gutiérrez (see p.689).

Baja California

The peninsula of **Baja California** is a unique part of the Mexican landmass. Its coastline provides sanctuary for a wide variety of marine mammals, including the major wildlife attraction of the area, the migratory **grey whale** (see box, p.882). The lagoons where these whales gather can also offer views of other whales, including blue, humpback, fin, minke, sperm and orca (killer whales). Dolphins, sea lions and a variety of sea birds (pelicans, ospreys, plovers and sanderlings) inhabit the lagoons too. The sparse vegetation provides roosting sites for jaegers (skuas) and peregrines, and coyotes may occasionally be seen wandering the shores.

Offshore, several small islands with protected status have been colonized by highly diverse animal communities. Furthest north is the island of **Todos Santos**, where the sandy beaches, festooned with the remnants of shellfish, are used as occasional sunning spots by the resident harbour seals. The atmosphere is ripe with an uncommon blend of guano, kelp and Californian sagebrush. The Pacific swell frequently disturbs the resting cormorants, which bask in the hot sunshine, and the skies are filled with wheeling western gulls.

Further south lies the island of **San Benito**, just northeast of the much larger Isla Cedros. San Benito provides ideal nesting grounds for migrating ospreys, which travel south from the US. The hillsides are covered by tall agave (century plants) whose brief, once-in-a-lifetime blooms add an attractive splash of colour to the slopes. These towering succulents produce a broad rosette of golden florets, which are a welcome supply of nectar for resident hummingbirds, and ravens soar above, searching for carrion. Along with Isla Cedros and the distant **Isla Guadalupe** (now a biological reserve), the island also provides a winter home to thousands of elephant seals, now happily recovering after years of overhunting. The large adult males arrive in December, and the pebbly coves are soon crammed with the noisy and chaotic colony of mothers, calves and bachelor bulls, all ruled by one dominant bull (or beach master) which can weigh up to two tonnes. The males make a terrifying spectacle as, with necks raised and heads thrown back, they echo their noisy threats to any would-be rivals.

The interior of the peninsula also has several areas of wildlife interest, many of which are now protected as nature reserves. Most significant are the national parks of the **Sierra San Pedro Mártir** and the **Desierto Central**. Here the chaparral-covered hills cede to Jeffrey pine forests and high meadows, interspersed with granite *picachos* (peaks) and volcanic mesas. The **Parque Nacional Constitución de 1857** is another green oasis in the arid lowlands, where the coniferous woodlands form a picturesque border to the central **Laguna Hanson**. These sierras are renowned for the numerous palm-filled canyons which cut deep into the eastern escarpment; they make spectacular hiking areas with their miniature waterfalls, ancient petroglyphs, caves, hot springs and groves of fan palms.

Durango

Durango lies within a dry, hilly area where the intermittent oak and pine woodland is surrounded by large expanses of low-lying scrub. These areas are frequented by large numbers of birds, whose presence is an extension of their North American range. Typical species include red-tailed hawk, American kestrel

Grey whale migration and breeding

Each year the **grey whale migration** attracts an estimated 250,000 visitors to Baja California. The whales' **migratory route** runs the length of the Pacific seaboard, from Baja to the Bering Sea and back; this is a round trip of some 20,000km – the longest recorded migration undertaken by any mammal. The whales spend the summer months feeding on the abundant krill in the Arctic and building up body reserves for the long journey south to the breeding lagoons. The migration begins as the days shorten and the pack ice thickens, with the majority of the whales arriving in January and February, though they can be observed here from December to April.

Nowadays human interest in the whales is purely voyeuristic, though times have not always been so peaceful; less than 150 years ago, the secret breeding grounds of the whales were discovered by **Charles Melville Scammon**. The Laguna Ojo de Liebre (renamed in recent times after the infamous whaler) was rapidly emptied of almost all of these magnificent beasts, and it wasn't until the establishment of **Scammon's Bay** as the world's first whale sanctuary in 1972 that their numbers began to rebound. The population in the area is currently estimated at about 20,000 – a dramatic recovery in a relatively short time span. The protected area now includes nearby San Ignacio Lagoon, forming an all-embracing national park, the **Biosfera El Vizcaíno**. San Ignacio Lagoon presents a daunting entrance of pounding surf and treacherous shoals, but inside its calmer waters flatten and spread inland for 15km towards the distant volcanic peaks of the Santa Clara mountains. Accessible points for land-based observation lie further north in the Parque Natural de Ballena Gris ("Grey Whale Natural Park").

and mockingbird. The denser, wooded areas provide the necessary cover for several more secretive varieties such as Mexican jay, acorn woodpecker, hepatic grosbeak and the diminutive Mexican chickadee. This is also an occasional haunt of the mountain lion (or puma) and the coyote. In the dry scrub, scorpions abound. Other nearby sites worthy of investigation include **El Salto** and **El Palmito**.

The Teacapán estuary

South of Mazatlán on the Pacific coast, the **Teacapán estuary** is an extensive area of sands with marshy margins: ideal feeding grounds for a variety of waders and wildfowl, including marbled godwit, greater yellowlegs and willet. Large numbers of herons and egrets feed in the shallow waters (including little green and Louisiana heron and snowy and cattle egret), while further out to sea passage birds include laughing gull, gull-billed tern and olivaceous cormorant. Most spectacular of all are the magnificent, aptly named frigate birds, which make a dramatic sight as they skim over the water's surface in their search for fish, with their long wings (sometimes more than 2m across), forked tails and hooked bills.

The rocks offshore provide a breeding site for both brown- and blue-footed boobies, and the pools at the northern end of the town, behind the large hotels, have some interesting water birds, including jacana, ruddy duck and canvasback.

San Blas

Immediately around **San Blas** are lagoons with wildlife very similar to that found in the estuary near Mazatlán; boat tours from San Blas take you out to see herons and egrets, with the possibility of seeing a caiman being the big attraction. Deeper in the wetlands the landscape forms areas of thicker scrub and at higher altitudes dense forest. In the lower-lying scrub, it is possible to see the purplish-backed jay, Gila woodpecker and tropical kingbird, while the skies above have the patrolling white-tailed kite. At higher altitudes, birdlife includes the San Blas jay, white-crowned parrot and cinnamon hummingbird. The town provides sufficient scraps for scavengers such as black and grey hawks and various rodents.

Veracruz and the Gulf coast

The eastern coastline of Mexico has attractions of its own, and none is more rewarding than the final remaining tract of rainforest on the Mexican **Gulf coast**, southeast of **Veracruz**. The vegetation is lush, the tended citrus orchards yielding to rolling tropical forest, with its dense growth of ficus, mango and banana trees and the occasional coconut palm. These trees provide cover for a colourful underlying carpet, including orchids, lemon trees, camellias, fragrant cuatismilla and gardenias. The roadsides are lined with banks of hibiscus, oleander and the pretty, white-flowered shrub known locally as *cruz de Malta*. At the centre of the whole area, **Lago de Catemaco** is outstandingly beautiful.

The surrounding forest has suffered much in recent times, and many of the larger mammals that once resided in this region are no longer to be found. One sanctuary which remains amidst this destruction is the ecological research station of **Los Tuxtlas**. Although the institute's holding is fairly small, it adjoins a much larger state-owned reserve of some 25,000 acres on the flank of the **San Martín volcano**. Despite problems of poaching and woodcutting, the area has the last remaining populations of brocket deer, black howler monkey, ocelot, jaguarundi, kinkajou and coati. It also boasts 92 species of reptile, fifty amphibians, thousands of insects and over three hundred species of birds. With patience, it is possible to see such outstanding avian varieties as the keel-billed toucan, black-shouldered kite, gold-crowned warbler, red-throated ant tanager, plain-breasted brush finch, red-lored parrot, ivory-billed woodpecker and the magnificent white hawk.

The Chiapas uplands and Palenque

In the **Chiapas uplands**, the absence of climatic moderation and coastal breezes creates dense, lush vegetation that makes it truly worthy of the name of tropical rainforest. The **Sierra Madre de Chiapas** is of particular interest, particularly the Pacific slopes at altitudes between 1500m and 2500m, as these are the last sanctuary of the endangered horned guan and azure-rumped tanager, and even the quetzal. **El Triunfo Reserve**, at 1800m in the very southeastern corner of the country, less than 50km from the Guatemalan border, makes an excellent base camp for exploration of the area. The cloud forest here is dense, and the tall epiphyte-laden trees grow in profusion on the slopes and in the valleys, in the humid conditions which occur after the morning fogs have risen (generally by early afternoon).

Another area of interest in eastern Chiapas is the **Parque Nacional Lagos de Montebello**, where more determined bird watchers may be rewarded with views of the azure-hooded jay and the barred parakeet. Human encroachment has substantially reduced the population of large mammals in the area, but small numbers of howler monkey, tapir and jaguar (known locally as *el tigre*) are a reminder of bygone days. Another speciality of the region is a vivid and diminutive tree frog, whose precise camouflage ensures that it is more often heard than seen.

At the archeological site of **Palenque** you're back among the tourists (and the howler monkeys), but the birding is unrivalled, and local species include the chestnut-headed oropendola, scaled ant pitta, white-whiskered puffbird, slaty-tailed trogon and masked tanager. In the area of marshland around the nearby **Río Usumacinta**, pinnated bittern, everglade kite and the rare lesser yellow-headed vulture have all been recorded.

The Yucatán Peninsula

The vegetation of the **Yucatán Peninsula** is influenced by its low relief and the ameliorating effects of its extensive coastline, which bring regular and fairly reliable rain along with year-round high temperatures. In the north it's predominantly dry scrub and bush, although large areas have been cleared for the cultivation of crops such as citrus fruits and henequen. To the south is lusher tropical and subtropical forest, where the effects of agriculture are less obvious and the dense forest of acacia, albizia, gumbo limbo and ceiba is in parts almost impenetrable. These form an ideal shelter for scattered populations of both white-tailed and brocket deer.

The **birdlife** on the peninsula is particularly outstanding. The abundant and spectacular birds which fill the treetops include squirrel cuckoo, citreoline trogon and Aztec parakeet, while circling in the skies above are the resident birds of prey such as the bat falcon, snail kite and the ever-present black and turkey vultures (these can be distinguished, even at great heights, as the wings of the latter are clearly divided into two bands – the darker primaries and the lighter secondaries being quite distinct). It is also possible to see all three species of Mexican toucan: collared aracari, emerald toucanet and the spectacular keel-billed. The denser areas of forest also hold small remnants of the original black howler and spider monkey populations.

Early-morning or late afternoon visits to the lesser-known **archeological sites**, where you may be the only visitor, are particularly rewarding: places like Sayil (p.785), Becán (p.762) or above all **Calakmul** (p.763). But even the most visited, like Cobá and Chichén Itzá, offer plenty of possibilities. The village of **Cobá** borders a lake with extensive reed margins along its eastern edge, which attracts a variety of water birds. Typical visitors, either migratory or resident, include the grebe, the elusive spotted rail, ruddy crake, northern jacana and the occasional anhinga – a cormorant-like bird which captures fish by spearing them with its dagger-like bill. The reed beds provide cover for several more-secretive species, including mangrove vireo, ringed kingfisher and blue-winged warbler, as well as several varieties of hirundine such as mangrove swallow and grey-breasted martin. The lake is also home to a variety of turtles and large numbers of Morelet's crocodiles.

At **Chichén Itzá**, save a little time at the end of the day for an exploration of the forested areas which lie to the south of the "Nunnery". The drier climate and lower altitude in this part of the peninsula encourage a sparser vegetation, where the oaks and pines are less obvious. The colours amongst the greenness come from a variety of splendid flowers, such as the multicoloured bougainvillea, the aromatic frangipani and the blue and mauve blooms of the jacaranda tree. Occasional splashes are added by the red bracts of the poinsettia and the brilliant yellows of golden cups. The resident birds appear oblivious to the tourists, and in the quieter areas to the south and southwest of the main site, the abundant birdlife includes the plain chachalaca, ferruginous pygmy owl, cinnamon hummingbird and turquoise-browed motmot and numerous brilliant vireos, orioles and tanagers.

Cancún, Cozumel and the Caribbean coast

Even the mega-resort of **Cancún** has wildlife-spotting possibilities: the lagoons that line the outskirts have a variety of birds (such as great-tailed grackle and melodious blackbird). These wetlands form an ideal breeding ground for a number of brilliantly coloured dragonflies and damselflies.

More importantly, the longest **barrier reef** in the Americas begins just south of the city, off the coast of **Puerto Morelos**, where the scuba diving and snorkelling are quite stunning. Formed by the limey skeletons of dozens of species of coral, the reefs show spectacular diversity, with varieties such as star, lettuce, gorgonian, elkhorn and staghorn being particularly widespread. The reefs provide food and shelter for more than four hundred species of fish, including several varieties of parrotfish, butterfly fish, beau gregories, rock beauties and porkfish; the blaze of colour is unforgettable. The coral also provides protection for other residents including spiny lobster, sea urchins, crabs and tentacled anemones.

Natural parks and nature reserves worthy of special mention include **Celestún**, on the west coast, and **Río Lagartos**, to the north. Both have spectacular flocks of migratory flamingoes, which winter here in the milder climate. The **Isla Contoy** bird sanctuary off the northeastern tip of the peninsula is a worthwhile and popular day trip from Cancún, and **Isla Holbox**, off the north coast, is the closest point to an annual gathering of more than one hundred whale sharks. The largest **botanic garden** in Mexico is near Puerto Morelos.

Playa del Carmen is frequented by various wetland species including American wigeon, and the ferry trip to **Cozumel** island produces sightings of sea birds such as royal and Caspian terns, black skimmer, frigate birds and Mexican sheartails. On Cozumel, the most rewarding sites are a couple of kilometres inland on the main road that runs across the island. The sparse woodland and hedgerows provide shelter for many typical endemics, such as Caribbean dove, lesser nighthawk, Yucatán and Cozumel vireo, the splendid bananaquit and a variety of tanagers. Elusive species which require more patient exploration (best through the mangroves which lie 3km north of **San Miguel** along the coast road) are the mangrove cuckoo, yellow-lored parrot, Caribbean ealania and Yucatán flycatcher. Cozumel, though, is better known for the **coral reefs** that ring the island, some of Mexico's finest.

The highlight of the peninsula's protected areas is the magnificent **Sian Ka'an Biosphere Reserve**, which includes coral reef, mangroves, fresh- and salt-water wetlands and littoral forest – possibly the widest range of flora and fauna in the whole of Mexico.

Music

Mexico has an enormous and vibrant music scene which made world headlines in the 1950s when the **golden age** of cinema immortalized songs like "*Bésame Mucho*" and artists like **Pedro Infante**. While Cuban and Brazilian music rode the crest of the world music boom in the late 1980s, however, Mexico largely missed out – with notable exceptions like Lila Downs and Los de Abajo. But there are signs that this is about to change with a growth of interest in Mexican *son* and the release of Paddy Malone and Ry Cooder's CD, 'San Patricio'.

This is a country where, whatever the crisis – political, social or economic – live music will always be central to survival and you'll come across local sounds wherever you go, from massive *banda* concerts in rural towns and villages, to *son* at family fiestas. Mexico has also become a major venue for **live music** on the international circuit: the likes of Buena Vista Social Club, Bob Dylan, U2, Shakira, Black Eyed Peas, Manu Chao, Eric Clapton, AC-DC and almost everyone in between, play huge concert halls and stadiums.

Son

Son is the music of the Mexican fiesta, the heart of a rural culture that stubbornly survives throughout the country. *Son* is where the story of Mexican music begins: the style that celebrated independence from Spain at the beginning of the nineteenth century and is still, today, a source of regional pride and identity. Although *son* survives on the margins of urban culture, more adventurous rock groups like **Café Tacuba** and divas like **Eugenia León** and **Lila Downs** have taken versions of this music to the big stage. *Son* is music for the more adventurous musical traveler: one who looks for intensity in the cross rhythms, who likes to hear falsetto voices above a fiery violin and who isn't expecting that it will all be over in a ninety-minute concert.

Like much of Latin American music, *son* is the bastard child of indigenous, Spanish and African parents. It is what musicologists call a "super-genre", meaning that there are eight or nine different styles of *son* that vary from region to region. In general, this is the music of country dances that begin at dusk – at the end of a celebration for a saint's day or a wedding – and last through the night. It is music to be enjoyed rather than listened to passively; the public adds a line of percussion with their **zapateado** foot-stamp dancing, and the musicians respond to their calls and comments with verses that are improvised on the spot. *Son* is played mainly by string bands but in some regions – especially in indigenous towns and villages – also by brass bands of twenty or thirty musicians. The different styles of *son* feature *copla* verses that are witty, sexual, poetic and proud.

Son Jaliscience

Probably best known outside Mexico are the **sones** from Jalisco, the west-coast state that is the home of the **mariachi**. This music became nationally and internationally popular in the 1950s, a time when regional music was recorded by major labels. A few of these treasures can be found in markets although the original country sound – played on a couple of violins and guitars and sometimes a harp – almost disappeared when Rubén Fuentes rewrote the **son jaliscience** repertoire for radio and cinema, introducing slick violin sections, trumpets and the portable bass known as the *guitarrón*. These groups, made up of twelve or even sixteen musicians, spectacularly dressed in tight trousers and large hats, played their show-business versions of the traditional repertoire ("Son de la Negra" and "El Cihualteco" are two classics) as well as a more simple accompaniment for the *ranchera* stars of the day. To hear the original *son jalisciense*, look out for Vol 1 of The Anthology of Mexican Sones and also for the CD by **Mariachi Reyes del Aserradero**, a post-Fuentes group that is still very much in touch with local tastes.

The stars of big-time mariachi music are **Vicente Fernández** and, for the past fifteen years or so, his son **Alejandro**, a mega-star who has taken the music so far down the commercial path that all that is really left are the lines of silver buckles down the trouser legs and some of the instrumentation. Look out too for **Aida Cuevas** and **Antonio Aguilar**; television has stripped away the original intensity of their music but the singing is still spectacular and the mariachi will always be a strong symbol of the Mexican passion to party.

Every year there is an enormous **mariachi congress** in Guadalajara (capital of Jalisco) where hundreds of bands gather from all over Mexico and the world – especially from Japan and the US, where there are countless mariachis of different genders and musical abilities. Many Mexican towns and cities still have a central square where the mariachis meet to offer their music on a nightly basis. Most famous of these is Plaza Garibaldi in Mexico City where hundreds of musicians serenade young girls and old ladies under the stars while hustlers bring in business for the many bars and food stalls that line the plaza. Mexicans come here at all hours of the day and night to hire bands for private parties; this is the real business for the mariachis since it is much better paid than playing to tourists.

Son Jarocho

After the *sones* from Jalisco, **son jarocho** from Veracruz is probably the best-known style. Many Jarocho musicians like **Andrés Huesca**, **Nicolás Sosa** and **Lino Chávez** tasted the big time in Mexico City before returning to the main square of Veracruz. Today, there is a new interest in *son jarocho*, especially in the country style from the south of the state, where there are some three hundred bands – many of them including fifth- or sixth-generation country musicians – playing a fairly traditional repertoire at local fiestas and on the national and international circuit.

The story of this huge revival of interest in *son jarocho* goes back to 1977 when a young *jarocho* from Tres Zapotes, a small town in southern Veracruz, emigrated to Mexico City and asked himself why the *peña* folk-clubs were full of urban musicians in ponchos playing Bolivian and Chilean music. Where was Mexican music and specifically the *son jarocho* that he had danced to as a child? **Gilberto Gutiérrez** formed a band called **Mono Blanco**, recording with some of the most outstanding musicians from southern Veracruz, setting up workshops, making records and giving countless concerts all over Mexico and the US and to some extent in Europe as well. His younger brother Ramón formed his own band, **Son de Madera**, also enormously successful on the roots circuit, and this helped to revive the *fandango* tradition of dancing within the same communities that had originally produced the music. Today, there is a huge following for *son jarocho* in Mexico City and musicians are fusing it with new and old styles so that now it's common to hear a *jarocho* band opening for a rock band or featuring in a programme of classical music.

Further north, in the port of Veracruz, the style of *son jarocho* that had made it to the big screen in the 1950s is still alive and kicking, although the worldwide success of the harpist **Graciana Silva**, "La Negra Graciana", has not been repeated by other bands. Graciana's style, like that of Nicolás Sosa and the legendary Lino Chávez, is faster than the *jaranero* style of the southern bands, and there is more African influence in the mix, whereas the *jaranero* bands (others include **Los Utrera** and **Los Cojolites**) reveal a gentle melancholy, associated with a more indigenous culture.

For *son jarocho* fans the *jaranero* festival held on February 2 in Tlacotalpan (see p.602) is a must: a huge fiesta dedicated to the Virgin of the Candelaria with a stage for *jaraneros* on which professional, amateur, local and foreign musicians have an open microphone in a party atmosphere.

Son Huasteco

A third style that is less well known internationally but which has a very passionate following in Mexico is **son huasteco**, from the Huasteca region in central and northern Mexico. The line-up, in contrast with the two previous styles, is always the same: a violin, a *huapanguera* guitar and the smaller, higher pitched *jarana* guitar. These three instruments, aided by the falsetto voice of at least one of the trio, creates a music that is surprisingly complete and which has a capacity to move audiences from a frightening melancholy, through to humour and to great joy. For the past ten years at least, the most important trio has been **Los Camperos de Valles**, led by the singer **Marcos Hernández** whose falsetto can be heard of Vol III of the Anthology of Sones CD set, in a recording that was made just before he formed Los Camperos. "El San Lorenzo", played by Los Camperos Huastecos, features Marcos' angelic falsetto as it sounded when he was 17. Today – forty years later – it is still worth taking a ten-hour bus journey from Mexico City to Ciudad Valles to hear Marcos, accompanied by Gregorio Solano on *jarana* and the outstanding violin of newcomer Camilo Ramírez.

Son huasteco is enjoying a huge revival which is almost completely driven by local tastes. There are hundreds of trios playing in the states of Hidalgo, Tamaulipas and San Luis Potosí, as well as many more who have emigrated to Mexico City. They have recorded countless CDs, some of which have local DJ-style introductions with synthesizers and extra-echo but, when the intro fades out, you are left with a perfect performance of the violin and two guitars playing the old repertoire. Apart from Los Camperos, look out for CDs by young Turks **Real Hidalguense** or the other classic trio **Armonía Huasteca**. There are many events in Mexico City and all over the Huasteca where it's possible to dance all night long to the *son* of different trios, but these are not usually announced beyond the local community so it can be hard to identify them. In February and April there are big local festivals in San Joaquín de los Minerales which are highly recommended. For the less adventurous, the Museo de Culturas Populares in Mexico City sometimes presents good trios from all over the Huasteca.

Other sones

Seldom heard in the city but enormously popular back home in the villages of the Sierra Gorda, the **arribeño style** is the most poetic form of *son*. Here, the *trovador* – who seems to be the natural successor of the medieval troubadour – is a country poet, often with no formal education, who composes verses about local heroes, the planets, the earth and the continuing struggles for land. Usually two *trovadores*, both playing the *huapanguera* guitar and each accompanied by two violins and the small *vihuela* guitar, confront each other on makeshift wooden platforms that are erected on two sides of the village square. The poets enter into musical combat, improvising verses which are interspersed with *zapateado* dancing. Each year on December 31, the greatest living *trovador*, **Guillermo Velázquez**, organizes a festival in his village, paying homage to the old musicians before starting a *topada* musical combat that lasts all night. Guillermo is an outstanding musician with a sharp wit that he uses to satirize the political situation and, in the sense of bringing a political message to deep-roots traditional music, he is unique in Mexico.

Based in the Mexican west, in the Tierra Caliente (hot lands) of the Río Balsas basin, the **son guerrerense** has a tradition of exceptional violinists, exemplified by **Juan Reynoso**, who died in 2007 at the age of 95. The first country violinist to win the prestigious National Prize for Arts and Science, Reynoso became the unwitting guru of a generation of Mexico City and US musicians who would travel to Guerrero and sit at his feet, learning to play his own compositions as well as the traditional repertoire. As an old man, Reynoso toured the West Coast of the United States, participating in fiddlers' festivals. In his own region he is remembered by the name given to him by a local poet: "The Paganini of the Hotlands".

Further west, in a region where the heat is so intense that it's known as "Hell's Waiting Room", **sones de arpa grande** (*sones* of the big harp) are one of Mexico's best-kept musical secrets. These bands – made up of a big harp, one or two violins and two guitars – don't thrive as they used to, but great harpists, like **Juan Pérez Morfín** and his band **Alma de Apatzingán**, can still be tracked down in the region. In the brothels of Apatzingán and in the region's country fairs, the sound boxes of the big harps are beaten in counter-rhythm by one of the band members or by a fan who pays for the privilege. The harpist, meanwhile, must hold onto the melody with *jananeo* vocals that can sound something like a shout from the soul. Concerts are often organized by stable-owners who pride themselves on their **dancing horses**: *conjunto* music is also popular in this region, but the horses only dance to the big harp music, and they do so on wooden platforms, beating out the rhythm and counter-rhythm with their hooves.

Although *son* is basically *mestizo* music, several **indigenous cultures** play *sones* to accompany their ritual dances. These are generally purely instrumental and are slower and more melancholy than those from other regions. Exceptions are the *sones* from Purépecha and Zapotec communities which are beautiful, bilingual songs that have been widely covered by urban stars. **Sones abajeños** are the frenetic party music of the Purépecha of Michoacán, played on guitars, violins and a double bass. Between the *abajeños*, the same musicians sing the hauntingly beautiful *pirecua* love songs, with words exclusively in Purépecha. Outstanding Purépecha *son* bands include **Atardecer** (Sunset), from the lake village of Jarácuaro, and **Erandi** (Dawn). This region is probably more famous for the dances that accompany the local *sones*; there is the athletic 'Dance of the Old Men' and the slow, incredibly beautiful dances of the *cúrpites* in which small, subtle steps are taken by elaborately costumed dancers. There is nothing folkloric about this tradition, which remains an important part of Purépecha fiestas. In the southern state of Oaxaca, the vibrant Zapotec culture has produced some of the country's great love songs and inspired mainstream Mexican romantic singers along the way. Sung in both Zapotec and Spanish, the **sones istmeños**, from the Tehuantepec Isthmus, are played to a slower, more melancholy 3/4 rhythm and boast some great solo passages on the *requinto* guitar. These *sones* can be accompanied by small guitar bands or by brass bands made up of at least eighteen musicians. Again, this is the music of fiestas and, to some extent, of cantinas.

Both of these styles are played by string bands but also by the **brass bands** which are incredibly popular over most of Mexico. In one Purépecha village, Ichán, there are eighteen professional bands for a population of only 4000 people. Each band has eighteen or twenty musicians, their own private bus and contracts all over the region, although there is also a very noble tradition of playing for free at the saints' days of other villages in order to have the compliment returned on the day that their own village is celebrating. **Banda La Michoacana**'s "El Sancho" is worth searching for and, if not available on CD, should be easy to download. There is a

On record

Mexican music is widely available online: try Amazon or Smithsonian Folkways (www.folkways.si.edu). A small selection from this enormous world of musical styles includes the following:

Compilations

Anthology of Mexican Sones (Discos Corasón, Mexico). The definitive survey of Mexican traditional music, featuring wonderful recordings of rural bands. Excellent accompanying notes plus lyrics.

Beso Asesino (Discos Corasón, Mexico). Traditional *trova* from the Yucatán and from Santiago de Cuba. An excellent celebration of the shared roots of the *bolero*.

Mexico – Fiestas of Chiapas & Oaxaca (Nonesuch Explorer, US). Recordings from village festivities in southern Mexico. Marimba *conjuntos*, brass bands, some eccentric ensembles and great fireworks on the opening track.

The Rough Guide to the Music of Mexico (World Music Network, UK). This set examines a wide variety of both traditional and contemporary music, including *rancheras*, *corridos*, *boleros*, indie rock and various stylistic fusions.

La Tortuga (Discos Corasón, Mexico). A heartfelt collection of the Zapotec *sones istmeños* from southwest Oaxaca; this repertoire has been successfully mined by urban artists but here it is in the original form.

Sones and Mariachi

Los Camperos de Valles *La Pasión*. The definitive CD by the definitive Huastecan *son* band and the last recording by violinist Heliodoro Copado who was the inspiration for the current generation of *soneros*.

Conjunto Alma Jarocha *Sones Jarochos*. First in a series of regional Mexican releases, featuring *sones* from Veracruz with harps and *jarana* guitars.

Juan Reynoso *El Paganini de la Tierra Caliente*. A cult recording in Mexico which led the great country violinist to gain national and international fame. Other CDs and DVDs followed, but this is considered the best.

Mariachi Coculense de Cirilo Marmolejo *Mexico's Pioneer Mariachis Vol 1*. Wonderful archive recordings from the 1920s and 1930s of one of the seminal groups.

Mariachi Reyes del Aserradero *Sones from Jalisco*. An excellent mariachi band from Jalisco state play the original *sones* from the region where mariachi was born.

Mariachi Vargas *20 Exitos*. Highly polished, big-band style mariachi from Silvestre Vargas, who has managed to stay at the top of his field for over fifty years.

Mono Blanco *El Mundo se va a Acabar*. The most ambitious record from the band that has led the revival of *son jarocho* in Mexico; although less traditional than their usual style, this is stunning.

Ranchera and Norteño

Banda del Recodo *Nuestra Historia*. This enormously popular band releases hit CDs rather than classics so possibly the best introduction is this 2003 release that brings together material from their long history.

Chavela Vargas *Noche Bohemia*. There has been a flood of CDs made since Chavela's return to the music scene in the late 1980s but nothing rivals this early recording with the legendary guitarist, Antonio Bribiesca.

Flaco Jiménez *Ay Te Dejo en San Antonio y Más*. The best of Flaco's many recordings; he's a huge name in the Tex-Mex world north of the border.

José Alfredo Jiménez *Homenaje a José Alfredo Jiménez*. Jimenez was the king of *ranchera* and an icon in Mexico: his classic repertoire of songs tells of the perfidy of women and the healing qualities of tequila. He may have created some of the worst clichés about machismo, but his music is irresistible.

Linda Ronstadt *Canciones de Mi Padre* and *Más Canciones*. *Ranchera* classics sung very convincingly by the Mexican-American vocalist, accompanied by Mariachi Vargas.

Los Lobos *La Pistola y El Corazón*. The East LA band's brilliant 1988 tribute to their Mexican roots, with David Hidalgo pumping the accordion on their blend of *conjunto* and rock and roll.

Los Tigres del Norte *Corridos Prohibidos*. A collection of *corridos* about Mexican low life and heroism from one of the best *norteño* groups.

Tropical and Música Romántica

Agustín Lara *Agustín Lara*. The legendary *bolero* singer and composer of classics such as "Rival" and "Noche de Ronda". There are countless recordings by him and the myriad of artists who have dedicated covers of his *boleros* to him (including Plácido Domingo and Pedro Vargas).

Armando Manzanero *20 Éxitos Originales*. A key figure for Cuban artists like Omara Portuondo, this Yucatecan pianist modernized the *bolero* and, now in his 60s, is still a huge figure who moves comfortably between the commercial and the alternative. Various artists (Tania Libertad and Alejandro Sanz are just two) queue up to sing duets with him. His voice isn't great but his songs are classics and this is a typical, very polished, selection of re-mastered classics.

Guty Cárdenas *100 Años del Ruiseñor Yucateco*. A collection of *trova yucateca* and other genres in the voice and guitar of a man who was an enormous star in the early years of recorded sound but who was assassinated in 1932. The tracks have been masterfully restored and are accompanied by a documentary.

Sonora Dinamita *Mi Cucu*. Mexican *cumbia* performed by a breakaway group of artists who took the name of the Colombian originals. Their lyrics, full of double entendres, are performed with a zest that has brought huge success in Mexico.

Toña La Negra *Antología*. A well-kept secret outside Mexico – where she was an enormous star in the 1950s – this *bolero* singer from Veracruz reveals how close Mexico is to Cuba (and vice versa). She died in 1982.

Rock and Pop

Café Tacuba *Re*. The second CD in a long list of successes from a band that has been at the top of the Mexican rock scene for more than twenty years, this is a highly recommended classic.

Eugenia León *Pasional*. The latest release by this great singer who has been much more successful on stage than on record. This CD celebrates the mature voice of a woman who has a powerful, emotional presence and has been at the top of the loosely-named "Latin American song" tradition for over 25 years.

Julieta Venegas *Sí*. The 2003 record that firmly established Julieta as a major figure on the pop-rock scene. There is something very attractive about her funky innocence which saves her from a closer association with mainstream pop.

Lila Downs *La Sandunga*. Not the most recent but an excellent CD by this singer who presents Mexican *sones* and *boleros* to a wider audience.

Molotov *Dónde Jugarán las Niñas?*. This aggressive, political hip-hop album was banned in Mexico for obscenity (and possible use of an underage model on its cover). Needless to say, it was a mammoth hit, and the band's "Gimme Tha Power" perfectly captures a moment in Mexican youth culture. Their songs about migrant workers, corruption and minibus drivers are contemporary classics.

Nortec Collective *Tijuana Sessions Vol 3*. More so than Vol 1 (which errs on the side of generic techno), this album shows off the funky potential of remixing blaring Mexican horns for the dancefloor.

direct line from these village bands playing local *sones* to the commercial **banda** phenomenon (see p.894).

Tropical

Mexico has had a very close musical relationship with Cuba and Colombia since the earliest days of the recording industry, and music that is born in one of the three countries tends to have a rebirth in another. It was in Mexico that **Damasio Pérez Prado** 'discovered' the **mambo**; **Celia Cruz** lived here, as did **Bienvenido Granda, Beny Moré, Rubén González, Enrique Jorrín** and **Miguel Matamoros** amongst others. All the different styles of upbeat and romantic music that these gods produced tend to be known in Mexico as **música tropical** and they are still much consumed, although the younger generation prefer **reggaetón**: a Latin version of hip-hop blaring from bars and radio all over the country.

Trova yucateca, a local style from the Yucatán, was present at the birth of the **bolero** in Santiago de Cuba and this romantic repertoire has a long history of coming and going between the two countries. This is hardly surprising since Mérida, the sleepy capital of Yucatán state, is geographically (and in some ways culturally) closer to Havana than to Mexico City. In the 1950s, trios like **Los Panchos** took the Cuban *bolero* and the Yucatecan *trova* and established the formula of a *requinto* guitar, two Spanish guitars and the harmony of three voices.

Such trios were enormously popular throughout the second half of the twentieth century and, although they are few and far between in Mexico City today, at least ten trios gather every night in the main square of Mérida to offer their local repertoire, performed in the style of Los Panchos, while in the theatres and clubs, there are a series of excellent groups that are fusing *trova* with Cuban *son* and other styles. **Yahal Kaab** offers an almost perfect contemporary fusion of the Yucatán and Cuba while the younger, more commercial group **Los Juglares** have a spectacular energy and stage presence. For people who (understandably) fall in love with the music, look for CDs by the grandfather of this style, **Guty Cárdenas**, who died in 1932 at the age of 27 but whose magic is still very much alive. **Armando Manzanero** was a *trovador* who emigrated to Mexico City in the 1970s and developed a new *bolero* style which has made him a favourite, not just in Mexico but all over Latin America and especially in Cuba.

Like the *bolero*, **danzón** is originally Cuban but the Mexican version, which is always instrumental and more formal than the original, filled oversized dance halls in Mexico City for more than half a century. It is still danced under the stars in the main square of Veracruz and behind the *Ciudadela* market in Mexico City: bastions of elderly couples who are masters of elegance and style and who won't let their age get in the way of a subtle sensuality that is...irresistible.

It is a similar story with the **cumbia**, a commercial style that was born in Colombia and became enormously popular in Mexico in the 1970s, when **Sonora Dinamita** came, saw and conquered and then fractured into several different groups, each with the same name.

Norteño

From Mexico's northern border came **norteño**, known in the US as **Tex-Mex**, traditional music that broke into the mainstream and became enormously popular in the early 1990s. This achievement is associated, above all, with **Los Tigres del Norte**, a band who had a mammoth hit with their 1988 Grammy winner "Gracias América sin Fronteras".

Norteño, the preferred style for accompanying the *corrido* ballads that are also played on the Pacific coast and in Morelos in central Mexico, has a history that long pre-dates its commercial breakthrough. The late 1920s were the golden age of the **corrido**, when songs of the recent Revolution were recorded in San Antonio, Texas, and distributed on both sides of the border. The accordion, which had arrived with German immigrants in the late nineteenth century, was introduced into the originally guitar-based groups by **Narciso Martínez** and **Santiago Jiménez** (father of the famous Flaco) in the 1930s, and the sound that they developed became the essence of *corrido* ensembles on both sides of the border.

Along with the **accordion** came the polka, and by the 1950s this had blended with the traditional duet-singing of northern Mexico and with salon dances like the waltz, mazurka and the *chotis* (the central European *schottische* that travelled to Spain and France before arriving in northern Mexico) to produce the definitive *norteño* style. The accordion pepped up the songs with lead runs and flourishes between the verses, but the *conjuntos norteños* needed to round out their sound to keep up with the big bands and so added bass and rolling drums – the basis of today's **conjuntos**.

The *corrido* ballads tell of anti-heroes: small-time drug runners, illegal immigrants, a thief with one blond eyebrow who defied the law. *Norteño* reflects the mood of a country that generally considers the government to be big-time thieves and hence has a certain respect for everyday people with the courage to stand up to a crooked system. Groups like Los Tigres del Norte and **Los Cadetes del Norte** take stories from the local papers and convert them into ballads that usually begin "Voy a cantarles un corrido" ("I'm going to sing you a *corrido*"; see box below) before launching into a gruesome tale sung in a deadpan style as if it were nothing to go to a local dance and get yourself killed.

Los Tigres are still the superstars of *norteño*, on both sides of the border. Quite early in their career, the band modified the traditional line-up by adding a sax and

El Gato Félix (Felix the Cat)

I'm going to sing a *corrido*
About someone who I knew
A distinguished journalist
Feared for his pen
From Tijuana to Madrid

They called him Felix the Cat
Because the story goes that
He was like those felines
He had seven lives
And he had to see them through

He came from Choix, Sinaloa
That was the place he was born
He stayed in Tijuana
Because it took his fancy
And he wanted to help in some way
With what he wrote in the paper

He made the government tremble
He went right through the alphabet
A whole rosary of threats
He made his paper *Zeta* popular
With his valiant pen

He pointed to corruption
He always helped the people
And more than two presidents
Had their eyes on him
In a treacherous way

The Cat met his end
Death, mounted on a racehorse
A real beast
Rode him down

Now Felix the Cat is dead
They are carrying him to his grave
He will be another one on the list
Of brave journalists
That they've wanted to silence

Candles burn for Felix Miranda
To you I dedicate my song
But don't you worry
There will be other brave people
To take your place

Enrique Franco
(*Los Tigres del Norte*, 1989)

mixed the familiar rhythms with *cumbias*; however, their nasal singing style and the combination of instruments identifies the music very clearly as *norteño*. The likes of **Ramón Ayala** continue to play the *norteño* repertoire and **Los Tucanes de Tijuana** get themselves into trouble with their narco-*corridos*, but most of the original bands have moved into the *conjunto* mould, playing romantic music as well as upbeat songs that combine elements of *música tropical* and *norteño*. Today the lines are very blurred between *conjuntos*, *norteño*, *banda* and a new favourite: the **duranguense**, which has its own, very popular dance and a range of artists such as **El As de la Sierra**, **Capaz de la Sierra** and **AK7** whose names confirm their origins in the narco-dominated mountain towns of the north.

The Banda boom

The enormous success of Los Tigres del Norte and their updated *norteño* sound resulted in a phenomenon that changed the face of Mexican music in the mid-1990s: **banda** music. This is a fusion of the *norteño* style with the brass bands that have played at village fiestas all over the country for the last century. There are now hundreds of *bandas* in Mexico – ranging in size from eight to twenty musicians – all playing brass and percussion, with just an occasional guitar. Their repertoire includes *norteño* polkas, *ranchera* ballads, *cumbia*, merengue and salsa. The most exciting of these groups is a fiery orchestra from Mazatlán, the **Banda El Recodo**. This is not a new band; indeed, its former leader, **Don Cruz Lizárraga**, had been in the business for half a century, starting out in a traditional *tambora* marching band (the *tambora* is the huge, carried side drum). However, Don Cruz had always had an eye for musical fashions, adapting his material to merengue, *ranchera* or whatever anyone wanted to hear. His great *banda* hit was a version of Cuban bandleader Beny Moré's classic "La Culebra". Other big-name bands include **Banda Limón** and the extravagant **Banda Cuisillos** that have been known to dress up in feathers and perform a neo-Aztec ritual before launching into the *banda* repertoire.

The *banda* boom dominated the national airwaves in the 1990s. Outside the big cities, it is still the *bandas* that fill the stadiums and village halls, and it's their names you'll see painted in enormous multicoloured letters on patches of white wall along the roads. The craze brought with it a series of new dances, too, particularly the *quebradita* – a gymnastic, very intimate combination of *lambada*, polka and even a little bit of swing and hip-hop, which is danced with particular skill in points north of Guadalajara. Despite its enormous following outside the capital, *banda* music is considered very unsophisticated by the urban elite. It exists as a parallel musical culture that has created its own aesthetics in terms of the slightly off-the-note vocal style developed by singers like **Julio Preciado**, cultivating the image of the Mexican macho in tight leather pants and a black cowboy hat with lines of ladies screaming at their feet.

Divas and Música Ranchera

Don't expect **women** in Mexico to take the macho culture sitting down. There is a very long and glorious tradition of female **divas** who share less in terms of their musical styles and more in terms of their fierce independence and the confidence to take on different influences and make them their own.

A forerunner who has inspired many of the later divas was **Lucha Reyes**, the remarkable singer of the **ranchera** repertoire which took the bucolic, upbeat *sones* and – in the flood of nostalgia that accompanied the growth of the cities in the 1940s – converted them into a sad lament for a lost way of life in which the woman was always the downfall and tequila the remedy. It was a man, **José Alfredo Jimenez**, who converted this music – so much more simple than the complex *sones* – into an art form. He composed songs like "El Rey" in which he sings of a man who has no money, no throne, nobody to maintain him and yet, despite that, he continues to be the king.

A close friend of José Alfredo's, **Chavela Vargas** was a remarkable figure in the 1950s as she continues to be today, at the age of 90. In a conservative, Catholic culture, she was proud to be gay, and she sang José Alfredo's songs in bars and nightclubs, changing the words so that she could lament and celebrate the love of a woman. Chavela retired early but, after giving up alcohol, she returned to professional life in the late 1980s and was serenaded by Pedro Almodovar, amongst others. She played at the Olympia in Paris, recording with the elite of Spanish superstars and then returned to Mexico, the home she had adopted after leaving Costa Rica as a young girl. At 90, Chavela is much loved and constantly celebrated in Mexico with books, concerts and TV specials. For 2010 she now plans to make a new CD because, she says, "she isn't afraid of anything".

One composer favoured by Chavela is **Agustín Lara**, "El Flaco de Oro", who fused the spirit of *ranchera* music with the Cuban *bolero*, creating a style that remains enormously popular in Mexico and all over Latin America where it coexists alongside the Cuban *boleros*. "El rival", "Amor de mis amores" and "Mujer" are amongst the many classics that have survived for more than fifty years. Each generation of mainstream Mexican artists reinvent Lara for their own glory and the countless CDs dedicated to his memory now include several recorded by flamenco singers from Andalucía.

Possibly the greatest contemporary diva is **Eugenia León**, who typifies the style with an exquisite voice that brought her fame first as a protest singer in the 1970s, later singing *ranchera boleros*, *norteño* and songs that were composed especially for her by writers like the late Marcial Alejandro. Despite her enormous following and more than thirty years at the top, she remains remarkably natural and is a generous artist who now spends much of her time promoting the talents of other musicians through her TV interviews and documentaries.

The next generation is led by **Lila Downs** who enjoys tremendous success both in Mexico and beyond. The daughter of a US filmmaker and a Mixtec mother from Oaxaca, she has carved an important place for herself on both sides of the border, using her admirable voice to project her own versions of music from Veracruz; *boleros*, *ranchera* classics in the style of Lucha Reyes and, more recently, a repertoire that is very much her own. With her neo-Frida Kahlo image, Lila has a tremendous stage presence and she was confirmed as a major international artist with her performance at the 2003 Oscar ceremonies. In the wake of Lila come **Julieta Venegas** from Tijuana, whose platinum-selling CDs are favourites on the pop-rock circuit but whose natural style and quirky innocence separates her from media-born artists, and two new names who have a fierce independence that distinguishes them from the mainstream. **Ximena Sariñana** and **Natalia Lafourcade** are both young, feisty singers who move in and out of the pop-rock world, according to their different moods.

Rock en Español

One reason that traditional forms such as *son* flourished in Mexico is that the country was closed to **rock** music until the late 1980s, when the government finally lifted import regulations and laws banning rock concerts. These had been in place since the 1971 Arándaro festival, dubbed the "Mexican Woodstock", scandalized the nation and effectively drove the country's rock music culture underground. When the borders opened in 1990, international rock music flooded the local market and Mexican rock began to flourish. The boom began in Mexico City, with middle-class rockers like **Los Caifanes** playing to middle-class audiences who knew about the outside scene because they, or their parents, travelled regularly to Europe and the US. Ironically, the Caifanes' massive hit was a 1988 cover of a traditional Cuban *son*, "La Negra Tomasa", which appealed to a public that understood *son* and salsa better than the British punk referenced in other songs. A little later, the eclectic **Café Tacuba** began to reach a bigger audience, with an interest, to some extent, in exploring Mexican roots and reinterpreting Mexican *son* in their own way. Then came **Maldita Vecindad** from Mexico City and **Maná**, from Guadalajara, and Mexican rock – now rather slickly produced – entered the superstar level.

In the late 1990s, the scene began to splinter into subcultures. The industrial town of Monterrey, home to a prestigious university and a lot of English-speaking, US-oriented youth, was a seemingly bottomless well of talent that drew comparisons to Seattle in the grunge years. Funky mix-masters **Plastilina Mosh**, ska band **El Gran Silencio** and **Control Machete**'s hip-hop went from here to Latin MTV. In Tijuana, meanwhile, **Nortec Collective** helped create an international club scene with its remixes of classic *norteño* sounds with techno beats. In Mexico City **ska** became immensely popular alongside **hip-hop**, with excellent bands such as **Molotov** making piercing social commentary in their songs about politics, corruption and what it feels like to live on the wrong side of the US border.

Mary Farquharson

Mary is co-founder of Discos Corason (Ⓦwww.corason.com) and was one of the original founders of World Circuit. She has lived in Mexico since 1987.

Books

Mexico has attracted more than its fair share of famous foreign writers, and has inspired a vast literature and several classics. Until very recently, however, Mexican writers had received little attention outside the country; what translations exist are mostly published by small US presses, and few authors are well known north of the border. Most big US bookstores will have an enormous array of books about, from or set in Mexico, plus a few novels. In the rest of the English-speaking world there's far less choice, though the best-known of the archeological and travel titles here should be available almost anywhere. In the lists below, o/p means a book is out of print, but may still be found in libraries or second-hand. Books with a ✱ symbol are highly recommended.

Impressions of Mexico

Sybille Bedford *A Visit to Don Otavio*. An extremely enjoyable, often hilarious, occasionally lyrical and surprisingly relevant account of Ms Bedford's travels through Mexico in the early 1950s.

Jeff Biggers *In the Sierra Madre*. Biggers juxtaposes the history of the Copper Canyon region – with all its indigenous tribes and foreign treasure-hunters – with his present-day experiences living there amid the Rarámuri, the drug-runners and other colourful characters. Really lively story-telling from someone with an obvious love of the place.

Frances Calderón de la Barca *Life in Mexico*. The diary of a Scotswoman who married the Spanish ambassador to Mexico and spent two years there in the mid-nineteenth century.

Tony Cohan *Mexican Days: Journeys into the Heart of Mexico*. Cohan, an American novelist, relocated to San Miguel de Allende in the 1980s; this is a travelogue of his explorations into small towns after some twenty years in Mexico – a perspective that's both respectful and informed.

Charles Macomb Flandrau *Viva Mexico!* (Eland, o/p). First published in 1908, Flandrau's account of life in turn-of-the-twentieth-century Mexico is something of a cult classic. Though attitudes are inevitably dated in places, it's extremely funny in others.

Carl Franz, Lorena Havens and Steve Rogers *The People's Guide to Mexico*. Not a guidebook as such: more a series of anecdotes and words of advice for staying out of trouble and heading off the beaten track. Perennially popular with old hippies of all ages (2006 saw the publication of the thirteenth edition), and deservedly so.

Thomas Gage *Thomas Gage's Travels in the New World* (o/p). Unusual account by an English cleric who became a Dominican friar chronicling his travels through Mexico and Central America in the early seventeenth century, including fascinating insights into colonial life and some great attacks on the greed and pomposity of the Catholic Church.

Richard Grant *God's Middle Finger: Into the Lawless Heart of the Sierra Madre* (published in the UK as *Bandit Roads: Into the Lawless Heart of Mexico*). A British journalist's adventures as he finds himself caught up in the north-east's drug wars and barely escapes with his life; a thoroughly entertaining read

Graham Greene *The Lawless Roads*. In the late 1930s Greene was sent to Mexico to investigate the effects of the persecution of the Catholic Church. The result (see also his novel on p.900) was this classic account of his travels in a very bizarre era of modern Mexican history.

Katie Hickman *A Trip to the Light Fantastic: Travels with a Mexican Circus* (o/p). Enchanting, funny and uplifting account of a year spent travelling (and performing) with a fading Mexican circus troupe.

Aldous Huxley *Beyond the Mexique Bay* (o/p). Only a small part of the book is devoted to Mexico, but the descriptions of the archeological sites around Oaxaca, in particular, are still worth reading.

D.H. Lawrence *Mornings in Mexico*. A very slim volume, half of which is devoted to the Hopi Indians of New Mexico, this is an uncharacteristically cheerful account of Lawrence's stay in southern Mexico, and beautifully written – although his characterizations of native culture will likely strike modern readers as condescending.

John Lincoln *One Man's Mexico* (o/p). Lincoln – the pen name of British Council officer Maurice Cardiff, whose identity was only revealed after his death in 2006 – travelled through the Mexican jungles in the late 1960s, producing an entertaining and offbeat read that you'd never guess was the product of a civil servant. Graham Greene called it the best book about Mexico of the twentieth century.

Jules Siegel *Cancun User's Guide*. Siegel, a freelance journalist, moved to Mexico in 1981, then worked for the tourism ministry in the nascent resort city. His self-published tome (widely available online) is as much an ode to this under-appreciated city and the people who built it as it is a practical guide: affectionate, opinionated and guaranteed to change your outlook on Cancún, as well as Mexico as a whole. The shopping and eating recommendations seem like an afterthought.

John Lloyd Stephens *Incidents of Travel in Central America, Chiapas, and Yucatán*. Stephens was a classic nineteenth-century traveller. Acting as American ambassador to Central America, he indulged his own enthusiasm for archeology. His journals, full of superb Victorian pomposity punctuated with sudden waves of enthusiasm, make great reading, especially as companions to the great Maya ruins, many of which he helped uncover. The best editions include the fantastic original illustrations by Frederick Catherwood; you won't have trouble finding inexpensive paperback versions in Mexico.

Paul Theroux *The Old Patagonian Express*. The epic journey from Boston to the tip of South America by train spends just three rather bad-tempered chapters in Mexico, so don't expect to find out too much about the country. A good read nonetheless.

John Kenneth Turner *Barbarous Mexico*. Turner was a journalist, and this account of his travels through nineteenth-century Mexico exposing the conditions of workers in the plantations of the Yucatán, serialized in US newspapers, did much to discredit the regime of Porfirio Díaz.

Ronald Wright *Time Among the Maya*. A vivid and sympathetic account of travels from Belize through Guatemala, Chiapas and Yucatán, meeting the Maya of today and exploring their obsession with time. The level of detail makes this a complex read – best for readers with a specific interest in ancient Maya culture.

Mexican fiction

Mariano Azuela *The Underdogs*. The first novel of the Revolution (finished in 1915), *The Underdogs* is told through the eyes of a group of peasants who form a semi-regular Revolutionary armed band; it relates their escapades, progress and eventual betrayal and massacre. Initially fighting for land and liberty, they end up caught in an uncontrollable cycle of violence and descend into brutal nihilism. The book set many of the themes of post-Revolutionary Mexican writing.

Carmen Boullosa *The Miracle Worker* (o/p). One of Mexico's most promising contemporary writers, Boullosa focuses on traditional Mexican themes, often borrowing characters from history or myth. *The Miracle Worker* explores Mexican attitudes to Catholicism through the eyes of a messianic healer and her followers. The story can be seen as a parable about the Mexican political system, where ordinary Mexicans petition a distant government for favours, which are granted or refused in seemingly arbitrary decisions. You may be able to find Boullosa's novel *Leaving Tabasco* more readily; it's not as strong a work, but an interesting vision of small-town life (and trauma) through the eyes of a child.

María Amparo Escandón *Gonzalez & Daughter Trucking Co*. A story within a story, told with gusto by an inmate at a women's prison in Mexicali – borderline pulp, with cliffhangers and campy drama, but heartwarming and funny in its treatment of loyalty and freedom. Escandón's earlier work, *Esperanza's Box of Saints*, is a charming, quick-read tale of female emancipation.

Laura Esquivel *Like Water for Chocolate*. Adapted to film, Esquivel's novel proved a huge hit in Mexico and abroad. The book is even better: funny, sexy, sentimental (schmaltzy, even), it deals with the star-crossed romance of Tita, whose lover marries her sister. Using the magic of the kitchen, she sets out to seduce him back. The book is written in monthly episodes, each of which is prefaced with a traditional Mexican recipe. The author's 2006 novel, *Malinche*, is not nearly as successful, but presents a sympathetic version of Cortés's courtesan and translator, whose name is synonymous with "traitor" in Mexico.

Carlos Fuentes *The Death of Artemio Cruz* and *The Old Gringo*. Fuentes is by far the best-known Mexican writer outside Mexico, influenced by Mariano Azuela and Juan Rulfo, and an early exponent of magical realism. In *The Death of Artemio Cruz*, the hero, a rich and powerful man on his deathbed, looks back over his life and loves, from an idealist youth in the Revolution through disillusion to corruption and power. *The Old Gringo* takes place during the Revolution, imagining that vanished American writer Ambrose Bierce has joined Pancho Villa's army; it's shorter, but no less carefully crafted. These are the classics, but Fuentes is a prolific writer and you'll find plenty of others if these pique your interest.

Jorge Ibargüengoitia *The Dead Girls*, *Two Crimes* and others (o/p). One of the first modern Mexican novelists translated into English (and unfortunately now left to languish), Ibargüengoitia was killed in a plane crash in 1983. These two, published just before his death, are both blackly comic thrillers, superbly told, the first of them based on real events.

Mónica Lavín (ed) *Points of Departure*. A collection of short stories from some of the country's most respected contemporary writers – the selection is a little uneven, but it may be interesting and refreshing to read stories that *don't* involve magical realism.

Octavio Paz (ed) *Mexican Poetry*. Edited by Paz (perhaps the leading man of letters of Mexico's post-Revolutionary era) and translated by Samuel Beckett, this is as good a taste as you could hope for of modern Mexican poets. Some of Paz's own poetry is also available in translation.

Elena Poniatowska *Here's to You, Jesúsa!* One of Mexico's best-known essayists and journalists lightly fictionalizes the life story of her cleaning lady to create a lively "autobiography" covering her marriage, involvement in the Revolution and the postwar period. Some of Poniatowska's other excellent works available in English include *Massacre in Mexico*, a collage of testimonies of those present at the 1968 massacre of students in Tlatelolco, and *Tinisima*, a portrait of Communist organizer and photographer Tina Modotti.

Juan Rulfo *Pedro Páramo*. First published in 1955, this is widely regarded as the greatest Mexican novel of the twentieth century and a precursor of magical realism. The living and spirit worlds mesh when, at the behest of his dying mother, the narrator visits the deserted village haunted by the memory of his brutal father, Pedro Páramo. Dark, but ultimately very rewarding. Rulfo's short-story collection, *The Burning Plain and Other Stories*, is rated by Gabriel García Márquez as the best in Latin America.

Ignacio Solares *Yankee Invasion*. An account of the 1847 US capture of Mexico City from the perspective of an ageing journalist, looking back at his youthful involvement. A sometimes uneasy mix of romance, psychology and history, but ultimately an enjoyable read. Solares is one of Mexico's leading men of letters.

Foreign fiction

There are hundreds of novels by non-Mexicans set in Mexico, all too many in the sex-and-shopping genre. Apart from those below, others to look out for include a whole clutch of modern Americans, especially **Jack Kerouac**'s *Desolation Angels* and several of Richard Brautigan's novels. And of course there's **Carlos Castaneda**'s *Don Juan* series – a search for enlightenment through peyote.

Tony Cartano *After the Conquest* (o/p). An extraordinary fictional account of a fictional author who believes he is B. Traven's son and sets out to discover the truth about his father (see p.901). A psychological thriller that is also full of Mexican history and politics.

Eduardo Galeano *Genesis*, *Faces & Masks* and *Century of the Wind*. Together forming the *Memory of Fire* trilogy, these anthologies of Indian legends, colonists' tales and odd snatches of fictionalized history by a Uruguayan writer take a sideways look at Latin America from the earliest times to 1984. Not specifically Mexican, but wonderful, relevant reading nonetheless.

Graham Greene *The Power and the Glory*. Inspired by his investigative travels, this story of a doomed whisky priest on the run from the authorities makes a great yarn and a wonderful movie.

Gary Jennings *Aztec*. Sex and sacrifice in ancient Mexico. The narrator travels around the Aztec empire in search of his fortune, chancing upon almost every ancient culture along the way, and sleeping with most of them, until finally the Spanish arrive. Perfect beach or bus reading, and informative too; if you're hooked, the story continues in *Aztec Autumn* and *Aztec Blood*, and in further instalments featuring our hero's descendants at key points of Mexican history.

D.H. Lawrence *The Plumed Serpent*. One of Lawrence's own favourites, the novel reflects his intense dislike of the country that followed on from the brief honeymoon period of *Mornings in Mexico* (see p.898). Fans of his heavy spiritualism will love it.

Haniel Long *The Marvellous Adventure of Cabeza de Vaca*. Two short stories in one volume – the first the account of a shipwrecked conquistador's journey across the new continent, the second the thoughts and hopes of Malinche, Cortés's interpreter.

Malcolm Lowry *Under the Volcano*. A classic since its publication, Lowry's account of the last day in the life of the British consul in Cuernavaca – passed in a mescal-induced haze – is totally brilliant. His *Dark as the Grave Wherein My Friend Is Laid* (o/p) is also based on his Mexican experiences.

James A. Michener *Mexico*. Another multi-generational family epic from Michener. Fans will love it.

B. Traven various works. In the 1920s and 1930s, the mysterious Traven – whose true identity is itself the subject of a series of books – wrote a series of compelling novels set in Mexico. Among the best-known are *Treasure of the Sierra Madre* (later a film starring Humphrey Bogart) and *The Death Ship*, but of more interest if you're travelling are such works as *The Bridge in the Jungle* and the other six books in the *Jungle* series: *Government*, *The Carreta*, *March to the Monteria*, *Trozas*, *The Rebellion of the Hanged* and *General from the Jungle*. These latter all deal with the state of the peasantry and the growth of revolutionary feeling in the last years of the Díaz dictatorship. Will Wyatt's *The Secret of the Sierra Madre: The Man Who Was B. Traven* (o/p) is the best of the books on the quest for the author's identity.

History

The sources below are all entertaining and/or important references; more standard general histories include *Fire and Blood: A History of Mexico*, by T.R. Fehrenbach; *Gods, Gachupines and Gringos: A People's History of Mexico* by Richard Grabman, with an easily accessible, non-academic approach; and *The Course of Mexican History*, by Michael Meyer, William Sherman and Susan Deeds.

Inga Clendinnen *Ambivalent Conquests: Maya and Spaniard in Yucatán 1517 to 1570*. A product of meticulous research that documents the methods and consequences of the Spanish Conquest of the Yucatán. The ambivalence in the title reflects doubts about the effectiveness of the Conquest in subjugating the Maya, and the book provides insights into the rebellions that followed: more than three hundred years later, the Maya rose in revolt during the Caste Wars, and almost succeeded in driving out their white overlords. Later editions also comment briefly on the 1994 Chiapas uprising.

Hernán Cortés *Letters from Mexico* (Yale UP). The thoughts and impressions of the conquistador, at first hand. Less exciting than Díaz, though.

Bernal Díaz (trans. J.M. Cohen) *The Conquest of New Spain*. This abridged version is still the best available of Díaz's classic *Historia Verdadera de la Conquista de la Nueva España*. Díaz, having been on two earlier expeditions to Mexico, accompanied Cortés throughout his campaign of conquest, and this magnificent eyewitness account makes compelling reading.

Adolfo Gilly *The Mexican Revolution*. Considered the classic work on the Revolution, this was written in Mexico City's notorious Lecumberri jail (Gilly was later granted an absolute pardon). Heavy going and highly theoretical though.

John Mason Hart *Empire & Revolution: The Americans in Mexico since the Civil War*. A fascinating study of the relationship between the US and Mexico, and in particular US imperialist aspirations and involvement in Mexican financial affairs. Hart's *Revolutionary Mexico* is a detailed history of the Mexican Revolution following the same theme of US involvement. Both are serious works of history, heavy-going in parts.

Enrique Krauze *Mexico: Biography of Power*. First published in Spanish, this sprawling history covers most of the nineteenth and twentieth centuries – the biography format makes it very readable, and easier to dip into if you can't weather all 896 pages. Street names and public holidays will make a lot more sense, at the very least.

Richard and Rosalind Perry *Maya Missions* (o/p). One in a series of expertly written guides to the sometimes overlooked treasures of Mexico's colonial religious architecture. *More Maya Missions* covers Chiapas. Both are illustrated by the authors' simple but beautiful drawings. These specialist offerings, ideal for travellers who want more information than most guidebooks can provide, are not widely available, though you can sometimes find them in tourist bookshops in the areas they cover.

William Prescott *History of the Conquest of Mexico*. Written in the mid-nineteenth century, and drawing heavily on Díaz, Prescott's history was the standard text for more than a hundred years. It makes for pretty heavy reading and has now been overtaken by Thomas's account – but as a classic history (written by someone who had never even visited Mexico) it's a fascinating work of scholarship, ranking with Gibbon's *The Decline and Fall of the Roman Empire*.

John Reed *Insurgent Mexico*. This collection of his reportage of the Mexican Revolution was put together by Reed himself. He spent several months in 1913 and 1914 with various generals of the Revolution – especially Villa – and the book contains great descriptions of them, their men and the mood of the times.

Nelson Reed *The Caste War of the Yucatan*. Reed's book is the authority on this tumultuous and defining era in Yucatán history, with great detail on the Talking Cross movement. A must-read for anyone intrigued by this period.

Jasper Ridley *Maximilian & Juárez*. This comprehensive, highly readable account of one of "the great tragicomedies of the nineteenth century" charts the attempt by Napoleon III to establish Archduke Maximilian as the emperor of Mexico. The colourful narrative brings to life an unmitigated political disaster with huge consequences, including the execution of Maximilian, the insanity of his wife Carlota and the emergence of the US as a world power.

Hugh Thomas *Conquest: Montezuma, Cortés, and the Fall of Old Mexico* (published in the UK as *The Conquest of Mexico*). A brilliant narrative history of the Conquest by the British historian previously best known for his history of the Spanish Civil War. A massive work of real scholarship and importance – much of the archive material was unearthed only in the 1980s and 1990s – but also humorous and readable, with appendices on everything from Aztec beliefs, history and genealogy to Cortés's wives and lovers.

Ancient Mexico

There are thousands of studies of **ancient Mexico**, many of them extremely academic and detailed, plus any number of big, highly illustrated coffee-table tomes on individual sites. Those below are of more general interest, and any of them will have substantial **bibliographies** to help you explore further.

Ignacio Bernal *Mexico Before Cortez* (o/p). The leading Mexican archeologist of the twentieth century, and one of the inspirations behind the Museo Nacional de Antropología (see p.419), Bernal did important work on the Olmecs and the restoration of Teotihuacán, and has written many important source works. This book covers much the same ground as Davies's, though in less detail, and is more dated, but it has the advantage of being widely available in Mexico. A more scholarly version is available in *A History of Mexican Archeology: The Vanished Civilizations of Middle America* (also o/p).

Warwick Bray *Everyday Life of the Aztecs* (o/p). An informative volume about Aztec warfare, music, games, folklore, religious ritual, social organization, economic and political systems and agricultural practice. Although the book is now showing its age, and some of its conclusions are a bit dubious, its attractive comprehensiveness more than makes up for this. An excellent general introduction.

Inga Clendinnen *Aztecs: An Interpretation*. A social history of the Aztec empire that seeks to explain the importance – and acceptance – of human sacrifice and other rituals. Fascinating, though best to know something about the Aztecs before you start.

Michael D. Coe *The Maya*. The best available general introduction to the Maya: concise, clear and comprehensive. Coe has also written several weightier, academic volumes. His *Breaking the Maya Code*, a history of the decipherment of the Maya glyphs, owes much to the fact that Coe was present at many of the most important meetings leading to the breakthrough that demonstrated how the glyphs actually did reproduce Maya speech. It is a beautifully written, ripping yarn, though the attacks on Eric Thompson become a bit wearisome. In *Mexico: From the Olmecs to the Aztecs*, co-authored with Rex Koontz, he introduces Mexico's other early cultures.

Nigel Davies *The Ancient Kingdoms of Mexico*. Although no single text covers all the ancient cultures, this comes pretty close, covering the central areas from the Olmecs through Teotihuacán and the Toltecs to the Aztec empire. An excellent mix of historical, archeological, social and artistic information, but it doesn't cover the Maya. Davies is also the author of several more-detailed academic works on the Aztecs and Toltecs, including *The Aztecs, A History*.

Munro S. Edmonson (trans.) *Heaven Born Merida and Its Destiny: The Book of Chilam Balam of Chumayel*. The *Chilam Balam* is a recollection of Maya history and myth, compiled by the Maya over centuries; this version was written in Maya in Latin script in the eighteenth century. Although the style is not easy, it's one of the few keys into the Maya view of the world.

Joyce Kelly *An Archaeological Guide to Mexico's Yucatán Peninsula*. Detailed and practical guide to more than ninety Maya sites and eight museums throughout the peninsula, including many little-known or difficult-to-reach ruins; an essential companion for anyone travelling purposefully through the Maya world.

George Kubler *Art and Architecture of Ancient America*. A massive and amazingly comprehensive work, covering not only Mexico but Colombia, Ecuador and Peru as well. It's rather old-fashioned, however, and fails to take into account the groundbreaking epigraphic findings in Maya scholarship.

Diego de Landa *Yucatán Before and After the Conquest*. A translation by William Gates of the work written in 1566 as *Relación de las Cosas de Yucatán*. De Landa's destruction of almost all original Maya books as "works of the devil" leaves his own account as the chief source on Maya life and society in the immediate post-Conquest period. Written during his imprisonment in Spain on charges of cruelty to the Indians, the book provides a fascinating wealth of detail. Various other translations are widely available in Mexico.

Simon Martin and Nikolai Grube *Chronicle of the Maya Kings and Queens*. A more graphic approach to Maya history, replete with photo illustrations, timelines, hieroglyphics and the like, making the complex dynasties a little easier to grasp.

Mary Ellen Miller *Maya Art and Architecture*. An excellent survey of the artisanship of the Maya, organized by media, from stelae to pottery. Her *The Art of Mesoamerica: From Olmec to Aztec* gives a broader view.

Mary Ellen Miller and Karl Taube *An Illustrated Dictionary of the Gods and Symbols of Ancient Mexico and the Maya*. A superb modern reference on ancient Mesoamerica, written by two leading scholars. Taube's *Aztec and Maya Myths* is perfect as a short, accessible introduction to Mesoamerican mythology.

Chris Morton and Ceri Louise Thomas *The Mystery of the Crystal Skulls*. Intriguing, if somewhat sensationalist investigation into an ancient Amerindian legend that tells of a number of life-size crystal skulls said to contain vital information about the destiny of mankind. Following the discovery that such a skull actually exists, film-makers Morton and Thomas set off on a journey through Mexico and Central America, meeting experts in Maya culture, archeologists and modern-day shamans and reaching their own conclusions.

Jeremy A. Sabloff *Cities of Ancient Mexico*. An easy-to-digest introduction to ancient Mexico, with excellent photos by Macduff Everton – the main text focuses on daily life, with the end of the book explaining how these conclusions are deduced from the archeological record. Up-to-date and easy to digest. Also worth reading is his *New Archaeology and the Ancient Maya*.

Linda Schele, David Freidel et al. *A Forest of Kings: The Untold Story of the Ancient Maya*. The authors, at the forefront of the "new archeology", have been personally responsible for decoding many Maya glyphs, revolutionizing and popularizing this field. Although their populist writing style is controversial, it has also inspired a devoted following. They have shown that, far from being governed by peaceful astronomer-priests, the ancient Maya were ruled by hereditary kings, lived in populous, aggressive city-states and engaged in a continuous entanglement of alliances and war. The story continues in *The Blood of Kings*, by Linda Schele and Mary Ellen Miller.

Linda Schele and Peter Matthews *The Code of Kings*. Illustrated with Macduff Everton and Justin Kerr's "rollout" photography of Maya ceramics, this examines in detail the significance of the monuments at selected Maya sites.

Robert Sharer *The Ancient Maya*. The classic, comprehensive (and weighty) account of Maya civilization, now in its sixth edition. Required reading for archeologists, it also provides a fascinating reference for the non-expert.

Popol Vuh The Quiché Maya bible, a fascinating creation myth, is available in two main translations (many others can also be found): the classic version by Dennis Tedlock is arguably still the most readable; Allen J Christenson's two-volume approach gives a literal translation as well. The Maya obsession with time can be well appreciated here, where dates are recorded with painstaking precision.

J. Eric S. Thompson *The Rise and Fall of Maya Civilization* (o/p). A major authority on the ancient Maya during his lifetime, Thompson produced many academic works; *Rise and Fall*, originally published in 1954, is one of the more approachable. Although researchers have since overturned many of Thompson's theories, his work provided the inspiration for the postwar surge of interest in the Maya, and he remains a respected figure.

Ptolemy Tompkins *This Tree Grows Out of Hell*. An interesting attempt to piece together the mystery of Mesoamerican religion, synthesizing and making readable many of the late twentieth-century findings in the area. The latter half of the book is a thoroughly unconvincing apology for the brutality of the Aztecs.

Richard F. Townsend *The Aztecs*. Companion in the series to Coe's *Maya* book (see p.903), this attempts to be an introduction to all aspects of Aztec history and culture, but if you haven't done some prior reading, the details of names and battles may be overwhelming. That said, it's a comprehensive reference, newly updated in a third edition.

Society, politics and culture

Taisha Abelar *The Sorcerer's Crossing*. The extraordinary true story of an American woman who joins an all-female group of sorcerers in Mexico and undergoes a rigorous physical and mental training process, designed to enable her to breach the limits of ordinary perception.

Rick Bayless *Rick Bayless's Mexican Kitchen*. Aimed at the ambitious chef, this weighty tome has more than 150 recipes but no photos. The country's gastronomic heritage is explored in detail with a special focus on the myriad types of chile that form the heart of Mexican cuisine. More accessible is his *Mexico One Plate at a Time*, which focuses on the classics of the cuisine, with careful instructions and thorough coaching, including a testimony in favour of lard.

Fernández de Calderón Candida *Great Masters of Mexican Folk Art* (o/p). An ambitious and gorgeously photographed coffee-table book produced by the cultural wing of Banamex, with portraits of the artisans alongside their works.

Macduff Everton *The Modern Maya: A Culture in Transition*. Everton's black-and-white photographs document Maya village life with affection and dignity, with an eye to socioeconomic issues.

Clare Ferguson *Flavours of Mexico*. All the classics are here: tortillas, enchiladas, empanadas, *flautas* and tamales, along with party-food suggestions and a few vegetarian recipes. A colourful and straightforward cookbook that will inspire you to keep feasting on Mexican cuisine once back home.

Judith Adler Hellman *Mexican Lives*. A compilation of interviews with fifteen Mexicans on the eve of the signing of NAFTA in 1994, offering poignant insight into how rich and poor alike cope with life on the brink of enormous political and social change. The interviewees' personalities and emotions stand out from the pages. Underlying all the accounts is the reality of institutional corruption, which affects every sector of society but falls most heavily on the poor. Worth reading by anyone who wants to understand what modern Mexico is like behind the headlines.

Hayden Herrera *Frida: A Biography of Frida Kahlo*. This mesmerizing biography brings to life a woman of extreme magnetism and originality. Starting with her childhood in Mexico City, the account describes the crippling accident she had as a teenager that left her in chronic pain, her tempestuous marriage to Diego Rivera and the various men with whom she had affairs including, most notoriously, Leon Trotsky. The book contains numerous colour reproductions of her paintings.

Diana Kennedy *From My Mexican Kitchen: Techniques and Ingredients*. Kennedy was a pioneer in bringing the multifaceted cuisine of Mexico to the attention of Americans, when she published her first cookbook in 1972. This book is a good starting point for anyone new to Mexican cooking. Her many other titles are good too: look out for *My Mexico: A Culinary Odyssey with More Than 300 Recipes*, which has a great travelogue element.

Dan La Botz *Democracy in Mexico*. Examines the political landscape of modern Mexico and puts it into historical context by equating the rise of civil society and political consciousness with the major defining events of recent decades – the 1968 student massacre, the 1985 earthquake and the 1994 Zapatista uprising, among others.

Peter Laufer *Wetback Nation: The Case for Opening the Mexican–American Border*. An impassioned argument for revision of the current US immigration system, first published in 2004, even before the contentious border-fence proposal, and since updated to respond to that concept.

Daniel C. Levy and Kathleen Bruhn *Mexico: The Struggle for Democratic Development*. Quite academic, but one of the more up-to-date analyses of Mexico's political and economic situation – revised edition published in 2006.

Oscar Lewis *The Children of Sanchez*. These oral histories of a working-class family in the Mexico City of the 1940s are regarded as a seminal work in modern anthropology. The book is totally gripping, and doesn't read in the least like an anthropological text. Lewis's other works, including *Five Families*, use the same first-person narrative technique. All are highly recommended.

Patrick Marnham *Dreaming with His Eyes Open: A Life of Diego Rivera*. A gripping account of the extraordinary life of the great Mexican muralist in which truths are revealed and myths are unravelled.

The Mexico Reader An exceptionally wide-ranging selection of essays and articles, song lyrics and photos, that does as good a job as any title of bringing together the many aspects of Mexico, from a historical and cultural perspective. Many of the pieces are translated from Spanish for this edition.

Octavio Paz *The Labyrinth of Solitude*. An acclaimed series of philosophical essays exploring the social and political state of modern Mexico. Paz, who died in 1998, won the Nobel Prize for literature in 1990 and was universally regarded as the country's leading poet (see p.900).

Sam Quiñones *True Tales from Another Mexico: the Lynch Mob, the Popsicle Kings, Chalino and the Bronx*. Snappy, absorbing essays and reporting about Mexican popular culture and heroes, from a Oaxacan basketball team to the scrappy force behind the Michoacana ice-cream shops.

Gregory G. Reck *In the Shadow of Tlaloc*. Reck attempts a similar style to that of Oscar Lewis in his study of a Mexican village, and the effects on it of encroaching modernity. Often seems to stray over the border into sentimentality and even fiction, but interesting nonetheless.

John Ross *Rebellion from the Roots*. A fascinating early account of the build-up to and first months of the 1994 Zapatista rebellion, and still the definitive book on the subject. Ross's reporting style provides a detailed and informative background, showing the uprising was no surprise to the Mexican army. His *Zapatistas: Making Another World Possible: Chronicles of Resistance 2000–2006* updated the ongoing saga.

Guiomar Rovira *Women of Maize*. Rovira, a Mexican journalist, witnessed the Zapatista uprising in Chiapas on New Year's Day, 1994. This book, which interweaves narrative, history and the personal recollections of numerous women involved in the rebellion, provides an extraordinary insight into the lives of indigenous people. The women interviewed reflect on how their previously traditional lifestyles were transformed when they joined up with the Zapatista National Liberation Army and gained access to education and other opportunities they'd never even dreamt of.

Chloë Sayer *Arts and Crafts of Mexico*. Sayer is the author of numerous books on Mexican arts, crafts and associated subjects, all of them worth reading. *The Skeleton at the Feast*, written with Elizabeth Carmichael, is a wonderful, superbly illustrated insight into attitudes to death and the dead in Mexico.

Joel Simon *Endangered Mexico*. Eloquent and compelling study documenting the environmental crisis facing Mexico at the end of the twentieth century – now slightly dated, but still essential reading for those wanting to know how and why the crisis exists and why no one can offer solutions.

David Rains Wallace *The Monkey's Bridge*. When the Panama Bridge formed between North and South America three million years ago, plants and animals surged back and forth across it in an evolutionary intermingling that created one of the world's richest natural environments. This engaging account of Central America's role as an evolutionary link between the two continents, out in a new paperback edition, cleverly interweaves natural history, human history, travel writing and personal reflection.

Mariana Yampolsky *The Traditional Architecture of Mexico*. The enormous range of Mexico's architectural styles, from thatched peasant huts and vast haciendas to exuberant Baroque churches and solid yet graceful public buildings, is encompassed in this inspired book. While most of Yampolsky's superb photographs are in black and white, a chapter on the use of colour emphasizes its importance in every area of life; the text by Chloë Sayer raises it above the level of the average coffee-table book.

Nancy Zaslavsky *A Cook's Tour of Mexico* (o/p). Great guide to outdoor markets and street food, by region, with recipes. A little dated, but a good starting point for people looking to focus on food during their trip.

Wildlife and environment

Rosita Arvigo *Sastun: My Apprenticeship with a Maya Healer*. The author established an organic herb farm in Belize, then studied with the region's best-known medicine man for five years. Her story is fascinating for anyone interested in herbal treatments; more detail can be found in her *Rainforest Home Remedies*.

Les Beletsky *Travellers' Wildlife Guides Southern Mexico*. An excellent, if rather bulky, field guide, with colour plates of not just birds but also reptiles and mammals found through the Yucatán, Oaxaca and Chiapas.

Steve Howell and Sophie Webb *A Guide to the Birds of Mexico and Northern Central America*. A tremendous work, the result of years of research, this is the definitive book on the region's birds. Essential for all serious birders, though a bit hefty to use in the field. Howell's *Where to Watch Birds in Mexico* details more than a hundred sites, where some 950 bird species can be seen.

Paul Humann and Ned DeLoach *Snorkeling Guide to Marine Life: Florida, Caribbean, Bahamas*. A handy, spiral-bound field guide to corals, fish, plants and other underwater life off the Caribbean coast. The same authors have individual titles on *Reef Fish Identification*, *Reef Creature Identification* and *Reef Coral Identification* for the same area, and a separate *Reef Fish Identification* title for the Pacific coast.

Eugene H. Kaplan *Coral Reefs of the Caribbean and Florida*. Part of the Peterson Field Guide series, a useful handbook on the abundant wildlife off the coasts of the Yucatán Peninsula.

Victoria Schlesinger *Animals and Plants of the Ancient Maya: A Guide*. More than a field guide, this book also examines the cultural significance of more than a hundred species in the ancient Maya world.

R.J. Secor *Mexico's Volcanoes*. Detailed routes up all the big volcanoes, and full of invaluable information for climbers.

Ber Van Perlo *Birds of Mexico and Central America*. Compact and comprehensive field guide; illustrations are tiny, which can make identification tricky, but otherwise the best of its kind to carry with you.

Language

Language

Mexican Spanish

Once you get into it, **Spanish** is a straightforward language, and in Mexico people are eager to understand and to help even the most faltering attempt. **English** is widely spoken, especially in heavily visited areas, but you'll get a far better reception if you at least try to communicate with people in their own tongue. You'll be helped by the fact that Mexicans speak relatively slowly, at least compared with Spaniards.

Rules of pronunciation

Relative to English, the rules of **pronunciation** are clear-cut and, once you get to know them, strictly observed. Unless there's an accent, words ending in d, l, r and z are stressed on the last syllable, all others on the second last. All vowels are pure and short.

A is between the A sound of "back" and that of "father".

E as in "g**e**t"

I as in "pol**i**ce"

O as in "h**o**t"

U as in "r**u**le"

C is spoken like S before E and I, hard otherwise: *cerca* is pronounced "SER-ka".

G is a guttural H sound (a little softer than the ch in "loch") before E or I, a hard G elsewhere: *gigante* becomes "hi-GAN-te".

H is always silent.

J is the same sound as a guttural G: *jamón* is pronounced "ham-ON".

LL sounds like an English Y: *tortilla* is pronounced "tor-TEE-ya".

N is as in English unless it has a tilde (accent) over it, when it becomes NY: *mañana* sounds like "ma-NYA-na".

QU is pronounced like an English K.

R is rolled; RR, doubly so.

V sounds more like B, *vino* becoming "BEE-no".

X has an S sound before consonants; between vowels in place names, it has an H sound, like México ("MEH-hee-ko") or Oaxaca ("wa-HA-ka"). In many place names from indigenous languages, the X is pronounced as S – as in Xochimilco ("so-chee-MIL-co"); in Maya, however, X sounds like SH – Xel-Ha is pronounced "shel-ha".

Z is the same as a soft C, so *cerveza* becomes "ser-VAY-sa".

Useful words and phrases

Although we've listed a few essential words and phrases here, if you're travelling for any length of time some kind of **dictionary** or **phrasebook** is obviously a worthwhile investment: the *Rough Guide to Mexican Spanish* is the best practical guide, correct and colloquial, and will have you speaking the language faster than any other phrasebook. One of the best small Latin American Spanish dictionaries is the University of Chicago version (Pocket Books), widely available in Mexico, although the Langenscheidt pocket dictionary is also handy because its yellow plastic cover holds up well. If you're using an older dictionary, bear in mind that CH, LL and Ñ are traditionally counted as separate letters and are listed after the

Cs, Ls and Ns respectively; most current dictionaries, however, follow more familiar alphabetizing procedures, though Ñ retains its own section.

Basics

Yes, No	Sí, No
Open, Closed	Abierto/a, Cerrado/a
Please, Thank you	Por favor, Gracias
Push, Pull	Empujar, Tirar
Where?, When?	¿Dónde?, ¿Cuándo?
With, Without	Con, Sin
What?, How much?	¿Qué?, ¿Cuánto?
Good, Bad	Buen(o)/a, Mal(o)/a
Here, There	Aquí *or* Acá, Allí *or* Allá
Big, Small	Gran(de), Pequeño/a
This, That	Éste, Eso
More, Less	Más, Menos
Cheap, Expensive	Barato/a, Caro/a
Today, Tomorrow	Hoy, Mañana
Yesterday	Ayer
Now, Later	Ahora, Más tarde

Greetings and pleasantries

Hello, Goodbye	¡Hola!, Adiós
Good morning	Buenos días
Good afternoon/night	Buenas tardes/noches
How do you do?	¿Qué tal?
See you later	Hasta luego
Sorry	Lo siento/disculpeme
Excuse me	Con permiso/perdón
How are you?	¿Cómo está (usted)?
Not at all/You're welcome	De nada/por nada
I (don't) understand	(No) Entiendo
Do you speak English?	¿Habla (usted) inglés?
I (don't) speak Spanish	(No) Hablo español
What (did you say)?	Mande?
My name is...	Me llamo...
What's your name?	¿Cómo se llama usted?
I am English	Soy inglés(a)
...American*	...americano(a)
...Australian	...australiano(a)
...Canadian	...canadiense(a)
...Irish	...irlandés(a)
...Scottish	...escosés(a)
...Welsh	...galés(a)
...New Zealander	...neozelandés(a)

*Mexicans are from the Americas too, so describing yourself as American can occasionally cause offence. Another option is "estadounidense" (or, more simply, "de Los Estados Unidos", from the United States) if you are a US American.

Needs: hotels, transport and directions

I want...	Quiero...
I'd like...please	Quisiera...por favor
Do you know...?	¿Sabe...?
I don't know	No sé
There is... (Is there...?)	(¿)Hay...(?)
Give me... (one like that)	Deme... indent (uno así)
Do you have...?	¿Tiene...?
...the time	...la hora
...a room	...un cuarto
...with two beds/ ...double bed	...con dos camas/ ...cama matrimonial
It's for one person (two people)	Es para una persona (dos personas)
...for one night (one week)	...para una noche (una semana)
It's fine, how much is it?	¿Está bien, cuánto es?
It's too expensive	Es demasiado caro
Don't you have anything cheaper?	¿No tiene algo más barato?
Can one...?	¿Se puede...?
...camp (near) here?	¿...acampar (cerca de) aquí?
Is there a hotel nearby?	¿Hay un hotel cerca de aquí?

How do I get to...?	¿Por dónde se va a...?
Left, right, straight on	Izquierda, derecha, derecho
This way, that way	Por acá, por allá
Where is...?	¿Dónde está...?
...the bus station	...la camionera central
...the nearest bank	...el banco más cercano
...the ATM	...el cajero automático
...the post office	...el correo (la oficina de correos)
...the toilet	...el baño/sanitario
Where does the bus to...leave from?	¿De dónde sale el bus para...?
Is this the train for Chihuahua?	¿Es éste el tren para Chihuahua?
I'd like a(return) ticket to...	Quisiera un boleto (de ida y vuelta) para...
What time does it leave (arrive in...)?	¿A qué hora sale (llega en...)?
What is there to eat?	¿Qué hay para comer?
What's that?	¿Qué es eso?
What's this called in Spanish?	¿Cómo se llama éste en español?

Numbers and days

1	un/uno/una
2	dos
3	tres
4	cuatro
5	cinco
6	seis
7	siete
8	ocho
9	nueve
10	diez
11	once
12	doce
13	trece
14	catorce
15	quince
16	dieciséis
17	diecisiete
20	veinte
21	veintiuno
30	treinta
40	cuarenta
50	cincuenta
60	sesenta
70	setenta
80	ochenta
90	noventa
100	cien(to)
101	ciento uno
200	doscientos
500	quinientos
700	setecientos
1000	mil
2000	dos mil

first	primero/a
second	segundo/a
third	tercero/a
fifth	quinto/a
tenth	decimo/a

Monday	Lunes
Tuesday	Martes
Wednesday	Miércoles
Thursday	Jueves
Friday	Viernes
Saturday	Sábado
Sunday	Domingo

Food and drink terms

On the table

Azúcar	Sugar	**Pimienta**	Pepper
Cuchara	Spoon	**Queso**	Cheese
Cuchillo	Knife	**Sal**	Salt
Cuenta	Bill/check	**Salsa**	Sauce
Mantequilla	Butter	**Servilleta**	Napkin
Pan	Bread	**Tenedor**	Fork

Cooking terms

A la parilla	Grilled over charcoal	**Barbacoa/pibil**	Wrapped in banana leaves and steamed/baked in a pit
A la plancha	Grilled on a hot plate	**Con mole**	In a thick, rich sauce of chiles, nuts, spices and chocolate
A la tampiqueña	Strips of grilled meat served with guacamole	**Empanizado/a**	Breaded
A la veracruzana	Stewed with tomatoes, onions, olives and chile	**En mojo de ajo**	Fried with slow-cooked garlic
Al horno/horneado	Baked	**Frito**	Fried
Asado/a	Broiled	**Poco hecho/a punto/bien cocido**	Rare/medium/well-done

Breakfast

Huevos...	Eggs...	**...rancheros**	...fried, on a tortilla, smothered in a red chile sauce
...a la Mexicana	...scrambled with tomato, onion and chile	**...revueltos**	...scrambled
...con jamón	...with ham	**...tibios**	...lightly boiled
...con tocino	...with bacon	**Pan dulce**	Pastries
...motuleños	...fried, served on a tortilla with beans, ham and cheese		

Soups (*sopas*) and starters

Caldo	Broth (with bits in)	**Sopa...**	Soup...
Ceviche	Raw fish pieces, marinated in lime juice	**...de fideos**	...with noodles
Entremeses	Hors d'oeuvres	**...de lentejas**	...with lentils
		...de verduras	...with vegetables

Tortilla and corn dishes (*antojitos*)

Burritos	Wheat-flour tortillas, rolled and filled
Chilaquiles	Tortilla chips stewed with meat and tomato sauce
Enchiladas	Rolled-up tacos, covered in chile sauce and baked
Enchiladas suizas	As above, with green chile and cheese
Flautas	Small, filled, fried tortillas
Gorditas	Small, fat, stuffed corn tortillas
Machaca	Shredded dried meat scrambled with eggs
Molletes	Split roll with beans and melted cheese
Quesadillas	Toasted or fried tortillas topped with cheese
Queso fundido	Melted cheese, served with tortillas and salsa
Sincronizadas	Tortillas with melted cheese and ham
Sopes	Bite-size tostadas
Tacos	Soft corn tortillas with filling
Tacos al pastor	With spicy pork
Tacos dorados	Deep-fried tacos
Tamales	Corn husk or banana-leaf packets of steamed corn-meal dough with a savoury or sweet filling
Tlacoyo	Fat tortilla stuffed with beans
Torta	Filled bread roll, often toasted like a panini
Tostadas	Flat crisp tortillas piled with meat and salad

Fish and seafood (*pescados y mariscos*)

Anchoas	Anchovies
Atún	Tuna
Cabrilla/Corvina	Sea bass
Calamares	Squid
Camarones	Prawns
Cangrejo	Crab
Caracol	Conch
Filete entero	Whole, filleted fish
Huachinango	Red snapper
Langosta	Rock lobster
Merluza	Hake
Ostión	Oyster
Pez espada	Swordfish
Pulpo	Octopus
Robalo	Bass
Sardinas	Sardines
Trucha	Trout

Meat (*carne*) and poultry (*aves*)

Alambre	Kebab
Albóndigas	Meatballs
Arrachera	Skirt steak
Barbacoa	Barbecued meat
Bistec	Steak
Cabrito	Kid
Carne (de res)	Beef
Carne adobado	Barbecued/spicily stewed meat
Carnitas	Pork cooked with garlic until crispy
Cerdo	Pork
Chivo	Goat
Chorizo	Spicy sausage
Chuleta	Chop (usually pork)
Conejo	Rabbit
Cordero	Lamb
Costilla	Rib
Filete	Tenderloin/fillet
Guisado	Stew
Hígado	Liver
Lomo	Loin (of pork)

Milanesa	Breaded escalope
Pato	Duck
Pavo/Guajolote	Turkey
Pechuga	Breast
Pierna	Leg
Pollo	Chicken
Salchicha	Sausage
Salpicón	Shredded meat with vinegar
Ternera	Veal
Tripa/Callos	Tripe
Venado	Venison

Vegetables (*verduras*)

Aguacate	Avocado
Betabel	Beetroot (often as a juice)
Calabacita	Courgette (zucchini)
Calabaza	Squash
Cebolla	Onion
Champiñones/hongos	Mushrooms
Chícharos	Peas
Col	Cabbage
Elote	Corn on the cob
Espárragos	Asparagus
Espinacas	Spinach
Flor de calabaza	Squash blossoms
Frijoles	Beans
Huitlacoche	Corn fungus, "Mexican truffles"
Jitomate	Tomato
Lechuga	Lettuce
Lentejas	Lentils
Nopales	Cactus leaves
Papas	Potatoes
Pepino	Cucumber
Rajas	Strips of mild green *poblano* pepper
Zanahoria	Carrot

Fruits (*fruta*) and juice (*jugo*)

Albaricoque/chabacano	Apricot
Cherimoya	Custard apple (sweetsop)
Ciruela	Plum
Coco	Coconut
Durazno	Peach
Frambuesa	Raspberry
Fresa	Strawberry
Guanábana	Soursop
Guayaba	Guava
Higo	Fig
Limón	Lime
Mamey	Large fruit with sweet pink flesh
Melón	Melon
Naranja	Orange
Papaya	Papaya
Piña	Pineapple
Pitahaya	Dragonfruit, a type of cactus fruit
Plátano	Banana/plantain
Sandía	Watermelon
Toronja	Grapefruit
Tuna	Prickly pear fruit
Uva	Grape
Zapote	Sapodilla, fruit of the chicle tree

Sweets (*dulces*)

Ate	Quince paste
Cajeta...	Caramel confection often served with...
...crepas	...pancakes
...churros	...cinnamon fritters
Ensalada de frutas	Fruit salad
Flan	Crème caramel
Helado	Ice cream
Nieve	Sorbet

Glossary

Ahorita diminutive of *ahora* (now) meaning "right now" – but seldom applied as literally as a visitor might expect.

Alameda city park or promenade; large plaza.

Ayuntamiento town hall/government.

Aztec the empire that dominated the central valleys of Mexico from the thirteenth century until defeated by Cortés.

Barrio area within a town or city; suburb.

Camino blanco unpaved rural road, so called because it is paved with limestone gravel.

Camioneta small truck or van.

Cantina bar, traditionally men-only, but increasingly open to women.

Cenote underground water source in the Yucatán, a natural sinkhole in the limestone surface.

Chac Maya god of rain.

Chac-mool recumbent statue, possibly a sacrificial figure or messenger to the gods.

Comal large, round flat plate made of clay or metal used for cooking tortillas.

Comedor cheap restaurant, literally dining room; also called a *cocina económica*.

Convento either convent or monastery.

CTM central union organization.

Cuauhtémoc the last Aztec leader, commander of the final resistance to Cortés, and a national hero.

Descompuesto out of order.

Don/Doña courtesy titles (sir/madam), mostly used in letters or for professional people or the boss.

Ejido communal farmland.

Enramadas palapa-covered restaurants.

EPR Ejército Popular Revolucionario, the Popular Revolutionary Army. Guerrilla group, not allied to the Zapatistas; their first appearance was in Guerrero in 1996.

EZLN Ejército Zapatista de Liberación Nacional, the Zapatista Army of National Liberation.

Feria fair (market).

Finca ranch or plantation.

FONART government agency to promote crafts.

Fonda simple restaurant or boarding house.

FONATUR government tourism agency.

Fray Spanish word for friar.

Gringo not necessarily insulting, though it does imply North American – said to come from invading US troops, either because they wore green coats or because they sang "Green grow the rushes oh!..."

Guayabera embroidered Cuban-style shirt, usually for men.

Güera/o blonde – very frequently used description of Westerners, especially shouted after women in the street; again, not usually intended as an insult.

Hacendado plantation owner.

Hacienda plantation estate or the big house on it.

Henequen a variety of agave cactus grown mainly in Yucatán, the fibres of which are used to make rope.

Huipil Maya women's embroidered white smock dress or blouse, worn over a white petticoat, usually with a small checkered scarf.

Huitzilopochtli Aztec god of war.

I.V.A. fifteen percent value-added tax (VAT).

Kukulkán Maya name for Quetzalcoatl, the plumed serpent god.

Ladino as applied to people, means Spanish-influenced as opposed to Indian; determined entirely by clothing (and culture) rather than physical race.

Licenciado A common title, literally meaning "graduate" or "licensed"; abbreviated Lic.

Malecón seafront promenade.

Malinche Cortés's Indian interpreter and mistress, a symbol of treachery.

Mariachi quintessentially Mexican music, with lots of brass and sentimental lyrics.

Marimba xylophone-like musical instrument, also used of the bands based around it; derives from northern Mexico.

Maya people who inhabited Honduras, Belize, Guatemala and southeastern Mexico from earliest times, and still do.

Mestizo mixed race, of Indian and Spanish descent.

Metate flat stone for grinding corn; used with a *mano*, a grinding stone.

Milpa a small subsistence farm plot, usually tended with slash-and-burn agricultural practices.

Mirador lookout point.

Mixtec people from the mountains of Oaxaca.

Moctezuma Montezuma, the leader of the Aztec empire when the Spanish arrived in Mexico.

Muelle jetty or dock.

NAFTA the North American Free Trade Agreement including Mexico, the US and Canada; see also TLC below.

Nahuatl ancient Aztec language, still the most common after Spanish.

Norteño literally northern – style of food and music.

Palacio mansion, but not necessarily royal.

Palacio de Gobierno headquarters of state/federal authorities.

Palacio Municipal headquarters of local government.

Palapa palm thatch. Used to describe any thatched/palm-roofed hut.

Palenque cockpit (for cockfights).

PAN Partido de Acción Nacional (National Action Party), conservative party that first took power when Vicente Fox became president in 2000.

Paseo a broad avenue, but also the ritual evening walk around the plaza.

PEMEX the Mexican national oil company.

Planta baja ground floor – abbreviated PB in lifts.

Porfiriato the three decades of Porfirio Díaz's dictatorship.

PRD Partido Revolucionario Democrático (Party of the Democratic Revolution), the left-wing opposition formed and led by Cuauhtémoc Cárdenas.

PRI Partido Revolucionario Institucional (Party of the Institutional Revolution), the ruling party for eighty years, until the PAN upset in 2000.

PT Partido del Trabajo (Workers' Party), small party but with opposition seats in Congress.

PVEM Partido Verde Ecologista de México (Green Party), small opposition party.

Quetzalcoatl the plumed serpent, most powerful, enigmatic and widespread of all ancient Mexican gods.

Romería procession.

Sacbé ancient Maya road, paved with limestone; plural *sacbeob*.

Stele freestanding carved monument; plural *stelae*.

Tenochtitlán the Aztec capital, on the site of Mexico City.

Teotihuacán ancient city north of the capital – the first major urban power of central Mexico.

Tianguis Nahuatl word for market, still used of particularly varied marketplaces.

Tlaloc Toltec/Aztec rain god.

TLC Tratado de Libre Comercio, the Spanish name for NAFTA (see above).

Toltec tribe which controlled central Mexico between Teotihuacán and the Aztecs.

Tope speed-bump or other barrier on rural roads for slowing traffic.

Trova Romantic Yucatecan song style popular in the early twentieth century, still played by *trovadores*.

Tula the Toltec capital.

Tzompantli Aztec skull rack or "wall of skulls".

Virreinal from the period of the Spanish viceroys – ie colonial.

Wetback derogatory term for illegal Mexican (or any Hispanic) in the US; *mojado* ("wet") is the Spanish slang term, without the negative connotations.

Zapotec tribe which controlled the Oaxaca region to about 700 AD.

Zócalo the main plaza of any town.

Small print and
Index

A Rough Guide to Rough Guides

Published in 1982, the first Rough Guide – to Greece – was a student scheme that became a publishing phenomenon. Mark Ellingham, a recent graduate in English from Bristol University, had been travelling in Greece the previous summer and couldn't find the right guidebook. With a small group of friends he wrote his own guide, combining a highly contemporary, journalistic style with a thoroughly practical approach to travellers' needs.

The immediate success of the book spawned a series that rapidly covered dozens of destinations. And, in addition to impecunious backpackers, Rough Guides soon acquired a much broader and older readership that relished the guides' wit and inquisitiveness as much as their enthusiastic, critical approach and value-for-money ethos.

These days, Rough Guides include recommendations from shoestring to luxury and cover more than 200 destinations around the globe, including almost every country in the Americas and Europe, more than half of Africa and most of Asia and Australasia. Our ever-growing team of authors and photographers is spread all over the world, particularly in Europe, the US and Australia.

In the early 1990s, Rough Guides branched out of travel, with the publication of Rough Guides to World Music, Classical Music and the Internet. All three have become benchmark titles in their fields, spearheading the publication of a wide range of books under the Rough Guide name.

Including the travel series, Rough Guides now number more than 350 titles, covering: phrasebooks, waterproof maps, music guides from Opera to Heavy Metal, reference works as diverse as Conspiracy Theories and Shakespeare, and popular culture books from iPods to Poker. Rough Guides also produce a series of more than 120 World Music CDs in partnership with World Music Network.

Visit www.roughguides.com to see our latest publications.

Rough Guide credits

Text editor: Lucy Cowie
Layout: Jessica Subramanian
Cartography: Swati Handoo, Rajesh Mishra
Picture editor: Nicole Newman
Production: Rebecca Short
Proofreader: Jennifer Speake
Cover design: Dan May, Chloë Roberts
Photographer: Dan Bannister, Jason Clampet, Sarah Cummins
Editorial: London Ruth Blackmore, Andy Turner, Keith Drew, Edward Aves, Alice Park, Lucy White, Jo Kirby, James Smart, Natasha Foges, Róisín Cameron, James Rice, Lara Kavanagh, Emma Traynor, Emma Gibbs, Kathryn Lane, Monica Woods, Mani Ramaswamy, Harry Wilson, Alison Roberts, Joe Staines, Peter Buckley, Matthew Milton, Tracy Hopkins, Ruth Tidball; **Delhi** Madhavi Singh, Lubna Shaheen
Design & Pictures: London Scott Stickland, Dan May, Diana Jarvis, Mark Thomas, Sarah Cummins, Emily Taylor; **Delhi** Umesh Aggarwal, Ajay Verma, Ankur Guha, Pradeep Thapliyal, Sachin Tanwar, Anita Singh, Nikhil Agarwal, Sachin Gupta.
Production: Liz Cherry
Cartography: London Ed Wright, Katie Lloyd-Jones; **Delhi** Rajesh Chhibber, Ashutosh Bharti, Animesh Pathak, Jasbir Sandhu, Karobi Gogoi, Alakananda Roy, Deshpal Dabas
Online: London Faye Hellon, Jeanette Angell, Fergus Day, Justine Bright, Clare Bryson, Aine Fearon, Adrian Low, Ezgi Celebi; **Delhi** Amit Verma, Rahul Kumar, Narender Kumar, Ravi Yadav, Debojit Borah, Rakesh Kumar, Ganesh Sharma, Shisir Basumatari
Marketing & Publicity: London Liz Statham, Jess Carter, Vivienne Watton, Anna Paynton, Rachel Spracket, Laura Vipond; **New York** Katy Ball, Judi Powers; **Delhi** Ragini Govind
Reference Director: Andrew Lockett
Operations Assistant: Becky Doyle
Operations Manager: Helen Atkinson
Publishing Director (Travel): Clare Currie
Commercial Manager: Gino Magnotta
Managing Director: John Duhigg

SMALL PRINT

Publishing information

This eighth edition published June 2010 by
Rough Guides Ltd,
80 Strand, London WC2R 0RL
11 Community Centre, Panchsheel Park,
New Delhi 110017, India
Distributed by the Penguin Group
Penguin Books Ltd,
80 Strand, London WC2R 0RL
Penguin Group (USA)
375 Hudson Street, NY 10014, USA
Penguin Group (Australia)
250 Camberwell Road, Camberwell,
Victoria 3124, Australia
Penguin Group (Canada)
195 Harry Walker Parkway N, Newmarket, ON,
L3Y 7B3 Canada
Penguin Group (NZ)
67 Apollo Drive, Mairangi Bay, Auckland 1310,
New Zealand
Cover concept by Peter Dyer.
Typeset in Bembo and Helvetica to an original design by Henry Iles.
Printed in Italy by L.E.G.O. S.p.A, Lavis (TN)

936pp includes index
A catalogue record for this book is available from the British Library
ISBN: 978-1-84836-487-5

1 3 5 7 9 8 6 4 2

Help us update

We've gone to a lot of effort to ensure that the eighth edition of **The Rough Guide to Mexico** is accurate and up-to-date. However, things change – places get "discovered", opening hours are notoriously fickle, restaurants and rooms raise prices or lower standards. If you feel we've got it wrong or left something out, we'd like to know, and if you can remember the address, the price, the hours, the phone number, so much the better.

Please send your comments with the subject line **"Rough Guide Mexico Update"** to Ⓔmail@roughguides.com. We'll credit all contributions and send a copy of the next edition (or any other Rough Guide if you prefer) for the very best emails.

Have your questions answered and tell others about your trip at Ⓦwww.roughguides.com

Acknowledgements

John Fisher would like to thank everyone who helped along the way and has contributed over the years, and especially, as ever, thanks to A and the two Js for putting up with it all.

Daniel Jacobs would like to thank Stephen Keeling, Zora O'Neill, Armida Durán and Axaya Rosales.

Stephen Keeling would like to thank Dulce Herrera Solis in Acapulco, Ricardo Collins García in Ensenada, Gina Machorro in Puerto Escondido, Pat Cordes and Jane Onstott at ⓦwww.mexicoguru.com, Rosie Glover in Puerto Peñasco, Lucy Cowie back in London for doing an excellent editing job, and finally Tiffany Wu, whose love and support made this possible.

Zora O'Neill would like to thank: Lee Christie at Genesis, Sofi and Daniel at Marionetas, Pedro and Eyal at Las Anclas and Rob and Joanne Birce at Alma Libre Books, for keeping me in the loop and offering me hospitality; mi chofer, Peter, for keeping his eye on the road; Lucy Cowie, for meticulous editing; and all the readers who took the time to send in corrections, tips and criticism.

SMALL PRINT

Readers' letters

Thanks to all the readers who have taken the time to write in with comments and suggestions (and apologies if we've inadvertently omitted or misspelt anyone's name):

Nolberto Abarca, Rob Adès, Elvira Anton Centenera, Joe Bowbeer, Stephanie Clark, Kyle Dromgoole, Bernard Houdmont, Erlend Ingebrigtsen, Petra and Ivar Inkapool, Jan and Marianne Knoblauch, Lars Kuipers, Nick Magnan, Ana Ortiz Monasterio, Ketta Morris, Paul Nash, Mike Phelps & Maria de Boer, Mary Ponsford, Nigel Pottle, Megan Ross, Mike Sparling, Paul Sportelli, Wanda and Barry Syner, William van der Veer, Tom Winnifrith, Siye Wu, Cody Wofsy.

Photo credits

All photos © Rough Guides except the following:

Introduction

Paseo de la Reforma, Mexico City © Walter Bibikow/photolibrary

Puerto Escondido, Baja California © Rinaldi Roberto/SIME-4Corners

Kayaking, Alseseca River © Lucas Gilman/Corbis

Mexican rodeo, Puerto Vallarta © Mark Callanan/photolibrary

Museo Nacional de Anthropología © Egmont Strigl/photolibrary

Chac-mool figure, Cancún © Chris Cheadle/photolibrary

Things not to miss

01 Woman Crouching in a cave near Valladolid © ML Sinibaldi/Corbis

02 El Castillo, Tulum © Jose Fuste Raga/Corbis

03 Performer from Papantla hangs over water © Guido Manuilo/Corbis

04 Fresco Paintings, Bonampak © Charles Lenars/Corbis

05 Mural depicts scenes from the revolution © Paul Harris/Corbis

06 Coffee beans, Veracruz © Leonardo Romero/photolibrary

07 Maya ruins, Palenque © Ignacio Guevara/photolibrary

08 Playa del Carmen © Cris Haigh/Alamy

09 Swinging bridge, Copper Canyon © Douglas Peebles/Robert Harding

10 El Lago de Pátzcuaro © Travel Ink/Alamy

11 View of Guanajuato © Jose Fuste Raga/Corbis

12 El Tajin, Veracruz © SuperStock

13 The Atlantes, Tula © Ken Welsh/photolibrary

14 Aztec Stadium © Aerial Archives/Alamy

15 The Zócalo, Mexico City © Walter Bibikow/photolibrary

16 Cowboy © SuperStock

17 Pre-Maya clay figure, Museo Nacional de Antropología © Mira/Alamy

18 Religious statue, underwater, Cozumel © Danita Delimont/Alamy

19 Turquoise and silver jewelry, Taxco © David R. Frazier/Alamy

20 Xochimilco © Hervé Hughes/photolibrary

21 Las Pozas Sculpture Garden © Angelo Hornak/Corbis

22 People dancing, Veracruz zócalo © Hauke Dressler/Corbis

23 La Quebrada cliff divers, Acapulco © eye ubiquitous/Alamy

24 Mexican musicians © SuperStock

25 Calakmul, Campeche © Leonardo Romero/photolibrary

26 Baja California Sur, Bahía Concepcion © Danita Delimont/Alamy

27 Museo Frida Kahlo, Mexico City © Lightworks Media/Alamy

29 Bird at Sian Ka'an Biosphere Reserve © SuperStock

30 Grey whale © Mark Conlin/Alamy

31 Interior of Iglesia de Guadalupe © Danny Lehman/Corbis

32 Market, Oaxaca © Carlos S. Pereyra/ photolibrary
33 Man wearing a headdress during the festival of the Virgin of Guadalupe, Mexico City © Oliver Gerhard/photolibrary
34 Monarch Butterflies, Michoacan © Phyllis Greenberg/Corbis
35 Chichén Itzá © Chris Cheadle/photolibrary

A taste of Mexico colour section
Chicken with *Mole Poblano* © CarverMostardi/ Alamy
Tequila © Bonhommet/Corbis
Day of the Dead candy © RFoxPhotography/ Alamy

Festive Mexico colour section
Our Lady of Guadalupe Statue, Zihuatanejo © Richard Cummins/photolibrary
Carnaval parade, Morelos © photolibrary
Semana Santa, Capomos © Blaine Harrington/ photolibrary
Tarahumara dancers, Semana Santa © Robert Cundy/photolibrary
Festival International Cervantino © David Bolaños/Corbis
Traditional clothing, Independence Day © Ann Summa/Corbis
Zacapoaxtlaz march, Independence Day © Ulises Ruiz/Corbis
Dancers perform during the Pocho festivities, Tabasco © Jaime Avalos/Corbis

Ancient Mexico colour section
Tulum, Yucatán © Peter Adams/Corbis
Olmec statue © Carlos S. Pereyra/photolibrary
Mural of Tenochtitlán, Mexico City © photolibrary
Tula, Hidalgo © Jim Zuckerman/Alamy
Tulum ruins from the air © Guido Alberto Rossi/ photolibrary
Fresco paintings in Mayan Tomb, Bonampak © Charles Lenars/Corbis
Sculpture of woman writing © Werner Forman/ Corbis
Monte Albán © Bob Krist/Corbis
Aztec Piedra del Sol calendar © Peter Horree/ Alamy

Black and whites
p.72 Restaurant next to the fish market, Ensenada © Thomas Shjarback/Alamy
p.136 Copper Canyon railway © Douglas Peebles/Robert Harding
p.150 Nuestra Señora de Concepción, Álamos © CuboImages srl/Alamy
p.181 Two men in a boat, Mexcaltitán © imagebroker/Alamy
p.184 Casas Grandes, Paquime © Tom Bean/ Corbis
p.202 Cathedral, Durango © Witold Skrypczak/ Alamy
p.220 Betsabeé Romero exhibition, Museum of Contemporary Art, Monterrey © Tomas Bravo/ Reuters
p.232 Guanajuato © Bruno Perousse/photolibrary
p.252 Plaza de Armas, Zacatecas © Michele Falzone/Alamy
p.263 Barra Cunningham murals, Palacio de Gobierno, Aguascalientes © Martin Siepmann/ photolibrary
p.290 San Miguel Allende © Bruno Perousse/ photolibrary
p.300 Statue, Querétaro © Ethel Davies/ photolibrary
p.314 Farm worker cutting agave plant © Aaron Ansarov/Corbis
p.326 Mural of Father Miguel Hidalgo by José Clemente Orozco © Danny Lehman/Corbis
p.353 Waterfall in Parque Nacional Eduardo Ruíz © Danny Lehman/Corbis
p.362 Fishermen, Lago de Pátzcuaro © Travel Ink/Alamy
p.378 Cathedral, Zócalo, Mexico City © Demetrio Carrasco/Corbis
p.399 Murals of Diego Rivera © Frans Lemmens/ Alamy
p.408 Palacio de las Bellas Artes, Mexico City © Mario Guzman/Corbis
p.421 Aztec calendar, Museo Nacional de Anthropoligía, Mexico City © Bertrand Gardel/ Corbis
p.438 Boats, Xochimilco © Eliana Aponte/Corbis
p.462 Pirámide del Sol, Teotihuacán © Egmont Strigl/photolibrary
p.484 Dome of the Capilla del Rosario, Iglesia de Santo Domingo, Puebla © Moreleaze Tropicana/Alamy
p.494 Palacio de Cortés, Cuernavaca © Frans Lemmens/Alamy
p.516 Aerial view of beach, Acapulco © Serdar/ Alamy
p.530 Humpback whale, Puerto Vallarta © Gerard Soury/Corbis
p.545 Nevado de Colima © Reuters/Daniel Aguilar/Corbis
p.560 Beach hotels, Acapulco © Anne Rippy/ photolibrary
p.570 Women dressed for Carnaval, Veracruz © Lindsay Hebberd/Corbis
p.575 Climbing El Pico de Orizaba © Daniel H. Bailey/Corbis
p.594 A kayaker on the Alseseca River, Veracruz © Lucas Gilman/Corbis
p.612 Surfer, Puerto Escondido © Jim Russi/ Corbis
p.622 Santo Domingo de Guzmán, Oaxaca © Bob Krist/Corbis
p.640 Mitla ruins, Oaxaca © JTB Photo/Corbis
p.664 Sea turtle, Mazunte © Tomas Bravo/Corbis
p.674 Olmec head, La Venta, Villahermosa © photolibrary
p.691 Dancers and musicians prepare for the Festival Maya-Zoque, Chiapa de Corzo © Pablo Virgen/epa/Corbis
p.719 The ruins at Palenque © Massimo Borchi/ Corbis
p.733 Great blue heron © Patricio Robles Gil/ Corbis

Index

Map entries are in colour.

H

I

INDEX

INDEX

N

O

P

Q

R

S

Map symbols

maps are listed in the full index using coloured text

International border
State border
Chapter division boundary
Highways
Major road
Minor road
Unpaved road
4-wheel drive road
Pedestrianized street
Steps
Railway/subway
Funicular
Path
Ferry route
River
Wall
Cable car and stations
Metro station
Reef
Cliff
Gorge/canyon
Volcano
Hill shading
Mountain range
Mountain peak
Cave
Waterfall
Spring/spa
Bridge

Point of interest
Fuel station
Internet access
Information centre
Post office
Hospital/medical centre
Phone office
Viewpoint
Arch
Lighthouse
Airport
Gate
One-way arrow
Gardens
Museum
Parking
Archeological site/ruins
Accommodation
Eating & drinking
Bus/taxi stop
Metrobús
Church/cathedral (regional maps)
Church/cathedral (town maps)
Building
Market
Cemetery
Park
Beach
Swamp